Twentieth-Century Literary Criticism

Volume 5

Twentieth-Century Literary Criticism

**Excerpts from Criticism of the
Works of Novelists, Poets, Playwrights,
Short Story Writers, and Other Creative Writers
Who Lived between 1900 and 1960,
from the First Published Critical Appraisals
to Current Evaluations**

**Sharon K. Hall
Editor**

**Gale Research Company
Book Tower
Detroit, Michigan 48226**

STAFF

Sharon K. Hall, *Editor*

Dennis Poupard, *Associate Editor*

Thomas Ligotti, James E. Person, Jr., *Senior Assistant Editors*

Marsha Mackenzie Check, Catherine E. Daligga, Thomas Gunton,
Ada Morgan, Lizbeth. A. Purdy, Anna C. Wallbillich, *Assistant Editors*

Phyllis Carmel Mendelson, *Contributing Editor*

Carolyn Bancroft, *Production Editor*
Lizbeth A. Purdy, *Assistant Production Editor*

Robert J. Elster, *Research Coordinator*
Carol Angela Thomas, *Research Assistant*

Linda M. Pugliese, *Manuscript Coordinator*
Marie Lazzari, *Manuscript Assistant*

Earlene M. Alber, Ann Kathleen Crowley, Francine M. Melotti-Bacon, Denise Michlewicz,
Gloria Anne Williams, Robyn V. Young, *Editorial Assistants*

L. Elizabeth Hardin, *Permissions Coordinator*
Filomena Sgambati, *Assistant Permissions Coordinator*
Janice M. Mach, Mary P. McGrane, Patricia A. Seefelt, *Permissions Assistants*

Copyright © 1981 by Gale Research Company

ISSN 0276-8178

Library of Congress Catalog Card Number 76-46132

ISBN 0-8103-0179-2

CONTENTS

PREFACE

It is impossible to overvalue the importance of literature in the intellectual, emotional, and spiritual evolution of humanity. Literature is that which both lifts us out of everyday life and helps us to better understand it. Through the fictive life of an Emma Bovary, a Lambert Strether, a Leopold Bloom, our perceptions of the human condition are enlarged, and we are enriched.

Literary criticism is a collective term for several kinds of critical writing: criticism may be normative, descriptive, textual, interpretive, appreciative, generic. It takes many forms: the traditional essay, the aphorism, the book or play review, even the parodic poem. Perhaps the single unifying feature of literary criticism lies in its purpose: to help us to better understand what we read.

The Scope of the Book

The usefulness of Gale's *Contemporary Literary Criticism (CLC),* which excerpts criticism of current creative writing, suggested an equivalent need among literature students and teachers interested in authors of the period 1900 to 1960. The great poets, novelists, short story writers, and playwrights of this period are by far the most popular writers for study in high school and college literature courses. Moreover, since contemporary critics continue to analyze the work of this period—both in its own right and in relation to today's tastes and standards—a vast amount of relevant critical material confronts the student.

Thus, *Twentieth-Century Literary Criticism (TCLC)* presents significant passages from published criticism on authors who died between 1900 and 1960. Because of the difference in time span under consideration *(CLC* considers authors living from 1960 to the present), there is no duplication between *CLC* and *TCLC.*

Each volume of *TCLC* is carefully designed to present a list of authors who represent a variety of genres and nationalities. The length of an author's section is intended to be representative of the amount of critical attention he or she has received in the English language. Articles and books that have not been translated into English are excluded. An attempt has been made to identify and include excerpts from the seminal essays on each author's work. Additionally, as space permits, especially insightful essays of a more limited scope are included. Thus *TCLC* is designed to serve as an introduction for the student of twentieth-century literature to the authors of that period and to the most significant commentators on these authors.

Each *TCLC* author section represents the scope of critical response to that author's work: some early criticism is presented to indicate initial reactions, later criticism is selected to represent any rise or fall in an author's reputation, and current retrospective analyses provide students with a modern view. Since a *TCLC* author section is intended to be a definitive overview, the editors include between 30 and 40 authors in each 600-page volume (compared to approximately 100 authors in a *CLC* volume of similar size) in order to devote more attention to each author. Because of the great quantity of critical material available on many authors, and because of the resurgence of criticism generated by events such as an author's centennial or anniversary celebration, the republication of an author's works, or publication of a newly translated work or volume of letters, an author may appear more than once.

The Organization of the Book

An author section consists of the following elements: author heading, bio-critical introduction, principal works, excerpts of criticism (each followed by a citation), and, beginning with Volume 3, an annotated bibliography of additional reading.

- The *author heading* consists of the author's full name, followed by birth and death dates. The unbracketed portion of the name denotes the form under which the author most commonly wrote. If an author wrote consistently under a pseudonym, the pseudonym will be listed in the author heading and the real name given in parentheses on the first line of the bio-critical introduction. Also located at the beginning of the bio-critical introduction are any name variations under which an author wrote, including transliterated forms for authors whose languages use nonroman alphabets. Uncertainty as to a birth or death date is indicated by a question mark.

- The *bio-critical introduction* contains biographical and other background information about an author that will elucidate his or her creative output.

- The *list of principal works* is chronological by date of first publication and identifies genres. In those instances where the first publication was other than English language, the title and date of the first English-language edition are given in brackets. Unless otherwise indicated, dramas are dated by first performance, not first publication.

- *Criticism* is arranged chronologically in each author section to provide a perspective on any changes in critical evaluation over the years. For purposes of easier identification, the critic's name and the publication date of the essay are given at the beginning of each piece of criticism.

- A complete *bibliographical citation* designed to facilitate location of the original essay or book by the interested reader accompanies each piece of criticism. An asterisk (*) at the end of a citation indicates the essay is on more than one author.

- The *annotated bibliography* appearing at the end of each author section suggests further reading on the author. In some cases it includes essays for which the editors could not obtain reprint rights. An asterisk (*) at the end of a citation indicates the essay is on more than one author.

Each volume of *TCLC* includes a cumulative index to critics. Under each critic's name is listed the author(s) on which the critic has written and the volume and page where the criticism may be found. *TCLC* also includes a cumulative index to authors with the volume number in which the author appears in boldface after his or her name.

Beginning with Volume 2, *TCLC* includes an appendix which lists the sources from which material in the volume is reprinted. It does not, however, list every book or periodical consulted for the volume. Beginning with Volume 3, *TCLC* includes an annotated bibliography for additional reading. Beginning with Volume 4, *TCLC* includes another new feature—portraits of the author.

Acknowledgments

No work of this scope can be accomplished without the cooperation of many people. The editors especially wish to thank the copyright holders of the excerpts included in this volume, the permission managers of many book and magazine publishing companies for assisting us in locating copyright holders, and the staffs of the Detroit Public Library, University of Michigan Library, and Wayne State University Library for making their resources available to us. We are also grateful to Fred S. Stein for his assistance with copyright research and Louise Kertesz for her editorial assistance.

Suggestions Are Welcome

If readers wish to suggest authors they would like to have covered in future volumes, or if they have other suggestions, they are cordially invited to write the editor.

AUTHORS TO APPEAR
IN FUTURE VOLUMES

Ady, Endre 1877-1919
Agate, James 1877-1947
Agustini, Delmira 1886-1914
Alain-Fournier (Henri Alban
    Fournier) 1886-1914
Aldrich, Thomas Bailey
    1836-1907
Annensy, Innokenty
    Fyodorovich 1856-1909
Anstey, Frederick 1856-1934
Arlen, Michael 1895-1956
Barea, Arturo 1897-1957
Baring, Maurice 1874-1945
Baroja, Pio 1872-1956
Barry, Philip 1896-1949
Bass, Eduard 1888-1946
Belloc, Hilaire 1870-1953
Benét, Stephen Vincent
    1898-1943
Benét, William Rose 1886-1950
Benson, E(dward) F(rederic)
    1867-1940
Benson, Stella 1892-1933
Beresford, J(ohn) D(avys)
    1873-1947
Bethell, Mary Ursula 1874-1945
Biely, Andrei 1880-1934
Binyon, Laurence 1869-1943
Bjørnson, Bjørnstjerne
    1832-1910
Blackmore, R(ichard) D(odd-
    ridge) 1825-1900
Blasco Ibanez, Vicente
    1867-1928
Bojer, Johan 1872-1959
Bosman, Herman Charles
    1905-1951
Bottomley, Gordon 1874-1948
Bourne, George 1863-1927
Broch, Herman 1886-1951
Bromfield, Louis 1896-1956
Buchan, John 1870-1953
Bunin, Ivan 1870-1953
Byrne, Donn (Brian Oswald
    Donn-Byre) 1889-1928
Cabell, James Branch 1879-1958
Caine, Hall 1853-1931
Campana, Dina 1885-1932
Cannan, Gilbert 1884-1955
Capek, Karl 1890-1938
Chapman, John Jay 1862-1933
Churchill, Winston 1871-1947
Corelli, Marie 1855-1924

Corvo, Baron (Frederick William
    Rolfe) 1860-1913
Crane, Stephen 1871-1900
Crawford, F. Marion 1854-1909
Croce, Benedetto 1866-1952
D'Annunzio, Gabriele 1863-1938
Davidson, John 1857-1909
Davis, Rebecca Harding
    1831-1910
Day, Clarence 1874-1935
Delafield, E.M. (Edme Elizabeth
    Monica de la Pasture)
    1890-1943
DeMorgan, William 1839-1917
Doblin, Alfred 1878-1957
Douglas, Lloyd C(assel)
    1877-1951
Douglas, (George) Norman
    1868-1952
Doyle, Sir Arthur Conan
    1859-1930
Dreiser, Theodore 1871-1945
Drinkwater, John 1882-1937
Duun, Olav 1876-1939
Eluard, Pual 1895-1952
Fadeyev, Alexandr 1901-1956
Feydeau, Georges 1862-1921
Field, Michael (Katharine Harris
    Bradley 1846-1914 and Edith
    Emma Cooper 1862-1913)
Field, Rachel 1894-1942
Flecker, James Elroy 1884-1915
France, Anatole (Anatole
    Thibault) 1844-1924
Freeman, John 1880-1929
Giacosa, Giuseppe 1847-1906
Glyn, Elinor 1864-1943
Gogarty, Oliver St. John
    1878-1957
Golding, Louis 1895-1958
Gorky, Maxim 1868-1936
Gosse, Edmund 1849-1928
Gould, Gerald 1885-1936
Grahame, Kenneth 1859-1932
Gray, John 1866-1934
Grey, Zane 1875-1939
Guiraldes, Ricardo 1886-1927
Gumilyov, Nikolay 1886-1921
Gwynne, Stephen Lucius
    1864-1950
Haggard, H(enry) Rider
    1856-1925
Hale, Edward Everett 1822-1909

Hall, (Marguerite) Radclyffe
    1806-1943
Harris, Frank 1856-1931
Hearn, Lafcadio 1850-1904
Hergesheimer, Joseph 1880-1954
Hernandez, Miguel 1910-1942
Herrick, Robert 1868-1938
Hewlett, Maurice 1861-1923
Heyward, DuBose 1885-1940
Hichens, Robert 1864-1950
Hilton, James 1900-1954
Holtby, Winifred 1898-1935
Hope, Anthony 1863-1933
Housman, Laurence 1865-1959
Howard, Sidney 1891-1939
Howells, William Dean
    1837-1920
Hudson, Stephen 1868-1944
Hudson, W(illiam) H(enry)
    1841-1922
Ivanov, Vyacheslav Ivanovich
    1866-1949
Jacob, Max 1876-1944
Jacobs, W(illiam) W(ymark)
    1863-1943
James, M(ontague) R(hodes)
    1862-1936
James, Will 1892-1942
Jerome, Jerome K(lapka)
    1859-1927
Jones, Henry Arthur 1851-1929
Kipling, Rudyard 1865-1936
Kuzmin, Mikhail Alekseyevich
    1875-1936
Lang, Andrew 1844-1912
Lawson, Henry 1867-1922
Leverson, Ada 1862-1933
Lewisohn, Ludwig 1883-1955
Lindsay, (Nicholas) Vachel
    1879-1931
London, Jack 1876-1916
Lonsdale, Frederick 1881-1954
Louys, Pierre 1870-1925
Lowndes, Marie Belloc
    1868-1947
Lowry, Malcolm 1909-1957
Lucas, E(dward) V(errall)
    1868-1938
Lynd, Robert 1879-1949
MacArthur, Charles
    1895-1956
Macaulay, Rose 1881-1958
Manning, Frederic
    1887-1935

Marinetti, Filippo Tommaso
    1876-1944
Marriott, Charles 1869-1957
Martin du Gard, Roger
    1881-1958
Martínez Sierra, Gregorio
    1881-1947
Mencken, H(enry) L(ouis)
    1880-1956
Meredith, George 1828-1909
Meynell, Alice 1847-1922
Milne, A(lan) A(lexander)
    1882-1956
Mistral, Frédéric 1830-1914
Mitchell, Margaret
    1900-1949
Monro, Harold 1879-1932
Moore, George 1852-1933
Moore, Thomas Sturge
    1870-1944
Morgan, Charles 1894-1958
Morley, Christopher
    1890-1957
Murray, (George) Gilbert
    1866-1957
Nervo, Amado 1870-1919
Nietzsche, Friedrich
    1844-1900
Norris, Frank 1870-1902
Noyes, Alfred 1880-1958
Olbracht, Ivan (Kemil
    Zeman) 1882-1952
Orczy, Baroness (Emmuska)
    1865-1947
Pinero, Arthur Wing
    1855-1934
Pontoppidan, Henrik
    1857-1943
Porter, Eleanor H(odgman)
    1868-1920
Porter, Gene(va) Stratton
    1886-1924
Powys, T(heodore) F(rancis)
    1875-1953
Proust, Marcel 1871-1922
Quiller-Couch, Arthur
    1863-1944
Rappoport, Solomon
    1863-1944
Reid, Forrest 1876-1947
Riley, James Whitcomb
    1849-1916
Rinehart, Mary Roberts
    1876-1958

Authors to Appear in Future Volumes

Roberts, Elizabeth Madox
1886-1941
Rölvaag, O(le) E(dvart)
1876-1931
Rolland, Romain 1866-1944
Rostand, Edmond 1868-1918
Roussel, Raymond
1877-1933
Runyon, (Alfred) Damon
1884-1946
Sabatini, Rafael 1875-1950
Santayana, George
1863-1952
Scott, Duncan Campbell
1862-1947
Seeger, Alan 1888-1916
Service, Robert 1874-1958
Seton, Ernest Thompson
1860-1946

Shiel, M(atthew) P(hipps)
1865-1947
Slater, Francis Carey
1875-1958
Sologub, Fyodor 1863-1927
Squire, J(ohn) C(ollings)
1884-1958
Stockton, Frank R.
1834-1902
Supervielle, Jules 1884-1960
Sutro, Alfred 1863-1933
Swinburne, Algernon Charles
1837-1909
Symons, Arthur 1865-1945
Synge, John Millington
1871-1909
Tabb, John Bannister
1845-1909
Tarkington, Booth
1869-1946

Tey, Josephine (Elizabeth
Mackintosh) 1897-1952
Thurman, Wallace
1902-1934
Tsvetaeva, Marina
1892-1941
Turner, W(alter) J(ames)
R(edfern) 1889-1946
Twain, Mark (Samuel
Langhorne Clemens)
1835-1910
Vachell, Horace Annesley
1861-1955
Van Dine, S.S. (Willard H.
Wright) 1888-1939
Van Doren, Carl
1885-1950
Vazov, Ivan 1850-1921
Verne, Jules 1828-1905

Wallace, Edgar 1874-1932
Wallace, Lewis 1827-1905
Wassermann, Jakob
1873-1934
Webb, Mary 1881-1927
Webster, Jean 1876-1916
Welch, Denton 1917-1948
Wells, Carolyn 1869-1942
Wells, H(erbert) G(eorge)
1866-1946
Werfel, Franz 1890-1945
Wister, Owen 1860-1938
Wren, P(ercival)
C(hristopher) 1885-1941
Wylie, Francis Brett
1844-1954
Zamyatin, Yevgeniy
Ivanovich 1884-1937
Zangwill, Israel 1864-1926

Readers are cordially invited to suggest additional authors to the editors.

Henri Barbusse

1873-1935

French novelist, poet, short story writer, essayist, biographer, and journalist.

Barbusse was devoted to pacifism and human rights. He is best known for the harrowing realism of his war novel, *Le feu* (*Under Fire*), but very few of his other works, particularly his later political writings, are available in English.

Barbusse began his literary career as a journalist and a poet. The poems in his first book, *Pleureuses*, were influenced by the aestheticism of the *fin-de-siècle* symbolist poets, and give little indication of the political commitment central to his later works. Barbusse's first novel, *Les suppliants*, like *Pleureuses*, reveals little concern with social problems. Lyrical and semi-autobiographical, it examines the pursuit of happiness and truth.

L'enfer (*Inferno*), Barbusse's first major novel, marked a new stage in his literary development. Breaking from the lyrical concerns of his early works, Barbusse, in *Inferno*, sought a philosophical and moral basis for human life. Influenced by the naturalism of Zola, Barbusse depicts the agony and isolation of modern existence. Pointing to the futility and disappointment inherent in human relationships, *Inferno*'s violent realism yields only pessimism and despair.

Barbusse's World War I experience was crucial to the reorientation of his views. Although he joined the French Army believing patriotically in the righteousness of its cause, he quickly became disillusioned by the filth and horror of war. In his masterpiece, *Under Fire*, Barbusse vividly recalls his life in the trenches and portrays, as no one had before, the realities of modern warfare. Characterized by precise attention to detail, moral fervor, and daring realism, *Under Fire* is praised as one of world literature's most powerful indictments of war.

Under Fire marks the beginning of Barbusse's commitment to world peace and human progress, and indicates the direction of his remaining works. Following the publication of *Clarté* (*Light*), a less successful war novel, Barbusse's writings were motivated entirely by his desire to benefit humanity. He joined the French Communist Party in 1921, and for the remainder of his life devoted himself to ideological writings, including studies of Lenin and Stalin. As Barbusse's writings became increasingly propagandistic and militantly communistic, his literary stature declined. None of Barbusse's postwar works ever received the acclaim of *Under Fire*.

PRINCIPAL WORKS

Pleureuses (poetry) 1895
Les suppliants (novel) 1903
L'enfer (novel) 1908
   [*Inferno*, 1918; published in England as *Hell*, 1966]
Nous autres (short stories) 1914
   [*We Others*, 1918]
Le feu (novel) 1916
   [*Under Fire*, 1917]

Clarté (novel) 1919
   [*Light*, 1919]
Jésus (biography) 1927
   [*Jesus*, 1927]
Staline (biography) 1935

STEPHEN GWYNN (essay date 1917)

[M. Henri Barbusse's *Le Feu*] is a grim book with a vengeance, and what discriminates it from any other that I have read is its entire freedom from convention. . . . [It is not] an improvisation suggested by the truth; [M. Barbusse] has made for the truth itself, and what lies behind it. Of course, the truth is truth as he sees it; the facts are presented under a prepossession, so ranged as to lead to a conclusion, or a group of thoughts—would it otherwise be a work of art? At any rate, of this purpose there is no concealment; the opening pages are symbolic, a kind of vision, and in the last chapter,

An asterisk (*) at the end of a citation indicates the essay is on more than one author.

out of all the desperate realism there comes an echo of this vision and its hope.

Yet so little underlined or explicit is the teaching that a hasty reader might easily accept the book for a casually strung series of episodes and impressions, and fail to detect the underlying motive which gives unity to the whole. Certain things, too, are episodic, illustrations as it were of matters peculiar to France; whereas the whole is in a sense international, or, more properly, human in its outlook. It is a study of Frenchmen at war, yet as the theme progresses it is seen with how little difference the whole could be true of Germans. (p. 805)

How far [his] interpretation of the common soldier's mind will be accepted by those for whom M. Barbusse speaks, I cannot say. . . . But this I do know—that he does not and cannot, even with his Southern's special hatred of that muddy watery torment, overstate the greatness and the obscurity of their sacrifice. And if in all his book there is no trace of flinching, the reason is, first, that he rings true to France; but secondly and chiefly that, knowing what war means to the man on the firestep, he holds to his faith that the man on the firestep will make an end of war. (p. 817)

> *Stephen Gwynn, "The Man on the Firestep" (reprinted by permission of the Estate of Stephen Gwynn), The Nineteenth-Century, No. CCCCLXXXVIII, October, 1917, pp. 803-17.*

FRANCIS HACKETT   (essay date 1917)

It is unnecessary to have been at the front to judge of M. Barbusse's veracity. One does not need to have killed a woman to accept *Crime and Punishment. Under Fire* . . . impresses its veracity in revealing its saturation with the war. There are other experiences of the war, as there are other men, but this is invincibly complete. It is a book that is no more to be questioned than the diary of Captain Scott or the deathless pages of Tolstoy. It composes the war for our understanding, making us familiar at the beginning with the men who are going to die, initiating us into trench life before the charge is launched over the top, ending the book in a supreme symbolism. But the wise composition that unites *Under Fire* is no more artificial than the due supervision of words as they stream from one's own brain to the penpoint. The facts have been disposed, even as a pointilliste disposes colors, only to keep them true.

Against the tale that M. Barbusse has told there is the conspiracy of a thousand conventions. He is a Frenchman fighting for France, la belle France, in what many consider the last extremity of her effort to remain a "first-class" power. To sustain that effort it is vital, even if untruth is required, to give a good account of the organization of the army and its esprit. . . . A good patriot is not supposed to tell the world of filth, of lice, of corpses in ridiculous attitudes, of bad food, of muck in language, of bloodshed sought and enjoyed. If a man tells these things or breathes a word contrary to the unanimity of national purpose, he is treasonable. The facts are of no consequence. The impossibility of keeping them suppressed is of no consequence. If the sun rises on a national delinquency or ineptitude, it is the sun that is treasonable. From the guns of such a conspiracy M. Barbusse is also under fire.

But when one has faced machine-guns, it appears, it is not impossible to face machine-minds. One can feel in M. Barbusse a disdain for those feeble men of Europe who, within boundaries insisted upon by themselves, brought about a war that is the crashing bankruptcy of all their theories, all their pretensions, their idols, their sanctity. . . . [They] ask M. Barbusse to take his mind from the actuality he has experienced, and disregard the war as a harvest of their statesmanship. But the author of *Under Fire* is too sure of war not to be sure of something about peace which is more than nonwar. He is for peace, not a peace that will save his own skin now but a peace that will be embodied in the plans of a society which takes full stock of its own bestiality, its own madness.

It is not the picturesque beginning of this book that lets one see M. Barbusse the accusant of war. He is content at the beginning to give us the mucky trench, the rag-bag cave-dwellers who are his comrades, the Falstaffian humor of their masculinity, the jocularity that is the jewel in the toad. . . . It is at [the] point, perhaps, with the disaster to Poterloo, that one is gripped by the inhuman remorselessness of all too human device.

No description of bombardment surpasses M. Barbusse's, even in translation. And no description of going forward, so it seems to me, can equal his chapter *Under Fire*. To quote from it is unfair. It is like giving one stilled picture of a terrific movement. (p. 358)

[Only by] profound acceptance of his comrades is M. Barbusse enabled to speak as he does in the concluding chapter, and also in that moment of superb magnanimity at the end of the advance when the dignified Bertrand permits himself to say, "It was necessary." . . .

It was necessary! One does not doubt that M. Barbusse has himself said so, in the face of all it means. But in the domicile that his mind gives this war there is no mysticism, no patriotism, no acquiescence. He knows that the war is evil. He has accepted it as the lesser of two evils. His book is great because it is able to encompass everything, even the necessity of living by dying. (p. 359)

> *Francis Hackett, "A War of Men," in The New Republic (© 1917 The New Republic, Inc.), Vol. 12, No. 156, October 27, 1917, pp. 358-59.*

ROBERT HERRICK   (essay date 1918)

[Barbusse's **"Le Feu"** is] the most searching, the most revealing statement of what modern war means both morally and physically. The book has all those intimate signs of truth that carry immediate conviction even to him who has had no personal experience with which to corroborate its record (as all vital literature convinces—as Dostoevsky or Gorky convince millions who know nothing personally about Russia and Russians). I have read many books, private as well as published diaries, which attempt to reveal what men suffer and endure in this most hateful of all wars. Not one of them— and there are many honest revelations, unaffected, simple, and sincere efforts to put into words the meaning of this monstrous calamity—has approached **"Le Feu"** in perception, in sheer capacity for truth. Nothing since heard or read has effaced its stinging impression. Others deal with familiar surfaces, with personal and incomplete reactions, often noble and sensitive, humorous and philosophical; but Barbusse gives the thing itself—War. (p. 133)

Barbusse has shown us soldiers, not only as dirty and un-idealistic, degraded by the occupation to which they are condemned, but also as too obviously the blind sport of life—human sacrifices of human society, killing and being killed in a war that is insanity, whose origin and conclusion they cannot affect. (pp. 133-34)

[What] Barbusse believes and what the person who thinks in terms of newspaper and politician formulae cannot see, is that War is most of all an awful process of religious conversion through which the minds of all men will be awakened to the recognition of supreme sin. It must drag on its dreary, blood-stained course until all whose selfish, thoughtless conduct in times of peace, all grasping and power-loving statesmen, journalists, business men, indifferents, have received sufficient vision to recognize their errors, which cause wars. (p. 134)

> *Robert Herrick, "Unromantic War," in* The Dial *(copyright, 1918, by The Dial Publishing Company, Inc.), Vol. LXIV, No. 760, February 14, 1918, pp. 133-34.*

LOLA RIDGE (essay date 1918)

Seen through that opacity that training and environment spreads before them like a curtain, men are essentially alike. This is a truth Barbusse brings out in *The Inferno* as well as in his famous book *Under Fire*. And not only in the debate between the doctors, where even the old traditionalist admits: "man is more closely knit to man than to his vague compatriots," and that "the cult of the fatherland" is the cancer of the world, but in the mere depiction of the vivid and flitting characters of *The Inferno*. For these French souls grope in barren spaces, clutching and rebuffing each other, bored and unhappy as Chekhov's Russians. Totally unlike the Slav writer in temperament and style, Barbusse yet sees with him eye to eye.

How often one walking at night stares avidly at curtained windows, longing to open those crystal cases where life burns so secretly, and watch the gesticulating figures in the abandon of their unconsciousness.

This is what Barbusse's *Inferno* has done.

Through a hole in the cracked plaster of the wall, he watches the people that come and go in the room with its common furniture "and the window like a human face against the sky." (p. 262)

In reading *The Inferno* one somehow thinks of [Frank] Swinnerton's *Nocturne*—perhaps because he, too, sounds, though not so poignantly, that note of eternal isolation. But we see Mr. Swinnerton's extraordinarily vivid characters as through an open door, and we are conscious always of the rank opacity of their flesh. The Frenchman's creations are like naked spirits—spirits seen through the pale luminosity of that *I* that enfolds them like an aura. This astounding ego encompasses and absorbs all that it envisions. The result is that we do not look through "a hole in the wall" at substantial people walking about, but through the lighted rift in a soul where strangely glowing shadows pass and repass. . . .

Eternal isolation, and yet eternal miracle—immensity within us—all the vast circumference of life, and all divine that

is. . . . This is the essence of the author's final illumination. If it be true, men are lonely Gods, incapable of fusing with each other, yet each seeking completion in the outward shadow of what lies within. And so it would seem that there can be no end to the human conflict, but that souls must go on crashing into each other's orbits like contending worlds. (p. 263)

> *Lola Ridge, "A Book of Souls," in* The New Republic *(© 1918 The New Republic, Inc.), Vol. 16, No. 204, September 28, 1918, pp. 262-63.*

JOHN MANNING BOOKER (essay date 1919)

Americans consumed [Henri Barbusse's] *Under Fire* by the tens of thousands; thrilled, throbbed, and ached over it; went the full length of its implication that all was wrong with the world; and would, perhaps, have fallen into its melancholia had they not set about putting things to rights.

What will they make of the stories written in peace times by the same author—such as those in *We Others*? (p. 146)

[These] stories of pity that Barbusse has written either throw a pitiful object against a pitiless world or reveal pity awakening in a hardened nature (the awakening is generally caused by a stroke of apoplexy—a rather radical cure). In both cases the reader is led to turn from the pity of a particular instance to face the pity of life in general.

Such a quality of pity may be typical of modern French literature or it may be exceptional in it: that is not our present concern. In English literature such pity is exceptional, and it is on English literature that the American reader is reared. He meets in Barbusse a kind of pity that for him is even more of a depressant than a purgative, and, therefore, distasteful. He turns away from it with the feeling that these stories of pity do not match experience.

And he will turn away from the whole of such a collection of stories as *We Others* with the same feeling. You cannot make him believe that Fate always works unhappily, that the madness of love always ends tragically, that pity always remains unconsoled—in short, that life is such a desperately sad affair. The pessimism in which *Under Fire* is steeped is justified by the catastrophic nature of the war that gave it birth. The average American will accept that pessimism as a war product, but he will not accept it in peace. It does not match his experience—actual or imaginative. He will "pass it up." (pp. 147-48)

> *John Manning Booker, "Barbusse in Peace and War," in* The New Republic *(© 1919 The New Republic, Inc.), Vol. 20, No. 252, September 3, 1919, pp. 146-48.*

MALCOLM COWLEY (essay date 1922)

There is something a little paradoxical in the attitude of Henri Barbusse toward the war [in his novel **"Under Fire."**] He hates it as much as St. Augustine hated the Devil, and yet the war was his salvation. Not because it made his name a common-place all over the world—fame has affected him very little—but because it resolved his difficulties as a man and as a writer. The books he wrote before 1914 were so blackly pessimistic that Schopenhauer beside them seems a booster for the Rotary Club. They deny every possibility of happiness; they deny even the reality of the world. They are nightmares, dreamed by a great artist. **"Under Fire"** may also be a nightmare, but after reading it one feels that some things are good: work, comradeship, peace. And by 1919, when he wrote **"Clarté"**, Barbusse had come to believe in the possiblity of a better world, a possibility that is even now within the grasp of struggling mortals. He had received a new vision of life, and he owed it to his experiences in the trenches. (p. 180)

Barbusse is irritated when he hears himself dismissed as a propagandist. He says, for example, "I never intended 'Under Fire' for propaganda. My enemies made it political, and not my friends." On the other hand he will never write a book without some bearing on contemporary ideas. "The sort of literature", he says, "that exists in a fourth dimension and has no connection with modern life: 'pure literature', as people call it, is dead. But the literature of ideas is always living."

He has a surprising sympathy with the experiments of younger writers. Most novelists who call themselves "advanced" are content to be advanced in politics alone; their prose has developed no further than that of Voltaire or Macaulay. Examples are numerous. Anatole France is by far the greatest. . . . That is not the fashion of Barbusse. He watches with interest each new experiment in prose or verse, and even makes bold experiments himself. "It is ridiculous", he says, "to try to cast the present age into molds which we have inherited from the eighteenth century." (p. 182)

> *Malcolm Cowley, "Henri Barbusse," in* The Bookman, *New York (copyright, 1922, by George H. Doran Company), Vol. LVI, No. 2, October, 1922, pp. 180-82.*

BRIAN RHYS (essay date 1926)

[Henri Barbusse's first book, *Pleureuses*, is] a slender volume of verses. Slight, light even, delicately artificial, they take us into the atmosphere of the drawing-room; it would be difficult indeed to find here any trace of the real Barbusse. (p. viii)

In *Les Suppliants* we are at the parting of the ways. The young man relives the sensitive, reluctant hours of his childhood, but the emotion so long pent up begins to flow in a rhythmical prose, surcharged with poetic imagery. . . . [In *L'Enfer* Barbusse] declares his fierce and sombre powers, affirms himself as a poetic realist. . . . *L'Enfer (Inferno)* is a terrible book. At first glance it might be taken for one of those *livres hardis* which constantly appear to prick on the Parisian's appetite for sensation. The theme frankly lends itself to the crude naturalism of a Zola. . . .

Its violent realism only ends in emptiness and blackness of mind. (p. ix)

[In *Nous Autres* (*We Others*)] a number of short stories are brought together and grouped under three headings: Fate, the Madness of Love, Pity. Barbusse does not reveal himself as a master in the art of the short story. Those in the first section are violent, rapid in surprise, often improbable. In the second, however, there are one or two—*The True Judge*, for instance—that a Guy de Maupassant might have approached from a slightly different angle and worked out to an inevitable close. In the third section Barbusse seems at first surer of himself and is near to abandoning realism. But in the later pages the story tends to dwindle away and become

a moral. We are reminded that mere artistry never appealed to Barbusse. . . .

We are far away enough now from [World War I]. It is time to look back dispassionately to the books which were written then, and to separate the true from the dross. The conviction comes that *Under Fire* will remain on record as the greatest novel of its kind. Other books seem to tell us *about* war, about our emotions in war-time. *Under Fire is* war. In the trenches Barbusse finds himself. The noise and horror seem to give calmness and counterpoise to his mind. The tenderness that was unexpressed in childhood and marriage finds its object in the men—the children—who live and suffer around him. These men do not think, talk, laugh or feel as we do; their very irritations are not ours. They seem to have been fighting for years. They have none of our illusions about bravery; and though they can pay passing homage to the man who dies for an idea, they do not waste words on patriotism. But when their sufferings are past human endurance, cries burst from their lips, and they curse their destiny. (pp. xi-xii)

[The] picture is carefully, admirably composed; it spares us some of the "raggedness" of modern warfare, though none of its fearful intensity. Yet there is a noble restraint in the words that Barbusse places at the end of this book: "If the present war has advanced progress by one step, its miseries and slaughter will count but little." (p. xii)

> *Brian Rhys, in his introduction to* Under Fire *by Henri Barbusse (copyright 1947 by J. M. Dent & Sons, Ltd.), Dent, 1926, pp. vii-xii.*

HENRI BARBUSSE (essay date 1927)

My purpose [in writing the biography *Jesus*] was . . . to address myself to the restless and tormented spirits of our own age—an age in which the march of economic and social events, of political and moral events, is inciting man to follow a sacred example which he has been permitted only to glimpse, and to become a breaker of idols.

My purpose was to display, for the sake of all those who live in waiting, the great parallel which can be rigorously drawn between the decadence of our own world, now at its summit of material progress, and that of the ancient world; between the beginnings of Christianity and the new levers which are setting themselves to raise the universe. (p. 11)

> *Henri Barbusse, in his note to his* Jesus, *translated by Solon Librescot with Malcolm Cowley (copyright, 1927, by The Macaulay Company), Macaulay, 1927, pp. 9-13.*

COLIN WILSON (essay date 1956)

At first sight, the Outsider is a social problem. He is the hole-in-corner man.

> In the air, on top of a tram, a girl is sitting.
> Her dress, lifted a little, blows out. But a block
> in the traffic separates us. The tramcar glides
> away, fading like a nightmare.
>
> Moving in both directions, the street is full
> of dresses which sway, offering themselves
> airily, the skirts lifting; dresses that lift and
> yet do not lift.

In the tall and narrow shop mirror I see myself
approaching, rather pale and heavy-eyed. It
is not a woman I want—it is *all* women, and
I seek for them in those around me, one by
one. . . .

This passage, from Henri Barbusse's novel *L'Enfer*, pinpoints
certain aspects of the Outsider. His hero walks down a Paris
street, and the desires that stir in him separate him sharply
from other people. And the need he feels for a woman is not
entirely animal either, for he goes on:

Defeated, I followed by impulse casually. I
followed a woman who had been watching me
from her corner. Then we walked side by side.
We said a few words; she took me home with
her. . . . Then I went through the banal scene.
It passed like a sudden hurtling-down.

Again, I am on the pavement, and I am not
at peace as I had hoped. An immense confusion bewilders me. It is as if I could not see
things as they were. *I see too deep and too
much.*

Throughout the book, this hero remains unnamed. He is the
anonymous Man Outside.

He comes to Paris from the country; he finds a position in
a bank; he takes a room in a 'family hotel'. Left alone in his
room, he meditates: He has 'no genius, no mission to fulfil,
no remarkable feelings to bestow. I have nothing and I deserve nothing. Yet in spite of it, I desire some sort of recompense.' Religion . . . he doesn't care for it. 'As to philosophic discussions, they seem to me altogether meaningless.
Nothing can be tested, nothing verified. Truth—what do they
mean by it?' His thoughts range vaguely from a past love
affair and its physical pleasures to death: 'Death, that is the
most important of all ideas. Then back to his living problems:
'I must make money.' He notices a light high up on his wall;
it is coming from the next room. He stands on the bed and
looks through the spy-hole. . . . (pp. 11-12)

The action of the novel begins. Daily, he stands on the bed
and stares at the life that comes and goes in the next room.
For the space of a month he watches it, standing apart and,
symbolically, above. His first vicarious adventure is to watch
a woman who has taken the room for the night; he excites
himself to hysteria watching her undress. These pages of the
book have the kind of deliberate sensationalism that its descendants in post-war France were so consistently to be
accused of (so that Guido Ruggiero could write: 'Existentialism treats life in the manner of a thriller').

But the point is to come. The next day he tries to recreate
the scene in imagination, but it evades him, just as his attempt
to recreate the sexual pleasures with his mistress had evaded
him:

I let myself be drawn into inventing details
to recapture the intensity of the experience.
'She put herself into the most inviting positions.'

No, no, that is not true.

These words are all dead. They leave untouched, *powerless to affect it, the intensity
of what was.*

At the end of *L'Enfer*, its nameless hero is introduced to a
novelist who is entertaining the company with an account
of a novel he is writing. A coincidence . . . it is about a man
who pierces a hole in his wall and spies on all that happens
in the next room. The writer recounts all of the book he has
written; his listeners admire it: Bravo! Tremendous success!
But the Outsider listens gloomily. 'I, who had penetrated
into the very heart of mankind and returned, could see nothing human in this pantomimic caricature. It was so superficial
that it was fake.' The novelist expounds: 'Man stripped of
his externals . . . that is what I wish to show. Others stand
for imagination . . . I stand for truth.' The Outsider feels that
what he has seen *is* truth.

Admittedly, for us, reading the novel half a century after it
was written, there is not so much to choose between the
novelist's truth and the hero's. The 'dramas' enacted in the
next room remind us sometimes of Sardou, sometimes of
Dostoevsky when he is more concerned to expound an idea
than to give it body in people and events. Yet Barbusse is
sincere, and this ideal, to 'stand for truth', is the one discernible current that flows through all twentieth-century literature.

Barbusse's Outsider has all of the characteristics of the type.
Is he an Outsider because he's frustrated and neurotic? Or
is he neurotic because of some deeper instinct that pushes
him into solitude? He is preoccupied with sex, with crime,
with disease. (pp. 12-13)

The Outsider's case against society is very clear. All men
and women have these dangerous, unnamable impulses, yet
they keep up a pretence, to themselves, to others; their respectability, their philosophy, their religion, are all attempts
to gloss over, to make look civilized and rational something
that is savage, unorganized, irrational. He is an Outsider
because he stands for Truth.

That is his case. But it is weakened by his obvious abnor-
mality, his introversion. It looks, in fact, like an attempt at
self-justification by a man who knows himself to be degenerate, diseased, self-divided. There is certainly self-division.
The man who watches a woman undressing has the red eyes
of an ape; yet the man who sees two young lovers, really
alone for the first time, who brings out all the pathos, the
tenderness and uncertainty when he tells about it, is no brute;
he is very much human. And the ape and the man exist in
one body; and when the ape's desires are about to be fulfilled,
he disappears and is succeeded by the man, who is disgusted
with the ape's appetites.

This is the problem of the Outsider. (pp. 13-14)

Barbusse has suggested that it is the fact that his hero *sees
deeper* that makes him an Outsider; at the same time, he
states that he has 'no special genius, no message to bestow',
etc., and from his history during the remainder of the book,
we have no reason to doubt his word. Indubitably, the hero
is mediocre; he can't write for toffee, and the whole book
is full of clichés. It is necessary to emphasize this in order
to rid ourselves of the temptation to identify the Outsider
with the artist, and so to oversimplify the question: disease
or insight? Many great artists have none of the characteristics
of the Outsider. (p. 14)

Barbusse has shown us that the Outsider is a man who cannot
live in the comfortable, insulated world of the bourgeois,
accepting what he sees and touches as reality. 'He sees too

deep and too much', and what he sees is essentially *chaos*. For the bourgeois, the world is fundamentally an orderly place, with a disturbing element of the irrational, the terrifying, which his preoccupation with the present usually permits him to ignore. For the Outsider, the world is not rational, not orderly. When he asserts his sense of anarchy in the face of the bourgeois' complacent acceptance, it is not simply the need to cock a snook at respectability that provokes him; it is a distressing sense *that truth must be told at all costs,* otherwise there can be no hope for an ultimate restoration of order. Even if there seems no room for hope, truth must be told.... The Outsider is a man who has awakened to chaos. He may have no reason to believe that chaos is positive, the germ of life (in the Kabbala, chaos . . . is simply a state in which order is latent; the egg is the 'chaos' of the bird); in spite of this, truth must be told, chaos must be faced. (p. 15)

[Like the protagonists of other modern novels, such as Roquentin of Sartre's *La Nausée,* Barbusse's Outsider] alone is aware of the truth, and if all men were aware of it, there would be an end of life. In the country of the blind, the one-eyed man is king. But his kingship is kingship over nothing. It brings no powers and privileges, only loss of faith and exhaustion of the power to act. Its world is a world without values.

This is the position that Barbusse's Outsider has brought us to. It was already explicit in that desire that stirred as he saw the swaying dresses of the women; for what he wanted was not sexual intercourse, but some indefinable freedom, of which the women, with their veiled and hidden nakedness, are a symbol. Sexual desire was there, but not alone; aggravated, blown-up like a balloon, by a resentment that stirred in revolt against the bewilderment of hurrying Paris with its well-dressed women. 'Yet in spite of this I desire some compensation.' In spite of the civilization that has impressed his insignificance on him until he is certain that 'he has nothing and he deserves nothing', in spite of this he feels a right to . . . to what? Freedom? It is a misused word. We examine *L'Enfer* in vain for a definition of it. (p. 26)

The Outsider tends to express himself in Existentialist terms. He is not very concerned with the distinction between body and spirit, or man and nature; these ideas produce theological thinking and philosophy; he rejects both. For him, the only important distinction is between being and nothingness. Barbusse's hero: 'Death, that is the most important of all ideas.'. . .

Barbusse's approach can be called the 'empirical'. His hero is not a thinker; he accepts *living*; it is its values he cannot accept. (p. 27)

> *Colin Wilson, "The Country of the Blind" and "World without Values," in his* The Outsider *(copyright © 1956 by Colin Wilson; reprinted by permission of Houghton Mifflin Company), Houghton, 1956, pp. 11-26, 27-46.**

MARTIN SHUTTLEWORTH   (essay date 1966)

[In *Hell*, Barbusse demonstrates that] men are lonely and lost, but also that man is magnificent; that he carries his remedy within him. For Barbusse this remedy was political: somehow mankind should get together, because there is no God; because the universe is terrible. This is the cry of a tormented man who is trying to find a political answer to a question that he is asking despite himself in religious terms. *Au Feu,* his book about the trenches, is an even more tormented cry. Barbusse is a deeply unsettling writer, because he is just not quite a great one: if you deny the existence of God; describe man as a God, then put all the blame for the predicament he is in on a God you protest does not exist, something, somewhere, has gone wrong with your logic. But, logic or no logic, his books remain among the most passionate and sincere cries against the tears of things that have risen from the earth this century.

> *Martin Shuttleworth, "Old and New Novels: 'Hell'," in* Punch *(© 1966 by Punch Publications Ltd.; all rights reserved; may not be reprinted without permission), Vol. CCLI, No. 6568, July 27, 1966, p. 162.*

JOHN DANIEL   (essay date 1966)

[*Hell,* by Henri Barbusse,] is sex as Divine Service, Apocalyptic Revelation and all. . . . [It] tells how a young bank clerk staying in a hotel finds a hole in his bedroom wall, through which he watches the occupants in the next room. This promising beginning is unfortunately the last touch of realism in the novel. Everything happens in the next room, and it happens in a semi-mystical prose that becomes increasingly more gorgeous. The steady parade of adulterers, lesbians, fumbling adolescents, old men and young women is sadly unerotic, and hardly discernible through the philosophy. A woman gives birth to a child; a man dies; a priest storms over religious truth and a poet reads a full-length epic poem.

What were breathtaking assertions against patriotism and Catholicism have gathered dust, and even the long descriptions of women undressing have a coy and perverted flavour. It is understandable that the sight of a human knee in 1908 was worth half a page, but one can't help feeling that the author's paeans to eternal beauty owe a lot to the prudery of the bourgeoisie. Still, the book was scandalous at the time . . . and retains a period interest.

> *John Daniel, "Rake's Progress," in* The Spectator *(© 1966 by* The Spectator; *reprinted by permission of* The Spectator*), Vol. 217, No. 7207, August 12, 1966, p. 210.**

THE TIMES LITERARY SUPPLEMENT   (essay date 1966)

Barbusse's first reactions to the martyrdom of man were concerned, in his own words, more with harmony than precision. In the poems of *Les Pleureuses* . . . , having taken stock of the miseries and disappointments of earthly life he retreats, as the age rather demanded, into the twilight of a bedroom or the shade of a fountain, to sing, but not too loudly, of his sadness. With such certainty did the young poet depress all the right keys it was inevitable that the clubbable Symbolists of the day should shuffle a little closer together on their sacred slopes in order to make room for him. . . .

[But] of course there are signs in *Les Pleureuses* of the ambition that ultimately turned Barbusse into an embattled director of consciences. . . . [In] some of the poems he looks forward to the day when an "implacable" truth may be asked of him, and when he will be able to speak on behalf of the inarticulate, a precise forecast of his relationship to the human material of his best-known book *Le Feu*. . . . Even at this stage Barbusse could not write like a man wholly trapped within the neurotic limits of his pessimism, but turned his sense of futility into a sort of narrative, making it that much more exemplary. . . .

Yet even when he produced his first novel, *Les Suppliants* . . . , he had found no sort of philosophy that offered to transform a sick world, still seen as independent of the afflicted mind. His young hero, Maximilien Desanzac, the useless luxury of whose name shows which way the wind was still blowing for Barbusse, is secure in his belief that his bourgeois environment can never be changed. . . .

Read simply as a novel, in isolation of what came before and after, [*L'Enfer* (*Hell*)] is rather forbidding, thick with the cobwebs of an earlier mannerism, but seen as a bridge between the torments of decadence and the simplicities of Revolution, *Hell* becomes of great interest. It contains all Barbusse's old disgust with the ways of God and of a majority of men, but the assault is made with a new ferocity and a new precision. For all that the social topography of the book is so vague and the conversations so tiringly biblicized, *Hell* has a far more direct revelance to an actual state of society than anything Barbusse had written before. But above all *Hell* was an important book for Barbusse because in it he brings Heaven down to Earth (and Hell, one might add, up to it). He exposes with force the conjuring trick of our emotions, whereby we can cause the present moment to vanish between regret for the past and hope for the future. In *Hell* Barbusse rivets his attention finally on the possibilities of the here and now, and rejects the ephemeral and self-indulgent policies of the heart for the more enduring ones of the intelligence.

There is a sound reason then why this novel should contain a lot of what one critic called "exasperated sensuality." . . .

What matters about the sensuality in *Hell* is that it *is* exasperated, that sex is here shown at the end of its tether. . . . Barbusse is out to tour the limits of sensual possibility because he wants to work out a final equation between the love life and the transience of all emotions. . . .

Hell is intended to show the fraud of basing our life on an emotional involvement with another individual, for such a relationship will oscillate between expectation and regret. Barbusse makes the same point perhaps more succinctly at the end of *Clarté*, where the acknowledgment of Simon Paulin that he no longer feels sexual desire for his wife, together with the confession of all his adulteries, immediately precedes the statement of his new-found socialism. Barbusse would say that this is what facing the truth about life entails.

What he has done with his hole in the wall in *Hell* of course is to try and cloak with plausibility the old, more openly magical devices used in the past to convince us that now we are seeing people as they really are. In his other books he seeks the same conviction with interesting variations or repetitions of this particular structure. *Le Feu* for example begins and ends with chapters that barely even nod in the direction of realism, "La Vision" and "L'Aube". In the first the imminent war is seen from on high by the patients in a Swiss sanatorium, in the second Barbusse's own hopes for the postwar period are orchestrated into a litany for anonymous French and German voices, scattered on isolated mounds of earth in flooded Flanders. Throughout the book the soldiers are shown merging helplessly with the mud and dark of the battlefields, capable only of the partial view of those who have indoctrinated them. The writer's job is to make them see, and so he finally frees them from their prison and places them where they can glimpse the dawn. . . .

[*Le Feu*] contains one or two other peculiar episodes which go right to the heart of [Barbusse's] final philosophy of how we should live. There is the magical adventure of a soldier called Poterloo, for instance. . . . Learning that his wife is now in a town just behind the German lines Poterloo contrives to see her. He achieves the necessary invisibility with a German uniform, procured for him by some Alsatian troops in the lines opposite, and enters the town at night. Through a window he sees into a lighted room where his wife, together with the widow of one of his regimental comrades, is sitting laughing with two German soldiers. Poterloo of course does not intervene, but his first disgust is suddenly replaced by a sort of exaltation, which sustains him into his death a day or two later. He has had a vision of inconstancy but also one of the irresistible resurgence of life; he has made the simple discovery that the real enemy in war is war itself, and not another army, that the real confrontation is between life and death. Like the narrator of *Hell* Poterloo has been shown the truth because he has been reduced for a moment to a single way of communicating with the world, through his eyes, the one organ that can be asked to turn chaos into geometry.

The intuition which Barbusse's privileged bystanders have is one of simplicity. Those who groan that life is so complicated are really making an excuse for keeping things as they are. Injustice comes in two forms; it is built into a universe that is not run the way we would run it, and it is present in the exploitation of one man by another. Barbusse clearly believed that if everyone became properly aware of the injustice we have got to accept then they would work together to suppress that which we could easily avoid. It is therefore the darkness that surrounds and mocks our aspirations which makes us divine and which ought to make us active revolutionaries. But if the revolution is to come we must give up the sterile complacency of worthy feelings and choose the pragmatism of reason. In *Hell* Barbusse swims far enough down to be overcome now and again by rapture of the deep, and so it is when he finally consecrates the human mind, in a thumping profession of philosophical idealism, which strips the divinity from Jesus Christ and bestows it on Kant.

> *"Militant Pulpiteer," in* The Times Literary Supplement *(© Times Newspapers Ltd. (London) 1966; reproduced from* The Times Literary Supplement *by permission), No. 3377, November 17, 1966, p. 1044.*

FRANK FIELD (essay date 1975)

[Barbusse's] work in the period before 1914 . . . is nearer in spirit to the tortured existentialism of the German Expressionists than to the harrowing, but ordered, world of the French Naturalists. This can be seen in the novel with which Barbusse made his greatest impact on the French literary scene in the years before the outbreak of the First World War, *L'Enfer*. . . . (p. 31)

Barbusse makes it clear that man's solitude in the universe is the source of his grandeur as well as of his misery, and there are passages in *L'Enfer* in which the author indicates that in a certain sense men *can* achieve some kind of fraternity if they experience suffering or if they are willing to use their powers of reason to recognise the fundamental absurdity of their existence. There are also passages which show that Barbusse was not entirely lacking in views on political questions. . . . In the years before 1914 Barbusse subscribed to a vague form of anarchistic socialism and a vague form of pacifism but he had little confidence that the rest of mankind could ever emancipate itself from its selfishness and greed. (p. 32)

It must be admitted that, partly because of the haste with which it was written, *Le Feu* is not the kind of book that can greatly impress the present-day reader. Despite the visionary power that the novel still retains, its style seems over-emphatic, its characterisation two-dimensional, and its plot difficult to follow. The propagandist element in the novel, an element which becomes particularly prominent in the closing chapters where Barbusse entirely abandons the techniques of Naturalism for a kind of Expressionism, is yet a further factor which helps to explain why it has lost much of its original appeal. Barbusse's contemporaries might have acclaimed *Le Feu* as the first successful attempt made by a writer to depict the First World War in truthful terms. What strikes the reader of today, however, is the way in which the book combines a great deal of indisputably authentic and realistic detail with passages of undisguised rhetoric, rhetoric which, far from enhancing the impact of the author's message, positively diminishes it. (p. 38)

At first sight Simon Paulin, the hero of the novel *Clarté*, is very similar to the leading character of *L'Enfer* in feeling himself to be a victim of the soullessness that characterised bourgeois society before 1914, a mere cog in a social machine that destroys love and understanding between human beings. But whereas *L'Enfer* ends on a note of despair the atmosphere of the closing chapters of *Clarté* is quite different. By now in fact Barbusse is an openly propagandist writer. Paulin is caught up on the First World War and although he is at first appalled by the brutality that he witnesses he eventually comes to realise that his experience has been a blessing in disguise: by uniting with his fellow soldiers in the struggle against militarism he can at last experience that sense of human brotherhood that had eluded him in the past. (p. 47)

In *Jésus* and *Les Judas de Jésus* (and in the unpublished play *Jésus contre Dieu* which he wrote at the same time) he attempted to demonstrate that a distinction should be made between the idea of 'the Christ', a theological abstraction invented by St Paul in order to prove that the founder of Christianity had been the Son of God, and Jesus the man who was a revolutionary atheist and rationalist whose primary concern had been that of alleviating the lot of the poor and the downtrodden. Once this essential distinction is made, Barbusse argued, the activities of Jesus became more comprehensible to modern man. Jesus appeared at a point in time when the corrupt and evil society of the Ancient World was in the process of disintegration—just as the capitalist world was moving towards its final collapse in the twentieth century. Seen in this light there were many parallels between the early Christians and the present-day Communists: both were groups of men who were determined to overthrow the existing order and to replace it by one founded on justice. (p. 67)

Perhaps it was in *Jésus* and in the collection of short stories that he published . . . under the title of *Force* that Barbusse most clearly revealed the nature of the fear that haunted him.

In *Jésus*, which he dedicated 'to all the troubled and tormented souls of our time,' he makes it plain that even if all the material problems of the poor were capable of solution men would still be lonely and unhappy, and in *Force* he gave an even more unambiguous statement of his conviction that the misery of the human condition is irremediable. (pp. 75-6)

Frank Field, "Henri Barbusse and Communism," in his Three French Writers and the Great War: Studies in the Rise of Communism and Fascism *(© Cambridge University Press 1975), Cambridge University Press, 1975, pp. 19-78.*

JONATHAN KING (essay date 1976)

Barbusse's *Le Feu* marks a key moment in [the development of social realist fiction]. The writer who wished to provide some kind of realist treatment of the First World War was confronted with . . . problems in a peculiarly concentrated form. The masses were now present in vast numbers as protagonists in the outcome of history. The worker, the peasant, the bureaucrat was lifted out of his normal environment and made the lynchpin of the various armies. Not so much tactical brilliance or technological superiority, but the sheer weight of numbers would largely determine the outcome of this war. On the other hand, this most plebeian and democratic of wars was also the most obviously apocalyptic, representing, in both its material and spiritual aspects, a genuine crisis of civilisation, not just another shifting of pieces in the diplomatic chess game of Europe. . . . [The] writer—novelist or poet—found himself, due to the sociological promiscuity implicit in a mass conscript army, at very close quarters with representatives of those strata of society which previously may have formed the object of rather more detached 'research'. His record of the war would tend simultaneously toward documentary and toward epic, his style oscillate between the demotic and the matter-of-fact required by documentary, and the symbolic and visionary required by his sense of proximity to the apocalypse. . . .

Barbusse's novel contains what can almost be thought of as two separate pieces of literature: a documentary about men at war and a poem about the landscape of war, much as [Emile Zola's] *Germinal* is both a documentary about the life of miners and a poem about destruction and fecundity. But Barbusse was less able than Zola to maintain an organic connection between the two, because the dualism of his material was more extreme. (p. 46)

What artist would be capable of conveying the wholeness of the experience, of encompassing within a single style what the soldiers did individually and the consequences of their actions as a mass? Where was the connection between the mundane humanity of the ordinary soldier's response to war and the destruction the war was bringing to life and to nature? The stylistic duality of *Le Feu* reflects the difficulty of expressing the connection, if indeed the connection exists.

To convey the horrific landscape of trench warfare Barbusse employs an imagery and a vocabulary which are highly figurative, tending always away from description towards symbolism; while to convey the way of life of the soldiers he uses a style which is objective and colloquial. Landscape and men—the tableaux which make up *Le Feu* alternate regularly between the two. Descriptions of actual combat are comparatively rare.

And yet the landscape is formed in part from the flesh and bone of the soldiers themselves. As, on the morning after an engagement, the dawn casts some light on the battlefield, the sentries glimpse the petrified remains of their fellow soldiers.... The vocabulary becomes increasingly figurative and employs more and more conventionally 'literary' images.... (pp. 47-8)

Pestilence and flood—the archetypal images of disaster and punishment—lend to the descriptions their intensely apocalyptic tone.... The ground between the trenches is an 'unearthly resting-place', a naked arm protrudes from the mud, the arm of a soldier drowned before he could move out of his shell-hole....

A war where the soldier may as easily die from drowning as from gunfire obviously has an unprecedented and unnatural quality. In trying to destroy each other, two vast armies are destroying the world itself, laying the ground bare like a skeleton, inundating it with floods, setting it on fire, changing its shape, corrupting its subsoil with putrefying flesh. This observed reality can most readily be conveyed with imagery which is apocalyptic and visionary.... (p. 48)

In his other war novel, *Clarté* ..., Barbusse allows this apocalyptic tone to get quite out of hand, merging it with a grandiose imagery and a religiosity which are no longer controlled by a firm documentary purpose. The soldiers of *Le Feu,* up to the closing chapter of the book at least, by their very ordinariness throw the landscape of war into horrifying relief. But in *Clarté* the commitment to realism surrenders almost totally to prophetic pretensions. The hero of *Clarté* has a vocabulary and a sensibility all too easily in tune with his surroundings. The tension between humanity and historical crisis is destroyed, as the cataclysm is no longer perceived as alien, but accepted and almost revelled in.

In *Le Feu,* however, the divorce between the soldier and the war, between the men crouching in the opposing trenches and the lunar wasteland confronting them, is absolute and daunting. One chapter in particular in Barbusse's novel expresses powerfully this divorce. This chapter is entitled simply 'Le Barda', or 'The Pack'. Set between two apocalyptic battle-scenes, it shows Barbusse's documentary gifts at their best. It is a good example of one of mimetic realism's most valuable qualities: humane attention to the concrete details of existence. The contents of the soldier's pack, the painstaking inventory of the paraphernalia he carries around with him, tells us more about the realities of life in the trenches, its squalor and its superstitions, than pages of dialogue or narrative. (pp. 48-9)

In a note, Barbusse refers to one of his aims as being to 'deepen the tragic aspect of the banality of war'.... This he achieves effortlessly by juxtaposing chapters like 'The Pack' or 'Matches' with settings of epic violence and destruction. These chapters are masterpieces of documentary realism. But we can already see, from the remarks of Barbusse at the end, that he is deeply bothered by the tensions implicit in the contrasting aspects of war.... By being a scrupulous observer of material reality, faithful recorder of the demotic, Barbusse is writing within the traditions of social realism. But he is also within its traditions in his sense of the epic, his grasp of evolutionary forces, his awareness of a society collapsing, of a civilisation on the brink of apocalypse, in his sense of a 'great light'. And all this he expresses through his evocation of the setting of war, through the highly sym-

bolic vocabulary and prophetic tone of the descriptions of the deathly landscape of no-man's land. Not until the very end of the novel, in the chapter called 'The Dawn', does Barbusse attempt to fuse within a single style both events and actors, and he does so in a way which is obviously fraught with danger. He abruptly endows the soldiers of the squad with a visionary sense equal to his own, with an improbable articulateness and sense of history, with a vocabulary commensurate with the magnitude of the events they are involved in. This eloquence is clearly incongruous.... (pp. 50-1)

That ingredient of social realism which requires scrupulous verisimilitude is sacrificed to its visionary proclivities, its sociological sensitivity to its historical sensitivity. It is not so much that the ending of *Le Feu* represents an abandonment of social realism; rather it represents the surrender of one of its elements to the other, as Barbusse's novel as a whole reveals the mixture of styles implicit in the genre. The chapter 'The Pack' and the chapter 'The Dawn' are equally representative of that genre. In the same way as *Germinal,* though of course far more blatantly, *Le Feu* ends with a statement of faith which, in manner as well as substance, is somewhat at odds with what has gone before. Furthermore, to clinch his belief in the possiblity of historical and evolutionary progress, Barbusse, like Zola, is forced away from people towards an image drawn from nature, from reality to abstraction, from observation to prophecy.... One way of seeing *Le Feu* then, is as a work which marks a critical point in the history of social realism. Indeed, one might almost see it as a terminal work. The 'proletarian' and 'populist' schools of fiction which proliferated in France and elsewhere in the nineteen-twenties and nineteen-thirties produced little of value. If the writer within these groups was politically committed, the prophetic and epic sweep of the genre degenerated into the mouthing of Communist orthodoxy. Otherwise, history was banished altogether and the writer concentrated on the apotheosis of the 'common man'. In other words, social realism became a decadent genre, and both these forms of decadence are, in a sense, prefigured in *Le Feu,* but there rendered almost imperceptible by the novel's astonishing documentary force. But neither the strengths nor the weaknesses of Barbusse's novel can be appreciated, still less explained, unless one stops seeing it purely as a 'war novel' and attempts to place it in the history of realist fiction. (pp. 51-2)

Jonathan King, "Henri Barbusse: 'Le Feu' and the Crisis of Social Realism," in The First World War in Fiction: A Collection of Critical Essays, *edited by Holger Klein (© The Macmillan Press Ltd 1976; by permission of Barnes & Noble Books, a Division of Littlefield, Adams & Co., Inc.), Barnes & Noble, 1976, pp. 43-52.*

GUESSLER NORMAND (essay date 1977)

Although generally ignored or only briefly mentioned by literary historians, Henri Barbusse's contribution to literature both as a novelist and journalist warrants consideration.... Barbusse emerges as one of the earliest of committed artists. Along with Romain Rolland he became one of the leading figures among French writers who insisted upon the artist's responsibility as a spokesman in defense of human rights. (p. 449)

The notion of commitment—as we know it today—is directly related to social responsibility and involvement, and is not merely devotion to an intellectual abstraction. It is strongly characterized by militancy, and it demands that fundamental moral issues be examined in the light of present-day problems. . . . The literary artist is not merely a spectator in the drama he depicts, but he is a conscious actor in it. . . . Thus, the literature which such an artist writes fulfills a *social* function and aims to change the world, for he is seeking not to foster illusions but rather to destroy them. (pp. 449-50)

Barbusse's early writings give surprisingly few—if any—indications of what he was to become later. In the poems of *Pleureuses*, . . . he is concerned primarily with his own emotional disturbances. His first novel, . . . *Les Suppliants,* is the semi-autobiographical, lyrical confession of "l'état d'âme" of the young men of the post-Symbolist period. The author is little concerned with social problems, and he rejects doctrines and religious tendencies. What he is seeking is simple happiness and truth. Barbusse's subsequent literary works took a new direction—no doubt somewhat as a result of the Dreyfus Affair—and in his next novel, . . . he turned to exterior reality in a search for a philosophical and moral basis for human life. His protagonist constantly raises basic questions about the causes of human suffering and misery, and he repeatedly probes the problem of the existence of man and society. In *L'Enfer* Barbusse focused his attention on the human milieu and showed the beginnings of that interest in social problems which later became the main preoccupation of his life.

Barbusse's experiences in the trenches as an infantryman in the First World War were crucial in the reorientation of his whole existence. His . . . masterpiece, *Le Feu,* vividly recalls these experiences and clearly marks his evolution from an idealist pacifist to a staunch revolutionary. In this book, Barbusse dared to condemn war and all it causes, calling upon men everywhere to work toward forming a society free of exploitation and of the armed conflicts to which oppression inevitably gave rise. He was the first writer to do what others were not sufficiently gifted to do, or who were too uncertain, fearful, or weak to express. . . . *Le Feu* marked Barbusse's dedication to humanity and launched him as a public figure who became a mouth-piece of his time. This novel was the preface of his commitment, and an indication of the path he was to take. After *Le Feu.* Barbusse wrote *Clarté* and other works that reveal his increasing preoccupation with contemporary social and political problems. The vaguely Symbolist poet of *Pleureuses* and *Les Suppliants* was dead. For the next twenty years he was an artist in the public arena, and his dedication to *Monde* during this period clearly illustrates the dimensions of his life of commitment.

Founded in 1928 and published for seven years, Barbusse's *Monde* marks a major period in his life. It was the organ through which he expressed his ideas on literature and civilization, on society and on politics. A close examination of this international periodical reveals the extent to which Barbusse was totally involved in the cause of humanity. *Monde* was a part of the crusading search for new reasons for existence during the inter-war period, and it was apparently able to influence public opinion to a considerable degree. Significantly, it was one of the first organs calling for active participation of intellectuals in contemporary social problems, and was one of the rare independent voices that forsaw and denounced the fascist danger that increasingly threatened human dignity. Barbusse's "enfant chéri," this periodical is particularly characteristic of his life as a totally committed intellectual; the ideas reflected in it parallel and illuminate those presented in his booklength works. Moreover, *Monde* played a definite role in the revolutionary movement during the inter-war period, and it was one of the first newspapers in France to advocate an art of the masses—one which would depict a total social reality, and which would be oriented toward serving in the best interests of humanity as a whole. (pp. 451-52)

While some of Barbusse's post-war works can perhaps be criticized as being too blindly documentary, his life-long sincerity, generosity, and genuine commitment to human progress and peace have been recognized by even his most severe critics. Clearly, he stands as a supreme example of the committed artist; one for whom literature was not a pasttime, nor an amusement, but a necessity, an action, a weapon serving to liberate men. Because he directed his life and writings primarily toward a "worldly" goal, because he transformed his thoughts into action, he exemplified a new type of writer, one who was the mouth-piece of the masses and who completely dedicated himself to the cause of humanity.

That *Monde* was primarily a revolutionary periodical expressing strong Marxist beliefs seems clear. However, in spite of this and in spite of the fact that Barbusse was a card-carrying Communist during its publication, it would be inaccurate to consider the paper as little more than a propaganda sheet. . . . To the extent that it and its editor were among the first in France to define the dimensions of commitment, they stand as prophetic voices of a literature which is their monument. In a very real sense, Malraux, Sartre and Camus can be considered their legitimate progeny, and the echo of Barbusse's voice can still be heard today. (pp. 458-59)

Guessler Normand, "Henri Barbusse and His 'Monde': Precursors to the Littérature Engagée Movement," in Kentucky Romance Quarterly *(© University Press of Kentucky; reprinted by permission of* Kentucky Romance Quarterly*), Vol. XXIV, No. 4, 1977, pp. 449-59.*

ADDITIONAL BIBLIOGRAPHY

"Letters and the Arts: Henri Barbusse—1873-1935." *The Living Age* 349, No. 4430 (November 1935): 269-72.
    A concise overview of Barbusse's life and literary career.

Schwartz, Kessel. "Henri Barbusse and the Ecuadorian Novel." *Romance Notes* 1, No. 1 (November 1959): 33-5.
    Briefly examines Barbusse's influence on the Ecuadorian novel.

(Enoch) Arnold Bennett

1867-1931

(Also wrote under pseudonym of Jacob Tonson) English novelist, short story writer, dramatist, essayist, critic, editor, and journalist.

Bennett is credited with bringing techniques of European realism to the English novel. Out of a mass of work, his reputation rests almost exclusively on *The Old Wives' Tale* and the *Clayhanger* trilogy, realistic novels set in his native Midlands district and intended to illuminate the extraordinary in dull characters and everyday life.

Bennett was born into a middle-class family in Hanley, Staffordshire, one of the Midlands towns which he incorporated into his Five Towns novels and stories. The son of a solicitor, Bennett began work at the age of eighteen in his father's office, intending to earn a degree in law. At twenty-one Bennett fled Hanley for London, where he worked temporarily for a solicitor until securing a position as an assistant editor with the ladies' magazine *Woman*, writing beauty hints and advice for the lovelorn. Although he never again lived in his home province, his best work grew out of his fictional rendering of the Midlands environment which as a young man he had found intellectually stifling.

Bennett's early models were the French writers Zola, Flaubert, and Maupassant, and his expressed intent in writing his first novel, *A Man from the North*, was to imitate meticulously the characteristics of the French novel. Bennett also admired the work of George Moore, then regarded as the leader of the British school of realism, and credited Moore's *A Mummer's Wife* with opening his eyes to "the romantic nature of the district that I had blindly inhabited for twenty years." Although Bennett eventually came to prefer the Russian novel, he never integrated its techniques into his own as he had those of Moore and the French naturalists and realists.

The panoramic technique of Bennett's finer works results from his great interest in human activity and organization. Using a simple vocabulary, disciplined objectivity, and exhaustive description, Bennett deftly portrays provincial life. While *The Old Wives' Tale* and *Clayhanger* are widely acclaimed for their meticulous construction and evocation of the passage of time, the sequels to the latter, *Hilda Lessways* and *These Twain*, are considered by some critics to be uneven, repetitious, and saturated with trivial detail. After finishing the *Clayhanger* trilogy Bennett ceased to write of the Five Towns.

Although Bennett is primarily noted for the realism of his Five Towns stories, much of his work consists of novels which he labeled "fantasias," essays designated as "pocket philosophies," and an assortment of undistinguished dramas. The "fantasias," written solely to entertain, are humorous novels generally structured around one improbable incident involving wealth, luxury, and adventure. Critics who hailed *The Old Wives' Tale* as a masterpiece of English realism disdained Bennett's willingness to cater to popular taste. However, in recent years critics have reevaluated these novels and have come to regard *The Card*, *The Grand Babylon Hotel*, and *The Pretty Lady* worthy of consideration with the best of Bennett's realistic fiction.

Bennett viewed himself as a professional craftsman whose duty it was to conscientiously produce a certain number of words every day. Adhering to his system, he created an unusually large body of work and achieved great success. While many of his titles are now forgotten, his realistic novels, particularly *The Old Wives' Tale*, insure Bennett's reputation as an important force in early twentieth-century English literature.

PRINCIPAL WORKS

Journalism for Women (essay) 1898
A Man from the North (novel) 1898
Anna of the Five Towns (novel) 1902
The Grand Babylon Hotel (novel) 1902
The Gates of Wrath (novel) 1903
Leonora (novel) 1903
A Great Man (novel) 1904
Sacred and Profane Love (novel) 1905; published in the
    United States as *The Book of Carlotta*, 1911
Tales of the Five Towns (short stories) 1905
Whom God Hath Joined (novel) 1906
The Ghost (novel) 1907
The Grim Smile of the Five Towns (short stories) 1907

Buried Alive (novel) 1908
How to Live on Twenty-Four Hours a Day (essays)
   1908
The Old Wives' Tale (novel) 1908
The Glimpse (novel) 1909
*Clayhanger (novel) 1910
Helen with the High Hand (novel) 1910
The Card (novel) 1911; published in the United States
   as *Denry the Audacious,* 1911
*Hilda Lessways (novel) 1911
The Matador of the Five Towns (short stories) 1912
Milestones [with Edward Knoblock] (drama) 1912
**The Great Adventure (drama) 1913
The Regent (novel) 1913
The Price of Love (novel) 1914
*These Twain (novel) 1916
The Pretty Lady (novel) 1918
The Roll-Call (novel) 1918
Judith (drama) 1919
Mr. Prohack (novel) 1922
How to Make the Best of Life (essay) 1923
Riceyman Steps (novel) 1923
The Bright Island (drama) 1924
Elsie and the Child (short stories) 1924
Lord Raingo (novel) 1926
The Imperial Palace (novel) 1930
The Journals of Arnold Bennett. 3 vols. (journals)
   1932-33

*These three novels were published as *The Clayhanger Family* in 1925.

**This work is a dramatization of *Buried Alive*.

––––––––––––––––––

THE ATHENAEUM (essay date 1898)

It is undeniable that, in good hands, the commonplace may be made to yield very charming material for fiction. But this result can only be obtained by emphasizing the poetry that may—that does—underlie the dreariest and most sordid lives. Mr. Bennett's method is the reverse of this. [In *A Man from the North,* he] supplies, not the poetry of the commonplace, not the romance of the commonplace, but the veriest commonplace of the commonplace.... [The story] is told in language that is invariably cultivated and frequently artistic; it is all perfectly truthful, widely typical; but there is nowhere any indication of the force by which alone such a subject could be justified.

> "New Novels: 'A Man from the North'," in The Athenaeum, *Vol. MDCCCXCVIII, No. 3673, March 19, 1898, p. 370.*

WILLIAM MORTON PAYNE (essay date 1909)

Unhappily named and ungainly in appearance, filling nearly six hundred pages of close typography, opening in a way that promises to tax the reader's endurance, and concerned from beginning to end with mean or commonplace characters, not one of whom is tricked out with the attributes that are commonly thought necessary to arouse sympathy and retain interest, **"The Old Wives' Tale,"** by Mr. Arnold Bennett, is nevertheless a remarkable work of fiction, a book of such

sincerity, truthfulness, and insight as to make the ordinary novel seem hopelessly shallow and artificial by comparison. (p. 236)

Just life, real and unadorned, a futile affair for all concerned, is what is portrayed in its pages. It is life viewed with microscopic vision, described with absolute fidelity, distorted by no trace of caricature, and commented upon, as we pass from phase to phase, with grave, sardonic, sometimes almost savage, irony. There is not a character in the book that is ennobled or glorified by the devices dear to the romantic novelist; there is no alluring heroine and no conquering hero, there is no indulgence in empty rhetoric, and there is no apparent effort to heighten either motive or situation. Yet with all this restraint, or perhaps just because of it, the final impression is deep and the resultant force overwhelming. As the figures pass before our eyes, and their lives one by one gutter out, we are made to know them better than we know most of the human beings of our actual acquaintance. This is true not only of the half dozen chiefly concerned, but also of the minor figures in almost equal degree. If we were transported by some magic carpet to mid-Victorian Bursley, we should have the advantage over their neighbors in our intimate acquaintance with these people. We understand them as we understand Balzac's men and women, and the great French novelist never shaped more authentic creations.... [The novel] is animated and even vivacious, for the most part cheerful in tone and shot through with gleams of humor. Its texture is so finely wrought that it is not to be read by leaps and bounds without serious loss. It extends to nearly a quarter of a million words, and few of them are superfluous. If it be censured for defect of ideality, it must be praised all the more for shrewdness, for accuracy of observation, and for the deep note of human sympathy which only the most careless of readers could miss. Moreover, although in its essence it is impressive of the futility of the average life, we gather this message only in our reflective moments of semi-detachment; we do not brood over it, any more than do the characters themselves. To them, life is an affair of ups and downs, no doubt, but it is also too closely packed with immediate interests to permit of their viewing it in broad perspective. The author will probably be charged with pessimism, but one has only to contrast his method with that of a genuine pessimist like Mr. Thomas Hardy to realize that the term is hardly elastic enough to cover both cases. (pp. 236-37)

> William Morton Payne, "Recent Fiction," in The Dial *(copyright, 1909, by The Dial Publishing Company, Inc.), Vol. XLVII, No. 559, October 1, 1909, pp. 236-38.*

F. G. BETTANY (essay date 1911)

There are [writers] who adopt the course of providing the public with "what the public wants," only to discover eventually that their capacity for achieving any nobler aim has somehow disappeared. There lies the danger of being too indulgent to the moods of the "great beast"; doing the second best may impair a faculty for doing the best—the material may react on the artist. Mr. Bennett in his time has written plenty of "popular" fiction, but he could always switch off his Muse, at will, to the service of serious art.... How has he contrived to keep the two sides of his fiction so long in tandem? Partly, I conceive, through his exceptional will power. The most methodic of writers, he has trained himself, when at his desk, to act like a machine. Partly through his never permitting himself the least relaxation of style. You will not light upon a single slovenly phrase in **"The Grand Babylon Hotel"**; its language is as carefully wrought as that of **"Clayhanger."** Moreover, Mr. Bennett has the knack in his sensational novels of getting hold of spacious ideas. . . . Even on this class of fiction Mr. Bennett leaves his special mark.

But there is a world of difference between the stories of the Five Towns and the other Arnold Bennett novels. . . . Mr. Bennett is not the same man away from the Potteries. They give quality to his novels—depth and certainty of effect, roundness of characterisation, colour and vivacity, along with a hardly definable intimacy of touch. . . . [For Mr. Bennett's] readers the main recommendation of his Midland origins is that he is able thereby to afford them a fresh view of life and human nature, to exhibit these in an unfamiliar setting, and, by a magic of his own, to make what to the average observer would have seemed commonplace and drab profoundly interesting and full of variety.

To analyse Mr. Bennett's technique is by no means easy. It is a matter of the multiplication of detail, and seems to betray the influence of Russian models. With stroke added to stroke the author proceeds till he has brought up before our eyes, first his leading figure or figures, next the family and shop or factory, then the street and neighbourhood and local society. But all the time you are looking at the microcosm thus gradually developed through the medium of one or more temperaments. Mr. Bennett will not be hurried over his detail. . . . It would be absurd to style Mr. Bennett's method photographic, yet it deals with innumerable small things. I am not sure that half its success does not depend on the author's leaving nothing out. He is singularly precise and microscopic in his observation. . . . It is obvious, [a critic] may say, that **"Clayhanger"** ought to be half as short as it is, and that **"The Old Wives' Tale"** could do with compression. He may urge, and quite rightly, that the novelist should be more selective, and use the blue pencil more resolutely on his work. . . . But is it much use quarrelling with a novelist's method when it is so deliberately adopted as is Mr. Bennett's, and when it is so successful? For when all is said, this author manages somehow to secure what he aims at—the suggestion of realism—as well as much besides—thus an individual interpretation of life, and at any rate his detail is always made interesting and contributory to the general scheme. (pp. 265-68)

Emphatic as is Mr. Bennett the critic on a story being the first requisite of fiction, it is life itself, rather than a story, which he presents to us as a novelist in his best work. The pageant of life, from its early promise to its eclipse in decline and death—that is his subject, and surely it is big enough. Because this subject is so admirably covered in **"The Old Wives' Tale,"** . . . I regard the story of the Baines' sisters, who met with such different destinies, as far and away the completest and most striking thing Mr. Bennett has done. **"Clayhanger,"** clear cut as is its battle between the old and the young, suffers from being but the first part of a trilogy, and from possessing a heroine whose personality is in the clouds and whose marriage to a man other than the one she loves is a mystery "to be explained in our next." **"The Old Wives' Tale"** labours under no such disadvantages. Within the range of a single novel we watch the progress of two girls from the age of fifteen till they sink into their graves. . . .

There you have one of Mr. Bennett's most urgent morals—the difference between the spring and the winter of life. Sophia is so full of vitality in her youth, Constance so sweet and good-natured; at the end both have become fussy old women who are fluttered and rendered miserable by the moods of a maid-servant. Disillusionment is the key-note of the novels; the revolt of youth against age furnishes their drama. Conceive the young rebelling against the tyranny of their elders, and then picture youth becoming old in its turn and bewildered before the assault of the next generation, and you have the secret of the irony of Mr. Bennett's fiction. (pp. 268-69)

There is indeed an element of hardness about his attitude towards life. . . . Love is for him a passion that is sure to end in disappointment, and the "common sense" which sacrifices it to material advantages has his sympathy. He does not sentimentalise this passion any more than he does the pathos of age. The old he makes lag, like veterans, superfluous on the stage. . . . In point of fact, Mr. Bennett is a realist of great imaginative power. We must not look to him perhaps for poetry or romance. But if we can bear the prose of life refracted through a very practical and unillusioned temperament, we may trust him about that confidently. (p. 270)

> *F. G. Bettany, "Arnold Bennett: An Appreciation,"*
> *in* The Bookman, *London, Vol. XXXIX, No. 234,*
> *March, 1911, pp. 265-70.*

H. G. WELLS (essay date 1912)

[While the current English spirit in novel-writing] is toward discursiveness and variety, the new French movement is rather toward exhaustiveness. One who is, I think, quite the greatest of our contemporary English novelists, Mr. Bennett, has experimented in both forms of amplitude. His superb *Old Wives' Tale,* wandering from person to person and from scene to scene, is by far the finest 'long novel' that has been written in English in the English fashion, in this generation; and now in *Clayhanger* and its promised collaterals he undertakes that complete, minute, abundant presentation of the growth and modification of one or two individual minds, which is the essential characteristic of the continental movement toward the novel of amplitude. While the *Old Wives' Tale* is discursive, *Clayhanger* is exhaustive; he gives us both types of the new movement in perfection.

> *H. G. Wells, "The Contemporary Novel," in* The
> Atlantic Monthly *(copyright © 1912, by The At-*
> *lantic Monthly Company, Boston, Mass.), Vol. 109,*
> *No. 1, January, 1912, pp. 1-11.*

FREDERIC TABER COOPER (essay date 1912)

[Arnold Bennett] has recorded with evident satisfaction the keen joy of the day when at last he sat down to write his first novel, [*A Man from the North*], under what he called "the sweet influences of the de Goncourts, Turgenev, Flaubert and de Maupassant." The purpose uppermost in Mr. Bennett's mind, so he tells us, was to imitate the physical characteristics of the French novel. There were to be no poetical quotations, no titles to the chapters; the narrative was to be divided irregularly by Roman numerals only. In short, the book was to be a mosaic of imitations of Flaubert and the de Goncourt brothers. Life being gray, sinister and melancholy, his first book should similarly be melancholy, sinister and gray. (pp. 208-09)

[Because of mixed reviews, it] was not strange, under the circumstances, that this first novel brought a certain amount of disillusionment, and that Mr. Bennett temporarily laid aside his theory of art for art's sake, and determined to write a serial of the kind that yields a revenue. (p. 209)

As to the ethics of debasing a talent of high order to pander to the popular demand of tawdry sensationalism, a good deal has already been said, and a good deal yet remains to say. Over and over again comments have been made, with all the varying degrees of irony, upon Mr. Bennett's versatility in appearing before the public "in a dual capacity as a writer of lucrative trash and as an artist". . . . (p. 211)

Mr. Bennett, in his dual capacity, always suggests to me the two familiar classical masks of Tragedy and Comedy, neither of them seeing life as a whole, but each viewing the outside world with its own characteristic grimace. Now, it is a notorious commonplace that the man who spends the better part of his life as a paid buffoon, the court jester, the harlequin, the circus clown, sees life through the eyes of a confirmed misanthrope; the merrier the jest that he cracks in public, the more impossible it becomes in private to stir the lips into the wraith of a smile. And that is precisely what I think is the trouble with the whole series of Mr. Arnold Bennett's stories of the Five Towns. It is not that they are untrue; it is simply that the joy of living has been sucked out of them. . . . [Mr. Bennett] exhausts his power of perceiving the reds and yellows, the joyous notes of life, in his purely negligible productions, and the consequence is that his mental faculties are too strained and too weary to perceive, in *Anna of the Five Towns*, in *The Old Wives' Tale*, in *Clayhanger*, any glint of those brighter, warmer colors without which, we all know, life would be too monochrome, too hopelessly gray for human endurance, even to those inured to the smoke-laden atmosphere of the Five Towns.

None the less, it is the inalienable right of every artist to choose his own pigments. . . . Mr. Bennett is an unrivaled expert in mixing leaden tints. . . . He makes us behold life, raw, anguished, hopeless life, through glasses, smoked not so deeply as to dull any of the poignancy, but sufficiently to rob us of the symbolic blue of hope. He is within his rights. He tells the truth about life—only, it must be borne in mind that he does not tell the whole truth. (pp. 212-214)

[Mr. Bennett's purely commercial productions, which some remnant of artistic conscience compels him to label "Fantasias,"] are all built on much the same formula; there is a taint of megalomania in their conception and development, a hugeness of setting and environment, an unparalleled and inexhaustible opulence of color and light, of ostentation and gaiety, of thronging men and women, and the glitter of jewels and the sheen of priceless fabrics. (pp. 214-15)

Between his riotous melodramatic "Fantasias" and the Five Towns Series, on which his reputation is solidly built, Mr. Bennett has produced a miscellaneous lot of volumes ranging from serious to farcical and difficult to classify otherwise than by the unsatisfactory generalization that they are not cheap enough to be profitable merchandise nor fine enough to be literature. As specimens of this intermediate class, it will be sufficient to comment briefly on . . . *Buried Alive*, *Denry the Audacious* and *The Glimpse*. The first of these three is a book towards which it is not difficult to be indulgent, for

it not only represents an honest effort to be humorous, with the further merit of succeeding, but it has an undercurrent of satire regarding the vanity of pompous obsequies, the elusiveness of fame. . . . [*Buried Alive* is] an extravaganza which is never tedious, never vulgar, but from beginning to end permeated with that brand of British humor already made familiar to us through the Gilbert-and-Sullivan librettos. (pp. 217-18)

[Of plot *Denry the Audacious*] is very nearly guiltless. In so far as it has any, it belongs to the *picaresco* type. Denry's adventures are practically all of one kind and they might have been expanded and multiplied to fill a dozen volumes or curtailed to the dimensions of a short story. His audacity amounts to this: whenever he finds himself in a position menacing him with failure . . . , he drives boldly, even brazenly ahead and wrenches a colossal triumph from the very jaws of disaster. A quite simple formula, you see, and one permitting of infinite variations. Add to this the fact that Mr. Bennett has a genuine sense of humor and the ability to make the most out of a paradoxical situation and you have the whole explanation why a book like this, which would have been a flat failure at the hands of ninety-nine writers out of a hundred, proves in this case to be very good fun indeed. (pp. 218-19)

[*The Glimpse*] is evidently meant by Mr. Bennett as a serious piece of work; and while it is not to be put for a moment in the same class with *Clayhanger* or *The Old Wives' Tale*, it is none the less a work of distinct originality. (p. 219)

[This] is undeniably an unusual story, and an uncomfortable one as well; but no one would ever infer from it that the author had the power to produce works of such real importance as *Anna of the Five Towns*, *Leonora*, and the several subsequent volumes that have for their setting a string of ugly, busy manufacturing centers in the pottery district of Staffordshire. In *Anna of the Five Towns* Mr. Bennett for the first time set his feet firmly on his rightful path. It has the same pervading grayness, physically and morally, the same overhanging veil of grimy smoke, the same dull helplessness of lookout that characterize what has come to be known as his distinctive work. . . . (pp. 220-21)

Leonora is another similar story of the same sordid life, constructed with the same solid and ambitious craftsmanship. (p. 222)

But it is with *The Old Wives' Tale* that Mr. Bennett achieves for the first time a work that beyond all dispute or cavil is of the first magnitude. . . . It is only at long intervals that a piece of fiction appears which conveys an impression of such magnitude, such finished workmanship and such a fund of reserve power. There are many books which impress one with a sense of amplitude, a sense of being spread over a very broad canvas. It is much rarer to find, as in the present case, a book which gives a sense of depth as well as breadth, a book that has a wonderful, far-reaching perspective, making you feel that you are looking not merely upon the surface of life, but through and beyond the surface into the deep and hidden meanings of human existence. As in the case of all novels which really deserve the attribute of bigness, *The Old Wives' Tale* achieves its effects without the aid of a spectacular background or of exceptional and exalted characters. Indeed, it would be difficult to imagine anything more essentially mediocre and commonplace, more uniformly dull and gray than the whole external atmosphere of this strong and poignant story. . . . Narrow, hopelessly conservative, unspeakably bourgeois in their attitude toward life, the Baines family, nevertheless, stand out in this story as fair average representatives of the human race, sufficient exponents of the three great mysteries of life: birth, marriage and death. . . . [The plot of this volume] has the multifold and wonderful intricacy of actual life. It is enough to say that there are very few books in English which mirror back so truly and with such a fine sense of proportion the relative amounts of joy and sorrow that enter into the average human life. . . . Naturally the book is, with all its merits, a depressing one. It leaves behind it a sense of grayness and loneliness and personal loss, and all the more so because it possesses that rare power of making us feel the brotherhood of these commonplace people that fill its pages. . . . Undoubtedly, a Touch of Poetry, that is to say, a strain of romanticism, idealising the meaner traits of character, the harsher blows of fate, would lighten the gloom and relieve the tension, but inevitably it would have shorn the book of its chief strength, the incomparable strength of literal and fearless truth. It stands out conspicuously as the one volume in which Mr. Bennett has justified his practice of painting in verbal *grisaille*.

When *Clayhanger* first appeared, it was announced as the first of a trilogy of novels dealing with the Five Towns, the central theme of which was to be the breaking down of the old spirit by the new in the central provinces of England. . . . [Structurally, *Clayhanger*] is undeniably an unwieldy, disproportioned piece of work, as full of loose ends and projecting corners as a chance fragment from a puzzle picture. . . . *Hilda Lessways,* instead of helping the situation, complicates it. Instead of sustaining the high standard set by *Clayhanger,* as a human document, it falls emphatically below the level of that volume; and instead of beginning the task of rounding out and filling in, it simply adds just so many more loose ends and projecting corners. . . . [If] we set aside completely the question of construction, and consider *Clayhanger* in just one aspect—the aspect in which, one suspects, the author himself would prefer it to be considered—namely, as a study of the unfolding and maturing of a single human character, it would be rather difficult to overpraise it. . . . It is the prerogative of just a few writers of Mr. Bennett's caliber to remain within the limits of their native village and yet at the same time to make their theme universal. . . . [*Clayhanger*'s] value as a human document lies, first, in the untiring fidelity with which Mr. Bennett convinces us that his people are so constituted that they must inevitably have said and done precisely what he records, and not otherwise; and, secondly, making due allowance for local differences, that his people are much the same as people everywhere else, with the same hopes and fears, the same futile efforts, the same disappointments. (pp. 222-29)

No writer is definitely placed during his lifetime; but Mr. Bennett is, up to the present time, peculiarly and exceptionally misjudged and alternately overrated and underpraised. . . . I could name offhand at least a score of novelists who may be trusted to provide quite as much pleasure as Mr. Bennett, to be equally true to the realities of life, and to be, in some respects, better craftsmen, and possessed of a higher ideal of art, a greater reluctance to prostitute it to the demands of expediency. But this does not alter the fact that Mr. Bennett is an exceedingly interesting product of the modern tendencies in English fiction, as contrasted with the American variety; and one shrewdly suspects that he has in him the capability of doing even bigger things. (pp. 230-31)

Frederic Taber Cooper, "Arnold Bennett," in his Some English Story Tellers: A Book of the Younger Novelists *(copyright © 1912 by Henry Holt and Company), Holt, 1912, pp. 208-31.*

F. J. HARVEY DARTON   (essay date 1915)

[There are primarily] three elements in Arnold Bennett's character as an artist. He is a Five Townsman—keen, interested, exceedingly shrewd, very practical and efficient, limited in certain directions, rather coarse-fibred in others. He is a trained manipulator of words. And he is highly strung, which means that in spite of a most efficient self-control—indeed, as the result of it—he is always (whether he wishes it or not) expressing some aspect of his experience, opening some tiny window of his soul, speaking out (however faintly) some whisper of personality. (pp. 43-4)

The classification of his writings which Arnold Bennett afterwards adopted (he was either the first modern novelist or one of the first to invent such a valuable guide to his intentions) includes six headings—Novels, Fantasias, Short Stories, Belles-Lettres, Drama and In Collaboration. (p. 51)

[The sensational novels] were not named "fantasias" fantastically. I take it that the title really conveys the author's opinion of the books. . . . [These] books are to be regarded as vivacious, skilful exercises upon certain central ideas in each case: exercises calling for high spirits, technical facility, and exuberance of ornament. . . . [They] are something more than frivolous improvisation—more responsible, more deliberately composed, written with a critical smile rather than a spontaneous laugh. You might say they were the handiwork of a literary "Card," showing off in a characteristically surprising manner.

That implies that there is a good deal of conscious and unconscious pretence about them. Arnold Bennett is as capable of pretence as any man. (pp. 52-3)

[The fantasias] were all written for pleasure and for profit, motives indissolubly mingled. They are novels of ideas vigorously worked out, but not of great ideas. They deal each with a characteristic phenomenon of material civilisation, raised to its highest power. It must be a phenomenon plain to the average man, but not fully and gloriously realised. The author takes it, and shows every conceivable splendour of it, and some inconceivable splendours as well. He brings in, in a grandiose spirit of intensive culture, every possible illustrative ornament. He adds profuse excitement, suddenness of transition, rapidity of movement, and a worldly, caustic humour. That is the whole prescription. (pp. 54-5)

Arnold Bennett is infinitely and splendidly subtle when he is working upon Five Towns material, and he is occasionally subtle also in these minor novels. But his intellect and his spirit and his literary sense alike (so far as they are revealed in his books) are inadequately tempered to fine issues. (p. 57)

[All of these novels] are, so to speak, pastimes: experiments, efforts at self-expression, which Arnold Bennett made concurrently with his more deliberate work upon his native raw material. It must be taken as a self-evident proposition that the Five Towns novels are far higher achievements. These works are merely clever. (p. 62)

The Old Wives' Tale appears, to a cursory glance, a formless chronicle; it is in reality a miracle of constructive genius and eclectic self-restraint. . . . It is the whole story of many lives; youth, marriage, the inexorable swift passage of the devouring years, adhesion to a place, death. Arnold Bennett tells it in such a manner that he never comments upon the two old wives; he never criticises the society in which they live; he never dwells upon any figure or thing in such a way that it stands out disproportionately from its environment; his own opinions, his sequence of ideas, his arrangement of the successive incidents, are wholly concealed. The book is just a chronicle, told with such profound art, equableness and perfection of construction, that it might be written by some spirit in another world a thousand years hence.

A man who can thus set down the pages of change that make up the continuous book of existence, who can withhold himself from a philosophy of what he tells so austerely, who can excite pity with the use of never a pitiful word, is a great novelist. There is no English novel quite like *The Old Wives' Tale.* (pp. 75-6)

In no other of his novels has Arnold Bennett reached the same height of passionless austerity. Even *Clayhanger* and its companion, *Hilda Lessways* . . . are not quite on the same plane as *The Old Wives' Tale*, fine though they are. *Clayhanger*, indeed, is written from the outside. But it is written by one plainly tolerant and amused, not dispassionate and far away. It has the defect of personal intrusion by the author. *Hilda Lessways* is much more objective. (pp. 77-8)

The isolation of the author's personality from his subject is better seen in *Anna of the Five Towns*, a work often underrated, and of very high value. Its weaknesses are a certain lack of control over the digressions (an imperfect welding—it was the author's first novel of large "scope") and what would in a lesser book be a virtue—a dramatic plot, which shows a tendency to let action dominate psychology too conveniently. . . . In the conclusion, in particular, the abstinence from compassion and the utter simplicity of language excite pity more forcibly than any emphasis could. *Leonora* . . . is a work of distinction on much the same level as *Anna of the Five Towns*, and subject to the same criticism. *Whom God hath Joined* has the defects of both the modern and the Victorian novel. . . . It is neither entirely dramatic (not a *story*, that is), nor entirely realistic. It suffers from a certain unevenness of execution and irresolution of aim, though it contains some remarkable passages.

The Price of Love, from a technical point of view, is admirably constructed, but not dispassionate enough. In scope, it is almost an artistic relapse. It is a particular, not a universal, book. . . . On every page the author is clearly enthusiastic; he is intensely interested in every shade of feeling, every reaction to stimulus, every logical foundation of emotions obscure and dumb. He has never shown a surer mastery than in the picture of Rachel's attitude to Mrs Maldon and the abominable Batchgrew, of her quarrel with Louis, of Louis's brief glimpse deep into his own mean soul when he is found out. (pp. 78-80)

So far, then, Arnold Bennett is seen to have tried, and tried more successfully than not, to set down his vision of life without explicitly adding his views of it—to chronicle soberly, seriously, things as they are, allowing local conditions to create their own atmosphere; for, prosaic, detailed, photographic as they may seem, the Five Towns novels are full of atmosphere. (pp. 81-2)

The Card is also really a fantasia. But it is something else as well. It is what painters used to call "The Portrait of a Gentleman"—a picture, that is, of someone whom they regarded as at least admirable. *The Card* is a very disturbing book. The man who could write it is a complete master of technique. It is episodic, but perfectly constructed, and the manner of it exquisitely suited to the humour of the conception. Ironic commercialism, the crafty triumphs of an alert, yet unconscious, financial genius, have never been so vivaciously and faithfully rendered. Nor is an occasional gentleness lacking. (p. 84)

Except Edwin Clayhanger, Denry Machin [of *The Card*] is Arnold Bennett's most completely and carefully studied male character; and he is, on a census of the persons in these novels, a more typical Five Townsman than Clayhanger. (p. 86)

[Of the old men in Bennett's novels, there] is not one who is not ignorant and cruel, domineering and boorish, physically nauseating and socially nonexistent. And yet they are powerful figures, not unworthy of respect; hard men facing a hard world proudly.

The female differs, and is on the whole more pleasing. She seems to fulfil one or other of two implied natural laws—that woman is the plaything, the adored plaything of man, often broken, or that she is the huntress, generally successful but always pursuing, with the arts of allurement and victorious concession highly developed.

The men in Arnold Bennett's books enjoy themselves in their way; I cannot recall one of his women who is really happy, except perhaps the delightfully drawn Mrs Sutton in *Anna of the Five Towns*. Their nearest approach to joy is humourless acceptance of comfort. The middle class is still predominantly Victorian in the habits of life; and the women have to be domestic, whether aggressively or receptively, whether hunter or hunted. They have, like the men, their own freemasonry. The men know their own vices, and never give one another away. The women never give away to the men their universal tolerant perception of male weakness.

Such is the society of that remarkable district of England, and so do the egotism and mentality of Arnold Bennett unite to picture it. He rises above his subject in the better part of all these novels, and entirely in *The Old Wives' Tale;* he identifies himself with it, takes its aggressive, defiant point of view, sinks with it, in other parts, chiefly when he achieves humour. (pp. 91-3)

The union of impersonal strength and personal bravado in Arnold Bennett . . . is his most characteristic trait. It makes it, however, very difficult to assess his outlook upon life justly. If we had not *The Old Wives' Tale*, and certain passages in *Clayhanger*, and the conclusions of *Anna of the Five Towns* and *The Price of Love*, the verdict would be hopelessly unfair. It would convict Arnold Bennett of knowingly accepting the egotistical, self-assertive, unlovely ideals of a community wholly commercial in thought and deed. In fact, one side of that community's existence is so far obscured by its commercial activity that Arnold Bennett fails to give it reality. He takes no account of what is still a powerful thing in middle-class life—religion in one form or another. . . . However superficial a religion may be, it is the framework of some sort of philosophy of existence in those who hold to it. It is a defect of sympathy in Arnold Bennett that he does not appreciate that philosophy; or if he does, does not deal with it in a series of novels which covers almost every other aspect of the middle class.

But the ignoble half of life, happily, is not Arnold Bennett's chief or sole preoccupation. He has become, by taking thought, a great novelist in regard to technique. He can, moreover, see life steadily and whole, as all great novelists must; even though he turns Card now and then and plays with it. He has also an individual gift which sets him apart from other novelists—his extraordinary power of analysis. . . . Very seldom does Arnold Bennett show his characters as searching their own souls. He shows what is much more profoundly true than any amount of introspection—that the middle class are incapable of searching their own souls; that Five Townsmen (like most Englishmen) act upon a balance of considerations, but seldom think the considerations out; that impulse and inhibition are for ever struggling on the surface; that action is character, and character, in people like these, is only the habitual, inveterate surface of an imperfectly exercised mind.

It is, then, as a Five Townsman that Arnold Bennett uses his genius, and it is upon the material of the Five Towns middle class that he works most happily. But just because he has genius he rises far above local conditions; and just because he is a Five Townsman he enjoys himself thoroughly—not least when he is privately laughing at those who would like him to do otherwise—in flouting the social and even the literary standards of persons born and bred in less favoured regions. (pp. 94-7)

"My aim in writing plays," [Bennett] affirmed in 1900, "whether alone or in collaboration, has always been strictly commercial. I wanted money in heaps, and I wanted advertisement for my books." It is only to be expected, in such circumstances, that the *Polite Farces* should not be works of genius. Nor are they worthy of consideration as works of art. . . . Emotions change in them with the rapidity and slickness peculiar to farce, where a door has but to slam to alter any train of causation. The dialogue has the stilted gentlemanliness also peculiar to farce of the drawing-room type. . . . They are not intelligent and they are not imaginative. They are effective in an entirely conventional way. (pp. 98-9)

[*Cupid and Commonsense*] is, of all Arnold Bennett's performed plays, the one which contains the most profound single or main idea—that of the conflict between sense and commonsense, feeling and reason. All his plays *are,* as a matter of fact, plays with main ideas, even that delightful fantasia, *The Great Adventure. Cupid and Commonsense* goes deeper than any. Its failure comes from the fact that its depth is uneven, shifting, and not to be charted—at one moment "dramatic," at another mental. (p. 104)

[Arnold Bennett] has really, as yet, made no mark upon the drama. He is too uneven a worker. He is always competent or skilled, but he does not climb the steep ascent of imaginative triumph. He brings intelligence to bear, but not imagination or strong effort. He does not even, in his plays, force an intellectual discussion of the potential problems with which he deals. He does not bring to the theatre what other men could not bring equally well. (pp. 111-12)

[Bennett's work] belongs to a marked epoch of industrial evolution. Now neither that epoch nor that society has ever appeared in English fiction before; nor has any novelist of middle or higher industrial life ever presented his material with such a literary equipment and outlook as Arnold Bennett

possesses. That is the great and new importance of his work. (p. 114)

[No] one hitherto, so far as I know, has not merely portrayed the life of the middle class manufacturer but spoken with his voice. . . . In the Five Towns novels there is no ideal. There is no criticism. There is no tradition or philosophy of society. There is nothing but life as the people described live it and see it and feel it. (pp. 114-15)

[It] is very much for the good of English literature that a writer can so profoundly master his art as to present this passionless panorama of life. . . . [Arnold Bennett's efficiency] is a Five Towns virtue, appreciated and desired by Five Townsmen. But it must not be confused with this infinitely higher artistic inefficiency—this selflessness, this steady, inexorable, faithful comprehension of mind and power of expression. (pp. 115-16)

It is not in all his books, not even in a majority of them, that Arnold Bennett reaches this height. Perhaps only one writer living to-day has shown the power of being always at the same pitch of soul (I say nothing now of expression or subject): Thomas Hardy, with whom Arnold Bennett has much more in common than the utter external dissimilarity of their books suggests. If all his novels were on the same plane as *The Old Wives' Tale,* Arnold Bennett would have recreated English fiction. . . . (pp. 116-17)

[He] has the little weaknesses of his individual virtues. He is so efficient that he economises details, as I have pointed out. He is so skilled that he may not always realise the unevenness of labour easily accomplished. He has that occasional cocksureness of a Card, that inability to perceive local or provincial limitations. . . . By education and training he relies upon a vocabulary that is unrelievedly plain: a primrose is a primrose to him—I am not sure that it is even yellow; and he employs words for what they denote, not for what they connote. The result is to make his victories more difficult, and (a curious irony) to necessitate the use of a great many severe grey words where another writer might have done as well with one purple one. There is no beauty in his English, no majesty: yet there is beauty and majesty in some of the thoughts he suggests—thoughts which will exist, for every reader, in other words than those he uses. (pp. 117-19)

When one has considered all the pettiness and coarseness and gloom of the Five Towns, there still remains something deeper, some quality not described, not mentioned, which makes Arnold Bennett's characters human. I should say that it is the spirit of freedom in them. . . . (p. 120)

> *F. J. Harvey Darton, in his* Arnold Bennett *(reprinted by permission of the Estate of F. J. Harvey Darton), Henry Holt and Company, 1915 (and reprinted by Scholarly Press, 1971), 127 p.*

STUART P. SHERMAN   (essay date 1917)

[It seems to me an] untenable assumption that Mr. Bennett, the popular novelist, and Mr. Bennett, the popular philosopher, are distinct and non-communicating beings. I shall attempt to show that the novelist's treatises on conduct are related to his artistic representation of it.

The beginning of wisdom, according to this philosophy, which runs counter to our current naturalism, is the recognition of a fundamental duality in human experience. Mr.

Bennett presumes not God to scan. He is as completely emancipated from religious metaphysics as any of his contemporaries. Like a true child of his scientific age, he takes nothing on authority; he brings everything to the test of his experience. But looking into himself as a microcosm, he sees and reports that the universe consists of a controlling power, which is the quintessence of man; and of a power to be controlled, which is nature. The zest, the object, the compensation of existence lie in the possibility of extending the dominion of the human over the natural power, the voluntary over the involuntary impulses, the conscious over the unconscious agents. (p. 108)

The responsibility for extending the dominion of man over his own nature and, indirectly, over his remoter circumstances, Mr. Bennett, in opposition to our popular sociological doctors, places primarily upon the individual. While Mr. Wells, for example, urges us to cast our burdens and our sins upon society . . . , Mr. Bennett fixes his eye upon plain John Smith. . . . (p. 109)

In dealing with the relations of John Smith to Mrs. Smith, the Victorian Bennett feels obliged to say, in opposition to those who hold out for these plain people the prospect of a life of freedom and sustained ecstasy to be attained by upsetting the established order, that most of our ideas of freedom and ecstasy are romantic will-o'-the-wisps. . . . "Passionate love," he insists, "does not mean happiness; it means excitement, apprehension, and continually renewed desires." . . . "Real happiness consists first in an acceptance of the facts that discontent is a condition of life, and, second, in an honest endeavor to adjust conduct to an ideal." (pp. 109-10)

[In] the face of the present naturalistic invasion, when humanistic ideas are in the trenches, under fire, fighting for existence, a novelist who paints men in preference to tigers, supermen, or scientific angels, has interestingly taken sides. (p. 111)

The general theme of Mr. Bennett's masterpieces, determined by the central interest of his philosophy, is the development of character in relation to a society which is also developing. He has no foolishly simple mechanical formula for the process. He has rather a sense that this relationship involves an interplay of forces of fascinating and inexplicable complexity.

His sense of the marvelous intricacy of his theme explains his elaborate presentation of the community life in which his principal figures have their being. He is bent upon bringing before the eye of the reader every scrap of evidence that may be conceived of as relevant to the "case." . . . One's first impression before this spectacle is of admiration at the unrelenting artistic energy which keeps this presented community life whole and steady and yet perceptibly in motion through a long span of time.

One's second impression is of admiration at the force of composition which keeps the principal figures from being "swamped" in the life of the community. . . . [Somehow] they are made to emerge above their "environment" as its creators and preservers—its plain, grim, but enduring heroes. The secret of this "somehow" is that Mr. Bennett implicitly recognizes as an artist what he explicitly declares as a popular philosopher, namely, the existence in the individual of something deeper than the body, deeper than the mind—an ultimately responsible, independent, spiritual, self with the power to control, in some measure, its circumstances. (pp. 112-13)

Constance and Sophia, the two heroines of *The Old Wives' Tale,* appeal to tragic compassion not because they were young and have grown old and grotesque but because they hungered for life and love, yet quietly and proudly starved in their respectability rather than touch a morsel of forbidden food. . . . Mr. Bennett portrays persons with various powers of inhibition; but he does not give the place of hero or heroine to a slave of instinct. . . . By the very design of his novels Mr. Bennett reveals his admiration for the prudent, foresighted, purposeful people. The man who has himself in hand he makes, by his compositional emphasis, a measure of the subordinated figures.

The Clayhanger trilogy, triumphantly completed by the publication of *These Twain,* expresses with the moving force of dramatic representation the ideas more simply exposed in *The Plain Man and His Wife.* (pp. 114-15)

It is clear that Mr. Bennett has attempted to present in the completed trilogy an adequate account of the fiery conflict, with typical antagonists, of the Eternal-Feminine and the Eternal-Masculine. If you are a man, you will writhe, or you ought to writhe, at the exposure in Edwin of your own obstinate conviction that you think straight and that your wife does not, and at the exposure of your hot fits of indignation at her shifty evasions of your flawless argument. If you are a woman, you will blush, or ought to blush, at the exposure in Hilda of your own illogicality and your willingness to gain ends—commendable no doubt—by perfectly unscrupulous means. (p. 116)

[Edwin ultimately finds] content by accepting discontent as a condition of life, and by honestly endeavoring to adapt his conduct to an ideal. In his recognition of the need of a more flexible intelligence and a stiffer backbone he embodies at once the principle of progress and the principle of conservation. He is a hero of his generation, not victorious but conquering. (p. 118)

[Mr. Bennett's philosophy] seems to support an altogether decent theory of human conduct. And this in turn underlies an artistic representation of life remarkable for its fullness, its energy, its gusto, its pathos, its play of tragic and comic lights, its dramatic clashes, its catastrophes, and its reconciliations—in short, for its adequacy. (p. 119)

> Stuart P. Sherman, "The Realism of Arnold Bennett" (originally published in a different form in The Nation, *Vol. 101, No. 2634, December 2, 1915), in his* On Contemporary Literature, *Henry Holt and Company, 1917, pp. 102-19.*

VIRGINIA WOOLF (essay date 1924)

I believe that all novels . . . deal with character, and that it is to express character—not to preach doctrines, sing songs, or celebrate the glories of the British Empire, that the form of the novels, so clumsy, verbose, and undramatic, so rich, elastic, and alive, has been evolved. (p. 102)

[Mr. Arnold Bennett] says that it is only if the characters are real that the novel has any chance of surviving. Otherwise, die it must. But, I ask myself, what is reality? And who are the judges of reality? A character may be real to Mr. Bennett and quite unreal to me. (p. 103)

The most prominent and successful novelists in the year 1910 were, I suppose, Mr. Wells, Mr. Bennett, and Mr. Galsworthy. Now it seems to me that to go to these men and ask them to teach you how to write a novel—how to create characters that are real—is precisely like going to a boot maker and asking him to teach you how to make a watch. Do not let me give you the impression that I do not admire and enjoy their books. . . . But the Edwardians were never interested in character in itself; or in the book in itself. They were interested in something outside. Their books, then, were incomplete as books, and required that the reader should finish them, actively and practically, for himself.

Perhaps we can make this clearer if we take the liberty of imagining a little party in [a] railway carriage—Mr. Wells, Mr. Galsworthy, Mr. Bennett are travelling to Waterloo with [a certain] Mrs. Brown. (pp. 104-05)

Mr. Bennett, alone of the Edwardians, would keep his eyes in the carriage. He, indeed, would observe every detail with immense care. He would notice the advertisements; the pictures of Swanage and Portsmouth; the way in which the cushion bulged between the buttons; how Mrs. Brown wore a brooch which had cost three-and-ten-three at Whitworth's bazaar; and had mended both gloves—indeed the thumb of the left-hand glove had been replaced. . . . And so he would gradually sidle sedately towards Mrs. Brown, and would remark how she had been left a little copyhold, not freehold, property at Datchet, which, however, was mortgaged to Mr. Bungay the solicitor—but why should I presume to invent Mr. Bennett? Does not Mr. Bennett write novels himself? I will open the first book that chance puts in my way—*Hilda Lessways*. Let us see how he makes us feel that Hilda is real, true, and convincing, as a novelist should. She shut the door in a soft, controlled way, which showed the constraint of her relations with her mother. She was fond of reading *Maud;* she was endowed with the power to feel intensely. So far, so good; in his leisurely, surefooted way Mr. Bennett is trying in these first pages, where every touch is important, to show us the kind of girl she was.

But then he begins to describe, not Hilda Lessways, but the view from her bedroom window, the excuse being that Mr. Skellorn, the man who collects rents, is coming along that way. (pp. 106-07)

One line of insight would have done more than all [of the many] lines of description; but let them pass as the necessary drudgery of the novelist. And now—where is Hilda? Alas. Hilda is still looking out of the window. Passionate and dissatisfied as she was, she was a girl with an eye for houses. She often compared this old Mr. Skellorn with the villas she saw from her bedroom window. Therefore the villas must be described. (p. 108)

At last [it seems] we are coming to Hilda herself. But not so fast. Hilda may have been this, that, and the other; but Hilda not only looked at houses, and thought of houses; Hilda lived in a house. And what sort of a house did Hilda live in? Mr. Bennett proceeds [to describe her house at length]. (pp. 108-09)

What can Mr. Bennett be about? I have formed my own opinion of what Mr. Bennett is about—he is trying to make us imagine for him; he is trying to hypnotize us into the belief that, because he has made a house, there must be a person living there. With all his powers of observation, which are marvellous, with all his sympathy and humanity, which are

great, Mr. Bennett has never once looked at Mrs. Brown in her corner. There she sits in the corner of the carriage—that carriage which is travelling, not from Richmond to Waterloo, but from one age of English literature to the next, for Mrs. Brown is eternal, Mrs. Brown is human nature, Mrs. Brown changes only on the surface, it is the novelists who get in and out—there she sits and not one of the Edwardian writers has so much as looked at her. They have looked very powerfully, searchingly, and sympathetically out of the window; at factories, at Utopias, even at the decoration and upholstery of the carriage; but never at her, never at life, never at human nature. And so they have developed a technique of novel-writing which suits their purpose; they have made tools and established conventions which do their business. But those tools are not our tools, and that business is not our business. For us those conventions are ruin, those tools are death. (pp. 109-10)

[The Edwardian tools] have laid an enormous stress upon the fabric of things. They have given us a house in the hope that we may be able to deduce the human beings who live there. To give them their due, they have made that house much better worth living in. But if you hold that novels are in the first place about people, and only in the second about the houses they live in, that is the wrong way to set about it. (pp. 112-13)

> *Virginia Woolf, "Mr. Bennett and Mrs. Brown" (originally a paper read to the Heretics, Cambridge, on May 18, 1924), in her "The Captain's Death Bed" and Other Essays (copyright 1950, 1978 by Harcourt Brace Jovanovich, Inc.; reprinted by permission of the publisher; in Canada by the Author's Literary Estate and The Hogarth Press), Harcourt, 1950, pp. 94-119.*

J. B. PRIESTLEY (essay date 1925)

[When] we come to think narrowly of Bennett the novelist, it is possible that we shall feel impelled to discuss him only as the author of three stories, *The Old Wives' Tale, Clayhanger,* and the recent *Riceyman Steps,* for these stories undoubtedly contain his best work. But frequently flimsy and faulty as some of the other novels may be, such light-hearted things as *The Card* and *The Regent, Buried Alive, Helen with the High Hand,* and *Mr. Prohack,* we should do their author an injustice if we left them entirely out of consideration, not only because they have entertained vast numbers of intelligent readers, but also because they represent a very important side of his work. Indeed—if I may be allowed to touch at once the very core of the argument—the principal weakness of this very able novelist is that he has never combined in one book the virtues of these two sides of his work; he has never combined the art and sweep of *The Old Wives' Tale* with the genuine humor and high spirits of, say, *The Card.* He makes a strict division between what we might call, somewhat superficially, the lighter and heavier chronicles, and this division has done him an ill service, for the whole Arnold Bennett never makes his appearance in any one book. (p. 261)

A good deal of his lighter fiction is really nothing but very clever journalism, touching lightly but surely any number of amusing "topics." . . . No one has studied the colored and glittering surface of modern life with more zest and gusto; instead of trying to escape from life, as so many clever moderns wish to do, he cannot have enough of it, he cannot have too many facts about this world of ours forced upon his attention. (p. 262)

Bennett may be called the poet and rhapsodist of this roaring, seething, glittering life of our great cities. But in the middle of it all there is nearly always some half-sophisticated, simple, wondering soul, some middle-aged man or woman from the provinces, busy fulfilling old dreams just as our author himself has fulfilled old dreams. He is showing us . . . Wonder in a hard hat and a business suit, Romance with an excursion ticket to London. (p. 263)

He is seeing the poetry and romance in something that is usually considered, by more timid or more sophisticated writers, the very enemy of poetry and romance. In these lighter stories of Bennett's, the dreams and aspirations of a whole host of people are seized upon for the first time. He is the romancer of what had hitherto appeared the least romantic class in the United Kingdom, the middle-aged members of the middle class. He sees life from their angle. Not only when he is describing their encounters with the glittering metropolis, but also when he is describing their personal relationships. . . . He can make more capital out of a little scene between a middle-aged husband and wife who are examining a new hat or setting out for a little holiday than most romancers can out of storms and revolutions and duels in the moonlight and meetings in far, fantastic islands. But hard on the heels of this virtue there follows a notable defect. He is content too easily with what we might call the "average" in character and motive and relationship; he describes not so much individuals as a kind of common denominator; he does not dig deep enough nor model with sufficient subtlety. He gives us the result of observation rather than creation. The relations between his men and women are always too general, so that the latter are not so much women as The Sex; the situations are touched off with extraordinary cleverness, but they are always, so to speak, typical, an approximation, the kind of thing that makes its appearance in his amusing and sensible little talks on Life and Marriage and what not. Everywhere the emphasis is laid on the constant factors in sexual relations, so that we are given love and marriage as they would appear to a clever psychologist and social historian rather than to an artist. His journalism . . . has tricked him into generalizing in places where generalizing is fatal. The result is that, though these stories please everybody, for everybody is compelled to recognize their rough approximation to truth, they do not succeed in mirroring anybody's secret self, do not go down to the roots, and have no abiding hold upon our imagination.

Just as the lighter fiction can be seen in the light of his provincial upbringing and of his work in London as a journalist, so his more serious fiction, *The Old Wives' Tale* and *Clayhanger,* can be seen in the light of his provincial youth and of the French influences. . . . These novels, we may say, are the children of an Anglo-French union, a marriage between English life and French literature. . . . [The realists] emphasized the drab and bleak aspects of this life, insisted upon inconclusive or deliberately unhappy endings, and tended to cast about for unpleasant characters and incidents just as the romanticists cast about for pleasant ones. Bennett, under the spell of naturalism, did not do this, but he did lay the stress upon the average, he did begin with the commonplace, and saw himself as a kind of social historian, whose business it was to touch in a large background, to sketch a whole epoch, to show the individual in his or her relation to the whole environment. (p. 266)

It would be difficult to overpraise the skill with which [*The Old Wives' Tale* and *Clayhanger*] have been devised and executed. . . . [Despite] their drab setting, their deliberate insistence upon prosaic matters, and their uneasy skepticism, which makes their author appear an ironical spectator of this life—despite all these things, they are really the work of a thorough romantic. Bennett is an English romantic working in an alien method, a method that suggests anything rather than the romantic outlook and temper. . . . He hustles away all the usual romantic trappings, the tinsel and the limelight and the sobbing violins, brings before us the most commonplace people in the dingiest and dreariest setting it is possible to imagine, and then proceeds to evolve romance. There is always present in his mind, and if it is not in the reader's too then the whole significance of these fictions has been missed, the piquant contrast between what we might call the "outward" and the "inward" views of his creatures' lives. . . . [Unless] the reader keeps this contrast in mind, the romantic significance of these stories is lost. Modern life is peculiarly suitable for this method of treatment because, with all its bewildering and intricate organization, it presents to us a mass of fellow-creatures who are not, so to speak, realized as fellow-creatures at all except at odd moments; we see them as economic units and what not, and their real humanity is lost. . . . Because we see them in terms of tags and labels, we are apt to forget that their lives to them are as exciting and wonderful as are our lives to us. In earlier times, the common brotherhood of men was ever present in men's minds—a universal religion never allowed them to forget the fact; but in our great modern cities we need to be ever reminded, and it says a good deal for Arnold Bennett that . . . he has revealed and stressed this common humanity. So far, so good. And yet something is wrong. . . . It is not enough that he should run a kind of romantic obstacle race; he should give us a personal vision of this world. The same fault we remarked in his lighter work is present in a slightly different form here too; he is too general, too easily satisfied with a broad average; he does not dig deep enough. We feel a want in him of values, a certain insensitiveness to the finer shades of feeling, the more subtle traits of character, the more poetical and mystical states of mind. He lacks the philosophic imagination that is necessary to all works of art on a great scale. He takes his old woman in the provinces, his dead miser in Clerkenwell, and, running back over their lives, contrives to tell us more of the truth about them than all the newspaper reports or the works of the social historian; but, we feel, he does not tell us the whole truth about them, not because he does not wish to but simply because he cannot. . . . [He] is a great journalist, who has an unflagging zest for and curiosity about the surfaces of this life; but while he has the virtues, the very solid virtues, of the great journalist, he has also the serious limitations. Whole sides of life and states of mind, and these not the least important, some of them perhaps the most important, seem to mean nothing to him; he can humanize the world of the newspapers, but cannot even enter the world of the poets and the saints and the philosophers. It is only right that he should have become one of the most successful men of letters of his time, if only because he is very much a creature of his time who has exploited, with extraordinary skill, the modern world as perhaps no other novelist, with the possible exception of Mr. Wells, has exploited it. An ordinary man of talent could not have done it; a great man of genius would have done something more. (pp. 266-68)

*J. B. Priestley, "Modern English Novelists: Arnold
Bennett," in* English Journal *(copyright © 1925 by
the National Council of Teachers of English), Vol.
XIV, No. 4, April, 1925, pp. 261-68.*

ELIZABETH A. DREW (essay date 1926)

[If] we judged [Arnold Bennett's] literary personality by the
lay sermons christened by him **"Pocket Philosophies,"** his
vision of life, though full of sound common sense and honesty
of outlook, is nothing but a restatement of maxims and aphorisms already better expressed by the sayings of Christ, Ep-
ictetus, and Marcus Aurelius. There are nine **Pocket Philosophies** and they may be distinguished—by their titles.
Otherwise they are a triumph of saying the same thing, very
often, at considerable length, in a variety of different ways.
Their message is an excellent one. . . . But again, the **"Pocket
Philosophies"** are journalism. What they say is true, but what
literature does and what journalism does not is to give the
truths of life *adequate and memorable expression* in artistic
form. (pp. 200-01)

Probably the main reason for this failure is the difficulty of
making the truths of life appear as living truth in so general
a fashion—the intensest interest in the study of living, being
the struggle, fresh born in every individual soul, between
personality and environment, the ceaseless effort of the ego
to harmonize itself with its surroundings. Once plunged into
the excitement of watching *this* spectacle, once concerned
more with the limitations than with the potentialities of human
existence, we find the real Arnold Bennett. (pp. 201-02)

[There] is no one with a keener sense of the immense importance of the correlation of all phenomena in the judgment
of any individual and of any event. But though all phenomena
excite him, he stands first and foremost as the creator of one
very specified set of phenomena, those connected with the
industrial and midland district of England known generally
as the Potteries, and christened by Arnold Bennett the Five
Towns. If any one thinks of Arnold Bennett, he inevitably
thinks of the Five Towns. Of course Bennett constantly creates whole stories outside that setting. . . . But no one thinks
of such books as typical Bennett books. (p. 202)

[Bennett takes] drab human beings in their drab surroundings
and shows how the eternal laws of humanity fulfil themselves
in them: how they face, or fail to face, the eternal problems
and the eternal experiences, and how, from the highest to
the lowest, irrespective of class or calling, life invariably
tricks the individual, filling him or her with ever blossoming
hopes and expectations, smiting him in the end with the
common lot of apparent futility. (pp. 203-04)

The meaning of life to Bennett, in so far as the word "meaning" can be applied to so diffused an impression as he leaves,
seems to be simply that, though life never fails to cheat the
individual, and though the onlooker cannot fail to be filled
with an overwhelming sense of the ironic hopelessness of it
all, life is nevertheless worth living, simply because each
individual instinctively and tenaciously holds it to be so. . . .
[No] life is dull unless the liver of that life feels it to be
purposeless—a frame of mind very rare among simple people.
Arnold Bennett's genius is original in the double vision which
he brings to his creation of human consciousness, in his
power to combine the sense of ironic detachment from the
lives he presents, with, at the same time, a complete identification with them. On the one hand we are made keenly

conscious of how environment has warped and prejudiced
these minds, how imperfectly they are exercised and trained,
how inadequate and superficial and impoverished they are,
how much they miss of the potentialities of existence. . . .
Having shown us these lives as they appear in the light of
a sophisticated, cultivated experience, he proceeds to identify himself with his creations, to show how these lives appear
to themselves, and how, viewed from that standpoint, nothing
is lost to them, because the whole perspective is entirely
altered. (pp. 205-06)

Arnold Bennett's sensitive curiosity of mind delights to probe
all the myriad secrets of impulse and motive, all the myriad
effects of emotion and intensity of life which lurk under the
most forbidding externals, the most apparently impenetrable
disguises, and his especial genius as an artist is seen by the
skill with which he communicates his own excitement to the
reader. (p. 207)

It is not possible to claim that Arnold Bennett can suggest
the pinnacles and abysses, the heights and depths of human
passion. He is not master of these, but of the common path-
ways of average experience; his emotional power is in his
creation of the atmosphere of ordinary happenings to ordinary people, in his reminting of the commonplace event, in
his discovery of the living truth in platitude. (p. 209)

Though Arnold Bennett always has a great air of omniscience
on the subject of the normal relations of men and women in
love and marriage, I think he is, in fact, less successful with
that theme than with any other. He will convey flashes of
insight into general truths . . . , or he can produce a stabbing
sense of reality in individual scenes. . . . But his treatment
of the central relationship, though he suggests extraordinarily
well its basic quality in human affairs, is nevertheless stereotyped. He seems almost obsessed by what one critic has
called the "formidableness" of the female; a wife is simply
Woman to him, and though there is variety in his husbands,
women, once married, seem all the same. Hilda Lessways,
Helen Rathbone, Mrs. Prohack, Lilian, and the heroines of
many short stories are all simply The Sex—plausible, dishonest, wheedling, affectionate, unscrupulous, crooked, and
clinging!

Indeed, this point might be pressed further into a statement
that Bennett always succeeds far better in conveying broad
effects or in diffused analyses of developing states of mind
than in the direct clash of personality or the moment of intense
emotion. (pp. 211-12)

It is the same bias for amplitude rather than intensity of
imagination which makes Bennett so skilful a summarizer of
the general in the particular, of universal human problems
in individual instances. . . . Part of the same gift, too, on a
lower plane is his faculty for a pungent summing up of typical
things or persons so that they are instantly recognizable. (pp.
212-13)

Another illustration of his genius for broad effects is what
is perhaps his greatest achievement in the presentation of
life, the brilliance with which he suggests the atmosphere of
general environment, of the forces with which the individual
is ever, consciously or unconsciously, at grips. He assembles
every scrap of evidence which goes to the making of a personality what it is. We see every detail of the time and the
place and the human background against which his characters
play their parts. . . . Yet with all the wealth of atmosphere
which Arnold Bennett creates about his human figures, they

are never lost in it. He insists not only on the truth that environment influences character, but on the far bigger and more interesting truth that character triumphs over environment. (pp. 214-15)

It needs very little reading in the novels of Arnold Bennett to conclude that he is supremely interested in the practice rather than in the theory of life. The perception of a fact thrills him as the conception of an idea thrills Wells. . . . Bennett illustrates Change simply as change, infinitely interesting to mark and analyze in the process of examining man in his environment, but not a matter to theorize about. Wells sees each step as a possibility in the evolution of Utopia. Change as change means nothing to him unless it be a stage in development; the present or the past is only of interest in so far as it may affect the future. . . . Bennett, again, can bring home as vividly as Wells the horror of poverty and squalor. . . . But he does not use such descriptions for any purpose of propaganda. There is no comment on such conditions: no passionate insistence on their crying injustice to the dignity of man: no appeal to our pity for suffering fellow creatures: no insistent determination that such things must cease. (pp. 215-17)

No, Bennett loves to recount detail simply because he loves to mark, with patient acuteness, everything which makes humanity as it is, and which humanity has made as it is. (p. 217)

Arnold Bennett's aim has been to render in writing as much of human life as he is capable of rendering. . . . He has done a mass of second-rate work, but I doubt if there is a single novel of his which does not contain scenes which no one but himself could have created so well, and in his finest books, in *The Old Wives' Tale*, in *Clayhanger*, in *Riceyman Steps*, he is a great sustained literary artist. On the one hand a brilliant craftsman, and on the other a man with a width of tolerant sympathy which perhaps has not been met in English fiction since Fielding. (p. 219)

> *Elizabeth A. Drew, "Arnold Bennett," in her* The Modern Novel: Some Aspects of Contemporary Fiction *(copyright 1926 by Harcourt Brace Jovanovich, Inc.; copyright 1953 by Elizabeth A. Drew; reprinted by permission of the publisher), Harcourt, 1926, pp. 197-221.*

REBECCA WEST (essay date 1928)

All our youth they hung about the houses of our minds like Uncles, the Big Four: H. G. Wells, George Bernard Shaw, John Galsworthy and Arnold Bennett. They had the generosity, the charm, the loquacity of visiting uncles. (p. 215)

Why is Uncle Bennett as good an uncle as any of them? Why, one might ask, does he count as an uncle at all? For it is not at all easy to chalk up what he has done for us. The mark of the visiting uncles, we have decided, is charm, and generosity and loquacity. Now Uncle Bennett has, superficially, very little charm at all. Very rarely does he attain that flash of phrase which is to the literary personality what brightness of eye and lip are to the physical personality. He is often a flat writer. Not a quiet writer, or a sober writer, or a restrained writer. Just a flat writer. His loquacity is neither spontaneous like Uncle Wells's, nor artful like Uncle Shaw's, nor poignant like Uncle Galsworthy's. It is never urgent. There are innumerable occasions when one suspects that he writes, not because he has something to say, but because of that abstract

desire to write, which is hardly ever the progenitor of good writing. His generosity certainly does not lie in the direction of general ideas, for he rarely refers to any, not to an extent that must be almost without parallel among the greater novelists in the invention of character.

Hardly any of his figures remain alive in the memory. There is certainly Elsie in *Riceyman Steps*, and Denry in *The Card*, but the one is an exquisitely drawn abstraction of tenderness and the other no more than a comic gesture. . . . [Even *The Old Wives' Tale*] gives us no characters. And the worst of it all is that his books are so often isolation hospitals full of the most feeble qualities.

All the Uncles have written twaddle in their time. . . . But Uncle Bennett does it again and again. *The Book of Carlotta, Lilian, Elsie and the Child, Our Women*—these are mere runnings of the pen. And the plays—*Judith, the Bright Island*. That last set a whole London theatre whimpering with boredom.

Yet the man is great. We must, indeed, count him as one of the Uncles of the English-speaking world who have more influence on innumerable young people than anybody else save their fathers and mothers; who fix thereby the colour of their times. He does not give what the others give, but he gives.

And one can see what his gifts are, and how lavish he is with them, and why he is incapable of giving what the others do, if one turns to *Lord Raingo*. That book is a failure and it is a success. It is a success because one likes it to the extent of carrying it about with one all day, reading and re-reading little pet half-pages. It is a failure because it does nothing at all with its subject. It distils no significance from it; it merely makes a bungling statement of it. (pp. 220-22)

[The love affair] is so awkwardly presented that when one closes the book one is left with no picture of it save poor old Sam Raingo clumping up the steps to the aerie where he keeps the lady and being either embarrassed by finding her with her sister, the bus conductor, or desolated by not finding her at all. Almost as little is done with the climax of the story. He gives no explanation of the girl's cruel desertion of her old lover for death except an innate melancholic taint, acted upon by the appearance in the casualty list of a former lover. But he does not convince us beforehand that she had that melancholic taint. It is perfectly true that he tells us so several times, but only by flat statement. . . . But never once does he invent the phrase, the speech, the incident, that would be the right hieroglyphic to stamp on our minds for ever the conviction that this creature, though young and beautiful and passionate enough to make an ageing man feel that his age was an adjustable defect like something a little wrong with the eyesight, had nevertheless looked on the waters of life and seen them dark.

Lord Raingo himself is treated almost as perfunctorily. The physical circumstances of his death are magnificently described. . . . But the obvious poignancy of his mental situation, the despair which must have crept over the old man as he realized that the woman he had chosen to wipe out the fact of death with her abounding life had betrayed him and gone over to the side of the enemy, is simply not stated. One gets not the slightest sense, in between the paragraphs which are tersely devoted to its manufacture, that he was saturated with love for this woman and distress at her fate; without which sense there is no subject at all.

And there is Gwen. Deplorably there is Gwen. . . . [She] makes insane, explosive interruptions into the story, repeatedly casting herself on Lord Raingo's death-bed, or fainting round it, and failing throughout to establish any sort of organic connection with the theme. In her, and in the equally irrelevant Mrs. Blacklow, who wanders through the story, being the most explicitly expectant mother in fiction, though having none of the characters to thank for it, is made manifest the curious hectic incompetence which comes upon Mr. Bennett so long as *Lord Raingo* is faithful to its main subject.

Yet the book is full of exquisite things. Once he steps out of the romantic circle of his principal characters, he has beauty at his finger-ends. (pp. 224-26)

[There are lots of things throughout the book] that have the rich air of not having been looked for, of having happened to the author; or rather, so independent of him do they seem, to his manuscript, of having inscribed themselves on the paper without the intervention of the pen by virtue of their fidelity to life, their propriety to the theme they illustrate. They are little presents given to the book by the unconscious. (p. 228)

Mr. Bennett's unconscious clearly reveals to us in *Lord Raingo* by its alternate meanness and lavishness, what its preferences are, and why he is one of the most unequal writers who ever attained to eminence. It does not do a hand's turn for him when he is dealing with his romantic theme. It refuses to present him with one felicity. And it leaves him as severely alone in the other part of the novel which deals satirically with the quarrels and intrigues of our statesmen during the war. The thing is competently done, but there is nothing over and above the unsurprising findings of logic.

But once Mr. Bennett deals with subsidiary themes that lead him away from the great ones of the earth to the humble, that lead him from what are considered the high lights of life to its obscurities, then these gifts are showered on him. (pp. 228-29)

[Mr. Bennett's unconscious] distrusts pomp and picturesqueness. . . . It hates the elevation of one man above another. Mr. Bennett can never work happily on a character which is not socially and personally mediocre. It wants to skip all the moments in life that are traditionally splendid and roseate in favour of the moments that are simply pieces of the general texture of life. Whensoever a Bennett character embraces a physically pleasing female his prose crumbles in cliches, in which the words, bland, superb, delicious, tender, are apt to occur. It is when an old clerk grumbles at his employer, a housemaid pokes her head over the banisters, that Mr. Bennett's unconscious softens, warms, glows in a transport of generosity, and gives him such inspirations as this sullen, loving vigil of Wrenkin in the power-house.

And that is why Uncle Bennett ranks as an Uncle; as one who brings gifts to the minds of the young, who is fixing the colour of his times. For there is a great deal in this Protestant art. It is quite true that if pomp and picturesqueness are cut away from worship the thoughts of the worshipper may turn to simpler and deeper issues. It is quite true that there is a glory about all men, about the flock as well as its leaders. It is quite true that life unlit by excitement is nevertheless a light shining in the darkness of the universe.

That is what Uncle Bennett's art proves to us. (pp. 229-30)

He can show us a man going into a shop to buy shoes as one who performs a wonderful ritual, beautiful because all those participating in it follow grooves so patiently worn down by those who, in following them through the ages, have served certain human necessities, certain human ideals of duty. He can see the tram-car passing through a suburb at twilight as the chariot of fire it veritably is. Like Wordsworth, he has triumphed over the habitual; he has not let it disguise the particle of beauty from him. Though he might never produce one single perfect or even imperfect work of art, or never produce a work of art at all, he remains an artist. (p. 231)

> *Rebecca West, in an essay in* The New York Herald Tribune *(copyright 1926 by the New York Tribune, Inc.; copyright renewed © 1954 by Rebecca West; reprinted by permission of Viking Penguin, Inc.) October 10, 1926 (and reprinted as "Uncle Bennett," in her* The Strange Necessity, *Doubleday, Doran & Company, Inc., pp. 215-33).*

WILBUR L. CROSS (essay date 1930)

[Those novels which Arnold Bennett designated as "fantasias"] are light and humorous structures, built as a rule upon a single bizarre incident lying outside the realm of probability. What would the consequences be, Bennett asks himself, should the incident with which he sets out actually occur? Fantasy, realism, and social satire gaily mingle in the story he has to tell. (p. 67)

Reading the best of his fantasias, from the earliest onward, one sees a genuine artistic sense winning against the purveyor of words. As Henry James remarked of Balzac, the man of business is doubled with the artist.

The man of business was a product of the Five Towns, where he was born and bred, and where, with few exceptions, he has placed, in whole or in part, the scene of his most characteristic novels. (pp. 68-9)

[The great Five Towns] novels, though not so entertaining as the fantasias, represent Bennett at his best. (p. 79)

No one had ever written novels much like these. . . . However much Bennett may have learned from his great predecessors, his art and procedure were his own. The Clayhanger trilogy and **"The Old Wives' Tale"** have, in the Aristotelian sense, no beginning, nor middle, nor end. And of plot as understood by the Victorians there are only traces. The villain is retained to work mischief and finally to pay the penalty for misdeeds by imprisonment, transportation, or miserable death. But except for this conventional blot, the idea of retribution is either absent or so concealed as to be barely visible. Nor is there a situation to be unfolded and brought to a conclusion. This form of novel, which Bennett had experimented with in **"Anna of the Five Towns,"** he discarded, presumably that the action of his characters might not be cramped by the restraint of a fixed frame of circumstance. (pp. 84-5)

In their art James and Bennett are as far from each other as the poles of the earth. For James in his mature manner the novel involved a psychological problem in the relationship between a small group of characters. Everything that did not contribute to the solution was ruthlessly excluded, so that there might be no confusion or misunderstanding in the artistic process. James hung his characters, as it were, in a vacuum. . . . In contrast Bennett leaves nothing unsaid. (pp. 86-7)

These details, it is admitted, will be of great value to the historian a century or two hence, who may wish to know about life in an industrial town back in the age of Queen Victoria. But, it is asked, what have they to do with a novel? It is, however, easy enough to see Bennett's drift. He was in reaction against the old narrow conception of the novel. . . . Bennett seems to say: Let us see if we cannot bring fiction into the very business of life. So he casts aside the conventional framework of the novelist's art—its logic, nemesis, and so-called "significant incidents" or "crucial moments," all of which are artificial devices for making life much more simple than it really is. After all, as [William] Hazlitt had remarked, our conduct is governed by the common occurrences of every day, which, though they once appeared trivial, assume significance in the long perspective of later years. Bennett's characters are placed in this long perspective. His masses of facts, statistics, and particulars, quite apart from the question of their relevancy in specific instances, are impressive when thus viewed as a whole. He accomplished his purpose, which was to throw over fiction the illusion of life as lived by ordinary men and women.

But his judgment sometimes failed him. Not often in "**The Old Wives' Tale,**" which is nearly perfect in its kind. It is in the trilogy that he lost artistic control of his material. There should have been here only one instead of three novels. The subject warranted no more. Bennett came to the end of "**Clayhanger**" with several loose threads in the story; and instead of going back over his manuscript to gather them up he went on to write another novel, perhaps for commercial reasons. Only incidentally is "**Hilda Lessways,**" as the author claimed for it, a re-telling of "**Clayhanger**" from the heroine's point of view. It is an appendix, in places literally repetitious, to explain Hilda's conduct where it was left mysterious. A few sentences here and there in "**Clayhanger**" would have made everything clear. "**These Twain**" is a second appendix, of five or six hundred pages of inordinate detail. . . . (pp. 89-91)

Bennett's novels are a record of what may be perceived, without much comment. In this respect he is like Homer, who does not stop to moralize. He adopts in places the mechanism of the psychological novel in that his characters are sometimes made to say to the reader what is held back from their associates, after the analogy of the dramatic aside and monologue. Their thoughts and emotions, however, lie close to the surface of the mind. Rarely do they reveal the depths. The author, one suspects, does not know what is going on below. . . . In general, innumerable details concerning the behavior of his characters have little or no discernible psychological import. His method is in direct contrast with Dostoevsky's, in whose novels whatever is said or done is an avenue to an underworld of impulse and emotion.

Equally objective is Bennett's treatment of environment. Nothing is left out of the account. One may easily draw a map of the Five Towns from Bennett's descriptions of them. The characters, it is assumed, belong to that industrial area and to no other. Its hold upon them is irresistible. . . . But wherein lies the magnetic force of the unlovely Five Towns? Bennett never tells. . . . With Conrad and Hardy character and environment become, by an imaginative process, one. Neither quite exists apart from the other. If Bennett has this imaginative grasp, he fails to exert it, and so leaves with the reader the labor of correlating a multitude of disconnected facts and perceptions. Compared with Conrad and Hardy, his is a looser and, at the same time, a more impersonal art. Of all English novelists Bennett comes the nearest to sheer objectivity.

His perceptions are recorded in an exact time sequence. . . . Time never moves backward as in Conrad; it is always going forward, bringing silently change to men and women and their institutions and at last bringing death. . . . A multitude of details gives the effect of a long lapse of time between youth and middle life and old age. In the course of years, time, symbolizing the life of man, wears him down. In "**The Old Wives' Tale**" nearly everyone dies or is brought near to death. (pp. 92-5)

Bennett's comment on death is as interesting for what it omits as for what it says. There is no moralizing on the brevity of life. . . . Neither is there insistence on the vanity of human life. The reader must decide for himself whether the lives of any of the characters are worth while as one generation treads upon the heels of another. . . . Bennett stops short with the death of his characters as the end of every man. There is no afterglow, as there was in George Eliot, of a world made better by ordinary men and women "who lived faithfully a hidden life and rest in unvisited tombs." In distinction, Bennett is a materialist in that he deals mainly with the outward aspects of material things, culminating in the fading away of the mind in senility and death. Here the book of life closes. (pp. 96-8)

> *Wilbur L. Cross, "Arnold Bennett," in his* Four Contemporary Novelists *(copyright 1930 Macmillan Company), Macmillan, 1930 (and reprinted by Books for Libraries Press, 1966; distributed by Arno Press, Inc.), pp. 63-102.*

W. SOMERSET MAUGHAM   (essay date 1931)

I was astounded to discover that [Arnold Bennett's *The Old Wives' Tale*] was a great book. I was thrilled. I was enchanted. I was deeply impressed. I had never suspected that Arnold was capable of writing anything of the sort. It would be impertinent of me to say anything in praise of it. I have read many appreciations of it, and I think everything has been said but one thing, and that is that it is eminently readable. I should not mention a merit that is so obvious except that many great books do not possess it. It is the greatest gift of the story-teller, and one that Arnold Bennett had even in his slightest and most trivial pieces. I thought at first that he owed it to his journalistic training, but . . . now I am under the impression that it is due to the intense interest the author has in what he is writing at the moment. (p. 416)

[Bennett] was neither mystic nor poet. He was interested in material things and in the passions common to all men. He described life, as every writer does, in the terms of his own temperament. He was more concerned with the man in the street than with the exceptional person. (p. 420)

The Old Wives' Tale is certainly the best book he wrote. He never lost the desire to write another as good, and because it was written by an effort of will he thought he could repeat it. He tried in *Clayhanger*, and for a time it looked as though he might succeed. I think he failed only because his material fizzled out. After *The Old Wives' Tale* he had not enough left to complete the vast structure he had designed. (p. 421)

W. Somerset Maugham, "Arnold Bennett," in Life and Letters, *Vol. VI, June, 1931, pp. 413-22.*

GEOFFREY WEST (essay date 1932)

[In both *The Old Wives' Tale* and *Riceyman Steps,* Bennett's] method, the formula by which he worked, is the same. Both are remarkable, among English novels, for their coherence and economy of construction, for their seeming detachment, their almost perfect suppression of the author's personality. The stories proceed by means of a succession of details, of tiny incidents often apparently unimportant in themselves. Life is presented, to use one of Bennett's own phrases, as a drama in ten thousand acts. . . . The characters have all, with few exceptions, a life of their own; and they move in a world the reality of which cannot be denied. And yet, quite beyond the question of their relative scopes, there is a considerable difference between the books. Where one moves to emotion, the other fails to move; where one is beautiful, the other is often almost inhuman; where one is significant, the other is unimportant; where one stands by general agreement as one of the great English novels of the present century, the other falls, by its lack of spiritual quality, below the level of the works of many lesser men. *Riceyman Steps* shows how tedious, even in a master's hands, the method of cumulative detail can become when uninformed by significance. In *The Old Wives' Tale* it is never so, for there the structure, the whole, is itself a living organism; life is breathed into it by an unfailing sense of the human tragedy of time and change. (pp. 12-14)

Riceyman Steps has no such pervading emotion. Page after page is dull, heavy with *dead* detail. The descriptions lack the vital quality of those in the earlier work, they photograph the actuality rather than portray the essential reality, and they are far too frequent and long. (p. 14)

The characters, too, of *Riceyman Steps,* for all their life, have little significance; one feels they do not matter very much, after all. Mr. Earlforward's extraordinary inner life and his commonplace outward appearance and behaviour remain unrelated. John Baines is twenty times as human though he appears in a few pages only. There is from every point of view a vast gulf between the two books. With one Bennett placed himself in the very first rank of English novelists; the other was a gallant effort, perhaps, to regain that height, but it did not succeed. It was as though there was now something "irrevocably dead" in his soul. (p. 16)

The essential qualities of Bennett's best books are fairly evident. . . . [Their] effort towards impersonality, their scrupulous construction, the easy movement of the prose, careful, though rarely rising above a level of exact statement and generally devoid of metaphor, . . . make evident his devotion to the French masters, and draw attention to certain psychological resemblances to Flaubert if no other. Despite some superficial differences, they have both the power of rendering appearances combined with very little of "the true faculty of metaphor." Both are devotees of a *controlled* art. Both exhibit evidences of documentation, however well justified, and at times a dependence upon a simple accumulation of material. Both hold composition to be the basis of art; in Bennett's phrase, presentment is more than the thing presented. It may, too, be said of Bennett, as of Flaubert, that whenever one is struck by the inexplicable beauty of a particular passage, the secret of its enchantment will be found

in its power of awakening in us a sense of the process of time. His range of sensibility, also, is small, or his interest restricted; he never departed far from normality, his heroes were essentially "average" men as Wells's (say) are not. . . . [Bennett] approaches the riddle of the humble, *un*conscious man or woman, to discern and reveal therein "the vein of greatness which runs through every soul without exception."

A yet more striking parallel with Flaubert might be found in their lack of inward growth, the absence in their books of any spiritual progression. In Bennett's case one could not even feel that his foundations, after a certain point, became stronger; he might concern himself with a larger extent of life, but with no new profundity. It would seem evident that his creative impulse was, like Flaubert's, never overwhelmingly powerful, always strictly under control. . . . (pp. 62-4)

But the intrinsic vitality or lack of vitality of the creative impulse apart, what was the personal, the fundamental, attitude behind that impulse? A clue is found in the general characteristics of Bennett's most satisfying work, [*The Old Wives' Tale*]. There is the steadfast avoidance in all his serious novels, of any unusual plot; the fact, too, that few of his characters are, in themselves, astonishing or even striking individualities. We have seen that he did indeed, in selecting his material, make a conscious rejection of those strands in the complex web of life which differentiated themselves from the general background, that the individual *as such* made little appeal to him, but rather the web itself, the eternal One which the numberless many compose. And it is just such an attitude that characterises *The Old Wives' Tale*. In fact, it may be said that without exception his writing at its finest induces this feeling of the *stream* of life flowing majestically, relentlessly, from eternity to eternity. (pp. 64-5)

Acceptance was his final wisdom and his constant theme. . . . During the whole period of [the writing of *The Old Wives' Tale*] that impulse sustained him, his vision did not fail; he looked upon his world with both charity and calmness, and its pattern, its unity, its harmony, was made clear to him. It has been suggested that the book displays a pessimistic attitude to life, as in the famous passage describing Sophia's feeling in confronting the dead body of her husband after a separation of nearly forty years. . . . (pp. 66-7)

[It] is certainly one of the great passages of English fiction. In itself it might seem the complete expression of the "purely" materialistic attitude to life, a resignation to despair. But the effect of the meeting upon Sophia is not necessarily the effect of the passage as a whole upon the reader. *Her* feeling may be one of revolt against the riddle of life, but in its place, and from the angle of a true appreciation, the scene is itself an answer to that riddle. (p. 68)

[It] was necessarily [Bennett's] task not to conceive and erect new worlds, but rather to turn all his "passionate intensity of vision" upon the world about him, until by peering into the depths beneath appearances he could regard all with universal and unfailing sympathy, and discern beyond its apparent chaos the pattern, complete and harmonious, of its essential unity. His impulse was not intense, nor was it compelling; it was, so to say, pitched on a low note—it had no overwhelming emotional source. Emotionally Bennett was aware of wonder in the spectacle of the universe; intellectually he was a materialist, and he was dominated by his intellect—or, to use a less definitive term, by his intellectual consciousness. (p. 70)

When he trusted—or thought he was trusting—his imagination (as in *The Glimpse*) he failed most lamentably of all.

Still, if imagination never forced him to authentic heights of ecstasy, nevertheless at his best it vibrated deeply through his being, at one continuous level. Rarely would it rise to the surface, so that it was quite possible for his outward personality to be altogether different from his inward and fundamental beliefs, and for his very best work to alternate with almost his very worst. . . . (pp. 72-3)

[The] crux of his attitude was acceptance, which implies perfect love, and in love there cannot be condescension. It was clearly his desire for justice that was instinctive: compassion, the greater, the *necessary* quality, was a conscious exercise. It pervaded *The Old Wives' Tale*, so long dwelt upon, absolutely. . . . Always a novelist rather of observation than of intuition (he did of course reveal at times remarkable qualities of insight), it was inevitable that he should, under the strain of continuous production, unable to wait upon "the language of the imagination," write more and more from the surface, that the artist should tend more and more to call in the aid of the efficient literary journalist, that more and more the sardonic, the capable, the knowing Mr. Bennett should become the voice through which the true self had to speak. He was, as man and as artist, hopelessly divided within himself, and the result was apparent in his works, the contrasting qualities of which can indeed only be understood in the light of that essential fact. (pp. 75-6)

[When Bennett] threw away the discipline of the French method he gained no compensating advantage. The failure of *The Clayhanger Family* to reach the highest level was due to diffuseness and repetition, an unevenness in the writing, the plain statements of the author's own feeling and judgment. *The Price of Love* was more than ever lacking in true detachment. (p. 78)

It may have been the consciousness of [Bennett's] clear decline which brought him to the renewed effort of *Riceyman Steps*. . . . With *Riceyman Steps* he strove to take up again a formula discarded (in faith if not in fact) ten years before. It failed, as it was bound to fail. The externals—the construction, the cumulative detail, the adherence to plain fact, the detachment—he could present with all the skill of the experienced craftsman, though it was significant, indeed, to see him, whose concern had always been essentially with the great normalities of life, turning to the grotesque. But the spirit had vanished, the impulse faded; he possessed no longer a secure knowledge.

The rest, on the spiritual plane, was *débâcle*. Death had always fascinated him, for obvious reasons. In the finite he sought to demonstrate the signature of the infinite, in mortality of the eternal. It was his faith that greatness is in all of us, that not one sparrow should fall to the earth unremarked. But deficient in "the sense of the sublime" it was no easy task; it was, however, least difficult of all when his characters approached the very gateway from time to eternity—Death. . . . All in all, he was never so impressive as when he wrote of it; his characters attained in their dying a dignity above their living. In *The Old Wives' Tale*, and even in *Clayhanger*, he could dominate death by the spiritual power that was in him. Compassion rose above despair to bestow nobility. But as the spirit died in him, death became a mortal terror, no more and no less. In *Riceyman Steps* and again in *Lord Raingo* he no longer triumphs but is triumphed over.

One feels here a fundamental morbidity; no more is death the natural sleep that rounds our life, but an obscene enemy whose lineaments must be told over and over, each creaking footstep of its approach recorded. Thereafter, defeated, he fled from it. He would wrestle with the antagonist no more. (pp. 79-80)

Bennett really reverenced all life. Every manifestation of the human spirit, in particular, seemed to fascinate him; just because a thing *was*, it therefore became worthy of attention and exaltation. "Everything on earth is beautiful." In a sense that is true, but it demands a tremendous and unremitting exercise of imagination to evoke the vision of pure being upon the plane of existence, to bring the illumination of eternity into the sphere of time. The effort was, after a point, beyond him. In place of the need to *show* the significance of things, he adopted the formula that things were of themselves significant, which was a totally different matter. In effect it meant that he abandoned the struggle, that he accepted contemporary standards. (p. 82)

In the divided self there must always be conqueror and conquered, and in Arnold Bennett the fundamental succumbed to the comparatively superficial. His once deep feeling for humanity became humanitarianism, and his "charity" an amiable benevolence. (p. 83)

[While] it seems necessary, or at least illuminating, to understand Bennett's psychology as artist and its effects upon his work as a whole, his positive achievement remains the final fact. (p. 85)

[He] sought very carefully to make his best novels true *to* if not *in* life, and his method was essentially realist, proceeding by naturalistic, almost photographic exactitude of description, striving to show the soul not above but within the common, the familiar thing. Thereby he carried forward the "revolutionary" tendency of art to exalt the humble and the meek, to reveal beauty where few had discerned it before—a *new* beauty added to life, therefore. . . . He bestowed a vision, that will not recede, of significance in the mundane. Towards the end that vision died from his writings; he gave the mundane, but the spirit had fled. But a man, ultimately, is judged by his best, his peaks. Bennett wrought one work as perfect as anything written in the English language in our century. (pp. 87-8)

That he failed to integrate or to sustain his own highest values, that he could reveal the spiritual in the material but intermittently, too rarely dynamically, is not very important. His was a *true* vision. (p. 90)

Geoffrey West, in his The Problem of Arnold Bennett *(reprinted by permission of David Higham Associates Limited, as literary agents for the author), Joiner and Steele, 1932, 94 p.*

ELIZABETH D. WHEATLEY (essay date 1934)

I do not believe there is any doubt about the fact that few of [Arnold Bennett's] novels compel a return. . . . One does not finger many of the Bennett novels with a loving hand, or seek them out with a companionable eye. As a matter of fact, nowadays, in spite of his tremendous, fleeting popularity, Bennett is read, with the exception of a few things, very little at all. More and more the middle and younger generations tend to be bored by him. The great part of [Arnold Bennett's] fictions belong to the tides of recreational literature that are forever being renewed by a tireless press. . . . The reason is to be found in the fact that Bennett wrote so much about what amused him rather than about what stirred his emotions or stimulated his mind. . . . [The] result of his amused preoccupation with the play books was that much of their quality and their contents slipped over into his serious work, faded their brightness, and confused the line between what Bennett candidly meant to be temporary and what he meant to be permanent. Moreover, his best self exists in some of his lightest work. This blending of the firm and the unstable makes the critic's task of seeking out his purely temporary work very difficult, makes that task more a matter of temperament than of judgment.

In so far, however, as it may be distinguished, the lighter work of Bennett falls roughly into two divisions, that which is undisguised fantasy, and that which is blithe, ironic realism. *The Grand Babylon Hotel, The Gates of Wrath, Hugo,* and *The City of Pleasure,* come in the first category: *Denry the Audacious, The Old Adam, Buried Alive, Mr. Prohack, Accident,* and *The Vanguard,* in the second. Both divisions exhibit certain marked characteristics in common. They are concerned, as I have said, with the things that it most pleased Bennett to contemplate; and these were, first of all, wealth, the appurtenances of luxury, and the adventurous ingenuity, the hitherto unexploited charms of clever, rich, middle-aged men. Bennett's interest in machinery, yachts, hotels, railways and haberdashery, crowds the lesser novels, and appears in one way or another in nearly all of the others. (pp. 180-81)

But wealth, luxury, and modern conveniences are things essentially of the kind that date, that are soon consigned, like old photographs, to an album of forgotten days. They have nothing to do with what is significant in human life; they satiate rather than sensitize, and thus change rapidly from fashion to fashion. (p. 181)

It is just in writing about such things as . . . the gauds of wealth, that Arnold Bennett is most incurably romantic after his own particular fashion. He is like a child lost in a dream of enchanted gardens, a changeling smothered, not in faery wilds, but in modern luxury, who will not awaken and grow up. . . . Nothing in the world loses its savor so quickly as luxury. Most of us soon tire even of the dream of it, for it is dryer than skepticism.

This is not to say, however, that Bennett's novels written solely for amusement, especially the more fantastical of them, have no place in the scheme of things literary. They have a very definite place in the satisfaction of a popular demand that will always exist, the demand, the universal desire, for wonders and marvels. (p. 182)

Bennett's typical hero is . . . a middle-aged, very commonplace individual. He is a man who has completed his battle with the world and emerged, if not a millionaire, at least safely in possession of more than enough money for his needs. He is a man, moreover, of provincial simplicity who accepts with joyous astonishment and childish thrills the new luxuries that his money provides. . . . [What Bennett means by the gaiety of the middle-aged is] the awakening of the boy mind and boy desires after a youth of laboring for fortune.

Since Bennett's rich man is invariably one risen from a lower level, he is not, in spite of his impeccable new garments, an aristocrat to the manner born. He fails in almost every crucial

instance of the tact, courage, and gentleness of the true gentleman. (pp. 183-84)

He is, however, by no means an entirely contemptible or even unlikeable being. He possesses an interesting freshness of vision with regard to things that have long become stale matters of fact for other people. (p. 184)

[*The Grand Babylon Hotel*] is the best of the fantasies. . . . This first novel of the group is a glorious riot of romantic gaiety, brightly colored comic opera personages, and money spread about like pirate treasure. Everything is a little overdrawn, but everything is consistent with the wild impossibility of the tale. One feels that it might be successfully set to the tunes of a Gilbert and Sullivan opera, for it is veritable light opera material. (p. 185)

The atmosphere of the whole is gaiety very slightly touched by Arnold Bennett's habitual irony. One of the chief requirements of a story of this kind is that we shall not become so attached to the characters as to regret any eventuality, or be confounded by any horror. . . .

Bennett's other stories of the same kind as *The Grand Babylon Hotel* have not the same happy success. They are more carelessly done as if Bennett felt too sure of himself. The mysteries are conceived upon a scale too grandiose and too fantastic for modern taste; the characters lack, in general, variety, and in particular, fidelity to themselves; and the mechanism is so crude that the reader is never carried away into an atmosphere of belief. (p. 186)

Bennett did not exert himself for perfection in work of this kind. Under all his writing is faintly to be seen his contempt for his audience, particularly in this. He believed too easily that the public was pleased. . . .

Throughout the second kind of play novels, those which are more realistic and probable than the first, and which are marked by an ironic observation, the same dominant, favorite personality seems to run. The alert, rich, middle-aged man of unlimited resource is still present. But in these books, of which the best examples are *Denry the Audacious* and *Mr. Prohack,* our rich man is treated with a kindly irony as if both he and his creator well knew the real worth of his pretensions to splendor. (p. 187)

This second type of play novel deals more largely in mental attitudes and processes of thought than do the fantasies. *Mr. Prohack* is one long soliloquy. . . . In the end, Mr. Prohack has not developed at all, with all of his much thinking. He is exactly what he was to start with, a shrewd, blind, decent, crude being with a few sentimental soft spots.

Denry, Hugo, Priam Farll, Allan Frith-Walter, and even, it may be said, Lord Raingo, are all slight variations of Mr. Prohack, the same mind, the same essential being with new names. The women that accompany the middle-aged rich man in his adventures have also a perceptible likeness to one another. There are a few set types that appear again and again like a company of stock actors who are not clever enough fully to assume the characters of their various parts. (pp. 187-88)

The most amusing of all Bennett's women are his mothers, patterned, if we believe his wife, on his own mother. She is the woman who cannot be deceived, who maliciously punctures all the bubbles of man's vanity, and who is the balance of common sense over against the flatulence of monied pride.

No doubt Bennett learned his types, both men and women, in the Five Towns during the years when his observation was most penetrating and embracing. But for all that he wishes to weave romance about them and to insist upon their unique importance, they fail, after *The Old Wives Tale* and *Clayhanger,* to be individually memorable. Each set of types is a series of portraits of the same person; their witticisms have a family resemblance; their mental states are surprisingly the mental states of Bennett himself. Like flatly colored pictures, they have no suggestiveness, and once looked at, are fully comprehended and forgotten.

The most important of all the play novels in the division of ironic comedy is probably *Buried Alive.* . . . *Buried Alive* contains some of the most charming passages in all Bennett's work, and represents him at his best as a romancer of contemporary life.

The structure of nearly all the play novels is loose and jerky, so that they seem to be a crudely amalgamated series of short episodes. The atmosphere of the fairy tale clings to the most realistic of them, for the good fortune of the hero is too bright and too sudden to be entirely credible. Emotion is thinned, or rather strained to sentiment, and the tales are told with a flying facetious touch that brushes surfaces as if there were nothing beneath.

But with all their obvious faults on their heads, the play novels are decent, jolly tales. They do not provoke to laughter, but they have quiet comedy, farcical gaiety, and a sprightly, rapid style, which, if it is sometimes forced and melodramatic, is yet well suited to its purpose. They have not the vitality of the great English works of humor. Denry will never take a place by Ferdinand Count Fathom, nor Mr. Prohack by Mr. Pickwick. The field of these novels is limited and they have often been excelled in contemporary light fiction. Nevertheless, journalistic and temporary as they are, they stand on a high plane as novels whose purpose is purely to amuse, and they balance with a kind of stubborn sanity the morbid affections of modern society. (pp. 188-89)

> *Elizabeth D. Wheatley, "Arnold Bennett's Trifles: His Novels for the Gay Middle-Aged," in* The Sewanee Review *(© 1934 by The University of the South), Vol. XLII, No. 2, April-June, 1934, pp. 180-89.*

GEORGES LAFOURCADE   (essay date 1939)

[Apart] perhaps from some early effusions, and novels admittedly written to order, [Arnold Bennett's] books exhibit a remarkable unity of purpose. Whether he created or criticized, took the pen of the novelist, dramatist, critic, journalist, diarist or even perhaps letter-writer, there was in his manner something deliberate and matter-of-fact, an "objectivity", a singular absence of contradiction which excludes doubt and imprecision. (p. 2)

What saves *The Old Wives' Tale* from being an amorphous mass of details loosely connected by the threads of three or four widely different narratives is [the] rigid "unity of time" which is preserved with unflinching rectitude through the surge of so many conflicting interests and events. The style of the first chapters may not be quite in keeping with that of the rest of the story; the psychology of the characters, the realism of the descriptions may occasionally prove superficial or highly conventional; but, the "time" is genuine and every event or bit of dialogue, however unreal, is firmly embedded into that uniform temporal texture which gives life and verisimilitude to all that it touches. But *Clayhanger* and *Riceyman Steps* have as good a claim to perfection. In fact the former is probably the most perfect of Bennett's novels, the latter the most artistic. As far as style, psychology and interest are concerned, they are superior to *The Old Wives' Tale*, whose realism is easily outstripped by *The Pretty Lady* or *Lord Raingo,* while its epic proportions are almost equalled by *Imperial Palace.* It is a masterpiece, but the first masterpiece of its author, and shows immaturity, or at least timidity as well as power. The view that this novel constitutes a solitary achievement is highly debatable. It suits manuals of literature and journalists in a hurry. It ignores the fact that, in his least auspicious novels, in his most mercantile moments, Arnold Bennett is apt to write admirably (some of his best prose can be culled from stray pages of his journalistic "inquiries" or "pocket philosophies"). It presupposes that the relative value of Arnold Bennett's one hundred and thirty-five novels or short stories has been settled once and for all. A clear case of begging the question. (pp. 3-4)

[Critics] agree in feeling that the art of Bennett is somehow incomplete and in regretting alleged wasted opportunities. They not unnaturally sigh for unborn masterpieces. The man to them was greater than the work.

Is then what he *did* do so negligible? Is it not, considering whence he started and how belated was his development, something wonderful, unhoped for? . . . I can conceive quite well an Arnold Bennett who would have written *A Man from the North,* the sensational and sentimental stories, *The Card,* perhaps *Buried Alive,* and perhaps, in an inspired moment, *Leonora* and *Whom God Hath Joined*—but nothing else. But that the author of *Sacred and Profane Love,* of *The Glimpse* should also have written *Clayhanger* and *The Death of Simon Fuge* is certainly surprising. What we know of the deliberate way in which at the age of forty he sat down to write what, he had made up his mind, would be his *magnum opus,* confirms one in the impression that with remarkable energy and critical sense he took himself in hand and by sheer force of will power lifted himself to a higher plane of art. This is true at least of *The Old Wives' Tale.* The qualities which are here revealed and which in the long run impressed the literary world were not splendour and variety of style or imagination; but care, patience, a minute accumulation and elaboration of details creating at long length the illusion of the remorseless passage of time. Here was genius, if ever genius was "an infinite capacity for taking pains". . . . Surely his genius, if genius it is, was slowly and laboriously manufactured. It was chiefly a matter of selection, rejection and organization. The style of his novels, their construction, their psychology all show the traces of gradual elaboration and patient development. There is in them little that is spontaneous, immediate. . . . [Of] the solidity, soundness and symmetry of his construction, there can be no doubt. From imperfect materials a manner of perfection has been achieved. (pp. 5-7)

By conquering and preserving a large circulation without giving up his honest realism, his honest style, his honest workmanship Bennett achieved a *tour de force:* he was that rare phenomenon, a cross between the Priest and the Purveyor. And yet (so complicated this "simple" writer may sometimes seem) I wonder whether the artistic faculty was not always with him supreme, whether his mercantile outlook, his readiness to sacrifice what the public might not like or approve of were not often in subtle accordance with his inner literary conscience. What he rejected for reasons of opportunity, perhaps the artist in him would not have tolerated, though he disliked to own to such timidity of taste. Hence the comparative moderation of his realism, that exquisite balance which saved him from the worst excesses of the French and English realists. (p. 13)

[Bennett's] real message, if any, would be found in his interest in all forms of efficient activity, in work well and ingeniously performed. Also, speaking more generally, in what he termed himself in his later career his enjoyment of "the savour of life", his zest, gusto, delight in the varying phenomena of everyday existence which . . . implied genuine interest and disinterested sympathy for the less attractive or sensational aspects of life: a dog run over by a bus, a street scene. . . . It may be that an inverted sentimentality thus occasionally found an expression and gave its unique flavour to those passages in his work where a dim emotion can be guessed at, where sympathy or admiration is displayed about some of the most commonplace aspects of life. (pp. 240-241)

His sense of the wonder of life was such, his gusto, his relish of existence so keen that the least promising themes became exciting to him. He thus shared in the wide sympathy, the Christ-like charity of mind which he found in his beloved Russians. What a wonderful gift for a realistic novelist! It may be that he exercised it a little too often and somewhat indiscriminately. . . . But it soon became an indissoluble association and a permanent feature of his literary self. He deliberately created interest for himself as well as for others. Like Dostoevsky, he is never blasé, superior, sophisticated. "Nothing in life is humdrum". That became one of the tenets of his artistic creed, and is his nearest approach to a message.

He would probably have mentioned imagination as his chief claim to greatness as a novelist. . . . It is chiefly in his description and analysis of the "discord between the sexes" which form the core of some of his major novels, in his subtle discrimination between the woman's and the man's side that [his] special form of imagination is seen to best advantage. This is all the more remarkable as his understanding of women's feelings does not proceed from any real sympathy with the woman's point of view.

This psychological imagination is of course conditioned by a power of detachment which must indeed exist in any novelist worthy of the name—detachment from others as well as from oneself—the legitimate selfishness of the creator who passes from one creation to another and beholds his work impartially. Bennett's humour, slight, unobtrusive, but very real proceeds from his unimpassioned, realistic at times cruel view of men and things; it leavens pleasantly the somewhat heavy substance of his more serious novels, but is neither charitable nor good-natured. It can even be grim. . . . (pp. 242-45)

Though of paramount importance to the success of his novels Bennett's psychological insight and realistic humour are not particularly original. Others though in varying degrees have shown exactly the same gifts; they are typical of more than one Victorian novelist. But there are two features in the psychology of his characters which are outstanding and mark him out as different from his predecessors and contemporaries.

The first is the introduction of contradiction or rather of emotional discontinuity in his characters. In *Mental Efficiency* he had warned us that a mother may hate and love her son

at the same time, that a man may hate his wife and yet be sentimentally interested in her. The practice of this theory is carried out in many of his novels. . . . It is chiefly in the description of love, this notoriously illogical passion, that Bennett gives free play to his realistic description of psychological inconsistencies. . . . [We] can experience feelings of hate for the people we love and respect, especially if we are closely associated with them in daily life; it is not true to say that the two feelings struggle with each other and that the stronger conquers; they coexist and develop side by side in one of the many contradictions of our heart.

The second feature of the psychology of Bennett's characters is repression. Here he had no master, he was in need of no model. Race, education, religion, natural tendencies all converged to the same end. Owing to the inevitable fund of autobiography from which the author must, as we know, build up his novels, Bennett had to depict heroes accustomed to conceal their feelings and even to deny their very existence. But with realistic honesty he was careful to describe the power of the tendencies thus suppressed, the secret havoc which they sometimes wrought in the conqueror's heart, and even their occasional victory which brings about one of those sudden psychological changes that illustrate the discontinuity of our sentimental life. Thus Bennett pays as much attention to what his heroes would do but will not permit themselves to do as to their actions; he thus refers to the subconscious or semiconscious life of the soul far more frequently than any of his contemporaries. The character ceases to be one whole and is split into at least two different and wrangling parts. While thinking one thing, he speaks words to a totally different effect. . . . Thus in the course of a conversation we hear two voices in every character, the unspoken one being often more important than the one that actually speaks. Bennett achieves effects of simultaneity which are dear to the modern school of novelists. (pp. 246-48)

[It] is interesting to note that his characters are far from being as highly conventionalized as Balzac's or Dickens's. In fact he does not select and emphasize essential traits from the beginning. He does not lay bare the mainsprings of action. . . . He accumulates the motives that his chief characters may have to act, or he reconstructs the causes of their past actions, but he gives us no permanent clue as to the inner secret of their soul. They are not clear themselves as to what they think or are and quite realistically Bennett preserves this uncertainty, which is the uncertainty of life itself, describing them "as they seem to themselves" and not as an almighty creator might know them to be. If we were asked how these characters would behave in given circumstances we should be at a loss to answer, though no such uncertainty would prevail as to Grandet, Micawber or Pecksniff. Bennett's technique is here nearer to that of the modern novelists than to the Victorians. (pp. 249-50)

[Bennett's choice of subjects] does not commend itself either by its freshness or arresting originality. His subjects are not devoid of interest, but it is interest of a permanent or classical, not imaginative kind. In fact most of them are frankly Victorian: marriage and the relation between the sexes, parents and children, money and worldly success. . . . In the "father and son" relation however he introduced a note of reckless realistic courage which is even more striking than the somewhat oversentimental preaching heard in [Samuel Butler's] *The Way of All Flesh*. Indeed the measure of his (very relative) originality is the measure of his realism. In the social satire of *Raingo* and chiefly in his treatment of the courtesan as a literary character he certainly went further (even though it was just a little further) than his contemporaries. His realism was not only frank; it was also admirably subtle and cleverly introduced. But it was chiefly in his treatment of money that he differed from the accepted tradition. Except perhaps in *Riceyman Steps,* money is to him not associated with tragedy and sordid realism, but creative of adventure and poetry. (pp. 250-51)

[If the plots of Bennett's great novels] often appear slow and uneventful it is because he feared to make them unreal by crowding them with incidents. As with Maupassant or Flaubert, reality was to him grey, dull, quiet, tragic only in its very lack of the fresh or the unexpected. . . . In some of his best stories the plot dwindles to a mere nothing and the story seems literally to stagnate. . . . This method, while rendering it difficult to sustain the interest, makes for realism and verisimilitude as the reader always has a tendency to discount as improbable any sudden event of great consequence.

Bennett's originality lies, not in his subjects, but in the background of his novels. . . . His originality as a writer of regionalist literature consists first in the very choice of the country described—a highly industrialized and on the whole wealthy district, yet narrow, provincial and with as marked idiosyncrasies as any country town of Scotland, Barsetshire or Central France; secondly in the markedly unsympathetic presentment of this picture of provincial life. He longs to escape from the scenes which he painfully reconstructs. (pp. 252-53)

To [his] subjects such as they were he applied an exceedingly minute and patient technique which he would probably have put forward as his chief claim to literary excellence. It consists of the selection and combination of a large number of details tending to create an impression of coherence and probability. All facts which would seem to obscure this general impression were ruthlessly pared off and eliminated. No incident was too trifling to be included if it could (sometimes merely by remaining in the subconscious mind of the reader) pave the way for another incident of slightly greater importance which would itself lead to the catastrophe. (p. 254)

Just as a mechanic or a chauffeur are responsible for the safety of the engine which they construct or they drive, Bennett felt himself responsible for the verisimilitude of the actions of the characters he had created. This unflinching honesty of technique—essential to the smooth working of the machine—he maintained throughout his books, the improbabilities and melodramatic tricks of his early novels being confined to a very definite portion of his work. In particular he applied this gift of patient and loving construction to two points of technique which have always exercised the talent of novelists. First the double narrative from different or opposite points of view. The difficulty had been attempted before, and it has become one of the chief methods of the detective stories. . . . But no such close correspondence of minute particulars, no sustained parallel description of the same scenes from the man's and the woman's point of view as are to be found in the last parts of *Clayhanger* and *Hilda Lessways* had ever been attempted. One may think that the result is not worth the trouble; that the correspondence is so close, that the indentations fit so closely into each other that repetition and futility cannot be avoided; but one cannot deny the extraordinary artistic conscience and the psychological power revealed by such an achievement.

The greatest triumph of Bennett's technique lies however in another field. He used his craft with as much patience and tenacity as ever, and to incomparably better purpose, to give in a natural manner the impression of the passage of time in the course of a long narrative. (pp. 255-56)

It remains to point out that the extreme precision and efficiency of Bennett's technique do not imply an undue abstraction, a semi-mechanical process of springs released and well-oiled wheels running in grooves, which would be fatal in work of realistic pretensions. His novels have the complexity of life; there is no arbitrary simplification about them. Bennett always tried to conceal the elaborate constructions of his technique; the more complex and the more extensive were his preparations, the more he strove to make his narrative appear casual and in fact sometimes almost formless. This he attained by strict suppression of the author's personality. . . . But he chiefly attained it by the accumulation of apparently unorganized details. (p. 257)

Bennett's influence is undoubted and will be permanent. He secured, by his courage but also by his skill, more freedom, moral and religious, for the novelist; he rendered a minimum of technique necessary, and taught the reader not to tolerate a certain kind of carelessness or effrontery on the part of his favourite authors; last but not least he helped in the transformation of the novel and in the advent of a new technique by introducing discontinuity in the psychology of his characters, by attempting a more subtle rendering of the passage of time, and by making the construction of the story less obvious, and therefore more artistic.

Thus he stands halfway between the Victorians he disliked and the young generation he mistrusted, related to both, a mighty link in the chain of the English novel. Not quite in the English tradition—he was too frankly realistic, too technically perfect, too unsentimental for that. . . . (pp. 262-63)

> *Georges Lafourcade, in his* Arnold Bennett: A Study, *Frederick Muller Ltd, 1939 (and reprinted by AMS Press Inc., 1973, 293 p.).*

WALTER ALLEN   (essay date 1949)

Bennett wrote four important novels before *The Old Wives' Tale: A Man from the North, Anna of the Five Towns, Leonora* and *Whom God Hath Joined.* They are all, in varying degree and with varying success, experimental. The least typical, in the light of his mature work, is naturally enough his first, *A Man from the North;* and the finest, *Anna of the Five Towns.* (p. 47)

[*A Man from the North*] is slight, it has few of the qualities that we associate with Bennett. It is tentative work, that of a man who has yet to find himself. But it remains an attractive work, because of its seriousness and honesty. . . . [It] is distinguished by an admirable detachment and lack of presumption, and by an austerity and quietness of style that Bennett was soon to lose.

Anna of the Five Towns is not at all a marginal book, nor is it tentative. It leads us directly and immediately into the heart of the Five Towns and because of this, because of the identity of background, critics have been drawn into assuming that it is merely a precursor of *The Old Wives' Tale* and *The Clayhanger Family.* In fact, it can exist in its own right, without reference to those novels. It is not simply a pointer to later excellence but itself an achievement in excellence. Of its kind it is a masterpiece, and it has never received its due in attention or praise because the kind is a kind that is not usually Bennett's. (pp. 48-9)

[*Anna of the Five Towns*] has a centre and a central character in relation to which everything in the book exists: it is a highly organised composition dramatically presented. Anna is seen from a comparatively narrow angle of vision, presented not full-face as are the characters in the later books.... (p. 51)

In *Anna of the Five Towns*, for the first and only time in his life, Bennett was writing at the tragic level.... The provincialism of *Anna* is no less evident than that of *The Old Wives' Tale* and *Clayhanger*, but the final impression *Anna* makes is not one of provincialism.... [In *Anna*] he is not exhibiting the Five Towns to an outside world, as he does later; he takes them for granted; they are simply his *mise-en-scène*, as Wessex was for Hardy or Warwickshire for George Eliot.... [Its prose is] of a kind that Bennett would not have written much later than *Anna of the Five Towns;* with its poeticisms, its heavily latinised vocabulary, it is much more literary, more rhetorical, more formal than his later style.... [Its] dignity confers dignity on the subject-matter; it enlarges the characters, not reduces them; while its content sets them not only in a locality but also in history and in a universal struggle; just as the dramatic method of presentation that Bennett adopts produces the most moving impact on the reader that he was ever to achieve, the most moving because the point of view and the emphasis disengage the story to a greater degree than in any of his other novels from the diminishing effects of the local and temporal.

None of the three serious novels that lie between *Anna of the Five Towns* and *The Old Wives' Tale* exists in the same class; while *Sacred and Profane Love* is best forgotten as a disastrous blunder, a signal example of what may happen to a novelist when he goes outside the range of his talent and experience. It is a dreadfully vulgar, tasteless work. For all that in it Bennett sacrificed art to propaganda, *Whom God Hath Joined* is a much more worthy book. It is an attack on the publicity attending divorce cases, and the message emerges with all the nakedness of a leading article.... The novel is sometimes moving, and the character of Mrs. Fearns is excellently drawn; but as a whole *Whom God Hath Joined* suffers from all the faults of the *roman à thèse*.

Despite the melodramatic plot imposed upon it, *Leonora* ... is a much more important link in the chain of Bennett's development. In theme at any rate it partly foreshadows *The Old Wives' Tale*.... Bennett seems to have seen the novel as a deliberate challenge to conventional notions of romance and romantic love. Leonora, a brilliant and solid creation, dominates the book. (pp. 53-8)

The core of the novel [is] the slow, relentless passage of time wearing down and imperceptibly changing human beings.... (p. 59)

There is a complete absence of pressure behind the writing and when Leonora is off the stage the novel has little more significance than a novelette. (p. 60)

[With the exception of *Anna of the Five Towns*,] *The Old Wives' Tale* is the most carefully, seriously and lovingly pondered of Bennett's novels. (p. 61)

The Old Wives' Tale, it seems to me, is in all essentials unassailable.

Certainly the passage of time has never been handled more skilfully or with greater brilliance in any novel. Bennett's thesis, that young girls grow into fat old women, may be of limited truth, but it is worked out with the fullest intensity; continuously throughout the novel the contrast between youth and age—and youth and age are always relative—is illustrated in a series of instances that only ends with the end of the book.... The theme and the contrast belong to the oldest material of lyric poetry; nothing could be further from the lyrical than Bennett's expression, and yet it seems to me that the final effect of *The Old Wives' Tale* is poetic. (pp. 65-6)

Bennett describes the paralysis of John Baines as "a tragedy in ten thousand acts." The use of the word tragedy is journalistic, but as Bennett employs it the phrase equally well describes *The Old Wives' Tale* itself. And never have the ten thousand acts which make a lifetime of daily life been more cunningly disposed. (p. 66)

The adjective that seems most usually applied to Bennett's attitude to his subject-matter in *The Old Wives' Tale* is "objective." (p. 67)

[Apart] from the objectivity in the great set passages, elsewhere the tone is one of what one must call, for want of a better term, facetious irony somewhat akin to the mock heroic.... It exists sometimes in the use of a single unexpected adjective; it is more often a tone pervading a whole passage or scene. Sometimes it is blatant.... (p. 68)

[In] *The Old Wives' Tale* Bennett is no longer in any real sense a follower of the French naturalists. He has retained their sense of form; but that is all. He has become an English humorist even though he is more disciplined than the English humorists tend to be. (pp. 70-1)

The Clayhanger Family is not in any strict sense a trilogy. Rather, it is a triptych.... And the three panels must be analysed and judged separately.

When this is realised, comparison with *The Old Wives' Tale* is impossible. Bennett was attempting something different, of a lower order of artistic creation perhaps, and on a smaller scale, but to be criticised on its own terms. In *Clayhanger* he is much nearer to his subject both in time and in his position relative to it. (pp. 75-6)

Bennett, who believed passionately in the "interestingness" of ordinary things and ordinary people, was never more successful in revealing the "interestingness" of an apparently perfectly ordinary man than in *Clayhanger*. (p. 77)

Clayhanger continually surprises; or rather, Edwin himself is continually surprised, and the reader with him. For while reading *Clayhanger*, we are living at the growing point of Edwin's mind. He lives as it were by a series of continual small revelations, discoveries about life, human nature and human relationships, which may be ordinary enough in themselves, part of universal experience, but which Edwin responds to with such open-mindedness as to make them absolutely fresh. (pp. 78-9)

Hilda Lessways, one feels, was a profound mistake. Reading it, one has a curious impression of a reversal of the usual process of creation; as though an artist, having caught intuitively a perfect likeness, had then gone on to work out from the miracle itself the rough sketches, the tentative drafts, the notebook scribblings which would normally have preceded it. Hilda—the Hilda of *Clayhanger,* whom one thinks of as the real Hilda—comes to life in *Hilda Lessways* only in a few isolated passages. . . . (pp. 83-4)

Imperfect though it is, *These Twain,* the story of the married life of Edwin and Hilda, is a much better novel than *Hilda Lessways.* (p. 85)

The weakness of the novel lies once again in the picture of Hilda. . . . The portrait of Hilda in *These Twain* is a masterpiece of observation; her behaviour is recorded in the most admirably accurate manner. But why she behaves as she does, that is a different matter. Never at any time does Bennett produce a satisfying explanation for her behaviour, and one is left with the feeling that he no more than Edwin understands her, that he has fallen back on some such inadequate generalisation as "All women are capricious," and has been content to leave it at that.

For there is this essential difference between the Hilda of *Clayhanger* and the Hilda of *These Twain.* In *Clayhanger* she is presented only as she comes into the view of Edwin; but she shares *These Twain* with her husband, she is presented full face. And as she is presented she appears no more than a maddeningly neurotic woman. . . . What could have made Edwin's and Hilda's marriage credible despite the constant friction, the tantrums of Hilda's neurotic caprices, is of course physical passion. But the suggestion of physical passion is precisely what Bennett cannot give us, and the substitute for it, "What a romance she has made of my life!" is completely inadequate.

Nevertheless, despite its serious central flaw *These Twain* is a rich book. In it Bennett exploited his vein of ironical comedy to an extent he was never to achieve again. And the comedy is rich and warm. (pp. 86-7)

[*The Card*] is much the best of Bennett's light novels. A picaresque novel, it recounts the adventures of Denry Machin. . . . Denry is a near-rogue, but a consistently amusing one. He succeeds by bounce, and the novel succeeds by bounce also. (pp. 88-9)

[Then there are] the three volumes of short stories, *Tales of the Five Towns, The Grim Smile of the Five Towns,* and *The Matador of the Five Towns.* For the most part based on anecdote, the contents of these books range from the farcical to the grimly pathetic. Bennett was not a natural short-story writer; his method of writing, the steady accretion of tiny details, demanded a bigger canvas than the short story could give him; and most of his stories are further vitiated by the fact, more obvious than in his novels, that he is as it were exposing the Five Towns for the edification of a cosmopolitan audience, explaining, commenting, illustrating. His two most famous stories, *The Matador of the Five Towns* and *The Death of Simon Fuge,* seem to me to have been much overrated. In each case, the point of the story is the impact made by the Five Towns upon the narrator, an intellectual from London. They are over-written, over-declamatory and . . . they are little more than conducted tours of the public institutions of the Potteries overweighted by Bennett's naïve belief in the "interestingness of things." (p. 90)

These Twain was the last of Bennett's Five Towns novels, and the fiction he wrote after that novel until the appearance of *Riceyman Steps* . . . is for the most part dreary in the extreme. . . . The best-known of the novels of this period, *The Pretty Lady,* on the life of a French prostitute in the West End, is nothing else but a triumphant exercise in vulgarity; it is Bennett at his least attractive and most flashy. . . . (p. 91)

Riceyman Steps is a remarkable novel, and the more one considers it the more remarkable it appears to be. It is as much outside the tradition of English fiction as *The Old Wives' Tale* and *Clayhanger* are at its centre. Certainly it has nothing of the universality of those books; its strength and its weakness both lie in the fact that it is a study of a special case, one might almost say a clinical study of a pathological case. It was a new departure for Bennett, and of a kind he did not again attempt. In the past he had needed space; he had described the life of a whole town over whole generations; his canvases were packed with figures and he had been lavish in creation of characters. *Riceyman Steps* represents a terrific contraction and a terrific concentration; instead of a whole town merely a square in Clerkenwell; instead of a whole generation not much more than a year; instead of a packed canvas only a handful of characters, not more than three of which are of real importance. In part it is a return to Bennett's earliest masters, but it is not a return to his early method; there is no resemblance to *Anna of the Five Towns.* . . . Much of the strength of *Riceyman Steps* comes from the fact it is a crystallisation of Bennett's abiding preoccupations, preoccupations with certain kinds of characters and situations evident in his work from its earliest days but here brought into the compass of a single novel. (pp. 91-2)

[The] great achievement of the book is certainly Earlforward. In the creation of his hero Bennett must have known exactly the task he was setting himself. The miser is one of the classic figures of fiction, and it is the measure of Bennett's success that he creates a new kind of miser. . . . His mania is to conserve rather than to get, for he is indolent, deficient in energy, characterised by an "extraordinary soft obstinacy." He is in a way curiously innocent and childlike; indeed, whether Bennett was acquainted with Freud's work or not, one can scarcely forbear seeing in Earlforward the child lovingly hoarding and playing with its fæces. In fiction, at any rate, Bennett's is a new conception of the miser.

Earlforward might have been a monster; he starved his wife, his servant and himself. But he is not; and he is not because of two qualities, his innocence and the irony in which the whole novel is bathed. . . . *Riceyman Steps* has usually been taken as an exercise in realism of the most intransigent order. The realism cannot be denied, but it is conditioned not only by Bennett's irony, which acts as an intermediary between the reader and the full horror of the story, but by a subtle distortion which the reader may not be conscious of but which surely acts upon him and prepares him to accept the unpalatable and the monstrous. (p. 97)

One would not, I suppose, normally describe *Riceyman Steps* as comedy, but it is the underlying pattern of comedy, with its necessary simplification of character . . . which makes the novel so remarkable and gives it so much the air of a *tour de force.*

It was the last of Bennett's great achievements. *Lord Raingo,* which followed it three years later, has the fascination of a *roman à clef,* but not much more. (p. 98)

Walter Allen, in his Arnold Bennett *(reprinted by permission of David Higham Associates Limited, as literary agents for Walter Allen),* Home & Van Thal, *1948, Alan Swallow, 1949, 107 pp.*

ANGUS WILSON   (essay date 1954)

Arnold Bennett's *The Old Wives' Tale* and, in a lesser degree, *Clayhanger* have all the marks of 'great' novels, yet they never for more than moments rise to greatness. It would be easy to say that the society out of which the 'great' novel had arisen was already dead and that Bennett's failure reflects that death. It is true, of course, that neither Bennett, Wells nor Galsworthy, for all their harping upon change, had any realization of the nature of the social cataclysm to come, no sense like Henry James of the inner decay at work. . . . Bennett reacted against the drab and, as he thought, hypocritical nonconformity of his early background. So, indeed, had writers of fifty years earlier. For him, however, the problem was to be very simply solved by eschewing the moralism of his predecessors, hence his adherence to the French naturalists.

The change in the world, however, went far deeper than this: for the writer, it affected, as any great change must, his whole conception of what people really were. It was no longer possible to regard 'character' in the same solid external way, or human motive as the simple conflict between desire and conscience or natural impulse and environment. It was no longer satisfactory to see personality moving against a background of passing time like some scenic railway against a backcloth of painted scenery. It is exactly in these fields of character and time that Bennett's most ambitious novels break down most completely. The later generation of Lawrence and Joyce and Mrs Woolf were to be preoccupied with these problems to an extent that now damages their work, making it, on occasion, seem too like the laboratory experiments that precede a great discovery. Bennett's work, however, suffers far more deeply from being so unaware. If he had not been a considerable artist, if he had been like Wells no more than a great journalist, it would not matter, but a great writer should, however unconsciously, be troubled by the mental agonies of his age. (pp. 61-2)

Bennett's presentation of character is largely monolithic. It belongs ultimately to the order of 'humours' which was the basis of all the great character drawing of the nineteenth-century novelists. Yet he was always trying to move away from what he clearly felt to be the exaggerated simplification which such a method gives. He lived at a time when it became fashionable to regard Dickens's characters as caricatures, yet his roots were still in Dickens's world. He painted his characters in the old simple colours and then, to avoid this simplicity, he fuzzed the outlines away with an elaboration of exterior detail. The result in the major characters . . . is a vague, indistinct blur interspersed with sudden clear, pictorial visions. . . . It is only in more minor figures . . . that Bennett allows himself the licence of drawing in clearer, bolder strokes, but even these characters are swallowed up in the vast maw of Bennett's fabulous monster—presenting 'life as a whole'.

I have no doubt at all after rereading his novels that the most successful is *Riceyman Steps*, and after that, though on a much smaller scale, *Anna of the Five Towns*. . . . *Anna* is an early production, still clearly hampered by over-conscientious pursuit of technique. The excellence of these two novels is directly connected with the problem of character presentation. It is only in these two novels of his serious work that Bennett gives up his obsession with an overall picture of life, for which his talents were so unfitted, and allows himself to write books in one dominant mood. *Anna of the Five Towns* and

Riceyman Steps have as a result an intensity and a cohesion which I find entirely lacking in *The Old Wives' Tale* or in *Clayhanger*. The hard finance of Anna's father Ephraim Tellwright is only exceeded by the insanity of miserliness found in Henry Earlforward, Bennett's greatest creation. Around Tellwright and Earlforward the rest of the characters group themselves, the profusion of observation and detail finds its place, and the results are works of art, minor but very satisfactory. In particular—and this is a striking quality of Bennett's work—somewhat negative figures like Anna herself or Violet Earlforward acquire true pathos by their attachment and subordination to the great grotesques of the books. In succumbing to a single mood, to such obsessive 'humours' as the misers, Bennett was, in one sense, following more closely the pattern of the Naturalists he admired . . . but through the element of the grotesque, he goes back beyond them to Balzac, and in greater degree than he would have consciously permitted, he so gives play to the great Victorian qualities which he disavowed. (pp. 63-4)

Character is only one element in the novel. Unfortunately, in Arnold Bennett's view of the novel this was not so. For him, the characters were the very core of his books, by them only could he convey 'life', by them, in large degree, therefore, his novels must stand or fall. But if 'character' was the means he needed to express 'life', the idea of life that he wished to convey was closely connected with time. (p. 65)

> *Angus Wilson, "Arnold Bennett's Novels," in* London Magazine *(© London Magazine 1954), Vol. 1, No. 9, October, 1954, pp. 59-67.*

FRANK SWINNERTON   (essay date 1961)

[Bennett's novels] belong to three orders; the realistic studies of men and women in their appropriate environment, the sensational or extravagant presentations of men and women in environments wholly fantastic, the humorous—some say facetious—comedies of character and circumstance of which *The Card* is the best example, although *Buried Alive*, the book on which his play *The Great Adventure* is based, has many delights. In every case the best of his novels has its main scene in the Potteries. This is true of *The Card* as of *The Old Wives' Tale* and *Clayhanger* and *These Twain* and *Whom God Hath Joined*. It was the life of his boyhood which gave confidence, fun, insight, and profundity to such work. (p. 19)

[Once] Bennett had assumed his natural style he was not afraid to allow humour to colour his most realistic work. He was still afraid of humour when he wrote the best of his early serious tales, *Whom God Hath Joined;* but by the time he came to *The Old Wives' Tale* he was entirely at ease with his own method. The humour was humane; he really liked men and women. (p. 20)

When he let his humour drop, and became very serious (or very French), as in *Sacred and Profane Love* or *The Glimpse*, the result was hard, superficial, and incredible. When he gave it rein, as in *A Great Man, Buried Alive, The Card, The Regent*, or *Mr. Prohack*, it was sometimes triumphant but sometimes, if the liveliness of composition had faded, less irresistible than it might have been. In *The Regent* it had lost all liveliness and become jocularity. When he carried it into adventure stories, such as *The Grand Babylon Hotel, Hugo*, and other, less successful, tales, it often robbed the adventures of danger. In plays it was almost always extremely effective in the theatre; such plays as *What the Public Wants, The Title, The*

Great Adventure were all delightful entertainment. No more than that. They represented the easiest of fun for Bennett. He did not attach the smallest importance to them, or to the more uniformly successful play in which he collaborated with Edward Knoblock, *Milestones.*

It was, however, the union of humour with resolute truthfulness which gave Bennett his distinction. He would lie in fun, and with extravagance; but the prime quality in his most ambitious writing is its integrity. There is no falsification. Those who suppose that he compromised, or wrote for money or popularity, do not understand that he was—what they are not—tolerant of defects in mankind. He was not tolerant of the petty vices of deceit, treachery, spitefulness, and censoriousness. For those he felt contempt. But he was tolerant of the faults of character. When he said, early in his life, that the characteristic of a great novelist should be a Christ-like compassion, he spoke for his whole history as a man and a writer. He could laugh—at, for example, the foibles of dwellers in the Five Towns—but he did not laugh cruelly. No less cruel man ever lived. And that freedom from cruelty in its every form, from bad conscience and from hatred and jealousy, is to be read in all his novels. All are humane.

The faults of his work, which, as in the case of all great, unequal writers, are many, can be briefly indicated. He wrote at several levels. He was, being a Staffordshire man, either incapable of showing passion or of feeling it; I think the latter. He could be grim, sardonic, accusing; but he had learned as a boy to be stoical, and I believe that, for all the virtues of restraint in literature, he could with advantage have been more emotional. When he tried to express an abandonment to emotion, as in *Sacred and Profane Love,* he failed. The weakest part of *The Pretty Lady* is the part relating to the lady's emotions. The weakest part of *The Old Wives' Tale* is the part in which Sophia ceases to belong to the Five Towns. And, finally, in his plays, his lesser books, and even in the *Clayhanger* trilogy, there is a meagreness or carelessness of design. I think this also arose from his Staffordshire upbringing; a mistrust of the grandiose, of, in fact, the tragic. 'In the county excess is deprecated.' For him, the nearest approach to tragedy is the pathos of old age. That pathos runs through all his books; but there is nothing in them of tragedy. . . . He would probably have insisted that life is not tragic, or that in literature tragedy is a manipulation of circumstance.

Within his range, however, which he perfectly understood and commanded, Bennett has a mastery not approached by any other realistic novelist of our age. His characters are there as people; they are there as types of the Potteries and as illustrations of the endless foibles and endurances of mankind. They live in time and space. . . . We see their shops and their bedrooms, their dogs, their mannerisms; but these things are not offered to us for their mere veracity, since each detail contributes to our knowledge of these and all people, to this way of life and all English ways of life. Bennett's novels will live, indeed, because future generations will see and feel in them the actual life of one part of England in a day that is already past. His scene is Staffordshire; but Staffordshire men think themselves the quintessence of the English spirit. If they are right, as I fancy they may be, Bennett expresses that spirit. (pp. 20-2)

Frank Swinnerton, in his Arnold Bennett *(© Frank Swinnerton 1961; Longman Group Ltd., for the British Council), British Council, 1961, 30 p.*

V. S. PRITCHETT   (essay date 1964)

It is a long time now since the earth seemed solid under the feet to our novelists, since caprice, prophecy, brains and vividness meant less than the solid substance of time and place. And Arnold Bennett, in books like *The Old Wives' Tale* and *The Clayhanger Family,* seems to be the last of the novel's four-square gospelers. . . . A book like *The Clayhanger Family* has the sobriety as well as the tedium of a detailed engraving; and there is, oddly, enough of the connoisseur in Bennett to induce our taste. He is not a dilettante in the ego's peculiarities and he is without interest in elegance; he is the connoisseur of normality, of the ordinary, the awkward. . . . We speak of the disciplines of belief, of art, of the spirit; Bennett speaks of the discipline of life itself, reveres its frustrations, does not rebel against them; kneels like some pious behavior to the drab sight of reflexes in process of being conditioned. He catches the intolerable passing of time in our lives, a passing which blurs our distinctiveness and quietly establishes our anonymity; until our final impression of him is as a kind of estate agent's valuer walking with perfunctory step through the rooms of our lives, ticking his inventory and treating us as if we were long deceased. He cannot begin—and I think this is his inheritance from the French Naturalists—until we are dead, until we and our furniture have become indistinguishable evidence. I find this very restful. Frustration—*pace* H. G. Wells—is one of the normal conditions of life, and calming is the novelist who does not kick against the pricks.

Fidelity and sincerity are the words one puts first to Arnold Bennett's work. . . . The very matter-of-factness of Bennett made him one of the best portrayers of women we have had. The vices of romanticism or of misogynist satire passed him by in his best work completely. What other words come to mind when we think of him? They are his own words: "detracting" is one, "chicane"—a great favorite—is another; but there is a sentence in the early pages of *The Clayhanger Family* which contains a volume of criticism on him. He is writing of young Edwin Clayhanger coming home from his last day at school in the Five Towns: "It seemed rather a shame," Bennett says of Edwin, "it seemed even tragic, that this naïve, simple creature, immaculate of worldly experience, must soon be transformed into a man wary, incredulous and detracting." The essence of Bennett's mind is packed into that awkward sentence with its crick in the neck at the feeble beginning and the giveaway of its three final words. . . . Timidity rather than conviction is behind the brevity of his address. The result is that the apostle of will, efficiency and success appears to us hesitant and uncertain; he is between two stools; he cannot make up his mind whether life is "rather a shame" or "tragic." . . . What Bennett observes will be truthfully, almost litigiously, observed. Hazard will set the points wrongly in the lives of humdrum people and push them off the rails. Time will get its teeth into them more deeply year by year. We shall feel, as Edwin felt, that we must "brace ourselves to the exquisite burden of life." We shall feel we are interpenetrated "by the disastrous yet beautiful infelicity of things." What we shall miss is the sense that life is conceived of as anything in particular, whether it be the force that makes the Five Towns or forms the bleak impetuosity of Hilda Lessways. We shall not feel that life is much more than a random collection of *things.*

Admitting the absence of a frame, allowing for some lagging of narrative which the modern novelist would speed up, everything else in *Clayhanger* is good. . . . [How easy it is] for the novelist to identify himself with the sixteen-year-old Edwin and to exaggerate that sense of being alone with the universe which the boy had when he sat in his room alone at night. Bennett collects that emotion, astutely yet compassionately—but he collects it, labels it—it becomes part of the collection of human samples which make up Edwin Clayhanger's life. Bennett's pursuit of the normal is even better illustrated by his treatment of the character of the hard, impulsive, passionate figure of Hilda Lessways. Here he uses a characteristic device: he makes two full-length portraits of her from two different points of view, a method which gives a remarkable suspense to the story. The first portrait of Hilda is romantic and mysterious outline. In the second, with enormous dramatic effect, he fills in the plain reality of her life. That second appearance of hers, as she cleans the house and quarrels with her mother about money, is a remarkable portrayal of the relationship of two women. As spectators of Hilda's character we might easily exaggerate, romanticize and misread her disaster; but Bennett's gift as a novelist is to abolish the role of spectator. He almost painfully domesticates the reader, puts him in the slow muddle, murmur and diurnal perturbation of a character's life, so that the reader knows no more than Hilda knows, where she is going or why she is going there. Where most novelists live by a sort of instinct for imaginative scandal, Bennett—by some defect of imagination which he is able to turn to advantage—clings like a cautious puritan to sober likelihood. He doesn't bet: "It's a mug's game." The result, in the portrait of Hilda, is a staggering probability. (pp. 169-73)

Bennett's characters have three dimensions; the slow but adroit changing of the light that is thrown upon them makes them stereoscopic and gives them movement. And this movement is not the swift agitation of the passions but the dilatory adjustment to circumstance.

One of the reasons why bad novels are bad is not that the characters do not live, but they do not live with one another. They read one another's minds through the author. In *Clayhanger,* we feel at once that the characters are living together because, quite without prompting and entirely in the course of nature, they misunderstand one another. Edwin never understands his father because he does not know his father's past. The father cannot understand the son because the father's whole attitude to life is that his rise from barbarous poverty is a primitive miracle. He is primitive, the son is rational. Each one bumps awkwardly along in the wonder of his own nature. . . . A writer with little poetic feeling, Bennett thinks of our awkwardness with each other, of the unbridgeable gaps of time, experience and faculty which separate us, and not of our ultimate isolation. That is why he is a pathetic and not a tragic writer; one who feels uncertainly that "it is rather a shame," that we have to bear time's burden of "beautiful infelicity." (pp. 173-74)

[The] virtues of Bennett lie in his patient and humane consideration of the normal factors of our lives: money, marriage, illness as we have to deal with them. Life, he seems to say, is an occupation which is forced upon us, not a journey we have chosen, nor a plunge we have taken. Such a view may at times depress us, but it may toughen us. Bennett really wrote out of the congenital tiredness of the lower middle class, as Wells wrote out of its gambling spirit and gift for fantasy; and in the end, I think, Bennett's picture, with its blank acceptance of the Sunday School pageants, the Jubilees, the Band of Hope, the fear of the workers, the half-

baked attempts at culture, is the more lasting one. It is history. History presented—when we glance back at Bennett's French masters—with the dilettante's and collector's indifference to any theory of what history may be about. (pp. 174-75)

V. S. Pritchett, "The Five Towns," in his The Living Novel and Later Appreciations *(copyright 1947, © 1964; renewed 1975 by V. S. Pritchett; reprinted by permission of Random House, Inc.; in Canada by Literistic, Ltd.), revised edition, Random House, 1964, pp. 169-75.*

OSWALD H. DAVIS (essay date 1966)

Arnold Bennett was artist to the marrow. His work, for those who understood, had that quality of inner loveableness which the great like Shakespeare, Tolstoi, Balzac, lack, but which the next great like Conrad, Stevenson, Daudet possess, a charm indispensable for readers' ranked and warm-hearted devotion, though not provocative of the warring activities of critics full of principle but without ruth. One grew to like Bennett in the same way that one became fond of an attractive member of one's family. His integrity of technique, his staunchness to actuality, were as the loyalty one admires in a favourite cousin; the deft workings of his prose, the rapid but sound masonry of his narrative, were the resourceful inventiveness of your kin-friend as entertainer; and then Bennett's breakaway from his besetting facetiousness, the sudden flitting to a haunted copse, the plunge into the phantom mere of his own impressibility, the easy cleaving of its mercurial wave, and the final volte-face back to your feet with the flashing motion of the perfect phrase, were the revelation that indubitably your blood-friend had authentic divine origin, that his wistfulness, Puckishness, fire and energy were the mark of the artist.

I will maintain that in the world of thrillers Bennett's Fantasias are rendered unique by frequent hints of the elusive artist in him. . . . [In] these Fantasias glimmers an uncanny radiance of invention. . . . Lucid, swift-moving, well-written, [*The Gates of Wrath*] invests scene and temperament with awe and terror as it is imaginatively propelled, by the fell stroke of character as much as by the swift fall of sensational deed, to its dread conclusion. But it is lightened by typical Bennett descriptive felicities, and it crackles up laughably now and then from the sprinkling of sparks from dry fun. (pp. 47-8)

In most of the thrillers I have read, character has been negligible. . . . With Bennett there is always adequacy of characterisation. The girls do live, though on their cheeks is perhaps artifice, in their speech a strut, and in their hearts an incredible weakness for bachelor philanthropist heroes aged fifty. (pp. 51-2)

The psychology of [Bennett's] Fantasias, bright and agile, or nervous and stressful where needed (as in *The Ghost*); the flashing and whimsical facetiousness (on this plane apt instead of clashing as clash it often does in the big novels); the ardent progress of narrative, like the glide of a bright and swift ship propelled by gay and clear-eyed youth: have the lilt and surge of spring. Bennett's Spring of life was in them as in the exquisite early novels. There is something Grecian in the debonair élan of these Fantasias.

And perhaps youth is the final note of them. Tonic aroma of vernal life is about one; diverting incident teems, seen with glad and sinless eye by the writer; life is wearing the raiment of love and laughter. Here, however, is not the ingenuous fervour of the virginally blundering, the fawn-like, flower-like young. . . . Bennett's light-heartedness is the exhilaration of a sophisticated mind able to use with the prodigality of youth an assured technique. Such excitation, operating through words, can be as interesting or attractive as the kick or sway of raw blood. And in these bravura blasts of technical ingenuity (for they are called *Fantasias*) there is a subtlety as good as the poetry of adolescence. . . .

Always behind these airy fabrications of Bennett, to give their texture weight, is the sense of impending storm, the lour of potential disaster; but apprehension, escaped by a romp through scorned difficulties, is finally seen as absurd instead of scaring, and mainly gives point to passionate attainment. Again we experience the feeling of exultation in escape that is so often the prerogative of youth. The man who can thus, by his narrative prowess, give us back the miraculous sense of youth, and give it us additionally, in his own individual way, by affecting us with his own blitheness in superbly overcoming technical obstacles, deserves our regard. (p. 54)

The admonisory bent present in Bennett's social articles was always enlivened by nimbleness of mind, and by his aim to get into his journalistic "turnovers" a "curve"—that is, form. I do not think Bennett, for all his competence, was a consistently good article writer, whether in homily, travel sketch, or observer-commentary of the style of *Things that Have Interested Me*, in the sense that I consider he was a consistently good short-story writer. He had his flat moments; he could not be dubbed invariably brilliant. . . . In many of his articles, Bennett's eye was too fixed on the public and the value to be given in terms of price paid, for his spirit to take free command of his pen. (p. 59)

The fairness, independence, courage, self-giving of [Bennett's] war-time articles are for me an indestructible memorial of Bennett's generous humanity. Their style is well indicated in the brochure *Liberty*, in which the case against the war-provokers is put with characteristic clearness, firmness, unflinchingness. (p. 60)

Of all the English books on journalism and fiction-writing that I have read, I have found the best-written and most informative to be the four by Arnold Bennett—*Journalism for Women, How to Become an Author, The Author's Craft*, and *The Truth about an Author*. The books have been cherished by me because they combined, with frequent passages of literary brilliance, mordant précis of the facts most relevant to authorship. (p. 62)

What is lacking in the 130 pages of *The Author's Craft* . . . in intricacy of texture, is made up for by pithiness of thought and rapidity of illumination. An inspired delving into the art of seeing life and interpreting it, a turning over of the old soil in the accustomed area of enquiry till the under becomes the upper and has the reek of newness and almost the strangeness of treasure, animate the book. (p. 67)

I do not think Arnold Bennett was a great playwright. Mainly he saw his facts and people with the mind, and manoeuvred them with puppet wires of the intellect. Such vision is excellent for novels, where action can be supplemented with psychology, with the responsiveness of the author to various interests, with the fascinating secrecy involved in a slow unfolding of human nature, with the social or national interest

of some vital locality. The Bennett temperament is desirable for the creation of a play like *The Bright Island*, where a comedy of ideas functions freely, the treatment of a bare Biblical subject like *Judith* or a traditional theme like *Don Juan* [*de Marana*,] or an idea through which time can be embodied, as in *Milestones;* in such productions ideas, personified and disciplined in figures of the stage, are magnificent marionettes through which an able and salient mind displays itself in glorious objectivity.

But for the greater play the dramatist must be not only emotionally responsive to the facts and scenes of life, and endeavour, being moved, to transfer his sensitiveness to the stage; he must also have in himself the kind of emotional drive that Shakespeare had. . . . A play is brief; execution should be brief and tense. This is not to cut out intellect in the creation of a play. Intellect and wit are used to select and crystallise character, to forward events by device, to season and divert by contrast. But the sustaining, vital ether of great drama should be emotional momentum; and in that atmosphere, considered as the energising force of the stage, Arnold Bennett constitutionally failed. (pp. 97-8)

The inventiveness, the humour, the graphic quality of many of [Bennett's short] stories is amazing. There are but two which are study or sketch: *The Glimpse*, later expanded into the novel of that name, and *The Dream*, which was the seed of his unfinished novel. Particularly in the three Five Towns volumes *Tales, The Grim Smile*, and *The Matador of the Five Towns*, is his wit and invention cascading from his native soil like a fling of local springs, sprightly and rife. . . . [The] gamut of normal human experience is his material. In the early stories I would expressly mention the wistful and humorous *Mimi*, the technical skill of *Catching the Train, The Cat and Cupid*, and *An Unfair Advantage*, and the musical touches in *Why the Clock Stopped* and *Hot Potatoes*. . . . (pp. 99-100)

The later stories are neither so sprightly nor boisterous but are more temperamentally subtle. . . . Some of the phrasing, as in the typical piece of virtuosity, *Nine o'Clock To-Morrow*, makes one exclaim with delight. *A Place in Venice, Toreador, Middle-Aged*, and indeed most of the minor stories in *The Woman Who Stole Everything* are delightfully constructed narratives, fine-drawn and accurate studies of mirth-provoking comedies. The title story and one or two others in *The Night Visitor* are weak; but *The Cornet Player* (singled out by Bennett as his most original short story), *The Wind, Murder, The Hat, The Seven Policemen, Second Night, Mouse and Cat*, are excellent. (p. 100)

To my mind [*The Matador of the Five Towns*] is a good English short story because in its weaknesses, its powers, its substance, it is interestingly expressive of the English. . . . For me there is in this story, amorphous and meandering though it be, a mysterious vital power emanating from its revelation of the dramatic pulsing of event that goes on within the ordinary round of British existence and under the commonplace ugliness and futility of our everyday life. Making banality wear the favours of art is a truly Bennettian trick.

The Mysterious Destruction of Mr. Ipple (in *Elsie and the Child and Other Stories*) is a good example of the occasional failure of Bennett in short stories, when handling a good idea, to lift the piece of work, by means of psychological constructiveness sufficiently subtle or sound, to the plane of the great instead of the merely lightly entertaining. (pp. 101-02)

The true drama of the defeat and destruction of Mr. Ipple, who is self-deluded as to the actual measure of his worth, would have been the revelation to himself, via his own self-realisation, of his limitations and falsity as a critic. That would have been devastating and desolating and final. When we realise we are nothing then indeed we are miserable. Ourselves we make, ourselves we kill. But the main defeat of Mr. Ipple, though he has two spasms of misgiving during the story, is not by self-knowledge and its tragic accusal. . . .

[It is possible] that the brief collisions with Miss Betty Brik would have caused the catastrophic rush of insight which alone could finally destroy a self-complacency so smug and sophisticated as Mr. Ipple's. But we are not fully convinced and our lack of conviction, coming on top of an occasional unfastidiousness of wording in the tale, mars our enjoyment of this ingenious example of the delightful theatre stories. (p. 103)

In [*The Death of Simon Fuge*] is localised once for all the thesis of the prophet without honour in his own country, and in a quarter peculiarly apt, since one has but to visit the Five Towns to find that even now they will not admit there the greatness attributed to Bennett by many others. In this matter the Potteries people behave toward Bennett exactly as they are described as acting with regard to Fuge.

But there is more in the story. If you care to lift the theme from the local to the universal, from the individual to the general, isn't this tale the story of art itself, of its central mystery? In the Five Towns the name of Fuge was in the melting pot. Isn't art always making and unmaking itself—showing itself as never truly known? (pp. 106-07)

The artist usually stresses the value of art; Bennett here emphasises the value of the gross and the secular. The picture hangs in the memory of the Bennett devotee like a star. Is it overwhelmingly great or not? Fuge's canvas is symbolic of the mystery of art, of life. But the Sphinx-like riddle of the picture is left unsolved, as are the problems of art and life left unsolved, with just the hint from Loring that though in art the perception of beauty (let us call it in life, the spiritual) has to run the gauntlet of scepticism before its validity is recognised, its final acceptance is to be counted on. (p. 108)

> *Oswald H. Davis, in his* The Master: A Study of Arnold Bennett *(© Oswald H. Davis, 1966), Johnson, 1966, 206 p.*

JOHN WAIN   (essay date 1967)

The early Bennett, having coolly rejected the Sunday-school religion of his childhood, has a tendency simply to leave religion out of account in his portrayal of human character. He presents people as simple organisms, propelled by this pressure and that incitement, moved hither and thither by the predictable demands of their appetites and what they take to be their self-interest. What we miss in them is that streak of the crazy, the unexpected, the fanatical, that makes ordinary people pour energy and passion into things that might have been expected to leave them cold. In particular, we miss the religious impulse: not necessarily a formal religious faith, but an assent to the power of the dark and mysterious, the intangible, the unbiddable. It is true that in *Anna of the Five Towns* . . . , which stands out among his novels for its unusually complete documentation of Potteries life both industrial and social, there is a description of a revivalist religious meeting. But it is seen entirely from the outside: pho-

tographed in words, not imagined. This cold objectivity was, so far, all he could manage.

Thus, in *The Old Wives' Tale,* we find almost no mention of religious feelings. Of the entire roll-call of characters, there is hardly one who is motivated by them. And when, at the end of the book, Constance contemplates the wreck of Sophia's life, and some faint religious reflex (it is hardly more) stirs in her mind, Bennett feels obliged to apologize for mentioning anything so vestigial and archaic. (pp. 28-9)

That such feelings might be permanent in the human animal, that Divine retribution for mockery might be something perpetually present to the human consciousness despite all the modifications wrought by "evolution," simply does not occur to him. . . . But Bennett moved on from this to a deeper and more sympathetic awareness. In *Clayhanger* . . . we have the famous set piece of the Sunday School Centenary. The main function of this scene in the novel is that Edwin takes Hilda to witness it, and certain features of Hilda's character are thrown into relief by the experience. But it also has considerable thematic importance. Throughout the novel, Edwin is shown as belonging to a fragile social layer, a thin, delicate shell of middle-class refinement which supports itself, somehow, over the dark and seething mass of the populace. This mass, which is too dangerous to explore, pulses with a rich and violent life of its own. . . . The people have their own life, from which he must be excluded. . . . And the people also have their own religion, from which Edwin, being thoughtful and to some extent educated, is also excluded. This religion is violent, orgiastic, absurd, but it is powerful. (pp. 29-30)

The faces of the massed fanatics are "stupid and superstitious," but at least Bennett does not apologize on their behalf for the way they are lingering on the stage instead of making way for more modern attitudes. In this orgiastic rite, he seems to be acknowledging, there is something permanent in humanity, however regrettable we may find it. The forms of religious belief may be altered, but the impulse to believe will remain; common sense will not, after all, prevail, at any rate among the populace.

This awareness must have readied Bennett for the explosion of 1914-18. . . . And Bennett's reaction was to write a novel in which the central character is a religious believer, however tainted and however lapsed.

This was *The Pretty Lady*. . . . It was a courageous book to write, not only because it dealt with the life of a prostitute . . . , but because of the imaginative boldness it required. To project himself imaginatively into the life of a woman is always a risk for the male novelist; Bennett had taken this risk successfully in *The Old Wives' Tale* and more or less successfully in *Anna, Leonora,* and *Hilda Lessways,* but there still remained the problem that Christine was a Frenchwoman, and with all his long experience of France Bennett had, understandably, never so far ventured to introduce French characters in other than tangential roles. That he succeeded so well (for *The Pretty Lady* is the most unfairly neglected of all his novels . . .) is very largely due, I think, to his newly increased insight into the nature of the religious emotions.

Christine, being an ordinary Frenchwoman (the fact of her being a prostitute only intensifies her ordinariness, confining her as it does in a narrow, stuffy little world), is naturally a Catholic. In drawing her character, Bennett could not in any case have avoided this element, but in fact he chose to make it central to the book, and the action pivots on it. (pp. 32-3)

Plying her trade, she deals with many men, but there are two with whom her involvement is genuine. One, who shares the central spotlight of the novel, is G. J. Hoape, an aging bachelor of settled habits and materialistic, rational, benevolent attitudes. Hoape in fact represents the old steady Edwardian England, trying to keep its coarse-grained sanity in this new apocalyptic world. He lives the kind of life that the young Bennett, twenty years earlier, had planned for himself as he grew older; his flat in Albany is irreproachable, his books and china enviable, his life selfish and secure. One theme of the book, and very ably Bennett handles it, is the ruthless destruction of these habits of mind. By the end, Hoape has realized that the world in which he must live out the rest of his life has no place for the old certainties of a prosperous bachelorhood. (p. 33)

Hoape's commerce with Christine is in fact a relic of his former life; he has found this the best method of satisfying his sexual nature without becoming involved in family life and thus having to revolutionize his habits. (p. 34)

To have gone fifty years without being in love with a woman argues a detachment from emotion, an ability to take life skillfully on the level of satisfaction and self-interest, that the younger Bennett might, in some moods, have admired and wished to emulate. The older Bennett did not. Hoape's position is described with an irony, and demolished with a completeness, that leave us in no doubt of the author's standpoint. Starting from this premise, it is inevitable that Hoape's dealings with Christine will come to an end; they are too mechanical, too sheltered from the rough and prodigal winds of real love. In fact, the debacle comes because of her involvement with the second man in the story, the officer whose name is given simply as Edgar.

Edgar, though also a mature man, is sharply contrasted with Hoape. He is doomed, mystical, tragic, an inhabitant of the apocalyptic landscape of the war. What binds Christine to Edgar is precisely that she has religious emotions and that he becomes the focus of these emotions. He comes into her life just after she has paid a Sunday morning visit to Brompton Oratory; there, she experiences a renewal of devotion for the Virgin Mary; Chapter 16, "The Virgin," is devoted entirely to this visit and should be studied carefully by anyone concerned with Bennett's development. For all his long experience of French Catholicism, he could not have written that chapter at any earlier point in his career. The attitude to Christine's religion is as skeptical and detached as the attitude to Nonconformism in *Clayhanger;* Bennett sees it as a complex and interesting form of superstition, a faith but hardly a philosophy; the difference, however, is that this time the religious feelings are a central motivation in a central character, and accordingly the novelist makes the effort of seeing them from the inside. (pp. 34-5)

Bennett's view of religion, any religion, is evidently that it is magic, an affair of lucky charms and talismans. But at least he realizes, as in the old comfortable days he did not, that human beings can use this magic as a means of keeping on going in impossible situations. Christine's situation is impossible; so, for different reasons, is Edgar's. Hoape, who is still clinging to the middle of the road, can do without magic; they know that they need it, and the knowledge brings them together. (p. 38)

The Pretty Lady is Bennett's principal war-novel. It is his agonized response to the insensate violence and cruelty of those years, and his intuitive acknowledgment that the old settled Europe had gone for ever. With a prostitute as its heroine, the dismembering of a comfortable man's life as its main theme, it is a lurid story, lit by the flames of burning cities; it is full of images of horror. . . . Looking ahead in Bennett's work, we see that his best stories will, from now on, mirror this jaded civilization that has looked too much on death. . . . (p. 39)

John Wain, in his Arnold Bennett *(Columbia Essays on Modern Writers Pamphlet No. 23; copyright © 1967 Columbia University Press; reprinted by permission of the publisher), Columbia University Press, 1967, 47 p.*

ARNOLD KETTLE   (essay date 1967)

[Arnold Bennett's *The Old Wives' Tale,*] for all its solidity, for all the fidelity of backcloth and detail in its setting, cannot adequately be described as a documentary. It has within it a more profound typicality, the kind of quality one associates rather with Dickens, which produces in the end a significant and moving pattern. (p. 78)

If *The Old Wives' Tale* has something of Dickens in it—betrayed perhaps by the tone and frequent facetiousness of the author's comment—there is also an austerity, a conscious concern over presentation, which is scarcely Dickensian.

The great problem of *The Old Wives' Tale* is why, fine and impressive novel as it is, it is not just that shade finer. It is almost a great novel—that is agreed—and yet, somehow, before the final affirmation of complete confidence one holds back. (p. 79)

The Old Wives' Tale seems to me to miss ultimate greatness because it presents a number of particular lives as Life and, in so doing, achieves the effect of 'reducing' life. As a picture of the life of Constance and Sophia Baines it is wonderfully successful. The Baines's shop, the relationships of the family, the development of the surrounding characters, are superbly done. We come to *feel* every stairway and passage, to relish every piece of furniture in that stuffy house on the corner of the Square in Bursley. . . . And Sophia's rebellion too we feel upon our pulses. We understand precisely her discontent and her vague but powerful aspirations; with ever-increasing admiration for Bennett's insight and honesty we watch her cope with her disillusionment and pay her subtle homage to the bourgeois virtues against which, insufficiently armed, she has once fought. We admire the remarkable lack of sentimentality with which Cyril Povey, Constance's 'artistic' son, is presented. One has only to compare him with George Eliot's Ladislaw or Galsworthy's Bosinney to grasp here the quality of Bennett's honesty. And finally we are moved, profoundly and bitterly, by Sophia's vision of her wasted life as she stands over the dead body of her worthless husband.

This much, then, of *The Old Wives' Tale* is wholly successful. What, bound up inextricably with it, limits our surrender is our sense that we are being asked here to contemplate the unrolling of Life itself. 'What Life Is' is the title of the fourth and final book of Bennett's novel and there is a pretension here which the novel for all its quality cannot fulfil. For to present the passage of time simply in terms of bitter, wasted aspiration, to claim for Sophia's tragedy a universal validity, is not good enough.

The Old Wives' Tale fails, in the end, to transmit a sense of the resilience of human experience, of the complexity of life's processes. (pp. 79-80)

The historical development of the Five Towns, for instance, though much is made of it in the latter part of the book, is seen *only* from Constance's point of view. We see the changes in the Square, the movement from the old independent trades-men to the new chain-store, from craft traditions to mass-production, the breakdown of the old civic spirit, the gradual encroaching from all sides of monopoly. All this is admirably caught. But because Bennett, for all his sympathy with the poor and the servants, conveys across to us nothing of the other side of the coin, the beginnings of trade union organ-isation for instance, the total effect of his picture of the Potteries is bound to lack something in vitality, is bound to give a certain sense of life's running down like a worn-out spring, which no doubt corresponds to Constance's own feel-ings but which is less than adequate as an expression of 'What Life Is'.

Similarly there is a weakness in the French section of the novel. In one way this book is a very remarkable achieve-ment. What Bennett succeeds in creating is a world, a way of life, emphatically not the Bursley way of life, so that when Sophia finally comes home and then looks back upon her life in Paris as she surveys the scene from Bursley Square, we have very effectively the sense of colour, brightness, a world of smart if brittle vivacity which throws into relief the grey and smoky provincialism of the Potteries. Parisian middle-class life is, in fact, contrasted with the middle-class life of North Staffordshire and the contrast is brilliantly effective. The weakness is that it is a limited contrast. Sophia's Paris remains essentially the tourist's Paris. This does not matter (it is from the point of view of Sophia herself quite credible) as far as Sophia's story is concerned. But for the larger claims of the novel it is inadequate. A great novelist who elected to deal with it would have seen for instance in the Paris Commune something that Arnold Bennett did not see. (pp. 80-1)

I am not suggesting that *The Old Wives' Tale* would necessarily have been a better novel if Bennett had included fuller de-scriptions of the Paris Commune or the rise of the Labour Movement in the Potteries. What I am suggesting is that a novelist must have a really rich imaginative understanding of anything that he writes about and that if his subject in-volves, as Arnold Bennett's did, a sense of broad social change and development, the novelist's own understanding of these issues is most relevant. He must convey somehow the sense of them even if it is outside the scope of his novel actually to describe them. One would not wish Sophia to understand what was happening in Paris in 1871—it is one of her characteristics that she could not; but Arnold Bennett should have understood and have conveyed across in some way that understanding. And if Bennett *had* understood or sensed something of the significance of the Paris Commune, then *The Old Wives' Tale* would have been artistically a better novel, for we should not then have had that uneasy sense of a false pretentiousness. The weakness of *The Old Wives' Tale* is that life itself is too closely identified with Sophia's and Constance's vision of life, so that when Sophia realises that her life has been wasted we are invited not simply to experience human pity and indignation but to say 'Ah, yes, Life's like that altogether'—which it isn't. (p. 81)

Arnold Kettle, "Mr Bennett and Mrs Woolf," in his An Introduction to the English Novel: Henry

James to the Present Day, Vol. II, *second edition, Hutchinson University Library, 1967, pp. 59-148.**

WALTER F. WRIGHT (essay date 1969)

[With] the illumination cast on mundane affairs by the spirit of romance, Bennett often went in search of the comic, or what is now fashionably called the absurd. In fact, both by comic implication and by explicit statement he was a critic of life in general and specifically of the life he had personally known in Victorian and Edwardian England.

Though Bennett was not a highly philosophical writer, he had certain guiding principles. His preoccupations might be summed up in the question, How can one make sense out of a universe and a human condition which seem in no way arranged for man's spiritual comfort? (p. 35)

As he put it in one of his "pocket" philosophies, *How to Make the Best of Life*, . . . "The biggest things in life depend on the smallest things." In its context the disarming remark reads like a truism, but in it is the clue to Bennett as nov-elist. . . . [For Bennett], it meant that one and the same in-cident could be romantically wonderful and acutely comic. The romance lay in the fact that the seemingly unimportant partook of the infinite, the comedy, of course, in the fact that events and persons of seemingly great magnitude could be reduced to miniatures. (pp. 35-6)

[Over] the years Bennett rang variations on the comic ser-vitude of the masters, the helplessness of the men of power. And, of course, as any good satirist has always done, he exposed the discrepancy between the actuality and the pre-tense. Consequently, much depends on what he has not said but implied; for around a situation there is always hovering a set of values whose presence, whether from ignorance, spiritual lethargy, or sheer obstinacy, the characters do not apprehend. (p. 36)

What were the subjects over which Bennett let the spirit of comedy range? Many were social in nature. A given character might be comic, but he reflected the influence of his relatives and neighbors in the Five Towns or in London. He was caught in a web of politics, of traditional religious sentiment, and of conventions of moral and cultural respectability. Even such a quality as obstinacy was contagious in the Five Towns; the atmosphere bred it. And the gloom and sterility of in-dividual lives was at least accentuated by the oppressive-ness of a Wesleyanism that had become perverted. . . . Wesley-anism as Bennett had known it represented a fear of pleasure and, even more, a fear of being suspected of irresponsible enjoyment. (pp. 36-7)

For Bennett the negative, repressive religious atmosphere and the inhibiting concern for respectability were inseparable from a general cultural barrenness. His criticism was not limited to the Five Towns. One of his most satiric, though rather good-natured, attacks, in *Buried Alive*, . . . has its scene in London. (pp. 37-8)

What occurred in London was, for Bennett, accentuated in the Five Towns. Cultivated individuals do live there, but the musical evenings initiated at the Clayhangers are considered outlandish; the good citizens have better things to do than to import foreign ways from London. The most pointed satire is in **"The Death of Simon Fuge."** . . . We catch glimpses of the world associated with Fuge, glorious, magical, intensely alive. Then we are jolted back to the drab reality, where bad art is preferred and Fuge is remembered as an eccentric. It is the juxtaposition of facts that provides the droll commentary.

If a single word could be used to cover what disturbed Bennett, it would perhaps be ''malaise.'' Indeed, the sensation comes through in work after work. Men are not happy, and their social institutions and customs reflect their feeling of insecurity, their inability to live honestly and enthusiastically. Again Bennett's commentary is usually not obviously comic, but at the center is the incongruity between the actuality and what good sense would dictate.

Conservatism was especially ludicrous, whether in politics, business, or social traditions, for it meant holding firmly not only to outmoded ways, but to ways that had never been good. (p. 38)

In fact, the complete picture of society offered by Bennett reveals a great waste. Men and women repeatedly exhaust on trivial matters the creativity which could have dealt with significant enterprises. (pp. 38-9)

The comedy that stems from one's undue sense of his own righteousness and dignity was, of course, most obvious in marriage. The absurdity of marital quarrels appears in story after story and is conspicuous in certain pocket philosophies. (p. 39)

Nevertheless, Bennett regarded marriage as the epitome of romance. There was something rather wonderful in the ability of human beings to work together despite the egoism innate in each. . . .

Life for Bennett entailed, indeed, a constant effort of adjustment, and part of the value of comedy was to show the absurdity of clashes and to suggest the art and grace required if existence were to remain civilized. Hence the serious overtones of the domestic comedy. . . .

Above all, humor, either ebullient or wry, provided a perspective. Bennett's most famous novel, *The Old Wives' Tale,* has both kinds. But apart from the details, the very theme of the book and the outline of the plot are concerned with life's ironies. Sophia Baines lives through one of the most exciting of times—the siege of Paris and the commune—yet returns to Bursley as limited in her horizons as if she had never left it. She and Constance are immersed in the trivia of their immediate lives, and each carries her universe within herself. Bennett reduces the vast questions of philosophy, politics, and the search for knowledge to their actual meaning for the two daughters of John Baines, draper on St. Luke's Square. . . .

[Bennett] was a man with a melancholy sense of the loneliness and harshness of life and of the paucity of beauty. For him comedy, whether light or satiric, gave freedom to the imagination to make of the very limitations of existence a subject of creative interpretation, and it helped to make that existence not glorious, but somewhat more than merely acceptable. (p. 40)

> Walter F. Wright, "The Comic Spirit in Arnold Bennett," in Kansas Quarterly (© copyright 1969 by the Kansas Quarterly), Vol. 1, No. 3, Summer, 1969, pp. 35-40.

JOHN LUCAS (essay date 1974)

'I finished *A Great Man* at 11.30 this morning', Bennett notes in the *Journal* (13 March 1904), and he adds: 'I am more satisfied with it than I thought I should be. I began it with an intention merely humorous, but the thing has developed into a rather profound satire.' . . . *A Great Man* is certainly not a rather profound satire. It is, however, extremely funny, and Bennett was right to be struck by his own accomplishment. For in writing the novel he fashions a comic style which seems to me peculiarly his own: it is a style at once bland, laconic, matter-of-fact. *A Great Man* does not use or depend on extreme situations or characters. On the contrary, it feels disarmingly low-key, even flat. The style reappears at moments in all Bennett's major works and it can become gratingly insensitive—especially in *Mr Prohack*. But it also lifts such otherwise minor works as *The Card* and *The Price of Love* into a class of their own. And it points to a fact about Bennett which is too often forgotten—that he can be a very funny writer.

A Great Man is about an utter mediocrity, Henry Knight, who cannot avoid converting into gold everything that he touches. In particular, he succeeds as an author. From birth, indeed, he has had the suspicion that he might be destined for greatness as a writer. (p. 57)

At school Henry wins a prize for his essay on 'Streets',—part of which is declaimed by his irreverent cousin, Tom, who is a genuinely talented artist: 'Some streets are longer than others. . . . Very few streets are straight. . . . But we read in the Bible of a street which is called Straight. . . . Oxford Street is nearly straight. . . . A street is what you go along. . . . It has a road and two footpaths.' . . . Tom turns up from time to time, always mocking, needling and troubling Henry. But Henry is no fraud. He is entirely innocent. It is simply that he lacks any kind of talent and cannot help succeeding because of it. His first work is written while he is ill in bed. . . . It is to be called *Love in Babylon,* and is in fact a spoof on the kind of romance which at that time was bringing Elinor Glyn so much money and fame. Not that Henry thinks of his novel as a spoof. He is convinced of its worth. . . . *Love in Babylon* is published. The critics trounce it. It becomes a bestseller.

Henry is now famous. (p. 58)

By the end of the novel Henry is making increasingly vast sums of money, and he is happily married. 'Upon the whole the newspapers and periodicals were very kind to Henry, and even the rudest organs were deeply interested in him.' . . . True, cousin Tom remains ruthlessly sceptical, but then as Henry points out, for all that Tom may be admired and honoured as a sculptor, he can't pay his creditors.

A Great Man is a highly professional novel. It is clearly and crisply told. Bennett moves the story forward at a splendid pace, cutting just the right number of corners, feeding us just the right amount of information. It may lack the exuberance of Wells's *History of Mr Polly,* but it is very much better written. It isn't of course a satire on the literary life, since Bennett's stance of wry, stoical acceptance, his acknowledging that this is the way things are, goes quite against any satiric bitterness of feeling for how things might be. . . . But the novel is certainly comic and informative about the poseurs, frauds and sharks with whom Henry Knight comes into contact. Those parts of it which deal with the flotsam of the literary world are done very much from the inside.

With Henry himself, however, one feels twinges of unease. He is done very much from the outside, and although it would be quite wrong to make too much of this, since *A Great Man* isn't one of Bennett's major fictions, there is a *kind* of implausibility about Henry that is carried over into novels which Bennett himself seems to have intended as altogether weightier works. I say 'seems', because anyone reading through Bennett's work soon discovers that a very odd tone plays over some of his fiction. At moments more than one of his novels develops an air of diffident self-mockery, as though Bennett himself isn't always quite sure how serious he wishes to be. Such a tone makes itself very strongly felt in *A Great Man*, and indeed much of the novel's charm depends on it. Yet it also produces false moments. . . . It isn't of course of much consequence in *A Great Man* and it would be wrong to make heavy weather of the matter. But I think it important at least to note Bennett's readiness to leave us in a state of ignorance about his character's inner life, because it can become decidedly irritating in such a novel as *Buried Alive*. *Buried Alive* is *A Great Man* turned upside down. It is about a painter of real genius who decides to seek anonymity. But as with Henry so, and much more damagingly, with Priam Farll: we know far too little about him to find Bennett's fiction at all convincing.

A Great Man is interesting for two reasons. On the credit side, it employs a comic manner which seems to me one of Bennett's important achievements. But against that, it exhibits a curious tactlessness in the handling of its main character. Bennett, one feels, is quite ready to make fiction out of lives about which he knows and can imagine nothing. I do not think that such tactlessness is the product of professional cynicism, a determination to go through with a 'well-made fiction', and hang the artistic consequences. On the contrary, it stems from an innocence that is really remarkable in so shrewd, intelligent, sensitive and critically astute a man. The fact is that Bennett often seems not to have the least idea of when he is writing badly or inadequately. Or perhaps any tremor of doubt is to be disarmed by self-mockery. (pp. 60-3)

[Another comic novel, *The Card*, is also] one of Bennett's best-known and most popular novels. Yet he himself was very uncertain of its worth. He noted in the *Journal:* 'Yesterday I finished three-quarters of *Denry the Audacious*. I think that in book form I shall call it *The Card*. Good honest work, vitiated by my constant thought of a magazine public.' . . . When *The Card* was finally published in book form he noted laconically, 'Reviews of the *Card* much too kind on the whole.'

It may come as a surprise to find Bennett admitting to these doubts, even in the privacy of the *Journals*. Surprising, too, that he should consider having to think of his magazine public as vitiating. True, *The Card* is episodic in structure and therefore fits neatly enough into serial form. But then its tale of the rise and rise of Denry Machin is by nature episodic (it is a good example of Bennett's use of the technique which he had first mastered in *A Great Man:* the telling of a story in separate but neatly joined incidents—Scenes from the Life of). Yet perhaps his reference to the magazine public provides an important clue to something that rightly worried Bennett. For I think that *The Card* is vulgar and complacent, and its brand of humour is a long way from the bland, laconic acceptance of things as they are which had characterized the tone of *A Great Man*. *The Card* strikes a note that is new in Bennett's fiction, though it will sound increasingly in later work, especially *The Regent* and the execrable *Mr Prohack*. It is at once boorish and philistinic, and at this stage at least

must have come as a troubling surprise to Bennett himself. After all, the hero of *The Card* was based on an old acquaintance . . . and Bennett obviously felt enough lively sympathy with the Card to share with him his own date of birth, 27 May 1867. Besides, he enjoyed the notion of the 'Card', the Five Towns type about whom he had already written on a number of occasions but who hadn't so far been put at the centre of a novel. Yet now that he has been, Bennett is not altogether pleased with the result. For on close inspection the Card turns out to be a kind of character who will inevitably appeal to a 'magazine public'—with all that that phrase implies of unthinking guffaws and uncritical acceptance. To put it rather differently, I think that when Bennett came to write *The Card* he discovered that he was writing about a kind of life which he could not admire, and that he used humour to fend off any really severe questioning about his hero, though in its complacency the humour itself indicates an uneasy conscience.

These are severe words and they must not stand on their own. For there is much to enjoy in *The Card*. The novel establishes a feeling of continuity with other Five Towns novels. . . . There are marvellous moments of detail, as for example when Henry has to put his coat on in his mother's kitchen, because the passage isn't wide enough. And always, of course, there is the feel for the place, its energies, squalors, amusements and scandals, its generations moving rapidly up and down the social scale. (pp. 123-24)

Denry is on the rise. Others fall. Chief among them is Councillor Cotterill. He has built up a business to the point where it has made him a rich man. Now it crashes and he is forced to emigrate to Canada, aided, but very perfunctorily, by Denry, who refuses to help Cotterill shore up his tottering business affairs. And it is here that one's doubts about Denry swell into a real uneasiness. For the blunt truth is that at this point he is quite plainly a ruthless, cynical person. He dismisses Cotterill's plea for a loan. . . . [In doing so he crassly reflects] that it is a mistake to be a failure: 'You could do nothing with a failure.' Such a reflection is meant to be redeemed by the fact that Denry pursues the Cotterills to Liverpool, pays for them to be moved from steerage to second class, and then whisks their daughter, Nellie, off the ship because he intends to marry her—and does. All this comes of his being a Card and it no doubt anticipates the 'magazine public's' approval.

But what exactly is a Card? Denry has two visions. The first comes to him when he attends a grand ball: 'The thrill of being magnificent seized him, and he was drenched in a vast desire to be truly magnificent himself.' . . . The way to magnificence is paved by money. And this leads to Denry's second vision, which has to do with himself.

> He did not consider himself clever or brilliant. But he considered himself peculiarly gifted. He considered himself different from other men. . . .
>
> And he knew of a surety that he was that most admired type in the bustling, industrial provinces—a card. . . .

The rest of the novel is taken up with Denry's achievement of magnificence through amassing wealth. By honest ingenuity? If honest means lawful, yes. Denry never steps beyond what the law allows. But it is an impoverished definition, just as his vision is impoverished. The problem for the novel is that Bennett half knows as much. At Llandudno Denry is, we are told, 'much impressed by the beauty and grandeur of the sea. But what impressed him far more than the beauty and grandeur of the sea was the field for profitable commercial enterprise which a place like Llandudno presented.' The tone is unruffled, neutral. Yet without wanting to be unduly heavy-handed—for *The Card* is a comparatively unambitious comedy, whose success probably surprised Bennett himself—I think it proper to suggest that its characteristic tone is an attempt to deflect unsympathetic responses to Denry. True, the 'magazine public' might not respond to him unsympathetically, but he could well end up by being unpopular with a more discriminating, sensitive observer—Arnold Bennett, for instance. . . . We are asked to admire without thought Denry the Audacious, the man of honest ingenuity; and when deflection becomes impossible—as in the treatment of Cotterill—the strategy nearly falls apart. It certainly isn't put together again by the plea made at the very end of the novel. Denry is now mayor and is being discussed by his fellow councillors. '"And yet," demanded Councillor Barlow, "what's he done? Has he ever done a day's work in his life? What great cause is he identified with?" "He's identified," said the speaker, "with the great cause of cheering us all up."' That is no more than a final deflection, though it does remind us that *The Card* shows us hardly anything of the inevitable ruthlessness that accompanies Denry's vision, so that we do not have to worry about the consequences—for others—of his honest ingenuity.

If the novel doesn't become entirely distasteful it is because Denry possesses qualities that really are attractive. He is audacious, he is funny, he is alive with energy and wit; he has, in short, qualities which Bennett brings out well enough to compel our affectionate liking for his hero. . . . Such scenes abound in *The Card* and they give Denry a proper and valuable comic gusto. But what Bennett won't bring out are the dubious ways in which that gusto has so often to express itself. To have done so would, of course, have strained our sympathies with Denry, perhaps to breaking point. It would perhaps have made *The Card* what it most certainly isn't, fiercely sarcastic. And it would certainly have made it another and a better novel. (pp. 125-27)

> *John Lucas, in his* Arnold Bennett: A Study of His
> Fiction *(© 1974 by John Lucas), Methuen & Co.,*
> *Ltd, 1974, 235 p.*

ADDITIONAL BIBLIOGRAPHY

Barker, Dudley. *Writer by Trade: A Portrait of Arnold Bennett.* New York: Atheneum, 1966, 260 p.
  Detailed account of Bennett's life and literary career.

Bellamy, William. *The Novels of Wells, Bennett, and Galsworthy: 1890-1910.* New York: Barnes & Noble, 1971, 257 p.*
  Critical study of *A Man from the North, The Old Wives' Tale,* and *Clayhanger.*

Bronson-Howard, George. "Arnold Bennett as a Melodramatist." *The Bookman* (New York) XLII, No. 2 (October 1915): 147-54.
  Chronicles Bennett's serialized fiction and its reception by his contemporaries. This essay also offers speculation on the significance of these writings in relation to Bennett's better-known works.

Cox, Sidney Hayes. "Romance in Arnold Bennett." *The Sewanee Review* XXVIII, No. 3 (July 1920): 358-66.
  Discussion of romantic elements in Bennett's novels.

Drabble, Margaret. *Arnold Bennett: A Biography.* New York: Alfred A. Knopf, 1974, 396 p.
  A thorough, well-informed biography which explores the overlapping influences of Bennett's ancestry, personal life, and literary career.

Forster, E. M. "The Story." In his *Aspects of the Novel,* pp. 44-69. New York: Harcourt, Brace and Co., 1927.*
  In a much-quoted essay, Forster briefly discusses time as the true hero of *The Old Wives' Tale.*

Hall, James. *Arnold Bennett: Primitivism and Taste.* Seattle: University of Washington Press, 1959, 159 p.
  Examines the conflict between primitivist and aristocratic values in Bennett's major novels.

James, Henry. "The New Novel." In his *Notes on Novelists, with Some Other Notes,* pp. 249-87. London: J. M. Dent & Sons, 1914.*
  Examines what James calls the problem of "saturation" of insignificant detail in Bennett's novels.

Lynd, Robert. "Arnold Bennett as Critic." In his *Books and Writers,* pp. 257-61. London: J. M. Dent & Sons, 1952.
  Discussion of Bennett's critical essays.

Pound, Reginald. *Arnold Bennett: A Biography.* London: William Heinemann, 1952, 385 p.
  Detailed study of Bennett's life and literary associations, including excerpts from his journals and personal correspondence.

Scott, Dixon. "The Commonsense of Mr. Arnold Bennett." In his *Men of Letters,* pp. 119-32. London: Hodder and Stoughton, 1916.
  Brief critical analysis of *The Card, The Regent,* and *Those United States.*

Tillyard, E.M.W. "Middlemarch and Bursley." In his *The Epic Strain in the English Novel,* pp. 168-86. London: Chatto & Windus, 1967.*
  Discussion of epic characteristics found in *The Old Wives' Tale* and the *Clayhanger* trilogy, including comparison with George Eliot's *Middlemarch.*

Wagenknecht, Edward. "Novelist of Being: Arnold Bennett." In his *Cavalcade of the English Novel: From Elizabeth to George VI,* pp. 441-57. New York: Henry Holt and Co., 1943.
  Categorization and critique of Bennett's novels and short stories. Wagenknecht discusses the value of Bennett's varied body of work and the reasons for its deserving a permanent place in English literature.

Ward, A. C. "Novelists." In his *Twentieth-Century Literature: 1901-1950,* pp. 21-86. London: Methuen and Co., 1956.*
  Examination of the conflict between romanticism and naturalism in Bennett's work.

West, Rebecca. *Arnold Bennett Himself.* New York: The John Day Co., 1931, 21 p.
  An intimate profile of Bennett.

Woolf, Virginia. "Modern Fiction." In her *The Common Reader,* pp. 207-18. New York: Harcourt, Brace and Co., 1925.*
  Classification of Bennett as a materialist who wrote with great skill on unimportant matters.

Young, Kenneth. *Arnold Bennett.* Harlow, England: Longman Group, 1975, 54 p.
  Overview of Bennett's life and work.

Ugo Betti

1892-1953

Italian dramatist, poet, short story writer, novelist, essayist, journalist, screenwriter, and translator.

Betti is often considered Pirandello's successor as the leading dramatist in modern Italian theater. Unlike Pirandello's pessimistic dramas, however, Betti's works offer a positive, humanist perspective. Paradoxically, his most typical plays depict violence and moral chaos as the essential human condition. Often his characters represent self-centered humanity turning its back on religious salvation, which is the difficult, sometimes unnattainable, goal of the Bettian hero. A frequent conflict is the difference between human and divine justice, the nature of justice acting as a major theme in the plays. Betti himself defined his persistent concern: "We are restless creatures distinguished from an indifferent universe by one trait only: a longing toward something that can be called harmony, that can be called justice."

Early in his life Betti revealed his literary inclinations, publishing a translation of Catullus in 1910. But his father, a physician, urged him to follow a more conventionally useful career, and Betti entered the University of Parma to study law. After World War I, Betti attained judgeships in Parma and then in Rome, his experience on the bench directly emerging in the themes of guilt and responsibility in such plays as *Frana allo scalo nord* (*Landslide*) and *Corruzione al palazzo di giustizia*. An officer during the First World War, Betti was captured and interned in a German prisoner-of-war camp, where he wrote many of the poems in his first collection, *Il re pensiero*. These have been characterized as "escapist" fantasies, their mood at variance with the moral struggles and misery treated later in the dramatic works.

Betti's first play, *La padrona*, won a dramatic competition and became a popular success, as did many of his other dramas. With *Landslide*, his sixth play, Betti began to acquire the critical standing which led to favorable comparisons with Pirandello. Critics praised Betti's stagecraft and the ambition of his themes, which compassionately reflect upon a degraded humanity and upon the nature of evil. He has been critically faulted, however, for a tendency toward didactic abstraction, his moral messages often detracting from the dramatic values of the plays. Betti's dramas are well-known for universalized, quasi-allegorical character types who exist in an indefinite time and place. In many of his works, but especially in his highly acclaimed tragedies of the 1941-53 period, Betti pursued a symbolic art akin to the mythic tales of Franz Kafka. *Corruzione al palazzo di giustizia*, *Delitto all'isola delle capre* (*Crime on Goat Island*), and *L'aiuola bruciata* (*The Burnt Flower-Bed*) dramatize humanity's striving to overcome evil in the form of corruption and natural weakness.

In addition to plays, Betti also published a novel and several collections of poetry and short stories. His reputation, however, is based almost exclusively upon his dramatic works. Betti's tragedies, in particular, support his high rank in modern Italian theater, for although he wrote a number of comedies, such as *Il paese delle vacanze* (*Summertime*), he made his most distinguished artistic and philosophical statements in his dramas

P. Fuller

of human suffering. In contrast to the nihilistic agony of the Theater of the Absurd, the suffering in Betti's works is relieved by the possibility of redemption inherent in his essentially Christian world view. Critic Harold H. Watts concisely defines Betti's dramas as the "theater of salvation."

PRINCIPAL WORKS

Il re pensiero (poetry) 1922
La padrona (drama) 1926
Caino (short stories) 1928
La casa sull'acqua (drama) 1929
Canzonetta (poetry) 1932
Un albergo sul porto (drama) 1933
L'isola meravigliosa (drama) 1933
Frana allo scalo nord (drama) 1936
   [*Landslide* published in *Three Plays on Justice*, 1964]
Una bella domenica di settembre (drama) 1937
I nostri sogni (drama) 1937
Il cacciatore d'anitre (drama) 1940
Il paese delle vacanze (drama) 1942
   [*Summertime* published in *Three Plays*, 1956]
Il diluvio (drama) 1943

Ispezione (drama) 1947
  [*The Inquiry* published in *Three Plays*, 1966]
Corruzione al palazzo di giustizia (drama) 1949
Lotta fino all'alba (drama) 1949
  [*Struggle till Dawn* published in *Three Plays on Justice*, 1964]
Delitto all'isola delle capre (drama) 1950
  [*Crime on Goat Island*, 1960]
Irene innocente (drama) 1950
Spritismo nell'antica casa (drama) 1950
Il giocatore (drama) 1951
  [*The Gambler* published in *Three Plays*, 1966]
La regina e gli insorti (drama) 1951
  [*The Queen and the Rebels* published in *Three Plays*, 1956]
L'aiuola bruciata (drama) 1953
  [*The Burnt Flower-Bed* published in *Three Plays*, 1956]
La fuggitiva (drama) 1953
  [*The Fugitive* published in *Three Plays on Justice*, 1964]
Acque turbate (drama) 1955

GEORGE JEAN NATHAN (essay date 1953)

[*The Gambler*] is another in the lengthy line of plays concerning themselves with the protagonist's defeated attempt to make logic triumph over emotion, but in the process so runs up and down the side-alleys of metaphysics, theology, ethics, morals, mysticism, Freudianism and other topics and accompanies the running with such ceaseless, lofty rhetoric that any drama that might conceivably be in the materials is completely talked out of them. What the plot line of the play, if any such motionless concoction may be called one, treats of is the murder of a hated wife through her husband's apparent connivance, his guiltlessness of the actual crime in the eyes of earthly law, and his conscience, reinforced by the operations of divine law, that drives him to a realization of his factual culpability. But the story is so cluttered up with interminable excursions into the subjects mentioned, almost all of them couched in such an excess of oratory that they sound like a battle royal among a lot of graduate and overly voluble German university students, that it becomes lost in the din, which in turn involves so much circular and conflicting argument that the whole takes on the flavor of double-talk. (p. 173)

The whole enterprise, indeed, is conducted on that resplendent plane and confounds confusion with an abstinence from any possible lightness worthy of a voodoo doctor suffering from his patient's disease. Where a Shaw in *Don Juan In Hell* dealt with some of the items in Betti's philosophical catalogue not only with a likelier intelligence but with simplicity, compulsion and wit, the Italian author. . .brings to them [solemnity, portentousness and depressive fog]. . . . (pp. 173-74)

The so-called play, in sum, is another of those fiercely intellectual exhibits exposed from time to time by Continental Europeans determined to unload their philosophies in dramatic form, for which they have little or no talent, and resolves itself finally and only into a watery chowder of the thought of Pirandello, Strindberg, Dostoievski, Anouilh, [and] Sartre. . . . (p. 174)

George Jean Nathan, "Sample Continental Imports," in his The Theatre in the Fifties (copyright © 1953 by George Jean Nathan; reprinted by permission of Associated University Presses), Knopf, 1953, pp. 161-84.*

J. A. SCOTT (essay date 1960)

[Pirandello] had concluded his examination of life's problems with a stalemate: man, according to him, is irreparably condemned to spiritual isolation and misunderstanding. Betti, on the other hand, while offering us a no less profound investigation, reaches a hopeful, Christian solution. He scorns to produce a miraculous panacea—his religion is no opium for the spirit—, but he does portray a fundamentally optimistic vision of life, wherein he shows great concern for the wounded soul of modern man, bewildered and led astray by his illusion of Progress. . . . (p. 44)

[In *Ispezione*] we are shown a family of displaced persons who are staying in a boarding-house in some unidentified country. Two detectives have come to question the various members of the family. . . . As in any other play that obeys the dramatic 'law' of the three unities, the characters have reached a point of maximum psychological tension.

The dramatic function of this police-visit is much the same as that of the inspector in J. B. Priestley's *An Inspector Calls:* it brings forth the hidden feelings and sores that are to be found beneath the surface of the family bond. . . . We have a terrifying impression of the moral vacuum in which these people lead their lives, and of the confusion and despair brought about by war. Each member of the family accuses the others, revealing the atmosphere of hatred and frustration that is destroying their souls. Above all, everyone in the family hates Egle, the old woman, . . . who attempts to tyrannize the rest by the power of her money. By making them financially dependent on her, she pathetically tries to bring herself to their notice. It is the only way in which she can claim their attention, if not their affection. Otherwise, old people no longer exist in this society. She is in many ways a harrowing portrait: selfish, grasping, domineering, despising all about her, whilst craving for their love. Nevertheless, even she retains some memory of the innocence and beauty of her childhood, the Eden of the soul, as do so many of Betti's characters—a melancholy longing for lost purity, the legacy of Original Sin. This is even more strongly marked in the characters of Emma and Andrea, who is tormented by the promise of his earlier years. Another characteristic typical of our author to be found in this play is the confession to a 'judge' that all these persons make—in this case, to a police inspector who is the helpless representative of that Supreme Judge whom they unknowingly seek to reach.

Ispezione is, however, an exception in Betti's work, for it ends with a completely negative answer. . . . The end, as in Chekhov's plays, is that there is no end, no solution for these tormented creatures. They will continue to lead their sordid, muddled lives without ever coming to an effectual conclusion. (pp. 44-6)

[*La Regina e Gli Insorti*] is yet another variation on the Romantic concept of the redeemed prostitute. This hackneyed theme, however, is renovated by Betti's treatment and conception of moral regeneration. For it is not love or religion that saves the fallen woman, but the rediscovery of faith in herself, in her own dignity. (p. 46)

L'Aiuola Bruciata is perhaps the greatest of Betti's dramatic achievements. It is certainly the most profound. (p. 47)

Betti, in his dramas, is constantly worrying at the questions: why is Man condemned to solitude? Who is responsible? Will Man ever find Justice or Peace? His plays are concerned with "le vibrazioni profonde" of Man's spiritual life. Working through them, we can see the answer that gradually unfolded itself in the mind of our author, and which he asserted with such force in his last plays. He sees Man, expelled from Eden, crushed by the curse of Original Sin, and driven towards crime and illusion. For him, as he wrote a short while before his death, the theatre of our times is best able to show to Modern Man, the Child of Progress, that this age is nearer in spirit to the Middle Ages than to the confident optimism of the Renaissance.

As far as dramatic technique is concerned, Betti undoubtedly learned a great deal from such predecessors as Ibsen. . . . Like Ibsen, Betti, in a number of his plays, works within the confines of 'realism', and we have the same result as in the works of the former: a hidden poetry, which is concerned, not so much with a series of actions or events, as with the hidden movements of the soul. Human actions have little immediate significance for Betti's purpose. We understand and feel that the words and actions of the characters are brought into the play, primarily in order to afford the sonorous counterpart to the ineffable conversation that is carried on between the souls of the various protagonists, or between their individual souls and the Great Judge of whose presence they are so agonizingly aware. (pp. 51-2)

All of Betti's characters feel the need to explain their lives to a third person. . . . In this need, we see the pitiful attempt of these people to speak to the Supreme Judge, the hope that they will eventually find someone who will understand their petty, sordid actions—even though understanding may mean condemnation. As we have seen, they are oppressed by their heritage of Original Sin. But their darkness is mitigated by hope. Man's true role in life, as we are told in *Acque Turbate*, is to discover the small grain of gold that is his and to wash it clean of all the mud surrounding it. Both—the mud and the gold—are part of his heritage. (p. 52)

Betti takes up and expounds the concept of the theologians, that redeemed man is more precious to God than if the curse of Original Sin had never been placed on him. It is the paradox of creation: that this imperfection in man, his first act of rebellion, was turned into potential good by the sacrifice of his Redeemer. (p. 53)

Betti, then, tells us that it is precisely those who are without faith, the helpless, the weak, that should be the concern of our modern society. It is this society that is put to the test in *Ispezione*, *La Regina e Gli Insorti* and *L'Aiuola Bruciata*, and is found to to be wanting. Progress, with its vague humanitarianism, is but a poor compensation to offer to the soul that is tormented by doubt and overcome by the problems of Life. (p. 54)

Giovanni, in *L'Aiuola Bruciata*, points an accusing finger at us all, when he tells us that we—the whole of society—are responsible for his son's suicide. . . . Society has failed in the education of its members, if it leaves them unprepared for the true battle of Life, which takes place within the soul.

Nevertheless, in this same play, Betti states his faith in Man, and his possible redemption through innocence. He tells that the leaders of our society must remember the importance of the life of the spirit, the essence of the individual, and, above all, they must never crush Man's self-respect. The sacrifice of Rosa, who goes out to meet her death in order to save the lives of her fellow-men, and thereby puts an end to the discussions and inaugurates a new age of peace; this sacrifice warns us all that it will not profit mankind to look at the flower-bed in which humanity can commit suicide. Instead, we must act and turn back to the path of goodness and generosity. We must heed the voice of innocence preparing itself for the supreme sacrifice: "Greater love hath no man than this, that a man lay down his life for his friends." The burnt flower-bed of Creation can be turned into a garden, in which Man can be happy, if he wills to be. (pp. 54-5)

> *J. A. Scott, "The Message of Ugo Betti," in* Italica, *Vol. XXXVII, No. 1, March, 1960, pp. 44-57.*

G. H. McWILLIAM (essay date 1960)

In his preface to *The Mistress*, Betti writes of "this solemn crown, called conscience, which rests upon our heads," and he asserts that all men are poor, restless creatures, longing for an explanation of the "monstrously grotesque incongruity between the way we live and the way we ought to live, granted the possibilities of the mind with which we are endowed." . . . Man's instinctive desire for harmony and justice is in perpetual conflict with his inner conviction that he has been unjustly condemned to a life of suffering and degradation. Against this second feeling, which obviously—though Betti never actually employs this terminology—is closely related to the doctrine of original sin, man's reason is powerless. And thus our actions are frequently directed, not towards our own ultimate advantage or even towards the advantage of our closest associates (our wives, parents, children) but along a completely different, often opposite, channel. In Betti's view, the true inner motive for a wide range of human behavior defies logical explanation. The psychoanalyst can follow its twisting roots to a certain depth, but it is eventually engulfed in shadow. Hence the temptation to endorse the hypothesis that man is eternally destined to atone for the first disobedience of his earliest ancestor. The symbolism of Betti's plays is all directed at emphasizing man's loss of Eden.

There is of course a danger that one may read too much into the somewhat cryptic comments of the preface to *The Mistress*. But it is at any rate evident that, even at the dawn of his career as a dramatist, Betti was willing himself towards the belief that there is a divinity which shapes our ends. (pp. 21-2)

[What] his plays demonstrate is the state of bewilderment and uncertainty of a man who thinks more deeply than most about the moral implications of human behavior and who longs to possess a positive belief in a higher, transcendent justice without ever being fully capable of bridging the chasm between reason and faith. If there is any conclusion to be drawn from Betti's plays, it is that, far from being a cogent champion of Christian beliefs, he is a disillusioned observer of human behavior to whom the possibility of a higher order of things offers the only escape from complete despair. Betti's general appraisal of human motive is reminiscent of Machiavelli's, who described men (in a famous passage from *The Prince*) as "ungrateful, fickle, dissimulating, cowardly and avaricious." But Betti's pessimism arises, of course, out of different circumstances. The intellectual climate of the early years of the present century, which produced works like Georges Sorel's *Reflections on Violence* and gave birth to the Futurist movement with its eulogies on warfare and its savage attacks on conventional values, is in part responsible for the uncompromisingly bleak assessment of human motive which we find in the plays of Betti. . . . It is [a] tiny, inexplicable spark of moral awareness which Betti seeks to uncover in his drama. (pp. 22-3)

> *G. H. McWilliam, "Interpreting Betti," in* The Tulane Drama Review *(copyright,* © *1960, The Tulane Drama Review; reprinted with the permission of the MIT Press, Cambridge, for the School of Arts, New York University), Vol. 5, No. 2, December, 1960, pp. 15-23.*

FRANK W. WADSWORTH (essay date 1961)

It is Ugo Betti's virtue that while he views life with the pessimism typical of the most sensitive writers of his era he never quite loses confidence in the essential dignity of mankind, a confidence unusual in a theatre inclined today to see man as an abomination. Like the author of *King Lear*, Betti can recognize the terrors of the world without completely losing faith in its inhabitants. . . . This faith is dramatized most strikingly in *The Queen and the Rebels* [(*La Regina e gli insorti*)], where a selfless act of will shines brightly in a world otherwise evil, selfish and shorn of traditional values.

From the point of view of his dramaturgy Betti is also significant. With their vividly human quality his plays recall the rich, complex texture of Miller's and Williams' best work more than the simpler patterns of most European playwrights. Continental drama has tended recently to be presentational, but Betti typically builds upon a firm foundation of concrete, realistic action, coloring this with an admixture of theatricalism which both deepens and broadens the implications of the basic dramatic movement much as do the nonrepresentational interludes of *Death of a Salesman*. His theatricalism ranges from such obvious devices as the appearance of dead men at the trial in *Landslide at the North Station (Frana allo Scalo Nord)* to the subtle undertones of *The Queen and the Rebels*, where Christian allegory points up the parallels between the heroine's sacrifice and Christ's Passion. In addition, the voice of Betti the poet is frequently allowed to break the realistic illusion, being especially noticeable in the verbal richness of parts of the dialogue and in the long flights of poetic rhetoric with which certain characters are indulged.

Both his view of humanity and his dramatic methods are revealed in *The Queen and the Rebels*. . . . More severely realistic than some of the earlier dramas, it nevertheless embodies Betti's fundamental approach to theatre, while revealing those thematic qualities responsible for his unusual distinction among recent dramatists. As so often with Betti, the essential narrative is richly melodramatic. (pp. 167-68)

The story of *The Queen and the Rebels* is potentially sensational, but Betti's actual handling of it is not. (p. 169)

Betti's realism relieved by the devices of theatricalism results in a rich and complex dramatic texture. As much as Jean Genêt, he is aware of life's evils. His heroine is no softhearted prostitute from the pages of sentimental fiction, but a scheming, sexually debased woman who has not hesitated to sell herself as bait for the traps of the secret police (a

character not unexpected from the author of so gripping a study of sexual degeneration as *Crime on the Island of Goats* [(*Delitto all'Isola delle Capre*)], Betti's view of human nature is unfashionable only in that it entails a belief in man's responsibility for bringing about the harmony implicit in the universe. Argia dies because she realizes that one must fully accept one's role as a human being in order to give significance to life. Through an act of will she becomes a person, finding salvation in a Sartrean effort of commitment. (p. 170)

Just as Betti's melodrama is muted, so is there little sentimentality in the play. Life for him, as for Genêt, Beckett, or Ionesco, is a grim absurd affair, a bitter struggle waged by people who "don't believe in equality; except over toothpicks" and hope only "to get rich, little by little." The despair that is so much a part of modern drama is clearly present, but in Betti's case it is a nobler sentiment, based upon a deep if hidden pride in mankind and on the conviction that man, any man, is capable of something better. Thus, inevitably, *The Queen and the Rebels* is a tragedy in the classic manner. It has a stark, simple quality, emphasized by the slightly stylized laconicness of the dialogue, and underscored by Betti's strict observance of the unities of time, place, and action. In the last analysis it is not Argia's sacrifice that bespeaks Betti's view of life, but the firm architectonics of his drama which reflect his innate belief in the meaning of life as surely as the chaos of a Ionesco play reflects hopelessness. Betti's voice deserves to be heard, not only because he has deepened and amplified the chords of realistic drama by his poetic approach, but also because he speaks with positive power at a time when too many dramatists can chant only the threnody of passive despair. (pp. 172-73)

It was inevitable that an Italian dramatist concerned with human conduct in an alien and unfriendly world should respond to the influence of Pirandello. Although the Pirandellian conflict of illusion and reality is present in most of Betti's work, it achieves its clearest focus in *Night Wind (Il vento notturno . . .)* where a man and a woman use an imagined father-daughter relationship as a shield between themselves and the harsh realities of their everyday lives. Their desperate need to assume protective roles, a need so great that the mask eventually becomes the face, recalls the older dramatist's *Henry IV,* as also does Betti's later play, *Spiritism in the Old House (Spiritismo nell'antica casa . . .).* And it is this same tragic search for identity which provides the central unity of *The Queen and the Rebels*. The political context in which Argia's search takes place may make it appear that the tragedy indicates a significant shift in Betti's view of life. But actually only the setting is new; the basic ideas reflect Betti's lifelong concerns. As the most effective synthesis of his major themes, *The Queen and the Rebels* marks the culmination of Ugo Betti's career as a dramatist.

By moving into the vaster arena of international tensions at the close of his career Betti parallelled the expanding vision of a number of contemporary European dramatists. His most explicit political comment is contained in *The Burnt Flowerbed (L'aiuola bruciata . . .)* written a year before his death. Argia has become Giovanni, a retired political leader and the dupe of former colleagues who plan to use his death as a pretext for starting another war. In his effort to escape, Giovanni allows a young girl to sacrifice her life for him, a sacrifice that results in his own reluctant recognition of the impossibility of avoiding human responsibility. As in *The Queen and the Rebels,* a selfless action redeems an otherwise meaningless world. The faceless evil of totalitarianism is brilliantly communicated by an unseen rifleman who waits across a mountain pass with orders to fire at the first person crossing the threshold of Giovanni's house. Too distant to see anything but the white flag the victim is supposed to be carrying, he becomes a frightening symbol of impersonal efficiency and an effective contrast to the tragically uncertain and therefore tragically human men and women within the house.

The Burnt Flower-bed, like *The Queen and the Rebels*, is one of the finest dramatic treatments of the conflict between a collectivist society and the lonely, defiant individual to be written in our day. However, it lacks the formal perfection that distinguishes the earlier play, and thus is inferior to it. *The Queen and the Rebels* embodies in its own artistic design the beauty and dignity of the human spirit. It is fashionable today to approve of the fragmented and the casual. *The Queen and the Rebels* reminds us that even though chaos has come again, high seriousness and a formal ordering of experience are still not impossible. (pp. 176-77)

> Frank W. Wadsworth, "Magnanimous Despair," in Drama Survey (copyright 1961 by The Bolingbroke Society, Inc.), Vol. 1, No. 2, Fall, 1961, pp. 165-77.

PAUL A. MANKIN (essay date 1962)

There are no happy endings in Betti's plays. Yet he avoids the innate pessimism of his great predecessor Pirandello. "Pirandello's characters reason because they suffer, Betti's characters suffer because they reason," is the distinction that Achille Fiocco makes. A clever quip that is easy to remember and difficult to prove, although it is true that remembrances of things past are a major preoccupation in Betti's theater. But it is seldom reason that provokes the reconstruction of former misdeeds, rather a justification that shows the immutable weakness of man. Betti's worth lies in his ability to identify himself with our times in terms of their negative aspects: anguish, moral decay, lack of communication, endless search, melancholy and suspicion. This suspicion is the fear of having been deceived, and the gap that exists for man between intention and realization had become the very form of his own drama. Throughout the plays certain themes recur: justice vs. pity, redemption through suffering, hope beyond death, and a powerful central irony: It is the function of the couple to make man become conscious of his loneliness. (p. 132)

Like Bertolt Brecht . . . , Betti wrote dramas to teach us how to survive. Unlike Brecht, who looks down on humanity, Betti often casts a tender glance beyond it to some undefinable cause.

Facts are barely outlined in the plays. Betti's heroes wear indistinct halos, his villains lack the conviction of their misdeeds. What matters most is the tragic vibration set off by a deed, ranging from an innocent boating party to a fifteen year old boy's mysterious suicide because he had lost faith in the world.

"Landslide at North Station" is the story of a disaster and of the inquest that follows it. In the process of pinning down responsibility and guilt the whole of modern society is accused and found guilty, and yet the final word of the play is "Pietà." If all are guilty, all are somehow innocent. All

men suffer, Betti says, but they want to suffer because they breathe, because they are men, because they want to live, to weep, to hope and to push their heavy burden forward. . . . There are some echoes of the Sisyphus myth here, without the ennobling qualities that Camus gives to his hero. The rungs of the ladder of indictment are peopled with very ordinary men, whose frailties evoke more compassion than disgust.

"Corruption in the Palace of Justice" discusses the problem of guilt where it would be least likely to appear, in a high tribunal, among respected judges. . . . The atmosphere of fear and suspicion is reminiscent of Kafka, the entire action takes place in one room of the Palace of Justice, and such a feeling of claustrophobia is created by constant confrontations and accusations between the three principal judges, that an innocent girl's suicide—she had begun to doubt her father's honor and righteousness—is almost a welcome escape to freedom. And yet the play's conclusion is not entirely negative: Elena, the young woman, has not died in vain, since the guilty judge, haunted by a sense of sin, confesses (we never find out just what) and redeems his soul. He will at last tell the truth, although he does not have to speak up at all. The curtain falls on his last, prosaic words: "I am a little scared. But I know that no one can help me." . . .

[Ugo Betti] touches the heart, as few dramatists have done in our century. (p. 133)

> Paul A. Mankin, "The Role of Ugo Betti in the Modern Italian Theater," in Books Abroad (copyright 1962 by the University of Oklahoma Press), Vol. 36, No. 2, Spring, 1962, pp. 131-33.

GINO RIZZO (essay date 1963)

[Too] many critics have fallen short of an understanding of Betti's art and have failed to account for the power of his dramatic vision through an honest analysis of his work.

Such an analysis would have to begin with the realization that the answer is contained, as far as Betti's plays are concerned, in his dynamic use of a "regression-progression" pattern. By unfolding this pattern through the psyche of his characters, he gives dramatic form to the awakening of those irrational needs which slowly rise from the depths of our unconscious and finally succeed in determining the direction of our moral conscience.

In his drama, the "bewildering incongruity" of our existence draws the psyche toward the memory of gratification (and the Proustian gratification of memory) in a retrogressive movement which has as its final goal a spiritual progression. More accurately, the regression is the means of the progression, for the backward movement of the psyche originates in its clash with the present reality and aims at transcending it. Betti's characters are restless creatures who cannot reconcile themselves to the unjust sentence weighing upon them, and must therefore turn inward and reexamine the chain of their existence in all its links until they can discover the primal cause of their present anguish. And such a retrogressive movement is hindered by the forward movement of life.

The resolution of these two antithetical movements—backward, to obliterate life and recapture its initial stage, and forward, to follow the flux of existence—transcends the confines of human life and time. Betti's metaphysical inquiry originates in the psyche's regression to that pre-conscious stage where *eros* and *thanatos* conjoin, and is projected into his plays by the child-motif. (pp. 102-03)

The child-motif is by its very nature the symbolic terminal point of the psyche's movement both backward and forward. In the regression-progression path followed by the playwright in reenacting the drama of human regeneration, the child-motif lends its manifold significance to the embodiment of this experience in artistic form. The child archetype, says Jung, "is both beginning and end, an initial and terminal creature. The initial creature existed before man was, and the terminal creature will be when man is not. Psychologically speaking, this means that the 'child' symbolizes the pre-conscious and the post-conscious nature of man. His pre-conscious nature is the unconscious state of earliest childhood; his post-conscious nature is an anticipation by analogy of life after death." (pp. 103-04)

As Betti saw in the world "a pressing need to be convinced on a new basis in the face of certain new objections," he found in the regression-progression pattern—and the child-motif which projects it into his plays—a means of moving from the alienation of modern man toward the core of an age-old religion. Through the symbolic significance of the image of childhood he could embrace all levels of human experience—biological, psychological, mythical, religious—and thus encompass the totality of life. He could reinterpret, in the light of modern psychology, the religious myths of the Christian world and revitalize them through the medium of a contemporary idiom. The challenge posed by the new science of psychology to the honored but timeworn Aristotelian-Thomistic rationalization of human instincts, motives, and purposes could only be met by accepting the postulates of the new rationalization and by attempting to reconcile these with the ultimate demands of the spirit. Betti understood and accepted this challenge. As a poet, he found in the image of childhood the "objective correlative" for his sublimation of a psychic pattern into a religious experience of universal significance. (pp. 104-05)

[In *La Padrona (The Mistress)*] the regression-progression pattern is present, but still in embryonic form. There are moments, if only during a pause in the dramatic action, in which the characters become cognizant of their isolation in an impassive universe and attempt to evade the forces and laws of a life which they feel foreign to their will. Both the impulse to evade and the motivating force which might enable these characters to transcend a genetic distinction between "red-blooded" and "thin-blooded" individuals (strongly reminiscent of Andreyev), are felt through memory, through the spontaneous return to the conscious mind of images buried in the past. . . . The haunting memory of childhood, the echoing appeal of lost innocence, and the unquenchable thirst for the fresh waters of felicity, which distinguish Betti's voice from those of his contemporaries, are not sufficient to free his characters from the laws of biological necessity.

With the exception of an occasional escape into a fairy-tale world charged with overtones of an exemplary fable, the concern of the artist in the plays written between *The Mistress* and *Frana allo scalo nord (Landslide at the North Station . . .)* is consistently focused on this same psychic region, dominated by primordial instincts, dimly reflecting a spark of moral identity and freedom. Especially in *La casa sull'acqua (The House on the Water . . .)*, the attempts of the characters to assert themselves through some positive action is set in

motion in opposition to their profound dissatisfaction with life. Once again, these attempts are prompted by the sudden illuminations which their consciences receive from the dark recesses of memory. In *Un albergo sul porto (An Inn on the Harbor . . .)*, the child-motif appears at the very center of an atmosphere of vice and corruption. But there the motif takes the variant form of "mother and child," and the dramatist seems unable to represent it in such a way as to transcend the animal instinct of procreation. He still fails, therefore, to achieve that integration of personal and moral responsibility which was inherent from the beginning in both his vision of life and his poetic imagery.

If the order and progression of a writer's work is seen as a symbolic projection of his inner world, then in these early plays one may follow almost step by step the re-enactment of Betti's spiritual regeneration. And read at this level, the "landslide" of *Landslide at the North Station* is what occurred in the dramatist's vision, the scattered elements contained in his previous attempts falling into place and converging on a single pole of attraction.

In *The Mistress* . . . neither the genetic and physical predispositions of his characters nor the force of brute instinct were adequate to penetrate the opaque materiality that marks the world of the play. Betti's plays continue to focus on these primal impulses of man's nature, but all the while his art moves towards a gradual integration of motive with purpose. As this integration is approached, the suffocating world of his first play yields to a world of liquid flux—*The House on the Water* and *An Inn on the Harbor*—where, underneath "the slimy mud," we can see the hidden presence of life. From the hellish atmosphere of these early plays, Betti arrives, in *Landslide*, at a sort of limbo, where man awaits judgment but still is allowed to make a final plea for salvation. (pp. 105-08)

L'aiuola bruciata (The Burnt Flower-bed . . .), one of Betti's last plays, demonstrates this final stage of the regression-progression pattern. Moreover, the unfolding of this pattern links here the private life of the protagonist to his public, political role. An individual instance of redemption thus becomes a message of social regeneration. (p. 122)

Betti's statement in this play is precisely this: that the seemingly ineluctable course of human events can be altered, because of its freedom from the laws of causality, by the presence on this earth of a *deus ex machina*. Individually, we may or may not recognize the presence of Christ in our midst. If we do . . . our individual existence will be re-oriented—and an individual redemption will offer a pattern of salvation of universal validity. But for the social body to be re-oriented, it takes no less than an active intervention by Christ. (pp. 123-24)

In *The Burnt Flower-bed* the regression-progression pattern underlying Betti's drama is given its maximum scope. The dramatist has unfolded his theme in all its cathartic potentialities: from *Landslide*, where this pattern of moral cognition had led him, by accepting evil as divinely ordained, to the first affirmation of a purposive universe; through [*Corruzione al Palazzo di giustizia (Corruption at the Palace of Justice)*] where it enabled him to re-live the paradox of the "fortunate fall" and the mystery of the Incarnation as means of personal salvation and individual redemption; to *The Burnt Flower-bed*, where an individual experience of rebirth is transformed, through the immanence of Faith, into an active program of social regeneration. He has chosen consistently and coherently to employ the child as the *irrational third* that can reconcile the opposites of life and provide a link between a primordial past and an unknown future. He has found in the child the most appropriate vehicle for the fusion of biological impulses, psychological manifestations and spiritual needs, thus transcending the limitations of clinical case-histories through the metapsychology of religious myth.

Both the regression-progression pattern and the child-motif that embodies it are at the center of Betti's dramaturgy. They are not only woven into the structure of all his major plays, determining the varied form taken by the dramatic action in each one of them, but they also indicate in their progression from play to play the total development of the dramatist's vision. Through them, he has given concrete expression to those "strange" and "illogical" needs which he himself experienced and which he could recognize, from the bench, even in the most abject of his fellow men. By presenting these needs in dramatic form, he has enabled us—which was the goal of his creative life—"to perceive a glimmer of light even in the most opaque things . . . to love a little this life that we must live." (pp. 128-29)

> Gino Rizzo, "Regression-Progression in Ugo Betti's Drama," in The Tulane Drama Review *(copyright,* © *1963,* The Tulane Drama Review; *reprinted with the permission of the MIT Press, Cambridge, for the School of Arts, New York University), Vol. 8, No. 1, Fall, 1963, pp. 101-29.*

G. H. McWILLIAM (essay date 1964)

Landslide is the culminating achievement of the first phase of Betti's activities as a dramatist. . . . His first five plays include two studies, in predominantly realist vein, of human passion and violence; a fable in high-flown, D'Annunzian verse; a broad farce which calls to mind the preoccupations of Italian writers of an earlier age, like Boccaccio and Machiavelli, with the dubious pleasures of cuckoldry; and a drama, set in a dingy seaport hotel catering to poor emigrants, in which the playwright, using a heightened, slightly sententious prose, attempts the allegorical presentation of certain human vices and virtues. All these early plays are experiments in which Betti seems to be groping his way towards a personal dramatic form. He oscillates bewilderingly between escapist fantasy and social realism, verse and prose, broad farce and high seriousness, symbolism and straightforward observation.

In *Landslide,* his sixth play, Betti succeeds for the first time in bringing the various strands of his creative and intellectual faculties together into a harmonious relationship, and becomes a dramatist of European stature. The main idea of the play—the terrible inadequacy of earthly justice and the consequent need for reciprocal compassion—is not exactly a new one in the annals of literature. But Betti's treatment of this idea *is* new, and powerfully so. For a practicing judge to concede the weaknesses of human justice is in itself somewhat surprising, particularly in a police state, although the same point is made with even greater force in a later play, ***Corruption at the Palace of Justice.*** . . .

However, the fact that Betti was himself a judge is of relevance only in so far as it explains why, in this play as in others by Betti, the peculiar atmosphere—as distinct from the formal procedure—of an Italian law court (with its predisposition to believe in a prisoner's guilt rather than his

innocence, its confrontation of witnesses, its odd combination of petty pomposity and extempore informality) is so authentically reproduced. The naturalism of the play is, of course, only skindeep: following his usual practice, Betti provides just sufficient realistic detail to anchor his play firmly in a recognizable environment, and for the rest he draws liberally on his rich, poet's imagination. His characteristic refusal to specify, noticeable not only here but elsewhere in his plays, annoyed some of his critics. But it is all part of his endeavor to seek out truths which are universal, and his attempt to liberate his thinking from the restrictions imposed by references to a precise time and a particular place. Thus there is a liberal helping of fantasy in all of Betti's plays. (p. x)

The fantasy elements in *Landslide* are of two distinct kinds. The first group consists of certain deliberately antinaturalistic devices such as the presence of a sort of *deus ex machina* figure—Goetz—who keeps a constant watch on the proceedings and guides Parsc, the representative of human justice, along paths which normally he would have had no intention of following. Also in this category we may place the three wraithlike figures who, in a brilliant *coup de théâtre,* are conjured out of the mist at the close of the second act. The second group comprises all those elements in the play which contribute in transmuting what is essentially a routine and ordinary investigation into a poetic statement about man's search for meaning, order, and harmony. In this connection we may mention the sudden appearance of sunlight at a crucial moment in Act One and the intense vertical lighting at the beginning of the final act, indicating the judges' determination to disperse, once and for all, the shadows which are obscuring what one of the characters calls "the heart of the matter." (p. xi)

In his handling of these technical features, Betti shows himself to be a theatrical craftsman of considerable skill. But while he remains constantly alive to the special possibilities of his chosen medium, he never loses sight of his main purpose, which is to offer a convincing and poetic presentation of man's instinctive search for true justice. In the later plays, this becomes more explicitly a search for a higher, divine justice, and the evolution of the Bettian hero is towards a figure tenaciously searching for God in a world which has lost its faith. In *Landslide,* however, the judge who is the play's central character goes no further than a humanistic appeal for universal, reciprocal compassion—thus echoing exactly the plea which was expressed by a great Italian poet of the nineteenth century, Giacomo Leopardi. As a consequence, the ending of *Landslide* seems to carry greater conviction than some of the endings of Betti's later plays, where very often the hero or heroine appears to endorse rather too readily Wordsworth's affirmation that "Our souls have sight of that immortal sea which brought us hither."

It would be no exaggeration to describe *Landslide* as the most important play to come out of Italy since Pirandello's *Six Characters in Search of an Author.* (pp. xi-xii)

[*Struggle Till Dawn*] is a drama that reflects the anarchy and destruction of the war years in Italy, at the same time relating these aspects to the deeper moral and spiritual chaos of modern society. Here we have the story of Giorgio's determination to settle a personal debt which has remained outstanding since the first day of the war, when he was seriously injured in a street accident. Betti is concerned here, as elsewhere, with the operation of conscience and the problem of responsibility, and he captures our attention the more readily by placing Giorgio's resolve to balance his account against a background of discussions in lawyers' offices about war reparations. We may note incidentally that Betti is very fond of employing monetary symbolism in his investigations into religious belief, which one might describe as his principal concern in his later plays. We shall meet it again in *The Fugitive,* where the heroine recklessly piles up enormous debts in playing at cards with her husband's employer, her actions being symbolic of an even more hazardous gamble with her chance of eternal salvation. The same kind of symbolism is also seen in a play which Betti wrote in 1950 and which is actually called *The Gambler.*

Struggle Till Dawn offers a good illustration of a type of dramatic writing to which Betti was increasingly attracted in his later plays, and which is possibly best described as a sort of parable in which characters, passions, incidents and dialogue are all presented in a densely concentrated form. There are moments in *Struggle Till Dawn* where Betti falls a victim to his deliberately stylized manner of presentation, and the action becomes melodramatic and uncomfortably sensational. But if we can remember that Betti is not writing in the naturalistic tradition, and that he is concerned with the dramatization of states of mind rather than with the photographic reproduction of surface reality, then these weaknesses are seen to be of marginal relevance.

At the simplest level of interpretation, *Struggle Till Dawn* is a new variant on the eternal-triangle theme. In each member of the triangle, the dramatist subjects a particular set of feelings to an intensive examination, allowing them complete freedom of development: in Giorgio, remorse and the desire for atonement; in Tullio, the thirst for revenge; in Delia, the determination to follow at all costs the bidding of the senses. The fourth main character, Elsa, embodies the less spectacular qualities of unswerving conjugal devotion, and she is therefore the least colorful. However, none of these characters is perfectly rounded in the traditional sense—their gestures are emphatic, their attitudes are intense, their language is formalized—and one experiences some hesitation about accepting them as creatures of flesh and blood unless one bears in mind that Betti's art, like Dante's, is allegorical, and that the stylization is as natural within its context as the stylization of medieval painting or sculpture. The comparison with medieval art gains meaning if we consider a passage from Betti's essay on *Religion and the Theatre,* where he wrote, among other things, that "if our epoch has affinities with any other, it is more with the passionate Middle Ages than with the brilliant and tolerant Renaissance. In some respects, our epoch, too, is eager for universal systems, and it is not so much preoccupied with living and prospering in them, as in fighting for them, in asserting that they *are* universal and absolute: in a word, religious."

Whether one agrees or not with this interpretation of the age in which we are living, it does, I think, help to explain the allusiveness which is so striking a feature of Betti's manner and which, unless its motivations are properly understood, stands in some danger of being mistaken for empty rhetoric. (pp. xii-xiii)

The plays of Betti's "middle" period, of which *Struggle Till Dawn* is a fair specimen, all explore the question of sexual morality, which Betti takes (with reason) to be intimately related to the question of religious belief or unbelief. In those plays, he places man's libidinous impulse under close and exhaustive scrutiny. But his preoccupation with sexual matters should not be mistaken for a narrow puritanism. He shows no desire to preach the virtues of chastity or to lay down rules of behavior. On the contrary, Betti accepts the libidinous impulse as a natural and inalterable element in man, and from this premiss he proceeds to enquire whether a belief in survival after death is justified. Occasionally, as in *Crime on Goat Island . . . ,* the conclusion he reaches is a bleak and despairing negative. But his plays more usually end on a note of optimism, which is sometimes, however, inclined to ring a shade falsely. The ending of *Struggle Till Dawn* will leave unsatisfied those who fail to accept Betti's view—and it *is* a poet's view—that man's first disobedience is a present reality, and that we are all exiles from a primeval state of happiness and innocence, to which we instinctively long to return. It is, I think, unnecessary to explain in detail why Betti has been called "the dramatist of Original Sin." But we might perhaps point out that the symbolism of his plays is indeed directed at emphasizing man's loss of Eden. How often, for instance, do we find Betti's characters referring to a garden, one which is usually associated with childhood?

Each of [Betti's] three "posthumous" plays [*The Fugitive, Troubled Waters,* and *The Burnt Flower-Bed*] examines a particular human relationship. In *Troubled Waters,* it is the relationship between a brother and sister; in *The Burnt Flower-Bed,* which is primarily an appeal for sanity in the conduct of political affairs, it is the relationship between a child and its parents; in *The Fugitive,* it is the relationship between a husband and wife. Thus Betti returns, in his last play, to a subject which had occupied his attention in his earliest work for the theater, and by which he was fascinated almost to the point of obsessiveness throughout his writing career: the nature of the conjugal bond.

The "fugitive" of the play's title is of course the wife, Nina, in whom Betti seems intent on portraying what he once described as "that freezing sense of isolation" which is a necessary concomitant of human life. We are like rabbits caught in a trap, furiously struggling to avoid final oblivion. Nina is not a "sympathetic" character: she is neurotic and hysterical, basically unintelligent, spiteful, disloyal, feckless, egocentric. Betti has deliberately painted her in these harsh, unattractive colors in order to test to the full the plausibility of a belief in spiritual survival. For if God exists, and if He is all-merciful, then His mercy will extend even to the most abject and misshapen of His creatures. Betti once stated that in writing a play, he liked to place his characters, alone and naked, at the foot of a giant staircase, and then discover whether they were capable of ascending by their own, unaided efforts. In this play, the heroine reaches the top of the staircase, but not under her own steam, and the almost complete absence of character development in the case of Nina is perhaps to be regarded as the play's major weakness. It certainly accounts for the difficulty one experiences in accepting the final solution. But against this, we must set the play's considerable positive qualities; the feast of dialectic in the speeches of the Doctor, who is a magnificent Mephistophelian figure; the penetrating exploration of Daniele's character; the novel and exciting structure of the play, which offers a stimulating challenge to the producer in all three acts; the interesting use which Betti makes of the two chorus figures; the cleverly organized interrelationship of the two separate scenes in Act I; and finally, the pointing of the action through a subtle arrangement of symbols. (pp. xiv-xv)

[Betti] is one of the few playwrights of the present century to have written cogently and with unflagging power and insight on the theme which inspired the best work of major dramatists of the past: the theme of justice. In his twenty-five plays, he provides excellent food for thought on this and a wide range of allied topics, among which the ones that come immediately to mind are ambition, pride, responsibility, predestination and freewill, and sexual morality. Whether or not one agrees with what Betti has to say, one cannot help being impressed by the dedicated manner in which, during the whole of his playwriting career, he approached the problems which he felt to be important. . . . [It] is our duty to place him firmly where he belongs, in the company of the major dramatists of the present century: Shaw, Pirandello, Eugene O'Neill, Bertolt Brecht. But one really has to go back to Ibsen before finding a dramatist of comparable heroic stamp. (p. xvi)

> *G. H. McWilliam, "Introduction" (copyright © 1964 by Chandler Publishing Company; reprinted by permission of the author), in* Three Plays on Justice: "Landslide," "Struggle till Dawn," "The Fugitive" *by Ugo Betti, translated by G. H. McWilliam, Chandler, 1964, pp. vii-xvi.*

G. H. McWILLIAM (essay date 1965)

A chronological survey of [Betti's] output reveals the fact that the six plays which remain the least characteristic of the author account for exactly half of his work for the theatre up to 1938. These six plays are all characterized by a flippant, occasionally pretentious mood which is almost totally absent from the remainder of his drama. They range in form from the dramatic fable [to bourgeois comedy and pure farce]. . . . They must be regarded as minor compositions, but they are nevertheless interesting to the student of Betti's drama both because they evidence the difficulty which the dramatist experienced, in the earlier phase of his playwriting career, in discovering a form, and because they offer confirmation of Betti's unusual technical competence from the purely theatrical viewpoint. (p. 78)

Let us begin with an examination of the dramatic fantasy, *L'isola meravigliosa.* . . . (p. 79)

Betti has chosen worthwhile themes—the loneliness of kingship and the eternal elusiveness of happiness—but he forfeits our serious interest in his exploration of those themes by employing a forced and pedantic style, at times similar (though more jarring) to that of the fables in *Caino*, at times recalling that of his earliest poems. Indeed, one of the play's chief shortcomings is its total lack of stylistic uniformity. Some characters speak in verse (generally facile, with emphatic rhythms, and having assonance in preference to rhyme), whilst others speak in a heavy, sententious prose containing a rich leavening of archaisms. These bizarre means of expression inevitably cloud our apprehension of the play's meaning. . . . (p. 80)

The total impression conveyed by *L'isola meravigliosa* is that of a play whose author is experimenting, unsuccessfully, with language. The main literary influence is D'Annunzio, but Betti's language here lacks the qualities which make D'Annunzio's prose and poetry tolerable: their imagery and musicality. It is D'Annunzio in pedant's clothing. (pp. 80-1)

[*Il diluvio*] is without any real parallel in the remainder of Betti's literary work. (p. 84)

[Although] basically the play is a critique of contemporary bourgeois morals, it is also a critique of mankind in general. An unkind observer might say that Betti looked upon the earth, and, behold, it was corrupt. For the play's symbolism is related firmly to the biblical myth of Noah and the flood. It is the hero of the play, Arcibaldo, who prophesies the impending doom of a corrupt world in the wordy treatise entitled *Il diluvio,* to which for years he has been devoting his moments of comparative leisure. . . . But if Archibaldo, with his awareness of the world's corruption, is projecting the dramatist's own feelings, it is to be noted that he too is tainted by the common evil. For he lends himself after a merely token resistance to the scheme for ensnaring the millionaire and relieving him either of his freedom or of at least a part of his fortune. And when Arcibaldo, through a misunderstanding, locks up his wife with Bemoll instead of her cousin, he becomes in a sense the victim of his own moral apathy. So that if Arcibaldo *is* a mouthpiece for the dramatist (and it is not only his final speech which suggests that he is) then Betti's is not a 'God's-eye-view' but the view of one who is at the same time observing and participating. It is this sense of involuntary participation in a corrupt world which humanizes and lends authority to Betti's moralizing, making it acceptable.

Il diluvio fails as a play, however, because after the central situation has been led up to and reached towards the end of the second act, the comic inspiration flags perceptibly. From a theatrical standpoint, the first two acts are as perfect an example of the writing of farce as one is likely to meet in the whole of the Italian comic repertoire. . . . On the other hand, it is no use trying to pretend that *Il diluvio* is any sort of masterpiece. Where Betti fails, I suggest, is in attempting to graft on to the farce, more especially in the third act, the social satire to which we have already referred. The farce is too unsteady a vehicle for the communication of a serious statement on contemporary ethics. The farce is in fact an inferior form of dramatic composition, because in its purest form it entertains but it does not instruct. (pp. 86-7)

And so to the comedies. (p. 88)

[In writing *Una bella domenica di settembre*] the author was motivated by more serious intentions than the mere demonstration of his technical ability in that *genre* of light, bourgeois comedy to which his own drama was basically antithetical. But although *Una bella domenica di settembre* is the most 'serious' of the four comedies, the message of the play . . . is lacking in true conviction. The protagonist, Adriana, chooses to remain with her egoistical husband and children, not because the family provides the only source of true happiness, but because she realizes that happiness—as defined by her young, idealistic suitor, Carlo—is in fact unattainable. The ending of the play, where Adriana thrice repeats the word 'Nonna' in a tone of regret and bewilderment, is suffused with a melancholy that reminds one forcibly of the plays of Chekhov. (p. 89)

Una bella domenica di settembre contains many elements which are characteristic of Betti's drama as a whole. Had the dramatist desisted from flirtation with the 'gran pubblico,' and lavished the same attention upon the other characters as he devoted to Adriana, the play might well have been one of his best.

The same cannot be said of *I nostri sogni.* . . . (p. 95)

I nostri sogni has all the appearance of a hastily assembled pastiche, and to expatiate on all its weaknesses (carelessness over details, introduction of superfluous characters, deliberate attempts to provoke laughter through devices unrelated to the main action, etc.) would be to employ the proverbial sledgehammer on what is certainly no more than a nut. It is more to the point to enquire in what relationship the play stands to the remainder of Betti's drama. Stylistically, it is rather uneven, but at some moments there are distinct traces of the characteristic Bettian manner. In the speeches of the store-manager, Posci, in the first act, there is that comical, inflated, enumerative style, which Betti used successfully in some of his short-stories (particularly in the fables in *Caino*). . . . (p. 98)

I nostri sogni, for all its shortcomings as a work for the theatre, has a special significance in Betti's evolution as a writer because, along with the previous play, *Una bella domenica di settembre,* it aims to show that concrete, everyday reality is is finally more substantial and more relevant than the world of fantasy. Henceforth, Betti will be seen to concentrate more and more on an investigation of the real problems that man has to face. . . . Betti made two further essays in the field of comedy.

The first of these, *Il paese delle vacanze,* is without question his happiest experiment in the *genre*. . . . Here Betti seems to be fully aware of the limitations of this type of play, and works within them. No attempt is made to equip the play with a serious 'message,' as in the other two plays that we have examined. And we are left with a piece of pure escapism, a simple love story in which feminine skill and patience do battle with masculine indifference, and secure their ultimate reward. (p. 100)

It is unnecessary for us to dwell at any length on the fourth and last of these 'bourgeois' comedies, *Favola di Natale,* since it is undoubtedly the weakest of them all. (p. 103)

Favola di Natale falls in the final analysis between too many different stools. At one moment it is broad farce, at another it is redolent of the worst type of music-hall, at another it attempts to become sophisticated comedy, and at yet another (in the final act) it has pretensions to earnestness which cannot be seriously entertained because the serious outcome of the piece has not been organically led up to, in the play's first two acts. Betti's other comedies show a tendency towards pastiche. But in *Favola di Natale* it is no longer a tendency but a *fait accompli.*

The connection between Betti's four comedies and serious dramatic art is of course somewhat tenuous. Yet with these plays (and especially *Il paese delle vacanze*) behind him, Betti could . . . return to the path that he had already (with *Frana allo Scalo Nord* and *Il cacciatore d'anitre*) begun to trace out for himself in the history of the drama. (p. 106)

None of the plays which we have examined in this essay is likely to stand the test of time. These six pieces represent the *marginalia* of Betti's work for the theatre. Nevertheless, they illuminate a facet of Betti which remains hidden in most of his drama, they provide confirmation of his unusual all-round technical competence as a playwright, they offer glimpses of a steadily maturing, characteristic dramatic style, and they show how deeply Betti felt about the salient themes of his more serious drama, since even in his lighter moods he is drawn strongly towards them. (p. 107)

> *G. H. McWilliam, "The Minor Plays of Ugo Betti,"*
> in Italian Studies, *Vol. XX, 1965, pp. 78-107.*

GINO RIZZO (essay date 1965)

With the advantage of historical perspective, it is now possible to see how closely the development of Betti's drama follows that of European existentialism. Leaving the question of influences and chronology to more exhaustive studies of the playwright's work, one can readily indicate the similarity of issues, themes, and even resolutions. First of all, one must point to that fragmentation of reality which is Betti's rendering in dramatic form, of the existentialist dissolution of being. Starting with *Landslide,* and in the fifteen plays written between 1938 to the year of his death, Betti presents the moral universe of man in a state of flux, in which the solidity of moral structures gives way to the subjectivism of human existence. It is in the face of this absence of moral absolutes that the great themes of his drama unfold—the fallibility of human justice, the search for moral freedom, and the speciousness of all human bonds, especially conjugal love.

Betti's indictment of human justice brings within his scope the socio-political structure of his society. Rather than apologize for the man's adherence to Fascism—tenuous as it was—the critic must state quite bluntly that Betti is the only Italian writer who accepted Fascism to have produced works of high artistic merit. His dramatic production begins in 1926—the year Fascism established itself as a one-party regime. From 1929 to 1932 it reflects the economic chaos of the Depression, turning to evasive comedy around the years of the Ethiopian campaign and Spanish civil war. But at the prelude of World War II it reverts, in tragic form, to its major themes, reaching its point of greatest intensity during and immediately after the war. Finally, its conclusion coincides with the rise of new political alignments at the aftermath of the country's ordeal and painful recovery.

Unlike Camus in *State of Siege, Caligula,* and other works, Betti almost never presents political situations as the scene of his plays. Actually, *The Queen and the Rebels* [and *The Burnt Flower-bed*] . . . , both minor works, are the only exceptions. (pp. xiv-xv)

A seismograph of his own time no less than Pirandello, Betti reflects in his drama the double conscience of Fascist Italy, its ambigous courting as well as innate distrust of authority, its moral flux and profound feelings of guilt. The resolution in his plays, especially during the war years, is often suicide— a symbolic ambivalence of acceptance-rejection which parallels once more the position of existentialist writers in Resistance France.

But if the bulk of Betti's drama falls within the mainstream of European existentialism, one must not lose sight of those traits which are particularly his own. First of all, Betti's existentialism is more akin to the Christian search of Mauriac and Bernanos than to the moral nihilism of Sartre, or even the *religion laïque* of Camus. It is the insertion of Christian myths into the framework of existentialist thought which gives his drama its unique metaphysical dimension. (pp. xv-xvi)

Betti's drama is religious in that it is universal. Seeking after God—or, what for Betti is the same, moral certainty—its focus is on man and his contradictory mixture of good and evil, faith and disbelief, hope and despair. Through a merciless indictment of moral ambiguities and social evils, his drama offers, at an equal distance from nihilistic pessimism and facile absolutions, the compassion and consolation which is the gift of art. (p. xviii)

Gino Rizzo, "Introduction" (1965), in Three Plays
by Ugo Betti, *edited by Gino Rizzo (reprinted by
permission of Hill & Wang, a division of Farrar,
Straus & Giroux, Inc.; copyright © 1966 by The
Ugo Betti Estate and Gino Rizzo), Hill & Wang,
1966, pp. vii-xviii.*

GEORGE G. STREM (essay date 1966)

In irony and gloom, the playwrights of the so-called theatre
of the absurd or of anti-theatre proclaim that man has come
to an impasse. Ugo Betti . . . offers a different perspective.
He presents the human drama as essentially the same since
the beginning of time: Man, born frail, tumbles through life;
his existence represents a duel between his earthbound body
and his high aspirations. More often than not, this duel is
marked by victory for the material forces in man; but death
erases his defeat. Life and death become meaningful when
the spiritual is affirmed in man through love or self-sacrifice.
In Betti's world, self-sacrifice has a redeeming value; it allows
mankind to continue, it enables the spirit to illuminate the
human struggle. He who surpasses himself asserts by his act
his solidarity with all mankind; in each single case, the individual's victory erases the defeat of all of his fellow men.

Betti's theatrical legacy comprises twenty-four plays, several
of which are true masterpieces. All derive their power from
the author's belief in a universe predicated not upon the
traditional concept of justice but on hope and charity. Beyond
the immediate dramatic tissue they reflect the dualism of
creation and destruction, while holding out the hope that a
father, not a stern judge, awaits man at the end of his road.
(p. 112)

Betti's sympathy with human frailty derives from his conviction that the power of the senses on man is so great that
it is beyond the average person's strength to resist it. In the
struggle between flesh and spirit, the dice are loaded to the
former's advantage. (p. 113)

Seen in the perspective of Betti's theatre, all his plays end
happily, whether the conflict, caused by the failings of the
protagonists, is resolved favorably according to our notions
or whether death obliterates it and peace is restored through
its action. If life is deterioration, decay of the soul and of the
spirit, then the end of it is a charitable solution, a return to
clarity and purity.

What could more forcefully affirm this theme than the very
moving, very poetic drama of *Irene the Innocent (Irene Innocente)*? In Irene the author paints a truly Dostoievskian
figure of a crippled girl, a helpless victim of the selfish exploitation of her parents, who allow the men of the village
to take advantage of her in order to pursue their financial
manipulations. A stranger shows a degree of respect and
affection toward the girl; immediately, her heart overflows
with gratitude and love. She awakens to her human dignity,
becomes aware of the shame that she can bear no longer.
She too, leaps to her death, but before she dies, the man she
has come to love has the charity to go through the marriage
ceremony with her. In her life she had been reduced to an
object of lust; she ends her life in the glory of innocence and
love. (pp. 113-14)

[The] act of salvation repeats itself eternally. This is what
makes mankind worthy of grace, and grace is indispensable
to the moral universe, to prevent evil from triumphing.

It is astonishing how this simple tenet of a mystical faith
inspires Betti to produce works of great variety within their
fundamental unity. (p. 116)

[Betti] proclaims from the beginning to the end of his dramatic
career his sympathy for man's plight. At the same time, he
expresses his belief that man's great adventure, his life and
death, can be rendered meaningful; that, in fact, it is meaningful because man is capable of surpassing himself, because
the spirit, through its striving alone, assures its ultimate victory over matter. If life is sin, life is also expiation; death is
a haven, also a point of departure. The cycle of sin, struggle,
and redemption continues, eternally. (p. 120)

Betti's theatre is as real or as unreal as faith is, as poetic as
the vision of the Very High.

It is a theatre of hope; no contempt or rejection, but encouragement and charity are held out to man. This theatre
proclaims no doom but offers the solace and solution of love.
(p. 121)

*George G. Strem, "Death and the Will to Redeem:
The Theatre of Ugo Betti," in* The Texas Quarterly
*(© 1966 by The University of Texas at Austin), Vol.
IX, No. 2, Summer, 1966, pp. 112-21.*

ERIC SALMON (essay date 1968)

[Ugo Betti's] plays are dangerously overloaded with mere
ideas, which seem often to exist independently of the play's
central experience or even of the essential nature of the
characters themselves: not that the ideas are precisely irrelevant, but that they usurp by outside comment the theater's ultimate purpose of a re-creation of the reality of experience. They tend to super-impose opinionated and
intellectual solutions on particular problems, rather than allowing the plays to reveal, by the sudden juxtaposition of
unrealised and previously unperceived relationships of things,
the truth of being humanly alive. (p. 97)

[Theater], like all art, is *abstracted* from life, not copied from
it and . . . speech, therefore, in a so-called naturalistic play
must somehow take this abstraction into account and invent
for itself a way of talking that can preserve the illusion of
existing in the everyday convention and yet give the characters the opportunity and the right to say, apparently easily
and naturally, those things for the saying of which the play
exists. It is precisely in this regard that Betti too often fails.
In his best plays, he demonstrates over and over again that
he has the largeness and the boldness and the vision needed;
he is instinctively a poet—but with a dearth of language. The
result is, too often, a series of flaccid images and a distended
and pretentious style.

Not that the falsity is entire and general. In Act III of *Troubled
Waters*, Betti has for Giacomo a magnificent, taut image which
springs naturally from the underlying poetry of the play.
Giacomo is seeking to confront his sister, Alda, with the fact
of her own sensuality, which he himself has only recently
come to recognize and which, being recognized, horrifies
him. He says to her:

> You know, Alda, I've been having the same
> dream over and over again. I open a drawer,
> but for some reason I am suspicious. It's clear
> that I expect something to happen. And some-
> thing comes out of it, moving forward with

natural poise. It's not a rat; not a cockroach. More than anything else it resembles a hand; a soft, fleshy hand. Its movements are comical, but also cunning. It's obvious that the hand is clever; it struts about, and swaggers, and hops; it caresses the air, makes grasping gestures . . . vague, vulgar . . . obscene gestures. Obscene. And you, Alda, you laugh, and then run; then you turn around again . . . and laugh; your hair comes loose and droops over your eyes. It becomes obvious that you really won't be able to escape. Again you laugh, and then you wink at that ugly thing. It's not easy for you to run or jump; you are fettered by your own knees, your sweat, your hair; your skirts, breasts, your hips . . . full hips, heavy breasts, thick thighs . . . it's horrible. How I suffered, Alda, when I watched you turn from a girl into a woman. You should have died before that . . . and now all this was weighing you down, making you like some ripe fruit . . . and you stand there, hypnotized, swollen, flushed with an animal-like fertility. Impersonal and practical. Already experienced, and submissive, and your face . . . ugly . . . ugly . . . ugly . . . and convulsed, over-blown. . . .

This is not a piece of metaphorical language chosen by Giacomo and designed to illustrate his argument and ideas as some of his speeches are. It is the recounting of an actual experience, simple and horrible. The image which it creates for *us* (as distinct from images which the *character* sees) springs authentically from the play's substance and is therefore compelling. (pp. 98-9)

[Language apart, Betti] reveals over and over again, in the structure of the plays, it seems to me, a sense of the world which is naturally dramatic and poetic. In *Troubled Waters* this is shown most clearly in the subtly judged shifting of the relationships of the three central characters, Alda, Giacomo and Gabriele. Giacomo's "protection" of his sister, which is established as his posture at the beginning of the play and is reflected in the ironic sub-title ("The Brother who Protects and Loves") has the sense of rightness about it. It is real for him but unreal for her, as a doctrinaire opinion enforced upon a natural impulse would be. The impingement of Gabriele upon each of them is accurately felt, too, and represents a strand of reality: his cautious empiricism and sardonic refusal to believe anything that does not respond to the test of immediate touch is properly represented as driving Giacomo's dogmatism immediately to a more extreme position while finding a warmth or response and attraction in Alda's strictly amoral sensuality. It is the clash of existentialism with Received Faith and in Betti's play it rings absolutely true at both the personal level of the imagined characters and at the deeper level of symbol and image in the macrocosm of total human experience. But it does so in spite of, rather than because of, some of the dialogue. (p. 100)

The overtly Christian context of the play—and indeed of all Betti's plays—strikes me as curious, and in some ways constitutes a difficulty of handling in actual production. There is, again, the language problem: much of what the characters say about their own religious impulses and belief is couched in language too conventionally "religious." But this is not

the core of the problem. There seems to be an odd paradox at the very heart of Betti's use of Christian belief in his plays: the general thrust of the plays, both individually and collectively, leads convincingly to a non-Christian, existentialist, cautiously empirical, position, a position which accepts no standards as absolute, no goals as declared and obvious, but gives to man the right and the compulsion to explore with his sensory perceptions the facts of his experience while acknowledging that this experience may not be in any way significant, a position which automatically regards courage as the only certain virtue and the Heroic as automatically open to intense suspicion; yet the conscious images employed—not simply the language, but the images deliberately invoked—operate constantly in terms of formal Christianity and contradict this mainstream of the plays' thought. Giacomo, for example, sets up very firmly, in relation to his sister Alda, the equation Chastity = Purity = Goodness and all his metaphors in support of this equation are Christian ones: in a word, he sees his sister idealised as another Virgin Mary. To take Giacomo seriously and to give him the stature which he must have in order to sustain the tragic implications of the play (without which central pillar the play disintegrates), one must believe not only that he means what he says, but that what he says is true outside of his believing it, true for *us* as well as for him. Yet it is not: the equation as such is eminently challengeable at both its stages. And the general sense of the play does, by implication at least, both challenge and demolish it. (Alda liberates herself from the dead weight of dogma and fully realises herself only through unchastity, which is, in the Christian convention, sinful). (pp. 101-02)

Though the play—if labels have any value at all—is a tragicomedy rather than a pure tragedy of the classical pattern, the central figure of Giacomo must be given full tragic stature if the play is to work. His errors of thought must be identified as his and shown for errors, but there must be no mockery of his motives, either in the way the actor represents him or in the way others talk about him. Though he himself sees, on occasion, that the posture he strikes is one which invites a derisive and belittling approach from others—and in my view it is well to allow us to see that Giacomo is capable of laughing at himself (though in the production we had some disagreement about this)—it is a mistake to allow the play, in total, to belittle him. He is a sensitive, noble and deluded man. And in the end, the moment of realization and reconciliation which completes the tragic pattern must unequivocally be allowed to mean that Giacomo's nobility has been accepted into the world's pattern and that he himself has, in death, accepted the faith he has resisted all his life, faith in the natural forces of life, of which Alda's urge towards the reproductive act and her instinct for warmth and communication through physical love was one expression. Giacomo signifies his final acceptance of life by dying. The moment of death comes, according to the script, after one of the two men (the general, 'chorus,' players of all the small parts), appearing now as what we must take to be a kind of supernatural figure, an Eternal Onlooker, says "The crescent moon is just now beginning to shed its light; the solitary sound of the river is nearer now. The troubled waters are almost stilled; the animals, the grass, everything in its way is saying "yes" to the night. The world is at peace. It has faith, Giacomo; you too have faith." His drying on these words is an act of acceptance, a releasing of his fierce and proud desire to control and to know, a sudden access of humble confidence: his life is mingled with the general life of the world. (p. 107)

Eric Salmon, "Ugo Betti's 'Troubled Waters'," in Modern Drama *(copyright © 1968, University of Toronto, Graduate Centre for Study of Drama; with the permission of* Modern Drama*), Vol. XI, No. 1, May, 1968, pp. 97-108.*

HAROLD H. WATTS (essay date 1969)

[The] religiousness of Betti is, in its essentials, a traditional one. It is one that can spell the name of deity in capital letters; it is one for which the central fact of religious experience is a divine awareness which both judges and loves, one which is best known in the person of Christ.

The difficulties of the plays result not from any great complexity in the divine vistas which man may choose to enter; they result from the countless subterfuges—the "many inventions"—which express man's unwillingness to respond to the obvious: that divine love and judgment are the focus of man's universe rather than man's own will for himself. Non-pietistically, the plays represent the enduring focus indirectly, by a chair in a hotel corridor which is hauntingly a place of judgment (*The Gambler*) or by a voice which reaches a man who is about to fall to his death on a mountain-side (*Troubled Waters* [*Acque Turbate*]) or simply by a stairway which leads to the unseen presence of a court authority (*Corruption in the Palace of Justice*). Occasionally there are direct echoes of material from Holy Scripture: the sufferings of Job, the struggle of Jacob with the Angel (from this narrative Betti derives the title of one of the plays, *Struggle Until Dawn* [*Lotta fino all'Alba*]). and the projected sacrifice of Isaac by Abraham. But these *loci classici* are understood in a perfectly conventional way; Betti is not writing a *Fear and Trembling* for the twentieth century.

What Betti is writing instead is a drama that, if successful, drives modern awareness to a resumption of relationship with such *loci classici*. The problem to which the religious dramatist must address himself is that of showing their relevance to gamblers, cheats, adulterers, and—most difficult task of all—respectable people like judges and members of loving families. The difficulty lies not in the increasing obscurity of divine revelation as it reaches modern temperaments—an obscurity expressed for Betti in the effort of T. S. Eliot. The difficulty lies in man's root indifference to truths that at present continue to be just as simple and saving as they were in past ages. "Mercy, harmony, solidarity, immortality, trust, forgiveness. . . ." These words are not basically mysterious and obscure; mystery and obscurity lie in man's resolute rejection of them. This being Betti's estimate, his plays mount attacks on this resolute rejection; they make little effort to embroider and complicate the truths that some of his personages finally respond to. "GOD" is simple; man is not. In consequence, what is most compelling in Betti's dramas is his sketch of human capacities, a sketch at odds with much that is believed or known about man at present. It is true that, on the basis of what he finds out about man, Betti makes a modification of traditional theological definitions that is startling (justice is primarily man's province and love and mercy God's). But this revision is not, one judges, a result of theological finesse in Betti but expresses his sense of what lies in modern man himself and what is absent. (pp. 65-6)

[Is] Betti just a talented repeater of effects in Pirandello? That is, does he offer us no more than the scant comfort we may draw from a play like *As You Desire Me*, where the husband has to accept the fact that his wife, rescued from her German ravishers, is nothing real in herself but is, at best, only the object that responds to the beliefs and hopes that are projected on her from his own mind?

Despite such parallels, the Betti world parts company with the Pirandello one when Betti's characters say: "I am ashamed." (It is a point which leads Betti to enter vistas—religious vistas—about which Pirandello is incurious.) Linked with growth in self-knowledge (which is also inevitably growth in self-disgust) is Betti's insistence on responsiblity. In play after play, when the depths of personal hell have been sounded, the key-phrase in question bursts out almost unsummoned from the lips of the suffering and guilty person: "I am ashamed."

The Betti character does not utter the phrase so habitual in many a modern French play where a character is undergoing a similar frustrating catharsis; he does not say, "I suffer." (Some such phrase would seem to be the proper end-point in the Pirandello theater also.) When a character comes to a terminus represented by "I suffer," he in effect implores those who witness his agony to offer complicity rather than judgment upon what events and analysis have revealed. (p. 69)

In contrast, "shame" can find its justification only in an acknowledgement that one has created—in part or in its entirety—the plight one endures. "Shame" rests, further, on a full concession that one has had, if unthinkingly, the power to shape the predicament that makes one wince. So, whatever else one chooses to say of the theater of a judge-dramatist like Betti, one must grant that it is made up of penalities justly assessed, not of agonies entirely imposed from outside. (p. 70)

Harold H. Watts, "Ugo Betti: The Theater of 'Shame'," in Modern Drama *(copyright © 1969, University of Toronto, Graduate Centre for Study of Drama; with the permission of* Modern Drama*), Vol. XII, No. 1, May, 1969, pp. 64-79.*

ANTONIO ILLIANO (essay date 1975)

In Ugo Betti's original vision man is a poor restless creature, unjustly deprived of his primeval innocence and condemned to bear the heavy cross of instinct, sin, and guilt. From this vision, which is partly akin to certain aspects of romantic victimism and of decadence, Betti draws the characters and issues of his dramaturgy. He concentrates on the elemental levels of existence, the hard core reality of abjection and degredation. His dramatic production forms a rich and colorful repertoire of human depravity and wretchedness ranging from the unrelenting drive of instinct to various forms of crime, maliciousness, foul play, perversion of the legal process, political ruthlessness, betrayal, cynicism, cruelty, and the like.

Within the context of the overburdening presence of evil, Betti also perceives the elements of the absurd and the incongruous, the sense of dread, uncertainty and alienation, the searching need for causes and purposes, the all-too-ineffectual and unavailing doubts of an existence he calls "this calm marvelous iniquity". But while the writers of the absurd are often resigned to a static contemplation of despair, to a kind of non-committal *nolle prosequi*, Betti's perception immediately becomes a center of tension, a dynamic nucleus of possible developments beyond the stricture of labels and definitions. Betti's alienated hero feels exiled from a condition of harmony which was his original lot, but this condition of exile may not, or needs not, always be beyond relief and remedy. There can be a redeeming principle in the negative. Both the attitude of total negation and of blindly absolute affirmation coincide with the attitude of motionlessness, or non-life.

In spite of, and often because of, all the abominations of living and dying, the ideological posture of the Italian playwright rejects any form of contemptuous denigration of man and reaffirms the value of dignity and the need for compassion. It proposes a view of destiny based on the conviction that man has a will, which responds to obscure and often totally disinterested impulses. . . . [The author attempts] to dramatize the plight of human beings who, finding themselves entangled in the mire of life or in their own abjection, will eventually recognize themselves and will attempt to rise above their predicament and reshape their destiny. (pp. 22-3)

It is no accident that Betti's major plays make recurrent use of such mystical symbols as the stairs, the pit, and the mountain. In *Corruziona al palazzo di giustizia* . . . , Cust, the guilty judge, cannot escape the awareness of his crime. He realizes that he is fearfully alone and that he alone can restore the forsaken harmony of justice by going up the stairs to confess to the supreme judge. In *Delitto all'isola delle capre* . . . , Agata, the protagonist, leaves Angelo to die at the bottom of a pit in spite of his desperate calls for help. Agata, a tragic heroine of indomitable character, is a modern personification of the will to evil, a will that is capable of menacingly standing up to God. In her, the Italian dramatist postulates the possibility of the human will to be free deliberately to choose non-redemption, and, on the artistic level, the necessity to understand, believe in, and even like, evil. (pp. 23-4)

Corruzione al palazzo di giustizia and *Delitto all'isola delle capre* are powerful dramas. Never again will Betti achieve such cogent intensity, such coordination and unity of intent and diction.

In the last plays [*Acque turbate, La regina e gli insorti, Il giocatore, Aioula bruciata*, and *La fuggitiva*] Betti yields to a compelling search for the absolute, which leads him to extend the logical confines of tragedy by introducing a system of religious messages and rituals. (p. 24)

Betti's mysticism, though essentially Christian, is not dogmatically based on revelation and it is not identifiable with any particular theological doctrine or current of thought; and it is not Jansenistic, as has been suggested, for its search for certainty is based on the value of doubt. Betti's mysticism stems from what may be called a human (not humanistic) immanence of the idea of God. Man is always at the center of the struggle; God is hope to know God, need to understand God; God is man's reaching out for God through his own personal hell.

The problem is that, in the last plays, the mystical drive can be misconstrued as a form of righteous pietism and edifying devotion two of the contaminations that Betti himself deplores in modern religious writing. On the artistic level, Betti's mysticism is not easily absorbed in, or reconciled with, the stylistic and technical configuration of the plays.

It adds a new dimension which seems to counteract the ascetic tranquillity and the classic sense of control and composure that characterize the earlier tragedies. In those dramas Betti had achieved a balanced and well orchestrated progression of movements: dramatization of the struggle—intuition of fear and aloneness—self-recognition—cathartic resolution. In the last plays, instead, there is a fundamental dichotomy between the dramatizations of the struggle and heightened metaphysical solutions, and between what should be the spontaneous evolution of the characters and the author's emphatic call for redemption. (pp. 27-8)

Antonio Illiano, "Ugo Betti's Last Plays," in Perspectives *(copyright © 1975 by The University Press of Kentucky), Vol. 1, No. 1, May, 1975, pp. 22-30.*

CHRISTOPHER CAIRNS   (essay date 1977)

[Ugo Betti is] Italy's foremost dramatist since Pirandello. His central preoccupations are certainly moral and sometimes implicitly religious. In his most famous plays—*Frana allo scalo nord, L'Aiuola bruciata* and *Corruzione al Palazzo di Giustizia*—Betti exhibits a concern for the dualism of human and divine justice that was the fruit of a legal career. Like Pirandello, Betti shows the moral dilemma of modern man, the difficulty of choice. Human justice, about which Betti's plays speak with the obsession of a professional, is a weak expression of divine justice. The conflicts facing modern man are those between the social and moral desire for harmony, and the individual and selfish desire for self-advancement.

In his *Corruzione al Palazzo di Giustizia,* Betti depicts the trial of magistrates accused of having abused the privileges of their position. The net of culpability also catches the accusers, being themselves not entirely without blame, and widens further to enmesh even the relatives of the inquisitors. . . . The corruption of the institution symbolises a universal impossibility of freedom from guilt. No one is immune; even those raised to positions of authority and responsibility—and those raised even higher to inquire into the conduct of that responsibility—carry with them the burden of imperfection, of human error and the pangs of conscience that result.

Frana allo scalo nord is also a play with a legal context and setting: an inquiry into the circumstances of a landslide at a construction site. It portrays the attempt to assess the blame for shoddy work and misconduct, and the unmistakable courtroom framework—the collection of evidence, calling of witnesses, official pronouncements of tired officialdom—is typical of Betti's drama. Self-justification becomes confused with expiation in the emotional statements of witnesses; the contrast between individual human anguish and the legal and scientific search for an absolute and impartial truth from which society must exact its tribute is also strongly marked. The furniture of this courtroom context provides Betti with this confessional; witnesses demonstrate their guilt far beyond the specific events of the inquiry; the judge's mask of impartiality gradually falls away to reveal his own guilt feelings, and the appearance of supernatural witnesses emphasises the universal nature of original sin. In the end, the character of Parsc comes prominently to the fore in his telling verdict of compassion for human error rather than justice in society's retribution for sin in accordance with defined laws.

In the third of Betti's well-known plays, *L'Aiuola bruciata,* the setting and context are again deliberately unspecific, underlining the questions of principle at the root of the author's preoccupations. As in *Frana allo scalo nord* where the characters have un-Italian, and therefore stateless, names and ranks, so in *L'Aiuola bruciata* the exact nature of the political cause being fought for is obscure. The play appeals for tolerance and moderation in a world torn by strife. It juxtaposes the devotion of men to political causes or ideologies with that to home and family, showing the tragedy that may result when the former replaces the latter. The outcome of political struggle is war, and Betti points out that the duties of political commitment may lead men into conflict for reasons which are trivial and far removed from fundamental human, moral and ethical values. These values, on the other hand, inform the duty to home and family. From these contrasts, Betti draws powerful drama. The death of the small boy is symbolic of this misplaced system of priorities; responsibility is again the key principle of the play: to people or politics? The sacrifice of the innocent Rosa becomes, not the sacrifice to a cause, but the impelling tragedy of humanity betrayed. (pp. 164-66)

> Christopher Cairns, *"The Dissection of Man: The Twentieth Century," in his* Italian Literature: The Dominant Themes *(© Christopher Cairns 1977; by permission of Barnes & Noble Books, a Division of Littlefield, Adams & Co., Inc.), Barnes & Noble, 1977, pp. 152-74.**

ADDITIONAL BIBLIOGRAPHY

Lumley, Frederick. "Italy: Ugo Betti." In his *New Trends in 20th Century Drama: A Survey since Ibsen and Shaw,* pp. 362-65. London: Barrie and Rockliff, 1967.
> Descriptive overview of Betti's major dramas, distinguishing his positive vision from the pessimism of Pirandello.

MacClintock, Lander. "Ugo Betti." *Modern Language Journal* XXXV, No. 4 (April 1951): 251-57.
> Plot outlines of the major plays. The critic calls Betti "the outstanding serious dramatist now writing in Italy."

Usmiani, Renate. "Twentieth-Century Man, the Guilt-Ridden Animal." *Mosaic* III, No. 4 (Summer 1970): 163-78.*
> Examines the judgement theme in Betti, Franz Kafka, and Frederich Dürrenmatt.

Algernon (Henry) Blackwood

1869-1951

English short story writer, novelist, autobiographer, and dramatist.

E. F. Bleiler calls Blackwood "the foremost British supernaturalist of the twentieth century," and most commentators agree that his best work entitles him to a prominent place in the field of fantasy literature. His major writings deal with the usual themes of the supernatural genre: haunted houses, nonhuman entities, reincarnation, psychic experience, and various other occult phenomena. The way he treats such themes, however, lifts his novels and short stories above the level of merely exotic or sensationalistic fiction. Devoted to investigating the mystical faculty in human nature, Blackwood conveys an acute personal feeling for the unseen and transcendent. Consequently, his work is singled out by critics as evidence that the supernatural tale can be a serious form of literary expression.

Blackwood experienced a strict religious upbringing in which the spirit of play was unusually inhibited. His early studies took place under the instruction of the Moravian Brotherhood in the Black Forest, Germany, a background that appears in the story "Secret Worship." He later attended Wellington College and Edinburgh University. In his autobiography, *Episodes Before Thirty*, Blackwood recalls that at twenty he was sent to Canada, where he failed in various business ventures and gained familiarity with the Canadian backwoods, which became the setting for "The Wendigo." Afterward he worked in New York as a reporter for the *Evening Sun* and the *New York Times*, but it was not until his return to England that he began his career as a fiction writer.

Blackwood's first works, *The Empty House, and Other Ghosts* and *The Listener, and Other Stories*, are collections of fairly orthodox ghost stories, a form to which he returned throughout his career. In his next book, *John Silence, Physician Extraordinary*, scientific research is introduced, some critics say overused, to account for the uncanny manifestations which are the subjects of these tales. John Silence is the first of a succession of Blackwood protagonists who willingly seek confrontations with the supernormal. These confrontations sometimes end in the protagonists' discovery of a higher order of reality, and other times in their horrified retreat back into a world of conventional routine.

For the most part, however, Blackwood is not a horror artist in the same vein as Poe or Lovecraft, who confront the reader with thoroughly fearful viewpoints. Instead he describes a character's experience of supernatural terror to underline the alienation of modern humanity from the spirit of the natural world, a world in which human life is inferior and irrelevant. Even in his most frightening narratives Blackwood achieves what Jack Sullivan defines as a "'cosmic' fusion of horror and ecstasy," and most critics have pointed out the basically positive outlook of the author's work. Particularly in his children's stories, such as *Jimbo*, Blackwood emphasizes the child's innocent sense of wonder in the face of the unknown, and the superiority of this vision in approaching a universe of mystery.

With the revival of occult and fantastic literature in the past decade, Blackwood has been acknowledged as an inspiration

Culver Pictures

for contemporary "seekers of wonder." The cosmic quests of such works as *The Human Chord* and *The Centaur*, as well as the profound eeriness of tales like "The Willows," are now familiar in both serious and popular fiction. Blackwood can be seen as a progenitor of this movement, his work representing the wide range of artistic possibilities latent in supernatural themes.

PRINCIPAL WORKS

The Empty House, and Other Ghosts (short stories) 1906
The Listener, and Other Stories (short stories) 1907
John Silence, Physician Extraordinary (short stories) 1908
The Education of Uncle Paul (novel) 1909
Jimbo (novel) 1909
The Human Chord (novel) 1910
The Lost Valley, and Other Stories (short stories) 1910
The Centaur (novel) 1911
Pan's Garden (short stories) 1912
Prisoner in Fairyland: The Book That "Uncle Paul" Wrote (novel) 1913

Julius Le Vallon (novel) 1916
The Wave (novel) 1916
The Garden of Survival (novel) 1918
The Promise of Air (novel) 1918
The Wolves of God, and Other Fey Stories (short stories)
    1921
Episodes Before Thirty (autobiography) 1923
Shocks (short stories) 1935
The Doll, and One Other (short stories) 1946

THE NEW YORK TIMES (essay date 1909)

"**John Silence**" is possessed of unusual charm and originality. Its hero is a doctor, a doctor whose interests lie with the psychic portion of man, with those spiritual diseases which are ruled out of court by the majority. Having himself passed through deep and occult experiences, conducted solely for love of others, he is able to oppose to the powers of evil a purer power, the invincible strength of unselfish good before which hate falls down defenseless.

In a certain way John Silence makes one think of Sherlock Holmes. Not as to temperament, but because he tracks down the evil spirits who are working their inimicable spells on their victims, much as that renowned detective hailed the villains of mortal wrongdoing. He is an expert, called in when every one else fails, and he has his peculiar methods and perceptions, and even a secretary whose god he is; but Hubbard is a more intelligent and likable man than Watson, with his eternal amazement at Holmes's genius. The book contains five "adventures," and each one of them is breathlessly interesting. Moreover, the sense of horror before the unknown which is experienced by the characters in each of these stories is shared by the reader.

Mr. Blackwood writes with a master's art, and conveys with power the impression he intends to produce. The spell of the old French town, for instance, in the tale "**Ancient Sorceries**" is strong upon you as you read. Its odd inhabitants, with their stealthy movements and cat-like glances, produce a curiously vivid effect, and you sit curled up in your chair before the fire believing every word of the strange adventure with all your soul. In his touches of description and of character drawing Mr. Blackwood is most felicitous; but perhaps the most marked quality of the book is the effect of peace it leaves. You are led through dark and even terrible experiences, where the human spirit is in sore travail with the spirits of darkness. But the serene and lofty note struck by Silence himself is what finally abides, inducing a sense of harmony and of the immense power residing in intelligent and unselfish goodness that is full of delight. You do not lay down the book until it is finished; and when you do it is with distinct regret that it must come to an end at all.

> *"Appealing Force of Ghostly Tales,"* in The New
> York Times (© 1909 by The New York Times Com-
> pany; reprinted by permission), March 20, 1909, p.
> 160.

THE SPECTATOR (essay date 1909)

Mr. Blackwood has on more than one previous occasion proved his capacity for making our flesh creep by excursions,

more or less legitimate, into the realm of the uncanny. [*Jimbo*] is not easily classified, nor can it be referred to any of the normal categories of fiction, but it marks a distinct advance in subtlety and delicacy of imagination upon his earlier achievements. It will not please every one, although it is a novel with a most laudable purpose, for a very simple reason. It deals largely with the entirely unmerited sufferings of a child, and there are quite a number of old-fashioned people who hold that while the miseries of grown people are fair game, those of children are not the proper subject of fiction. *Jimbo* is not a book for children, and tender-hearted parents will find it almost unbearably painful, in spite of its comparatively happy end. But as a fantastic exposition of the psychology of fright, as an attempt to illustrate the workings of the mind in the spectral world of delirium, it is of engrossing interest. (p. 619)

Jimbo is something more than a *tour de force*. The sense of being in an unreal, but not an artificial, world is sustained with remarkable cleverness; the pictures of Jimbo spinning dizzily through space, "ruining along the illimitable inane," are done with extraordinary vividness; and the whole conception of the House of Fright is unusual and poetic. But, for reasons which we have already set forth at the beginning of this notice, we cannot unreservedly recommend a romance which deals so largely in gratuitous anguish. (p. 620)

> *"'Jimbo',"* in The Spectator (© 1909 by The Spec-
> tator), Vol. 102, No. 4216, April 17, 1909, pp. 619-
> 20.

THE NEW YORK TIMES (essay date 1910)

[It is] the road through fairy land to spiritualism that Algernon Blackwood has tried to make practicable for the feet of grown-ups in his curious, insidious, and to many respects charming volume entitled "**The Education of Uncle Paul.**" The author of "**John Silence**" has undertaken no less a task than to follow the backtrack over those trailing clouds of glory which, according to [Wordsworth's] "Ode on Intimations of Immortality," we bring with us as children from God.

Inspiration, one guesses, is borrowed from Peter Ibbotson no less than from Wordsworth, and method from Carroll. But Mr. Blackwood's goal is the goal of the Psychical Researchers, and, for all the poetry and lovely fancy of much that he writes, the thing written as a whole is subtly poisonous and decadent. The last word is employed with reluctance because it means so much and so little—but it carries taint in its syllables. And the taint is here.

In reality the little girl who leads Uncle Paul—who is already a sort of wood faun—through the miraculous Crack between Yesterday and To-morrow to where time is not and peace and joy dwell always, is as little like Alice who adventured in Wonderland as night is like the day. Her voice, indeed, is the voice of childhood, her talk has the accent of the nursery—but she is a sprite, a being from the poet's land of shadows and the mystic's house of dreams—worse, she is that will-o'-the-wisp of the morbid sentimentalist—the soul mate. And somehow that sort of relation between an uncle past forty and a niece not thirteen—even though the niece be now a true inhabitant of shadow-land—being dead—seems inappropriate, to say the least.

These philosophical and moral aspects apart, there is rare magic, white as well as black, in many passages of the story of the man who returned from his solitary life in the woods of North America to share the make-believe and fantasies of his sister's children in an old country house in England, to be made one of a weird fellowship with them, and to share with them, "verywonderfulindeed adventures" in dream-land.

"Fairyland Road to Spiritualism," in The New York Times *(© 1910 by The New York Times Company; reprinted by permission), April 23, 1910, p. 223.*

GRACE ISABEL COLBRON   (essay date 1915)

[Algernon Blackwood's stories] haunt one after reading. . . . His imagination and insight are as rare as his choice of subjects is unusual. (p. 619)

At first it seems that it is the subject which enthralls, then comes appreciation of rare insight and finally a realisation of remarkable stylistic power, rich and exuberant, a rush of words like a mountain torrent, suiting sound to sense poignantly, hypnotising like some Eastern drug. The reader's progress to understanding follows the writer's progress of achievement. In his earlier books the subject sometimes taxes his power of expression. But with growing practice the gift of interpretation in words grows and grows—until his tendency to linger over the soul conflict and hurry with a sentence past actual happenings is handled with such mastery that it gives the chosen theme its greatest charm. There are few others who dare to do this. (pp. 619-20)

Algernon Blackwood's chosen theme is the Unknown, the great realm that lies beyond the world of the Known and the Obvious. He finds it in many places, in the forest depths of pathless Canadian wilds, in Egyptian desert sands, in smiling mountain valleys, and even in London streets and offices. It comes to the adult with a tinge of horror, because the adult dislikes and fears all that will not fall in line with his notions of what the world should be like. It comes to the child as something exquisitely sweet, in dreams of Star Dust Caverns, of beautiful beneficent Beings that understand one's play. And it comes to the cat—but then the cat is half in that world always and often has to come back from it when we would call her attention to our humble human selves! For Algernon Blackwood is one of those rare adults who can so sink his own consciousness of self that he can find his way into the psychology of the little child and the cat. They have taken him into the secret garden where they really live and he has interpreted it for us in tales of poignant sweetness. The child and the cat are the supreme non-conformists of a world which spends its energies trying to conform to some set pattern changing with the decades. They simply *don't* try; that's why so few adults understand them. In *A Prisoner in Fairyland; Jimbo;* some of the stories in *Pan's Garden* . . . , and *The Education of Uncle Paul* . . . , Blackwood has given us lyrics of childhood that will last. Children themselves may not understand them until they grow up, and then only if they are the sort of children that never grow up. But the adult who Knows will find great store of riches, and the lover of cats will find much delight, in these books.

But when the adult mind finds itself approaching or crossing the borderland that parts the Known from the Unknown, sorrow or horror even take the place of joy. And in the expression of this creeping horror that chills the heart when the human comes face to face with what is not human, Algernon Blackwood excels. It is not done sensationally, it seems to come from the man's inmost heart, as an expression of personal beliefs and experiences, and his stories have little dealing with organised or accredited spiritualism. He has only scorn for such futile mental debauches, he has no interest in ghosts that are ticketed and classified, and have even become fashionable. He lays no claim to "scientific research," but he can enthrall the reader until the sweep of unseen or dimly glimpsed Presences crowd thick upon us in the silent room and we long to get back, in sheer shrinking fear, into the "sweet wholesome business of To-day." Every degree of emotion felt by the mind and heart under stress of such experience figures in the many stories that deal with this subject. For sheer naked concentrated horror, unexplained and unexplainable, such tales as ["**The Wendigo**" and "**The Willows**"] . . . may be said to lead among the stories of the supernatural. But many others are a gorgeous, haunting riot of imagination and creepiness, mingling terror and a sense of splendid free life, Real and Unreal, in bewildering confusion. "**The Regeneration of Lord Ernie**" and the stupendous "**Descent into Egypt**" in the book *Incredible Adventures* . . . , "**Ancient Sorceries**," "**Secret Worship**," and "**The Camp of the Dog**" in *John Silence* . . . are some of the most noteworthy among these, although many others have power to hold and thrill unendurably. *The Centaur* . . . has sustained power of imaginative writing equal to the best Blackwood has produced. (pp. 620-21)

And yet through all these tales of the power of What Lies Beyond to act upon human lives, there is a note of splendid courage in the appeal to the mind of man to understand that he may control—by controlling himself—all these powers, and take their strength into himself to form it over for Good. It is this note and the sincerity of the style which free the tales entirely from any reproach of desired sensationalism, and which also relieve the strain of horror, that might otherwise prove too strong to be wholesome. Algernon Blackwood stands in a class by himself. (p. 621)

Grace Isabel Colbron, "Algernon Blackwood—An Appreciation," in The Bookman, New York *(copyright, 1915, by George H. Doran Company), Vol. XL, No. 6, February, 1915, pp. 618-21.*

ROBB LAWSON   (essay date 1918)

There is just a chance that much of what has been said about Algernon Blackwood, and what he has himself written, may be regarded as slightingly as the abracadabra of the vaudeville magician whose purpose is rather to impress with his cleverness than illuminate with the clarity of his vision. It is solely to those who believe that the imagination is not a state of consciousness but human existence itself, that his work comes as a refreshing gospel. Frankly speaking, it is to the poet that has died young in most of us that his constant appeal is made. For the human who does not class himself in that category I fear Mr. Blackwood's message will be regarded as wasted breath. (pp. 228-29)

Blackwood seeks no converts. The Dedication to one of his books reads significantly: "To Those Who Hear." The message of his books, despite various attempts to link him up with the mystical horrors of Edgar Allan Poe, is to those of the elder race. It is the Ideal of an older time he holds—an ideal which may be expressed thus: In the beginning was feeling—not thought. The ancient mind did not crystallize into a hardened point, but, remaining fluid, knew that the mode of knowledge suitable to its nature was by intercourse and blending. Its experience was that it could blend with intelligence greater than itself—that it could have intercourse with the gods.

Mr. Blackwood's greatest attempt at stating the faith he holds is contained in that much misunderstood story of his, **"Julius Le Vallon,"** which devotes itself to a daring exposition of the theme of rebirth. As to its purport I may be permitted to adumbrate somewhat of the ideas that Blackwood has set himself to interpret. In remote times Humanity lived so close to Nature that the elemental activities of Nature were actually shared by them. Nature worship was the communicating chord which the Invisible Brain and reason had not developed. Men *felt* rather than thought. They read Nature like a written script. By *feeling with* the elemental powers they could even share those powers. Such powers might then be regarded as gods. And in the Nature worship of that day they evoked these gods and shared their strength and beauty.

To those who have not made acquaintance with the Blackwood books, perhaps, in naming **"Julius Le Vallon"** I am doing its author an injustice in counseling that this should be their first adventure into the realms of the Unknown. There are . . . others. Each is alive with a tense spirituality. For Blackwood the true Shekinah is the soul of man, and in pursuit of his subject (his whole material possessions contained in three trunks) he has wandered throughout Europe, the pantheist pilgrim visiting every possible shrine where Beauty might be. For **"The Wave,"** . . . Egypt became his resting-place; the idea of the book of strange wonders, **"The Centaur,"** came to him in the Caucasus Mountains; **"A Prisoner in Fairyland,"** with all the madness of its dreams and the wild largeness of its outlook, was born in the Alps; **"Pan's Garden,"** that eerie collection of nature stories, was evolved in the Jura Mountains, to which he again returned in the rushing splendor of **"The Human Chord."** (pp. 230-31)

The ordinary mystic is well content if his vision may conjure up from the dim shadowland that lies at the Back of Beyond, the pale, ineffectual ghosts of yesterday—ineffectual shapes forever pathetically dumb. There are no vaguely moving shadows in the realms of Blackwood's world—his transcendent imagination rising to the *n*th sense invests his characters with the contours of living beings. For, above all, he is a practical mystic with a message for this generation. Arnold Bocklin, the Swiss painter, had the same vivid, uncanny imagination, and had these two met I do not doubt they would have joined hands and, wandering together in that ancient Garden of the World-Soul, have evolved together some immortal work, whose purpose would have been to take away the ache of the World. (p. 231)

Robb Lawson, "Algernon Blackwood," in The Living Age, *Vol. IX, No. 3838, January 26, 1918, pp. 228-31.*

LOUISE MAUNSELL FIELD (essay date 1921)

The last few years have witnessed a deep and vivid increase of interest in all that lies on and across the borderlands— borderlands of consciousness, borderlands of the physical and the tangible. . . .

In these borderlands Algernon Blackwood has long since made his spiritual home. Of them all he writes as few if any have ever written, with a power, a dramatic vividness, a sheer beauty of imagination as well as of style which render him unique among present-day writers. Inheriting no small amount from our American genius, Edgar Allan Poe, he cannot be called in any way an imitator or even a follower. Mystic as in a sense he certainly is, he is as certainly a man of the present day, using present-day knowledge, the results of modern psychology and modern research, scientific and historical, as familiar tools—and using also the lore of ancient Egypt, Indian legends, folktales of werewolves and disincarnate spirits, of diabolical possession, and the rites of those hideous sacrifices offered to the gods when the world was young. A master of horror, uses the properties of the charnel house but seldom, and then sparingly, suggesting rather than describing; it is rarely a physical horror he depicts, physical horror being employed by him principally to intensify that other horror which is a thing of the spirit, not the flesh. And when, as sometimes happens, he does depict the physical, it is always transfused with a poetic quality which lifts it far above brute pain or terror.

Consider **"The Wolves of God,"** the opening story of [**"The Wolves of God and Other Fey Stories"**]. . . . The naked dead body, its flesh "torn but not eaten," is from one point of view the culmination, the awful, gruesome culmination, of that which happened on the black night of rain and wind when old John Rossiter invoked justice, not mercy. But he must be indeed a crude and dull-natured reader to whom the physical fact seems of paramount importance. For the forces let loose on that terrible night were near akin to the Eumenides of the Greeks. Their coming "howling in deep, full-throated chorus * * * above yet within the wind" is a thing to shudder at. But as it was a look of "mystical horror" which those others saw upon the face of the guilty man as he strode out into the fearful darkness, so is it a thrill of mystical horror the reader feels while watching him go. They were forces of the spirit which manifested themselves in **"The Wolves of God"** that night when justice battled against love.

But this instance of the defeat of love is almost unique in Mr. Blackwood's work, where, again and again, presented in every imaginable form and in every sort and kind of guise, the theme is the triumph of love—its victory over hate and fear and cowardice, over ancient, discarnate powers of evil, over death itself. The exquisite little tale of **"The Call"** in this latest volume is a lovely example of such a victory—the kind of victory shown in other of Mr. Blackwood's tales, and especially in his short novel **"The Garden of Survival."** The sense of a spiritual presence, invisible, inaudible, intangible, yet somehow realized, somehow felt, which grows and develops through that remarkable book is a marvelous making real of what we usually regard as outside reality. But to Algernon Blackwood it is always these intangible forces which count most, though they may reveal their presence in ways as different as those shown by the woodland powers who drew to themselves **"The Man Whom the Trees Loved"** and the purely malignant activities of the **"Elementals"** in **"The Nemesis of Fire"**—that thrilling tale of Egyptian magic which could control "the active force behind the elements." . . . The old nature worship, of which all this was to some extent a portion, is a theme which has a notable attraction for Mr. Blackwood. Again and again do we find it in his work. It is one, though of course but a minor factor, among the many which set that work apart. Sometimes it takes a form almost, if not perfectly, Greek, as in the remarkable story of **"The Man Who Played Upon the Leaf"**; sometimes there is terror in it, and menace, such as we find in the symbolical **"Vengeance Is Mine,"** which closes the present volume. Mr. Blackwood has an unusual ability to call up vivid images of ages long since dead; witness **"The Tarn of Sacrifice."** . . .

This, of course, is a story of reincarnation, and reincarnation plays an important part in many of Mr. Blackwood's tales, especially in his novels, two of which, **"Julius Le Vallon"** and **"The Wave,"** tell how those who had sinned and suffered, loved and hated in their former lives, met again to finish or to expiate what had then been begun. This ancient doctrine, all but completely ignored for so long, has shared in the new interest in religions and religious speculations brought about by the World War. Mr. Blackwood's use of it is no impersonal theory of Karma; it is of Brahma, rather than of Buddha. A personality essentially the same is reincarnated, bringing with it the loves and antipathies of a former existence, of which it is conscious, at most, only in the moment of death, through the intervention of some initiate seer or in such vague flashes as came to the hero of **"The Wave,"** who when first he came to Egypt realized that in some indefinable way he belonged there—there in that Egypt which, though dead, sometimes "came back." No quotations could possibly do justice to the effect Mr. Blackwood produces in his descriptions of that most ancient and majestical land where sometimes and at night the old gods still walk, striding mightily across the country they ruled in its time of greatness.

But such personal memories are not the only ones Mr. Blackwood invokes; he draws, too, on those remote depths of the subconscious where lie the racial memories which link man with his brute ancestors. (p. 18)

Those old, slumbering impulses and desires and fears, which most of us have felt rather than perceived, when alone in the midst of great solitary spaces—forest or plain, desert or the shores of the sea—are matters which Mr. Blackwood understands and depicts as no one else has done. But there is another kind of subconsciousness, and the power of it is described in that extraordinary novel, **"The Promise of Air,"** where for Joseph Wimble "to rely upon inner, subconscious guidance was to rely upon that portion of his being—that greater portion—which obeyed spontaneously an immense rhythm of the mothering World-Spirit. * * * The subconscious powers, knowing nothing, yet approached omniscience." Mr. Blackwood, who has so often taken us into the realms of the past, shows us here a vision of the realm of the future, which will be that of the ether, foreshadowed already by airplanes and wireless, by restlessness and dissatisfaction with ancient conventions and ancient creeds. The book seems flooded with sunlight, for Mr. Blackwood can use sunshine as well as shadow, and, master that he is of fear, and especially of that fear which is a thing of nerves and sensibilities, not of reason nor of bodily peril, he is among the least pessimistic of writers. "The Garden of Survival," that perfect story of a man lifted to the best of which he was capable by the power of a woman's love, love which had survived death, closes triumphantly. And if **"The Empty Sleeve," "Confession," "The Decoy,"** and several other tales in this present volume are full of a shuddering horror, **"Egyptian Sorcery"** works beneficently, and **"The Lane That Ran East and West"** unites the faithful lovers at the last.

The sense of brooding, unseen forces, forces kindly, indifferent or inimical, lurking somewhere just behind the veil of the tangible, of personality leaving its impress upon an apparently empty house, of memories that keep slipping just beyond the reach of our conscious minds—all these Mr. Blackwood has vividly and dramatically expressed, he who is so eminently the expressor of the all but inexpressible, who can crystallize into word and phrase what most of us can at best but dumbly feel. This type of expression belongs of course to the very essence of poetry, and Mr. Blackwood is in truth a poet, far more of a poet than are many of those to whom we unhesitatingly give that title. Beauty of thought, beauty and flexibility of phrasing, a sense of rhythm, of the perfect word—all these are his to a very exceptional degree. And with them he has, too, the gift of dramatic narrative, the attention-holding power of the born story-teller. . . . Mr. Blackwood has never "written down," never lowered the high standards of his fine and beautiful art. (p. 20)

> *Louise Maunsell Field, "The Prose Poet of the Borderlands," in* The New York Times Book Review *(© 1921 by The New York Times Company; reprinted by permission), December 18, 1921, pp. 18, 20.*

H. P. LOVECRAFT (essay date 1927)

[Amidst Algernon Blackwood's] voluminous and uneven work may be found some of the finest spectral literature of this or any age. Of the quality of Mr. Blackwood's genius there can be no dispute; for no one has even approached the skill, seriousness, and minute fidelity with which he records the overtones of strangeness in ordinary things and experiences, or the preternatural insight with which he builds up detail by detail the complete sensations and perceptions leading from reality into supernormal life or vision. Without notable command of the poetic witchery of mere words, he is the one absolute and unquestioned master of weird atmosphere; and can evoke what amounts almost to a story from a simple fragment of humourless psychological description. Above all others he understands how fully some sensitive minds dwell forever on the borderland of dream, and how relatively slight is the distinction betwixt those images formed from actual objects and those excited by the play of the imagination.

Mr. Blackwood's lesser work is marred by several defects such as ethical didacticism, occasional insipid whimsicality, the flatness of benignant supernaturalism, and a too free use of the trade jargon of modern "occultism." A fault of his more serious efforts is that diffuseness and longwindedness which results from an excessively elaborate attempt, under the handicap of a somewhat bald and journalistic style devoid of intrinsic magic, colour, and vitality, to visualise precise sensations and nuances of uncanny suggestion. But in spite of all this, the major products of Mr. Blackwood attain a genuinely classic level, and evoke as does nothing else in literature an awed convinced sense of the imminence of strange spiritual spheres or entities.

The well-nigh endless array of Mr. Blackwood's fiction includes both novels and shorter tales. . . . Foremost of all must be reckoned *The Willows*, in which the nameless presences on a desolate Danube island are horribly felt and recognised by a pair of idle voyagers. Here art and restraint in narrative reach their very highest development, and an impression of lasting poignancy is produced without a single strained passage or a single false note. Another amazingly potent though less artistically finished tale is *The Wendigo,* where we are confronted by horrible evidences of a vast forest daemon about which North Woods lumbermen whisper at evening. The manner in which certain footprints tell certain unbelievable things is really a marked triumph in craftsmanship. In *An Episode in a Lodging House* we behold frightful presences summoned out of black space by a sorcerer, and *The Listener* tells of the awful psychic residuum creeping about an old house where a leper died. In the volume titled *Incredible Adventures* occur some of the finest tales which the author has yet produced, leading the fancy to wild rites on nocturnal hills, to secret and terrible aspects lurking behind stolid scenes, and to unimaginable vaults of mystery below the sands and pyramids of Egypt; all with a serious finesse and delicacy that convince where a cruder or lighter treatment would merely amuse. Some of these accounts are hardly stories at all, but rather studies in elusive impressions and half-remembered snatches of dream. Plot is everywhere negligible, and atmosphere reigns untrammelled.

John Silence—Physician Extraordinary is a book of five related tales, through which a single character runs his triumphant course. Marred only by traces of the popular and conventional detective-story atmosphere—for Dr. Silence is one of those benevolent geniuses who employ their remarkable powers to aid worthy fellow-men in difficulty—these narratives contain some of the author's best work, and produce an illusion at once emphatic and lasting. The opening tale, *A Psychical Invasion,* relates what befell a sensitive author in a house once the scene of dark deeds, and how a legion of fiends was exorcised. *Ancient Sorceries,* perhaps the finest tale in the book, gives an almost hypnotically vivid account of an old French town where once the unholy Sabbath was kept by all the people in the form of cats. In *The Nemesis of Fire* a hideous elemental is evoked by new-spilt blood, whilst *Secret Worship* tells of a German school where Satanism held sway, and where long afterward an evil aura remained. *The Camp of the Dog* is a werewolf tale, but is weakened by moralisation and professional "occultism."

Too subtle, perhaps, for definite classification as horror-tales, yet possibly more truly artistic in an absolute sense, are such delicate phantasies as *Jimbo* or *The Centaur.* Mr. Blackwood achieves in these novels a close and palpitant approach to the inmost substance of dream, and works enormous havoc with the conventional barriers between reality and imagination. (pp. 404-06)

> *H. P. Lovecraft, "Supernatural Horror in Literature" (1927), in his "Dagon" and Other Macabre Tales, edited by August Derleth (copyright 1965 by August Derleth; reprinted by permission of Arkham House Publishers, Inc.), Arkham House, 1965, pp. 347-413.**

STUART GILBERT (essay date 1935)

No living writer in the English tongue has done more than Algernon Blackwood to quicken [the] sense of wonder and open our eyes to the conscious vitality of much that we habitually regard as inert matter, and to the miraculous nature of what we call causation—a purely abstract concept. (p. 91)

In the world of to-day the very existence of . . . mythological values is usually denied; they are taken for figments of the primitive mind, or, at the best, as obsolete; and their manifestations, lying outside the focus of our normal vision, pass unrecognized. Yet, in all ages, there have been men who apprehended them, poets and philosophers who gave us glimpses of that "something infinite behind everything" perceived by Thomas Traherne. It is noteworthy that quotations from many such writers—Novalis, Edward Carpenter, William James, Fechner and others—are prefixed to the chapters of 'The Centaur'; indeed the whole novel is a magnificent and, as nearly as such attempts can be, successful attempt to revive a sense of the consciousness of the Earth, through the experiences of O'Malley, the protagonist. Yet even O'Malley, for all his gift of speech, admits his incapacity fully to describe his great adventure. "Far behind words it lies, as difficult of full recovery as the dreams of deep sleep, as the ecstasy of the religious, elusive as the mystery of *Kubla Khan* or the Patmos visions of St. John. Full recapture, I am convinced, is not possible at all in words." (p. 92)

It might be said that the true protagonist of 'The Centaur' is not Terence O'Malley, a man "of mingled Irish, Scotch and English blood", "forever deciphering the huge horoscope of Life, yet getting no further than the House of Wonder, on whose cusp surely he had been born," but the *Urwelt* itself, made manifest in one of its most singular yet typical denizens. We accompany O'Malley on a voyage to the Eastern Mediterranean. . . . As the voyage proceeds the feeling of tension, the imminence of some supernatural event, grows almost unbearable. Mr Blackwood does not, like many writers dealing with 'occult' subjects, shirk the issue, or hide it in a mist of wordage. He goes as far as words can reach, and when, somewhere in the Caucasus, the strange adventure moves rapidly towards its climax, we participate, to the measure of our intuitions, in O'Malley's return to a primordial world. . . . The effect of Mr Blackwood's prose is cumulative; by some strange and gradual alchemy of words and an intuitive felicity he recalls to consciousness a world of memories "so deepseated and so foreign to our present life that this latter for a moment seems something unreal and conventional."

In 'The Human Chord' the central idea is as unusual and seemingly unpalatable to modern minds as that of 'The Centaur'; yet, as a critic observed when the book appeared, there is a rush and splendour about the narrative that sweeps the reader off his feet. (pp. 93-4)

In a lonely house in the Pontwaun Mountains of Wales four people—an elderly man, a young man, a motherly middle-aged housekeeper and a young girl—participate in a unique experiment: an effort to find and formulate the Great Names whose utterance makes men like gods. . . .

> "The properties of things . . . are merely the 'muffled utterances of the Sounds that made them.' The thing itself is its name."

And, for the utterance of the Tetragrammaton, "the name that rusheth through the universe", a human chord is needed; four voices—soprano, alto, tenor and bass—must combine to make the perfect chord. As the novel advances, the feeling of suspense, of sublime peril, steadily increases, and though, at the crucial moment, Skale "utters falsely" and the consummation is not reached, the catastrophe that follows is so prodigious that the book leaves no sense of anticlimax in the reader's mind.

The secret of Algernon Blackwood's pre-eminence over such of his contemporaries as essay this most difficult and precarious type of fiction is, I think, his absolute sincerity, coupled with an unusual command of language and a feeling for the numinous word. I use the term *sincerity* in something wider than its usual application to works of art. An author is often said to be sincere when he writes with genuine conviction, states his views frankly, or uses his art as a medium for expressing a deeply felt belief. Applied to Mr Blackwood the word "sincerity" involves an ampler connotation. He has, it seems, a power of second sight and a clarity of vision allied—what is more and rarer—with an equal clarity of expression. He neither formulates a belief nor points a moral; all the experiences he describes are particular experiences—neither universal, nor symbolic, but intuitive—and intuition is the 'sincerest' form of knowledge. Yet, as Porphyry said of Homer, "it must not be denied that he has obscurely indicated the images of things of a more divine nature in the fiction of a fable." Our outlook on those diviner things has been occluded by the overgrowth of civilisation and the dark forest of desires, psychic and material, which hems in the modern man; hence the aptness of the word "occult" to Mr Blackwood's work. (pp. 94-5)

It is because Mr Blackwood himself has this gift of clairvoyance—in a word, sincerity—that he can open windows which so many exponents of the occult leave shut, or merely feign to open. "To him philosophy was to be something giving strange swiftness and double sight, divining the sources of springs beneath the earth or of expression beneath the human countenance, clairvoyant of occult gifts in common or uncommon things, in the reed at the brook-side, or the star which draws near to us but once in a century." Pater's description of Leonardo's philosophy is applicable word for word to Mr Blackwood's—if philosophy it can be called, this intuitive knowledge of things unseen. Reading such novels as **'The Centaur'** and **'The Human Chord',** or such an amazing story as **'The Wendigo',** we have so keen a sense of an authentic experience, of participated swiftness and double sight, that we seem to see the world invisible, partaking for a fugitive but splendid moment in "the only kind of knowledge that is everlasting." (pp. 95-6)

> Stuart Gilbert, "Algernon Blackwood: Novelist and Mystic" (reprinted by permission of the Estate of Stuart Gilbert), in transition (copyright, 1935, by transition), No. 23, July, 1935, pp. 89-96.

PETER PENZOLDT   (essay date 1952)

Stuart Gilbert called Blackwood a 'mystic', and despite the frequent misuse of the term, it is that which describes him best. Writing a short story of the supernatural means to Blackwood exactly the opposite from what it means to most other authors. While they are merely seeking a new field in which to try their skill, Blackwood has a message, and for him experiment is limited to technique. This must be kept in mind throughout an analysis of Blackwood's stories, else the critic may fail to understand when the mystic occasionally gets the better of the artist. (pp. 228-29)

[It] is extension, and even 'change' of consciousness that Mr. Blackwood seeks. His message is of the beauty or possible dangers involved in this extension of consciousness.

Yet his work has no didactic purpose. He detests the idea of teaching anybody. He has a message, but no dogma. His pleasure lies in dreaming or living through a new adventure in the other-worldly regions, and as the travellers of bygone

centuries brought home sketchbooks from their journeys, so he brings back the written image of what he has seen. (p. 229)

Blackwood's stories are usually longer than the average short story of the supernatural. The lengths of his first five important stories, published . . . under the common title of *John Silence,* vary between fifty and one hundred pages, while the average length of a ghost story in a good anthology such as *Great Tales of Terror and the Supernatural* is about twenty pages. Accordingly the expositions are rather long. Usually they contain the description of the scene in which the action is going to take place. This part of the story is more important in Blackwood's tales than in those of most authors, because the preternatural he describes is usually a deeper aspect of nature, which commonly remains unperceived, but which may reveal itself in moments of 'extended consciousness'

In **'The Willows',** for example, the story begins with a long poetical description of the Danube, as it is seen by two tourists, who follow its course in a canoe. One night they arrive at the marshes below Pressburg—the country of the willows. Then, imperceptibly, a new note is introduced into the almost lyrical description of the river. The author's main interest has shifted from the landscape itself, to its effect on his actors—one of them is the narrator himself. The scenery, of course, remains outwardly unchanged, but in the eyes of the person who is supposed to tell the story, every detail gradually acquires a new significance, and these hitherto concealed qualities of simple objects gain in importance, until a new world, that of extended consciousness, is realised, and entirely replaces reality. (pp. 230-31)

[Almost] every one of Blackwood's stories contains more than one supernatural appearance [at its climax]. This may of course become rather disturbing and in one of his earlier stories, **'A Nemesis of Fire',** from *John Silence,* his use of the climax is open to all the objections made to the employment of several climaxes in one story. Yet most of Blackwood's tales do not give one the feeling that the author is 'overdoing it'. There are probably two reasons for this. One is the impression of sincerity that emanates from Blackwood's work. His visions seem too authentic to be altered for the sake of mere effect. The second is that his climaxes, though they certainly inspire terror, are never loathsome. Blackwood describes no rotting corpses, or slimy monsters as do [F. Marion Crawford, Arthur Machen and H. P. Lovecraft]. His apparitions fill us with awe, while those of so many others fill us with horror akin to disgust. Blackwood's spirits have some of the beauty of the elements they symbolise. They are gods, rather than ghosts or goblins. We accept them not only as the climax of a thriller, but also as a poetic reality, and maybe even a reality beyond that of poetry.

Possibly we come closest to truth in saying that Blackwood's apparitions are the personified atmosphere of certain places—the 'spirit of place' as S. M. Ellis calls it. In his tales the indefinable atmosphere of a landscape materialises into individual beings, gifted with thought, speech, and a will of their own. A river, a forest, a house, each has for him an intense and aggressive personality. In **'A Descent into Egypt'** ancient Egypt absorbs George Isley's personality, until there is nothing left of him but a 'human shell'. Ancient Egypt captures him, and steals his spirit away into the past. In **'The Glamour of the Snow',** the snow-ghost nightly lures her victim to the freezing white hills. (p. 232)

Blackwood's spirits do not merely come out of nature, they are nature herself, nature surprised, as it were, in her deepest secrets.

It would nevertheless be essentially wrong to mistake Blackwood's approach to nature for that of a lyrical poet, who peoples the empty groves and meadows with a host of nymphs and fairies. His experience lies much deeper. It is that of a true mystic, for his message is the extension of consciousness, and the world reached by this extension is nature, the essence of nature, and all her hidden aspects.

To be exact, Blackwood's interest is divided between two great fields for the exploring of which the extension of consciousness is merely a refined tool. One of these themes is nature, the other is the atmosphere of houses, and the way in which their 'spirits' are permanently affected by the thoughts and deeds of former occupants. As will be shown, nature to Blackwood is by far the more important theme, but in both his approach is linked to certain early experiences in his life. . . .

Blackwood's father was an ardent revivalist, who though certainly not devoid of a genuine good-heartedness, had appallingly narrow religious ideas. . . . Blackwood was to meet the same religious intolerance again, though in a slightly different form, among the 'Brüder' of the Moravian school in the Black Forest, where he was sent to learn German. Early on, he developed a gradually increasing resistance to the teachings of religious intolerance. Books certainly helped him to create his own vision of the universe. (p. 233)

But it would be a great mistake to pretend that these books suggested the deeper meaning which most of Blackwood's tales contain. Their influence is always superficial. They called upon and helped to awake the author's dormant genius, which rose up to meet them. H. P. Lovecraft [see excerpt above], who otherwise was a great admirer of Blackwood, completely failed to understand this when he wrote that,

> Mr. Blackwood's lesser work is marred by several defects, such as ethical didacticism, occasional insipid whimsicality, the flatness of benignant supernaturalism, and a too free use of the trade jargon of modern occultism.

Lovecraft here refers to certain technical deficiencies which are visible in Mr. Blackwood's earlier books. Being of a purely materialistic temperament, Lovecraft was evidently unable to recognise the truly mystical impulse which even Blackwood's earlier works show to a certain extent. . . .

Nature became Blackwood's God, the deity that saved him from the perils of religious intolerance. . . . In the puritan atmosphere in which he was brought up, which considered instinct, passion, and every kind of worldly joy as sinful, nature was the only master who could teach Blackwood that instinct and Law were not opposites, but formed a unity, and which could dispel the awful nightmare of a 'personal Satan and an actual Hell'. Without nature for his guide, his gift of second sight, and ability to describe what he had seen, might well have led him to write of such hideous monsters as one finds in Crawford's, Machen's and Lovecraft's tales. The splendid visions might never have been born. (p. 234)

Blackwood's idea is that nature is good, beautiful, right and healing. In his autobiography [*Episodes Before Thirty*], he again and again tells us how nature was his only dear companion when the world of men failed him. It may therefore

seem astonishing that in his tales he often describes it with a certain amount of anguish, showing how men who fall under the spell of nature lose themselves, so to say, or to quote his favourite expression, are 'absorbed' by the particular part of nature, or the 'God' they worship. In **'The Sea Fit'**, for example, a man offers himself as sacrifice to the ancient but eternal Gods of the sea; a splendid, unbloody sacrifice, in which the 'victim' becomes one with the Deity, is 'absorbed'. A wave of preternatural dimensions catches the worshipper while he is kneeling to the sea, and 'the body was never recovered'. In **'The Man whom the Trees Loved'**, the hero's soul unites with the spirit of the forest. . . .

Such stories as these . . . must not be taken to show a second and negative attitude of Blackwood towards nature. They are rather the expression of the culmination of the author's mysticism. The mingled fear and desire to become one with the worshipped deity is typical of all mystics. It will be noted that Blackwood, who so often uses the first person to relate his experiences, uses the third person when he describes such an 'absorption'. This is logical, because such tales can only express a hidden desire, but cannot possibly refer to any experience, even if it were of a mystical order.

Nature provides most of Blackwood's themes, but a second source is the intense and mysterious atmosphere of certain human habitations; the spell which rooms, houses or entire cities may throw on a sensitive mind. Here, as in his stories on nature, Blackwood avoids ugly climaxes. He still regards repulsive physical horror as a primitive device to create atmosphere. Yet in his tales on 'haunted houses', a new element is introduced, personal, aggressive evil. In nature, he well understood, there was no evil. Nature as he describes it in his tales may be overwhelmingly beautiful, terrifying, 'absorbing', and thus even dangerous, but it knows not the passion of hatred. Blackwood finds evil in those who believe in it: in men. There are early attempts in his work to show how the influence of evil deeds and evil thoughts may remain and even accumulate in certain places. A story entitled **'The Empty House'** gave its title to Blackwood's first volume of short stories. . . . It is still a rather poor tale, hardly more than an ordinary ghost story about a haunted house. The theme, as in **'A Case of Eavesdropping'**, in the same volume, is the repetition of a murder scene, each time the atmosphere of a haunted room or house becomes strong enough to allow a materialisation of the evil forces. But in *John Silence* . . . we find the theme in a more involved form. (pp. 236-37)

Yet it is only in **'The Damned'** (*Incredible Adventures*) . . . that Blackwood's conception of the 'haunted house' is fully apparent, and that the intimate connection between the motif and his own life becomes most obvious. 'The Damned' is a fascinating tale about a house haunted by the evil presences of those who have undergone the only form of damnation that Blackwood will admit; the imprisonment of men in their own narrow intolerant ideas. The story is an appalling vision of the sort of damnation that Blackwood himself might have undergone if he had remained the slave of the narrow selfish creed to which his education had tried to chain him. It is a portrait of that world from which he had escaped through nature. The house, haunted by the evil of men, becomes a symbol of all that is opposed to nature. To Blackwood, it means everything that used to shut him off from the spiritual freedom he finds in nature. It is the prison which the Moravian school, and even to a certain extent his father's house, had become for him; the above of intolerance and spiritual slavery. Is it not natural, therefore, that the house should nearly always appear in his writings as the shelter of evil and ugliness, while nature reveals beauty? (p. 237)

I have said that Blackwood's first tales on haunted houses are still very close to the orthodox form of this type of ghost story, and that only later he chose the evolved form we have described. This was to be expected. The haunted castle, house, or room are among the oldest traditional forms of the ghost story. They provided the favourite main motifs for the Gothic novel. Naturally, it is more difficult to create something new if tradition already furnishes a set pattern. In his stories on the mysterious hidden aspects of nature Blackwood discovered an entirely new field, and in those tales his originality is therefore apparent from the very beginning. Nor was Blackwood's idea that strong thinking never dies and in certain places may survive the physical existence, particularly new. We find the theory in Bulwer Lytton's 'The Haunted and the Haunters', and later in such famous stories by Henry James as 'The Turn of the Screw' and 'Sir Edmond Orme', as well as in Oliver Onions' 'The Beckoning Fair One'.... Compared with Henry James and Bulwer Lytton, Blackwood's originality lies rather in the use he makes of a more spiritual approach to the subject, than in any perfectly new conception. He simply avoids all physical horror, and the terror lies in the vision revealed by second sight.

More interesting would be a comparison of **'The Damned'** with Oliver Onions' masterpiece 'The Beckoning Fair One'.... Onions and Blackwood are contemporaries, and Blackwood's story was written not long after 'Widdershins' was published. This comparison is especially useful, because it allows one to measure the gulf that separates the psychological from what might be called the 'psychical' ghost story, and of which Blackwood's works are probably the only examples.

'The Beckoning Fair One', like Blackwood's **'The Damned'**, is the story of an invisible presence—the ghost, or spirit of a person or persons, whose intense personality allowed the psychic part of their being to continue after death, and exert an evil influence. In both **'The Damned'** and Oliver Onions' story, the presence of the ghost or spirit is felt rather than actually perceived by the senses. The theme of both stories is the spell that a house may exercise over a sensitive temperament. But the essential difference between the two is appreciated when attention is focused on the principal actors. Mr. Onions' tale is about a young man, who, living alone in the haunted house, falls in love with the invisible presence of a woman. ... The 'ghostly lover' may then be considered as a dangerous symptom of a certain type of neurosis. 'The Beckoning Fair One' is merely a tale based on this type of neurosis. Only the 'ghostly lover' is not described as a symptom, but as the real being for which the patient takes her. Thus the story becomes a ghost story. In Blackwood's tale the narrator himself is the central figure, he tells his own experience. The experience he says he has had in the haunted house shows a complete sublimation of the problems he had met with in his earlier life. Everything is transposed into a purely spiritual world. There are no descriptions of typical symptoms, because these have long since lost all reality for the author. Blackwood speaks as one who has already conquered. This is why he may talk in the first person. The story no longer bears any direct relation to his own experiences, a state of full consciousness has intervened between them and the story. The story, one might say, is their echo, in a

world that is purely spiritual. What is interesting is that **'The Damned'** shows a sublimation of a struggle with precisely those forces that tried to prevent Blackwood from sublimating his own problems by creative writing.

In an analysis of Blackwood's style, one must always keep in mind his earnestness about his subject, about the 'something God had whispered to him'. He naturally sought to reproduce his experience as exactly as possible, and this tendency is reflected in his style, as well as in the structure, of his tales, and his choice of themes.

Blackwood had a choice between two different methods of achieving his purpose. He could either have used what Sean O'Faolain called 'suggestive language', or with infinite care, revealed every detail, and then let the whole suggest something beyond the reach of words. Blackwood chose the second method. In this he was not alone. Many ghost-story writers rightly believed that if the scene the words were to depict lay beyond the range of common experience, it was better not to use a language which, for all its charm, already demanded an intellectual and imaginative effort from the reader. Nevertheless, Blackwood seems more conscious of the problem than others. Many passages in his work are concerned with the struggle the writer of short stories of the supernatural has in finding the appropriate means of expression. (pp. 239-41)

Algernon Blackwood is probably, both as a personality and as a writer, the most impressive figure among contemporary writers of supernatural short stories. A few of his earlier tales remind us of the current crop of ghost stories, but the main part of his work shows that in every respect he refused to tread the beaten path. It is wholly impossible to place him in any school. His work bears no resemblance to the orthodox form of the ghost story, nor did he follow the recent fashions in science fiction and the psychological ghost story. He is one of the few authors in this field who are completely free of E. A. Poe's influence, nor does he in any way seem indebted to the great English masters, with the one exception, perhaps, of Henry James. He refuses to write simple tales of horror, but he also neglects the purely poetical approach and suggestion of a strong but indefinite atmosphere as one finds in Walter de la Mare's inconclusive tales. He scorns the rigid rules of construction that Dr. M. R. James so brilliantly put into practice.

His writings are rather the accounts of personal experience, the epic of a spiritual odyssey, which doubtless began in a whirlpool of neurotic conflicts, but soon brought him out into regions of light and happiness. The scenes he describes inspire terror and awe, but never horror and disgust. His tales have, therefore, a higher literary standing than those of most writers who deal with the same subject. They reflect the achievement of spiritual freedom, and of a deeper knowledge, both of which we miss in the works of those authors who consciously or unconsciously were unable to conceive the supernatural except as a symbol of direct and clearly defined neurotic conflicts. Therefore Blackwood is a lonely but outstanding figure, in a genre which is already restricted. (pp. 247-48)

Peter Penzoldt, "Algernon Blackwood," in his The Supernatural in Fiction *(copyright 1952 by Peter Penzoldt; reproduced by permission of The Hamlyn Publishing Group Limited), P. Nevill, 1952 (and reprinted by Humanities Press, Inc., 1965), pp. 228-53.*

E. F. BLEILER (essay date 1973)

Blackwood worked in many different subforms within the range of fiction loosely called the ghost story or supernatural story. He wrote tales of terror, intended to thrill the reader; stories that embodied elements of weird science; occult detective stories; psychological-supernatural stories; conventional ghost stories; mystical stories; light fantasies and many other kinds of stories that cannot be labeled easily.

All of these forms Blackwood handled superbly. To the tale of terror he brought a subtlety, a craftsmanship and a maturity of outlook that it had seldom enjoyed before. In "**The Willows**" he makes a remarkable use of a scientific idea, interpenetrating dimensions of existence, to create one of the most sustained situations in supernatural fiction. "**The Wendigo**" expands a small point in Algonkin folklore—which may ultimately be nothing more than cannibalism—into a cosmic situation. Many of his lesser stories in this same vein show a skill at handling old themes and motives that raises them above their predecessors.

While Blackwood's terror stories are often great, the stories that are his most personal are those that must be called mystical for the want of a better term. In these the common theme is an empathy between man and the forces of the universe, the elemental powers that are above, around, apart from yet within man. This is not religious mysticism, nor occultism, but a loosely philosophical pantheism of a sort, nature constituting the Godhead. This Divinity could be called the Great God Pan, as long as it is remembered that Pan is not the goat-footed piper, but Everything. Numinous for Blackwood were the dark forests of Canada, the rushing wind from the Caucasus into the Black Sea, the crags of the Alps, and other aspects of the Universe, man subtracted. Many of his stories are built upon this emotional feeling; outstanding among them is his novel *The Centaur*. . . . Other facets of this mystical thought appear in such works as *The Human Chord* . . . , in which the ancient Pythagorean wisdom of sound is worked into a moving fiction. The basic concept of traditional mysticism, too, is represented in the Julius LeVallon novels, *The Bright Messenger* . . . and *Julius LeVallon* . . . , in which an elemental spirit, trapped in a human cage, strives for release. Two of his collections of short stories, *The Lost Valley* . . . and *Pan's Garden* . . . , present many stories that develop shades of these situations. (pp. vi-vii)

Blackwood's supernatural short stories are spread through several volumes. *The Empty House* . . . and *The Listener* . . . contain mostly stories of supernatural terror, while *John Silence, Physician Extraordinary* . . . records the cases of a psychic detective, certainly the most important occult detective since LeFanu's Dr. Hesselius. [*The Lost Valley* and *Pan's Garden*] . . . present mostly nature mysticism, while *Incredible Adventures* . . . offers several long nouvelles that are difficult to categorize. Most of the stories in these earlier collections are fully developed in the late Victorian manner, occasionally leisurely in their progress, but at best as powerful and homogeneous and embracing as a wave. His later collections, such as [*Ten Minute Stories, Day and Night Stories, The Wolves of God, Tongues of Fire*, and *Shocks*] . . . are usually briefer, sometimes more conventional in subject matter. But if the themes they develop are sometimes traditional, they are handled with mastery.

Blackwood did not limit himself to the ghost story, however, even though it was his primary interest. In addition to a little poetry and a couple of plays, he wrote a considerable amount of fiction for children, much of which was published in periodicals or annuals, and is now forgotten. Some of it, like *How the Circus Came to Tea* . . . , deserves revival, for at its best it is whimsical, charming, and dryly humorous, the amiable personality of the author emerging more visibly than in his supernatural fiction. He also wrote a single major work that is not fiction, his autobiography *Episodes Before Thirty*. . . . This is a brilliant memoir of the New York tenderloin as of about 1900, but the reader who is interested in Algernon Blackwood the fantaisiste may find it disappointing for its reticence. As Blackwood concludes: "Of mystical, psychic, or so-called 'occult' experiences, I have purposely said nothing."

Several things Algernon Blackwood, in his best work, could do better than anyone else. He could arouse a sensation of terror in the reader, and sustain it at high pitch until the end of the story. The suspense of "**The Willows**," for example, is hard to match anywhere. It has often been rated as the finest single supernatural story in English. Blackwood could also impart to his readers a sort of cosmic experience, and could impel the reader to perceive otherwise invisible powers and stirrings in the universe, inexplicable sensations, and the ineffable bliss of *natura naturans*. In these areas only Gustav Meyrink, the Austro-Hungarian writer, could match him, though on a different level. Blackwood could also write a fantasy of pathos and tenderness without mawkishness, as in his *Dudley and Gilderoy* . . . , the experiences of two friends, a cat and a parrot.

Faults, of course, Blackwood had. He wrote because he had to, at word rates, and he did not always resist his natural tendency to say things the full way. His novels suffer from this flaw, on the whole, more than his short stories. In his later short stories, possibly at editorial prodding, he tried to be concise, but the scanty raiment of the 1920's did not suit him as well as Edwardian full dress. Not all of his experiments, too, were successful, such as his attempts to create an implied supernaturalism of mood within a social-psychological framework, but the attempt at least was admirable. On the verbal level, sometimes, he did not always match the splendor of his ideas, and occasionally his ideas were simply incommunicable. But all in all, no writer of fiction has written better individual stories or spoken better about the ineffable.

Historically Blackwood offered much to the development and continuity of the ghost story. He widened the range of its subject matter greatly, and showed that the myriad rooms of the human mind were teeming with a strange, hidden life. He brought into the supernatural story the realms of philosophy, serious Oriental thought, modern psychology and new areas of magical lore. He demonstrated that the supernatural story did not have to be a revenge story nor a primitive justice drama, nor detritus of ancient wickedness, nor the crudities of the lower-level fiction of his day. While the comparison should not be pushed too far, since there are significant differences, Blackwood in some ways was the heir to J. S. LeFanu, the greatest of Victorian supernaturalists. With the work of Blackwood, it seems safe to say, the ghost story was finally recognized as a legitimate, respectable literary form—not a hypocritical Christmas entertainment nor a horror-bludgeon for the dull—but a thought-provoking work that had something to say to an intelligent reader. (pp. viii-x)

E. F. Bleiler, in his introduction to Best Ghost Stories of Algernon Blackwood, *edited by E. F. Bleiler (copyright © 1973 by Dover Publications, Inc.), Dover, 1973, pp. v-x.*

JULIA BRIGGS (essay date 1977)

The psychic doctor fulfilled in fiction a need that was strongly felt in fact, by providing psychic or psycho-therapy before the advent of the analyst. The transference of this role of exorcist from priest to doctor which took place before and during the nineteenth century is represented in [Joseph Sheridan] Le Fanu's story 'Green Tea' by making the victim who consults the psychic doctor, Hesselius, a priest himself—the Reverend Jennings. (p. 60)

In effect the career of this first and most intriguing of psychic doctors had begun and ended with 'Green Tea'.

It was to Blackwood's John Silence that the mantle of Hesselius fell, but not till more than thirty-five years had elapsed, and that most spiritual of detectives, Mr Sherlock Holmes, had been created for much the same sort of audience as enjoyed ghost stories—the sober, respectable middle class who delighted to imagine their familiar environment transfigured by fearful mysteries. Algernon Blackwood had published two volumes of ghost stories before *John Silence, Physician Extraordinary*. . . . According to Blackwood's account, it was his publisher, Eveleigh Nash, who suggested that he grouped five separate studies of various 'psychic' themes 'under the common leadership of a single man, Dr John Silence'. Blackwood was a far more careful and conscientious writer than Le Fanu, and on the whole he integrated Silence into the five stories fairly successfully, though one story, 'Ancient Sorceries', has no real connection with Silence.

This is a tale of seventeenth-century witchcraft, and it belongs to a type of ghost story in which the strong atmosphere of a particular place (or object) is used to summon up the past. Blackwood describes how Laon, in Northern France, possessed his imagination: 'The picturesque little town, perched on its hill, had an extraordinary atmosphere, and though I dare not pretend that the inhabitants turned into cats, they certainly betrayed all the feline characteristics.' Blackwood's imagination is often at its most powerful when it is animated by a vivid impression of a particular place. It is his talent for evoking his surroundings, both visually and atmospherically, which gives his work its distinction. **'The Camp of the Dog'**, a variation on the werewolf theme, badly flawed both by sentimentality and the technical error of giving too much away too early, is the weakest story in the volume, yet its vivid setting redeems it to some extent—a bleak island in the Baltic provides just the kind of wild and alien landscape that Blackwood describes most tellingly. He had a strong, almost gnostic sense of the forces immanent in nature, which he dramatized in ghost stories set in the Canadian forests, the Swiss Alps, the Danube, Egypt and even the Caucasus. (p. 61)

'Secret Worship' is the best story in *John Silence,* and again much of its strength comes from the vividly remembered setting—'a Moravian school at Koenigsfeld in the Black Forest, where . . . I spent rather an unhappy eighteen months learning German'. The power of the story lies in its employment of such familiar dream elements as the return to one's old school, the growing sensation of being trapped, the failure to communicate one's intentions adequately, a sense of being increasingly misunderstood, and the final closing-in of threatening figures before the moment of waking. There is a strong emphasis throughout on language, and distorted meanings of certain words contribute much to the surreal effect of the whole. The final explanation given by Silence, that the school had once been the haunt of Satanists, and that 'your deeply

introspective mood had already reconstructed the past so vividly, so intensely, that you were *en rapport* at once with any forces of those days that chanced still to be lingering', seems to suit the dream-like character of the piece. Even the calm of the October morning after conveys a sense of release and the enhanced beauty of the familiar, which often follows nightmare or delirium.

The first tale in the volume, **'A Psychical Invasion'**, concerns a haunted house dominated by an evil spirit. Like [Edward G. Bulwer-Lytton's] 'The Haunters and the Haunted' it is a tale of possession, but as in [Joseph Sheridan Le Fanu's] 'Green Tea' the victim has laid himself open to the invasion by taking a particular drug. Unlike Mr Jennings, however, Mr Pender has taken this drug (*cannabis indica*, as familiar to us as it was mysterious to Blackwood's original audience) deliberately, in order to increase his sense of humour—he makes his living by writing humorous stories. The story falls into two parts, the first an imaginative account of the combination of hysterical laughter caused by the drug and the deepening terror produced by the 'invasion'. The second part describes the haunting primarily through the reactions of Silence's cat and dog. In general Silence emerges as a rather different figure from [Le Fanu's psychic doctor] Hesselius— gentler and more approachable, and far more English. When Le Fanu was writing it was no doubt still necessary to convey a 'Germanic' atmosphere if a character was to be considered 'deep' and knowledgeable about strange psychological states. Silence on the other hand is very much an Englishman, a gentleman who loves outdoor life—a walking tour in Germany, or a turn about Colonel Wragg's estate—an animal-lover and a philanthropist. And if these traits seem to sort a little oddly with his familiarity with the black arts, the Egyptian Book of the Dead, and Eliphas Lévi, such dubious knowledge is softened by his benevolent use of it. On the whole this surprising mixture works precisely because it is unexpected. Silence's 'speaking brown eyes' seem to contrast sharply with those cold grey eyes of Sherlock Holmes, and his bearded features with the latter's lean, clean-shaven ones, yet there are some similarities. Like Holmes, Silence works only from choice. **'A Psychical Invasion'** begins with a dialogue with an acquaintance who is trying to persuade him to take the case—several Holmes stories begin in a similar way. The narrator, Hubbard, is his friend and assistant, who may hear the case at second hand or may himself be an eye-witness. In **'The Nemesis of Fire'** Hubbard is summarily brought to Waterloo, armed, in preparation for a journey into the unknown. When Silence, having dropped a few sinister hints and shown him the letter that has summoned them, then lapses into a brooding silence in his corner of the railway carriage, the shadow of Baker Street seems to fall heavily over the story. Significantly, Silence is here revealed in more of a detecting role than usual. (pp. 61-3)

Julia Briggs, "A Scientific Spirit: Mesmerism, Drugs and Psychic Doctors," in her Night Visitors: The Rise and Fall of the English Ghost Story *(© 1977 by Julia Briggs; reprinted by permission of Faber and Faber Ltd.), Faber and Faber, 1977, pp. 52-75.**

JACK SULLIVAN (essay date 1978)

Algernon Blackwood's **"The Transfer"** is perhaps the strangest of all vampire tales. The vampire is not a demon, a corpse, a bat, or even a rapacious Wellsian plant. Rather, the vampire is an ugly, barren, somehow "hungry" patch of earth. . . . (p. 112)

"The Transfer" represents a movement out of the claustrophobic world of old houses, churches, and mausoleums into the cosmic world of outdoor ghost stories, a world where ghosts and demons are apparitions of primal forces in nature. The patch of earth is the "emissary" of an unseen life-force which can be glimpsed only through constant experiments in metaphor: "It was like a gulp; it was deep and muffled and it dipped way into the earth. . . ." The language alone tells us that the narrator is not a stuffy Jamesian antiquary who is only in touch with books. This is the language of a visionary who is in touch with a living universe.

It would be schematically easy simply to classify Blackwood as the master of the outdoor ghost story; he not only wrote more of them than anyone else, but he managed to create at least two authentic masterpieces, **"The Willows"** and **"The Wendigo."** But Blackwood also wrote more than a few claustrophobic haunted house tales, some of them (such as **"The Listener"**) worthy to stand beside [Joseph Sheridan] Le Fanu's "Strange Disturbances in Aungier Street" and [H. R.] Wakefield's "Blind Man's Buff." In addition, he wrote intermediary tales such as "A Haunted Island" which move in and out between the freedom of nature and the oppressiveness of old houses.

What binds Blackwood's work together is not a common setting, but a distinctive use of language and a distinctive vision. The vision is peculiar in that it is announced decisively but is undermined by the structure of the stories until it seems strangely unsure of itself. This ambivalence adds tension and intellectual credibility to the stories, which would be impossibly dull were they as programmatically "mystical" as they pretend to be.

Unlike the mundane characters of Le Fanu and [M. R.] James, Blackwood's heroes are visionaries who feel oppressed by everyday reality and who deliberately seek out other worlds. What they discover usually encompasses both ecstasy and horror, though sometimes only horror. In either case, the "other" reality is as unmanageable as the first, and the character often spends the rest of the tale desperately negotiating a reentrance into what was renounced in the first place. Rarely, however, is there the slightest verbal retraction of the initial renunciation. Because most of Blackwood's heroes do make it back, he has been seen to be an uncharacteristically "positive" writer for this genre. There are few upbeat endings in Wakefield, M. R. James, or [L. P.] Hartley, and almost none in Le Fanu. On the other hand, Blackwood's characters, while they live to tell the tale, usually end where they started; the stories read like unresolved circles.

Blackwood's fiction is part of an intensively subjectivist tendency in modern British fiction. Reacting against Victorian scientism and technology, his characters are constantly indicting the outer world and plunging into inner vision. . . . M. R. James also expresses an alienation from the modern world, but more through implication than authorial statement. Blackwood belongs to a more didactic tradition of ghost story writers which includes Yeats, Arthur Machen, Oliver Onions, E. F. Benson, and (somewhat ambiguously) Walter de la Mare. (pp. 112-14)

[Blackwood] seemed to possess an endlessly fertile imagination, creating more conceptual variations than any of his rivals. Though his fiction lacks the unity of Machen, Chambers, or [H. P.] Lovecraft (writers who use a central, organizing mythos), it has far greater variety. Like Poe's Roderick Usher, who speaks of "the sentience of all vegetable matter," Blackwood envisions a world in which everything is alive and anything can be a ghost: trees, bushes, earth, snow, even the wind (which in **"The Wendigo"** becomes one of his most unusual demons). His indoor apparitions are also nicely varied: the old gentleman from the eighteenth century in **"The Other Wing,"** who has a gracious smile and impeccable manners; the leprous thing in **"The Listener,"** who has very poor manners, leaving putrid odors wherever he appears; the Satan figure in **"Secret Worship,"** who appears in a haunted monastery; the emaciated spectre in **"Keeping His Promise,"** who, having starved himself to death, returns to haunt a kitchen, stuffing himself with endless amounts of food. Though Blackwood's human characters behave in predictable patterns, his ghostly characters do not.

Unlike his admirers, who view his work with a kind of religious awe, Blackwood is not unaware of the element of farce in these stories. His characters are often tuned into it as well: the narrator of **"With Intent to Steal"** speaks of the "element of the ludicrous" in the ghostly experience, an element which produces "empty laughter." Laughter is empty because it attempts, unsuccessfully, to exorcise the absurdly grim situation which provoked it in the first place (in this case, the situation of being trapped in an old barn with a ghost whose sole function is inducing people to commit suicide). Blackwood's humor is more closely akin to Le Fanu than to M. R. James. Lacking James's understated wit, Blackwood relies on outright farce. (pp. 115-16)

Unlike [Le Fanu and Lovecraft] (and M. R. James as well), Blackwood was a committed believer in psychic experience and ghostly phenomena. (p. 118)

Blackwood indulges in the "expanded consciousness" rhetoric of the Order of the Golden Dawn. . . . [The impulse is] to transcend the "homespun 'ghost story'" by subjecting the supernatural to the rigors of a quasi-scientific discipline. The desire to have it both ways—to be both mystical and scientific—is characteristic of much of the supernatural fiction of the late Victorian and Edwardian periods. . . . In Blackwood's case, the desire is symptomatic of a thematic ambivalence which sometimes undermines his style. Although the works of his contemporaries are self-sabotaging in much the same way . . . , the problem is easiest to see in Blackwood in that the felicities and flaws in his style exist in almost manic relation to each other. (pp. 118-19)

[In] Blackwood, the [creative and didactic] impulses are continually at war. At his worst, he is guilty of "a too free use of the trade jargon of modern occultism," a charge levelled by an astute H. P. Lovecraft in 1927 [see excerpt above]. John Silence's endless disquisition on the "etheric Body of Desire" in the otherwise compelling **"The Camp of the Dog"** is a particularly wearisome example. Whenever the good psychic doctor appears on the scene, we can expect some heavy going. We suspect that Dr. Silence can indeed "conquer even the devils of outer space" . . .—by boring them into a catatonic state.

But even the private moments of mystical awakening by the Man in the Street are often marred, not only by the "diffuseness" cited by Lovecraft, but by a tendency to be too literal. . . . (p. 119)

Blackwood is clearly part of the "moment" tradition in modern British fiction, but his moments seldom amount to much.

Rather than evoking the experience and allowing us to flow with it, he feels compelled to preach at us, lest we explain the whole thing away with "some shallow physiological label."

This is an odd flaw in a writer whose enduring strength is precisely the power to evoke. The stylistic split between Blackwood the guru and Blackwood the ghost story writer suggests that he is better off when he sticks to writing ghost stories. Despite his protestations about being classified as "the ghost man," his best scenes are his ghost scenes. It scarcely matters whether we regard his apparitions as "psychic" or "homespun": they are as enchanting and chilling as anything in the literature.

An unforgettable example is **"The Willows,"** Blackwood's most frequently anthologized tale. The elusive forces which besiege the campers on a Danube island also besiege the reader; they emerge as a deeply felt experience of "bewildering beauty" and escalating terror. The story has its dull, jargonistic passages, but Blackwood mercifully keeps these to a minimum. In the apparition scenes, Blackwood is a freewheeling pantheist: he envisions nature as an altogether ambiguous divinity, impossible to pin down, both enticing and insidious, spreading out into everything. The deadly willow bushes, the strange sand-funnels, and the otherworldly sounds which vibrate sometimes like gigantic gongs, sometimes like "the whirring of wings" and sometimes like "a swarm of great invisible bees" are not lethal deities in themselves, but satellites of larger unknowable powers. Like symbols in a Symbolist poem, they progressively suggest or evoke each other without defining what they are moving toward.

In this important sense, Blackwood is part of the Le Fanu tradition which opts for suggestion over definition. His best stories (**"Confession"** and **"The Haunted Island"** are other notable examples) are the ones which know how to keep a few secrets: **"The Willows"** moves us precisely because we never quite know what the Willows are. In classic Le Fanu fashion, the story builds intensity through a slow accretion of detail: the willow bushes which each day seem a little closer to the tent; the otter-like creature "turning over and over in the foaming waves" of the Danube; the "flying apparition" which makes the sign of the cross as it glides by; the unexplainable destruction of the canoe; the "nude, fluid shapes" which materialize in the patterns of the trees at night; the multiplying sand funnels; the otherworldly gongs—all build toward a conclusion that is at once climactic and mysterious. Although interconnections between details gradually clarify themselves, the larger structure of the "unearthly" region remains a mystery. (pp. 120-21)

Both the strengths and weaknesses in Blackwood are largely functions of his consuming interest in what Lovecraft calls "atmosphere." For Blackwood, "atmosphere" is fundamental and thematic rather than decorative. His dialogue and characterization often fall flat because he is more interested in recording intimations of the "beyond region" than in recording credible interactions between people.

Thematically, Blackwood's nature stories represent an early version of what D. H. Lawrence calls the "nonhuman." Indeed Blackwood has several things in common with Lawrence, the most noticeable of which is a repeated use of Lawrentian terms—"nonhuman," "otherness," "separateness," "the beyond"—before Lawrence codified them in

The Rainbow and *Women in Love.* Though not on the same level of achievement, Blackwood's rendering of nature is strikingly similar to Lawrence's in one crucial respect. Romantic poetry generally propounds the notion that interaction with nature enhances the individual's humanity. In the romantic universe, the emphasis is on the human. But Blackwood and Lawrence are part of a reactionary, anti-human thread which twists through writers such as Conrad, Yeats, Eliot, and Pound. Rather than putting us in touch with our larger possibilities, communion with nature in Lawrence and Blackwood shows us that nature is a distinctly "other" form of life to which humanity is profoundly irrelevant. In **"The Willows,"** nature is "another evolution not parallel to the human." While nature is not always this "alien" in Blackwood, it generally has the effect of making us aware of our smallness, our "utter insignificance." . . . (p. 123)

Blackwood's fiction, like Lawrence's, represents a militant assertion that the outer world *does* exist—sublimely apart from human psychology. Although the unconscious is an active force in Blackwood's stories, it is not Freudian, not limited to human beings (or even "collective" human beings in a Jungian sense); it is a pre-human energy which infuses not only Lawrence's birds, beasts, and flowers, but patches of dirt.

This is somewhat of a departure from Le Fanu and Lovecraft, who present the alternate reality as an evil conspiracy. In Blackwood, the world beyond space and time is simply irrevocably *there*—not to be tampered with, but not evil either. Blackwood's distinctively "cosmic" fusion of horror and ecstasy occurs in this context: what the willows represent is alluring to people because it is superior; it is also deadly because it is saturated with a "primeval" intensity which "materialistic" modern man can no longer match.

Fortunately, Blackwood the Edwardian primitive is often belied by Blackwood the story-teller. His tendency to sentimentalize nature, even when nature does outrageous things, usually occurs in labored soliloquies by Blackwood personae (see **"The South Wind"**) or in passages of thinly disguised omniscient narration. "Blackwood's idea is that Nature is good, beautiful, right and healing," says Peter Penzoldt [see excerpt above]. But it is difficult to reconcile this notion with **"The Wendigo,"** a creature of the wind who snatches sleeping campers out of their tents at night, propels them for huge distances through the sky, and redeposits them on the ground as drooling idiots. This is peculiar behavior for something "beautiful, right and healing." The willows too, with their "sacrificial" habit of arbitrarily puncturing people to death with hideous pock marks, behave rather badly. If not evil, nature can at least be extraordinarily nasty. Ostensibly, human apparitions in old houses are evil (precisely because they are human), whereas "primeval" apparitions in nature are merely menacing. For the pursued character in the story, however, the distinction is likely to seem a dubious one.

Though more Gothic and "scary" in the usual sense, the indoor tales are similar in style and theme to the outdoor tales. In the better passages, they have the same hallucinatory vividness; in the weaker passages, the same lapses into pontification and repetitiveness. An example is **"The Listener,"** an overlong but frequently powerful tale of a man haunted and possessed by the ghost of a suicidal leper. (pp. 124-25)

[**"The Listener"** is] useful as a structural paradigm of Blackwood's work. Frequently a character will begin by revolting against the every day world of empirical facts, with much fanfare about the visionary "path of real knowledge" and many regrets about having spent so much of life "in the pursuit of false knowledge, in the mere classifying and labelling of effects, the analysis of results." The character then gradually propels himself into the experience of an alternate reality, only to find it necessary to flee back to the old "false" reality he has already declared to be an illusion of the senses. Worst of all, he usually finds that in order to make it back, he must enlist the aid of the "skeptical" character with whom he has been arguing throughout the story. (p. 128)

This is a typical Blackwood reversal in which the man of no imagination saves the visionary from his own visions. . . . It is the skeptics who survive—and enable the visionaries to survive as well. We are left with an ambivalence between vision and sanity that the stories never resolve.

The closest Blackwood comes to facing this ambivalence is, ironically, in one of his weakest, most bombastic stories, **"May Day Eve."** As usual, the character sees the dilemma and makes the decision by default. The difference is that this narrator makes the decision with an exact notion of the price he is paying: "I must escape at all costs and claim my old self again, however limited. I must have sanity, even if with

limitations, but sanity at any price." The "price" is a heavy one in Blackwood—a deadening of the imagination, the destruction of "the delicate woof of a vision." It is paradoxical that so many of the stories of this most mystical of ghost story writers should end on a ruthlessly pragmatic note. But since Blackwood's visions have a way of turning into horror stories, "sanity at any price" is not a bad bargain. (p. 129)

> *Jack Sullivan, "The Visionary Ghost Story: Algernon Blackwood," in his* Elegant Nightmares: The English Ghost Story from Le Fanu to Blackwood *copyright © 1978 by Jack Sullivan; reprinted by permission of Ohio University Press, Athens), Ohio University Press, 1978, pp. 112-30.*

ADDITIONAL BIBLIOGRAPHY

Hudson, Derek. "A Study of Algernon Blackwood." *Essays and Studies* (1961): 102-14.
   Biographical sketch and descriptive survey of the major works.

"Sound Made Visible: The Occult Theme of Algernon Blackwood's *The Human Chord." The New York Times* (6 August 1911): 483.
   Criticizes the novel for its heavy use of occult terminology.

Aleksandr (Aleksandrovich) Blok

1880-1921

Russian poet, dramatist, essayist, critic, and autobiographer.

Blok was the foremost poet of the Russian literary flowering called the Silver Age. During the first decade of the twentieth century he was the acknowledged leader of the Russian symbolist movement, and he is remembered today as the creator of the controversial *Dvenadsat (The Twelve)*, the greatest poetic celebration of the October Revolution. His poetry is infused with what he called the spirit of music: an emotional and intellectual sense of exaltation and vivacity, the fount of all creativity, "which the artist finds in his inspiration and the ordinary man in his moments of absorbed energy and all-sufficing activity," according to C. M. Bowra.

Raised in the intellectual and literary atmosphere of his family's Petersburg home, Blok began writing poetry as a young man. Initially a romantic of the order of Mikhail Lermontov and Afanasi Fet, Blok believed that the poet should trust his own visions and feelings, working unbound by social responsibility. Focusing on his lifelong obsession with the feminine ideal, his early poems were inspired by the mystic-philosopher Vladimir Soloviev's writings on Sophia (the Eternal Feminine and embodiment of Eternal Wisdom), as well as by his wife Lyubov Dmitrevna, in whom he found Sophia reborn. With the publication of his first volume *Stikhi o prekrasnoi dame*, in 1905, Blok was hailed as Russia's most important symbolist. He became the center of an admiring coterie, who worshipped his wife as the Beautiful Lady of his first book. Blok and the Russian symbolists were concerned with the metaphysical tension between an individual and the universe and viewed the artist as a mystic able to penetrate to the essence of things and reproduce the hidden music of life. The symbolists viewed their work as more than a literary movement; they considered their doctrine to be a philosophy of life and a new way of apprehending reality.

The ethereal wonder of Blok's early verses gave way to earthbound pessimism after Lyubov and Blok's friend and fellow symbolist Andrey Bely fell in love. Blok's essays became decidedly antiintellectual, while his poetry and ventures into drama revealed his self-destructive bitterness and his attempts at rediscovering his feminine ideal in the various Petersburg actresses and prostitutes with whom he consorted. In the 1906 drama *Balaganchik (The Puppet Show)*, Blok's Eternal Feminine is reduced to a cardboard doll, an image that disturbed his fellow symbolists and dealt a death-blow to the future of Russian symbolism. Blok eventually abandoned mortal women in his search for Sophia, and his subsequent work mirrored his disillusionment with life's ugliness.

Blok turned to Russia itself as his new ideal, and from 1908 until the Revolution his verse evidenced the poet's concern for his country's culture and destiny. An exception to his new direction was his strongest drama, the chivalric *Rosa i krest (The Rose and the Cross)*. Blok began work on the ambitious poem *Vozmezdie* in 1910, a narrative examining Russia's fate and the destruction of his generation. His belief that "the terrible world" needed a blizzard's destructive cleansing culminated in *The Twelve*. Written shortly after the Bolsheviks'

ascension, *The Twelve* caused controversy throughout Russia's political spectrum; the image of a communist Jesus in the last line enraged traditionalists, drew the scorn of Marxists, and became a common point of departure for Blok's critics to this day. His *Skify*, a threatening call for Western support of the new regime, was published at the same time as *The Twelve*, but is considered much the weaker of the two works. Blok wrote little for the rest of his life, telling his friends that due to the hunger, violence, and devastation caused by the Russian Civil War he could no longer sense the "music" of his earlier life.

Many eminent critics consider Blok Russia's leading poet of the century. His importance for Russian literature and culture lies in his successful transversal of two epochs; as Marc Slonim has stated, "the last poet of Imperial Russia is the first poet of its triumphant Revolution."

PRINCIPAL WORKS

Stikhi o prekrasnoi dame (poetry) 1905
Balaganchik (drama) 1906
  [*The Puppet Show* published in journal *Slavonic and East European Review*, 1950]

Korol na ploshchadi (drama) 1907
  [*The King in the Square* published in journal *Slavonic Review*, 1934]
Nechayannaya radost (poetry) 1907
Snezhnye maski (poetry) 1907
Zemlya v Snegu (poetry) 1908
Pesnya sudby (drama) 1909
  [*The Song of Fate* published in journal *Poet Lore*, 1938]
Nochniye chasy (poetry) 1911
Neznakomka (drama) 1913
  [*The Stranger* published in journal *Slavonic and East European Review*, 1948]
Solovyinny sad (poetry) 1913
Stikhi o Rossii (poetry) 1916
Dvenadsat (poetry) 1918
  [*The Twelve*, 1920]
Rossiia i intelligentsiia (essays) 1918
Skify (poetry) 1918
Rosa i krest (drama) 1920
  [*The Rose and the Cross* published in journal *Slavonic and East European Review*, 1936]
Vozmezdie (poetry) 1922
Selected Poems (poetry) 1968
Alexandr Blok: The Journey to Italy (essays, sketches, and poetry) 1973

*These works were published together in a single volume in 1918.

LEON TROTSKY (essay date 1924)

Blok belonged entirely to pre-October [Revolution] literature. Blok's impulses—whether towards tempestuous mysticism, or towards revolution—arise not in empty space, but in the very thick atmosphere of the culture of old Russia, of its landlords and intelligentsia. Blok's symbolism was a reflection of this immediate and disgusting environment. A symbol is a generalized image of a reality. Blok's lyrics are romantic, symbolic, mystic, formless and unreal. But they presuppose a very real life with definite forms and relationships. . . . Blok's starry, stormy and formless lyrics reflect a definite environment and period, with its manner of living, its customs, its rhythms, but outside of this period, they hang like a cloud-patch. This lyric poetry will not outlive its time or its author.

Blok belonged to pre-October literature, but he overcame this, and entered into the sphere of October when he wrote **"The Twelve"**. That is why he will occupy a special place in the history of Russian literature. (p. 116)

Blok did not "go over to the Revolution", but he took his spiritual course from it. . . . The first Revolution entered his soul and tore him away from individualistic self-contentment and mystic quietism. . . . The second Revolution gave him a feeling of wakening, of movement, of purpose and of meaning. Blok was not the poet of the Revolution. Blok caught hold of the wheel of the Revolution as he lay perishing in the stupid *cul de sac* of pre-revolutionary life and art. The poem called **"The Twelve"**, Blok's most important work, and the only one which will live for ages, was the result of this contact. (pp. 117-18)

This poem is unquestionably Blok's highest achievement. At bottom it is a cry of despair for the dying past, and yet a cry of despair which rises in a hope for the future. The music of the terrible events inspired Blok. It seemed to say to him: "Everything which you have written up to now is not right. New people are coming. They bring new hearts. They do not need this. Their victory over the old world signifies a victory over you, over your lyrics, which voiced only the torment of the old world before its death." Blok heard this, and accepted it, and because it was hard to accept, and because he sought support for his lack of faith in his revolutionary faith, and because he wanted to fortify and convince himself, he expressed his acceptance of the Revolution in the most extreme images, that the bridges behind him might be burned. Blok does not make even a shadow of an attempt to sugar the revolutionary change. On the contrary, he takes it in its most uncouth forms and only in its uncouth forms . . . and, he says, *I accept this*, and he sanctifies all this provocatively with the blessings of Christ, and perhaps tries even to save the artistic image of Christ by propping it up with the Revolution.

But none the less, **"The Twelve"** is not a poem of the Revolution. It is the swan song of the individualistic art that went over to the Revolution. And this poem will remain. The twilight lyrics of Blok are gone into the past, and will never return, for such times will not come again, but **"The Twelve"** will remain. . . . (p. 119)

> *Leon Trotsky, "Alexander Blok" (1924), in his* Literature and Revolution, *translated by Rose Strunsky, Russell & Russell, 1925 (and reprinted by Russell & Russell, 1957), pp. 116-25.*

D. S. MIRSKY (essay date 1926)

The greatest of all the Symbolists was Alexander Alexandrovich Blok. His work is at once very typical of the whole school—for no one carried farther the realistic mysticism of Russian symbolism—and very peculiar, for he has a definite air of kinship with the great poets of the Romantic Age. His poetry is more spontaneous and inspired than that of his contemporaries. . . . He was the meeting-point of several lines of traditions—he was both very Russian and very European. (pp. 210-11)

Blok always insisted that his poetry can be really understood and appreciated only by those who are in sympathy with his mystical experience. This assertion is especially true in regard to his first book. Unless one understands the mystical "setting," one is apt to take it for mere verbal music. . . . *[Stikhi o prekrasnoi dame (The Verses about the Beautiful Lady)]* is the history of a mystical "love affair" with a Person whom Blok identified with the subject of Soloviev's *Three Visions*—Sophia, the Divine Wisdom, a feminine hypostasis of the Deity. . . . Blok's mystical friends and himself always insisted that these *Verses* are the most important part of his work, and though the ordinary poetry-reader may be inclined to prefer the mighty numbers of the third volume, these early *Verses* are certainly very interesting and biographically important. In spite of the influence of Soloviev (in the matter) and of Zinaida Hippius (in metrical form), they are quite original and their style is strangely mature for a young man of twenty to twenty-two. The principal feature of this poetry is its complete freedom from everything sensual or concrete. It is a nebula of words, and affects the uninitiated reader as mere verbal melody. It answers better than any other poetry to Verlaine's rule *"de la musique avant toute chose."* Nothing can be "*plus vague et plus soluble dans l'air*" than this poetry. Afterwards, in his play [*Nezkomka (The Stranger)*], Blok makes a poet (who is obviously a parody of himself) read out his verse to a waiter in a public house, and the waiter's verdict is: "Incomprehensible, but exceedingly refined, sir." Apart from the few initiated, the attitude of Blok's early admirers was much the same as the waiter's. (p. 212)

[The] inner literary circles at once realized the importance of the new poet.... [Two] young Muscovites, Andrey Bely and Sergey, the son of M. S. Soloviev, discovered in it a message that was akin to their own spiritual experience, and Blok became to them a prophet and a seer, almost the founder of a new religion. (p. 213)

But this did not last. *Verses about the Beautiful Lady* was still in the press, and the Blokists were at the height of their ecstasies, when a change came over Blok's visionary world. "The Beautiful Lady" refused herself to her lover. The world became empty to him, and the heavens clouded in darkness. Repelled by his mystical Mistress, he turned towards the earth. This change made Blok certainly more unhappy and probably a worse man than he had been, but a greater poet. Only now his poetry begins to acquire human interest and becomes comprehensible to others than the elect few. It becomes more earthly, but at first his earth is not a material earth. His heaven-bred style succeeds in dematerializing the world of common experience when it first comes in contact with it. His world of 1904-1906 is a drapery of fata-morganas, thrown over the more real but invisible heaven. His immaterial and purely musical style was admirably suited to evoke the mists and mirages of Petersburg, the illusionary city which had haunted the imagination of Gogol, of Grigoriev, and of Dostoevsky. This romantic Petersburg, the dream city arising in the unreal misty atmosphere of the North on the uncertain quagmire of the Neva delta, becomes the background of Blok's poetry ever since he touched the earth after his first mystical flights. "The Beautiful Lady" disappears from his poetry. She is replaced by the Stranger (the Strange Woman—Neznakomka), an immaterial but passionately present obsession that haunts the poems of the second volume of this collected verse (1904-1908). She appears with particular vividness in [*In Vino Veritas*] (perhaps, next to [*Dvenadsat (The Twelve)*], the most widely popular of all Blok's poems) written in 1906, which is characteristic for its combination of realistic irony with romantic lyricism. (pp. 213-14)

To the same period belongs a series of exquisite poems where, for once, Blok displays an unexpected gift of homely and whimsical humour. The series is entitled, in a phrase from *Macbeth*, "the Earth's Bubbles." It is about the homely and mischievous spirits that live in the woods and fields. Few poems have won more popular feeling for Blok than the *Little Priest of the Bogs*, a mysterious, impish, and good-natured creation of his fancy.... (p. 215)

The defeat of the Revolution, which followed in 1906-1907, added to his despair and pessimism and emphasized the growing gloom of his soul. His poetry becomes, once for all, the expression of that "fatal emptiness" (of which he speaks in a poem of 1912) which was familiar to many men of his generation. This "emptiness" has much in common with [Leonid] Andreev's. The difference is that Blok was a greater genius, and a man of greater culture—and that he *had* known a state of mystical bliss of which Andreev could have no suspicion. An impotent desire to return into the Radiant Presence he had been expelled from, and a bitter resentment of

the way he had been treated by "the Beautiful Lady," form the subject of his "lyrical dramas" written in 1906-1907—*Balaganchik (The Puppet Show)* and *Neznakomka (The Stranger)*, which are among his earliest and most charming masterpieces. *Balaganchik* is a "pierrotic" comedy.... It contains much of Blok's very best lyrical matter, but it is in essence a satire, a parody, and a piece of grim blasphemy. It is a parody on Blok's own mystical experience, and a satire on his own mystical hopes and aspirations.... The lyrical charm and capricious symbolism of *Balaganchik* may obscure from most readers its terrible pessimism. But it is in essence one of the most blasphemous and gloomiest things ever written by a poet.

The Stranger is a dreamy and romantic visionary drama developing the subject of the poem of the same name. It has less lyrical charm than *Balaganchik* but it shows at its best Blok's ironic and grotesque realism, which only serves to enhance the visionary romanticism of the main theme.... Even those who will not sympathize with the romanticism of this play, will yet appreciate the unique mastery of the prose dialogues and the skilful structure of the first and third scenes, which are built along parallel lines, so that the conversation in the drawing-room every moment reminds the spectator in a startling and uncanny way of the conversation in the public house. Public houses henceforward become the frequent setting of Blok's poetry. It becomes full of wine, women, and gipsy song, and all this against a background of passionate despair and hopeless yearning after the irretrievably lost vision of "the Beautiful Lady." This state of passionate and hopeless disillusion is the atmosphere of all Blok's subsequent poetry. Only at rare moments is he seized and carried away from his slough of despond by the whirlwind of earthly passion. Such a whirlwind is reflected in [*Snezhnye maski (The Snow Mask)*], an ecstatic lyrical fugue.... (pp. 216-17)

Blok's genius reaches its maturity about 1908. The lyrics written between that date and 1916 are contained in the third volume of his collected poems [*Stikhi o Rossii*], which is, together with *The Twelve*, certainly the greatest body of poetry written by a Russian poet within the last eighty years. He was a man neither of great brains nor of great moral strength. Nor was he really a great craftsman. His art is passive and involuntary. He is a recorder of poetical experience rather than a builder of poetical edifices. What makes him great is the greatness of the poetical spirit that fills him, coming, as it were, from other worlds. He has himself described his creative process in one of his most remarkable poems, *The Artist* ..., as a purely passive process very much akin to mystical ecstasy as it is described by the great Western (Spanish and German) mystics. The ecstasy is preceded by a state of boredom and prostration; then comes the unutterable bliss of a wind from other spheres, to which the poet abandons himself, will-lessly and obediently. But the rapture is interfered with by "creative reason," which forces into the fetters of form the "light-winged, benevolent, free bird" of inspiration; and when the work of art is ready, it is dead to the poet, who subsides into his previous state of empty boredom.

In the third volume Blok's style pulsates with a more intense and nervous life than in his earlier work. It is more tense and full-blooded. But, as in his earlier work, it depends to such an extent on the "imponderables" of diction, sound and association, that all translation is hopeless. The more purely lyrical poems can be read only in the original. But another group of poems, more ironical and consequently more realistic, are less completely untranslatable. (pp. 217-18)

The gloom and despair expressed in his *Danse Macabre* are characteristic of most of Blok's poetry since 1907. Yet for a while, and intermittently, Blok seems to have discovered a ray of hope, which was to replace "the Beautiful Lady"; this was his love for Russia. It was a strange love, intensely aware of all that was base and vile in the beloved one, and yet reaching sometimes to veritable paroxysms of passion. The image of Russia identified itself in his mind with the Stranger—the mysterious woman of his dreams—and with the passionate and ambiguous women of Dostoevsky, Nastasia Filipovna (*The Idiot*) and Grushenka (*The Brothers Karamazov*). Another symbol and mystical counterpart of Russia became the snow-storm and the blizzard, which in *The Snow Mask* had been a symbol of the cold and scorching storms of carnal passion, and which forms the background of *The Twelve*. This Russian wind of passion is again associated with the songs of the gipsy choruses of Petersburg and Moscow. Many great writers (including Derzhavin, Tolstoy, and Leskov) had understood before Blok the lure and glamour of the gipsy chorus. . . .

Blok's love of Russia expressed itself in an acute sensibility for the destinies of his country, which sometimes verges on a genuine gift of prophecy. In this respect the lyrical fugue *The Field of Kulikovo* . . . is especially remarkable: it is full of dark and ominous presentiments of the great catastrophes of 1914 and 1917. (p. 220)

It is impossible to give any detailed enumeration of Blok's shorter poems written between 1908 and 1916. Suffice it to mention such unforgettable masterpieces as *Humiliation* . . . —the humiliation of venal love; *The Steps of the Commander* . . . , one of the greatest poems ever written on the eternal subject of retaliation; that terrible cry of despair, *A Voice from a Chorus* . . . , and *The Nightingale Garden* . . . more "classical" and austere in style than most of his lyrics, a symbolical poem, unexpectedly reminiscent of that other great symbolical poem, Chekhov's *My Life*. Apart from the lyrics contained in the third volume stand two longer works of the same period: the narrative poem *Retaliation* and the lyrical tragedy [*Rosa i krest (The Rose and the Cross)*].

[*Vozmezdie (Retaliation)*] was begun in 1910 under the impression of his father's death. It was planned to include three cantos, but only the first was completed. It is realistic in style and attempts to approach the methods of Pushkin and Lermontov. It is the story of his father and of himself, and Blok intended to make it a work of vast significance, illustrating the law of heredity and the consecutive stages of the disintegration of the Old Régime in Russia. Blok was unable to master his task, and the poem as a whole is not a success. But it contains many vigorous and beautiful passages. (p. 221)

[*The Rose and the Cross*] is more conventional and less immediately striking than anything Blok ever wrote. The scene is laid in Languedoc in the thirteenth century. The play is very well constructed and the lyrical quality of the poetry is on Blok's highest level. (p. 222)

The Bolshevik Revolution with all its horrors and all its anarchy was welcome to him as the manifestation of what he identified with the soul of Russia—the soul of the Blizzard. This conception of the Bolshevik Revolution found expres-

sion in his last and greatest poem, *The Twelve*. The Twelve are twelve Red-Guardsman patrolling the streets of Petrograd in the winter of 1917-1918, bullying the bourgeois and settling their quarrels among themselves for their girls, with the bullet. The figure twelve turns out to be symbolic of the Twelve Apostles, and in the end the Figure of Christ appears, showing the way, against their will, to the twelve Red soldiers. . . . [The poem serves as a] testimony to the essentially irreligious character of Blok's own mysticism. Those who are familiar with the whole of Blok's poetry will know that the name of Christ did not mean to him the same as it does to a Christian—it is a poetical symbol which has its own existence and its own associations, very different from those of the Gospels as well as from those of Church tradition. . . . [But] it is not its intellectual symbolism that makes *The Twelve* what it is—a great poem. The important thing is not what it signifies, but what it is. Blok's musical genius reaches in it its highest summit. From the point of view of rhythmical construction, it is a "miracle of rare device." The musical effect is based on dissonances. Blok introduces the rhythm and the diction of the vulgar and coarse *chastushka* (factory song) and draws from them effects of unutterable vastness and majesty. The poem is built with wonderful precision. It develops with a tremendous swing, passing from one rhythmical form to another, and fusing its dissonances into a superior harmony. In spite of its crude realism and of its diction bordering on slang, one is tempted to compare it with such another masterpiece of lyrical construction as *Kubla Khan* or the first part of *Faust*. (pp. 222-23)

In the same month as *The Twelve* . . . , Blok wrote [*Skify (The Scythians)*], a piece of intensely rhetorical invective against the Western nations for their not wanting to join in the peace proposed by the Bolsheviks. It is a powerful piece of eloquence but can hardly be called very intelligent, and is on an entirely inferior level as compared with *The Twelve*.

This was Blok's last poem. . . . His death became a signal for his recognition as a national poet of the first magnitude. That Blok is a great poet, there can be no doubt. But great though he is, he is also most certainly an unhealthy and morbid poet, the greatest and most typical of a generation whose best sons were stricken with despair and incapable of overcoming their pessimism except by losing themselves in a dangerous and ambiguous mysticism, or by intoxicating themselves in a passionate whirlwind. (p. 224)

> *D. S. Mirsky, "Blok," in his* Contemporary Russian Literature, 1881-1925 *(copyright 1926 by Alfred A. Knopf, Inc.; Canadian rights by permission of Alfred A. Knopf, Inc.), Knopf, 1926, G. Routledge & Sons, 1926, pp. 210-24.*

C. M. BOWRA (essay date 1943)

[Blok's *Verses about the Beautiful Lady*] are undeniably mystical and have even an Orthodox Christian air. They are poems of prayer, of meditation, of religious joy. The object of his devotions is, it is true, addressed in the language of love but of love so deeply respectful and devoted that it can hardly be intended for a human being. It has some parallel in Dante's cult of Beatrice, but is more formless, more instinctive, more emotional. Beatrice symbolises much that Dante honoured; the Beautiful Lady exists almost on the edge of consciousness, and is hardly even a vision. For the poet she absorbed his being and filled his verse. In it there are no clear outlines. All is mist and solitude, but in this vague world the poet waits anxiously for her, hears at dawn or sunset her footsteps in the infinite sky, feels her withdrawal into vast orbits of space, shuts his eyes or cries to her, hoping that she will answer him. There is no direct revelation, no contact. The poet hovers in rapt expectation on the brink of some unimaginable event. This is the poetry of a young man who concentrates all his thoughts and feelings on a single experience, a single hope. (pp. 146-47).

By the mysterious quality of his verse, by his symbols adapted to this middle state between dream and waking, by his cadences and choice of words for their expressive subtlety, Blok re-creates in his readers the indefinite emotions which he had for the Beautiful Lady. Valéry has said that a poet's task is simply to transfer to another his own state. That is what Blok does. Through his rhythms and the power of his words he conveys his own unique, extremely private state.

For Blok . . . the Beautiful Lady was not a poetic fancy but a real fact. She became almost a cult and aroused incalculable expectations. . . . [Blok] waited for some overpowering revelation to come. It never came. . . . The end of this extraordinary marvel was a turning-point in Blok's life and poetry. He had to make a fresh start, haunted by the gnawing conviction that he had been tricked, that he had failed in a task which had absorbed his whole being. . . . But because his attention was now turned to reality, because he knew the bitterness of defeat, the gain for his poetry was inestimable. He had been subtle and delicate; he became powerful and profound.

The contrast between vision and reality determined much of Blok's later poetry. . . . His second volume began with the words

Gone to the meadows, you will not return

and was his farewell to the Beautiful Lady. . . . He found substitutes for her, but they were not entirely satisfactory. In one of his most famous poems, *The Stranger* . . . , he paints a realistic scene of a pleasure resort near Petersburg. Here he sees a woman, entirely modern and fashionable in her clothing. He does not know if she is real, is fascinated by her, seems to look through a dark veil and see an enchanted horizon. He feels that he has a unique treasure, and that he alone holds the key. The vision certainly means much to the poet, despite the worldly setting and despite his own final admission that "Truth is in wine". The poem gives the contrast between his dream and the reality which he was beginning to know. But it is noteworthy that the dream is what really counts.

Blok's first reactions to his loss of the Beautiful Lady may be seen in his first lyrical plays. His natural gift for the drama was extraordinary. With no apparent preparation he created his own kind of play, intensely poetical and yet full of wit and irony. His dramatic world makes no claim to be realistic. Its characters are not tied down by the ordinary rules of behaviour or even of the physical universe. But the effect is brilliant, so brilliant indeed that we may not at first see the cruel spirit which informs the plays. In *The Puppet Show* . . . Blok produced a comedy of the old pantomimic kind with Pierrot, Harlequin and Columbine. Under its gay appearance it is a satire on Blok's mystical experiences. . . . What once meant so much to him, now means nothing. He can make fun of it and show how absurd it is. (pp. 147-49)

The irony of his plays had helped to assuage Blok's particular grievance about being tricked. In his lyrical poetry he still kept much of his old visionary self and Symbolist methods. Moving between contrasts of dream and reality he saw that he must still use symbols for what was still visionary, if not mystical, verse. But now he used them not for a single metaphysical scheme but because they conveyed his complex, often irrational states of mind. (p. 150)

With his mystical temperament Blok came more and more to find symbolical importance in things and to interpret ordinary happenings as instances of mysterious divine laws, and developed his Symbolism in new ways. He sees, for instance, a woman growing old in her hut after her daughter has died, sitting and sewing with needle and thread. The scene is perfectly simple, but in it Blok finds an ulterior meaning. The thread is associated with the thread of life, and through this the old woman is a symbol of the cosmic process which eternally fashions new shapes. This method could be extended, and in *Son and Mother* Blok uses it to great effect. The Son leaves his Mother for a glorious life, is persecuted and wounded and comes home to die. The myth stands for the poet who leaves his home for great adventures, suffers and fails and finds that in the end his only peace is at home. . . . The symbolical story is [Blok's] own. It tells of his romantic dreams, his sufferings and his final peace.

By 1909 Blok's new manner was complete. His whole style had changed. Diffuseness and vagueness have given place to a hard outline, an economy of effects and a boldness of imagery unique in Russian verse. The varied rhythms of his earlier verse are succeeded by more regular and more resonant forms. Blok now says in four lines what before took eight, and the concentration is a great gain. There is now little place for rhetoric or the lesser emotions. All is clear, grand, direct and powerful. (pp. 151-53)

Blok had found himself as a poet. . . . What he felt, he transposed into song so powerful and so direct that it is unique in this century. This poetry is entirely personal. Blok was not prevented by shyness or irony from writing in the first person about himself. In many of his poems there is a deep gloom, the result of his disillusionment. (p. 154)

Blok found various ways of escape from this numbing gloom. His powerful temperament swept him into most of the excitements known to the human soul, and much of this passed directly into poetry. He had a gift of seeing only one thing at a time and concentrating his powers on it. He is usually economical of imagery, but when his images come, nothing can withstand them. The brilliant pictures which he introduces lift the passions into the realm of pure art since they give exactly the right emotional note. Through them the poem finds its individuality, takes its readers by storm and makes them catch the poet's intonation. He places some compelling, concrete image as the keystone of a poem and makes it coordinate the lines and carry their weight. It contains what is most important and subdues the details to the unity of the main design. (p. 155)

No less remarkable than the power of presentation is the great range of subject, the endless variety of these poems. In his poems of love Blok has struck more chords than any writer of our time. What Yeats has done in depth and intensity, Blok has done in variety and range. No doubt he was helped by his lack of false shame and of other civilising qualities inimical to genius. (pp. 155-56)

[In Blok's] poetry there is often a variety of content, a movement from one mood to another, especially when Blok indulges the pleasures of memory and surveys in retrospect what has happened. His strong undeceived intellect did not shrink from contrasting the promise of a great occasion with its actual end. He can convey both the illusion which was once his, and his later knowledge of its falsity. Such a contrast need not imply any great hope or disaster. (p. 157)

[The] extremes of happy vision and dark gloom are to be [commonly] seen in Blok's . . . poetry. He was capable both of losing himself in a rapturous vision and of being crushed by cosmic despair. For each kind he found an appropriate style. The first called for his decorative gift, his use of the senses, the second for grand imagery of prophetic import. He knew what happiness was, especially in his imaginative life, and at such times he doubted the reality of the world about him. (p. 158)

At other times Blok looked out from his own depths onto the world and foresaw some fearful disaster ahead, far worse than anything he had suffered himself. At such moments he took on the full stature of a prophet who neither warns nor denounces but pities the victims of a cosmic disorder. In *A Voice from the Chorus* he warns his friends of the dark future that lies before them. . . . When he wrote these lines Blok was not turning his own defeats into a vision of universal disaster. This was his authentic insight into the future, his interpretation of the limited life, with its dramatised emotions and petty pretences, which he saw around him. (pp. 159-60)

Pity and tenderness, pity for a generation doomed to disaster, tenderness for those who cannot defend themselves against the blows of chance, these are outstanding qualities of Blok's poetry when he wrote in a prophetic vein. Abandoned by his dreams, he wrote from the excitements of his varied life and forgot his own disappointments in the sorrows of others. He looked on himself with dispassionate eyes. His poetry records his tempests and torments, but it is controlled by an intelligence singularly candid and free from prepossession. We feel no suspicion that he is ever dramatising himself in the cause of literature or adding anything for effect to the pure originating emotion. In his high creative moments he possessed a vision so vivid that he can call up almost any scene and present it to the inner eye. He often makes his point by some specially appropriate picture and sums up in it exactly what he feels. His imagination moved naturally in such scenes. (p. 160)

[In such] strong, straightforward poems [as *A Voice from the Chorus*], Blok's qualities have passed outside his own time and he writes, as great poets have written, of fundamental things in masterful words. (p. 161)

More than any Russian poet, more than any European poet of his time, Blok gives the impression of being literally inspired. The extraordinary originality of his poetry, its endless surprises and startling strength, its inexhaustible music, seem to have been given to him by some power outside himself and to owe little to painstaking workmanship. Even its occasional oddities, its turns of phrase or imagery which surprise by their quaintness, support the impression. Blok believed that a poet must trust in his visions and write in accordance with them. He was a mystic, a seer. The experience which he found in poetic creation was the fundamental reality to him. . . . He believed that a poet must write out of his intuition, his emotional and imaginative experiences,

that he must rid himself of the deceptive processes of logic and dialectic. . . . His poetry stands by its truth to his visions and to his feelings. It is a powerful record of a nature which felt deeply and saw clearly many secrets of the heart and soul. He was entirely faithful to his standards, and his poetry is always poetry, powerful to recreate in his hearers that almost audible music which he knew when inspiration descended on him and he lived outside time in a region of unspeakable joy. (pp. 178-79)

> *C. M. Bowra, "Alexander Blok," in his* The Heritage of Symbolism *(reprinted by permission of St. Martin's Press, Inc.; in Canada by Macmillan, London and Basingstoke), Macmillan, 1943, pp. 144-79.*

MARC SLONIM (essay date 1953)

'What is a poet? A man who writes verse? Of course not. A poet is the bringer of rhythm. And it is the waves of rhythm that direct the universe and the human spirit.' . . . 'At the beginning,' Blok contends, 'was Music. Music is the essence of the world. The world grows in resilient rhythms.' The poet is bound to clash with the multitude, the mob. Their clash is inevitable, and so is the destruction of the poet. He perishes—but this is only the breaking up of the instrument; the sounds continue to ring. In the history of mankind there are non-musical epochs, when the bark of matter is thick and heavy, and music is exiled to the nether regions. Then man is alienated, divorced from music. Revolutions, cataclysms change this situation and bring forth the spirit of music from prison and out into the open.

This philosophy determined the character of Blok's work. The precision of Pushkin's sensuous perception, the harmony between his eye and his ear explain in part the plastic quality of his imagery as well as the fullness and vitality of the older poet's work. Blok's hearing, however, was more perceptive than his sight. He was guided by sound and grasped its slightest nuances—and he renders in the changing tonalities of his lilting melodious verse a wide range of phenomena, from the forest's murmur to the storm's roaring. Most of his similes and symbols are of an auditory nature. It is also typical of him to speak of 'elemental' sounds: 'the wild howl of violins,' 'the tune of the wind,' 'the harps and strings of the blizzard.' The dynamic substance of the world is revealed to him in the polyphonic peals of thunder, in the surge of the surf.

Two other elements molded his style more specifically: the refined and highly literary tradition of the Symbolists, and the low trend of popular poetry. He borrowed from the Symbolists all the technical devices of musicality and often lapsed into that 'eloquence' which he at last came to reject and despise. His less successful poems are pale and wordy; they are no better than the verses of the average twentieth-century Symbolist poet. But when he abandons the nebulous eloquence of the Symbolists, the mellowness and passionate anxiety of his poems exhibit high individuality. Blok's lines are immediately recognizable by the flow of his euphonic rhythms, by his antithetic metaphors ('hot snowy sob,' 'resounding silence'), by his change of inflections, and by the emotional intensity, often poignancy, of his expressions. 'A poem is a canopy stretched on the sharp points of several words. Those words shine like stars,' he wrote, and this explains the parallel structure of his poems.

A poem by Blok is seldom a mere description, a narrative, or a statement: it is either an inner monologue or a conversational address, and this gives it its dramatic quality. Even in his odes, such as **'The Scythians,'** . . . Blok exhorts or threatens; the figure of speech and the exclamatory turn are everywhere. This strongly inflected and accented poetry (often with an uneven number of syllables in each line) incorporates not only the classic meters of which Blok was fond, but also the melody or the texture of the old drawing-room ballad, of folklore poetry, and of the gypsy song. . . . The lilting rhythms of the gypsy song, with its uneven beat and abrupt alternation of fire and melancholy, suited Blok perfectly; many of his best lyrics are a curious transposition of gypsy tunes into the moods, forms, and vocabularies of modern Symbolism.

The folklore ballad and the rollicking, racy quatrains of the streets, factories, and villages were also molded into refined lines, particularly in *The Twelve,* in which the popular and literary currents meet and merge into musical unity. This is . . . a deliberate attempt to achieve the reunion of two currents: that of the intelligentsia and that of the people—or, as Blok would say, of culture and of nation. This poet of the cleft spirit, who had passed from demonism to spirituality and had arrived through the squandering of his passions at the adoration of Beauty and the Motherland, is the personification and the culmination of Russian romanticism; in his sufferings, wanderings and contradictions he is a descendant of Lermontov. But like all Russian romantics—including Gogol and Dostoevsky—Blok was not satisfied with a truth that is above and beyond men. He looked for moral and social values he could assert in his life and in his poetry. Thus, in his own evolution, he repeated not only the development of Symbolism but of Russian literature in the nineteenth century. (pp. 206-08)

> *Marc Slonim, "Blok and the Symbolists," in his* Modern Russian Literature from Chekhov to the Present *(copyright © 1953 by Oxford University Press, Inc.; renewed 1981 by Tatiana Slonim; reprinted by permission of the publisher), Oxford University Press, New York, 1953, pp. 184-210.*

F. D. REEVE   (essay date 1958)

The poem [*Retribution*] is epic and lyric at once. It is description of a society's manners. It is the story of love between a series of two men, between fathers and sons, and between these men and their society. It is a psychological self-study of a liberal opposed to the history of his time. It is an effort to realize a man's consciousness in a self-generating—a "musical"—form. Morally, it is an analysis of the war that is revenge. (p. 176)

The poem's epigraph—*iunost'—eto vozmezdie* (Youth—that is retribution)—comes from one of Solness's speeches in the Russian translation of *The Master Builder.* "The younger generation—it means retribution," Solness says to Hilda in the first act and keeps repeating throughout the play. . . . Ibsen's play is a passionate attempt to penetrate the psychological masks of the obsolete mind of a powerful man, a mind and a man supported by status and profession but challenged by the impulsive, intuitive brilliance of actuality.

The penultimate line of *Retribution*—"Than the *quantum satis* of Brand's will"—refers to what Ibsen intended as a great poem. Ibsen's [*Brand*] is a poem of ethics and passion, an

innovation to which Blok considered his poem more than adequate successor. Ibsen's is a national poem, the epitome of a society, of an era, and of a consciousness, which Blok, fifty years later, thought he readvanced (that is, refined, redefined, and reanimated). The antibureaucratic protest Ibsen makes in *Brand* Blok makes more pervasively—bureaucracy being by then more pervasive—in *Retribution*. Ibsen said, as Jaeger quotes him: "The State crushes Individuality; away with the State. . . . Undermine the notion of the State, let free will and spiritual affinity be the only recognized basis of union, and you will have a liberty worthy of the name." This represents Blok's politics not only in *Retribution* but also in other poems. . . . The name Brand is an obvious identification of the rebel, the new prophet of "being oneself," as given in *Peer Gynt* also. Ibsen said, "I have studied men and human fate and drawn the philosophy out of them for myself." Blok argued that, by the objectivity of his poem's masks, he had made the same understanding of experience.

The irony in Blok's poem is reinforcement of the perceptions of that conciousness which requires faith but finds none available. An example of it is Blok's use of Brand's tag "quantum satis," which Blok ties in with the will of God and the over-all plan of the world. It is a dramatic tag; it functions as the priestly or professional label; it identifies that bourgeois satiety which Blok, like Ibsen, hates; it marks the child of sin and, therefore, a child lost or at least a victim, a sacrifice; it equally suggests the effort to penetrate frustration in the name of self-validation. The complexity of life requires more real responses than the assertion of ego or merely political protest. The meaning, unlike the perceptible beauty, is a remote artifact, the object of this poem. (pp. 179-80)

The poem is, like Pushkin's *Evgenii Onegin,* a portrait of a society and its most representative individualities bound and exposed, like the poem itself, in terms of all their qualifying properties and modified by the possibilities presented by narration as a literary form and by the lyric expression following as necessity from the poet's alienation. The poem is a study of the meaning of a society as revealed in its essential manners. The poem's success continues to be the similarity between it and its referents. (p. 182)

Retribution is shaped by the rhythmic recurrence of themes and variations. Lexical repetitions, repeated images and metaphors (especially of light, color, size, shape, and time) as in all Blok's poems, help establish the pattern. Unlike his other poems, however, this poem is built on the combination of variations of iambic meter and the idea of the mazurka rhythm, which Blok described in preparing the poem as a series of three triplets and a final two-beat burden: tsýnt-syrny—tsýntsyrny—tsýntsyrny—tsytsy. Each chapter is, or was to be (the second chapter was never written) a three-movement tone poem in which the first movement presents the dominant theme and the burden is interposed as either a lyric or rhetorical contrast to the syncopated development of the dramatic and narrative themes. In narrative or descriptive passages, the iambic meter approaches conversational rhythms. The syntax is colloquial, and the verse, which throughout the poem is not organized in formal stanzas, tends to form paragraphs. . . . (p. 184)

[The mazurka is] a mobile and infectious dance music. . . . It has beauty, opulence, speed, elegance, and ebullient passion. . . . The movement of the mazurka is an analogy to the movement of history, a developing spiral of moments always moving toward the present in which choice and judgment are real: "The life of the old is going down."

The introduction to *Retribution* is a warning on how to read the poem: namely, one should read it, as if experiencing music, as a response, alien to its provocation, which assumes in its emotional order reality of events and the moral efficacy of a nonlogical form. In other words, we are warned against a nondramatic reading of a formally lyric poem. In this sense, the poem, like any moral narrative, is an extended effort to define the assumptions epitomized arbitrarily by the title. Locating the title in its context takes us to drama. (p. 187)

The "musical" organization of events establishes satisfactory aesthetic correspondences but not necessarily ethical or philosophic. The musical organization is incapable of organizing such an expanse of thoughts and things. Also, the fact that the author is the protagonist, in some places technically and in others emotionally, limits the poem to lyric experience. That is, the poem's dramatic material does not contain self-sustaining images that infallibly transmit the equivalent of the required emotion. There are symbols in the poem, but, like the figure of the father or the semivisualized concept of retaliation, they are bundles of meaning or perceptions or interpreted emotion. The chief limitation of the poem is the limitation of the lyric attitude of a half-illusioned idealist who, because there is no community of values on which he can rely and because he is not in a position to invent a system, cannot extend the essential drama of experience beyond the modes which he discovers in himself. Although he presents them objectively in his poem, as if eliminating his personality through his art, the delimited frame of reference continually forces him back on himself. What may on the surface seem to be self-celebration is actually only a use of self as agent in an aesthetic attempt to expunge the self in definition of a real, transcendent, meaningful scheme.

The first line of *Retribution,* a kind of epigram, moves us to dramatic experience itself—

Life is without beginning or end.

—provided we follow it, as Blok does, as closely as possible into an experience of life. Unlike us, the artist is required, the poem says, to believe in beginnings and ends and to describe the indifferent environmental forces that, if unopposed or uncontrolled ("chance," line two, versus "hell and heaven," line seven), prevent meaning. The poet is judge, and his art is conscious standard. Intuition is irrelevant after the fact, which is the poem or any part, regardless of its involvement beforehand. By making beginnings and ends the poet creates something which cannot be wholly explained by anything prior to the poem itself. In . . . lines referring to the poet's responsibility, . . . Blok makes his attitude toward the poet's function and the function of poetry as concrete and as general as possible. Poetry is its own efficient form and content. Because a poem is the focus of all relevant experiences and the only center of meaning, the poem, like a fact, is what holds good for all observers. (pp. 188-89)

Blok intended *Retribution* to be a great poem. . . . The poem was to be an analysis of the habits and values of a nation at a turning-point in world history. . . . History is present in contemporary time. By studying a moment, one studies all previous moments also. History is terrible and inexorable. Like an ancient Greek, Blok believes that it is a personal force—he uses the second person singular—hostile or indifferent to individuals and, worst of all, unwinding into irrel-

evant details, into what seem to be "real" historical moments but are meaningless, harmless accidents. . . . Men and women behave like marionettes. Intellectually, they have run down, and the classical system demonstrating absolute value remains only as a "humanistic haze." Even war has become impersonal and, consequently, absurd. . . . The image of Roland and his horn symbolizes both the fallen hero and the impossibility of heroism after Roland's death.

Despite the restriction on meaningful life and communication, the poet wishes to make his poem large enough to break the restrictions. Roland, for example, is also a romantic figure. The world also is perceived as emotionally animated. . . . The romanticism is the romanticism of disillusionment, of the impotency of the individual by feeling or by reason to provoke response. One's job is limited to apprehending and properly interpreting the signs: . . .

> The terrible apparition up above
> Of a menacing and caudate comet.

Those signs are terrifying which, although ostensibly manufactured to help men, function in such a way that they can have no meaningful interpretation. Unlike the indifferent comets, . . .

> Why does the propeller, howling, cut
> The cold—and empty—fog?

The image is competent and complete. It is ineffable. The question is unanswerable.

We are encouraged to read the poem as being as "big as life" not only by its literary and political references and by the recurrent motifs from Blok's earlier work which are expanded in it, but also by its specific use of *Evgenii Onegin,* which Blok, by stylization in his own poem, wished to reinvoke for his reader. (pp. 191-92)

The parallel between *Retribution* and *Evgenii Onegin* is apparent in several general respects: "epic" presentation of an age in terms of generalized characteristics—the study of the meaning of social activity by confrontation of patterns and manners, human involvement in natural events, and the motion of a central individual within a social context; everyday detail and commonplace response to actualize central events of the poem; lyric and moral digressions from the plot; admixture of historical and national material; development of character from the author's viewpoint or as aspects of the author himself; use of the classic, Russian iambic tetrameter (including similar ironic or punning rhymes). At moments, both poets show a common attitude: in many descriptive passages, in which the personae are located by lyric description and moral judgement so that setting, actor, and meaning are perceived as interdependent; in asides; and in instructions to the reader. (pp. 193-94)

Pushkin's poem, basically classic in form and intent, tends to please; Blok's basically dramatic and skeptical, tends to teach. Pushkin tells two stories: one about a love quadrangle and one about his own artistic life. *Evgenii Onegin* is Pushkin's effort to guarantee his own social function as a poet and the social function of art. Blok had a moral provocation. He presents his information as a fable or a series of incidents pointed to the justification of his own sensibility and, by analogy, of meaningful life. The poem is Blok's effort to prove the importance of the existence of men. To do it he must go through what is trivial and irrelevant, as similarly Pushkin went through social gestures contradictory to the

values of art: superficial conversation, intellectual pretension, self-indulgence, conspicuous consumption, confusion,
selfishness, egotism, and merely arbitrary behavior designed
to conform to social norms. These unreal gestures become
real through the poems. Both poems take on further reality
by doubling back on the gestures with formal devices: puns,
irony, ambiguity, alteration of context, transfer of response
or of emotion, literary reference, and so on.

Essentially it is an issue of form. Blok wrote in his diary
toward the end of his life that "Classicism, as distinguished
from Romanticism and Naturalism, consists in the fact that
the observer is presented a firm carcass. Observers such as
myself, who know how to look, fit out this carcass with
various kinds of figures." *Evgenii Onegin* has a firm carcass
defined by specific metric, stanzaic, and structural organization. *Retribution* is organized on a principle of perception,
epitomized by the musical development of themes. It is less
formal than *Evgenii Onegin*. . . . (p. 194)

In *Retribution* the content—what the poem is "about," the
autobiography, the geography, and the history—are made to
stand for or to inform on a total understanding. . . . How
Blok proceeds from autobiographical description to a generalization in which the autobiographic moment takes on a
symbolic function is seen in the . . . passage about the father's
burial in Volia, a suburb of Warsaw, in a large cemetery also
called Volia—which means "will" or "freedom." . . . Blok
overcomes the limits of history by using a historical discovery
of reality, symbolized by the Copernicus statue in Warsaw,
which he takes as analogous to the one he himself is working
on. . . . Blok was overcome, and wanted his reader to be,
by the terrible indifference and power—the terrible void he
associates with Copernicus and Copernicus's brilliance—of
the world outside the self. To come to reality is to come, like
Hamlet, to revenge. . . . If to come to reality is to take revenge, then to hope is to have the continual possibility of
discovering another provocation and another method of satisfaction. Simplified, the "idea" seems conventionally Romantic—the self-justification of the individual against an indifferent, self-satisfied, and conventional world—and the
"images" of Copernicus, the chimera, the frozen cast-iron
world of the nineteenth century may be squeezed into representations of a conventional attitude. Left complex, as
given in the poem, the images work out among themselves
from image to idea the sense of horror that Blok identifies
as reality and that we must identify afresh. (pp. 195-97)

> *F. D. Reeve, in his* Aleksandr Blok: Between Image
> and Idea *(a revision of a thesis given at Columbia
> University in 1958; reprinted by permission of the
> publisher),* Columbia University Press, 1962, 268 p.

RENATO POGGIOLI (essay date 1960)

[No] modern poet has ever consecrated to [the cult of the
Eternal Feminine] so vast a body of poetry as the youthful
Aleksandr Blok. . . . Blok called the being whom his poetry
evoked, or rather invoked again, by the designation of Beautiful Lady, which is deceivingly simple, being at once mystical
and courtly, as well as chivalric and popular, in both sense
and tone. (p. 192)

Blok's first collection of poems takes its name from that icon
and is entitled *Poems on the Beautiful Lady*. . . . [The] spiritual
atmosphere throughout is one of expectation and initiation
rather than of mystical revelation. The Beautiful Lady is

surmised, rather than seen: she is not so much a presence
as a dream or a longing, a hope or a desire. All too often the
poet has no visions but forebodings; occasionally, he sees,
or better feels, portents and signs.

From a psychological, and perhaps also an aesthetic, standpoint, one might find natural the poet's inability to envisage
the ideal figure after which he strives. It is obvious that Blok
fails in the attempt to project and to reshape into reality the
phantasm he carries within himself. That phantasm is perhaps
but a reflection of the femininity of his own psyche; yet the
fantasy itself is rooted in innocence and purity. It would be
unfair to accuse Blok of perversion or morbidity; ghostly as
she is, the Beautiful Lady never takes such ambiguous and
perfidious forms as the Morellas and the Ligeias resuscitated
by the poetic necromancy of Edgar Allan Poe. A psychoanalytical critic might well see in the Beautiful Lady the
sublimation of a Narcissus complex. But the diagnosis would
be wrong, at least in literary terms: the childish naïveté of
Blok's mystical *Sehnsucht* is such as to dispel the suspicion
that his youthful muse is affected by decadent vices or decadent ills. Yet the very paradox of his first collection of
poems may be seen in the poet's failure to grasp or reach
that feminine image, to embody in the outside world what
Jung would call his *anima,* or the womanly archetype which
is rooted within his soul.

The whole of Blok's early verse is a realm of gleams and
shadows, flickers and *frissons,* resonances and hints. Its
mood and taste are not so much symbolistic as neoromantic.
(p. 193)

Blok does not fix the intellectual content of his inspiration
into firm images: rather, he dissolves that content into reverie
and fantasy, into the vague and fluid atmosphere of fancy
and dream. In this book he is the poet of the indefinite, rather
than of the infinite: even when he feels the presence or the
proximity of the Beautiful Lady he merely says that "somebody," or even "something," is beside or near him. Blok
sees shadows, not creatures or things: what he contemplates
is above all the reflection of his own dream. His psyche is
constantly in a state of trance, which never turns into full
rapture or transport. In brief, what motivates this poetry is
not a manly will to believe, but a sentimental impulse, a naïve
mystical wish. If Blok rests his faith mainly on ritual and
liturgy, it is because the ultimate grace of religious belief is
denied to him. . . . Often the poet prays not as one who
expects a miracle, or at least a sign, but as one afraid that
the miracle will fail, that the sign will never come. (p. 194)

The development of Blok's early poetry may be described
as a crescendo of incertitude and distrust. It is doubt, and
doubt alone, that dominates the inspiration of the poems
closing his first book. . . . What he now anticipates is not the
presence but the absence of the Beloved, not an imminent
revelation but an impending failure.

The *Poems on the Beautiful Lady* ignores the concrete world
of reality, and evokes in its place an unsubstantial aura, a
rarefied atmosphere. The images do not stand in clear and
firm outline against the sky, but waver and hover, bodiless
and shapeless, at midair. When we pass to Blok's second
book, *The Unexpected Joy,* however, we witness a change of
locale and climate, of vision and imagery. The change itself
is well suggested by the title of the opening cycle, "Earth's
Bubbles," which Blok took from the words by which Banquo
tries to explain away to Macbeth and himself the witches

who have just appeared and disappeared before their eyes. In this book, and especially in that cycle, the realm of shadows and fitful cross lights is thus replaced by a landscape which is a recognizable part of this earth, even if it is inhabited by creatures which are inhuman or nonhuman, by a spectral flora and a bloodless fauna.

The new landscape is but a transfiguration of the delta of the Neva, of that Petersburg countryside which looks like a Northern *campagna,* a desert spotted with marshes and lakes. Everything here is grassy and watery, humid and misty, fading and formless. From the unearthly Paradise of the first book we have now descended into a kind of limbo, halfway between life and death. Dreamland is now a marshland. Here, for the first time, the poet foreshadows the human and the worldly through animal legends and floral myths. (pp. 194-95)

Nothing could be more natural for the poet, as soon as he enters this world of fens and pools, to embody the Beautiful Lady in a vegetal fetish, in a pale flower of the bogs. Such a metamorphosis, which is also a metempsychosis, takes place in the long poem *The Night Violet.* (p. 195)

The full title of *The Night Violet* defines the poem as "a dream," while a poet's note claims that the poem is "the exact reproduction of an actual dream." The oneiric vision begins, however, as soon as the poet abandons the metropolis which appears at the beginning of the poem, and enters what is at once a marshland and a dreamland. The marshland itself exists also on this earth, not just in the geography of the mind: it is a real landscape as well as a mirage. There is no doubt that the subtitle of the poems alludes not only to the content of the vision, but also to the style of the composition, to the lullaby quality of its rhythms, to the poet's obvious intent to transcribe verbally the state of the psyche between sleeping and waking. Metrically, *The Night Violet* is one of Blok's most successful experiments in the field of free verse. Yet, despite its varying length, the line keeps an even and regular beat: hence the poem's impression of insistent monotony, like the sound of water dripping or the tick-tock of a clock.

The background of the opening lines is not so much the metropolis as its outskirts: a street or avenue where two men walk silently together. One of them is the poet, seeking escape from the prose of life, from the world of the city and of people, in that marshland that he apprehends as a dreamland. In a symbolic or mystical sense, one could say that the poet's is only a "vegetative soul." His companion is a wretched creature, consumed by blind impulses of the senses, and, as such, an "animal soul." Soon enough, he disappears alone into somewhere and nowhere, probably to play the beast. Allegorically speaking, these two figures are but a single person, and represent two parallel and different aspects of man. In a sense the poem presents from its very beginning one of Blok's main themes, that of the *dvojnik* or Alter Ego. . . . (pp. 196-97)

No sooner does the poet reach the region of the bogs than the metropolis suddenly fades away, with all its lights and shadows, from the horizon. It is now that the poet really enters that marshland which is also a dreamland: and he considers his entry therein not as a fancy of the mind or an illusion of the senses, but a spiritual awakening, as the sudden bestowal of a "second sight." Blok tells us that the revelation took place "when consciousness unclosed itself." Yet the new revelation does not imply a denial of the real world, the world of the city and daily life. The poet's attitude seems to be that of a double quixotism, now viewing the castles as if they were more real than the inns, and now the inns as if they were more real than the castles.

The dual vision of the poet distinguishes the two opposite spheres of his experience not only through the category of space, but also through the category of time. The city stands for "today," for a present from which to escape; the marshland, a "yesterday," or a past to go back as to a refuge. The symbolism of language describes the future as an ascent and the past as a descent in time. In the *Poems on the Beautiful Lady,* the dream was a beyond, an after, an *ultra.* Here the dream is rather a before, or an *infra.* One of the conscious motifs of this poem may well be the Platonic doctrine of knowledge as recollection and reminiscence, and its very locale brings to mind [Plato's cave]. . . . (p. 197)

This descent into the abyss of time is symbolized by the sudden discovery on the part of the poem's protagonist of all his remote ancestors, grouped together in a mysterious hut. . . . Thinking perhaps of both heredity and fate, the poet calls back from a buried and submerged past the creatures in whom his destiny and fate, his passions and dreams, were already sealed. . . . [One of these] is a young hero sitting in a corner, seemingly absorbed in a single idea, an all-pervading thought. The poet recognizes in him his spiritual Alter Ego, his "intellective soul." The young warrior is immovably chained to his ageless meditation, with "limbs made wooden by time. . . ."

Wood is but a petrification of vegetal life, and it represents here a form of being which endures by losing its very vitality. A dream which survives itself is like flesh ossified. Yet here too there is a living creature, who, in a world like this, cannot be but a flower. That creature is indeed both woman and flower. She is another incarnation of the Beautiful Lady: the only sort of incarnation possible in this underworld. The flower is colorless, and the woman without glamor. Here the Beautiful Lady is neither beautiful nor ladylike, but, as the poet says, "a homely maid, with an invisible face." It is through the very invisibility of her countenance, as well as through her name, Night Violet, that we recognize in this creature the nature or essence of a flower. . . . [By] stripping the traditional attribute of beauty from this new version of the Eternal Feminine he transfigures her into a strange and novel vision. The transformation of the Beautiful Lady into the Night Violet, into a flower of the bogs, is a concrete and literal metamorphosis, not merely an abstract allegory.

Such a metamorphosis, which reflects the poet's changed view of dream and reality, carries within itself a sad and a lucid message. What the poet seems now to imply is that dream-life too may be shallow and mean, vulgar and ugly, formless and faceless; that it may be a gray and dark prison no less than waking life. (pp. 198-99)

Blok's subsequent poetry was largely consecrated to the theme of man's existence within the walls of his modern prisons of stone and brick. To this theme he devoted an entire cycle of poems entitled *The City.* (p. 199)

Like a character from Dostoevskij's fiction, Blok now pursues the ideal of the Eternal Feminine among the creatures of the city, among the daughters of Eve, the slaves of fashion and sin. They too are flowers: flowers of evil. But in order that he may learn to rediscover his ancient ideal in those vessels of perdition and grief, the poet must first pass through the stages of another initiation; he must achieve that visionary state which Rimbaud sought to attain through *le dérèglement de tous les sens.* Blok achieves this state of grace through the cheapest and basest of all "artificial paradises": alcohol. It is alcohol that enables the poet to recognize for an instant a new incarnation of the Beautiful Lady in a feminine figure who momentarily appears before his bleary eyes in a public place, in a cheap café on the outskirts of the capital.

The transcription of this experience constitutes one of the most beautiful and perhaps the most popular of his lyrics, **"The Unknown Lady."** . . . Blok successfully expresses, even in the rhythm, that psychological state which Dostoevskij called *nadryv,* that feeling of "laceration" experienced by the human heart when torn between opposite forces, good and evil, foul and fair. The vulgar, impure atmosphere of the place is suggested with such evocative power that it brings to mind the art of Van Gogh, the greatest of the *fauves,* and especially such paintings as his "Café in Arles." Suddenly the apparition occurs. This time the woman is not a phantom or a vision, but a warm, living creature both hiding and revealing her soulless and sinful nature under her fashionable veils and ostrich feathers. But again, as in the case of the Night Violet, her countenance cannot be clearly seen. Yet we feel the presence of beauty, and it is in an attempt to capture that loveliness that the poet cries out, in a despair which is a longing to see and believe: "I know it: truth is in wine."

In the ensuing collections, Blok is the poet of the soul's perdition in what he calls, by the title of one of his new cycles, **"The Terrible World."** . . . Like many a Dostoevskian character, he now seeks redemption through degradation, by that mercenary love which is only the defilement of the self. (pp. 200-01)

Every so often oases appear even in Blok's "terrible world." Such is certainly the case with *The Nightingale Garden.* . . . The poem is a kind of legend or fairy tale, at once wise and naïve, designed for children and grown-ups alike. (p. 202)

Like all fables, *The Nightingale Garden* has its moral, although in remains unuttered. . . . Without daring to affirm that a work of art as pure as this contains a social message, one may still claim that here Blok translates poetically some of the ideas he had been expressing in his essays on the conflict between the Russian intellectuals and the Russian masses. By writing this poem Blok wished perhaps to proclaim that the homecoming of the artist was overdue, that the poet should finally return to earth and the world of man. This charming tale seems to say that the poet too is an artisan and a worker, and that he should not abandon for the sake of any dream . . . the poor, good-hearted Russian people.

The poet is now on the road that will lead him to the pieces which from the title of a later collection may be called the *Poems about Russia;* some of them are genuine songs of love for a fair and gentle motherland, sound and simple as a woman. It is Russia herself that now replaces Night Violets and Unknown Ladies, and with them all the other incarnations of the Eternal Feminine. (pp. 202-03)

Technically speaking, *The Twelve* is one of Blok's most perfect and mature works. A supreme harmony is achieved by way of a chaotic confusion, by means of an uninterrupted series of dissonances. Structurally, the poem is a succession of fragments of unequal length, varying greatly in meter,

diction, and tone. . . . Many a section is constructed like a mosaic, with the insertion and juxtaposition of factory songs, political slogans, and revolutionary refrains. . . . A series of sketches and vignettes acts as a prelude, producing the black-and-white effect of the opening scenes. A set of figurines appears and disappears in pantomimic tableaux, culminating in gestures and words that are in themselves diminutive dramas, microcosmic catastrophes. Everything seems to contribute to an impression of cinematographic technique, from the harsh chiaroscuro of the vision to the foreshortening of the perspective, from the interplay between backgrounds and foregrounds to the tempo of the action, from the sharpness of the images to the brutality of the plot. (p. 205)

[For] Blok the Revolution is not so much a messianic vision as an apocalyptic one. The poet views that upheaval not as a social and human catastrophe but as a cosmic cataclysm. This is the reason why he does not symbolize the Revolution in the traditional image of fire, of a flame that burns and destroys but also lights and warms. Ice alone is the proper emblem for the demonic and monstrous, for all those blind and chaotic forces which are neither divine nor human. . . . In many of the poems he had written in the preceding years Blok had already asserted that life was identical with cold and winter. Now he tells us that history is prehistory: that in the natural history of man we are still in the ice age. Hence the symbolic significance of Russia, which becomes a Siberia of the spirit. Like Sleeping Beauty, Russia lies in a desert of frost, under a quilt of snow.

It is evident that even the final appearance of Christ reflects the same vision of life as a frozen wasteland. Here the Saviour manifests Himself as a kind of Snow Guest. Blok may have been led to such an image or intention by the heterodox theology of Rozanov, who saw in the Father a solar god, and in the Son a lunar deity, pale and cold, virginal and sterile. But the Christ of *The Twelve* is Blok's unique creation, even though he may recall the Jesus of Tjutchev, treading on the soil of Holy Russia and blessing that soil with His hand. This identification of Christ with Russia may well explain why the Son of God is here but another embodiment of Blok's feminine conception of the divine: a novel mask or disguise for the Beautiful Lady, or at least for the "Virgin of the Snows."

Any disrespectful interpretation of this feminine metamorphosis of the figure of Christ would be not only in bad taste, but also false. It is true that here the Savior wears a wreath of white roses rather than a crown of thorns. And it is also true that the halo surrounding His head is made not of bright rays, but of pale snowflakes. But man always conceives of the divine in his own image, and the poet has mirrored himself and his sense of life in the sacred image painted by his hands, in this icon of a bloodless and frozen God. Yet by doing so Blok simply reveals his ability to turn to his advantage some of the traditional details of the Orthodox iconography of the Saviour. The image so produced is distorted; yet in this case we have to do not with the "deformation" of Decadent or advance-guard painting, but with the stylization of Gothic or Byzantine art. The femininity of His effigy gives the person of Christ a feeling of immaculate purity, a sense of inaccessible spirituality. The Redeemer is here not the Lamb but the Dove. The complexity of this figure tends to prove that Christ's final appearance is no mere *deus ex machina.* Jesus does not intervene in order to calm the troubled waters: here He too is wind and storm. What His visitation means is that Jesus is present everywhere, in nature and history, even where and when men hoist flags which do not carry the sign of the Cross. Yet by marching before the Red flag He seems to say *In hoc signo vinces* to every man of good will. He is the great fisher of souls; behind Him, blindly and unknowingly twelve Red Guards become his vicars on earth. No man except the poet is aware of His presence, yet the artist, like Leonardo painting the Last Supper, was unable to draw the face of the Lord. The reason for this failure may well be that the poet could not avoid putting even this last epiphany to the test of doubt. During one of the moral crises of the last years of his life, Blok alluded to the Christ of *The Twelve* in words that reveal his awareness of the ambiguity of that figure: "sometimes that feminine ghost is deeply hateful even to myself. . . ." In this avowal there is also the acknowledgment that the feminine being, half-divine and half-human, that had haunted him all his life, from beginning to end, had been a nightmare as well as a dream. (pp. 207-08)

> Renato Poggioli, "Aleksandr Blok," in his The Poets of Russia: 1890-1930 *(copyright © 1960 by the President and Fellows of Harvard College; excerpted by permission), Cambridge, Mass.: Harvard University Press, 1960, pp. 179-211.*

HELEN MUCHNIC (essay date 1961)

[Blok] had no desire for popularity, but neither had he any patience with "pure aestheticism," and he frequently expressed such sentiments as the following:

> I fear every manifestation of the tendency of "art for art's sake," because such tendencies contradict the very essence of art and because in following it we would, ultimately, lose art. For it is born of the eternal interaction of two strains of music—the music of the creative individuality and the music which sounds in the depths of the people's soul, the soul of the *masses*. Great art is born only of the union of these two electric currents. . . .

And so, although his poems, like those of other Symbolists, are allusive, mysterious, evocative, although they make use of private imagery, and convey the indeterminate meanings of music rather than the precise ones of logic, the "dead poets, his ancestors" who "assert their immortality" in his lines are the readily understandable Pushkin, Gogol, and Dostoevsky, rather than the "difficult" Baudelaire, Verlaine, or Mallarmé. Not method so much as aesthetic purpose and moral conviction distinguish him from the masters of French and English Symbolism. Unlike Baudelaire, he was not driven by a desire to escape banality and shock the philistine; unlike Verlaine, he was not absorbed in sensations; unlike Mallarmé, he was charmed neither by obscurity nor the urge to express nonexistence. And Pater's famous phrase, "Not the fruit of experience, but experience itself is the end," could not have been his credo. It was neither experience nor its fruits that he was after, but Truth, some permanent, eternal value that might lend meaning to experience. Obscurity seemed to him a mark of vanity or of poetic deficiency, as he says in one of his early poems, drawing a distinction between the laureled "singer" of strange songs who delights in misty verse, and "the poet," whose goal is Truth, and whose reward is not a laurel wreath, but the glimpse of unknown light beyond new horizons. (pp. 175-76)

But the fundamental difference between Blok and other modern Symbolists is this: that whereas their perception was based on a sense of irreconcilable dualities—"the absolute laws of the mind and the limiting contingencies of life" for Valéry, existence and nonexistence for Mallarmé, Earth and the Beyond for the early Yeats—Blok's derived from an innate sense of wholeness, a feeling for a unifying principle that he called "music."

> In the beginning was music. Music is the world's essence. . . . Culture is the musical rhythm [through which the world grows]. . . . The whole brief history of man, that has remained in our poor memory, is, it would seem, the alternation of epochs—in one of which music dies down, sounds muffled, to gush forth with willful pressure in the one that succeeds it.

So he wrote in his diary in 1919, and developed this theme in "The Decline of Humanism," making explicit what all his work had said by implication, emphasizing, as Tolstoy had done in a different way, the reality of the unanalyzable *substratum* of existence, the matrix of life and the motion of the universe which man's mind cannot grasp, although his whole being is intuitively aware of it.

Blok's attention was centered primarily on the "music" of his emotions, and in his work he found concrete visual equivalents and rhythms to express it. If genuine lyricism is a translation of initial, recondite experience that has no language of its own, Blok's initial experience is the powerful and undirected flux and reflux of emotion, which seems limitless in strength, depth, and duration, principally because it is in essence aimless and larger than its cause. . . . Like Mallarmé, and other Symbolist poets, he sought to transmit what was "hardly expressible," but unlike the others, he did not see the "hardly expressible" as the fleeting and the momentary, but on the contrary as the universal and enduring. Music and imagery were to him something other than a means of suggestion or evocation. He had no such theory as Mallarmé's, that poetry must never *paint* but only *allude* to objects, and that its proper dominion was not creation or statement, but the unveiling of the interconnections between aspects of things. And if his poetry is also a study in relations, there is this difference between it and that of the French Symbolists: that the end of this study Blok conceived to be not an understanding of interconnections but a metaphysical insight that such understanding could yield. What gave him joy was not the pattern of relations itself, but knowledge of what lay back of them, meaning rather than emotion, insight rather than pleasure. He believed in the reality of the imperceptible and the unattainable, and the significance of his life lay in his quest of this; but, unlike Valéry, he was not afraid to realize a dream lest the delight of dreaming vanish, and unlike Mallarmé, he had no desire to express the existence of non-existence. Mallarmé's, theory was the product of an analytic turn of mind of a kind that was distasteful to Blok, whose whole bent was away from the questioning, the skeptical, the rational—which accounts for the immediate, dramatic quality of his lyrics and the clear-cut lucidity of his images, which have nothing of the intermelting mobility of Mallarmé's. For Blok did not value indefiniteness, and the effect of melting and fusing in his poetry is not designed—not even in *The Snow Mask*—to emphasize imprecision but to create an impression of exactitude, just as the frequent extravagance of his imagery is not merely rhetorical but appropriate to the turbulence it symbolizes. His method was direct rather than allusive; his whole attitude tended toward affirmation rather than denial; and the symbols in which he wrote were the expression not of aesthetic theory but of a kind of habit of soul, an emotional and intellectual predisposition to see disparate elements as units. Thus the essence of life *was* music to him, not *like* music; his bride not *like* the Beautiful Lady but, actually, her earthly aspect; an Enchantress was Fate, or a shooting star.

Blok was never consumed, as Valéry had been, for example, with the "mad desire to understand." The mad desire that consumed him was to attain something which he knew existed, without the help of thought; and if Valéry, in the words of Marcel Raymond, sang "a hymn of gratitude to the forces which are active only in the shadow," Blok extolled forces of mystery that were revealed to him in a blinding light. There is something primitive in his sense of the fusion of the natural and the supernatural, in the way the hardest actualities of earth are to him translucent, as if permeated by the light from the realm of the Beautiful Lady. (pp. 177-79)

The cadences and images of Blok's poetry are an intimate revelation not only of this fundamentally nonanalytical, affirmative quality of his nature, but of the very traits of temperament that must have shaped it, the pattern itself of his personality which, through varied modulations, displays an essential consistency from the beginning to the end, from the *Verses on the Beautiful Lady* to "The Scythians." All through, like the tempests of his poems blowing over an indestructible land, the forces of passion and of enduring calm weave the basic design of his life and of his poetry: the onward rush and circular return in the rhyme scheme of his early lyrics; the mounting waves of struggle that fall from crest to trough in the poems of 1907; the moments of infatuation—with Faïna, Carmen, and the Revolution—followed by periods of dejection; and always, throughout the tension and the lassitude, there remains the devotion to Russia, to the Beautiful Lady, and to Lyubov Dmitrevna, always beneath the raging variations there breathes a lasting quietness, as intense as the moment of passion. (pp. 179-80)

His poetry reconciled the antagonisms of his nature, and its imagery is as organic as its rhythms—the visual counterpart of the musical ebb and flow that unites the romantic and realistic aspects of his vision, as his cadences combine violence and calm. Thus the shrines and trappings of chivalric romance, which stand for desires beyond those life can satisfy, occur along the roads of a familiar landscape; the fires and abysses of wildest Romanticism, which symbolize mad passions, flame and yawn on city streets; the ships of thought come sailing into imaginable harbors; the bewitching Stranger retains her mystery in an ordinary restaurant; [and] Christ leads men through an actual blizzard in a real city. . . . And so close were the instruments of poetry to his thoughts and feelings, to his intuitive apprehension of life, that Blok could think of them as the language itself of historic periods. Thus, for example, having drawn a picture of the age of which he was writing in *Retribution,* he explained as follows his selection of the meter for it: "The simplest expressions of the rhythm of that epoch, when the world, preparing itself for unheard-of events, was so intensively and continually developing its physical, political and military muscles, was the *iamb.*" Could anyone but Blok perceive a whole epoch in terms of pulsations, and these as equivalent to a poetic meter? (pp. 180-81)

Blok has often been called a mystic and a prophet, but it seems to me that he was not a mystic at all. . . . His poetry is hardly the poetry of trance or vision, nor of "spiritual revelation," and only occasionally, like "Kubla Khan," the product of "unconscious cerebration." It is the result, rather, of a habit of ardent, exclusive concentration on the remote reaches of the self, a listening to its most secret motions, and the skill to reproduce these motions in language that renders them in their complex rhythms, colors, forms, and suggested meanings. It is as if the Platonic archetype had here become the middle term, not the origin of the creative process; and ultimate reality, not universal ideas but private experience— a characteristically Russian process that one is tempted to call Platonic Realism. Nor is there anything mysterious or miraculous in the way some of his poems seem to foretell the future. In their "prophetic" aspect, they are, really, statements of desires or fears that were fulfilled in his life. For little of importance happened to Blok through chance alone, and if his life seemed sometimes to have imitated art, it was only proof that his desires as poet were urgent, and his will as man was strong. (pp. 181-82)

Helen Muchnic, "Alexander Blok" (originally published in somewhat different form in The Russian Review, *Vol. 12, No. 1, January, 1953), in her* From Gorky to Pasternak: Six Writers in Soviet Russia *(copyright © 1961 by Helen Muchnic; reprinted by permission of Random House, Inc.), Random House, 1961, pp. 104-84.*

VICTOR ERLICH (essay date 1964)

[In the essay] **"The Soul of a Writer"** Blok insisted that the earmark of a literary artist is the incessantly intent inward hearing, the ability to listen to a distant music. . . . [On] February 11, 1913, he wrote in his diary: "The morality of the world is unfathomable and quite different from what is usually meant by this word. What makes the world go round is music, passion, prejudice, power." The same note was sounded in one of the latest entries: "In the beginning was Music. Music is the world's essence. Culture is the musical rhythm through which the world grows."

These persistent intimations were borne out by Blok's life as actually lived and as stylized in his lyrical verse. The driving force of this *agon* is the view of poetry as an act of total (i.e., rapt, unceasing, strenuous) listening to elemental rhythms surging below, a view in which the spirit of music and the motif of self-sacrifice are fused organically. The bulk of Blok's poetic achievement adds up to a *sui generis* passion play about the poet's self-imposed ordeal. The three acts of the drama correspond to three successive phases of the chief protagonist's never-ending search for salvation. (pp. 102-03)

"The Fair Lady," "The Stranger" and **"The Native Land"** sequences, held together as each of them is by the unity of the love object, can be said to represent respectively: a) seraphic innocence, b) self-destructive, Dionysian eroticism and, c) an ambivalent, guilt-ridden involvement with Russia's national destiny.

It is essential to note that at each juncture we are dealing with erotic poetry, though the target varies drastically from period to period. The theme of love, or rather of being-in-love remains constant. "Infatuation," a very inadequate English equivalent of *vliublennost',* is characteristically one of Blok's favorite words. It serves as the title for two poems written during his middle period. The mistily romantic 1905 poem whose opening line is "The princess lived on a high mountain," proclaims being-in-love as the poet's destiny, the law governing his life. (p. 103)

[The esoteric "Fair Lady"] appears in Blok's early verse within a fairy-tale setting, now as a mysterious maiden, now as a princess living in an enchanted castle upon a snow-capped mountain peak. Whatever the guise, she is invariably exalted, inaccessible—a legend rather than a blood-and-flesh woman, an object of timid adoration and futile longing. All that remains to the younger worshipper is to burn incense and to wait for a miracle.

The tenor of this disembodied love poetry is one of enraptured anticipation of "love and agony." . . . The fear which we detect in [certain] lines is not one of rejection, of being spurned by the Fair Lady, if and when she deigns to appear, but of disenchantment or betrayal. It is a metaphysical, a religious doubt. The vague yet insidious presentiment that the long-awaited encounter would lead to a tragic let-down may well have been a projection of the poet's growing sense of his own unworthiness and corruptibility. . . . Blok's apprehension was borne out. . . . In such cycles as **"The City,"** and later, **"The Terrible World,"** the landscape of the poet's soul undergoes a drastic transformation. The medieval ballad-like settings are supplanted by sordid, tawdry, urban imagery—"taverns, by-streets, electric nightmares" of a vice-ridden, teeming metropolis.

Apparently the quivering innocence of the first period could not be sustained. In the process of a painful maturation of the man and the poet, the adolescent worship of the Fair Lady had to give way to a more complex and tragic vision of life and love where mysticism alternates with blatant realism, intermittent bliss of being-in-love with blasphemous irony and self-mockery, Dionysian intoxication with a spiritual hangover. The moments of total surrender to a dark passion, of a near-complete breakdown of ego controls, at once irresistibly tempting and terrifying, are objectified in one of Blok's most haunting poems, in an image of a charger racing across a bottomless pit. . . . The aftermath is apathy, stupor, self-disgust. (pp. 104-06)

Yet this phase could not last indefinitely either. . . . He needed an escape from lyrical isolation, a way out of narcissism into the wide open spaces of a great national theme. Thus a new myth is born, and with it a new lyrical cycle, **"The Native Land."** . . . In 1908 a new feminine symbol starts haunting Blok's poetry, now alternating with, now superseding, a Carmen or a Mary. Her name is Russia. Georgii Adamovich, the dean of Russian *émigré* critics, observed judiciously that Blok's Russia was a metaphysical entity rather than a cultural or political actuality. One might add that in Blok's verse, **"The Native Land"**—be it the "beggared Russia," "the drunken Russia," or "my fatal country"—is an idiosyncratic, personal myth or, to put it differently, another female protagonist in Blok's lyrical drama, another object of a fervid and ambivalent passion.

In Blok's early verses the motif of Russia appears within a quasi-Slavophile *ambiance*. "Rus'" is an epitome of purity, an object of reverence—in short, a Fair Lady writ large. Yet the heroine of Blok's civic poems in the decade immediately preceding the Revolution is neither the radiant maiden nor the traditional "Mother Russia." Instead, she is a wife . . . or, more frequently, an ardent wild mistress, a Carmen with

Tartar eyes. Not unlike Gogol or [Fyodor] Tiutchev, Blok is irresistibly drawn to Russia thus stylized in spite of, if not because of, her failings. The murky romance can be strained yet it will not be destroyed either by Russia's bleakness and poverty—qualities which the mid-nineteenth-century Slavophiles hailed as proof positive of their country's truly Christian essence—or, for that matter, by the tawdry or meretricious traits which the image of the native land occasionally displays. At times the poet seems to chafe at the bit as he rails against the savagery and primitivism of his accursed lover. . . . Yet the revolt remains futile and short-lived. The fatal bond will not be broken. For one thing, the very darkness, so abhorrent to the poet's "free soul," holds an irresistible attraction to his id—the irrational, Dionysian, self-destructive facet of his psyche. For another thing, the Symbolist poet's determination to listen, whatever the cost, to the discordant music of the elements is compounded here by an acute sense of social responsibility strongly tinged with an upper-class sense of guilt vis-à-vis the people.

This anguished social awareness assumed an increasingly important role in Blok's writings during the last pre-revolutionary decade, especially in his controversial essays and lectures. In **"The Intelligentsia and the People,"** **"The Elements and Culture,"** **"Three Questions,"** he keeps sounding the same dark warning. The world in which we live is a castle built on sand. The Russian intellectual dwells in a fool's paradise: his sheltered world is precarious and doomed. (pp. 107-08)

[Blok's] Cassandra-like utterances stirred a lively controversy among the Russian literary elite. The acid poet-critic, Zinaida Gippius spoke somewhat disparagingly of Blok's cryptic stammering. Fëdor Sologub, one of the older Symbolist poets and a distinguished novelist, opined: "Blok is wise when he writes verse, but he is not so wise when he attempts to write prose." (p. 109)

These criticisms were not altogether unwarranted. Clearly the discursive mode was not Blok's forte. His natural element was music rather than logic. In precision, rigor and cogency Blok's expository prose was vastly inferior to [Valery] Briusov's, [Vyacheslav] Ivanov's or [Andrey] Belyi's in his most sober moments. In fact, Blok could not effectively argue with his opponents since even as an essayist he dealt in lyrical metaphors rather than in concepts. He could merely project a mood, a stance, a vague presentiment.

Yet this was only part of the story. On balance, some of the literati may have been a bit too hasty or complacent in rejecting his urgent message. The author of **"The Twelve"** was not a sustained thinker, but he was admittedly a superb listener. His single-minded dedication to music entailed an uncanny alertness to the rhythms of history. In Blok, the faculty which Lionel Trilling has called the "imagination of disaster" was developed to the highest possible degree. No poet of the Silver age gave a more striking expression to the "ever-present sense of catastrophe," the brooding anticipation of an impending cataclysm. (pp. 109-10)

There is an element of irony in Blok's impassioned dialogue with his contemporaries. A visionary in quest of a miracle, of a personal salvation, an introspective lyrist who saw in poetry primarily a projection and a vehicle of a unique creative personality, Blok was the very epitome of Romantic individualism. Yet few of his programmatic essays written during the fear- and hope-ridden decade of 1908-18 fail to contain a scathing attack on the individualistic fallacy.

Is it necessary to urge that this apparent contradiction was fully consistent with Blok's notion of the artist's calling? If, as he argued in his 1908 essay, "the poet's soul must move the contemporaries by the sincerity of his self-sacrifice," is not the creator's sacred duty to renounce his supreme values, to deny himself the satisfaction of his fundamental emotional and ideational needs? The motif of self-immolation acquires a special poignancy on the eve of the Revolution when Blok declares his readiness to surrender unconditionally the rarefied culture, of which he was one of the finest products, to the elemental rhythms of an imminent cataclysm. (pp. 111-12)

> Victor Erlich, *"The Maker and the Seer: Two Russian Symbolists," in his* The Double Image: Concepts of the Poet in Slavic Literatures *(© 1964, by The Johns Hopkins Press), The Johns Hopkins University Press, 1964, pp. 69-119.**

JAMES B. WOODWARD (essay date 1968)

Blok regarded the creation of a poetic work as an act of total sacrifice. It signified to him complete self-abdication to forces infinitely more powerful than the individual, to that 'elemental music' of universal life which . . . he compared to a wind blowing from worlds which lie beyond the perception of the ordinary mortal, but which are revealed to the poet in his moments of inspiration. A few months before his death he wrote in his diary: 'The poet is the bearer of a rhythm. In the infinite depths of the human spirit, which are beyond the reach of morality, law, society and the state, move soundwaves akin to the waves embracing the universe. . . .' Repeatedly he emphasized that constant receptivity to this 'cosmic music' was an unfailing condition of the writer's existence, for true art, he claimed, is itself the voice of the elements, a reflection of 'elemental, natural rhythms'. Expressing himself, as was his custom, in vague, metaphorical images, he defined the poet's mission and *raison d'être* as the restoration of the 'creative rhythm' from which the modern world had become divorced and without which life stagnates and disintegrates. He urged the poet to seek this 'rhythm' wherever it might reveal itself—in art, in erotic passion, in revolution, on every level of life, whether it be good or evil, for, as he put it in [his diary] . . . the source of both God and the Devil is the one Simple Unity and the extremes of good and evil are part of the same Infinity. In his quest for the infinite the poet must place no limit on his demands on life. Like Dante, he must pass through the circles of Hell and feel the flames on his cheeks. (pp. 2-3)

But all the torment, anguish, and tedium of the unrelenting search, which are reflected so vividly in Blok's verse, were more than compensated by the sensation of timeless rapture which came to him with the brief flashes of insight, when chaos was transformed into harmony and he felt himself transported into a world beyond that of contingent affairs. . . . [The] actual experience of such moments of creative vision was of far greater importance to him than the concrete poetic forms in which they were crystallized, and this experience became the basis of his metaphysical system. Yet he himself was aware that without the protection of poetic discipline his personality could hardly have survived the recurrence of this ecstatic type of experience, and the despair, self-contempt, and sense of anticlimax which invariably ensued. 'I strive increasingly to strengthen artistic form', he wrote in August 1912, 'because for me (for my "ego") it is the only defence.'

In poetry he found a refuge from the irrational forces which imperilled his sanity and a purpose which gave meaning to his life. (p. 3)

The normal, referential function of language is of secondary importance to the symbolist poet. His main concern is with the emotional, connotative or allusive power of the word, and in his verse he seeks to enhance this power at the expense of its conventional meaning in order to communicate his individual vision of the Absolute. It follows, therefore, that one of the fundamental devices of symbolist poetry is metaphor, or, more specifically, the type of metaphor which forms a symbol, i.e. one which offers an insight into the transcendental world of the poet's vision.

No Russian symbolist made greater use of metaphor than Blok or went as far as he in the process of emancipating it from the norms of logical or conceptual language. (pp. 19-20)

The unity of most of Blok's lyrics derives not from any thematic framework but from their centralization in a specific emotion or mood generated by the choice and juxtaposition of words and images, by the rhythm and sound of the verse, and by the interchange of intonations. Various structural devices were used by Blok to reinforce the emotional unity of his poems, and one of the most important of these is, . . . in rhetorical terminology, epanadiplosis. In the simplest terms, it denotes the repetition of the beginning at the end, and it was used to enclose both individual stanzas and entire poems. (p. 21)

[Blok's] predilection for repetitive devices, which partly reflects the influence of popular poetry, was shared by all the symbolists. They regarded them as a vitally important means of enriching the musical quality of their verse. Repetition (often consecutive) is also used by Blok to heighten the emotional tone of a poem. . . . (pp. 22-3)

The abundance of imperatives in Blok's verse, especially in his declamatory style, gives it one of its distinctive intonations and contributes significantly to its emotional intensity. Since most of his verse is either explicitly addressed to some person or personalized entity, or . . . devoted to exhortation, his repeated use of this form is not surprising. The frequent recurrence of questions is explained by the same characteristics of his poetry. Two or more questions often appear consecutively. (p. 25)

The last type of repetition to be considered is perhaps the most important of all—the repetition of sounds, i.e. alliteration and assonance. Naturally, the symbolists were not the first Russian poets to use euphonic devices, but they were the first to make the question of sound-organization a fundamental poetic principle. Their concern for the expressiveness of sound was firmly rooted in their aesthetics, in their whole conception of the function of poetry.

When reading Blok one is always conscious of the central importance of the sound of the verse, of the great care taken by the poet in arrangement of vowels and consonants, and of his striving to evoke through sound a specific mood. Alliteration is used by Blok with considerable restraint. . . .

Assonance plays a more conspicuous part in the sound-structure of Blok's poetry and is a major factor in its remarkable fluidity. 'No other poet', Chukovsky has truly observed, 'had so heightened a sensitivity to vowels.' . . . In assonance, as in alliteration, however, the excessive and prolonged predominance of an individual sound is rare. (p. 26)

James B. Woodward, in his introduction to Selected Poems of Aleksandr Blok, *edited by James B. Woodward (© Oxford University Press 1968; reprinted by permission of Oxford University Press), Oxford University Press, Oxford, 1968, pp. 1-32.*

EWA M. THOMPSON (essay date 1970)

There is no doubt that Blok did not intend to voice in *The Rose and the Cross* any new philosophical outlook of his. . . . As he stated in his diary, he was working with words rather than with ideas. . . . The dramatization of Bertran's experience, then, unlike the longing for the Beautiful Lady expressed in the earlier works, seems not to have weighed on Blok's philosophical conscience. Thus *The Rose and the Cross* shows us Blok as the artist who is less concerned with Romantic self-expression than is generally assumed. (p. 345)

The story on which *The Rose and the Cross* is based is simple and conventional: a young and bored countess, a knight in love with the countess, she pining after another knight, an old and jealous husband, plus an array of flattering courtiers. (p. 346)

Bertran does not aspire to the "beyond." He does not even aspire to Lady Izora's love. The manifestations of his devotion to her are full of humility. . . . It originates in the feeling of gratitude toward Izora who then showed him sympathy. . . . In *The Rose and the Cross,* the mystery of the Feminine and of "the world beyond" is replaced by the mystery of the influence of one human being on another.

Bertran displays human . . . sensitivity. He is open not to the messenger from "beyond" but to the signs of sympathy or abuse from other humans. He desires to fulfill his duty, not to possess. His unselfishness salvages him from despair twice: first, when he resigns himself to the fact that he will never be able to claim Izora as his Lady; second, when the unworthiness of Izora is unambiguously revealed, i.e., when she asks him to keep guard near her chambers, so that no one could disturb her tête-à-tête with Aliskan. The protection which he offers his Lady during her amorous night with the page is the dying Bertran's last act of sacrifice. And, because the sacrifice is so enormous and done for Izora's sake, it creates the possibility of raising her, from her solitude and desire to possess, through suffering, to the fulfillment similar to that reached by the dying knight. It also breaks down Bertran's patterns of reacting and comprehension, and he grasps the sense of the song about joy and suffering and their inevitable interrelation.

These changes come to life through Blok's manipulation of the requisites of the play: the black and the red rose, and the cross. These requisites, like the changes of clothing in *Macbeth,* denote various stages of action and of Bertran's relation to other characters.

Izora is the red rose of the play, and at first, Bertran admires this particular quality in her. She, in turn, yearns for some immaterial ideal sprung from the books of romance she has read. She projects her longings into the person of the mysterious troubadour, the author of the song about joy and suffering. In Act Three, she throws a dark purple rose on the breast of the sleeping Gaètan. The dark color of the rose signifies, for her, her burning desire. . . .

The flower falls on the cross which Gaètan wears on his breast. When Bertran sees the flower in the morning, the rose does not *seem* black any more, it *is* black, having acquired this quality from the cross it covered. The mystery of human relationships is subtly underlined: Izora wanted to give love to Gaètan and instead gave suffering to Bertran.

At first, Bertran associates the color of the rose not with the cross on which it lay but with his dark-eyed Lady. Then, he notices that the black rose does not fade, while the red ones nearby do. Here the symbol begins to expand. It now encompasses not only Izora but also suffering and the force of spirit reached through suffering properly accepted. With the cry "The Holy Rose!" Bertran rushes into the battle with the Toulousian rebels who had just attacked the castle. Thanks to him the castle is saved. Mortally wounded, Bertran does not complain of the ingratitude he meets upon return from the battlefield. . . . Before death he becomes fully conscious of the reversal of meaning of the rose symbol, as well as of the kind of struggle he participated in during his life: that between desire and deterrence, so that he might enter meaningful relationships with others. (pp. 346-47)

The requisites of courtly love are only too obvious in the play. Bertran is a knight; he is devoted to a lady of great beauty and high station. Like Andreas Capellanus, he asserts at the outset of the play that love is a form of suffering, that it brings no joy. . . . The transformation of the rose, however, indicates the beginning of the transformation of Bertran's attitudes. During his last conversation with Izora he still expresses his admiration for her. . . . [Shortly afterwards,] he voices his growing awareness that Izora is by no means an embodiment of all that is worthy of admiration. He even detaches himself so much from his previously overwhelming love that he is able to assume a mentor-like attitude toward his once-idolized Lady. . . . Bertran hints at the possibility of redemption for Izora. The "dark days"—the days of suffering—may bring it to pass that Izora's rose, like Bertran's, "will not fade." As the night goes on, Bertran speaks of joy and suffering ("Oh, what pain! And sweetness, after this pain! . . . Joy and suffering are one."), of God and death, and does not even mention the subject of love for Izora, or his yearning to fathom the "radiant depths" of the world beyond, to which he once aspired in his conversation with Gaètan. At the pivotal moments of the play little is left of the apparent homogeneity of the courtly love attitudes. . . .

Izora is left in the world of the red rose, of thinking that "Joy means love, suffering—lack of love." She disregards the human and continues to yearn for the superhuman. . . . And so to a large extent does Gaètan, the poet-knight. It is characteristic that it is Bertran who voices the final interpretation of Gaètan's song. He relates it not to the revelation coming from "the other world" but to the long-range effects of one's relationship with other humans. Gaètan fades away from the picture after his performance at court, while Bertran's importance as a character grows steadily until the end of the play. (pp. 347-48)

The Rose and the Cross approaches [the miracle play *Théophile* and the works of Calderón] in its tone, in certain technical devices, and in the dramatic solution it proposes. . . .

[*Théophile, Devotion to the Cross* by Calderón,] and *The Rose and the Cross* share the device of placing the main hero, or heroes, apparently ordinary men (whose power of action seems, at first, to be equal to ours, just as in a realistic play) in an equivocal milieu. At first encounter with Bertran, Théophile, Eusebio, and Julia the realistic touch about them appears unmistakable. Yet, we are not surprised that in spite of it, they sometimes rise to the power of action far exceeding that of the characters in a realistic drama. Bertran, a sorry if sympathetic creature at the outset, has a major influence on the lives of all first-plan characters, and is the only one to grasp the significance of the transformation of the rose. . . . It is significant that the device of endowing the realistic hero with superrealistic power of action is accompanied, in all three plays, by the hero's renunciation of the object of immediate desire: Izora's courtly love for Bertran, wealth and position in the world for Théophile, vengeance for Julia and Eusebio.

Converging with a different tradition, Blok also perfected the dramatic quality of his work. Drama is born out of two basic elements of human reality: the wish for immediate happiness, and the human situation which thwarts the satisfaction of this wish. If the character rushes headlong to achieve happiness . . . there is little drama, and the character merely represents various stages of self-knowledge. The latter is good material for lyrics and prose fiction, but seldom can be made into a good play. If, however, the protagonist consciously recognizes his limitations and acts according to this recognition, there arises a conflict, i.e., drama. Bertran is such a man. Like a Claudelian hero, he comes to grips with life's incompatibilities in an increasingly mature manner. This struggle, and not the standard vicissitudes of courtly love to which he is subject, constitutes in my opinion the dramatic conflict of *The Rose and the Cross*. (pp. 349-50)

> Ewa M. Thompson, "The Development of Aleksandr Blok as a Dramatist," in Slavic and East European Journal (© 1970 by AATSEEL of the U.S., Inc.), Vol. XIV, No. 3, September, 1970, pp. 341-51.

JANKO LAVRIN   (essay date 1973)

The old romantic in Blok . . . came out in his attitude towards the Revolution, but this time with a definite view about the creative value of the hurricane which—according to him—brought into history a 'different, a new spirit'. Carried away by the sway of this spirit, he felt the stirring of new hopes and visions. It was in January, 1918, i.e. during the cruellest ordeals, amidst hunger, cold and chaos, that he wrote his *The Twelve (Dvenadtsat')* and *The Scythians (Skífy)*, both echoing the Revolution in a quasi-Apocalyptic manner.

The first of these two creations is the high-watermark of Blok's poetry. Simple at first sight, it is full of ingenious rhythms and devices, some of which were even taken from street jargon and factory ditties. Blok the romantic, the realist and the symbolist collaborate here on equal terms, accompanied by his bitter hatred of the old world, the collapse of which he had been more than ready to welcome.

> The wind reels, the snow dances;
> A party of twelve men advances.
> Black rifle-slings upon their backs.
> And flame, flame, flame upon their tracks.
> With crumpled caps, lips smoking fags,
> All should be branded as prison lags.

This is how the poet introduces the twelve Bolshevik guards, patrolling the streets of Petrograd, at night, during the days of turmoil and hunger. The poem has twelve parts, each of

them composed in a different rhythm and adding different motifs. The language, too, is appropriate to 'prison lags', who mix it with half-digested revolutionary slogans and clichés. The narrative incident is deliberately crude and could have been taken from any police chronicle. One of the twelve patrolling soldiers, infatuated with the street-girl Katya . . . accidentally shoots her dead—while aiming at his own rival in love. Throughout the poem we can follow his reactions to the crime, but this personal drama is cunningly interwoven with the ordeals of a bleak northern winter and the Revolution. The tension of the conflicting social strata is suggested by the rhythm, the tone and the accent of each verse, as well as by Blok's own sallies against the old 'bourgeois' order. . . . (p. 235)

Nothing that belongs to the old world matters any longer. Even the 'Holy Russia' of yore can be blasphemed and, hooligan-fashion, trampled underfoot for the sake of a new era. . . .

The fury of destruction, with 'no Cross', fills the air. But however un-Christian its external ravages, a revolution in the name of justice and brotherhood may yet be based upon a Christian impulse, which in the end must win—provided the revolution itself be imbued with [the] 'spirit of universal music.' . . . This is where the creative element of the revolution comes in, no matter whether the participants are aware of it or not. And so 'the twelve' (a reflection of the twelve Apostles) march on. And in the midst of all the desolation, crime and chaos they are suddenly joined by [the apparition of Christ] which confers upon the poem a final message and meaning. . . . (p. 236)

The Twelve is pervaded with the pathos of revolution and yet remains elusive enough to be interpreted in a number of ways. Christ as protector and leader of the twelve Bolshevist guards may appear to some people a blasphemy and to others a *deus ex machina*—the more so because nothing in the poem makes one expect such a dénouement. On the other hand, He can be explained as a Messianic symbol of that creative era which ought to follow upon the Inferno of suffering, blood and destruction. A revolution devoid of inner meaning remains only a calamity which has not been deepened into a purifying tragedy; and a mere calamity is always crushing and sterile. Blok knew that an event of such magnitude as the cataclysm of 1917 could not have been of this sterile kind, and he said so. *The Twelve* was a final attempt on his part to regain his faith in humanity and life—an attempt expressed in strains of which only great poetry is capable.

Less elusive and somewhat programmatic is his other poem, *The Scythians*. It was written during the peace negotiations at Brest-Litovsk and represents a platform counterpart to *The Twelve*. Here Blok challenges the luke-warm bourgeoisie of the Western world to join the universal brotherhood inaugurated by the Revolution. In terms redolent of aggressive Slavophilism and speaking both as a revolutionary and a Russian, he reproaches the nations of the West. . . . (pp. 236-37)

And in case the challenged Western nations should refuse to join, he threatens them with the 'Asiatic face' of Russia (or rather with the Asiatic half of her face), as well as with her indifference to their fate even if another Mongolian invasion, headed by an up-to-date Genghis Khan, should come from the Far East. (p. 237)

'Life is only worth living when we make immense demands upon it.' Blok wrote in an essay at the time of his two revolutionary rhapsodies. 'All or nothing! A faith, not in what is not found upon earth, but in what ought to be there, although at the present time it does not exist and may not come for quite a while.' Approaching the Revolution with such an attitude, he saw its scope as nothing less than a gradual remaking of man and the world. . . .

His own maximalist demands made him impatient to see the economic and political upheaval completed by an adequate inner change of men, but this change was either too slow, or else entirely different from what he had expected. It must have been the discrepancy between the external and the inner revolutions—a discrepancy which assumed unexpectedly ugly aspects during the ravages of the Civil War—that eventually damped Blok's hopes and enthusiasm. (p. 238)

> *Janko Lavrin, "Alexander Blok" (originally published in a different form in his* From Pushkin to Mayakovsky: A Study in the Evolution of Literature, *Sylvan Press, 1948), in his* A Panorama of Russian Literature *(copyright © 1973 by J. Lavrin; reprinted by permission of Barnes & Noble Books, a Division of Littlefield, Adams & Co., Inc.),* Barnes & Noble, 1973, pp. 226-38.

HAROLD B. SEGEL (essay date 1979)

Blok's entry into the drama dates from 1906 when his *Fairground Booth* was first staged. Two years later, this play together with *Korol na ploshchadi (The King on the Square)* and *Neznakomka (The Unknown Woman)* were published under the common title *Liricheskie dramy (Lyrical Dramas)*. (p. 89)

In the Preface to his cycle of *Lyrical Dramas* Blok defines a lyrical play as one which presents the experiences of an individual soul, its doubts, passions, failures, and falls. Ideological, moral, or other inferences have no place in it. The common link of the three-play cycle (and *The Song of Fate* as well) is the search "for a beautiful, free, and luminous life, one capable of removing from weak shoulders the unendurable burden of *lyrical* doubts and contradictions and of dispelling importunate and illusory doubles." These doubts, contradictions, and phantoms are distributed among male characters who represent different aspects of the soul of a single person: the comically unsuccessful Pierrot in *The Fairground Booth;* the morally weak poet in *The King on the Square;* the Poet whose dream eludes him in *The Unknown Woman;* and the vacillating Gherman in *The Song of Fate.* These men are variants of what could be called the Masculine figure in Blok. In each case, the search for the beautiful life centers on a woman, representing what Blok himself refers to as the Eternal Feminine. For Pierrot, it is the luminous Columbine; for the Poet in *The King on the Square,* the daughter of the architect; for the Poet in *The Unknown Woman,* it is the Unknown Woman herself; for Gherman in *The Song of Fate,* it is the singer Faina.

On a first, more immediate level of meaning, these plays dramatize the restless quest of a particular type of personality (a projection of Blok himself?) for an ideal life of beauty and meaningful self-fulfillment and the weaknesses and inadequacies which cause the ideal to be lost even when it is within grasp. But the quest for the beautiful also assumes a transcendent significance. Dissatisfied with the banality and vulgarity of society, the sensitive Masculine figure (a poet or

someone of poetic sensibility) yearns for an existence of beauty and meaning necessarily equatable only with the spiritual. The world as he knows it becomes distasteful to him and he seeks a way out of its self-intoxicating clamor and superficial brilliance, suggested by the ball in *The Fairground Booth*, the excitement attending the arrival of the ships in *The King on the Square*, the tavern and intelligentsia party scenes in *The Unknown Woman*, and the International Industrial Fair in *The Song of Fate*. That is why the Feminine figure symbolic of the Ideal not only is presented in all instances as in some way linked to or emergent from "above" or "beyond" or the "other world" but also is dualistic in the sense of combining the life-giving and life-taking. If the Eternal Feminine has to be understood as the spiritual life . . . she must also symbolize the leavetaking of the physical, earthly life—death, in other words—which man must first undergo before entering the spiritual.

In his Preface to the *Lyrical Dramas* Blok also mentions the mocking tone of the plays as another element making for a certain unity between them. He associates this tone with the romanticism of the first half of the nineteenth century and, more specifically, with what he refers to as the Romantic "transcendental irony" or what we understand more commonly as Romantic irony. This Romantic irony is often self-ironizing—the dispelling of personal demons through a process of artistic transmutation. There is, to be sure, much of this in Blok's early plays: the *fin de siècle* world-weariness, the exaggerated sense of alienation, the relentless search for an ideal, for an absolute, the self-indulgent fantasizing, the weakness of will when the time for decision making is at hand, the inability to distinguish illusion and reality—all collectively the malaise of the age to which Blok gave expression in the early plays and which he could bring himself to ironize over at a time when he was able to perceive their grip on his own psyche.

But there is also a sociopolitical dimension in the early plays which Blok says nothing about in his Preface and about which it may have been politic, in fact, for him to remain silent. *The King on the Square* and *The Song of Fate* acquire an additional significance from precisely this point of view. In the first play the weaknesses of the Poet are observed against and set into relief by a successful popular revolt against a king. The inhabitants of the kingdom anticipate the arrival of ships symbolizing hope, abundance, and salvation. The long delay in the ships' coming intensifies their sense of frustration and adds fuel to their grievances. When the ships finally arrive, it is already too late. Unable to bear further their frustration, the people rise up against their king, destroying the Poet, the architect's daughter, and a number of their own in the process. When the king is toppled from his pedestal, it is discovered that he is only a *statue;* fearful for the future without a leader, without someone to guide them, the people ask the architect whom can they now turn to for sustenance, both physical and spiritual. He replies in such a way as to suggest that the only master that they need recognize is God. The political sense of the play, coming only a few years after the Revolution of 1905 (which had a profound impact on Blok), seems sufficiently clear. The masses cannot continue to be fed on vain hopes and empty promises (symbolized by the ships) created for them, by and large, by an effete, spiritually crippled intelligentsia and any ruler toppled will prove to be no more than a shattered statue.

Blok's repudiation of the intelligentsia and his crystallizing enthusiasm for the mystique of the great as yet untapped reservoir of national strength represented by the Russian masses—which brings him ideologically (if indeed not aesthetically) close to Gorky—is less obliquely expressed in *The Song of Fate*. Here Gherman's pursuit of the dynamic life force embodied in the character of Faina leads to the Seventy-seventh International Industrial Fair at which he and Faina will finally meet. During the Fair (scene 4) a Man in Spectacles addresses the crowd. He speaks of the gulf between the intelligentsia and the people (who are characterized throughout the play as a slumbering, potentially explosive mass) and the ever increasing irrelevance of the former. Faina appears to him as a symbol of the national spirit and as such he contrasts the weakness of his own voice, as a representative of the intelligentsia, with the strength of hers. When Faina leaves Gherman at the end of the play telling him that the time is not yet ripe for their union, her words extend meaning on several levels.

Blok's three *Lyrical Dramas* together with *The Song of Fate*, which belongs to the cycle in all respects but that of formal link, carry the same problems of stage-worthiness as much essentially poetic neo-Romantic drama. Blok himself was aware of this at least with regard to the *Lyrical Dramas* and in his Preface to them he speaks candidly of their deficiencies and weaknesses from the point of view of stage production. The exception, among the early plays, was *The Fairground Booth*, [to be discussed later in this essay.] (pp. 89-92)

Many of the weaknesses of Blok's early plays disappear, however, in *The Rose and the Cross*.... Set in thirteenth-century Languedoc and Brittany, the play reflects the poet's long-standing interest in medieval French culture....

The advance in dramaturgy represented by *The Rose and the Cross* relates to both technique and point of view. Prose and verse mingle as in the early plays, but characters (above all, the knight Bertran) become more than poetic symbols and a more lucid and coherently developed plot structure makes for greater dramatic interest.

At the center of the play is the knight Bertran's hopeless love for Isora, the wife of the master of his castle, Count Archimbaut, and her search for the author of a haunting song whose meaning she does not fully comprehend. Song as lyrical interpolation is a recurrent motif in all of Blok's plays. But it is only with *The Rose and the Cross* that song, character, and plot are brought together in an integral relationship of dramatic effectiveness.

The whole sense of the song, which Bertran recites at the beginning of the play, is contained in the words: "Serdtsu zakon neprelozhny—/Radost—Stradanie odno!" ("The heart's immutable law—/Joy and suffering are one.") Although neither realizes it, the song defines the relationship of Bertran and Isora. (p. 92)

Bertran suffers because of his hopeless love for Isora, but in this suffering there is also joy in the ability to love fully, without the hope of fulfillment, to love enough to be able to sacrifice oneself so that one's beloved may find what she believes to be her own happiness in the arms of another. Blok's own discovery of this "verity" of life expressed in *The Rose and the Cross* comes as a significant departure from the transcendent Neo-Romantic quest for ideals of truth and beauty dramatized in the early plays.... The result is an outward reaching instead of upward-striving play of richer human understanding and superior design.

Blok's more concentrated and less ambiguous dramatic method in *The Rose and the Cross* still accommodates the symbolic.... The rose and the cross of the title signify, respectively, happiness and suffering. Throughout the play two types of rose are contrasted: the red, which is associated with Isora and suggests merely fleeting happiness; and the black, which symbolizes the happiness that knows suffering as well and is derived from the dark-red rose tossed by Isora at one point in the play on the sleeping trouvère's breast. It is this rose that Bertran wears into the glory of his victorious defense of the castle and into the ignominy of his night vigil beneath Isora's window. In taking the black rose unto himself Bertran opens his consciousness to the meaning of Gaetan's song. Preferring the red rose which will fade, unlike the black, Isora at once relegates herself to a lower level of awareness. (pp. 93-4)

In their desire to move drama and theater away from the representationalism (the "illusionism," as they saw it) of realism and naturalism as well as from the metaphysicality of symbolism, the theatricalists [of early twentieth century Russia] often fell back on "older" theatricalist techniques. These included . . . the device of the play-within-a-play, the masks of the commedia dell'arte, pantomime, motifs borrowed from marionette performances, . . . and stage directions calling for the absence of curtains and/or set changes in full view of the public.

In making use of several of these techniques within the limited space of a play no longer than a traditional one-acter, Aleksandr Blok's first dramatic work, *The Fairground Booth*, broke new ground, becoming thereby the first important manifestation of theatricalism in early twentieth-century Russian drama. (pp. 123-24)

The innovative character of *The Fairground Booth* is established virtually from the outset by what seems to be a double-edged parody of Maeterlinckian symbolism and St. Petersburgian mysticism. I say "double-edged" because Blok appears to be both parodying and satirizing not only Symbolist drama itself but the mystic symbolism of his own earlier writing as well. With *The Fairground Booth* Blok is declaring, in effect, his liberation from the mystic orientation of his previous writing and, on the launching of his career as a playwright, from the style of Maeterlinckian dramaturgy. Abandoning "Maeterlinckianism" Blok seems to suggest that henceforth the direction he intends to follow is that of theatricalist drama, a promise unfulfilled in his later plays. (p. 124)

Short as it is, *The Fairground Booth* has several layers of meaning. With one, involving the mystics, Blok proclaims his repudiation of mystical otherworldliness and, in terms of dramatic tradition, of the Maeterlinckian "static" theater of death. Through the "inner drama" of Pierrot, Columbine, Harlequin, and the author, and the scenes with the masked lovers he projects the desire to accept life realistically rather than to make it palatable and hence "unreal" by spiritualizing and romanticizing both life and love. The failure of Pierrot and Columbine to unite and the frustration of the author's original scheme mark the abandonment of idealization and the acceptance of the unpredictability of human experience. The author's plan for a conventional "happy ending" play of romantic love is constantly thwarted and *The Fairground Booth* ends with Pierrot's loss of Columbine.

The third layer of meaning of Blok's play—and perhaps the most important in view of the form of the work—is its patent theatricalism, a conscious planned assault of a very specific sort on the illusionistic drama of realism and naturalism and on the mystico-metaphysical drama of symbolism. It was to point up the underlying theatricalist premise of the play that Blok introduced the figure of the author, masked actors and actresses in costume ball attire, traditional figures of the commedia dell'arte, the physical buffoonery of the Italian improvised theater, the partial extension of an actor (the clown) beyond the proscenium into the audience, and the baring of the stage by the rolling up of the scenery near the end of the play. (pp. 126-27)

Harold B. Segel, "The Revolt Against Naturalism: Symbolism, Neo-Romanticism, and Theatricalism," in his Twentieth-Century Russian Drama: From Gorky to the Present *(copyright © 1979 Columbia University Press; reprinted by permission of the publisher), Columbia University Press, 1979, pp. 51-146.**

ADDITIONAL BIBLIOGRAPHY

Annenkov, George. "The Poets and the Revolution—Blok, Mayakovsky, Esenin." *The Russian Review* 26, No. 2 (April 1967): 129-43.*

Reminiscences of life among Russia's pre-revolutionary *literati*, featuring quotations of Blok which illuminate his beliefs on poetry and the Revolution.

Banjanin, Milica. "The Problem of Evil in the Poetry of Aleksandr Blok." *Essays in Literature* 1, No. 2 (Fall 1974): 236-47.

A study of Blok's vision and his treatment of the city as the spawning ground of evil.

Bowlt, John E. "Aleksandr Blok: The Poem 'The Unknown Lady'." *Texas Studies in Literature and Language, Special Russian Issue* XVII (1975): 349-56.

A close study of "Neznakomka"—a poem which preceded the drama of the same title—focusing on the paradoxical unity of seemingly disparate motifs within the work.

Gorky, Maxim. "Reminiscences on Alexander Blok." In his *Reminiscences*, pp. 204-13. New York: Dover Publications, 1946.

Memoir of a conversation with Blok, in which that author revealed his mistrust in the utility of reason. Gorky relates this mistrust to similar attitudes expressed by Tolstoy, Dostoyevsky, and others.

Kembell, Robin. *Alexander Blok: A Study in Rhythm and Metre*. Slavistic Printings and Reprintings, edited by C. H. Van Schooneveld, vol. XXXIII. The Hague: Mouton & Co., 1965, 539 p.

An examination of the rhythms and cadences of Blok's poetry, and comparison with the meter of selected English poems.

Lednicki, Waclaw. "Blok's 'Polish Poem'." In his *Russia, Poland and the West: Essays in Literary and Cultural History*, pp. 349-99. New York: Roy Publishers, 1954.

Traces the Polish theme in *Vozmezdie (Retribution)*. Lednicki examines the poem in the light of previous Russian literary treatment of Poland and its fate.

Lewitter, L. R. "The Inspiration and Meaning of Aleksander Blok's *The Rose and the Cross*." *The Slavonic and East European Review* 35, No. 2 (June 1957): 428-42.

An examination of the origins of *The Rose and the Cross* finding Blok's drama an original treatment of the theme of courtly love, "full of intense subtlety and based on a sound knowledge of medieval life and literature."

Masing, Irene. *A. Blok's "The Snow Mask."* Stockholm Slavic Studies, vol. 4. Stockholm: Almquist & Wiksell, 1970, 100 p.

An explication of the thirty poems composing *The Snow Mask*.

Nilsson, Nils Åke. "Strindberg, Gorky and Blok." *Scando-Slavica* 4 (1958): 23-42.*

A short study of August Strindberg's role in shaping Blok's outlook.

Pyman, Avril. Introduction to *Selected Poems*, by Alexander Blok, edited by Avril Pyman, pp. 1-53. Pergamon Oxford Russian Series, edited by C.V. James. Oxford: Pergamon Press, 1972.

A cogent biography and critique of Blok and his work.

Sendich, Munir. "Blok's *The Twelve*: Critical Interpretations of the Christ Figure." *Russian Literature Triquarterly*, No. 4 (1972): 445-61.

A survey of the critical reception and interpretation of the controversial figure of Christ in *The Twelve*.

Vogel, Lucy. "A Symbolist's Inferno: Blok and Dante." *The Russian Review* 29, No. 1 (January 1970): 38-51.

An essay examining the curious poetic kinship between Blok and Dante which is revealed in the former's poems "Ravenna" and "Canto of Hell."

Weidlé, Wladimir. "The Poison of Modernism." In *Russian Modernism: Culture and the Avant-Garde, 1900-1930*, edited by George Gibian and H. W. Tjalsma, pp. 18-30. Ithaca: Cornell University Press, 1976.

An essay probing Blok's quarrel with Russian modernism.

Zhirmunskij, Viktor. "The Passion of Aleksandr Blok." In *Twentieth-Century Russian Literary Criticism*, edited by Victor Erlich, pp. 117-37. New Haven: Yale University Press, 1975.

A critical overview of Blok's poetry, presenting its several phases as an expression of Blok's evolving preoccupation with love and the search for love, a treatment of the poet's work later developed by Victor Erlich (see excerpt above).

Wolfgang Borchert

1921-1947

German dramatist, short story writer, and poet.

Borchert is known as the voice of post-World War II Germany's disillusioned "lost generation." His artistic stature was elevated by his powerful drama *Draussen vor der Tür (The Man Outside)*, the story of a soldier's return from war to a spiritually empty existence. Borchert's work, rooted in early twentieth-century expressionism, depicts a world in which God, nature, and humanity are united only in their mutual indifference and cruelty. Despite his insistent nihilism, Borchert's brief canon is suffused with compassion and hope for humankind.

His native Hamburg provided the background for many of Borchert's poems and stories; there he began an acting career that was cut short by his conscription into the Nazi Wehrmacht in 1941. As a soldier he lived a nightmarish life on the Russian front: he was wounded in action, subjected to bitter cold and recurring sickness, and repeatedly imprisoned for criticizing the Third Reich. Borchert's works, most of them written during his brief postwar years under the strain of ill health, define human existence within the framework of war and its blighted wake. All people are life's victims, he claims; all are oppressors as well.

The day after his death the premier stage performance of *The Man Outside* established Borchert as the first important literary voice to rise from spiritually devastated Germany. The play served as an important link between the prewar expressionist drama and the postwar Theater of the Absurd and parable plays. His other work is noted for its style rather than its content. Although popular interest in *The Man Outside* has faded in the years of Germany's recovery, the antiwar message and pacifist sympathies in such works as the short story "Billbrook" ("Billbrook") and the poem "Dann gibt es nur eins!" ("Then There Is Only One Thing Left") continue to find an audience with young people.

PRINCIPAL WORKS

Laterne, Nacht und Sterne: Gedichte um Hamburg (poetry) 1946
An diesem Dienstag (short stories) 1947
Draussen vor der Tür (drama) 1947
  [*The Man Outside* published in *The Man Outside: The Prose Works of Wolfgang Borchert*, 1952]
Die Hundeblume (short stories) 1947
Das Gesamtwerk (drama, short stories, and poetry) 1949
  [*The Man Outside: The Prose Works of Wolfgang Borchert*, 1952]
Die traurigen Geranien und andere Geschichten aus dem Nachlass (short stories) 1962
  [*The Sad Geraniums*, 1973]

MARIANNE BONWIT (essay date 1951)

Borchert was the heir of Expressionists like [Klabund, Alfred Döblin, and Christian Morgenstern]. He delighted in unex-pected contrasts and was addicted to punning, not only because play on words was all the play left in a world full of menacing things and mortally serious people, but perhaps even more because language, like the world to which it belonged, was bursting at the seams, because it was simultaneously fixed and footloose, seemingly serious and yet fundamentally irresponsible. Rhythms once hallowed by tradition or authority occur in his tales—ironically, since their original meaning, far from signifying what it once did, only serves to heighten some particularly glaring contradiction: patriotic ditties accompanied slow death before Stalingrad, gay marching songs were muttered in the suffocating snow. Traditional syntax gives way to emotionally charged staccato, gradation to repetition and accumulation. There are hardly any subordinate clauses, since everything may be important within a scope in which everything may also be completely absurd.

It all depends on a man's point of view. And this man was alone. In his aloneness, he was curiously like his contemporaries similarly alone in other lands. For him, as for the Existentialists, Nature was hostile, God questionable, Man a pitiful outcast, redeemable only inasmuch as he appears able to choose and to act according to his choice, whatever the choice and whatever the consequences. It may be the decision to pick a "dog-flower" in a prison-yard, to bequeath one's last shirt to a fellow-prisoner, or not to jump back into the Elbe river after all. Borchert describes "extreme situations," frequently those of a concentration-camp-like universe in which a man is utterly alone—and yet not without a queer and lowly dignity. . . . (p. 15)

Borchert's writings are not faultless but have that innocence which forms part of the highest talent. They are as simple—perhaps as deceptively so—as some of Klee's and Picasso's drawings.

Take the story of the dog-flower. This yellow weed has sprouted in the yard where the prisoners—as anonymous, as legally guiltless as any of Kafka's heroes—take their daily exercise. For the hero, this flower represents the beloved goal of all longing, flowering of all life, most of all a potential companion in his cell. . . . After all, the flower is picked by the hero. It is his, and during one night it means to him his home, his family, his world. He falls asleep and dreams that he is earth—life annihilated and revivifying—giving birth to just such miracles, such "tiny, unpretentious suns." And that is the end of the tale in which the once blue flower of the Romanticists has become dreadfully common and, yet, perhaps even more than to the Romanticists, a matter of life and death. (pp. 15-16)

Borchert scorns not only the relationship of causality and time, but he neglects all traditional perspective. He distorts distance too. Any of his short stories might illustrate this, but the one which brings it out most forcibly is perhaps *Billbrook.*

A Canadian sergeant-major, Bill Brook, discovers after D-Day that a suburb of Hamburg bears his name. Despite his comrade's mockery, he visits "his" suburb and finds after wandering through bombed wasteland that people in Billbrook are either unconcerned or hostile, and that only *things* speak to him, empty telephone booths, leaning bill-boards, bent and darkened street-lamps. Things seem articulate, while man is uncommunicative. . . .

In Borchert's eyes, *things* can be of tremendous importance: they survive because they can be mended like the kitchen clock which is all that remains of a bombed-out man's past. Things may also be all we have at present as a voucher for the future—a pink shirt, a green bottle of gin, a sheet of paper with a poem on it, a dandelion, a street-lamp, anything, even a man when he has become a corpse in the Russian snow, or a woman whose body is expendable for one night. For, except possibly in the observer's mind, these things lack ambiguity, multiple meanings, the dreadful self-willed propulsion of life. They are safe and at rest.

But if Borchert is a poet who delights in things, he is no less a poet for that. His vision animates them, he is their crucible, and in this way the true successor of Rilke and Morgenstern. His vision of the world around him is manifested most clearly in his lyrics. There his favorite companions appear: street-lamps shining green or red or golden in the night; his beloved city of Hamburg, its wind, its fog, its quays; children who are children and not, as in his short stories, either absent or distressingly like adults. His prose reflects what he hated or suffered from; his play shows the tensions which puzzled him; but in his poems we meet the living beings and objects he loved. These poems vibrate with a highly personal sen-

sitivity continually in conflict with the social forces of his age. (pp. 16-17)

Borchert derived much from tradition and shared much with his generation. There seem to be echoes to Matthias Claudius and answers to Albrecht Haushofer. However, there is a personal note in Borchert's writings, discernible at the beginning as at the end of his career: despite the inhumanities of man, despite the cruelty of circumstance, Man is free to fight against inhumanity and cruelty. This appears nowhere more clearly than in the early tale *Shishiphush* and in one of the last sketches **"Then There Is Only One Thing Left."**

Shishiphush is the story of a little waiter who, because of a speech-defect—he pronounces "s" as "sh"—is apologetic to the point of self-debasement, but can still be furious when he thinks that his speech-defect is mockingly copied. Upon learning that such seeming parody need not spring from contempt but may be due to the very same defect as his, the waiter gains courage and becomes a different person. The other handicapped man may be more self-confident than the little waiter, more capable of surmounting what is, after all, with him a war injury; he never was laughed at during his school-days for transforming "Sisyphus" into "Shishiphush"; he belongs to the upper class; he is indomitably cheerful. Yet, he feels so brotherly toward the waiter that he is concerned with imbuing "Thish shorry rashcal" with his own sense of inner freedom. And Borchert is too restrained an artist to allude to the meaning of the Sisyphus, albeit "Shishiphush," myth in connection with human frailty.

None of those mentioned in **"Then There Is Only One Thing Left"** enjoy particularly favorable circumstances. Machinists, office girls, research-workers, doctors, pilots—any of them and most of all, mothers—may be instrumental in another war, and Borchert, out of the depth of his experience, appeals to them. He asks them to say "No" to any war, to use their human prerogative in saying "No." The survivor of Stalingrad conjures up apocalyptic visions of what may happen unless there is such generally uttered *"Nein."*

Compassion for all mankind, for the conquerors as well as for the conquered, is Borchert's most significant contribution to German literature of the war period. At all times free from self-pity, this compassion is not part of any discernible religious or philosophical conviction, but, rather, pervades the atmosphere of a world in which all convictions are shaken. (p. 17)

Marianne Bonwit, "Wolfgang Borchert, 1921-1947,"
in Books Abroad *(copyright 1951 by the University*
of Oklahoma Press), Vol. 25, No. 1, Winter, 1951,
pp. 15-18.

ADOLF D. KLARMANN (essay date 1952)

In considering Borchert's *Weltanschauung* we must keep in mind three important physical factors: his youth, his state of health, and the fact that all his writing was crowded into two hectic disease-ridden years. [*Draussen vor der Tür*] was written in one week. To expect a well-defined consistency under such conditions would be illogical. One thing is certain: the easy materialistic panacea of the dictatorship of the proletariat holds no attraction for him and does not even receive mention. With things as they were a nihilistic outlook is tempting, and, as we [know,] Borchert apparently subscribes to it. However, there seem to be strong indications in this play and even more so in some of his prose that nihilism was not his ultimate solution. (pp. 109-10)

The stories of [*Die Hundeblume: Erzählungen aus unseren Tagen*] were written in 1946, the title story in the winter of 1945-46. . . . [This] collection shows a time-space progression in its subdivisions. *Die Ausgelieferten* consists of four stories. A thin thread ties them together: prison, wandering in the streets, hungry loneliness, despair, and yet assertion of life. *Unterwegs* has five stories with the important symbols of trains and stations. It conveys the irrepressible nostalgia for and the magnetic pull of Hamburg. And finally the last group *Stadt, Stadt: Mutter zwischen Himmel und Erde* contains three stories set in Hamburg. As there is no political statement and the war is barely mentioned the stories are imbued with a timelessness and universality which they derive from the author's profound identification with his own time. The intensity of experience is so strong that the normal epic flow of narrative is obliterated. The impact of each moment, the vibration of a sensitive soul, the ebb and flow of a hectic mind, the undulations of repeating scenes, images, sentences, words, emotions, all this is caught in a unique weaving, musical style which never really tells a story but which creates a full scale of moods: moods of loneliness, of despair, of hate, of disillusion, and yet a bit of hope and faith.

Borchert is an intense talker. It is as if he held the reader by the button and would not let go of him until he had his ardent, incoherent, jerky, honest say. . . . [His many ideas] merge into a whole and thereby create Borchert's remarkable art. Its effect is frequently so strong that the reader is submerged in a complete identification with the author. (p. 112)

[The title story, *Die Hundeblume*, is] one of the best though not most typical, inasmuch as it almost tells a story. (p. 113)

[What starts] out as a depressing story of futility and despair turns deftly into a mildly optimistic acceptance of life through the miracle of existence. As in *Draussen vor der Tür* God is drawn into the picture, but as yet the youth of the godless age does not have the courage to will a faith that would dispel frustration, loneliness, and fear, and he sidesteps the issue by turning to a sort of agnosticism.

The musical basis of Borchert's literary experience is strongly present in this work. The author hears with a keen and painfully sensitive ear. The structure of the story is that of a symphonic poem, and the technique of leitmotiv and repetition becomes evident. As with the Expressionists the verbal forms prevail and the monologue solo is established, tendencies which will increase in his other prose. Rilke, whose influence was missed in the poetry, is felt in the author's relation to things, and Kafka in the anonymous existential guilt.

The remaining stories, though independent in themselves, seem to evolve from the first, which sets the basic mood. [In *Die Krähen fliegen abends nach Hause,*] even more than in *Die Hundeblume,* we encounter Borchert's prose technique in full array. A simple epic thought is woven into an intricate musical pattern of variations, codas, and fugues, progressing on a spiral line; a mood is indicated by a situation, an image, an observation, and then like a spiral (or a thread in a cloth) it winds through the prose, recurring in variations, monotonous, yet ever heightening the effect of the original mood, reducible to a series of a few words or short sentences which provide theme and variations. The mere enumeration practically tells the story. But it is not the story that is important,

it is the mood and the extraordinary effect that is created by the music and rhythm of words. . . . A strange, tantalizing, frustrating rhythm is achieved in a heartless staccato of chopped-off, jerky, weighted, short sentences or word-sentences. (pp. 114-15)

Here, as almost invariably, Borchert starts with an introduction, an overture, creating a totality of mood before he settles on a specific narrative incident which frequently concentrates the mood or occasionally contrasts it.—Though this particular story, if such it is, does not rank with Borchert's best, it serves well as a model for his style.

An interesting example of Borchert's monodramatic technique is *Gespräch über den Dächern*. Its essence is not at all narrative but confessional. It is a refutation of a futility of existence arising from self-preoccupation, cosmic self-pity, and a rhetorical pathos of frustration, and it culminates in a self-redemption. (p. 115)

Borchert juxtaposes here two modern youths, the one intellectually corroded by his time, by too much thinking, too much doubting, too much asking, too much concern with life in the abstract, a compendium of fear, insecurity, frustration, isolation and futility; the other silent, warm, secure, sound and at peace with himself and the world. His very presence lends affirmation to the answer: man is caught within himself yet he can will a new tomorrow. Beckmann's outcry at the end of *Draussen vor der Tür* finds here one response.

In its style *Gespräch über den Dächern* follows an interesting pattern. At first there is the overture of short, choppy, staccato sentences. . . . Then sets in the incantation of futility counterpointed now and then by motifs from the introduction, the city at night, and underscored from the very beginning by the obbligato of the silent man of contentment. We remain constantly aware of his presence in spite of his silence as though a low, warm cello monotone had been assigned to him which hums throughout the incantation until its shrill descant becomes unbearable. Then the silent man breaks in with the motif: Why don't you hang yourself? The incantation is picked up again in a major key with the motif: No, I am in love with life . . . blending now with the cello obbligato in a harmonious duet. The piece ends piano on the confident note of the victorious morning.

In the five brief stories of the next section, *Unterwegs*, we are on the way; on the road of insecure restlessness and a hopeful search for a place of rest. For Borchert this can only mean Hamburg. *Generation ohne Abschied* is part a rhapsodic poem of resignation and hope, part a proclamation of the new generation. (pp. 115-16)

The third and final section *Stadt, Stadt: Mutter zwischen Himmel und Erde* opens with an overwhelming ode to Hamburg. The prose has become completely rhapsodic. Whitmanesque outpourings sing of the joy at being again in Hamburg, in the city so different from all others, yet so akin to all its sister harbors throughout the world. Enumerative and alliterative lines abound in this great proclamation of love. (p. 116)

An interesting departure is *Bilbrook*, Borchert's longest story and the only one in which one of the occupying forces is brought into play and in which the author does not identify himself with the protagonist. The ruins of Hamburg are highlighted by the contrast with the memories of the peaceful, unscathed Canadian town, Hopedale.

The Canadian soldier starts out on a jaunty walk to that silly little town that bears his name. On the way he soon is engulfed by war's desolation. There is no life, only ruins, miles of them. A cosmic panic chokes him. At last, he finds a tiny human settlement, an oasis, rescued from the desert of rubble. Relieved, he joins two men fishing there. But the cold and unrelenting stare of hatred of the younger, legless one chills him and drives him back, through the dead city, back to the barracks. In a letter home that was to be so chatty he finds no words to tell of his experience.

Borchert uses here a realism which one is tempted to call metaphysical. His meticulous observation becomes transparent to symbolism, as every object, every gesture becomes fraught with hidden life, explosive with emotion, and filled with the unsurmountable hostility of man against man and thing against man. As in a surrealist nightmare the tortured world turns on its unwilling torturer, man. In a headlong flight, like a frightened child, he senses instinctively his desperate aloneness in a hostile cosmos and his own unincurred share of universal guilt, in a universal crime, which enmeshes him in its inextricable net. The naïve Canadian from Hopedale joins the line-up of fate. (pp. 116-17)

The collection ends with *Die Elbe,* another Whitmanesque paean of the river and its city, both beautiful in their living ugliness. It sums up the moods of the book in a soberly enthusiastic acceptance of the present for the sake of the future, for the sake of life that is mightier than death and destruction. (p. 117)

The nineteen short prose pieces of the collection *An diesem Dienstag,* written between the fall of 1946 and the summer of 1947, were published shortly after Borchert's death. They fall into two sections, *Im Schnee, im sauberen Schnee,* ten Kurzgeschichten of the Russian war experience; and *Und keiner weiss wohin* nine stories of the homeless return. On the whole this collection is more homogeneous in mood and form than the first. A uniform air of bleakness and despair, of futility and fatalism pervades the book. Hardly a relieving note of protest, or defiance, or hope, just a resigned acceptance of a cold fate in a heartless world. (pp. 117-18)

Yet even in this bleakness there are touching moments, as in *Die drei dunklen Könige,* a stirring version of the story of the Three Wise Men, or in *Radi* the gripping sympathy with the dead who cannot find peace in a strange earth.

In these depressing Kurzgeschichten of the first part Borchert's stylistic virtuosity at times dangerously borders on mannerism. To be sure, we do not find aberrations of taste like those which occasionally marred a story in his first collection. . . . Borchert plays expertly every instrument in his orchestra. His greater mastery is evident in the deft handling of the short sentence and its concentrated explosiveness. It is an attempt to reproduce in vitality and cruel terseness the enormity of the war experience which defies expression. In one of his later prose pieces of this book Borchert despairs of his ability to cope with it. . . . This ineffability may also explain the relatively small number of accounts from the war.

In the second section of this book *Und keiner weiss wohin* we are closer to the world of his only drama. In nine stories of varying length the tragedy of post-war Germany unfolds. The moods vary considerably, as does the style. Borchert is groping here for the right articulation and a greater poetic projection by developing from a primary concern with his own image toward an understanding objectivity. His sphere of sympathy reaches out beyond his ego. Yet, the epic situations are not changed; on the contrary, stark loneliness, human, all too human ego-centricity, inertia of the heart, futility, they are all there, and hardly the minutest ray of hope breaks through all this darkness. Fate is still cynical, chance omnipotent, and man's attempt at escaping as effectual as a worm's running away from a bird. For God has no face and no ears, and man's agonies cry out in the deaf void. (pp. 118-19)

One of the best of Borchert's prose pieces, *Im Mai, im Mai schrie der Kuckuck,* is one of his most musical and most moving, yet told without pathos. It opens with a rich overture on the theme of night: nights in their many variations. . . . [There are] nights when man feels utterly abandoned and excluded, and envies people in the streetcars, for they know their destination and have a shelter.—Yet, there are always the streets, the roads with their stars, and rains, and echoes; and once in a long while a window, and in it a light, and a woman.

The mood is set, the overture is finished, and now starts the lonely solo of the youth with his yearning for a rest on his endless road of restless escape, for warmth, for love, a woman's love. A loaf of bread opens the door, bread for her children. Awkward boyish playing at being a man. But his tiredness is too obliterating, and a boy falls asleep on a mother's shoulder. . . . And then the last sad finale. An embarrassed awakening, awkward silence, awkward empty words, good-by, a short hesitation at the door, and again the endless lonely road. (pp. 119-20)

If Borchert could have been expected to be consistent, and if an appreciable time of gestation had elapsed between the two volumes, one could, with considerable justification, conclude that his last *Erkenntnis* was total nihilism. This idea cannot be lightly brushed aside. However, before arriving at any conclusions we must still consider *Das Holz für morgen,* which for some reason was not included in the *Gesamtwerk,* and finally the *Nachlass.*

The undated *Das Holz für morgen* tells the simple story of a man returned from war who wants to commit suicide because he has come back to a world in which, he thinks, he is an unwanted stranger even to those who love him. . . . As he is about to open the attic door he hears from below his mother's voice instructing the washer-woman to bring the soap powder tomorrow; her boy has come home and he will fetch the wood, as such chores are getting to be too hard for father. The would-be suicide descends the stairs again. How could he have forgotten the wood?—Some very decisive things have happened to the youth in these short moments. Memories of a childish transgression have brought home to him the existence of unknown guilts and have opened to him the idea of reparation and expiation. His mother's voice pulls him out of his egocentric self-commiseration and makes him realize his obligation to others. He has found his place in the world, he knows he is wanted, he is needed, he belongs. This is, as far as I could ascertain, the only Borchert story with such a positive ending. It touches upon the double crux of German youth, as Borchert sees it: the overwhelming feeling of an unknown or unadmitted guilt, and the sense of living in a void from which no bridges reach out. In the liberation from such fears and in the humble acceptance of one's place in the order of things, whatever it may be, lies the possibility of a cure.

The *Nachlass* is primarily important for its two manifestos. *Das ist unser Manifest* is a positive declaration of the avowed nihilist who is not a nihilist, an unreserved acceptance of life as it is, of the world, of Germany as it is, and above all an unconditional dedication to love, in spite of all.... This powerful document carries out what *Das Holz für morgen* promised. It rises far above any self-pity to a sobered acceptance of life through love. (pp. 121-22)

Adolf D. Klarmann, "Wolfgang Borchert: The Lost Voice of a New Germany," in The Germanic Review *(copyright 1952 by Helen Dwight Reed Foundation), Vol. XXVII, No. 1, February, 1952, pp. 108-23.*

STEPHEN SPENDER (essay date 1952)

[Borchert's] appears to be the life of a perfect victim of our times, a man whose soul must bear simply the impress of the world of dictatorship and war and post-war horror into which he was born. It is in some ways like the life of a man born and bred in a prison cell.

It is therefore not surprising that his writings are like those of a man who sees hardly a day before his time or beyond it, and for whom a world outside his experiences seems completely shut off. The war which he describes is not the one for which German leaders bore, in the opinion of the rest of the world, a certain responsibility. (p. v)

Borchert's soldiers are the doomed race of the Russian winter of 1941, and of Stalingrad. Nothing existed for them before they went to Russia. They are filled with the sense that if there are other soldiers, they must feel the same, and be equally passive victims of their time. The Russians are only a background to their own misery and to the German doom which is regarded as universal doom.

Borchert's post-war Germany is a universal apocalypse seen in the language of symbolic horror of the ruin of German cities. For him war is simply the affirmation by mankind of a spirit of destruction in the world. (pp. v-vi)

The limited truth which Borchert creates within his prose is not only literature; it is useful to us. Of course, the wider truth is that although if people stopped acting in a way which contributed to war, wars would cease, they will not do so. (p. vi)

We have to look longer and further for a cause of war which, if it is grasped, may prevent further wars. That cause is guilt, with ensuing responsibility. It is this which the German mind seems to find it peculiarly hard to grasp: perhaps largely because when most people say 'guilt', they mean German guilt. Borchert does not create any picture of guilt and responsibility in his preoccupation with apocalyptic doom.

There is, though, a danger of people who talk about the causes of war, forgetting the reality itself. What Borchert does do most memorably, is create the doomed, horrible reality of the victims who are just nothing but victims; who feel no responsibility for the situation in which they are ruined; and whose widest sense of humanity is a feeling that on the other side of the barbed wire fence which surrounds them, there are other victims. (pp. vi-vii)

But in Borchert's world there is something beside the trap itself: there is a mysterious sense of Otherness, of a World Outside....

This Otherness is the central point of conflict in Borchert's mind. Is it dream? Is it reality? Or is it just a name for the persistent courage which can go on creating again and again the illusion that life is worth while.

Sometimes Otherness is just the point where human happiness merges into a human dream. It is the little piece of pink cloth cut from his sweetheart's petticoat, which the soldier on the Eastern Front carries in his trouser pocket. In that remarkable prose poem drama *The Man Outside*, it is The Other, the soldier who has been at Stalingrad, the one who goes on struggling while his neighbour gives in, who remains present in the consciousness of Beckmann the suicide who has thrown himself into the Elbe. It is also, of course, nature, and the beauty of the world everywhere. (p. vii)

There is no sense in conjecturing how Borchert would have developed had he lived. In the manifesto which is printed among his posthumous works, he has reached a stage of accepted nihilism on which he proposed to rebuild a world— or at least, a Germany—of love. "For we are no-men," he declared. "But we do not say No in despair. Our No is a protest. And there is no peace for us in kisses, for us Nihilists. For into nothingness we must again build a Yes. Houses we must build in the free air of our No, over the abysses, the craters and the slit-trenches and over the open mouths of the dead." (p. viii)

Since Borchert did in fact die, his work stands completely enclosed within the world in which he grew and which he saw destroyed. To read him is—to change the metaphor from that of the trap or prison—to study the sensibility of a man who is the victim of a machine which is itself destroyed, tearing his life down with it. His vision is entirely confined by this machine, and except once for the vague mention of 'Hindenburg' he does not seem to see the men who were the makers of the machine or the faces of those who destroyed it.

The world of Borchert is not very far from that of George Orwell's *1984*. (pp. viii-ix)

As description of a moment of European history, it is difficult to think that anyone has excelled Borchert's invocations of Hamburg and the Elbe. For a young writer he has an astonishing discipline in his use of many details of observation; and a poet's gift in making the inanimate significant and personal. (p. ix)

Stephen Spender, "Introduction" (reprinted by permission of A D Peters & Co Ltd), in The Man Outside: The Prose Works of Wolfgang Borchert *by Wolfgang Borchert, translated by David Porter, Hutchinson International Authors Limited, 1952, pp. v-ix.*

KARL S. WEIMAR (essay date 1956)

The hero of Wolfgang Borchert's radio play, *The Man Outside* ..., has lost all contact with his fellow human beings; his efforts to reënter society are thwarted, for he is misunderstood and rejected by all save one, and from this creature he flees in distraction, believing he has innocently sinned against her husband. The three figures of Jean-Paul Sartre's play, *No Exit* ..., are irremediably alone, and, although they are sentenced to be forever together, they will never be able to bridge the distance between them nor to share in each other's lives. Borchert's man, Corporal Beckmann, remains always outside society; Sartre's trio is forever sealed within the walls of society. The closed door of the original titles, **Draussen vor der Tür** and *Huis Clos,* is an unmistakable symbol of isolation and loneliness. Yet in each play the hero makes stubborn and frenzied attempts to find some justification, some meaning for his existence; the goal in each case is what is described in existential philosophy as authentic existence. Both heroes are impelled in the same direction; the one, despite his frantic drive, is irremediably closed off from existence, and the other is ironically walled in toward existence. Both citified heroes know only the approach through human society; they fail to recognize the possibility of reaching authentic existence through the experience of nature and to realize that man is an integral part of the natural world. (pp. 153-54)

Both writers accept man's existential guilt. Both are apparently pessimistic in their emphasis on the pain and disillusion, the grief and despair of existence; yet they reject death as a choice for man and deliberately commit their heroes to live on, thus affirming their belief in man's potential to realize the ''possibilities of being'' (Heidegger). In both plays the characters are stranded in unrelieved solitude, for they fail to reach the ''being'' (existentially expressed, the ''Mitsein'') in their fellow human beings. Common to both writers is the experience of confronting the void, of the silent absence of a Divine Being. Into this void Sartre has elevated man and considers this aspect of his *Weltanschauung* humanistic. Borchert, on the other hand, may have been leaning toward an ontocentric view, in the spirit of Heidegger....

The extreme situation in Borchert's play is a living hell: the bomb-blasted, cold, selfish, post-war world as experienced by the returning soldier, whose reintegration is frustrated by the indifference of his fellow men and by his own existential guilt. He recognizes, with the help of the Other One, that the world is part of man's fundamental state of being, that it exists inasmuch as he exists, and that he must establish the relationship. These are basic aspects of Heidegger's concept of *Erschlossenheit.* Beckmann's frantic actions are directed toward gaining access to existence, to other people, to home. But all doors are closed, one after another, all save one, the door to death; and although Borchert's hero had slipped through and been ejected, he is unwilling at the end to choose death again. (pp. 154-55)

And in this respect Borchert and Sartre seem to deviate strikingly from Heidegger, who conceives death as the last and most authentic possibility of that which is existentially impossible. But more of this later. At this point, cold, wet, alone, half corpse, half living thing, Beckmann is confronted by the Other One, the same one who knew him as schoolboy and soldier, the inescapable One of yesterday and tomorrow, whose voice is known to every man; the One who always affirms, always answers. And now that Beckmann wants to say No to life, he is there to counter with a calm persuasive Yes. Again and again on Beckmann's way he appears to summon him back from self-destruction to life, to try one more road home, until finally he too falls silent. (pp. 156-57)

In utter despair he cries out: ''Tell me why are you silent? Why? Is no one going to give me an answer? Will no one answer??? No one, no one answer???.''... The sound of closing doors heard throughout the play is now effectively transposed to the anguished outcry of man, the lonely outcast.

The *Weltanschauung* of Borchert's play seems to be unreserved nihilism. (p. 157)

Beckmann's tragic situation is so appalling because he is left in a vacuum with the old world in ruins about him and no indication of a new world before him. (p. 158)

But is there really nothing in the play which might be interpreted as a sign, as a possibility of some new value upon which to rebuild? The figure of the Other One immediately suggests itself, for in contrast to God, ''in whom no one believes any more,'' the Other One is introduced as one ''whom everyone knows'' (dramatis personae). His existence is real, and his influence upon Beckmann is demonstrated again and again. And yet who he is or what he is, remains a matter of speculation. He is obviously not the Christian conscience; nor can he represent some Schopenhauerian Will, for he seems to expire while Beckmann continues to exist. (pp. 158-59)

Beckmann has been ''thrown'' into life, into the vortex of war, and the waste land that followed. He sought to flee into death, without ever having realized any of his possibilities and without even knowing dread of death. His return to life is a merciless maneuver, but it is nevertheless an opportunity for Beckmann to become what he is. The voice of the Other One now persists in calling him back to life, again and again. In some significant respects Heidegger's conscience suggests lines of interpretation. When the Other One states, ''You can't get rid of me''... he clearly indicates the essential indissoluble relationship between himself and Beckmann, for the call of conscience originates in man himself; and when he makes his first question, ''Who are you?''... he raises a fundamental issue which refers to man's true foundation. At first glance the Other One seems to be directing Beckmann toward absorption in other people, in the general public; but actually he is leading Beckmann back to himself, through the girl, and in the last analysis away from the general public (the Colonel and his family, the Cabaret Director, and Frau Kramer) by evoking a stinging revulsion in Beckmann. Beckmann's sense of guilt is, to be sure, not as subtle or as profound as Heidegger's analysis; but after all he is only a bewildered soldier, neither a poet nor a philosopher. (pp. 159-60)

Beckmann never comes to the state of resoluteness, although what he experiences ultimately is no longer fear but dread, the dread of the nothing and the nowhere which is yet something. It is true, of course, that Beckmann is overwhelmed by the world; however, his situation is not only existential, that is, inasmuch as it represents a man's search for his position in the world and in society, but also ''essential,'' insofar as it is a search for his authentic home, which is Being. From this same perspective of existential philosophy as proposed by Heidegger, we might interpret Borchert's play also as an illustration of the futility of existential engagement which is not predicated upon ''essential'' engagement. This play may very well represent an anguished attempt to find a substitute for the silent impotent God so often encountered in Borchert's work. Beckmann's final indeterminate position with respect to the ultimate questions parallels Heidegger's speculations in the closing paragraph of his incomplete work, when he raises the question: can the study of human existence serve as an approach to the understanding of Being as such?

Borchert, however, did not always raise unanswered or unanswerable questions in the darkness of doubts and despair.

He was at times a lantern in the night, no matter how feeble and flickering. . . . [Passing] mention might be made here of the very interesting sketch, *Thithyphuth,* of early origin but included in the posthumous writings, which Meyer-Marwitz finds noteworthy because of its "abgründigen Humors.". . . Although he only suggests the myth, Borchert emphasizes, somewhat grotesquely and yet also somewhat hopefully, the comic aspect of the absurd situation rather than the tragic, as Camus, for instance, interprets it. This work is a striking example of the triumph over existential guilt effected by laughter. Two men are brought together in a beer garden, each with the same speech defect; embarrassment, anger, humiliation, laughter, tears, and reconciliation follow. This is, in a sense, the tale of deliverance from an original fault, a deliverance given by the laughter of a man who had himself overcome a similar fault. The bridge from man to man is built, and because it is such a rare event in Borchert, it is doubly noteworthy. The writer's uncle is the protagonist, an ebullient, massive Apollo of a man who had lost a leg and part of his tongue in battle. He lisps, but "loud, laughing, lively, colossal, confident, Croesus" that he is, he acts as if he had no lisp at all. When a pathetic little waiter lisps his order, he is enraged; but his wrath is quickly converted to tender compassion when he learns that the poor man was born with this defect, and his booming laughter dissolves the tension and evokes tears of timid joy from the waiter's eyes. . . . [The] waiter is last pictured wiping away with his napkin "the whole gray world, all the beer gardens of the world, all the waiters, and all the speech defects of the world forever out of his life." In Borchert's world, so circumscribed by sickness, war, and early death, there are many little "waiters" but hardly any "uncles." (pp. 160-61)

The contrast between Sartre and Borchert, so strikingly evident in the diverse matrices and polar aspects of existential philosophy, is also apparent in their antithetical techniques. Sartre's control of form, his technical skill in unfolding the histories of his characters and in developing the tense situation, are evidence of his intellectual detachment, one might say, of his philosophic objectivity. On the other hand, the loose construction and episodic nature of *The Man Outside* attest to its author's impassioned subjectivity and his poetic frenzy.

Sartre has constructed his one-act play logically and incisively. . . . Borchert's technique is more fluid; the Other One appears in every scene, except the third, like a constantly recurring theme; three times the locale shifts from an interior to the street, and the change is effected not so much by stage directions as by the sound of a closing door. The play is introduced by a prologue, where the identity of the speakers is transposed from the concrete to the abstract, and by a very brief dream colloquy between Beckmann and the river Elbe, which all but defies staging. . . .

Two plays, one a brilliant philosophic exercise, the other an impassioned outcry; both born of despair, yet sustained by a stoic will; one an expression of a new humanism, the other gravitating toward Being; while for both writers there remains no faith, no love, only hope. (pp. 164-65)

> Karl S. Weimar, "No Entry, No Exit: A Study of Borchert with Some Notes on Sartre," in Modern Language Quarterly (© 1956 University of Washington), Vol. 17, No. 2, June, 1956, pp. 153-65.*

HANS POPPER (essay date 1964)

[We must agree with Bernhard Meyer-Marwitz]—and not least with the poet himself—that [Borchert's] lyrical output served as a preparation for the really important works, which came into being in the period January 1946—November 1947: the prose pieces and the play, *Draussen vor der Tür.* . . .

Only two prose pieces had been written by him before that time, *Die Blume* . . . and *Requiem für einen Freund.* . . . They are hardly of any interest, except to the student of the poet's development. (p. 272)

The lyrics already contain many of the motifs, which Borchert was to work out more thoroughly in his prose pieces and in the play. And these two early prose pieces thus form a bridge between the two phases of the poet's work. In them we may also detect flashes of that concreteness in the presentation of setting and action, in the visual field, which makes his prose writing so effective. And we find beginnings of one of the most important characteristics of Borchert's style: the device of juxtaposing objects, or even words and short sentences, which appear, outwardly, to be totally disconnected, and which result in forming a rhythmic and visual pattern, having an atmosphere and a psychical unity of their own. But the relation to the observer—whether of such patterns, or even of single objects—is put on a new basis. Sometimes the poet uses, as it were, the style of a schoolchild's essay, or of an *ingénu,* so that the object the poet presents should be able to make its impact and impart its message, independent of our preconceived notions of it. (p. 274)

A study of Borchert's life and personality shows, that pairs of opposites in his attitudes, moods, thoughts and in his reaction to his environment are clear-cut to quite an extraordinary degree. This is also reflected in his manner of writing. Persons, actions, situations, are all set in a well-defined town or landscape, and the events, with their motivation, are made manifest to the reader in the form of sense impressions. Yet by means of alienation we are taken to the very heart of the issues at stake—we relive the action, we re-experience its joys, its sorrows, its problematic. (p. 276)

[It] is surprising, how rarely his sense of timing fails him, even in such highly rhetorical pieces as *Die lange lange Strasse lang,* or *Im Mai, im Mai schrie der Kuckuck.* And the reason for this great buoyancy may be sought in the dialectic nature of the poet's attitude. For while the reader (or, in the case of the play, *Draussen vor der Tür,* the audience) is made to participate in the inner experience which the work in question presents, by watching and listening, even smelling and tasting, the poet himself moves in the *opposite* direction: he detaches himself, and views, even the most deeply felt sentiment, critically, even ironically. [An example can be taken] from the story, *Der Kaffee ist undefinierbar,* which is set in the desolate atmosphere of a station waiting-room. Men are reduced to mere functions designed to fill the gap between birth and death, hung over chairs and tables like drapery, playthings of a God without eyes and ears, simply covering, like cloth, the "chairs, bars, tables, gallows and immense abysses", over which they have been hung ("hingehängt"). Their isolation from each other is complete. But their supreme desolation is due to their isolation from this God without eyes and ears, whose impotent playthings they are, who lets them breathe—just that and no more!—and who reduces their cries—by this very loneliness—to the thin-voiced tinkling of a bell.

The point at issue is this *absence* of seeing, communicating and hearing, the *remoteness* of man from man, so that the responsible coexistence of persons in community gets reduced to the chance togetherness of biological functions, and the *presence* of God, his vital breath, his powerful Word of Truth, gets veiled behind this cruel mask of deaf and blind facelessness. The *ruach adonai*, the *Logos* has become the mere originator and sustainer of bodies which breathe, which exercise their instincts "savagely, greedily, omnivorously" ("wild, gierig, gefrässig"). Four people sit at a table, three men and a girl. Suddenly, but in the most matter-of-fact way, the girl says that she is going to commit suicide. In this very situation, but also in the ensuing conversation, again and again, the opportunity presents itself of being truthful, of talking in a responsible, truly personal manner. The opportunity is missed every time, until the men discover that the girl has, in fact, carried out her intention. One of the characters, an intellectual ("der Buchmann"—"the man with the book"), suddenly recognises his and the other two men's irresponsible attitude: the girl had been lonely, and they had simply talked about her, then about their own concerns, as if she had not been present. (p. 277)

[Let us now refer to Borchert's letter of February 27, 1947 to Dr. Gantz]. In the penultimate paragraph he comments on the end of his play [*Draussen vor der Tür*]. Beckmann, the poet says, does not throw himself into the Elbe, but cries out for an answer, asks after God, after love, after the neighbour, after the meaning of life on this earth.

> . . . And he does not receive an answer. No answer exists. Life itself is the answer. Or do you know of one?

"No answer exists" is almost dynamic. The paradoxical "Life itself is the answer" is a retrograde step. It suggests the same immanentism as appears in the previous paragraph, which we considered above, and which appears again and again throughout the poet's work. It has its value, but is inadequate. (pp. 291-92)

[The] opposition between the prison, which human society has built (*Die Hundeblume*), with its locked doors, its barred windows, and its uniformed guards on the one hand, and primitive nature on the other, is of only secondary importance. It is true, the prison yard, where the *planks* in a human *fence* go round and round, *encompassed* by *barking dogs* . . . , is the very antithesis of living growth, even of such a humble plant as the dandelion, which convict No. 432 manages to pluck surreptitiously one day, to have in his cell as a token of the universal breath of life. Again, earth is good and tastes sweet (*Radi*); but snow is, again and again, described as nauseating, giving rise to anxiety—even disorienting one's whole sense of time and space (esp. *Mein bleicher Bruder* and *Der viele viele Schnee*). "Rain is an angel" (*Liebe blue graue Nacht*), but wind is cunning and destructive (*Die Mauer, Tui Hoo*); and the combination of physical strength with the instincts unleashed in man can crush a sensitive soul as effectively as the indifference of the men round the coffee table in *Der Kaffee ist undefinierbar*: Elsie in *Alle Milchgeschäfte heissen Hinsch*. As for self-sufficiency, the spider in *Die Hundeblume* is the perfect example. It produces its own scaffolding by excreting the necessary substance, and it would seem that the motto of the story: "And who catches us in mid-air? God?" is quite inapplicable. Furthermore the spider's web is a symbol for prison-bars, already in the *Moabit* lyric included in the section, *Nachgelassene Gedichte*, in the

Gesamtwerk: Der Mond lügt; in Das Holz für morgen the glass roof over the top of the landing of a block of flats is covered with wire netting, which looks like a spider's web, breaks up the light, obscures it. The hero of the story notices it at the beginning, when he intends to commit suicide. At the end, when he has given up the idea, because he has discovered that he is wanted and loved by his family, it is no longer noticed. It seems, in fact, not to harbour, but to *exclude* the divine quality in life. And in *Im Mai, im Mai schrie der Kuckuck* it adds its touch of dreariness and neglect to the institutional green of the lampshades, which the all-powerful All-Provider, the Fatherland, has placed in railway stations and lavatories for the benefit of its children.

It is true, on the other hand, that when personal community (*Das Brot*) or divine hope (*Die drei dunklen Könige*) is experienced, the terms must be those of natural or human objects and of personal living. And yet its dynamic transcends nature. It is rooted in the human soul (*Nachts schlafen die Ratten doch*), but again, its provenance is as mysterious as the sweetness and brightness of the burning timber, or the spontaneous giving and receiving of hospitality together with the presenting of gifts, which has nothing to do with that resentment that makes the father of the new-born child wish he had somebody's face to push in (*Die drei dunklen Könige*).

And ultimately, the problematic of life is not to be found in among the elements, plants, animals, or even the actions and sensations of the human world, but in the loneliness for which there are no words, to an awareness of which we are recalled by the cry of the cuckoo. This is the true "vocabulary" of the world, before which all else must keep silent. (*Im Mai, im Mai schrie der Kuckuck.*) But its full realisation in human terms is rare and full of terror. We find it in the child's impotence when faced with the cod's eye (*Gottes Auge*), which, although supposed to belong to God, is utterly inactive and unresponsive. We find it again in *Die Kegelbahn*, when two soldiers obediently liquidate piles of enemy lives, until the realisation of what they are doing costs them their sleep. So they talk about it, and their argument sways to and fro. (pp. 292-93)

[The] non-existence of God is linked with the existence of men, with moral responsibility. The word *existence* is charged with the same potential force, as when Borchert tells Dr. Gantz, that no answer *exists*. It tears down such idols as "our good German truth", or the "impregnable civilian prosperity" of the Colonel and the Manager respectively (*Draussen vor der Tür*, scenes 3 and 4), and drives Beckmann into a void, where he asks questions, to which he does not receive an answer; for God, to change the metaphor (*Der Kaffee ist undefinierbar*), is without face. The man with the book *closes his eyes* and realises that the girl, whose face he can no longer visualise, has killed herself because she had been bypassed in conversation. Her absence exists as powerfully as the deafness of the God, who does not hear [her glass poison container] drop on the floor and smash. And this deafness reappears, even more terrifyingly, at the end of *Dann gibt es nur eins, . . .* where the last blasphemy, the last accusing "Why?" drains away in the wasteland, because man has been as irresponsible as the soldier in *Der Kaffee ist undefinierbar* when he lets the glass tube roll across the table till it smashes on the floor.

This is as far as the actual text of the works takes us. Attempts at making Borchert either into a "nihilist"—except in the very special meaning of the word as used in *Das ist unser*

Manifest, where love is seen to be rooted in suffering and evil; or, on the other hand, into a *positive* writer with a comforting message, are one-sided. The poet certainly intended his work to be read as a message—hence his series of manifestoes. But the comfort is no more than a hope. God is hidden. And the only trace of the Logos is in the poet's utter truthfulness in his statements regarding human responsibility in the face of this hiddenness. (p. 294)

Hans Popper, "Wolfgang Borchert," in German Men of Letters: Twelve Literary Essays, Vol. III, *edited by Alex Natan (© 1964 Oswald Wolff (Publishers) Limited), Oswald Wolff, 1964, pp. 269-303.*

KURT J. FICKERT   (essay date 1966)

Borchert concerns himself not with the events of life, but with its essence.... One of Borchert's short stories which presents the poignantly asked question, "What is life all about; who are we?" and which can also be regarded as typical of Borchert's work in its simple façade and labyrinthine interior is **"Billbrook."**

Bill Brook, an Allied air force sergeant, comes shortly after the end of the war to Hamburg from the land of innocence and hope, specifically Hopedale, Canada. He is immediately confronted by a situation, the very illogicality of which forces him to try to fathom its meaning, a situation which, furthermore, centers about his most inviolable possession, his identity, his name. In the Hamburg railroad station he sees a signpost spelling out "Billbrook." The shock of recognition is so great that in trying to light a cigarette, Bill singes a bit of his vanity, his little red mustache; also he feels frightened, quite out of proportion to the mystery of the situation, the solution of which (that Billbrook must be a place name, a suburb of Hamburg) lies readily at hand.... [On] the next day he sets out impatiently to explore those acres of a strange city which seem somehow an extension of himself. He never reaches Billbrook, which is much too far away from the start of his journey. He comes instead to the bombed-out part of Hamburg, the endless vistas of rubble. Now he is no longer engaged in a search; rather, the city is happening to him.... Standing in relief against the vast panorama of waste, a few mementos of a thriving life somehow left perpendicular, now completely meaningless in any objective sense, act as symbols and address themselves to the awakened consciousness of the wanderer.... Finally Bill encounters a few living beings in the void. These, too, have their existence only in relation to the inner world of Bill Brook.... He has not found Billbrook, but he has had a revelation.... The once mildly vain and generally simple-minded Bill Brook has changed, he knows; he has had his eyes opened to the true nature of life, its accretion of guilt, the desolation of its inexplicableness. When he reaches his hotel and in the quiet of the night sets about writing home, he finds that he can tell nothing of his search for Billbrook, but he can write knowingly, appreciatively of the trivia of life in Hopedale, because he did find a Bill Brook, a sentient self, among the ruins. (pp. 31-2)

Bill Brook becomes a man, any man, in search of a soul, and the flux of objects around him comes into focus—they become meaningful. (p. 32)

The message pertaining to the revitalization of the self contained in the depths of Borchert's **"Billbrook"** can be deciphered on the basis of symbols generally understood; they are not the particular language of Borchert, nor of any author. They are universal and address themselves to a general understanding, dissociated from the paraphernalia of literary appreciation. **"Billbrook"** is an effective story on this intuitive, mystic level. It also explores successfully the crisis in the life of the fictional character Bill Brook. Lastly it recreates vividly the world of postwar Germany, devastated and defeated, and pictures the conquered and the victors. Borchert's ability to create such a multi-leveled structure, coupled with a brilliant style, was his genius. (p. 33)

Kurt J. Fickert, "Wolfgang Borchert's 'Billbrook' as a Search for the Self," in Books Abroad *(copyright 1966 by the University of Oklahoma Press), Vol. 40, No. 1, Winter, 1966, pp. 31-4.*

A. LESLIE WILLSON   (essay date 1968)

Considerations of form and incident show that fantasies in the mind of a drowning person ... may be presumed in Wolfgang Borchert's *Draussen vor der Tür.* Such a presumption may lead to the reappraisal of a play which has perplexed and fascinated critics since its first presentation on the German radio in 1947. (p. 119)

[The] work's presentation first as a radio play cannot be ignored, and it seems certain that Borchert's composition of the play for radio guided both form and content. Both seem to have been shaped in accordance with a basic premise: the action takes place in the mind of a drowning man.

What is there in the structure and the content of the play to support the suggestion just made? The original conception of the piece for radio presentation accounts for the strong level of sound in the play: the repeated leitmotiv of the creaky door slammed shut, the gurgle of a bottle, the whish of a street cleaner's broom, the tick-tock, clock-like stomp of a one-legged man, labored breathing, and the repeated use of onomatopoetic words, such as *knirschen, piepen, flüstern, gluckern, kreischen,* and *knistern.* Sound heard under water is also magnified. The character of radio drama also permitted Borchert to give free play to his fantasy in regard to structure and content. Inextricably linked with the content is the temporal sequence of events in the work. In a kind of inverted and twisted parabolic spiral, Beckmann relives his encounters with those persons whom he visited on his return from war: the colonel, the cabaret director, and the callous, shallow Frau Kramer in his parent's former apartment. His most distressing encounter—that with his wife—is not depicted except in hearsay. The meetings depicted in the play occur only in Beckmann's imagination. In his drowning delirium he sees again those persons who were standing on the bank of the Elbe when he plunged in: the street cleaner who resembles an undertaker, a personification of death, and the old man, a forgotten and helpless God. The scenes with the colonel, the cabaret director, and Frau Kramer are vivid though distorted recollections of actual meetings, re-experienced by a drowning Beckmann. It is significant that although he has not re-entered the river but imagines that he lies dying on the street during his re-encounters with the colonel, the cabaret director, and Frau Kramer, he nevertheless accuses them of having driven him to suicide in the Elbe. At this time, too, he calls each of their comments his obituaries. The re-encounter with his wife—the only time they meet in the play—is with a woman who remains mute, utterly unaware of his presence, the consequence of his having blotted the actual first meeting from his memory and of his having substituted for it a chance and almost idyllic meeting with a girl. The girl is simply a figment of his fantasy, a wish-fulfillment and wife-substitute who befriends him in the phantasm of his drowning. She is the only one whom he does not accuse of his murder on their re-encounter. The wraithlike figure of the one-legged man is his own double, whom he murders by his suicide, becoming paradoxically the murdered and the murderer. When the enigmatic figure of *der Andere* fades away upon Beckmann's command to be gone, Beckmann's last gasp is a resounding No to life. (pp. 121-22)

The prologue of the play sets the scene for the entire hallucinatory action which transpires in the mind of a drowning man, an action which undoubtedly is easier to represent with the facilities of radio production than on the stage. Although Beckmann is not named in the prologue, his close-cropped hair readily identifies him with the man who jumps into the river. The following scene, the dream—in which the Elbe's nixes throw him out at Blankenese, where he imagines his corpse will wash ashore . . .—justifies his further illusions, first that of the conjuration by his will to live of the girl who befriends him on the river bank at Blankenese, a scene which is a surrogate for the meeting he had with his wife, a meeting which he cannot bear to recall, and then the further scenes in which he recapitulates the meetings of the foregoing day. That he must have leaped into the river after his conversations with the colonel, the cabaret director, and Frau Kramer is evident from his remark to each as they pass by while he supposedly lies in a dreamlike state in the street; he accuses each of having driven him to his death. . . . Even in the heightened reality of dream it would be incongruous for a river suicide to accuse his persecutors from the muck of a city street. (p. 123)

Beckmann's *Doppelgänger*, the one-legged man, the reproachful projection of his own Self, says that he jumped into the Elbe himself on the previous evening. . . . Of course, these exchanges, too, take place in the mind of Beckmann as he drowns.

The question of the identity of *der Andere* is pertinent to both the structure and to the content of the play, particularly to one thesis presented in this paper: namely, that Beckmann is not the typical soldier returned home from war to find himself isolated by rejection. The typical soldier got along somehow, even as a street dweller or a drunken bum. The typical soldier was more resourceful than Beckmann, who is totally crushed by his rejection, who finds no haven, even with God; Beckmann's spark of life surrenders to an imperious will for extinction. That the whole action of the play is the hallucination of a drowning man reinforces the inevitable fact of Beckmann's suicide. It is not Beckmann at the end of the play who raises his voice in a vain plea for contact with the world; Beckmann has already shouted No to existence. It is the author who pleads for others like Beckmann who may be inescapably doomed. (p. 124)

Der Andere is inextricably involved in the life of Beckmann, a positive power, Protean, obstinately affirmative. (p. 125)

The thesis that the whole action of the play transpires in the fervid fantasy of a drowning man is supported by the sinuous texture of exterior form and details of interior vocabulary and incident. Repeated reference to the physical sensations associated with submersion is made. Since the sense of sight becomes secondary under water to the sense of hearing,

underwater sounds are magnified to a submerged ear, although articulation is reduced. Sounds abound in the drama, in part because it was written as a radio play; but sounds lend themselves well to a role in the underwater realm. The creaking and slam of a door resound repeatedly in Beckmann's ear. The absence of sound creates a stillness which is yet incomplete under water, for the liquid rhythm of the flowing river instills a monotony more dreadful than total silence. . . . The tick-tock gait of the one-legged man resembles the inexorable sound of time, but the recurrence of the tick-tock rhythm at the end of the play heralds, with the strenuous beat of an expiring heart, the monotonous eternity of death. In the last scene Beckmann begins to yawn, a characteristic physical reflex to increase the body's intake of oxygen. . . . When the struggle of his own lungs for air creates a rasping which he senses, Beckmann complains that he cannot go on. *Der Andere* contradicts him, however, and suggests that the sound is that of a street cleaner's broom. The power of conjuration native to *der Andere* then produces a street cleaner, who in a dialogue with Beckmann, however, becomes symbolic of death. . . . The chief physical sensation of submersion is coldness and wetness. . . . The girl calls him a cold, wet fish . . . or a gray, wet, cold ghost. . . . To the cabaret director Beckmann speaks of himself as a ghost of yesterday. . . . The epithets of fish and ghost used by the girl in reference to Beckmann emphasize both his struggle in the liquid element and its outcome. (pp. 126-28)

Lack of air leads to murder, he says to *der Andere*, and at the end of the play, in the airless river, he has murdered himself. The use of the term *ersaufen*, both in the sense of "to intoxicate" and "to drown," is made again and again in the play . . . , often in a completely ambiguous context.

Beckmann's frequent remark on his desire to nap (*pennen*) has the character of a leitmotiv as an allusion to death. The theme of *pennen* is struck in the dream scene. When the Elbe asks Beckmann what he is doing under water, he replies: "Pennen." . . . His eyes keep closing . . . and he feels enormously weary . . . , until finally darkness engulfs him. (pp. 128-29)

The total effect of the play has been felt by some critics to be negative, nihilistic. . . . Beckmann cannot be exonerated of a nihilistic persuasion by being oversimplified into a nonentity, or by being made too much of a symbol for any sort of homecomer, or by being reduced to a Christ-figure subjected to a heroic and tragic passion. He is another casualty of war, but not simply that. The wretchedness of his end, the hopelessness of his fate is cast in such horrifyingly and piteously nihilistic circumstances that the reader, the listener, the spectator flinches, forewarned, and involuntarily generates his own hope with a determination that what he has witnessed should not happen again.

Beckmann is at the moment of his suicide a nihilist, and the moment of his suicide encompasses the whole work; yet the play is not nihilistic. Beckmann, whose spark of life-force insists that he wander in his drowning moments through a world he has already abandoned, has irrevocably committed himself to death. His surrender to weary sleep in the gutter heralds the cold, wet, suffocated, deeper sleep in the river which he accepts with a final No to life. The reader feels compassion for the individual Beckmann, but has no wish to emulate him. Beckmann is nihilistic, but the work itself—ending as it does with a desperate plea for an answer to a piteous cry for help—is not nihilistic. The paradox is resolved because the appalling fate of Beckmann increases the positive force of *der Andere* in every man. Beckmann, however, does not survive, but is from the beginning of the play a drowning man. (pp. 130-31)

A. Leslie Willson, "The Drowning Man: 'Draussen vor der Tür'," in Texas Studies in Literature and Language *(copyright © 1968 by the University of Texas Press), Vol. X, No. 1, Spring, 1968, pp. 119-31.*

JOHN PICKFORD (essay date 1973)

[Wolfgang Borchert] died a martyred symbol of yet another of the 20th century's 'lost generations' and this accounts, in part, for his great popularity in the immediate post-war years. More recently, his reputation in Germany has waned. For the generation of 1968 he is too bewildered by oppression, too politically naive, too much the bourgeois humanist. . . .

[The selection of stories titled *The Sad Geraniums*] reflects these criticisms. The stories are statements about suffering and alienation. They do not explore the economic and political background to the deprivations they describe. They do not contain neat Marxist explanations for the chaos of events. Political assertiveness is not Borchert's natural territory: he writes instead of a collision he has himself experienced between the flabby warmth of people and the austere abrasiveness of mechanistic systems, be they totalitarian states or the unfeeling power of industrial production lines. Somewhere in almost every story a round, soft creature—the human—is trying to squeeze into a sharp, angular space—the non-human. A dead man is appositely described as a 'broken rod'; the instrument of his death, 'a piece of metal'. We meet people with 'watery, fish eyes', 'horribly sickly sincere eyes', the vacuity of their faces emphasising the hopelessness of any struggle against the agents of oppression. They choose oblivion instead. The oblivion of a flickering screen in a crowded cinema, the oblivion of 'the blue-grey night hours (grey for cats and blue for women)'. The oblivion that signifies an escape, like the young man's laugh of relief in the title story, **'Sad Geraniums',** when he finally says good-bye to the girl with the deformed nose who wanted to be his lover.

There may be an element of moral apathy in this sort of response to a brutal and depressing reality. For all that, Borchert writes, or rather composes, his stories with real care and concentration. They are actually stories in miniature, often dominated by just one or two evocative and sometimes voluptuous images. They have the smell of experience. Their impact is strangely dependent on our belief in Borchert's profound sincerity. Taken together, they make up a moving personal allegory.

John Pickford, "Hard and Soft," in New Statesman *(© 1973 The Statesman & Nation Publishing Co. Ltd.), Vol. 86, No. 2232, December 28, 1973, p. 978.**

DONALD F. NELSON (essay date 1975)

In his *Myth of Sisyphus* Albert Camus insists on the primacy of the question whether—in man's discovery of and confrontation with the absurdity of existence—life is or is not worth living. . . . For Camus, it is not the *discovery* of the absurd—the yawning chasm between human nostalgia for

meaningfulness and reasonableness of existence and the unreasonable silence of the world—that is so interesting, but rather the *consequences* of this discovery. . . . [Pushed] to the very limits in the waterless desert, it is up to man to choose how he will relate to the world, the absurd world; that is, whether he will confront the absurdity in implacable opposition and unremitting struggle or whether he will succumb to the escapist solution of suicide.

Viewed in the context of Camus' formulation of the problem, it becomes evident that Borchert's protagonist Beckmann vacillates throughout between these two poles. . . . Even though Beckmann himself never declares it to be so, his wavering between the existentialist and the romantic solutions, and the dialectical tension that prevails in the tug-of-war with "Der Andere" make it sufficiently clear that to live or not to live is the question upon which the plot turns. . . .

To my knowledge, . . . no investigation [of Borchert's work] has as yet seriously considered Camus' philosophy of the Absurd as a frame of reference. In the present essay this orientation to Camus is intended to enlarge the scope of existentialist motifs in *Draussen vor der Tür*. (p. 343)

[Returning home from the wars,] Beckmann finds himself in a position of standing *outside* the round of accustomed existence. He finds himself outside his bedroom door after discovering another man in his bed, and eventually outside his own house. His one-year-old boy has been killed in the bombing. Thus upon returning home, Beckmann discovers something quite the contrary of what he had expected. This contradiction corresponds in essence to what Camus calls the Absurd. (p. 345)

On a conscious level, Beckmann wants to commit suicide, and sees this as a solution. Beckmann no longer masters life—life masters him. But on the deeper level of unconscious motivation, it is significant that Beckmann chooses water as a medium in which he will disappear definitively from life. Keeping in mind that this action is unconscious to Beckmann, we may say that the water of the Elbe is to be equated with the amniotic fluid of the uterus. Unconsciously, Beckmann desires to return to a state of intrauterine security. . . . But Beckmann's solution is not a mature solution, and the Elbe knows it. She proves this by rejecting him. The Elbe, the Mother, expels him from the womb and forces him to come to grips with life once more. (p. 346)

Borchert has split Beckmann's ego in two, leaving Beckmann dominated by the death-instinct and relegating the self-preservative or life-instinct to "Der Andere." In this way he personifies the conflicting forces in the mental life of the protagonist. The tension between the two, the constant pendulation between the primacy of the one and the domination of the other, is an artistic embodiment of Freud's metapsychological speculations on the life and death instincts in his *Jenseits des Lustprinzips*. I see no reason to attribute omniscience or any superhuman quality to the figure of "Der Andere"; this needlessly complicates matters. As the personification of an instinctual force he possesses, to be sure, a corresponding degree of autonomy, but like all instinctual forces, he undergoes vicissitudes. "Der Andere" stands for the life instinct. His function is that of countering the domination of the death-instinct which is operative in Beckmann in the form of an impulse toward suicide.

Eros is a major component of the life instinct. . . . Eros is unification, not destruction. Man owes his existence to Eros.

Accordingly, the function of "Das Mädchen" is that of working in alliance with "Der Andere" to make the life instinct predominant in Beckmann. . . . With Beckmann's departure in the company of the girl, "Der Andere" still exists as a force, but as a force which Beckmann for the time being no longer needs, since he is now, though somewhat hesitantly, dominated by the life instinct (Eros). (pp. 346-47)

"Das Mädchen" finds Beckmann at the water's edge, and by taking him home with her and giving him warm clothing, she saves him from death, either from exposure or by suicide. (p. 348)

The new faith which Beckmann must accept is that life is worth living. Beckmann must be converted from the death-cult, from Thanatos, to life (Eros). "Das Mädchen" succeeds in bringing about this conversion, at least temporarily. Through her kindness and love Beckmann becomes a human being again after he had been discovered half-dead and fish-like, exiled to an existence in the sand, the death-element of the fish. (pp. 348-49)

Beckmann's despondency is progressively intensified by each of his encounters with a bourgeois type well-entrenched behind a bulwark of complacency. Dead serious in his efforts to arouse and convert the others to a sense of responsibility for the disasters of the war, he succeeds only in convincing them that he is a clown. His appeal to ethics encounters a deafness in his audience which reaches the proportions of an epidemic. His only chance to be heard, it seems, is on the stage, not as a preacher, however, but as a clown. Beckmann follows the Colonel's advice and turns to the Director for a chance at "engagement." Beckmann wants to become *engagé* in the Sartrean sense of moral commitment, whereas the Director's sense of "engagement" is strictly one of play for play's sake, of non-commitment. The Director represents the type of the equivocal opportunist. (p. 349)

At the end of the fourth scene Beckmann expresses finally the desire to return home to his mother. We are no longer dealing now with a mother symbol, but with the real mother. The mother still signifies security and protection against the brutal and insensate life with which Beckmann has not been able to cope. Instead of struggling with the absurd, he wants to withdraw once again into intrauterine security. But a fresh disappointment is in store for him. In the same way that he returned home earlier to find another man in his bed, so now he returns to his parental home to find it inhabited by someone else. Instead of his mother Beckmann stands face to face with a horrendous substitute: Frau Kramer. Such are the vicissitudes in the aftermath of the war and its dislocations. Beckmann's return to his mother is denied him. Learning of her departure from life, his only possible recourse—if he still desires reunion—is to follow her into death. And it is the romantic escapist solution, to which Beckmann is again drawn, which occasions the emergence of "Der Andere."

The tug-of-war between the life and death instincts begins anew. "Der Andere" is relentless in his appeal to Beckmann to opt for life. Beckmann's confrontation with the absurdity of post-war society makes him regard life as meaningless, human beings as cruel and without pity. "Der Andere" counters this indictment with the assertion that humans are good, they have a heart, but they are so naïve . . . ; life, furthermore, will now allow them to show their heart.

Beckmann remains unconvinced. Like Shakespeare, he compares life to a play. In his account of life as a drama in five acts we see a recapitulation of his own fate in which his life assumes transpersonal significance in a mythic sense. It is not only Beckmann's fate, it is the fate of *Everyman*. Act One: somebody gets hurt—Beckmann returns home and discovers his wife in bed with another man. Act Two: the person who is hurt hurts somebody else—Beckmann causes the one-legged man the same hurt that was done to him: he allows himself to be found in a situation suggesting intimacy with the one-legged man's wife. Act Three: the gray sky, which has prevailed through the first two acts, becomes dark and it is now raining; this corresponds to Beckmann's lugubrious moods. Act Four: it grows still darker, but a door is visible—that is the door leading to Beckmann's parental home; as such it stands for a symbol of hope, but Beckmann cannot enter through this door, for he would run—not into the arms of his mother—but into those of the ghastly Frau Kramer. Act Five: dark night prevails and Beckmann is still standing outside the door, outside all integration into human existence. His impulse is to take the anti-existentialist leap into the water, into the arms and womb of the Elbe. But we already know that the Elbe is not in the least inclined to grant him this infantile wish.

Beckmann cries out in distress, but both human and divine ears are deaf. Beckmann is confronted with what Camus calls the "benign indifference" of the universe at the conclusion of his novel *The Stranger*. (pp. 350-51)

The conclusion of the play remains open. Beckmann asks urgent questions, but receives no answer. Once again the universe is mute and benignly indifferent. In the unreasonable silence of an absurd world he will receive no answer. He will have to rely on himself. The mind, Camus says, when it reaches its limits, must make a judgment and choose its conclusions. Beckmann stands in that waterless desert where thought has reached its limits. He will have to choose between life and death. "Der Andere," the eternal answerer, is mute. He is no longer there. Since his emergence and disappearance have, throughout the play, been connected with the dominance of the death and life instincts respectively, we must conclude that his disappearance here means that Beckmann will choose life. (p. 353)

Donald F. Nelson, "To Live or Not to Live: Notes on Archetypes and the Absurd in Borchert's 'Draussen vor der Tür'," in The German Quarterly *(copyright © 1975 by the American Association of Teachers of German), Vol. XLVIII, No. 3, May, 1975, pp. 343-54.*

ADDITIONAL BIBLIOGRAPHY

Mileck, Joseph. "Wolfgang Borchert: *Draussen vor der Tür;* A Young Poet's Struggle with Guilt and Despair." *Monatshefte* LI, No. 7 (December 1959): 328-36.
    A brief biography and critical examination of Borchert's canon, focusing on his drama. Mileck traces the author's changing attitudes on existential guilt and despair.

Pritchett, V. S. "Books in General." *The New Statesman and Nation* XLIII, No. 1098 (22 March 1952): 349-50.
    An essay covering *The Man Outside: The Prose Works of Wolfgang Borchert*. Borchert is praised as "a poet who never loses his quickness, never fumbles an image, never sags in power, never loses precision."

Spaethling, Robert H. "Wolfgang Borchert's Quest for Human Freedom." *German Life & Letters* n.s. 14, No. 3 (April 1961): 188-93.

A study of Borchert's nihilism, finding it to be a sign of spiritual rebirth—a rejection of the world's jaded "business as usual" attitude to violence and destruction.

Wellwarth, George E. Introduction to *Postwar German Theatre*, edited and translated by Michael Benedickt and George E. Wellwarth, pp. ix-xxvii. New York: E. P. Dutton & Co., 1967.*

A short introduction to *The Outsider*, Michael Benedickt's translation of *Draussen vor der Tür*. The critic finds the play important because it is an excellent drama in itself, it resoundingly voices Germany's postwar disillusionment, and it successfully utilizes the Expressionist style.

(Ignatius) Roy (Dunnachie) Campbell

1901-1957

South African poet, translator, and autobiographer.

During his lifetime Campbell was primarily considered a satirist of contemporary culture but has since been recognized as an accomplished lyric poet. He has been called the most purely natural rhymer since Byron. Campbell regarded himself as a modern romantic, and assumed the poetic pose of a lonely rebel cast out by society. Much in the tradition of the romantic poets, his work celebrates individualism and rejects the influences of civilization which threaten individuality.

Born in South Africa, Campbell grew up amidst the wilds of the Veldt. He often used the beauty and terror of the South African landscape in his poetry to denote the power of nature; throughout his work the animals of the Veldt symbolize grace, freedom, and independence. Campbell left South Africa as a young man and spent most of his life in England and Europe. He worked at a variety of occupations including soldier, journalist, bullfighter, and horsebreeder; because of this colorful and adventurous background, Campbell was able to portray himself as a poet of experience.

Campbell's first work, *The Flaming Terrapin*, was highly praised on publication. A Miltonic epic describing the regeneration of a decadent society through destruction and spiritual rebirth, *The Flaming Terrapin* reflected Campbell's lifelong concern with violence as a way of solving social problems. Critics now view the poem as an interesting but hollow piece of work. His lyric poetry, however, was more accomplished and continues to receive critical praise. Campbell's most important work as a lyric poet appeared in *Adamastor*, although he continued to produce excellent lyrics in later books, such as *Mithraic Emblems* and *Flowering Reeds*. Like many of the romantic poets he emulated, Campbell viewed the world through his senses and emotions, relying on intensity of feeling, not intellect, to determine his responses to life.

Campbell considered his satires more important than his lyric poetry. The power of his heroic couplets and the force of his invective are undisputed, but critics note that the bitterness and lack of subtlety in his attacks often inspire sympathy for his targets rather than ridicule. His best known satires are *The Georgiad*, an attack on the writers of the Bloomsbury set, and *The Wayzgoose*, a satire of provincial South African journalists and intellectuals.

Campbell became embroiled in controversy for supporting Franco and the Fascist cause during the Spanish civil war, and his antiloyalist views colored the critical reaction to his poetry for some time. When political passions died, critics were able to assess his work more judiciously. Today Campbell is recognized as a minor lyric poet whose desire to write satire compromised his talent as a lyricist.

PRINCIPAL WORKS

The Flaming Terrapin (poetry) 1924
The Wayzgoose (poetry) 1928
Adamastor (poetry) 1930

Choosing a Mast (poetry) 1931
The Georgiad (poetry) 1931
Flowering Reeds (poetry) 1933
Mithraic Emblems (poetry) 1936
Flowering Rifle (poetry) 1939
Talking Bronco (poetry) 1946
Light on a Dark Horse (autobiography) 1951

EDWARD GARNETT (essay date 1924)

"The Flaming Terrapin" . . . offers a nest of nice problems to critics. Only professors, gentlemen who compete with the pen, prosaic people, and those who have their eyes set in the back of their heads, to wit the majority of readers, will disdain or deride "**The Flaming Terrapin.**" It would be easy for me to pull the poem to pieces, to quote passages inspired by extravagance of manner, and it is true that a cold and correct taste may be repelled by the poetic rhetoric, and by the naive inconsequence of the Argument. But the beauties are so many, the poet's imagination so daring, his descriptive powers so fresh and triumphant, his imagery so strong and often so delicate, that the very immaturity and wildness of his Muse will interest the discerning. It is evident that the poem is the work of adolescence—of those early years when the senses run delicious riot, when the perceptions are thrilled by the incredible largesse of life and nature, when the mental horizon seems boundless and the sun reveals afresh each day's teeming delights and miracles. It is evident, also, that, though the poet's imagination seems unbounded, he is indebted to the classics for a number of his inspirations. But obviously also his familiarity with the flora and fauna of the South African Veldt, and his experience of his sailoring days, have inspired his strongest passages. . . . (pp. 323-24)

One would need to cite at least a dozen passages to give an adequate idea of the strange stature of the poem, of its reach, its fantasticality, its artistic lapses and shortcomings. It is obvious that it was not planned originally as an ordered whole, but that it is a piecing together of diverse fragments sustained by a loose general Argument. The central idea introduces the Flaming Terrapin as the elemental force of primeval earth, Leviathan, the system of active things. Then Noah, who stands for Heroic man, appears and builds the Ark, and when the great Terrapin, rising from the deep, rushes to meet it, Noah heaves his great stone anchor at the monster and impales his shell. The Ark is now dragged into the living sea by Leviathan, and so all round the drowning earth. This simple Argument leaves the poet's gorgeous imagination to disport itself at will in a series of descriptions of earth, heaven, and hell, of extraordinary daring. It is the mixture of realism, romantic naïveté, and classic allusiveness that endows the piece with its peculiar quality and great wealth of colouring. The poet's imagination leads us, indeed, an extraordinary dance. He is not content with chanting the progress of the Ark round the world, hurrying from the Coloradoes to the Amazon, and then to the Congo and the Horn, but he must needs foreshadow suddenly the Great War and the Devil's part therein, introducing flaming passages, filled with Miltonic echoes, in which the Terrapin puts to rout the old Serpent and his anarchic crew, and Noah is left to chant his creed on the top of Ararat. It is absurd, of course, to try to measure the poetic treasure-house by the yardstick of prose. The poet's achievement lies in the leaping fountain of imagination, in its profusion of invention, in its lavish exuberance, and wealth of emotion. Its pictures are so concentrated and its transitions so abrupt that it is not easy to grasp the effect of the whole, even at a second reading. One must add that though there are many reverberations from the seventeenth-century classics, such as Dryden and Milton, and also of Shelley, and even of moderns, the original feeling of the whole transmutes these borrowings, and the poet's youthful, magnificent audacity sweeps all before it. (p. 324)

Edward Garnett, "A South African Poet," in The Nation and The Athenaeum, *Vol. XXXV, No. 10, June 7, 1924, pp. 323-24.*

F. L. LUCAS (essay date 1926)

[*The Flaming Terrapin*] is a book of sins against the laws of poetry: and yet—'it is so full of youth.' . . . [It] is excellent that such work should win its recognition; but it throws also a strong light on the shabby gentility of modern poetry as a whole, that this book should have been immediately so feverishly praised and overpraised. Yet it is natural that this

should happen; we are so tired of the confessions of second-rate sensitive minds with nothing to confess and no gift for confessing it, of lyrically bleeding hearts on every sleeve, which the poor daws can scarcely summon the appetite to go on pecking. There are times when niggling subjectivity becomes an infliction and whoever breaks a window in that stuffy salon earns gratitude beyond his due. (pp. 217-18)

The Flaming Terrapin has no form worth the name; its philosophy is neither deep nor new; why then does it stand apart from the usual abortions of modern poetry? Partly because Mr. Campbell has lungs, imagination, and an ear; but much more because he has a personality—the charming, laughing, laughable earnestness of youth, that vigour which is still unwearied, that intensity unblunted by too much experience, that spontaneity which has not learnt to suspect. You can feel most of our versifiers feeling their audience, perspiring under their evening dress with self-consciousness and solicitude to please. Hence the blessed relief of a writer who has clearly written to please himself, and enjoyed it, because he loved shouting his thoughts in galloping rhythms that he liked none the less for being—like all the things that move us most deeply—old as the changeless hills to which men lift their hearts. (pp. 218-19)

[A brief summary of *The Flaming Terrapin*] can give little idea of the gallimaufry of the original, with its wild digressions, its mixture of the atmospheres of *The Apocalypse,* Lucan, and *The Ancient Mariner, Moby Dick,* Dryden, and the Sitwells. This amorphousness is a fault that will escape no reader; no reader, indeed, will be able to escape it. It is the redeeming qualities that matter—the mere sound of the verse . . . , the imagination which can drag by main strength likenesses from the uttermost ends of thought to flash and combine in some thunderous metaphor; the vividness of vision that can prod the sleepiest mind awake and make it feel and see. Often enough Mr. Campbell's taste fails him, his ambition overleaps itself, and the reader relaxes to a smile, as

> Enormous lice, like tiger, hog and bear,
> Go crashing in the jungles of his hair.

or

> Gigantic copulations shake the sky.

Quite a number of our contemporaries could have written that, with one smirking eye upon their audience; whereas Mr. Campbell, I suspect, wrote it just because his eye was not on his audience, because it gave him a childish amusement to say it. And that makes all the difference in the world. And in any case these *bêtises* are forgotten in the hollow thunder of the trees that fall to build the Ark . . . , or in the whistling of the Antarctic gales . . . , or in the silence of Corruption's descent upon the smoky cities of the earth. . . . Things such as this do not make *The Flaming Terrapin* a great poem; but they make it a very interesting and hopeful one. Time will calm that vehemence which at present makes even his nightingales 'ferocious'; experience may teach him to send into the world poems with backbones, not unlicked bears' whelps. If he can learn without losing his spontaneity, we shall hear more of Mr. Campbell. (pp. 220-21)

F. L. Lucas, "Turtle and Mock-Turtle," in his Authors Dead & Living (*reprinted by permission of the Estate of F. L. Lucas*), *The Macmillan Company, 1926, pp. 217-23.**

ALLEN TATE (essay date 1931)

"**Adamastor**" is a distinguished book: it is not, I believe, receiving the attention it deserves. "**The Flaming Terrapin**" was merely interesting; it caused a sensation. It was facile, brilliant and hollow, owing to the failure of the poet to bring more than a pictorial rhetoric to bear upon a subject that required a little philosophical subtlety. It was, for these times, a very long poem. The new poems are short, well written and formally complete. . . .

There are brilliant passages [in "**The Flaming Terrapin**"] and yet the grasp of the subject is almost entirely pictorial. A harder, more intellectual approach would have arranged the theme in its high and low points, and spaced out the emphases: there are, in Mr. Campbell's early style, no climaxes, but simply a constant opportunity for the highest flights of rhetoric. Now, far from being "modern," this defect is characteristic of the worst eighteenth-century poets; Mr. Campbell is more often nearer to Blackmore and Ambrose Phillips than to Rimbaud, to whose work for some reason "**The Flaming Terrapin**" has been compared. . . .

The poetry in "**Adamastor**" is much better. It is uneven, yet Mr. Campbell has found a way of relating his genius for imagery to a genuine center of feeling. The new poems are intelligently conceived, and the imagery is not decorative, but inherent. For the first time in Mr. Campbell's work, after the talk about it is over, there is a similarity to Rimbaud—not in any specific sense, but generally in the sense that his logic of imagery does not rest on a rational theme or argument, but rather on an emotion below (or above) reason which he succeeds in presenting with remarkable purity. Because the duration of this kind of emotion is necessarily brief, the best poems in the book range from fifteen to forty lines; beyond that length Mr. Campbell seldom knows where he is going, but within it he has written five or six poems that are among the best of their kind in this period. "**Rounding the Cape**," "**The Zulu Girl**," "**African Moonrise**" and notably "**The Sisters**" are unsurpassed by anything like them since the War—unless by Hart Crane's "**Black Tambourine**," which was written about ten years ago. Mr. Campbell's new poetry is extremely well written; it is versatile and charming; it is often witty, even when it is not distinguished. One hopes that he will write a great deal more poetry.

> *Allen Tate, "Roy Campbell's Poetry," in* The New Republic *(© 1931 The New Republic, Inc.), Vol. LXVI, No. 850, March 18, 1931, p. 133.*

GEOFFREY STONE (essay date 1936)

Romanticism continues to dominate the literature of our day. Fashions change, of course, and the postures and figures of the first half of the last century are no longer the style; but of essential change there has been little, and the noble savage is the same man despite his Moscow uniform of latest cut. Whether the poet has retreated into the cloud-cuckoo land of aestheticism, or taken his stand on the meaner plane of a "collective society", he is still the beautiful soul in revolt against an evil society, whose restraints hamper the expression of his natural goodness. . . . Both aesthete and leftist share the romantic view of man; they hold that if only the stopper of accepted ways can be removed, the land will be flooded with milk and honey from the well of the noble (and natural) self.

In the midst of this drably similar crew, Roy Campbell occupies a curious place; for he wears proudly the outmoded garments of romanticism and speaks in the loud tones of its lusty youth, rather than in the tired whimper of its sick old age. At a time when half our poets speak so cryptically that they are not understood even by the critics who enumerate their obscurities, and when the other half seek to identify themselves with the voice of the subhuman creature to which industrialism has degraded the workman, Mr. Campbell declares:

> I will go stark: and let my meanings show
> Clear as a milk-white feather in a crow
> Or a black stallion on a field of snow,

and declares it on horseback, wearing a broad-brimmed hat. His posture is certainly the stock romantic one, but he is worthy of notice because he has invested it with vigor and even with dignity.

Now the romantic posture is intrinsically one of defiance toward society, though everyone join in it and grow weary in its stance. But Mr. Campbell is defiant of the latter-day romantics who surround him; he takes the position of the forebears to belittle the descendants. He began with the customary bourgeois-baiting and exaltation of the poet. . . . He has found, however, that the great public are not the only ones who cannot "learn to look on beauty unashamed"; the self-appointed intellectual élite are in no wise better, perhaps even worse, for they profane the shrine they profess to serve. Doubting them, he has examined sceptically their intellectual premises, and in the end rejected most current notions, to establish himself on a groundwork of ideas decidedly classical in view of the frank romanticism of his own poetry. The disparity between critical ideas and poetic practice is fairly common in an age whose prevailing sensibility often runs counter to the strictest logic. Messrs. Eliot and Wyndham Lewis have both been accused of this failing—unjustly, I think—and Mr. Campbell is an ardent follower of the second. In the case of Mr. Campbell, where the disjunction seems actually to exist, a personal explanation is perhaps to be sought; and this seems justified for the "I" of his poems is plainly to be identified with a young South African who lives in Provence and earns his living by fishing and bull-fighting. (pp. 164-66)

The terminology of the bull-ring is frequent in his poetry, and life itself assumes the aspect of a cunning and powerful beast, against whom man must pit his skill and whom he must slay, though life is not "bestial"—the bull himself is noble and an object of beauty; his death is justified only because it can be the occasion of a superior beauty and nobility. Here, of course, might be seen a sort of blood mysticism . . . , anti-rational in tendency. (p. 167)

The equestrian figure also bulks large in his poetry, and he sets off the mounted man, skillful, physically strong, and accustomed to wide horizons, against the hiker, the dweller in cities, and the tourist by train. Certain other figures turn up again and again in Mr. Campbell's verse, and represent a fairly coherent symbolism: the bull has been mentioned, and sometimes merges into the figure of the sun, which . . . may be Mithras or Christ, and the whole notion of light is, as it was with the mystics, bound up with the idea of the final aspect of reality. Occasionally in his latest book, *Mithraic Emblems*, the symbolism degenerates into an unpleasant sentimentality, as when the Crucifixion is called the "final toss'' on ''the black horns of the cross''. And the expression of religious concepts in cowboy language often strikes the falsely hearty note of manufactured *genre* poetry. Yet in the title-poem of *Mithraic Emblems* this symbolism is combined into a strangely effective work, perhaps open to the accusation of a Keatsian lushness, but reinforced by a philosophy that Keats's youth did not achieve. The emblems referred to are figures on the fountain at Tourne described by Mistral, whose words serve as an epigraph: a bull beset by a dog, a serpent, a youth with a sword, over whom presides a raven. Symbolism is by its nature indefinitely extensible; it conveys a manifold meaning beyond the rational limits of language; so that a prose interpretation of what Mr. Campbell intends by his sonnet sequence cannot be much more than a parody. . . . (pp. 168-69)

Mr. Campbell's imagery, while distinctly his, is not especially peculiar; allowing for the figures derived from the bull-ring, from herding, and from life in South Africa, his imagery belongs to that tradition of style in English verse which springs from Milton and which, by its grandeur and sense of spaciousness, appealed to the earlier romantic poet. . . . Mr. Campbell's first book, *The Flaming Terrapin,* is a sort of mythology of the creation of the world, an account of the cruise of a great terrapin through wilderness of water, but the real purpose served by the poem's story is to provide a framework on which is hung a crowded series of gigantic tropes and metaphors. . . . *The Flaming Terrapin,* despite its formlessness, is not merely a great wind of verbiage. Beyond poetry lies the problem of belief, and much modern verse has been vitiated because the poet has not looked on a meaningful universe, and what might have served as the objects of poetic experience have been only stocks and stones, given no significance by place in a larger scheme. Such a difficulty is not Mr. Campbell's, who renews the depleted word by his belief in what formerly gave it significance; the fury of his speech is not in its sound alone, but comes from a fervently held view of nature as intelligible. (p. 170)

[His most accomplished satire, *The Georgiad,*] revolves around a hero called Androgyno, who is reminiscent of Mrs. Woolf's Orlando, and of fifty other literary figures in England who exist off paper, if not with much more reality. Androgyno's adventures result in satire of a strength and accuracy that only Wyndham Lewis (in another medium) equals today. Mr. Campbell employs the couplet of Dryden and Pope, and, as a careless though naturally very gifted craftsman, must suffer by the comparison, but he does convincingly show that satire is not in need of new forms to preserve its vigor; once more he suffuses the traditional forms with life by the very vitality of his own belief and shows that, while it is something consciously imposed from without, form is dead if it is not a reflection of the spirit. His satire, indeed, I would rank above his lyric pieces; but, given a poet of varied talent, it is perhaps inevitable in an age of numerous and conflicting standards that his satire should prove superior to other forms of verse, allowing as it does a greater didactic content by which to indicate its intellectual bias and straiten the interpretation to be set upon the poem's meaning. The intellectual nature of satire makes it depend less than the lyric upon words from which a common emotional response is expected. (p. 173)

Mr. Campbell has a lot to account for on the debit side. His verse is plainly written in haste, and speed is a worthier attribute in the arena than in the muses' garden. For all his facility in language, he is apt to repeat too often a good phrase, as when in three different poems a train at night is found stitching the world with threads of fire. His scorn of the unworthy at times degenerates to mere bravado, bringing in its train statements that are not poetry but noisy rhetoric. Relying on a romantic intensity of feeling rather than a classical balance of form to sustain his poems, his verse too often tends to collapse under its own weight, or dissolve in the mind after the first impact of its rich imagery has passed. He has imposed his own rhythm on a fairly regular iambic line, but not always with that imagination which can convert a standard meter into something peculiar to a single poem. His emphatic rhyme is not without monotony, and to achieve a rhyme he will on occasion resort to strategems that even Browning would not have condoned. As a result of all this, his verse is distressingly uneven, and will descend from a pure and perceptive lyric note to he-man swashbuckling. These things, of course, are consequent upon his romantic posture: though he inveighs against those who gaze into mirrors, his own verse bears too little testimony to interior discipline and partakes of the fitful nature of the moment's inspiration, with the inevitable attempt to justify the work simply because it is something personally and deeply felt. Yet in balancing the ledger, the ultimate figures must be on the credit side, I believe, and the reason, paradoxically enough, is romantic and personal. For the small residue of fine poetry that is to be found in Mr. Campbell's work comes, as it were, out of his native sanity, uncorrupted by our dominant industrialism and the morbid intellectual fashions it breeds. From his pose of romantic defiance has grown his defiance for all that originally supported that pose, and his vision of the poet as the lonely wayfarer seems to have led him back to the haunts of men. (pp. 175-76)

Geoffrey Stone, ''Roy Campbell: Romantic Paradox,'' in The American Review *(copyright 1936 by the Bookman Pub. Co.), Vol. 8, No. 1, November, 1936, pp. 164-76.*

G. S. FRASER (essay date 1949)

Mr. Campbell is that hard nut for the reviewer, a poet of striking and successful obvious effects. His tone is usually that of the harangue or even of the tirade. [As seen in his *Collected Poems*, there] are no hesitant, implicit ironies, no shy layers of meaning. He presents the poet not as the uneasy conscience of our sick society but as the fierce, rejected tribal hero of a simpler day:

> A God has touched him, though with whips:
> We only know that, hooted from our walls,
> He hurtles on his way, he reels, he falls,
> And staggers up to find himself a king
> With truth a silver trumpet at his lips.

Ought that not, with its melodrama and its stock properties— ''truth a silver trumpet''—to be mere sounding fustian? Yet any fool, if not every critic, can recognise that is poetry: of, naturally, an unfashionable sort. We have to think of Victor Hugo and of Byron, who have the same art of turning what looks, at a first glance, like padded declamation into muscular verse. Such poetry is saved by the very risks it takes. Mr. Campbell swings from line to line like an athlete on a trapeze. His level of utterance is far above the safe ground; one miss or fumble will bring the poem crashing fatally down. So reading him is a nervous and alert, not a soothing, pleasure.

He is at his best with things in motion: in conveying sheer physical exhilaration, the sea waves like wild horses, the wild horses like sea waves. . . . He is not so good when he has to bring a poem to the point of reverberating rest. Exhilaration will keep breaking in. . . . His poems cannot stop long enough to explore the "still centre"; they present, rather, Mr. Campbell's active, outward role. It is that of the man on horseback who is at once *caballero* and *vaquero*, the noble knight and the simple cowboy, and who, doubling as it were the parts of Don Quixote and Sancho Panza, can speak at once for the high romantic tradition and for coarse common sense. We get to know this figure as a character very well, yet the intimacy of Mr. Campbell's poems is an oddly gregarious and public intimacy; to the solitary, troubled inner man in his reader (and perhaps in himself) Mr. Campbell has little to say. He cannot be accused of posing, since the poetic role he has chosen represents his convictions, and convictions he is ready to act on; but it might be said that he hardly ever relaxes from performing, with great gusto, the public part of himself.

Sometimes, and especially in his satires, it seems to me that he rather hams this part. He is an excellent satirist when he has a proper target: as in the generous anger of his epigram on a South African statesman . . . or as in that exuberant, jovially contemptuous poem about "colonial culture," *The Wayzgoose*. But in his later poems, I sometimes feel that he is lashing out at random, hammering dummy heads:

> Jock Stot's the same—but when the bullets whistle
> Up goes the White Flag, and down comes the Thistle. . . .

The Scottish people offer a wide flank to satirical darts of various kinds. They have not, so far as I know, been previously accused—and certainly not by a poet of Scottish ancestry—of lacking physical courage. Here, Mr. Campbell's passion for trailing his coat (and perhaps the temptation of a rhyme) have run away with him. Naturally, such writing makes him enemies. The anger which I, for instance, as a Scotsman, feel at that couplet is not the anger properly induced by satire—anger at being pinked in a vulnerable spot—but the anger that is aroused by unprovoked rudeness. Mr. Campbell is, I think, sometimes betrayed by his skill and fluency in writing rhymed invective into mere vulgar abuse. And I think that his personal feuds sometimes rob him of a craftsman's sense of proportion. Yet, when the dust has settled on these quarrels—and on wider political quarrels, on which I have not touched—Mr. Campbell's place, I would think, among the dozen or so more important poets of our time is assured. Future readers will not go to him for insights into a troubled civilization to which, as a nostalgic rider of the outlands, he has never really belonged; they will not go to him for psychological subtlety or contemplative wisdom; but is there another lyrical poet of our time who combines, just as he does, vigour, directness, technical control, and the most vivid sense of natural beauty? With the man, whose generous, muddled, sometimes rancorous, sometimes wrongheaded attitudes are woven into the poetry, we may often properly lose our patience; but never with the poet, the pure poet. . . .

G. S. Fraser, "The Solitary Horseman," in The New Statesman & Nation *(© 1949 The Statesman & Nation Publishing Co. Ltd.), Vol. XXXVIII, No. 980, December 17, 1949, p. 738.*

THE TIMES LITERARY SUPPLEMENT (essay date 1950)

It could hardly be said that Mr. Roy Campbell did not enter our pre-war poetical bathing-place, our well-mannered "Parsons' Pleasure," with a notable splash. But in another sense he made little impression there. The ripples and the indignation subsided; the outsider was accepted as a "regular." Nevertheless, he collected no following, and nobody seemed anxious to learn his particular tricks with the medicine-ball.

He was by nature solitary, a South African who found himself out of sympathy with the two main schools of English poetry between the wars. The Georgians aroused his contempt, and he had quite as little in common with the followers of Mr. Auden. Where they were of the Left, he was of the Right; where they were obscure, he was lucid; where they were cerebral, he was muscular. Their potted psychology, their private jargon, their bloodless subtleties meant nothing to him. . . .

D. H. Lawrence being dead, only in Mr. Wyndham Lewis, it seems, did he find a spiritual ally of importance, and this alliance had little effect on poetry. But taste has been altering to his advantage. He is a romantic, he is sensuous, and he is violent; and to that extent he is now more "contemporary" than he used to be. When, in the further revolution of taste, clarity itself returns to favour, as return it inevitably will, Mr. Campbell will reap the benefit.

His reputation has passed through several phases since he arrived in England. First the "white hope" of poetry, he was soon the *enfant terrible*, savaging the hand that perhaps too condescendingly patted him. . . .

The earliest of his collected poems is **"The Flaming Terrapin,"** . . . a work which revealed the presence of a new poet whose qualities could be distinguished from anyone else's. It tells of a vast mythological beast that towed the Ark on its voyage of destiny; but the poem is more truly an expression of lyrical rapture, in epic form, of abounding youthful delight in sensual existence, a hymn to energy. Re-reading it now, one finds it monotonous in vehemence, the declamatory tone of voice too seldom varied, the narrative far too slender to support such cornucopias of high-coloured imagery as tumble relentlessly upon it. . . . [Yet] the cornucopias spilled out fruit that was inviting, if not of the first quality. . . . [**"The Flaming Terrapin"**] is unmistakable Roy Campbell, but to readers in 1924 it was something new; the promise, at least, of a striking talent for descriptive writing. Notice how the images are almost exclusively kinetic. This gave a novel gusto to the writing, but was also a prime cause of monotony, from the virtual exclusion of all quieter ingredients. Here, too, is already the typical Roy Campbell line— "Heaved the superb Olympus of his head"—"Toppled the white sierras of the sea"—a type of construction vigorously effective when sparingly used, but rendered wearisome through sheer repetition in some of his later poems, where an active Muse appears to have become muscle-bound.

That satire was in his blood might already be observed; and four years later he published a long work ridiculing the culture of his native land, South Africa. **"The Wayzgoose"** invites comparison with Dryden and Pope, not merely in the choice of metre, but in the handling of the theme, with its invocation to a personified "Dullness." There is amusement here; but judgment is passed on this work as a whole if we say that its victims are too remote and obscure to support our interest. . . .

Much better was the bang with which five years later, and three years after the publication of **"Adamastor," "The Georgiad"** exploded, spattering ridicule far and wide on the literary "government" of England, and covering a good many other aspects of English life in the process. Restrained by no gentlemanly feelings, the satirist was sometimes frankly offensive. . . . It was unpardonable; but it was also undeniably funny. . . . It has to be acknowledged that he had chosen most (though not all) his victims out of the second-rate, like Pope before him. . . .

There, however, the similarity ends. **"The Georgiad"** is a part of literary history, and will long be read for enjoyment; but place its finest passages alongside Pope, and how knockabout, how slap-dash they are seen to be! The resemblance is more to the satires of Byron, and indeed there is much in his lyrical poetry which suggests an un-patrician Byron, less versatile and less sophisticated than the author of *Don Juan,* but at the same time richer in his gift of sensuousness.

This is notably true of **"Adamastor,"** on whose magnificent lyrics especially, together with some of those in **"Flowering Reeds"** and **"Mithraic Emblems,"** Mr. Campbell's reputation stands firm. The poet regards himself as a lonely figure, a superb rebel, at once the castigator and outcast of the loutish multitude who fear and reject him. . . . Insolence and conceit play their part in the "build-up" of this pose, but if the poet "gets away with it," and he does, it must mean that the claim is not wholly empty. And he *has* an imaginative energy and a zest for living that are exalted. . . .

But there are implications that invite further analysis. Mr. Campbell is a poet of violence; he delights in violent images, violent themes. . . . Quite in a minority are the "quiet" poems he has written, and even in these the reader may look far for any evidence of loving-kindness. Compare **"The Serf"** with the great poem it immediately recalls, Thomas Hardy's on the very same theme—"Only a man harrowing clods." Both are outstanding: the first empty of compassion, the second steeped in it. Perhaps only in one poem, **"The Dead Torero,"** do we find any real compassion. . . . [And even here] the poet is engrossed in the manner of the dying. . . .

Whether pity, affection, tenderness, or another shade of emotion might have been expressed, it is this lack of feeling which gives to most of his quieter poems, and to most of his love poems within that category, a hollow ring. We may be offered the *circumstances* of poetic emotion: something may be beautifully observed, and likened revealingly to something else—glimmer of light on hair or skin—but the observation and the simile are all. We enter the poem, we admire the skill of its construction; but in the end the shrine seems vacant, the grotto untenanted.

Well, a poet is not obliged to be compassionate like Hardy. Yet there is a positive attached to this mere negative—this lack which merely proves Mr. Campbell's genius to operate best elsewhere. Some of his writing has, without doubt, a distasteful ingredient, an element of brutality, of hatred uninspired by moral judgment, of pleasure in suffering. This is not easy to illustrate, though noticeable enough, for it is apt to be found in the mood or tone of a complete poem, more than in any one particular statement. . . .

"A poet of limited ambition, like Tennyson," wrote Mr. Campbell in **"Taurine Provence,"** "remains in the precincts of the croquet lawn: but a great poet like Shakespeare will wrestle with the phantoms of terror, fear, jealousy, hatred,

madness, and death." Pacing the shrubbery is not the only way of limiting one's ambition—and one's humanity.

Limited he is. How many contemporary poets are not? The admission helps us little towards a judgement. "When an author is yet living," said Dr. Johnson, "we estimate his powers by his worst performance, and when he is dead we rate them by his best." We ought always to resist that inclination. Mr. Cambell's best performance has been to extol, in memorable and shining words, all sorts of bravery—and in an age of versifiers far more justly described as croquet-playing than the noble Tennyson.

"The Poetry of Statement," in The Times Literary Supplement (© *Times Newspapers Ltd. (London)* '1950; reproduced from The Times Literary Supplement *by permission), No. 2,512, March 24, 1950, p. 184.*

HUGH KENNER   (essay date 1953)

Mr. Campbell's name turns up in lists, and his verse goes mechanically into the bigger anthologies, but the location and magnitude of what he does don't seem to get plotted. His verse, one gathers, is found stirring by rather inarticulate people. This isn't to say that it is written down to a public, or that Mr. Campbell is either unintelligent or dishonest. He writes to please himself, and he isn't a dull man. He has, however, a good deal more "biography" on his record than most poets, and, to complement it, rather less poetry in his verse than his talents would lead one to expect. This needn't be an inexorable equation; one doesn't write by abstaining from living. But the man of courtly and ritualistic action has been so much an anomaly in the lustrum 1920-50 that Mr. Campbell's muse has used up her energy being, so to speak, astounded at her own existence. She speaks most of the time in borrowed accents—rather absent-mindedly borrowed: Pope's, Rimbaud's, Baudelaire's. In a trance of astonishment she chants, astonished at the things that go on before her eyes, not caring especially whether the subject really gets caught up into the verse so long as we stay aware that she and Mr. Campbell are alive-oh.

This diagnosis is sustained in detail by Mr. Campbell's engaging and colorful autobiography [*Light on a Dark Horse*] but it can be illustrated from the verse itself, especially from the *Georgiad* and the *Wayzgoose,* where the author has provided occasional notes to assure us that absurdities of the order the verse alludes to have really occurred. (p. 169)

Mr. Campbell's life, one may say without irony, has been a pretty good poem. Here matters of technique have really absorbed him; not merely the techniques for mastering specific situations—you kill an octopus, he has found, either by turning it inside out or by biting the nerve between the eyes—but the techniques that constitute "style" and enable you to carry off your adventures with an air of ease, of knowing where you are heading. The autobiography has soft spots but no fractures, not because a superb technician plotted it (though a man with swift sensitivity to words wrote some of the paragraphs) but because Mr. Campbell's life seems by a miracle of good management to have had no dull stretches worth mentioning. Indeed the last chapter (Spain in 1935) manages to achieve a climax of the sort that invites a second volume . . . without either truncation or rhetoric.

It is the interest of the material that carries the reader along, and when the material is being interesting the words never get in its way. It is hard to say how much of this prose transparency is technique, how much simply the author's absorption in what he has to say; but the contrast with the verse is instructive. When he writes verse, Mr. Campbell's interests are divided between his relish of epithets . . . and his compulsion to set himself in a rhetorical relation with the subject . . . When he writes prose, the epithets convey information and the self-consciousness gets absorbed into a loosely colloquial convention: he is talking to you about things that happened to *him,* so he finds himself quite satisfactorily present in recalling them. (pp. 170-71)

Light on a Dark Horse scatters whole cornucopias of lore. . . . (p. 172)

On the other hand, if knowledge is, in Confucian phrase, ''To know men,'' Mr. Campbell must be accounted an ignoramus. There is no sign, where he drops the name of my friend x or my friend y, that his relation with these celebrities consists of anything but undifferentiated awe masquerading as camaraderie. . . . People whom he assures us mean a great deal to him get marginally characterized as ''that lazy and pleasant American,'' ''that lovable Jewish giant;'' ''a very nice girl who had been my partner in the grape harvest,'' ''that splendid man,'' while the sensed and valued presence through the anecdotes that include these people continues to be that of Mr. Campbell. (pp. 172-74)

Awareness of himself in action, detailed knowledge of the animal and vegetable kingdoms, and an assortment of impressive athletic skills may be said to constitute Mr. Campbell's poetic equipment; and the first is constantly blurring the other two. ''I am able to address the barrack-square as a Sergeant-Major, and explain the parts of a machine gun, speaking as one ranker to another in English, Swahili, or Chinyanja; I can address the English Society at Oxford or Cambridge from the same platform as T. S. Eliot or Sir Osbert Sitwell: confer ceremoniously in flowery Zulu or Sintabele with delegations of headmen: I can join a knot of stokers in a pub in Glasgow or Liverpool as one of them . . .'' and so on and so on. The stuff of a limited kind of poetry inheres in accomplishments like these, if only the protagonist were less aware of their rarity; . . . we never get the poem, only the versified statement that Mr. Campbell's life has touched on poetry in the raw. His prose makes similar statements, rather better, and so is a better *substitute* for poetry than his verse is.

These defects of knowledge and defects of character don't much detract from the excitement of the autobiography, or from our being heartened by the mere existence of Mr. Campbell (shades of Cunningham-Grahame!) in the mid-twentieth century. But they emphasize the narcissism, whether hearty or stultified, into which a time with no use for poetry drives minor talent. ''Love at first sight'' (which has happened to Mr. Campbell three times) gives him ''needles and pins that you get down your back after reading a superb line of verse, or making a good pass in front of a bull, or seeing a picture like the *Assumption* of El Greco or the *Surrender of Breda* by Velasquez,'' and all four experiences seem for him to be on the same footing. There has been no way for him to learn about the autonomy of art, the need for a poetic fiat, for an act of transfer and recreation in which the energies of life are *imitated* by the energies images and words will set up. It is enough for him to allude to life, where emotion has been strong, and trust that he has tapped some of that strength in

the process of alluding. It happens sometimes in his prose, and the result is surprisingly fruity. . . . (pp. 174-75)

It is a real detraction from the pleasures of an absorbing book, that one feels the experiences it chronicles ought to have fed so much poetry. (p. 175)

Hugh Kenner, ''A Narcissist of Action,'' in Poetry *(© 1953 by The Modern Poetry Association; reprinted by permission of the Editor of* Poetry), *Vol. LXXXII, No. 3, June, 1953, pp. 169-75.*

G. S. FRASER (essay date 1953)

[Roy Campbell is an] important poet whose approach to the world is through his senses and emotions, and one should add emphatically his will, rather than his intellect. He is notable among modern poets for his strict traditionalism of form and vocabulary, only mitigated (but more often in his satires than in his lyrical poems) by a certain expansiveness and a vigorous use of colloquial expressions, particularly army slang. (p. 225)

Roy Campbell has lived an adventurous life, . . . and has therefore a direct and simple approach to life which makes him impatient of the subtleties and hesitations, the qualifications and self-corrections, which are so typical of the tone of much modern poetry and criticism.

Mr Campbell's attitude, in fact, to the modern urban scene is a little like that of Rousseau's 'noble savage,' though at the same time, as a satirist, he perhaps deliberately exaggerates the naivety of his responses for rhetorical effect. Campbell's very great gifts as a poety tended to be denigrated in the 1930s, partly because, almost alone among the English poets of his generation, he espoused the cause of General Franco in Spain and indeed fought on that side. He was denounced as a 'Fascist,' though his fine war record with the Allies in the last war shows that to have been an unfair accusation. It would be truer to describe him as a strong traditionalist (he is a fervent Roman Catholic), who has an instinctive dislike of all sorts of political interference with healthy local habits and customs. His feeling about politics, he wrote in a recent article, is that there should be as little politics as possible . . . He likes the common man and distrusts intellectuals, and when he was once asked in a questionnaire in what ways he differed, as a poet from the ordinary man, he wrote, 'In nothing at all . . . in which, however, I differ very much from *the ordinary poet.*' Campbell has a strongly combative temperament and in the last five years, since he left the Army, has been briskly continuing his feud with the English radical poets of the 1930s, in spite of the fact that in the last ten years most of these have fundamentally revised their former attitudes. This combative attitude is his strength and weakness as a poet. He has wonderful vigour, but everything he writes is very much on one note, and his poems never work up to the passages of concentrated meditation which, in poets like Yeats or Eliot or Graves, give one an impression of deep contemplative wisdom. The verse goes at a steady and exhilarating gallop but never comes to a halt from which we could take in Mr Campbell's whole spiritual landscape at a glance. Mr Campbell presents himself dramatically, as a figure in action, in conflict with others, but if this man on horseback has ever any inner doubts and worries, they are not communicated to the reader. A lack of inwardness and concentration in this sense is Mr Campbell's great limitation. It breeds a certain hardness. One of his most striking lines is,

> I learned to inflict and suffer pain,

but, in spite of his Christian beliefs, there are few passages in his poems which suggest that he has learned to inflict or suffer forgiveness. Mr Campbell has nearly all the gifts of a major poet, but it can be questioned whether he has sufficiently chastened his irascible appetite to make the tenor of his thoughts and feelings a sufficiently noble content for the grand vehicle of his verse. (pp. 226-27)

> G. S. Fraser, "Poetry," in his The Modern Writer and His World, *Derek Verschoyle Limited, 1953, pp. 185-284.**

JOHN CIARDI (essay date 1955)

Roy Campbell's **"Selected Poems"** appear in his fifty-third year and offer themselves as a sort of retrospective show that might accurately be billed as Three Decades of the Muscle Man. No poet writing in English has equaled Campbell's violence, though Robinson Jeffers must be entered in the competition. None has presented a mind—to me at least—more despicable, a mind compounded of storm-trooper arrogance, *Sieg Heil* piety, and a kind of Nietzschean rant sometimes mixed with a ponderously uncomical sense of satire.

The center of that mind—and of its poetic style—is all sledgehammers. It would be comforting to one's sense of liberalism to report that the result is all merely thud-thud. What must be reported instead is that the sledgehammers are sometimes magnificent. . . . But if this adulation of brute splendor shines as a magnificence in the physical world, the same muscularity applied to human orders becomes a disaster. No poet in English has come nearer composing the entire litany for the storm trooper—the mystique of the superman, the paean to muscular arrogance, even the sentimental piety of the romantic thug. So, in the Dedication to Mary Campbell, the poet is described as born of his own disdain, emerging from the rabble to live by sterner laws and a god superbly stronger; he is plotted against and hated by the small ones, is murdered at last by their leaden blows, but dies trailing his scorn and knowing that in death the Valkyrie will descend to him. (p. 515)

Small wonder that Campbell fought for Franco; only the accident of writing in the wrong language could have kept him from being drafted as Poet Laureate of the Third Reich.

"A poetic tornado," as Edith Sitwell calls him? At least that, or perhaps the wind seems more impressive when it blows through the chinks of the Stately Homes. "A poet of genius," as Dylan Thomas called him? Beyond argument: Campbell can make an English line hammer beyond belief, or tune a simple and persuasive lyric. Yet in everything his limitations are inescapable. A bull can startle, but no bull sings entirely like a man. In time one tires of so much noise, and in art there is no apology for boredom. (pp. 515-16)

> John Ciardi, "Muscles and Manners," in The Nation *(copyright 1955 The Nation* magazine, *The Nation Associates, Inc.), Vol. 181, No. 24, December 10, 1955, pp. 515-16.**

HOWARD SERGEANT (essay date 1957)

Despite Roy Campbell's long absence from his native country, and his own disclaimers, it can truly be said that he is a poet with South Africa in his blood. In his poetry the brooding elements, the violent climatic and geographical contrasts, the rich colour and the uncontrollable natural forces of the environment, as well as the conflicting qualities of its inhabitants, seek and find expression as in the work of no other poet. Despite his isolation and individual style . . . without abandoning his roots or making any concession to the ideas he has opposed from the beginning of his career, he has compelled the attention of all discerning critics. (p. 105)

Wild creatures such as those of the South African veld, with their grace of movement and untamable spirit, have always served for Campbell as symbols of the life of freedom and independence which he would have for human beings, and his physical contests with them have been a source of spiritual exultation. This proud vision of beauty "volted with delight" is probably South Africa's most valuable gift to him. It is revealed in his scornful attitude towards the smugness and unadventurous mediocrity of modern city life, its meaningless pursuits and activities, its mechanical patterns and drab order of society, in both his prose [and his poetry]. . . . It is also responsible for his glorification of the cattleman, the matador, and similar representatives of the desirable way of life, in **Taurine Provence** and **Broken Record** and so many of his poems. Campbell's ideal community would be a "gymnasium of athletic personalities", though presumably a community which would, at the same time, be susceptible to the appeal of the creative arts. (pp. 105-06)

Most of the South Africans who resented his unbridled ridicule of "Banana-Land" in **The Wayzgoose** and the caustic lines of **Adamastor** have never appreciated the real motive behind these attacks. When he made them Campbell was still immature enough to take it for granted that what provoked his anger was typical of South Africa alone. It was not long before he discovered that spiritual poverty was by no means so confined, before he was tilting at his real enemies—the materialism, the littleness, and the herdlike propensities of urbanized and industrialized humanity.

Danger, hardship, beauty and love, filling every moment with their particular excitements—these are the attributes of the life he extols. Together they inspire him to a sense of worship, which gives the finer edge both to his activities and his poetry. In its freedom from romantic hyperbole, **Mass at Dawn** conveys this religious experience as well as the zest for vigorous action. . . . Thus life is measured by its intensity and becomes at once a communion, an adventure, and an exaltation to which the physical world, the senses, emotions and intellect alike contribute.

Unlike many of his English contemporaries, Campbell gazes outward upon the world rather than inward upon himself, and the pettiness and materialism he perceives appal him. He seems to be preoccupied with the two contrasted modes of existence which, by means of an extensive range of symbols, he is never tired of presenting in his poetry—the life of the independent personality revelling in freedom, and that of the conventional, herd-minded, half-blind and already half-dead citizen. When others speak of freedom, he sees only a progressive humiliation of mankind. The typical figure on the one side is the horseman or herdsman; on the other "Charlot", Charlie Chaplin, shuffling in his thousands through city streets. And these have given rise to a whole series of representative figures with which the reader soon becomes familiar: equestrian—pedestrian; cattleman—shopkeeper; Sons of Cain—Sons of Abel; cowboys, toreros, vaqueros—Charlies, Tommies, Pommies, wowsers. The city itself is placed in opposition to "The Hill, the Pampa, and the Tide" by which humanity may perhaps be regenerated. Another term for those whose equestrian qualities may cleanse and revitalize society is "The White Commando". Christ, though sometimes represented as a great Albatross, is usually a great equestrian figure, the Prince of Herdsmen, the Herdsman King, or the red Torero. (pp. 106-08)

The kinetic power and muscular rhythms of [*The Flaming Terrapin*] took the literary world of the 'twenties by storm. It scintillates with brilliant lines, and is constantly lit with original and breathtaking images. . . . If *The Flaming Terrapin* vibrates with energy and the kind of high-pitched exuberance that usually lends itself to overwriting (and Campbell does not always escape the dangers surrounding this type of work), the style is remarkably individual and one which, though it has since been pruned and toned down, we have come to recognize as characteristic of Campbell's entire output. (p. 109)

The theme, woven around the biblical story of the Flood, is such as might be expected from a poet of Campbell's susceptibilities—the regeneration of a sick and decadent society through a spiritual rebirth and a re-peopling of the earth by free creative spirits and pastoral heroes. (p. 110)

The machinery of the poem creaks at times, and the verse is occasionally marred by an over-dependence upon the old device of personification. The chief fault, however, is the poet's intoxication with words and ideas. Like one of his "riders of the air" of Part V, "lariat twirling, cracking whips", he gallops madly through the poem without restraint or pause for reflection, driving image after image before him and scattering his verbs in all directions. . . . That Roy Campbell has a most energetic mind is demonstrated by his verbal prodigality. A reading of *The Flaming Terrapin* leaves no doubt concerning his capacity for activizing the language; passage after passage, taken at random, shows the same vitality and enthusiasm. (pp. 111-12)

Yet because the exuberance is seldom abated throughout the whole poem, the total impact is weakened. The reader is carried breathlessly along on the crest of a tidal wave that neither breaks nor loses its impetus until it reaches the final exclamation-mark. In some of his subsequent lyrics this exuberance has been transformed into speed; and the same lack of control, in spite of the obvious lingual mastery, gives the impression that the poet has lost his sense of direction, so that one's attention is distracted from the experience he is attempting to communicate. Nevertheless, with all its faults, *The Flaming Terrapin* is a poem to be enjoyed. (p. 112)

[*The Wayzgoose*] is cleverly and amusingly written, with Dryden as the model, and casts ridicule upon most of South Africa's literary, artistic and political figures—indeed upon almost all the white population. . . . *The Wayzgoose* makes entertaining reading, and will probably take its place in South Africa's literary history as a curiosity rather than as a work of art. Its victims do not come to life as do those of either Pope or Dryden. (pp. 113-14)

In *Adamastor* [Campbell] reveals himself as a thorough-going romantic, and most of all he romanticizes himself, the poet.

Influenced by Baudelaire and the French Symbolists, he employs symbols which relate largely to the poet and the poet's relationship to the society in which he lives. He translates Baudelaire's *L'Albatross;* he dwells upon the suffering and glory of the poet in the tale of *Mazeppa.* The young rebellious steer driven from the herd, the solitary cobra of the Kalahari, the palm tree of the desert, and the parallel drawn with the lonely island fronting the Atlantic surges in the magnificent *Tristan da Cunha* . . .—all emphasize the cycle of rejection, lonely suffering, heroism, and ultimate glory and power of the outcast from society.

The Georgiad, another venture into satire, . . . was obviously intended for those who had more than a casual acquaintance with the feuds and the conditions of the English literary scene of the 'twenties rather than for the general reading public, for it is crammed with allusions to private incidents, poems and characteristics of various writers and editors of the time. Yet the general direction of Campbell's thrusts is unmistakable, and the reader is compelled, at least, to re-examine his standards of value. As its title suggests, *The Georgiad* is modelled upon Pope's *Dunciad* and is aimed at the Georgian poets and their followers. (pp. 114-15)

It was the bloodlessness and affectation of their work which provoked Campbell to flay the Georgians so mercilessly; and in some of his comments he completely overstepped the Georgian idea of good literary taste. All the Georgian traits were remorselessly exposed to ridicule. . . . [When] Campbell was writing this satire Georgian influences were sadly on the wane. *The Georgiad* will hardly bear comparison with the polished satire of Pope; nevertheless, it is extremely amusing, and, for that reason, will continue to provide entertainment for some time to come.

From *The Flaming Terrapin* and *Adamastor*, through the poems of the 'thirties, to *Mithraic Emblems* . . . can be traced a clear line of development. There is little of the earlier egotism or arrogance in *Flowering Reeds*. The love songs in this collection are imbued with a deep passionate quality that is communicated through a more subdued tone and a more selective range of imagery than his earlier exuberance permitted, but the discipline of *Choosing a Mast* and *La Clemence* was prefigured in *Mass at Dawn* and *Horses on the Camargue*. (pp. 117-18)

For [Campbell] the war in Spain represented an open conflict between the Christian tradition and Communist materialism (the Christ or crucifix image appears again and again in the war poems of *Mithraic Emblems*). Being both a man of action and a practical idealist, he was compelled by his very nature to take sides in that conflict, and there could be no doubt in his mind as to which was the enemy "when all the world was Red with hate!"

The Second World War found him fighting again, this time for Democracy, "though by his age, race, domicile, description, Exempted from all service or conscription", and in his next volume, *Talking Bronco* . . . he had a great deal to say in his satirical style about the Left-Wing poets who were not in the fighting forces. For this purpose he invented a composite mythical character, MacSpaunday (the name obviously derived from those of four well-known English poets [Auden, Day Lewis, Spender, and MacNeice]), and this figure appears in several of the poems. (pp. 118-19)

The most impressive pieces in *Talking Bronco*, however, are not the mordant satires, but the translation from St. John of the Cross (one of the Spanish poets by whom Campbell has been influenced), the philosophical *The Skull in the Desert,* and the sonnets *San Juan de la Cruz* and *Luis de Camões.* . . . It may seem odd that so active a man and so vigorous a poet as Campbell should be drawn to the mystic and saint, St. John of the Cross, but it is in keeping with the conflicting elements which go to shape his outlook. Perhaps this profound reverence is the obverse side of his character and is obscured, to some extent, by his natural zest and vitality. There is certainly an affinity between the two poets, or Campbell could never have communicated the essential qualities of the Spanish poet's work so perfectly as he has. In his translation of *The Poems of St. John of the Cross* . . . , Campbell displays another aspect of his remarkable talent—and succeeds in suppressing his violent and aggressive personal moods without impeding the spontaneous flow of imagery normally at his command. (pp. 119-20)

The discerning student of Campbell's life and work will observe yet another paradox. Despite all his gibes at people in the mass and at the herd instincts of the crowd, Campbell can truly say, ''Let me be there to share the strain And with the poorest pull my weight.'' If he belongs to the aristocratic rather than the democratic tradition, as has been stated, he certainly does not squeeze himself into the seats reserved for the privileged classes, but rides with the cattleman and fights with the ranker. It is this capacity for identifying himself with the individual members of the most primitive orders of society which has enabled him to catch the spirit of Africa itself, as he does in *The Zulu Girl.* (pp. 120-21)

At the same time it encourages a tendency towards overstatement when the poet is expressing his contempt for life in towns and cities. . . . It seems to me that Campbell reacts so hotly against the artificial values of modern civilization and has been so forced to defend his political ideas that, with his naturally boisterous and aggressive manner of utterance, he has been inclined to exaggerate what he actually feels or believes.

It would be unwise to attempt a final assessment of his poetry at this stage of his career, for his best work may be yet to come, when his varied experience has been properly assimilated—always providing that his love of danger and excitement will allow him the opportunity to develop his medium to its full capacity. Nevertheless, I feel that his poetry has, so far, been undervalued, and that political and personal feuds have served to obscure his real stature as a poet. If I may venture upon an interim judgement I would say that, despite the fact that satire comprises a large proportion of his poetic output, the lyrical poems will be the most enduring. For, however amusing he may be, Campbell is too undiscriminating a writer to distinguish between genuine satire and mere abuse; rich invective streams from his pen in a constant flow, but does not always reach a valid target. Some of his statements fall quite wide of the mark. Moreover, the characters lampooned are not always delineated sharply enough to stand out as living people. He has the Byronic flow, but not the Byronic relevance.

Campbell's most valuable contributions to English poetry of today are undoubtedly his vitality and power. At a time when young poets had almost become afraid of exhibiting strong emotions, and when traditional forms were out of favour, Campbell pursued his own unpopular way, speaking without ambiguity, responding to natural beauty unashamedly if unsentimentally, yet attaining a technical mastery possessed

by few of his contemporaries. Among the poems which will probably last beyond our own age are *Tristan da Cunha, The Serf, The Zulu Girl, Choosing a Mast,* a few of the Toledo sonnets, *Luis de Camões, The Skull in the Desert,* one or two lyrics from *Flowering Reeds,* and the translations from St. John of the Cross; and it is likely that extracts will be taken from his satirical poems to illustrate the peculiar conditions of his time. How many contemporary poets can match such an achievement? (pp. 121-22)

Howard Sergeant, ''Restive Steer: A Study of the Poetry of Roy Campbell,'' in Essays and Studies *(© The English Association 1957), n.s. Vol. 10, 1957, pp. 105-22.*

KENNETH REXROTH (essay date 1961)

Roy Campbell was hardly a writer at all. He was a professional personality, a rowdy bully and creator of scenes. (p. 225)

[Campbell's] ideas were all outrageous, and they did not have the excuse that they issued from a government hospital for the insane. But they were more than that—they were tawdry and cheaply antihumane. He didn't only despise Einstein, I am sure he despised Erasmus . . . or Florence Nightingale.

So too, his verse. I am all for simple, sensuous and passionate utterance. I am sure Racine had a good idea when he read his stuff to his cook and rejected what she couldn't understand. . . . But this is not the verse of William Barnes, or Toulet, or Robert Frost, or whoever you like who writes simply. It is doggerel. It is not conscious doggerel, of the type Goethe or Heine once wrote, and Mr. Auden sometimes uses so skillfully today. It is just plain doggerel. Not even like Robert W. Service (a much better poet with somewhat similar tastes in life if not in politics). What distinguishes it is its persistent, insistent ill-temper. This has given Campbell a reputation as a satirist. To most vulgar people, Pope sounds like doggerel, and abuse sounds like satire. But this just means that there are a lot of people in the world like Roy Campbell—a lot of very coarse-grained people with tin ears. They just haven't worked it out in a political theory and they don't have a facility for rather clumsy rhyming, but there are lots and lots of people every bit as vulgar. Ill-temper is not satire. Ill-temper is not ''savage indignation.'' . . . Rocking-horse couplets that go bump at the end are not ''skillful verse in the great traditions of English Poesy.'' You can't learn that in any manual. In the long run it requires sensibility to tell Campbell from Kipling.

That brings up a necessary comparison of Campbell and better poets with whom he might easily be confused. Hilaire Belloc and Oliver St. John Gogarty were professional belligerents. . . . They wrote conventionally structured verse about all the old-time great themes. They wrote a great deal of satire and some very funny epigrams and limericks. Belloc was a very good poet indeed. His verse is actually extremely subtly put together; his ideas, in the days when he thought them up, were original, and underneath his bluster was a powerful, magnanimous mind. Gogarty was in every way a lesser man. He was corny and sentimental, like an Irish barfly, but like so many barflies, he was very winning sometimes, and he had a great way with the ladies. There is no magnanimity whatever in Campbell, and less charm. The first requisites for satire are greatness of soul, and a certain ironfisted charm. (pp. 226-27)

There is no vestige of these in Roy Campbell. He early learned that the British—inveterate bird watchers and amateur entomologists—will buy anything odd. In a nation of polite snobs he made a career of being a rude boor.... Had he been able to grow two heads, or at least four ears, he would have been even more successful. The islanders would have said, ''What jolly fun!'' and lined up for tickets, until they grew bored and newer oddities invaded Bartholomew Fair. (p. 227)

> *Kenneth Rexroth, "Poets, Old and New: Roy Campbell," in his* Assays *(copyright © 1961 by Kenneth Rexroth; all rights reserved; reprinted by permission of New Directions, Agents), New Directions, 1961, pp. 225-28.*

ROWLAND SMITH (essay date 1972)

The explicit moral of [*The Flaming Terrapin*], and its plot, loosely organized around a description of the revitalization of the earth after the flood, are less impressive than its local effects. The impact of *The Flaming Terrapin* mainly depends on its energy, which embodies the positive moral value the poet sets out to describe didactically through his mythical plot. To the reader the plot seems in many passages to be only a convenient external framework for the evocation of natural strength and beauty in descriptions of the sea and the elements. But the poet himself regarded his plot as organic to the whole poem. In a letter to his parents he explains an early draft of *The Flaming Terrapin:*

> My dear Father and Mother,
>
> You wrote to ask me about the meaning of my poem, or rather its purpose....
>
> I'll try to explain. The whole moral of the poem is contained in Christ's words, ''Every tree that bringeth not forth good fruit, is hewn down and cast into the fire,'' and again in His words, ''Ye are the salt of the earth but if that salt shall have lost its savour it shall be scattered abroad and trodden under the feet of men'' (I have possibly misquoted it). Christ was one of the first to proclaim the doctrine of heredity and the survival of the fittest. Nietzsche [*sic*] was too dull to understand the aristocratic outlook of Christ, he slangs Him for inventing a religion for the weak and the wretched. But in this he was wrong for Christ in his gospels is continually emphasising how hard it is for anyone to enter into the Kingdom of Heaven, or as we would say the Kingdom of Man....

Such a fundamental belief in self-reliant, aristocratic heroism is central to Campbell's outlook from this point until his death. The often ostentatiously ''enlightened'' humanism of *The Flaming Terrapin* in no way affects his passionate belief in rugged vitality as the solution to the malaise of a shell-shocked world. This same belief is basic to the poet's later tributes to the aristocratic, equestrian world of the pious and self-reliant vaquero who will ''anachronise'' the sordid industrial values of modern civilization. The latter views are often couched in an aggressively reactionary tone, or become part of a fervid Christian mysticism, but they are still based on Campbell's instinct to identify himself with the vigours of an intuitive, natural world.

In the letter to his parents he goes on to give formal expression to the regenerative heroic principle which is suggested throughout the poem:

> However, to continue my explanation: in a world suffering from shell-shock, with most of its finest breeding-stock lost, and the rest rather demoralized, it is interesting to conjecture whether a certain portion of the race may not have become sufficiently ennobled by its sufferings to reinstate and even improve on the pre-war standard, and in the end to supplant the descendants of those who have become demoralised and stagnant, like the Russians for instance. I have taken this more cheerful view, as I would much sooner feel that I was a Simian in the state of evolution into something higher, than a fallen angel in a state of decline. So, with the deluge as symbolising the war and its subsequent hopelessness, I have represented in the Noah family, the survival of the fittest, and tried to describe the manner in which they won through the terrors of the storm and eventually colonised the earth. The Terrapin is the symbol for masculine energy.

There is an element of insensitivity suggested by the detached tone with which he discusses the loss of the world's ''finest breeding-stock,'' and the possibility of a ''certain portion of the race'' being able to ''improve on the pre-war standard.'' This suggestion of insensitivity is not part of the poem itself, which is free of sociological theory. Nevertheless, here his serene theoretical discussion in nonhuman terms of race and breed gives an ominous hint of the poet's own predilection in his polemical writings for social theory and abstract social values.... Still, youthful ebullience, and not insensitivity, is the main impression given by the letter.

Just as the poem itself does not embody the regenerative theory in anything like the formulaic clarity which Campbell explains in his letter, so too its ''symbolism'' is far less consistently developed than would be expected from his explanation to his parents. The flexibility of the use to which he puts the Terrapin alone can be seen in the letter, when, after describing it as ''the symbol for masculine energy,'' he adds in a second postscript: ''P.P.S. Throughout China, Japan and India the tortoise is the talisman which represents strength, longevity, endurance and courage. It is also the symbol of the Universe, the dome representing the heavens and the body the earth.'' ''Strength, longevity, endurance and courage'' are all qualities suggested by the Terrapin in the poem. The additional explanatory detail—that it also represents the ''Universe''—is typical of his tendency to overload the symbolic effects in *The Flaming Terrapin* until they become too general and all-embracing. (pp. 21-3)

[Dazzling] descriptions stamp Campbell's personality on the poem. His ability to create so compelling an un-European wildness justifies the praise with which *The Flaming Terrapin* was greeted. There is also an inherent danger in the ''foreign'' quality of his responses and values. As he grew older, it became increasingly difficult for him to abandon the role of the outsider with a down-to-earth heroic answer to most problems.... It is a tribute to its poetic vitality that the exuberant evocations of primitive force are convincing, and not quaintly colonial. The poem is exciting and refreshing.

Not surprisingly, it is at its best when his vivid imagery supports the basic regenerative moral, and less convincing when he is trying to describe abstract moral qualities.

The vagueness at the core of many of his depictions of moral values can be seen in an early passage describing Samson, roused by the Terrapin to perform heroic feats:

> Tigers he mauled, with tooth and ripping nail
> Rending their straps of fire, and from his track
> Slithering like quicksilver, pouring their black
> And liquid coils before his pounding feet,
> He drove the livid mambas of deceit.

Samson's physical prowess is being described in the first lines, and the tigers he mauls are real. Similarly the description of the snake is a typically vivid picture of an observed detail from Campbell's African background, and the mambas, like the tigers, are still physical opponents. A new element is suddenly introduced in the last line when the snakes are described as "mambas of deceit." The addition of the specific moral concept can only weaken the snaky quality of the preceding lines; from the real tigers and realistic writhing of the snakes we have suddenly moved to snakes which symbolize an abstract quality. (pp. 25-6)

In the best passages there is a brilliant vividness which depends both on suggestions of vastness and on the reality of specific details. (p. 26)

Campbell's descriptions are often playful. Without weakening his central impression of the vigour of the natural forces around the ark and Terrapin he continually achieves a charming lightness of effect. . . . A similar control informs the openly satirical moments when he exaggerates the very epic effects on which his poem depends at other points. . . . A feeling of the poet's own mental alertness is one of the most appealing features of *The Flaming Terrapin*. Its changes in mood, together with the extraordinary vividness and colour of so many moments, provide an interest which the poet's overt moral intention does not always realize. As a first poem the work shows the rare quality of demonstrating an originality and distinctly personal style, which Campbell in his twenty-third year could legitimately claim to be his own. At the same time, both the wild delights and the controlled vitality of *The Flaming Terrapin* give it a permanent value which is not simply that of showing a promising poetic quality. (pp. 31-2)

> *Rowland Smith, in his* Lyric and Polemic: The Literary Personality of Roy Campbell *(© McGill-Queen's University Press 1972), McGill-Queen's University Press, 1972, 249 p.*

JOHN POVEY (essay date 1977)

It is the collection entitled *Adamastor* . . . that is Campbell's most significant achievement. It is in fact the one volume upon which must rest any justification he may have for being considered a major poet. (p. 59)

It is in *Adamastor* that we discover Campbell's most famous, often anthologized African poems, **"The Serf,"** **"The Zulu Girl,"** and **"The Zebras."** These three poems describe the African scene with an accuracy that equals love. It is impossible to be so intensely aware of these African places and animals and not demonstrate that one is bound to that continent in some close emotional reaction. This remains true

even for poems which perhaps have apparent evidence of South African racial attitudes implicit in them. A contemporary Nigerian poet, John Pepper Clark, suggested that a poem such as **"The Zulu Girl"** has nothing to do with Africa, since although it is full, as he puts it, "of breast-feeding babies in the sun," it is an outsider's poem, it is a white man's exterior vision of Africa. There is a deliberate flaunting exaggeration in such a remark, yet there also is some truth. Obviously Campbell does not share that Zulu identification with the African scene and the African emotion any more than Joseph Conrad could in writing his Congo stories. Yet self-inclusion is not the only manner of perceiving the scenes of this continent. Identification is not the only source of poetic compassion. In Campbell's exactness there is an accuracy we share and a lyricism we can admire.

"The Zulu Girl" . . . describes simply the common enough scene of an African mother feeding her child. It is possible, I think, that we may feel a faint qualm of moral disapproval in the image in this poem that compares child to puppy, evocative as it may be. But this requires only passing comment. Our primary awareness here is of a most exact and precise record of this Zulu landscape, the area which Campbell knew so well as a boy. The scene is constructed for us with careful sensuality. The use of color words, the purple blood, the darkness of shadow, evoke the scene supported by sounds. The "sharp electric clicks" produce an onomatopoeic effect that reinforces the visual observation. There is also an accuracy in that grunting feeding, a record of that moment when a child, hungry for the breast, is no more human than any other greedy life-seeking animal.

Beyond this setting of scene Campbell carries us into another area which shows his understanding and his sympathetic recognition. He knows this "curbed ferocity." The "solemn dignity" makes clear that however much the system maintains serfdom for the Zulus and the Zulu girl, there has been no spiritual defeat, and there is a sharp note of warning in the last lines. In this poem Campbell has moved beyond the point of description which has so often been asserted to be his major forte. He exhibits an intellectual awareness and, if not identification, at least a recognition. It is this profound knowledge of a situation in which he lives which can stand against the possible accusation that there are tourist photograph aspects in his African poetry. The success of this poem in moving beyond such merely colorful description is strengthened by the technical skill with which he handles these lines. In particular, one notices the rhythmic reinforcement between the topic and the stressed patterns of the lines. The broken, bouncing consonantal syllables of "Tugs like a puppy, grunting as he feeds," audibly indicate that seeking, nudging of the child. There is a controlled transition to those "deep languours ripple / Like a broad river sighing through its reeds," where not only the obvious device of the repeated sibilants indicate the moving water, but the extremely slow phrases suggest more exactly the movement of those slow-running, languid African rivers.

Very similar in tone and very commonly coupled with **"The Zulu Girl"** in anthologies is his sonnet **"The Serf."** . . . Here again we have a description of an African scene which could bog down into the merely picturesque like a color slide, extended into a potent feeling for the African. Again Campbell shows his awareness of the veneer by which this South African society maintains its existence.

The first four lines set the scene with great evocation, particularly for those who have ever witnessed the plough cutting into the brilliant red earth of Africa. This crimson furrow, exposed by the sharp blade of the plough, is seen as a blood-stained gash. The inevitable drought has so desiccated the earth that little puffs of dust appear with each step, as the African ploughs his dry and infertile patch. The blood suggestion of the red earth provokes Campbell into a continuing development of this extending metaphor. He comprehends that this serf labor which the African is compelled to do is a repudiation of the old brave warrior life which the Zulus once lived as the great military people of southern Africa. There can be a special identification here because, black or white, Campbell comprehends this loss of soldier prowess, the elimination of individual bravery, for such feeling motivated much of his later life. Campbell avers that there is a dual wound; the wound in the earth is the symbolic replication of the heart's wound in the man, linked by the blood color of the soil. (pp. 59-61)

The foregoing poems, which have been primarily praised for their lyric descriptive qualities, can be shown to carry us forward into quite a different area. This discovery is equally true when Campbell goes on to descriptions of African animals which he admired and enjoyed so much.... **"The Zebras"** is certainly perhaps the most colorful and effective poem of Africa that Campbell achieved. It is another sonnet and gives evidence both of the love with which he reacted to the African scene and African animals, and also supplies us, in microcosm, with evidence of the techniques which he regularly employed in order to describe that emotion.

What is significant here is a classic example of the techniques which Campbell employs throughout his collection. Most potent is the way in which his brilliant use of color is reinforced by his deliberately chosen verbs of action and of movement. To describe these zebras who wander in their striped herds across the African high veldt, he not only uses the evocative color adjectives ''gold,'' ''scarlet,'' ''fire,'' and ''rosy,'' but also chooses his verbs to give a sense of participating action. It is not enough that the scene is pictorial; in a sense, it becomes cinematographic, a moving picture. When he describes the striped effect of the zebras, he uses the term ''zithering'' to impose the idea of the rapidly moving strings of that harplike instrument. The sunlight is not seen simply as a static golden glow but flashes with the movement of these animals. Their coats are barred in a design similar to the contrasted lines of sun and shadow, in the landscape. But zebra stripes form ''electric'' tremors, and suggest vibration. It is movement that constitutes the effect of these lines. The sight of the wind slipping across the elephant grass ''Like wind along the gold strings of a lyre'' is an image of transient movement.

Action within the poem is continued even farther and more extravagantly when we have the description of the actual beasts in their ardent mating maneuvers where ''the stallion wheels his flight.'' The zebra's movement is seen as exploiting the freedom, the unrestrained movement of a bird.... The action and color are precisely brought together in the last line where the copulation, representing its most complete of unions, is splendidly and eagerly performed among the lilies of the scene. The handling of the verbs to create this degree of movement is appropriate. This is because where the scene has its own physical violence, Campbell's somewhat violent language is not excessive, does not set up a discordant discrepancy in our minds between what is appropriate in the scene and what is exact in the language.

When he describes the color of Africa, we know the exotic hues of Africa are themselves as brilliant as Campbell writes. It is when he later chooses to apply these terms to England that they become bombastic metaphors that only surprise rather than delight. (pp. 62-3)

There are many other poems than those discussed which could equally exemplify Campbell's poetic qualities. The ones which I have critically examined show that . . . Campbell was developing a lyric gift that was unmatched in the contemporary English tongue. I do not think this is too excessive a statement. No one else had achieved this vivid, virile note, this authoritative power, coupled with the sensitivity to sensory experience. Everything appeared to suggest that this man was going to be a new force in English poetry, an invaluable antidote to the prettiness and etiolated intellectualism which had so filled the style of poetry at this particular period. On the one hand, T. S. Eliot had made his own revolution by asserting that the nonpoetic could be the substance of poetry, that the damp souls of housemaids were as appropriate a subject for poetry as the women breast-high amid ripening corn. . . . Campbell came with his own revolution which, as it turned out, appeared to be an antagonistic one, but could well have been coupled with Eliot in introducing a change in English poetry. Campbell was asserting the possibility of sensual vehemence, of intensity for a poet, but not deriving this from the shallow and falsely poetic excess that had cluttered the remnants of Victorian verse. Campbell was trumpeting that it was possible to create a new and modern poetry which did not have the dry, prosaic, deliberately conversational flatness which was the calculated basis of Eliot or Pound's style.

The significant point is that at this time Campbell could have brought to English poetry a new vision. (pp. 88-9)

Here was a direction for Campbell to take. It was in one sense the road that Eliot had chosen. This is not to pretend that Campbell was even at this stage in his poetic career as potentially significant as Eliot. It is equally true that nothing that Campbell ever wrote could equal the power of ''Gerontion'' or the social impact of *The Waste Land*. Nevertheless, theirs was an identity; in Campbell too there was a new voice. If he could have been true to the intellectual ideal, the clarity of his African vision, then his success as a poet would have been assured, and through this success his influence and prowess would have been recognized and admitted. Unfortunately, many dominion poets from new lands come to the mother country, in the same way as people from parochial and minor areas of this nation go to the great metropolitan center, New York. Such travelers bring with them this same sense of the inferiority of their own environment, the sense that somehow they must adjust so that they can become part of the literary scene, or react in a grieved display of petulant bravado. . . . Campbell himself, in fact, did not allow himself to be swamped or changed directly by the disparagement which, to his anger and humiliation, he met with from the leading literary figures in the English Georgian movement, but his reaction drove him to write poetry of shrill satiric excess. It allowed him to dissipate his talents, quarreling and feuding with the minor literary figures which he should have had the good sense to ignore as being unworthy of his concern or interest. It also led him to take more and more virulent stands, both in his political and intellectual beliefs, and more specifically, in the poetry which he wrote, straining to gain the effects which would more than ever shock and dismay the poets whom he despised.

In a way this is doubly sad because it occurs in such an early volume; but one might insist that his first collection represents possibly the poetic climax of his career. After this, although there are many successful individual poems and poems which reflect the qualities which he achieves at his best in this volume, they are often isolated examples among a matrix of excess, of absurd satire, of ugly anger. The vision which he had as he recapitulated the Africa of his youth, the Africa of his intense feeling was lost, as was the skill which he brought to his poetry and which so illuminated and inspired these powerful emotional effects.

Campbell's potential was lost by being exchanged for another determination, a belief that the London literary scene could be conquered within its own odious, narrow terms. Its terms were those which he had the good sense completely to despise and reject. But the unconscionable arrogance, the certainty of these people was sufficient to drive him into rebellious assault upon their assured citadel. In doing so, he lost his integrity, lost his vision of himself as a poet, and became only a shrill, angry man, humiliated, defiant and, as a poet, irretrievably lost. (pp. 89-90)

> *John Povey, "The Making of a Poet: 'Adamastor'," in his* Roy Campbell *(copyright © 1977 by Twayne Publishers, Inc.; reprinted with the permission of Twayne Publishers, a Division of G. K. Hall & Co., Boston), Twayne, 1977, pp. 59-94.*

ADDITIONAL BIBLIOGRAPHY

Abrahams, Lionel. "Roy Campbell: Conquistador—Refugee." *Theoria*, No. 8 (1956): 46-65.
    Explores the poet's relationship with nature as seen in his earliest works, briefly describes his major works, and discusses his place in South African literature.

Bergonzi, Bernard. "Roy Campbell: Outsider on the Right." *The Journal of Contemporary History* 2, No. 2 (April 1967): 133-47.
    Explains why Campbell's background had such an impact on the poetry he wrote.

Hamm, Victor M. "Roy Campbell: Satirist." *THOUGHT* XXXVII, No. 145 (Summer 1962): 194-210.
    Discusses the satiric art in Campbell's works, especially with regard to *Flowering Rifle, The Wayzgoose,* and *The Georgiad.*

Joost, Nicholas. "The Poetry of Roy Campbell." *Renascence* VIII, No. 3 (Spring 1956): 115-20.
    Discussion of the several kinds of poetry that Campbell wrote, such as Churchillian satire and political verse.

Krige, Uys. "Roy Campbell As Lyrical Poet: Some Quieter Aspects." *English Studies in Africa* 1, No. 2 (September 1958): pp. 81-94.
    Excellent study of Campbell as a lyric poet which finds him to be "one of the few really powerful lyrical voices of his generation."

Parsons, D.S.J. "Roy Campbell and Wyndham Lewis." *PMLA* VII, No. 4 (Fall 1971): 406-21.
    Compares Campbell's work to Lewis's and discusses the influence that Lewis had on Campbell's writing.

Paton, Alan. "Roy Campbell: Poet and Man." *Theoria*, No. 9 (1957): 19-31.
    Bio-critical study.

Seymour-Smith, Martin. "Zero and the Impossible: Roy Campbell; Wyndham Lewis; Joyce Cary; John Middleton Murry." *Encounter* IX, No. 5 (November 1957): 38-51.*
    Considers the inhumanity of Campbell's poetry. Seymour-Smith believes that Campbell's aggressive style, a compensation for his sense of inferiority, is the type of emotion that fuels authoritarian regimes.

Thomas, Dylan. "Flamboyants All the Way." *The Observer* (16 December 1951): 7.
    Review of *Light on a Dark Horse* in which Thomas calls Campbell "a poet of genius."

Wright, David. *Roy Campbell.* London: Longmans, Green & Co., 1961, 43 p.
    Criticism and personal reminiscence by a South African poet.

Charles Waddell Chesnutt

1858-1932

American short story writer, novelist, biographer, and journalist.

Known primarily as a short story writer, Chesnutt was the first black American fiction writer to receive serious critical attention. He sought to transcend the limitations of the plantation school, such as condescending characterizations of blacks and nostalgia for the antebellum days of slavery in the South, without alienating his white readership and publishers.

Chesnutt's youth in Fayetteville, North Carolina, provided him with many of the themes in his fiction. He absorbed the dialects and folktales of the region and observed the social structure based on color within the black community. As a light-complexioned Negro, he was able to explore the moral ramifications of "passing" into white society. Although he was a successful school principal, Chesnutt felt circumscribed by Southern apartheid policies and moved his family to his birthplace, Cleveland, Ohio, where he studied law and established a profitable legal stenography business. Dissatisfied with the bucolic portrayals of slavery in American fiction, he decided to write stories that would show plantation life from the slave's point of view.

In his first work, *The Conjure Woman*, ex-slave Julius McAdoo tells stories of metamorphosis, voodoo, and conjuring that exploit the local color and dialect of the Southern plantation tales popular with white readers, while ironically illuminating the horrors of slavery. Contemporary critics, who often missed the subtle use of protest in the stories, applauded *The Conjure Woman*, but became disenchanted with Chesnutt when he began to treat taboo themes such as miscegenation and racial hatred.

In *The Wife of His Youth and Other Stories of the Color Line*, his second collection of short stories, Chesnutt portrayed the dilemma of mulattoes who felt alien in the black community and excluded from the white. He satirized the race-conscious Blue Veins of Cleveland (people of Negro descent with skin light enough to show the blueness of their veins) for snubbing their darker-skinned relatives, and mimicking middle-class whites.

Disturbed by violence and discrimination against blacks in the South, Chesnutt began to write propagandistic novels espousing racial harmony and understanding. His sympathetic treatment of erotic love between blacks and whites in his first novel, *The House behind the Cedars*, outraged critics of his day. Pessimism pervades his later work, prompting William Dean Howells, an early champion of Chesnutt's, to criticize *The Marrow of Tradition* for its bitter tone. Modern critics have attacked the heavy melodrama, facile coincidence, and overt didacticism of the novels. However, some critics praise Chesnutt's objectivity in the so-called propaganda novels, citing his willingness to portray a broad cross section of the black community, including accommodationist professionals, sycophants, and rebels.

Critics generally agree that Chesnutt's novels are artistically inferior to the earlier short stories. While some contend that

The Granger Collection, New York

he made too many concessions to the white book-buying public, he is, nevertheless, considered an important figure in the early history of black literature in the United States.

PRINCIPAL WORKS

The Conjure Woman   (short stories) 1899
Frederick Douglass   (biography) 1899
The Wife of His Youth and Other Stories of the Color Line   (short stories) 1899
The House behind the Cedars   (novel) 1900
The Marrow of Tradition   (novel) 1901
The Colonel's Dream   (novel) 1905

FLORENCE A. H. MORGAN   (essay date 1899)

The keynote of the [seven stories in *The Conjure Woman*] is the blind superstition and duplicity of character fostered by the life of servility and cringing to the master. These stories stand out as an impartial picture of the life of the slave in the Southern States. Uncle Julius is a fine type of the old slave devoted to his master, never lacking in dignity and courage, but withal possessing an indifferent code of morals, the result, most likely, of his close association with the white man whose ethics were, to say the least, pliant. All the wrongs of the race are in these simple tales unfolded, but with never a complaint, a strict justice being displayed in the drawing of the good and bad master, the good and bad slave, each having a fair showing. Mr. Chesnutt does not strive for any dramatic effects, nor does he ever introduce any unnecessary harrowing situations; there is a surprising absence of false sentiment. Love, hate, jealousy and cruelty are dealt with in a thoroughly sane, good-natured, sensible manner. No hysterics, no posing, mar the simple recitals of Uncle Julius as he happens to talk to the Northern man and his wife who have come to North Carolina. . . . (p. 372)

Between the introduction of slavery into the South and the Civil War lies a picturesque period, something more than dramatic and less than tragic, fraught with wonderful possibilities for just such a facile, discriminating pen as Mr. Chesnutt's. As we of this day look back over that shadowed bit of history, such a transaction as is set forth in **"Sis' Becky's Pickaninny"** seems absolutely incredible, and moves our hearts to an outspoken rebellion that such things could ever have been, and yet the author does justice to every one in the tale. . . . In this story more than in any other of the group does Mr. Chesnutt place before his readers the two kinds of masters, and a strong wave of irrepressible compassion sweeps over us as we grasp the tragical undercurrent of those lives bowed down with ignominy and shame. Through the medium of **"The Gray Wolf's Ha'nt"** and **"Po' Sandy"** the author pictures the every-day, pathetic side of the negro's life, and forcibly brings out that peculiar mysticism which may be the black man's inheritance from the Orient; the beliefs and superstitions which have been transplanted along with the race. But across the darkest phase of the slave's life there flashes that quaint humour which saves even the most tragic scenes from too heavy a shadow of horror. So clever a master of literary skill, so keen a student of human nature is Mr. Chesnutt, that he never allows himself to drift into too great gloom, but plays with an artistic touch on our emotions and our sense of humour in an equal degree. (pp. 372-73)

The Conjure Woman is a collection of quaint tales, with an admirable Southern setting, replete with the humour and tragedy of slavery, so skilfully blended that often one does not know where the one begins and the other ends. The dialect in which the story-teller speaks is smooth and readable, evidently a means and not an end, and Mr. Chesnutt's English is remarkable for its literary style and quality. (p. 373)

> Florence A. H. Morgan, "Novel Notes: 'The Conjure Woman'," in The Bookman, New York (copyright, 1899, by George H. Doran Company), Vol. IX, No. 3, May, 1899, pp. 372-73.

NANCY HUSTON BANKS (essay date 1900)

[To Mr. Chesnutt] may perhaps be given the credit of the first publication of a subtle psychological study of the negro's spiritual nature, the first actual revelation of those secret depths of the dusky soul which no white writer might hope to approach through his own intuition.

The depth of the revelation [in **"The Wife of His Youth"**]—its width and completeness—are scarcely apparent at a glance, the little story is so short and so simply and quietly told. The author extenuates nothing. The man is drawn as he is—vain, conceited, puffed up over his small measure of success, thinking over-much of his white blood, and looking forward to an ambitious second marriage, without troubling himself as to whether the wife of his youth be living or dead. The woman also stands in full light, a mere withered atom of old plantation life—ignorant, bent and black—"so black that her toothless gums, revealed when she opened her mouth to speak, were not red, but blue"—with tufts of wool, instead of hair, protruding around her ancient bonnet. Such are the actors in the humble tragedy that Mr. Chesnutt has written, yet neither they nor their lowly environment ever touch the absurd or even the commonplace. There may be a smile at the sidelights of the quiet beginning, but the long shadow of slavery still stretches too far across the lives of the emancipated for the smile to last. From its very simplicity, its quiet, its reserve, comes the force of its great appeal.

All this and more may be said in praise of the first and the shortest of the nine stories forming the volume. The others are hardly worthy of mention in comparison with the first. The single partial exception is **"Uncle Wellington's Wives,"** but even this is readable chiefly because of its kind, mellow humour and its photographic portrayal of a familiar type of the negro. As fiction it has little if any claim to consideration, and a graver fault than its lack of literary quality is its careless approach to the all but unapproachable ground of sentimental relations between the black race and the white race. Touching this and still more dangerous and darker race problems, Mr. Chesnutt shows a lamentable lack of tact of a kindred sort, an incomprehensible want of the good taste and dignified reserve which characterises his first beautiful story and the greater part of all his work. **"The Sheriff's Children"** furnishes, perhaps, the most shocking instance of his reckless disregard of matters respected by more experienced writers. In saying this there is no intention to deny the too probable truth of the untellable story, nor any wish to dispute its tragic importance as legitimate literary material. On the contrary, it is the recognition of that terrible truth and its mighty weight which cause the protest. Had the author recognised these things, it would seem that he must either have left them alone or have approached them more carefully, and with greater strenuousness; that he must have felt the need of laying hold of them with far surer, firmer, larger grasp, if he touched them at all. It may be, however, that Mr. Chesnutt earnestly tried to reach beyond his grasp, and failed.

Be that as it may, it is much to be regretted that he has not held to the themes well within his scope, where the surety and strength of his touch needs no better proof than the faithfulness and beauty of *The Wife of His Youth*. (pp. 597-98)

> Nancy Huston Banks, "Novel Notes: 'The Wife of His Youth'," in The Bookman, New York (copyright, 1900, by George H. Doran Company), Vol. X, No. 6, February, 1900, pp. 597-98.

W. D. HOWELLS (essay date 1900)

The critical reader of the story called **"The Wife of his Youth"** . . . must have noticed uncommon traits in what was altogether a remarkable piece of work. The first was the novelty of the material; for the writer dealt not only with people who were not white, but with people who were not black enough to contrast grotesquely with white people,—who in fact were of that near approach to the ordinary American in race and color which leaves, at the last degree, every one but the connoisseur in doubt whether they are Anglo-Saxon or Anglo-African. Quite as striking as this novelty of the material was the author's thorough mastery of it, and his unerring knowledge of the life he had chosen in its peculiar racial characteristics. But above all, the story was notable for the passionless handling of a phase of our common life which is tense with potential tragedy; for the attitude, almost ironical, in which the artist observes the play of contesting emotions in the drama under his eyes; and for his apparently reluctant, apparently helpless consent to let the spectator know his real feeling in the matter. Any one accustomed to study methods in fiction, to distinguish between good and bad art, to feel the joy which the delicate skill possible only from a love of truth can give, must have known a high pleasure in the quiet self-restraint of the performance; and such a reader would probably have decided that the social situation in the piece was studied wholly from the outside, by an observer with special opportunities for knowing it, who was, as it were, surprised into final sympathy. (p. 699)

It is not from their racial interest that we could first wish to speak of [Mr. Chesnutt's stories], though that must have a very great and very just claim upon the critic. It is much more simply and directly, as works of art, that they make their appeal, and we must allow the force of this quite independently of the other interest. Yet it cannot always be allowed. There are times in each of the stories of the first volume [*The Conjure Woman*] when the simplicity lapses, and the effect is as of a weak and uninstructed touch. There are other times when the attitude, severely impartial and studiously aloof, accuses itself of a little pompousness. There are still other times when the literature is a little too ornate for beauty, and the diction is journalistic, reporteristic. But it is right to add that these are the exceptional times, and that for far the greatest part Mr. Chesnutt seems to know quite as well what he wants to do in a given case as Maupassant, or Tourguénief, or Mr. James, or Miss [Sarah Orne] Jewett, or Miss [Mary Eleanor] Wilkins, in other given cases, and has done it with an art of kindred quiet and force. He belongs, in other words, to the good school, the only school, all aberrations from nature being so much truancy and anarchy. He sees his people very clearly, very justly, and he shows them as he sees them, leaving the reader to divine the depth of his feeling for them. He touches all the stops, and with equal delicacy in stories of real tragedy and comedy and pathos, so that it would be hard to say which is the finest in such admirably rendered effects as **"The Web of Circumstance," "The Bouquet,"** and **"Uncle Wellington's Wives."** In some others the comedy degenerates into satire, with a look in the reader's direction which the author's friend must deplore. . . .

[However, the stories in *The Wife of his Youth*] are new and fresh and strong, as life always is, and fable never is; and the stories of *The Conjure Woman* have a wild, indigenous poetry, the creation of sincere and original imagination, which is imparted with a tender humorousness and a very artistic reticence. (p. 700)

[These stories] are Mr. Chesnutt's most important work, whether we consider them merely as realistic fiction, apart

from their author, or as studies of that middle world of which he is naturally and voluntarily a citizen. We had known the nethermost world of the grotesque and comical negro and the terrible and tragic negro through the white observer on the outside, and black character in its lyrical moods we had known from such an inside witness as Mr. Paul Dunbar; but it had remained for Mr. Chesnutt to acquaint us with those regions where the paler shades dwell as hopelessly, with relation to ourselves, as the blackest negro. (pp. 700-01)

He has sounded a fresh note, boldly, not blatantly, and he has won the ear of the more intelligent public. (p. 701)

W. D. Howells, "Mr. Charles W. Chesnutt's Stories," in The Atlantic Monthly *(copyright © 1900, by The Atlantic Monthly Company, Boston, Mass.), Vol. 85, No. 511, May, 1900, pp. 699-701.*

JOHN CHAMBERLAIN (essay date 1930)

Negro fiction in America properly commences with Charles Waddell Chesnutt. . . . One goes back to the archaic, quaintly-flavored novels and stories of this pioneer with mingled appreciation and esthetic blankness. Most of the Chesnutt plots hinge on such adventitious circumstances that the works of Thomas Hardy seem the very soul of the natural by comparison, but even in the stretches where the antique machinery creaks the loudest one reads with nothing but admiration for Chesnutt as a man. If his plot structure is definitely dated, the fault resides with the white models with which he worked in that era when the novel was designed to tell a story at all costs; and the spectacle of a Negro of the time working with any models at all and producing fiction with many good points is sufficient to compel applause. (p. 603)

Chesnutt is at his happiest, from a modern point of view, in the whimsical, poetic folktales that comprise *The Conjure Woman*. (p. 604)

The worst side of the writer crops up in the short stories of *The Wife of His Youth and Other Stories*. The tales of *The Conjure Woman* are the stock in trade of an old Negro Machiavelli, Uncle Julius, who tells them with ulterior motives. For example, he regales his white masters with some nonsense about the "goopher" placed upon a grape vine with the end view in mind of preserving the income he has been deriving from the scuppernong wine made from the fruit. Julius is a lovable old liar with a fine imagination; and, as J. E. Spingarn says, every story he passes on adds a stroke to his self-portrait—something that cannot be said for Joel Chandler Harris's entertaining Uncle Remus. We accept queer twists from Uncle Julius.

But in **"The Wife of His Youth"** we cannot accept queer twists. For instance, when the dean of the Blue Veins of Groveland is confronted by the forgotten wife of his plantation days, a little black wizened woman, we cannot believe in the wrench whereby Chesnutt makes it possible for the confounded man to accept the situation and present "the wife of his youth" to the assembled Blue Veins [a term applied to very light complected Negroes] at a ball originally intended to mark his betrothal to a charming young woman. The inner conflict of Mr. Ryder is totally missing. **"A Matter of Principle"** is the best of the Chesnutt short stories in the realistic genre; it is too plotted, but irony saves it. **"The Sheriff's Children,"** a story of North Carolina, is effective as melodrama, for the sheriff who saves a prisoner from the lynching mob finds himself confronted by his own mulatto son, a son who is willing to kill him to make good his escape. In other stories, such as **"The Bouquet"** and **"Ciceley's Dream,"** Chesnutt can become as sentimental as any of the cheaper fiction writers of his day or ours; but it is a tribute to his artistic conscience that he lapsed only occasionally. (pp. 604-05)

> John Chamberlain, *"The Negro as Writer,"* in The Bookman, *New York (copyright, 1930, by George H. Doran Company), Vol. LXX, No. 6, February, 1930, pp. 603-11.**

STERLING BROWN   (essay date 1937)

[Charles Waddell Chesnutt] deserves to be called a pioneer.... Chesnutt is the first to speak out uncompromisingly, but artistically, on the problems facing his people. (p. 78)

Whether he was pessimistic about his crusade or not, his achievements in fiction were worthy. Answering propaganda with propaganda, he might be expected to have certain faults. He was overinclined to the melodramatic, to mistaken identity, to the lost document turning up at the right or wrong moment, to the nick of time entrance. His characters are generally idealized or conventional. His "better class Negroes" speak too literary a language and are generally unbelievable models in behavior. Although attacking the color line within the race, he makes great use of the hero or heroine of mixed blood, and at times seems to accept the traditional concepts of Negro character. Even so, however, his characters stand nearer to the truth than those of Thomas Page or Thomas Dixon; he does not force them into only two grooves. There is no gainsaying his knowledge of the southern scene, or of the Negro upper class in northern cities. Unlike Dunbar he is opposed to the plantation tradition, sharply critical of southern injustice, and aware of the sinister forces at work in Reconstruction. Deploring the abuses of that era, he still sees . . . that the story of a South victimized by carpet-baggers and scalawags is only a convenient half-truth. He gives high praise to the Yankee schoolmasters and schoolmarms who swarmed over Dixie to lift a second bondage from the freedmen. He shows exploitation, riots and lynching mobs, as well as the more refined exercising of prejudice. Often pompous and roundabout, in the manner of his times, he nevertheless knew how to hold a reader's interest. We must concede that he was melodramatic in plotting, but evidences of a skillful master's hand can still be found. He knew a great deal, and all things considered, he told it well. (pp. 81-2)

> Sterling Brown, *"Reconstruction: The Not So Glorious South,"* in his The Negro in American Fiction *(copyright 1937 by Associates in Negro Folk Education), Associates in Negro Folk Education, 1937 (and reprinted by Kennikat Press, 1968), pp. 64-83.**

J. SAUNDERS REDDING   (essay date 1939)

Charles W. Chesnutt is a transitional figure. He drew together the various post-Civil War tendencies in Negro creative literature and translated them into the most worthy prose fiction that the Negro had produced. . . .

In one stroke Chesnutt had achieved [in *The Conjure Woman*] what others had striven for interminably. Written around a central framework, the care with which the stories are done bespeaks the writer's artistic sincerity. The tales, concerned with the deeds and misdeeds of a conjure woman, are connected with each other in such a way as to give them more than the superficial unity which the framework supplies. The plan is very simple. Uncle Julius, a frosty-headed Negro who has lived through and absorbed all the romance and reality of slavery, tells the seven folk tales to a northern white couple recently moved to North Carolina. (p. 68)

For sheer accomplishment . . . he never surpassed *The Conjure Woman,* and none of his later stories ever equaled the folk tale **"The Gray Wolf's Ha'nt,"** that dark and cruel tragedy of jealousy and love. Nearly all the stories of this first collection are tragic with the fatal consequences of human actions and prejudices. It is not the weak pseudo-tragedy of propaganda, it is not pathos and tears in which Chesnutt deals—it is the fundamental stuff of life translated into the folk terms of a people who knew true tragedy.

Chesnutt's first volume proved two important points. It proved that the Negro could be made the subject of serious esthetic treatment without the interference of propaganda; and it proved that the Negro creative artist could submerge himself objectively in his material. It must not be thought, however, that the tradition of buffoonery was broken by *The Conjure Woman.* The buffoon had two faces. He grinned and danced and capered as a minstrel Sambo and in the stories of certain popular authors, while Joel Chandler Harris saw the other face, the blandly kind and childish smile, the improvident generosity and loyalty. But he was still a Negro, lazy, ignorant, dependent. Both faces showed him as a woefully inferior being, and that was the very core of the tradition. Like a Jewish actor in pre-Christian Rome, he might be the instrument of tragedy, but he was never tragic. Beneath the mask there grinned the Negro. (pp. 68-9)

The struggle between Chesnutt the artist and Chesnutt the man (not immediately resolved) is evident in *The Wife of His Youth.* In these stories Chesnutt discards folk material to deal with the lives of a certain Negro type in Cleveland, the "Groveland" of his stories. These people represent the special and important group of Negroes with a large admixture of white blood. Because the peculiar situation of the near-whites was (and is) considered ideal for the purposes of propaganda, their lives had been used by nearly all the Negro novelists prior to [Paul Laurence] Dunbar. This put upon such characters a certain stamp, and in that stamp lay danger for Chesnutt the artist.

The moods in which Chesnutt approaches his material are puzzling. In only a few of these stories is the reader sure of the author's point of view, his convictions. In **"A Matter of Principle,"** for instance, a story of the color line in which the daughter of a well-to-do quadroon family loses a brilliant marriage because her father mistakes a stout, black gentleman for the lover whom he has never seen—what is the author's point of view? Based on the tragic absurdity of colorphobia, the story is a comedy of manners in the Molière sense. But what is Chesnutt's conviction as an artist? Does he sympathize with the existence of a color caste within the race? Is he holding his characters up to ridicule? Of what is he trying to convince us? In this and other stories one seems always at the point of making a discovery about the author, but the discovery never matures. (pp. 70-1)

The title story, **"The Wife of His Youth,"** is an exception. The delicacy of its mood, the tempered sharpness of its point, and the subtle simplicity of characterization remind one of Hawthorne. Indeed, it might have been conceived and executed by the author of *Twice Told Tales*. . . . It is not character that is of most interest here. The characters are flat, two-dimensional. Situation, circumstance—and beyond these, the whole complex social structure—draw our attention. Only Chesnutt's brooding sympathy for the problems present in the society of which he writes makes the story at all possible. One feels here something more of his personality than that which ordinarily belongs to creative writing. One finds here a key to him, the ever-coiling spring of his future creativeness.

Whether written in the spirit of comedy or tragedy, all the stories in **The Wife of his Youth** deal with the entanglements resulting from miscegenation. They are stories of situation. They represent a new approach to the Negro character in fiction. They argue artistically and not too obviously . . . of the way of life to which the Negro might attain were it not for the bugaboo of color. The picture of life which Chesnutt draws is not exaggerated. The Negro characters are simplified beyond any that had appeared other than as types in American fiction. This simplification and the fact that the characters are limited to a certain group makes them less than ever representative. But they are people. **The Wife of his Youth** thrust into Negro literature a brace of which it was sadly in need.

In his first novel, **The House Behind the Cedars,** Chesnutt the Negro emerges more distinctly outlined, with a greater consciousness of social kinship. This self-consciousness is seen nowhere more plainly than in the story material itself. Chesnutt had used the bi-racial elements in American life before, but he had put the Negro in the relationship of servant to the white master. No violence had been done the standard American concept. In an exploratory way he had reviewed the product of miscegenation. Now he was to probe the infinitely dark ways in which miscegenation worked. Without doing injustice to either racial group, he had to bring them together on a plane of intimacy never before attempted, save for purposes of propaganda, in American fiction. He succeeded remarkably well.

As in the shorter tales of the color line, **The House Behind the Cedars** is a situation story. Situation that does not develop from the inescapable strength or weakness, love or hate, weal or woe of character is likely to be too doctrinaire, and its assumptions much too general. Even when such stories avoid this danger, they are likely to become melodramatic. Skillful and dispassionate handling is necessary to bring them safely between the rocky shore and the shoals. It is in this that Chesnutt shows his craftsmanship. . . . [When] George Tyron, the aristocratic scion of an old southern family, falls in love with Rena we come face to face with the immediate and personalized problem of race. All this happens through situation. But it is at this point that character, aided by Hardian twists of fate, comes in to play its part. Rena faces the same problem that faced Hardy's Tess—whether to disclose her secret (of Negro blood) on the chance that her happiness would not be destroyed thereby. Like Tess, she sees the problem as a moral issue. The Hardian flavor is strong: the primary sin which was, however, not her sin, the struggle between the desire for happiness and the propulsion to truth, the innumerable circumstances that work for and against,

and finally the stark, bare tragedy and the resolution in death. For downright power, no novel of the Negro race quite equals **The House Behind the Cedars**.

Not the least important consideration in Chesnutt's first novel was the treatment of George Tyron. Numerous white writers, including George Cable, Thomas Dixon, and Mark Twain, had treated of love (of one sort or another) between black and white. But they followed the convention. They made such love always a degraded thing, a bestial thing, bitch and hound. Chesnutt manages differently. The relationship between Tyron and Rena is as free from moral turpitude as the love-life of goldfish. (pp. 71-3)

[Beneath] all the skillful management of character and situation one can feel the author losing the delicately balanced objectivity of his short stories. Sometimes it shows through the characters, through sharp thrusts of ironic dialogue. . . . (p. 74)

Chesnutt worked in hazardous elements—elements that in any moment of unawareness might prove his undoing.

In his second novel, **The Marrow of Tradition,** Chesnutt stumbled headlong into the dangers that had lurked for him in his earlier books. **The Marrow of Tradition** is definitely propaganda. All the reasonable sympathy, so marked in his previous books, and so necessary to fine artistic accomplishment, is gone. In a passion of hatred, he writes of insult, injustice, and ignorance, piling "scorn and contumely and hard words," not upon a situation, a way of life or thought, as he would have had perfect right to do, but upon the white race, "a people of our common race—the human race." Nothing of artistic sanity saves the novel from its melodramatic madness. Chesnutt no longer sees the white and the black with equal eye. He is no longer content to let the story tell itself or to let the characters live in the free air of their own inclinations. Possibility and probability find no kinship here; truth and reality are confused. (pp. 74-5)

More delicately wrought is **The Colonel's Dream,** also a novel of purpose. It is a clear but partial exposition of the deadly social forces that were at that time at work in the South. It is tragic in the overwhelming defeat of the good intentions of Colonel Henry French. The Colonel represents for Chesnutt that modicum of intelligence and humane feeling to be found in every social situation. (p. 75)

[Chesnutt] brought Negro creative literature much further along. His early career was a great artistic success, for he did the one thing needful to the American Negro writer: he worked dangerous, habit-ridden material with passive calm and fearlessness. Considering more than the emotional factors that lay behind the American race problem, he exposed the Negro to critical analysis. . . . No less can be said of him than has been already implied: he is the most solid representative of prose fiction that the Negro could boast before the 1920's, and even now his work in its kind has not been equaled. (p. 76)

J. Saunders Redding, "Adjustment," in his To Make a Poet Black *(copyright © 1939 by The University of North Carolina Press), The University of North Carolina Press, 1939 (and reprinted by McGrath Publishing Company, 1968), pp. 49-92.**

ROBERT A. BONE (essay date 1965)

Charles Chesnutt and Paul Laurence Dunbar were the first Negro novelists to attract the attention of the white literary world.... Both had launched their literary careers by exploiting the plantation tradition; both brought them to fruition with the help of white patrons. Dunbar, however, continued to write in the plantation tradition, or avoided controversy by making his main characters white. Chesnutt, on the other hand, pioneered in his "problem" novels, pressing his publishers for freedom to treat the color line from the Negro point of view. His novels are therefore of considerable historical if not literary importance. (p. 35)

In all important respects, *The House behind the Cedars* conforms to the prototype of the early Negro novel. Structurally speaking, Rena's social aspirations are played off against the constraining effects of caste, in a manner calculated to arouse the reader's indignation. The stereotype of the tragic mulatto is employed, with all of its moral and aesthetic limitations. Nor is *The House behind the Cedars* immune from the literary infirmities of the period. The novel is incredibly overwritten in spots: "Rena, my darlin', why did you forsake yo'r pore old mother?" The dramatic conflict never transcends the plot level; there is no characterization worthy of the name; and in the end, Chesnutt avoids his artistic responsibilities by arbitrarily putting his heroine to death.

In *The Marrow of Tradition* ..., Chesnutt comes to grips with the violence of the post-Reconstruction repression. (pp. 36-7)

Fundamentally the novel raises the issue of retaliation in the face of direct provocation from the whites. (p. 37)

The novel is heavily overplotted; the maze of characters precludes adequate motivation; the style is excessively formal and unsuited to the highly emotional quality of the theme, and an element of melodrama pervades the whole novel. To a large extent the fiction is merely a scaffolding through which Chesnutt can present his views on contemporary race relations. In the theme of retaliation he has the makings of a good novel, but he fails to cast his theme in an appropriate dramatic mold.

Chesnutt's third novel, *The Colonel's Dream* ..., can best be described as the work of a pamphleteer.... [It] is conciliatory and ingratiating in tone, for it represents that phase in Chesnutt's development in which he means to talk business with the Southern whites. The novel depicts the struggle of Colonel French, a progressive white Southerner, against Bill Fetters, a former poor white who represents the survival of the spirit of slavery. Perhaps nowhere in the early Negro novel is the bourgeois spirit so manifest. (pp. 37-8)

An appraisal of Chesnutt's novels is hardly a fair measure of his talent. On the strength of his short stories alone, he raised the standards of Negro fiction to a new and higher plane. These short stories—especially the conjure tales—can be judged on their own merits, and in this department Chesnutt's reputation seems secure. In his novels, however, he became an overt propagandist, to the detriment of his art. Furthermore, he never succeeded in mastering the aesthetic requirements of the longer genre. (p. 38)

> *Robert A. Bone, "Novels of the Talented Tenth: Charles Chesnutt," in his* The Negro Novel in America (© *1965 by Yale University Press, Inc.), revised edition, Yale University Press, 1965, pp. 35-8.*

ROBERT M. FARNSWORTH (essay date 1969)

[*The Conjure Woman*] illustrates the terms under which the white American reading public at the end of the nineteenth century was willing to let an Afro-American put his foot on the ladder of literary success. (p. v)

While Charles Chesnutt abandons the sentimental fantasy of plantation life projected by such writers as Thomas Nelson Page, he was deliberately cautious in what he said to a white audience whom he suspected of being hostile and knew to be uninformed.... Chesnutt wrote stories deliberately contrived to condition or enlighten a white audience without forcing a direct emotional confrontation.

The tales of *The Conjure Woman* are all narrated by a white Northerner who has gone South after the War in search of a suitable place of business for himself and a hospitable climate for his ailing wife.... At the heart of each tale is a story within the story told by Uncle Julius, a shrewd old ex-slave who recalls pre-War incidents of conjuration. The white narrator retells these stories, always making clear to the reader that he is aware that Uncle Julius usually has a lurking personal interest in his entertaining tales. (pp. vii-viii)

But there is much in the stories that the narrator himself never seems to recognize. The narrator is preoccupied with his business interests and his immediate family responsibilities, and Uncle Julius quickly recognizes that he has a more sympathetic and intuitively perceptive listener in the narrator's wife. (p. ix)

It is in this area that Chesnutt makes his points. Both the narrator and his wife are Northerners; therefore, their sympathies can be counted upon as antislavery; but as she tries to measure the impact of slavery on blacks, the woman's heart reaches much further toward Uncle Julius' world than does the man's mind or social conscience. (pp. ix-x)

[Consider] the differing response of John and his wife Annie after Uncle Julius tells the tale of ["**Po' Sandy**," in which a conjure woman turns her husband into a tree so that he will not be forced to work on other plantations]. (p. xi)

The narrator's preoccupation with the practical and the immediate is a limitation. It causes him to see only a farfetched amusing story told as a rather shrewd contrivance to protect some covert interest of his employee. Annie's sympathies sweep past the difficulties of believing in such activities as conjuration and point to the response Chesnutt hoped his larger reading audience would share—"What a system it was."

The inner stories of Uncle Julius convey the indictment Chesnutt wanted to make of the master-slave relationship in implicit rebuttal of the sentimental picture that had become current in the magazine fiction of the time. Chesnutt, probably remembering the powerful impact of *Uncle Tom's Cabin*, plays strongly on the theme of slavery violating the ties of love between man and woman and between mother and child. The slave becomes a piece of property, and on one level Uncle Julius more than once indicates to his male employer that slave masters often were bad businessmen who didn't know how to take care of their capital. But at a deeper level he clearly appeals to Miss Annie for a stronger response of repugnance to a system in which human beings are reduced to objects or *mere* capital. (pp. xiii-xiv)

In these stories Chesnutt evokes a strong sense of discreteness between the black world and the white. The slaves may resort to occult natural powers to help them overcome particular difficulties, but the white man's arbitrary power is stronger and more destructive.... The slave may call upon the trees, birds, animals, even the seasons to help him, but he has no ultimate defense against the master's legal and economic power. It determines life and death at the white man's whim. But as the reader progresses through the tales he gains a sense of the power of the black world, the mysterious natural world that challenges his common assumptions of the supremacy of the white man's world.

By the end of the book Uncle Julius emerges as a shrewd and wise old man. He understands the principles of husbandry and business, but more than that he knows something of the nooks and crannies of the human heart. He knows all about the world John, his employer, likes to pretend does not exist or which he consigns to women. With this knowledge Julius gains power, not the economic and social power John can take for granted with his whiteness but a power over the more intimate and mysterious secrets of life itself.

Thus, as John patronizes Julius, he testifies to his own limitations and to the white world's fumbling inability to appreciate the wisdom, humor, and heart of a black man's experience, rooted in the cruelties of the slave experience. John's limited sympathy, his inability to fathom Julius' experience, is a hauntingly familiar projection of the white response to America's racial problem. Julius' various efforts to engage his employer's imagination, to arouse his sympathy, and to focus his indignation reflect Charles Chesnutt's own many-sided efforts to reach the imagination and the heart of his largely white audience. (pp. xiv-xvii)

> *Robert M. Farnsworth, in his introduction to* The
> Conjure Woman *by Charles Chesnutt (copyright ©
> by The University of Michigan 1969), University of
> Michigan Press, 1969, pp. v-xix.*

RICHARD E. BALDWIN (essay date 1971)

In *The Conjure Woman* Charles Chesnutt analyzes with balance and subtlety the paradoxes and tensions of American racial life. The penetrating insights of these stories he never matched in his realistic fiction. Here Chesnutt avoids stifling stereotypes while criticizing the myths of white supremacy and demonstrating the range and quality of black experience. Other early black writers sought to do the same, but not until *Uncle Tom's Children* did any succeed as fully as did Chesnutt, for in *The Conjure Woman* he developed and exploited a finely balanced technique which solved the major artistic problems faced by early black writers. (p. 385)

Chesnutt aimed to modify white minds to feel the equality of the black man, and with the conjure tales he developed a perfect vehicle for his artistic needs. Chesnutt's genius shows in the certainty of touch involved in the choice of Uncle Julius as his central character. Choosing a character so close to widely current pejorative stereotypes was a stroke as significant as [Richard] Wright's choice of Bigger Thomas, for only by confronting and thus destroying the stereotypes could the black artist hope to alter the public mind. Further, Uncle Julius resolves for Chesnutt the black artist's problem of creating a black character in a situation in which significant dramatic incident is possible. To demonstrate the equality of blacks and whites, a black character must be presented in dramatic conflict with whites in a situation which allows the black not only to survive but to succeed with dignity. (p. 386)

The tales which Uncle Julius tells stand in the tradition of subterfuge, indirection, and subtle manipulation of whites developed by the slaves as a strategy for surviving in the face of oppression. Chesnutt's conjure stories turn the strategy of "puttin' on ol' massa" into effective dramatic action through parallels and tensions between the frames established by the white narrator and the tales told by Uncle Julius. (p. 387)

"The Goophered Grapevine" gains . . . richness through the complicated nature of Julius's motivation. While he wants very much to preserve his vineyard, he simultaneously wants to strike out at the racial superiority assumed by the narrator. The tale which he tells consistently presents white men bested by blacks or acting in ways whose folly is clearly perceived by the blacks. Both in the broad outline of his tale of the goophered grapevine and in numerous minor points . . . Uncle Julius asserts the humanity of the black and his equality with, or superiority to, whites. Julius thus has the pleasure of effectively calling the white man a fool to his face, yet he fails to make any impression because the narrator is too blinded by racism to be able to perceive what Julius is up to. Ironically, that failure, while it underscores the truth in Julius's point, is vital to his success at preserving his livelihood, since the narrator would not likely have hired Julius had he perceived the insults. The concluding frame thus generates multiple ironies which illuminate the complex tension between the black's need to deny and attack white supremacy and the hard fact that while whites are not superior beings they nevertheless have very real power.

Chesnutt's success in dealing with this tension in *The Conjure Woman* depends not only on the complex motivation of Uncle Julius but also on the two white characters of the frame, the Northern narrator and his wife Annie. . . . The narrator, a basically decent sort of man, takes a typical paternalistic attitude towards Uncle Julius and his tales. He accepts Julius's attempts at manipulating him yet remains blinded by his own sense of superiority. His understanding of black life has been molded more by Uncle Remus and the plantation school than by Uncle Julius. (pp. 388-89)

The narrator's posture has immense rhetorical value for Chesnutt, for it enables him to present his stories with detachment from the point of view of any of his characters. The framing narrative voice is that of a typical white American liberal, an unconscious racist who seems free of bigotry. In his reactions to Julius's tale the narrator is not so dull as to miss all that the black is up to, yet he misses enough that he can report the tale of slavery with no sense of the range of its meaning, especially those portions directed against him. The narrator thus appears as a mixture of sensitivity and callousness, and he can be treated sympathetically while his blindness to Uncle Julius's character and to the implications of his tales provides ironic commentary on his own character and on America's racial absurdities. (p. 389)

While the narrator has sufficient curiosity to listen to [Uncle Julius's] tales with pleasure he has no patience for discovering meanings in them; rather than revelations about American life he sees only an "Oriental cast of the negro's imagination." Annie, on the other hand, instinctively leaps to at least some meanings. The resulting contrast helps Chesnutt bring a white audience to perceive events from the black point of view, for while the narrator reacts with a typical white obtuseness, Annie, by seeing through the surface of fantastic and supernatural machinery, points the reader to the vital human life behind.

Chesnutt uses this contrast most effectively in **"Po' Sandy."** (pp. 390-91)

The narrator as usual sees nothing but the surface of the tale, but with his insensitivity as a contrast Chesnutt needs no more than Annie's murmured "Poor Tenie" to alert us to the story of the pain caused by the inhuman violations of personal life and the brutalities endured by slaves. The narrator believes in the beauty of the Old South and the quaintness of Negro folktales, but through Annie we see the horrors of slavery. (p. 391)

> *Richard E. Baldwin, "The Art of 'The Conjure Woman'," in* American Literature *(reprinted by permission of the Publisher; copyright 1971 by Duke University Press, Durham, North Carolina), Vol. XLIII, No. 3, November, 1971, pp. 385-98.*

WILLIAM L. ANDREWS (essay date 1974)

Unlike almost every black writer before or contemporary with him, Chesnutt achieved his initial fame without reference to either his own racial identity or to the current racial issues of his time. He did not present himself as a "race author." He presented himself as a literary craftsman, and he won recognition because he met the standards for fiction by which his white contemporaries were judged. Thus Chesnutt's familiarity with and mastery of the accepted modes and traditions of the American short story in the 1880s and '90s should be recognized as the basis for his popular success and his place in American literary history. But Chesnutt was not merely an assimilator and imitator of prevalent trends. Though he attempted no innovations in either style or structure, he did widen the perspective of the conventional short story to include his peculiar subject matter and his individual thematic concerns. In this respect Chesnutt's conjure stories take on additional historical significance, for they reflect both his understanding of literary tradition and his ability to use the tradition as a means of approaching his readers with untraditional themes. An accurate assessment of the significance of Chesnutt's conjure stories in both American and Afro-American literature depends on two realizations: that Chesnutt achieved popularity in his own day through his adherence to tradition, and that he maintains his distinction today because of his expansion and occasional transcendence of tradition.

The literary tradition that Chesnutt followed when he wrote his conjure stories was the local color tradition, the predominant mode of the American short story during the period in which Chesnutt was primarily a writer of short stories. . . . Local colorists satisfied their readers with superficial renditions of the life, manners, and environment of people whose day-to-day experience seemed simpler and less trying than that of the reader or the writer himself.

For this sort of reader the subject, the central characters, the tone, and the style of *The Conjure Woman* were designed. . . . Through the comments of the white Northern businessman from Ohio, who functions as narrator of the stories, the physical appearance of the countryside and the manners and attitudes of the people of the region, especially the blacks of the region, are brought out.

This use of an outsider to report on life in an unfamiliar region was a standard convention in local color writing. The narrator from Ohio does not present an extensive study of his new North Carolina residence, but he gives his reader the kind of surface details and superficial realism that local color writing usually provided. . . . These details, presented by a detached but interested observer, contribute much to the success of the conjure stories as local color stories.

More central to the success of the conjure stories, however, was Chesnutt's use of the ex-slave Julius as a delineator of life on the ante-bellum "plantations" of the sandhills region. . . . The ex-slave's testimonies to the power of a "goopher" or a rabbit's foot augment the quaintness of his character and the interest of his tales. Moreover, through Julius's descriptions of the activities of various slave conjurers in the affairs of blacks and whites on the plantation, the ex-slave's memories of ante-bellum days receive a distinctly local color cast. The transformation of the peculiar customs of an isolated group of people into the materials for fiction was a familiar method of local color writers. It was also the method Chesnutt used to provide his stories of plantation life with a background and a principle of action that stemmed directly from the little-known, but fascinating culture of the slave. (pp. 79-82)

In his conjure stories Chesnutt did not attempt to expand Julius into a fully-rounded character. To a significant extent, the possibility of Julius's development is limited by the role he plays in the frame story in which his tales are placed. Popularized first by Thomas Nelson Page and later employed by his imitators in plantation fiction, the narrative structure which Chesnutt used in his conjure stories was not designed to delineate the ex-slave's character except insofar as his storytelling talents were concerned. . . . Chesnutt altered the conventional Page frame story by adding to it an ironic conclusion which grows out of the unusual presence of ulterior motives in Julius. But the repeated incidence of the ironic conclusion in Chesnutt's conjure stories, derived consistently from the same source, Julius's hidden economic motives, serves only to heighten the formulaic quality of those stories. Within that formula Julius remains a stable and familiar quantity, the black storytelling functionary of some charm and interest, but essentially a static character whose major purpose is to reaffirm his ingenuity in tale after tale. (pp. 85-6)

Within the confines of the local color tradition, Chesnutt depicted the situation of the average slave on an average plantation with greater care and sympathy than any of his white fiction-writing contemporaries. This does not mean that Chesnutt created rounded, complex black characters in his conjure stories; the brevity of his genre prevented this. Nor does it claim for Chesnutt an early realistic examination of the everyday experience of those who suffered most under slavery. The pervasive use of conjuration and supernatural events in the tales of Uncle Julius removes Chesnutt's characters from the mundane world and places them at varying distances from the reader's powers of sympathetic identification. But the reason for resorting to conjuration by the slave heroes and heroines in Julius's stories points back to the chief distinction of these tales vis-à-vis the slave.

If the central black characters of Julius's tales do not possess a complex human identity, they usually evidence rather early in their stories some quality or trait or obsession which motivates them and brings them eventually into conflict with the white slaveholding institutions. Tenie and Sandy in **"Po'**

Sandy" are hardly individualized at all until their marital love and devotion moves them to defy the plans of their master. Then Tenie resorts to her conjure powers as a means of preserving their relationship. (pp. 92-3)

While not every story told by Uncle Julius pits slave ingenuity and voodoo against the established power of the slaveholder, almost all the stories portray conjuring as a means by which a slave expresses and attempts to preserve his most deeply felt emotions, human relationships, or identity. Lacking the space in his Uncle Julius tales to create complex human figures, Chesnutt concentrated on depicting slaves whose motives—love, hate, jealousy, envy, and pride—and pathetic or even tragic actions gave incontrovertible evidence of their humanity. By de-emphasizing physical descriptions and personal idiosyncrasies of his characters, Chesnutt avoided the dangers of local color caricature of blacks. He portrayed the slave's essential humanity beneath the accidents of his peculiar ethnic background and social status. . . . In Chesnutt's conjure stories the most disturbing aspect of slavery is not the possibilities of physical abuse, which occurs very rarely, but the likelihood of a more profound threat to the slave's dignity, his capacity to feel, his human identity. (pp. 93-4)

By showing slavery not as a protected, sheltered condition of existence tailored to meet an inferior race's ample needs but as a difficult and fortuitous way of life in which great determination, courage, and quick-wittedness were needed in order to survive, Chesnutt proved his essential theme in the Uncle Julius stories—that in the midst of his degradation the black man had affirmed his human dignity and purpose. Chesnutt also left little doubt that having endured the crucible of slavery, the black man and woman could overcome the problems of a free status. (pp. 95-6)

The significance of these early stories by the first important black American writer of fiction lies in the objective balance that Chesnutt maintained in them between the demands of popular local color realism and the obligation of the artist to reveal ''truth to nature'' despite the traditions, conventions, and prejudices of the literature of his own day. (p. 99)

> *William L. Andrews, ''The Significance of Charles W. Chesnutt's 'Conjure Stories','' in* The Southern Literary Journal *(copyright 1974 by the Department of English, University of North Carolina at Chapel Hill), Vol. VII, No. 1, Fall, 1974, pp. 78-99.*

J. NOEL HEERMANCE (essay date 1974)

A great literary artist is one who possesses deep, significant ideas and feelings and who commands, as well, the technical ability to present those ideas and feelings effectively within an artistic medium. Such a man was Charles W. Chesnutt. (p. 181)

Perhaps the most impressive embodiment of Chesnutt's technical artistry was his last novel, *The Colonel's Dream*. (p. 184)

The skeletal structure of *The Colonel's Dream* is a kind of missionary travel novel, which operates on the framework of a national allegory, as Colonel French travels South with Northern ideas and attempts an economic conversion. French himself is a national American hero ''type'': a figure of military bearing who is also a successful businessman. He is also a man who represents the ''whole country,'' coupling a Southern past with a Northern present and attempting to unite the two under the banner of his industrial Northern

way of life. The geographic movement and semiallegorical characterization are essential elements of the plot structure: both are important, not only for the traditional elements contained, but also for the innovations which Chesnutt added.

The Colonel's Dream uses a ''visiting narrator,'' travel novel technique, the sort that was so widely in use at the end of the nineteenth century in this country. (p. 185)

[Most] of the novels in this subgenre were barefacedly unrealistic in their basic structure. They were ''vacation'' novels in which the narrator had little real motivation for the trip and just seemed to appear somehow on the scene with only the barest of structural mechanics to assist our belief in him. In one way *The Colonel's Dream* shares some of this artificiality in order to establish its national allegory. For French is really too young, handsome, rich, and free from entanglements to be realistically believable. Moreover, his son Phil is also overdrawn in fairytale fashion, having a perpetual ''sweet temper'' and ''loving disposition.'' Yet we need only look at the characterization of French to see how hard Chesnutt has worked to break the stereotype feeling which often accompanies a symbolic national allegory. We note first how French faints at the end of the tense opening chapter, thereby destroying the rugged, successful, nonchalant American hero who everyone from Cooper to James had symbolically delineated before Chesnutt. In fact, not only does he faint, but he then loses his allegorical aura by sheepishly trying to joke his way out of it. Finally, even more realism creeps in when French's partner, in an explanatory aside, tells us how hard the latter has worked and how little sleep he has had. Clearly this hero is a real man.

Equally significant is the fact that French is a man with a tragic flaw stemming from his personality, and not just an allegorical hero who is defeated by a hostile, looming society. . . . French has been accustomed to hand-to-hand combat among single individuals or corporations who all shared the same monetary values. Therefore the persistence and drive which have made French successful in the North now greatly harm him in Clarendon; and he is too insensitive to realize this fact. As Chesnutt realistically portrays him, the Colonel is not only too weak to be victorious everywhere, but he is even blind at times. (pp. 185-86)

Now let us look at Chesnutt's deft use of characters as indirect spokesmen for his own intellectual position. Essentially a technique to keep the novelist from having to make pointed or poetic statements that would appear didactic or mawkish in his own mouth, this device approaches T. S. Eliot's conception of the ''objective correlative'' and is especially valid in an allegorical novel where the symbols occasionally need to be explained or commented upon. Clearly the novelist can't very well comment on his own symbols, so he lets his characters amplify his meanings for him. (p. 188)

Chesnutt uses this device . . . to open the novel to large, ''wondering'' questions of cosmic significance. We note, for example, the delicacy of feeling and statement in little Phil's question to his father about the family cemetery plot (''eternity,'' in a sense, even as it is also a piece of Southern sod) and the faithful ex-slave, Peter.

> ''Papa,'' he said, upon one of those peaceful afternoons, ''there's room enough for all of us, isn't there—you, and me, and Uncle Peter?'' . . .

What is happening here is that Chesnutt is asking these large, eternal, and therefore often cumbersome questions through the mouth of a pretty and poignantly naive child—in whose mouth they lose their overbearing complexity and become somehow charming, even as they retain their deadly significance.

Even more interesting in *The Colonel's Dream* is Chesnutt's development of background symbols for the narrative—a tonal and structural device revealed in his use of Viney and her paralysis. Within the framework of the plot itself, Viney is a peripheral character. She is the mulatto slave woman who has been housekeeper and mistress to old Malcolm Dudley at the period when his uncle supposedly hid a million dollars somewhere on the Dudley estate. (pp. 189-90)

There is, however, an accompanying string attached to this key. For if Malcolm is mad, Viney's tongue is correspondingly paralyzed, and she is therefore unable to tell where the money is. The paralysis itself, symbolically enough, is the result of a beating which Malcolm let another white man inflict on her at that time; and since that beating she has remained paralyzed—as the Southern Black in general has been paralyzed by the violence inflicted upon him. (p. 190)

The symbolism so far is clear and powerful. Sociologically truthful and correct, it forms a very substantial background subplot. Then, all of a sudden, we receive an ironic jolt in this relationship between white master and mulatto mistress. One hundred pages after we thought we had the symbolic progression solved and subsumed into the recesses of the novel, we suddenly learn that Viney could speak—can speak in fact. For twenty-five years she has feigned paralysis, keeping her master vainly searching for a pot of gold which she knew had never been left there. It has been revenge and the justified spite of a woman scorned, and it is the major moment of the novel. Not only is it still psychologically and symbolically as true as the earlier assessment of the paralysis, but the moment of revelation also leads us to an explosive power and pathos so searing and turbulent that, in this fourth from the last chapter, we suddenly see a fiercer and more psychologically incisive Chesnutt than we would have ever guessed could develop from a travel novel structure. (p. 191)

Having discussed Chesnutt's technical skill and craftsmanship, we come now to the more important analysis of his themes. Basically, the ideas in, and purposes behind, his greatest writings were three. First, there was his concern for attacking and changing racial evils in this country, especially in the South. More subconscious, but equally pervasive, was his felt need to work out his own personal identity within the framework of some of his stories. And finally, overarching these two purposes was Chesnutt's deep desire to present to the world his philosophy of man's universal relation to the cosmos and to his fellow man. . . .

The Marrow of Tradition is clearly the best example of [Chesnutt's work as a social crusader], especially in its comprehensive treatment of the physical, literary and overall scenes against which Chesnutt found himself pitted. (p. 192)

The story takes place in Wellington, a small Southern seaport town concerned most with tobacco and turpentine; and the situation comes very close to duplicating Chesnutt's own remembrances of Wilmington. The time in question is clearly that of the 1890s when whatever social and political progress Reconstruction had made was being rapidly eroded and destroyed by white reactionaries in the South. (p. 193)

Chesnutt presents us with a historical spectrum of those unreconstructed Southerners who formed the basis of the chicanery and violence which led to this period's being called the ''nadir'' of Reconstruction in the South. Indeed, Wellington's ''Big Three,'' as they saw themselves, are spelled out for us in detail through direct moments of character exposition.

[Carteret] is introduced to us as something close to the New South's middle class aristocrat. A man with ''an old name'' in the State, Carteret finds, with the birth of a son, that ''all the old pride of race, class, and family welled up anew'' in him. (pp. 193-94)

The other two members of the triumvirate . . . form the two extremes of the spectrum: General Belmont, the shrewd but courtly old aristocrat and Captain McBane, the sadistic ''poor-white'' who is graspingly fighting his way up in the New South's economy and social strata. (p. 194)

Whatever else it may also include, then, *Marrow* is clearly . . . a historical novel. . . .

[The] ''Big Three'' divide up their roles in fomenting their White Supremacy ''revolution'' and riot, and once more Chesnutt is historical in his assigning of roles to these allegorical characters of his. (p. 196)

Perhaps the most bitterly treated aspect of racial discrimination in the novel is that of ''Southern justice.'' On its least emotional level, there are several allusions to the South's brutal system of hiring out convict labor to men like McBane, whose methods, as we have seen above, ''had not commended themselves to humane people,'' with the result that ''charges of cruelty and worse had been preferred against him.'' . . .

Far more upsetting to Chesnutt was the basic Southern sense of justice that conceived of solving crimes by immediately pinning the guilt on any available Black man who happened along. (p. 198)

What finally galls Chesnutt the most is the incredible air of sadism and violence which pervades the whole Southern system of justice when relating to the Black man. . . .

With Sandy in jail under the sheriff's phlegmatic ''guard,'' the town has already started making plans for its traditional pretrial lynching. It is to be a social affair for sadists, and Chesnutt describes the preparations and mood for us in caustic, incisive precision. (p. 201)

And lest we think that Chesnutt's tone here is merely an accidental occurrence in the novel, we need merely move to the conclusion of the novel to see that it isn't. For there he describes the indiscriminate, wholesale murder of Blacks during the riot with a similarly bitter, caustic metaphor. . . . (p. 202)

As he goes on even further [in his description], it becomes clear that the historian in Chesnutt is also a moral philosopher, for on occasion the time tense of his verbs changes and moves into the present tense—and ultimately into the future, with a sense of fearful moral prophesy presaging Malcolm X's ''chickens coming home to roost'' metaphor by fifty years. ''The great steal was made,'' he tells us. (p. 205)

[The] distorted, brutal world, then, was the basis of Chesnutt's constant protest and social crusading, and *The Marrow of Tradition* was where he made his strongest, most direct case. Significantly enough, *Marrow* was the novel that was most strongly denounced for its subject matter and tone by Southern and Northern reviewers alike. . . . (p. 207)

At the same time that Chesnutt was obviously fighting the above physical conditions which the freedman faced during the period, he was also, as we have noted already, fighting the psychological and literary distortions which the Black man faced throughout the country. Stereotypes and myths, romances and rhetoric; all were barriers to the Black man's attaining his rightful place in American society and ascertaining his identity in his own mind as well. Chesnutt's role in fighting this literary-psychological battle was twofold. On the one hand he wanted to call attention to the amount of myths and stereotypes being propagated throughout the country; on the other, in their places he meant to supply the truth about real Black characters—their feelings and their thoughts. (p. 208)

This accounts for the wide spectrum of Black characters which the novel offers: ranging from the subservient, shuffling character of Jerry to the strong, courageous and militant figure of Josh.

The obvious use of contrasts and spectra here is significant, since it represents Chesnutt's attempt to create a historical-allegorical novel as well as a personal, romantic one. Just as we saw various characters like McBane, Carteret, and Belmont arrayed together in order to represent whole segments of white Southern society, so do Chesnutt's realistic Black characters play equally large roles, in addition to their unique personalities. Indeed, so important is this spectrum of characters that we can see Chesnutt's own ambivalent position towards some of them as he implicitly assesses his own role in fighting racial injustice in this country, a point which we will examine in greater detail later. It is obvious that this spectrum and contrast of Black characters is as much meant to be read by Black readers searching for a positive, identifiable role in the movement towards freedom as it is meant for the detachedly or marginally interested whites who might be interested in the story as a piece of contemporary history. (pp. 211-12)

[Indeed] the question of identity with the common people was always a major one for the isolattoe, intellectual in Chesnutt; and it was partially this inner conflict which was externalized in his spectrum of Black characters in *Marrow,* as he was deeply torn between the moderate, practical, professional Dr. Miller and the more heroic, but less sophisticated and analytic, Josh Green.

There are, then, three different kinds of Black characters in the novel: embodied by the subservient Jerry, the progressive professional Dr. Miller, and the courageously heroic, essentially "reckless" Josh Green. At one extreme of the spectrum, Jerry is Major Carteret's porter and is content—and almost intent—on retaining this "august" position in the Southern white man's world no matter how much humbleness it entails. (pp. 212-13)

Jerry's grandmother, significantly, is also from this mold and tells us of her and Jerry's ambitions in the Southern white man's world. In discussing the modern generation of young Blacks whom Mrs. Carteret thinks are "too self-assertive," Mammy Jane agrees whole heartedly. . . . (p. 213)

[The] ultimate irony is, of course, that, when the riot finally does break out, both Jerry and Mammy Jane are killed in the

day's brutality: shot randomly as common "niggers," far from the thoughts—and protection—of their supposed benefactors. . . .

Early in the novel, Dr. Miller learns of Josh's ultimate desire to kill McBane, and he attempts to dissuade Josh from the act. Josh's answer is almost classic in its honest realism, and the reader cannot help but feel that seventy-five percent of Chesnutt's own nature at this moment is aligned with Josh, in preference to the alter ego Miller with whom Chesnutt usually identifies. (p. 214)

With this sense of fatalism and realistic insight into the South as it is, Josh becomes the most heroic and magnificent figure in the novel. When the riot begins, therefore, it is he who attempts to organize the Blacks for physical self-defense. (p. 215)

The majesty, courage and almost mystical power of Josh . . . are clearly visible. Eons away from Jerry on the human spectrum and several levels above Miller as well, Josh dies like a man and Chesnutt applauds his transcendent courage even as he doubts and debates the pragmatic wisdom of his action. This, then, is the range of Black characters in *Marrow,* and they are meant to dispel the world of stereotypes and offer a world of realistic and even heroic Black men. . . .

The ultimate basis of Chesnutt's protest in *Marrow*—spanning both the brutal physical and distorted literary conditions of the South—was his bitter realization of just how little the Southern white man's friendship could be counted on when the chips were down. If there is an underlying theme in the novel, this is clearly it.

On a most artistic, indirect level, Chesnutt makes this point in a softly delicate, if caustic, manner. Three times in the novel a basically "good" but weak white figure fails to stand up for his principles of justice, and each time his semiacknowledgment of failure is delicately couched by Chesnutt in a Pontius Pilate allusion. (p. 217)

In such a way does Chesnutt powerfully, yet artistically, establish this underlying theme. Yet should we have missed the theme through its indirect sense of placement and allusion, he has two of his responsible, moderate Negro characters blast the truth to us directly—in a way that is all the more forceful because the characters involved are so essentially moderate. (p. 219)

[The] Black lawyer Watson accidentally meets Miller outside the town limits, as Watson himself is fleeing for his life. Caught unprepared and almost killed before he could escape, Watson scathingly denounces his nominal white "friends" who could have warned and easily saved him. . . .

[It] marks the strongest cry of outrage and protest which Chesnutt will ever utter as a writer—which is why *Marrow* is his strongest and most savagely honest novel dealing with the racial situation in America. This is why it struck his white readers so forcefully and seared their collective guilt so fiercely that they were afraid to acknowledge any truth in the novel at all. This is why they frenetically attacked it in any and every way they could. It was that good. (p. 220)

On the third and ultimately highest level of his art, Chesnutt was no longer a man intent on ambivalently exploring and working out his social and political position here in America; instead he was an artist who deeply understood his position in the universe and his relationship to his fellow men as they all fit into the same cosmos.

On its most tangible level, Chesnutt was deeply sure of the Black man's just and inevitable place in American society. As he has Colonel French proclaim in *The Colonel's Dream,* the success and progress of any society like America's depends on the interwoven, combined success of all the groups in that society. (pp. 225-26)

It is not surprising that Chesnutt saw the overcoming of racial problems and the establishment of humanity and social cohesion in this nation not merely as a specific national goal but as the essential goal and future of all human endeavors. (p. 227)

In his treatment of individual, human characters outside of this national-allegorical aspect, Chesnutt showed great sensitivity for an extremely large range of individuals. In fact this is where his sense of universalism first shows itself. . . .

Black characters, of course, are the ones with whom Chesnutt is basically identified; "the Laureate of the Color Line" was, of course, a deserved title. Yet what is most important here is the range of Black characters portrayed. (p. 228)

[The range] reaches all strata of rural and urban society at the turn of the century.

In terms of racial attitudes, Chesnutt also covered the full spectrum of character positions. In *Marrow* alone he gave a fairly detailed account of contemporary Southern white feelings on the subject, with the "Big Three" on the bottom, the mass of ordinary people in the middle, and such a lonely "concerned" figure as Ellis anemically at the top. As for Northern white attitudes, his next novel, *The Colonel's Dream,* gave us the concerned industrialist who deeply cares about this country's social problems; and throughout so many of his works Chesnutt constantly introduced committed Northern white teachers who came south in the early days of Reconstruction in order to help educate freedmen (**"The March of Progress"**) and poor white (*Evelyn's Husband*) alike. (pp. 228-29)

Throughout all this we should further note the great range of tones which Chesnutt brought to all these characters: from satire to bitterness to compassion, all with sensitivity and feeling. Most significant, perhaps, is the fact that he was able to feel a close sympathy for, or understanding of, the essence of all his characters—even those whom he basically despised, like Captain McBane in *Marrow,* or those whom he satirized, like the "Blue Vein socialites." (p. 229)

[Even] in the midst of Chesnutt's strongest novel of historical bitterness, the brotherhood of men—and, most especially, the sisterhood of women—is the final theme of [*Marrow*]. This major assertion is what allows Julia Miller (who has been disinherited all her life by Mrs. Ochiltree and Olivia Carteret, even though she is Olivia's legitimate half-sister) to tell her husband to perform the operation that will save the Carteret's son and only child. Most dramatically, this decision by Julia comes immediately after the Millers have just seen their own son and only child killed in the Wellington riot which Major Carteret ignited. Thus, somehow, the shared brotherhood and sisterhood of all peoples here on earth tran-

scends for Julia and Chesnutt whatever differences and conflicts may lie between individuals: and this then becomes his final dramatic assertion in this novel, which in so many other ways has stressed a real pessimism and bitterness in its historical discussions. In a sense it is almost as if Chesnutt's universal faith has somehow overcome his more specific historical analysis. (p. 232)

> *J. Noel Heermance, "The Greatness of Chesnutt's Art: Techniques, Themes and Purposes," in his* Charles W. Chesnutt: America's First Great Black Novelist *(© 1974 by The Shoe String Press, Inc.), Archon Books, Hamden, Connecticut, 1974, pp. 181-235.*

ADDITIONAL BIBLIOGRAPHY

Ames, Russell. "Social Realism in Charles W. Chesnutt." *Phylon* XIII, No. 2 (1953): 199-206.
> Analyses critical opinion of Chesnutt's work in light of the date and prejudices of the source.

Britt, David D. "Chesnutt's Conjure Tales: What You See Is What You Get." *CLA Journal* XV, No. 3 (March 1972): 269-83.
> Argues that the dual narrative structure of *The Conjure Woman* allows the story to be interpreted according to the reader's particular bias.

Chesnutt, Helen M. *Charles Waddell Chesnutt: Pioneer of the Color Line.* Chapel Hill: The University of North Carolina Press, 1952, 324 p.
> Biography by Chesnutt's daughter. This book offers little critical interpretation but contains many early reviews of his work and interesting letters between Chesnutt and his publishers.

Gloster, Hugh M. "Negro Fiction to World War I." In his *Negro Voices in American Fiction,* pp. 23-100. New York: Russell & Russell, 1965.*
> Includes a brief survey of Chesnutt's work.

Hemenway, Robert. "Gothic Sociology: Charles Chesnutt and the Gothic Mode." *Studies in the Literary Imagination* VII, No. 1 (Spring 1974): 101-19.
> Examines the Gothic elements in *The Conjure Woman,* concluding that, since Chesnutt uses images of darkness and the supernatural to symbolize good, the stories do not fit into the Gothic tradition.

Hemenway, Robert. "'Baxter's Procustes': Irony and Protest." *CLA Journal* XVIII, No. 2 (December 1974): 172-85.
> Contends that Chesnutt wrote "Baxter's Procustes," "one of his most subtle short stories," in reaction to an exclusive Cleveland literary society's refusal to grant him membership.

Render, Sylvia Lyons. Introduction to *The Short Fiction of Charles W. Chesnutt,* by Charles W. Chesnutt, edited by Sylvia Lyons Render, pp. 3-56. Washington, D.C.: Howard University Press, 1974.
> Discusses character portrayal, point of view, tone, themes, and style in Chesnutt's fiction.

Turner, Darwin. Introduction to *The House Behind the Cedars,* by Charles W. Chesnutt, pp. vii-xx. London: Collier-Macmillan, 1969.
> Good introduction to Chesnutt's life and works.

Wideman, John. "Charles W. Chesnutt: *The Marrow of Tradition.*" *The American Scholar* 42, No. 1 (Winter 1972-73): 128-34.
> Study of *The Marrow of Tradition,* which Wideman contends has been unjustly maligned in previous criticism.

Kate (O'Flaherty) Chopin

1851-1904

American novelist, short story writer, poet, and critic.

In her day, Chopin was regarded as one of many popular local colorists noted more for skillful regional depiction than for insight into human nature. Critics now attach more importance to her work, particularly *The Awakening*, praising her psychological realism, astute characterization, and careful attention to detail. After being neglected in the early twentieth century, Chopin's works were reassessed and began to receive serious critical attention in the late 1950s.

Although Chopin did not begin writing until she was in her late thirties, her earlier life formed the basis of her fiction. For the first ten years of her marriage to Oscar Chopin, she lived in New Orleans forming impressions of Creole society. These impressions, as well as her experience as a young mother, were later to become crucial to the themes and setting of *The Awakening*. When her husband's business failed, the family moved to a plantation in Cloutierville, Louisiana, where Chopin gathered the material later developed in her short stories.

For a short time after the sudden death of her husband, Chopin maintained the plantation, but then at the urging of her mother returned home to St. Louis. Encouraged by friends who praised the vividness of her letters, Chopin began writing poems, short stories, and her first novel, *At Fault*. To develop her style, she studied such contemporary French writers as Flaubert and Maupassant, whose directness and precision she admired. Their influence is easily discerned in the objectivity, polish, and restraint of her prose. Chopin wrote quickly and rarely revised, preferring, as she once stated, "the integrity of crudities to artificialities."

The short stories collected in *Bayou Folk* and *A Night in Acadie* established Chopin as an important writer of local color fiction. Set primarily near the Red River in the Natchitoches parish of Louisiana, these tales of Creole and Cajun life are noted for their meticulous description, precise rendering of dialect, and objective treatment of emotional states. "Désirée's Baby," often named as one of Chopin's most poignant stories, is praised for its directness of approach and skillful psychological exploration. Like many of Chopin's stories, "Désirée's Baby" builds to an ironic reversal reminiscent of Maupassant. Although some critics claim that Chopin's frequent dependence upon this device weakens her art, others defend its effectiveness. In the stories of *Bayou Folk* and *A Night in Acadie*, Chopin was already treating the themes of marriage, infidelity, and sexual freedom which she was to fully explore in *The Awakening*.

Publication of *The Awakening*, Chopin's most ambitious work, prompted an indignant critical response that ended her literary career. Contemporary critics failed to give the novel the complex consideration it deserved and dismissed it as a perverse and wasted effort. In her native St. Louis, the novel was withdrawn from library circulation, and although she was considered one of the city's finest writers, Chopin was refused membership at the Fine Arts Club. As a result of the adverse criticism, her publishers rejected a third collection of stories said to contain some of her best work. Stung by the reaction to *The Awakening*, Chopin wrote little else.

In contrast to the disdain and condescension of her contemporaries, modern critics praise Chopin's objective treatment of sexuality and feminine psychology in *The Awakening*. Chopin's somewhat narrow interpretation of the female protagonist in her first novel, *At Fault*, had matured into the convincing and complex characterization of Edna Pontellier. Filled with vivid images and unifying symbols, *The Awakening* is noted for its detailed and sensuous prose. This novel, in addition to her best short stories, assures Chopin's permanence in American literature.

PRINCIPAL WORKS

At Fault (novel) 1890
Bayou Folk (short stories) 1894
A Night in Acadie (short stories) 1897
The Awakening (novel) 1899
The Complete Works of Kate Chopin. 2 vols. (novels, short stories, poetry, and essays) 1970

THE NATION (essay date 1891)

It is not quite clear who is cast for the title-rôle in [Kate Chopin's] 'At Fault,' since all the characters have valid pretensions to the part. There is the lady who drinks and the gentleman who gets a divorce from her, the widow who loves and is beloved by him, but who persuades him to remarry his divorced partner and bring her to the Louisiana plantation, where she (the widow) may have a fostering care of the two and help them do their duty to each other. There is also the young lady of many engagements, the negro who commits arson, the young gentleman who shoots him, the Colonel who shoots the young gentleman, the St. Louis lady who goes to matinées and runs off with the matinée-going gentleman. It may not be amiss, in deciding who is **"At Fault,"** to consider as well the claims of the author, the publisher, and the reader. The reverse side to all this is a graphic description of life on a cotton plantation, an aptitude for seizing dialects of whites and blacks alike, no little skill in perceiving and defining character, and a touch which shows that the array of disagreeables was born rather of literary crudity than of want of refinement.

"Recent Fiction: 'At Fault'," in The Nation *(copyright 1891 The Nation magazine, The Nation Associates, Inc.), Vol. 53, No. 1370, October 1, 1891, p. 264.*

THE ATLANTIC MONTHLY (essay date 1894)

Mrs. Chopin shows us a most interesting group in her [collection **Bayou Folk**]. Her reproduction of [Acadian] speech is not too elaborate, and the reader who at once shuts up a book in which he discovers broken or otherwise damaged English would do well to open this again; for the writer is discreet enough to give suggestions of the soft, harmonious tongue to which the Bayou folk have reduced English speech, and not to make contributions to philology. What he will find, both in speech and manner, is a sensitiveness to passion, a keen feeling for honor, a domesticity, an indolence which has a rustic grace, and a shiftlessness which laughs at its penalties. . . .

[Mrs. Chopin is not] a writer who is afflicted with a purpose to add to our stock of knowledge concerning obscure varieties of the human race. Mrs. Chopin simply deals with what is familiar to her, and happens to be somewhat new in literature. She deals with it as an artist, and the entire ease with which she uses her material is born not less of an instinct for story-telling than of familiarity with the stuff out of which she weaves her stories. . . . All of the stories are very simple in structure, but the simplicity is that which belongs to clearness of perception, not to meagreness of imagination. Now and then she strikes a passionate note, and the naturalness and ease with which she does it impress one as characteristic of power awaiting opportunity. Add to this that a pervasive humor warms the several narratives, that the persons who appear bring themselves, and are not introduced by the author, and we have said enough, we think, to intimate that in this writer we have a genuine and delightful addition to the ranks of our story-tellers. It is something that she comes from the South. It is a good deal more that she is not confined to locality. Art makes her free of literature. (p. 559)

"Recent Fiction: 'Bayou Folk'," in The Atlantic Monthly *(copyright © 1894, by The Atlantic Monthly Company, Boston, Mass.), Vol. LXXIII, No. CCCCXXXVIII, April, 1894, pp. 558-59.*

THE CRITIC (essay date 1894)

It is the folk that inhabit [the] taciturn [Louisiana bayou] wildernesses that Miss (?) Chopin introduces to us in her unpretentious, unheralded little book [**Bayou Folk**]. She is evidently familiar at first hand with the illiterate Creoles, the old broken-down plantations, the queer *patois* people, the bayou landscapes to which she leads us in these simple tales, whose very simplicity increases their verisimilitude and makes in some cases a powerful impression on the imagination. She takes Middle-Upper Louisiana, as distinct from 'Cadjen country and New Orleans, as the scene of her little dramas, and reproduces for us, often very realistically and pathetically, the oddities in life and character which she has observed there. In her sheaf of twenty-three sketches some are like rude cartoons whose very rudeness brings out a more vivid effect. . . . If we are not mistaken, Louisiana has another remarkable observer in this "unannounced" lady, whose keen eyes see even through the green glooms of her prairies and cane-brakes, and see things well worth bringing into the light. . . . Miss Chopin's work is true to nature and often singularly dramatic in substance. There is not . . . the subtlety of [George Washington] Cable, or the delicious humor of Ruth McEnery Stuart, but there is photographic realism, shrewdness of observation and a fine eye for picturesque situations: which is only saying that Miss Chopin is herself, and nobody else. (p. 300)

"Literature: 'Bayou Folk'," in The Critic *(© The Critic 1894), Vol. XXI, No. 637, May 5, 1894, pp. 299-300.*

THE CRITIC (essay date 1898)

"A Night in Acadie" is the title-tale of a collection of short stories by Kate Chopin who, in **"Bayou Folk,"** has already made us familiar with the simple, childlike southern people who are the subjects of her brief romances. **"Athénaïse,"** the longest of the stories, is written with much delicacy and understanding of both man and woman, and is only marred by one or two slight and unnecessary coarsenesses. . . . All the stories are worth reading. The author is sympathetic and tender, and shows a knowledge of the human heart, young as well as old, as **"Polydore"** and **"Mamouche"** prove. She is never very exciting or dramatic; there is even a slight feeling after reading about six of the stories, that one has read something very like the seventh before; but to anyone who wants to be quietly and soothingly interested for an hour, they are to be recommended. A breath of warm summer air, the hum of insects and the scent of flowers seem to hover round the reader, and the pleasant, low-toned 'Cadian patois lingers in his ear.

"Literature: Mrs. Chopin's 'Night in Acadie'," in The Critic *(© The Critic 1898), Vol. XXIX, No. 843, April 16, 1898, p. 266.*

WILLA CATHER (essay date 1899)

A Creole *Bovary* is this little novel [**The Awakening**] of Miss Chopin's. Not that the heroine is a Creole exactly, or that Miss Chopin is a Flaubert—save the mark!—but the theme is similar to that which occupied Flaubert. There was, indeed, no need that a second *Madame Bovary* should be written, but an author's choice of themes is frequently as inexplicable as his choice of a wife. It is governed by some innate temperamental bias that cannot be diagrammed. This is particularly so in women who write, and I shall not attempt to say why Miss Chopin has devoted so exquisite and sensitive, well-governed a style to so trite and sordid a theme. She writes much better than it is ever given to most people to write, and hers is a genuinely literary style; of no great elegance or solidity; but light, flexible, subtle, and capable of producing telling effects directly and simply. (p. 697)

Edna Pontellier [the heroine of *The Awakening*] and Emma Bovary are studies in the same feminine type; one a finished and complete portrayal, the other a hasty sketch, but the theme is essentially the same. Both women belong to a class, not large, but forever clamoring in our ears, that demands more romance out of life than God put into it. . . . The unfortunate feature of their disease is that it attacks only women of brains, at least of rudimentary brains, but whose development is one-sided; women of strong and fine intuitions, but without the faculty of observation, comparison, reasoning about things. Probably, for emotional people, the most convenient thing about being able to think is that it occasionally gives them a rest from feeling. Now with women of the Bovary type, this relaxation and recreation is impossible. They are not critics of life, but, in the most personal sense, partakers of life. They receive impressions through the fancy. With them everything begins with fancy, and passions rise in the brain rather than in the blood, the poor, neglected, limited one-sided brain that might do so much better things than badgering itself into frantic endeavors to love. . . . These people really expect the passion of love to fill and gratify every need of life, whereas nature only intended that it should meet one of many demands. They insist upon making it stand for all the emotional pleasures of life and art; expecting an individual and self-limited passion to yield infinite variety, pleasure, and distraction, to contribute to their lives what the arts and the pleasurable exercise of the intellect gives to less limited and less intense idealists. . . . They have driven the blood until it will drive no further, they have played their nerves up to the point where any relaxation short of absolute annihilation is impossible. Every idealist abuses his nerves, and every sentimentalist brutally abuses them. And in the end, the nerves get even. Nobody ever cheats them, really. Then ''the awakening'' comes. Sometimes it comes in the form of arsenic, as it came to Emma Bovary. . . . Edna Pontellier, fanciful and romantic to the last, chose the sea on a summer night and went down with the sound of her first lover's spurs in her ears, and the scent of pinks about her. And next time I hope that Miss Chopin will devote that flexible, iridescent style of hers to a better cause. (pp. 698-99)

> Willa Cather, "Four Women Writers: Atherton, Ouida, Chopin, Morris," (originally published under a different title in Leader, July 8, 1899, in The World and the Parish, Vol. II: Willa Cather's Articles and Reviews, 1893-1902, edited by William M. Curtin, University of Nebraska Press, 1970, pp. 694-99.*

THE NATION   (essay date 1899)

[Mrs. Chopin's] **'The Awakening'** is the sad story of a Southern lady who wanted to do what she wanted to. From wanting to, she did, with disastrous consequences; but as she swims out to sea in the end, it is to be hoped that her example may lie for ever undredged. It is with high expectation that we open the volume, remembering the author's agreeable short stories, and with real disappointment that we close it. The recording reviewer drops a tear over one more clever author gone wrong. Mrs. Chopin's accustomed fine workmanship is here, the hinted effects, the well-expended epithet, the pellucid style; and, so far as construction goes, the writer shows herself as competent to write a novel as a sketch. The tint and air of Creole New Orleans and the Lousiana seacoast are conveyed to the reader with subtle skill, and among the secondary characters are several that are lifelike. But we cannot see that literature or the criticism of life is helped by the detailed history of the manifold and contemporary love affairs of a wife and mother. Had she lived by Prof. William James's advice to do one thing a day one does not want to do (in Creole society, two would perhaps be better), flirted less and looked after her children more, or even assisted at more *accouchements*—her *chef d'œuvre* in self-denial—we need not have been put to the unpleasantness of reading about her and the temptations she trumped up for herself.

> "Recent Novels: 'The Awakening'," in The Nation (copyright 1899 The Nation magazine, The Nation Associates, Inc.), Vol. 69, No. 1779, August 3, 1899, p. 96.

PERCIVAL POLLARD   (essay date 1909)

Another lady who proved to us that dear Thackeray's scruples no longer worried her sex was Kate Chopin. The book I have in mind was called **"The Awakening."** Like many others that may be named in these pages of mine, it is doubtless utterly forgotten; but it would be illogical for me to proclaim that we had a deal to thank the ladies for, if I had not the documents at hand to prove it.

Again this seemed a subject for the physician, not the novelist. So skilfully and so hardily does the book reveal the growth of animalism in a woman, that we feel as if we were attending a medical lecture. In the old days,—when men, mere men such as Balzac or Flaubert or Gautier, attempted this sort of dissection,—we were wont to sigh, and think what brutes they must be to suppose women made of this poor clay. Surely it was only the males who harbored thoughts fit only for the smoking-room; surely—but, Pouff! Kate Chopin dispelled those dreams. . . . (pp. 40-1)

"The Awakening" asked us to believe that a young woman who had been several years married, and had borne children, had never, in all that time, been properly ''awake.'' . . . She had to wait until she met a young man who was not her husband, was destined to tarry until she was under the influence of a Southern moonlight and the whispers of the Gulf and many other passionate things, before there began in her the first faint flushings of desire. So, at any rate, Kate Chopin asked us to believe. (p. 41)

However, taking Kate Chopin's word for it that *Edna* had been asleep, her awakening was a most champagne-like performance. After she met *Robert Lebrun* the awakening stirred in her, to use a rough simile, after the manner of ferment in new wine. *Robert* would, I fancy, at any Northern summer resort have been sure of a lynching; for, after a trifling encounter with him, *Edna* became utterly unmanageable. She neglected her house; she tried to paint—always a bad sign, that, when women want to paint, or act, or sing, or write!—and the while she painted there was ''a subtle current of desire passing through her body, weakening her hold upon the brushes and making her eyes burn."...

All this, mind you, with *Robert* merely a reminiscence. If the mere memory of him made her weak, what must the touch of him have done? Fancy shrinks at so volcanic a scene. (p. 42)

We were asked to believe that *Edna* was devoid of coquetry; that she did not know the cheap delights of promiscuous conquests; though sometimes on the street glances from strange eyes lingered in her memory, disturbing her. Well, then those are the women to look out for—those women so easily disturbed by the unfamiliar eye. Those women do not seem to care, once they are awake, so much for the individual as for what he represents. Consider *Edna*. It was *Robert* who awoke her. But, when he went away, it was another who continued the arousal. Do you think *Edna* cared whether it was *Robert* or *Arobin*? Not a bit. (pp. 42-3)

Ah, these married women, who have never, by some strange chance, had the flaming torch applied, how they do flash out when the right moment comes! This heroine, after that first flaming torch, went to her finish with lightning speed. She took a walk with *Arobin*, and paused, mentally, to notice "the black line of his leg moving in and out so close to her against the yellow shimmer of her gown." She let the young man sit down beside her, let him caress her, and they did not "say good-night until she had become supple to his gentle seductive entreaties."

To think of Kate Chopin, who once contented herself with mild yarns about genteel Creole life—pages almost clean enough to put into the Sunday school library, abreast of Geo. W. Cable's stories—blowing us a hot blast like that! (pp. 43-4)

Robert had gone away, it seems, because he scrupled to love *Edna*, she being married. But *Edna* had no scruples left; she hastened to intimate to *Robert* that she loved him, that her husband meant nothing to her. Never, by any chance, did she mention *Arobin*. But, dear me, *Arobin*, to a woman like that, had been merely an incident; he merely happened to hold the torch. Now, what in the world do you suppose that *Robert* did? Went away—pouff!—like that! Went away, saying he loved *Edna* too well to—well, to partake of the fire the other youth had lit. Think of it! *Edna* finally awake—completely, fiercely awake—and the man she had waked up for goes away!

Of course, she went and drowned herself. She realised that you can only put out fire with water, if all other chemical engines go away. She realised that the awakening was too great; that she was too aflame; that it was now merely Man, not *Robert* or *Arobin*, that she desired. So she took an infinite dip in the passionate Gulf.

Ah, what a hiss, what a fiery splash, there must have been in those warm waters of the South! But—what a pity that poor *Pontellier*, *Edna's* husband, never knew that his wife was in a trance all their wedded days, and that he was away at the moment of her awakening! For, other men failing, there are, after all, some things that a husband is useful for, in spite of books like **"The Awakening."** ... (pp. 44-5)

[Kate Chopin] was already distinguished for charming *contes* of Creole life. **"The Awakening"** was a deliberate case of pandering to what seemed the taste of that moment. (p. 45)

Percival Pollard, "Women, Womanists and Manners," in his Their Day in Court *(copyright © 1909 by The Neale Publishing Company), Neale, 1909 (and reprinted by Johnson Reprint Corporation, 1969), pp. 17-144.* *

FRED LEWIS PATTEE   (essay date 1923)

[In] American short-story chronicles [Kate Chopin] must be rated as a vivid episode, as brief and intense as a tropic storm. . . . [Her] name is forgotten save by a few, and yet there are few pieces in the American short-story collections that surpass in restrained intensity, in finesse, in the inevitableness of startling climax, some of the best of her tales.

To no novelist of her period . . . was fiction-writing a more spontaneous thing. . . . She must be rated as a genius, taut, vibrant, intense of soul, yet a genius in eclipse, one, it is to be feared, that is destined to be total.

The materials in Mrs. Chopin's two volumes [**Bayou Folk** and **A Night in Acadie**] are more strange even than those used by [George Washington] Cable and Miss [Grace] King, but the tales are far more than mere strange materials. Without a thought, undoubtedly, of what she was really doing, she struck always universal chords. The tales are more than mere snapshots in the Red River canebrakes: they are glimpses into the universal heart of humanity. (pp. 325-26)

Local color she used with restraint only to intensify her characterization. Here, as with Miss King, was a chief source of her strength. Like Dickens, she could make even the most insignificant of her characters intensely alive. The reader knows them and feels them and sees them. . . .

Her sense of dramatic values was strong. Unconsciously to the reader, she worked ever toward some unforeseen climax. (p. 326)

Without models, without study or short-story art, without revision, and usually at a sitting, she produced what often are masterpieces before which one can only wonder and conjecture. (p. 327)

Fred Lewis Pattee, "The Revolt of the 'Nineties," in his The Development of the American Short Story: An Historical Survey *(copyright 1923 by Harper & Row, Publishers, Inc.; renewed 1950 by Fred Lewis Pattee; reprinted by permission of Harper & Row, Publishers, Inc.), Harper, 1923, pp. 309-36.* *

DANIEL S. RANKIN   (essay date 1932)

[Kate Chopin's] *At Fault* is a study of character development and disintegration. It is a domestic drama enacted in sharply contrasted sections of this country—the city of St. Louis and the Place-du-Bois Plantation in central Louisiana. A novel with the scene laid in the Cane River region of Louisiana was a novelty. . . . Kate Chopin was the first to weave the customs and traditions of its people into fiction. (p. 117)

By the force of its own vitality the plot works itself out to a highly colored, tragic climax. In compassing Fanny's death—the point where under a less clever hand mechanism would have supplanted nature—although there is nothing artificial, there is meager art. In its preparation and accomplishment this startling episode might have been a clever exhibition of artistic skill in maintaining dramatic and excluding melodramatic interests. This it is not. (p. 118)

There are delightful gleams in this novel of real plantation life without the gaudy glamor usually associated with it in fiction. . . . *At Fault* takes its incidents from the reality of Louisiana plantation life. . . . Kate Chopin's skill portrayed the lives of the whites and blacks as partly segregate, partly intertwined. If any special link is needed, Grégoire's position supplies it. Her portrayal of the southern negro character and dialect shows knowledge learned gradually, and she treats them with the sympathy of one who has caught with exquisite skill the real side of their lives. (p. 127)

The story is written with a refreshing reserve. . . . Both in style and structure there is a break and a drop toward the end. These are faults of detail. What first novel reveals an author's surest skill and literary cunning? (p. 128)

Partly through her remarkable skill with dialect Kate Chopin in *Bayou Folk* gives some very vivid glimpses into a life that seems alien to what passes for modern civilization. . . . *Bayou Folk* is one of those books that the reader of American literature runs across, only to ponder upon the great difference in life, civilization, indeed, in the entire point of view, that may be found in this widely extended nation. (p. 138)

The word *vignette* would be an apt characterization of the sketches and of several of the stories. They are neither episodic nor dramatic in the accepted sense of these words; they are extraordinary delicate and human glimpses. "A Very Fine Fiddle" is one of the most quietly moving fragments in modern writing. The entire story **"In Sabine,"** of the rescue of a pretty Acadian wife from a brutal husband, is a glittering weave of humor.

The most noticeable feature in these stories or sketches is the author's clear perception of the characteristics of her subject, the good understanding of her people. She seems to have gone straight to the heart of the Natchitoches folk. She has heard their little confidences of joy and grief, and relates them with the directness and naturalness of the finest art. And there is a delicacy of touch, a sureness of handling. In the moderation and economy of expression, in the power only half displayed, there is an almost austere adherence to art. With no affectation of theories, no message to the dissatisfied, no sentimentality, they are only simple stories simply told.

Kate Chopin never gives a mere factual transcription of life; her realism is always poetic realism, in the sense that it does not only reflect, but illuminates the narrowly circumstantial lives she portrays.

Translated into terms of painting, the art in *Bayou Folk* manifests quick, sharp, effective brushwork, lavish color, and effective composition. She has the knack of telling a story, which is not a common gift, but she has with it the touch of an artist so that each little study is perfect and satisfying. She communicates without saying much about it, the charm of the tropical air and the languor and life of the plantation; and her few words of description have an added value from the very fact of her frugal use of them. The strong individuality of these narratives gives impressive testimony to the genius of their author, who with unerring hand produces vivid pictures without wasting a line or misplacing a single stroke of coloring. In them art and truth are blended in a way that make a harmonious whole.

They differ in their subject-matter and points of view but the quality is the same in all. They are full of life, warmth, color, ardor, fire—artistic versions of pathetic, poetic, tragic, heroic, and comic episodes and customs in the lives of her people. The pathos is bred of sympathy. It is not the curious morbid pathos of mental dissection, later to be exhibited in Edna of *The Awakening*. (pp. 138-40)

In style and design her writing is not art that conceals art. It is spontaneous success. Without any of the tricks of style she achieves the effect of style through simplicity and deftness.

The universal appeal of her motives, the tenderness and depth of her varied sympathy, the strenth of her dramatic expertness, the intense aliveness of even her insignificant characters, the spontaneous humor, and the art of prose in her writing as a whole assure the lasting importance and significance of Kate Chopin's *Bayou Folk*. (p. 140)

Now and then in her stories after 1894 she strikes a passionate note that is not revealed in her previous work. Her curiosity about life, her instinctive perception of the sheer actuality of passion, loom larger and with a more compelling presence in the stories written after *Bayou Folk* was given to the public. Not that this fact, in itself, is a criterion of her art, but the naturalness and ease with which she did this conveys the impression of power awaiting opportunity. And the opportunity came with *The Awakening*. (p. 161)

Simplicity and directness of treatment combined with an invariable verity of motive are the characteristics of the stories in [*A Night in Acadie*]. The hand of the artist is apparent in every one of them. The hopes and loves of her lowly single-hearted Acadian or Creole folk create an indulgent sympathy; the mingled humor and pathos of their brief histories move to laughter or tears.

From story to story, each so different from the other in the conditions of life surrounding the characters, and yet all alike in their strict adherence to the finished literary method of the author, the mind is more and more moved to an enthusiasm of intellectual gratification over the assured touch, the perfect balance of values, the flashes of insight, and the keen artistic sense that holds back the word too much. (pp. 167-68)

The stories in *A Night in Acadie* show the same admirable handling of the patois of the Louisiana bayou country, the same clear delineation of the life of that region. But Kate Chopin's gifts as a writer go deeper than mere patois or local description of background. There is truth in all her writings. She knows the characteristics of the negro race through and through and strikes an elemental note now and then to prove it. (p. 168)

Self-sacrifice and devotion are constant motives in these short stories. Simple, sincere, and unconscious goodness reveal the better side of human nature through many of her characters. (pp. 168-69)

["**Nég Créol,**" the] exquisite vignette of the French Market of New Orleans illustrates one of Kate Chopin's characteristic literary touches—that of surprising the reader with a climax that *is* a spiritual illumination. Not even De Maupassant, whom she most suggests, is more clever at this. (p. 169)

Visions of the bright, languorous Southland, with its magnolias and jessamine, its mockingbirds warbling through the night, its air fragrant with the odors of flowers, are conjured up in the stories of *A Night in Acadie*. It is a greater book than *Bayou Folk*. In the earlier volume the grace and delicacy of her art is paramount; in the later an intellectual and spiritual quality is added which keeps one brooding long after the spell of charm has passed.

Kate Chopin belongs to the artistic realism of today, as well as to her own generation. This generation sees life, or reality, differently from any generation before it. The literary artist in his absorbing process is no longer a discoverer, no longer a refiner, still less a dictator, but an observer at best, with an impulse to state his impressions clearly. And if one were to ask in what way after all Kate Chopin differs from a past-master in the short story art, say, de Maupassant, the answer may be that she blesses while he bewailed the terrible clear-sightedness which is the strength and the anguish of every good writer. (p. 170)

The Awakening follows the current of erotic morbidity that flowed strongly through the literature of the last two decades of the nineteenth century. The end of the century became a momentary dizziness over an abyss of voluptuousness, and Kate Chopin in St. Louis experienced a partial attack of the prevailing artistic vertigo. . . .

In *The Awakening* under her touch the Creole life of Louisiana glowed with a rich exotic beauty. The very atmosphere of the book is voluptuous, the atmosphere of the Gulf Coast, a place of strange and passionate moods. . . .

The Awakening is exotic in setting, morbid in theme, erotic in motivation.

Kate Chopin felt most profoundly and expressed most poignantly in *The Awakening* facts about life which to her were important, facts which easily might be overlooked, she thought. Being a woman she saw life instinctively in terms of the individual. She took a direct, personal, immediate interest in the intimate personal affairs of Edna's daily life and changing moods. But the questions arise, "Is it at all important? Did Kate Chopin by her art reveal a fresh beauty or vision or aspiration?" (p. 175)

The reader, following Edna as she walks for the last time down to the beach at Grand Isle—well, what does he feel? Merely that human nature can be a sickening reality. Then the insistent query comes—*cui bono?* (pp. 175-76)

The theme was not an easy subject to treat, for morbid states of mind and motives need endurance and a resistant restraint on the author's part. Kate Chopin's extraordinary tact enabled her to produce a book which tells the truth without offense, with detachment, and with just that gleam of humor which makes even the nasty digestible, illuminates the agreeable and gives a grace of movement to the whole. But was the theme deserving of the exquisite care given it? (p. 177)

> *Daniel S. Rankin, in his* Kate Chopin and Her Creole Stories *(copyright 1932 University of Pennsylvania Press), University of Pennsylvania, 1932, 313 p.*

JOSEPH J. REILLY (essay date 1942)

Optimists like to believe that, in the long run, justice is accomplished [in literary history], the unworthy dislodged, the truly great seated among their peers and the neglected recalled to their place in the sun. Among these last must be remembered . . . Kate Chopin, whose work included two striking volumes of short stories, [*Bayou Folk* and *A Night in Acadie*]. . . . What Hamlin Garland did for the middle west, Mary Wilkins Freeman for New England, Thomas Nelson Page for the middle south, and Miss [Mary] Murfree for the Tennessee mountain country, Mrs. Chopin did for the dwellers along the sluggish marshy streams that meander among the sugar plantations of upstate Louisiana. . . . [She] sought her material without distinction of class and among people whose knowledge of ante-bellum opulence was largely a tradition. (p. 130)

[Mrs. Chopin] was a student of Maupassant. Her Celtic warmth of blood and romantic spirit rejected his icy cynicism, and her human sympathy kept her point of view from the rigorous impersonality of his. But she enriched her innate talent for story telling by studying his virtues and making them her own: economy of words, beginnings which start the reader off like a shot from a pistol, and infallibly "right" endings.

Mrs. Chopin knew before setting pen to paper exactly whither she was bound and her conclusions bear proof of it. They are never flat, trite, weak, or forced. They seem to be there not as the result of a clever device or for a calculated effect or—as with O. Henry—to startle the reader, but as if they were inherent in the situation or in the psychology of the chief character. . . .

Mrs. Chopin's people are not mere names. She endows them with three dimensions in a sentence or two. (p. 131)

The important thing with Kate Chopin as with Maupassant is character rather than situation, the response of men—and even more of women—to the passion of love. Maupassant's interest is in the blasé, the sophisticated, when confronted by the ingenuous and unspoiled (or the reverse), while Mrs. Chopin's is chiefly in young men and women in the first blush of romantic passion. . . . [The elderly appear], but youth is almost always at their side, softening their decline with tenderness, profiting by their experience, or implying the onward flow of life and its unquenchable hopes.

Kate Chopin's youths and maidens are unspoiled. They have not toyed with their emotions until they become their victims nor are they afraid of the promptings of their hearts. . . .

For them love is the great, the crucial and transfiguring experience, the door swinging open to whatever earthly paradise there be, glorified by nothing but the abiding satisfactions of the heart. (p. 132)

Mrs. Chopin touches passion with a deft hand. In the case of young women she is sensitively aware of its revelations, its hesitancies, its fears, while she senses how deeply young men are troubled by its bitter sweet torment and bewildered by its divine illogic, and always she treats them with a certainty and convincingness which owe as much to reverence as to art. . . .

Of course Mrs. Chopin does not confine herself to this sole *motif* nor, when treating it, does she limit herself to a single formula. Love dawns and its loyalties find expression in infinite ways; in recounting them she sometimes hints at twists of thought whose subtleties she, like Maupassant, leaves the reader to divine. (p. 133)

The emotions which for the most part concern Mrs. Chopin are elementary even when their roots are struck in hidden places, and it is not surprising that the maternal instinct should provide the theme for some of her finest stories. . . . Most notably this theme appears in the tale of Athénaïse [in **"Athénaïse"**] who, scarcely out of school and married to the widower Cazeau, resents his having married her and hides away from him in a kindly city *pension*. (p. 135)

None of Kate Chopin's short stories is told with greater beauty or more exquisite understanding than this, and only one, **"Désirée's Baby,"** outranks it. Here is a tragedy, miniature in proportions, overwhelming in effect, told in a bare 2000 words, every one significant, from the incisive opening sentence to the final startling one, which matches O. Henry's "Furnished Room" in the suddenness of its surprise and in the irony and pathos of its revelation. All Mrs. Chopin's gifts are here in their perfection: directness of approach, sureness of touch, and delicate shading, and the swift strokes which provide the setting create the atmosphere and introduce and realize the characters. With unerring instinct and an amazing economy of words which even she never equalled and Maupassant never surpassed, she probes the psychology of Désirée and her husband to the quick. . . . (pp. 135-36)

As one reads recollections of other short story masters arise with whose revelations of power and skill in evoking the spirit of tragedy this perfect tale takes its place, Poe, Hawthorne, and Thomas Hardy.

From Kate Chopin's two volumes of short stories a modest book could be made containing half a dozen tales which her only American superiors in that field would not disdain to own, a volume which those most proud of American literature would gladly proclaim an addition to its masterpieces. (p. 136)

> *Joseph J. Reilly, "Something about Kate Chopin," in his* Of Books and Men *(copyright 1942, 1970 by Joseph J. Reilly; reprinted by permission of Julian Messner, a Simon & Schuster division of Gulf & Western Corporation), Julian Messner, Inc., 1942, pp. 130-36.*

ROBERT CANTWELL (essay date 1956)

Mrs. Kate Chopin's *The Awakening* seems to me to be the finest novel of its sort written by an American, and to rank among the world's masterpieces of short fiction. (p. 489)

Some of her stories are wonderful; a few like *Désirée's Baby,* which tells of a country girl who learns from the birth of her child that she is of Negro blood, are unforgettable; but they are fragmentary, and her mastery of the Cajun idiom is an example of her facility and her inclination toward prevailing literary trends rather than of her ability to distill imaginatively the life she herself had known. They more often seem translations of experiences from the sophisticated world into the backwoods than evocations of that backwoods life itself. Mrs. Chopin had an extraordinary distaste for the elementary mechanics of fiction—getting people into and out of rooms, the *he saids* and *she saids* of romance. She tended to skip over them entirely if possible, and the result is a lack of continuity, and a broken effect of many-faceted brilliance rather than a sustained narrative control—an impression which often results from a writer's attempt to take over a subject and a setting not his own.

But *The Awakening* is a great novel. . . . Turgenev is the novelist whom Mrs. Chopin most strongly suggests, and where the novel falls short it is Turgenev's fault—the book is too good a work on the Turgenev pattern to be true to Louisiana in its quietly melodramatic conclusion. Mrs. Chopin also tried to emulate George Washington Cable's stories of New Orleans' Creole society. . . . [She] tried to equal the almost incredible charm and vivacity of Cable's French-American conversations, the rattling inconsequent talk, and the high-spirited worldly humor that is so magically free of malice. Mrs. Chopin did well enough, better than anyone except Cable himself, but the achievement was still secondary, and not her own native gift.

That gift was rather a heightened sensuous awareness, awake and alive. (pp. 490-91)

> *Robert Cantwell, "Kate Chopin: 'The Awakening'," in* The Georgia Review *(copyright, 1956, by the University of Georgia), Vol. X, No. 4, Winter, 1956, pp. 489-94.*

KENNETH EBLE (essay date 1956)

The claim of [*The Awakening*] upon the reader's attention is simple. It is a first-rate novel. The justification for urging its importance is that we have few enough novels of its stature. One could add that it is advanced in theme and technique over the novels of its day, and that it anticipates in many respects the modern novel. It could be claimed that it adds to American fiction an example of what Gide called the *roman pur*, a kind of novel not characteristic of American writing. One could offer the book as evidence that the regional writer can go beyond the limitations of regional material. But these matters aside, what recommends the novel is its general excellence. (pp. 262-63)

In a way, the novel is an American [*Madame Bovary*], though such a designation is not precisely accurate. Its central character is similar: the married woman who seeks love outside a stuffy, middle-class marriage. It is similar too in the definitive way it portrays the mind of a woman trapped in marriage and seeking fulfillment of what she vaguely recognizes as her essential nature. . . . And too, like *Madame Bovary*, the novel handles its materials superbly well. Kate Chopin herself was probably more than any other American writer of her time under French influence. . . . But despite the similarities and the possible influences, the novel, chiefly because of the independent characteristics of its heroine, Edna Pontellier, and because of the intensity of the focus upon her, is not simply a good but derivative work. It has a manner and matter of its own. (p. 263)

The Awakening excels chiefly in its characterizations and its structure, the use of images and symbols to unify that structure, and the character of Edna Pontellier.

Kate Chopin, almost from her first story, had the ability to capture character, to put the right word in the mouth, to impart the exact gesture, to select the characteristic action. An illustration of her deftness in handling even minor characters is her treatment of Edna's father. (p. 265)

Characterization was always Mrs. Chopin's talent. Structure was not. Those who knew her working habits say that she seldom revised, and she herself mentions that she did not like reworking her stories. Though her reputation rests upon her short narratives, her collected stories give abundant evidence of the sketch, the outlines of stories which remain unformed. And when she did attempt a tightly organized story, she often turned to Maupassant and was as likely as not to effect a contrived symmetry. Her early novel *At Fault* suffers most from her inability to control her material. In *The Awakening* she is in complete command of structure. She seems to have grasped instinctively the use of the unifying symbol—here the sea, sand, and sky—and with it the power of individual images to bind the story together.

The sea, the sand, the sun and sky of the Gulf Coast become almost a presence themselves in the novel. Much of the sensuousness of the book comes from the way the reader is never allowed to stray far from the water's edge. . . . The way scene, mood, action, and character are fused reminds one not so much of literature as of an impressionist painting, of a Renoir with much of the sweetness missing. Only Stephen Crane, among her American contemporaries, had an equal sensitivity to light and shadow, color and texture, had the painter's eye matched with the writer's perception of character and incident. (pp. 265-66)

[Mrs. Pontellier] has the power, the dignity, the self-possession of a tragic heroine. She is not an Emma Bovary, deluded by ideas of "romance," nor is she the sensual but guilt-ridden woman of the sensational novel. We can find only partial reason for her affair in the kind of romantic desire to escape a middle-class existence which animates Emma Bovary. Edna Pontellier is neither deluded nor deludes. She is woman, the physical woman who, despite her Kentucky Presbyterian upbringing and a comfortable marriage, must struggle with the sensual appeal of physical ripeness, with passion of which she is only dimly aware. Her struggle is not melodramatic, nor is it artificial, nor vapid. It is objective, real and moving. (p. 268)

The Awakening exists, as do most good novels, as a product of the author's literary, real, and imagined life. . . . [Having] added to American literature a novel uncommon in its kind as in its excellence, [Kate Chopin] deserves not to be forgotten. (p. 269)

> *Kenneth Eble, "A Forgotten Novel: Kate Chopin's 'The Awakening'," in* Western Humanities Review *(copyright, 1956, University of Utah), Vol. X, No. 3, Summer, 1956, pp. 261-69.*

EDMUND WILSON (essay date 1962)

There is a good deal of marital instability in the fiction of Kate Chopin, whether she writes of Acadians or New Orleans Creoles. . . . The situations in her first novel [*At Fault*] were already rather uncomfortable from the point of view of conventional morality; but in the central one she followed the then standard procedure of getting rid of an undesirable wife by having her accidentally drowned so that the lovers might be finally united. In 1899, however, she published a novel, *The Awakening,* quite uninhibited and beautifully written, which anticipates D. H. Lawrence in its treatment of infidelity. . . . It is a very odd book to have been written in America at the end of the nineteenth century. It is not even a "problem novel." No case for free love or women's rights or the injustice of marriage is argued. The heroine is simply a sensuous woman who follows her inclinations without thinking much about these issues or tormenting herself with her conscience. Even her death is hardly a tragedy, hardly a deliberate suicide. "How strange and awful and delicious!" she thinks, standing naked on the sand, and the description of her fatal swim has the same sensuous beauty as all the rest. (pp. 590-91)

> *Edmund Wilson, "Novelists of the Post-War South: Albion W. Tourgée, George W. Cable, Kate Chopin, Thomas Nelson Page," in his* Patriotic Gore: Studies in the Literature of the American Civil War *(reprinted by permission of Farrar, Straus & Giroux, Inc.; copyright © 1962 by Edmund Wilson), Oxford University Press, New York, 1962, pp. 529-616.**

LARZER ZIFF (essay date 1966)

The most popular of Mrs. Chopin's stories, while they make full use of the charming lilt of Creole English and the easy openness of Creole manners, concern themselves, as do Maupassant's, with some central quirk or turn in events which reverses the situation that was initially presented. (p. 297)

But more important to Kate Chopin's art than such plotting was her acceptance of the Creole outlook as the ambiance of her tales. The community about which she wrote was one in which respectable women took wine with their dinner and brandy after it, smoked cigarettes, played Chopin sonatas, and listened to the men tell risqué stories. It was, in short, far more French than American, and Mrs. Chopin reproduced this little world with no specific intent to shock or make a point. . . . Rather, these were for Mrs. Chopin the conditions of civility. . . . But for Mrs. Chopin they were only outward signs of a culture that was hers and had its inner effects in the moral make-up of her characters. Though she seldom turned her plot on these facts, she showed that her women were capable of loving more than one man at a time and were not only attractive but sexually attracted also. (pp. 297-98)

[The] open delight in the difference between the sexes was not a mentionable feeling until Mrs. Chopin brought to American literature a setting in which it could be demonstrated with an open geniality.

In almost all her stories, however, Kate Chopin conventionalized the activities of her passionate characters, and even in some cases betrayed them for the sake of exploiting the quaintness of it all. The ambiance of sensuality was rarely permitted to permeate the actions on which the stories turned. But she was obviously growing in that direction. (p. 298)

In her unsuccessful first novel, *At Fault,* Kate Chopin used the successive-marriage plot in a rather wooden fashion to explore the responsibilities of the sexes toward each other, and it contains little that should have made it a success. She was trying her hand at full-length works too soon after beginning to write, and her characters refuse to take on the life she learned to give them after a longer apprenticeship in story-writing. . . . [The novel] proceeds by contrivance rather than psychological analysis, and, since the theme is the nature of self-fulfillment, analysis is urgently needed.

The stories Kate Chopin wrote after she destroyed her second novel [*Young Dr. Gosse*] showed an increasing deftness of style and a greater daring in relating the open sensuality of her characters to their inner cravings and their actions. But the editorial policy of the magazines to which she contributed would not have permitted her a full exploration of such themes, so that, after ten years of writing, she again turned to the novel form to bring together the Creole environment and the theme of feminine self-awareness which she had approached tangentially in *At Fault* and stories such as

"Athénaise." The result was *The Awakening* . . . , a novel of the first rank.

Like *Madame Bovary, The Awakening* is about the adulterous experiments of a married woman, and while Mrs. Chopin did not have to go to Flaubert for the theme, she obviously was indebted to him for it as well as for the masterful economy of setting and character, and the precision of style which she here achieved. . . . [Flaubert's] Emma Bovary is a foolish, bored woman, while Mrs. Chopin's Edna Pontellier is an intelligent, nervous woman, but Edna's salvation is not to be found in drifting back into relation with her environment. Rather, the questions Mrs. Chopin raises through her are what sort of nature she . . . possesses, and how her life is related to the dynamics of her inner self. (pp. 299-300)

The Awakening was the most important piece of fiction about the sexual life of a woman written to date in America, and the first fully to face the fact that marriage, whether in point of fact it closed the range of a woman's sexual experiences or not, was but an episode in her continuous growth. It did not attack the institution of the family, but it rejected the family as the automatic equivalent of feminine self-fulfillment, and on the very eve of the twentieth century it raised the question of what woman was to do with the freedom she struggled toward. The Creole woman's acceptance of maternity as totally adequate to the capacities of her nature carried with it the complements of a fierce chastity, a frankness of speech on sexual matters, a mature ease among men, and a frank and unguilty pleasure in sensual indulgence. But this was not, ultimately, Edna Pontellier's birthright, and she knew it. She was an American woman, raised in the Protestant mistrust of the senses and in the detestation of sexual desire as the root of evil. As a result, the hidden act came for her to be equivalent to the hidden and true self, once her nature awakened in the open surroundings of Creole Louisiana. The new century was to provide just such an awakening for countless American women, and *The Awakening* spoke of painful times ahead on the road to fulfillment.

Kate Chopin sympathized with Edna, but she did not pity her. She rendered her story with a detachment akin to Flaubert's. At one point Edna's doctor says, "Youth is given up to illusions. It seems to be a provision of Nature; a decoy to secure mothers for the race. And Nature takes no account of moral consequences, of arbitrary conditions which we create, and which we feel obliged to maintain at any cost." These appear to be the author's sentiments. Edna Pontellier is trapped between her illusions and the conditions which society arbitrarily establishes to maintain itself, and she is made to pay. Whether girls should be educated free of illusions, if possible, whether society should change the conditions it imposes on women, or whether both are needed, the author does not say; the novel is about what happened to Edna Pontellier. (pp. 304-05)

Kate Chopin, a wise and worldly woman, had refined the craft of fiction in the nineties to the point where it could face her strong inner theme of the female rebellion and see it through to a superb creative work. *The Awakening* was also an awakening of the deepest powers in its author, but, like Edna Pontellier, Kate Chopin learned that her society would not tolerate her questionings. Her tortured silence as the new century arrived was a loss to American letters of the order of the untimely deaths of [Stephen] Crane and [Frank] Norris. She was alive when the twentieth century began, but she had been struck mute by a society fearful in the face of an uncertain dawn. (p. 305)

Larzer Ziff, "An Abyss of Inequality: Sarah Orne Jewett, Mary Wilkins Freeman, Kate Chopin," in his The American 1890s: Life and Times of a Lost Generation *(copyright © 1966 by Larzer Ziff; reprinted by permission of Viking Penguin Inc.), Viking Penguin, 1966, pp. 275-305.**

GEORGE ARMS (essay date 1967)

[In **The Awakening** Kate Chopin basically] writes as a non-intrusive author but principally presents her material with a sense of constant contrast, partly in the whole social situation, partly in [the heroine, Edna Pontellier], but essentially as the author's way of looking at life. . . . Mrs. Chopin is unwilling to present Edna as simply struggling between two opposites, later remarking that her emotions "had never taken the form of struggles." . . . (p. 217)

On the whole, as she reveals herself, her aimlessness impresses us more than her sense of conflict. . . . Edna appears not so much as a woman who is aware of the opposition of two ideals but rather as one who drifts—who finally, even in death, is drifting when she again recalls having wandered on the blue-green meadow as a little girl. . . . Edna is sensitive to many states of mind as the author describes her after the consummation of her affair with Arobin: irresponsibility, shock, her husband's and Robert's reproach, but not shame and not remorse, though regret that she has yielded from erotic longing rather than from love. Still, there is an "understanding" that hints of a polarity: "She felt as if a mist had been lifted from her eyes, enabling her to look upon and comprehend the significance of life, that monster made up of beauty and brutality." . . . (pp. 217-18)

[One] of the oppositions which the author develops throughout the novel is that of romance and reality, and she suggests that Edna remains a figure of romantic ideals in spite of her acting with a sexual freedom that the common reader would call realistic or even naturalistic. . . . [One] can summarize that instead of identifying herself with Edna's actions, Mrs. Chopin tends to regard them as romantically motivated rather than as realistically considered. Yet, as if to say that there are other kinds of romanticism, the author introduces Adele Ratignolle, Edna's friend who is completely in love with her husband. . . . (pp. 218-19)

In all, the author presents these contrasts suggestively rather than systematically. Perhaps if she takes any stand at all it is to favor individualism against social obligation. . . . (p. 219)

In treating Edna's awakening, the author shows irony and even deviousness. We look upon Edna's awakening as archetypal in marking her passage from death to rebirth, but we many also look upon her awakening as not a rebirth but as another kind of death that is self-sought. Amusingly enough, the author, quite consciously I am sure, allows Edna to do an inordinate amount of sleeping throughout the novel, in spite of her underlying vitality. . . . It is almost as if the author were saying: here is my heroine who at the critical points of her progress toward an awakening constantly falls asleep.

An even grimmer irony, of course, is in her awakening to an erotic life not through Robert, whom she truly loves, but through Alcée, whom she uses merely as a convenience.

Though Edna recognizes this, she hardly does so in the sense that the novel does. . . . We cannot help suspecting that Edna simplifies and melodramatizes her view of herself far more than the author does. (pp. 219-20)

Finally, the underlying awareness of contrasting forces in the novel is exhibited in its use of children. . . . Again we are somewhat perplexed as to whether or not the author approves of Edna's attitude toward her children. I suppose that those who look upon the novel as a defense of the New Woman would feel that Mrs. Chopin regards freedom from children as a necessary basis for complete freedom. But again I am doubtful, for Mrs. Chopin delights in the contraries which are present in Edna's response toward her boys. (p. 220)

[We] observe her constantly returning to her children as a kind of penance whenever she displays most markedly her love outside of marriage. When she suspects that Robert goes to Mexico to avoid her, she shows an unusual intimacy with her children by telling them a bedtime story. . . . She had already coddled and caressed one of her sons immediately after her day spent with Robert. . . . After her second night with Alcée she visits her children in the country . . .—one would think more as an act of penance than of affection. Just after Edna had fully admitted her love for Robert to a friend, she sent her children "a huge box of bonbons." . . . (pp. 220-21)

Perhaps it would even be better to treat [the children] as bringing another contrast into the story. Like those contrasts of purpose and aimlessness, of romance and realism, and of sleep and awakening, this one is not of absolute opposition but is complex and even blurred. . . . [Precisely] this complexity may be what Mrs. Chopin is trying to achieve. She presents a series of events in which the truth is present, but with a philosophical pragmatism she is unwilling to extract a final truth. Rather, she sees truth as constantly re-forming itself and as so much a part of the context of what happens that it can never be final or for that matter abstractly stated. (p. 222)

> *George Arms, "Kate Chopin's 'The Awakening' in the Perspective of Her Literary Career," in* Essays on American Literature in Honor of Jay B. Hubbell, *edited by Clarence Gohdes (reprinted by permission of the Publisher; copyright 1967 by Duke University Press, Durham, North Carolina), Duke University Press, 1967, pp. 215-28.*

LEWIS LEARY (essay date 1968)

Like *The Awakening*, [Kate Chopin's first novel, *At Fault*,] speaks of marital unhappiness and of dangers which lie in wait for people who do as they want to do without concern for other people. It is more cluttered than the later novel, with characters and with convolutions of plot; its thesis is more overtly but less expertly enforced. (pp. 176-77)

Mrs. Chopin was not finally able to turn her tune, to make whatever point she had to make come effectively through. Manifestly something or someone was at fault. Perhaps it was everyone, for one distinguishing mark of this first attempt at long fiction is that no one is free from fault, and that the world is indeed spoiled with "rut and mire" for every "pinioned spirit" who submits to "earthy needs." Something lurks behind these words which Mrs. Chopin in 1890 could not or dared not express. Sexual overtones are sensed rather than heard.

For Mrs. Chopin evidently had something which she wanted to say about self-fulfillment, its possibilities and its cost, which she would say better and more simply, with deeper psychological insight, in *The Awakening*. Melicent's imperious selfishness, her desire to be free from restraint of convention, and her dabbling in "culture" may be recognized as foreshadowings of the more intense fumblings toward freedom of Edna Pontellier in the later novel, and Hosmer in some sense can be supposed to anticipate Edna's businessman husband, who leaves his wife too much alone, but neither is fully nor consistently realized—in fact, no character in *At Fault* (except perhaps Grégoire) is presented convincingly in depth. Throughout much of the action focus is unsteady, plot is choked with incident, contrivance usurps the place of motivation, and themes so jostle one another that none is ultimately articulated.

But for all its faults of occasional melodrama or shrillness, *At Fault* need not be dismissed as simply another bad novel. There is too much good in it, for an artist can be seen at work, learning her trade, to be sure, and often fumbling, but with a touch which is sometimes sure. She was to do greatly better, in a few short stories and in her second novel, but this other novel also deserves something more than casual remembrance. (pp. 188-89)

[The] elements are all there: the freshness of perception, the acknowledgement that flesh demands its share from living, the eye for scene, the ear for dialect. What is lacking is a sense of timing, of economy, of focus. Contrivance is imperfectly masked. Superfluous characters come and go. Reasons for resolution are harshly improvised—arson, murder, drunkenness, drowning. The richness of Mrs. Chopin's mimic imagination is dissipated through scenes which are often more pictorial than necessary. But the principal fault, and one so magnificently overcome in the portrayal of Edna Pontellier in *The Awakening*, is that of not being able effectively to present any convincing reason why any character acts as he does. In her second novel, Mrs. Chopin displays the gradual awakening of a woman to the gratification and the peril of extramarital sexual satisfaction. Edna Pontellier's fumbling toward freedom elicits sympathy, disapproval perhaps, but understanding certainly. Given what she is and where she is and how she reacts, she could not have done otherwise. In *The Awakening* a master handles her tools with expert skill in analysis of a single character—nothing is wasted, the focus remains sharp; in *At Fault* she is experimenting, producing rough first designs of what later would be fashioned to art. (p. 191)

> *Lewis Leary, "Kate Chopin's Other Novel" (originally published in* Southern Literary Journal, *Vol. 1, No. 1, December, 1968), in his* Southern Excursions: Essays on Mark Twain and Others *(reprinted with permission of Louisiana State University Press; copyright © 1971 by Louisiana State University Press), Louisiana State University Press, 1971, pp. 176-91.*

PER SEYERSTED (essay date 1969)

[Many] similarities might justify us in calling *The Awakening* an American *Madame Bovary*. Mrs. Chopin did not use the French classic as a model, however, but only as a point of departure, giving the story an entirely new emphasis. Flaubert paints the manners and the mediocrity of bourgeois life. A major part of Emma's motive power stems from her belief that the fortunate ones—the elite, the Parisians—lead charmed lives, and, to a large degree, she stands for both sexes in her self-dramatization and her frenetic attempts to escape her dull environment. Edna, meanwhile, is socially secure and satisfied with her upper middle class position, and she even has certain means of her own. This constitutes a basic difference between the two women, and, unconcerned with her protagonist's social and economic situation, Kate Chopin could focus very sharply on the truly fundamental problem of what it means to be a woman, particularly in a patriarchy. Edna's revolt against her conventional roles as a wife and mother and against her biological destiny is naturally more representative for the female than the male mind, and it is possible to see *The Awakening* as a woman's reply to a man's *Madame Bovary*.

The common starting point of the two heroines is that both have grown up on romanticism with its exalted ideas of transcendent love. (p. 138)

In their attempts to realize their visions, the two women illustrate a second basic dissimilarity. In her fight for the fulfillment of her dreams, Emma persists in trying to conform to models, blaming others rather than herself when she is disappointed in her roles, and gaining little insight into her own nature. . . . "Pontellierism," on the other hand, represents a wish for clarity and a willingness to understand one's inner and outer reality, besides a desire to dictate one's own role rather than to slip into patterns prescribed by tradition. (pp. 138-39)

Edna's emancipation starts with her physical attraction to Robert. . . . When she vaguely feels the first suggestions of desire, her will blazes up, and her tacit submissiveness to Léonce comes to an abrupt end. But conditions restrict her, and her dreams only leave her dejected.

What dominates her imagination during this period is not so much a feminist revolt as the idea of a transcendent passion for Robert of the kind suggested by romantic literature; and not seeking help from any source, external or internal, to check it, she dreams about such a love, lending herself to any impulse as if freed of all responsibility. (p. 141)

[After Alcée kisses Edna], the author—in a single, crucial paragraph—explodes the romantic myth of the noble, undivided passion. Leaving behind all traits of the maudlin heroine of the dime-novels, Edna now realizes that the physical component of love can stand apart from the spiritual one, that sensuous attraction is impersonal and can be satisfied by a partner she does not love. (p. 142)

Yet she cannot give up Robert, and while realizing that he might consider her "unwomanly," she takes the initiative toward him when they next meet, giving him the voluptuous kiss which sets him on fire. Refusing to be what she regards as the inessential adjunct to man, she has something of the emancipated woman who wants to play the man's role as a taker. It is not his role *per se* that she wants, however, but only those aspects of it which make the creation of one's own essence, as Jean-Paul Sartre terms it, easier for the male than it is for the female. (p. 144)

Edna's sexual emancipation is so completely interlocked with her spiritual breaking of bonds that she insists on both with equal force. Even so it is a remarkable feature of *The Awakening* that the protagonist thinks nothing of disregarding her traditional duties toward her husband and of challenging the sacred concept of matrimony. . . . It is as if Edna's creator considers these aspects of woman's emancipation too elementary for further comment and wants to move on to the really fundamental—and more taboo—factor which her predecessors had shied away from: the children. (p. 145)

Edna had for many years been a tolerably good mother. . . . But now she sees her boys as opponents and refuses to live for them rather than for herself. When Edna parts from Robert to go to [Adèle's] childbirth, she still believes that she has a certain power to direct her own life. But Adèle's reminder of the mother's duty toward her children; her own reflections as she watches her friend's birth agonies, and Dr. Mandelet's comments as he walks her home after the ordeal, change her view of her possibilities for a self-directed, emancipated life. (pp. 145-46)

Edna realizes that sex is not only separate from love, but also largely independent of our volition, being a fundamental force of nature which spurs us blindly on toward procreation. This is the function of the brutal juxtaposition of the love-scene and the childbirth: to suggest how pleasure and pain, conception and delivery are inextricably intertwined. She sees how sex and pregnancy represent nature's play with woman, and she concludes that a woman's links, or chains, to her children make her hopes for independence illusory. She realizes that patriarchal society is quick to condemn particularly a freedom-seeking woman who neglects her children since she—rather than her husband—is "intended by nature" to take care of them.

The note which Edna finds when she returns to her house is a further illustration of woman's situation in a man's world. Robert's words signify to her not only that he is afraid of braving conventions, but also that "he would never understand" her, or ever accept that kind of independence and equality without which she cannot exist. He is Kate Chopin's example of the ordinary man who cannot tolerate the unusual woman, and his reactions emphasize the reasoning which relentlessly leads Mrs. Pontellier to her final exertion of responsibility and of her will as she pays the price of freedom. (p. 146)

As appears from Mrs. Chopin's notebook, she originally titled her novel "A Solitary Soul." When she did this she was no doubt referring in part to Edna's awakening to the loneliness of imperative sexuality, of illusory, evanescent love. But the term refers even more to another aspect of the human condition: the curse of freedom. . . . The attitude she lets Mrs. Pontellier illustrate comes close to that of existentialism. She seems to say that Edna has a real existence only when she gives her own laws, when she through conscious choice becomes her own creation with an autonomous self. But while such a developmental freedom may strengthen the self, it is accompanied by a growing sense of isolation and aloneness, and also anguish. (pp. 147-48)

[Kate Chopin] seems to see no happy end to woman's quest for freedom. Edna wants to decide over her own life, but this urge brings her despair rather than happiness. She appears to need all her strength to want freedom *from* rather than freedom *to*, and to be too weak both to break the chains and to justify her non-conformist existence through positive performance. The note of pessimism which runs through the book may be due in part to the romantic syndrome which Edna mirrors in her passion, her anguish, and her occasional passivity and desire for nothingness. The ultimate reason for the heroine's feeling of hopelessness, however, is her urge for spiritual emancipation which is so strong that there is no turning back for her. . . .

Edna is defeated in the sense that she cannot meaningfully relate herself to the people around her and in some way integrate her demands with those of society, a society, to be sure, which is responsible for the fact that emancipation is her goal rather than her birthright. Not attempting to come to terms with her selfish drives, she is unable to reach that harmony, that feeling of creative cooperation and companionship with the people around her at which Athénaïse apparently arrives. Yet she is not defeated like Emma Bovary: Her death is not so much a result of outer forces crowding her in as a triumphant assertion of her inner liberty. (p. 149)

Edna's victory lies in her awakening to an independence that includes an act of renunciation. The novel is something of a landmark in nineteenth-century American literature in that it reaches out beyond woman's obtaining equality in law and love to the existentialist demand for dictating one's own destiny, and even beyond that to the horror of freedom, the immutable affliction for both the women and men who venture that far. What is most important, however, is that the book is a great artistic achievement. . . .

The Awakening shows that the author had learned, now also in a longer work, to eliminate irrelevancies and to make everything contribute to a single, strong effect. (p. 150)

Even though Mrs. Chopin devotes only little space to the setting, she gives an unmistakable sense of place. With a few, quick strokes she manages to evoke powerfully the whole scene, to create an ever-present Southern atmosphere. We see the Lebrun pension and the bent oaks, the sandy path and the Gulf caressing the beach. We feel the luscious charm of the summer. . . . But above all, there is the sea itself. . . . (p. 151)

[The] emphasis on the passion which peoples the earth is entirely natural in a novel which covers two gestations and births. *The Awakening* is a finely wrought system of tensions and interrelations set up between Edna's slow birth as a sexual and authentic being, and the counterpointed pregnancy and confinement of Adèle.

There is also the interaction between the heroine and her men and a constant interplay between Edna's passion and her attitude to her boys. We find the latter already in an early incident in which her still only lightly suggested attraction to Robert is offset by Léonce's reproach that she neglects her children. When she later is able to show greater tenderness toward them on occasion, it is apparently both a result of her emotional thaw and an expiation for her affairs. (p. 153)

The children themselves are somewhat anonymous. . . . It seems as if the author wants to show that while the boys may be living realities to the heroine, they are so more in their capacity of demands put upon her than as living individuals who directly influence the awakening that is the subject of the book. . . .

As Edna's counterpart, Adèle is presented more at length. We are shown her total devotion to her family, and the domestic harmony in her home. But there are shades in this picture of a mother-woman who has a baby every two years and is always talking about her ''condition'': Though she is the embodiment of unselfishness in her care for the children,

she also uses them as an excuse to draw attention to herself. (p. 154)

Edna's half-hearted attempt at becoming an artist is one of her means to escape from [her] oppression. Mlle. Reisz, the musician, is therefore another natural foil to her. She is far from the Bible's idea of woman. She objects to babies, and she is rude and self-assertive, with ''a disposition to trample upon the rights of others.'' But this disagreeable and unpopular person is at least an individual, and this fact—together with her music—attracts Edna as she struggles with her own individuation. (pp. 154-55)

Adèle's ''hour of trial'' gives the author . . . [an] opportunity to fuse Eros, birth, and death. The confinement scene is set between a real and an imagined embrace, and its core is a double birth which leads to death. When Adèle's agony starts, Edna's throes begin in the form of a vague dread as she thinks of her own births. In this recollection, Mrs. Chopin again unites the sensuous with the beginning and the end of existence, adding a touch of the sadness of eternity, and suggesting the theme of a waking up to a responsibility. . . . Adèle's words complete her birth: She has determined what character of a woman she is, and her unwillingness to give up her new-won essence can only lead to the determination which drives ''into her soul like a death wound.''

The title of the book is singularly appropriate. The dualities of sleep (or drowsiness)-awakening and bewilderment-understanding are introduced early and thereafter frequently approached from shifting angles. Edna's intermittent anguish and the voices which speak to her ''without promise'' also prepare us for the denouement. . . . There will always be physical partners for the heroine, but none to understand or accept her spiritually. Thus as she develops from bewilderment to clarity and from egocentricity to a kind of responsible renunciation, she also moves from quasi-attachment to solitude. (pp. 157-58)

Edna's action of casting off her garments [before walking into the sea] symbolizes a lifting of the veil with which conventional ethics have draped the true meaning of existence. She is new-born in the sense that she comprehends and accepts life's basic urges in all their nakedness. At the same time she also wants the spiritual freedom which is sought mostly by men; but, while the man may believe that the bird of male freedom *can* fly, she has learned that the woman's wings are broken when she attempts such a flight. (p. 159)

The Awakening can be seen as a eulogy on sex and a muted elegy on the female condition. From its appearance, it has been read as a novel on a woman's gradual arousal to passion. But the book is not just another love story. . . . We miss its richness and deeper meaning if we overlook the vision which is evoked at the end, a vision which is reflected in the novel's focus, tone, and point of view. (pp. 160-61)

[There] is hardly anything inessential in the novel. Everything contributes to the effect: setting, characters, and symbols; atmosphere and tone; parallels and contrasts. Such a seeming contrivance as having Edna called away when she is to possess Robert is a highly conscious means to an end. The book shows a rigorous selectivity in description and dialogue, and a concentration which makes everything play together in a functional unison. The work is simple and clear in conception. Its structure is complex, yet completely coherent, making full use of the realistic and symbolic elements, and bringing all strands together at the end. Its texture is rich, with a wealth of images, a warm Southern color, and a resonant tone, in which the pessimistic note is offset by a basic vitality reflecting man's authentic, immutable heart-beat.

The Awakening may echo both Flaubert and Darwin. Yet it is entirely independent, and fundamentally not dated. Edna's sexual awakening is as valid and full of reality today as it was when *Hippolytus* was written, and her basic existentialist quest is as modern now as it probably will be in a still patriarchal tomorrow. But the mature author does not force her views upon us. Edna's story is given with a detachment which joins with the general artistic excellence to make it into a convincing and deeply moving experience and a balanced and highly accomplished work of art. (pp. 162-63)

[In the short story **"The Storm,"** there] is complete correspondence between theme, on the one hand, and setting, plot, and character, on the other. The elements of this piece are inextricably fused as the tale moves relentlessly forward, in one sustained, effortless sweep, toward the inescapable outcome of the cyclone. With a minimum of characterization this highly effective story gives a convincing picture of the figures—at once representative and individual—who are influenced by the storm. The tone greatly contributes to the artistic impact: detached and unsentimental, yet warm, and serenely free.

Artistically, **"The Storm"** is a first-rate story. It is important also for its daring. The frankness about sex of such books as *Madame Bovary* and *Nana* was of course slowly having an impact even on American fiction. But with this tale, Kate Chopin not only outdistanced her compatriots, but also went a step beyond the Frenchmen. That her description of physical union is more open than theirs is a relatively minor point in this connection; what is important is its "happy," "healthy" quality. (pp. 167-68)

Kate Chopin was not interested in the immoral in itself, but in life as it comes, in what she saw as natural—or certainly inevitable—expressions of universal Eros, inside or outside of marriage. She focuses here on sexuality as such, and to her, it is neither frantic nor base, but as "healthy" and beautiful as life itself.... In **"The Storm,"** there is exuberance and a cosmic joy and mystery as Alcée and Calixta become one with another and with elemental nature. With its organic quality, its erotic elation, and its frankness, the story almost makes its author an early D. H. Lawrence. (p. 168)

[Though] what could be called her feminist stories are so greatly important in Kate Chopin's *œuvre,* they are rather few in number, and the rest of her writings show a detachment on the relationship between the sexes. The man-woman relationship of **"The Storm"**—the most intimate possible—is a crucial touchstone for objectivity....

There is no antagonism or competition between Alcée and Calixta, no wilful domination in his manner or subservience in hers, even though he is higher up in society than she. In short, Mrs. Chopin appears to have achieved that thing—comparatively rare even today: to become a woman author who could write on the two sexes with a large degree of detachment and objectivity. (p. 169)

The fact that Kate Chopin tried to place a number of her nearly fifty poems would suggest that she attached a certain importance also to her efforts in this medium; nevertheless, most of her poetry is undistinguished, when it is not downright awkward or trite. Though she admired Whitman, she

seems to have been satisfied to use in her own verse only conventional diction and meter.... Typifying its period, Mrs. Chopin's poetry comprises both quatrains accompanying gifts and the inevitable imitations of the Rubaiyat. Particularly in her early verse, she uses archaic words like "list" and "hath"; her imagery is traditional, including birds and flowers, the moon and the stars, and her use of them has little freshness or originality. (p. 171)

She often shows true feeling, but in many instances she is defeated by stale language or by a certain monotony of form. Her earliest fairly good effort—**"In Dreams throughout the Night"** is also the first in which not all lines are rhymed. As she gained in self-confidence, she was on occasion able to fuse all elements into a successful whole, particularly in **"If Some Day"** ... and **"The Haunted Chamber,"** her two best poems. (p. 172)

Mrs. Chopin was at least a decade ahead of her time.... [She] can be seen not only as one of the American realists of the 1890's, but also as a link in the tradition formed by such distinguished American women authors as Sarah Orne Jewett, Mary E. Wilkins Freeman, Willa Cather, [Edith Wharton and Ellen Glasgow]. One factor uniting these writers is their emphasis on female characters. Another is their concern with values, but here we see a difference between the St. Louisian and the others in that she is less interested than they are in preserving these values.... [Kate Chopin] was no celebrant of the aristocratic qualities of her own distinguished background.

The one value that really counted with her was woman's opportunity for self-expression.... She was sensitive, intelligent, and broad enough in her outlook to see the different basic needs of the female and the various sides of her existence and to represent them with impartiality. Her work is thus no feminist plea in the usual sense, but an illustration—rather than an assertion—of woman's right to be herself, to be individual and independent whether she wants to be weak or strong, a nest-maker or a soaring bird. (pp. 195-96)

The great achievement of Kate Chopin was that she broke new ground in American literature. She was the first woman writer in her country to accept passion as a legitimate subject for serious, outspoken fiction. Revolting against tradition and authority; with a daring which we can hardly fathom today; with an uncompromising honesty and no trace of sensationalism, she undertook to give the unsparing truth about woman's submerged life. She was something of a pioneer in the amoral treatment of sexuality, of divorce, and of woman's urge for an existential authenticity. She is in many respects a modern writer, particularly in her awareness of the complexities of truth and the complications of freedom. With no desire to reform, but only to understand; with the clear conscience of the rebel, yet unembittered by society's massive lack of understanding, she arrived at her culminating achievements, *The Awakening* and **"The Storm."** (p. 198)

She obviously does not come near the breadth and stature of Dreiser, but among the American authors of second rank she occupies an important and distinctive position. In her best writings within her particular field, she not only equals Dreiser's courage, but shows an independence, a directness of purpose, a deep understanding, and a sensitive artistry which make them into minor masterpieces. With *The Awakening* and a handful of her stories, such as **"Regret," "Athénaïse,"** and **"The Storm,"** she deserves to be permanently included, not only in her country's literary history, but also in its body of living fiction. (pp. 198-99)

Per Seyersted, in his Kate Chopin: A Critical Biography *(reprinted by permission of the author; copyright © by Per Seyersted 1969), Louisiana State University Press, 1969, 246 p.*

GEORGE M. SPANGLER (essay date 1970)

Mrs. Chopin tells [the story of *The Awakening*] with impressive technique. Rarely abusing the privilege of authorial omniscience for the sake of special pleading or didactic comment, she combines a detached tone with a sensuous prose that strongly enforces the point of Edna's awakening. Central is the characterization of Edna, and, until the final pages, it is very well done. For Mrs. Chopin is able to convey dramatically the ultimately terrifying emergence of Edna's passional self, a self whose needs are not to be denied by social custom, conventional morality, or domestic obligations. Never much inclined to self-scrutiny, Edna at the start of the novel is only vaguely aware of an equally vague sense of discontent, a discontent which is apt to bring her to tears for no apparent reason. As her frustration increases and her longing fixes itself on Robert, the first practical result is an unreasoning, stubborn resistance to the will of her husband, whose very presence reminds her of the false role of devoted wife and mother which impedes the expression of her latent selfhood. . . . Her rebellion against conventional obligations reaches its first climax when she decides to establish a home apart from her husband. Indifferent to appearances and indefinite about her future, she also rejects sentimental qualms about her children. . . . Later on, her assertion of self becomes a matter of principle as well as the basis of her daily behavior: "but whatever came, she had resolved never again to belong to another than herself." . . . Even as she and Robert confess their mutual love, romantic sentiment must make way for her determination to protect and express her independent selfhood. (p. 251)

Finally there is a disturbing, even alienating ruthlessness about Edna, but a ruthlessness which eludes moral categories because it is no more and no less than the reflection of her passional nature's drive for fulfillment. This is the heart and the great triumph of Mrs. Chopin's characterization—that the relentless force that compels Edna is felt—and felt insistently—rather than analyzed, explained and, least of all, condemned. That what Edna awakens to is simply and ineluctably a fact of nature, whatever its implications for the individual and society is conveyed metaphorically through the pervasive linking of her desire with images of the sea. . . . [The] sea becomes more and more clearly the symbol of sexual desire itself. . . . (pp. 251-52)

Just as skillful, though of course far less conspicuous, is Mrs. Chopin's presentation of Edna's husband. Here the crucial point is that Mr. Pontellier is not a hopeless boor whose nature would provide easy explanation and justification for his wife's rebellion. Rather he is portrayed as a thoroughly likable man of good nature and intention, successful in his business, popular with his peers, devoted to his wife and children. Though more than a little smug, he is immediately sensitive to the change taking place in his wife. . . . But concerned and sympathetic as he is, he is also uncomprehending and, at times, more than a little exasperated. Indeed he never really understands what has happened to his domestic life.

Instead he must simply confront more and more evidence that he and his children are no longer of consequence to his wife; and his bafflement, not at all comic, generates a pathos which few readers could ignore and which further enriches the novel. For a man who clearly wants nothing more of home than that it be comfortable, a wife who longs for "life's delirium" is no minor trial. (p. 252)

[He] will drop out of the narrative as inconspicuously as he has passed from her consciousness. In a sense, however, Mr. Pontellier is not alone; finally none of the men in the novel is prepared to cope with Edna, a point that requires some consideration when the conclusion is examined. . . .

Mrs. Chopin gives added density to the texture of the novel through the contrast she draws between the backgrounds of the husband and wife, that is, through provision of a cultural dimension. Born and raised among "sound old Presbyterian Kentucky stock," . . . Edna can never feel completely at home with the Creoles among whom her marriage has placed her. What is most disconcerting to her is "their entire absence of prudery," which allows a frankness of conversation that often causes her to blush. The Creole women are chaste and their husbands free of jealousy, yet their talk easily and naturally turns to matters Edna has been taught to consider the most intimate. Of course, once Edna puts aside her repressions, her behavior goes far beyond the limits Creoles, not to mention Kentucky Presbyterians, accept. Mrs. Chopin is not, however, hinting at a cultural explanation for Edna's predicament. The contrast of cultural attitudes toward sex serves rather to enforce the image of Edna's isolation and to make the more difficult her quest for fulfillment; for she is really at ease in neither milieu, and both in their different ways enforce standards that would frustrate the expression of what she comes to feel is her essential nature. . . .

[One] can easily and happily join in the praise that in recent years has been given to *The Awakening*—one can, that is, until one reaches the conclusion of the novel, which is unsatisfactory because it is fundamentally evasive. (p. 253)

Its great fault is inconsistent characterization, which asks the reader to accept a different and diminished Edna from the one developed so impressively before. Throughout the novel the most striking feature of Edna's character has been her strength of will, her ruthless determination to go her own way. In thought and act she has rejected unequivocally the restraints of conventional morality, social custom and personal obligation to her husband and children. . . . Yet in the final pages, Mrs. Chopin asks her reader to believe in an Edna who is completely defeated by the loss of Robert, to believe in the paradox of a woman who has awakened to passional life and yet quietly, almost thoughtlessly, chooses death. Having overcome so much in the way of frustration, Edna is destroyed by so little. As well, the reasonings and feelings attributed to her as motivation at the end do not bear scrutiny. Her brief affair with Arobin hardly proves the certainty of a host of future lovers, but it has clearly shown her what is missing from her life; and since she has long been indifferent to convention and domestic ties, she could well expect to find someone less shoddy than Arobin and less scrupulous than Robert. Equally perplexing is her sudden concern for her children, who previously have seemed to matter little as long as they were out of the way. Increasingly strong, practical and sure of herself and her needs through most of the novel, Edna suddenly collapses, and what the reader gets in the way of explanation does not follow from what he has witnessed before. . . . (p. 254)

What happened was that Mrs. Chopin provided a conclusion for a novel other than the one she wrote, a conclusion for a novel much more conventional and much less interesting than *The Awakening*. Specifically it is a conclusion for an ordinary sentimental novel, not for a subtle psychological treatment of female sexuality. If the rest of the novel existed only at the sentimental, romantic level, then Edna's suicide would be conventionally appropriate and acceptable: a woman surrenders her chastity and death is the consequence. In such a novel Robert would be the single great love of her life, a great romantic passion, finally doomed and destructive. But despite its conclusion *The Awakening* is not such a novel; indeed its relation to the conventional sentimental novel is not apparent until the final pages. For Mrs. Chopin was concerned not with seduction and retribution, but with woman's passional nature and its relation to self, marriage and society. Yet at the end she transformed a character who has embodied these complex issues into one who simply dies from disappointed, illicit love. In a word, a complex psychological novel is converted into a commonplace sentimental one. (pp. 254-55)

If, then, the conclusion Mrs. Chopin chose for *The Awakening* allows for pathos and poetic justice to please the sentimental and moralistic—a dubious accomplishment indeed—it also leads to a painful reduction in Edna's character. For in the final pages Edna is different and diminished: she is no longer purposeful, merely willful; no longer liberated, merely perverse; no longer justified, merely spiteful. And the painful failure of vision (or, more likely, of nerve) implicit in the change prevents a very good, very interesting novel from being the extraordinary masterpiece some commentators have claimed it is. (p. 255)

> *George M. Spangler, "Neglected Fiction; Kate Chopin's 'The Awakening': A Partial Dissent," in* Novel: A Forum on Fiction *(copyright © Novel Corp., 1970), Vol. 4, No. 3, Spring, 1970, pp. 249-55.*

ROBERT D. ARNER (essay date 1972)

[Kate Chopin's] **"Désirée's Baby"** gives evidence of a careful craftsmanship that goes well beyond formal elegance and fuses theme, structure, and imagery into one of the most successful of her works. (p. 132)

Far more is at stake in [its] ending than the simple discovery that the parent who has driven his wife and child to exile and death on the suspicion that his wife had Negro blood is himself the tainted and guilty party. That indeed might satisfy our sense of justice, but Kate Chopin has more to say on the issues of race and slavery. For one thing, the story makes a point made by a number of other Southern writers both before and after Mrs. Chopin: that there is no absolute distinction between white and black, but rather an imaginary line drawn by white men and crossed at their own choosing. . . . Of the two discoveries Armand makes at the conclusion of the story, that he is part Negro and that the idea of white racial purity is a myth, the second is the harder to live with, since it deprives him of all semblance of justification for his treatment of Désirée and the baby. He learns, in fact, that his relationship to his father is precisely the same as the one he imagined existed between his son and himself. It is

this profound irony of sacrificer become the sacrifice, a reversal of racial identity, that underlies the story and determines—in fact, almost necessitates—the ironic reversal at the end. Form is wed inseparably to theme, and both originate in the realities of the Southern social system.

The antidote to the poison of racial abstraction that destroys Désirée, the baby, and Armand is love, a deeply personal relationship which denies the dehumanizing and impersonal categorization of people into racial groups. The possibility that love may offer individual salvation from the evils of racial definition is suggested first of all by Armand's father's marriage to a Negress and, second, by Madame Valmondé's open acceptance of Désirée and her child even after she believes that the girl is part black. Love demands that people be seen as individuals, not as members of a social caste or as extensions of one's own ego. But the story makes clear that Armand does not really love Désirée; he thinks of her as a possession, a rich prize to display to his friends and to flatter his vanity, and when he thinks that she is black the value of the prize entirely disappears. . . . Armand's passionate intensity and his pride in possession make him a willing agent of his own destruction. . . . [A] pride nurtured by artificial racial distinctions ultimately destroys Armand's chances for happiness and personal salvation. Character and environment unite to produce one part of the tragic denouement of the tale.

The several racial themes of **"Désirée's Baby"** are reinforced by two major patterns of images which, circulating throughout the story, unobtrusively contribute both unity and density of meaning. The first of these is the contrast between light and shadow, whiteness and blackness. Armand is associated with darkness from the outset. His estate is a place of terror and his house inspires fear. . . . In contrast, Désirée is surrounded by images of whiteness. (pp. 133-35)

A third important color in the story is yellow. Armand's plantation house is yellow and, in view of the association between his personality and the atmosphere surrounding the house, this fact acquires significance. . . . [All] the Negroes mentioned by name in the story are "yellow" rather than pure black. That so much yellow color is associated with the Aubigny estate, both with its buildings and more important, with its slaves, is another means of foreshadowing the revelation of Armand's true racial identity. (pp. 135-36)

Armand makes a most excellent earthly representative of Satan. His treatment of his wife is an act of defiance against both God and man (not, of course, against man in Armand's artificial social environment, but as a denial of the human power of love). He shares with Satan the sin of pride: racial and aristocratic pride specifically, but also a pride in his own power to rebel against God. (p. 137)

Armand's darkness is associated with sensuality and aggressiveness, in contrast to Désirée's whiteness, which represents purity and, in spite of her marriage, inviolability and gentleness. Désirée is unmistakably Kate Chopin's version of the Pure Maiden, the Saviour Woman; she suffers at the hands of a villain to whom, for all his villainy, she is powerfully attracted. Her suffering and her death, however, seem unimportant in the end. The reader has little doubt that she will be rewarded in heaven (whence she came?), that Armand will be punished. . . . For a brief while she acts as the civilizing and humanizing consciousness for his primitive and animalistic unconscious. She provides him with a socially accepted and sanctified outlet for his brutal passions, a sexual surrogate as it were, for his will to dominate. During this brief period of marital felicity, significantly, Armand stops mistreating his slaves. But when he discovers, or thinks he discovers, that Désirée is tainted with the blackness that confirms in his mind her essential similarity to his inner sensual and aggressive self, she loses her efficacy for him as a means to grace. Marriage to her was not salvation but, in both racial and psychological terms, surrender to the self within and therefore damnation. Predictably, Armand reverts to his old ways; if anything he is more cruel to his slaves than formerly, linking them to his "betrayal" by a woman but unaware that they are projections, literally and symbolically, of the darkness that lurks within him.

Combining as it does racial themes with a transmuted seduction theme . . . , **"Désirée's Baby"** turns out to be a surprisingly rich and complex story, one of the best of its kind in American literature. (pp. 139-40)

> Robert D. Arner, "Pride and Prejudice: Kate Chopin's 'Desiree's Baby'," in The Mississippi Quarterly (copyright 1972 Mississippi State University), Vol. 25, No. 2, Spring, 1972, pp. 131-40.

CYNTHIA GRIFFIN WOLFF (essay date 1973)

[The] contemporary readings of [Kate Chopin's *The Awakening*] which stress Edna's position as a victim of society's standards do not capture its power; for although it is not a great novel—perhaps it is even a greatly flawed novel because of the elusiveness of its focus—reading it can be a devastating and unforgettable experience. And such an experience can simply not grow out of a work whose importance lies in the fact that it anticipates Lawrence or that it is a sort of American *Madame Bovary*. Such evaluations are diminishing. The importance of Chopin's work does not lie in its anticipation of "the woman question" or of any other question; it derives from its ruthless fidelity to the disintegration of Edna's character. Edna, in turn, interests us not because she is "a woman," the implication being that her experience is principally important because it might stand for that of any other woman. Quite the contrary; she interests us because she is human—because she fails in ways which beckon seductively to all of us. (p. 450)

It is difficult to define Edna's character as it might have existed before we meet her in the novel, for even at its opening such stability as she may have had has already been disrupted. We do learn something of her background. She is the middle child of an ambiguously religious family. "She comes of sound old Presbyterian Kentucky stock. The old gentleman, her father, I have heard, used to atone for his weekday sins with his Sunday devotions.". . . The family has two faces, then: it "sins" (during the week) with its racing and landgrabbing; and it "atones" (on Sundays) with pious condemnations. . . . Edna, caught between the two extremes, can live comfortably with neither portion of the family's double standard; instead she tries to evolve a habit or manner which will accommodate both.

The attempt to internalize this contradiction combines with other of Edna's psychic needs to produce an "identity" which is predicated on the conscious process of concealment. In some sense there are two Ednas: "At a very early period she had apprehended instinctively the dual life—that outward existence which conforms, the inward life which questions."

. . . Therefore she is very little open to sustained emotional relationships because those elements of character which she might want to call her "real" self must remain hidden, revealed only to herself. . . . Not that Edna *wants* to be so entirely alone. On the contrary, the cool distancing tone of her "visible" character conceals an ardent yearning for intensity, for passion. So Edna provides the passion she needs in the only manner which seems safely available to her— through daydreaming. (pp. 450-51)

Given the apparent terror which genuine emotional involvement inspires in Edna, her marriage to a man like Léonce Pontellier is no accident. No one would call him remarkable; most readers might think him dull, insensitive, unperceptive, even callous. Certainly he is an essentially prosaic man. If one assumed that marriage was to be an intimate affair of deep understanding, all of these qualities would condemn Léonce. Yet for Edna they are the very qualities which recommend him. . . .

The marriage to such a man as Léonce was, then, a defensive maneuver designed to maintain the integrity of the two "selves" that formed her character and to reinforce the distance between them. Her outer self was confirmed by the entirely conventional marriage while her inner self was safe— known only to Edna. An intuitive man, a sensitive husband, might threaten it; a husband who evoked passion from her might lure the hidden self into the open, tempting Edna to attach her emotions to flesh and blood rather than phantoms. Léonce is neither, and their union ensures the secret safety of Edna's "real" self. (p. 452)

It is hard to cast such an ultimately insignificant man [as Léonce] in the role of villain—compared with a man like Soames Forsyte or with some of the more brutal husbands in Chopin's short stories, Léonce is a slender vehicle to carry the weight of society's repression of women. Yet Edna sees herself as his possession, even as she sees herself the prisoner of her children's demands. . . .

Possession, as descriptive of any intense emotional involvement, is both tempting and terrifying. To yield to possession is to become engulfed, to be nothing. (p. 454)

One solution for the problem [of possession and self-preservation] Edna faces would be to formulate a way to have her relationship with Robert without ever *really* having it. Temporarily she does effect such a solution, and she does so in two ways. First, while she is at Grand Isle, she systematically denies the possibility of an adult relationship with him; this denial takes the form of her engulfing him "possessing" him, perhaps) by a kind of incorporation of his personality into her own. . . . Only after he has left can she safely *feel* the intensity of passion that later comes to be associated with him; and she can do so because once physically absent, he can be made magically present as a phantom, an object in her own imagination, a figure which is now truly a part of herself. . . .

[She] evolves a second solution by which she can have a relationship with Robert without being forced to fuse the outer and the inner "selves" that comprise her identity. This stratagem is the affair with Arobin. She can respond sensually to the kiss which initiates their relationship precisely because she has no feeling for him. Her feelings are fixed safely on the *image* of Robert. . . . (p. 455)

Robert's return and his sensuous awakening to her kiss . . . precipitates the final crisis from which she must flee. She cannot, in the end, yield her "self" to the insistence of his passionate plea to stay; and his own subsequent flight destroys the fantasy lover as well. Both of Edna's selves are truly betrayed and barren, and she retrenches in the only manner familiar to her, that of a final and ultimate withdrawal. (p. 456)

One wonders to what extent Edna's fate might have been different if Robert had remained. Momentarily, at least, he might have roused her from her despondency by offering not ecstasy but at least partial satisfaction. The fundamental problem would have remained, however. Life offers only partial pleasures, and individuated experience.

Thus Edna's final act of destruction has a quality of uncompromising sensuous fulfillment as well. It is her answer to the inadequacies of life, a literal denial and reversal of the birth trauma she has just witnessed, a stripping away of adulthood, of limitation, of consciousness itself. If life cannot offer fulfillment of her dream of fusion, then the ecstasy of death is preferable to the relinquishing of that dream. So Edna goes to the sea.... She is a child, an infant again. "How strange and awful it seemed to stand naked under the sky! how delicious! She felt like some new-born creature, opening its eyes in a familiar world that it had never known." ... And with her final act Edna completes the regression, back beyond childhood, back into time eternal. (p. 471)

> *Cynthia Griffin Wolff, "Thanatos and Eros: Kate Chopin's 'The Awakening'," in American Quarterly (copyright, October, 1973 Trustees of the University of Pennsylvania), Vol. XXV, No. 4, October, 1973, pp. 449-71.*

BERT BENDER (essay date 1974)

If she is mentioned at all, Kate Chopin is safely categorized in literary histories as a local colorist. Some of her own titles [**"Bayou Folk,"** and **"A Night in Acadie"** and that of her first biography (**"Kate Chopin and Her Creole Stories"**)] . . . imply that the classification may be just. But it is bitterly ironic that she should be so classified; for her fiction probes far more deeply into human nature than "local color" implies, and her entire career represents a struggle to break through restricting classifications. Her works, themselves, were the ultimate breakthrough: in the face of genteel traditions of the 1890's, she wrote of people who break free from traditional moral and social structures to experience and express socially unacceptable feelings. Her stories are lyric celebrations of life. In them, a character's feelings are associated with natural "songs" and "voices" or with images of objects and events in nature. In these celebrations, typically, a character awakens to ecstatic knowledge of his own sexual being; or a wife, having become aware that she resents the restricting presence of the husband and children whom she nevertheless loves, experiences at least fleeting moments of ecstatic freedom.

Such sentiments were disturbing to American readers at the turn of the century. As two other minority writers, Paul Laurence Dunbar and Charles Chesnutt, found, the public preferred harmless dialect stories to serious fiction of protest. Like them, Kate Chopin found that her stories of the quaint life on the Louisiana bayous were more acceptable than the more serious and searching fiction that she dared to write during the last part of her career. Her last novel, **"The Awakening"**. . ., shocked many of its reviewers (one said that it was "too strong drink for moral babes, and should be

labeled 'poison'"), and others simply refused to review it at all. (pp. 257-58)

The best of Kate Chopin's stories are thematically as unconventional as **"The Awakening."** And—at a time when American short fiction was dominated by formal prescriptions for what Brander Matthews called the "Short-story," her lyrical stories were unconventional in their form. Toward the end of the nineteenth century, the production of the "Short-story" in America was a substantial industry. In a perversion of Poe's idea that composition should proceed "with the precision and rigid consequence of a mathematical problem," the "Short-story" was mass-produced; its essential element was plot, and it culminated in O. Henry's stories with snap endings. (p. 259)

The lyrical voice embodied in Kate Chopin's short fictions is the antithesis of both the formal rigidity and the genteel, comic tone of the "Short-story." Variations on the theme of awakening to ecstatic self-realization, her stories are fictional songs of the self. In them, she affirms aspects of the self that conventions denied, affirms them in a way that resembles Whitman when he sings approvingly of "forbidden voices, / Voices of sexes and lusts." But her stories do not locate, as *Leaves of Grass* does, a mythic self as the synthetic, integrating center of a larger democratic context. The characters depicted in her fictions are tragically cut off from their social surroundings, because, like D. H. Lawrence's characters, their awakened identities are at odds with social conventions. The original title of *"The Awakening"* was "A Solitary Soul," and it suggests that for Kate Chopin, the freedom and ecstasy of self-affirmation are necessarily accompanied by isolation. Her characters transcend their socially limited selves by awakening to and affirming impulses that are unacceptable by convention. (pp. 259-60)

Many of her characters are like the typical nineteenth-century romantic characters whose impulsive, unmediated awareness is approvingly opposed to traditional learning and knowledge from books. (p. 260)

The central figure in the story **"A Vocation and a Voice"** . . . is a youth who frees himself from the restricting conventions of work and orthodox religion to achieve a knowledge of his intuitive, animal self. The mythic dimension of his quest for self-knowledge is evident in the first words of the story when he asks, trying to find his way back to his place of work, "Is this Adams Avenue?" Told that he is in "Woodland Park," he begins to wonder and to relish his freedom in nature. He lapses into a "blessed state of tranquility and contemplation" and realizes repeatedly how good it is "to be out in the open air": "He belonged under God's sky in the free and open air." But in meeting the girl Suzima, a travelling fortune teller, he comes to feel the disturbing excitement of sexual arousal. . . ."... He shrank from trusting himself with this being alone. His soul turned toward the refuge of spiritual help, and he prayed to God and the saints and the Virgin Mary to save him and to direct him." He finds refuge from his frightening self-knowledge in a monastery, where symbolically he is granted permission "to build, with his own hands, a solid stone wall around the 'Refuge.'" Inevitably, though, while working one day "out in the open air," he succumbs to his animal impulses. He suddenly stops his work on the wall and lifts "his head with the mute quivering attention of some animal in the forest, startled at the scent of approaching danger." Having sensed the presence of Suzima, he comes finally to a full knowledge of himself:

"He knew that he had pulses, for they were clamoring, and flesh, for it tingled and burned as if pricked with nettles."

The opposed forces in this story are, on the one hand, work, conventionality, orthodox religion, and the will; and on the other hand, idleness, unconventionality, a kind of pantheistic religion, and impulsiveness: or, as in the title of the story, **"A Vocation and a Voice."** For the natural impulses that work on the youth are represented primarily by Suzima's voice, the tracing and echoing of which embody the lyric quality of the story. The lull of her voice awakens in the youth the lull and hum of his own soul's voice, and the repeated sounding of Suzima's voice reminds the reader that in Kate Chopin's world, the throb of man's natural but often unrecognized impulses is as beautifully mysterious as D. H. Lawrence's blood consciousness. (pp. 260-61)

Like the men in . . . [her stories], Kate Chopin's women must struggle to know and accept themselves, but their predicament is more excruciating because of what she called the "matrimonial yoke." Her stories openly criticize the unnaturalness of institutionalized marriage, but her characters do not contend with marriage in a uniform way. Some accept it after considerable anguish; some flee from it. . . , and some manage to find illicit but naturally innocent nourishment outside of the marriage. Regardless of the outcome, the predicament of the lonely, restricted women in these stories is like that of the lyric poet who in his loneliness turns his back to his audience. And in each case, Kate Chopin consoles herself by lyrically associating her character's disruptive impulses with such natural and sanctifying impulses as a bird's song or a flower's blossoming.

"Athénaise" . . . is the story of a girl who, having yielded to custom by marrying prematurely, finds the "galling matrimonial yoke" unbearable. Incapable of either "patient resignation," a talent born in the souls of many women" or of "philosophical resignation," she is given to a kind of innocent rebelliousness. Her husband, Cazeau, is not unusually abusive; it is simply that she has married before having come naturally to know herself. . . . That there is no *reason* for her discomfort in her marriage merely adds to the exasperation of her husband and her father. Only her brother understands, for—since he has no authority over her—they relate freely, albeit with incestuous overtones. . . . The institution of marriage, itself, is oppressive to her—the simple fact that her husband (as his name suggests) is head of the household. . . . Even though Cazeau is not harshly authoritative, he has, as Athénaise's father happily realizes, "a master hand, a strong will that compels obedience." And the nature of their relationship (and of marriage in general for Kate Chopin) is suggested by the repeated mention of Cazeau's spurs and by a scene in which the institutions of slavery and marriage are symbolically linked. (pp. 262-63)

Athénaise finally does come to herself when, alone in a New Orleans boarding house, she has time and freedom. She is helped to her self-knowledge by the gentle wisdom of a newspaperman who, though he woos her, knows that he has "no right to her" until she wants him. Ironically, his very gentleness works against him and for Athénaise, for she "could not fancy him loving anyone passionately, rudely, offensively, as Cazeau loved her." So in a way she is prepared for the miraculous change that comes over her "as the song to the bird, the perfume and color to the flower": she is stunned to learn from a black maid that she is pregnant, and,

breathing unevenly, she begins to feel an immediate change in herself. . . . (p. 263)

Athénaise's awakening to an ecstatic knowledge and acceptance of her biological destiny is by no means Kate Chopin's general solution for woman's anxieties. Athénaise's nervous and impulsive discomfort with the lack of freedom in marriage is, however, for Chopin, a general condition in the institution; and Athénaise's salvation in pregnancy is certainly the most socially acceptable of Kate Chopin's solutions to the problem. In other stories, some of which were not published during her lifetime, she writes more openly and perhaps more truthfully of socially unacceptable feelings about marriage and of equally unconventional developments from these feelings. (p. 264)

["**The Storm**"] is another treatment of unconventional, impulsive behavior in marriage; and again, the impulses are associated with (and sanctioned by) larger impulses in nature—with the storm of the title. An actual storm strands Calixta's husband and son while they are away to town, and it parallels a "storm" of sexual energy that brings Calixta together with Alcée Laballiére, a former suitor who in passing by seeks shelter from the storm. With its 1,800 words, the story moves with the pace and rhythm of a natural change of weather. . . .

There is no suggestion that the marriage of Calixta and Bobinôt is in any way unhappy. Bobinôt is gentle and unauthoritative. . . . When Bobinôt and Bibi arrive home after the storm, the return is genuinely joyful for all three; there are kisses, exclamations of relieved concern. . . . (p. 265)

Calixta's adulterous encounter had been accidental and innocent. It is simply that mysterious natural forces larger than the individuals or the marriage institution have worked to refresh all the parties of both marriages, Laballiére's as well as Calixta's. Kate Chopin's principle here, as usual, is that freedom nourishes. . . . **"The Storm"** is remarkable not only for the freedom it asserts in the face of the suffocating conventionality of the 1890's, but for the lyrical ease with which it unites human and universal rhythms to celebrate "the procreative urge of the world." The story realizes Kate Chopin's dream of woman's renewed birthright for passionate self-fulfillment. But surely it is a tragic comment on her life and work that only recently—with a gradual but widespreading awakening of woman's consciousness, nearly three-quarters of a century after her death—has our culture been prepared to see Kate Chopin's dreams as anything but nightmares. (pp. 265-66)

Bert Bender, "Kate Chopin's Lyrical Short Stories," in Studies in Short Fiction *(copyright 1974 by Newberry College), Vol. XI, No. 3, Summer, 1974, pp. 257-66.*

CARLEY REES BOGARAD (essay date 1977)

[Kate Chopin's *The Awakening*] presents the basic conflict in the *Bildungsroman* of the twentieth century: the heroine experiences sexual initiation in a struggle for self-assertion and identity. As a consequence of growth, the central character—almost always an aspiring artist—becomes profoundly alienated from traditional roles required by family, country, church, or other social institutions and is unable to reconcile the desire for connection with others with the need for self-expression. In novels written by men the hero finally chooses an apostasy which promises both personal and artistic fulfillment. . . . Almost always in novels written by women, however, the same struggle ends in madness or suicide. This significant difference between male and female images in literature reflects and reinforces the cultural roles which men and women assume. . . . Kate Chopin's *The Awakening*, though placed in the highly structured New Orleans' Creole Society at the turn of the century, is still the clearest statement of the feminine dilemma that we have. I contend that it is an early and central statement of a developing twentieth century literary tradition which gives apt phenomenological description to female experience and presents a break from the male tradition which Lawrence and Joyce, among others, have defined. (p. 15)

Before the republication of the novel [in 1963], critics viewed Edna Pontellier as a woman, like Emma Bovary, who gets caught in a web of romantic illusion which she has spun for herself. Consequently, they argued that she should pay for her sins with her life; for she fails both her family and her society. . . . I would describe *The Awakening* in diametrically opposite terms. (pp. 15-16)

Even though Kate Chopin was forced to renounce her positive attitudes toward her novel and for Edna specifically, we can now see that she intended Edna as a courageous woman who wants both union and freedom and gets crushed in a lonely effort to be lover and artist. . . . What remains to be understood now is the exact nature of Edna's self-discovery and the motivations for her final defeat.

I want to argue that Edna's awakening is a double one. The first is her awareness that she wants autonomy as a human being. . . . At the same time, however, she also conceives of a kind of union with a lover that would provide emotional connection and intimacy and permit external validation in support of her search for an authentic self. This initial awakening takes the form of a growing awareness of the conflict between her life as a conventional wife and mother and her emergent sense of self, and its consequences are rebellion and hope because she conceives of a choice. However, at the point of Edna's move to the Pigeon House a second awakening begins; and its consequences are despair and death. At first her decision to reject her traditional marriage seems to free her to love another and to be loved in return. However, her candidates for lovers are bound by the same categories she seeks to reject. Arobin clearly adheres to the double standard and Robert seeks to save her honor by leaving her. Since she is defining not only a new self, but also a realization of what is possible to her through living as an autonomous person, she is again rebuffed. (pp. 16-17)

At first Edna's decision to begin a new life as artist seems to free her, but she learns that she cannot be both a sexual person and a successful person.

Edna realizes that the human possibilities opening to her ought to permit a reconciliation of the contradiction that she exists as an "either-or": either self or other, lover or artist, lover or wife, angel or whore. However, the men she meets, upon whom she becomes emotionally dependent for her sense of herself as lover, themselves reimpose the conflict. Thus, the second awakening is the knowledge that the first awakening is illusory—at the least, forever elusive, that the radical choice she has conceived is untenable and that she is unwilling to compromise, either through isolation as Mlle. Reisz does or through connection as Adele Ratignolle does. Therefore, her only resolution is suicide.

Edna Pontellier begins her awakening at Grand Isle during the summer of her twenty-eighth year. At that time she has already been married for ten years, and she has two children. This situation is very different from male characters in novels of development, for they are almost always unmarried, and they never have to face the complications of marriage and parenthood in the process of achieving self-determination. (p. 17)

[If we see Edna] as a woman who has held her feelings in check for twenty-eight years, who has chosen friends and a husband who have reinforced her reticence, then we can understand her ripeness and intensity when she does begin to allow herself to feel and to act on those feelings. We can also understand her vulnerability. On the one hand, her reserve is a strength because she is not accustomed to have others affirm her and this provides a base for self-determination. On the other hand, because she has lived so long without real warmth and connection with others, she is unable to conceive of giving up the desire for community once she opens to it.

Edna's first real moment of openness comes during her walk to the beach with Adele Ratignolle. . . . When she touches Edna as they sit on the beach, Edna suddenly opens and begins to talk of her childhood "sea of grass" memories. . . . Edna's first awakening is two-fold: she experiences personal rebirth, and she opens to others. For the first time, she risks genuine connection. Strange that Adele who represents all that Edna is trying to rebel against—the oppression of having her life defined by her husband and children—should be the one who gives her the first real moment of liberation. Adele serves both as contrast and catalyst. She understands Edna well enough to reach her deepest feelings, to warn Robert to be careful, and to support her efforts to become an artist; but she does not understand well enough to encourage Edna's actions which run counter to her own presuppositions about a home-centered life.

Edna Pontellier's second moment of emotional release comes from the music of Mlle. Reisz. An unpleasant, quirky, spirited woman, Mlle. Reisz knows that Edna is the only person on Grand Isle who understands and appreciates her music. Therefore, she plays only for Edna who responds to the music with direct intensity. (pp. 18-19)

The "mystic moon" swim suggested by Robert is the central event in Edna's emotional growth. Touched by the music and by Robert's presence, she finally learns to swim, an art she has longed to master. Like the bird/flying images in the novel, swimming also represents rebirth, freedom, and wholeness to Edna—it requires overcoming the split she feels between her mind and her body, between thought and feeling, between conception and acts. (p. 19)

The union of body and soul that comes with her oneness with the sea gives Edna courage and a sense of independence; and her dormant sexuality is finally awakened when she feels the power of her own body. Finally she permits herself to acknowledge her attraction to Robert. (p. 20)

Her first effort to assert herself, her first act of rebellion is to refuse to make love to her husband for whom she has never felt desire. This action, I think, shows integrity; finally she begins to connect idea and feeling; and she is unwilling to violate herself or another person by doing something she does not feel.

Edna's constructive efforts to open herself to others with honest emotion prove that the comparisons made by critics to Emma Bovary have distorted our view of Edna's awakening. Too much emphasis has been placed on her sexual experience and not enough attention has been paid to her other efforts to become a person in her own right. . . . To assume that the expectation of loving someone who returns that love is a belief in "great romantic passion" is the ultimate cynicism. Edna's desire for the first time in her life is directed at someone who returns it and who has been fulfilling her emotional needs. She finally has evidence from the way Robert has been treating her and from her own emerging sense of self that she might choose to live in a more meaningful, constructive and active way. She does not lose her sense of responsibility; she redefines it.

Unfortunately, Robert cannot fully return the love which Edna gives him. Creole, with a strong sense of honor and duty, Robert feels free to love Edna only when there is no risk involved. . . . He loves Edna; but given the narrow confines of his social code, he cannot conceive of consummating that love. Robert is clearly not a courageous person; Edna is. (pp. 20-1)

[Just] as Edna develops a new sense of sexual awareness and integrity when she refuses to sleep with her husband, she also changes her social responsibilities—I think the change is constructive. First, she decides to become a serious artist. Since her painting fulfills her need for creative expression and since the sale of her sketches helps her to become economically independent, this decision is wise. (p. 22)

Kate Chopin obviously realized that women have difficulty becoming professional artists; yet she characterizes two women in her novel who manage to receive recognition for their achievements. Like Edna, Mlle. Reisz achieves independence through her art. But her freedom is not without a price. As a pianist, she is seen as a performer of great excellence. As a person, she is seen as an eccentric, unpleasant "old maid." The presuppositions behind her isolation are apparent: 1) She is a pianist because she is unsuitable as a mate. Any woman should choose love instead of artistic expression. 2) The only way to be a true artist is to give oneself totally to Art. . . . Mlle. Reisz embodies all of the myths we have created about art and artists—myths which have excluded women or forced them to choose between art and connection with others—like Mlle. Reisz and Lily Briscoe in Virginia Woolf's *To the Lighthouse*. Edna attempts to demystify all of these myths, and this struggle is partially responsible for her final defeat.

As a contrast to Mlle. Reisz, Adele Ratignolle represents another way which women have succumbed to myths about the expression of their creativity. . . . Her talent is only important to her in the context of her roles of wife and mother. She has no way of conceiving of herself as a separate person— indeed, she rarely is a separate person because she is always pregnant. (pp. 22-3)

[Neither Adele nor] Mlle. Reisz provide an adequate model for Edna. Because she is in the midst of a total awakening, she cannot accept a view of art or self as isolating and consuming. The new life energy which gives her motivation and courage to paint is the same energy which propels her into the world of feeling; she needs to be both whole and connected with others. Thus, she is an artist and woman in a society with no adequate models to follow. Yet she manages

to conceive of a way of life which would reconcile the contradictions. This is the completion of the first awakening. (p. 23)

[When Edna kisses Alcée Arobin] she has an insight about sexuality—she realizes that sex and love can be separated. Until she meets Robert, she has repressed her sexual responses or lived them in fantasy; her love for him brings her the first open and total feeling of her life. Arobin, who she knows is a man-about-town, rekindles the desire which emerged the night she learned to swim. . . . The explosion of life energy which she feels is triggered by the release of her sexuality; she begins to hope that she might have her own physical and emotional needs met for the first time.

However, when she kisses Alcée Arobin, she initiates a new fragmentation of her being. She separates her sexual need from her feelings for Robert in order to have an outlet for all her pent-up desire. (p. 24)

Originally Edna chooses to be wife and mother at the expense of identity and real love. Her relationship with Arobin represents another kind of denial—she chooses sexual connection at the expense of identity and real love. Either way she has no opportunity to be free or whole. Because she does not understand that her affair with Arobin is not and cannot be emotionally satisfying, depression continues to plague her. . . . Because she is unable to identify her pain, she keeps searching for ways to express herself. She remains unsatisfied because all of the choices available to her are destructive. (pp. 24-5)

By the time she decides to move out of Pontellier's house, she has already begun to fragment herself sexually. Therefore, her chances for success are diminished before she starts her new life. The dinner party is a central symbolization of the danger. The decor of red and gold represents the lush sensuality which has awakened in Edna and which will split her from her love for Robert. . . . [Edna] had hoped that her friends would help her move with strength and happiness; instead she feels alienated and alone. The group of people she has invited form an odd company, and no one really connects with anyone else. The party is a disaster; a shadow on her present, a bitter omen for the future. Here begins the second awakening.

Edna's belief that she can define an authentic self and love another in support of that definition begins to crumble. Edna enjoys the company of Arobin because he is a charming man, attentive, amusing, a person of the world. He is a sexual partner who does not ask for, expect, or give love. Consequently, Edna need not feel that she is compromising him because she loves another. What she slowly discovers is that there is no way to separate what the body does from what the mind or heart is feeling without creating a violation of self. . . . In reality, the men in her life split her—Robert sees her as the angel, and Alcée sees her as the whore. (p. 25)

[Because Edna] has cast aside traditional roles and broken Creole social and religious custom in order to define herself, she cannot find others who understand and support her. She has chosen not to live for others, but she refuses to choose to live without others. She views such isolation as an unacceptable compromise of her emotional needs.

These iconoclastic actions place Edna on the periphery of her society. Robert leaves to save her; Léonce is only interested in saving face; her children are visiting their grandmother; Adele only offers limited and traditional answers to her problems; Mlle. Reisz does not know how to be intimate except through music; and Arobin cannot in some final measure be trusted.

When Robert returns, he provides the one hope she has for real connection in the world. Her love for him has helped to get her through the profound loneliness inherent in her radical departures from Creole life. Yet Robert, whose social and personal belief is Creole, can hardly be expected to choose Edna. He loves and wants Edna, but he cannot bring himself to join her in rebellion against the sacrament of marriage. Worse than that, he does not understand her. . . . Robert cannot understand or believe that she can assume power over her own life. When Edna finally admits that her first assessment of Robert's ability to love and accept her as an autonomous person is mistaken, the second awakening is complete. (p. 26)

When Edna concedes to herself that she cannot achieve either autonomy or connection with others, she surrenders and stops struggling. "Nor was there hope when she awoke in the morning." . . . When she moves from what Chopin calls "despondency" to indifference, her life takes on a new feeling of unreality. She has awakened to consciousness from "a life long dream" only to find her reality a nightmare. Consequently, she finally retreats from her second conscious awakening—first through withdrawal and then through suicide. Because she is so totally alone at the end, because no one understands her desire to redefine herself outside of traditional societal roles for women, because no one is meeting her newly felt needs, because she is unwilling to compromise, because she has not yet had time to develop inner resources to sustain her through such alienation, she is defeated and returns to the womb-like embrace of the sea, "the consummation of her passion." (pp. 27-8)

What really are her alternatives in her historical moment? Chopin has shown the only ones available—the consuming life of Adele Ratignolle or the lonely existence of Mlle. Reisz. For Edna these choices are equally impossible; they are compromises of the radical vision she has conceived. She has not the patience or masochism for the former or the ascetic discipline for the latter. In male novels of development the hero is expected to make the stoic choice which Mlle. Reisz has accepted; in female novels of development the heroine is expected to come to her senses and return to the cycle of marriage and motherhood which she has rejected. Edna will choose neither of these alternatives, and that is precisely the point of book. (p. 28)

> *Carley Rees Bogarad "'The Awakening': A Refusal to Compromise," in* The University of Michigan Papers in Women's Studies *(copyright © 1977 Women's Studies Program, The University of Michigan, Ann Arbor), Vol. II, No. 3, 1977, pp. 15-31.*

ADDITIONAL BIBLIOGRAPHY

Allen, Priscilla. "Old Critics and New: The Treatment of Chopin's *The Awakening.*" In *The Authority of Experience: Essays in Feminist Criticism,* edited by Arlyn Diamond and Lee R. Edwards, pp. 224-38. Amherst: The University of Massachusetts Press, 1977.
>   Assesses the changing critical interpretations of *The Awakening* since its publication, with particular emphasis on modern evaluations.

Arner, Robert D. "Kate Chopin's Realism: 'At the 'Cadian Ball' and 'The Storm'." *The Markham Review* 2, No. 2 (February 1970): 1-4.
>   Traces the development of Chopin's realism through a comparison of "At the 'Cadian Ball'" and "The Storm."

Fletcher, Marie. "The Southern Woman in the Fiction of Kate Chopin." *Louisiana History* VII, No. 2 (Spring 1966): 117-32.
>   Examines the progression of Chopin's fictional interpretation of southern womanhood.

Lattin, Patricia Hopkins. "Kate Chopin's Repeating Characters." *The Mississippi Quarterly* XXXIII, No. 1 (Winter 1979-80): 19-37.
>   Traces the recurrence of three families throughout Chopin's fiction. Lattin argues that this repetition contributes to the complexity and sophistication of Chopin's art.

May, John R. "Local Color in *The Awakening.*" *The Southern Review* VI, No. 4 (Autumn 1970): 1031-40.
>   Examines the effect of the New Orleans environment on Edna Pontellier, the protagonist of *The Awakening.*

Quinn, Arthur Hobson. "Place and Race in American Fiction." In his *American Fiction: An Historical and Critical Survey,* pp. 323-73. New York: D. Appleton-Century Co., 1936.*
>   A brief discussion of Chopin's fictional rendering of Creole society and individuals.

Rocks, James E. "Kate Chopin's Ironic Vision." *Louisiana Review* 1, No. 2 (Winter 1972): 110-20.
>   A study of Chopin's literary methods and themes, focusing on the irony present in her authorial objectivity.

Rosen, Kenneth M. "Kate Chopin's *The Awakening:* Ambiguity as Art." *Journal of American Studies* 5, No. 2 (August 1971): 197-99.
>   Discusses the ambiguity inherent in the character of Edna Pontellier.

Schuyler, William. "Kate Chopin." *The Writer* VII, No. 8 (August 1894): 115-17.
>   An early biographical sketch which reflects the contemporary regard for Chopin and her work.

Seyersted, Per. Introduction to *The Storm and Other Stories,* by Kate Chopin, pp. 7-18. New York: The Feminist Press, 1974.
>   A concise overview of Chopin's life and literary career.

Stafford, Jean. "Sensuous Women." *The New York Review of Books* XVII, No. 4 (23 September 1971): 33-5.
>   A review of Per Seyersted's critical biography, *Kate Chopin,* and *The Complete Works of Kate Chopin.*

(Sidonie-Gabrielle) Colette

1873-1954

French novelist, short story writer, and journalist.

Colette is recognized as one of France's leading twentieth-century novelists. Critics praise her warm, subjective style, her keen observation of nature, and the lyrical beauty of her prose. The central theme in much of her work is the reconciliation of women's struggle for independence with the insistent demands of physical passion. Many of her characters yearn to abandon the conflicts of adult life to return to the protected innocence of childhood.

The vicissitudes of Colette's life are mirrored in her novels and short stories. She spent an idyllic childhood in the region of Burgundy where her mother instilled in her a lifelong love for the countryside. At the age of twenty she married a much older hack writer, Henry Gouthier-Villars, who introduced her to the enervating decadence of the Paris demimonde. Under her husband's insistence she began to record her memories of her childhood and school days. The results were the "Claudine" series. The first, *Claudine à l'école* (*Claudine at School*), which her husband published under his pen name, "Willy," enjoyed tremendous popular success. After divorcing Gouthier-Villars, Colette embarked on a career as a music hall dancer and mime. During her second marriage, she devoted her full energies to her literary career, firmly establishing herself in French letters. Having gained the respect of her contemporaries, she was elected to the prestigious *Académie Royale Belge* and *Académie Goncourt*.

Critics generally divide Colette's work into four phases: the "Claudine" novels; novels dealing with life in the theater; novels of love; and, toward the end of her career, her touching and sensitive reminiscences of her youth and family. Although many critics consider the "Claudine" novels to be little better than pot-boilers, they still praise her fluid prose style and sensitive portrayal of character. Her work of this period also reveals her special affinity to nature and an almost mystic understanding of animals. After the "Claudine" novels, Colette abandoned the cheap titillation Gouthier-Villars had encouraged and wrote *La vagabonde* (*The Vagabond*), a novel that skillfully evokes the seedy atmosphere of backstage life, and the spiritual torment of a young actress's search for dignity and self-reliance. All of the novels of the subsequent theatrical cycle explore the problems inherent in a woman's pursuit of self-realization.

The subject of Colette's third phase is love and its politics. Thus in *Chéri* (*Chéri*) and *La fin de Chéri* (*The Last of Chéri*), considered the masterpieces of this period, Colette contrasts the dissolution of a pampered young gigolo, Chéri, with the growth and self-acceptance of his lover, Léa, a rich middle-aged cocotte. In *The Last of Chéri*, Cheri's inability to cope with the responsibilities of life away from Léa leads to his nihilism and suicide, while Léa's withdrawal from men and sex results in deep internal peace. As if to echo the serenity Léa found late in life, Colette became increasingly concerned with reenacting scenes from her childhood. Many critics judge the novels of this, her last period, to be her finest achievements. In her rapturous descriptions of plants and animals in *La*

The Bettmann Archive

Maison de Claudine (*My Mother's House*), and in her loving portrait of her mother in *Sido* (*Sido*), Colette idealizes childhood and nature, which to her represent primordial innocence and purity.

Although some critics regard her work as naive and sentimental, the excellence of her style, her fresh use of metaphor, and her intensity of feeling have earned Colette an esteemed place in French literature.

(See also *TCLC*, Vol. 1)

PRINCIPAL WORKS

Claudine à l'école (novel) 1900
 [*Claudine at School*, 1930]
Claudine à Paris (novel) 1901
 [*Claudine in Paris*, 1958]
Claudine en ménage (novel) 1902
 [*The Indulgent Husband*, 1935; also published as
 Claudine Married, 1960]
Claudine s'en va (novel) 1903
 [*The Innocent Wife*, 1934; published in England as
 Claudine and Annie, 1962]

L'ingénue libertine (novel) 1909
   [*The Gentle Libertine*, 1931; also published as *The Innocent Libertine*, 1961]
La vagabonde (novel) 1910
   [*The Vagabond*, 1954]
L'entrave (novel) 1913
   [*Recaptured*, 1931; published in England as *The Shackle*, 1964]
Mitsou (novel) 1919
   [*Mitsou*, 1930]
Chéri (novel) 1920
   [*Chéri*, 1929]
La maison de Claudine (autobiographical novel) 1922
   [*My Mother's House*, 1953]
La fin de Chéri (novel) 1926
   [*The Last of Chéri*, 1932]
La naissance du jour (autobiographical novel) 1928
   [*Break of Day*, 1961]
La seconde (novel) 1929
   [*The Other One*, 1931]
Sido (autobiographical novel) 1929
   [*Sido*, 1953]
La chatte (novel) 1933
   [*The Cat*, 1936]
Duo (novel) 1934
   [*Duo*, 1935; published in England as *The Married Lover*, 1935]
Gigi (novel) 1944
   [*Gigi*, 1952]
Le fanal bleu (diaries) 1949
   [*The Blue Lantern*, 1963]
Earthly Paradise (autobiographical writings) 1966
Letters from Colette (letters) 1980

RICHARD HAYES (essay date 1952)

[Far] more significant than any question of social or intellectual range is [Colette's] greatest gift: the ability to create parables of experience with the conciseness, the exact correspondence of image and idea, of the finest poetry. Nothing will suffice for her but the total imaginative act; the breath of perfection is on all her work.

What Colette can do in the middle register of her art is displayed most brilliantly in *Chéri*, a *nouvelle* of some hundred odd pages, which is essentially an extended metaphor of human love, perhaps the most exhaustive and remarkable in contemporary literature.

Against a background of the Parisian *demi-monde*, peopled by rapacious discarded courtesans who have relinquished beauty but not their fierce and tensile hold on life, she poses the figures of her tragedy: Léa de Lonval, blonde and sexually opulent, with her magnificent, lustrous arms ("what lovely handles for such an old urn"), somehow of a finer grain and more generous spirit than the others, but like them, aging, and bound to the intolerable daily judgment of the mirror; and Chéri, handsome and spoiled—stunted, rather—breathing forth "the melancholy of perfect things."

Léa takes Chéri in self indulgence, with full knowledge that the love affair can be sustained only a few years; but when she must release him to the inevitable, well-arranged marriage, it is more terrible for her than ever she could have imagined. (pp. 536-37)

In *Chéri*, and particularly its sequel [*The Last of Chéri*], Colette moves throughout on two levels of absolutely controlled, totally disciplined meaning. There is, of course, first and foremost, the sensuous world of Colette's personal discovery. Her art is grounded in the springs of sensation; *nihil in intellectu quod non prius in sensu* might serve as her epitaph. She conveys marvelously, as no one else quite can, the turning of life, the opulence of nature, with its glory and irremediable pathos.

But this historian of fine senses is also the moralist in spite of herself; unless that paradox is grasped, it is impossible to trace her art to its secret and intimate source. *Chéri* is, to be sure, a poem of the senses, but it is also a serious study of the wound of love, "with all its intrigue, its calculated unselfishness, its passionate violence." It possesses a moral substance that is rich, complex and enigmatic. . . .

What has been gained is a morality, a whole world of obligations exceeding those of self-indulgence. When Léa, rejecting Chéri and her own last hopes of natural happiness, says to him: "If I'd really been so fine, I'd have made a man of you instead of thinking merely of the pleasure of your body and mine," she moves into the climate of sin and grief where few novelists choose to go. A kind of silence falls over the page; all that is gross and trivial drops away; we have the sense that a soul has undergone change, that some hard bit of knowledge has been gained, that a spiritual advance of permanent consequence has been made.

To Léa and Chéri, because they have loved generously, much is forgiven, but Colette never absolves them of the consequences of their actions, or of their characters. She is not deceived, nor does she deceive us, about her people. Through defiance, false pride, stubbornness, self-indulgence, they come to grief, but it is not a literary contrivance—it is the way of the world. Above all, love never saves them: it is the hardest thing of all here, the most difficult—as much a corruption as a salvation—coming in a thousand devious and treacherous disguises. Perhaps, after a point, one no longer even desires love: serenity, strength, repose—the stoic virtues—may well be what we will request in the end. (p. 537)

[Colette's] art has celebrated, as surely as any of this century, a knowledge of the world's beauty and delight; it has rendered the highest kind of justice to the life of nature, recording not only the glory, but also the taint of inadequacy, of human hopelessness, which poisons its sweetest springs. (p. 538)

Richard Hayes, "The Wisdom of Colette," in Commonweal *(copyright © 1952 Commonweal Publishing Co., Inc.), Vol. LVI, No. 22, September 5, 1952, pp. 536-38.*

JEAN COCTEAU (essay date 1956)

I insist strongly, and I can never insist enough, on the fact that the greatness of Colette is due to an inability to distinguish between good and evil which placed her in a state of innocence; it would be unworthy to substitute for this a voluntary, artificial and conventional purity totally unrelated to the terrifying purity of nature, which men destroy by the disorder of their own order and the ridiculous verdicts of their own law-courts.

I have seen Colette in pain yet refuse to take aspirins as though they were the devil's own pills, demanding that there should occur within herself, without any assistance, the mysterious mixtures and dosages of herbs and simples which the synthetic reconstitution of science can perhaps imitate but only superficially and without recreating their virtues.

Let us honour in Colette a sage who stopped her ears in order to shut out the sirens' song and refused nothing of the rich corruption of life. Like a true countrywoman she sensed that everything in nature that seems topsy-turvy possesses a secret significance and that the slightest alteration to any figure entails fatal errors in the total. . . .

I admit then that I cannot confirm the picture that people want to create, of a woman born from a cabbage, unaware of getting and spending and set in the margin of our terrible world like a small flower in a flower-bed. First of all it is important to realize that this humble flower probably has its own thoughts, and that its thoughts are perhaps different from what one might believe. Those accelerated films, which we believe to be in slow motion, have revealed that a garden engages in fierce struggles, erotic gestures and murders; if the country priest, as he waters his flowers, could observe all this at human tempo, he would take to his heels.

While admitting that Colette belongs to the animal and vegetable kingdom, it would be wrong to find a place for her in a fine, brave, motionless universe, in a false serenity of nature whose extreme slowness of movement, in comparison to our own, caused our innocent philosophers to be deceived for centuries on end.

Further, one should not confuse the protective cloud which Colette maintained round her person, like the smoke screen round warships, with the indifference of a spectator who is tired by the spectacle and falls asleep. Liveliness never left Colette's mind and there was no end to the curiosity she felt for every kind of thing, big or small. (pp. 20-1)

That inner eye, always at the service of a shameless sensibility or sensuality, freedom from all politeness and the formal dance of social life, a mania for truth at any price, even within untruth, a passion for describing oneself in minute detail and above all the rehabilitation of idleness and disorder, for fear of obeying the hypocritical rules of bourgeois respectability, an incredible mixture of sentimentality and filthy rubbish, these fragments of broken bottles planted round the mind, this careless spitting, those cigarette ends which remain alight beneath the heel that crushes them, those sentences torn up from the depths with their roots, soil and all, the declarations of love which consist of saying unpleasant things to each other, that marshy iridescence like the Venetian canals where cabbage stalks, orange peel and lovers' gondolas float along together—all that, extraordinary though it may seem, is the legacy of Colette. This conclusion makes me think of the time when these unusual combinations of words, and these images as juicy as fruit and insolent as blows put us all on a régime of cold showers. We were tempted to believe that boldness of this sort would soon cease to be bold, would acquire the period charm of 'modern-style' curves.

Embossed leather thistles, pokerwork irises, brass chestnut leaves from Maxim's, these are the decorations we imagine on the bed where Léa sips her chocolate and beaten egg-yolks, watching extremely severe elderly baronesses in impeccable dinner-jackets, with cigars in the corner of their mouths, with very large feet and hunting stocks, playing cards.

But we must not confuse a piece of furniture and the person who paints it, Gauguin's armchair and the same chair painted by Van Gogh, a concierge and the same concierge painted by Toulouse-Lautrec, a broom and Vermeer's painting of a broom. What matters is not Léa's bed, but the fact that Colette paints it, and projects it outside fashion, space and time, that it collects our wretched human mud and fashions iridescent soap bubbles from it. . . . (p. 23)

[In] Colette's famous immorality, and even because of that fresh innocence which constitutes its charm and transcends it, there lay the germ of that monstrous frankness with which our lady novelists mix the sexes. Colette was certainly the first who was not ashamed of her body, that maternal heap of entrails possessed by Rimbaud's sisters of charity and the *chercheuses de poux,* the first to model herself on nature and its countless attacks against modesty. Is she responsible for social disorder? No, and Goethe was right when he described the people who committed suicide after reading *Werther* as fools.

We should certainly honour in Colette the liberator of feminine psychology which had been caged by the scruples of the Princesse de Clèves and Madame de Chasteller, and certainly, when she renounced the pride which made these ladies value their virtue so highly, Colette made this virtue change places and opened horizons more subtle and vast than the rectangular canopy over a bed.

There is no need to whitewash Colette, because she is white. She disliked black as much as did the Impressionists, with whom she is in sympathy, although she never belonged to their group and was probably blindly indifferent to their researches. She is alone. Alone she was and alone she remains. And I emphasize this because strangely enough it was through belonging to no school and playing truant that she brought every school together. (p. 24)

Jean Cocteau, "A Speech on Colette," translated by Margaret Crosland, in London Magazine (© London Magazine 1956), *Vol. 3, No. 5, May, 1956, pp. 16-24.*

ELAINE MARKS   (essay date 1960)

Next to the narrator, "Colette," Colette's greatest literary creation is "Sido." And it is in those three works which owe their existence both to "Sido" and to "Colette" that the "Colette-Claudines" and the "Colette-Sidos," at last stripped of their fictitious trimmings, emerge as both real and mythical beings, embodying what is, at least in the western world, the very essence of childhood and motherhood. Although different in form and content, *La Maison de Claudine, Sido* and *La Naissance du Jour* are all suffused with the wisdom of "Sido," that wisdom which could only attain effective literary transposition when sufficient time had passed for Colette to begin, undisturbed, her long dialogue with her mother.

Two of Colette's major themes, childhood and the conquest of self, reach their fullest expression in these works. With Sido as the starting point, Colette attempts to explore past, present and future. Her aim would seem to be twofold: to evoke the past through the perspective of the present in *La Maison de Claudine* and *Sido;* and to foresee the future with the aid of the past in *La Naissance du Jour.* Also, however, one feels in these three works that Colette has a need for lucidity, a need to understand her mother, her past and herself, a need to commune with a presence and a world which had a certain "purity" and strength, "a world of which I have ceased to be worthy." (pp. 200-01)

La Maison de Claudine is one of the books which best convey the poetry of childhood. *Maison,* as Colette uses the word in her title, refers specially to the house itself, the large house "topped by a lofty attic," in which the narrator and her family lived. *Maison* has a broader significance, as well. It is also the family of Claudine, the *pays natal* of Claudine, the childhood of Claudine. The first appearance of "Sido" in the opening chapter, following the description of the house and the silent, invisible presence of the children, establishes between "Sido" and the house both a real and a symbolic intimacy. (p. 201)

The narrator of *La Maison de Claudine* is both the child and the woman, and because of this, there is a poetic stylization both of incident and character which attests to the dominating presence of the older, the writer Colette. (pp. 202-03)

There is no significant arrangement in the order of the stories. The narrator is ten years old in one story and fifteen in the next and then again ten or nine or eight. Each story, each short drama, illustrates, illuminates another aspect of her childhood, either her own private world of odors, colors, words and games, or the world of her family, of her village. These unrelated stories nevertheless form patterns: the repeated patterns of everyday family life, familiar patterns which make the period of childhood seem eternal. The narrator is the major link between these stories. Much of the poetry of *La Maison de Claudine* owes its origin to the narrator's double perspective: sometimes completely involved in the past, reliving the incident she is relating as if it were actually occurring; sometimes stepping out of the story to comment on the past from the point of view of the present. There is also a constant movement from the third person to the first, as the ubiquitous narrator becomes a character in her story. Colette employs, in *La Maison de Claudine,* the techniques of both her first-person and her third-person writings.

More than in the other short stories, however, the density of Colette's prose, the extreme degree of condensation, make the small world of *La Maison de Claudine* expandable, make it a symbol for the ideal world of childhood. The mere mention of such words as "my mother," "my province," "my house," evokes a series of poetic images which carries the reader beyond *La Maison de Claudine* to his own real or imagined childhood. (pp. 203-04)

Although slightly different in form, *Sido* is, in theme and atmosphere, very close to *La Maison de Claudine.* In the three parts which compose this work—"Sido," "Le Capitaine" and "Les Sauvages"—the first-person narrator attempts even more intensely than in *La Maison de Claudine* to understand her past, to understand her parents and their relation to each other, to understand that heritage which they passed on to her and to her brothers and sister. (p. 206)

In Colette's evocations of her childhood and her family, as in her fictional world, it is the female element that predominates. Father and brothers, too, are relegated to inferior roles, they are part of the setting necessary for the main actors, who are Sido and her younger daughter. (p. 207)

In *La Naissance du Jour,* Colette attempts, with Sido's aid, to create her own values for herself. *La Naissance du Jour* is the account of a woman who, having arrived at a certain age, is forced to set new limits to her world. It is a spiritual odyssey, the story of the creation of a way of life by a woman who is forced to abdicate and who, guided by the examples found in her mother's letters, discovers that even in abdication there is joy. From the beginning of *La Naissance du Jour,* Sido is taken as a model of "purity," as a storehouse of that wisdom for which the narrator, in her long monologue, is searching. (p. 211)

In this work . . . Colette is not describing a present state, she is projecting a future one, she is attempting, in advance, to come to terms with herself, with love and with life, she is reconciling herself to the inevitable. (p. 213)

Colette dramatizes the narrator's renunciation of love in a dialogue with Vial, a dialogue which begins in the evening and ends with the birth of a new day. In refusing Vial, the narrator has refused all men, she has definitely rejected the world of physical love.

Into the almost uninterrupted monologue, Colette has succeeded in interweaving all her themes: Sido, childhood, animals, death, the beauty of nature and love. Her prose is here at its best. (p. 214)

At the end of the monologue, the narrator is on the threshold of a new life. She has witnessed the birth of a new day in the splendor of Provence, she has witnessed her own slow rebirth. . . . (p. 215)

Never again did Colette achieve that perfect balance of form and content, that delicate relation between fact and fiction, between poetry and prose, which make of *La Maison de Claudine, Sido* and *La Naissance du Jour* her indisputable masterpieces. (p. 216)

> *Elaine Marks, "The Masterpieces," in her* Colette *(copyright © 1960 by Rutgers, The State University; reprinted by permission of Rutgers University Press), Rutgers, 1960, pp. 200-19.*

MARGARET DAVIES (essay date 1961)

Some of the very best of Colette's writing is inspired by memories of her childhood. Throughout her earlier works she repeatedly turns back to the Burgundian village of Saint-Sauveur-en-Puisaye, her house and garden, the surrounding wooded hills, the village school, as a refuge from the miseries of her married life. It soon comes to symbolise for her a whole lost world of savage innocence from which she has most sadly fallen: and it is always on a note pitched passionately high, sometimes to the level of incantation, that she celebrates what are, for her, the magical qualities of her native countryside. (p. 1)

[Nobody] better than she has succeeded in conveying so acutely the physical sensations of remembered time. Proust, who saw fit to address her as "Maître," may have submitted it to a more cerebral research on a wider scale, but Colette remains unsurpassed in her powers to communicate her own vibrating, sensual awareness of the particular quality of a moment of childhood experience.

It was in middle age that she began to apply herself systematically to re-creating her childhood: until then her impassioned, lyrical outbursts about it had tended to be a sort of safety valve. But in the nineteen-twenties, when she had gained increased self-control, as well as a sense of definite aesthetic purpose, and, of course, the accompanying mastery of her craft, she produced three books on this theme, which are to be regarded amongst her masterpieces: *La Maison de Claudine, La Naissance du jour* and *Sido.* Here her intention is explicit: now that all of her family, except one brother, are dead, she feels it is her duty to repay them for giving her such a rich and happy childhood, and the subtle tenderness which informs her portraits of them proves to be one of her most endearing traits as a writer. (pp. 2-3)

[*La Maison de Claudine* and *Sido*] are an admirable series of impressionist sketches, a technique which she had managed to bring to a state of near-perfection. She highlights certain images that emerge from the past, brushing in the central figures of her mother, the incomparable Sido and her father, the Captain, sometimes humorously, sometimes with a sort of filial piety, but always lightly and with a fine precision, and places them against the changing background of the house and garden and country through the seasons, a whole kaleidoscope of light and colour and scents and sounds. (p. 3)

[One] of her major problems, and indeed another of the dominant themes of her writing [is] how an exceptional human being adapts herself to the additional burden of being a woman in a predominantly male world. Her sense of deprivation and humiliation in being forced to exchange the proud independence of her childhood for the inevitable female weaknesses is acute, and constantly chimes out. (p. 7)

[*Claudine à l'école*, Colette's first book, which appeared under her husband's name "Willy,"] had an enormous popular success. . . . (p. 13)

[The major defect is] the way in which she obeyed Willy's injunction to "liven things up a bit and put in some saucy details," the self-conscious wink, the raising of the skirts at the reader, so that the natural hilarity of the schoolgirl giggles ends up on a note of strident hysteria in a completely melodramatic scene where the headmistress of the village school is found in bed with the inspector during the annual village dance. In like manner, the theme of Claudine's schoolgirl pash bifurcates into a full-blown Lesbian affair between the vicious red-haired headmistress and her tarty little assistant, with prolonged kisses in the classroom and in the dark at the top of the stairs, and the sado-masochistic relationship between Claudine and Luce, the assistant mistress's little sister, the tart in embryo. Not many pages are free from Willy's *voyeur* influence: the chatter of the schoolgirls about the goings-on in the hedgerows, the young schoolmasters weighing up the charms of their flock, the inspector, that paternal pedagogue with the straying hands and the indiscreet questions, and Claudine herself, full of what Colette called "all the ugly desires of the adolescent."

The plot is a mere series of incidents strung together. (p. 14)

The characters, too, other than Claudine, who stands out like all Colette's first-person heroines in isolated relief, are shadowy, two-dimensional caricatures. . . . Her writing in the early days is so intensely subjective that the other characters, especially the male ones, are consigned to a blurred periphery.

But—and there is obviously a "but," because mere salacity is not enough to explain the book's continued success—right from the beginning, the authoritative tone of the born writer

is there. It is the style, that style which was to become ultra-famous, indeed one of the national glories of the French, which redeems everything. Words bubble out as irrepressibly as ink from an over-full fountain pen: she says exactly what she thinks, and proves, right from the start, that she can say absolutely anything and get away with it. Already, with only an occasional lapse into the young woman's favourite purple patch, she shows abundantly her flair for finding just the right words to convey her animal *joie de vivre,* her passionate ingurgitation of nature, her sudden bursts of wild, irreverent hilarity. Here was that rare specimen in the literary showcases, a completely natural writer. (pp. 14-15)

The second Claudine, *Claudine à Paris,* . . . was even more of an indelicate prank than the first, and, what was worse, much more self-conscious. It depends largely for its effect on a yet stronger dose of sexual titillation, tracing a sort of figure-of-eight of inversion with Claudine as the travestied male and Marcel, her young homosexual cousin, as the female, and little Luce, up from the country, and busy crawling obediently about on all fours for her septuagenarian uncle. Colette herself judged that this and the fourth *Claudine* were the ebb-points of the series. The plot here is even less existent than in *Claudine à l'école*—Claudine falls in love with the handsome, mature Renaud and agrees to marry him—and the natural exuberance of the style tends to degenerate into exclamations and asides and apostrophes. But there is still Claudine, and she, because she has so much of Colette herself, is genuine enough to keep up a certain interest. (p. 16)

Colette was now on the treadmill. The next year . . . another *Claudine* appeared, and this one even more shocking than before. . . . And yet *Claudine en ménage* is unquestionably the best of the series. Colette has stopped her self-conscious, Willy-inspired larking about with provocation, and is writing now out of a sincere emotion; which no doubt is why it was considered so shocking. A sly snigger at two rather ridiculous schoolmistresses embracing in the shadow of the blackboard is one thing, but to be taken right into the motives for a genuine Lesbian experience was more than most readers of the day bargained for. In actual fact the moralists should not have minded. In the end Claudine is amply punished for her aberration and a state of normalcy reigns supreme. . . .

[The] experience which the book relates has been perfectly imagined, and . . . Colette is beginning to show considerable skill in her treatment of it. In form it follows classical French tradition of the *roman d'analyse,* the intrigue depending entirely on the tightly-knit relationships between a limited number of characters. (p. 18)

It is in this book that Colette first seems to have found her strength, like a child who, after making all the motions of walking for some time, at last moves upright alone. By the process of "digging into herself," she has discovered a rich source of subject-matter for her subtle and penetrating powers of analysis.

Another noticeable development is the evolution of her highly personal kind of lyrical prose, full of poetic images and governed by an infallible sense of rhythm. . . .

After the definite achievement of *Claudine en ménage, Claudine s'en va* . . . makes depressing reading. In fact, a cynical reader might be tempted to think that its chief merit lies in the title's indication that this will be the end of a character who has had all the life written out of her. (p. 20)

Claudine has been pushed into the back seat, leaving the steering-wheel in the ineffectual hands of a new heroine, Annie.... It was, in fact, Colette's first attempt to create a central character who was not basically like herself, although she did at the time share some of Annie's preoccupations, and there are moments of insight and sympathy which at times make Annie into quite a touching figure. But she is too passive to give enough flavour to the whole book.... (p. 21)

At this stage in her life she began to be aware of one main duty—to use gifts that had become obvious even to herself in writing something other than a *Claudine,* and about a subject other than love. (pp. 22-3)

It is significant that when she turns in to herself to discover a subject both entirely personal, and honourable, she should choose animals. *Dialogues de bêtes* [is] the first book under her own name of Colette Willy, and therefore in the eyes of the public her one and only book so far.... All her life Colette had an unusually strong feeling for animals of every kind.... (p. 23)

Later it becomes obvious that the theme of animals is one of the strands in her personal mythology of the lost paradise, and is accompanied by a nostalgia for an impossible ideal—childhood, a complete integration with nature, primitive purity—as a refuge from the impure but inevitable demands of adult human relationships. Here her first and rather naïve contribution is to make her two animals, the cat Kiki-la-Doucette and Toby-Chien into two little persons who speak and behave as if they were cat-and-dog-like human beings. The result is charming, full of humour and fantasy, and her own characteristically lyrical evocation of nature. (p. 24)

[Her first major work, *La Vagabonde,*] is of all her books the most passionately subjective, and the figure of its heroine, Renée Nérée, is of all the fictional heroines the one who most resembles the Colette of the time. The compulsion of the theme drums out in every line: it is a book which had to be written before Colette could free herself finally of the shade of Willy and set herself to rights both in her life as a woman and her career as a writer. This almost totally autobiographical *cri du coeur,* in imposing itself, helped her to realise her own potentialities as both, so much so that never again after this book and its sequel *L'Entrave* did she feel the obsessive need to pour all her own turbulent feelings directly into the mould of her main character in a work of fiction.

At the beginning of the book Renée Nérée, like Colette, has just emerged from the long humiliation of her marriage, and the portrait of her ex-husband, Adolphe Taillandy is the spit image of Monsieur Willy, that "genius of deception". (pp. 32-3)

Like Colette, Renée Nérée has been a writer and has known the slow "voluptuous process of tracking down words as one tracks down an animal, lying in wait, motionless, then pouncing." Like Colette, she finds in the harsh business of earning her own living an occupation not without its comforts: the need to work has become an active fever.... (p. 33)

It is with the arrival of another man who literally lays siege to her, that her conflict begins; and conflict it is, as acute and as self-conscious as those in *La Princesse de Clèves* or in Corneille, although the terms are very different and uniquely Colette's own. For at no stage does Renée love Maxime, love, that is, in the absolute sense of *l'amour-pas-*

sion which is generally and classically opposed to the will and to duty. (p. 34)

[Refuse] him she eventually does both as lover and as husband, although not without the most poignant suffering. (p. 35)

[Colette has] taken us to the heart of one of the recurring crises of her *vie de femme,* and Renée's solution is only one of many which she herself tried. It is the anomalous position of the superior woman choosing or not choosing to subjugate herself to the inferior man.... Colette's achievement here is that she has managed to portray a situation, universal enough to be significant, but heightened and aggrandised because of the two extreme poles of her own nature: on the one side, ability, strength, self-discipline amounting to something like genius; on the other, a burning sensuality and a definite penchant for feminine submissiveness. Renée may be tough and clever, but she is never a shrew.

The dramatic tension which makes *La Vagabonde* into such an exciting narrative is due to the force of these two extremes, and to the extent of the eventual sacrifice. (pp. 35-6)

Certainly in *La Vagabonde* [Colette] has succeeded in her set task of creating a work of art, and, illuminating though it may be from the autobiographical point of view, it finally merits appraisal on this other plane. At last Colette has achieved one of the most perfect examples of the *roman d'analyse*—so far her chosen form. But now everything extraneous has been omitted, the choice of detail limited to the essential, the secondary characters more sharply defined than before and grouped so as to bring the figure of Renée into relief. Renée herself stands out with a poetic intensity in the floodlighting of Colette's analysis, and the music-hall décor behind her has for the first time given Colette an opportunity to paint a background which is not only picturesque, but which also awakens her sympathy and pity for her fellows. (pp. 36-7)

It was immediately obvious when *La Vagabonde* appeared that it was a major achievement. Colette had harnessed her gifts for composition and surface decoration to a profound and moving study of a real human being. She had also, for the first time completely successfully, managed to discipline her desire to say all about herself to the exigencies of a work of art, which exists quite independently from the vagaries of her own existence. (p. 39)

Just as Claudine had become a type, and later Chéri and Léa and the adolescents of *Le Blé en herbe* and Gigi were to be universally recognised as types, so Renée Nérée sums up the new sort of woman who is struggling, often at odds with her femininity, to make her way alone: in short, the prototype of the career-woman. Not only that, but the whole atmosphere of the book ... generates a new and special kind of sadness which later reached its climax in Existentialist writings. The anguish of Renée's lonely stance on the edge of the void, the intense conviction that she and she alone is responsible for her destiny, the whole of the last remarkable section, when she seems to be spinning around in a meaningless, arbitrary world, her tension so extreme that she is completely dissociated from what she sees—all these symptoms, noted well before the First World War, herald in a peculiarly modern feeling of unrest.

L'Entrave, her next novel, ... is another example of her discreet participation in the spirit of the time. It is a corollary to *La Vagabonde* in which Colette has exercised the feminine prerogative of changing her mind. With *La Vagabonde* we were left with a Renée Nérée who is as heroic as Moses on his lonely mountain: in *L'Entrave* she comes down to earth and the worship of the Golden Calf of man. (p. 40)

It is as if, in this reversal of Renée Nérée's previous attitude, Colette was trying to get to grips finally with this thing called love, to finish off the wild beast which gave her so much trouble by dissecting it, and isolating its basic, component parts. It is for this reason that I say that she shows herself, even if unwittingly, again in tune with the spirit of the times. In *L'Entrave* she approaches love as analytically as the Cubist painters of the time were approaching visual forms, splitting it up into its simplified factors—desire, companionship, and what she can only call "the rest"—then trying to rebuild them into her own arbitrary composition. (p. 41)

[Renée] has now become so self-conscious, burrowing down ever further into the split hairs of emotion, so aware of her superiority, so determined not to give more than her body, that even when she is really suffering she forfeits most of the sympathy she had won so easily in *La Vagabonde*. Her previous strength of character has become sheer egotism. (pp. 42-3)

It seems obvious that Colette had now reached the end of one particular path—that of the subjective *roman d'analyse*. Analysis has led away from the novel into the realms of the psychological treatise, art has given way to therapy. It is the stage when introspection grows obsessive to the point of destruction. Small wonder that it was seven years before she produced another major work; nor that, with her particular faculty of turning deadends into thresholds, she should then achieve the perfect synthesis of a series of masterpieces. (p. 43)

Naturally the Léa of *Chéri* is Colette, as Madame Bovary is Flaubert, that is, enough one facet of her creator to be blown-up into a life-size solidly-imagined character in her own right. (p. 47)

The [characterization of Chéri] was so successful that Colette pulled off once again the same trick as with Claudine and Renée. She had created a type. (pp. 47-8)

Superficially he is nothing but a spoilt, handsome boy, who never looks at women in the street because he is sure that they will look at him. (p. 48)

Underneath—inevitably, for his materially pampered childhood has been as empty as if he had been an orphan—he is a lost soul, disorientated and a prey to anguish. . . . He is a mysterious figure. Sometimes Colette even seems to hint that he is the vehicle for strange, diabolical forces. At his first appearance he is only a shadow, "a graceful devil jumping about against a furnace of light": at the end Léa calls him a little Satan. He is elsewhere an "inaccessible carrier of light." These references must not, I think, be ignored, for Colette was always susceptible to the supernatural. Chéri is to be regarded as ill-starred, the sort of person who brings not only temptation but bad luck in his wake, a damned soul, almost a representative of the spirit world. (pp. 48-9)

Léa, the well-made, well-fed, well-breeched blonde courtesan, who appears at the beginning to regard the beautiful boy with nothing more than a mixture of animal, maternal solicitude and sheer *gourmandise*, has certainly met her match in Chéri. On its purposefully modest level the story is nothing less than the chastisement of *hybris*, not in its antique form

but as the modern pride of little people made up of self-satisfaction and complacency. (p. 49)

[Colette] has given to this greedy, almost seedy, woman [Léa] something like an archetypal significance. She appears as a heady combination of Circe and Ceres, representing the two cults of pleasure and security both united in an apotheosis of material comfort. Nobody better than Colette, significantly a Frenchwoman, has known how to convey the poetry of luxury and good living. Contrasted with Charlotte's empty barn of a place, Léa's lovely house becomes a symbol of comfort, with its shining brass and silver, the discreet ring of crystal, the exquisite food and wine, the warmth and glow and softness everywhere, and at the heart of it her rose-pink, womb-like bedroom. . . .

But as well as moving in this poetic atmosphere, Léa has an extraordinary physical magnetism. She is, like no other fictional heroine, always wholly present to all one's senses, even when she is not on the scene. She is a superb literary creation, immediate and real as few women have ever been in fiction. (p. 51)

In *Chéri* [Chéri] had been a little swamped by the full-blooded Léa, who had obviously grown in importance as Colette wrote the book. In *La Fin de Chéri* he takes on even wider implications; for, once again, Colette manages to reflect and to anticipate in one of her main characters the whole spirit of the time. Chéri is now the vessel for all that feeling of aimless unrest and anguish which seem to be the inevitable backwash of a war; and it is no accident that his state of mind is akin to those depicted in [Camus's] *L'Etranger* and [Sartre's] *La Nausée*, novels written in a later but similar period. (p. 55)

The kernel of the book is the magnificent and horrible scene in which Chéri, in search of the heart-breaking impossible—lost time, ruined childhood, the ideal womb-enfolded existence which Léa had given him—goes back with an almost religious fervour to meet her after an absence of seven years. It is one of the best pieces in all Colette's writing. . . . (p. 57)

Change of character is, of course, at the basis of any plot: the human being needs to be surprised by his own capacities for transformation, for better or worse. Here the metamorphosis of Léa stuns, not only because of the extreme contrast, from luscious beauty to red-faced gendarme, a new variation on the age-old Belle Heaulmière theme, but because it is the sudden crumbling of Chéri's last pipe-dream, the first muffled clang of his death-knell. (p. 58)

The undercurrent of symbolism in Colette's works has not, I think, been sufficiently stressed. It runs all through her later works, but never with more integrated effect than in these two *Chéri* books. There is significance in the choice of every single detail of colour, shape, and weather. Chéri's wife, Edmée, that polished, competent lady, is always in shiny black or shiny white, reflected in a mirror in a shining hall; her face is cut in sharp angles. Chéri, too, who at the beginning in Léa's bedroom was black and white and hard, disintegrates into dead sculptured marble. The two old *cocottes*, his mother and Léa, are cubic and ruddy, Edmée's lover is equally solid and ginger and red. Paris, after being bathed in grey torrid heat, is then traversed by grey rain-clouds, illuminated only occasionally by the pink and golden light of Chéri's fading illusion. (p. 61)

Throughout it is the women who represent solid practicality, the limitless strength of sheer resistance, as opposed to Chéri who simply cannot cope with life. This basic toughness of women was a point which Colette never ceased to make. (p. 62)

[Love] had been, and would be until the end as her choice of the great cathartic agent, the process which strips down the human being to its bare bones.

But in her non-fictional work it was a different matter. Here there was no need to choose a subject which would engender the drama of emotional conflict, or charge a tightly-knit plot with the explosive qualities of suspense and irony and shock, no need even to create characters outside herself. She could, with her charmed pen, explore herself, and what she knew about other people and about life, write of all the myriad things that absorbed and delighted her—love, of course, among them, but so many others as well that her later works can be regarded as manuals in the art of enjoying life. After *La Fin de Chéri*, she wrote only four other novels, properly speaking, although there were also several volumes of short stories like *La Femme cachée, Bella Vista, Chambre d'hotel*. But it is the whole other current that now comes into its own, dealing with the variety and spread of life, in works which are hard to define—essays, articles, memoirs, diary, sketches—except by saying that each one is a work of art in its own right. (pp. 69-70)

[*La Maison de Claudine*] is perhaps, of all her works, the most accomplished and the least controversial. This delightful recreation of her childhood and of the dearly-loved figures of her family is artistically a *chef d'œuvre*, and *Sido*, as Colette herself knew, was one of her finest literary creations.

Some critics have thought that she wrote these books mainly as an atonement for the grossly caricatured picture of her native land in the *Claudines*. She had certainly not dared to touch the figure of her mother in that rather questionable period. The return to childhood at this specific point in her life could, however, well be of deeper significance. Once the young Claudine had recovered from her early nostalgia for childhood, the mirage of the Lost Paradise had receded somewhat in Colette's trek through the complicated business of her "life as a woman." Now, however, at the age of fifty she obviously was beginning to feel that she had worked through the main problem of her life, that she was coming out of the delicious but murky labyrinth into a wider world. . . . [It] is by scrutinising carefully the Lost Paradise of her memory that she makes yet another of her astonishing leaps forward into a new, untramelled attitude towards life. From now on all her works seem to be the stages in a quest to make herself worthy of that lost, ideal world. (pp. 70-1)

[During] the whole of the War period she never ceased to work actively to remind people what France had meant and still could mean. She gave regular broadcasts to France and to America, she wrote articles in daily and weekly newspapers. . . . In these articles, many of which are collected in *Paris de ma fenêtre*, it is obvious that she felt it was her patriotic duty to make others, and especially the women of France, participate in her own creative, adventurous spirit which by sheer will-power she managed to keep alive through the greyest days.

It seems to me that it is this same spirit which informed the choice of her last fictional work, the work which has perhaps enjoyed the widest popularity of all: *Gigi*. As opposed to the gnashing of teeth and the grimace of anguish which were reflected in the works of nearly all other writers of this period,

Colette chose to tell a luminous fairy story in modern dress. It is as if she had consciously decided to pick on all the qualities which could be of the greatest comfort to her compatriots at this time. The story is set in a period of particular glamour and frivolity when France was paramount among civilised countries. Even its most amoral members, the old *cocottes,* are models of dignity and good taste, and in their dishonourable, unreasonable lives exercise a healthy respect for their own particular code of honour and reason and hygiene; what Colette calls "the honourable habits of women without honour," the recognition of quality in its every guise. It is against their sophisticated, elegant corruption that she draws in relief the figure of the young girl Gigi. Youth, hope, life, irrepressible high spirits, a typically French irreverent humour, intransigent idealism, inherent purity, all these crowned in this story of virtue more than rewarded, a dream made true. It must, at that time particularly, have fulfilled symbolically the secret hopes of all her readers.

But of course there is no need to see *Gigi* only in this narrow context. Its repeated popularity today is a proof of that. Colette, at seventy, with her gossamer pen had netted the ephemeral butterfly of youth.

Claudine had come full circle. (pp. 100-01)

[In] the eighth decade of her life she produced a series of works: [*Belles Saisons, L'Etoile Vesper, Journal à rebours, Pour un herbier,* and *Le Fanal bleu,*] which are among the most heart-warming and magical of all. (p. 102)

Out of the prison imposed by her ailing flesh, with the ingredients just to hand—her flowers and books, buds and berries, her lamp, her crystal objects, her butterflies, and, most precious of all, her inexhaustible treasure-house of memories—she managed daily to create her own kind of paradise, still following as best she could the pattern of that ideal one of childhood. And it is this paradise, bounded by the evening star and her blue-shaded reading lamp, which she recreates for us in her two last great works, *L'Etoile Vesper* and *Le Fanal bleu*, works which, for want of a better definition, I can only call, in her own words, manuals of "the supreme *chic* of *le savoir décliner.*" The human race might be well served if these two books were handed out to all those who are embarking upon old age, as glucose sweets are given to aeroplane passengers before take-off. (pp. 103-04)

She herself called *L'Etoile Vesper* "souvenirs." Reminiscences, diary, what you will, this and its sequel *Le Fanal bleu* follow her life day by day, her thoughts, her impressions, her memories, and all on the tone of the most polished conversation. She invites the reader into her personal paradise with the politeness of the experienced hostess begging him to look and taste and smell all the good things she has gathered around her. But under the guise of this casual chat, there come all the *mots justes* marshalling themselves, as if on their own accord, into perfect order. Her style, which began so lushly, has now been pared down to the unemphatic, exquisite precision, the quiet but complex harmony of a late Beethoven quartet. (p. 104)

[In her work Colette] had created a universe entirely her own, one which is not merely autonomous but which has the power so to radiate the sense of wonder which informs it that the face of our own reality is changed. After reading Colette, one never looks at a flower, or an animal, or even one's own possibilities, in quite the same way again. Life, which has been a dish of boiled mutton and cabbage, is now full of the most delicate and heady spices. (p. 108)

Margaret Davies, in her Colette *(reprinted by permission of Grove Press, Inc.; copyright © 1961 by Margaret Davies), Grove Press, 1961, 120 p.*

JOHN WEIGHTMAN   (essay date 1966)

The fact is, surely, that a fair proportion of Colette's writing is quite bad, and that her range at all times is rather narrow. Her obvious fault is that she overwrites and gushes and enthuses in a way which is less reminiscent of great literature than of a popular columnist doing an ''In My Garden'' or ''These You Have Loved.'' Admittedly, Nature poetry is difficult to manage; it has to be discreet and glancing if it is going to be tolerable at all, because sentimental admiration of the universe can be just as vulgar and silly as sentimental rejection of it. But Colette often plunges in with the shamelessness of a tourist guide and quite turns the stomach. . . . At any moment, Colette is liable to fall into this style when she is writing in the first person and not expressing herself through the medium of objectified characters. She never cured herself of it and, if anything, it got worse as she grew older; it is combined, for instance, with sententiousness, in her last volumes of essays, *The Blue Lantern* (*Le Fanal bleu*) and *L'Etoile Vesper*. . . . In short, I would be prepared to jettison the Colette who rushed at Nature too ardently, who used the vocative in addressing gardens, who claimed to speak the language of the animal world and who wore sandals all the time. . . . She was not alone in this Panic enthusiasm; after all, she was a contemporary of D. H. Lawrence, Llewellyn Powys, and André Gide, as well as of the vegetarian, Jaeger-clad Bernard Shaw. All this was no doubt part of the historical mood of emancipation and being a woman and therefore, needing to be doubly emancipated, she was especially sensitive to it. But it has not worn well and it may put off younger readers who are approaching Colette for the first time . . . , and who take the enjoyment of Nature for granted.

Nevertheless, she is a great writer, or at least unique in her subtlety, when she combines psychological perceptiveness with her awareness of the moods of nature, as she does in some of the stories of *The Tender Shoot* and in the short novel, *The Other One* (*La Seconde*). Here she has the qualities of her defects, i.e., she continues to react violently to material phenomena, but instead of rendering them for their own sake in cloying prose, she subordinates them to human relationships, and even achieves a degree of self-satire. The central character in *La Seconde*, Fanny, who seems to be a version of herself during her marriage to the unfaithful Henri de Jouvenel, is always exceptionally aware of the landscape, the temperature, the light, her degree of comfort or discomfort, fatigue or freshness, yet she is not allowed to wallow in sensation; she is always being brought up short by the astringent reactions of the other characters. . . . The same virtues are to be found in the stories of *The Tender Shoot*, apart from the lamentably saccharine one called *The Sick Child*. They usually present some psychological, preferably sexual, drama in a clearly defined physical setting. Colette is so good at suggesting the precise quality of the light, the feel of the wind, or the taste of food that the effect is of an Impressionist painting containing a slowly evolving plot. When she is at her best, the plot is completely amoral, in respect of conventional morality, yet relates to a deeper

morality which is suggested rather than stated. . . . Nothing much happens in the novel, except that Fanny gradually achieves a *modus vivendi* with Jane instead of flying off the handle with jealousy, but the book is unforgettable because of the shimmering rightness of the physico-psychological notations. The technique is not unlike Virginia Woolf's, except that her characters have only souls and artistic sensibilities, whereas Colette's have genitals and digestive systems in addition to the higher feelings. Because she gets the details absolutely right, the book swells in the memory and one is surprised, on re-reading it, to see that a great many things that one had remembered as part of the story and that can be quite legitimately inferred from the text, are not actually said. Farou himself, the charming, sloppy, egotistical womaniser, who is a successful but superficial playwright and rather less intelligent than either Fanny or Jane, is an excellent characterization, although the number of words specifically devoted to him is very small. It has been said that Colette is not very good at describing men, and this is true if by men we mean intellectuals or active individuals in the exercise of their extra-sexual functions. She is not really interested in ideas and collective phenomena as such, i.e., the truly masculine domain. . . . She sees men only as they impinge on women, and therefore her recurrent male characters are womanisers, gigolos, *amants de coeur*, ponces or semi-ponces, in other words the male inhabitants of the *demi-monde* or the artistic or delinquent fringe that she was introduced to by Willy, and where she clearly felt more at home than in respectable or conventional society.

The explanation may be that she was fundamentally bisexual, and so was naturally drawn to an area of society where masculine and feminine behavior overlaps and the same person can move, almost at will, from the masculine to the feminine role, or vice versa. . . . At her best, Colette never thinks or feels monosexually; her men are men and her women are women, yet their sexual attributes wax and wane with wonderful accuracy, according to the tensions of the moment. (pp. 9-10)

John Weightman, "Earth Mother of the Demi-Monde," in The New York Review of Books *(reprinted with permission from* The New York Review of Books; *copyright © 1966 Nyrev, Inc.), Vol. VI, No. 10, June 9, 1966, pp. 8-10.*

HENRI PEYRE   (essay date 1967)

The one woman writer who, up to a few years ago, would have been claimed by most Frenchmen as the glorious paragon of literary talent, if not of genius, was Colette. Our own conviction is that she was always grossly overrated and that she may well, more than any other cause, be responsible for the sad plight of feminine writing in France up to the fourth decade of the present century.

Her skilled workmanship is of course not to be denied, even if it was ridiculously overpraised by gallant French critics. . . . She could chisel swift, sensuous sentences admirably, convey the color of an adolescent girl's eyes or the earthy fragrance of rain-soaked gardens, the lusciousness of pears or peaches melting in the mouth. She possessed the classical art of omission. . . . Colette, like Proust with whom she has not a few points in common, hunted the adjective, 'the chatoyant, evanescent, entrancing adjective,' as she calls it somewhere in an adjectival triad worthy of Proust. She could conjure up the very special taste of tears gliding down a powdered cheek or the feel of male muscles pressing on a pliant body. But she seldom reached that naturalness in style which has obliterated effort. She seldom prefers her prose and its sobriety to the pleasure of displaying her skill in welding it expertly. Too many women writers in France have been lured by her example into a new preciosity. She and Giraudoux may well appear some day as the most insidious corruptors of taste in our age and as antediluvian writers cherishing allusions and quaint, far-fetched comparisons. (pp. 276-77)

Antediluvian, Colette also is in the subject of her stories. She is at her best when she harks back to her childhood and to her roots, and she and many a critic have erred, or led us into error, by dismissing the early *Claudine* volumes as youthful sins inspired by her first husband. Even as a little girl, Colette was already experienced, adorned, mature, and attracted by naïveté, as slightly corrupt sensibilities can be. She entertained our grandmothers through her insolent boldness and the audacity with which she rent the veils covering 'those pleasures that are lightly called physical.' But her implicit ideals never endangered bourgeois values. She reveled in stories of marriages arranged by prudent families, of aging roués caught in the contrivedly naïve nets of a cool-headed girl, in courtesans aping the women of the middle class, and in interiors which are as respectable, as stuffily rancid as in any 'nineteen hundred' novel for model 'jeunes filles.' Her world is one of boudoirs and of bedrooms, with no genuine joy and no tenderness ever emanating from those unconvincing love gymnastics attempted by Antoine and Minne at the end of *L'Ingénue libertine* or by Léa and her child lover, Chéri. It is typically a pre–World War I microcosm, in which outward nature itself appears adorned and powdered as in some Alexandrian tale retold by Pierre Louÿs. The only men who are loved are brainless gigolos who would not be so relentlessly pursued, 'loved they honor a little more.' In a volume on her laborious sentimental and professional education entitled *Mes Apprentissages* . . . , Colette made a melancholy avowal: 'I have not come near those men whom others call great. They have not sought me.' It is not surprising that many males should refuse to recognize themselves in those men who have little brain and less heart and whose introspective life is so elementary. 'I do not like you to be subtle. [*fin* is hardly translateable.] You are subtle only because you are unhappy,' the woman remarks to her partner in *Duo*. It is hardly less surprising that French girls of 1966 should feel totally estranged from those creatures who were all slightly venal, never forged bonds of comradeship with men, never discussed politics, ideas, ethics, aesthetics with them, never tried to found a loving relationship on candidness and on loyalty, and accepted deceit as the condiment to their love life. (pp. 277-78)

> *Henri Peyre, "Feminine Literature in France," in his* French Novelists of Today *(copyright © 1955, 1967 by Oxford University Press, Inc.; reprinted by permission), revised edition, Oxford University Press, New York, 1967, pp. 275-307.**

MARY KATHLEEN BENET (essay date 1977)

The *style Colette* is one of the national possessions of France: it represents a fusion of the two most striking French cultural preoccupations, rigid intellectual formality and immersion in the life of the senses. Colette's stories are as stark and self-contained as a drama by Racine, with no unnecessary

characters or action. But what are they about? She has abandoned the conflict between love and duty, between the intellect and the senses, that the classical French dramatists took as their theme; her books are about the many varieties of love, and the unending conflict between men and women. (p. 237)

The heroines in Colette's books are often actresses or courtesans, and it seemed to her that making one's living by writing was essentially similar. The reader, the client, must be charmed and even bamboozled; self-revelation, though crucial, must take place on the performer's own terms; there must be a careful control underlying even the most apparently spontaneous moments.

This tension is part of what gives Colette's books their fascination, their mesmerizing quality. But it also means there is something ultimately unsatisfying about them, once the immediate spell dissipates. Just as she was always too guarded with men to be completely happy in marriage, so she is guarded in her work. The stories she tells are strangely at odds with the way she tells them. (p. 238)

[There are two] striking things about the *style Colette*. First, . . . her propensity for "feminine" imagery where it is least expected, an entirely open mind about appropriate metaphors that gives her imagery its freshness. Nothing is too humble to be used: she has the freedom trained out of most writers by the very academic process that supposedly qualifies them to write. (pp. 240-41)

[The second striking thing is a] sense of balance, of the blending of disparate elements into a unified whole, [which] is as typical of the *style Colette* as it is of Frenchness. . . . Here is Colette's own credo of nationality: balance, organic relation with the natural world, and the popular basis of the arts of living. The things she discusses—wine, cheese, cuisine, couture, perfume—are all matters of art and nature combined, and to Colette's public all are universally accessible, have their basis in the fact that they are necessities of life.

All the world agrees that the French painters, too, practised their art in this way, and Colette always felt closer kinship with painters than with the writers who have given France a reputation for literary coldness and formality. The Impressionists and their successors were her spiritual kin. . . . Her bond with the painters is that she celebrates the same France, the same rich and fruitful world. The male writers of France, from whom she consciously dissociates herself, have been sidetracked and misled by the cold and classical intellectual tradition of the country: the tendency to systematize, categorize, and work with antitheses. Although Colette too has a taste for antithesis—which appears in such facile Colette-ish phrases as "cette Bretagne doux et amer"—her terror of general ideas helps to save her from it, as it saves her from falling into the tendency to intellectualize of such writers as Gide, Sartre, and Camus.

Colette felt the strongest bond with the few French writers who also escaped this trap—Balzac, Baudelaire, and (among her own contemporaries) Proust. Outsiders, satanists, renegades, they saved their own spontaneity and capacity to respond to life by remaining alienated from the intellectual establishment. Telling the truth about money and sex preoccupied them, as it did Colette; they all saw conventional high culture as an attempt to cover up these truths. (pp. 241-43)

The theme of renunciation in Colette's novels, and her persona as the old wise woman, enable her to treat the many varieties of love dispassionately. . . . (p. 247)

Colette was able to face head-on the fact that the relation of marriage includes most of the hues in the emotional spectrum, and to paint these hues one by one. This is why she always seems to stay on the periphery of her great subject, to circle around it, viewing it from one angle after another, and never to sum it up. She sees quite clearly that there is never an ideal that is more or less approximated, but spoiled by the failures and paradoxes of imperfect human beings; instead, each human relation is a summing up of various needs, drives, influences; the mixture is different in each case; and there is no such thing as a "norm." There are conventions, true enough—but adherence to them can be the most abnormal thing of all, the essence of hypocrisy, cruelty, and exploitation. The "conventional" man who keeps Luce as his mistress is a monster compared to the moral but unconventional Claudine; the "conventional" politician in *Julie de Carneilhan* is far less admirable than the straightforward Julie, even though it is she who is the outcast of society. In one of her subtlest books, *La Chatte*, it is the husband who behaves properly, and the wife who gives way to bizarre and unaccountable behavior—but it is he who is the monster of the two.

To say that love of a sexual nature has elements of parental love, homosexual love, hostility, dependence, ambiguity, is to express a truism of psychoanalysis; but to place these elements at the center of the stage, and to say that instead of being flaws in some nebulous, perfect love, they are love itself—this is Colette's profoundest insight.

Colette's best work achieves its strength by making no distinction between the normal and the abnormal, by reversing the categories of the pure and the impure.

Though Colette has often been considered one of those writers totally unrelated to her own time, who could have existed in any era, these psychological techniques make her very surely part of the modern movement that was the ultimate heir of romanticism. Her exploration of the world by means of her own psyche, her search for the roots of human experience and emotion, her broadening of the definition of literary subject matter, are the main characteristics of the literary history of the first half of this century. She is in the same class as Katherine Mansfield and Virginia Woolf—and as in their case, the fact that she was a woman has something to do with her modernism. The "feminine" sphere of psychological understanding, of human relations, was at the center of the literary stage; and women who had been barred from the aridities of conventional male letters were superbly equipped to delineate it. (pp. 247-48)

The relation in Colette's work between money, sex, and fame or notoriety is very central. The transactions of a writer are implicitly compared to those of an actress, or a wife, or a mistress; some are conventionally moral and socially acceptable; others, and usually the purest, are outside of convention, law, or acceptability. In fact, she seems to say that one touchstone of pure emotion is its freedom from any taint of business—and marriage, sex, and the exercise of an artistic profession are all businesses. Only among the "pure" outcasts in *Le Pur et l'Impur* do we find emotion for its own sake, sufficient unto itself; there is no doubt in her mind who are the pure and who the corrupt.

Her critique of relations with men (including marriage) as business transactions of a more or less sordid kind is as strong as that of the other two women; like them, she tries to isolate the transcendent theme of love between men and women from its accretions of worldliness. How can she purify it, isolate it, and see it in its most basic form? Only in the loves of outsiders, unisexuals, or those mismatched in the world's eyes by disparity of age (*Chéri*), social standing (*Gigi*), experience (*Le Blé en herbe*), is love at all pure. (pp. 250-51)

Mary Kathleen Benet, "The Style of Colette," in her Writers in Love *(reprinted with permission of Macmillan Publishing Co., Inc.; copyright © 1977 by Mary Kathleen Benet), Macmillan, 1977, pp. 237-54.*

WILLIAM H. GASS (essay date 1978)

Love. Always *that* in these silly French novels. Isn't there another subject, Jouvenel [Colette's second husband] had complained, beside incestuous longing, adultery, absence? Well, not really. Look at how this tiny boudoir mirror reflects all the larger relations! Because novels about love are inevitably about its failures, and the failure of love leads directly to the need for an alternative salvation which can lie nowhere else but in one's work, although most work is as impermanent as pleasure, often even hurtful, and pointless to boot; still for a fortunate few (and if they are women they are very few and fortunate indeed), there is the chance for a redeeming relation to some creative medium—in Colette's case, as Fate finally settled it, the written word.

The better word, as she suggested her hunt was—the better word. But the better word did not fall toward her out of space like a star, nor did the untranslatable rhythms of her prose dance like urchins in the street beneath her flat. Words arose, came to her, fell in line, principally as she reflected upon her life, whether it was fiction she was writing or something else. Experience was her dictionary, and what we can observe, as we read through the *Claudine*s, is the compiling of that dictionary, and how, out of that large scrawly book of girlish words, is finally shaped an art of grave maturity, subtlety, perception, grace; one which is at once so filled with Colette's own presence and yet so open to the reader, so resolutely aimed, that it masters a mode: *le style intime,* one would be tempted to dub it, if that didn't suggest it was a naughty perfume.

The memory transcribes loops. It begins here where I am; it departs for the past, then returns to me through possibly fancy slips and spins like a Yo-Yo to the hand. Colette was fond of mimicking such motion, beginning a chapter with Claudine breathless from an outing or a visit, and then returning the narrative through some carriage ride or concert until Claudine is once more at home. In this way the event is bracketed by endings at both ends (and ends as it began). The immediate moment can benefit then from the play of reflection, although there is little benefit from reflection in the Claudine books, which are for the most part shallow indeed. Plunged into iniquity, Claudine emerges as clean as a washed doll.

Events are naturally related in the first person. Even *Chéri*, which is written in the third, has every quality of the quiet "I." The tone is of course girlish in these girlish books, but it is that of the confidential exchange in almost all of them: the personal letter, the intense tête-à-tête, confessions passed between chums like shared toys, or at its most innocent, it has the character of a daughter's report of what happened on her first date. . . .

Colette will copy the manner of the diary or journal too, but also include a great deal of designedly empty and idle yet lively chatter. Opportunities will be manufactured for the exchange of confidences, though the effect is nothing like that of Henry James. Equally contrived, the result is merely artificial, and unfortunately often cheap. Verbal voyeurism is the rule. Claudine enjoys hearing how it is to be a kept woman from her former school chum, Luce. . . . (pp. 140-42)

It is not the promise of dirty details which makes [Colette's] style so personal and beckoning. Confessions can be as public as billboards, and our bookstores are as cluttered by be-seechments and soulful outcries as our highways. (pp. 142-43)

[But] Colette is always carefully *en déshabillé*. There is the unguarded expression of emotion (the all-too-frequent exclamation and oo-la-la!); there's the candid opinion dropped as casually as a grape, the gleefully malicious judgments, . . . the broken phrases, sentences darting in different directions like fish, gentle repetitions, wholly convincing observations, . . . and above all the flash of fine metaphor . . . or sometimes an image which is both accurate summation and continuing symbol . . . and when we look down the length of her sentences, we see the energy which rushes up through them like the bubbler in the park—they are alive—even when otherwise they are callow and jejune, or even when they move with an almost Jamesian majesty, as they often do through the stories which make up *The Tender Shoot*, or reveal the pruned, precise lyricism, the romantic simplicity of a finely shaped head beneath a haircut. . . . (pp. 143-44)

Colette did not invent so much as modify her memory, thus her work required continual return; yet retracing well demands forgetting too, or the early line will soon be overlaid with other lines and lose all definition. None of us now matches her skill at rendering the actual contours of experience. How far can we see out of raised eyebrows? How straight can we speak with a curled lip? Irony, ambiguity, skepticism—these aren't attitudes any more which come and go like moods, but parts of our anatomy. However, Colette could recall a young girl's innocent offer of commitment and not dismay it with the disappointments and betrayals which she knew were sure to follow. She did not feel obliged to insist that the confusions of the loving self rise from their depths to trouble every feeling just because she knew they were there and wanted us to know she knew. Our illusions, when they shattered, spilled affection like a cheap perfume which clings to our surroundings, overscenting, so that the sick smell of ourselves is everywhere, however frantically we move. In English, how many genuine love stories have we had since Ford wrote *Some Do Not?*

Colette is being pushed to pen it; nevertheless, *Claudine in Paris* is often a sadly meretricious book. Despite its causes, and despite the fact that she, herself, has suffered seven years of Willy like the plague, Colette can still remember what her hopes were—how it was—and can render Claudine's feelings for this older man (handsomer than her husband to be sure, but close enough in every other way to guarantee discomfort) with a rare and convincing genuineness. In the best of these books, *Claudine Married*, there are many unreal and merely

fabricated things, but the passion is real: at the sight of her beloved's breasts, she aches and fears and trembles, is full of the gentlest and most giving hunger. (pp. 144-45)

[The late books tell us that] in a life of love and even melodrama, a life that was lived within the skin and nerves as few have been, it was her work which won—loved her and won her love; and that finger which once held down sentences for Willy helped write others which need no help and hold themselves. The moral isn't new or arresting. Philosophers have been saying the same thing for centuries. (p. 146)

William H. Gass, "Three Photos of Colette," in his The World within the Word *(copyright © 1977 by William H. Gass; reprinted by permission of Alfred A. Knopf, Inc.), Knopf, 1978, pp. 124-46.*

DIANE JOHNSON (essay date 1981)

Robert Phelps explains in his preface [to *Letters from Colette*] that he has followed his "own taste, trimming freely and trying simply to show Colette in her daily zest. . . . Letters and memoirs to come will certainly deepen the image this book makes, but it is unlikely that they will radically alter it." His taste leads him to emphasize a zestful, simple Colette and to ignore the more prudent, calculating, and interesting woman who emerges from the complete texts of her letters. It is of course the defect of all collections of trimmings that the idea of the editor about the writer controls our understanding of his subject, the more particularly in cases of translated letters, which have the usual problems of translations in addition, among them that we are far less likely to go ourselves to the originals to see what is missing. Mr. Phelps, the editor and translator of *Earthly Paradise*, a compendium of Colette's autobiographical writings, and of *Les Belles Saisons*, a picture book, has had considerable influence on our view of Colette. . . .

Since her death in 1954, Colette's literary reputation has followed the usual curve, at its apogee during her last years, by which time she had received the medal of the Legion of Honor, been elected to the Academie Goncourt, and much else. A dozen years after her death, the august Henri Peyre would pronounce "our own conviction that she was always grossly overrated and that she may well, more than any other cause, be responsible for the sad plight of feminine writing in France up to the fourth decade of the present century." . . .

Today we again admire her candor and penetration—the superb style has never been questioned—and assume her to have been an astute observer of her society. (p. 6)

In her fiction, as well as in the letters, Colette's preoccupation with advice is striking—it is her great subject. She is interested above all in the protégé(e) and in the emotional plight of the protector, and in the communication of experience, especially of love and its economics. And she moved in her own life from beloved child to protégée to protectrice, so are the characters in her books arranged. Each person is in some sense the creation of someone else in a natural hierarchy. She seems not to have minded, really, being locked in the room by the awful Willy, so much as she minded his infidelities. Locked in the room, she learned the rudiments of self-creation.

Her view of men in her fiction is a little harsher than the sympathetic tone of her letters to male friends. . . . (pp. 6, 8)

On the other hand, Colette's women often get revenge—the fate of Chéri, the uppity independence of the Vagabonde. Colette's view of the relations of the sexes fundamentally in opposition was founded upon observation and experience. At the outset of her affairs with both Jouvenel and Maurice Goudeket, her third husband, she had to deal with jealous rivals who threatened scenes, scandal, and even murder. She sees the real conflict of interests of men and women—alien creatures involved like spiders in some painful but inevitable biological conjunction which would lead to the extinction of one or the other; but like a biologist or a UN observer she can keep a certain sympathy for both sides; she's a man's woman and a woman's woman both, and feels herself to have "a genuine mental hermaphroditism." (p. 8)

Colette was very much as one would expect, a writer of her own day, influenced by the visual aesthetics of Wilde, Gautier, Proust, the senior writers of her youth. Her rapturous passages of natural description owe as much to art as to nature—remind, even, of the descriptions in Huysmans of art objects or perfumes: "one must live here to appreciate the four colors of figs: the green with yellow pulp; the white with red pulp; the black with red pulp; and the violet, or rather the mauve, with pink pulp." Colette's nature writing is a little *à rebours*, an attraction to style like her attraction to those turn-of-the-century lesbians, triumphantly stylish, whose wonderful evening costumes and dramatic decor she would so meticulously describe. (pp. 8-9)

> *Diane Johnson, "Colette in Pieces," in* The New York Review of Books *(reprinted with permission from* The New York Review of Books; *copyright © 1981 Nyrev, Inc.), Vol. XXVIII, No. 5, April 2, 1981, pp. 6-9.*

ADDITIONAL BIBLIOGRAPHY

Cottrell, Robert D. *Colette*. New York: Frederick Ungar Publishing Co., 1974, 150 p.
    General introduction to Colette's life and work.

Crosland, Margaret. *Colette: The Difficulty of Loving, a Biography*. London: Peter Owen, 1973, 200 p.
    Biography of Colette, with chronology and bibliography.

Mitchell, Yvonne. *Colette: A Taste for Life*. London: Weidenfeld and Nicolson, 1975, 240 p.
    Richly illustrated biography.

A(lfred) E(dgar) Coppard

1878-1957

English short story writer and poet.

Coppard is recognized primarily as an innovator of the English short story. In an era when the norm for the short story was the formula piece written for magazines, Coppard introduced a new short story convention, rich in the English rural tradition and poetic in mood and style. It was due to his influence that the short story was reappraised in his time as a significant literary form.

Born into a working-class family, Coppard grew accustomed to a life of hard work; he was removed from school at the age of nine and apprenticed to a London tailor. His education thereafter was self-acquired and included reading the works of such writers as Chaucer, Shakespeare, Keats, and Whitman. When Coppard took a clerical position at Oxford, befriending a number of literature students including Roy Campbell and Aldous Huxley, he was stimulated to write.

The influence of Chekhov and Maupassant, masters of the short story, is seen in Coppard's early prose style, while his later works reveal a Jamesian sophistication. Throughout his career, Coppard focused on the emotional reactions of his characters rather than their social, religious, or scientific background or bias. His prose is essentially poetic and Coppard's ability to convey what he saw and imagined is complemented by his use of a rural vernacular to describe what he heard. Coppard hoped to recreate the oral tradition of the folktale: the story heard and not read. The supernatural "Adam and Eve and Pinch Me" and "Dusky Ruth," found in the collection entitled _Adam and Eve and Pinch Me_, exemplify his best writing.

His poetry, of which _Hips and Haws_ and _Pelagea_ are representative collections, has few distinctive qualities. Citing the influence of the Irish poets, Robert Herrick, and many others on Coppard's work, critics have noted that he failed to achieve his own poetic style. Not surprisingly for an accomplished short story writer, his successful poems were his ballad stories, such as _Yokohama Garland_. Coppard evidenced his greatest poetic effect, however, in his short stories.

PRINCIPAL WORKS

Adam and Eve and Pinch Me (short stories) 1921
Clorinda Walks in Heaven (short stories) 1922
Hips and Haws (poetry) 1922
The Black Dog (short stories) 1925
Fishmonger's Fiddle (short stories) 1925
The Field of Mustard (short stories) 1926
Pelagea (poetry) 1926
Yokohama Garland (poetry) 1926
The Collected Poems (poetry) 1928
Cherry Ripe (poetry) 1935
The Collected Tales (short stories) 1948
It's Me, O Lord! (autobiography) 1957

THE TIMES LITERARY SUPPLEMENT (essay date 1921)

[If, as the publishers of _Adam and Eve and Pinch Me_ say,] Mr. Coppard acknowledges his debt to Tchehov and Mau-

A. E. COPPARD
By Powys Evans

passant, we are constrained to add the comment that he has still a great deal to learn from these two masters. As a matter of fact, in reading most of these short stories, the names of neither would have occurred to us, for the most obvious influence on Mr. Coppard is that of the Irish school, with its rather voluble style of narrative, its elaborate similes, and the elusiveness of its meaning. The last story in the book is called "an arabesque," and the impression that Mr. Coppard gives nearly always is that he is evolving a quaint design in words rather than a short story which appeals to the intelligence, a thing which Tchehov and Maupassant would never have thought of doing. Life to them was far too real and too tragic. To Mr. Coppard life seems to be a blend of fantasies from which wraiths of deep meaning float away just in the moment of apprehension.

"Marching to Zion," "Piffingcap," "The King of the World," and "The Princess of Kingdom Gone" are purely fantastic, and, regarded as such, very agreeable. In other stories, however, Mr. Coppard mixes this fantastic attitude with something more like realism, and the result is an unavoidable impression that he is deliberately straining for effect. In **"Dusky Ruth,"** for instance, which relates an amorous passage at an inn, the real delicacy of the emotion is spoiled by the flamboyance of the rhetoric, and in **"The Angel and the Sweep"** the effects of incongruity are too artificial to be convincing. When Mr. Coppard writes soberly he ascends into quite another plane of excellence. The stories called **"Communion"** and **"The Quiet Woman"** are admirable, and the disagreeable little study unaccountably called **"Weep not my Wanton"** is all the more vivid for its sobriety of statement. In the Hibernian mood **"The Trumpeters"** gave us most pleasure, but even that came dangerously near to becoming a parody.

> *"New Novels: 'Adam and Eve and Pinch Me',"* in The Times Literary Supplement (© *Times Newspapers Ltd. (London) 1921; reproduced from* The Times Literary Supplement *by permission), No. 1004, April 14, 1921, p. 243.*

MALCOLM COWLEY   (essay date 1921)

[In some of the stories in *Adam and Eve and Pinch Me*] Coppard becomes an out-and-out realist, deriving obviously—but not entirely—from Maupassant and Chekhov. . . . He is at his best when his stories, instead of marching off to an immediate blare of ghostly trumpets, begin with a matter-of-fact narration and slip quite insensibly over the borders of experience. (pp. 93-4)

He uses both landscapes and people in obtaining his effects, and he uses them both in the same way. They are the materials with which he builds; he shapes them skilfully and dispassionately. (p. 94)

The unity of his stories is emotional; it does not depend on time or space. The first few pages are spent in creating an emotion; the last in maintaining it; when the emotion dies, the story comes to an end, without much reference to plot or character. The result is sometimes an air of perverse incompleteness, and the psychoanalysts, to explain it, will refer hastily to their texts. To no avail, for Coppard's workmanship is not subconscious. The apparent difficulty is explained by the fact that his handling of a plot depends on aesthetic judgements and not on journalism or its recent ally, psychology.

The beauty which he attains (I use the work in its technical sense) is satisfyingly restrained; unlike his romantic forebears he has made the necessary compromise with the imperfections of the actual. (pp. 94-5)

It is to [Emma Bovary's] modern prototypes that we are indebted for the novel of nerves and for the development of the cult of the disagreeable. Coppard is not healthier, perhaps, but he is saner; he has nerves, but he does not allow them to be rasped continually.

In fact, he makes a habit out of not falling into pitfalls. He works in dangerous mediums; at any moment he might stumble into the bog of the Freudian novel or, on the other side, into the quicksands of [Maurice] Maeterlinck, but he keeps his feet on the firm way. To attain this surety he must either struggle a long time with his stories or else he tears up most of them. He is a careful workman and a sure workman, and a pleasant reminder that the short story, unlike the autobiographic novel, is not yet a dead form. (p. 95)

> *Malcolm Cowley, "Book Reviews: 'Adam and Eve and Pinch Me'," in* The Dial *(copyright, 1921, by The Dial Publishing Company, Inc.), Vol. LXXI,*

> *No. 1, July, 1921 (and reprinted by Kraus Reprint Corporation, 1966), pp. 93-5.*

LUDWIG LEWISOHN   (essay date 1922)

Mr. Coppard is concerned with moods, visions, legends, and with these primarily as they permit him to draw all possible variations of melody from the instrument of style. He is, first of all, a lover of words and rhythms—the large, orchestral rhythms of prose. He cultivates by turns the majestic harmonies and grave imaginative altitudes of the seventeenth century prosemen, writing of the god with "bright hair burning in the pity of the sunsets and tossing in the anger of the dawns," and the wild, earthy, naked sweetness of Synge, speaking, then, of "eyes that were soft as remembered twilight," and of a "welt that would have bruised an oak-tree." He cares very little for story interest and weaves the rich and soft or strange and stirring patterns of his imaginative moods and visions as though there were no such things in the world as machinery or magazines. He is that rare thing—an almost quite pure, quite disinterested artist to whom the deep forms of beauty have a mystical finality of value. And one cannot conceive of him as even discussing in any theoretical manner this to him at once primal and transcendent truth. Among his actual twelve legends it is a little unjust to discriminate. Each renders the visionary mood from which it grew. Perhaps most memorable are the rich, dreamy passion and pity of **"Dusky Ruth,"** the picture of immemorial and recurrent fate in **"The King of the World,"** the superb arabesque **"The Mouse"** with its strange excursion into the beauty of cruel and monstrous things.

> *Ludwig Lewisohn, "The Return of the Short Story," in* The Nation, *Vol. 114, No. 2956, March 1, 1922, p. 261.**

THE TIMES LITERARY SUPPLEMENT   (essay date 1923)

Among the diversely mannered tales which make up *The Black Dog* . . . the greater number will be found to develop the distinctive character of Mr. A. E. Coppard's two previous volumes. But the remainder serve no purpose more useful than a makeweight; for such stories as **"Simple Simon,"** **"Tanil,"** and **"The Man from Kilsheelan"** are excursions, admirably conducted, into regions of fantasy where there is nothing to nourish Mr. Coppard's earthly imagination. Whilst it is good to see a writer attempting to extend his range, the tales we have named are, in observation and sympathy, far behind the rest of the book, and smack of the literary apprenticeship.

The greater part of the book, however, testifies to a personality which is at the same time sensitive and robust. Mr. Coppard does not look outside the ordinary people of the villages for his characters, he does not choose idiots or introverts for his heroes, but he gives a vitality to country life which is strange to our usual vision of it. It is the strangeness which comes from suddenly seeing *with* people one has long been merely looking at. This gift of vision is intermittent, of course, but it is sure to appear whenever Mr. Coppard is writing of the country, and it is steadiest when his stories are in the open air. There is nothing sentimental in his treatment of the country; he does not idealize it, and has no illusions as to the wisdom of those who inhabit it. But sensuously it has deeply affected him, so that the emotions he describes stand out like motives from a rich texture, from a profound inheritance of 'memoried images'. Such stories as **"The Black Dog"** and **"The Poor Man"** have a unity closer than that of plot or style (though sometimes style is immoderately loosened), the unity we look for in a poem and may call inadequately atmosphere, though it comes from within and is personal rather than objective. The title story relates the love of a country girl and a man of birth. With this simple situation Mr. Coppard is at his best. He has avoided making an idyll of it, yet it is idyllic, in an honest sort of way. The sensibility of the man, over-refined by the habit of wealth and town life, provides him with just the contrast he needs to bring out the full pungency of his sense of country life. . . . **"The Poor Man"** is a very different kind of tale, the story of a villager to whom a measure of success came too easily. . . .

These two stories (with which **"The Handsome Lady"** and **"Mordecai and Cocking"** have much in common) are the fullest expressions of the peculiar blend of poetry and realism which distinguishes Mr. Coppard among his contemporaries and the direction in which we shall expect his gift finally to mature.

> *"New Novels: 'The Black Dog'," in* The Times Literary Supplement *(© Times Newspapers Ltd. (London) 1923; reproduced from* The Times Literary Supplement *by permission), No. 1119, June 28, 1923, p. 438.*

BABETTE DEUTSCH   (essay date 1928)

Coppard treats of poetic commonplaces: love and death, gardens and night skies. Coppard is sometimes so old-fashioned as to use not merely traditional metres but even inversion and antiquated stresses. But this lack of originality has not impaired the quality of his work. He can bestow upon the tritest of themes—the betrayal of a lover, the oncoming of evening, youth's vanishing— words and cadences that give it new values. A nice choice in phrasing, a sardonic abruptness, a fine sense of melody, combine to give a fresh lustre to the oldest story. As for his occasional employment of a style that would and does suit the verse of Donne and Herrick, Crashaw and Webster, that, too, fails to offend because Coppard shares with those poets not merely certain technical mannerisms but a unique vigor of attack a rich sweetness of tone. . . .

Not that Coppard always uses the traditional forms. Frequently he writes in a fluent free verse, innocent of rhyme, but never unmusical. Indeed, what one notes first about his poems is that they are all compact of music. Not for nothing does one find such titles as **"A Carol for Margaret Chester,"** **"Andante,"** **"Autumn Song,"** **"Crazy Girls Song,"** **"Nocturne,"** One can readily conceive of hearing them sung, to melodies written by Brahms, or Schumann, or it might be Hugo Wolff. And there are several that should be performed by such a company as the English singers, with all the delicacy, all the flourish with which they enhance the simplest tune.

But pure melody, however delightful is insufficient ballast to carry poetry to the far shores that Coppard reaches. . . . Perhaps it would be more nearly just to describe Coppard, in so far as his poetry reveals him, as one who believes in the sensual apprehension of truths beyond the understanding. Here is no Wordsworth, waiting for the heavens and the hills to utter universal truths. Here is a skeptical comtemporary,

who so profoundly possesses the seen that, in communicating it, he touches the fringes of the unseen. Nothing can destroy his feeling for the life about him. . . .

At the same time, he has a benign acridity. It flavors not only that bitter piece on the war entitled **"The Glorious Survivors,"** and the poem called **"The Conscript,"** and the ballad of **"The Unfortunate Miller."** It is present even in songs of defeated love such as most poets are content to dress in the garments of tender melancholy. (p. 5)

Disillusion, fear, pain, are as real to Coppard as beauty, laughter, and health. His eye for the noble and the lovely has been sharpened because he has lived with the evil and the ugly. Whatever he has looked upon he has seen with an intensity of vision that approaches the supersensuous. Is not the ability to convey such an experience the essence of the poetic gift? (p. 6)

> *Babette Deutsch, "The Essence of Poetry," in* New York Herald Tribune Books *(© I.H.T. Corporation; reprinted by permission), Vol. 88, No. 29960, November 25, 1928, pp. 5-6.*

HAMISH MACLAREN   (essay date 1928)

Mr. Coppard's book [*Collected Poems*] is published for the sound and sufficient reason that his two earlier volumes of poetry, *Hips and Haws* and *Pelagea,* are now no longer obtainable. . . . [Whilst] Mr. Coppard is recognized in two continents as a short story writer of, to say the least, durable quality, up to the present his poetry has remained practically unknown to the public. One can only hope that, coming perhaps at a more fortunate time than *Hips and Haws* did . . . , and containing as it does the whole of the poet's output, it will receive the attention from the public that it deserves. It is not enough that a few poetry readers of discernment should be left to appreciate such work. Mr. Coppard is as definitely a poet as a short story writer, getting into his verse the same effects of life crystallized with gem-like precision and clarity, the same apparently casual and yet deliberate music, and the same deep compassion and understanding as the finest of his stories show. . . . Mr. Coppard, although he prefaces his poems with a most refreshing and challenging *Advertisement,* is not himself an advertiser. He does not howl his verse through a megaphone, and not for one stanza will he descend from his own high, chosen point of outlook to be merely "different," or to echo popular ideas that he obviously cannot feel. He has no master in the making of verse but the rich tradition of the English language. And he works from life, not books. . . .

Mr. Coppard is modern in the only intelligible sense of the word, he is himself: and not less modern because he so frequently reminds one of Herrick, a poet who will be up-to-date so long as the English language exists. If he is not read now, Mr. Coppard may take some slight consolation in the fact that he very likely will be in the second, third, or twentieth generation after us.

> *Hamtsh Maclaren, "Joints of Cunning Workmanship," in* The Spectator *(© 1928 by* The Spectator; *reprinted by permission of* The Spectator), *Vol. 141, No. 5241, December 8, 1928, p. 873.*

MORTON DAUWEN ZABEL   (essay date 1929)

Readers of *The Black Dog* and *Fishmonger's Fiddle* have set A. E. Coppard down as one of the best tale-tellers of our day. He is no rapid narrator with a hundred stories up his sleeve, but a sly and crafty fabricator who has fashioned some of the most adroit fables of recent days. Like T. F. Powys, he has confined himself rather closely to the folk tradition of the English country; but his genius is humorous, not tragic, and his frail allegories and legends are alive with his own witty fantasy. (pp. 48-9)

[His poems] do not ring out across the fields of modern literature with high voices. They are likely to win the ear of those readers who already know their author for his other work, and who make up that small group which admires the bric-a-brac of art. They lead us into a narrow plot of ground which Mr. Coppard has cultivated carefully: it includes a small patch of woodland populated by gnomes and grandmothers; a neat garden full of wrens and robins; a tavern where greybeards are forever retelling village yarns; a tiny heath for little tragedies; ponds for dace and alewives; and a house full of ragged books. (p. 49)

Mr. Coppard's verses must have caused him much amusement. They show a variety of meters and rhythms; they use refrains and choruses and all the characters and symbols of popular allegory. Probably the most successful (at least to their author) are those which give us ballad stories: *Betty Perrin, The Innkeeper's Handkerchiefs, Pelagea,* and the exquisite tale of *Yokohama Garland.* Some of the poems define types in a way which reminds us of Hardy. The best, however, are probably those which reduce the intricate devices of Mr. Coppard's art to simple lyric elements. . . . In *Crazy Girl's Song, Country Sabbath,* and *Geography on the Jew's Harp,* Mr. Coppard invites—and suffers by—comparison with Walter de la Mare. And his literary personality is strong enough not to desire confusion with any other writer's. He has a bright little niche of his own. (pp. 49-50)

> *Morton Dauwen Zabel, "Dainty Devices," in* Poetry *(© 1929 by The Modern Poetry Association; reprinted by permission of the Editor of* Poetry*), Vol. XXXIV, No. 1, April, 1929, pp. 48-50.*

GEORGE BRANDON SAUL (essay date 1931)

[The] enduring qualities of the Elizabethans and their wayward kin have unquestionably colored the strands of [Mr. Coppard's] thought, though that fact need not embarrass the poet, who stands on thoroughly good legs of his own, and who has merely interpreted in the light of his own individuality moods which the "sons of Ben", as well as the brothers, could have shared. One feels that here is a man who would have been as welcome in the pastoral loneliness of Herrick, or the boisterous give-and-take of the Mermaid, as he is in his own local inn.

For Mr. Coppard is—save in a few instances which insist on recognition—eminently natural throughout his poetry, and entirely frank in personal revelation. He is, fundamentally, neither innovator nor experimenter; whether his verse be "free" or "regular", he is concerned with the old tranquillities, the old ecstasies. And he is an artist to the bone. . . . [Like] Mr. Yeats, he likes to rework his verse (generally to its improvement). Yet he is one who . . . finds it difficult to be confined by highly artificial lyric forms (which may account for his frequent use of free verse). Technically, Mr. Coppard is almost invariably satisfactory, and often hauntingly so . . . . consider the meditative quality of his merely cadenced verse . . . , the fantastic arpeggios of "Geography

on the Jew's Harp", the delicately imperfect rhyme to be found in "Betty Perrin", the unforgettable perfection of "Night Piece", "Stay, O Stay", "Curfew", "Winter Field", "Complaint of Time", or "A Carol for Margaret Chester". . . . Yet there are things in Mr. Coppard's poetry that one could wish away, if only to prevent contrast with the indubitably finer things he offers in rich profusion—and thus assure greater evenness of impression. (pp. 39-40)

It seems unfortunate . . . that Mr. Coppard has indulged so immoderately in free verse . . .—unfortunate because free verse tempts vague and easy moods into mild expression as disciplined verse seldom does, and because it too readily becomes a habit rather than the necessity of a given impulse. . . . What better explanation than Mr. Coppard's too ready yielding to the temptations of an easy and casual form, then, need be sought for the dilettantism untrue to his real nature, but inevitably suggested by poems like "The Sapling"; or for the brittle artificiality of the opening of "The Young Man under the Walnut Tree". . . . (p. 41)

[Also] certain mannerisms are legitimately to be observed. For example, one notes the frequent use of inversions, as in "Andante":

> Sways not the lilied stem,
> The rose not sways; . . .

inversions which do not invariably enrich the cadence, though they do in the "Carol" and certain other poems. Similarly, one is aware of the occasional imitation of a kind of Anglo-Irish; of a tendency toward exclamation and apostrophe; of a fondness for grave accents and abstractions like "love", "truth", "beauty", "wisdom", and so forth; and of a constant preoccupation with time and the idea of time—a preoccupation which, however often it insinuates itself into the reader's consciousness, is, strangely, never tiresome, and is mentioned here merely because it has the quality of a mannerism—or manner—of thought.

But Mr. Coppard, whatever his faults or strikingly recurrent peculiarities, is never commonplace. Certain pieces, naturally, have less appeal than others—but here the matter of individual taste inevitably asserts prejudices. . . . I cannot help feeling that Mr. Coppard should avoid the rightly-or-wrongly-so-dubbed "metaphysical" species of poetry: his gift lies in the simple and clear—in suggestion by overtone and implication, not in profound deduction—as the ineffectiveness of "Mendacity" and "The Well", compared with the complete success of "Curfew" and "Night Piece", should testify. (pp. 43-5)

It seems true to observe that Mr. Coppard's great general qualities are the pictorial and descriptive; indeed (in "Pelagea", "Yokohama Garland", and "Country Sabbath", for example) one sometimes feels that a given poem is really a draft for a prose tale. It is also true that—in Mr. Frost's phrase—one has to be "versed in country things" to comprehend Mr. Coppard completely . . . : but this fact need disquiet not even the most perversely urban of possible readers, who can disregard the question of whether bats have a "trickling flight" with small loss of enjoyment. It merely happens that, so far as diffused qualities are concerned, this poet is at his best when, in pastoral mood (and sometimes mode), he is writing of night, rusticity (country gardens—country characters), and the incongruities of love. (pp. 48-9)

His most memorable utterances on love consist in four lyrics—"Stay, O Stay", "The Trick of Change", "Complaint of Time", and "A Lover".... (pp. 50-1)

Poems like these do much by way of revealing a personal philosophy and characteristic ideas.... (p. 53)

[There is a robust quality in] Mr. Coppard's vocabulary. The man loves words for their own sake; he likes to savor them.... Generally the unusual words or coinages to which he inclines give a delightful effect of originality and freshness: never do they suggest pedantry, bookishness, or unjustifiable daring, and only in a few cases does too-obvious choosing injure personal element or pictorial effectiveness.... And the poet has the wit seldom to press language so hard as he does in "The Sapling", where he speaks of an "unthrift tree".

He has the wit, too, to indulge his gift for imagistic writing, as poems like "Dusk", "Quiet", "The Oracle", and "To One Unknown and Gone" abundantly testify. Consequently he gives us an interior like that in "The Streams", with its lovely close, warm with simple life.... or a changing canvas like that of "Storm on the Heath"; or, again, an exquisitely delicate projection of pictorial sensuousness like that of "Midwinter Night's Dream".... (pp. 54-5)

No less fresh than his imagistic qualities are Mr. Coppard's figures and comparisons. The poet who says the moon is [so] clear . . . that the mist coils "like a subtle wrestler round the hill", that the sunlight "pounds" "soft rocks" of cloud "like an axe", or that death is "the shore of idle waters" . . . assuredly—and rightly—does not suggest the reviver of trite phrases and stereotyped figures, but does suggest the sane individualist and the original artist that Mr. Coppard unquestionably is.

Finally, it may be remarked that while this poet is . . . more memorable for lyrics as entities than for lyrics as mere frameworks on which striking "readings of life" are hung, "readings of life" are by no means absent from his work. But these readings (most frequent in the free verse) do not have the lyrical spark, the sudden revelation, of such lines as Meredith's . . . they have, rather, like Mr. Frost's, the quality of having been deliberately thought out.... Yet Mr. Coppard, being always a fine poet at bottom, has his full share of memorable phrases and effective figures—phrases like "besieging sleep", figures like that which compares the sound of a weir to "the cry of a little everlasting train" or like those already mentioned.... He has called poetry "instant and simple and clear": his own best lyrics are precisely and undeniably that in eminent degree.... (pp. 56-8)

> *George Brandon Saul, in his* A. E. Coppard: His Life and His Poetry to the Publication of the "Bibliography," *a thesis given at The University of Pennsylvania in 1931 (copyright © 1932 by George Brandon Saul), printed in Philadelphia, 1932, pp. 39-58.*

H. E. BATES (essay date 1941)

Katherine Mansfield and A. E. Coppard, for all their faults and their debt to Tchehov, succeeded more than any other writers of their day in assisting the English short story to a state of adult emancipation.... [It] will remain eternally to the credit of Katherine Mansfield and A. E. Coppard that both attempted to bring to the short story some of the fancy, delicacy, shape, and coloured conceit of the Elizabethan

lyric—a comparison especially true in the case of Coppard—and that when they left it the short story had gained new vitality and new design and above all, perhaps, a certain quality of transparency. (p. 124)

Coppard, who had spent some years of his life in business, had waited rather longer than most writers before opening up the literary shop. It is not surprising, therefore, that the first contents of that window should have had a certain maturity of finish.... Coppard's first window display, in fact, was like a show of well-made, bright-coloured handicraft: strong in texture, bold and fanciful in design, carefully finished, fashioned from excellent native materials which, like oak and wool, had their own sweet earthy and enduring flavour. For Coppard, like Sherwood Anderson, had recognized the beauty and value of indigenous materials.

Coppard's work is contained, except for a little verse, in a dozen volumes of stories. Of these only the first six or seven are outstanding; the work between *Adam and Eve and Pinch Me* and *Silver Circus* contains the cream of Coppard. In each of these volumes there meet a number of conflicting elements which are both the actual and the theoretical essentials of all Coppard's work: on the one hand realism, vivid factual description, earthiness, a home-brewed strength and simplicity; on the other hand fantasy, fairy-tale impossibility, exoticism, psychological trickery and hypothesis, sophistication; on the one hand buffoonery, punning, heartiness, bawdiness, good rounds of belly-laughter and low comedy; on the other hand a certain literary dandiness, pretty play of words, elaborate metaphorical crochet-work, a love of subtle conceits for their own sake. As time goes on the elements of the first group are forced into secondary place by the elements of the other; the home-brewed earthy simplicity is ousted by a kind of twilit fantasy; the trick of telling a tale rather than of writing a story reaches a stage where it is all too patently the result of a carefully elaborated theory.

For this too must be noted about the work of Coppard: his pieces are not stories but, as he is very careful to emphasize on every fly-leaf, tales. Behind this lies Coppard's theory that the art of telling stories, since it originates by the primitive camp-fires of unread peoples far back in time, is an oral and not a written one.... Such a method of tale-telling, having much in common with folk-lore, local legend, and the spoken parable (note that Coppard delights in allegory), would depend for its effect largely on pictorial simplicity, the use of homely metaphor, and the entire absence of literary language.

Unfortunately for Coppard's theory his work shows the strongest signs—increasing rather than decreasing as time goes on—that he is in reality a very literary writer, influenced in turn by other very literary writers, notably Henry James. Throughout Coppard's work may be observed, in fact, the consequences of a strange battle between tale-telling at its simplest and tale-telling at its most sophisticated. And in this battle Henry James is the major—and regrettably I think—the winning combatant.

This corruption of Coppard's work by sophisticated influences seriously detracts from what originally promised to be a very stout, yeoman achievement, very much of the English earth, closely akin to the lyric poetry of the Elizabethans. As Coppard began speaking, in the early twenties, through such volumes as *Clorinda Walks in Heaven, The Black Dog,* and *Fishmonger's Fiddle*, it was clear that a poet had taken up the short story, choosing as his backgrounds the countryside of middle England, the pubs, the provincial towns with their faded breweries and gloomy old-fashioned lawyers' offices, even the East End of London and the shops of tailors' pressers. A man with ripe powers of description, an uncanny knack of weaving a tale, a keen eye for lyrical colour, a sense of both humour and tragedy, Coppard had both strong and delicate gifts. The results excited attention, as they were bound to do, for Coppard's way was refreshing and the English short story had never known such pieces as *Dusky Ruth, The Poor Man, The Higgler, Fishmonger's Fiddle*—stories as sturdy and sound in grain as oak, as delicate and oddly scented as hawthorn. Coppard's peculiar achievement in such stories was never subsequently surpassed. (pp. 134-36)

Coppard wrote with great care, piecing his stories together rather than writing them, noting down metaphors as they flashed on him, storing up oddities of description, odd names, odd situations, until a suitable niche was found for them in the final framework of the tale. All this gives his work the effect, at times, of being the product of an arts-and-crafts shop. Its apparent boisterous spontaneity is in reality studied; the shop window with its homespun cloth and rough carving has been set out by a West End hand. Coppard cannot escape, I think, the charge of pretentiousness even in some of his best work—yet that work, as seen in *The Higgler, Dusky Ruth, Fine Feathers, The Cherry Tree, The Field of Mustard*, is as English and as sturdily beautiful as the Cotswold Hills and the Buckinghamshire beech-woods that are so often the background of Coppard's tales. On these achievements, and a dozen or so like them, Coppard's reputation may safely rest. The worst of his work can never detract from their craftsmanship or their very English beauty.

Unlike Wells and Kipling, Coppard had no sociological axes to grind. He was interested only in the tale for the tale's sake; in his stories there is no social, religious, scientific, or imperialistic background or bias. Coppard was interested in what happened to people once they got on to the merry-go-round of emotion, and indeed his stories, half-real, half-fantastic, have something of the atmosphere of the fair-ground; behind the well-lit exteriors lurks a certain air of gipsyish fancy and romance, and it is interesting to note that Coppard for some years chose just that gipsyish mode of life, living as he did in an isolated caravan in the Buckinghamshire woods and writing many of his best stories there.

But Coppard, forty when the Great War ended, hardly belongs to the generation of writers that cut its teeth on bullets and found the future beyond 1920 a very sadly disrupted prospect. Coppard, though always regarded as a writer young in spirit, belongs essentially to the generation of Conrad and Maugham. His significance to the new generation lay in the fact that he alone of his generation sought his expression solely in the short story. . . . (pp. 138-40)

> *H. E. Bates, "Katherine Mansfield and A. E. Coppard," in his* The Modern Short Story: A Critical Survey *(© 1972 by Evensford Productions Ltd.), T. Nelson and Sons Ltd.; reprinted by permission of Lawrence Pollinger Limited, as agents for The Estate of H. E. Bates), 1941 (and reprinted by Michael Joseph Ltd, 1972, pp. 122-47).*

FRANK O'CONNOR (essay date 1963)

Coppard was a Georgian in the same way that Robert Frost, Edward Thomas, Edmund Blunden, and a score of others were Georgians, and he shared their obsession with personal freedom—freedom from responsibilities, freedom from conventions—particularly sexual conventions; freedom from duties to state and church, above all, freedom from the tyranny of money. (pp. 171-72)

In the early books of stories, particularly **The Black Dog** . . . and the magnificent **Fishmonger's Fiddle** . . . , the sense of personal freedom creates the feeling of a country being looked at again in an entirely new way. It even creates the feeling of the form itself being handled in a new way. Most storytellers see the short story first as a convention that appeals to them: the convention of Chekhov, the convention of Maupassant—in America nowadays, the convention of Joyce—and it is only as their work develops that they create a convention of their own. Coppard knew Chekhov and Maupassant backward, but he never settles for one convention rather than the other, or indeed for any convention other than his own need to grip the reader by the lapel and make him listen.

As a result, his formal range is remarkable—greater I should say than that of any other storyteller. A story like **"The Field of Mustard"** might be an exercise in the manner of Chekhov; others suggest Maupassant; others still seem to be folk tales like those of Hardy: **"At Laban's Well"** could be a prose version of a poem by Robert Frost, while **"Mr. Lightfoot in the Green Isle"** is merely a skittish description of a walking tour in Ireland which might have appeared in a travel magazine. (pp. 173-74)

One can trace his feeling of freedom even better in his tendency to prefer quality—in the painter's sense of the word—to design. What this meant in practice to Coppard was that whenever a character entered a restaurant or a railway carriage there should be someone or something there for him to observe, even when this distracted from the character's own preoccupation. He might have just visited the hospital where his sweetheart was dying or the prison where his only son was awaiting execution, but having a bit of Coppard in him, he could never resist a momentary interest in an old gentleman with a passion for Hittite. This is perfectly true and within the experience of everybody. (pp. 174-75)

Technically what it means is that to write a story resembling the best of Coppard we should have to carry a notebook and jot down the details of every moment of interest and pleasure—the appearance of a house of landscape, the effects of lighting, the impression of characters glimpsed in passing, with their actual words. Then we should have to work these notes into the texture of whatever story we happened to be writing until every paragraph tended to be a complete work of art. . . .

[In the early Coppard stories] the surface of the story is always exquisitely rendered—the glimpses of landscape, the snatches of conversation overheard, the odd names of villages and people, the illiterate shop signs—even the comments in the visitors' book in country inns. (p. 175)

The landscape, too, seen in sudden vivid flashes like jottings from a painter's notebook is surely the moment caught and held in a brilliant sentence or two. "Oppidan was startled by a flock of starlings that slid across the evening with the steady movement of a cloud." . . .

But though Coppard may have thought that he wrote for every sort of magazine and in every sort of manner, there was one kind of story that he wrote again and again as though he were in the grip of some inner compulsion. That is the story in which the motivation is given by some woman's secretiveness. (p. 176)

He was fascinated primarily by women's secretiveness: it is the theme of most of his great stories, and I fancy one could almost trace his decline as a writer by confining oneself to the stories in which it recurs. In *Fishmonger's Fiddle* . . . , which is probably Coppard's finest book, it occurs in several forms. (p. 177)

[In both **"The Watercress Girl"** and **"The Higgler"**] we catch a glimpse of Coppard's preoccupation with money, but a glimpse only, for it is kept in its proper place as part of the necessary condition of life.

But in **"The Little Mistress"**—an enchanting story—money, which has been a mere incidental in the other stories, intrudes, and with it an excess of what I have already described as "quality." (pp. 178-79)

[In *The Field of Mustard* the treatment of the money problem] is even more casual. It is a fine story, but I have to put my finger on passage after passage in which Coppard's mania for quality has run away with him and played hell with the design. I know that in earlier stories he has made fun of it, but the digressions were sufficiently amusing to justify the joke. (pp. 181-82)

[With **"Olive and Camilla"**] I find myself reaching out for a very soft black pencil. It is not, God knows, that I want to eliminate the thing that delights me in Coppard, the accidental and incidental. . . . It is because all the characters are being taken out and replaced by Coppard himself; because the wonderful sense of personal freedom that for a time penetrated and leavened the dull mass of Necessity has begun to get out of hand and the necessary daily bread has started to blow up into a thin feathery pastry. To be quite so much at ease with the logic of circumstance—the power of things, which the Spanish poet tells us can do more than Hercules himself—is to be a thoroughgoing romantic, and, what is more, a romantic with an independent income. (pp. 182-83)

It is obvious that Coppard is deeply attracted by the woman [in **"Emergency Exit"**] and admires the perfect freedom of her behavior . . . , but it never seems to have occurred to him that from the point of view of the suspicious reader what he seems to be admiring is a very large income indeed. . . . Freedom and necessity—those two poles between which we mortals must live—are getting far too close to the old poles of wealth and poverty we know from Victorian romances. (p. 184)

I begin to wonder whether Coppard's favorite subject is not one best suited to comedy, or even farce; whether, in fact, the particular sort of freedom he longs for is really personal freedom at all and not merely a new form of the old naturalistic compulsion that put a man's nose to the grindstone and never admitted the possibility of his raising it again. Coppard . . . , being a man of the people, knew what the grindstone was, and when he describes people of his own class, like Frank Oppidan and the Higgler, each with his dream of a nice girl with a little money, the personal freedom Coppard had himself achieved gave him a new perception of the possibilities of their lives; but when he turned it on people of the leisured classes it tended to become a romanticism of wealth and position. (p. 185)

In this metamorphosis Coppard's greatest virtues become faults in their own right. His uncanny perception of a woman's secretiveness, her mystery, the thing that lures men, continues, but the mystery gradually seems to require a larger and larger income to support it in the style to which it is accustomed, until the dullest, plainest housewife begins to seem more attractive. The quality—the packing of the story with fascinating though largely irrelevant detail—becomes more irritating, as though Coppard were not really performing an impudent pirouette but indulging some nervous tyranny. Freedom and necessity are not abstractions but different poles of the human condition, and too much emphasis on one can only result in some inhuman form of the other. (p. 186)

> *Frank O'Connor, "The Price of Freedom," in his*
> The Lonely Voice: A Study of the Short Story *(©*
> *1962, 1963 by Frank O'Connor; reprinted by permission of Joan Daves, Literary Agents), World*
> *Publishing Co., 1963, pp. 170-86.*

DORIS LESSING (essay date 1972)

These short stories [*Selected Stories*] are as fine as any we have. In friends' houses, on the shelves where the books stay which will be kept always, you find Coppard. Talking to people, not necessarily literary, who have read their own way into literature, and who use books for nourishment and not debate, Coppard's tales are found to be treasures. He wrote a good many, some now in collections hard to come by. They are not widely known or quoted. Yet that they can have a general appeal was proved when recently they were adapted for television: like Lawrence, Coppard tells a good story.

He was an exquisite craftsman, and wrote well-made tales. But their shape was that of the growth of people or events, so that watching one unfold, you have to cry 'What else? Of course!' as you do in life. Coppard's work owes everything to this quality of knowing how things must be, how they have to work out. He understands growth. Nowhere are cataclysms or marvels, not so much as the whiff of a foreign port or an exotic person. If there's a sailor, then he has come back from somewhere and will be off again. (p. vii)

[Coppard] was the most lovable of people, and it is evident in every word he wrote. (p. xii)

> *Doris Lessing, "Introduction" (© 1972 by Doris*
> *Lessing), in* Selected Stories *by A. E. Coppard,*
> *Jonathan Cape, 1972, pp. vii-xii.*

GEORGE BRANDON SAUL (essay date 1976)

After the appearance . . . of *The Black Dog*, there was no question in competently critical minds as to the significance of Alfred Edgar Coppard . . . as a teller of prose tales. Not that sufficient argument had not been implicit in the contents of the two earlier collections—[*Adam and Eve and Pinch Me* and *Clorinda Walks in Heaven*] . . . : it is only that *The Black Dog*, an exuberant blend of humor and tragedy, rich in colloquial speech as in make-believe, proved especially revelatory of imaginative scope and range of human concern. And the long—and at least through *Polly Oliver* . . . exciting—series of prose volumes that followed unquestionably won their author every right to recognition as a leading writer of short stories (he preferred the label "tales") in his day, and as a worthy member of that line of outstanding, albeit sometimes anonymous, yarn-spinners which in British antiquity begins beyond old Chaucer's time. For what we find here—at best, as a result of preoccupation with what George Meredith calls "tragic life"—is a wizard joy in the telling of tales that will hold not only old men "from the chimney corner," and an achievement perhaps justifying the garrulous Ford Madox Ford's claim: "Mr. Coppard is almost the first English writer to get into English prose the peculiar quality of English lyric verse . . . the fancy, the turn of imagination, the wisdom, the as it were piety and beauty of the great seventeenth century lyricists. . . ."

America has at date of writing yet to pay a tribute of critical appreciation to the genius of Coppard consonant with that accorded by his fellow Britons. . . . (pp. 104-05)

> *George Brandon Saul, "Complaint of Time: A. E. Coppard's Verse," in his* In Praise of the Half-Forgotten and Other Ruminations *(© 1976 by George Brandon Saul), Bucknell University Press, 1976, pp. 104-18.*

ADDITIONAL BIBLIOGRAPHY

Jehin, A. *Remarks on the Style of A. E. Coppard.* Buenos Aires: Talleres Graficos Contreras, 1944, 15 p.
> Thorough study of Coppard's techniques of contrast, inversion, and transposition.

"Latest Works of Fiction: *The Black Dog.*" *The New York Times Book Review* (21 October 1923): 8.
> Briefly explores the theme of death found in the stories in *The Black Dog.*

(Harold) Hart Crane

1899-1932

American poet and essayist.

Although he left only a small body of work, Crane is important as a lyric poet in the tradition of the romantic visionary. As such, his work is often compared to that of Blake, Coleridge, and Baudelaire. A man acutely conscious of the transitory nature of life, Crane sought salvation from the spiritual pains of existence through art. His poetry chronicles a quest for love and beauty that would lift him above life's miseries. Thus, his work is at once an expression of despair over the disintegrative processes of life and a cry of exultation for his occasional transcendence of despair through art. Crane's greatest poems are ecstatic celebrations of life reminiscent of Whitman.

As the only child of estranged parents, Crane was often the victim of their mutual antagonism. Never sure of his parents' love, he sought affection from friends, but his needs were often greater than their emotional capacities. Consequently, Crane reacted with bitterness over what he considered to be betrayal, a response which regularly colors his poetry. Because he left high school without a diploma, Crane found it difficult to hold a job. His life was further complicated by his aggressive homosexuality and his alcoholism. Financial and emotional difficulties, including despair over what he considered to be failing poetic powers, led him to commit suicide.

Crane's poetry is often difficult to comprehend, primarily because of his poetic theory. According to Crane, logic should not be allowed to divest experience of its complexity, for "the entire construction of the poem is raised on the organic principle of a 'logic of metaphor,' which antedates our so-called pure logic." Thus his poems are often laden with private symbolism and emotions inspired by the sounds of words. He was more concerned with the illogical connotations and associations inspired by words than he was with their rigid definitions, which he felt would limit the perceptions of his poems. Throughout his career Crane aimed at spontaneity of expression and crystallization of feeling through rich imagery; to achieve this effect he often wrote while drinking and listening to jazz. This type of composition best served his lyric poetry, which was unencumbered by any philosophical abstractions requiring careful logical development. Of the poems in *White Buildings*, "Voyages," an evocation of lost love, stands out as his lyrical masterpiece.

Crane's major work, *The Bridge*, planned as a reply to T. S. Eliot's *The Waste Land*, is essentially a series of lyrics on a single theme. *The Bridge* was meant to counteract the pessimism of Eliot's poem with an exuberant affirmation of experience. Crane intended to provide a myth for American life, but his lack of formal education resulted in social analysis and criticism that displayed a deficient knowledge and understanding of the American past. Early critics, while recognizing the greatness of individual passages, considered the poem as a whole to be a failure. Most found *The Bridge* to have no formal unity or logical exposition of its ideas; its symbolic structure was considered incoherent and poorly conceived. Later critics, however, have reassessed the poem. They agree that as an epic expression of American history and an affirmative myth of

American experience the poem fails. But they contend that *The Bridge* succeeds admirably as the portrayal of a spiritual quest for a new mythic vision. The poem's subject is thus the quest itself and the necessity for such an intense examination of experience by every individual. Whether or not the quest succeeds in providing a new vision is of secondary importance. Though uncertain about its ultimate merit, most critics agree that *The Bridge* is a major achievement in many of its parts and that Crane is one of the most important American poets since Whitman.

(See also *TCLC*, Vol. 2, and *Dictionary of Literary Biography*, Vol. 4)

PRINCIPAL WORKS

White Buildings (poetry) 1926
The Bridge (poetry) 1930
The Collected Poems of Hart Crane (poetry) 1933
Complete Poems and Selected Letters and Prose (poetry, letters, and essays) 1966

HART CRANE and HARRIET MONROE (essay date 1926)

[The following correspondence between Hart Crane and Harriet Monroe, editor of *Poetry*, refers to the poem **"At Melville's Tomb."**]

From the editor to Mr. Crane:

Take me for a hard-boiled unimaginative unpoetic reader, and tell me how *dice* can *bequeath an embassy* (or anything else); and how a *calyx* (*of death's bounty* or anything else) can give back a *scattered chapter, livid hieroglyph;* and how, if it does, such a *portent* can be *wound in corridors* (of shells or anything else). . . .

All this may seem impertinent, but is not so intended. Your ideas and rhythms interest me, and I am wondering by what process of reasoning you would justify this poem's succession of champion mixed metaphors, of which you must be conscious. The packed line should pack its phrases in orderly relation, it seems to me, in a manner tending to clear confusion instead of making it worse confounded. . . .

From Mr. Crane to the editor:

Your good nature and manifest interest in writing me about the obscurities apparent in my Melville poem certainly prompt a wish to clarify my intentions in that poem as much as possible. (p. 35)

[Though] I imagine us to have considerable differences of opinion regarding the relationship of poetic metaphor to ordinary logic (I judge this from the angle of approach you use toward portions of the poem), I hope my answers will not be taken as a defense of merely certain faulty lines. I am really much more interested in certain theories of metaphor and technique involved generally in poetics, than I am concerned in vindicating any particular perpetrations of my own.

My poem may well be elliptical and actually obscure in the ordering of its content, but in your criticism of this very possible deficiency you have stated your objections in terms that allow me, at least for the moment, the privilege of claiming your ideas and ideals as theoretically, at least, quite outside the issues of my own aspirations. To put it more plainly, as a poet I may very possibly be more interested in the so-called illogical impingements of the connotations of words on the consciousness (and their combinations and interplay in metaphor on this basis) than I am interested in the preservation of their logically rigid significations at the cost of limiting my subject matter and perceptions involved in the poem.

This may sound as though I merely fancied juggling words and images until I found something novel, or esoteric; but the process is much more predetermined and objectified than that. (p. 36)

Its paradox, of course, is that its apparent illogic operates so logically in conjunction with its context in the poem as to establish its claim to another logic, quite independent of the original definition of the word or phrase or image thus employed. It implies (this *inflection* of language) a previous or prepared receptivity to its stimulus on the part of the reader. The reader's sensibility simply responds by identifying this inflection of experience with some event in his own history or perceptions—or rejects it altogether. . . . Much fine poetry may be completely rationalistic in its use of symbols, but there is much great poetry of another order which will yield the reader very little when inspected under the limitation of such arbitrary concerns as are manifested in your judgment of the Melville poem, especially when you constitute such requirements of ordinary logical relationship between word and word as irreducible. (pp. 36-7)

You ask me how a *portent* can possibly be wound in a *shell*. Without attempting to answer this for the moment, I ask you how Blake could possibly say that "a *sigh* is a *sword* of an Angel King." . . . I ask you how Eliot can possibly believe that "Every street *lamp* that I pass *beats* like a fatalistic *drum!*" . . . [My] metaphors may fall down completely. I'm not defending their actual value in themselves; but your criticism of them . . . was leveled at an illogicality of relationship between symbols, which similar fault you must have either overlooked in case you have ever admired the Blake and Eliot lines, or have there condoned them on account of some more ultimate convictions pressed on you by the impact of the poems in their entirety.

It all comes to the recognition that emotional dynamics are not to be confused with any absolute order of rationalized definitions; ergo, in poetry the *rationale* of metaphor belongs to another order of experience than science, and is not to be limited by a scientific and arbitrary code of relationships either in verbal inflections or concepts.

There are plenty of people who have never accumulated a sufficient series of reflections (and these of a rather special nature) to perceive the relation between a *drum* and a *street lamp*—via the *unmentioned* throbbing of the heart and nerves in a distraught man which *tacitly* creates the reason and "logic" of the Eliot metaphor. They will always have a perfect justification for ignoring those lines and to claim them obscure, excessive, etc., until by some experience of their own the words accumulate the necessary connotations to complete their connection. (pp. 37-8)

If one can't count on some such bases in the reader now and then, I don't see how the poet has any chance to ever get beyond the simplest conceptions of emotion and thought, of sensation and lyrical sequence. (p. 38)

Not to rant on forever, I'll beg your indulgence and come at once to the explanations you requested on the Melville poem:

> "The dice of drowned men's bones he saw bequeath
> An embassy."

Dice bequeath an embassy, in the first place, by being ground (in this connection only, of course) in little cubes from the bones of drowned men by the action of the sea, and are finally thrown up on the sand, having "numbers" but no identification. These being the bones of dead men who never completed their voyage, it seems legitimate to refer to them as the only surviving evidence of certain messages undelivered, mute evidence of certain things, experiences that the dead mariners might have had to deliver. Dice as a symbol of chance and circumstance is also implied.

> "The calyx of death's bounty giving back," etc.

This calyx refers in a double ironic sense both to a cornucopia and the vortex made by a sinking vessel. As soon as the water has closed over a ship this whirlpool sends up broken spars, wreckage, etc., which can be alluded to as *livid hieroglyphs*, making a *scattered chapter* so far as any complete record of the recent ship and her crew is concerned. In fact, about as much definite knowledge might come from all this as anyone might gain from the roar of his own veins, which is easily heard (haven't you ever done it?) by holding a shell close to one's ear. (pp. 38-9)

From the editor to Mr. Crane:

No doubt our theories and ideals in the art differ more or less fundamentally, yet I would not deny to the poet the right to take certain of the liberties you claim. I think he can take as many as he succeeds with without mystifying his particular audience; for mystery is good, but not mystification.

I think that in your poem certain phrases carry to an excessive degree the "dynamics of metaphor"—they telescope three or four images together by mental leaps (I fear my own metaphors are getting mixed!) which the poet, knowing his ground, can take safely, but which the most sympathetic reader cannot take unless the poet leads him by the hand with some such explanation as I find in your letter. . . .

I don't get this effect from Blake or Eliot in the lines you quote or others that I have read. . . .

My argument comes down, I suppose, rather to your practice than your theory. Or, more specifically, your practice strains your theory by carrying it, with relentless logic, to a remote and exaggerated extreme. You find me testing metaphors, and poetic concept in general, too much by logic, whereas I find you pushing logic to the limit in a painfully intellectual search for emotion, for poetic motive. Your poem reeks with brains—it is thought out, worked out, sweated out. And the beauty which it seems entitled to is tortured and lost. (p. 40)

> *Hart Crane and Harriet Monroe, "A Discussion with Hart Crane," in* Poetry *(© 1926 by The Modern Poetry Association), Vol. XXIX, No. 1, October, 1926, pp. 34-41.*

EDMUND WILSON (essay date 1927)

Mr. Crane has a most remarkable style [as exhibited in *White Buildings*], a style that is strikingly original—almost something like a great style, if there could be such a thing as a great style which was, not merely not applied to a great subject, but not, so far as one can see, applied to any subject at all. . . . One does not demand nowadays of poetry that it provide us with logical metaphors or with an intelligible sequence of ideas: Rimbaud is inconsecutive, his imagery is sometimes confused. Yet, with Rimbaud, whom Mr. Crane a little resembles, we experience intense emotional excitement and artistic satisfaction; we are dazzled by the eruption of his images, but we divine what it is he is saying. With Mr. Crane, though he can sometimes move us, the emotion is oddly vague. . . . (pp. 200-01)

His poetry is a *disponible*, as they say about French troops. We are eagerly waiting to see to which part of the front he will move it: just at present, it is killing time in the cafés behind the lines. (p. 201)

> *Edmund Wilson, "The Muses Out of Work" (originally published in* The New Republic, *May 11, 1927), in his* The Shores of Light: A Literary Chronicle of the Twenties and Thirties *(reprinted by permission of Farrar, Straus & Giroux, Inc.; copyright 1952 by Edmund Wilson; copyright renewed © 1980 by Helen Miranda Wilson), Farrar, Straus & Giroux, 1952, pp. 197-211.**

WILLIAM ROSE BENÉT (essay date 1930)

[None] of the more recent male American poets has received greater encomia than has Hart Crane. And this arose immediately with the publication of his "White Buildings." We ourself derived very little from "White Buildings" save the impression of a wild talent which might make itself articulate when it chose to submit to some of the means of communication afforded by a proper use of the English language, which has proved quite flexible enough for greater writers who chose to use and not abuse its syntax. Undoubtedly a gift for imagery appeared in this newcomer, undoubtedly as an intensity of feeling and a sensitivity to mood. And there was always the reckless reach for striking phrase which more than half the time eluded the grasp. Rhetoric there was in abundance, and rhetoric there is in abundance in Mr. Crane's latest, and second, volume, "The Bridge," which is the most ambitious flight he has yet attempted. It endeavors to wrest from its breast the full significance of Northern America, the utilitarian grace and beauty of the Brooklyn Bridge—such grace and beauty as always abides in great engineering—being its myth and symbol. . . .

The total impression made is that the author is an outstanding modern writer. He has, perhaps, a touch—how slight or great it may be we are not prepared to say—of the thing called genius. He has the fire in his bowels. And he does things to the English language that make us wish to scream in torment.

The use of intransitive verbs as transitive verbs, the use of nouns as verbs, the jarring of mismated adjectives and nouns, the typographical tricks, so many wild phrases like "Who grindest oar, and arguing the mast Subscribest holocaust of ships," a great deal of sound and fury in reality signifying very little, cannot negate the fact that on occasion the cascading fervor of this poet's speech sweeps aside his obvious faults and raises the rainbow of his vision before our eyes. Nor may one scientifically analyze the spectrum of that rainbow, except to say that, in spite of his homage to Whitman, it seems to be his own. He has borrowed technical devices here and there, and has not thoroughly assimilated them. He is, once more, but half articulate. He has failed in creating what might have been a truly great poem, failed through the impatience and overconcern with mere impressionism which are characteristics of this age. One feels that though he has observed keenly and sometimes minutely the life about him, though he has read history with intuition, and though he has grasped swiftly some of the potencies of the tongue he speaks, he has need of a mental discipline that would teach him organization and control of his material.

One hesitates to say this of a young poet, because one of the virtues of the early work of a man who has not yet quite come into his own lies often in blazing his own trail and learning from the mistakes of his ambitions. And some of Mr. Crane's most successful moments are due to his sheer recklessness; he is an unbaffled though not always a successful Prometheus. . . .

[To] realize the force of this poem one must not read it piecemeal. One must make the best of certain apparently undecipherable passages. . . .

And, to speak for ourself, we found it all quite fascinating. Our demurrer is entered against too great haphazardness in the organization of the material and against phraseology that often clots against all sense and that even sometimes descends to the banal. But there is a sweep to this poem; it is a most interesting failure; and it reveals potencies in the author that may make his next work even more remarkable.

William Rose Benét, "Round about Parnassus," in The Saturday Review of Literature (copyright © 1930 by Saturday Review), Vol. VI, No. 50, July 5, 1930, p. 1176.*

BABETTE DEUTSCH (essay date 1935)

In the game that the poet is committed to play, reason and fantasy, sense and spirit perpetually act upon one another, producing in the end something which seems as natural and inevitable as a flower or a rock. The genius is one whose subconscious mind gives him the richest materials to work with, whose conscious mind is in the most complete control of those materials.

An American who closely approximates this definition, one who plunged adventurously into life and desperately to his early death, was the author of that superb symbolist poem of our own time and place: *The Bridge*. A mystic, like Yeats, deprived, like him, of a religious tradition in which he could be at ease, longing, like him, for a sacred myth acceptable to his compatriots and contemporaries, but far more keenly alive to the disruptive elements of our urban, industrial civilization, Hart Crane found in the Brooklyn Bridge a symbol adequate to his purpose. The bridge became for him the key, not alone to the spanning of a continent, but to the ultimate union of mankind. It was the outward and visible sign of man's dynamic nature, the mechanical extension of his being which pointed to vaster ideal horizons. Where Crane telescopes sensations and emotions, or with a cinematographic touch allows the close-up of a remembered moment to open into scenes rapidly shifting time and place, he presses upon the nerve of modern sensibility. Where the light of intellectual beauty sheds its radiance on the given experience, the poet transcends all his contemporaries. (pp. 140-41)

Crane could more easily soar than saunter. Of the eight parts which compose the whole, the least successful are the *Three Songs* and the short canto, *Quaker Hill*, which center, like the lyrics, upon a personal reminiscence. *Powhatan's Daughter* identifies the Indian princess with the American earth, traversing its history since the white men took possession of it. *Cutty Sark* is the résumé of a shore leave which tenders exciting, half pathetic, half romantic intimations of journeys through the seven seas and fairer adventures of the mind. *Cape Hatteras* recalls the slow growth of the continent, lifting its peaks out of the ancient waters; the rapid rise of commerce and industry, changing the aspect of empire; the conquest of the air-ways, enormous with promise, but sowing death; the hope Walt Whitman cherished: the dream of a bridge across the gulfs of man's consciousness. . . . *The Tunnel*, one of the major parts of the poem, sees the poet descend into the subway, with its cumulation of sordid horrors, its evocation of Poe's mechanic infernos, but as he makes his exodus to the harbor, his dream revives, crossed with the pain of all he has suffered. The final section, *Atlantis*, completes the transfiguration of the bridge into a symbol of ineffable beauty and dynamic thrust. . . . (p. 142)

The epigraphs from Blake and Plato help to elucidate the mystic strain which marks the whole poem, and particularly the line from the *Symposium* which Crane renders: "Music, then, is that which relates to love in harmony and system." This suggests Rimbaud's prophecy: "Always full of *Number* and *Harmony*, poems will be made last. At bottom this should have in it again something of Greek poetry." . . . Neither Crane nor Rimbaud relied much on reason, but both were in search of reality, and both revered the immaterial beauty of ideal patterns.

There are several passages in *The Bridge* which read like a fulfillment of the extravagant prophecies of Rimbaud, whom Crane professed himself unable to read in the original (a piece of mockery which one is at liberty to doubt). The poem is an apotheosis of the stormy voyages and far explorations, the energy, the agony, the exaltation evoked by the author of *The Drunken Boat* and *A Season In Hell*. (pp. 142-43)

In spite of the debt to Rimbaud, the poem has a native indigenous character which separates it from work centered, as so much contemporary poetry has been, more upon literary than upon personal experiences. The American element in Crane's performance is emphasized. . . . The scene is America: the Atlantic coast, the harbor of the empire city, . . . the country through which the Twentieth Century whizzes over the rails, and the Mississippi mightily moves. The spirit is American: the spirit of Walt summoning his comrades to more generous loves. . . . (pp. 144-45)

One of the reasons why *The Bridge* is so full of interest is that the poem draws together three significant elements in American poetry: it opens upon the democratic vistas of Whitman; it employs the symbolist method of Poe to record his nervous terror; it celebrates the inviolable self to which Emily Dickinson clung. (p. 145)

The poem is not without flaws. It is unnecessarily obscure, sometimes because of the too private nature of the references, sometimes because of too great compression of meaning, aggravated by the use of a technical nautical terminology. The exalted character of the writing is not always sustained at the right level, but occasionally produces a strained, rhetorical effect. Yet, like the best symbolist poetry, it yields richer meaning with each re-reading. Such a sleight as the transformation of "dreams weave the rose" to "drums wreathe the rose" is more than a technical trick: in its context the twist of the phrase suggests the whole complex of sensations, ideas, and emotions which agitate a modern Platonist drinking with a sea-worn sailor in a South Street café to the sound of a mechanical piano grinding out *Stamboul Nights*. (pp. 146-47)

Crane, in his impatience to meet death, forwent the fruits of maturity. He did not achieve the ripeness which belongs to Yeats, the technical felicity of Eliot (it is worth remarking that a posthumously published poem, *The Hurricane*, bears the stamp of Gerard Manley Hopkins). But he escaped exhaustion and staleness, and his influence upon his contemporaries continues to be felt, as the work of Horace Gregory, Lola Ridge, Louis Grudin, Yvor Winters, variously attests. Before he was undone by the pressure of immediate evils he found the symbol which would survive him, to bear to later comers his intimations of a brave new world. (pp. 147-48)

Babette Deutsch, "Heirs of the Symbolists," in her This Modern Poetry (reprinted by permission of W. W. Norton & Company, Inc.; copyright © 1935 by W. W. Norton & Company, Inc.; copyright renewed 1962 by Babette Deutsch), Norton, 1935 (and reprinted by Kraus Reprint Co., 1969), pp. 108-48.*

STANLEY K. COFFMAN, JR. (essay date 1951)

I should like here to add a note upon an aspect of *The Bridge* which, as far as I know, has not been more than mentioned. . . . Perhaps the shortest way to what I propose is through Ezra Pound's definition of the Image: "that which presents an intellectual and emotional complex in an instant of time." As symbol providing a logical meaning for the poem, the Bridge has been examined and judgment delivered; but the pattern of language through which Crane hoped to make his symbol effective as intellectual and emotional complex, or, to use his terminology, a "new *word*, never before spoken and impossible to actually enunciate," has been left almost untouched.

The remark has frequently been made that the Bridge as object lent itself admirably to the symbolic use Crane meant it to serve: its qualities were just those which could be translated into the metaphors that would express concretely the central abstractions of his poem. His belief in the continuous, organic growth of human history, in which each period is a source of the next; or his idea that the American, and particularly the modern, industrial American, period is to lift us over into an even greater future; or the purpose he sees in the poem itself, which is to link the reader, and the poet, to their own past, present, and future—all are effectively objectified in the figure of the Bridge. Again, each of the several human achievements dealt with in the poem may, by the nature of Crane's (and Whitman's) myth, be seen symbolically as bridge: Columbus' voyage of discovery, the transcontinental routes of the frontier settlers, and then the accomplishments of industrial science exemplified in the national highway and railway, and the airplane.

This, however, leaves the symbol to be apprehended only in terms of concepts, leaves it, in fact, with only the kind of logic Crane wanted his poetry to replace. The Bridge was not just to symbolize a particular belief but to reproduce all the qualities of experiencing that belief; it was to fuse the intellectual and emotional components of a belief so completely that the poem as a whole, dominated by this symbol, would become metaphor translating this particular aspect of the poet's consciousness. There is, for example, the pattern of language which conveys an exhilaration that is part of Crane's mysticism and grows out of an imaginative approach to the Bridge as object: the Bridge is seen vaulting the sea (transcending and including it, but with the transcending and including expressed in such a way that they can be felt); its counterpart, the highway, *leaps* from Far Rockaway to Golden Gate; the railway *strides* the dew, *straddles* the hill; the wires *span* the mountain stream—each verb giving the symbolic action human and therefore immediately apprehensible character. Emphasizing further the religious and emotional, the Bridge's outline suggests an "arching path / Upward," an image repeated in "arching strands of song" and "spiring cordage." In the *sweep* of the Bridge, in the petition that its "lariat sweep encinctured" descend and enfold us within its embrace, Crane is further drawing upon the affective powers of the object. The Bridge is Love's paradigm, revealing its inflected forms (aspiration, exhilaration, all-inclusiveness) through the motions of spanning, spiring, sweeping, which evoke these feelings.

The Bridge is also "arc synoptic," which not only strengthens the religious connotations, but shows how closely Crane was allying himself with the particular mysticism that was Whitman's religion. Like the concept of reality as Love, this of the object as microcosm recalls Whitman, but where Whitman is content to allow philosophic conviction to carry the poetry and thus strings out his catalogues of metonyms, Crane turns his relief in philosophic unity into a technique of expression, somewhat in the manner of the French Symbolists, and unifies his poem by showing how the universe will repeat its patterns and images, especially one so expressive as that discovered in the configuration of the Bridge. Love itself surveys the world with a "*diametric* gaze"; the world is God's "teeming *span*." Both day and night reveal the Bridge's form: night is a "sapphire *wheel*," dawn appears as "dayspring's spreading *arc*," and the Bridge lifts night to day's "*cycloramic* crest." The planes of Cape Hatteras are launched into "abysmal cupolas of space." The larger phenomena of nature reflect this basic configuration in other ways; one notes, for example, the rainbow's arch, an image that occurs at four widely separated places in the poem, [and] the crescent of the moon. . . . (pp. 65-6)

"Proem" opens, in fact, with the flight of the gull, whose wings trace "white rings of tumult" and who disappears from sight with "inviolate curve," a spiring, sweeping motion which is intensified by the sudden contrast with the "chained bay waters" and which inevitably merges into and enforces the qualities of the Bridge's own *curveship*. In **"The River,"** carrying out the pattern, eyeless fish *curvet*, and in **"Ave Maria,"** the sails are mustered in "holy rings," just as the image of "Pennants, parabolas" reappears in appropriate guise in **"Cutty Sark."** Ironically, the same motion is repeated in the horror of man's machine world, concentrated in the subway hell of **"The Tunnel"**: as the car rounds a bend for the dive under the river, newspapers on the cluttered floor "wing, revolve and wing." All nature writes the figure of the curve or, by extension, the circle; and the universality of its appearance adds persuasiveness to the symbolic meaning of the Bridge. The Bridge thus speaks, through this one of its properties, a universal geometry, an "unfractioned idiom," and argues, by what can best be called a logic of metaphor, the fundamental point which the poem was to present: its man-made configuration, repeated by nature, is given a kind of divinity, and the mathematical thinking which planned it a like sanctity. (pp. 66-7)

Clearly this Bridge is not a symbol in the conventional sense, as an object which can, by virtue of certain properties, be translated into terms of an abstraction. Crane has conceived of it rather as the French Symbolists did, working out, for example, correspondences between the object and other phenomena of the natural or civilized world, and between the object and a state of consciousness existing in the poet. . . . That it becomes metaphor (or myth as the Symbolists understood it) for a complex state may perhaps be confirmed by a glance at a further pattern of imagery through which it speaks to the reader. **"Atlantis"** opens with an epigraph from Plato, "Music is then the knowledge of that which relates to love in harmony and system," and the use of this quotation seems to parallel Symbolist insistence upon the musical potentialities of language and upon approximating poetry to music. There was a generous measure of Platonism in Symbolist theorizing about the aims of poetry, and the function of music as suggesting the harmony of the Ideal world figured largely in this theorizing. Though the poetry of *The Bridge* seldom approaches music in the Symbolist manner, through special attention to the pitch and rhythm of language, Crane reveals a correspondence between his symbol and an Aeolian harp whose music by its harmony recalls the harmony between man and his universe, the harmony within the universal plan.

As Brom Weber has pointed out, Crane prepares for this climactic transformation of his symbol in **"Proem,"** where the Bridge is "harp and altar," whose choiring strings could not have been aligned by mere toil of man. (It is *altar* as bridge between human and divine.) Other musical reference is infrequent until the closing section. (pp. 74-5)

But in **"Atlantis"** the music imagery is dominant, fusing the other patterns that have been mentioned and giving them a greater intensity than they have had before in the poem. Here the Bridge is not only harp but accompaniment to "Sibylline voices" which "waveringly stream / As though a god were issue of the strings. . . ." The Bridge is light, motion, sound. . . .

These are "orphic strings," entrancing, Dionysian, and thus mystic, oracular (Sibylline). But Orpheus (though his music saved the Argonauts from the lure of the Sirens) appears not without connotations of tragedy for, almost in sight of the upper regions, he turned back to look at Eurydice, and thus lost her. Intended or not, this overtone of meaning agrees with the questioning of these final lines: "Is it Cathay . . .?"; and the last image leaves considerable doubt concerning the mystic or any but the ecstatic quality of the poet's or the Bridge's song. It is a song suspended in air: "Whispers antiphonal in azure swing." (p. 76)

There are, of course, dangers in the approach that I have used. It tends to isolate the symbol, whereas Crane in most cases works his symbolic pattern carefully into the texture of the separate sections. It does not measure the extent to which his effort in this direction falls short of success; where his interest in a passage wavers, the effectiveness of the Bridge imagery wavers. . . . The primary value of this approach, however, is in its emphasis upon Crane's brilliant elaboration of symbolic meaning, even though the brilliance is vitiated by failure to cope philosophically with his material. While the qualities of the symbol do not evenly permeate the poem, while the symbol itself betrays its confusion, one ought not attempt an estimate of *The Bridge* without understanding Crane's grasp of a fundamental Symbolist technique. (pp. 76-7)

> *Stanley K. Coffman, Jr., "Symbolism in 'The Bridge',"* in *PMLA, 66 (copyright © 1951 by the Modern Language Association of America; copyright renewed © 1979 by the Modern Language Association of America; reprinted by permission of the Modern Language Association of America), Vol. LXVI, No. 2, March, 1951, pp. 65-77.*

VINCENT QUINN (essay date 1963)

[Crane held the] conviction that a poet is a seer, an inspired creature who is permitted a more profound glimpse into reality than men ordinarily experience. (p. 21)

This conviction marks the tradition of Blake, Coleridge, Poe, Emerson, Baudelaire, Rimbaud—and Hart Crane. In this tradition the creative experience of the poet is regarded as a gratuitous visitation far beyond his conscious power and control. The poem resulting from this experience is a verbal report of an inspiration. . . .

Crane believed that his poetic visions contained implicit knowledge about man and nature that could be obtained in

no other way. He felt that these experiences offered an objective insight into reality. . . . From this point of view, the poet's vision is objectively valid, even though he experiences it through the channel of his subjectivity. Not only did Crane believe that poets are among the few human beings who realize their opportunity to make unique, interior discoveries about what exists, but he also valued poetry as virtually the expression of a mystical experience. (p. 22)

Crane considered himself the fortunate recipient of this aesthetic experience. It came unbidden, suffused him, and left him under the compulsion to articulate, however imperfectly, what he had experienced. It was a rich and powerful epiphany that he joyfully accepted but could not control. He saw himself as merely the channel or vehicle of an experience as real as breathing, but he could not "know" it until it had been defined in poetry. (p. 23)

The obligation to achieve a verbal equivalent for a unique experience demanded the utmost semantic freedom. The denotations of words had to be kept from overwhelming their far-ranging connotations. The restrictions of discursive logic had to be transgressed when they made experience less true to its actual complexity, even though more manageable. In an unpublished essay **"General Aims and Theories,"** . . . Crane stated that "the entire construction of the poem is raised on the organic principle of a 'logic of metaphor,' which antedates our so-called pure logic." This principle allowed him to create a work adequate to the complexity of his intuitive experience. His poetry might violate ordinary logic and, to that extent, be nonrational, but it could not be antirational because it was governed by the same experience that reason handles with less completeness.

Crane recognized that practicing this principle made his poems frequently seem obscure and thereby limited his audience. . . . Nevertheless, immediate clarity was not to be achieved by sacrificing the fidelity of the work to its intuition. When his intuition violated logic, Crane himself, along with his readers, had to be permissive and trust that its organic impact on the imagination would establish its coherence. He saw that this method might bemuse him into mistaking subjective confusion for objective illumination, but he accepted this possibility as an unavoidable risk. (p. 24)

The result of these efforts and attitudes is a body of work— *The Collected Poems of Hart Crane*—that stands in the vanguard of twentieth-century American verse beside the poems of Frost, Pound, Eliot, Williams, and Stevens. It is a small volume—fewer than a hundred poems, even if the sections of *The Bridge* are counted separately—but one marked by the eloquent rendering of a passionate, far-reaching imagination.

The earliest group of Crane's poems is *White Buildings*, a volume of twenty-eight lyrics. . . . Containing poems written from 1917 to 1926, *White Buildings* offers a splendid sampling of Crane's lyricism. There are the best of his early work— poems like **"Chaplinesque," "My Grandmother's Love Letters,"** and **"Praise for an Urn";** his first major poem, **"For the Marriage of Faustus and Helen"** . . . ; and the deeply moving, confessional lyrics of disappointment and hopefulness, like **"Possessions," "Lachrymae Christi," "The Wine Menagerie,"** and **"Voyages."** (p. 28)

[Next is *The Bridge*,] his most widely known work and the one Crane regarded as the proof and pinnacle of his career. In all respects a capital literary achievement, it joins *The Waste Land, The Cantos,* and *Paterson* as one of the most ambitious modern American poems. It has magnitude of size—fifteen sections extending over twelve hundred lines—and intention. (pp. 28-9)

Crane ranges over the entire span of American history in urging a single vision of the past that anticipates the nation's glorious spiritual destiny in the future.

Finally there are the single lyrics written after the publication of *White Buildings*. They are in two groups: *Key West*, a volume of twenty-two poems that Crane had ready for publication at the time of his death; and twelve poems found among his worksheets after his death. . . . These two groups generally reveal the darkening and weakening of Crane's talent.

The poems of *Key West* were written from 1926, when Crane was getting *The Bridge* under construction, through the four years he spent completing it, to the end of his life two years later. **"The Broken Tower"**—the finest poem of the collection—was concluded just a few weeks before his death. . . . They are mainly poems of fear, written either when *The Bridge* was temporarily abandoned and he feared he lacked the faith or the talent to finish it or, following its publication, when he feared that he had failed and could not bear the thought of the future. In addition to **"The Broken Tower,"** the best of these poems are **"Key West," "O Carib Isle!",** **"The Idiot," "Royal Palm,"** and **"The Hurricane."**

The atmosphere of *Key West* is violent and alien to man. Reality is felt under the pressure of heat, storms, waste, and death; there is a frightening mingling of fecundity and desolation. Although sensuality is offered a gross and pointless parody of itself, its presence is so intense that faith in anything superior to it is discouraged.

Crane conceived many of these poems under the influence of such a climate. . . . Crane was losing his battle to preserve an idealistic vision in the midst of a sensual jungle. His self-awareness remained clear and honest, but it doomed him to the consciousness of imminent defeat. (pp. 29-30)

Altogether, Crane's poems present an unusually powerful lyric voice. Its identifying feature is his brilliant command of metaphor. His imagination fixed upon images of tremendous energy. (p. 30)

These charged and rhythmical images constitute the magnificence of Crane's poems; their abundance often creates a bewilderment of plenty. A succession of compressed, richly connotative images accompanied by little or no discursive statement—as in **"Lachrymae Christi"**—dazzles the reader but may leave him uncertain in his response. He may feel that the poem possesses a unity that he has not been able to discover. The form of the poem is usually familiar—frequently blank verse arranged in quatrains—but the images may not seem to cohere.

This difficulty results from Crane's particular sensibility and his poetic theory. His imagination was vividly responsive to the associations of images: connotations that often lie below the threshold of consciousness. He thought and felt in images; his references to a logic of metaphor accurately describe his intellectual equipment. Moreover, he believed poetry to be the concrete evidence of an experience. The poet was not to tell about an experience but to convey it to the reader in the sensual terms in which he had received it. (pp. 30-1)

[Unhappiness] is at the core of Crane's themes. A vein of misery runs from his earliest poems to his last. His disposition

is fearful; his relationships with family and friends, melancholy; his attitude toward society, hostile.

Several poems suggest a generally troubled, anxious temperament. (p. 33)

Anxiety is expressed [most] successfully in **"Poster,"** . . . later published as **"Voyages I."** The weakness of his other poems on this theme is that they suggest merely a personal, childish terror. In **"Poster"** a universal relevance is attained by his use of the sea to symbolize the unavoidable painfulness of life. The poem is also strengthened by his dramatic invention: the poet, whose innocence has been lost, utters a warning to "bright striped urchins," who, "gaily digging and scattering" sand and shells at the shore, are unaware of any danger. . . . At the same time he knows that such a warning is never heeded. As he wistfully regards their still unspoiled joy, he suffers the foreknowledge of their inevitable discovery of suffering.

In choosing the sea as a symbol of the apparent benevolence masking the terror of life, Crane was especially fortunate. He used it for the first time in this poem and responded to it richly. It provided him with a metaphor that could bear the heaviest pressure of his own experience without becoming sentimental or eccentric. Its universal significance was quickened by his personal response but not overcome by it. His further exploration of the resilience of this symbol led to the **"Voyages"** sequence and to some of the best sections of *The Bridge*. It also drew him close to the earlier American writers with whom he was most congenial—Melville and Whitman. . . .

Crane's fear of nature is more grimly expressed in two later poems planned for *Key West*—**"O Carib Isle!"** and **"Hurricane."** Both poems bespeak his astonishment at the violence of the tropics. In **"O Carib Isle!"** he is frightened by the predominance of waste and death. . . . He also observes that, although death abounds, there is no mourning. Life seems to be reduced to a wanton mingling of fecundity and destruction.

He wonders about the metaphysical implications of this stark drama. "Where is the Captain of the doubloon isle?" he asks. He questions the nature and even the existence of its creator. (p. 34)

"The Hurricane" presents a different but no more comforting view of nature. The violence of a tropical hurricane is evoked in couplets that burst furiously. Although the storm is addressed as God and Lord, it has no personal consciousness. It is absolute, raw power, lacking all awareness and discrimination. Everything is ripped and swept before it. . . . Crane's use of archaic forms to suggest biblical usage—"Lo," "Ay," "Thou," "e'en"—and his reference to "Scripture" are both appropriate and ironic. They suggest the harsh God of the Old Testament, or even the apotheosis of nature itself. It is as though the whirlwind of the Book of Job were not subject to God's control but asserted itself blindly. . . .

Undoubtedly, Crane's anxious forebodings were conditioned by his unhappy family life. His letters document his difficulties; his poems attest to them in that every reference to a family relationship is sad. (p. 35)

Crane's poems about friendship are equally melancholy. In **"Praise for an Urn,"** one of the most successful elegies in American poetry, he confronts the fact of death with his desire for a lasting relationship. Several impulses incline him to believe in the presence of his deceased friend. There is his affection, of course, but also his recollection of the large spirit of his friend. . . . Just as men of the past lived on in the consciousness of his friend, so his friend may live on in him. . . . Tranquil, moon-charged evenings intimated the immortality of the soul to both of them and directed their conversation toward this possibility. Under the spell of nature's serenity and their spiritual intimacy, all reality seemed united and harmonious.

Now the confidence they felt together collapses as the lone survivor faces the fact of death. The funeral with its bold assertion of lifelessness and, even more, the cremation of his friend break the poet's faith. He realizes that even while he and his friend had been speaking of immortality and believing that nature sustained their faith, the clock "perched in the crematory lobby" had been ticking ironically toward that moment of dissolution. The poet's faith in personal immortality cracks under the mechanical flux of matter.

His resolution of this conflict is plaintively uncertain. The funeral and its aftermath of loneliness have dangerously weakened the poet's confidence in a deathless relationship but not destroyed it. Images of his friend return insistently and by their invincibility keep his hope alive. . . . This slim basis for hope holds the issue in tension, but it is in discouraging contrast to the trust he has felt while his friend was alive. He can only assert his desire; objective support is not available. So the poem ends meekly. "Well-meant idioms" are all that remain of their earlier "assessments of the soul." . . . He fears that the same ashen fate that claimed his friend's body will be suffered—and perhaps deserves more to be suffered—by his poetic tribute to "what the dead keep, living still."

Crane's other poems about friendship speak of infidelity and alienation. (pp. 37-8)

Crane's references to society reflect the same unhappy strain. Disappointed by family and friends, he is repelled by the harsh, materialistic ways of his era. In two sections of *The Bridge*—"The River" and "The Tunnel"—he expresses his revulsion. "The River" presents a kaleidoscopic nightmare of advertisements seen from a transcontinental railroad. . . . In "The Tunnel" chaos is represented by a subway descending beneath the East River. Disconnected tags of vulgar conversation mingle with gongs, hissing doors, and cars screaming around curves. (p. 38)

Feeling alien to these conditions, the poet in "Chaplinesque" identifies himself with the lonely, abused tramp of the movies and uses him to symbolize the fate of human values in his time. The familiar cop who always chases Charlie away from some innocent enjoyment represents society. His prohibiting thumb is "inevitable"; he sees life through a "dull squint" and opposes all more liberal views.

Upon this foundation of unhappiness, Crane strived for fulfillment and joy. In his personal life his hopefulness persisted almost to the end—his resolution was "to keep saying 'YES' to everything and never be beaten a moment, and I shall, of course, never be really beaten." Similarly, in his poems a dominant theme is his faith in the possibility of happiness. (p. 39)

His ability to aspire to happiness in the midst of misery depended upon his trust that suffering may be the gateway to peace. He believed that pain might be redemptive and

enlightening, that "between black tusks the roses shine," as he wrote in "The Wine Menagerie." Believing that the brave endurance of suffering can instigate profoundly satisfying insights, he expressed this faith in several poems about triumphant sufferers, most notably about Jesus, in "Lachrymae Christi." . . . [The] sufferings of Christ, the birthpangs of spring, and the anguish of the poet are presented as analogous instances of torment. From this gathering of pain, a chorus of triumph emerges. (pp. 39-40)

Less fervid but thematically similar to "Lachrymae Christi" is "At Melville's Tomb." Melville is praised for having borne the torments of human experience with honesty and courage. He did not coddle himself with illusions; he dared to face the terror of life. (p. 41)

Crane associated the achievement of serenity through suffering with the creative agony of the artist. He regarded his poetry as the justification for his life as well as the fulfillment of his literary talent. His sufferings were to lead to higher insights which would be fully realized only when expressed in poems. Crane attempted to illustrate this relationship between wisdom and art in all his poems, and he made it the subject of several. Among the best of these are two that appear in *White Buildings:* "Legend," and "Passage." (p. 42)

Related to these themes is Crane's persistent faith in the joyfulness of love. He knew that love means suffering through self-surrender and that it involves the risk of betrayal, but he also believed its requital to be the supreme fulfillment of body and spirit. His noblest aspirations and his strongest creative intuitions centered upon the articulation of this conviction. In the "Atlantis" section of *The Bridge*, the sublime role of "the bridge" is to persuade men to accept the guidance of love in diverting their energies from mundane to spiritual satisfactions. (p. 45)

[Similarly] the "Voyages" sequence is a celebration of the transforming power of love. "Permit me voyage, love, into your hands" is the theme of the entire poem. Its metaphor is the sea, and its movement is from the lover's dedication to a human and therefore changeable lover to a beloved beyond time and change.

Crane was even optimistic enough at times to see traces of nobility in contemporary society. He believed that America had become a slave to materialism, but he contended that this condition was not in keeping with either its finest tradition or the needs of human nature. He felt that his need as a person and his opportunity as a poet were to demonstrate a vision of life more worthy of the human spirit. Both "For the Marriage of Faustus and Helen" and *The Bridge* were intended to realize such a goal. "Faustus and Helen" asserts that even in the midst of urban chaos and the destructiveness of war a sensitive person may discover grounds for dedicating himself to love and beauty. (pp. 45-6)

The Bridge offers the same encouragement. The Brooklyn Bridge seemed to Crane the finest product of modern times. It not only represents the most advanced stage of technology and serves the most practical purpose but also satisfies the beholder's aesthetic and spiritual hunger. Crane saw it as an incarnation of beauty and a pledge of man's aspiration for the sublime. No man could see this bridge, he felt, and dismiss the age as vulgar.

On the impetus of this insight, Crane devoted the remainder of *The Bridge* to demonstrating the presence of similar evidences of idealism throughout American history. In each age he recognized signs sufficient to sustain faith in noble ideals. He hoped that the presentation of these signs would quicken his readers' faith in the fundamental spirituality of society.

As we might expect, Crane's combination of unhappiness and hopefulness creates considerable tension in his work. (p. 46)

This conflict is intense . . . in several of the shorter lyrics. In them he made clear that, although his strongest desire was to enjoy the happiness of love and creativity, he feared that he had failed to do either. He felt that he had sacrificed love to lust and that his creative skill had not grown properly. Yet, even in his most melancholy utterances, hope persists. (p. 47)

Why is this poet important? What are the dimensions of his achievement?

Crane's poetry is important for several reasons. First, he possessed an extraordinary gift for metaphor. . . . His poems, of course, present a harmony embracing more than single images, but their greatest intensity—their brilliance—is located in particular phrases. His distinguishing trait is the pitch of eloquence that he often achieves several times in a single poem through the startling aptness of his imagery. . . .

His work is significant, too, because of its irresistibly moving theme: man's quest for enduring love and absolute beauty. He expresses moods varying from exultant trust that the fulfillment of his quest is imminent to a downcast premonition of continued failure, but his desire never deviates from the true north of his idealism. This preoccupation gives a dignity and a universality to his poetry. (p. 127)

Another appealing feature of Crane's poetry is its passionate involvement with life. It bespeaks his total commitment—body and soul—to human experience. He wanted love and beauty; no renunciation or sublimation was ever possible. In striving for the satisfaction of his personal hungers, he activated destructive forces that ultimately overwhelmed him, but his desire was positive and life-loving. Even when imbued with grief and failure, his longing for the attainment of full human stature is more inspiring than the expression of a life made comfortable by evasion or by lack of appetite.

These traits comprise Crane's poetic strength; they are best exemplified by his short lyrics of intimate self-revelation, like **"Lachrymae Christi," "Possessions,"** and **"Voyages."** His work is less impressive when he attempts to bring society within his range. His indictment of the vulgarity of modern times is overdrawn. His acquaintance with society seems too narrow for the intensity of his criticism. Moreover, the presence of vulgarity must be assumed in all times; the test of idealism is whether or not it can flourish in spite of this handicap. Similarly, his exploration of America's past in search of encouragement for his idealism is lyrically moving but historically unconvincing. His knowledge of the past seems spotty; his judgments, self-willed.

Ironically, Crane's exhortations to hopefulness are not persuasive. Their shrillness betrays a lack of confidence. Either the evidence he offers is too weak for the pressure he puts upon it or a passage of yea-saying is followed by a more powerful passage which is frankly melancholy. Yet his poetry arouses hopefulness, not by virtue of his advocacy but because, despite all setbacks, he never loses hope himself. Crane's ability to sustain his dream in the teeth of defeat and to give eloquent expression to both his humiliation and his revival of confidence is the height of his achievement. (p. 128)

Vincent Quinn, in his Hart Crane *(copyright © 1963 by Twayne Publishers, Inc.; reprinted with the permission of Twayne Publishers, a Division of G. K. Hall & Co., Boston), Twayne, 1963, 141 p.*

R.W.B. LEWIS (essay date 1967)

Taken as a whole, **"Voyages"** is undoubtedly Crane's lyrical masterpiece. . . . (p. 148)

"Voyages" from its beginning to its end unfolds a story—a love story, needless to say—that in its rhythm and content is altogether familiar and expertly conventional.

"Voyages," that is, presents a clear enough and a continuing action, and one that belongs recognizably to an age-old tradition of romance. In it, by convention, the experience of earthly love reaches its peak of excitement only to be broken off by the departure or death of the beloved, whereupon the poet-lover finds consolation and a more permanent kind of gratification in a vision of transcendent beauty or of God or paradise; and in his own poetic narrative of the entire affair. Petrarch and Sidney come to mind as notable early practitioners of this genre; Keats's "Ode on a Grecian Urn" and Whitman's "Out of the Cradle Endlessly Rocking" are perhaps the later poems in English with which **"Voyages"** has most in common. . . . Crane's sequence . . . was rooted in the joy and pain of a homosexual love affair and its culmination; and it similarly described, in a series of highly metaphoric projections, the experience of psychic death leading to the discovery of the language of vision—that is, to poetry. At times, **"Voyages"** almost dissolves this "story" in the sheer flow of its sensuous imagery; at other times, its suggestive allusions, taken out of context, seem to carry us into the realm of myth, or into some boundless domain of splendid un-reason where opposites consort and nameless forces or disembodied pulsations dance out their uninterpretable allegory. But we should hang on to the traditional, even the archetypal, story in it; to do so may, at any given moment, seem to reduce the poem's range, but it is in fact and over all to perceive more fully the beauty, the poignance, and the power with which the entire work is endowed.

"Voyages I" introduces the theme of experience—represented, for Crane as for Herman Melville, by the dangerous but inviting sea and taking the specific form of a sea-journey which at the same time is and stands for a journey into love. The heart of the poem is in its final stanza, in the poet's would-be address to the "bright, striped urchins" he sees—evidently in a picture or poster of some sort—playing on the beach. . . . The urchins, as we see, are swiftly transformed by metaphor into ships alerted for departure: their bodies are "spry cordages" or lively ship's rigging. But Crane urges them *not* to put out to sea—not to voyage into a crueler and more encompassing love, but to stay safely on shore or in harbor; to be satisfied with "fondl[ing]" their playthings in innocent affection, and not to submit to caresses from a sea which, in its largeness and power, may dash them against the lichen-covered rocks. (pp. 150-52)

But this was only a warning to the uninitiated (Crane called it a "'stop, look and listen' sign"). It was no more Crane's final exhortation about experience than it had been Melville's. We recall, in **"Faustus and Helen II"** the invitation to make the daring plunge into life: "to fall downstairs with me / With perfect grace and equanimity"; or, closer to the symbolism of **"Voyages,"** to "scud past" those "shores" where the trimmers sit in pious safety. Just such bold "shoreless" venturing was commended by Melville. . . . (pp. 153-54)

Melville, of course, was speaking about a voyage of thought, of "deep, earnest thinking"; the daring effort of the mind to retain its freedom and to journey through the tempestuous appearance of things to the nature of ultimate reality. Crane was speaking about a (for him) no less daring voyage of love, the effort of flesh, feeling, and imagination to travel to the last reality and meaning of the erotic life. And for Crane, the sea plays a more ambiguous and shifting role. In **"Voyages II,"** it is a still mightier being than in **"I,"** but it is no longer the cruel and destructive lover of the human who submits to it. Instead, as the actual love affair—*"our* love"—gets under way, the sea becomes an imperious rival in love, an absolute and godlike monarch (evidently a queen) whose boundless love and huge embrace of the moon at first make mockery of the limitations of the merely human lovers. The new identification of the sea emerges . . . from the "combination and interplay" of the connotations of words as they impinge on our consciousness; and from a rhythmical energy that, as against **"Voyages I,"** seems suddenly supercharged. In **"I,"** however effective its content, the tone was flat and prosaic, and kept at a low key by a number of monosyllabic grammatical binders . . . that in his later and more highly pressured verse, such as **"Voyages II,"** Crane would do without. The rhythm in **"II"** is a remarkable mixture of the sense of flowing and that of marching: or better, it suggests a flowing movement that has been stiffened and accentuated into a march—just as the coined word "processioned" visually transforms the rising and breaking waves into disciplined figures marching by in some pageant or parade.

"Processioned," meanwhile, is also one of the important words whose impinging connotation interacts with others to beget the new image of the sea. . . . What is being stressed about this royal lover in the opening stanza is the absolute nature of her love and the derision she visits, in consequence, upon the finite love-possibilities of man. (pp. 155-56)

But the authority and the arrogance of the sea do not, after all, overpower or disempower (through laughter) the human love. The action in **"Voyages"** is, as I have suggested, an interlocking double action: the progress of the human affair as it is dialectically involved with the shifting relation between the poet and the sea. This is Crane's dazzlingly original treatment of an old, essentially a Romantic, convention of love poetry: whereby "nature" (here, chiefly, the sea and the sky) reflects or frustrates, sympathizes with or opposes the movements of human emotion. In **"Voyages III,"** the sea as lover will become the reverent mimic of human sexual behavior; here, in the second stanza of **"Voyages II,"** the two elements—the infinite lover and the finite—grow matched and even. (pp. 156-57)

Human love is mortal: it exists in time, and time is passing; the relentless passage of time is just what the sea-tides, timeless as they are, continuously measure—"her turning shoulders wind the hours," like a clock. And so. . . .

> Hasten, while they are true,—sleep, death, desire,
> Close round one instant in one floating flower.

Those lines have the kind of utter finality—as of some deep and serious emotion perfectly realized in language and ca-

dence—that a lyric poet would be lucky to achieve half a dozen times in his life. The rhythm that hurries briefly and then slows to the solemn tread of "sleep, death, desire," continuing in the soft funereal count of the second line; the countering of imperative and statement; the play, almost the wash, of words against each other; the alliterations and repetitions; even the dimness of syntax and allusion—all gives us poetry in intimate touch with a feeling (about love and death) that is on the far side of logical formulation but that communicates immediately. The entire experience and all its many elements are quietly concentrated in a single entity or image: "one floating flower."

And yet the very beauty of the lines has, I believe, caused a certain misapprehension about **"Voyages II"** and, by their influence, about a larger range of Crane's poetry. It is true that in the sequence "sleep, death, desire," sleep and death determine the reference of desire—which becomes, exactly, a desire *for* sleep and death; a yearning for oblivion. Crane is indeed saying in some untranslatable way that he and his lover must hasten to enjoy their love while the sea's bounty is still available ("while they"—the bent foam and wave—"are true")—as the setting which gives their love its ultimate and awesome nature. For he knows that, like Keats, he is half in love with easeful death, and perhaps all men are; before death closes sweetly upon them, they must seize the day of love. But, to put it as unequivocally as possible, **"Voyages II"** is not a *Liebestod;* it is not an expression of the so-called death-wish; it is no evidence of a suicidal impulse. It gives rise, quite on the contrary, to a remarkably firm prayer for life. . . . (pp. 158-60)

This prayer would be very definitely answered in the conclusion of the **"Voyages"** sequence—when, in **"Voyages VI,"** the poet passes through a kind of death (symbolized as death at sea), through the grave of his love, to rest his own visionary gaze upon a paradise of timeless beauty, an unearthly shore called Belle Isle. . . . [Then] the floating flower of death would become the "petalled word" of creation.

It occurs to me that the presumptive manner of Crane's actual death in 1932 has been a blinder on the understanding of his poetry. Because he died by his own hand as it seems, and at so relatively young an age, there has been a temptation to find in his writing the constant expression of a suicidal urge, or at least a yearning for nothingness; a profound and dominant desire to be released from this mortal world. But the proudest imperatives of his characteristic poems are directed against the escape from the temporal world and toward the praise of it. . . . That Crane had a fervent consciousness of death is undeniable; he would scarcely have been a very interesting poet without it. But the force and beauty of [his poetry] come directly from his committed *resistance* to that consciousness. (p. 161)

The life he spoke for, and we cannot insist upon it too often, was life enlarged and illuminated by a divine energy: or by a human energy raised to a higher power. This is the life realized as the intoxicated fulfillment of love in **"Voyages III,"** where death is mentioned only to be utterly denied. **"Voyages III"** is the most riotous poem, emotionally, in the whole sequence. . . . The poet's sea-journey is now a journey *to* his beloved (the title of the sequence, we remember is **"Voyages"** in the plural); a movement—toward perfect union—that becomes enormously accelerated. The poetry swirls with gerunds of breath-taking activity, and at a speed too great for normal punctuation. And where, at the start of

"**Voyages II**," the human love saw itself derided by the boundless erotic swellings of the sea, now on the contrary it is magnified beyond measure—since the erotic act of the lovers has become the model imitated by the universe at large. (pp. 161-62)

The poet's love for his friend is blood-brother to the love discernible between the elements of nature throughout infinity: at once a model for and portion of that love. The sea mounts the sky's proffered breast in a sexual union identical with that of the lovers. . . . The image is huge and startling; but the convention, sometimes and disapprovingly called the pathetic fallacy—natural elements behaving in sympathetic imitation of human beings—is probably as old as love poetry. . . . But perhaps never have the elements engaged in so fierce a mimicry of human sexual combat as in "**Voyages III.**" . . . (pp. 162-63)

All the forms of love—as it were, the various and strenuous embraces of the universe—reach their culmination in the sexual embrace of the beloved. This is the end of the journey: which, through the preceding lines, had been steadily gathering momentum. (p. 163)

"**Voyages III**" represents the peak of the love experience, and the moment when the sense and the sound of song are most powerful. With "**IV**," a change sets in; and soon the poetic attention will shift from love to loss, and from song to vision. (p. 165)

The general sense of "**Voyages IV**" we make out without undue exertion; but there is in it a notable slackening of poetic muscle. The compact vigor of "**III**" is dissipated; and the first and third stanzas in particular seem for all their brevity to thicken interminably, piling phrase upon phrase with a loss rather than an accumulation of meaning and intensity. Crane seems here to be poetically grinding his gears, as though he were trying to move the action forward but had not found the way to do so. (p. 166)

Homosexual symbolism also hovers inescapably in the imagery of "**Voyage III**" and infuses "**Voyages V**"; it is present wherever hands or oars are referred to, and in one perspective it can be seen pervading the whole sequence. This is perhaps the moment to remark that "**Voyages**," despite its flaws, is not only that rarity in American literature—genuine and personal love poetry; it is also the only truly moving and beautiful poetry of male homosexual love in English with which I am acquainted. It is so because Crane has succeeded in making the passionate love of male for male representative of every kind of human passion: "the secret oar and petals of *all* love." (p. 168)

"**Voyages VI**" is in its own right one of the truly splendid poems in English; and it concludes the "**Voyages**" sequence with a poetic splendor so appropriate as in effect to provide the subject matter of this final moment. It is a poem of intense visionary straining, sight and blindness are of its essence, and eyes constitute its key reference; and it is a work of the utmost rhetorical magnificence. Vision and poetry: these are what "**Voyages VI**" is about; vision and poetry as the answer to the death of love and the shattering bewilderment it produced. Out of the vortex of love's grave, the shipwreck of his love, the poet sees and hears the long-awaited answer to "the seal's wide spindrift gaze toward paradise." And the answer ("**Voyages VI**" consists, structurally, of a prayer and an answer, an "unbetrayable reply") is a glimpse of the paradise of the poet's own aspirations—his creative aspira-

tions; for as he comes to perceive Belle Isle, he also hears issuing from it the "petalled word" of "creation." In Crane's compelling treatment of this greatly traditional movement, the sea is again a decisive agent. The sea that had threatened and laughed at him, that had rivaled, imitated, and turned against him, that had wrecked or drowned him, now exerts its power to rescue and restore the poet. (p. 172)

We have moved, geographically and spiritually, from the warm Caribbean to icy northern waters; as it turns out, from the heat of emotional and physical experience to the cool zone where emotion may be recollected in tranquillity. . . . As "**Voyages VI**" opens, the poet finds himself in a region and within a complete poetic figure where swimmers struggle through chill ocean rivers toward morning, under skies that are strange to them, and with "eyes" that are "lost." The poet is one of those swimmers, or like them. He too is lost; he does not recognize the new surroundings, the shifting borders; and he has lost his ability to see—that is (again, as it turns out), his capacity to understand the actual world, its excitement and its pain, in the light of an envisioned ideal world. "**Voyages VI**" begins on the note of desolating incomprehension with which "**Voyages V**" ended.

It also begins with a tight paradox and an eloquent prayer. The poet is like a drowned and eyeless swimmer; two stanzas later, he is also like a blind sailor on an abandoned ship—he is even that ship itself. . . . He had, against all the warnings of "**Voyages I**" embarked on the dangerous love-journey; he had trusted his "spry cordage," the vessel of his body, to the cruel sea—had, in "**Voyages III**," descended to the depths of the sea to experience the whole fierce grandeur of human love; but after that grandeur had come the separation and with it the sense of psychic incarceration and death. And yet it is exactly that imprisoning and destructive sea whose *guest* the poet is, and whose "dungeons" (according to the poem's surprising syntax) can "lift" the "lost morning eyes" of swimmers like the poet. The sea possesses the power to restore life and light and vision, which is why its icy dungeons are also "bright"; for it is through just such a descent, just such a sea-death, that the adventurous and questing spirit may reach an ultimate perception forever denied to the emotionally landlocked. One must lose one's vision in order to find it. In the poem, the poet knows this; even as Crane knew it to be the inevitable outcome in the poetic tradition he was following; and the voice in "**Voyages VI**" prays to the ocean rivers that he too may be resurrected and re-enlightened. . . . (pp. 172-74)

It is a prayer for an end to the exhaustion of voyaging, a prayer for peaceful rest (later: "unsearchable repose"); for a spiritual haven and a phoenix-like rebirth. It is above all, a prayer for spiritual vision that can once more give rise to poetic utterance. In lines that surge and fall, that pound almost audibly to a turbulent oceanic pulse, the poet urges the sea-waves to "rear" for him an immense poetic theme. . . . [The] new subject is the death or fragmentation of poetic vision itself: it is "a splintered garland for the seer" which at the same time, by transposition, is a garland for the splintered seer.

This endlessly reverberating passage contains, among other things, as direct and dramatic a statement as one can find about the nature of the Romantic tradition—one is inclined to say, about the nature of modern poetry, and of a large range of modern literature generally. It bespeaks what is probably the key historic event in that tradition: the emergence of the poet—replacing the king or prince—as the hero of poetry; and of the exacting processes of the creative imagination as the drama that most absorbs the poet's attention. No less in the Romantic tradition . . . , the prayer is in great part answered in the very eloquence by which it gets uttered. The sweeping intensity of the poet's address to the waves indicates how far he has recovered his lost powers. (pp. 174-75)

As the voyage and the **"Voyages"** sequence approach their ending, the language and cadence slow and soften, a profound quiet enters into them. But on Belle Isle, the poet does not forget or repudiate the actual world he has left behind. On the contrary, he finds there the means of understanding it and the terms for describing and rejoicing in it, even . . . as he will—for this would essentially be the theme of Crane's epic—in *The Bridge*. The goddess who rises smiling from her lounge (her "floating dais," Belle Isle itself) is no doubt the goddess of dawn. . . . [But] she is also the poet's muse and [her] blithe word is a word *about* creation. Even as she says, "Let there be light!" she also says, "Let there be poetry!" For if the human union has been betrayed and dissolved, poetry will yet emerge from the union between the poet and his goddess; that union is exactly the "dialogue" which her eyes "concede." And in the poetry—that is, of course, in the entire love suite the poet is now enabled to compose— the human world and the human love affair find their identity, their meaning, their justification. (pp. 176-77)

By the end of **"Voyages,"** there can be little doubt about the nature and content of Crane's so ardently sought after "vision." One has heard it remarked that Crane was occupied with the tactics and intensity of vision, with the excitement of pursuing it, rather than with its definable substance. But about **"Voyages"** there can hardly be any uncertainty. It is a vision of this human life, of the loves we experience, the sufferings we endure, the kinds of deaths we undergo—and of the splendor and beauty of that life when it is viewed under the aspect of eternity and illuminated by the language of poetry. (pp. 178-79)

> *R.W.B. Lewis, in his* The Poetry of Hart Crane: A Critical Study *(copyright © 1967 by Princeton University Press; reprinted by permission of Princeton University Press), Princeton University Press, 1967, 426 p.*

NORMAN D. HINTON and LISE RODGERS   (essay date 1980)

Hart Crane's early poem, **"The Moth that God Made Blind,"** is most often dismissed with a word or two by critics. Their consensus is apparently that it belongs among Crane's juvenilia. . . . (p. 287)

Indeed, **"The Moth that God Made Blind"** seems at first glance to show us little more than the work of a promising youth who has not yet been able to find his own poetic voice and is still, regrettably, under the spell of Swinburne. We intend to show, however, that rather than representing the last of Crane's uninteresting early writing, the poem makes a fit beginning to his *oeuvre*, and that it grows . . . from a state of mind and an aesthetic which he never outgrew. That aesthetic, one of equilibrium between opposing forces, refusing to produce confident answers to major questions about existence, truth, beauty, and the like, is often identified with the "modern (i.e., 20th century) sensibility": if our suggestions are correct, it is likely that Crane should be thought of

as one of the early members of that group of poets who developed "modern poetry," rather than one who joined the group later and with reluctance.

The poem is generally read as an allegory of the young poet's growing up in a world of Philistines, finding a way to escape momentarily, but ultimately finding destruction. But this easy analysis is not supported by the text. The lives of neither the oasis-bound nor the blind moth are attractive, nor is the theme of the poem an easy one to specify.

A first reading yields logical conclusions: The moth is metaphor for man. One man, of extraordinary beauty and uniqueness of soul, dares to risk his life, to break from the chains of convention and darkness. In so doing, he experiences the ecstasy of freedom, and the beauty of knowledge and truth, but death is the consequence. The narrator identifies himself with this creature, indicating that he has searched for, and seen, beauty, and has suffered because of it: "These things I have: —a withered hand;—dim eyes;—a tongue that cannot tell."

The ambiguities within the poem, however, though perhaps not apparent on first reading, reveal a more complex and obscure situation. Basic questions are raised about a 'correct' interpretation—even about the very *possibility* of a final and logical explication of the poem.

One important problem in the poem is the association of the daylight and the desert with a truth and knowledge that are indeed beautiful and desirable. Such an association seems inevitable in the context of the poem's narrative—the blind moth exchanges imprisonment and blindness for freedom and sight in the desert. The reader can accept the moth's death; it seems an inevitable fate for someone who uncovers the mysteries of the universe. But the imagery associated with desert and oasis within the poem is less easy to explain, and too pervasive and insistent to ignore.

The desert, rather than seeming beautiful and desirable . . . , seems instead dry, barren, searing, and even ghastly. . . . The moths, on the other hand, are "born in mosaic datevases," they "emerge black and vermeil from yellow cocoons," they are all "countless rubies and tapers," "myriad jewellries of night." Their land, the oasis, is fertile and lovely, with "cocoa-nut palms . . . conceived in the light of Arabian moons," and is surrounded by a "halo of light" from the moon itself. The blind moth is superior to all others because that part of him associated with the *oasis*—his beautiful coloring—is exaggerated. . . . And his blindness, rather than his sight, is here associated with the desert, and unfavorably so. . . . Within this context, the sight that greets the moth when he momentarily achieves vision is negative. "Great horizons and systems and shores all along / Which blue tides of cool moons were slow shaken and sunned." "Great horizons and systems" connote vastness, emptiness, perhaps impersonality while the "blue tides of cool moons" are at a disadvantage in such an environment: "shaken" suggests a sort of trauma, and "sunned" is hardly favorable in its context. There is nothing paradisal about this world.

Besides the ambiguity concerning the oasis/desert antithesis, other questions are raised by the final stanza. Can the narrator, in fact, be identified with the blind moth, as a first reading of the poem implies? If so, why does the narrator search for the moth in the sand? . . . The previous stanza has described the moth falling to the desert; and earlier, of course, the moth is described as a "ruby brightening ever." This first line, then, strongly implies that the moth is something—or has something—that the narrator is searching for. This invalidates an identification of moth with narrator. (pp. 287-89)

There remains a crucial question. Why is the one moth who is, upon a simple reading of the poem, the creature with the greatest sensitivity—or genius, or courage, or knowledge—at first *totally* blind? Why is he initially *less* capable than his fellow-creatures? This fact seems to make his sojourn into the desert a simple act of unwitting self-destruction, rather than an act of autonomy or courage. . . . Perhaps related to the question of motive is the question of the title. What place does God have in the poem? The poem itself gives little indication that God is important to its meaning; but the reference to him seems to suggest that a power outside the blind moth's autonomy is at work to some extent. What significance is it, if any, that the God in the title makes the moth blind, while the "god" in the poem, the sun, enables him to see? Is the poem, to some extent at least, an attempt to comment on the cold indifference of a deity—a very modern theme—or on the beauty in store for God's special creatures despite the injustices of life?

We suggest that in the world of this poem all of these questions are unanswerable. There is no satisfactory solution to be found for its most basic themes: beauty, truth, freedom, and suffering. To say that all of these ambiguities equal a message directly opposed to the surface reading of the poem is as much an oversimplification as the surface reading itself. To say, for instance, that the moth does not represent an extraordinarily gifted creature, but merely a blind misfortunate, is to ignore the envy and awe that his beauty excites. To say that the knowledge of truth is a totally undesirable thing is to ignore the exhilaration, power, and freedom that the blind moth experiences, however fleetingly, in pursuit of that knowledge. To say that blindness—and security—are preferable to sight within the poem is to ignore the lines of of stanza 12: "sight burned as deep / As his blindness before had frozen in Hell." Equally unsatisfactory is the contention that this passage indicates the poem's message is relativistic; this does nothing to explain the very puzzling questions raised by the final stanza.

One must of course ask *why* the questions are, in fact, unanswerable. The immediate temptation is to dismiss the poem as a work filled with ambiguity in the worst sense of the word: an uncontrolled, and perhaps unintentional, ambiguity. We do not believe, however, that this is the case. The ambiguities or inconsistencies within the poem are not only numerous, but fundamental to the poem's meaning. (pp. 290-91)

All critics who have written on the poem agree that the blind moth is a figure of the poet and, more specifically, of Crane. We would not quarrel with this, but the ambiguities discussed above raise some questions. Assuming that the poem is not marred by juvenescent bungling, can these doubts and paradoxes, these hesitations as to which life is better, the blind moth's or the "ordinary" moths', represent young Crane's feelings about himself? It might be reasonable for the poem to suggest dubiety about the narrator's poetic abilities at this stage of his fledgling career. But the doubts in the poem are deeper, and apparently addressed to the vocation of poet itself—is it, after all, better not to be a Daedalus, not to be an aesthetic hero? On the other hand, one can hardly claim victory for the moths of limited vision. There seem to be

claims made for and against both sides, and the narrator is left at the end of the poem with a genuine dilemma as he hunts the desert sands for a "spark."

Such a state of mind does in fact represent Crane's personal dilemma, one that he never totally escaped, and this dilemma speaks directly to the ground of his aesthetic, which he was about to encounter or perhaps already had encountered when **"The Moth that God Made Blind"** reached the state in which we have it. (p. 291)

[Crane's mentor, Carl Schmitt,] taught Crane that "moral experience" and "sensual experience" must balance each other, that man's life is always compounded from a mixture of good and evil, beauty and ugliness," and Crane himself wrote his father "I have powers which, if properly balanced, will enable me to mount to extraordinary latitudes. There is constantly an inward struggle, but the time to worry is when there [sic] is no inward debate. . . . There is only one harmony, that is the equelibrium [sic] maintained by two opposite forces, equally strong." (Notice the metaphor of flight and the insistence on the equal strength of each side or "power".) The theory so clearly matches much of the poem that it would be most unusual if Crane had worked out such theories at the age of 15, before he had even met Schmitt.

This sense of equilibrium through struggle was to stay with Crane all his life, expressing itself over and over, in such famous instances as his "serpent with the eagle in the grass," his juxtaposition of rural America and the Brooklyn Bridge, his scenes of agony and love at once in **"National Winter Garden,"** to cite only *The Bridge*. (pp. 293-94)

"The Moth that God Made Blind" is an important radical departure from poetry as popularly conceived in the early years of the century. In its refusal to see beauty (however painfully attained) as a glorious end in itself, in its ability to balance, not between good and evil alone but between ironically perceived goods and evils in both tribes of moths, the poem speaks to the emerging spirit of Pound and Eliot, not to the departed ones of Swinburne and Dowson, Johnson and Wilde. It is impossible to explicate this poem as those of the late 19th century are explicated. No matter where one turns in the poem, it exhibits both a measure of solace and a larger measure of ironic disappointment. The extended vision of the blind moth is countered absolutely by his fate, and the happier (and also, in its own way, beautiful) life of the other moths is countered absolutely by their circumscription. The resultant personal and cultural ironies are not so different from the more famous ones of [Pound's] *Hugh Selwyn Mauberly*, with its "botched civilization" and its "tawdry cheapness." (p. 294)

Norman D. Hinton and Lise Rodgers, "Hart Crane's 'The Moth that God Made Blind'," in Papers on Language and Literature (copyright © 1980 by the Board of Trustees, Southern Illinois University at Edwardsville), Vol. 16, No. 3, Summer, 1980, pp. 287-94.

ADDITIONAL BIBLIOGRAPHY

Crane, Hart. *Letters of Hart Crane and His Family*, edited by Thomas S.W. Lewis. New York & London: Columbia University Press, 1974, 675 p.

    Large collection of Crane letters.

Horton, Philip. *Hart Crane: The Life of an American Poet*. New York: Norton, 1937, 352 p.

An early critical biography.

O'Connor, William Van. "The Employment of Myths." In his *Sense and Sensibility in Modern Poetry,* pp. 7-30. New York: Barnes & Noble, 1963.*

Discusses *The Bridge* and its relationship to T. S. Eliot's *The Waste Land.*

Paul, Sherman. *Hart's "Bridge."* Urbana: University of Illinois Press, 1972, 315 p.

Close study of Crane's poetry.

Schwartz, Joseph. *Hart Crane: An Annotated Critical Bibliography.* New York: David Lewis, 1970, 276 p.

The most complete bibliography to date.

Sugg, Richard P. *Hart Crane's "The Bridge": A Description of Its Life*. University: University of Alabama Press, 1976, 127 p.

Important reading of *The Bridge*.

Unterecker, John. *Voyager: A Life of Hart Crane.* New York: Farrar, Straus and Giroux, 1969, 787 p.

The most thorough biography of Crane.

Vogler, Thomas A. "A New View of Hart Crane's *Bridge.*" *The Sewanee Review* LXXIII, No. 3 (July-September 1965): 381-408.

Important reassessment of *The Bridge* which discusses its success as the study of a search for a mythic vision.

W(illiam) H(enry) Davies

1871-1940

Anglo-Welsh poet, novelist, essayist, and autobiographer.

Noted for his lyrics inspired by nature and for the direct simplicity of his prose, Davies occupies a modestly secure position among English poets. Although Davies's poetry is uneven, it is often praised for its sincerity.

Since Davies's father died when the poet was very young, Davies, a difficult child, was raised by his grandparents. As a young man, he chose to live the life of a tramp until he lost a leg while attempting to jump a train. After his accident, Davies renewed an early interest in literature; he began writing while supporting himself as a peddler in London.

Davies published his first collection of poetry, *The Soul's Destroyer and Other Poems*, at his own expense. He sent copies of the book to several critics in an attempt to gain recognition; the first important review came from George Bernard Shaw who saw great merit in the work. Shaw brought it to the attention of other critics who noted that despite roughness in some poems, *The Soul's Destroyer* contained some of the freshest and most beautiful poetry of the day.

Davies also received recognition from critic and poet Edward Thomas, who became his mentor. Thomas gave Davies financial support and provided him with a house in the country, where Davies wrote his highly respected *The Autobiography of a Super-Tramp*. This prose work is the story of Davies's wandering years and is noted for its frankness as well as its descriptive passages. The *Autobiography* made Davies well-known to the public.

Following the *Autobiography* Davies wrote poetry profusely; *New Poems* and *Nature Poems and Others* are two of the most important collections. Both his lyric poems, reminiscent of the delicate verse of the Elizabethans, and his nature poems, in the style of Robert Herrick, are found in these volumes. The success of his nature poems is due to his peculiar powers of observation, which Lawrence Hockey attributed to Davies's practice of "stopping and staring." Through this intense study, Davies presented the reader with a complete picture: a scene with a primary focus and a detailed background.

"The virtues of Davies's poems" writes critic Ralph J. Mills, Jr., "are those of the author himself—unaffected simplicity, directness, intuitiveness, coupled with a genuine and marvelous lyric gift."

PRINCIPAL WORKS

The Soul's Destroyer and Other Poems (poetry) 1905
New Poems (poetry) 1907
The Autobiography of a Super-Tramp (autobiography) 1908
Nature Poems and Others (poetry) 1908
Farewell to Poesy and Other Poems (poetry) 1910
A Weak Woman (novel) 1911
The True Traveller (prose) 1912
A Poet's Pilgrimage (autobiography) 1918
True Travellers: A Tramps' Opera (opera libretto) 1923

Later Days (autobiography) 1925
My Birds (essay) 1933
My Garden (essay) 1933
Love Poems (poetry) 1935
The Loneliest Mountain and Other Poems (poetry) 1939
Collected Poems of W. H. Davies (poetry) 1943
The Essential W. H. Davies (poetry, prose, and autobiography) 1951
The Complete Poems of W. H. Davies (poetry) 1963
*Young Emma (memoir) 1981

*This work was written in 1924.

THE ATHENAEUM (essay date 1905)

['**The Soul's Destroyer**'] is in all respects a remarkable book, singularly lacking in the tags and conventionalities which go to the making of minor poetry. That the personal note should predominate is, perhaps, natural; neither is it surprising, in view of the peculiar circumstances of the book's production, that the verses should show a certain crudity of technique, a few shaky rhymes and some grammatical lapses; but these are surface faults, and by no means numerous. It is the work of a nature-lover, compelled to dwell in the unsavoury regions of the town; of one with an intimate and first-hand knowledge of the life of the very poor, and, withal, possessed of a genuine gift of poetry. The poems are numerous, and, naturally, of varying merit. That which gives its name to the volume, **'The Soul's Destroyer,'** suffers in the main from a certain brutality of detail and a lack of restraint. . . . The rest of the poem is almost unnecessarily sordid, and the blank verse is apt to be monotonous, though there are many beautiful and striking lines. . . .

The author is more uniformly successful in his rhymed poems, particularly in the shorter of them. . . .

[The] verses dealing with life in a common lodging-house, describing the inmates, the miseries of existence in such a place, the foul surroundings, and the hopelessness of it all, constitute the distinctive feature of the book. . . . There is grim humour in [the] descriptions of **"Old 'Barge' Bill," "Brummy Tom," "Sailor,"** and the rest of them; while **"The Lodging-House Fire,"** . . . has real pathos and a note of despair. . . .

The faults of the book . . . are not such as should seriously interfere with a full appreciation of its force, sincerity, and poetry. It is to be hoped that the poetry-reading public will give it the welcome it deserves.

> *"Verse, Old and New: 'The Soul's Destroyer'," in* The Athenaeum, *No. 4062, September 2, 1905, p. 300.*

BERNARD SHAW   (essay date 1907)

In the year 1905 I received by post a volume of poems [*The Soul's Destroyer and Other Poems*] by one William H. Davies. . . . (p. viii)

An accompanying letter asked me very civilly if I required a half-crown book of verses; and if so, would I please send the author the half crown: if not, would I return the book. This was attractively simple and sensible. Further, the handwriting was remarkably delicate and individual: the sort of handwriting one might expect from Shelley or George Meredith. I opened the book, and was more puzzled than ever; for before I had read three lines I perceived that the author was a real poet. His work was not in the least strenuous or modern: there was in it no sign that he had ever read anything later than Cowper or Crabbe, not even Byron, Shelley or Keats, much less Morris, Swinburne, Tennyson, or Henley and Kipling. There was indeed no sign of his ever having read anything otherwise than as a child reads. The result was a freedom from literary vulgarity which was like a draught of clear water in a desert. Here, I saw, was a genuine innocent, writing odds and ends of verse about odds and ends of things, living quite out of the world in which such things are usually done, and knowing no better (or rather no worse) than to get his book made by the appropriate craftsman and hawk it round like any other ware.

Evidently, then, a poor man. It horrified me to think of a poor man spending his savings in printing something that nobody buys: poetry, to wit. . . . I wrote him a letter telling him that he could not live by poetry. Also, I bought some spare copies, and told him to send them to such critics and

verse fanciers as he knew of, wondering whether they would recognise a poet when they met one.

And they actually did. (pp. x-xi)

My purchase of eight copies of the book enabled him, I gathered, to discard all economy for about three months. It also moved him to offer me the privilege (for such I quite sincerely deem it) of reading his autobiography in manuscript. . . .

All I have to say by way of recommendation of the book [*The Autobiography of a Super-Tramp*] is that I have read it through from beginning to end, and would have read more of it had there been any more to read. It is a placid narrative, unexciting in matter and unvarnished in manner, of the commonplaces of a tramp's life. It is of a very curious quality. Were not the author an approved poet of remarkable sensibility and delicacy I should put down the extraordinary quietness of his narrative to a monstrous callousness. Even as it is, I ask myself with some indignation whether a man should lose a limb with no more to-do than a lobster loses a claw or a lizard his tail, as if he could grow a new one at his next halting place! (p. xii)

It is to be noted that Mr. Davies is no propagandist of the illusions of the middle-class tramp fancier. . . . He does not tell you that there is honour among tramps: on the contrary, he makes it clear that only by being too destitute to be worth robbing and murdering can a tramp insure himself against being robbed and murdered by his comrade of the road. (pp. xv-xvi)

Mr. Davies is now a poet of established reputation. He no longer prints his verses and hawks them: he is regularly published and reviewed. . . . That the verses in *The Soul's Destroyer* and in his *New Poems* will live is beyond question. . . . Though it is only in verse that he writes exquisitely, yet this book, which is printed as it was written, without any academic corrections . . . , is worth reading by literary experts for its style alone. And since his manner is so quiet, it has been thought well by his friends and his publishers to send a trumpeter before him the more effectually to call attention to him before he begins. I have volunteered for that job for the sake of his poems. Having now done it after my well known manner, I retire and leave the stage to him. (pp. xvi-xvii)

> *Bernard Shaw, "Preface" (1907), in* The Autobiography of a Super-Tramp *by William H. Davies (copyright © 1917 by William H. Davies; copyright renewed © 1944 by Helen Mitilda Davies; reprinted by permission of the Executors of the W. H. Davies Estate and Jonathan Cape Ltd, Publishers), Knopf, 1917 (and reprinted by Alfred A. Knopf, 1938), pp. vii-xvii.*

STEPHEN GWYNN   (essay date 1910)

Life held two adventures for [William H. Davies]—one the adventure of the open road with its infinite variety, the other the adventure of poetry with its grinding climb. (p. 490)

[What] kind of poetry was the outcome of these thirty odd years of a life whose adult period has been spent among tramps and sturdy beggars, street-singers, fish-porters, sellers of flypapers, cadgers of every category. . . .

[In] shorter pieces the life of the doss-house is sketched—sometimes with humor, sometimes shot through with beauty, called into memory by an unseen singer's voice, and once and most terribly in the description of the poisonous coke fire. That is hideous—hideous as anything that Mr. [James] Stephens calls up before us—yet it is human. We enter into it, our life also fights against the stupefying vapor: Mr. Stephens sees his garbage-littered street, the black cave of the lodging-house door, his blear-eyed cabman; but he sees them from aloof and apart. Where he breeds in us disgust only, Mr. Davies evokes a human ruth.

Yet—and here is the essence—no poet was ever less inclined than Mr. Davies to dwell on ugliness. While he lived in the reek of that squalor it pervaded his vision; he scarcely could be unconscious of it for a moment. But the goal once achieved, Mr. Davies was a free man: he had made his footing, and now he could afford to set his face for home. He left London for Wales.

In the second volume, *New Poems,* we still find him dwelling here and there upon those years of slavery. . . .

But in the third book, *Nature Poems,* all this has gone from him; it is only the shadow against which he sets his joy—his **"Happy Life."** (p. 492)

It is only in this third book that we begin to get echoes of the earlier days when Mr. Davies was vagrant by choice, not by necessity. That is the vagrancy out of which comes poetry. . . .

I should hardly go back to Mr. Davies's poem on the lodging-house fire, in spite of all its tragic force, and certainly not to the lines on **"Hope Abandoned."** It is for the sake of that elemental joy, like the joy of the earth over rain, or of the dam licking her new-born cub, which is the poet's deepest attribute, and which I find in many of his poems, that I should always return to Mr. Davies. . . . The ultimate and crowning need in the making of a poet is a wise heart. (p. 493)

> *Stephen Gwynn, "The Making of a Poet," in* The Living Age *(copyright 1910, by the Living Age Co.), Vol. XLVII, No. 3437, May 21, 1910, pp. 484-93.**

THE TIMES LITERARY SUPPLEMENT (essay date 1916)

Mr. Davies's new book is called **"Child Lovers,"** but its real title is **"And other Poems."** He bade **"Farewell to Poesy"** in 1910, but she ran after him with **"Songs of Joy,"** and they have met again and again under the dappling shadow and sunshine of **"Foliage"** vocal with wholly indigenous **"Birds of Paradise."** Apart from her clear, smooth cheek, her small, sweet, round voice, it is easy to say what there is not in Mr. Davies's work—or rather play. It has a Caroline grace and ease, but no "elegance." It expresses no more mystery, nor criticism of life, than a buttercup or a goldfinch, since it shines and sings and rejoices in answer only to its own impulse. Mr. Davies can paint an almost Hogarthian picture of actuality in **"The Inquest,"** but his fellow-jurymen would have hesitated to declare his rider, and it would have scandalized the coroner. . . .

Mr. Davies rarely says anything but for that thing's sake, and seldom in a syllable more than enough for his purpose, whether he tells of May finding him inexplicably mute, "My lips, like gills in deep-sea homes, Beat time, and still no music comes"; of "The white cascade, that's both a bird and star

That has a ten-mile voice and shines as far"; or of the winter song of the robin. . . . One is apt to call such things naïve and simple, but they are simple only in the sense that an essence is simple. Was it merely a happy five minutes or half a close, strange, sensitive lifetime that went to the making of **"This Night"**? . . . We use the word originality, too, as if, like Oxford marmalade, it were a delectable addition to a literary breakfast. But life cannot be neatly potted like that. The very Self in every man is all original. Now and then comes one who, like Mr. Davies, can be at times that naked self *and* can express it. . . . It is either poetry or nothing; and first we must accept Mr. Davies's mood, his quiet, happy, and serious outlook. He fails when he writes heedlessly, merely as he has written before, or with his eye straying towards the sophisticated. But the wonder is that after so much writing of verse he still can cry, "Come, thou sweet Wonder . . . Come to my heavy rain of care And make it weigh like dew," and that his call is heard.

> *"Two Poets," in* The Times Literary Supplement *(© Times Newspapers Ltd. (London) 1916; reproduced from* The Times Literary Supplement *by permission), No. 751, June 8, 1916, p. 269.**

EZRA POUND (essay date 1917)

William H. Davies writes in a curious traditional dialect—that is to say in a language that is more or less the tongue of Burns and Blake and the Elizabethans; he puts his words "hind-side to" as the ancient writers were wont, and he says "did go" and "did sing" and so forth. . . . Also Mr. Shaw once introduced him as a curiosity and all these things put one off. Having found out this much, one has also found about as much fault as one can find with Mr. Davies, or at least all the fault that he would not find with himself. (p. 99)

Davies uses his verse as a vehicle for a philosophy as well as for communicating his mood. Certainly he does talk *about* things quite as often as he presents them, possibly more often; still he does now and again present men or things without comment: as, for example, a drunk who has done time watching school-house after school-house in the hope of finding his children. . . . The poem is possibly sentimental. There are flaws in its technique. "But you know it's only about one thing in thirty I do that's any good," is the author's own summary criticism of his poems, so we may as well take the good with the flawed for a moment. Poet Davies is without any doubt, if one will but read enough of him for conviction. Despite the ancient speech . . . there is here and there the fine phrase and the still finer simplicity. (p. 100)

Frankly I do not think that most of Davies' poems are so good as [*Sweet Youth* and *A Lovely Woman.*] Yet sometimes he uses the "classic-English" manner to perfection. In *Dreams of the Sea,* for example, are lines and strophes which I think we would accept without quaver or question if we found them in volumes of accepted "great poets." . . . (p. 101)

Robustezza! This verse is not in the latest mode, but compare it with verse of its own kind and you will not find much to surpass it. Wordsworth, for instance, would have had a deal of trouble trying to better it. The sound quality is, again, nearer that of the Elizabethans than of the nineteenth-century writers. The philologist will find scarcely a Latin word in the . . . verses: "Armada" is a proper name, and "gentle" is so tempered by mediaeval French popular usage that one forgets its Latin derivation. I do not wish the reader to imply from this that the use of Latin words in English is taboo. Simply: certain effects are very often due to the omission of Latin words from the verse.

There is a resonance and a body of sound in these verses of Davies which I think many vers-librists might envy.

I am by no means attempting a full examination of Davies in this brief annotation. I think . . . he should be considered at least as much for his verses as for his better known prose, *Autobiography of a Super-Tramp.* (p. 102)

> Ezra Pound, "William H. Davies, Poet," in Poetry (© 1917 by The Modern Poetry Association), Vol. XI, No. II, November, 1917, pp. 99-102.

HAROLD WILLIAMS   (essay date 1919)

The extravagant praise which greeted Mr. W. H. Davies on the appearance of his first book, *The Soul's Destroyer* . . . , was due less to the merit of his poetry than the interest of his story, which had spread abroad. . . . Mr. Davies' story was romantic; but this did not justify foolish over-praise of his verse. He was compared to James Thomson (B.V.), Crabbe, Wordsworth, the Elizabethans, and described as "a lord of language." Comment is needless. In his first collection those poems of the doss-house, 'Saints and Lodgers' and the reverie, 'The Lodging-house Fire' contain good writing, but the blank verse 'Soul's Destroyer' is metrically monotonous, and, beyond betraying a genuine feeling for natural beauty, it has small vestige of the stronger emotion of poetry. And vulgarisms—for example the poet's notice of the bird that "twittered some"—which can never be made into poetry are unpardonable even in a tramp-poet. The one poem of distinction in this volume is 'The Lodging-house Fire.' . . . In [*New Poems* and *Nature Poems*] . . . he uses to far better purpose the two faculties that chiefly are his—a vision of beauty and happiness in life and nature as clear and direct as the child's and an unfailing strain of effortless song. Nearly all his poems are fresh, springing from a mind which sees the world not as others see, but individually. Women and children, bird-song and sunset, ale and the vagrant life, the characters of doss-house and slum—of these he sings for the joy and interest of seeing and feeling. And he wisely forswears cumbering his poetry with intellectualisms. There is nothing sophisticated in his thought or style. In restrained simplicity he is sometimes not far from Wordsworth, in the fleeting beauty of his word-music not unlike Herrick. And the next two volumes, [*Farewell to Poesy* and *Songs of Joy*] . . . , exhibit even greater gain in melody and felicitous simplicity. Perhaps in *Foliage* . . . he sings a little less spontaneously of the themes from which he rarely departs, but his poems retain their charm of artless grace in imagery and style. Mr. Davies' genius as a poet is limited; he has neither the strength nor intellectual force of Mr. [Alfred] Williams, nor can he successfully embark on a long poem. He has no message, no strong thought for his generation. He is content if he may sing in his own words the changeless and simple facts of life and nature, and he rarely fails to render these sincerely and with a clear music. (pp. 129-31)

> Harold Williams, "The Passage of the Centuries," in his Modern English Writers: Being a Study of Imaginative Literature 1890-1914, *Sidgwick & Jackson, Limited, 1919, pp. 55-139.**

ALBERT EDMUND TROMBLY   (essay date 1920)

In reading the poems of Mr. William H. Davies one is struck by their revelations of character. Robust and virile, he is tender-hearted without being mawkish. His are songs of joy; and joy and beauty he finds in all healthy activities. In a graceful analysis of Fancy he tells us that its roots are contentment, innocence, and wonder: the three things which we find to be the prime elements in his own being. Content with the common things of day, he finds in them a perennial source of wonder, and in his joy of them he remains as innocent as a child.

There are no large perspectives in his landscapes,—no mountains, no forests, no great noisy waters; but sheep and cattle feeding, butterflies, flowers, brooks, and birds. He loves, understands, and pities the poor; pities them as only one who knows and is one with them can. That is his Christianity. . . . He would feel guilty and ashamed at having fled the misery of the city could he not console himself with the thought that he can help his fellows best only when he is light-hearted, and light-heartedness for him is not to be found in the dismal city. He is sometimes betrayed into preaching too openly; but a sermon which pleads for brotherly love is not very likely to prove offensive. In so genial a personality one might expect to find a visionary, a man full of illusions touching the innate goodness of men. That note does arise now and then, but it is offset by others of disillusionment and even cynicism. . . . The predominant tone, however, is that of faith in men. Even when that faith is shaken, there remain an understanding sympathy and pity. There are also moments of revolt, moments when the inequalities of society seem unjust, when the luxuriousness and callousness of the rich seem to mock the misery of the poor.

Although the poet has no children of his own, we are constantly meeting with children in Mr. Davies's poems, true children, understandingly and appreciatively presented. But perhaps nothing speaks more eloquently of his large humanity than his tender love of animals. (pp. 414-15)

One is constantly aware that Mr. Davies loves and delights in animals, not because he finds them in any way symbolical of this or that, but for themselves. I am reminded, in reading these poems, of nothing quite so often as of those calm and restful landscapes of the Dutch masters wherein we see cattle and other domestic animals serenely still or browsing. Whether I find them in the poems or not, I see, as I read, sheep grazing contentedly on a hillside, cows standing knee-deep in meadow-streams, horses gazing idly from the corner of a pasture or rubbing their noses and necks on the fence-rails. How pleasurable to meet a man who, without concerning himself too much with discovering or establishing a mystical brotherhood between himself and the so-called lower animals, actually is their brother! For such an one the fields are a storehouse of pure joys. . . . (pp. 415-16)

Mr. Davies is eminently a poet of birds, and preëminently the poet of butterflies. He is no indoor poet ruminating the pleasant memory of what he has observed outside. His birds are caught on the wing and his butterflies are hardly to be distinguished from the flowers. Here are butterflies which might be wind-blown petals. . . . [His] bees, also, are very much alive and hardly to be confused with those which one keeps and observes under a glass globe. . . . Butterflies are forever fluttering in and about these poems, simply because the poet has thrown open his heart to them and let them in.

They belong to the out-of-doors, and none but an out-of-door poet can know and sing them. (pp. 416-17)

I never feel that Mr. Davies goes a-hunting for poems with a note-book. That is not his method. He finds, after having been out, that he has lived songs, and inevitably he sings them. A day in the fields fills his heart with the songs of blackbird, cuckoo, thrush, and even with the mute song of the grasses; and when, in the evening, he returns home he finds in his heart both the songs he has heard and one that is all his own. This man with a child's heart, who shares his bread with a robin singing in the cold, who enjoys listening to the wren as she dominates with her clear note the chatter of numberless starlings, is the man who finds April a season. . . .

His understanding and love of lesser aspects of Nature are equally marked. There are beauty and song for him in flowers, grasses, the wind, the moon, and the sea. He has written but very few sea-poems, yet a single couplet from one of them is an earnest of his deep and native love of the sea. . . . (p. 417)

No subject is worn threadbare of poetry so long as poets can endow it with fresh beauty. I am not implying that Mr. Davies imitates, for he does not; but in *Autumn,* responding to the same sense of haze, drowsiness, fullness, and decay which moved Keats and [Thomas] Hood in their odes, he gives us the Autumn feeling anew. . . .

How poignantly the simplest song will thrill the hearer, if the poet, too, has been deeply moved! (p. 418)

Mr. Davies is particularly delightful in his love-poems. Here, as elsewhere, he appeals by being natural, simple, spontaneous, homely, and picturesque. His love is no more a thing of the indoors than are his birds and butterflies. It is airy, boyish, always wholesome, and the poet can speak of it with entire frankness. Now he tells of what his sweetheart means to him . . . now he sings the praises of her hair, roguishly stealing up behind her, pulling out a long pin, and all but drowning in the flood that is loosened and shaken about him. Again, in another poem, he warns the fairies against getting lost in the forest of his lady's hair and thanks Puck for having knotted the grass in such a way that it threw the sweet maiden into his arms. And how charming is *Love's Coming,* wherein the lady's bird, which has been silent during her absence, cocks his head as she enters, begins to sing at the sound of her voice and sings so loudly that the lovers must leave the room to hear each other speak. But nothing quite equals *My Lady Comes,* in its fanciful and original conceits, in its intrinsic beauty, and in its mingled extravaganza and sanity. . . . (pp. 418-19)

Mr. Davies's manner is no less interesting than his matter; in fact, the two are as one, for if he writes delightfully it is because he has delightful things to say. A shrewd observer, a careful reporter of what he observes, he is always natural without being prosaic, and we never feel that his simplicity is a forced or conscious naïveté. He is fond of symbolism, as when, seeing children at play,—the boy digging in the sand for gold, the girl knitting stockings for a bird,—he thinks of the one as digging his grave, of the other as making her shroud. He is often suggestive of Herrick and the Elizabethans, as in [*The Boy*]. . . . His poems are rich in quaint and delightfully surprising figures, figures wrought of keen observation and delicate fancy. . . . (pp. 419-20)

A lover and singer of the little things of life, it is perhaps natural that Mr. Davies should be a poet of fancy rather than of imagination. I have spoken of a certain resemblance which he bears to Herrick. For myself, I think him an even finer poet. He is more authentic, and he is much more spontaneous. He has more to say than Herrick had, breathes a larger and a more wholesome atmosphere, is less artful, and fully as charming. If a poet is to be measured by his world, Mr. Davies will not loom very large, for his is a small world of small things; but within that world he is a master; and it may be that we should judge a man, not by the magnitude of his task, but by the manner in which he accomplishes it. (p. 420)

Albert Edmund Trombly, "The Poems of William H. Davies," in The Sewanee Review *(© 1920 by The University of the South), Vol. XXVIII, No. 3, July, 1920, pp. 414-20.*

J. C. S[QUIRE] (essay date 1922)

A few years ago, Mr. Davies published a volume of *Collected Poems,* which was a selection of what he thought his best, a selection very well made. The next edition might profitably be expanded, for each new book he issues contains a few poems as good as his best. There was a marked development in his art between the first and the third of his twelve books of verse; from the third onwards he has not changed at all. He found his materials and his tools; he has been happy with them ever since. Occasionally he experiments with some novel theme or manner, but never with success. The great majority of his poems are short lyrics in iambic measures about the elementary features of the landscape and human nature, and the simple joys and sorrows of ordinary life. The difference between the good ones and the others is the difference between verse which is written under inspiration and verse which is not. When Mr. Davies is not in the mood he may express his usual sentiments in his usual words and his usual metres, but the result is cold. When he is really moved to write he cannot help succeeding; he has only to be natural and he has done all that is necessary, so frank and easy is his expression, so comprehensible his emotion, so keen his eye, so charming the images which leap to his mind. One flash of vision, one jet of emotion, one momentary strangeness seized, and Mr. Davies has made a little poem which nobody else could have written, said an arresting thing in an unmistakeably individual voice which is very difficult to define but very easy to recognise. What he could do he can still do: his curiosity is unabated, he is still as surprised as he ever was by men and women, the grass is still as green for him and the lambs as innocent; experience does not take the edge off his observation or retard the movements of his heart; he does not learn, but he does not lose. . . . [The] great thing about Mr. Davies [in *The Hour of Magic*] is that when he is at his best we do not mind his awkwardnesses. *Impudence,* in which Mr. Davies indulges in his odd habit of rhyming "cold" and "world," is a delicious picture of a young girl, and *Lamorna Cove* has one of those odd effective images which Mr. Davies alone can use. Of the rest, the best are *Grief of Others, The Collar,* and one or two love-poems, tinged with that naive sensuality, akin to a delight in stuffs, which has always been characteristic of Mr. Davies in this vein. (pp. 95-6)

J. C. S[quire], "Poetry" (reprinted by permission of the Estate of J. C. Squire), in The London Mercury, *Vol. VII, No. 37, November, 1922, pp. 94-6.**

FRANK LUCAS   (essay date 1926)

It may seem absurd to say of a poet as firmly established as Mr. Davies that his work shows less performance than promise. In a rather undistinguished age his verse ranks high; and yet the basis of his reputation is not metrical subtlety, or distinction of style, or profundity of thought. . . . (p. 198)

His prosody, never ambitious, is not invariably respectable; . . . [it] scans hideously; and one had 'rather be a kitten and cry "mew,"' than rhyme 'converse' with 'hoarse,' 'looked' with 'sucked,' 'sweet' with 'mute.' Assonance is one thing, rhyme another—they do not live happily together in the same poem. Similarly with his diction; the comparison of a kiss to a dead fly has indeed ceased to blot **'The Portrait'** in its latest form, but the worm-simile of **'The Grief of Others'** . . . is almost as intolerable. There is no intrinsic objection to worms, creatures with a peculiarly distinguished poetic past; and after the recent plethora of birds, let the worms have a turn by all means; but not disconnected worms dragged in anyhow. And there is much more evil than genius in the spirit that moves Mr. Davies to write. . . . Whence, then, Mr. Davies' reputation; and his real promise? It is, partly, that he has an extraordinarily happy, though fickle, fancy, and the mob of his more superficially accomplished contemporaries have not. It is a far cry from Mr. Davies to Aristotle; but the stress laid by that ancient on the gift for metaphor (and, it follows, simile) above all else in poetic style—'since this alone cannot be taught and is a mark of genius, for it entails a real eye for resemblances'—is itself by now one of the platitudes of genius. That eye lives in Mr. Davies' head and its visions form his greatest charm. . . . [If] Mr. Davies' work is as full of holes as a net, it is a net full of butterflies; and a symbolist might find a subtle fitness in the recurrence through his work of this emblem at once of frivolous light-heartedness and of the soul. His own first poem indeed takes no other emblem of the recurrence of his thoughts from 'higher themes' to those he loves from of old. (pp. 198-200)

The other thing about Mr. Davies is that genuine spontaneity of his feelings which, though too often he tries (surely not with great success) to make Mrs. Grundy's flesh creep, is the secret of much of his appeal. (p. 200)

The pity of it all is that there should be so many good lines, good verses, good ideas; and yet so few good poems here. In these reviewing days, the fool in Hierocles who carried about a brick as a sample of what his house was like, is become the type of us all; we are cultivating a pretty taste in bricks rather than in architecture, and it would be particularly easy to write a convincing 'puff' of Mr. Davies. But it is a commonplace literature that caters only for commonplace books. And that is Mr. Davies' besetting sin. He can begin a poem with a quiet distinction . . . and then allow it to gutter out in a fourth verse of utter banality. With a repetition of this sort of *felo-de-se* the reader grows embittered. We cannot trust Mr. Davies not to let us down in midstream; and this feeling that we must be perpetually prepared to wince spoils the enjoyment of the happier moments. Mr. Davies' success is one more testimony to the truth of Ruskin's paradox, 'the utmost a man can do is that which he can do without effort.' But having lustily hammered the iron while hot does not dispense from the after-use of the file when it is cold. 'A great statesman must have two qualities—the first is prudence, the second imprudence. So with poets.' That is true enough: all the same, Mr. Davies' imprudence is too imprudent and his artlessness too like the real thing. It is

futile to leave the winnowing of his work to the casual reader's pencil, and it may be fatal to leave it to Time. Nothing is quite so dead as promise never fulfilled.

The trouble is that though other modern poets have more admirers, none has more adorers than Mr. Davies. They have erected their conception of him into a sort of idyllic idol, an inspired natural, a poetic Peter Pan of bucolic complexion, contemplating, with poesy and a straw in his mouth, the loves of the butterflies. Infant prodigy, *enfant terrible*—both aspects are dear to jaded dowagers of either sex in this our middle-age. Mr. Davies is *so* original—no one else rhymes 'power' and 'fire,' 'ever' and 'together.' . . . (pp. 201-02)

The best thing about *Secrets* is that it contains some charming poems that are not in this overworked and overflattered vein, that are not naïve at all, without being for that, the less characteristic. . . . (pp. 202-03)

Something has certainly brought here a new majesty into the democracy of Mr. Davies' style. It is a happy restoration, that with him will never become a tyranny. Nor need this dignity prove out of place; for I do not believe that the real Mr. Davies is, after all, quite so simple. When his muse sings, straw in mouth, her most ingenious praises of infinite beer and skittles, one has often felt that she had also—ever so little—tongue in cheek. She had merely discovered that a certain exaggerated *simplesse* in the manner of expressing feelings, genuine in themselves, ravished a section of the public, who can discern no new thing in poetry unless it is underlined six times. *Secrets* is better than its recent predecessor, because it has less mental morris-dancing and more thought, less thumping on the table with a beer-jug and more of that wide human pity which is one of the deepest and most enduring springs of the world's poetry. In **'Earth Love,'** the poet contrasts his own light-hearted joy in living things, in the dancing boughs of green, with the darker thoughts of another at his side. . . . But it is just because Mr. Davies at times ceases to flutter about surfaces, because he himself can go groping deeper among the roots of things and the sweet dignity of their sorrow, that he here wins new successes worth winning, with poems like **'Pity'** and **'The Two Heavens.'** How well his writing will last, it is even harder than usual to prophesy; if it proves ephemeral, it will be largely because Mr. Davies has been taken too seriously by his public, not seriously enough by himself. (pp. 203-04)

> *Frank Lucas, "Bedlam and Parnassus," in* New Statesman (© *1923 The Statesman Publishing Co. Ltd.), Vol. XXI, No. 525, May 5, 1923 (and reprinted in a different form as "Mr. W. H. Davies," in his* Authors Dead & Living, *The Macmillan Company, 1926, pp. 198-204).*

EDMUND BLUNDEN   (essay date 1932)

There is always a refreshment and a renewal of poetic sympathies in the arrival of a new volume by Mr. Davies, and one is not disappointed in the reading; some delightful things are there; to thank the poet in extended critical terms, to analyse what he has accomplished, to paraphrase his songs, is doubtful work. The mention of some predecessors who in manner or in mood or point of view resembled Mr. Davies occasionally is allowed us. We may iterate that there is in our contemporary a bright free melody such as the Elizabethan song-makers have given us, and an elemental joy comparable with the sudden intuitions of [Henry] Vaughan or Blake. Yet such suggestions of kinship leave us still aware rather of the difference of Mr. Davies. His sheep are neither with Blake's "Little Lamb" nor Vaughan's "harmless beast" when, having closed the poet's actual books, we let them all leisurely pass by.

Such poems as Mr. Davies, with few exceptions, has written are so brief, and involve so few images and considerations, that they may be said either to win or lose. There is no space in their swift transit for a "number of things," which in poetry of another plan may create interest in spite of some general defect. Mr. Davies sometimes appears not to notice details which clash with the clear purpose of a poem in a few lines. When he rhymes "place" with "dice" in a series of steady, correct rhymes, a Cockney pronunciation is almost sure to force itself on a reader's attention and damage the process of persuasion. Similarly with "leave" and "breathe."

Such awkward coincidences or suggestions of the ludicrous impair the short type of poem which Mr. Davies practises so well. The **"Epitaph on John Keats"** is one of his failures, because it concludes with an ambiguity of which he was obviously unaware. . . . [It] almost inevitably reduces Keats's tragedy to the figure of a boy with his nose against a confectioner's window.

So, occasionally, Mr. Davies does not bring off the "short swallow-flights of song"; he runs the risk. He continues to increase the number of his successful poems, thoughts that shine and ring with some pretty metaphor (or it may be a grim one when he is in the mood). He continues to defy the larger forms of poetical activity, and to produce the illusion: "This is enough, why should poets ever strive for anything more complex?" Perhaps the new volume contains an enlarged number of verses with an autumnal tint about them, a shadow, a trouble; indeed, one of the best pages is that called **"Old Autumn,"** and the last stanzas emphasize what is elsewhere hinted among these poems. . . . But this is not to say that Mr. Davies has resigned his position as the laureate of light and joy in these hard times; as before, his cheerful note is heard and hailed. He communicates the sense of alert and early enjoyments—"a rainbow and a cuckoo," the sunbeam and the missel-thrush, a spring day and a sailing-ship. The mind that hears him on such themes recaptures others. He leads the way. . . . His directness must not be mistaken for something entirely unpremeditated. In **"A Fleeting Wonder"** he appears to indicate his deliberate method, contrasting his "little horse" (a good Welsh pony one supposes) with another's temporary ambitious Pegasus. . . . Other poets will leave the portrait of these times, expressing our great dilemmas and strained questionings in verse for long contemplation; standing apart, Mr. Davies will hold those who range with his many songs of the fresh world and of the plainer battles of life. There will not be many commentators on him. He gives his meanings at once.

Edmund Blunden, "Mr. Davies' New Lyrics," in The Spectator *(© 1932 by The Spectator; reprinted by permission of* The Spectator*), Vol. 149, No. 5450, December 9, 1932, p. 840.*

EDITH SITWELL (essay date 1934)

Mr. Davies' poems are among the beauties of nature, and are therefore disliked by persons to whom travelling in the country means a ride upon a motor bicycle.

These lyrics are exquisite as are those of Herrick, but they are on a rather larger scale and their loveliness, even when many images are used, is never of an artificial nature. Those images, indeed, are but reflections seen in a kingfisher's lake. Mr. Davies, to quote himself, is a "starer." He stares longer, and more intently, than starers who are not poets. He stares with more comprehension than most poets. And so he gives us the world as it is, but after it has been bathed in the radiance and the dew of a strange innocence.

The beauty of these poems is due mainly to their fresh and lovely fancy, and this is enhanced, often, by the shape, which is clear and rounded as an apple, or has the soft perfection of a bullfinch's rosy feathers. The beauty, indeed, lies more in the exquisite images—those reflections in a lake, in the roundness of the dew-clear apple—than in the texture, which often has a kind of homely and pleasing country roughness, like that of certain leaves—raspberry leaves, for instance—or of cool country sheets and of home-baked bread.

Yet in such a poem as **"The Kingfisher,"** there is an extraordinary beauty of texture as well as of fancy and of shape. . . . (pp. 90-1)

The poignance of the vowel-sounds in the first lines give the lovely colour of the kingfisher's feathers. The deep and changing vowels, the alliterative liquids . . . the change from the sound of "choose" to the deeper plunging sound of "haunts," and the change from the long clear O in "lonely" to the assonances "choose" and "pools"; these sounds, echoing each other, or producing some clearer reflection of each other, seem like reflections in deep water. . . . [There is] a lovely secrecy, the sound of a gentle withdrawal into some green solitude, because of the shrinking vowels of "quiet" coming after the long dewy "qu." (pp. 91-2)

This amazing visual beauty and clearness, as of something that has been washed in heavenly dews, is natural to all Mr. Davies' poetry. (p. 92)

A clear light and colour surrounds all these poems, and often it cannot be explained. . . .

How clear are the eyes that perceive these beauties, how keen is their perception. To Mr. Davies every flower holds the secret of Heaven, and he stares at it with the knowledge of which he has written in ["**Starers**"]. (p. 93)

There are moments when, reading Mr. Davies, we believe in reincarnation. ["**Smiles**"] we feel, must have been written by a poet living in the same age as Herrick, yet there is nothing derivative in manner or feeling. The poem has been born of the poet's blood. . . . (p. 94)

How great is the contrast between this happiness and such a poem as . . . [**"The Heap of Rags"**]. Where could we find a more terrible simplicity, than in the sound of this uncomplaining voice coming from the depths, and, in its very uncomplainingness, loading our souls with guilt? (pp. 94-5)

It is not possible to find a more poignant poem of the kind, or one more deeply experienced. If it is possible to hazard a criticism, however, I believe the poem would have been even finer without the last two lines:

> Too many bitter fears
> To make a pearl from tears,

which seem to reduce the poem in scale.

The same deep compassion and understanding shines in such poems as **"Night Wanderers."** . . .

[Some of the lines] so heart-piercing and so true, shame the cold heart of the world. Mr. Davies almost invariably attains to an extraordinary compression, arriving at this largely by the means of a pure outline, and also by the simplicity which is one of the great beauties of his poetry. This simplicity, this compression, pure outline and poignancy, are particularly remarkable in [**"Body and Spirit"**]. (p. 96)

Mr. Davies with his poems reminds me of a bird-fowler. Indeed, once when I complained to him that a poem of my own was not working out as I wished, he said: "You sit quietly, and it will come. A poem is like a bird in a wood." He sits quietly then, surrounded by all the birds of the wood, singing to him—or he wanders amongst the clearly seen beauties of Nature, looking at them with the eyes of the Happy Child, in his own poem—of a Blake-like innocence and radiance. . . . (pp. 97-8)

In these days, when any clotted and incompetent nonsense is recklessly encouraged by the Press, as long as it is dressed in overalls and masquerades as a messenger of the new age, it is discouraging to find this great lyrical poet treated with a certain indifference. Whilst we have such a poet amongst us, we ought to honour him. But he has been consistently misunderstood and underrated from the first—simply because he is on traditional lines, and because his poems have a radiant innocence and a rare physical beauty. (p. 98)

> *Edith Sitwell, "William H. Davies," in her* Aspects of Modern Poetry *(reprinted by permission of the Estate of Edith Sitwell), Duckworth, 1934 (and reprinted by Books for Libraries Press, 1970; distributed by Arno Press, Inc.), pp. 90-8.*

LOUIS KRONENBERGER (essay date 1935)

W. H. Davies has published fifty books, yet aside from his prose I should guess that his reputation is founded mainly on anthologies. His own volumes, so far as I know, have never had their day with the reading public. But in spite of all this, his name for a quarter of a century has been well known, the special quality of his verse has been well apprehended, and the praise—however careless—of poetry readers has been warm and sympathetic. If he has never been hailed with ardor, he has always been mentioned with respect. He has, as they say, his niche.

To become suddenly intimate, through reading his collected work, with a man half of whose charm has resided in our knowing him casually at odd moments, is not altogether for the best. Savoring food is not the same as eating it. Nor is there anything less charitable than a collected edition just off the press; it shrieks the arrival of something presumably important, and trumpets the idea that the Day of Judgment is at hand. Author and reader, both, are left without a loophole. The author has destroyed any evidence he does not wish used against him, and marshaled all that he believes will weigh in his favor; and the reader plainly must bring in a verdict.

The W. H. Davies I had savored hitherto seemed like a simple, winsome fellow with a heart close to nature, loving little things and seeing large things in them, and singing in a fresh and happy voice that sometimes broke with artless charm. Nor is the W. H. Davies of these many pages alto-

gether different from what I had supposed him. The man is as likable as he appeared to be; as much in love with life and in tune with nature; as sweetly humane and as vibrantly indignant. Himself satisfied by the permanent things which are not sold and bought, he has yet not retreated from a rapacious, dishonest world without replying to it. If Davies has a child's sense of beauty, he has not a child's easy way of ignoring squalor. He hates what he has seen of poverty and injustice, and cries out constantly with a moral fervor that takes by surprise those of us who remember him best as writing playfully about bees and butterflies, or prettily about flowers, or whimsically about love.

Thus in this man whom we think of only as a minor poet there is a genuine concern with the major subject-matter of life. Unfortunately, however, Davies altogether lacks the poetic vision and power to cope with it. It is not only that he is naïve (and he is very naïve); it is that whenever he seeks to be a large-scale poet he becomes hopelessly crude. A sentimentalist to begin with, he turns at once into a moralist defeated by his own sincerity. Neither the note of pathos nor the much deeper note of tragedy is ever piercingly sounded; a vision of life is never cleanly projected; there is for much the most part only clumsiness or didacticism. "Oh, who can love thy slums with starving ones!" is how Davies sometimes writes, and it would perhaps be impossible to write worse.

Indeed, poverty of style which aside from other things does so much to injure Davies's singing in a major strain, does much to wreck him as a minor poet also. One hates to inflict upon him the epithet of birdlike, but birdlike he often is, and it means of course that along with something fresh and sweet goes something else which is dangerously uneven, which is likely to turn flat, and which is completely worthless when it is anything less than pure song.

And that is just the sort of poet Davies is—simple in the truest sense, and able now and then to hit the bullseye by his simplicity; but, when inspiration fails, quite without anything else to fall back upon, Davies has no carrying power of style, and style is of vast importance when one's choice of subject-matter is not less truistic than true. Thus that grace and point of utterance which have given us, from Elizabethan and Caroline poets, so many gems, or that unerring ability to fuse words with music which makes A. E. Housman—no better a philosopher at bottom—an enchantment, is quite lacking in Davies. . . .

In a man of Davies's small powers, writing of himself or of love or of nature, not profoundly but delicately, the touch is everything and Davies's touch is consistently shaky. I do not believe (thereby crossing swords with Sir John Squire, who speaks of "at least fifty lyrics pure and transparent") that there are two dozen really satisfactory poems among the near six hundred of [*The Poems of W. H. Davies* and *Love Poems*].

The good poems, in the main, are those with which we are familiar by way of the anthologies; they are fresh and lovely, and deserve to be remembered. A collected edition, on the other hand, and in particular a collected edition such as the present one, in which no selective tact whatever has been manifested, can only do Davies the worst of disservices. The good here is swallowed up in the bad; let us hope it will eventually be saved.

> *Louis Kronenberger, "An Evaluation of the Poetry of W. H. Davies," in* The New York Times Book

Review (© 1935 by The New York Times Company; reprinted by permission), July 21, 1935, p. 2.

BRIAN WATERS   (essay date 1951)

Davies is a poet of experience, and even in an age of literary candour few men have written about themselves in more direct and simple prose. There is no self pity in Davies's attitude towards himself and for this reason he wins and holds the reader's sympathy. (p. 10)

Though the story of the poet-tramp made Davies's poetry conspicuous to the public, and though his prose writings are the classics of English and American vagrancy, it is not as the tramp poet that he should be remembered. He was a born poet, but not a natural vagabond. He wandered because he was homeless and needed leisure in which to grow. He looked for something he knew not what, when he found it he was content to remain in one place, at peace with himself, and work. (p. 12)

His prose writings were for him interludes, brisk and swift departures from his life as a poet. He wrote them with remarkable speed, for while occupied on a book of prose he found it impossible to write poetry. On this account he completed his autobiography in the short space of six weeks; a great achievement for a first book by a man with the minimum of education. He told me that he had formed his clear, direct style through limiting his vocabulary by the simple expedient that when he came to a word he could not spell, he chose another and simpler one to take its place. He knew no word of any language other than his own and when one came his way as an interpolation to his native tongue, he ignored it as being unfit for English currency. He only enjoyed writing prose that was tinged with humour, and though he is not one of the English humorists the flicker of a smile often crosses his printed page or lurks upon the next. He realized, however, that humour, so effective in prose, must be used sparingly and with infinite subtlety in poetry. . . . (p. 15)

There have been many more voluminous poets in the English tongue, both narrative and dramatic. Davies was not one of these, but few have written a greater number of individual poems. With the passing of time these noble numbers tend to sort themselves out from the sequence in which they were written, regrouping themselves according to the range of the poet's achievement. He was in the great tradition of poetry and was never tempted to make experiments away from the discipline of rhyme and metre. His poems of town life show vivid power in his use of natural direct speech within the confines of the lyric. They also display a deep knowledge of human nature that comes from an understanding of the human heart. He is best known for his nature poems, which are marked by the daring imagery of his unique mind and in these he rises to his greatest height as an artist. As a love poet he is the robust and happy lover of former days. His verse carries the ecstacy of the moment. His mind was not querulous as to the way beyond life's journey, nor did he ask questions only to hear them answered by the baffled echo of his own voice. He was not a religious man, but accepted life calmly as it came. (p. 18)

Brian Waters, "W. H. Davies, Man and Poet," in The Essential W. H. Davies by W. H. Davies, edited by Brian Waters (reprinted by permission of the Executors of the W. H. Davies Estate), Jonathan Cape, 1951, pp. 9-20.

LOUIS UNTERMEYER   (essay date 1959)

A prolific and almost compulsive writer, Davies unquestionably wrote too much. His birdlike simplicities and almost mindless fluency made it difficult for critics to separate what was good, indifferent, and plainly bad. Davies sang ingenuously rather than ingeniously of happy mornings and evenings sweet with pleasant reveries. He regarded with an air of discovery things that everyone else took for granted. A butterfly sunning itself on a stone, a glowworm at dusk, a rainbow seen and a cuckoo heard at the same time—these were all Davies needed for a full life and the life of poetry. . . .

More than most poets of his time, Davies recalls his forerunners. He has sometimes been compared to the lyrical pre-Elizabethans, more often to Herrick, occasionally to Blake. But Davies, a charming rather than a passionate poet, could not frame burning images and prophetic visions. His poetry was at best a Child's Primer of Innocence, a Blake in words of one syllable. (p. 651)

Louis Untermeyer, "New Trends in England," in his Lives of the Poets: The Story of One Thousand Years of English and American Poetry (copyright © 1959 by, Louis Untermeyer; reprinted by permission of Simon & Schuster, a Division of Gulf & Western Corporation), Simon & Schuster, 1959, pp. 648-65.*

RICHARD J. STONESIFER   (essay date 1963)

Davies has been regarded as primarily a poet. He so regarded himself. He was restless when writing prose. Indeed, he claimed that he could not even think of poetry when writing prose, and he regarded his prose without affection. [The Autobiography of a Super Tramp] he regarded as a pot-boiler and a means to an end, a method by which he could get enough to live on so that he could write poetry. His novels he regretted, even offering to buy up stray copies to take them off the market. His other works of prose he produced to fit a particular need, either as money-getters or to satisfy a publisher's demand.

The careful student of Davies's work cannot overlook his prose or dismiss it lightly. Shaw, whose brilliance of style and dazzling wit made him prefer the same qualities in others, saw in the placid, quiet, and unvarnished manner of the Autobiography a style that, though opposed to his own, deserved special mention. 'This book', Shaw wrote in his preface, 'which is printed as it was written, without any academic corrections from the point of view of the Perfect Commercial Letter Writer, is worth reading by literary experts for its style alone.' It was the style, Shaw pointed out, of a genuine innocent, and he was particularly attracted by what one commentator has rather elegantly called Davies's 'feline litheness, that athletic irresponsibility and amorality, which detaches Mr. Davies from our civilization, and makes him an instinctive critic of it.' Certainly Davies's position in our literature will rest as solidly on his Autobiography as on his poems, for this book has been called one of the most notable human documents of our time, a beautiful, touching, and illuminating record of an unusual life (these are Osbert Sitwell's terms), and an amazing book (the adjective is Shaw's). Davies's casual dismissal of this masterpiece is proof of the fact that, in this case at least, he could not assess his own powers. Actually his powers are doubled in effectiveness because he was unaware of them and thus never pushed them too far. When he did become aware of his own distinctiveness, and conscious of the particular qualities that he had, his prose began to deteriorate in quality. That *Later Days* is not so good as the *Autobiography* is obvious to the most casual reader. Davies is far more charming when he is describing his tramp-companions than he is when he is talking about his literary acquaintances, whom he could not describe half so well. Not only does the subject-matter of the first prose book deal with more interesting material, but there is nothing in the *Autobiography* that gives us the unpleasant feeling of self-consciousness on the part of the author, the suspicion of pose, that marks the prose of *Later Days*.

Certainly, then, one of the main reasons for an analysis of Davies's prose is that in the *Autobiography,* and to a lesser degree in *Beggars, The True Traveller,* and *A Poet's Pilgrimage,* he achieved distinction because he was not self-conscious and wrote for the most part with a natural simplicity, while in *Later Days* he failed because what had been natural had become partly artificial, what had been casual had become forced, and what had been simple dignity in the man had given way to what is suspiciously like posturing, a conscious attempt to be naive. (pp. 155-56)

It is thus necessary to direct attention briefly to three things regarding Davies's prose: to the qualities which it has, to the failings and shortcomings of his two novels, and to the deterioration of his effectiveness in prose as his simplicity took on overtones of sophistication, self-consciousness, and egocentricity. (pp. 156-57)

The critics who have noted Davies's best prose have united in applying certain terms to it. We are told that it is direct, casual, quiet, simple, not self-conscious. Or we are told that it is characterized by ingenuousness, artlessness, and intensity. A few discerning critics have pointed out that there is great subtlety in it on occasion, that its very artlessness often indicates a very great deal of art indeed, and that the simplicity and dignity of it are due to the influence on Davies of the Elizabethans, Bunyan, and the Authorized Version of the Bible. . . . Everyone has united in saying that Davies's chief quality is natural simplicity, but not much has been done to explain that simplicity. Or, more to the point in a criticism of his prose, a host of people have compared him, for example, to Defoe, doing so in general terms only. (p. 157)

Both Defoe and Davies wrote material that can be called picaresque, both have created masterpieces in what might loosely be called the literature of roguery, and both are spokesmen for a class which they loved and understood thoroughly. Defoe took as his prose ideal a style that was always explicit, easy, free, and very plain, and this is exactly what Davies's also achieves, though he does so most gracefully only when he is not aware of his aims. Beyond this, the comparison cannot be pushed without danger. Defoe's vivid realism depends upon the tireless accumulation of petty detail, a process which reveals his skill as a pamphleteer; Davies's prose gives us an almost impressionistic effect by comparison. Defoe's sentences are extremely long . . . ; Davies's sentences are short, and there is never any complexity in structure because he was incapable of handling involved sentences and had no choice but to write as he did. (pp. 157-58)

[One] of Davies's stock devices is a kind of understatement, a deliberate omission of detail, the presentation of a scene or a comment in such fashion that we are tantalized into

reading between the lines for the full meaning. Often he does this with considerable humour. . . . [There are] a number of passages from the *Autobiography* that illustrate this, and there is another in *The True Traveller,* where Davies tells us of an experience he had in America. While washing and resting himself after a hard day's tramp through the flat Illinois countryside, he met a woman gathering sticks in the woods. She turned out to be a former Chicago prostitute, and the almost-inevitable happened. But how quaintly Davies gives us the story of this woodland meeting. . . . (p. 158)

It is not to be supposed that the incident really occurred as it is given to us here. Davies's verbal propriety is a well-known quality of his prose, though in private conversation he had a considerable taste for vulgarity coupled with a tendency towards almost unbelievable primness. But he also had what Ezra Pound has called a 'peasant's shrewdness' about him. He tells this simple incident in this way because it is more effective than it would be if told in any other. Detail is not needed. The reader's imagination can supply that readily enough; and it frequently pleased Davies to be sly. In this instance, one can almost see the wink of the eye, the chuckle, the admittance of the reader to the private joke—I'm not really as innocent, naive, and simple as I seem, Davies says to us, but make of me what you will! By the time this was published . . . Davies had begun to be thoroughly aware of the qualities which the public expected him to exhibit on command. The natural simplicity of his prose, which we see on the whole in the *Autobiography,* had begun to give ground to the subtle-simple, or to the synthetic simplicity which we see in *Later Days* most completely, or on occasion in *My Garden* or *My Birds.*

One of the most striking qualities of Davies's prose at its best is its spare quality. There is little mention of scenery or of background, a fact that immediately forces us to make reservations about Davies's status as a nature-writer. In the *Autobiography,* though one is delighted when he pauses to give us a commentary on the American landscape or details about a doss-house, one soon accepts the fact that Davies is a writer who reacts to objects only at the moment of seeing them. One reads not only the *Autobiography* but Davies's poetry with amazement that the American landscape has so little effect on him. To be sure, when he was tramping, his mind was of necessity concentrated on the grim business of getting food and shelter rather than on birds and the beauties of the woodland. But it is certainly valid to say of him, as an unnamed critic has said, that he looked at the world as if Wordsworth had never written. There is little in Davies's *Autobiography* that we can call thoughtful. He goes through a succession of adventures and he records them; he sees a variety of things and he reacts to them, simply, directly, often charmingly. But there is little evocation of background, little creation of mood. If he tells us things about the fields, if he takes us into the world of the doss-house to meet his colourful associates, he hardly ever tells us anything but the most obvious facts. (pp. 159-60)

It is impossible, then, to find purple passages in Davies as we find them in other writers on nature, Thoreau, for instance. Despite this, he often manages in his quiet way to give us the bare bones of a quite complete picture. Not frequently, but with success when he does attempt it, Davies manages a fine touch of description, sometimes in a single phrase, as, for example, when he describes the Wye as 'shining like a silver blade in a green handle' in *A Poet's Pilgrimage,* or, in more extended form, as in [a] bald description of the Mississippi, from the *Autobiography*. . . . Sometimes Davies attempts to describe something and fails, unable to manage the complexities of objective descriptions. (pp. 160-61)

Davies is at his best in describing simple things that have an element of quiet humour in them. In *Nature* he gives an account of the farmer on Elses Farm near Sevenoaks. The man, says Davies, had a sense of humour and, what was more to his credit, believed that animals had too, a belief which was also cherished by Davies. . . . (p. 161)

Trifles do not exist in Davies's world, for everything that happened to him was significant. Like a child, he reacted to everything with the same interest and wonder. Sometimes this childishness can become oppressive. . . . But usually, in the *Autobiography* and in the best parts of *Beggars, The True Traveller, A Poet's Pilgrimage,* and *Later Days,* Davies captures our interest with his observations, though occasionally his penchant for banality creates monotony. . . . Davies manages to interest us in things that we are astonished to find ourselves interested in, although there is certainly no other relationship between their prose styles. There is a freshness in the writing of these works that disarms criticism, for it is a freshness that might be mistaken for a real or assumed innocence only, whereas it is clearly a genuine simplicity allied to a keen natural intelligence, the 'peasant shrewdness' that Ezra Pound used as his label.

The thing that we read Davies for is this detached viewpoint. If he held W. H. Hudson entranced at a dinner-party by his account of the methods that tramps use to keep warm by wrapping newspapers around their bodies, he holds his reader by lifting the veil on a multitude of similar odd things. . . . Even his comments on his literary friends in *Later Days,* written up in a manner that reveals all Davies's limitations as an observer and all his quiet maliciousness—though he tells us that he does not intend anything to be malicious—even these sidelights on England's literary giants are valuable, because they come from an unusual viewpoint. It is as though a very shrewd child had put his observations about the great on paper. We read the book aware of its limitations in style, aware that this is not the simple, natural Davies of earlier days, but also aware that we are being given the opportunity of seeing familiar things from a completely unfamiliar point of view.

This simplicity, then, is by no means a simple thing, and it is certainly not an indication of ignorance. Rather, and particularly in Davies's prose, it is the result of a number of qualities interacting on each other: naivety, humour, irony, natural shrewdness—all these coupled together and working to produce a quality that is difficult to assess. When the interaction fuses perfectly we get passages that strike us with their simple forcefulness, the justness of their observation, the vividness and precision of their insight. When the fusion is not perfect, or when Davies is seduced into regarding something that is undeniably trivial as something that is startlingly and refreshingly new, we get banality and monotony.

Certainly Davies had no conception of the banality in his own work. In the first part of *Later Days,* he tells us that he hesitated to write the book because he did not want to attempt to 'make common ditchwater sing like a pure spring', which is what he actually does try to do in the greater part of the book. But Davies could not see this, for he reacted with intensity to everything, trivial and momentous alike. . . .

Since most of his life was spent in childlike breath-holding before objects of wonderment, Davies did not term things trivial and banal that we would so label. If a thing *was,* it was worthy of notice and comment. The result is that we are constantly amazed at the casualness and quietness of his approach, at the plain realism whose very economy has a force astonishing to the sophisticated reader. There is simplicity, naturalness, and an easy forcefulness, a purity and intensity about his writing that mark it as distinctive. One of the best passages in the *Autobiography* to illustrate this is Davies's description of a lynching he witnessed in a Southern town. Faced with an adventure that was not inconsequential, Davies still used the quiet, almost detached approach. . . . (pp. 162-63)

On one occasion Davies told Brian Waters that he had formed his simple style by limiting his vocabulary to those words that he could spell without recourse to a dictionary. (p. 165)

Davies pictures the real world, but he makes use of a great deal of romance in portraying his tramp-companions and their common experiences for us. We can never be sure where fact leaves off and fiction begins. Occasionally we can accuse him of sentimentality, the sentimentality that involves an oversimplification of an experience or a set of characters. . . . He has no illusions, however. In one place he tells us that while tramps are not, as a class, dirty physically, they are all dirty morally. . . . Davies's tramps are rooted in reality. They are shiftless and do not lead a poetic life. Although we are given a great deal about them that is humorous and idealized, the grim, sordid, squalid truth shines through his pages.

At best, though, it is unreal reality. These wanderers talk like students in a philosophy seminar, instead of illiterate, brutal men. . . . [However,] this really contributes to our delight in Davies. His curious point of view flashes light on his amazing companions. If we see them indistinctly because of his distortion, we see *him* all the more clearly for it. Sociologically, what he gives us is of great value even if we do have to readjust our perspective to take his colouring into account. He shows us the humorous and dignified side of these strange men, their great kindness and good fellowship as well as their failings and shortcomings. Robert Frost once remarked that there are two kinds of realist: the one who gives you a freshly scrubbed potato, and the one who gives you a potato with dirt plastered on it to prove that it is genuine. Davies is of the former school. If occasionally we question his presentation of the life of the open road, we realize it is done in this way because he himself was too much a creature of joy to remain preoccupied with stark reality. (pp. 165-67)

Richard J. Stonesifer, "The Quality of His Prose," in his W. H. Davies: A Critical Biography *(copyright © in Great Britain 1963 by Richard J. Stonesifer; reprinted by permission of Wesleyan University Press; in Canada by Jonathan Cape Ltd), Jonathan Cape, 1963, pp. 155-76.*

RALPH J. MILLS, JR. (essay date 1966)

This new, and apparently definitive, edition of the poetry of W. H. Davies [*The Complete Poems of W. H. Davies*] . . . supersedes the 1943 *Collected Poems,* which was selected by Davies himself before his death in 1940 but still unaccountably omitted a considerable number of good pieces. The latter have been restored here, making the present volume a very substantial one of seven hundred and forty-nine poems. (p. 406)

Yet Davies' poetry requires no critical prefaces or explanations. As a body of writing it stands completely outside the modernist or post-Symbolist movement in poetry; its closest kinship is to the work of the Georgians. The virtues of Davies' poems are those of the author himself—unaffected simplicity, directness, intuitiveness, coupled with a genuine and marvelous lyric gift. While he has been compared to Herrick and Blake—and, of course, the resemblances are sometimes there—he is really untutored, a wholly *natural* poet; his responses to experience seem to take the form of brief lyric poems, as if these composed his ordinary, accustomed mode of utterance. (pp. 406-07)

Much of Davies' experience derives . . . from nature or rural life; and at times, as we would obviously expect in a poet of so spontaneous a sort, the results deaden into convention, the responses become too mechanical. That is the cost, but it is certainly worth it for all the fine poems we get. And it ought to be emphasized at once that Davies is not merely a barely self-educated poet naïvely singing the joys of field and forest in total ignorance of the world's ways. His prose works chronicle his travels as a "super-tramp" in America and Canada . . . ; after his return to England he lived (until his books sold and he received a civil list pension and married) on a tiny inheritance from his grandmother in London doss-houses, printing and selling his own verses. A number of his poems deal, often fiercely, with the conditions of poverty and anguish he witnessed in that period. . . . (p. 407)

What is perhaps most amazing about Davies is that in spite of a profound personal acquaintance with human suffering, dereliction, evil, and abandonment, his own nature never hardened but remained sensitive and uncorrupted. He was a poet of real talent whose work should long remain with us, giving pleasure. (p. 408)

> Ralph J. Mills, Jr., "Two British Chronicles," in
> Poetry (© 1966 by The Modern Poetry Association;
> reprinted by permission of the Editor of Poetry),
> Vol. 107, No. 6, March, 1966, pp. 406-10.*

LAWRENCE HOCKEY (essay date 1971)

[Davies's first book, *The Soul's Destroyer*,] contains much that reflects the life and environment of Davies during his days of struggle and hardship; for he wished to reveal, through the medium of poetry, aspects of his own experience and that of others, and he attempted to expose some of the evils of the existing order of society as endured by the ignorant and suffering poor of the slums. Hence, a number of pieces in *The Soul's Destroyer* are poems of revolt against poverty and intemperance and, by implication, against a society which not only allowed those evils to exist, but tolerated them with complacency; and these poems are based not on theories but on actual experience—on what the poet knew. Much of the book is humanitarian in tone, sympathising with homeless men and describing their conditions of existence *from the inside;* and it may be considered, to some extent, as a social document in poetry; whilst there are also some nature poems, love poems and vivid flashes of descriptive poetry which give intimations of Davies's later powers in these directions. (pp. 28-9)

[In *New Poems*] the poet is revealed in a phase of transition from poems of revolt to poems of contentment—a phase in which the influence of the town gradually yields to the benign influence of the countryside. *New Poems,* as a whole, represents an advance in technique, promise and achievement on *The Soul's Destroyer,* though it contains a number of poems which are inferior to the best of those in the first book. . . .

Most of the London poems are sad, compassionate or angry poems of revolt in which Davies is revealed as a man with a mission to plead the cause of the underdog and to expose certain fundamental evils of society—poverty, privation, intemperance, meanness, cruelty and oppression; and many of these poems are depressing and unpleasant. . . .

However, once Davies had got these poems of revolt out of his system and had removed from the immediate environment of the slums, he was able to concentrate more and more on the pleasant themes of nature and country life which comprise the happier part of this book. These poems were written not from a great knowledge but from an intense love, and were founded on keen and fresh observation and clear-sightedness. Davies saw all things new, as does a child, and wondered about them, bringing an original and unorthodox mind to bear upon them, giving the unexpected instead of the obvious. Thus, he created his sweet and lovely lyrics of nature. (p. 36)

But not all the nature poems attain Davies's highest standard. Many of them are uneven. They are very good in part, but mediocre or bad elsewhere; for, though most of them contain some first-class lines and stanzas, they do not maintain such a high standard throughout. Thus, some poems contain excellent ideas by the side of bathos; for Davies had not yet attained thorough discrimination and critical judgement. In spite of this, the indications are that he was approaching his true *métier* as a writer of lyrical poetry. Yet, after the success of *The Soul's Destroyer, New Poems* was a comparative failure and sold very slowly; though many favourable opinions were expressed about the poet and his book. (p. 37)

[*The Autobiography of a Super-Tramp*] was Davies's most important prose work, and it has been reprinted many times. The *Autobiography* is a straightforward, chronological account of the first thirty-four years of the poet's life, narrated with a wealth and mastery of detail by a man of keen and lively perception, interested in his fellow-men, and with a love of adventure. The incidents are related just as they happened, almost casually, sometimes unexpectedly, yet with extraordinary skill, in a simple, conversational style, after the manner of Defoe. (pp. 38-9)

The book is packed with fascinating incidents and is alive with many full-blooded and unusual characters. (p. 39)

With genuine sympathy and understanding of human nature, Davies gives us an insight into the lives and characters of the poor people with whom he was forced into company during his tramping days and we are given glimpses of their free and independent way of obtaining a living. Full of human interest, the *Autobiography* is a clear guide to vagabondage, with all that it entails, and is a masterpiece of vagrant literature. The book became an immediate literary success, for it was very favourably reviewed and achieved a steady sale which has continued over the years and, during his lifetime, brought Davies a small but steady income. (p. 40)

In his books, *The Soul's Destroyer* and *New Poems,* Davies had written his poems of experience, many of them bitter;

but, in *Nature Poems,* a new spirit is evident, for here is a poet of experience singing many delightful songs of innocence. *New Poems* revealed Davies in a transitional phase in his art, a phase in which he was turning away from long narrative poems to short lyrical pieces, from themes of the town to those of the country, and in which his mood was changing from revolt to contentment. In *Nature Poems,* his mood is one of contentment and joy, his bitterness has almost disappeared, and he has discovered his true vocation as a writer of brief, but beautiful lyrics on simple themes—especially the themes of nature and of love.

This book is a revelation of the deep love of nature which absorbed Davies; and this is not surprising, for he was leading the life of a poet, in a country cottage, close to green nature; and he was deriving great benefit from the influence of his rural surroundings. (p. 41)

New Poems was a comparative failure due, I believe, to its preponderance of morbid and unpleasant themes; but *Nature Poems* was an outstanding success because of its happy and lovely songs and its freedom from depressing themes, while there are very few poems of revolt. In *Nature Poems,* Davies attained maturity of thought, technique and utterance; while an ever-growing confidence in his poetic powers and greater certainty of treatment are discernible. There are fewer faults and awkwardnesses, and many of the poems are incapable of improvement. This book, the precursor of many such, is important because it demonstrates that Davies was a poet of rare distinction, with an undeniable mastery of the English lyric. (p. 43)

[*The Loneliest Mountain and Other Poems* was his last book of new poetry.] This beautiful volume of twenty-nine short poems once again proves Davies's masterly power as a writer of exquisite lyrics; for there are poems in this book worthy to rank with his best work. . . .

The prevailing mood of the book, as revealed in such poems as *The Mind Speaks, Days and Years* and *The Last Years,* is a preoccupation with the passing of time and the approach of death. The serious mood is continued in the poems *Trust, The Deed* and *Armed for War.* But there is a contrasting mood in the love poems and nature poems which are truly *songs of joy;* whilst the poem which sums up the poet's general attitude at this time is *Life.* . . . (p. 86)

The poet's command of technique, depth of thought, finesse of phrase, and subtle simplicity of diction mark the whole book and make this a memorable collection of poems. (p. 87)

[In *The Poems of W. H. Davies,*] Davies is seen in the full range of his powers, an accomplished poet of sustained inspiration, writing on a wide variety of themes in a highly individual manner, a lord of language, an expert technician, and a master of the English lyric.

Davies was always a great humanitarian, the spokesman of the weak, the suffering and the oppressed and, in some respects, he may be regarded as a poet of revolt, especially in many of his early poems, when the squalor and misery of poverty were fresh in his mind. He was angry about the unequal distribution of material possessions, which allows one man to live in luxury while others are homeless and starving. He was in revolt against slums, against unnecessary poverty in a rich land, against the exploiters of the poor, against the idle rich who do not earn a living. (pp. 87-8)

It is not only in his early poems that he is in revolt against the evils of the existing order: his attitude of revolt is persistent, as it should be while the state of affairs is faulty. He just takes facts as he sees them and sets them down. There are many poems, scattered throughout his work, where this revolutionary attitude is expressed, but it is stressed most in his early work when he was nearer to the distress of poverty.

After Davies had cleared his conscience by writing most of his poems of revolt against the evils of society, the dominant mood of his poetry was one of ecstasy, which gradually yielded to a mood of serene happiness and contentment; but his poems assumed a deeper, more solemn tone as he grew older, becoming more serious in outlook and more profound in thought and significance.

It is as a poet of nature that Davies has become most famous; and it is not surprising that he should have taken nature as his main subject. He had lived close to the earth and in the open air, and had grown to love the countryside with its fields, woods and streams, its trees, hedges and flowers, its birds and beasts, bees and butterflies, it sunny and cloudy skies and capricious moods: in short, its infinite variety. Though a man of limited education, here he was at no disadvantage with an intellectual; for appreciation of nature is based not on the intellect but on love: and Davies loved nature deeply. His nature poetry is founded on his delight in nature, and he exulted in revealing the loveliness of heaven and earth and his interest in the creatures of the countryside. As does a little child, a pagan or a mystic, he glorified nature and never ceased to regard it with eyes of wonder. (pp. 88-9)

Davies's nature poems are as original as nature; for, though the poet took his themes from nature, he has such unique power of observation, such an original turn of mind and such marvellous expression that he made nature seem new and consequently enriched it. He obtained his results through *standing and staring,* until he could see. . . . (p. 90)

Thus, Davies wrote many lovely nature poems which *smell of the open air* and are imbued with the freshness of the countryside.

W. H. Davies was also one of the finest love poets of his time. From his earliest days as a poet, he revealed his subtle skill as a writer in this genre, for he possessed a natural gift for this kind of poetry and was an ardent lover. Nobody could express his feelings for his loved one better than he, and no-one could pay a prettier compliment; and Davies expressed many such sentiments and paid many tributes to the one he loved. . . . (p. 91)

The remainder of Davies's poetry may be classed as miscellaneous poems and songs on a wide variety of themes, based on incidents in his experience and random thoughts on many subjects. His general attitude towards religion is revealed in his poem, *Christ, The Man.* . . . Among his miscellaneous work are poems on the passage of time, life and death, joy and pleasure, and some rollicking drinking songs.

Original, unorthodox and individual in outlook, fresh in expression, startling and audacious, frank and unconventional, Davies's poetry reveals him as a complete master of his art, writing with sweet simplicity and, apparently, effortless ease.

In his treatment of his themes, Davies showed his great skill as a technician and his extraordinary power as a poet. He had a fine feeling for words and used language accurately, yet subtly. Much of his charm is that he used simple words, but that he used them cleverly, and endowed ordinary words with an unusual association, giving a new significance to them by using them in novel, original ways, thereby enriching their meaning. (pp. 94-5)

People often say that he is child-like in his writings, but his language is made to seem child-like when it is really very artful and cunning. Words, phrases and sentences fall so seemingly innocently, so child-like, that the poetry seems artless, due to the poet's great skill in making the artful appear artless. It is all so natural, so apt: the *real* word falls into place, and no other word will do. Davies was daring in his use of words, but was so sure and true in his judgement that he succeeded where another would fail. (p. 95)

Davies did not deal in rhetoric. It was not in resounding lines of magnificent majesty that he excelled, though his work contains such lines; but in magic of phrase, set in a simple sentence. . . . (p. 96)

There is no diffuseness: he does not waste words. At his best, Davies achieved that concentrated utterance which is the essence of lyrical poetry.

He was an expert in the art of versification—a first-class craftsman who was at home in all verse forms, but who generally employed the short line and a simple stanza form. He usually conformed to the accepted principles of versification, but he did not mind departing from the regular if it suited his purpose—if by so doing he could get the exact meaning or effect that he desired. Therefore, there is occasional laxity in the use of rhymes, as in: plays, noise; care, here; that, hot; leave, breathe; ever, together; chance and branch. In spite of this, the poems do not seem to suffer, for it would be impossible to alter them without detriment. With Davies, the idea or effect came first, and rhyme or versification was subservient to this. Doubtless, he tried to get proper rhymes, but was unable to do so without spoiling the effect that he wished to convey: therefore, the end justified the means. He did this, without scruple, or possibly because of super-scruples, throughout the whole of his career as a poet, just as and when necessary, but sparingly.

He was an adept in the use of lyric forms and metres, and learnt through study, imitation, experiment and practice. He stated that he did not deliberately choose his metre or stanza form, but was content to be chosen by it; for when an idea for a poem came into his head, it took its own shape or pattern as it developed and he allowed it to take its own course. His medium was not the line as such, so much as the poem considered as an artistic whole—an entity or complete work of art. Of course, he tried to make each line perfect; yet some of his poems contain weak lines, but considered as a whole or complete poem they are successful. In composing a poem, Davies worked around an idea or incident as a nucleus, bringing to bear upon it all the skill of language, observation, poetic fancy, imagery and thought of which he was capable.

Davies possessed the power of vivid description, which he used with telling effect in many of his nature poems, and this was based on his acute and sensitive observation. . . . (pp. 96-7)

Davies was alert all the time for material for his poems, noticing and observing what was going on round about him. . . .

This was literally true. His method was to *stand and stare* and listen until he assimilated the experience and so was able to fashion his poems. (p. 99)

Though Davies was an original and individual poet, he was no innovator; but was content to advance through the gradual assimilation of new ideas into traditional forms and modes. His poetry contains no obscurities, no incomprehensibilities, no undigested thought wrapped up in a mass of verbiage. He knew what he wanted to say, and said it in the simplest, clearest and briefest way, with economy yet sufficiency of language, so that there is no doubt about his meaning.

It is upon this fine simplicity of utterance, combined with clarity of vision and a marvellous gift of lyricism, that Davies's fame rests. (pp. 99-100)

Lawrence Hockey, in his W. H. Davies *(© Lawrence William Hockey, 1971), University of Wales Press, 1971, 108 p.*

ANN HULBERT (essay date 1981)

When W. H. Davies appeared on the English literary scene at the turn of this century, it seemed as though he had stepped out of a rustic Romantic poem or perhaps a low-life scene in a Shakespeare play. He had one wooden leg, a rough accent, and artlessly naive verses to show as well as a wayward past to recount. . . . Peddling his new poetic wares, he caught the attention of George Bernard Shaw, Arthur Symons, and others, who saw to it that favorable notices began to appear. The literary figures of the "Tramp-poet" was an entrancing one—an "idyllic idol, an inspired natural, a poetic Peter Pan," one critic wrote. The actual human character within was more mysterious. Just how mysterious is suggested by this short memoir [*Young Emma*], which none of his contemporaries except his publisher, Jonathan Cape, and G. B. Shaw ever got a chance to read. . . .

[*Young Emma*] tells the outlandish tale of how Davies took himself a wife in his 50th year. He wrote the account in 1924, two years after the odd wooing and wedding, dispatched it to his publisher, and then decided not to publish it, for fear of alarming "young Emma," his bride. (His publisher was more worried about alarming refined society.) Though Davies had been traveling in London literary circles for more than 20 years, charming the company and apparently enjoying himself, he found it "much more natural" to return to his tramping ways in his matrimonial search. "I made up my mind to trouble no more about respectable women," he declares at the beginning of the memoir, "but to find a wife in the common streets." In the same forthright, slightly archaic style in which he makes this announcement, he proceeds to tell the story of "how it was done"—how he found a thieving mistress on one corner one night, kept her for a few weeks; found a gentler woman on another stroll; and then at last on a different evening succeeded in his quest to "get one woman as a life-time companion." (p. 39)

Altogether this is a perplexing document. The facts of the bizarre marriage are stated plainly enough, but the man who recounts them remains a baffling character, despite his gestures toward self-revelation. As Shaw remarked in his letter to Jonathan Cape, the manuscript shows the signs of "a fully developed, vigorous, courageous, imaginative, and specifically talented adult" at work crafting words, a story, and a tone. Yet at the same time it betrays "the outlook of a slum boy of six or seven,'' a boy who chats cheerily about disease and poverty and thinks unabashedly about marriage in terms of a practical deal: security from loneliness for himself, safety from the streets for his partner. How much is true simplicity and how much disingenuousness on the part of this curious man, we can wonder but never know. *Young Emma* presents the kind of intriguing psychological mystery that is a rarity these days, when publishers make sure their authors tell all during their lifetime, and TV hosts then invite them to explain. And unlike so many sensational outpourings now, this one has far more in common with a strange and captivating short story than with a soap opera. (p. 40)

> *Ann Hulbert, ''Brief Reviews: 'Young Emma','' in*
> The New Republic *(reprinted by permission of* The
> New Republic; © *1981 The New Republic, Inc.),*
> *Vol. 184, No. 12, March 21, 1981, pp. 39-40.*

ADDITIONAL BIBLIOGRAPHY

Adcock, A. St. John. ''William Henry Davies.'' In his *Gods of Modern Grub Street: Impressions of Contemporary Authors,* pp. 62-71. New York: Frederick A. Stokes, 1923.
  Finds that Davies's poetry is ''not flawless, but its faults are curiously in harmony with its unstudied simplicity and often strangely heighten the beauty of thought and language.''

Church, Richard. ''W. H. Davies: The Man and His Work.'' In his *Eight for Immortality,* pp. 1-12. 1941. Reprint. Freeport, N.Y.: Books for Libraries Press, 1969.
  A personal reminiscence of Davies and his works.

Kernahan, Coulson. ''W. H. Davies, a Nature Poet.'' In his *Five More Famous Living Poets: Introductory Studies,* pp. 17-48. 1928. Reprint. Freeport, N.Y.: Book for Libraries Press, 1969.
  Discussion of the many aspects of nature included in Davies's writing.

Sitwell, Osbert. Introduction to *Collected Poems of W. H. Davies,* by W. H. Davies, pp. xxi-xxviii. London: Jonathan Cape, 1943.
  A biographical introduction to Davies.

Williams, Charles. ''W. H. Davies.'' In his *Poetry at Present,* pp. 70-81. Oxford: Clarendon Press, 1930.
  Comprehensive review of *Collected Poems.*

André (Paul Guillaume) Gide

1869-1951

French novelist, essayist, poet, diarist, and dramatist.

Though credited with introducing modern experimental techniques to the French novel, Gide is more highly esteemed for the autobiographical honesty of his work, which depicts the moral development of a modern intellectual. Although his work is diversified in both form and content, critics have noted that his characters are primarily manifestations of his own moral and philosophical conflicts. For this reason, Gide's critics often attach as much importance to biographical detail as they do to artistic method.

There were many contradictory influences in Gide's life which he drew upon to create his most important works. Gide had a strict Calvinist upbringing that strongly affected his perceptions of the world, but a journey to the Middle East when he was twenty-four exposed him to a more exotic way of life. The romantic surroundings inspired Gide to pursue previously denied sensual pleasures. On this trip he also confronted and celebrated his homosexuality. However, his early religious teachings continued to haunt him, and he became obsessed with resolving the struggle between the puritan and the libertine in his nature. Two works which explore this conflict in his personality are *L'immoraliste (The Immoralist)* and *La porte étroite (Strait Is the Gate)*.

Gide's marriage to his cousin Madeleine, whom he had loved since boyhood, was traumatic for both. Madeleine was a source of both stability and distress throughout his life; Gide's love for her was deep and unremitting, but her strict Christian values often conflicted with his unconventional lifestyle. Critics have remarked, and Gide supported the contention, that many of his mature works were inspired by conflicts that arose within his marriage.

One of Gide's primary artistic concerns was authenticity. He discussed his life in print in a way that has been called self-consciously candid and exhibitionistic. But even though he used forms conducive to telling the truth, such as first person novels, journals, and personal essays, Gide did not reveal himself completely in his works. His method was to create a character in part based on himself; his characters were abstracts of elements of his nature. And the nature of his characters varied widely from work to work. Gide was constantly reexamining his assumptions, so it is not uncommon for successive novels to portray contradictory beliefs and situations. His shifting concerns did not reflect indecisiveness, as early critics charged, but rather indicated a continual dialogue with himself.

Gide believed that style and subject matter were irrevocably linked; consequently his style changed from book to book. Early works, such as *Les cahiers d'André Walter (The Notebooks of André Walter)* and *Les nourritures terrestres (The Fruits of the Earth)*, are rich in metaphor and lyric beauty, as befits works concerned with an impressionable young man's first encounters with life. In several novels narrated in the first person, Gide altered his style to enhance the illusion that the novels were written by their protagonists. *The Immoralist* best exemplifies his work in this manner.

Les faux-monnayeurs (The Counterfeiters) is both his most interesting novel stylistically and his most elaborate creation. In *The Counterfeiters*, an experimental work that derives its structure from patterns in music, Gide abandoned linear chronology, creating instead a narrative in which several unrelated stories occur simultaneously. Though his innovations in *The Counterfeiters* were important to the development of the French novel, his work did not continue in that experimental vein. Instead, his later novels display a style of classic severity and restraint markedly different from the verbal lushness of his early works. This classic tone is particularly suited to his last work, *Thésée (Theseus)*, a study of the problems of the mature artist.

In addition to his major works of fiction, Gide also wrote literary criticism, studies of colonialism and communism, and a controversial defense of homosexuality entitled *Corydon*. He also helped found the influential periodical *La Nouvelle Revue Française*.

Though well received by fellow writers, Gide was unrecognized by the general public until the 1920s, when a postwar generation that had rejected social conventions embraced his restless search for spiritual values, and his belief that life should be lived to its emotional and intellectual fullest. His influence on the generation of Camus and Genet was enormous. The importance of his examination of private morality and its effect on society was recognized in 1947 when he received the Nobel Prize in literature.

PRINCIPAL WORKS

Les cahiers d'André Walter (novel) 1891
   [*The Notebooks of André Walter*, 1968]
Les poésies d'André Walter (prose poems) 1892
Le traité du Narcisse (essay) 1892
Le voyage d'Urien (novella) 1893
   [*Urien's Voyage*, 1964]
Paludes (novella) 1895
   [*Marshlands and Prometheus Misbound*, 1953]
Les nourritures terrestres (prose poems) 1897
   [*The Fruits of the Earth*, 1949]
Philoctète (drama) 1899
Le Prométhée mal enchaîné (novella) 1899
   [Published in England as *Prometheus Illbound*, 1919;
     published in the United States as *Prometheus
     Misbound*, 1953]
Le Roi Candaule (drama) 1901
L'immoraliste (novel) 1902
   [*The Immoralist*, 1930]
Prétextes (essays) 1903
   [*Pretexts*, 1959]
Saül (drama) 1903
La porte étroite (novel) 1909
   [*Strait Is the Gate*, 1924]
Isabelle (novella) 1911
   [*Isabelle* published in *Two Symphonies*, 1931]
Les caves du Vatican (novel) 1914
   [Published in England as *The Vatican Swindle*, 1925;
     published in the United States as *Lafcadio's
     Adventures*, 1928]
La symphonie pastorale (novella) 1919
   [*The Pastoral Symphony* published in *Two Symphonies*,
     1931]
Dostoïevsky (criticism) 1923
   [*Dostoevsky*, 1925]
Corydon (dialogues) 1924
   [*Corydon*, 1950]
Si le grain ne meurt (autobiography) 1924
   [*If It Die*, 1935]
Les faux-monnayeurs (novel) 1926
   [*The Counterfeiters*, 1927; published in England as *The
     Coiners*, 1927]
Voyage au Congo (travel essay) 1927
   [*Travels in the Congo*, 1929]
L'école des femmes (novella) 1929
   [*The School for Wives*, 1929]
Oedipe (drama) 1931
   [*Oedipus* published in *Two Legends: Oedipus and
     Theseus*, 1950]
Retour de l'U.R.S.S. (travel essays) 1936
   [*Return from the U.S.S.R.*, 1937; published in England
     as *Back from the U.S.S.R.*, 1937]
Journal 1889-1939 (journal) 1939
Thésée (novella) 1946
   [*Theseus* published in *Two Legends: Oedipus and
     Theseus*, 1950]
The Journals of André Gide, 1889-1949. 4 vols. (journals)
   1947-51

My Theatre (drama and essay) 1951
The Return of the Prodigal (essays and dramas) 1953

EDMUND GOSSE (essay date 1909)

Among recent imaginative writers, M. Gide is perhaps the most obstinately individualist. No subject interests him so deeply as the study of conscience. . . . Nothing vexes M. Gide so much as the illogical limits which modern discipline lays down for the compression of the human will. He has written in *L'Immoraliste* what I admit is an extremely painful study of the irritation and misery caused by a too-definite divergence from the comfortable type. He is impatient of the worry which is brought about by moral and religious abstractions, and this I take to be the central idea pervading some of his strictly symbolical work, such as the strange drama of **Le Roi Candaule** and the stranger extravaganza of **Philoctète**. These are books which will never be popular, which are even provoking in their defiance of popularity, which, moreover, bear the stamp of the petulance of youth, but which will always attract the few by the remoteness of their vision and the purity of their style.

The strength of M. Gide's genius consists, I believe, in the delicate firmness of his touch as an analyst. He has no interest in groups, or types; his eye is fixed on the *elected* spirit, on the ethical exception. . . . It is a most encouraging matter to the admirers of M. Gide that his progress as an artist has been definite and steady. He has grown from year to year in his sense of harmony, in his sympathy with human existence. In his early books, he gave a certain impression of hostility to ordinary life; his personal attitude was a little arrogant, tending a little to lawless eccentricity. The beautiful human pages of **La Porte Etroite** show how completely he has outgrown this wilful oddity of aim. (p. 349)

M. André Gide is more closely attuned in many respects to the English than to the French spirit. This is true, if we regard his attitude as a little belated. . . . English literature has, in this twentieth-century, set up a megaphone in the marketplace, and the prize is for him (or her) who shouts the loudest. But when we say that M. Gide is in sympathy with English ideas, it is of a slightly earlier period that we are thinking. He is allied with such tender individualists of the close of the nineteenth century as Shorthouse and Pater. Those who delight in the contrast between types of character, exhibited with great dexterity by a most accomplished hand, will follow the literary career of M. André Gide with curiosity. (pp. 349-50)

> *Edmund Gosse, "The Writings of M. André Gide,"
> in* Contemporary Review, *Vol. 96, No. 525, September, 1909, pp. 342-50.*

ADOLPHE-JACQUES DICKMAN (essay date 1933)

[In *les Faux-Monnayeurs* Gide] presents his characters with a certain brutality, in direct light, as we are struck by certain persons that we meet in life. We form a first impression which is rather strong and which is the only one that remains if we do not cultivate the acquaintance or friendship of these people. (p. 492)

Gide wished to come as near as possible to the idea of the pure novel which he has exposed in the book by Edouard, i.e., the conflict between reality as it is and reality as we think of it. That is why, since reality is never seen or understood in exactly the same way by different persons, Gide wishes to present it to us several times, under different angles, so that by our effort to "re-establish" it, our interest may increase. For this reason his novel cannot advance rapidly, it is rather a novel in depth, a continuous *mise au point,* a readjustment of the different characters. The book becomes then a very dense work, for nothing in it is indifferent; and seemingly secondary characters demand momentarily as much interest as the heroes . . . ; they come to the foreground, in the place of the heroes or besides them, and for the time being we are fully interested in them, as it happens in life, when we regret not to be able to deepen the acquaintance of someone who has occupied our thoughts for a while. It is then that we feel overwhelmed by the multiplicity of life. (p. 493)

The main interest of *les Faux-Monnayeurs* is its life. But it is not a mere exaltation of life, as we find in *les Nourritures Terrestres,* for the life of a man is more complex than the life of nature. It is true that the more complex the heroes in Gide, the more they feel attracted by simple, primitive life, represented variously by peasants, by rascals, by children, or by the Arab population of South Tunisian countries.

One of the most curious traits of Gide's writing is the freedom that he preserves in his various presentations. Although he does not ever judge his characters, he places them in certain positions, situations, or contrasts, such as life offers and such as give birth to the critical mind and develop the critical side of the intelligent man. In other words, Gide does not defend a cause, or any causes, he is not carried away by passions; this is why he is not a novelist in the sense generally given to that word. (pp. 493-94)

In *les Caves du Vatican* Gide's critical mind indulged in such a satire, a satire as many sided as the mind of Gide himself, for the atheists as well as the pious are exposed to the clear beams of his analysis. The very foundations of social morality and social hypocrisy are sapped. The central character, Lafcadio, he whose lack of traditions, illegitimacy, health, and adventurous spirit seemed to be placed as a judge or at least as a foil to the rest of society, is not spared either. He dared go to the logical end of his acts when he killed the colorless Fleurissoire. But how out of proportion is such an act with the spirit of Lafcadio. And, besides, Lafcadio cannot be wholly consistent even though he has rejected all bonds, all pretense at morality. He thinks of giving himself up to the police, because Protos, a man guiltless of this crime but guilty of a great many others, is indicted for the murder.

And so it might be argued that the whole social structure topples for lack of a moral basis. But such is not Gide's thesis, for it is upon the catholic faith and christian morality (deformed evidently and narrowed) that most characters have established their lives. The atmosphere is stuffy, close, unbreathable; the only gust of fresh air comes with Lafcadio, the heathen. (pp. 494-95)

La Symphonie Pastorale is the work in which [Gide's] satire is at once the most poignant and the most subtle. . . . One can easily see what a fine example of christian charity such a story could represent. In point of fact the worthy pastor thinks that he does offer such an example. But his solemn

ecclesiastical tone becomes slightly irritating, he is totally devoid of any sense of humor; the humor comes in the irony we feel in the pastor's total blindness at his own sentiments for the young girl, when they are evident to everyone around him. However, even at that it might be a touching story. But the critical demon of Gide has placed by his side his family, his wife especially. She says not a word about all this, unless covertly, and goes about the hard tasks of caring for the numerous family, Gertrude included, and of making both ends meet. Spiritually, the wife may seem somewhat of a dead weight at first, but gradually we become aware that she is full of common sense, and also that there must be on her face some sadness, a little bitterness, a tinge of irony. The love of the husband has gone to an ethereal creature, but meantime the wife bears all the responsibilities, which she accepts without revolt. It is a drama, and a most subtle one, brought on by a love that calls itself spiritual, charitable. But there is also a more evident drama: Jacques, the son, is in love with Gertrude; the father has forbidden this love for every sort of reason except the real one. And because of this the pastor will lose the creatures he loved best: Gertrude through death, and his son just as irrevocably, for he becomes a monk.

Thus, while the satire or critical spirit in Gide is never direct, it penetrates you, envelops you, it is contained in the atmosphere of the books, it is scattered, distributed among the different characters, not concentrated on one. This is all the more curious since in several of his characters, Gide has put a great deal of himself, slices of his life, events of his life, his tendencies, self-analysis, such as Edouard of *les Faux-Monnayeurs,* Michel of *l'Immoraliste.* But as Gide wrote in his *Journal des Faux-Monnayeurs,* it was easier for him to make a character speak than to express himself in his own name; all the easier that the character differed more from him. In writing his novels he had no respect for his own opinion; he no longer was a single individual, but became several. The thoughts, the emotion of others inhabited him, he abandoned the place of honor to them.

Thus he placed himself in the best position possible for a critic; the critic is the one that can understand all; a preconceived idea, a strong principle would hinder his understanding. He is not a moralist, for the moralist takes sides. A critic like Gide is most diverse, for, as all his characters are living, each is justifiable in his own eyes, in our own and in regard to life. Despite its complete lack of violence, criticism in Gide exists, but it is left for us to give it the quality and strength we wish. Gide will never become indignant with a few of us against his own characters, and neither will he mind the indignation of those few who will rise in virtuous wrath at the flouting of their principles. As for Gide, it is not principles he started from, but from sympathy with life and men. (pp. 496-98)

Adolphe-Jacques Dickman, "André Gide, the Critical Novelist," in The Modern Language Journal, *Vol. XVII, No. 7, April, 1933, pp. 491-98.*

JEAN HYTIER   (essay date 1938)

That Gide is a novelist is contestable. We shall have to decide the question apropos of *Les Faux-Monnayeurs.* Yet he is universally recognized as a master of the *récit. L'Immoraliste, La Porte étroite, Isabelle, La Symphonie pastorale* are four authentic masterpieces which enrich that magnificent tradition of French literature. . . .

These *récits* have often been misunderstood, primarily because they have been taken for more or less fictionalized confessions, secondly because they have been read without being "placed" in the ensemble of Gide's works, and finally because their hidden irony has not been discerned. (p. 73)

[The *récits*] constitute a part of the same series of tendentious works to which the *soties* belonged. They too are satires, although Gide has hedged a bit here (" 'Criticism' doesn't mean the same thing as 'satire' "), but of a special nature: they are serious and indirect satires. We all know that a portrait painted with great fidelity and complete submission to the model can be infinitely more cruel than caricature, especially since, being truthful, it leaves no margin for the illusion of a systematic distortion against which the model could protest. Gide's *récits* are like those implacable portraits in which the painter's very love for his subject serves only to reinforce—emotionally—the severity of his vision by a deliberate accuracy.

What further differentiates the *récits* from the *soties* is the role of irony. Whereas *Paludes* and the *Prométhée* are steeped in it, and though it circulates freely in *Les Caves du Vatican*, aiming even at Lafcadio in places . . . , there is no direct attack in the *récits*. The characters the narrator encounters may well be ridiculed by him, but only from his own point of view, not that of the author, who stubbornly remains in the wings. It is in order to attain a higher degree of objectivity that Gide has handed his pen to the four characters who tell these stories, and whose nature must indeed be ignored in order to mistake them for him; any comparison eloquently testifies to this separateness. . . . (pp. 73-4)

The surface interest of these *récits* has obscured their critical aspect; readers let themselves be carried away, and react naïvely to the story they are being told, and this is indeed part of Gide's intentions; but he also intends the reader to withdraw his identification, either by the story's end or, perhaps still more, as it is being told.

The extension of the adventures of these singular spirits in the reader's mind, and the accompaniment to them, is a critical reflection which detaches him from them and keeps him from granting a predominant, excessive importance to the total emotion he may be tempted to derive from them. . . . The irony consists in not accepting them, however human or superhuman they may be, and however touched we are by their motives or their condition, by value or virtue, by sanctity itself. We must, however much it goes against the grain, reject them. They are dangerous examples. The Gidean irony lies in this transcendence, which always costs us something, for there is a kind of horrible courage in Michel, an exalting appeal in Alissa's renunciations, a pietistic respect in Jérôme's inaction, a charm in Gérard's romanticism, an intoxicating seductiveness in the portrait of the unreal Isabelle, an evangelistic fervor and kindness in the pastor. It is a heroic irony. Hence the deep resonance of these unforgettable works, even after we have plumbed their secret. (pp. 74-5)

If this irony, sometimes muted, sometimes lightly etched upon the story's transparency, sometimes concealed in an intention that exceeds it, yields the secret of each of these *récits*, none gives us Gide's whole thought. To arrive at this, we must complete them by each other; and it is obvious, for

example, that the excesses of egoism in *L'Immoraliste* and of sacrifice in *La Porte étroite* counterbalance one another; but for a total view, we must actually take all of Gide's work into account, oppose the impotent exasperation of *Paludes* to the harsh energy of *L'Immoraliste*, the parody of sanctity in the *Prométhée* to the sublimity of *La Porte étroite*, the destructiveness of *Saül* to the enrichment of *Les Nourritures*, the altruism of *Le Roi Candaule* to the egoism of *L'Immoraliste*, etc. . . . The most cursory indication of these necessary comparisons suggests that Gide's entire work is a kind of symphony whose significance is not in this or that part, but in their harmony, their unison, and by this I mean their contrast as much as their concert. There are only two books in which Gide has tried to put all of himself—prematurely, in *André Walter*; at the peak of his maturity, in *Les Faux-Monnayeurs*. . . . [The] total of Gide's *récits* and *soties* would be the substance of a vast novel integrating them in a varied unity. *Les Caves du Vatican* might be said to afford something like a rough draft of this polyphony, with the contrasts of its double plot, the variety of its characters, their varied situations in society, but in tone and intention it is not so much a novel as a parody of a novel, the comedy of the novel—moreover, one admirably executed. And here again Gide has contrived a relation with another of his works: *Les Faux-Monnayeurs* corresponds, on the serious level, to this farcical work.

[*Les Faux-Monnayeurs*] allows us to see more clearly the nature of these *récits* without which Gide could doubtless not later have conceived and mastered such a network of intersecting intentions. Each of the *récits* is in fact remarkable for the purity of its line, the elegant singleness of its contour, the sobriety of its development and, for once to use this word in praise, its *unilaterality*.

I think that what distinguishes the tale from the novel is its minimum of intricacy, its continuous *melody*. Without proliferating incident or episode, Gide has admirably understood the technical purity this genre requires, as opposed to the novel, where only proliferation and interconnection can give the impression of total life. In the tale, one takes a sounding which of course respects divagations but must especially preserve, in its elegant abstraction, the separateness of its singular object. (pp. 76-7)

The art of the novel tends to create in the reader emotional states which approach those of poetry. In French this tendency is called, in fact, *le romanesque*. It would not be difficult to show that Gide's *récits* achieve powerful effects and that, on this point, he is a match for the most spellbinding storytellers. . . . The whole range of feelings, from the most powerful to the most subtly tinted, is explored by Gide. (pp. 77-8)

We realize how readily the novel may contain all genres: tragedy, comedy, poetry. And the tale can, precisely, isolate—whereas the novel must mingle—any one of these great fundamental emotions which are at the core of the ensemble effects by which the genres may be distinguished. From this point of view, then, these four *récits* of Gide's are tragedies: they are all determined by deaths, save one, *Isabelle* (not counting the deaths of the minor characters), which ends in a collapse of the heroine that is worse than death. As a bloodless tragedy, all things considered, it is Gide's *Bérénice*. And apparent in all of them, more than the *romanesque*, is a profound poetry consisting of our distressed sympathy for all these splendid themes of true suffering, for all these excesses of unchecked vitality, of elevation to the absolute, of the romanticizing of reality, of mortal hypocrisy. It is against this poetry—abjured yet so deeply felt—that resolute irony gains a footing, not without regrets, not without bitterness. [All four *récits* are also] narratives of *disappointment*. All touch us, distress and irritate us; but intellectually they show us characters imprisoned in a formula, captives of a rule, a law, a convention or a habit, and victims of themselves. They have all *chosen* and have found themselves prisoners of a choice—of a choice whose distinguishing mode is, respectively, harshness, narrowness, facility, or deception. The reader will recognize once again the horror of choice, a sign in Gide of rigidity and ossification in an attitude, a sign of thralldom, of impoverishment, and no doubt of imbecility, of weakness, of deficiency, whether its source is the absolutism of desire, the exaltation of virtue, the seduction of the imagination, or the complacencies of conscience. The fraudulence of his goal imprisons man in a fatality. If these tragic works are cruelly crowned by irony, it is because for Gide intelligence is an essential value; it is because the critical spirit is at the basis of all true progress and, no doubt, of all true love as well. That even the critical spirit is liable to distortions, Lafcadio has shown us. One might follow it at work in everything Gide writes, notably in his plays and above all in *Les Faux-Monnayeurs,* where I am tempted to see it, more than the devil in whom Gide has not succeeded in making us believe, as the true protagonist. (pp. 78-9)

The composition of [Gide's] *récits* shows great narrative mastery in the chronological organization of events, in the rhythm of the scenes, in the progression of effects. (p. 87)

Economy of means is another quality of this art of the *récit.* In Gide, every line counts. None is without its edge. From this point of view, *L'Immoraliste* is of a magnificent hardness and speed, whereas in *La Porte étroite* there are certain rare places that seem somewhat overworked, a little too satisfied with their own effects.

But where Gide excels is in the reverberation, the *reprise* of a detail; the reader will recall the scissors stolen by Moktir which are later found and returned to Michel by Ménalque. How one and the same sentence can affect the development of a soul according to the different values attributed to its meaning is shown in *L'Immoraliste* by a remark made by Marceline to Michel, and which he later addresses to Ménalque. The art of preparations, whose power is particularly prized in the theater, is no less necessary to the novel, but gains in discretion without losing any of its suggestiveness. Consider, for instance, how the second of these two passages is cruelly sensitized by the recollection of the first. . . . (pp. 88-9)

By making his main characters speak or write, Gide has obliged them to paint their own portraits. A method which admirably suits the tale and perfectly justifies (etymologically) the title *récit* that Gide affects. It was essential to lend each of these narrators a tone of his own. . . . His method seems indeed to have consisted of *listening* in himself to the voice of his characters. Hence that timbre, those particular inflections which make us recognize them so certainly, without Gide's having to bother with all those clumsy "he saids" which encumber the prose of novelists incapable of giving their protagonists a characteristic tone. (pp. 89-90)

We need not insist on the point. Gide's style here retains all the qualities we have discerned in his poetic prose. But since it is the expression of characters who say "I" but are not Gide, the language is barer, soberer, more direct, and carefully avoids those *recherché* turns of speech and those violations of syntax by which Gide inflects his own sentences. These are not artists talking; these are human beings. But here too Gide never forgets that art is transposition; and the perfect stylization of his characters' dialogue shows that while respecting the particularity of their personal idiom, the author purifies it in order to render it still more faithful to his meaning, and raises it, by the finish he imparts to it, to the level of art, whose truth is less that of reproduction than that of representation.

Passionate yet measured; their composition so clear and sober, their passion so contained, their *attention* so loving, their diligence so skillful; stripped of all superfluity (one only appreciates to what degree Gide's tales are without digression when one reads other storytellers), these *récits* irresistibly remind us of the great portrait painters of the French school, especially, perhaps, in their exclusion of pomp and prettiness and sentimentality, of the perfect honesty of a Clouet. (p. 92)

> *Jean Hytier, "The Récits," in his* André Gide, *translated by Richard Howard (copyright © 1962 by Jean Hytier; reprinted by permission of Doubleday & Co., Inc.), Editions Charlot, 1938, Doubleday, 1962 (and reprinted in* Gide: A Collection of Critical Essays, *edited by David Littlejohn, Prentice-Hall, Inc., 1970, pp. 73-92).*

GEORGES LEMAITRE (essay date 1938)

The powers of darkness have a favourite lurking place in man's subconscious mind. Gide has a special predilection for hunting them out, not in order to destroy them, but mainly for the sheer interest of discovering them and bringing them to the light. He experiences a strange pleasure in exposing in the most respectable and even most saintly people unsuspected and reprehensible phases of mentality. Quite often these workings of the subconscious mind are hidden, even from the person in whom they occur, behind a sophistry of well reasoned arguments. . . . Almost every man, according to Gide, has a definite ugly strain in him, perhaps limited to subconscious longings, or displaying itself in imagination only—more often finding an outlet in a secret life of shame, carefully concealed from all but his partner in guilt. Gide loves to pry into these most private affairs, not so much, as in the case of Proust, in order to study the intricate psychological mechanism involved but rather because he finds a specific moral—or immoral—interest in the cases themselves. A man whose life is devoid of these complications must, he thinks, have a very poor and empty personality. . . . Gide presents an insinuating picture of these tendencies in people. He seldom states facts plainly. He merely makes suggestions, awakening suspicions by implications and hints; he stirs the reader's curiosity and often sends the imagination wandering along forbidden paths. So he succeeds in conveying a half-veiled but all the more convincing impression of the hideous festering larvæ that are bred at the bottom of man's soul.

Yet love, according to Gide's experiences, appears to be singularly free from these unsavoury elements. He has retained a perfectly pure and almost immaterial conception of love. . . . It has its source in the innermost recesses of the human soul—in fact, is part of the very soul and therefore should live and endure as long as the soul itself. Its ethereal nature places it out of the reach of disappointment and decay. Such a pure and exalted sentiment naturally precludes any possibility of defiling relationship; and indeed the very idea of combining ideal love with physical pleasure appears to Gide to be a sort of profanation. Between the two there can be no compromise. Woman as an ideal of moral devotion fills him with respect and admiration. Woman as an object of desire inspires him with loathing and disgust. (pp. 187-89)

Gide does not deny that pleasure is permissible, even right; but it belongs to an entirely different type of experience from love. Just as sensuality would besmirch true love, love would hamper the free play of healthy sensuality. (p. 189)

The aspiration towards balance and harmony is fundamental in Gide's nature. . . . It is the final achievement of his life as well as of his art. In the intervening period all his writings have been impregnated and permeated by it.

For that reason, and also on account of the sheer clarity of his thought, of the dignified restraint of his expression, Gide's artistry has sometimes been compared to that of the great writers of the French Classical School of the seventeenth century. Gide's 'classicisme' confers on his writings a permanent and compact solidity. (pp. 201-02)

Gide's style forms the most typical characteristic of his art and is closely related to his general attitude towards life. Perhaps the most obvious feature of practically all his writings is the occurrence of sudden and unforeseen breaks in many of his phrases. Sometimes a sentence that the reader was unconsciously expecting to go on, stops short abruptly. Quite often a sentence which had begun in a certain rhythm halts and pauses, and then continues in another rhythm. Or again the grammatical sequence may be interrupted and the sentence may end with a different construction from that with which it began. All these abrupt changes seem to be connected with Gide's natural aversion to conventional, expected developments of thought—in short, to what might be called his hatred of eloquence. . . . This peculiarity shows that the author never permits himself to be carried away by the thoughts he is expressing, or tied down by a formula for rhythmic or grammatical reasons—or indeed for any other reasons—but that he is always on the alert, thinking independently and with continued freshness and vigour. This is the stylistic counterpart of Gide's refusal to submit obediently to the demands of conventional logic.

These sudden interruptions do not make for a limitation of outlook; on the contrary, they are a subtle invitation to the reader to let his own imagination pursue a direction hinted at occasionally by Gide. The same end is served by Gide's constant use of very simple and unpretentious terms, which however imply more than they actually express. This moderation in vocabulary and this conciseness in the combining of words, are but two aspects of the fundamental restraint which is one of the principles of Gide's conception of art. The aim is always to set the reader thinking for himself in order to complete, or perhaps simply to continue, the half-uttered thought. (pp. 202-03)

Gide's prose, as the most tangible part of his art, remains very close to real life. There is nothing theoretical or artificial about it, especially nothing conventional or ready-made. The sentences are not modelled on a set pattern, are not specifically well turned and displayed for our admiration in full and

splendid array. They give the impression of being formed and of taking shape under our very eyes. (p. 203)

Gide's style is both critical and poetical. It is critical inasmuch as it proceeds cautiously, never hurrying blindly forward, but always taking stock of its position, examining the ground ahead, sometimes wandering in search of a better path, stopping, or even retracing its steps. It is poetical because it keeps in close touch with reality, never allowing abstract intelligence to interpose a veil between human personality and the essence of things. Sometimes the brightest jewels are found in privileged moments of complete communion between mind and reality. Purely poetical moments are as rare in Gide's prose as they are in ordinary life; but a sort of dim poetical colour suffuses all his writings, precisely because he never loses sight of the actuality of things and never wanders into the theoretical or the conventional.

That sincerity towards himself and towards reality appears on the whole to be the fundamental feature of Gide's personality and his work. He is a sincere man, seeking his own interpretation of the world. He refuses to accept the ready-made images that are offered to him, and resolutely rejects those that are forced upon him. He wishes to discover his own truth. All his writing bears testimony to the manner in which he has achieved this; it sets an example of how the discovery may be made by any one of us. In fact it must be made, to some extent, by all those who do not want to be merely one of the herd, who refuse simply to repeat words and formulæ that have been taught them, who desire to live a life of their own. . . . His truth is not everybody's truth; his conclusions apply to himself alone. Gide is never eager that other people should adopt his own ideas, but he would have them go forth and seek the truth for themselves. (pp. 204-05)

> *Georges Lemaitre, "André Gide," in his* Four French Novelists *(copyright © 1938 by Oxford University Press, Inc.), Oxford University Press, New York, 1938 (and reprinted by Kennikat Press Corp., Inc., Kennikat, 1969), pp. 115-208.*

J. D. SCOTT (essay date 1945)

In his **Journals,** and in his critical writing, Gide has a good deal to say about [the] ubiquitous pressure of convention. He repeats over and over again, in different words, Schopenhauer's dictum—'we find, in fact, that most men's guiding star is the example of others; that their whole course of life, in great things and in small, comes in the end to be mere imitation . . .'. . . . [It] is one of his arguments in **Corydon** that we are heterosexual largely because it is the convention of society that we should be so. Gide sees us, therefore, as inverted Pinocchios, as human beings who are trying to become marionettes, trying to fasten ourselves by as many strings as possible to Society. The marionettes are all the same, similarity is in fact their *raison d'être.* They acquire the same virtues in order to be fit for the same duties. . . . The real personality is therefore—at least in the 'chosen'—always in revolt against the counterfeit personality. It is not responsive to the strings which move the marionette; it has its own quite different gestures. The submerged personality has other aims than the public personality, and those aims are exclusive. Between the two personalities there is an invincible antagonism. It is not difficult to hear . . . a muted and perhaps subtly distorted echo of the big guns of

Nietzsche. 'To create itself freedom, and to give a holy Nay even unto duty.'

It is, of course, to Nietzsche that Gide turns most frequently in acknowledgement, and the psychology of his character owes a great deal to Nietzsche. Lafcadio, for instance, is the Nietzschean hero—'courageous, unconcerned, ironical, coercive'. And after Nietzsche, Blake. . . . What Gide found in Nietzsche and Blake was a conception of the suppressed self, of the double nature of man, which enabled him to grasp the nature of his own experience and to impose its form upon life. (pp. 268-69)

[These ideas] provide the material for Gide's novels, and each of the novels is a variation on this theme of the true self and the false, of Appearance and Reality. . . . (p. 269)

> *J. D. Scott, "Novelist-Philosophers: IV—André Gide," in* Horizon (© *1945 American Heritage Publishing Company, Inc.), Vol. XI, No. 64, April, 1945, pp. 267-79.*

GAËTAN PICON (essay date 1946)

Thésée serves up to us once again all the "Gidean" problems—and it is fair to regard this book as, if not the masterpiece, at least perhaps the most complete expression of its author. When Theseus, impatient to assume the throne, forgets to put out the white sails on his ship, we hear again the old "Families, I hate you . . .". *Passer outre;* to go beyond—this is the imperative that governs the hero in all his adventures, his labors, his perils and amours; it is also the law of *L'Immoraliste,* and that of *La Porte étroite.* One can recognize here all of Gide's temptations. Theseus saved by Ariadne, then betraying Ariadne—what is this but the old confrontation between freedom and fidelity, adventure and order? Icarus defeated and Theseus triumphant—the struggle between prudence and excess. The seductions of the Labyrinth—constructed, Daedalus informs us, "in such a way not that one cannot . . . but that one does not want to escape"—are those of the passing moment; and the death of the Minotaur is the victory over those seductions. And finally, Theseus against Pirithoüs, Theseus against Oedipus— this is the affirmation, against pessimism and uncertainty, of a humanism that believes in man's perfectibility—and that terrestrial existence offers us all the meaning we need. (pp. 39-40)

It has always seemed to me that Gide's work was an instance of a *centered* work, a life's work built entirely around a perfectly firm and constant attitude; and *Thésée* only serves to confirm this impression. That Gide's thought is not something simple and unsubtle does not imply that it is necessarily indecisive. That he is able to entertain a contrary opinion, understand it, respect it, perhaps even envy it does not mean that he identifies it with his own. No doubt he does proceed by a form of dialogue, refusing to stifle brutally the voice of his adversary; but it is no less true that his own voice is always to be found on the same side of the dialogue. What we take for indecision, is it not rather a simple respect and consideration for the ideas of the opposition (so easy is it to confuse assurance with ignorance and incomprehension)? What seems a contradiction, is it not rather a tendency to reunite under a single attitude personal qualities more commonly dispersed? I think it inexact to present a Gide torn between the hedonism of *L'Immoraliste* and the first *Nourritures,* and the austerity of *La Porte étroite,* between the

seductions of the Labyrinth and the determination to conquer the Minotaur. Did not he himself describe *Nourritures terrestres* as a "Guide to Self-Deprivation"? Did he not tell his reader to throw the book away? The idea of momentary pleasure has never been for Gide an absolute, an acceptable resting-place. "Go beyond" is still the highest law; if it crosses the pleasure principle, it is the former that takes precedence. "Do not think of finding rest except in death, your destiny achieved," is Daedalus' advice to Theseus. Sensation is nothing but a moment in the limitless development of oneself, and to stop at that point would be to betray the greater exigence that aroused it. By conceiving of them as parallel paths, Individualism becomes for Gide a way to Humanism, far more than an absolute in opposition to it. It will be answered that Gide has no sense of incompatibles, that it is useless to try to reconcile the irreconcilable. But that is not the question. What is true is that Gide does not think from the point of view of the irreconcilable, and that this tendency of his mind allows him to choose one thing without brutally rejecting another. (pp. 40-1)

In great part, the value of Gide's work is coexistent with its *lack* of contemporary relevance. There is in this nothing surprising: it would be absurd to believe that we can admire only the things that move in our own direction. We are never so wholly satisfied with ourselves that we are not quickly tired of our own concerns. What we are is as much the result of pressures as of choice. The "non-contemporary" will benefit from that seductive attraction we feel toward things we have left behind: the potent nostalgia of time past. What moves us, what captivates us in Gide is, at least to some degree, the feeling that we are in the presence of a work the like of which we are not to see again—the belated and succulent fruit of a culture which is already beginning to take on the colors of a Golden Age. We love to puzzle out forgotten secrets in it, the traces of a lost happiness. Sometimes it looks to us like the last production of a freedom, a leisure, and a mental discipline that we cannot hope to recapture, so many and so fragile were the conditions that fostered them. It looks to us, too, like the final example of a truly classical work—I mean a work that is before all else *crafted,* constructed at the same time that it is written, the issue of a writer patiently working in his own unique style, and thereby identifying a particular moment in the history of the language. The work of Gide is the expression of neither a system of thought nor a fixed personality: it is first and foremost the search for, and the elaboration of, a style. . . . His work is at least as much the creation of a style as the expression of an established ego—and the style is the history of a personality that is in a parallel process of transformation. There is a young, a mature, and an old style in Gide, because his own youth, maturity, and old age are present in his work. The greater part of his contemporaries' works have an odd sense of fixity, resolution, definiteness. His own is perhaps that last instance we have of a collected work that can profitably be studied in chronological order, with distinctions drawn between successive stylistic and philosophical phases. And one may well wonder whether this is not one of the signs that a cultural revolution has definitely taken place. Because what this intimate relation between life and work in effect implies, if one studies it closely, is the attribution of a kind of incommensurable value to the work of art—since every stammering, every slightest variation in the life is willingly confided to the work, since the transposition into art suffices to validate all things. One may well believe that there will in future be few examples of a life that puts so high a value on the work of art that it is perfectly willing to be itself indistinguishable from it. (pp. 43-5)

When we grow tired of probing our metaphysical condition and examining ourselves from the outside as some kind of mundane object, the work of Gide will be able to recall for us the still-unblemished richness of the moralist tradition. Against the external and unitary image of man towards which we are tending it will set the value of the internal and the distinctive. Not that Gide's writings (however much they may be nourished with the subtle lyricism of a private interior life) are representative of the literature of introspection—not at all. . . . A classical writer, devoted to the study of man, he never made use of psychoanalysis. For aesthetic reasons, first of all: believing as he did in an art of suggestion and secrecy, Gide has always been shocked by the excessive clarity of analysis, by its exhibitionism, by the fact that it reduces to nothing the contribution of the reader. It says everything; it says too much. Secondly, it always seemed to him more easy to describe sensations and ideas, to note them in passing, than to gather them up and categorize them; art begins on the other side of analysis. But there are deeper reasons too. Gide is perfectly aware of the illusory character of introspection; in fact he was probably the first man to understand it. The ambiguous, vague, at bottom inconsistent, ultimately non-existent nature of the interior self—when considered as a substantial reality one is trying to describe, independent of the mind that is observing it, as a chemical reaction is independent of the chemist—this was hardly to be lost on the man who said that he could see no difference between what we feel and what we imagine we feel, the man who wrote, even more explicitly, ''I am never anything more than what I think I am.'' Which can only mean one thing: that there is no such thing as a true interior being, already formed, waiting for us to come and uncover it; that we are *not* something made, but something-in-making—the image that we believe in and want to be. One should speak not of self-consciousness, but of a consciousness of one's self-image, of a dream, a desire, a will, an interpretation of oneself. (pp. 45-6)

> *Gaëtan Picon, ''Actualité d'André Gide'' (1946), in his* L'usage de la lecture *(copyright © 1960 by Mercure de France; reprinted by permission of the author and the publisher), Mercure de France, 1960 (translated by David Littlejohn and reprinted as ''The Presence of André Gide,'' in* Gide: A Collection of Critical Essays, *edited by David Littlejohn, Prentice-Hall, Inc., 1970, pp. 36-48).*

HENRI PEYRE (essay date 1947)

Gide has nowhere expressed himself more informally and more fully than in his diary, kept more or less continuously for fifty years. One will find no ''personal'' revelations here, as in his famous and bold autobiography, **''If It Die.''** Indeed, the author's sentimental life is the one voluntary and notable omission from these **Journals.** But every literary problem, as well as many a moral or religious issue, is touched upon in these pages, sometimes in the desultory way and with the nonchalant verve of Montaigne, sometimes with the penetration of the fine aphorisms scattered in Goethe's memoirs and in his letters and *Gespräche*. Montaigne and Goethe are the men to whom Gide has been most often compared: both have been his life-long masters.

No principle, perhaps, has haunted Gide so constantly as that of sincerity in life and in literature. Nowhere, in his intimate notes thus jotted down from day to day, does the author pose, not even with the devilish coquettishness which tempts a writer of confessions to proclaim himself worse than he is. Nowhere does he even compose his own portrait for posterity. He eschews brutal revelations and the crude violence of which modern literature boasts with much naïveté. He does not seek originality at all costs: on the contrary, fully aware that the truest originality is that which is hardly conscious of being such, he multiplies his tributes to the molders of his thought, Nietzsche, Dostoevski, Blake. He renders his feelings without strain and never allows words to magnify, and thus betray, the thought or the emotion within them. His delicate prose, among the purest in modern French, is rich in undertones and suggestion.

Gide's sincerity goes farther. He rejects the shackles of logic and explores, more effectively than any other modern writer except Proust and Joyce, the delusions of wishful thinking. He delves into the subconscious with unfailing tact and shamelessly accepts his own contradictions as part of his truth. Sincerity, for him, does not lie in merely saying everything about oneself; it is reached through unceasing efforts to lay bare the most authentic of the several selves. One strives towards it, not by attempting to save one's personality from outside influences, but by submitting humbly to them, then outgrowing them and discovering one's deepest truth after much trial, error, and lopping off of borrowed foliage. Such sincerity entails the cultivation of one's plasticity, the refusal to be summed up into any kind of unity, into one book, one philosophy, one attitude, be it the one under which critics and readers insist upon recognizing an author. Two mottoes might thus be said to have served as guiding lights on Gide's winding path and in his struggles, related in these **Journals,** to be sincerely and authentically himself: one is the ancient Greek saying which Nietzsche revealed to him, ''Become the one who you are''; the other is the revered saying from St. Matthew, transferred by Gide from the religious to the moral and aesthetic plane, ''He that findeth his life shall lose it, and he that loseth his life . . . shall find it.'' (pp. 342-43)

> *Henri Peyre, ''Nobel Prize Recipient, 1947,'' in* The Yale Review *(© 1947 by Yale University), Vol. XXXVII, No. 2, December, 1947, pp. 341-43.*

LAWRENCE THOMAS (essay date 1950)

Charles Du Bos concludes, ''after innumerable hesitations, fifteen-years' study of Gide's work and of Gide himself'' that Gide is ''first and foremost an artist, and perhaps only an artist''. Gide himself insists repeatedly on the primarily artistic nature of his works. . . .

It is however obvious . . . that Gide's art, in spite of his insistence upon its purity, its gratuitiousness, is . . . emphatically tendentious in character; that there is woven into its texture a body of ideas which though complex and seemingly contradictory, have the consistency and emphasis of a doctrine. Strangely mingled with the Dionysiac lineaments of this essential artist, are clearly visible the sterner traits of the teacher and preacher. . . . (p. 221)

This doctrine, reduced to its bare elements, is composed of these cardinal notions: the paramount importance of the individual: individualism as the sole path to truth, to God; the individual conceived as an essence, an idea, to the expression of which he must subordinate personal well-being . . . at all costs; sincerity as the supreme virtue; individualism understood as self-abnegation as well as self-affirmation; "dépassement"—going ever beyond—with the corollary of effort as an end in itself; progress therefore more important than happiness, the future than the past, possibility than actuality; the moment of intense experience as the criterion of reality; spontaneity as the criterion of conduct; the rejection of the tragic view of life—joy as the supreme aim in living; Christianity understood as a doctrine of love and not of moral law; "dénûment" as the key to perfection in joy. The doctrine is clearly creative and cognate with the "creative" or "aesthetic" philosophies—those of, for instance, Nietzsche, Santayana, Bergson, Whitehead—produced by an age intensely conscious of the threat to individuality, to quality, to beauty, constituted by its own plethora of material productiveness, an age in which organism is lost in organisation. The emphasis in these philosophies does not therefore fall upon the idea of virtue, of the "good life", of the moral law, but on adventure, creativeness, impulse, and—in the case of Santayana—aesthetic contemplation. They are therefore in a literal sense non-ethical, if we take ethic in its root meaning, and their ambiguity lies in their assumption of creativity as the irreducible basis of all thought. In their idealism—deriving explicitly from Plato in the case of Whitehead and Santayana—are implicit the primacy of feeling, of instinct, sensation, the adequacy of sincerity as a guide to conduct, just as we find linked with the materialism of the preceding age of the notions of virtue, restraint, decorum, governing the prevalent ethic in a climate of sentiment dissolving readily into sentimentality.

Gide's doctrine is therefore, in part, a manifestation of the spirit of the age: its bivalence is no more contradictory than that of the fundamental assumption of the characteristic thought of the age—creativity. But Gide is no philosopher speculating abstractly—he is an artist embodying this thought in human actors of it, a teacher advocating a way of life, demonstrating, if not in his own life at least in that of his creations, the consequences of putting into practice the ethic implicit in the speculative conclusions of his contemporaries. . . . (pp. 222-23)

The broad fact that underlies Gide's primary concern with the individual, with the particular, is of course the fundamental individuality of the artist, of his temperament and outlook—Gide's whole work may be viewed as an attempt to solve the problem of the artist, to reintegrate him in society, to seek for him moral justification as a person. Now the vision of the artist is the vision of the particular by virtue of his preoccupation with form, with what defines, separates, isolates; moreover, the world in which the artist lives—the world of the imagination—is a world apart, discontinuous with his real environment; the life of the artist is discontinuous, unstable, because of the irregularity and unpredictability of his inspiration, because of the violent alternation between the rapture of inspiration and the despair of ennui. . . . There is an inherent discontinuity in the work itself of the artist, because each creative act is an act *sui generis,* unique, inimitable, which ignores other acts. . . . The acme of discontinuity is contradiction, and Gide not only exemplifies this discontinuity but is intensely aware of it, fosters it, exploits it, sharpens its edge, so to speak, so as to convert it into an incomparable instrument of moral surgery, of critical dissection. (pp. 224-25)

[Gide] is an artist first and foremost: the work of art does not, primarily, preach—it rather "invites the reader to reflect"; and Gide's art partakes fully of this interrogatory character of art in general, its problematical nature—"la mise en valeur d'une incertitude". Yet each of his works, while being more or less a question, is nevertheless a tendentious question and contains, delicately insinuated, an answer: the Gidian art is in the highest degree a rhetorical question of the order of "Que fera l'homme, si derrière chacun de ses désirs se cache Dieu?" . . . His whole art is a rhetorical tissue, brilliant, sensitive, ambiguous, less concerned with things as they are—and therefore unsuccessful as a transcript of reality, as a "slice of life"—than with things as he feels they ought to be in the light of a doctrine that emerges, not from consciousness of the nature of the whole activity of man, but from contemplation of one segment of it—that of artistic creation, the very segment to which logic, consistency, predictability are most foreign. His essential sophisticality lies not so much in the patent disingenuousness of his replies to the numerous attacks on the spirit of his works, the pathetic contradictions in which his ingenious eristics have involved him, but in his complete immersion in his function as an artist, his Narcissistic preoccupation with the *idea* of art—with the implications of the aesthetic consciousness whose data, perceived and analysed by his acute critical intelligence, he regards as valid for the whole field of experience. His individualism thus embodies in a doctrinaire, rationalised form, the sophisticated ethic which the artist is so prone to embrace—the belief that the complete freedom which he enjoys in his own solipsistic imaginative world may be enjoyed in the everyday world of fact, the world of whose logical laws the artist is ignorant precisely in proportion as his own imagination is ideal rather than factual. (pp. 251-52)

Gide's individualism is an "ethic" which is not an ethic, for ethic means a settled way of life, the preservation of identity and continuity in the welter of creative unrest, a meditation on the given and not the pursuit of the not-given. The work of art and the human being, for Gide's radically creative outlook are important less in themselves than as instruments of progress: he is the incarnation of the "principle of unrest" that underlies both cosmic and artistic creation, an artist born perhaps less to create than to "manifest" the essence of creativity. . . . Gide's uniqueness, his singularity as a writer lies in the skill with which he has blended doctrine and art into an amalgam in the consistency of whose composition the ingredients are no longer distinguishable, a feat only possible because the doctrine is the doctrine of art itself. Others—Yeats, Eliot—have fashioned art out of the artist's plight, made poetry, as it were, out of what it means to be a poet, speculated in verse on the craft of verse—they are representative figures of an age absorbed in process, experiment, and the creative idea, but none with [Gide's] . . . tenacity, persistence and resource in the pursuit and exploration of an idea in detachment from the "total of events, the truth, the reality." The fragmentariness of the ethic is matched by that of the characters—their exceptional psychology is that of the aesthetc, the artist. . . . [Gide's] "characters" are not seen in the round flesh, they are not concrete wholes but the intensely animated abstractions of a strange geometry of pure feeling in whose veins pulsates the ichor of a perverse idealism—the oblique Platonism that derives from his intimate and passionate understanding of the Idea of the artist. Gide's magnitude is to be found not on the plane of creative fecundity, for his art is in a sense poor in spite of its copiousness, or on that of its fragmentary if forceful ethic, but in the dimension of fidelity to this Idea, with the exclusions, the renunciations, the loneliness, which this fidelity involves. (pp. 256-57)

Gide's first-rate importance lies in his having, above all contemporary writers, conveyed the stimulation, the dynamic provocativeness of this philosophy with the force and concreteness of which art alone is capable, in having offered himself as a vehicle for the active currency of ideas which might otherwise have remained, remote and ineffectual, enthroned in an abstract empyrean. (p. 259)

Gide's is a high voltage art; its tenuous filaments bear a potent, a perilous charge, and the intensity of its creative heat, its illumination, is in ratio to the polarity of his mind. . . . Like all first-rate, serious art, it refines and deepens the zest for living, through the enlargement of consciousness simultaneously with the stimulation of feeling, through the extraction of moral overtones from the fundamental life of sensation, those overtones which, mingling gravity and pathos, are part of the seductive music of Gide's exquisite and unique accent, with its core of sensuous joy. (p. 260)

> Lawrence Thomas, in his André Gide: The Ethic of the Artist, *Martin Secker & Warburg Ltd., 1950, 260 p.*

GERMAINE BRÉE (essay date 1951)

Of the problems Gide's world raises, none recurs more persistently than the problem of time in relation to the shaping of a human destiny. All Gide's fictional works, récits, soties, novel, are carefully timed; they contain a definite chronology. . . . Though Gide may, on the surface, disrupt the time-scheme of his tales, the succession in time of the events themselves, or their relation in time is always clearly indicated. Past and present do not mingle in the Gidian world. In fact, the domain explored by Gide is conditioned by his constant meditations on what determines the ordering of a life in time, and on what makes that ordering seem, like the passage of time itself, inevitable. He does not, like the ordinary novelist, merely accept as a fact that in a story the time sequence is like the river bed which sustains the flow of a life.

In every tale, time is that which reveals the fundamental value of the human experience described. In all Gidian situations, intelligence, moral intention—good or bad—always fall short in their appraisal of the present and their prevision of the future; time alone reveals the nature of their inadequacy. It reveals that inadequacy by the form the individual's relations with himself and others eventually take as the tale develops. Since that form is a result of some inadequacy in his grasp of the situation, the individual can in no way foresee its development nor understand it. What Gide sets up for his characters is a plausible development in time, the significance of which escapes them, but which they see clearly was not fatal, uniquely determined. . . . However simple a Gidian situation may be it always puts to the reader one and the same question: how can a human being act in human situations in which no logical, preconceived, long-term rules can be laid down, situations in which, as on a crowded billiard table, each move can set a dozen other balls rolling unexpectedly? Is a calculated, systematic human course of action any better in time than a set of shots made at random? Gide sets up the adventures of his characters consciously so that they, in some way, present tentative solutions to that prob-

lem. The discrepancy between the individual's evaluation of his adventure and what really happens to him is rigorously determined by Gide's point of view on the solution offered. That point of view quite arbitrarily—and always rather ferociously—is what, step by step, carries the character, in time, to his real destination. (pp. 52-3)

In the récits the question raised is that of movement in time, of orientation in time. It is one of destination. The characters move toward a destination which, retrospectively, when they see the path they have walked as a whole and as it were "à contretemps," seems to them a predestination. Each moment of their lives appears, at the end, as consequent to the whole, not, however, as the inevitable consequence of the one before. Gide, in the récits deliberately dissociates the convenient assimilation of time sequence and consequence in the development of a human destiny. . . . Yet, though the ordering of events in time could have been different, their succession is irreversible, and its outcome all the more baffling because no inescapable preordained pattern of destiny slowly reveals itself as fatal. (p. 54)

In every Gidian tale the relation of the time sequence to the events narrated is the statement of a problem—a fundamental problem—the problem of the part played by chance, will, necessity, in the complex chain of consequences any action initiates. The relation, within the tale, of time sequences to consequences raises the question of human freedom in decision and action, and of human logic in evaluating decision and action. It therefore also raises the problem of the individual's responsibility—in virtue or guilt—towards himself and others. (pp. 54-5)

Gide is always concerned with the interplay of motivation and accident in the development of a human life. In the soties, however, he stresses that part of life which escapes all prevision, the "devil's share" as he himself calls it. He engages his characters in a complex web of related situations which overlap and react one on the other, precipitating in time chains of reaction of which no one is master. The situation of the characters is presented as seen from outside relatively to more complex situations which they do not know. (p. 56)

In the last analysis, all Gide's characters, in the récits as in the soties, are rather like players who, in a football game, persist in playing basket ball, with the conviction that that is the game being played. The "récit" is the tale of the basketball player as he sees the game; the "sotie" shows the basketball player in the middle of the football game. In both cases he is pathetic and absurd: explicitly pathetic and implicitly absurd in the récit; explicitly absurd and implicitly pathetic in the sotie. He does not know the rules of the game he is playing any more than a Kafka character; but unlike a Kafka character, he thinks he knows. With Lafcadio, Gide introduces into the human game the erratic player, who, like Zeus, acts without motivation, at random. . . . Time is the umpire which exacts from the Gidian player, consequential or inconsequential, penalties for which he is, like Lafcadio, unprepared. Time makes clear to the individual that his life is engaged, his and that of others. All Gide's tales imply that there is a certain sense to the game of life. To see none, or to mistake it is to err gravely. The game is arduous and complex but the rules cannot, in time, be bypassed. However cleverly a Gidian character counterfeits for his own benefit or for that of others, he never tricks life. Time inevitably reveals the counterfeit. One of the essential tasks of each individual therefore is to discern the real nature of the game, to compose his own part in it in harmony with the forces at play within and around him. But this he can only do in time, by trial and error, since even the most lucid cannot dominate the entire game, since the "devil's share" in it is so large.

The *inner* life therefore of each individual within the game is like a journey over some uncharted land where little by little he charts his path. The journey is an essential Gidian symbol, and the adventures of the Gidian characters in time—like those of Bunyan's Pilgrim or of Ulysses—have an allegorical or symbolic value. For the Gidian explorer, however, there is no eventual heaven or Ithaca. If one follows each character as he plots his course, one clearly distinguishes the Gidian point of view on life which, implicitly only, shapes their destiny, by qualifying what they become as they journey in time. (pp. 57-8)

Man's journey in time, in its most healthy aspect, appears to [Gide] as a search for an equilibrium, a form of harmony which, if sincere, can over a period of time chart, in an erratic world, a coherent human path. Each man therefore is responsible for what, in time, he becomes. Life asks of him that he have the courage to realize his form in time progressively, making of no error a fatality, of no idea a destiny. Gide's ethical preoccupation here turns into the aesthetic problem of form. It is not by chance that in all Gidian tales the central character is an author who struggles to give an account of the events he has lived successively, who tries to "relate" them, to order them coherently, to give them a shape in time. The Gidian author is not merely a projection of Gide himself, he is every man as Gide sees him. For each and all the problem in that ordering is essentially the problem of the novelist, the ordering of a life in a coherent sequence in time. It is no doubt Gide's modern view of the problem of time sequence and consequence which determined for him simultaneously the situations he chose to delimit and elaborate, and the nature of his search for an adequate form for the novel. (p. 59)

> Germaine Brée, "Time Sequences and Consequences in the Gidian World," *in* Yale French Studies (copyright © Yale French Studies 1951), No. 7, 1951, pp. 51-9.

THOMAS CORDLE (essay date 1951)

Gide, from the very beginning of his career had his eye fixed on the novel. *Les Cahiers d'André Walter* were in some degree an attempt at fiction, and their youthful author rather hopefully called them the notes for a novel, even though they represented at most only the states of consciousness that an author might experience in the composition of such a work. (pp. 91-2)

Though he claims only one novel, *Les Faux Monnayeurs*, his reasons for excluding certain other books from that category derive rather from his notion of the novel he wanted to write than from the general characteristics of the genre. He has, in fact, written six novels embodying two distinct novel forms: in one group are the "récits" or novelettes, *L'Immoraliste, La Porte Etroite, Isabelle* and *La Symphonie Pastorale*; *Les Caves du Vatican* and *Les Faux Monnayeurs* constitute the other.

L'Immoraliste, insofar as it was an attempt to shed egoism and reach a true, uncolored statement of a drama in his life, is rather a failure. His hero-narrator, Michel, is too much

like himself to provide the release, the detachment which he sought in a fictional character. Michel only becomes hampered by the pretence of self-consciousness; he inherits his creator's egoism, and the story he tells loses its sincerity, becomes dubious even, by the stuffy manner in which he relates it. It purports to be an oral narrative, recounted to a group of friends (and in view of its very intimate character that alone predisposes one to skepticism) but it has the pompous ring of a carefully prepared discourse.... As he proceeds, Michel's manner becomes increasingly self-conscious. He is enthralled by his own eloquence, and the narrative is often no more than a pretext for rhetorical exercise.... (pp. 92-3)

And Marceline, who is perhaps a more important figure in the drama than Michel ... is swallowed up by Michel's egoism. She appears only negatively in the story, a person whose character is never shown but simply attributed to her.

La Porte Etroite is in all things except the narrative form the reverse of *L'Immoraliste*. Its theme, its tone, its characters, all seem to counter the example of the earlier novel. The narrator, Jérôme, writes simply and directly; his style is polished but never lyrical. His eye looks outward, toward events and other people, seeking in them the truth rather than in himself; and when the occasion presents itself, he allows Alissa to speak for herself, especially in her letters and her diary.

But there is one serious deficiency in the book which hangs like a pall over its pages: the character of Jérôme is not at all what the circumstances oblige him to be.... The question which unfailingly comes up is: why does Jérôme choose to tell a story in which his rôle is one of passive incomprehension. There is a fundamental flaw in his character; which is to say, in his maker's conception of him. Michel was too conscious of the rôle he played in *L'Immoraliste*, so much so that he overplayed it, became a pompous story-teller instead of a real being engaged in a real drama. In the face of this error in the characterization of Michel—which he undoubtedly could see—Gide was naturally inclined toward restraint in picturing Jérôme. He visualized him objectively, without imposing his consciousness upon him, and in that effort succeeded in removing the positive stamp of egoism from the novel; but, going too far in the opposite direction, he failed at the same time to provide Jérôme with the consciousness to which the outward appearances of his character seemed to entitle him. Jérôme is a nonentity because he is not conscious of himself and of his place in the events he relates. The error of *La Porte Etroite* is not so grave as that of *L'Immoraliste:* there is an atmosphere of truth, albeit heavily veiled, in this novel which was lacking in the first; but the rôle which was palpably created for a hero remains unfilled. (pp. 93-4)

[*Isabelle* and *La Symphonie Pastorale*] follow the narrative model of *L'Immoraliste* and *La Porte Etroite*, but unlike the first two novels they contain nothing tangibly autobiographical and are, of all his novels, those in which the author's personality is the least in evidence.

Ramon Fernandez calls *Isabelle* a parody on the decorative romance which was popular in France around the turn of the century. The bizarre group of characters, the atmosphere of musty age, Isabelle's colorful history, and the tense wait for her appearance are all calculated romantic effects which lead to a conclusion whose flat realism is crushing....

La Symphonie Pastorale is, according to its subject, a throwback to the period of *La Porte Etroite*, but at the same time it illustrates amply Gide's reorientation toward a more imaginative type of fiction. His subject—the inclination of the Protestant, with no authority to guide him, to interpret the Scriptures according to the demands of temperament and circumstances; here specifically the error of disguising a guilty love in the name of charity—is in a sense the counterpart of the subject of *La Porte Etroite*. Alissa read the Scriptures too seriously and aspired to saintliness; the pastor reads them too liberally and falls into sin. In this book, however, he creates a character to illustrate the subject. The pastor is an extreme example; the last person who should be the victim of such an error, he is at the same time the most ignorant of his fault. Gide adopts the personality of the pastor in every word he writes and never allows his own understanding to influence a thought or action of his protagonist. The conflict between passion and ideal is here, as in *La Porte Etroite*, an undertone hardly audible beneath the placid surface of the narrative. (p. 94)

Les Caves du Vatican is a surprising book. In its form and tone it breaks away from the tradition which Gide had established in the novel; yet at the same time it reiterates in its own peculiar fashion many of the themes of his earlier work. The vein of parody which he had broached in *Isabelle* is exploited more extensively in *Les Caves*, with this important distinction: his tone in *Isabelle* was ironical, and was carefully hidden at that; in this book he is pointedly humorous and maintains for long stretches a tone of out-and-out buffoonery which is no mean accomplishment in itself alone. Humor is a necessary ingredient because Gide is not parodying here the tastes of his contemporaries but the cherished discoveries and beliefs of his youth. (p. 95)

The form of *Les Caves du Vatican* is a new venture. Told by an omniscient narrator, the story is made of a number of loosely connected episodes about a group of people who are related one to another by family ties, friendship, or hazard. They are united neither by the principal plot, the "Vatican swindle," nor by the hero, Lafcadio; but the novelist, Julius de Baraglioul, who has no very active rôle in the novel, comes in contact with each of the principal characters at some point in the narrative. His presence is of interest, however, not for the suggestion of unity which he gives the book, but because he is the tangible expression of the author's egoism. The egoist experiences the imperious need to hear his own voice and to react to his own thought. In a novel like this one, his easiest course is to speak out from his select position as narrator, but Gide could not be readily content with this solution, because after *L'Immoraliste* his efforts were visibly directed toward suppressing his own intrusions in the narrative. Julius is in no sense a direct reflection of Gide's personality; he simply acts as a soundingboard for the other characters, wondering at their eccentricities, speculating upon their motives, and finally being almost won to a new morality by Lafcadio. His steady reasoning and skepticism make him an admirable witness to the impulsive movements of the other characters, and through him Gide was able to prefigure their effect upon the sober mind of an ideal public and to hear an echo of his thought which would otherwise escape his ear. Julius is altogether a clever creation. (pp. 95-6)

The fact that *Les Faux Monnayeurs* is the only one of his books that Gide labeled "novel" has lent the work more of

a revolutionary character than it deserves, because in *Les Caves du Vatican* he had already established the formal structure he employs in *Les Faux Monnayeurs* and had more than suggested the vision of life he seeks to evoke in it. (p. 96)

It is primarily the character of Edouard, however, that makes *Les Faux Monnayeurs* a fuller, deeper work than its predecessor. Julius de Baraglioul was an episodic figure in *Les Caves;* his rôle was that of a bystander who offered good contrast for the other characters and gave Lafcadio someone to try his strength against. He was a partial replacement for the author's voice in the novel in that he remarked the things that Gide particularly wanted his reader to see. Edouard is everything that Julius was and a good bit more. He is an almost constant participant in the events of the novel, and he gives it an appearance of unity which its many characters and varied action would otherwise make impossible. Furthermore, his journal is integrated into the narrative for long stretches, and it is in this that his utility to the author becomes apparent; for his journal, concerned rather with the motives of the other characters and the meaning of their acts than with the action proper, is little more than a continual, but nicely disguised, intrusion of the novelist into the lives of his characters. . . . Edouard probes so deeply into the minds of the youths with whom he is in contact that he finally becomes a sort of superior consciousness ruling the whole group, turning them this way and that like so many puppets. He saps their life away until he alone remains, a very equivocal figure, as the substance of the novel.

It is a long evolution from *L'Immoraliste* to *Les Faux Monnayeurs*, in the course of which Gide worked more changes in his manner as a novelist than most fiction writers have ever attempted. All the more strange that it should be a path which led from one error back to that same error. *L'Immoraliste* was spoiled because Gide allowed Michel to assume a storyteller's personality which completely obscured the one he was supposed to have as the hero of the story. *Les Faux Monnayeurs* fails in essentially the same way: a second-rate novelist so dwarfs and twists the characters in the story that there is little reality or life remaining in them.

The interim stages of the evolution are represented by novels which come closer to the sort of truth which is the object of fiction; but even there, Gide, hampered either by the inability to endow his characters with a consciousness of their own, or by a concept of man in which consciousness is the property of the artist alone (which may be just two ways of saying the same thing), allowed only a glimpse of mute drama taking place before the uncomprehending eyes of his hero. Oddly enough, *Les Caves du Vatican*, which appears to aim at being just an elaborate amusement, comes nearest to offering a picture of living, feeling, thinking humanity, even though it is a caricatured humanity.

Gide had within his grasp one real hero, who was, like Proust's hero, an artist seeking the terms which would translate the crude reality of life into the ideal vision lying half-formed in his mind. He is the hero of *Les Cahiers d'André Walter*, of *Paludes*, and just possibly of *La Porte Etroite*. Gide, however, never found those terms in the novel, which was the medium of his choice. The reason for his failure lies less in his philosophy—which is less changing than he would have it appear—than in a temperament which drives him to seek forever a fresh starting point, which does not allow him to see the past objectively but always with reference to the present. To picture himself as the hero of the novel he needed to give himself up completely to a moment in the past, to rediscover the consciousness which was his at that time; but his egoism is so profound that the consciousness of the self writing the novel stifles the consciousness of the self depicted in the novel, and the hero who was to be loses his heroism and becomes the instrument of a force which he does not even recognize. (pp. 96-7)

Thomas Cordle, "Gide and the Novel of the Ego-ist," in Yale French Studies *(copyright © Yale French Studies 1951), No. 7, 1951, pp. 91-7.*

ALBERT J. GUERARD (essay date 1951)

Gide wanted to be, like Flaubert, a "demoralizer"—a destroyer, that is, of pragmatist pretense, of abstract or inherited authority, and of flattering self-delusion. He wanted to throw open all questions which men are tempted to consider closed; to challenge all received opinions, all restrictive institutions, all *a priori* notions concerning the nature of man. He had the puritan's horror of spiritual inertia, the scientist's skepticism of conclusions, and the optimist's faith that man achieves a higher destiny if he works it out unaided. Perhaps his most characteristic gesture is to refuse to profit from the *élan acquis;* from the acquired momentum of what others have discovered and codified, or of what one has himself discovered in the past. The ardently critical spirit thus advances into an always fresh, perilous, and unpredictable future, though constantly menaced by nostalgia for a comfortable and inherited past. . . . Temperamentally, Gide was inclined both to mysticism and to rationalism; to destroy both therefore required an unusually severe effort. He was harried as often by the nemesis of belief as by the nemesis of faith.

To "demoralize" meant to disturb faith in every institution which depends on compromise or submission and which is rooted in ancient habit: the church, family, and home most obviously, but also all political and intellectual "parties," the Cartesian and kindred traditions, and the elaborate ethics of custom. Gide believed in progress, but where others sought progress through provisional order, he preached provisional anarchy. Like Nietzsche he offered a startling parody of the golden mean. Rather than seek the midpoint between two extremes (which vary with each individual), man should cultivate both extremes, and hold them in precarious harmony. Suppression and fear may, paradoxically, induce comfort: the comfort of mediocrity and ignorance. But only the most ruthless and most adventurous *self-exploitation* can create new energy. "Descend to the bottom of the pit if you wish to see the stars." Gide called this a "Proverb of Hell," which by no means implied disapproval. Why did he insist on the educative value of what men normally call "evil"? Primarily because the "evil act" is often independent and insubordinate, and sometimes so spontaneous as to appear gratuitous. However dangerous in itself, it promises a possible progress to a different state of being. The lawless individual, if he does not rest in lawlessness, has a chance to transcend himself.

For Gide did not preach mere nihilism and anarchy; he criticized rather than transvalued values. What he wanted of course was to put the ethical problem, which concerned him more than any other, squarely to the individual. And he was persuaded that the emancipated individual could endure and survive his freedom. The price of success is eternal vigilance, which can be a weariness to both flesh and spirit. Gide's is essentially an ethics of reaction, the most sophisticated of

puritanisms. His famous adage—that *man should follow his slope* (his natural inclinations), *upward*—implies not merely that a goal of diversified harmony should be kept in mind, but that the hardest way is the best. The Apollonian by birth should explore and develop all his Dionysian impulses; the born Dionysian should seek coolness and wisdom. The extremes of traditionalism and experiment in art, and of order and anarchy in conduct, have no value in themselves, but are alike useful as educators and correctives. The true individualist cultivates a rich eclecticism of the inner life and respects the spirit's dialogue with itself. To suppress one voice at the expense of another is to cease to be fully alive. The great enemy of *individualism* (a personal complex of often heterogeneous tendencies) is *individuality* (the exclusive and tyrannical predominance of one tendency). But even the most rewarding state of being must be destroyed, *must die,* so that a new one can be born; even one good custom can corrupt the man. . . . The condition of man is one of restless change and courageous seeking; of institutions and values and selves incessantly dying, and incessantly being born. (pp. 30-2)

[*Le Voyage d'Urien*] has had few readers and almost no commentators; it demands a much fuller analysis than Gide's other early works. For this earnest prose-poem is one of the most tantalizing of Gide's works psychologically. . . . The voyage is a "voyage du rien" (Mallarmé had feared it would be the account of a real trip), yet contains everything. It is a Homeric *Pilgrim's Progress,* replete with sirens and other perils of the sea: a dream of life as a series of embroidered and sensuous dreams, and as the puritan rejection of those dreams. (p. 58)

As a Symbolist novel, *Le Voyage d'Urien* stands somewhere between the occult reality of *Arthur Gordon Pym* and the cloudy philosophizing of Novalis's *Lehrlinge zu Sais.* . . . The voyage of the "Orion" is a dream adventure through desire; an "invitation au voyage" of which the first condition is that the pilgrims leave their pasts and their books behind. These young men, wearied by fruitless studies, set out on an unpremeditated journey. Yet they dimly understand their "valor" will be tested, and vaguely long for heroism. . . . After the obvious sensuous enticements and pestilential languors of "The Dolorous Ocean" comes the ennui of "The Sargasso Sea": the ennui which follows not upon surfeit but upon the annihilation of desire. Here the pilgrims casually encounter Ellis (Urien's destined soulmate) or at least a woman who resembles her, and the ship passes over a submerged city. The same day they observe the first blocks of ice. A few, sick with ennui, must be left behind, but the eight who remain embark on the "Voyage to a Glacial Sea."

The goal proves to be a disappointing, "apathetic," and unfrozen little lake. The pilgrims wonder then whether it is perhaps better not to attain one's goal, but decide that the joy of effort and satisfied pride is reward enough. What then has been the voyage's and the book's meaning? That it is impossible to achieve genuine peace without having led the will through evil, through the temptations of passion and sluggish indifference? . . . It is perhaps better to avoid all intellectual paraphase; to admit that any ethical summary of *Le Voyage d'Urien* falsifies the impression it makes.

For the adventures seem truly gratuitous, unless interpreted psychologically. And here precisely lies the historic interest of *Le Voyage d'Urien,* which has never been fully recognized: it is a distinct and important episode in the transition from symbolism to surrealism; from the mysterious but somber soul-voyages of symbolism to the free absurdity of surrealist nightmare. Some of the gratuity reminds us vaguely of *The Ancient Mariner* and directly of *Arthur Gordon Pym.* (pp. 59-60)

It takes no psychiatric bias to see that *Arthur Gordon Pym* also dramatizes preconscious longings and fears. There is nevertheless a great difference between the two works, which brings Gide's much closer to surrealism. Except in the final pages, Poe is as careful to prepare and justify his mysteries as any Gothic novelist. Gide, on the other hand, does not even bother to explain how his pilgrims happened to set out. There is no logic in the connection of events, other than an inner logic of psychological necessity. Streams may flow backward; the *Orion* may "become" a felucca in an instant; a monument—"for some unknown reason"—may suddenly rise out of a plain. (p. 61)

"Souls are landscapes," says Gide's Preface to the second edition, and the landscapes of *Le Voyage d'Urien* are fluid and dissolving. Longing for fixity, the pilgrims travel past transforming shores evanescent as "insincere actions." They explore floating islands, and are lost among shifting dunes and moving knolls. . . . Some of the imagery of dissolution and putrefaction must be discounted as symbolist and decadent commonplace. This is perhaps least true where the dissolving agent is water—warm water, the recurrent menace on this voyage of the Puritan will. In the queen's grotto air and diaphanous water merge, and solid objects seem magically displaced. Icebergs melt in warm water at significant moments in the story. Can we not see in the corpse, imprisoned in a solid ice wall, a wishful image of fixity and unmenaced purity? (pp. 63-4)

The desire to dissolve the self . . . seems to take on several forms in *Le Voyage d'Urien,* and to have a multiple meaning. A verbalized and conscious longing for fixity is affronted by the spectacle of a dissolving universe. But what does this longing for fixity really signify, and does it not cover a less conscious longing to be one of the dissolving forms? And what would dissolution itself bring, if accomplished in these tepid waters: escape from the "miserable personality," or the riches of restored energy, or sexual release and expense? A passage from the *Lehrlinge zu Sais* [of Novalis] suggests that these impulses may be, at a given moment, inextricably connected: "He felt his miserable personality melt, submerged beneath waves of pleasure, and that nothing remained but a home for the incommensurable genetic force—a whirlpool in which everything is swallowed by the vast ocean. What does the flame ubiquitously offer? An intimate embrace, from which the sweet liquid trickles in voluptuous drops."

Compared with the diffuse *Lehrlinge zu Sais, Le Voyage d'Urien* has the density and economy of the most conscious art. Yet the fifth chapter of the first part—which conveys both the latent homosexuality and the fear of dissolution—must certainly have escaped any rational "intention" and all but the most rudimentary of unconscious censorship. It forces upon us not merely the equivalence of water, indulgence and dissolution, but also the very physical terms of the homosexual embrace. (pp. 66-8)

All this is conveyed in a little more than five hundred words. It should be emphasized that there are no logical connections between the four "episodes": the observation of the fish-

ermen, the swim in the magic pool and subsequent torpor, the evening restlessness on the ship, the coming of the vampires. There are no transitional phrases, yet not a single word breaks the prevailing and complex mood. Mere revery—which normally results in such diffuseness—has here imposed rather than destroyed unity by the very urgency of its demand: by its longing for a nevertheless dreaded relaxation, by its "selection" of particular and revealing imagery. However florid some of its pages, *Le Voyage d'Urien* already shows Gide's ability to record feelings exactly; to penetrate—more successfully than he knew—beneath the level of full consciousness. (pp. 68-9)

Certainly [*L'Immoraliste*] is the most frequently misunderstood of [Gide's] novels, partly because its deceptive simplicity of surface invites casual and very literal reading. Like the unread *Voyage d'Urien,* the misread *Immoraliste* demands a fuller analysis than books as well or better known. . . . *L'Immoraliste* brought to the French novel all the seriousness and much of the complexity of Dostoevsky's short novels—and did so first of all through its successful use of the "imperceptive" or self-deluded narrator as subject of the story he tells. *L'Immoraliste* is not, to be sure, *The Possessed,* or even *Crime and Punishment.* But it exists as a touchstone for shorter and less ambitious fiction. It helps us to define a level of achievement which autobiographical and subjective fiction can rarely hope to surpass: fiction which concentrates on one man's destiny (a shadow of the author's own) and which offers no comprehensive understanding of society. Michel's revolt reflects his age (the age of Nietzschean hopes and destructions) but reflects even more the timeless conflict of the unconscious life and the conscious. Already the psychological realism of *L'Immoraliste* seems more important than its critique of individualism; its anticipation of Freud more valid than its oblique reflection of Nietzsche. Its more personal triumph lies in the successful avoidance of lyricism, of confused or angry self-justification, of special pleading—of all the evasions, in fact, to which autobiographical fiction is tempted. The precarious balance of the author's sympathy and detachment remains to the end under minute control. (pp. 99-100)

In personal terms, *L'Immoraliste* was a symbolic act of dissociation from Michel. Had Gide not discovered himself so fully, he too might have been driven to such a harsh and aimless individualism. This is the book's "personal" subject. *L'Immoraliste* is also, of course, a critique (not rejection) of Nietzschean individualism. But most of all it is a study of latent homosexuality, of repression and compensation, of the effect preconscious energies may have on a man's acts, feelings, and ideas. It is no wonder, since the book was all these things, that it was little read and little understood at first. (p. 102)

L'Immoraliste is one of the first modern novels to deal at all seriously with homosexuality. But it is most important to keep in mind that Michel never participates in a homosexual act. The reader who assumes that such acts occur but are not mentioned, for reasons of discretion, is likely to misinterpret everything else. . . . Through many pages of a first reading we have every right to share Michel's bewilderment. We explore him with the same curiosity that he explores himself. And how much would be lost if the last revealing lines of the novel were its first ones! But on second and subsequent readings the ambiguities should dissolve. Not till then, perhaps, does the reader notice that Michel possesses

Marceline only after fighting with the drunken coachman; that he felt "obliged" (in an hour of frustration) to caress a strangely textured shrub; that his period of tranquillity at La Morimière ends abruptly with the coming of the boy Charles; that he longs to sleep in the barn because the boy Alcide sleeps there; that, in fact, he never proceeds beyond the stage of longing for these boys. The important fact about Michel is not that he is a homosexual, but that he is a latent homosexual, a homosexual without knowing it.

Thus *L'Immoraliste* is not a case study of a particular and manifest neurosis, but a story of unconscious repression. In the light of this, but only in this light, various unexplained ritual acts take on meaning: the shaving of the beard, or the ceremonial undressing, sun-bathing, and immersion in the pool near Ravello. The vengeance of what has been suppressed touches every fiber of Michel's intellectual and moral life; determines his self-destructiveness and his anti-intellectualism alike. Restrained from sexual satisfaction and even from self-discovery by an unconscious force, Michel rebels in other ways. The outburst may be sudden and specific, as when he leaps into the draining lake and takes a savage excitement in catching eels with Charles. More generally, Michel rebels against his early intellectual training in his philosophical defense of barbarism; against his inherited Norman prudence in trying to destroy the harmony and order of his farm. *L'Immoraliste* dramatizes as clearly as Dostoevsky's *Gambler* the compulsion to risk—and lose. Payment must eventually be made to the internalized parental authority. But the first impulse is to destroy not appease this superego. The harshness of Michel's individualism—and this, in general terms, is no less than the "subject" of the novel—is determined by the harshness of the repression.

The hidden victim of this hidden restraint reveals itself in a curious hostility toward the convention-bound and in an abnormal sympathy for the free. Michel's acts seemed to many early readers (and even at times to himself) unmotivated and "Satanic." Like *The Secret Sharer, Heart of Darkness,* and parts of *Lord Jim, L'Immoraliste* dramatizes unconscious or half-conscious identification. The lawless buried self is attracted to all whom the superego and the waking conscience deem guilty, and repelled by all the well-behaved. Even when he is most determined to lead a regulated life, Michel's affections go out to the unmoral, the corrupt, the unrestrained. . . . The movement toward discovery is not, to be sure, uninterrupted. The alternating and sometimes simultaneous impulses to concentrate and to destroy the ego—to use Baudelaire's terminology rather than Freud's—increase or weaken according to the self at the moment dominant and the self at the moment suppressed. The frustrated Huguenot as well as the frustrated homosexual may demand satisfaction. In the final chapters, however, the inward aggressions become frenzied as the "authentic self" nears the surface. (pp. 106-08)

One strength of *L'Immoraliste* lies in its awareness of the close interdependence of Michel's health, his degree of sexual adjustment, his moral heritage, and his intellectual interests. The novel's over-all "meaning" is reducible to the barest Freudian terms, but Michel as a character is not. His intelligence and will, however weak, do play some part. His tenderness toward Marceline develops into love at the same time as his cruelty toward her—and at the same time as his homosexual impulses. And if his ideas are determined by his unconscious needs, his arguments still demand attention. The

problem of individualism, though provoked in this instance by a specific sexual situation, nevertheless transcends neurosis.

For Gide knew that the problem of the emancipated individualist goes on, even after sexual adjustments have been made. Must one choose between a refusal to live and an individualism which makes others suffer? Marceline justly observes that Michel's doctrine may be a "fine one," but that it threatens to suppress the weak. And can the individualist cut himself off to be free, yet live in that rarefied air? "To know how to free oneself is nothing; the arduous thing is to know what to do with one's freedom." It is here, in its critique of Nietzschean individualism, that *L'Immoraliste* is necessarily imperfect—and first of all because Michel is an imperfect Nietzschean. Gide agreed with Michel and Nietzsche that the world is divided into the strong and the weak. . . . But Michel was incapable of the solution Gide elsewhere proposed: to become fully conscious of the inner dialogue between order and anarchy, and to suppress by an act of will whichever voice threatens to become too strong. The very fact that makes Michel so interesting dramatically and psychologically—his imperfect understanding of himself—makes him a poor vehicle for Gidean and Nietzschean ideas. His story could not answer the question raised in the Prologue: how is society to use the energies of the free man? "I fear the failures of individualism," Gide wrote in 1898. Michel is such a failure; he is not a free man.

Thus the aspect of *L'Immoraliste* most emphasized by critics is in fact unsatisfactory. The novel's strength lies rather in its art and psychological understanding, and in its controlled transposition of personal experience. . . . The triumph of intelligence reveals itself in the close pressure of form. . . . This required a conscious separation of the author's consciousness from Michel's, and a careful use of the "imperceptive" narrator as a technical device. . . . The problem for the novelist is to keep his narrator (or Jamesian "fool" and observer) self-deluded, imperceptive, blind; incapable of accurate self-analysis—yet have that narrator supply all the evidence necessary to the reader's understanding. He must say enough to convey his daily suffering and betray his true difficulties, but not say too much more. (pp. 108-10)

[Nearly] everything Michel says and nearly everything he sees has a direct bearing on his sexual problem. He keeps Moktir's theft secret not merely because he sees in it an acting-out of his own longing to rebel against accepted decencies, but because he here enters into a first clandestine relationship with a child. A large psychological situation is thus perfectly dramatized in the action or inaction of a moment; the "gratuitous act" of sympathetic identification is in no sense gratuitous. Yet Michel's prolonged compulsive need to spend all his money is, to the reader of Menninger and Freud, fully as convincing. The novel offers very little "neutral" or innocent imagery. Lassif's canals and Lachmi's gourd for collecting the sap from palm trees are images as primary, for this latent homosexual, as the eels he caught with Charles; clay and shrub alike have a fleshy texture. How could Gide, using so much significant imagery, yet contrive to give an impression of real life, of unselected experience? . . . One answer is that Gide's significant images also serve as casual images—*and so serve because never explained.* No single image or experience, but the cumulative effect of them all, drives us very slowly to an awareness of Michel's trouble. Everything in Michel's story leads to his revelation in the last line, yet no particular page seems to lead there in an obvious way. The minutiae of style and technique thus disguise an economy as extreme as any in modern fiction. Could Gide achieve a latent homosexual's vision of experience so exactly and so economically only because he had been, himself, a latent homosexual? To ask this is to take a very naïve view of the art of fiction—and to forget the imperfections of certain earlier books. In *L'Immoraliste* he reduced a most confused personal experience to an order which even the best-adjusted writers rarely achieve.

It is hardly the intention of this book to defend realism as such, and the anti-realism of *Les Faux-Monnayeurs* may have done more for the modern novel. But *L'Immoraliste* is a great realistic novel, and perhaps the best novel Gide would write. (pp. 116-17)

> *Albert J. Guerard, in his* André Gide *(copyright © 1951 by the President and Fellows of Harvard College; copyright renewed © 1979 by Albert J. Guerard; excerpted by permission), Cambridge, Mass.; Harvard University Press, 1951 (and reprinted by E. P. Dutton, 1963), 255 p.*

HENRI PEYRE (essay date 1955)

Gide the novelist should be judged by three volumes: [*L'Immoraliste (The Immoralist)*, *La Porte étroite (Strait Is the Gate)*, and *Les Faux-Monnayeurs (The Counterfeiters)*]. *La Symphonie pastorale (The Pastoral Symphony)*, . . . while exemplary within its limits, suffers from an excessive haste in the development of the plot and from some improbability in the denouement. The lyrical vein has been silenced by the author; sobriety and simplicity are carried almost to the point of asceticism. The symmetry between the spiritual blindness of the pastor and the gradual discovery of light, of love, of evil by the blind girl is too deftly contrived. The irony toward the ecclesiastical unctuousness of the clergyman undergoing a second youth and rationalizing his impulses is a trifle facile. (pp. 87-8)

L'Immoraliste was slowly and probably too laboriously composed by Gide. Several incidents, easily identifiable, are borrowed directly from life, obviously a legitimate procedure; but the author may have respected their literal data overmuch, instead of transfiguring them through some impetuous rush of an imaginary re-creation. . . . The preface, written in a somewhat stilted manner, offers the author's plea that he be dissociated from his hero and that his book be judged as an objective work of art, in which, as Flaubert had taught the young admirer of his correspondence, the artistry alone matters and no conclusion need be sought. The conclusion of the novel also betrays traces of imperfection. But Gide is fond of intriguing denouements that, untying little (the plot was frail in any case), seem to prolong the story into the reader's perturbed mind. But elsewhere, in the descriptions of Normandy, in the slow recovery of the hero in North Africa, and in his naïve egotism asserting itself at the expense of his wife's very existence, the book reaches one of the few summits of Gide's career. It is indeed, as Charles du Bos aptly called it, 'the masterpiece of luminous cruelty.'

The themes woven into the novel are complex, although they hardly enter into struggle with one another. Gide keeps sedulously shy of conflicts in his strangely anti-novelistic novels. On the surface, *L'Immoraliste* is the portrayal of the individualist who breaks free from his past, from his edu-cation, and from his environment and asserts his determination to live authentically. Such a subject was hardly original and has today become a current one in international fiction, from Franz Kafka to Georges Simenon. The liberated individualist in this case is a scholar who, like Gide in his earlier crisis, rapturously celebrated in *Les Nourritures terrestres*, bidding farewell to his youth, realizes that true life has passed him by. Michel decides to scratch beneath the varnish of culture and to embrace a more primitive mode of life, to flee both the aridity of scholarship and the effete existence of the salons. His journeys to more sunny climates are flights away from his earlier and tamed self, responses of a Faust hardly of epic stature to some Mephistophelic calls, and yearnings for some Walpurgis night. (pp. 88-9)

The second part of the novel, too symmetrically contrived in relation to the first, relates Michel's new passion for all that is primitive, robust, spontaneously vicious. . . . Ménalque, a predicating and not too witty Oscar Wilde, teaches Michel in ponderous formulas to believe in his own pleasure and to cultivate his own uniqueness. He incites the former archaeologist to forget all yesterdays and to welcome every hour that strikes as virginly novel. Meanwhile his wife falls gravely ill. . . . While she pines alone on her sick bed, distressed by the doctrine now preached by her husband, which advocates the suppression of the weak, he worships 'an unknown god.' He gives free rein to his homosexual bent and rises at last beyond conventional good and evil. 'In every being, the worst instinct appeared to me as the most sincere.' His wife dies in desperate solitude. Thus each man kills the thing he loves. Gide's message had not essentially varied since *Les Nourritures terrestres* and would vary but little in years to come: liberation is arduous and perhaps genuine only if it is bought with the suffering of others. One must not indulge possession after possession has ceased being an enrichment and has become a stale prison; for then one is in truth possessed by what one loved. (pp. 89-90)

Although Gide, in his Goethean ambition, always refused to let himself be summed up by one single work and coyly dissented from admirers who singled out one of his volumes for their eulogy, he may well remain for future ages the novelist of *La Porte étroite*. Once again, the book may be biblically said to be 'a bone out of his bones and flesh out of his own flesh.' There is little invention in it, as there was little in many eclogues and epics and tales of the classical ages; but the incidents and the dreams of his own youth are harmoniously fused by the author into one of the most restrainedly tragic novels of the century.

The elements Gide borrowed from his own peculiar inclinations are here transmuted into universal motives. . . . (p. 90)

Gide's limitations as a writer of fiction are here turned to actual advantages. The type of novel attempted in *La Porte étroite* required a minimum of incidents, few or no exterior intrusions, an extreme purity of structure, and the effective use of silent pauses. The souls of the protagonists had to be engaged in an inward exploration of their own depths in order to offer to each other the noblest of tributes: a clearer insight into themselves and a fervent striving after perfection, laid at each other's feet. It was thus natural for Alissa, Jérôme, and Juliette to avoid the brutal explanation or conflagration of scenes, to shun the harsh words, the swoonings, or the hysterical flow of tears dear to earlier fictional heroines or to Dostoevskian ones. Gide's rather easy device, the laying bare of the private diary invariably kept by the leading character, thus becomes fully natural here, as does the exchange of letters indulged in by the idealistic lovers. . . . Jérôme, the witness and recorder of the tragic story of failure, had to have, as seemed natural in his case, a discreet, modest, even a weak, personality. He had to be intelligent and analytical, but neither avidly possessive nor scathingly ironical. He only half understood the drama in which he was a semipassive actor, and Gide was thus able to launch his reader on several divergent tracks without ever imposing one set of symbols or of explanations upon him. The extreme brevity of the volume enhanced its beauty further; for, unlike Balzac and the novelists who insist upon leaving nothing unsaid, Gide wants to remain as far as possible from the perilous effect of saturation produced by Richardson, Zola, or Dostoevski. The past is subtly guessed. . . . *La Porte étroite* stands in some respects closer to some of the late nineteenth-century novels than to more recent ones, in which obstacles laid before the fulfillment of passion spring from physiological or psychoanalytical motives, seldom from spiritual aspirations. In very few of the great French novels (neither in *La Princesse de Clèves,* in *Manon Lescaut,* nor in Rousseau, neither in Stendhal, in Balzac, nor even Mauriac) did love enter into conflict with religion. It wrestled with honor, ambition, pride (Mlle de la Môle), maternal affection, social conventions, the fear of hell occasionally, or even the sense of duty to one's spouse, but seldom with the aspiration toward saintliness. . . . [Alissa's] idea of happiness is a steep and perilous one. It must, like true love, feed on the sacrifices that it entails. She cherishes difficulty, wants a human happiness that leads not away from Christ but closer to mystical love. The dream proves an impossible one, and she mutilates herself in pursuit of inhuman purity.

But Alissa is more complex than that. The fire that burns within her soul stirs also within her body. . . . Her acquired seriousness has not . . . killed her zest for life. There are dormant possibilities in her that love might awaken.

She has not yielded to them up to the present. Her implacable Protestant habit of soul-searching has taught her to be lucid and has given her the pride of dignified self-sacrifice in favor of her more earthly and less exacting sister Juliette. (pp. 91-3)

Jérôme is an essential agent in the development of the volume, even if a passive one. It would have taken the tricks of a coquette or the harmless poutings and whims of an average girl to stimulate him into less cerebral a passion and to hasten the marriage he steadfastly but shyly contemplated. . . . Gide has never written more heart-rending pages than those that follow the tragic misunderstanding between two exalted natures, perhaps not born for happiness, and too averse to anything low or vulgar ever to reach it at the expense of their spiritual or religious ideal. Alissa's slow death was a prefiguration of the premature aging and forlornness of Gide's own wife, as his posthumous revelation of Mme Gide has showed. Never did Gide explore the abysses of sorrow more tragically than when he turned her irretrievably away from him. But he knew the Goethean art of converting sorrow into art. 'We make out of the quarrel with others, rhetoric, but of the quarrel with ourselves, poetry.' (pp. 93-4)

[*Les Faux-Monnayeurs* is] a prolonged intellectual attempt and . . . a work that springs from will power as much as from inspiration. The mastery of the craftsman is evident. The elaborate organization and the utmost care spent over details

concealed under an apparent nonchalance have caused the novel to be compared with the three greatest works of the years 1920-26: *Ulysses, A la recherche du temps perdu,* and *The Magic Mountain.* The comparison, however, can only bring out Gide's lesser power. (p. 94)

The unity of a single plot and the intimacy of a narrative in the first person, which marked Gide's earlier novels—or *récits* as he was to call them according to a *distinguo* that we need not adopt—are gone. There are as many as five or six separate stories in *Les Faux-Monnayeurs,* and the links established among them remain tenuous. Gide sought new starts with every chapter and attempted very hard not to take advantage of any earlier and cumulative *élan.* The tone itself is no longer as clear and bright as that which irradiated Gide's early prose. There is something abrupt and disconcerting in the succession of the chapters and in the very last sentence, which does not close the book but with which Gide delights in appearing as the demoralizer. The structure of *Les Faux-Monnayeurs,* also, even judged by its own laws, is not above reproach. Far too much has to be presented through Edouard's diary and is colored through his tinted glasses. But there is much also that could not be thus encompassed, and the fusion of heterogeneous data is not felicitous. The omniscient author himself asserts his presence and pulls the strings of his puppets with some irony. One is too deeply conscious that he had earlier selected the material his characters have observed. The characters are very artificially linked to one another by the busybody Edouard. . . . (pp. 94-5)

The chief interest of the novel, next to its delineation of the complex psychology of adolescents, has been found to lie in its being a novelists' novel; its theme is 'the rivalry between the real world and the representation we make of it,' as Gide formulated it. (p. 95)

Stronger features of *Les Faux-Monnayeurs* are the central symbol of counterfeit coin and the dramatized position of the question that permeated all the meditations of Gide in his last thirty years and that will probably remain the most valued part of his legacy to the world, the question of sincerity. Most of the characters in the book are themselves counterfeit. . . . However, many people go through life without having ever been sincere in the sense of being authentically themselves. The true hypocrite, as Gide remarked in one of his many reflections on the subject, 'is he who is no longer even aware of a lie, who lies with sincerity.' (pp. 95-6)

Gide is the novelist of sincerity. Therein lies his chief claim to the gratitude of moderns who are determined not to live forged lives and who wish to throw away the forged coins of social conventionality, of religious conformity, of sexual Pharisaism, of literary and rhetorical embellishment. (p. 96)

Henri Peyre, "The Legacy of Proust and Gide," in his The Contemporary French Novel *(copyright © 1955 by Oxford University Press, Inc.; reprinted by permission), Oxford University Press, New York, 1955, pp. 67-100.**

PHILIP TOYNBEE (essay date 1956)

'Protean' was the word most favoured by Gide's admirers. It is a flattering word, and it was intended to convey a resourceful versatility, and even an ability to adopt opposing attitudes almost at will. It was often pointed out that *La Porte Etroite* was written soon after *L'Immoraliste* and that these two novels were each the pendant of the other, providing

228

between them a masterly and balanced demonstration of opposing attitudes to life.

But now, standing back a little and surveying the whole work of André Gide, it may seem that this protean dexterity is the very quality which has dissolved the apparent solidity, loosened the whole structure, weakened the effects. It is usual to think of Gide as a novelist—as a novelist who did many other things and had many other interests but nevertheless as a novelist first and last. Yet how many genuine novels did Gide write, and what do they amount to? *L'Immoraliste; La Porte Etroite; L'Ecole des Femmes; La Symphonie Pastorale; Les Caves du Vatican; Les Faux-Monnayeurs*. . . . I can only write here that they seem to me to make no sense as an *oeuvre* and that no book among them strikes me as an evident and permanently valuable achievement. Collectively and individually I feel that these books have been undone by their author's refusal to stand still. It is natural that any thinking and feeling man of our century should change his views and submit to strange processes of conversion. When we confront, in the *Journal* or the other books, Gide the near-Christian and Gide the near-Communist it is possible to sympathize with both. But there is, surely, in this changeability, an element of deliberate experiment with which it is much more difficult to sympathize. (pp. 46-7)

It is not that Gide was a frivolous man; he was admirably in earnest in nearly all that he wrote and said and did. But he strove too hard for a belief and never achieved that 'negative capability' which has become, since Keats invented the term, more necessary to the European writer every passing decade of faiths sadly lost or angrily recovered. There is something both desperate and calculating about Gide's intellectual profligacy—and the impression we get of it oddly resembles the impression we get of his profligacy in private life. . . . If Gide had been truly *in command* of his material he might have been able to deploy contrasting beliefs with great effect, lending to each in turn his partial but sufficient sympathy. That would have been the method of a classical master: it was the method of Goethe. But Gide, one of the most personal and romantic among modern writers, was blown off like a balloon by each successive gust of faith or speculation. He wilfully surrendered himself to 'experience', precisely as he had recommended us all to do in *Les Nourritures Terrestres*. And although this may be an exciting policy for living, the cautious writer must be more selective in his life as well as in his writing.

It seems to me, then, that most of Gide's books have the effect of cancelling each other out, so that nothing clear or effective emerges from the whole. But it might be said that writers should not be surveyed like this, pushing all their books together and seeing how they look collectively. How does Gide look when we take up his books one by one? Perhaps the individual books, happily illuminated by newly-adopted but self-consistent attitudes to life, are individually triumphant? (pp. 47-8)

If we are thinking in terms of individual books it is better, perhaps, to write about *Les Faux-Monnayeurs*. This was the only attempt Gide ever made to write a 'great' novel, in which a considered attitude should be embodied and a considered literary method should be employed. Here if anywhere in his fiction he was being himself, having discarded all temporary masks and rejected all previous stances. Yet the result, it seems to me, is even more unhappy than in those deliberately 'orientated' books like *L'Immoraliste* and

La Porte Etroite. Do what I may to remind myself of the immediate critical reaction and to guard against olympian judgements I cannot help writing that *Les Faux-Monnayeurs* is a very bad novel indeed. Its principal characters are intended to be credible, but remain stilted and lifeless projections which can win neither our sympathy nor our indignation. Its theme, when divested of an uninspired and too-obvious symbolism, is so familiar that only a brilliant novelty of treatment could have brought it to life again. There is, throughout this long novel, a painful impression of the author's constant and prejudiced intrusion. . . . And though we know by now that authors must always intrude on their own books, this kind of gross and prejudiced intrusion is still, surely, to be condemned. *Les Faux-Monnayeurs* is simply a piece of the *Journal* which lacks the *Journal*'s truth, sincerity and charm. (pp. 48-9)

Les Nourritures Terrestres will always remain one of the key books of its epoch. To-day we are as far as can be from its sensuous poetics, its fruity moralizings, its lush and humourless self-assurance. But it is not a book which can be laughed at or despised. We see that it does what it meant to do—that it is a triumph. I still find, as well, that *Les Caves du Vatican* is a comic success. The famous 'acte gratuit' looks silly and pretentious now, but the book still pleases as a *jeu d'esprit*. And no doubt if I now re-read all the books that Gide ever wrote I would find many others to remind me of his powers and to make more intelligible to me the gigantic reputation which he enjoyed for so many years.

From a literary point of view, then, I have not found that Gide looks very good to me now, whether I think of his books together or alone. . . . Is it possible, perhaps, to see Gide in such terms as these—as the prophetic representative of an epoch, of a climate of opinion, rather than as a writer whose works must be submitted to detailed criticism?

Seeing him thus I believe that we shall probably come closer to seeing him justly. If it was his fault as a writer that he submerged himself in too many diverse experiences and scurried too eagerly in search of a faith, it was his merit as a man to have remained honourably fluid in his beliefs and never to have closed his mind against the events and ideas of successive decades. To construct a work—even to construct a single, central book—a writer must stand calmly somewhere, even in the calm of a total disbelief. 'Negative capability' does not imply a ready suspectibility to new emotions and ideas, but a capacity to hold all emotions and ideas at a certain distance, perceiving them, appreciating them but never submitting to them. This was the capacity which Gide lacked as a writer. But his very lack of it made him the more efficient as a human weather-cock, or litmus paper. To contemplate him is truly to contemplate one kind of Hero of Our Times. (pp. 49-50)

What did they learn from him, those generations of young men who were submitted to Gide's intoxicating influence? In his prophetic rôle there was one issue which burned in him throughout his life, one cause which he served with scarcely a single doubt or reservation. Himself a homosexual, he was not only the passionate defender of sexual freedom but a powerful and deliberate propagandist for the superiority of his own accidental tastes. Though he rejected the exuberant sensuality of *Les Nourritures Terrestres*, though he made full use of that counter-balancing puritanism which was no less a part of his complicated nature, Gide was as consistent in his recommendation of sexual freedom as Voltaire had been consistent in the defence of intellectual freedom.

In this field, though he had many allies, Gide was the *primus inter pares*. It was his great cause and he served it with courage and devotion. . . . As a sexual emancipator I believe that Gide did good—or at least that he helped to create a situation which contained a greater potential for good than the one that existed before him. What we may say against him is that he was naïve in his conviction that the good was absolute. . . . But Gide often seemed to treat sexual indulgence as a sufficient end in itself, as if it were an absolute good instead of an added means for reaching the good. Few sillier books than *Corydon* were ever written in defence of anything. (pp. 50-1)

Gide was, as a prophet, consistently on the side of humanity and good sense in public affairs. His campaign against the iniquities of African colonialism was a noble episode in a life which was not lacking in such episodes. He became a Communist for the best of reasons and he rejected Communism for reasons no less good. He kept his head in both wars. He was a compassionate and sensible observer of the life around him.

It does not seem to add up to major prophetic stature. There were many other good liberals at the time. Many others were recommending new ways of thinking and helping to pilot us through strange new seas of thought. Gide served the mood of his period, and he served it, I think, for the good rather than for the bad. But his message, when we look back on it, may seem too easy a message; we may feel that he treated emancipation too much as an end in itself and self-indulgence as a good in itself instead of as a good only when other things are equal. (And there are so many other things!)

There remains still another rôle which he played for us and which may perhaps survive our present disrespect for the writer and suspicion of the prophet. In his long *Journal* and in many other of his books Gide diligently presented his own features for our inspection. We can see him not only as a writer and thinker but also as a personality. And few even of the great egotists of the past have given to the public a fuller description of themselves, a more detailed self-portrait. . . . [No] writer of our time has exposed himself to the public with such relentless candour. Will Gide survive, then, as one of the great introspectives and egotists of history—or at least as one of the great recorders? (pp. 51-2)

It is my own belief that he succeeded in both and that all that is best in Gide can be discovered in the seventeen hundred pages of the *Journal*. (p. 52)

His *Journal* will be read, surely, not only as a document invaluable to historians but as a work of desultory art in its own right. From that secretive 'Visite à Verlaine' which appears on the first page as the first entry for 1890 to Gide's final absorption, fifty-nine years later, in the *Journal* of Joseph Goebbels, we are conducted through a whole epoch of our history by a cunning, eloquent and tactful guide.

But the *Journal* is much more, of course, than a Guide to the Times. It is an introspective mining operation which has no equivalent in this century or any other, except, perhaps, in the work of Proust. Here the dominant characteristic of Gide—his incurable and conscious naïveté—is as much an advantage to him as it is a handicap when he tries so hard to overcome it in his novels. It is intolerable when the hero

of *Les Faux-Monnayeurs* emerges as Gide himself and is applauded by his creator. But Gide's own efforts to observe himself, to justify himself to present the truth but in a pleasant light, are deeply interesting to follow. He is determined to be 'sincere', and no word is so often on his pen. The sincerity which he achieves is not always of the direct sort which he was aiming at. Often we find ourselves reading Gide rather as we listen to the strange, purposive ramblings of an accused child. The truth comes out; it was always meant to come out; but it comes out, as it were, between the lines. It is not simply that Gide fails to tell us what would displease us. Often he beats his breast with dramatic zeal. But he has, nonetheless, a preconceived picture of himself to which he pays lip-service from the beginning of his long confession to the end of it. If we are to see him more clearly and more exactly we must learn to see him through this projected image. . . .

Devious in his naïveté, both innocent and guilty, a saint and an outrageous egotist, his greatest talent was for portraying himself against the carefully-delineated background of his time. His individual novels may seem, to us, at this time, so many successive and ineffective literary gestures. His message may seem to have evaporated—or at least to have been drowned by that general cry for emancipation which was sounded from so many throats during the years of Gide's lifetime. But his *Journal* retains, even at this dubious moment of his reputation, all the interest for us which can be earned by a patient sincerity, an eager curiosity, and a brilliant pen. (p. 53)

> *Philip Toynbee, "The Living Dead—III: Thoughts on André Gide," in* London Magazine (© London Magazine 1956*), Vol. 3, No. 10, October, 1956, pp. 46-53.*

WILLIAM W. HOLDHEIM (essay date 1962)

The title of Gide's *Caves du Vatican* is so strongly suggestive of the book's central conception that it should never have been changed in the English translation. . . . "Lafcadio's adventures" are important components of this book, but they are far from representing its basic conception. The image of the *caves*, suggesting imprisonment or hermetic enclosure, is much more appropriate. (p. 292)

Indeed the characters in the book are hemmed in by walls from which they cannot (or do not want to) escape. Instead of "cellars" let me speak of "systems," replacing the concrete image by a concept, for the sake of expository clarity. The earmark of a system is its closed nature, its perfect objective coherence that does not take account of subjective distinctiveness and spontaneity. Gide's characters are caught in systems that flatten their personal existence and strip them of individual substance. . . . The system may be social or intellectual. That of the Vatican, to which Julius is subject, happens to be both, since the Church is a hierarchized socio-political power which offers a complete systematic explanation of life. Anthime has taken his position at the opposite pole. Intellectually, he is a free-thinker, illuminating the mystery of life by facile explanations that are as comforting as Julius' fixed universe of meaning; socially and politically, he is a member of the powerful organization of Freemasonry. Another system is that of established bourgeois morality, yet another that of traditional French literary psychology (Gide's *bête d'aversion*), which undermines subjective spontaneity by reducing man's mind to a consistent mechanism intelligible in terms of unequivocal formulae. Catholic philosophy, bourgeois morality, and classical psychology all merge in the edifying *bien-pensant* novel as written by Julius, which is itself nothing but the systematic elaboration of pre-established formulae and which Gide parodies in his first chapter, the story of Anthime's conversion. (pp. 292-93)

I said that an air of unreality adheres to the "cellars" of the title. The systems, just like the individuals caught in them, are characterized by a lack of density. They do exist, but what they stand for, the way in which they arrange or explain life, makes little difference. What counts is their coherence, their comforting consistence. . . . The interchangeability of systems unites with the unreality of the characters to give this world its peculiar lack of gravity, so characteristic of Gide's *soties*. Quite obviously this is a parody of human inauthenticity, a familiar Gidian theme. And it is equally Gidian that the family, that "grande chose fermée," is the most important of all systems. It is, indeed, not just one more system, but the quintessence of all "systematic" life. (p. 293)

[What] of Lafcadio, the only one who creates an impression of freshness and spontaneity? As his illegitimacy indicates, he is conceived as the antipode of all systematic forms of existence. Lafcadio has to create himself, is not weighed down by any ballast, his point of departure is the *tabula rasa*—a fact amusingly symbolized by the shocking photograph in his room which shows him in the pristine state of nature. Therefore his "lifelike spontaneity" is in the first place a deliberate symbol, expressing his freedom from and antagonism to any system, his quest for authenticity. But the photograph stands not only for the authenticity of Lafcadio's *dénûment*, but also for the attractiveness of his nudity. It is in the last analysis this disquieting desirability which makes him more concrete as a character. A subtle irony lies in the fact that Lafcadio seems more "alive" than all the others, since his existence is in truth even more stylized and impossible than theirs. They, after all, represent modes of being that do exist in reality, although here in the exaggerated form of parody. But a creature that lives outside of all systems, that does not live "en situation," is inconceivable. Lafcadio's very existence, down to his spontaneity, is posited logically. He exists because the conception of the book required a personification of complete freedom, as an antithesis. He is a purely hypothetical being.

Lafcadio's vitality, therefore, is illusory. This fact is underscored by the crime he commits, the notorious "gratuitous act." It is conceived as a deed that is entirely his, an affirmation of his freedom and authenticity—an act in which the self and its expression merge in a living unity. But how could a deed that emanates from an artificial "self" be anything but artificial? This is not the psychologically credible action of a living character whose successive experiences mark an organic development: it is merely a logical necessity, for logic requires that a free being commit an act that is foreign to all systems. In fact, Lafcadio's crime must necessarily be precisely what it is. It must be a crime in order to be alien to the system of morality, and it must be unmotivated so that it may not be enmeshed by psychological consistency. Moreover, it is extraneous to the web of ramifications spun by the plot. Its spontaneity and concreteness is hypothetical. However, even this bloodless version of concreteness cannot be maintained. Lafcadio's act is drawn into a system of ramifications to which it was entirely foreign, and he ends up by being caught in the meshes of a well-organized society. . . .

Lafcadio's crime is not appropriated by an opaque and lifelike reality, but by a thin, constructed mechanism, and what is stressed is the falsity of this mechanism. It takes control and dissolves everything into a comfortable explanation. The falsification becomes complete when Protos, the man with the motive, is held responsible. It is this explanation which counts, as Julius suggests to Lafcadio: a confession would merely disturb the restored equilibrium of the universe. If Lafcadio toys with the idea of a confession, it is out of protest against the alienation of his act.

Let us return to the crime as such, whose hypothetical concreteness goes with the hypothetical vitality of the criminal. The fascination with unreasoned action, with spontaneous criminality, is a constant in Gide's work. In his Dostoevsky lectures, he distinguishes three zones in the human psyche: that of the intellect, that of action, and that of mystical experience. The third plays no role in our context, but it is clear that Gide's sympathies lie with action rather than intellection—with Dmitri rather than Ivan Karamazof. . . . Gide's theory grows into a veritable creed of vitalist anti-intellectualism. Lafcadio's act has to be viewed in this light. It is symbolic of vitalism, of *life* that crashes through a constrictive maze of rationality. Raskolnikof—as Gide argues in his Dostoevsky lectures—is not a superman because his crime is not sufficiently irrational: he reasons it instead of naïvely committing it. Gide would have us believe, at least provisionally, that Lafcadio's crime has the required naïveté of execution. (pp. 293-96)

This brings us to the paradoxical relation between freedom and necessity which has been touched upon before, and which should be further clarified. At first sight, we can distinguish two forms of "necessity" which may be designated as "psychological" and "conceptional." The second form has been described: we saw that in terms of the basic conception of the story as a critique of systems, Lafcadio's act is precisely what it had to be. This necessity clashes with the theoretical freedom of an action that is supposedly the self-expression of a free being. But even in the relation between Lafcadio and his act—i.e., within the psychological sphere—this ironic vacillation between spontaneity and necessity is carried through. The crime, supposedly gratuitous, is paradoxically shown to be determined by Lafcadio's character, to flow from the playful richness of his nature. Gide wishes to establish that an unmotivated crime could be (had to be) committed by precisely such a man. (pp. 296-97)

[Psychological] motivation is not the only factor in the development. Among others, the symbolic theme of departure from a constrictively systematic civilization is primarily conceptional in significance. But it is fruitless to make a clear distinction between psychological and conceptional components, since all are inextricably intertwined and cleverly blended and balanced to prepare the final effect. Thus a schematic psychology and a schematic plot merge in an act that presents itself as a necessary *sequitur*. This is another way of saying that all elements are treated as literary themes. If we look at the work as a whole rather than in detail, it is this literary dimension which is primary. Both psychological and conceptional necessity are integrated into a third type of "necessity" which is *aesthetic* and which may be more appropriately designated as "coherence." This is not just one additional component, on the same level as the psychological and philosophical content, but the very form in which this content has to appear. This form determines its substance, since the fundamental dimension of the content is its place in the coherent aesthetic whole. . . . In other words, the novel is another system, and whatever I have said about the *Caves* must be qualified and reinterpreted in this light. The book remains a parody of inauthenticity, a critique of systematic coherence, but first and foremost it is a critique of the one system in which all the others are here embedded and by which they were shaped: the aesthetic system of the novel. Julius the author wants to write a novel which defies such coherence and presents a breakthrough of life and spontaneity. Clearly a paradoxical enterprise, which can only be carried out in the form of irony. This is what Gides does in the *Caves,* the auto-critical novel. It is a perfectly organized construct that paradoxically exalts the asystematic spontaneity of life—but in such a way as to ironically demonstrate the paradox. (pp. 297-99)

This holds true for the reality of the characters as well. The ontological fallacy is exemplified when literary criticism is too exclusively concerned with psychological analysis. The characters are mistakenly imagined to be "real" whenever aesthetic prehension is equated with psychological cognition. Gide's "failure" to make Lafcadio's psychology convincing may well be intentional. Between the author's intention to motivate his hero and the hero's lack of psychological credibility, there exists an ironic tension which reveals the basic artificiality of any invented character. More generally, we saw that Gide's characters refuse to create the illusion of vitality. A related question is that of the emotional involvement of the reader: it can be said that a character is "living" when he attracts our sympathy. But Gide refuses to trap our feelings, he deliberately keeps us at a distance. The interest which his characters arouse in the reader remains cerebral. (pp. 300-01)

Gide's cerebral *sotie,* which exposes the illusory nature of novelistic "life," can tell us more about the novel than just another specimen of that genre. It is a novel stripped down to its technical and formal elements, a parody of fiction, and Gide is "not a creator but a destroyer of fictional worlds." (pp. 302-03)

William W. Holdheim, "Gide's 'Caves du Vatican' and the Illusionism of the Novel," in MLN (© *copyright 1962 by The Johns Hopkins University Press), Vol. 77, No. 3, May, 1962, pp. 292-304.*

E. SAN JUAN, JR. (essay date 1965)

Gide imposes on the theatre the task of a radical transvaluation. He decries the contemporary trend of the French theatre as a trivial mimicry of social conventions. . . . What afflicts the theatre today, says Gide, is precisely its paltry realism. Hopelessly paralyzed in conforming to what is normal, the theatre ceases to be a moral force. (p. 220)

Gide declares that the theatre today has forfeited its old privilege of providing the audience ideal examples of character. The proper function of the theatre is to create exalted models of humanity. It must inspire men to draw out of themselves their own hidden personalities, to develop their own native resources. Consequently, Gide contends that there is a need to react against realism if we would restore to the theatre the role of challenging man to fulfill himself. . . .

Gide intends to restore to the theatre its original task. He identifies his main intentions with that of Greek drama;

hence, his theatre evolves from the tragedy of classical antiquity. From this view point, Gide elects two modes of accomplishing the rebirth of the theatre: first, he affirms the Greek conception of each man's uniqueness; secondly, pursuing the Greek conception of man, he advocates the adoption of certain theatrical conventions. . . .

Gide's theatre concerns itself with the search of the individual for self-fulfillment. He who is engaged in this search is the hero-protagonist. . . . One's desires, so long as they rule one's actions, are the only true gods. Despotic reason falsifies desires and misleads the individual. To follow one's desires is to realize one's virtues. What Christianity regards as qualities of the soul, e.g. courage, goodness, etc., are simply the natural properties of the body. . . .

To obey one's temperament is to realize one's true character. To Gide drama is fundamentally sustained by passion; and since passion stems from character, drama is nothing else but character. . . . Tragedy cannot live without the presence of exemplary characters. Character, in furnishing the initial motivation, makes dramatic action possible. (p. 221)

Gide asserts that the playwright, in order to regenerate the theatre, must people the stage with heroic characters. But today you cannot draw exemplary characters from actual life, for everyone wills his own slavery to society. One must then separate the drama from actual life and the episodic. . . .

The main objective of Gide in arguing for conventions is to create a gulf, a distance between the audience and the figures on the stage. In this connection, he endorses Racine's view that tragic characters must be regarded differently from the persons with whom one associates in real life. (p. 222)

Like meter in poetry, theatrical conventions are employed to create a system of expectation and fulfillment. Moreover, they establish an atmosphere of remoteness in time. Temporal distance enables the playwright, by exhibiting new forms of heroism, to defy the hypocrisy of custom and morals. In the context of the plays, heroism may be defined as the individual's struggle to discover his identity by following his own temperament. For this purpose Gide appropriates historical personages and mythical figures [some examples being the protagonists of *Saul, Oedipus,* and *Philoctetes.*] Actually this borrowing or adaptation is only a device for creating aesthetic distance. . . . Gide contends that the constraint offered by certain restrictions allows freedom to the artist to the extent that, within a limited field, he can explore the maximum of human potentialities. (p. 223)

Gide's theatre is then the theatre of the individual struggling to find his own identity. In this struggle he becomes heroic. . . . Gide's aesthetics invests his drama with a prophetic tone of address. As a "criticism of life," his drama evolves as a confrontation of the human condition. Insofar as it is a reaction against society, Gide's theatre is also a reading and criticism of our own milieu. Premised on a certain interpretation of life's meaning, his theatre contrives solutions to the major moral problems that beset the theatre today. On the whole, Gide conceived of the theatre as a medium for integrating the chaotic elements of modern consciousness. Few can refuse to heed the importance of Gide's attempts to define the essence of man in his plays.

Since Gide views the theatre as a moral agent, he adopts a subjective approach to the drama, an essentially objective literary form. Objective circumstances and characters are used to embody or symbolize the inner dialogue of opposing moral values: the sensual, dionysian, diabolic potencies of man against the abstract god of his conscience. As a creature of dialogue, Gide recognizes that only in the inner dialectic of fundamental extremes can one attain psychic balance or self-integration. (pp. 223-24)

In the context of Gide's plays, self-completeness implies the balance of thought and emotion, of Dionysian and Apollonian tendencies in human nature. It signifies moral and aesthetic sincerity based on the unity of the conscious and subconscious aspects in man, the fusion of sensual vitality and puritan restraint. . . . [The] Gidean hero is he who, in sustaining an inner conflict, surpasses himself and arrives at a stage of harmony which is truly—to use Nietzsche's phrase—"beyond good and evil." (p. 224)

> E. San Juan, Jr., "The Idea of André Gide's Theatre," in Educational Theatre Journal (© 1965 University College Theatre Association of the American Theatre Association), Vol. XVII, No. 3, October, 1965, pp. 220-24.

WALLACE FOWLIE (essay date 1965)

[Gide's first important book,] *Les Nourritures terrestres,* like every other work of Gide, represented an effort to know himself. But this self was constantly changing. Each book is a quest, and *Les Nourritures* stands at the beginning of Gide's career as a guidebook to the pattern of self-inquest. (p. 34)

[Gide] calls his book a manual of escape, the book of a sick man or of one who has just recovered from a long illness and who feverishly longs to live again and know all the excesses of living. But Gide reproves those who see in his book only a glorification of desire and instinct. He himself sees it as an apology for asceticism or renunciation, and he describes three stages the reader should pass through. The reading of the book, the first stage, should turn the reader back to himself, to a new interest in himself. After this intermediary stage of self-interest, the reader should reach the third stage of engrossment in everything else in the world, everything that is *not* the book and *not* himself.

There is perhaps no adequate term for the literary genre which *Les Nourritures terrestres* illustrates. It has some affinity with the prose poem, as developed by . . . Baudelaire in *Spleen de Paris,* and especially by Rimbaud in *Les Illuminations.* And yet Gide's book has none of the narrative quality of Baudelaire's prose poems, and none of the condensed powerful imagery of *Les Illuminations.*

Neither can it be called a journal in any strict sense, although passages in it are extremely reminiscent of the *feuilles de route* and the *feuillets détachés* which Gide includes in his *Journal.* It appears to be a journal, but it lacks the usual journal notations. It appears also to be a kind of *récit* or tale, annunciatory of the more formal tales such as *L'Immoraliste* and *La Porte étroite.* But it would be a *récit* without the most important element of a *récit,* namely, events and episodes. *Les Nourritures terrestres* has only commentaries on events and episodes. It is a life recalled by commentaries from which the story is deliberately concealed. The commentaries that make up this spiritual autobiography follow no logical plan or coherence. (pp. 34-5)

The book might be defined as the absence of its story, the comments on a story that is willfully effaced or which is never allowed to form. The term "novel" would, of course, be even less appropriate than *récit,* because of the lack of characters engaged in anything that resembles action. In addition to the narrator, the "I" of the book, two characters are named, Nathanaël and Ménalque, but their existence is denied by the author-narrator. The narrator even refuses to define himself in any recognizable way. He is invisible. He refuses to *be.* There is no term for the kind of fiction where the hero is always dissolving. Only the vaguest outline of the narrator is given, because he is continually changing and is very much in love with this mobility, with his multiplying and changing sensations. (pp. 35-6)

What the book expresses is a personal experience, or a series of personal experiences, that have no logical or sequential relationship with one another. It is the account of a soul in the presence of many things—landscapes, gardens, deserts. The soul is one, unified and continuous, but it absorbs, in its peregrinations, a profound lesson on the instability of things and states of feeling. The ideas and emotions of the book are always expressed in the present. We never see their genesis nor their ending. It is a book of travel, but no progress is described because there is no goal to be reached. The various scenes are unrelated. They serve to generate and exalt different emotions, but they do not advance toward any point. With each scene, the book begins all over again. The soul of the narrator is always impatient to have new scenes presented to it, and eager to obey new impulses. The unity of the work is almost indefinable. It is the soul of Gide, multiple and exacting, welling up in constantly new thoughts. The soul is also the stage of a drama where sensations are minutely described, provoked and liberated. In this one soul, the entire universe, inexhaustible and multifaceted, has to be reflected and apprehended. Ideas and emotions are equally gratuitous, all spontaneously generated. Whenever an event is about to come into focus, it is quickly abandoned so that the author can concentrate on the hundreds of movements and impulses which an event would create.

In the midst of such wealth of sensory indulgence, Gide is unable to choose. His book is about his incapacity to choose. His passion is impartiality. The words which recur the most frequently in his text seem to be *fervor, waiting, moments (ferveur, attentes, instants),* and especially *disponibilité* or the freedom to welcome every new sensation, every new experience. . . . Much of *Les Nourritures* explores a doctrine whereby all action and all attachment is considered evil and debilitating because it will turn us away from ourselves. All that is necessary is the knowledge that we are. At the beginning of the third section, Gide speaks tenderly of the word *volupté,* and describes it as synonymous with *being.* Fervor can survive only if it remains constant in an inconstant world or in a perpetual flux. Such themes as these continue throughout the work of Gide. (pp. 36-8)

An overfacile definition of *Les Nourritures terrestres* has tried to pass it off as poetry. But Gide is not a poet, not even in this, his most poetically written book, of which the beauty is essentially a beauty of syntax. The text, when examined closely, proves to be without metaphor. What counts most is the literal transcription of the sentiment aroused in the presence of the object. Gide is not a poet in *Les Nourritures;* he is infinitely closer to being what he is in his other books, part-novelist, part-moralist.

Yet he disguises to some degree his real literary function by his poetic style, in which adjectives often precede their nouns, pronouns are widely separated from their antecedents and their verb, and sentences tend to be unusually long and undulating. The words seem to obey the length and the rhythm of the sentence. And the sentences unfold slowly and uncertainly as if the gestures and the desires they describe are only tentative. This is because the story of *Les Nourritures terrestres* is not one of action, in the usual sense, but one of a soul which is unknowing of its movement until it has created it. The book narrates a personal experience, which turns out to be less a personal experience than a means for metamorphosis. The soul remains one, but it is constantly undergoing changes of form and desire. It is a soul of velleities, and the kind of sentence that Gide has elaborated in the book is that best suited to the expression of spiritual metamorphosis.

Notwithstanding this unusual verbal form of expression, *Les Nourritures terrestres* inaugurated Gide's principal vocation of moralist. The book is a combined essay on things and an essay on the author. It completed the first period of his career. The second period begins with *L'Immoraliste,* and the main difference between them is one of style. In the style of *Les Nourritures* the reader becomes aware of a sensual delight in the flow and articulation of the sentences. Their form, a voluptuary form, holds the attention of the reader. The style of the *récits,* beginning with *L'Immoraliste,* and continuing with the one novel, *Les Faux-Monnayeurs,* is more bare and severe, more devoid of ornamentation. The actual subject matter of *Les Nourritures* and *L'Immoraliste* is much the same, but Gide's style of writing has so changed that the two books appear very different from each other. The final sentence of *Les Nourritures* is a good example of the troubled searching rhythms of the book; it also contains the subject matter of *L'Immoraliste,* the principal preoccupation of its protagonist Michel. This is nothing less than a proposal for the quest of total individuality, for the development of that part of us that is different from every other man. (pp. 38-9)

[The language of] *Les Nourritures terrestres* appears to unfold according to some magical accident. It never betrays any premeditated intention. The author knows that he is speaking, but he does not always know what he is saying; or rather, he is lost in some kind of ignorance concerning the matter of which he is speaking. If he learns anything about his subject matter, he learns it at the moment he is uttering it. (p. 41)

This definition of *Les Nourritures* as a work of dictation rather than of deliberate creation may explain the effect it has had on its readers of a liberating force. . . . Both the experience and the form have an absoluteness which liberated the author and which liberates the reader. The very unpossessiveness of the narrator, his *disponibilité* and freedom to welcome all experience and states of feeling, promotes in the reader a habit of suppleness identical with the experiences described in the book itself. Gide tested himself on those experiences, and the reader tests himself on the exercises of the book. What is constant is the doctrine of inconstancy, which means sincerity or the hatreds of lying, vitality or the love of life in all its manifestations, liberty or freedom from dogmas and influences. The composition of the book is so delicate and pliable precisely because it has espoused its subject matter. The form has so become the experience, that the reader is led to a self-liberation. Of all Gide's books, *Les Nourritures terrestres* would seem best to exemplify the power of literature to create of itself an absolute existence, which in turn is able to liberate the reader from himself. (pp. 41-2)

The most exalted of Gide's books in its style and its individualism, *Les Nourritures* marks the point from which the subsequent books descend in a progressive simplification of style and personal exaltation. (p. 42)

It continues to be for the new readers of each generation one of the most upsetting of books. It is of such subtle ambiguity that it answers two needs, one for those readers who have a sense of order and will profit from a salutary upsetting of order, and another for those readers lost in a sense of disorder who can find in it a new order. It has the quality that prophetic books possess, of supplying whatever remedy is sought. On the one hand, it sings of energy and plenitude of character, of self-realization and self-fulfilment; and on the other hand, it sings of a submission to the inevitable in life. The two themes of fervor and poverty are somehow reconciled. Gide makes both words, *ferveur* and *dénuement,* equally luminous and seductive. (p. 43)

> *Wallace Fowlie, in his* André Gide: His Life and Art *(reprinted with permission of Macmillan Publishing Co., Inc.; copyright © 1965 by Wallace Fowlie), Macmillan, 1965, 217 p.*

GEORGES I. BRACHFELD (essay date 1965)

Though it may appear as an exercise in intellectual narcissism, *The Counterfeiters* was intended by its author to be a "pure" novel. The reader will search in vain in its pages for plots that have a beginning and an end, for characters who linger long enough to be liked or known, for plans and aspirations that reach fulfillment or failure through logical progression, for love that falls within recognizable patterns, for a universe in which both God and Satan, not the Prince of Shadows alone, vie for the soul of man. It was not the writer's intention to create that kind of logical, satisfying reality. It would have been easy, he mused in his *Journal,* "to get the approval of the majority by writing *Les Faux-Monnayeurs* in the accepted fashion of novels, describing persons and places, analyzing emotions, explaining situations, spreading out on the surface everything I hide between the lines, and protecting the reader's sloth!"

The complexity of this "pure" novel is further increased by Gide's contradictory desire, within a narrow framework of self-imposed strictures, to "pour everything into it without reservation." He wished to fill it with all his thoughts on matters ethical and aesthetic, to convey all his aspirations, social as well as personal, to transmute his frustrations into art, to leave nothing unsaid that he felt he still had to say, to repeat that which had not been sufficiently heard, as if this work were to be his last major pronouncement, "the only novel and final book" that he would write. (pp. 153-54)

All through his life, the author of *The Counterfeiters* pursued his quest for authenticity and inner harmony. He often stated this essential preoccupation, in words such as these: "The only drama that really interests me and that I should always be willing to depict anew, is the debate of the individual with whatever keeps him from being authentic, with whatever is opposed to his integrity, to his integration. Most often the obstacle is within him. And all the rest is merely accidental." In alluding to the conflict between authenticity and whatever stands in its way, Gide was not echoing the Pascalian view that man, because of his limited faculties, faintness of heart, self-love, and delusions, and in general because of his debased nature, is incapable of reaching truth, or even of wishing to attain it. On the contrary, Gide's attitude was optimistic. (p. 158)

[Gide] wondered about the relationship of cause to effect in man's actions and whether it is true, as La Rochefoucauld propounded in his *Maxims,* that the acts outwardly most disinterested reveal, on examination, self-interested motivations. Could man, by a supreme act of freedom, escape the laws of determinism? Is man capable of a disinterested act, nay, of a gratuitous action? Many readers of Gide's *Prometheus Ill-Bound* and *Lafcadio's Adventures* were deluded into believing that these books described unmotivated actions, pure effects without causes, not detecting the irony surrounding each of the gratuitous actions. Whether it is Zeus's diabolically planned gesture in the mythological work, or Lafcadio's senseless murder of Fleurissoire during a moment of boredom and dejection, the act gives rise to infinite consequences. It would then appear that the lack of causes is compensated by the multiplicity of effects. But a closer analysis discloses a motivation on the part of each protagonist: a desire for diabolical tampering with human destiny on the part of God's ironical counterpart or a rebellious assertion of freedom by a young man ostracized from the society he wished to enter. There are no gratuitous actions, and rare are the disinterested acts through which man sacrifices himself for others in a selfless assertion of his limited freedom.

Basic to Gide's interest in the hypothetical gratuitous action is also his preoccupation with the extent of man's freedom. In novels that may be construed in this context as moral experiments, he imparted an insatiable thirst for freedom into two heroes he created somewhat in his own image, Michel who resembles him closely, and Lafcadio whom he patterned after his idea of the young man he might have wished to be. Both fail piteously to achieve their goals. Through the destiny he foisted upon them, Gide verified the axiomatic truth that freedom is defined by its limitations. (pp. 160-61)

[It is] from the Gospels that Gide drew the guiding aphorism of his life, "For whosoever shall save his life shall lose it; but whosoever shall lose this life, the same shall find it." This apparent paradox becomes luminous when it is understood that the two lives in question are not the same, one being the life of the flesh on earth, the other the eternal life of the soul. In a secular context, as Gide saw it, one is the insincere life oriented toward the acquisition of immediate advantages, whereas the other is devoted to the pursuit of higher goals at the expense of quick rewards. In *The Counterfeiters,* Vincent, like the legendary Faust, surrendered his soul to Satan in exchange for material gains, or, in other words, wasted his life for the sake of material pleasures. This aphorism also applies on the aesthetic level, for, according to Gide, aesthetics is the ethics of the artist. What matters to the true artist is his enduring art—his soul—not an immediately successful, sensational work that bears within it the seeds of decay, such as that which Passavant was writing in the novel. Moreover, in an act of abnegation which is a supreme affirmation, the writer must, in the manner of the French classicists or of Gustave Flaubert, efface himself before his work. Whatever his endeavor, man achieves the highest manifestation of himself through that which transcends him, as the work of art transcends the artist. (pp. 162-63)

The writer in search of his authentic self transferred his preoccupation into the creatures of his fictional microcosm. At the

risk of oversimplification, they may be divided into two broad families of minds: the Gidian and the non-Gidian. Those are Gidian who seek their true nature, whose essential quality is sincerity, whose inescapable need is to "be" rather than to "appear." Non-Gidian are those who live a counterfeit life, who conform to conventional morality and religion, who strive to "appear" rather than to "be." Gide's ethic is based on a distinction, not between good and evil, but between authentic and false. Many may start, like Michel and Lafcadio, in the Apollonian path of enlightened search for freedom and authenticity, but they fail or abdicate because of a flaw in their critical sense or a weakness in their will. Rare are those who, like Bernard, achieve a Gidian integrity before the last word of the book permanently fixes their posture. Others, from the moment of their inception in the writer's mind, are doomed to Gidian reprobation, as they clothe their weaknesses or self-interest in a complacent hypocrisy, for none of these can bear to be openly insincere. Their need for moral sanction is Gide's own, with this difference: social acceptance suffices them, whereas, more exactingly, he seeks his own approval. Still others, in a more restricted group illustrated by Strouvilhou in the novel, dare to be openly insincere: they are the true amoralists in Gide's imaginary world. The sincere character must go counter to the accepted morality of a society whose structure is based on insincere values. He must oppose religious beliefs which lull the mind to questions unanswerable by reason alone. According to the beliefs he rejects, he then falls prey to the very symbol of rebellion, Satan. (pp. 163-64)

[The] pervading theme of [*The Counterfeiters*] is authenticity. As a young writer meditating on his art [Gide] had said: "The symbol is the thing around which a book is composed." The symbol at the center of this novel is the false coin. This false coin, however, appears only incidentally at the center of the novel and briefly thereafter. Obviously, the yellow glass token. . .is merely a pretext, in this case a pretext for symbolic variations on monetary themes. "Ideas of exchange, of depreciation, of inflation, etc., gradually invaded his book." Gide tells us of Edouard's unwritten *Counterfeiters.* In Gide's book, the symbol is webbed into a parable, a simple tale fraught with a universal moral lesson and affording broad interpretations. People and events in *The Counterfeiters* are exemplifications of this parable.

On the surface, *The Counterfeiters* appears as the retelling of Bernard's revolt against his family and eventual return to it. It is again the story of the Prodigal Son, with a significant twist. As in Homer's long epic, in which a crucial episode of Achilles' life is the core around which the poet recreates the society and events of a fabulous period, Bernard's simple tale of revolt and submission is placed within a context that gives it meaning and affords a critical view of French society shortly before World War I. Without pursuing an analogy to which Gide himself invited us by revealing his desire to give his novel an epic quality, let it be noted that in both works the depiction of individual fates suggests universal comments on man.

Whereas what we may call the parable of the False Coin proposes a key to the interpretation of the psychological content of the novel, the parable of the Prodigal Son. . .may then serve as a guide to its framework. Bernard's escape from the House opens this chronicle and his return closes it. He is the adolescent who breaks away from the security of his family home in search of self. (pp. 166-67)

The House, from which all adolescents yearn to escape, is presented as a vipers' nest of shame, hypocrisy, and conformity. All families in Gide's fiction are thus portrayed as harboring shameful secrets beneath the glossy surface of respectability. . . . The family is to Gide the major obstacle to the adolescent on his road to fulfillment.

The adolescent is the object of Gide's predilection. Opening his eyes in a first awareness of the world about him, the youth is yet uncommitted, free as he never again will be. Better yet if, like Bernard, he is a bastard and therefore, according to Gide's poetic license with logic, unmarked by the determinism of heredity; he may then realize all the potentialities of his being, unhampered by authority or convention, and launch his soul on an uncharted course. (pp. 167-68)

Beyond adolescence Gide believed that our choice has been made, our postures have become fixed. We repeat the gesture that we first made sincerely, even when it has lost its meaning; we perpetuate a lie, in faithfulness to a credo once held, and because this is the way that others see us. We dare not disrupt this resemblance to ourselves. Edouard's attempt at avoiding this straitjacket in a vain clinging to adolescence is but another fixed posture. The dilemma of choice may be resolved, however, as Bernard's example purports to show. From the child to the adolescent to the young adult André Gide thus presents in his novel a study of the individual's personal evolution.

Moving on to the next generation, he focuses his gaze on the couple. There, all attitudes appear as frozen, and life together continues at two different levels, appearance and reality. This dichotomy is inescapable: love itself, which may have presided over the original union, is founded on a sort of lie. Gide endorsed Stendhal's profound analysis of the process of crystallization, whereby we endow the loved one with the gifts and qualities for which we love him. In simpler terms, love is founded on an illusion, and it is a near constant of Gide's fiction that women are the victims, men the objects, of this illusion. . . . When the veils are withdrawn, and reality gradually replaces illusion, a reverse process takes place, that of decrystallization. Faced with an unbearable reality, the wife may reject the sham, as Madame Profitendieu did only too briefly, or organize the family life around it. Life then becomes a succession of hypocritical acts. This is the life not only of the Profitendieus, but also of the Moliniers and of the old couple La Pérouse. (p. 169)

According to Gide himself, the multiplicity of principal characters in *The Counterfeiters* caused him great difficulty in its composition. It presents a like obstacle to a summarization of its plot. Indeed, each of the more than twenty highly individualized personae, endowed with a singular destiny, generates his own plot. All being Gidian creatures, their fates conform, however, to the same general movement: they are swept by a centrifugal force which projects them away from their homes or from themselves. Escape from home characterizes revolt; separation from self is a sign of submission achieved through a compromise between what one is and what one pretends to be. The only hero who submits without self-distortion is Bernard. This is why Bernard's progress through the events of this novel, proposing a positive lesson, imposes itself as one of its main plots. Another character eludes classification, as he seems to transcend any reduction to the norm: Edouard. But Edouard, in spite of his lucidity and of his efforts to do so, does not escape the stigma of

inauthenticity. It appears in his case that blindness to reality is a cause, rather than a consequence, of his hypocrisy. Thus, although his stated objective for the novel he proposes to write is to show the struggle between reality and what the novelist strives to make of it, he is unable to assimilate any rash intrusion of the real event into his fictional construction. . . . His hypocrisy, to be sure, manifests itself at an aesthetic level, as he shirks the uncompromising honesty that he professes. It is true also that, at times, he experiences the difficulty of "being," especially under the impudently pragmatic look of Bernard. What distinguishes Edouard is his awareness of sham and his effort to denounce and overcome it. He too is subject to the centrifugal force that sweeps the other characters, but, in a paradoxical way, he maintains himself in a constant state of self-dispersion, a state of tension between the limits of his being. . . . Edouard does not realize that the novel he envisions is impossible of writing, whereas Gide, ironically aware of it, writes the story of Edouard's failure. That is the second main plot of *The Counterfeiters*. Whereas the plot generated by Bernard centers on ethical questions, the core of Edouard's plot is in the aesthetic domain. The two intertwine like point and counterpoint in a Bach fugue.

The ethical and the aesthetic questions, content and form, reality and its fictional projection, are variations on the same theme: Gide's quest for authenticity in his art, his effort to write a "pure" novel. Of this effort, he made one of the main subjects of his novel. Wary of absolutes, he created a protagonist imbued with his own extreme aspirations and, as in all previous similar cases in his fiction, doomed him to failure. Gide stands in relation to Edouard like an artist painting his self-portrait. (pp. 173-74)

A fundamental decision that the novelist made bears on his relationship to his characters. Would he, like Stendhal or Balzac before him, and most other novelists, adopt the omniscient, omnipotent attitude implicit in a third-person relation?. . .Gide decided on a compromise. He used the third person, but with self-imposed limitations: rather than reading his characters' minds, he surmises what they are thinking and at times interprets their words and actions, in a constant dialogue with the reader. He wishes to give the impression that each character, acting according to his own nature, independently as it were, is observed rather than determined by his creator. He is most often overheard and his words repeated by the novelist, which explains the length and multiplicity of the dialogues. . . . It is as though Gide invited his readers to observe with him the comportment of his characters, addressing us directly in an occasional first person as he comments on it, and remaining somewhat detached, rejecting any complicity in their misdeeds. (pp. 174-75)

The characters are known by their deeds and words, as if they were on a stage and we the spectators. What A says to B, or of B, is revealing of both A and B. The truth about a character is at the point of convergence of several viewpoints, including the author's and the reader's. Likewise, events grow in significance, or reality, as they are retold by different speakers. (p. 175)

Gide solved the dilemma of the novelist baffled by the elusiveness of reality by presenting reality as an elusive thing which conforms, as it were, to the idiosyncrasies of the beholder. . . . For Gide, ideas, not people, are endowed with integral reality. It is as if ideas first imposed their existence on his mind, and then sought manifestation through characters. Or it may be said that the characters in his novel appeared to him first as embodiments of ideas. Thus, at the origin, there were not characters imposing their personalities, or events their necessity, but artistic and moral concepts seeking expression. . . . Thus Gide constructed what Edouard calls "a novel of ideas." (p. 176)

Gide knew, however, that what distinguished a "novel of ideas" from a "thesis novel" is that in the former ideas are manifested through characters. Ideas have reality, characters lend them life. If characters are not to remain allegorical figures, they must be given a convincing context: a place in society, a past and a family, friends and preoccupations, all the complex fabric of life. (pp. 176-77)

After breathing an idea into each of his characters, placing them in a lifelike context and at a given time and place, Gide endowed them with free will. Their freedom of choice places the responsibility for their acts on them, not on the author, so he would have us believe. He merely observes them as they follow their tortuous paths. (p. 178)

Most characters in the novel are only glimpsed, as the novelist briefly focuses his light upon them, and then they disappear, often without a trace. Even a highly individualized hero like Armand projects his distorted shadow only momentarily against the troubled background and then is withdrawn from the reader's gaze. Likewise, embryos of possible plots appear briefly and vanish into oblivion. . . . That is the image of life, which does not resemble the traditional novelist's neat constructions. Similarly, in this novel which pretends not to improve on life, many events simply fail to occur: an instant sooner, Olivier would have found Edouard, and their destinies would have changed. Words not spoken, as between Olivier and Edouard, gestures not made, as when Olivier failed to open the door behind which Laura was weeping, determine our fates as much as positive actions. It seems that it is Olivier especially who thus misses his destiny. In Gide's novel, as in life, cards were dealt out wrongly. But it is Gide who, deliberately, mixed the cards. (p. 179)

In writing *The Counterfeiters*, André Gide performed a masterful act of self-restraint. Through its wealth of ideas, characters, and events, the attentive reader becomes aware of what has been left unformulated and unfinished, and he accepts the author's invitation to fill in the silences and prolong the events, as if he had witnessed life itself. Edouard, Gide's ambiguous projection into the novel, raises questions to which Gide's book is an answer. Is that answer satisfying? The student of literature finds in it a subtle and dramatic analysis of the process of literary creation. To the moralist, beyond the depiction of moral decay, it proposes the luminous example of Bernard, the undaunted young man to whom the future belongs. By his quality of reserve, the universality of the questions raised, and his concern with man, André Gide rejoins the classical tradition of seventeenth-century France. *The Counterfeiters* is one of those books that raise essential questions for each generation of readers, the answer to which is in themselves. (pp. 180-81)

Georges I. Brachfeld, "Gide/'The Counterfeiters':
The Novel of Ideas," in Approaches to the Twen-
tieth-Century Novel, *edited by John Unterecker*
(copyright © 1965 by Harper & Row, Publishers,
Inc.; reprinted by permission of Harper & Row,
Publishers, Inc.), Crowell, 1965, pp. 153-81.

J. C. DAVIES (essay date 1968)

[Examined together, *L'Immoraliste* and *La Porte étroite*] provide an excellent introduction to the work of Gide. They are entirely representative of the most interesting period of his evolution—that which covers the first twenty years of his literary career, a period marked by the most intense conflict between opposing tendencies in his nature. This conflict gives to the creative works of Gide's youth and early maturity the tension of an inner *angoisse* which largely disappears from the later works. We feel that Gide at this period is driven by an inner compulsion to write, that his books are the necessary, though bitter, expression of personal suffering and anguish. . . . Gide, at this time, is torn between two violently opposing ideals—a tortured quest for God, amid a background of puritanical restraint and inhibition, on the one hand, and a frenzied lust for life and freedom on the other. *L'Immoraliste* and *La Porte étroite,* taken together and duly compared, present a more or less faithful image of the opposing forces at war in the mind of Gide at this troubled period of his life. (pp. 7-8)

In *L'Immoraliste,* the author took as his starting point the assumption that the end of man was, in fact, man, and showed the hero's attempt to discover his true personality and realise to the full his hidden potentialities. . . . But that man may increase, God must decrease, and *L'Immoraliste,* in three highly significant and symbolic episodes, shows the rejection of religion and a dependence on man alone. . . . *La Porte étroite* postulates the opposite point of view, assuming the all-powerfulness of God and the insignificance of Man. Alissa sacrifices man's claims to happiness in this world to a longed-for communion with God in the next world and places her whole trust in religion. (p. 8)

It is significant that both Michel and Alissa fail in their respective quests. Michel destroys both his wife and his own happiness. Alissa breaks her cousin's heart, and brings about her own death. This occurs because of the *excess* to which both protagonists carry their ideal, so that it becomes a dangerous obsession, almost a temporary insanity. . . . Both are hopeless romantics yearning for the unattainable, but at the same time dangerous fanatics who are to serve as a warning. . . . [Gide's] intention was to show that an excess of virtue or saintliness could be no less ruinous than an excess of independence and self-development. From this point of view, *L'Immoraliste* and *La Porte étroite* could be said to represent opposing swings of the same pendulum, the movement in one direction finding its counterpart, and its justification, in a corresponding movement to the other extreme.

Gide has continually stressed the fact that these books are in effect "des livres ironiques." . . . Not the least of these ironies is his attribution of typically human failings to these fanatics enamoured of the *inhumain.* They refuse the possibility of conventional human happiness, yet they remain attached, in spite of themselves, to a human being whom they love, and it is this attachment which is one of the reasons, if not the principal reason, for the failure of their quest. Alissa loves Jérôme, Michel loves Marceline, and a violent conflict is set up between their impossible ideal and an ordinary human being's need for love. The superhuman heroes become frail, ordinary mortals like ourselves. The purity of their ideal is further compromised by the mixed motives which the author assigns to them, not directly or explicitly, but by means of subtle hints and suggestions. Michel is engaged in a disinterested quest for self-realisation and self-understanding, but, beneath the surface, there is many a hint to suggest that egotism and the selfish pursuit of pleasure are equally strong incentives. The sublimity of Alissa's quest for God is similarly compromised by suspicions of an inordinate pride finding expression in self-sacrifice, and by suggestions even of a contrary motive—a basic fear of life, arising from strong sexual inhibitions, which causes her to seek refuge in God. The purity of the original ideal is thus diluted, but we can at least warm to Alissa and Michel as human beings. (pp. 8-10)

The supreme originality of Gide's early *récits* lies in their combination of intimate personal experience with a technique that strove to exclude entirely the presence of the author. . . . Gide's view is essentially that of the classical artist, whose aim is to present characters in action, who reveal themselves sufficiently by what they say or do, without any need for the author to intervene and explain motives or draw conclusions. (pp. 18-19)

Nowhere is Gide's objectivity more conspicuous than in *L'Immoraliste* and *La Porte étroite,* where the author deliberately refrains from passing any judgment on his chief characters and invites the reader's active collaboration in forming his own opinion from the events related. (p. 19)

The most striking way in which Gide achieves objectivity in his *récits* is by his use of the first-person narrator device. At first glance, it may seem something of a paradox that the use of the first person should achieve such an aim, but it will be seen that it is a borrowed first-person, and not Gide speaking in his own name. . . . No comments or explanations are provided by the author, who, as far as the reader is concerned, simply does not exist. He stands aside and effaces himself completely behind his narrator, who is also the hero, or one of the chief characters, of the *récit.* This character at once takes on an apparent authenticity, a third-dimensional quality which gives the story greater realism. At the same time, an illusion of greater intimacy is achieved, as a result of the direct *rapprochement* which is established between the narrator and the reader.

Here then, is an extremely economical, and subtle device for portraying the character of a fictional hero, and one which always proved tempting to Gide: to let the hero reveal his character *directly* by his narration of events which have had a decisive influence on the course of his life. Thus Michel's forthright, callous nature is revealed by his account of the tragic events of his marriage. The passive, spineless and highly suggestible character of Jérôme emerges clearly from his narration of the events that lead to Alissa's self-sacrifice and death. In *La Porte étroite,* however, the technique is more complex, for we have here really two complementary *récits* and two narrators—Jérôme's version of the story, and Alissa's version of a part of it, as recorded in her Diary. Illuminating flashes of light pass from one version to the other to reveal, and to expose inconsistencies in, the characters both of Jérôme and Alissa. (pp. 25-6)

It is above all the inconsistencies in his characters, and their unconscious distortion of the events, that Gide is eager to reveal by his use of the first person narrator device. . . . It is very important to note this fact for the two *récits* we are considering. The three narrators involved in the stories are all suffering from delusions about themselves, and these delusions inevitably affect, and even distort, each person's account of the events. It is for us to *rétablir,* with the aid of the scraps of evidence which Gide disperses throughout the *récits.*

We can, in addition, sense in the narratives of both Michel and Jérôme a subconscious desire for self-justification, a wish to prove to themselves, and to others, that they were right in acting as they did. Subtly, Gide has made it appear that one of their chief motives in undertaking the narration lies in this uncertainty about themselves, in this eagerness to *convince.* . . . It is for this reason that both narrators emphasise the factual accuracy of their account. Because they seek to draw their own justification from the *récit,* they are careful to insist that they are simply setting down the events as they occurred, without any falsification or any attempt to deck them out in the garb of art. . . . (pp. 26-7)

What, now, is the essential nature of [the] blindness, or self-delusion, that Gide imposes on each of his narrators? In each case, it resolves itself into that basic conflict which was so constant a preoccupation in Gide's work—between . . . the real self and the mask, between true motives, which often lie hidden in the sub-conscious, and apparent ones, which we deceive ourselves into regarding as real, and which make unconscious hypocrites of us all. . . .

One of Gide's chief preoccupations, in composing the two stories, was to keep his narrators at least partly deluded about their motives for action, so that, in the course of the narrative, they tend to incriminate themselves by what they either say or do. The attentive reader is thus invited to read between the lines and attempt to distinguish true motives from false. (p. 28)

The technique of the deluded narrator, as Gide understood it, inevitably led to a widespread use of irony in the *récit.* Since the author had deliberately absented himself from the narrative, and since the narrator was himself labouring under delusions about his role in the story or as regards the effectiveness of his actions, the sole method of enlightening the reader was precisely by the use of such a device. And Gide, throughout both stories, has made a most subtle use of irony. . . . [For example,] Jérôme's delusion, towards the end of the story, was that it was his effort alone which had been responsible for elevating Alissa to such dizzy heights of virtue. A close reading of Alissa's diary, however, makes it clear that the greatest efforts to attain virtue were made by Alissa herself and that these efforts were often accompanied by the most heartbreaking inner conflict. On the contrary, it was *she* who had urged on *Jérôme* towards virtue, as we see from the diary. . . . The irony, in this instance, clearly arises from the juxtaposition, within the same text, of two completely contrasting interpretations—one nullifies, and cancels out, the other; the second destroys the first by its implications, and much more subtly and effectively by bare statement than by lines of detailed analysis or explanation on the part of the author. (pp. 31-2)

Both works are stories of an ambitious quest which ends in failure, and related by narrators who deceive themselves about their motives for action or their responsibility for this failure. Both Michel and Alissa, though disillusioned, still believe in the validity, and even the nobility, of their mission, and it is the role of irony to destroy these illusions for the discerning reader. By reading the story carefully, the latter is thus enabled to substitute true motives for false, and to come to his own conclusions about the success, or failure, of each quest. This is achieved by the ironic juxtaposition of contrasting motives (as seen in the example above), by conflict between stated intentions and the actual events which transpire, or by ironic parallels which are set up between two similar sets of happenings. Nowhere does the author intervene with any comments, and the narrator himself is not conscious of the irony, but the facts related speak eloquently for themselves. (p. 32)

The technique of the first-person narrator implies, on the part of the author, some effort to reveal the character of the hero not only by what he says but also by his manner of saying it—in other words, the style is to be a revelation of the character himself, in the same way as it is normally a revelation of the author. For a writer with an ardent desire for objectivity, here is yet another way in which he may achieve the illusion of detachment and present his fictional world as a completely independent creation, existing in its own right. . . . Gide, in both *L'Immoraliste* and *La Porte étroite*, has sought to adapt his style to that of the narrator. . . . (p. 40)

The question of style, in a story involving the 'first-person narrator' technique, poses difficult problems for a novelist who is anxious both to preserve a classical detachment from his characters and at the same time to safeguard the artistic value of his work. The two are not necessarily compatible, unless the hero-narrator happens also to be a talented literary artist capable of imparting real stylistic and dramatic qualities to his *récit*, which is not the case with either Michel or Jérôme. . . . [Gide solved this problem by adopting] a style which respects, in its broad outlines, the character of the narrator, but which will constantly vary and fluctatute to harmonise with the lyrical and dramatic movement of the *récit*. (pp. 41-2)

In *L'Immoraliste*, then, let us not expect a style which will reproduce exactly the voice of Michel. If we demanded strict authenticity, we might ask Gide how it is that an archaeologist without especial literary pretensions, however brilliant he might be, could relate his story in a style so rich in literary merit, so full of excellent lyrical and dramatic qualities and containing such a wealth of suggestive images. (p. 43)

While resorting to a style which, in its essentials, is true to Michel's character and even, in general, to the mood of desolation and distress in which we find him, Gide has acknowledged the inability of the narrator to express adequately the great lyrical and dramatic moments of the story, and it is then that Gide, the great writer and stylist, has visibly taken over the narrative himself. Thus, there is, in *L'Immoraliste*, not one, but several styles, each corresponding to the ebb and flow of the varying moods of the story—in turn concise, brief and terse, even to the point of cruelty, yet eloquent, lyrical and dramatic at the great moments of climax. (pp. 43-4)

Much of Michel's story is told in the terse, clipped, uncompromising style of a man who, like many scholars, is not given to verbiage, one whose language is as precise as his thought. Such a tone is at the same time appropriate to the general mood of disillusionment and apathetic indifference in which we find Michel at the beginning of the story. Here is a man for whom life has lost all its lustre, and who, in spite of the compulsive urge he feels to tell his story, is in no mood for eloquence or artistic embroidery. . . .

But, at other times, usually at the great climactic points of the story, the style develops a passionate intensity, a lyrical movement, which, while hardly appropriate to the broken-spirited, apathetic figure who is now telling his story, nevertheless remains, in spirit, true to the feelings which Michel must have experienced at the time of his profound reawakening to life. (p. 44)

La Porte étroite has very little of the variety and richness of style which is to be found in *L'Immoraliste*. . . . [In] *La Porte étroite*, the comparative bareness of expression is largely due to a conscious effort on the part of Gide to place himself "within the skin" of the narrator and to render faithfully the character of Jérôme by a deliberately flat, and somewhat colourless style. Thus Gide's attempt at greater realism in *La Porte étroite* leads inevitably to a sacrifice in artistic effect, and from the rich multiplicity of styles characteristic of *L'Immoraliste*, we are reduced to the more sober unity of a single style—or rather, of two styles, that of Jérôme and that of Alissa. Gide has, indeed, been very careful to distinguish between the widely differing styles of Jérôme and Alissa, and we can only concur in his own personal view that the real artistic success of the book is to be found in the language of Alissa's letters and diary. Simple, unadorned, natural and, at times, profoundly moving in its simplicity, the style of Alissa provides a striking contrast to the more mediocre and uninspiring narrative of Jérôme. (p. 49)

Jérôme's style is, indeed, a faithful reflection of his character—at times, flat, lifeless and banal, at other times, pretentious, artificial, affected and slightly unctuous. Devoid of real literary talent and well aware himself of what he describes as "mon médiocre lyrisme" . . . , he is quite adequate to the task of narrator so long as he remains within his limits, but let him venture beyond these limits into the realms of creative style or metaphor, and the effect is nearly always *manqué*, if not disastrous. (pp. 49-50)

Gide's constant fidelity, in the style of *La Porte étroite*, to the character of the narrator, constituted a remarkable *tour de force*. . . . At the same time, the highly complex technique of the book, with its alternating succession of *récit*, letters and diary, enabled him to avoid the ever-present danger of monotony inherent in a technique of presentation from a single point of view. (p. 50)

Gide, even in his more complex works of fiction, like *Les Caves du Vatican* and *Les Faux-Monnayeurs*, is no creator of memorable and fully rounded living characters. This is still more apparent in works of narrower dimensions, such as the *récits*. In *L'Immoraliste*, in particular, the minor characters exist purely in terms of their functional purpose, which is to serve as stimuli for setting in motion the psychological reactions of Michel. They have little more than a symbolic value, reflecting the successive states of mind of the hero, and, as they take their place in the ever changing but symmetrical patterns of the work, they become themselves an integral part of these patterns. (pp. 63-4)

These characters, however, are but the accessories to the drama. The true measure of Gide's success must ultimately depend on his treatment of the chief protagonists of the two *récits*. And, to judge this, we must adopt different criteria from those which we usually apply to the criticism of characters in a novel. Let us not, then, expect, as in Balzac or Dickens, the creation of powerfully drawn and fully rounded characters, which as a result of their intensely living qualities, reach out from the particular to the universal and become "types". Gide does not belong to that class of novelists whose methods are founded primarily on a close observation of life around them. . . . Gide's basic starting point is from within himself—a feeling, emotion or idea which takes hold of his mind and seeks expression in the work of art. . . . The physical appearance of his heroes thus becomes irrelevant, for it is the original idea or emotion which counts, and even the addition to the character of other psychological traits can be considered an unnecessary complication of the issue. The result is a reduction to essentials and an idealisation or stylisation of the main characters of the *récit*. They each represent an idea—even an *idée fixe*, which so dominates their nature that they leave the bounds of everyday life and enter a rarefied world of their own. Michel and Alissa have very little link with the general run of humanity, with the external world so faithfully, if laboriously, constructed by the *romanciers naturalistes*.

They have a closer link with the world of the theatre, especially tragedy. We think of each of them not so much as a physical presence, but as a mind in the throes of a violent conflict. Like the great figures of tragedy, Phèdre for example, their lives are dominated by a single obsession, which, coming into conflict with natural human emotions, gradually poisons their minds and brings about their eventual downfall. And it is precisely through the dramatic portrayal of a mind in conflict that these characters, in other respects so removed from normal life, re-enter the living world of human beings. . . . As a result, the portrayal of the inner struggle in Michel and in Alissa takes on an intensity which is deeply moving. The conflict, in Michel, between the "old man" and the new, between the quest for individualism and love for Marceline, leads to anguished self-questionings and vacillations which carry all the conviction of a real-life struggle. The case of Alissa is even more poignant, as she struggles to assume, before Jérôme, a mask of impassive indifference, while, within, her mind is torn by a cruel conflict between her ideal and her overwhelming love for her cousin. Alissa's diary, as the tragic record of a human heart at variance with itself, represents, indeed, a living document almost without parallel in the history of modern French literature.

These characters, then, though idealised, remain true. Their inner contradictions, their inconsistencies, and their repressions, are those of real human beings, and bestow on Michel and Alissa a psychological truth which richly compensates for their lack of physical presence. (pp. 67-9)

> *J. C. Davies, in his* Gide: "L'immoraliste" *and* "La porte étroite" *(© J. C. Davies 1968), Edward Arnold, 1968, 80 p.*

DONALD WILSON (essay date 1971)

The real subject of [*La Symphonie pastorale*] is indeed the way in which a man's vision of himself and of reality is transformed and distorted, unknown to him, by his emotions. For Gide is more interested in the Pastor than in Gertrude. Making him tell her story is but an ingenious way of getting him to reveal his own. He is the real protagonist of *La Symphonie pastorale*. (p. 19)

Gide's main purpose in having the story told by one of the characters involved in it is not to give a greater impression of reality. It is rather that uncommitted to a single moral attitude he seeks to avoid imposing his own vision on the story—indeed he probably feels incapable of doing so. He therefore makes of his narrator someone whose point of view

is relative, even prejudiced, and recognised as such by the reader. Paradoxically the result of this is that the narrative point of view is neutralised. The author's presence is not felt, while the attitudes of the narrator are viewed by the reader with mistrust. (p. 20)

The Pastor, who slowly falls in love with the blind girl he has taken into his charge on a charitable impulse cannot see what is happening to him. . . . Outwardly he writes to illuminate the past, but subconsciously he is aware of how uncomfortable the truth would be for him if recognised. His deeper motive thus becomes to conceal the truth from himself. What begins as an effort of discovery turns into self-apology, an attempt to prove the innocence of his relations with Gertrude by portraying them as purely 'charitable', based on the Christian virtues of pity and love, even directly inspired by God.

It is particularly important to note that the first *cahier* of the Pastor's diary is a *retrospective* account of the adoption and education of Gertrude. . . . The second *cahier*, on the other hand, comprises the day-to-day record by the Pastor of his attempts to justify in moral and religious terms behaviour which normally he would reprove in another person. It tells finally of the tragic consequences to Gertrude and to himself of the Pastor's moral egoism. The self-deception is of a somewhat different quality from the first *cahier*. The intellectual dishonesty, the 'bad faith' of the Pastor is much more antipathetic than his earlier failure to achieve self-knowledge. Whereas he had been concerned to persuade himself only that he did not have feelings incompatible with his religious and moral tenets, now, having been obliged to recognise that he, a married man, father of a family, a Calvinist minister, is passionately in love with his blind protégée, he must persuade himself that such feelings are not inconsistent with his place in life. To do so he completely transforms the meaning of the Gospel until it becomes a justification for love under whatever form or in whatever circumstances. It is no longer a question of projecting a particular light on events, but of transfiguring beliefs and values. (pp. 24-5)

It is the heart which the Pastor obeys in all things. Any attempt at self-control by reason or by will is rejected; he blinds himself to true reality both within and without.

The central irony of *La Symphonie pastorale* is thus that the Pastor, like Gertrude, is blind, though in a moral as opposed to a physical sense. (p. 26)

Corresponding to this theme of 'blindness' is the image of darkness and night, used to underline the ironic parallel between Gertrude and the Pastor, since it can be used to describe both her condition at the outset, and the despair which is his in the end. There is of course nothing very original in using the image of darkness to describe either blindness or despair, as Gide well knew. Indeed, he chose it as one of the most common New Testament symbols, one which would come naturally to the pen of the Pastor. His art consists in the ironic meaning he gives to his commonplace image as it is used by the Pastor, who throughout remains unaware of its ambiguity. (pp. 26-7)

La Symphonie pastorale is more the portrait of a man than a story, a portrait which is painted by the man himself wishing to create a certain image of himself but by his style, by the texture of his brushstrokes, creating a truer picture. Gide's task was not to describe the Pastor's personality, but to create him, to make him speak, and to make his personality emerge from what he said and how he said it. (p. 28)

Gide gives the Pastor a style which is often stilted, rhetorical, self-righteous, that of a habitual preacher. It is not Gide's style, but one created to suit this fictional personality. And yet, thanks to the suppressed characteristics of the man, this style often achieves extreme beauty, particularly in its imagery. (pp. 28-9)

If to begin with the Pastor sets out to explore the truth, he soon becomes conscious that the truth is too uncomfortable for him, so that his journal becomes more an attempt to cover it up than to reveal it. The heavy conscientiousness with which he tells his tale contrasts ironically with the fundamental error underlying the narrative: his failure to recognise the development of his feelings for Gertrude. (pp. 29-30)

Even more fundamental to the structure of the *récit* is the irony which opposes a certain degree of moral lucidity in the blind Gertrude to the moral blindness of the sighted Pastor. . . . Basically Gertrude is better endowed with wisdom and moral sense than the Pastor, her teacher and mentor. She possesses the moral firmness and strength which he lacks and with which—more serious—he fails to credit her. (p. 31)

[As] the Pastor's 'blindness' grows, so does Gerturde's lucidity. The first time she speaks of the love existing between them she is quite unconscious of the implications of her words. . . . [It] is not until the recovery of her sight that Gertrude becomes truly aware in concrete terms of the meaning of sin. Until then she accepts passively the Pastor's arguments. Yet even at the very end of the book, after Gertrude's attempted suicide, the Pastor remains more blind than she to human realities. . . . (pp. 31-2)

If the Pastor would almost prefer to maintain Gertrude's happiness even at the cost of her continued blindness, physical as well as moral, Gertrude herself prefers lucidity, the acceptance of reality with all its imperfections, to a happiness based on ignorance, on innocence, on the accident of blindness. . . . (p. 32)

It is quite possible to find the Pastor's self-deception credible. The emergence of an adulterous love between a middle-aged Protestant pastor and a blind girl young enough to be his daughter is so unexpected, so unthinkable, that he himself fails for a considerable time to comprehend the precise nature of his feelings towards her. Drawn to her first by pity and by charity he falls victim to a passion which unfolds with her development into a real person. To him this passion is hardly distinguishable from his joy in what is virtually his own creation of a human being.

This failure to recognise the new nature of his emotions is helped by the ambiguity of the word 'amour', used to express the Christian ideal of charitable love (agape) and also the pagan ideal of physical passion (eros). Imperceptibly to the Pastor, perceptibly to the reader, he begins by using the word in its first sense, then with its precise meaning blurred, and finally in the second sense. At times he himself is made uncomfortable by this unconscious ruse, though never does he explore the reasons for his uneasiness. (pp. 32-3)

But the irony in the portrayal of the Pastor's love for Gertrude is not only that it is shown to be a 'romantic' rather than a 'charitable' love, but that it also emerges from the Pastor's narrative that despite his professions of charity he exercises this virtue in a most selective manner. The education of

Gertrude does indeed demand an effort of love and patience, but this contrasts all the more strongly with his failure of love, of patience and of understanding where his wife and children are concerned. The Pastor's charity is hence put in question because it is selective, because he excludes from it anyone who does not conform to his own wishes and desires. (p. 36)

When we get to know the Pastor better we realise that rarely if ever does he base his behaviour on Christian precept, but that on the contrary he changes his own concept of Christian morality to fit in with his own impulsive behaviour. . . . As he explores the past the Pastor thus grasps at every detail which might help to reassure and justify himself. But precisely because he relies on an external authority in this way, because he finds the justification for his acts outside the acts themselves, our suspicions are aroused.

Gide is careful to stress how *mechanically* the Pastor makes use of the Gospel as a systematic justification of himself whatever the circumstances—something particularly ironic in a man who insists on the spirit rather than the letter of Christianity. (p. 39)

It would of course be wrong to assume, however, that the Pastor does not himself believe in his justifications, in his divine mission. . . . Here indeed is for Gide the great danger of insincerity and self-deception inherent in the puritan type of mind—the ability to believe an urge, often selfish or egoistic, to be sent from God when it is just as likely to come from the Devil.

Religion thus becomes for the Pastor little more than a bastion against the discomforts of self-examination, a refuge from the claims his family puts on him, and a justification for his passion. (pp. 40-1)

The final tragedy is a cruel one for [the Pastor] and we pity him when he sees himself rejected by Gertrude. . . . Guilty in one sense, the Pastor is less responsible in the sense that none of his errors are entirely witting. But he is nevertheless deeply guilty. This guilt does not so much consist for Gide in his illicit love—Gide had too little sympathy with conventional morality to condemn him on such grounds. His fault is first of all a failure towards Gertrude: he seems to take advantage of her innocence to supplant her own vision of reality with his, and for Gide nothing was more sacrosanct than the integrity of the individual vision. In the second place the Pastor's fault is that he fails to make even his own vision a completely lucid and true one. He fails to confront reality and to come to terms with it, resorting to self-deception and insincerity, however unwitting. This constitutes the real object of the irony of *La Symphonie pastorale*. . . . [The Pastor] is guilty, but in the end it is himself he destroys together with Gertrude, and he seems in spite of all his unattractive characteristics as worthy of pity as she. (pp. 42-3)

Donald Wilson, in his A Critical Commentary on André Gide's "La Symphonie pastorale" *(© Donald Wilson 1971; reprinted by permission of Macmillan, London and Basingstoke), Macmillan, 1971, 85 p.*

KARIN NORDENHAUG CIHOLAS (essay date 1974)

One of the main themes expressed by the incidents in [*Les Faux-Monnayeurs*] is the critical development of the young and their desire to escape. (p. 50)

For the young people of the novel the theme can be stated as follows: Youth seeks to break the chains which imprison it under the authority of a past establishment, but once the chains are broken they are perplexed with the prospect of their own freedom, their dependence upon others to maintain it, and its consequences. They search for an ideal to follow and most often find that they have gone astray only to be able to return to the fold. Hence one of the central themes of the story expressed by the actual outcome of the incidents is resignation and acceptance. The young have experienced their moment of rebellion and are forced by circumstances beyond their immediate control to adopt a basic attitude toward life.

Among the middle-aged in the novel the central theme of resignation is continued. Albéric Profitendieu [for example] is resigned to his rôle in life, to his wife's momentary infidelity, even to accepting someone else's son as his own. (p. 51)

As for the aged of the novel a dimension of the tragic is portrayed which is all the more poignant, because the old no longer have the opportunity to change. They must reconcile themselves to the essence they have accepted as their own without realizing that this was not their true destiny. With this distinct impression of his failure, of having been duped, Monsieur La Pérouse's existence becomes a meaningless struggle between his desire to die and his failure to have the courage to kill himself. On the surface his struggle seems to be resolved when his only link with life, his grand-son Boris, dies, and he can enjoy the silence of subdued resignation once again. (pp. 51-2)

Every age of life is thus represented in *Les Faux-Monnayeurs* and we soon realize that Gide places all humanity in front of the same dilemma. Man sets out to solve the problems of reality and ends up resigned to the inevitable lack of any absolute solution. . . .

The novel is not just a story of forty individuals as they develop and react, but also as they interact and form into groups. There is the family group which disintegrates during the course of the novel into individuals going in opposite directions. Once the young peoples' interests have turned away from family to the larger world of society they split off into social, patriotic, or literary groups or into gangs with a criminal or carnal intent. Because the members of most of these groups are unstable as individuals the groups themselves fall easy prey to a dominant character. . . . (p. 52)

In the story the particular incident of counterfeiting propagated by Strouvilhou, the mastermind behind the swindle, and carried out by the group of boys, is subordinated to the universal application of values, whether it be the value of money, of an idea, or of a personality. Thus the way in which we perceive reality, the evaluation of appearances, is another theme of the story. Edouard, as the novelist, writing the book of the same title, claims the real subject of his work is the struggle between the reality presented by the facts and an ideal reality. This ideal reality becomes unattainable as he is constantly expounding his theory on a novel he is never able to write. The act of being creative, however, of actually producing a work of art, of being an artist in the world of conflicting realities, is the pervasive theme of the novel, theme as topic, and makes *Les Faux-Monnayeurs* in a very real sense a *Künstlerroman*. Inasmuch as Edouard's vacillation in between his idealistic concepts and reality presents man's universal predicament Gide has transposed the dilemma of the artist of Everyman's struggle to grasp reality.

First and foremost Edouard reveals himself in his Journal, but we soon learn through Edouard himself that he cannot distinguish between reality and illusion, what he imagines he feels and what he really feels, or even if he feels anything apart from his representation of that feeling. Hence his actions speak louder than his words, and his actions portray a man who is a failure. He is caught up in the dichotomy of being actor and spectator of his deeds at the same time, and in the end seems incapable of truly living. (p. 53)

Edouard does not have an independent personality; he is constantly being molded by those around him. His relationship to others is continuously placed in jeopardy by his need to analyze his own feelings toward them. . . .

Edouard's relationships to others show an uncomfortable erosion of contours, a lack of anything we can pin down and define. He is an idealist, but an idealist bound by an almost slavish realism in his observations of others. Bernard, on the other hand, conceives an idealistic love for Laura, a veneration and an esteem which inspire him to a higher reality. In direct contrast to his love for Laura is his degrading passion for Sarah which he abandons in disgust once he realizes what this passion has done, not to Sarah, but to Rachel and himself. Bernard has progressed from a dangerous feeling of absolute moral freedom (his liberation from his family, his attitude toward taking Edouard's suitcase and delving into his secrets) to a feeling of extreme solitude when he realizes after successfully passing his *bachot* that he has no one with whom to share his success, to a sense of moral responsibility for what he is to become in relationship to others as well as to himself. (p. 54)

At the start of the novel Bernard Profitendieu and Vincent Molinier have essentially the same potential opportunities as they face life. Their different reactions and encounters with life, however, soon lead them in opposite directions. . . . As Vincent is imprisoning himself in a diabolical relationship which will lead to his ruin , Bernard is liberating himself from all ties. He is free, outside. (p. 55)

Bernard and Vincent represent the two opposing forces in man. Bernard strives upward toward freedom; Vincent although he thinks he is freeing himself is irremediably bound to the demon that possesses him. (p. 56)

Laura and Lady Griffith are complementary figures to the characters of Bernard and Vincent. Both can be seen as fallen women, yet Laura has a depth of understanding which can inspire men to higher deeds, whereas Lilian lacks any depth whatsoever. (p. 57)

[Laura] is torn between her frantic search for happiness and the reality of a mediocre substitute, and only in the end does she resign herself to the fact that the passion of her dreams does not correspond to reality, that her dream-world does not exist. . . . [This dichotomy between reality and illusion suggests] another theme of the story, a pet preoccupation of Gide's, the theme of sincerity. (pp. 58-9)

[Everyone] plays a rôle, a rôle which he either thinks is expected of him or which he expects of himself. . . .

The assumption of rôles in society makes the counterfeit personality inevitable. Never at one time can a character in *Les Faux-Monnayeurs* say absolutely what and who he is.

Faced with the alternatives life offers, a balance becomes necessary between absolutes, between the extremes of complete resignation and complete rejection of life, because both extremes make life meaningless. (p. 59)

In between the two extremes lies the acceptance of life which, however, can be just as meaningless as resignation or rejection if such acceptance is based on the blindness of a faith which allows no questions or on the blindness of a doubt which allows no answers. In the former instance an acceptance based on the blindness of a faith which allows no questions is domonstrated by Vedel and Azaïs whose religion becomes a cowardly escape from the responsibilities of life. In the latter instance, an acceptance based on the blindness of a doubt.which allows no answer is demonstrated by Lilian, Vincent, Armand, and Passavant whose outlook on life also becomes a cowardly escape from life's responsibilities. In both extremes acceptance is only apparent and really serves to camouflage an underlying escapism whether they themselves are aware of it or not.

Edouard strives toward total awareness in order to base his attitude toward life on firmer ground, but total awareness is not possible. The effort he makes toward awareness however, deprives him of the very reality he seeks, in that during the time he takes to analyze the reality of what he is and does at a given moment, the moment passes, and he is stifled in it by the inactivity forced on his life by that very reflection. (p. 60)

In the end, the kind of attitude which leads toward a positive involvement in life is shown in Bernard's progression toward a dynamic acceptance which allows no stagnation, which meets each moment without the prejudice of a fixed and immutable goal. It is both idealistic and realistic at the same time. Bernard's acceptance of life is both a self-realization and a self-transcendence. . . . The reality of setting out upon the exciting journey of life is more important than knowing where he is going.

All of the characters are faced with the problem of their attitude toward life, of their identity in relationship to others, to their destiny and to the world, and in the end all of them fail to find an absolute truth to live by. In other words the thematic conclusion of the work lies in the fact that the world and we ourselves cannot be analyzed and explained unless we cease to search for absolutes and simply live our lives. Living our lives is the only reality. Life is an experiment. Since there are no ready-made formulas we can impose upon existence, existence itself must be our guide. If it is not we face the unavoidable fate of becoming counterfeit. (pp. 60-1)

> *Karin Nordenhaug Ciholas, in her* Gide's Art of the Fugue: A Thematic Study of "Les Faux-Monnayeurs," *U.N.C. Department of Romance Languages, 1974, 125 p.*

C. D. E. TOLTON   (essay date 1975)

[When we read *Si le grain ne meurt*] we are at first struck by the imbalance in the length of its two parts. André Gide often conceived works in two parts, as in the case of each of *Les Cahiers d'André Walter, La Porte étroite, L'Ecole des femmes,* and *Robert.* Sometimes (most notably in *La Symphonie pastorale*) his impatience to complete a work and get on with the next overcame his desire for classical symmetry, resulting in the second part's being shorter than the first. But in none of these works is the imbalance as glaring as the proportion of ten chapters to two in *Si le grain ne meurt.* . . . What Gide has done here is to take a lesson from fiction. He has structured his work in such a way that through the development of the first part the reader is drawn into such close contact with the personality of the young Gide that he is ready to linger with him over the most commonplace of remembrances. The reader is made to feel that a climax awaits him further on, and that this climax is not necessarily, as is the case with most literary autobiographers, just the publication or success of a literary work.

Gide's skill in building suspense here is entirely professional. The device he uses is the familiar one of foreshadowing. And he uses the device rhythmically. (pp. 39-40)

Foreshadowing is not the only device that Gide borrowed from fiction. . . . The structure of Gide's autobiography can be, and in fact should be, studied in the same way as that of a first-person novel. . . . The narrator of *Si le grain ne meurt* is André Gide, who appears in the pivotal role of protagonist as well as narrator. . . . [We may] consider the narrator of *Si le grain ne meurt* to be a *persona* of André Gide, in much the same way that we consider Henry Brulard to be a *persona* of Stendhal, or the poet of "Le Lac" to be a *persona* of Lamartine. André Gide's many-sided personality, his tendency to present only a portion of himself in each of his works, and his very specific purpose in writing *Si le grain ne meurt* invite us to say that the image of himself which Gide projects through his mode of narration is a selective one, and that certain sides of himself indeed have been masked, as the word *persona* suggests.

André Gide, narrator, then, is not to be confused with André Gide the man, who lived the life that is being described and analysed in the work. Nor is he to be confused with an intermediate entity, André Gide the author, who conceived the work and set the words on paper. André Gide the narrator is a creation of André Gide the author, a creation who sees the world in a way which André Gide the author has chosen for him. The voice which André Gide the narrator uses will also have been chosen for him. The material which will form his story will be the life of André Gide the man. One must also reckon with a fourth entity, André Gide the hero of the work. For we must be sceptical about accepting all the details of the life of André Gide the hero as the same as those of André Gide the man. Discrepancies in fact, magnification of incidental moments, omission of important events, must all be considered as not just possible but inevitable. And too many years have passed for the narrator to view all events in the same light as the young hero. We are, after all, witnessing in the story the evolution of this young hero. André Gide the hero, who seems to a reader to be an authentic recollection of André Gide the narrator, has actually been created (like the narrator) by André Gide the author. We are thus confronted with the following house-that-Jack-built situation: A man named André Gide lived a life which in his role as an author by the name of André Gide he has recreated in a book where a narrator (also named André Gide) tells the life of his younger self, the hero, who of course was also called André Gide. (pp. 40-2)

[In] spite of Gide's constant references to his "Mémoires" *Si le grain ne meurt* is an autobiography . . . [People] and places have taken on an importance in the work only in so far as they reveal truths about Gide himself. Such was the method of writing about his past which best suited his purposes. (p. 84)

If André Gide's autobiography reads like a novel, it could be argued that this is merely characteristic of the genre. However, *Si le grain ne meurt* reads like a *good* novel, a phenomenon that is not at all common to the genre, and which is attributable to the coincidence that its author is a first-rate novelist. The question arises, then, as to why a successful novelist chose to write an autobiography for his defence of homosexuality rather than use the genre to which he owed his reputation. There would seem to be several reasons.

The most obvious is that the expense of personally damning confessions leaves no doubt as to the importance which the author is giving to his subject. Contrary to advice from Wilde and Proust, and only too aware of the accusations that would be made, Gide *was* ready to use the pronoun "je" to reveal all. Moreover, he would not this time use any interposed narrator named Michel to put the reader off his track.

In the second place, as a propagandist, Gide was to use more than one literary genre. His autobiography would take its place beside the arguments of the *Corydon* dialogues and the example of Edouard's and Olivier's relationship in *Les Faux-monnayeurs* as yet another rendering of his request for understanding.

In the third place, as Gide uses the genre of autobiography, superficially it differs very little from what his *récits* had already been providing for his readers. The length of his work and its commitment to honesty are the most apparent departures from subject matter and a narrative technique with which he was already comfortable and which pleased his public. And this time, he was eased of the burden of creating a fictitious narrator or explaining how the narrator came to have the inclination, time, or talent to tell his story.

The fresh problems that autobiography imposed were not insurmountable. Gide soon recognized that total accuracy of recollection was neither possible nor necessary. The autobiographer's usual problem of appearing more reliable when treating recent events than childhood was not his, since even the end of his narrative had taken place in the fairly distant past. He had also had time to appraise the retrospective significance of events which may have seemed unimportant at the time, and even the relatively short time-span of his story allowed for sufficient evolution in his own character to keep the readers interested. The problem of characterizing himself both as a young boy and as a mature writer seemed to take care of itself, since personal traits linking his youth and his maturity were different enough to make the connection striking, yet similar enough to keep it believable. The sleepy childhood of the writer with encyclopaedic interests is, for instance, fascinating; yet their constant literary interests, sensitivity, and imagination make both the narrator and his subject unmistakably the same person. And finally, the usual pre-eminent handicap of autobiography becomes for Gide an advantage. For him, the fact that the only character whom the narrator can know thoroughly—if not completely—is himself relieves him of the responsibility of the full development of other characters, and allows him to concentrate on the single example he needs for his purpose, namely himself. Gide's pledge to his mission led to his painting his self-portrait with particularly consistent care, but still an impressive number of secondary figures populate the work. (pp. 85-6)

Now that the work can at last be regarded from an unobstructed literary perspective, let us begin by recognizing its genre correctly—literary autobiography. In 1926 it both reinvigorated the genre and set new standards for frankness. Since then, the number of autobiographies by French men of letters has proliferated, and authors like Jean Genet have far outdistanced André Gide in frankness. But over the years, Gide's work has never become just another crumbling landmark in literary history. Nor will it. *Si le grain ne meurt* has the lasting freshness of a classic; and it is time to acknowledge that it is not to its daring subject matter or to its biographical usefulness that it owes its durability, but to the unique personality and literary deftness of the artist who lived its story and recorded it. (p. 87)

> *C. D. E. Tolton, in his* André Gide and the Art of Autobiography: A Study of "Si le grain ne meurt" *(reprinted with permission of the author; © 1975 by C. D. E. Tolton), Macmillan Publishing Co., 1975, 122 p.*

CHRISTOPHER BETTINSON (essay date 1977)

The key note of Gide's first novel, *Les Cahiers d'André Walter*, is self-denial and wilful renunciation of the flesh. His obsession with an ideal, spiritualized love . . . was further tested in *La Tentative amoureuse* in which passion is clearly presented as self-consuming and destructive of the will. On the other hand, *Les Nourritures terrestres* preaches an unrestained joy in all physical experience, now seen as a positive means of glorifying God. Life must be seen as a succession of pregnant moments, each of which should be treated as a wondrous novelty. But self-gratification and egoism have no place in this Gidian vision: on the contrary, what is advocated here is a spontaneous, disinterested joy in creation, involving freedom of movement and the rejection of fixed attitudes and limiting social ties.

Such a tendency to move in an individual work towards one extreme attitude and then in another to draw back from it in a critical fashion is typically Gidian. . . . Most of his heroes are deliberately presented as logical extremes. In the light of their *hubris,* their *ivresse* or lyrical excess, Gide is able to clarify his own position. It is part of his attempt to bring such familiar impulses under control. In the effort to give expression to a dilemma, Gide strives for a form of detachment in order to illustrate that he has moved beyond the terms of the original moral problem.

However, the control Gide achieves can never be more than temporary. In each new work Gide looks at the same moral and intellectual problems again, posing fresh solutions and seeking new forms of balance. (pp. 6-7)

Gide's writing was experimental in a number of ways: he tested ideas in a variety of conditions; he subjected his linguistic equipment to ceaseless scrutiny and he experimented with many different styles and genres. But perhaps his main achievement lies in his thinking on the novel, based on his reactions to nineteenth-century realism. His Symbolist experience taught that it is the artist's duty to transcend the meaningless details of everyday reality. The work of art is a closed system of linguistic signs—an artificial world. While it will certainly suggest human truths and encapsulate human experience, it must never reflect life in a banal, descriptive way. In fact, a novel can only illustrate the complexity of life if the artist abandons any attempt to be a neutral observer and projects instead the uniqueness of his own point of view. By a heavy concentration on the particular truth, the artist can make it symbolize a universal truth even more forcefully. (pp. 11-12)

Gide was constantly alluding to the question of the relationship between literature and life. One of his favourite techniques is the first-person narrative convention, which he uses to approach reality from an oblique angle. Superficially, he deliberately absents himself from the action of his works, creating the impression that his narrator-heroes are free to express their own view of reality. But as the reader becomes aware of the extreme partiality of the self-justifying narrator, a new critical viewpoint comes into play, constantly judging and modifying the narrator's account of his life. (p. 12)

Gide makes the novel the focal point of different versions of reality. Events are not related directly but through a succession of partial viewpoints and it is the role of the reader to relate them to each other. Gide's reader must be prepared to follow him in his quest for new forms and assist in the creation of a multi-dimensional experience of life seen in the round. For Gide the role of the artist was to stimulate creative thought, to pose problems and not to present ready-made solutions. By itself a work of art has only a *potential* significance: it acquires its full status only when it is read, interpreted and experienced by a reader. . . . [*L'Immoraliste* and *La Porte étroite*] are marked by a kind of ironic detachment fostered by the simplicity of plot, an extreme economy of stylistic means and a relentless narrative rhythm, which emphasizes the tragic destinies of both Michel and Alissa. The reader is invited to sympathize with them and, at the same time, view them critically as they involve others in the implacable logic of their extremism.

Taken together, then, *La Porte étroite* and *L'Immoraliste* create a balance between opposing attitudes to life, each taken to a logical extreme. In the latter, Gide's fascination for individual, natural impulses is sympathetically examined and countered by a less sympathetic but realistic awareness of social demands. In *La Porte étroite,* on the other hand, Gide approaches the same social demands from the point of view of an attitude of extreme self-sacrifice, embodied in Alissa. Ultimately, a ferocious attachment to physical fulfilment is balanced against an equally strong impulse towards self-abnegation. (p. 15)

L'Immoraliste is divided into three unequal parts. The long first part . . . charts Michel's slow recovery from tuberculosis, through the exercise of his will and his discovery of the world of the senses. This culminates in the consummation of his relationship with his wife and in the apparent establishment of a new balance in his life. Part Two consists of three long chapters . . . in which Michel's marriage and his growing obsession for physical experience are seen in conflict. A significant encounter with Ménalque in the central chapter encourages Michel in his search for new experience, now clearly seen as incompatible with his responsibilities as husband and landowner. Part Three describes Michel's failure to revive the earlier intensity of his love for Marceline and his constant neglect of her needs as he systematically searches for physical satisfaction. With Marceline's death, the inevitable consequence of Michel's personal quest, he finds himself committed to his immoralism but without the will and energy to cultivate it. (pp. 15-16)

It is important to remember that, as in all autobiographical fiction, ambiguity arises from the confusion between the at-

tempt at an honest record of past events and the inevitable structuring and justification of the past in the light of subsequent experience. Thus the unmistakable callousness of most references to Marceline throughout the book seems to be an exaggeration of Michel's vague feelings in the past, conditioned by his present knowledge of where such feelings were in fact leading him. (p. 17)

The central chapter of Part Two sees Michel drawn towards a rejection of civilized culture and social values under the influence of Ménalque. At the outset Michel is determined to commit himself once more to social life but in his extreme self-confidence, as Michel hints in his retrospective account, a dangerous tendency towards extravagance and self-delusion is apparent. (p. 19)

[The] 'vagabond inclinations' which Michel tried to suppress for the sake of Marceline and their unborn child are very soon in evidence. He feels superior to his society friends in Paris, resents that he is forced to play a social role and, because of his intensely physical experience of death and life, feels isolated in a world of shallow artificiality.

Four crucial meetings with an old friend, Ménalque, further undermine Michel's attachment to his social and domestic duties and lead him to develop a more systematically individualistic attitude. (p. 20)

Ménalque's influence is immediately seen in Michel's dissatisfaction with his academic work . . . and in his even stronger sense of disgust at the artificiality of Marceline's *soirées* . . . , in contrast with his obvious attraction for Ménalque's physical appearance, leading to his admiration for Ménalque's systematic immoralism. . . . Michel's increasing interest in these ideas is symbolically connected with hints of Marceline's physical decline. (pp. 20-1)

Michel attempts to live [a] double life and reconcile his love for Marceline with his impulse towards individual freedom. The problem, and it is one that Michel is brutally self-critical about in his retrospective account, is that his personal quest involves estrangement from Marceline, as Ménalque had so carefully pointed out. At the end of Part Two Marceline's illness and reproachful words produce in Michel sudden feelings of guilt and the desire to recapture the love they had shared at Sorrento. Part Three, faithful to Ménalque's prediction, vividly charts Michel's failure to harmonize the contradiction between duty to Marceline and duty to himself. (p. 23)

Michel's attachment to life as an absolute has tragic consequences. It is all-consuming, destroying his wife and undermining his will power. It is this last effect that is stressed most strongly in the closing section of the book. Michel now lives like a prisoner in his isolated villa, fed by a sympathetic innkeeper and dependent for company on a young Arab boy. The clarity and vigour of Michel's account, and the relentless movement towards a tragic climax, give way to a static, expressionless prose, indicating the ultimate debasement of Michel's ideal.

As with Michel in *L'Immoraliste* we can detect in Jérôme's account [in *La Porte étroite*] a desire for self-justification by means of a subconscious re-ordering of events. . . . The effect of Gide's use of a first-person narrative technique is in fact to make the reader both sympathetic and hostile to Jérôme: on the one hand, it enables the reader to focus critically on the gap between superficial appearances and underlying, often subconscious, factors in the behavior of Jérôme and Alissa; but equally it helps to persuade the reader that their lack of self-knowledge and their possible self-deception are vital ingredients in the irreversible movement towards the tragic conclusion of the book. (pp. 25-6)

[Jérôme's restrained style in chapter one] is the literary reflection of a moral attitude—a life-denying Puritanism associated with his mother, with Flora Ashburton and notably with Alissa. Thus, despite Jérôme's obvious attraction for the exotic and beautiful outsider, Lucile Bucolin, there is an emphasis on her unseemly physical qualities. . . . (p. 26)

What is also clear, however, is that Jérôme's hatred of Lucile Bucolin is inseparable from his attraction for Alissa, whose physical qualities are deliberately played down and who is presented in the highly dramatic bedroom scene as the pathetic victim of her mother's immorality. And just as Jérôme had identified Alissa imprecisely with different forms of ideal beauty . . . , so his love for her, which starts from a physical base, is dominated by a mixture of innocent and transcendental impulses. . . . (pp. 26-7)

Despite their apparent love for one another, Jérôme and Alissa are exceedingly inhibited in each other's company. (p. 27)

[In] order to guarantee contact with Alissa, Jérôme has to forgo talk of marriage and becomes trapped in a platonic relationship. . . . Obsessed with her duty to God and with the idea that it is irreconcilable with earthly happiness, she is borne along on the wave of poetic mysticism. In this way her capacity for emotion and physical involvement is directed away from Jérôme towards God; even her contact with the world of sensation has all the accents of otherworldly requirements. (p. 29)

Thus, all things are subordinate to the need to prepare for salvation, and to that end Jérôme must not tempt her with the possibility of earthly happiness. In one way, we see Jérôme as the victim of Alissa's rejection of life, just as Juliette was rejected by Jérôme because of his attachment to the spiritual values represented by Alissa. On the other hand, we hesitate to condemn Alissa for her somewhat harsh treatment of Jérôme because her struggle to do what she believes to be right for her and Jérôme causes her so much pain. Still, however, the ambiguity remains: do her letters simply illustrate the tragic struggle between love to Jérôme and duty to God, or are they not equally a cruel reminder to Jérôme that his duty is self-imposed and that their love can only be maintained at a distance? (pp. 29-30)

In chapters five to eight the focus is on Jérôme as the victim of Alissa's mystical urge. He accepts her view of their relationship, partly because he shares it to a degree and partly because he believes that they will eventually be united. And whereas Alissa appears perverse in her desire to turn away from Jérôme and life, Jérôme finds it clearly impossible to suppress his natural feelings for her. . . . (p. 30)

In *La Porte étroite* there is, until the final revelations of Alissa's Diary, a superficial impression of diversity and disjointedness which mirrors Jérôme's constant feeling of puzzlement. But this apparent artlessness in the narrative technique is soon belied by the cumulative effect of symbolic descriptions (the garden at Fongueusemare), recurrent scenes (Alissa's bedroom) and symbols (doors, gates, paths), all defined in terms of a basic dichotomy between the values of a puritanical faith

and those connected with life and human experience. In addition, characters are grouped in relation to this basic conflict. One group of characters consistently turn their backs on life—Jérôme's mother, Alissa's father and pastor Vautier—and they are set against Lucile Bucolin, Félicie Plantier and Abel Vautier. In the middle are three characters—Jérôme, Alissa and Juliette—whose lives are destroyed, because of their interlocking destinies, by these irreconcilable values. The sense of fatality is on one occasion underpinned by the parallel between Alissa's father, Félicie Plantier and Jérôme's mother in their youth, and Jérôme, Juliette and Alissa. Also, in the contrast between Alissa and Lucile Bucolin it becomes clear how one extreme of behavior provokes another. Alissa systematically suppresses all that Lucile represents but, in the process, discovers both the force and the attraction of human nature in herself. Jérôme, too, initially suppresses his instinctive admiration for Lucile's physical qualities, only to become identified with physical demands in contrast to Alissa's extreme spirituality. Underlying the whole tragedy of the relationship between Jérôme and Alissa is the brilliantly suggested tragedy of Juliette. Her unrequited love for Jérôme and her sacrifice of it in her marriage to Tessières are movingly recalled in the closing lines of the book, as Jérôme's mixture of awe and admiration for Alissa's sacrifice reminds her brutally of her own, underlining the sense of tragic waste that Jérôme has experienced with Alissa. (pp. 32-3)

> *Christopher Bettinson, in his* Gide: A Study *(© Christopher Bettinson 1977), Rowman and Littlefield, 1977, 104 p.*

ADDITIONAL BIBLIOGRAPHY

Ames, Van Meter. *André Gide*. Norfolk, Conn.: New Directions Books, 1947, 302 p.
> Literary biography with particular emphasis on the predominant ideological and moral influences which affected Gide's work throughout his life.

Bonheim, Helmut, and Bonheim, Jean. "Structure and Symbolism in Gide's *La porte étroite*." *The French Review* XXXI, No. 6 (April 1958): 487-97.
> Close analysis of themes, motifs, and characterization in *La porte étroite*.

Carrier, Warren. "The Demoniacal in Gide." *Renascence* IV, No. 1 (Autumn 1951): 59-65.
> Discusses the function of the polarities of good and evil in Gide's fiction.

Cordle, Thomas. *André Gide*. New York: Twayne Publishers, 1969, 183 p.
> Critical survey of Gide's career.

Freedman, Ralph. "Imagination and Form in André Gide: *La porte étroite* and *La symphonie pastorale*." *Accent* XVII, No. 4 (Autumn 1957): 217-28.
> Demonstrates how the form of these novels allowed Gide to dispassionately examine his own inner crises.

Garzilli, Enrico. "The Myth of the Labyrinth and the Self" and "The Fictive Self and Identity." In his *Circles without Center: Paths to the Discovery and Creation of Self in Modern Literature*, pp. 89-117, 118-27. Cambridge: Harvard University Press, 1972.*
> Discusses the problems of reality, sincerity, and authorial presence in *Thésée* and *Les faux-monnayeurs*.

Haberstich, David. "Gide and the Fantasts: The Nature of Reality and Freedom." *Criticism* II, No. 2 (Spring 1969): 140-50.

A study of the way cubist, dadaist, and surrealist aesthetic principles are displayed in *Les faux-monnayeurs*.

Holdheim, W. Wolfgang. *Theory and Practice of the Novel: A Study on André Gide*. Geneva: Librairie Droz, 1968, 271 p.
    Study of the novels contending that Gide's "early discovery that life and art are incommensurate is one of the principle keys to the understanding of Gide's entire work."

Ireland, G. W. *André Gide*. New York: Grove Press, 1963, 120 p.
    Study which is primarily concerned with Gide's methods of creation, and the development of characters and ideas in various works.

Kloss, Robert J. "The Gratuitous Act: Gide's Lafcadio Reconsidered." *The Psychoanalytic Review* 64, No. 1 (Spring 1977): 111-34.
    Psychoanalytic reading of *Lafcadio's Adventures*.

Lynes, Carlos, Jr. "André Gide and the Problem of Form in the Novel." *Southern Review* VII, No. 1 (Summer 1941): 161-73.
    Examines the structural devices used by Gide in *Lex faux-monnayeurs*.

March, Harold. *Gide and the Hound of Heaven*. Philadelphia: University of Pennsylvania Press, 1952, 421 p.
    Biography of Gide which thoroughly explores both his influences and his intentions for each of his works.

McLaren, James C. *The Theatre of André Gide: Evolution of a Moral Philosopher*. Baltimore: The Johns Hopkins Press, 1953, 117 p.
    Close study and analysis of the plays of André Gide. Extensive quotation, in French, is incorporated into the criticism.

Merchant, Norris. "The Spiritual Dilemma of André Gide." *The Colorado Quarterly* VII, No. 4 (Spring 1959): 406-23.
    Examines Gide's emotional and spiritual conflicts, and the manner in which they are reflected in the protagonists of his novels.

Mitchell, John D. "André Gide, Rebel and Conformist." *The American Imago* 16, No. 2 (Summer 1959): 147-53.
    Examines the psychological dynamics of Gide's childhood environment and the consequences for his future characters and attitudes.

O'Brien, Justin. *Portrait of André Gide: A Critical Biography*. New York: Alfred A. Knopf, 1953, 390 p.
    A critical and biographical study of Gide. Much of O'Brien's information was gathered from interviews with Gide.

Painter, George D. *André Gide: A Critical and Biographical Study*. London: Arthur Barker, 1951, 192 p.
    Critical biography that also contains plot summaries of Gide's works and discusses the similarities of Gide's writings with his life.

Starkie, Enid. *André Gide*. New Haven, Conn.: Yale University Press, 1954, 63 p.
    Study which pays particular attention to Gide's works as examinations of modern morality.

Steel, D. A. "Gide and the Conception of the Bastard." *French Studies* XVII, No. 3 (July 1963): 238-48.
    Sees Gide's theme of "the flight from the family" crystallized in the figure and symbol of the bastard.

Storzer, Gerald H. "*Les Cahiers d'André Walter*: Idea, Emotion, and Dream in the Gidian Novel." *Philological Quarterly* 54, No. 3 (Summer 1975): 647-62.
    Psycho-philosophical reading of this novel.

Sypher, Wylie. "Gide's Cubist Novel." *The Kenyon Review* XI, No. 2 (Spring 1949): 291-309.
    Examines the experimental methods of depicting reality used by Gide in *Lex faux-monnayeurs*, and contrasts these methods to techniques and theories of the cubist painters.

Watson-Williams, Helen. *André Gide and the Greek Myth: A Critical Study*. Oxford: Oxford University Press, 1967, 200 p.
    Discusses Gide's use of classical Greek literature for thematic and symbolic motifs in a large number of his works.

(Karl Gustaf) Verner von Heidenstam

1859-1940

Swedish poet, novelist, short story writer, and dramatist.

Heidenstam's poetry, his most important literary achievement, initiated a revival of romanticism during a period when Strindbergian naturalism dominated the literary scene in Sweden. While Strindberg dramatized social issues of the day, Heidenstam composed poems that have been described by critics as rich, self-regarding, and melancholic. Later in his work Heidenstam shifted focus from his inner life to an interest in his country, though it was not topical modern problems he depicted but a romantic Sweden of the past.

Heidenstam came from an aristocratic family. In his youth he traveled around the Middle East, Italy, Greece, Germany, and Switzerland, where he met Strindberg. Heidenstam's first collection of poems, *Vallfart och vandringår*, conveys a sense of the exotic inspired by his travels. He also studied painting at the Ecole des Beaux Arts in Paris, and critics believe this contributed to the lush imagery of his early poems. Both the foreign themes and romantic style of these poems protested the contemporary trend of realism in literature. Heidenstam further portrays a remote world in *Endymion*, and in *Hans Alienus* describes a pilgrimage in quest of an ideal model for humanity.

In his second poetry collection, *Dikter*, Heidenstam develops the feeling for his homeland prefigured in the "Thoughts on Loneliness" section of *Vallfart och vandringår*. Such poems as "Home" display a transition in Heidenstam's attitude from somber introspection to a robust, affirmative spirit taking pride in the life of his country. This spirit had its most successful fictional presentation in *Karolinerna* (*The Charles Men*), to which commentators have given the highest critical approval as a work both national and universal in its human interest. Influenced by folklore and the Scandinavian sagas, Heidenstam continued to explore the romantic aspects of Sweden's history in *Heliga Birgittas pilgrimsfärd* and *Folkungaträdet* (*The Tree of the Folkungs*), which is often likened to Ibsen's *Peer Gynt*. The lyric genius of Heidenstam's last collection of poems, *Nya dikter*, is compared to that of Goethe. In 1912 Heidenstam was elected to the Swedish Academy and in 1916 was awarded the Nobel Prize in literature.

Though Heidenstam never achieved the international influence of his Scandinavian contemporaries Ibsen and Strindberg, he affected the course of Swedish literature in the late nineteenth century and remains historically significant as one of a number of prominent authors who moved away from the values of realism toward those of imagination.

PRINCIPAL WORKS

Vallfart och vandringår (poetry) 1888
Endymion (novel) 1889
Hans Alienus (novel) 1892
Dikter (poetry) 1895
Karolinerna. 2 vols. (short stories) 1897-98
  [*The Charles Men*, 1920]
Heliga Birgittas pilgrimsfärd (novel) 1901

Folkungaträdet. 2 vols. (novel) 1905-07
  [*The Tree of the Folkungs*, 1925]
Svenskarna och deras hövdingar. 2 vols. (short stories)
  1908-10
  [*The Swedes and Their Chieftains*, 1925]
Nya dikter (poetry) 1915
*Sweden's Laureate: Selected Poems of Verner von
  Heidenstam* (poetry) 1919
När Kastanjerna blommade (memoirs) 1941
Sista dikter (poetry) 1942
Samlade verk. 23 vols. (poetry, novels, short stories, and
  essays) 1945-46

CHARLES WHARTON STORK (essay date 1916)

At first thought it is surprising that Heidenstam's poetry is popular at all. His subjects are frequently exotic and his moods usually introspective; his style is always compressed and abrupt, and at first repelling. Gradually, after much rereading, the depth and power of the poet begin to fascinate the student. The sensation is something like looking down into the ocean through a confusion of waves and gloomy sea-weeds, until finally, far below, glimpses of something rich and strange begin to attract the eye. The chief fault in such a simile is that the style of Heidenstam, far from being always cold, is often shot through with intensity.

Above all, Heidenstam's poetry impresses one as being mainly the product of an isolated, self-conscious, and painfully sensitive mind. It is most often original in treatment and very seldom within the range of our ordinary feelings and interests. If the poet undertakes any given theme, he is more than likely to contradict the reader's expectations in his treatment. In a narrative poem, for instance, he seems to be deliberately undramatic, to disappoint in the climax much as do some of Meredith's novels. He at least resembles Meredith in caring nothing for action in itself, but only as it illuminates the soul of the actor.

In Heidenstam we discover two types of narrative: the exotic and more fanciful, and the native and more realistic. To the former class belongs the story of the Egyptian poet, Djufar, who, when he is expected to burst out into a glowing song in praise of the beauty of the Orient, merely sinks his head and weeps: "He paints the joy of the East on an empty, tear-wet page." Nor is this restraint less sincere in his well-known poem, "**Nameless and Immortal,**" in which the architect of the Temple of Neptune at Pæstum resolves not to chisel his name on the masterpiece, but to live by his deed alone. In "**Childhood Friends,**" where the scene is laid in Sweden, we have a careful analysis of character which makes the poem seem like a novel of Henry James irregularly compressed into verse. In this type of study, found in the poet's second volume, there is a realism not unlike that of our own poet, Robert Frost, himself doubtless to some degree a disciple of James. The poets differ, however, in that "North of Boston" reads like a veracious record of fact, whereas the style of Heidenstam reveals an artistic personality which colors, arranges, and generalizes. There are exceptions as to the involved character of Heidenstam's longer poems, notably in "**Songs from the Church-Tower,**" which is as direct as most of the others are complex. Here the bell-ringer, a man of the people, first rings in a future of class war; afterwards his wife changes the note to one of universal brotherhood. The whole poem is boldly conceived.

Passing from the narrative to the more exclusively lyrical poems, we come at once to the most characteristic phase of Heidenstam's talent in a number of very short subjective pieces. Few living writers are so concerned with their own spiritual secrets, and fewer still have put the problem with a simpler poignancy than may be seen in ["**Thoughts in Solitude**"]. . . .

I have noted that Heidenstam's style is usually abrupt as well as compressed; it consists often of a number of rapid, illuminating flashes, none of them long enough to display more than a fraction of the writer's meaning. The logic is evasive. Herein some will find the fascination of the poet, for his flashes correspond to one's insight into the most baffling moments of consciousness. (p. 509)

Heidenstam has Francis Thompson's sensitiveness, and in his lavish use of color is akin to Rossetti and to the Austrian philosophical poet of the present day, Hugo von Hoffmannsthal. He is, however, much less consistent in devel-

oping his thought than is any of the other three. Perhaps for this very reason he seems more earnest. He is too intense to work out the smoothly woven allegories of "The Hound of Heaven" and "Traum von Grosser Magie"; even a sonnet of Rossetti's would be impossible to him. He shifts from one picture or figure to another with an eagerness that is very confusing, yet rapidly as the pictures change, each is likely to be, for its purpose, a memorable stroke of artistry. As introspective as Poe, he is preoccupied with melancholy themes, especially with death, and not infrequently with the thought of his own death. There is, for instance, "**Let Us Die Young,**" or the "**First Night in the Churchyard,**" in the second of which the soul escapes from the coffin only to be hunted away from its former home, as though it were a stray dog. The daughter of Jairus, brought back to life, wishes to return to the bosom of her mother, Eternity. Heidenstam loves, too, to dwell on the isolation of the soul, or on the wandering of soul or body in strange lands. His poetry is only saved from overpowering morbidness by the vigor of the style, which tends to dispel the gloom inherent in the subject.

Yet why, with his many palpable defects, has Verner von Heidenstam won so high a place in the assembly of Swedish authors? The answer seems to lie mainly in the interrelated qualities of sincerity and freshness which have been noted. These make their strongest appeal in a sphere that I have not yet referred to: that of patriotic poetry in the widest sense. In a few fine lyrics Heidenstam escapes from his lonely, tortured self and throws his fervor into the celebration of all that is best in the landscape and the people of his native country. In "**Home**" we feel that a man's longing for the scenes of childhood has never been more beautifully rendered. And there are trumpet-notes of enthusiasm in "**Native Land,**" "**A Day,**" and particularly in "**Sweden**" that issue, as it were, from the breast of the earth and partake of its nobility. On this side Heidenstam suggests Masefield's "August, 1914," but has much more of a clarion ring. Who would recognize the morbid, introspective poet now? (p. 510)

Charles Wharton Stork, "Verner von Heidenstam: Winner of the Nobel Prize for Literature for 1916," in The Nation *(copyright 1916 The Nation maga-zine, The Nation Associates, Inc.), Vol. 103, No. 2683, November 30, 1916, pp. 509-10.*

CHARLES WHARTON STORK (essay date 1917)

Verner von Heidenstam first came into literary prominence in 1888 with a volume of lyrical poems entitled *Pilgrimage and Wanderyears*. This volume was the result of a long period spent in travel, principally in Italy and the Orient. The marked success of these poems was due not only to the sincere and individual personality of the author, but to the fact that they came as a relief in a period of exaggerated realism. Their remote setting and the romantic treatment of the material at once caught the Swedish imagination. People were glad to forget social questions and problem-plays of sex either by losing themselves in the colourful representation of the East, or by entering into the intimate recesses of the poet's own consciousness. For Heidenstam has almost equally the gifts of clear-cut objectivity and of deep self-analysis.

But it is not only as a poet that Heidenstam has won his high reputation. Shortly after the lyrical volume already mentioned he brought out a novel, *Hans Alienus,* much in the same idealistic vein, describing a pilgrimage through many lands in search of beauty. In the prose style, as in the poetry, there is an earnestness, a depth of vision that holds the reader even though he be out of sympathy with the immediate subject in hand. . . .

At first Heidenstam's appeal was chiefly to the clique of dilettanti. He was admitted to be a new phenomenon in literature, but his point of view was felt to be somewhat morbid and self-absorbed, and his style was characterised as "exotic." This impression was largely modified by the appearance of a second volume of verse, *Poems,* and of a second novel, founded on Swedish history, *The Carolines.* In both of these works, written after he had settled definitely in his native land, Heidenstam showed the growing love and understanding for Sweden which have since made him a popular idol. There is also a strong infusion of realism into his style; not the realism of the social statistician, but the realism of the fine-spirited artist who, as he develops, becomes more and more conscious of the need for observed fact as a basis for imagination. Always self-analytical, Heidenstam evidently began to appreciate the responsibility of his high calling. Consequently, striking his roots deeply into his native soil, he soon began to exhibit a forceful sturdiness which could never have been developed in a southern climate.

It is this national element in his work that Heidenstam has cultivated up to the present time. . . . Thus Heidenstam has come to represent to the Swedish people the principle of their new nationalism, of their new striving to be a great and united people. . . .

If we were asked to state in a few words the reason why the Nobel Prize for Literature in 1916 was given to Heidenstam, we should probably be right in saying that it was because he has become the recognised spokesman of Sweden. His vividness in the portrayal of beauty, his psychological insight, and his stylistic ability *per se* count for comparatively little in this connection. (p. 590)

But a knowledge of why Verner von Heidenstam has received the Nobel Prize does not by any means convey a full knowledge of his genius. There are . . . two distinct phases of his work: the first, personal and introspective; the second, national and self-dedicatory. His style in the former field is extremely difficult; being involved, compressed and very rapid in its changes from idea to idea or figure to figure. In marked contrast is the clear, direct style of the poet when he loses himself in thinking of his country. It is impossible to recognise two poems in these conflicting manners as being by the same author, unless perhaps we notice a certain tendency to over-compactness and an abrupt shifting of thought as common to both. Intensity is a constant quantity in Heidenstam's writing, but the intensity of, for instance, **"Thoughts in Solitude"** would never suggest that of **"Invocation and Promise."** . . .

["**The Dove of Thought**"] is like a glimmer in the twilight. Others of a similar kind make us fancy ourselves on the brink of a deep and narrow crater, gazing at the lurid gleams that pierce the darkness below. Gloom, hyper-sensitiveness, spiritual isolation—these are the moods induced by [Heidenstam's poems].

["**The Dove of Thought**"] is a rather morbid and complex, but in its way very affecting, poem. The difficulty of it lies in the entangling of the physical with the metaphysical world. The flaming of the earth in autumn colours is apparently identified with the feverishness of the restless human heart,

a not very apt metaphor. But the picture of the dove conveys with delicate skill the fluttering feeling of spiritual uncertainty to which all of us can bear witness. It is to this class of interest that most of Heidenstam's poems and much of his prose belong.

But the other class, though smaller, is of far wider significance. In it we are inspired not only by the author's love of Sweden but by his thorough democratic spirit. It is very remarkable that a man of aristocratic background and idealistic training should so fully sympathise with the common people. For instance, Heidenstam has said that no man did so much harm to Sweden as did Charles XII, one of the great national idols. (p. 591)

[The] spirit which has given Heidenstam his literary eminence . . . [is found in] the ringing summons to his people in the lines of "**Invocation and Promise.**" (p. 592)

> *Charles Wharton Stork, "The New Nobel Prize Winner: Verner von Heidenstam," in* The Bookman, *New York (copyright, 1917, by George H. Doran Company), Vol. XLIV, No. 6, February, 1917, pp. 589-92.*

SVEA BERNHARD (essay date 1917)

Heidenstam's first books were all written in prose, but a prose that lies far from that language of everyday conversation and newspaper style which so many of his contemporaries had religiously adopted as an expression for true realism. With Heidenstam begins the literary Swedish renascence in which are counted such names as Selma Lagerlöf, Per Hallström, E. A. Karlfeldt, Oscar Levertin, and Gustaf Fröding. (p. 36)

Heidenstam had passed the age of thirty before publishing . . . his first book, *Years of Wandering and Pilgrimage.* This was rapidly followed by the traveling sketches *From Col di Tenda to Blocksberg,* the novel *Endymion,* and the great heroic epos *Hans Alienus,* born out of a poet's inspiration and a philosopher's meditations about life, its ideal of happiness and its tragedy. Hans Alienus, the restless seeker of truth and beauty all over the globe and through all ages, is Heidenstam's own youth spent in worldwide travels, with the longing for home hidden half unconsciously in the depths of his soul; to return at last to the country of his birth, convinced of the vanity of any attempt to pursue happiness outside of his own soul.

Heidenstam then returned to the love of his early youth, lyric poetry, and published . . . his first volume of *Poems,* the most individual creation he had until then given. A "high song" in praise of high idealism, "of a national idealism so pure and full that the air itself sings with joyous expectation that every wife is to bear a Messiah."

Heidenstam's best known historic work is *The Carolins,* thirty-four short stories depicting the epoch, glorious in Swedish history, of Charles XII and his faithful warriors; but it is the masterly psychologic knowledge of human nature, from the fantastic and contradictory character of the King which runs like a red thread through the book, to the feelings of the small drum-boy, that gives to this work its chief interest.

Several other important historic works followed *The Carolins;* foremost among them *The Pilgrimage of Holy Birgitta.* In all these he has made Swedish history live anew in the hearts of his people, made it a real and cherished possession for old and young, not merely a dry science with innumerable dreaded dates and names.

But still, it is as a lyric poet that Heidenstam has given his country most. He has gradually reached a higher and wider horizon, but in spite of his aristocratic aloofness and the decidedly "unpopular vein" of his poetry, he has become the poet under whose banner the others have gathered in the last decades. His works have become classic. . . . Verner von Heidenstam and Gustaf Fröding, the two who wrought their intuitive philosophy of life into poetry of wondrous strength and beauty, and who incarnated the national character of their people in song and prose, stand foremost as representatives of the idealistic school of writers in Sweden. (pp. 36-8)

> *Svea Bernhard, "Verner von Heidenstam," in* Poetry (© *1917 by The Modern Poetry Association), Vol. X, No. 1, April, 1917, pp. 35-8.*

FREDRIK BÖÖK (essay date 1919)

The Charles Men is a timely work. The fall of the Swedish empire, the desperate contest of an inflexible ruler for what he believed to be true and right, the boundless suffering of an ill-fated people, the ravages of hunger which they endured, their growing despair and infinite fortitude, their inevitable ruin and eternal glory—such is the picture that appears before us in simple, majestic lines; a tragedy clear and compelling as one of the Greeks', composed by the very history of the world, and fitted to purify our hearts through terror and pity, as Aristotle taught. He who ponders the nature of war and the philosophy of history may win instruction from the epic which Swedish history and Swedish imagination together have formed about Charles XII and his men. It was no superficial romance of war, no rancorous and hypocritical chauvinism, that inspired Verner von Heidenstam. He saw before his eyes the misery and degradation of war; no pacifistic Barbusse has painted it in grimmer colors than he. He saw the problematic side of his hero; the rigid, petrified insensibility that misfortunes and spiritual torments wrought in the breast of the king. And yet he felt deeply the moral beauty, the human magnanimity, which these men of battle displayed, and which they gave to posterity as a noble, strengthening essence, extracted from withered herbs and crushed reeds, a *medicina mentis* for every one who must needs fight, endure, be vanquished and overpowered.

The highest praise one can give to *The Charles Men* is that this work, which was composed in deepest peace, has not lost its color and quality during the World War. Verner von Heidenstam has come forward among the pacifists side by side with Romain Rolland; but he does not belong to the superficial, blind zealots for peace of whom Paul Elmer More speaks in his profound and humane essay, *The Philosophy of War*. He belongs with those who have always seen mankind in all its contradictory profusion. . . . (pp. viii-x)

The Charles Men is a poem in prose. Heidenstam's technic has all the freedom, abandon, even caprice that belongs to verse. There is no steady and clear stream of narrative in his work; he leaps over what is inessential, and his imagination concentrates itself on the scene, the figure, the detail that strikes him as significant. This technic is in accord with the historical atmosphere. Uniform realism, methodical description, and painstaking motivation may be in place in a modern

novel; if, on the other hand, it is a question of conjuring up visions from the past, the poet must not bring his figures out into the full daylight—that can only lead to destroying the illusion, as when masks go about in the sunshine. We must have a broad river of darkness, which contains all the mystery of the past, and against this black background the figures and scenes may glimmer forth—symbolic flashes of that life whose depth and scope one cannot define, but only surmise.

That Heidenstam dreamed at one time of becoming a painter, to this every page of *The Charles Men* bears witness. What a mighty composition is the picture of Stockholm's castle in flames which closes the first narrative, *The Green Corridor!* Heidenstam has rendered the picturesque element of Charles XII's history with the most finished art: not only the gloomy scenes in black, gray, and white from the wintry land in the North, but also the variegated and highly colored representations of the wanderings in the war. The Queen of the Marauders among the Cossacks by the Beresina; the march of Mazeppa, surrounded by drunken Zaporogeans; the flaxen-haired Stupid Swede in the serail of the sultana, among gilded parrot-cages and black cypresses—one could not draw a more masterly contrast between the simple poverty of the Charles folk and the exoticism of the Orient.

The artist reveals himself everywhere, but so, too, does the aristocrat. The patriarchal idyl of the country manor is immortalized in the airy *Midsummer Sport*. The gay, care-free spirit of adventure that played through the centuries among the Swedish nobility is incarnate in the indomitable Grothusen who is always in debt; and when Rika Fuchs rides in front of his regiment to make an estimate of his property, every Swede must recognize the national sense of humor. The joking spirit has undergone an intimate union with a proud and taciturn sense of duty. (pp. xvii-xix)

Of the glittering conqueror, "King Charles, the youthful hero," illuminated by the sunshine of triumph and success, whom Tegnér celebrated a hundred years after, Heidenstam has not much to tell. Only for a brief second may we catch a glimpse of his boyish ardor as he steps ashore at Zeeland. It is in the time of adversity and defeat that he begins to interest Heidenstam. (p. xx)

The hero of this tragedy is, accordingly, not only the king, but the Swedish people as well. In *Poltava* Lewenhaupt says: "The wreath he twined for himself slid down upon his subjects instead." (pp. xxi-xxii)

[*The Charles Men*] is not only a monument over the fall of the Swedish empire, but also a hymn on the beauty in its destruction, the hopeless magnanimity of obedience to duty, the poetry of sacrifice. It expresses Heidenstam's deeply tragic philosophy of life. The highest that a man can attain is to fall with honor, and such is the fate of the best. Happiness is common and superficial; suffering is holy and great.

None of the stories in *The Charles Men* is more deeply characteristic of Heidenstam than *The Stupid Swede*. The parks and pavilions of the Turkish serail, with their roses and jewels, symbolize the oriental doctrine of pleasure and beauty that he celebrated in his youth. But at the moment when the awkward and joyless Swedish thrall stands among the glittering, soulless dancing-girls, who know nothing more of earth than that it is lovely, and dream of nothing else than of a kiosk with red damask hangings and perfumed fountains, her form suddenly takes on an exaltation that none of the others possesses; and when she seizes the basket with the snake in order to fulfil her duty, it is she who is the most beautiful. Beauty of self-sacrifice, of misfortune, of the soul, causes her to shine more brightly than even the odalisque Evening Starlight. (pp. xxii-xxiii)

The Stupid Swede is a legend of that soul-temper which transforms ugliness to grace and misfortune to harmony. That soul-temper is glorified in the concluding words of *The Charles Men*, where a benediction is called down upon the people who in their fall from greatness caused their poverty to be glorified before the world. (p. xxiii)

> *Fredrik Böök, "Verner von Heidenstam: Author of 'The Charles Men'" (1919), in* The Charles Men *by Verner von Heidenstam, translated by Charles Wharton Stork (copyright © 1920 by The American-Scandinavian Foundation; Canadian rights by permission of Jonathan Cape Ltd), American-Scandinavian Foundation, 1920, pp. vi-xxiii.*

THE NEW YORK TIMES BOOK REVIEW   (essay date 1925)

"The Tree of the Folkungs" spreads an enticing shade. Under its high and heartening spell the reader becomes gratefully aware that "The Mabinogian," the Arthurian cycle, the Nibelungen Lied, the Song of Roland, the old Norse sagas and even Homer are not of an order of literature which is altogether past. . . .

To call "The Tree of the Folkungs" a romantic history or a historical romance of Sweden, from the decline of the Age of the Vikings, about 1060, to the final triumph of Christianity over the dark and bloody old pagan rites, in 1275, would be at once simple accuracy and a gross understatement. "The Tree" is laden with magnificent treasure. It is a glimpse of furtive, cave-dwelling dwarves, delightfully reminiscent of a part of "Peer Gynt"—of the customs and robust daring of the Vikings, of the rise of a landed aristocracy, of the conflict between Christian priests and the earthy rituals of Thor, Odin, Loki, Frey, of desperate and hopeless romantic love, of honor and chivalry and falsehood. It might almost be said to run the gamut of human emotions. Yet it has a modern sense of complicated motive and personality. It is full of pageant and circumstance, battle, thrilling action, and it has an unforced density of inner struggle. (pp. 9, 16)

The book falls into two great divisions: "Folke Filbyter" and "The Bellbo Heritage." The foundation of the dynasty that is to be the Folkungs, enormously rich, fabulously greedy and strikingly of a mold in traits and habits, yet each individualized, is laid in the character and dogged singleness of purpose of Folke Filbyter. . . .

The influence of material possessions, in all its variations and inflections, upon human character is an unobstrusive yet potent ingredient in "The Tree of the Folkungs." The first Folke had pride of race, in the future, and a blank, relentless subordination of self to the larger biological purpose. He is a living ancestor. Yet Folke stands as enduringly and as inescapably, all dimensions of him, as that "barge of a man" in Knut Hamsun's "Growth of the Soil." The second generation has begun to know shame of the father and covetousness of his accumulations. With Folke's very recognition of the fulfillment of his impersonal design there comes a belated awakening of his personal yearning for that affection and intimacy which the whole direction of his life has excluded. He lies in the ashes and filth of his hearth, among the stolid serfs, and peers abashed at the resplendent con-

descension of his two sons and his crafty grandson, already deep in the councils of the king.

"The Bellbo Heritage" concerns the fortunes of the property whose nucleus was gathered by Folke in the period two centuries later, when the supremacy of the Folkungs is supreme and a Folkung is King of Sweden. (p. 16)

Arthur J. Chater presents what is apparently a plastic equivalent of the original in his translation. The prose is figurative, concrete and sonorous. It clusters delightfully in little nuggets of pithy and abstract wit. It strides along in the magnificent major chords of an epic, and it glitters and ripples in spontaneous lyricism. . . . "The Tree of the Folkungs" is monumental. (p. 19)

> *"After the Vikings," in* The New York Times Book Review *(© 1925 by The New York Times Company; reprinted by permission), April 12, 1925, pp. 9, 16, 19.*

THE SATURDAY REVIEW OF LITERATURE   (essay date 1926)

"The Swedes and Their Chieftains" is designed primarily for youth, though it is written in a manner that to a certain extent may alienate it from young people, and to a certain extent from their elders, for it lies on middle ground. It is often too simplified and naive for adults, it is often too literary and unexciting for adolescents. Where young and old should meet in heartiest unanimity is in a couple of rousing and spirited sagas and in the full-blooded stories of two or three really great Swedish heroes. Gustav Vasa, Gustavus Adolphus, and Charles XIII are inherently good characters for narrative, and in his clear, direct manner Heidenstam speeds them through pages of exploit which neither boyish impatience nor grown-up sophistication can withstand. So, too, in their way, but not to the same extent, will one or two stories from the repository of Scandinavian legend hit double targets, for they appeal strongly to the imagination, which is perennial.

Heidenstam manifests his primary desire to reach a youthful audience in a tale like "At Venerable Upsala," where the unisyllabic method of writing, with its questionable simplifications, gives a brief summary of the lives of several Swedish scientists. Here certainly is something for grown-ups to skip and for boys to find in watery contrast to the tales that precede and follow. The tale which immediately follows, concerning Gustav III, with its climactic assassination at a masquerade, makes very good reading. Of course Heidenstam has certain notable literary qualities, implicit rather than emphatic in a book like this—qualities of vigor, clearness, vitality, and imagination which are needed to revivify the past as "The Swedes and Their Chieftains" proves itself capable of doing. The technique of the book is simple and orthodox, far removed from the technique of our present-day sophisticated historians, but its aims are far removed also. Here are sagas and battle-pieces and chronicles simple and clear in their architecture and their style. They constitute an effective arrangement of the high points in Sweden's history. (pp. 531-32.)

> *"'The Swedes and Their Chieftains'," in* The Saturday Review of Literature *(copyright © 1926 by Saturday Review; all rights reserved; reprinted by permission), Vol. II, No. 27, January 30, 1926, pp. 531-32.*

ANNIE RUSSELL MARBLE (essay date 1932)

Verner von Heidenstam must be included on the lists of novelists as well as poets [beginning with his first romance, *Endymion*]. . . .

With a painter's glow of fancy he sought to depict, through a love story of moderate interest, the atmosphere of the East, when it is clouded by restraints of Western civilization. He had registered rebellion against the growth of naturalism in fiction: in *Pepita's Wedding* . . . he urged idealism, and search for inner truth. The term, "imaginative realist," which has been used to classify Heidenstam, is especially applicable to the fantastic, emotional tale, *Hans Alienus*. . . . As writer of fiction, however, the name of Heidenstam will always be linked most closely with *The Charles Men (Karolinern)*—stories of Charles XII and his wars—a series of prose-poems depicting Swedish heroism, written with fervor and artistic finish. . . . Among the best of several dramatic tales are **"French Mons," "The Fortified House,"** and **"Captured."** Like Rolland, Heidenstam is a pacifist yet he has written a vigorous tribute to this "King who lived his whole life in the field and died in a trench," the man who was a genius in war but, like his heroic men, gentle as well as brave, with lofty visions.

Other romances followed this major work, *The Charles Men*—tales and folklore, sagas and modern applications in *Saint George and the Dragon, Saint Birgitta's Pilgrimage,* and *Forest Murmurs*. In fiction and essays the writer has attacked naturalism that "lets the cellar air escape through the house." Some of his significant essays are collected as *Classicism and Teutonism*. It is unfortunate that so few of his works are adequately rendered into English. (pp. 193-94)

For older youths and adults he has embodied poetic legends with modern teachings in two plays [*The Soothsayer* and *The Birth of God*]. . . . The first play is located upon "An Arcadian Plain" with Apollo, the Soothsayer, the Fates, and Erigone, wife of the Soothsayer, as leading characters. . . .

The Birth of God is founded upon Egyptian mythology. (p. 195)

[*The Tree of the Folkungs*] is a romance, mingling history, sagas, fantasy, pageantry, action, and modern interpretation of some of the deeds and ideals of the Vikings. . . . This legendary romance-pageant has scenes of dramatic power . . . , and many customs of historical and imaginative past. It is an elaborate, well constructed revelation of Heidenstam's imaginative insight and vigor, united with his skill in interpreting the *past,* in history and sagas, to the problems of the *present hour*. He is, in truth, "the herald of a new epoch in our literature." (pp. 196-97)

> *Annie Russell Marble, "A Group of Winners—Novelists and Poets," in her* The Nobel Prize Winners in Literature: 1901-1931, *D. Appleton, and Company, 1932, pp. 189-205.**

ALRIK GUSTAFSON (essay date 1940)

[Though] in the middle of the '80's Heidenstam's view of the future of his own class is dark enough, he did not permit this view to lead him ultimately into either of the two characteristic blind alleys of *fin de siècle* decadence—the sordidly fatalistic hopelessness typified by [Hermann] Bang's *Generations without Hope* or the thinly veiled sensuousness parading as religious mysticism which runs through much of

[J. K.] Huysman's late work. Heidenstam . . . came finally to work out a new synthesis of the spirit of the age, a synthesis essentially optimistic in its tone, idealistic in its aims, critically constructive in its manner of procedure. He conceived this new synthesis as largely in opposition to the current naturalism and decadence. . . . Heidenstam was no mere dogmatic reactionary, any more than he was an irresponsible aesthete resting sensuously in the slumbrously mystical shades of a resuscitated Romanticism. His reinterpretation of Sweden's national past, first becoming manifest in the more mature portions of *Dikter* (*Poems* . . .), has proved to be one of the most solid, bracing contributions to Swedish literature and to Swedish culture in the last fifty years. In the best of his poetry and prose since 1895—and little of it falls below the best, so critical is his artistic self-judgment—he has given expression to an heroic national ideal with no less dignity and reserve than freshness and vigor. (pp. 129-30)

[When his first volume of poems, *Vallfart och vandringsår* (*Pilgrimage and Wander-Years*), appeared], it aroused immediate admiration. (p. 131)

Some of the acclaim of critics and public was perhaps occasioned by the exotic background of many of the poems in Heidenstam's first volume; but more significant, no doubt, was the vigorous freshness of tone which animated most of these poems. The imagery, brilliantly alive, was boldly conceived and not sparing in broad, vivid splashes of color—a startling contrast to the grays and blacks of the contemporary naturalism and decadence. And in the narrative poems, especially, the metrical technique was marvelously flexible, invariably appropriate to the diverse pattern of the themes. Most of the poems tended to glorify youth and beauty, the pleasures of the moment, the unlimited power of love. Strange themes these—strange, and seductively fascinating—to a literary generation which had been taught to admire rigid utilitarian ideals of social conscience and an art rigorously subordinated to immediate, observable fact.

Much, however, as Heidenstam's poems in this volume seemed to glory in undisciplined, spontaneously youthful responses to all the diverse wealth of life which the poet had experienced, this was not the only note struck in *Pilgrimage and Wander-Years*. Nor, in the light of Heidenstam's later development, was it the most important. The discriminating reader is aware of occasional notes of questioning, of skepticism even, in the zestful abundance of Heidenstam's oriental tales; and that these notes were neither accidental nor a pale reflection of an earlier Romantic nostalgia is suggested by the formal inclusion in the volume of a section of short, confessional lyrics entitled **"Thoughts in Loneliness."** [Oscar] Levertin had, indeed, in his review of the volume, dismissed this section with the phrase "uninteresting sentimental lyricism"; but his judgment was obviously hasty. In these poems we find the first genuine evidences of the *great* note that is to come more richly into Heidenstam's poetry in such mature later volumes as [*Dikter* (*Poems*) and *Nya Dikter* (*New Poems*)]. . . . (pp. 131-32)

Each of the poems in the section "Thoughts in Loneliness" is a highly concentrated, exquisitely beautiful expression of some mood or idea that had intimately and deeply moved Heidenstam in these early years: his loneliness in an essentially unfriendly contemporary world; his yearning for the homeland; his desire to identify his spirit with something outside itself, with nature or with the past; his proud rejection of Christianity in favor of an atheism more consistent with the modern temper—yet an atheism with its own deep humility, originating in Heidenstam's consciousness of the solemn human mission of the poet. The contrast is curious, and very marked, between the poetic extravaganzas of the oriental poems and the beautifully restrained lyric dignity of the **"Thoughts in Loneliness."** The former remind one in their vivid and glowing imagery and in their spontaneous romantic lyricism of Byron or the young Hugo, the latter in their epigrammatic concentration of phrase and their emotional restraint of Runeberg and Rydberg, or of Goethe in such a lyric as "Über allen Gipfeln." (p. 132)

[Before *Poems* appeared] Heidenstam was engaged in a rather prolific literary production, for the most part in prose, and largely conceived in the vividly colorful manner of the oriental tales from *Pilgrimage and Wander-Years*. In these works Heidenstam casts up accounts with his youth and with the Sweden of the '80's in a series of autobiographical fragments [*From Col di Tenda to Blocksberg; Endymion; Hans Alienus*] . . . and in two very important controversial essays ["Renascence"; and "Pepita's Wedding," written with Levertin]. . . . We find in these works that he is as severely critical with the extravagances of his own youth as he is with the sober, utilitarian spirit of the '80's against which in his youth he had so strongly reacted.

The critical essay **"Renascence"** and the autobiographical fantasia *Hans Alienus* are the most important of these works. *Hans Alienus* was obviously written as a discipline in thinking, despite the fantastic allegorical framework in which it is cast. In it Heidenstam was taking inventory of his spiritual resources at the close of his period of revolt in preparation for the more constructive period which was to follow. Hans Alienus, at the close of the novel, dies rather sordidly—a kind of aristocratic Wilhelm Meister who found no solution to the riddle of the universe at the close of his chaotic, strangely hopeless "wander-years." It is not to be so with the Heidenstam who is to come, however. The universe, it is true, always comes to retain for him its deep, inexplicable mystery. But this mystery he finds, ultimately, to be a bracing, invigorating challenge to the free human spirit, to the best instincts of man; and out of the mystery, even in its profoundly tragic aspects, man must inevitably grow in moral stature—dignified, heroic, noble to the very end. The mystery of the universe, Heidenstam's mature thought would suggest, is a deeply *moving* mystery—a mystery that can finally spell unity rather than chaos, a mystery that challenges a noble gathering of one's spiritual resources rather than one that precipitates hopelessness and despair and spiritual decadence.

The essay **"Renascence"** is to be looked upon as a preliminary statement of general literary aims and ideals rather than a carefully worked out aesthetics. It is a pronunciamento, more interested in sketching future possibilities for literature than in lingering over past accomplishments or failures, though its opening sections do concern themselves with the limitations of the prevailing naturalism. It proposes, in short, to give impetus to a new literary and cultural movement in Sweden; and it did just this. Its most immediate concern was to define with some care the limitations of naturalism as a literary method and to announce that the day of naturalism had passed and that a new aesthetics must be ushered in if Swedish literature was to retain vitality and lasting significance. Heidenstam does not in this essay condemn naturalism

and the spirit of the Swedish '80's *sub specie aeternitates*. He looks upon it rather as a passing phase in literary taste, which had in it something of good, though in its extreme manifestations as an art form, it had more of evil; and certainly it had run its course and should give way to a new literary form. He admits that naturalism had exercised an "extraordinarily salutary" influence on prose fiction, though for poetry it had perhaps chiefly a negative significance. He holds naturalism responsible for much of the false note of melancholy to be found in the chill "gray weather" poetry of the '80's. He insists that both this poetry and the contemporary philosophical pessimism, with which such poetry is closely related, must soon give way to other moods and other points of view. "The times thirst for joy," he maintains—though not, of course, for a superficial, hysterical joy. Man needs a deep, abiding joy—a joy that is to be made consistent ultimately with the spirit of resignation. . . . Particularly desirable, he finally argues, is a departure from naturalism, and its ultimate form, *fin de siècle* decadence, in the literature of Sweden; for the spirit and technique of naturalism are basically foreign to the Swedish national temperament. Sweden needs a new *national* literature, developing naturally out of the healthy, vigorous organism of its own basic racial and national temper. (pp. 133-35)

Though Heidenstam's true greatness must always be sought in the best of his lyric poetry, he wrote much prose, most of it in quality just short of much of his greatest lyric poetry. Practically all of his most significant prose falls within the score of years marked off by his two great volumes of poetry, [*Poems* and *New Poems*]. . . . He reveals himself in this prose as an essayist of sparkling epigrammatic power, as a short story writer of marvelous dramatic concentration, and as a novelist of very real distinction. During the years in which this prose was written he had "arrived" as an artist and thinker; the critical ideas which had been given preliminary expression in **"Renascence"** had by this time matured and deepened into a creative production of marvelous depth and power.

The subject matter of most of Heidenstam's poetry and prose tends to expand and illustrate the ideal of a Swedish national literature which had been proposed in the closing paragraphs of **"Renascence."** The volume of *Poems* . . . contained something more than hints of Heidenstam's movement in this direction. Some of the poems in it, to be sure, are closely related to his earlier work, particularly to *Pilgrimage and Wander-Years* and to *Hans Alienus*. Here is to be found the old theme of the poet's loneliness, his inability to identify himself with the immediate realities of contemporary life and thought. Here are poems also with the bold, vivid imagery of *Pilgrimage and Wander-Years*. Moreover two of the poems in *Hans Alienus* appear again, unchanged, in *Poems*. . . .

And yet how different on the whole are these new *Poems!* The old brooding, the old skepticisms bordering on pessimism are for the most part gone. They give way to a new spirit of optimism, restrained, dignified, characterized by a deep-flowing, quietly vigorous zest for life; and they suggest a new, constructive attitude toward life—an attitude filled with a warm, understanding humanity which finds its deepest roots in a feeling for Sweden's national past. (pp. 136-37)

His first important prose work was the two volumes of *Karolinerna* [*The Charles Men*]. . . . In the tragic-heroic figure of Charles XII Heidenstam came to find at one and the same time a constructive national ideal of the truly heroic and a point of departure for a severe critical analysis of the cultural materialism of Sweden at the turn of the century.

As early as 1892 Heidenstam had published "Fifty Years After," the first to appear of the tales that ultimately went into the pages of *The Charles Men*. In Heidenstam's early treatment of these tales he seems to have been largely fascinated by the romantic, robustly saga-like nature of his material; but the longer his genius occupied itself with the theme the more he became impressed with the sombre, tragic grandeur of the material. Heidenstam's final picture of Charles XII is, in consequence, a picture of heroic sacrifice, of magnificent resignation to a hopeless train of circumstance; and in this picture, characteristically, the humble, undying loyalty of the private soldier comes to serve as a fittingly heroic background for the central portrait of Charles himself—a Charles whom his soldiers worshipped even in the moments of their severest trials. (pp. 138-39)

The story of Saint Birgitta [in *Heliga Birgittas pilgrimsfärd* (*Saint Birgitta's Pilgrimage*)] led Heidenstam back to the fourteenth century, four hundred years earlier than the time of Charles XII. It led him also into religious concerns primarily, rather than into political and military activities; and yet here, as in *The Charles Men*, his chief preoccupation is with the heroic *character* rather than with historical detail in general, and one discerns in his finely imaginative conception of Saint Birgitta many of the same strengths and weaknesses with which he had previously invested Sweden's hero-king of the early eighteenth century. Here are the same heroic proportions, the same fanaticisms, the same gloriously feverish activity, the same ultimate tragedy—except that now all of this is placed over against a religious background.

And yet one notes a difference—a difference not in kind, but in emphasis; and the difference is very important. The great personality, the strong will, is treated with the same sympathy in *Saint Birgitta's Pilgrimage* as it is in *The Charles Men;* but it is to be noted that the domineering will of Saint Birgitta must ultimately undergo a cleansing transformation—its instinctive fanatical brutality must finally be transformed by humility, by resignation, by a profoundly human spiritual experience, before the great deeds of Birgitta can be anything more than a mere mockery of fate. This is a new note in Heidenstam, pointing the way to a new conception of the heroic and the tragic, and hinting a new ethics. It is, however, in *Folkungaträdet* (*The Tree of the Folkungs*, . . .)—the first part of which (*Folke Filbyter*) follows *Saint Birgitta's Pilgrimage* by only four years—that Heidenstam's mature ethics of heroic resignation is given its most complete and consistent expression.

The Tree of the Folkungs reaches still farther back into Swedish history than had *Saint Birgitta's Pilgrimage*. Its first volume, indeed, pushes us back beyond the pages of sober historical documents into that only half-historical region of the early Scandinavian sagas. Myth and legend, tradition and saga provide only partially complete materials to Heidenstam's historical imagination as he sketches in bold, realistic outlines the character of Folke Filbyter, that legendary peasant founder of a family which a couple of centuries after his death was to occupy the throne of Svea Land and Göta Land. The very tenuousness of the historical material permits Heidenstam the greatest imaginative freedom in his treatment of the origins of the Folkung family; and the result—as in the case of Shakespeare's Lear—becomes a tragedy of profound and moving power. (pp. 139-40)

[An] outline of the story contained in *The Tree of the Folkungs* provides only the faintest suggestion—if it does even that—of the narrative skill with which Heidenstam has developed tha tragic theme of the novel. It throws little light on his conception of the tragic as such, and only hints at the ethics upon which this conception of the tragic rests. It touches not at all, moreover, on the more purely aesthetic aspects of Heidenstam's fictional technique: his method of employing historical material; his occasional use of poetic symbolism to give to the novel a unity even beyond that provided by the plot; and his richly varied prose style, a prose style which is vigorous and idyllic by turns, which never draws back from the most bold realistic phrase if the action demands it and yet is always completely controlled, restrained, finely disciplined. (p. 148)

The approach to an adequate understanding of the ultimate greatness of *The Tree of the Folkungs* must in consequence by made primarily through an analysis of the guiding ideas of Heidenstam's mature general thought. Heidenstam's ethics is at the core of this body of thought. He found his way to the ethics of *The Tree of the Folkungs* only by a long and arduous route. We have seen that his earliest volume of poetry, *Pilgrimage and Wander-Years*, reveals little if any concern with social and moral problems. The poems in this volume, with the exception of those contained in the section entitled "Thoughts in Loneliness," are largely concerned with a spontaneous enjoyment of the immediate physical pleasures of life. And even the "Thoughts in Loneliness" are partly epicurean in tone, though it is the epicureanism of Romantic melancholy rather than the robust epicureanism of a glorified youthful sensuousness. Nowhere in *Pilgrimage and Wander-Years* is there any sympathetic response to the large world of humanity beyond the poet's own created world of beauty. The poems in the volume are essentially amoral in their point of view; they concern themselves primarily with the poet's own ego, and when a larger world outside this ego makes itself felt at all, the poet finds this world negative, disturbing, something from which to escape. In *Poems* . . ., a somewhat maturer note is struck; the poet has begun to identify himself with the world about him, and this identification, partial and fragmentary as it is, leads him inevitably to a consideration of broad social values—social values which in such a poem as "Home" take on the form of a nascent nationalism.

In *The Charles Men* . . . , Heidenstam's growing concern with the world outside himself takes on a much more definite form. In this novel he centres his attention primarily, as we have seen, on the character of Charles XII and the way in which this character represents in Swedish history a heroic moral ideal. Heidenstam finds the greatness of Charles XII to lie in a stern, self-sacrificing attitude toward his conception of duty. In striving to fulfill his destiny Charles XII found no personal sacrifice too great to make; and he expected the same ideal of sacrifice to actuate his people. The individual may thus be able to realize greatness, but only, in Heidenstam's view, as he identifies himself with the larger strivings of his people.

In *Saint Birgitta's Pilgrimage* . . . , Heidenstam's second venture into historical fiction, the figure of the famous Swedish saint seems at first conceived in precisely the same manner as Charles XII had been. She is on occasion inhuman, demanding of those about her the most undeviating loyalty to a harsh, almost brutal conception of duty; and her inhumanity is intensified by the driving motive of a severe religious fanaticism. And yet Birgitta is a character of a subtly complex, even of a paradoxical, kind. At times she yearns passionately for human sympathy, a sympathy which she had shut out from herself because of the fierce fanaticism that actuated her sense of duty. "If only people know," she burst out on one occasion, "how much more passionately I yearn to their hearts than they to mine!" . . . Saint Birgitta was great, her will had triumphed among her kind; but her greatness was not pure, unalloyed—in her devout spirit good and evil were both present, as it is in all of human life. She came to see this finally—this deep mystery which lies at the core of existence. And when she perceives it there sweeps over her a warm, intimately touching humanity, a humble resignation to the great mystery of life—a desire, finally, for peace rather than strife, for humble self-effacing prayer rather than for that vigorous aggressiveness of spirit which performs evil even when it yearns most intensely to do good. (pp. 152-54)

The ethical paradox contained in Saint Birgitta's final confession to her God becomes the basis for the ethics of *The Tree of the Folkungs,* though in this novel Heidenstam comes to apply the paradox more boldly and sweepingly to an interpretation of broad national and cultural issues rather than to an immediate personal religious experience. Gunnar Castien, a recent Swedish critic, sums up the ethics of this novel excellently when he writes that *The Tree of the Folkungs* "is a saga of large proportions about how culture has grown up from good and evil, from both the light and the dark powers in man's spirit. Culture is built upon meanness and greatness, upon egotistical greed and upon the ideal will to create, upon earthly envy and upon a deep yearning for purity. No one who has a purpose in life to realize can go through life blameless and without stain. But life can reconcile and ennoble." (p. 155)

Good and evil . . . so hopelessly intertwined in life, in individual men's lives and in the national structures which men try to build before they die. Can any good come out of conditions of existence so confused, so ominously chaotic, so ceaselessly at strife among themselves? Heidenstam does not answer the question definitely. He is too much of the critical philosophic mind to venture a dogmatic assertion; and yet as a poet he has a presentiment that good shall finally triumph, a profound historical intuition that man shall finally succeed, through aching lessons taught by trial and error, in building something approaching an ideal social and political structure which shall ultimately prevail. . . . The Folkungs themselves, we know, finally passed away, and evil days were to come again before their dynasty ceased to occupy the ancient throne of the Sveas and the Goths; but a Swedish national culture continued to exist, through evil hours and good, groping instinctively onward toward man's ultimate ideal—"Peace, peace, peace!" This is the burden of Heidenstam's ethical message in *The Tree of the Folkungs.* (pp. 159-60)

Heidenstam's greatest contribution to Swedish literature [is] the slender volume entitled *New Poems.* . . . [These poems represent] the most mature and perfect expression of Heidenstam's genius. For them the Swedish people have come to be deeply grateful. (p. 170)

[The poems in *New Poems*] occupy a peculiarly distinguished—if not an actually unique—place in the great flowering of lyric poetry which is the chief glory of Swedish literature since the 1890's. . . . In Heidenstam's poems Sweden has come to find, not without a deeply ennobling sense of humility, a profound national discipline—a discipline

which she may have needed even more than the perfect music of Fröding or the robustly virile tones of Karlfeldt. For *New Poems* . . . is essentially *a discipline:* an artistic and ethical discipline for Heidenstam himself, and a discipline of like kind for anyone who may come to linger long enough over these poems to fathom in some measure the deeper meanings which flow with nobly quiet dignity through them. Only the Swedish nation, to whom these poems were dedicated and directed, can hope to sense their finer, ultimate values.

What we find in these poems, fundamentally, is the quiet, meditative note of the "**Thoughts in Loneliness**" and of *Poems* . . .; except that now this note has taken on a new strength and richness, a new and arresting maturity. Its thought is infinitely more profound; its emotional overtones are more restrained, without losing their basic freshness and vitality; and its form is invariably exquisite, crystal clear, with no ornamental excrescences—in a word severely, nobly classical. (p. 171)

[In] the years after the appearance of *New Poems,* down to Heidenstam's death nearly a quarter of a century later, his voice was largely silent. . . . [He] became in the last analysis a prisoner of the 1890's, the literary program of which he was the first to define and whose rich efflorescence of poetry and prose found in Heidenstam one of its most representative figures. (p. 176)

> *Alrik Gustafson, "Nationalism Reinterpreted: Verner von Heidenstam," in his* Six Scandinavian Novelists: Lie, Jacobsen, Heidenstam, Selma Lagerlöf, Hamsun, Sigrid Undset *(copyright © 1940 by the American-Scandinavian Foundation), Princeton University Press, 1940 (and reprinted by the University of Minnesota Press, 1967), pp. 123-76.*

CHARLES WHARTON STORK   (essay date 1961)

[Heidenstam's *Pilgrimage and Wander-Years* (*Vallfart och vandringår*] was a brilliant debut, so much so indeed that it aroused a new vitality in the younger poets. . . . Professor Fredrik Böök, Sweden's foremost critic of the period, acclaims it as follows: "In this we have the verse of a painter; strongly colorful, plastic, racy, vivid. In a bold, sometimes careless, form there is nothing academic; all is seen and felt and experienced, the observation is sharp and the imagination lively. The young poet-painter reproduces the French life of the streets; he tells stories of the Thousand and One Nights, and conjures up before us the bazaars of Damascus. In the care-free indolence of the East he sees the last reflection of the old happy existence, and for that reason he loves it. And yet amid all the gay hedonism in *Pilgrimage and Wander-Years* is a cycle of short poems, "**Thoughts in Loneliness**," filled with brooding, melancholy, and sombre longing." (pp. 39-40)

"**Thoughts in Loneliness**" is . . . in sharp contrast with the others. It consists of fragmentary personal revelations. . . . A dominant motive is the poet's longing for his homeland and its boyhood associations. . . . He is utterly disappointed in himself and in the desultory life he has been leading. What he really wants is to find "a sacred cause" to which he can honestly devote himself. This restless individualism found its answer when he returned to live nearly all the rest of his life in Sweden. His cause was to commemorate the glory of her past and to incite her people to perpetuate it in the present. (p. 40)

Like his friend and contemporary August Strindberg he had little patience with collective mediocrity. He saw Sweden as a country of smug and narrow provincialism, indifferent to the heroic spirit of its former glory. Strindberg's remedy for this condition was to tear down the old structures and build anew from the ground up. Heidenstam's conception, on the contrary, was to revive the present by the memories of the past.

Whether in prose or poetry, all of Heidenstam's later work was concerned with Sweden. With the first of a group of historical novels, *The Charles Men (Karolinerna)* . . . , he achieved the masterpiece of his career. In scope and power it can only be compared to Tolstoy's *War and Peace*. . . . Though it centers around the brilliant and enigmatic figure of Charles XII, the true hero is not finally the king himself. Hence the title of the book, referring to the soldiers and subjects of the king. (pp. 40-1)

The Charles Men consists not of a connected narrative but of a group of short stories, each depicting a special phase of the general subject. Somewhat uneven in interest for an average reader, eight or ten of these are among the finest of their kind in literature. They comprise a great variety of scene and interest: grim episodes of war, idyllic interludes, superb canvases of world-shaking events, and delightfully humorous sketches of odd characters. The general effect is tragic. Almost nothing is said of Charles' spectacular victories, the central theme being the heroic loyalty of the Swedish people to their idolized king in misfortune and defeat.

To carry out this exalted conception the author has combined the vivid realism and imaginative power we have noticed in his early poetry and carried them out on a grand scale. His peculiar gift, as had been suggested before, is his intensity. (p. 42)

Heidenstam wrote four other works of fiction about earlier figures revered in Swedish memory. Excellent in their way, they lack the wide appeal of *The Charles Men*. . . . It is different with his volume *The Swedes and Their Chieftains (Svenskarna och deras hövdingar)*, a history intended for the general reader and particularly suited for high school students. Admirably written, it is a perfect introduction to Swedish history for readers of other countries. Some of the earlier episodes have touches of the supernatural, as suited to the legendary background. . . . The chief incentive to patriotism with Heidenstam, as has been noted all along, is faithfulness to the great memories of the past. . . . There is also the love of the land in all its aspects and in every season, especially of the old houses where men live so close to it. (p. 43)

Heidenstam was almost equally pre-eminent in poetry and in prose. The reason that his poetry has been so extensively dealt with was, first, that in it his personality is more intimately revealed, and secondly, that it had a more important influence on contemporary writers. . . .

The example of Heidenstam gave confidence to [Gustaf Fröding] to develop his natural genius. Fröding was closely followed by E. A. Karlfeldt, a gentler and mellower celebrant of peasant life, who was one of the very few recipients of the Nobel award for poetry exclusively. Since then poetry has continued to hold a leading place in Swedish literature. (p. 44)

> *Charles Wharton Stork, "Verner von Heidenstam," in* The American Scandinavian Review *(copyright 1961 by The American-Scandinavian Foundation), Vol. XLIX, No. 1, March, 1961, pp. 39-44.*

ADDITIONAL BIBLIOGRAPHY

Borland, Harold H. "Heidenstam and Nietzsche." In his *Nietzsche's Influence on Swedish Literature with Special Reference to Strindberg, Ola Hansson, Heidenstam and Froding*, pp. 82-111. Göteborg: Elanders Boktryckeri Aktiebolag, 1955.
> Describes Heidenstam's introduction to Nietsche through Strindberg and the Nietzschean ideas in Heidenstram's writings, especially *Hans Alienus.*

"V. von Heidenstam, Nobel Winner, 1916." *The New York Times* (21 May 1940): 20.
> Outline of Heidenstam's literary career.

"*The Tree of the Folkungs.*" *The Spectator*, No. 5070 (29 August 1925): 341.
> Praises this romance for its "tenderness of imagination and spirituality," reiterating Heidenstam's kinship with the English temperament.

Stork, Charles Wharton. Introduction to *Sweden's Laureate: Selected Poems of Verner von Heidenstam*, by Verner von Heidenstam, edited by Charles Wharton Stork, pp. 13-31. New Haven: Yale University Press, 1919.
> Biographical sketch and introduction to the major themes and styles of Heidenstam's poetry.

Nikos Kazantzakis

1885?-1957

(Also transliterated as Kazantzakes) Greek novelist, poet, essayist, travel writer, dramatist, autobiographer, and translator.

Kazantzakis, one of the most controversial of modern Greek writers, struggled throughout his life for a resolution of the conflict between mind and body. It has often been remarked that Kazantzakis's works, when viewed as a whole, form an integrated vision. Though obsessed with abstruse philosophic issues, Kazantzakis had a sensual love of life, which he best portrayed in his character Zorba in the novel *Bios kai politeia tou Alexe Zormpa* (*Zorba the Greek*). His novels are not dry philosophical tracts; rather, they are vivid examinations of ideas given life through his characters.

Kazantzakis, born in Crete, grew up in the midst of Cretan rebellion against Turkish rule, which culminated in a revolution in 1897. Kazantzakis was evacuated during the uprising and placed in a Franciscan school where he was introduced to Western philosophies, a discipline he pursued the rest of his life. He completed his education in Germany, Italy, and France, studying in Paris under the philosopher Henri Bergson. After taking a degree in law, Kazantzakis spent thirty years in government service. Throughout that period he traveled extensively, and his travel books are often praised for their understanding of people and places.

In Kazantzakis's works philosophic questions play a primary role; in fact, they can almost be called his protagonists. Kazantzakis was a philosophical syncretist who incorporated concepts from many forms of thought to create his own vision of life. However, he was most profoundly influenced by the works of Nietzsche and Bergson. From Nietzsche came a formal definition of the duality which lay behind all Kazantzakis's works: the opposition of flesh (the Dionysian) and spirit (the Apollonian), which was characterized in Nietzsche's *The Birth of Tragedy* as the fundamental conflict of human nature. From Bergson he accepted the concept of life as an ever-improving process. According to Bergson, every form of life represents a step in the evolutionary process toward a more perfect being who will eventually become one with the creative force, which Bergson termed the *élan vital*. In this schema, as humankind (the highest order in the chain of being) is further refined, it will move closer to absolute unity with the *élan vital*.

Kazantzakis utilized the two philosophies in this way: through his work he sought to unite flesh and spirit, believing that by harmonizing them humankind would achieve liberation from an eternal conflict and thus gain greater freedom and closeness to the creative force. Kazantzakis believed that the quest for such freedom should be the basis of life, though he knew that liberation was impossible to achieve, except in brief, isolated instances. He used the term the "Cretan glance" to describe this fleeting achievement of unity between opposing dualities, such as life and death, passionate action and passive reflection, the Apollonian and Dionysian, and Eastern and Western philosophies and ways of life.

The attempt to resolve the conflict between flesh and spirit is central to *Zorba the Greek*, and *Ho Christos xanastauronetai*

Pictorial Parade Inc.

(*The Greek Passion*), but it found its ultimate expression in his epic poem *Odyseia* (*The Odyssey: A Modern Sequel*). Kazantzakis's Odysseus is a confused modern man, stripped of his illusions, who searches for a meaning to life and freedom. Like most of Kazantzakis's heroes, Odysseus seeks self-knowledge and unity, but rarely succeeds in his quest. Kazantzakis regarded *The Odyssey* as his major work, and most critics agree.

In *Ho teleutaios peirasmos* (*The Last Temptation of Christ*), Kazantzakis took what he considered to be another mythic hero and examined the conflicting dualities in his life. Kazantzakis's Christ is a prototypical free man who achieves victory over evil and fear by his constant struggle with temptation. The Greek Orthodox Church considered this humanization of Christ heretical. Both the church and the press attacked Kazantzakis in an enmity which lasted until his death, when the church refused to celebrate a funeral mass for him.

But this wasn't the only controversy surrounding Kazantzakis's work. He wrote in Modern, demotic Greek at a time when it was still considered unpatriotic to write in a form other than the Classical Greek of Homer. Kazantzakis was often attacked for his use of the demotic, but critics believe that his work was better for it. The demotic is more richly metaphoric than the

Classic, more concrete than abstract, and it made possible the vivid imagery necessary to his examination of the conflict between flesh and spirit. Kazantzakis is often praised for his impressive descriptive talent. He was not a great craftsman, however, and his works are often politely described as having "uncontrolled energy." In fairness to Kazantzakis, it must be noted that he did not aspire to literary craftsmanship; he wrote a large amount and he wrote it quickly.

Kazantzakis examines life with the tragic optimism of a man who delights in the knowledge that strife is the pervading fact of existence. His work vividly portrays modern spiritual conflicts, and for that reason he is one of the most widely read Greek writers of his time.

(See also *TCLC*, Vol. 2)

PRINCIPAL WORKS

Ophis kai krinos (novella) 1906
  [*Serpent and Lily*, 1980]
Salvatores Dei (essay) 1927
  [*The Saviors of God*, 1960]
Toda Raba (novel) 1929
  [*Toda Raba*, 1963]
Le jardin des rochers (novel) 1936
  [*The Rock Garden*, 1963]
Odyseia (poetry) 1938
  [*The Odyssey: A Modern Sequel*, 1958]
Bios kai politeia tou Alexe Zormpa (novel) 1946
  [*Zorba the Greek*, 1952]
Ho Christos xanastauronetai (novel) 1951
  [*The Greek Passion*, 1954; published in England as
    Christ Recrucified, 1954]
Ho kapetan Michales (novel) 1954
  [*Freedom or Death*, 1956; published in England as
    Freedom and Death, 1956]
Ho teleutaios peirasmos (novel) 1955
  [*The Last Temptation of Christ*, 1960; published in
    England as *The Last Temptation*, 1960]
Ho phtochoules tou Theou (novel) 1956
  [*St. Francis*, 1962; published in England as *God's
    Pauper, St. Francis of Assisi*, 1962]
Anaphora ston Gkreko (autobiography) 1961
  [*Report to Greco*, 1965]
Hoi aderphophades (novel) 1963
  [*The Fratricides*, 1964]

EDMUND FULLER (essay date 1953)

Mr. Kazantzakis speaks with a voice distinctly different from the familiar diction of the American novel. ["**Zorba the Greek**"] is a book with so much sweep and vitality and excitement that although many additional reactions are possible, few will read it without fascination.

The story's narrator, who is nameless, is a somewhat pallid man of books, in his mid-thirties, addicted curiously to Dante and Buddha. (p. 4)

The book is Zorba's. The narrator performs his technical function, but there are times when his cerebration becomes tedious and his boasted detachment becomes irresponsible and even ugly.

But Zorba! He is funny, ferocious, ingenious, unscrupulous, indomitable, bawdy, sacrilegious and frenzied. Above all, he is terrifyingly, disconcertingly alive.

Zorba is an elemental. He is more demonic than comic. He is in a tradition that can be traced through Aristophanes, Plautus, Rabelais, Cervantes and Voltaire. In part, he is the *picaro*, the wily rogue and companion, but he has a wildness, a demoniac quality that the traditional *picaro* does not possess. (pp. 4-5)

Conceptually the novel gets nowhere. It is in the life force of Zorba himself that its uniqueness rests. Otherwise it is pantheism, paganism of the classic school, which is rather sterile to be celebrated as a modus vivendi. . . .

The appearance of "**Zorba the Greek**" . . . [is] evidence that there is genuine vitality in the contemporary Greek novel. (p. 5)

> Edmund Fuller, "The Wild and Wily Zorba," in
> The New York Times Book Review (© 1953 by The
> New York Times Company; reprinted by permis-
> sion), April 19, 1953, pp. 4-5.

ANTHONY WEST (essay date 1953)

[Nikos Kazantzakis's novel "**Zorba the Greek**,"] which is filled with the clear beauty of the Greek islands, is a portrait of a good and happy man and is of outstanding excellence. Its author was a pupil of Henri Bergson and, like Proust, he seems to have found an immense and lasting stimulus in his contact with the luminous mind of that strangely outmoded philosopher. Proust said that after reading Bergson he felt as though he were standing on a high hill, and one senses that Kazantzakis has also visited this summit, a vantage point from which life is seen as a whole, bathed in the warm sunlight of sanity. . . . This breadth of view, based on a truly civilized culture, gives Kazantzakis's novel an extraordinary richness and completeness; instead of dealing with a single sector of experience, isolated for a special aesthetic purpose, it seems to celebrate all life in a manner that is at once altogether realistic and altogether happy. (p. 126)

Every page is alive with ideas and limpid images that have the precision and the concentrated, vibrant quality of poetry. As the Cretan village they lived near and its people enter one's mind, with the aromatic air and the sights and sounds of Greek life about them, one feels the same excited stirring of awareness that comes from the best of D. H. Lawrence. The writing is alive in the same way, and the mind behind it has the same warm appreciation of life and appetite for its pleasures. But unlike Lawrence, Kazantzakis has no constricting chapel background to break away from and no repulsive class system to preach against; he inherits the Greek tradition and proceeds without distraction to his main aim, the portrayal of a free man with the courage to undertake the responsibilities of his freedom and the moral strength to make full use of it. There is another difference between them. Lawrence was under such pressure to fight against what oppressed him that he could rarely risk being funny and lightening his deadly seriousness with comedy, as Dostoevski and all other truly great writers have done. On top of his fire, Kazantzakis has a rich vein of humor, and his Zorba is as entertaining as he is good. "**Zorba the Greek**" is a delightful and memorable book by a writer of real importance. (pp. 126, 129)

Anthony West, "Happy and Happy-Go-Lucky," in
The New Yorker *(© 1953 by The New Yorker Magazine, Inc.), Vol. XXIX, No. 10, April 25, 1953, pp. 126, 129-30.*

LESLIE A. FIEDLER (essay date 1956)

Freedom or Death [is] another fat, untidy Historical Romance, prompted by the best of political intentions on the surface level, and trifling just beneath the surface, with the worn-out Romantic themes of nostalgia for the primitive.

I am not, of course, impugning Mr. Kazantzakis' patriotism, his love for the soil of Crete or his dedication to the cause of freedom. On these subjects he gets the highest marks; it is only as a novelist that he fails. Even if he had composed *Freedom and Death* 50 years ago, it would not have been a *new* book but an obvious pastiche of Byronic stereotypes and costume melodrama out of Sir Walter Scott. . . .

Surely, it should be clear by now that the novel has only one obligation, along with its unlimited privileges: "to carry the torch to the back of the cave," that is, to illuminate the dark underside of the psyche, to explore the duplicity of human motivation. But this is precisely what Mr. Kazantzakis does *not* do. He is quite prepared to give us everything else: all the sensual reality of a Cretan village from the musk under the armpits of the Turkish women to the mingled odor of thyme and dung in the streets, but not the psychological reality. . . .

In this book which repeats over and over that a man must be a man, there are no men, none at least that we recognize as such—no complex, contradictory creatures whose weakness is their glory and whose glory is a joke. No character is seen from the inside, for none has an inside; they are all only "Heroes," which is to say Tenors and Baritones got up as Noble Savages. And since there are no men, there can be no true actions, only operatic gestures—without lights or sets or music to justify them. One could forgive the book finally everything but this: its poor writing, its archaic form, even its obviousness. . . .

Historical Romance has traditionally been as lacking in irony as in psychological insight. Heroism is its subject *par excellence:* and heroism is for us no longer a fact but a problem. . . .

I do not mean that the subject of heroism cannot be handled in our time; but it must be handled psychologically rather than rhetorically. (p. 19)

From time to time, a token modern, troubled and educated, is permitted to enter the difficult but unproblematical world of Mr. Kazantzakis' hairy heroes; and briefly we hope that a double view will prevail, some human perspective be established so we do not have to take his *palikars* at their own evaluation. But such "moderns" either retire in confusion, like the English schoolmaster who faints when a Greek warrior presents him with the head of a freshly decapitated Turk . . . or, if a Cretan by birth, he is permitted at the last minute to slough off the debilitating wisdom and caution learned in the effete world of the French and become a killer—earn for himself the final ecstacy of death beside a bloodstained comrade. . . .

And so Kosmas, a writer returning from abroad (who seems at first the author himself about to judge rather than abdicate

before his berserker ancestors) manages to become in the book's last pages the image of the brutal father he has always hated and to be killed in futile resistance against the Turks. . . .

Once he has embraced that great Mother, who is death as well as freedom, all things are forgiven him (even foreign loves)—and all things granted, whether he live or die. . . .

These were, we are asked to believe, the values of *real* men, before the fall to philosophy and literature and tightfitting trousers. (p. 20)

Leslie A. Fiedler, "Horse-Opera in Crete," in The New Republic *(reprinted by permission of* The New Republic; *© 1956 The New Republic, Inc.), Vol. 134, No. 9, February 27, 1956, pp. 19-20.*

EMMANUEL HATZANTONIS (essay date 1963)

Kazantzakis' writings on Spain reveal his great familiarity with the country's literary, cultural, and socio-political traditions. . . . Of all the leading literary figures of Spain, however, Kazantzakis had the greatest esteem for Cervantes. . . . (p. 283)

Kazantzakis did not limit himself to lauding Cervantes, to the exegesis of *Don Quijote* as a synthesis of the virtues and weaknesses of Spain, or to the portrayal of the Manchegan Knight as a symbol of the destinies of the Hispanic race. His creative imagination was fired by Cervantes' *hidalgo* more than once, and in the *Odyssey,* Kazantzakis' "magnum opus," we find Captain Sole deliberately modeled on Don Quijote.

Captain Sole makes his appearance in Book XX of the *Odyssey.* He is tormented by nightly visions of suffering human beings who ask him to come to their aid. . . . He then mounts his camel and sallies forth. . . . (pp. 283-84)

His mission, however, soon comes to an end, for in the very first encounter he is uncameled and bound by a band of "black armed men." They are about to kill him and feast upon him, when Odysseus arrives. . . . Odysseus marvels, recognizes in him "a new friend," and sets him free from his captors. Captain Sole, however, insists that he and his liberator should free the other slaves who are still in the hands of the "blacks." Odysseus endeavors to explain to him that it is rather difficult, pointing out that they are unarmed, but Captain Sole exclaims: "I am not disarmed! Justice is my protective shield!" He then dashes out, while Odysseus, rejoicing in his heart, hails him. . . . (p. 284)

The background of this episode corresponds to that of the "primera salida" of Cervantes' *hidalgo,* and the quixotic overtones in Kazantzakis' conception of Captain Sole are discernible in many details. Kazantzakis does not state that Captain Sole "frisaba con los cincuenta años," but it is obvious that his life has passed its meridian. His physical characteristics ("he was lean gangly, gawky, his head flat as a pie") resemble those of Don Quijote. . . . Cervantes derides his knight's weapons as rust-eaten relics. . . . Captain Sole's armor is worthy of derision, too: a battered shield that is not feared by mice; a dull sword whose only ambition is to lie in a soft velvet sheath; a frightened spear that bends and quivers like a reed; a helmet with a thousand holes. But to the deluded eyes of their master, as to those of the Manchegan knight, they appear superlative and, of course, suitable for the great battles conceived in his inflamed imagination. (pp. 284-285)

These analogies and similarities are so apparent as to suggest that Kazantzakis wanted his readers to know that he was deliberately casting his Captain Sole after Don Quijote. This suggestion is further corroborated by the fact that he called his character "Captain Sole," a name given to Cervantes' *hidalgo* in a poem that Kazantzakis had written four years before the publication of his *Odyssey*. This poem is one of twenty-one *Cantos in Terza Rima* which he composed in order to extoll "the souls that nourished his own soul," that is, those immortals of history and literature who become spiritual symbols of mankind and of himself. . . .

Odysseus' encounter with Captain Sole, the embodiment of Don Quijote, is not as strange or as anachronistic as it may at first appear. Though Kazantzakis' poem is a continuation of the Homeric *Odyssey*, its plot is not circumscribed by any temporal or spatial limitations. As a result, Odysseus meets in his new peregrinations many of the most salient personalities of all times and places, thinly disguised under new and less familiar names. Furthermore, while the immediate inspiration stems from Homer, the spiritual dimensions of Kazantzakis' epic and of its protagonist are not Homeric. This latest Odysseus is, in fact, closer to Dante's and Tennyson's Ulysses than to Homer's Ithacan. . . . Many of the other characters that populate the poem, whether created ex-novo or revivals of historical, religious, and literary figures, are also searching indomitably for something beyond the common and the material.

Kazantzakis fashioned or re-created these characters as men who, maniacally possessed by an ideal, reject the status quo of their times and environment, and seek to elevate actuality to the level of their illusions. He seems to have had a twofold purpose: 1. to celebrate them as companions-at-arms and kindred souls of his Odysseus, and 2. to make them symbols. He was convinced that such monomaniacs embody man's creative force and that they have marked the progress of the human race through the centuries, continuing and often improving divine creation. (p. 285)

Thus conceived, the Manchegan knight was bound to find a place in Kazantzakis' *Odyssey*. As a man who transfigured the drab world of facts into the splendor of his fertile imagination, as a redresser of wrongs and champion of justice, he was singularly apt to inspire Kazantzakis, and to become a character in his *Odyssey,* a poem whose central theme is the rejection of all coercive orthodoxy and the quest of absolute freedom.

Kazantzakis' conception of Don Quijote as a dispenser of Justice and an apostle of Freedom is not, of course, original or new. Neither is Kazantzakis the first writer to forge a character after the image of Cervantes' *hidalgo*. He is, however, the first modern Greek writer to re-create Don Quijote as a major character in a significant work. Hence, he can be considered as the initiator of Don Quijote's "fortune" in Greece. (pp. 285-86)

Emmanuel Hatzantonis, "Captain Sole: Don Quijote's After-Image in Kazantzakis' 'Odyssey'," in Hispania *(© 1963 The American Association of Teachers of Spanish and Portuguese, Inc.), Vol. XLVI, No. 2, May, 1963, pp. 283-86.*

C. N. STAVROU (essay date 1964)

In his lifetime, Kazantzakis embraced and discarded many philosophies. From all and sundry, he sought the same thing: some logic, some means by which he might reconcile his passionate love of sensuous existence with the importunity of his spiritual yearnings. He esteemed the Self and was jealous of its prerogatives; at the same time, though he saw the danger in exalting Man far above man, he realized it is "sympathy" which makes the cosmos one. . . .

Kazantzakis recognized that the inherent duality in man is a condition of life. Yet he felt equally certain that man's duty was to strive incessantly to reduce the dissonance of duality to the harmony of unity. (p. 317)

Three facets of Kazantzakis' thought . . . merit attention because of the crucial role they play in his works. These are his antirationalism closely allied with his mysticism, his belief in struggle as an efficacious agency for ultimate salvation, and his conviction that the unceasing striving to secure internal harmony and an integrated personality on the part of every individual is a prelude to union with the One. (p. 318)

[Although] Kazantzakis shared many of Nietzsche's ideas, he was never at ease in any thoroughgoing naturalism or rationalism. For example, he preferred Bergson to Darwin and Lenin to Spengler because Bergson and Lenin, unlike the others, gave him assurances that the earth is not a fortuitous concourse of atoms but purposeful and progressive; that man is not an accident but part of a design; that the present is not the finale but only the prologue to a resplendent future. Whether it was his early training, his heredity, his artistic temperament, or his "daimon," Kazantzakis would have been unable to say; all he instinctively and deeply knew was that the road to salvation was not in reason but in ritual, not in logic but in intuition. (pp. 318-19)

To the question whether any certainty can supersede hopes which betray and despair which debilitates, his Odysseus answers: "Live without one single hope or fear." But, in *The Last Temptation of Christ,* this admonition becomes: "Live in Christ." Toward the end of his life, Kazantzakis was wise enough, and courageous enough, and honest enough, to admit that man's emotional and spiritual needs craved what amoral naturalism and scientific naturalism could never provide. . . . Others might reduce all human motivation to the drive for power, for equality, or for sexual experience. But even in his Nietzschean, Darwinian, or Freudian moments (and these abound in his verse epic) Kazantzakis still conceptualized human motivation, repressions, lusts, in terms of the eternal conflict between soul and flesh. . . .

Kazantzakis' Odysseus wishes to savor life to the fullest; he wishes his flesh to be refined away entirely in experiencing all aspects of existence so that when the Iceman cometh, he will find not an iceberg of a man but only an icicle. At the same time, however, his adventures and escapades bring him neither lasting satisfaction nor any profound sense of fulfillment. The termination of each experience brings in its wake no feeling of accomplishment but rather a rejection of the experience as vain and abortive. (p. 319)

The temptation motif—ever present in the work of Kazantzakis and as prominent in *The Odyssey: A Modern Sequel* . . . as in *The Last Temptation of Christ* . . .—is, in fact, a helpful clue to his thought; temptation is stressed strongly in Greek Orthodoxy. It is significant to note that, although Odysseus' ostensible and avowed goal . . . is to acquire the wisdom which enables one to live without hope and to remain true to the earth, his journey, insofar as it is a series of repudiations—and even though Christ's teaching is numbered among these repudiations—is not very different from the progress to Calvary. . . . When man perceives the futility and absurdity of existence, he is faced with two alternatives, which can readily be confused: he may renounce terrestrial imperfection for heavenly utopia; or he may stoically reason that life is worthwhile since it is all of joy and/or pain that man will ever know. Kazantzakis' Odysseus, of course, enunciates the latter view. But Odysseus' creator was not as far from the first alternative as he thought himself to be.

The mystical always figured importantly in the thought and life of Kazantzakis. It was the product of his dual heritage: the Greek peasantry and the Greek Church. Hope does not spring eternal in the breasts of a people barely subsisting under a foreign yoke. For such a people, hope is the staple of their diet. And such a hope can assume only one guise— the fantastical guise of the miraculous. (p. 320)

Kazantzakis, like Joyce, made some bold Icarian passes at the sun, but the wax on his wings never melted to the point of danger. Kazantzakis's Odysseus conceives of himself as a species of Nietzschean Superman and may be called an atheist. But the Kazantzakis of *The Last Temptation of Christ* accomplished a prodigal's return home in exemplary fashion—doubly secure, be it added, in the knowledge that he was saved and that his safety could not be attributed to a cloistered virtue. The godlessness of a James Joyce was completely antithetical to Kazantzakis' perception and response to life although he himself was not completely aware of it until relatively late in life. However, *The Poor Man of God*, a work about St. Francis, reveals the ancient mariner Kazantzakis, returning to the belief of the young boy raised by Franciscan monks and to the devoutness of the young man seeking enlightenment in the monasteries of Macedonia. Neither his exile from country nor his apostasy from Church was as final or as irrevocable as Joyce's.

Kazantzakis' solution to the inner conflict which rages in all men was indebted to Kierkegaard's *redintegratio in statum pristinum*. Every one of Kazantzakis' major works can be read as a portrayal of Man's seeking reintegration. Some succeed, some enjoy a partial success, some fail, others are completely indifferent or find integration by a repudiation rather than a reconciliation of the eternal duality. But there is never any question that in Kazantzakis' eyes the *desideratum* was the conciliation, not the subjugation of the opposing selves in the human psyche. In addition, Kazantzakis believed that whatever offered succor from the mental anguish and practical difficulties indispensable to achieving this conciliation was one more temptation to be foregone. That is why in his works more importance attaches to the struggle to arrive than to the fact of arrival itself. In Kazantzakis' prescription for salvation, Golgotha must not and cannot be circumvented. He called for immersion in the destructive element—not for circumvallated withdrawal. Significantly, his Christ's victory of self-conquest is consummated on the Cross—as are those of Manolios (the Christ of the passion play in *The Greek Passion*); of Odysseus (*The Odyssey: A Modern Sequel*); and of Captain Michales (*Freedom or Death*). Man must not remain mired in the abysmal depths of his personality; Self must transcend Self before Self can be fully realized.

I should like now to trace these ideas and their transmutations in the principal works of Nikos Kazantzakis. (pp. 321-22)

[*The Odyssey: A Modern Sequel*] is influenced to such an extent by Nietzsche's philosophy that some notice, however cursory, must be taken of this fact. (p. 322)

Surprisingly, the parallels between Kazantzakis' Odysseus and Nietzsche's Zarathustra are more numerous than those between Kazantzakis' hero and the latter's Homeric counterpart. Both are concerned in helping man but seldom find him willing to cooperate. Both periodically seek out a hermit existence amid mountains and forests although both preach against asceticism. Both are subject to frequent trances, dreams, and visions. Both conceive of death as the end of the festival, life; and both image death in terms of a sea voyage. Both soliloquize interminably, discourse garrulously, and harangue formidably. Both assail philosophies of quietism and passivity. Both speak out boldly and vehemently against the constraining chains of outworn conventions, dogmas, and creeds. Both refer their catechumens to the savage sources of life: to the fierce combats among jungle beasts, to the fructifying rays of the sun, to the Dionysian frenzy of the dance, and to the uninhibited laughter of the satyrs. Both implore men to attain to self-mastery, even to the conquest of hope and pity. Both castigate those who, through benighted mores, self-distrust, constitutional impotency, or reliance on superterrestrial Edens, are afraid of life and hence condemn it. Both pose the paramount question of our times—which is not whether man will survive but whether he deserves to survive. (pp. 322-23)

Odysseus' supreme triumph is supposed to proceed from the fact of his rising superior to all the fears and hopes which beset mortals and thereby preclude enfranchisement from arbitrary taboos, unrealistic mores, delusory imperatives, bigoted creeds, and perverse necrolatry.

Odysseus' freedom, however, is not very inspiring because the reader is never fully convinced of its meaningfulness. Inevitably, one wonders whether his Herculean labors, his Achillean derring-do, his preternatural cunning, his prodigious energy, his titanic imaginings are worthy of emulation if they vouchsafe only the bleak counsel of Buddhistic nirvana. (p. 323)

Undoubtedly, Kazantzakis' Odysseus often lacks conviction because his creator was troubled by second thoughts. . . . Kazantzakis' hero's ecstatic joy in the mere living is moving, to be sure, but underlying it is usually the disconcerting reflection, seldom completely rationalized, that life is a jest, death a certainty, and the grave the end of identity. . . . (p. 324)

[Kazantzakis] believed the autochthonous was an integral part of the personality and advocated its incorporation into the whole, not its extirpation. Yet, on several occasions, Odysseus' bestiality and cruelty call in question his author's wisdom. Granted, Odysseus' inability to rest from travel is to be construed not as wanderlust or Faustian insatiability, but rather as the noble quest for the meaning of life and the knowledge of how to live. Frequently, however, he loses sight of his estimable goals and gives way to unedifying displays of sadistic blood lust, depraved sensual orgies, wanton displays of his strength and craft, and senseless ventings of his wrath and indignation on all and sundry. He is as often Man Transmogrified as Man Transfigured. . . . [In addition, Odysseus himself] boasts that he has discovered that all heretofore acknowledged authorities are naught, that man's invincible mind alone is worthy of worship. . . . [It] is apparent that a doctrine as stern and suprahuman as that which Odysseus promulges can entice few adherents. Like Zarathustra, Odysseus is often listened to but seldom understood or heeded. (pp. 324-25)

He confidently promises that when we no longer hope for the impossible, when we no longer fear Macbeth's tomorrow, then, and only then, shall we savor fully true freedom's exhilaration. To Odysseus' way of thinking he who still has hope puts his great soul to shame; only he is free who strives on earth with not one hope. Odysseus does not dismiss Christianity as a childish toy. But, like Freud, he views it as a deleterious anodyne. For him the sole omnific agency is the human mind.

Together with his eagerness not to miss a single one of life's buffets and rewards is his eagerness to prove that through these and these alone can man cognize life, that through these and these alone can man know aught of life that he knows or needs to know. Odysseus, in fact, carries his subjective idealism to the point where he is ready to dismiss freedom as a scornful song, old age as a false dream, and death itself as a fantasy. (pp. 325-26)

A partial withdrawal from such desperate and impious self-sufficiency is noticeable in *Zorba, the Greek*. . . . In this novel, the author-narrator (more closely identified with Nikos Kazantzakis than even Odysseus) constantly berates his inability to espouse a life of the senses. But—significantly—he does not! Prufrock-like, he is always asking himself whether it would be worthwhile to live life instinctively and spontaneously like his companion and employee, the ebullient Macedonian Zorba. (p. 326)

There is no question . . . that Kazantzakis intends that he should be understood, in addition, as personifying the flesh: Zorba is exciting, irrepressible, prodigal, importunate, voracious, effervescing, culpable, rejuvenescent, and bawdy. He represents a high order of achievement in high comedy, and is one of Kazantzakis' best characterizations. He is as inimitably irresponsible, incorrigible, witty, rascally, convivial, and amorous as Sir John Falstaff. . . . Zorba's right combination of Falstaffian deference and impudence ingratiates him with all. His seriocomic cynicism, like Sir John's, whets, rather than curtails, his appetite for lusty pleasures. Like Shakespeare's jovial and jocose knight, he, too, evokes the spirit of eternal youthfulness; he, too, figures the Tempter whose temptation is set aside more out of fear than out of rectitude; and he, too, embodies a way of life his creator renounces in a later work.

The repudiation of Zorba's way of life is not explicit in *Zorba, the Greek*. For one thing, he is too attractive as a fictive creation to be rejected or even condemned. For another thing, Kazantzakis was not ready to find the way of life for which Zorba stood entirely bad. For that matter, Kazantzakis never disallowed the legitimate claims of the flesh in the moulding of the human personality. But, in time, he came to feel that he in whom the combat between flesh and spirit persisted longest represented a higher order of being than he who, tiring of the struggle, capitulated before the onslaughts of the flesh and thereby neglected the parallel development of his spiritual nature. There is no explicit deprecation of Zorba before the prologue to *The Last Temptation of Christ*. . . . At the same time, there is little doubt that, through his author-narrator, Kazantzakis voices some disapproval of Zorba's philosophy.

Autobiographically, *Zorba, the Greek* is valuable in making clear that, after a careful revaluation of the thought of Nietzsche and Buddha, Kazantzakis found both wanting. The entire novel portrays the author-narrator endeavoring—with Zorba's daily example before him—to discard the asceticism of Buddha and to espouse Nietzsche's *amor fati*. . . . [Quite] early in the novel, he tells us that his goal in life is to reconcile soul and flesh. He is painfully aware that he has been inclined—in his first enthusiasm for Buddha, no doubt—to cultivate the soul to the detriment of flesh. He knows he should try to balance matters more evenly. . . . (pp. 326-28)

The thought of Nietzsche is . . . echoed later in the novel when the effendi of Zorba muses: "I have always been consumed with one desire: to touch and see as much as possible of the earth and the sea before I die. . . . There is only one life for all men, there is no other . . . all that can be enjoyed must be enjoyed here. In eternity no other chance will be given us."

It seems that Kazantzakis is once again one with Odysseus. But there is a difference: the author-narrator of *Zorba, the Greek,* unlike the doughty Odysseus, is unable to implement these beliefs with any deeds. Nor is he committed to these ideas body and soul. He never puts his theoretical ruminations to the practical test because he is never really positive about their validity. Zorba often teases him good-naturedly about his vacillation and his distrust of his own convictions. Like Coleridge's Hamlet, his strength to act deliquesces in the energy of resolve. Dimly but surely he senses that Nietzsche is no more the whole answer than is Buddha. (p. 329)

Can Nietzsche live in harmony with Buddha? This question left unanswered at the end of *Zorba, the Greek* is considered again . . . in *The Greek Passion*. At this time, Kazantzakis was retired from active life, sixty-five years old, and more compatibly matched with a second wife. He finished the work in two months. As a matter of fact, his autumnal burst of creativity enabled him to complete within two years *Freedom or Death*, *The Last Temptation of Christ*, and *The Poor Man of God*. The progression, from secular to religious, indicated by these three titles, may be said to hold true also where Kazantzakis' thought is concerned. And, if we recall that *The Greek Passion* or *He Who Must Die* is also deeply religious, we may safely assume that in his twilight years Kazantzakis turned from Nietzsche and Buddha to Christ. The furor the first two of these four titles aroused among the Greek clergy—already incensed beyond patience by *The Odyssey: A Modern Sequel*—can be ascribed only to their realism and unflinching accuracy. (pp. 329-30)

The principal offensive passages in *The Greek Passion* and in *Freedom or Death* are the wrestling match between two priests—no holds barred—in the former novel and the Turkish exploitation of Greek prelates' avarice in the latter. There is no question that both episodes contain a plenitude of coarse ribaldry and scurrility. But it is also patent that the writer's design is to inspire reform, not to defame. Not the Church so much as man's inerrable turpitudes are Kazantzakis' target. (p. 330)

The Greek Passion again enjoins man to struggle continually to wed flesh and soul. More prominent here than in *The Odyssey: A Modern Sequel* or *Zorba, the Greek* is the conviction that this can best be done by always being mindful of Christ's example. . . . Manolios, who enacts the Christos in the Greek Passion Play, does just this: he endures Christ's trials, tribulations, and mortal agonies in every particular in actuality—even to a martyr's bloody murder—before the day for the dramatic representation even arrives. By documenting the lives of the men and women assigned roles opposite Manolios in a manner which calls attention to the parallels between them and those they are impersonating, Kazantzakis shows the significance, in contemporary terms, of Christ's Passion. Just as Faulkner did in *A Fable,* Kazantzakis informs the *New Testament* drama with compelling immediacy and forcefully demonstrates the potentiality of Christ in every man. Manolios, like Faulkner's Corporal, is both Manolios and more than Manolios. Like the actor who becomes what he portrays, who, in a sense, becomes more real than the reality itself, Manolios' personation becomes more than an Aristotelian mimesis, becomes, virtually, a mystical Imitation.

Manolios' search for identity yields him Kierkegaard's rather than Nietzsche's type of freedom. For Manolios accepts the discontinuity between faith and reason. Instead of trembling on the edge of the abyss and endeavoring to tell himself he is unafraid, nay, that he really rejoices in his peril, Manolios vaults the abyss and finds his rest in the certainty of the impossible's fulfillment and in the incomprehensible logic of divine injustice. (pp. 330-31)

Odysseus' freedom is in part freedom from Christ: it presupposes the right to refuse all sanctions and behests other than those of self, and to denominate evil whatever is inimical to the vital instinct. Manolios' freedom is in part freedom through Christ: it permits consideration of the origin, purpose, and goal of existence as well as the fact of existence, and it allows transcendence of self as a means of fulfilling self. Kazantzakis had evidently reached the conclusions that to reconcile flesh and spirit, one must refuse to reconcile faith and reason, and that for belief to be meaningful one cannot merely believe but must will to believe. . . .

Odysseus' way, however, is to yield to all temptations as a means of overcoming them. He must needs hear the Sirens' Song, yet be secured against the consequences of doing so. Manolios believes in the martyrdom embraced in behalf of man, principle, or faith; to Odysseus' mind, self-denials, sacrifices of life, and foolhardy heroics are possibilities one is not unprepared to face, but never deliberate choices over life. (p. 332)

One of Kazantzakis' themes is hinted at by the alternative title to the novel—*He Who Must Die*—or, as it is rendered in the Greek—*Christ Recrucified.* In other words, agony and sacrifice are conditions of salvation, of reintegration. They can never be said to be in vain. They bear witness to the earnest struggle man wages to wed his opposing selves. They recall Christ's travail, and, by so doing, teach man once again to endure afflictions with fortitude and piety, to covet the soul's permanent abode more in order that the dread of death might prove less, and to refuse to despair and deny in order that he might learn to love and live. Through the fate of Manolios . . . Kazantzakis teaches that, frequently, sacrifice of one's life for a temporarily lost cause is desirable, because frequently martyrdom is the price for ultimate freedom and because, without hope of ultimate freedom, life is empty and worthless.

This is precisely the theme of *The Last Temptation of Christ* in which the story of Manolios is retold, this time with authentic Biblical backdrops, names, places, together with some gratuitous embellishments of the author. Vastly inferior

as a work of art to *The Greek Passion,* and by no means as engrossing or engaging as the latter work, this novel is still another retelling of the life of Christ. . . . Christ is not a particularly appealing character. Perhaps he is too similar to Dostoevski's idiot Prince. And Kazantzakis' own Freudian touches are not especially happy. Christ is too transparently a Greek peasant, and his Jewishness consists only in his lack of a Greek peasant's attractiveness. In addition, the slight flaw in Milton's *Paradise Regained* assumes the proportions of a major fault in Kazantzakis' novel: not only has the author's temptation motif worn thin by this time, but history and hindsight naturally defeat all efforts to generate suspense and dramatic conflict. (pp. 332-33)

In all of his works, Kazantzakis is the uncompromising realist. He does not hesitate to transcribe the ugly and the terrible as well as the beautiful and the ineffable. More often than not his works show the defeat of love and liberty. More often than not his works recount tyranny's triumph over charity, loyalty, devotion, and honesty. What he seems to be telling us is that sufferings, defeats, and losses are relatively unimportant; what really counts is man's stubborn refusal to capitulate, man's ability to endure and survive. . . . If one is aware of any message in his work more than any other, it is the urgent appeal that a way to human harmony must be found, together with the quiet confidence that it can and will be found. (pp. 333-34)

> *C. N. Stavrou, "Some Notes on Nikos Kazantzakis," in* The Colorado Quarterly *(copyright, 1964, by the University of Colorado, Boulder, Colorado), Vol. XII, No. 4, Spring, 1964, pp. 317-34.*

FREDERIC WILL   (essay date 1964)

[Nikos Kazantzakis' *Odyssey*] has enlarged and deepened our notion of the modern Greek achievement.

That modern epic, in 33,333 lines, is based on Homer's *Odyssey.* It literally takes its beginning from the end of Homer's poem. Kazantzakis' Odysseus, furthermore, has much in common with Homer's hero. That is not all. Even the "godlike" vision of Homer is emulated. Here it is not a question of evaluating Kazantzakis: I, for one, am prepared so far only to speak of the work as huge in scope and impressive, not as a classic. It is simply that Kazantzakis strives for the history-and-essence-embracing wholeness of vision which we associate with Homer. (pp. 57-8)

From the beginning Kazantzakis' Odysseus differs in an obvious way from Homer's hero: he tends more toward change, toward becoming different in nature through the course of his wanderings. (p. 58)

From our first meeting with Homer's Odysseus . . . to our final encounter . . . , we find him essentially "unchanging." . . . [Something] which we may call Odysseus' vitality, canniness, courage, and pride remain consistently at the felt core of his behavior. They are changeless.

The hero of Kazantzakis' epic is somewhat different. "Something" in him is constant. Certainly the author's vision has been steady and persistent. But his Odysseus changes—essentially and variously—in a way Homer's hero does not.

That change takes the form of a gradual release from "society," in a broad sense, from the pressures of social conventions, from the constraints of family affection, from all routine social occupations. The progress of this release is not unilinear, does not head straight for the mark; but throughout it can be felt as a thrust. When Odysseus first returns to Ithaca, has destroyed the suitors, and presents himself to Penelope, he is still relatively involved in the social web. . . . But he can still wonder at not feeling the old love for Penelope. . . . His relation to Telemachus is similarly strained, tense between former fondness and present coolness. . . . [With his son Telemachus] as with Penelope Odysseus expresses a love, as though from a great distance, from the other side of pain and experience. But he feels his deepest relation to his father. (pp. 58-60)

Kazantzakis has carefully integrated heroic restlessness into these suggestions of Odysseus' lingering domestic feeling. There is little more than mention, in Homer, of Teiresias' prophecy that Odysseus must continue to wander, after he reaches home, and that he will settle down only in old age. That mention, which inspired Dante and Tennyson to the vision of Odysseus as an "eternal wanderer," becomes a seminal motif for Kazantzakis: he does not mention the prophecy, but he uses its spirit. Odysseus' antipathy to the bourgeois situation on Ithaca is brought out subtly. It is chiefly shown, as in the relationship with Telemachus and Penelope, by a dramatized sense that Odysseus has gone beyond, has transcended the kinds of existence he finds on Ithaca, where there has been no war, no heroism, no maturing. . . . In contrast to Homer, Kazantzakis brings out the impossibility of any real domestic reunion, precisely through the scene in which Odysseus retells his wanderings to Penelope and Telemachus. During this narrative, in Book II, there is little rapport between Odysseus and his hearers. . . . But it is not until the end of his narrative that we realize how completely he has convinced himself, in telling of his former freedom, of the importance of remaining free. (pp. 60-1)

Surrounded by a group of fellow adventurers, Odysseus leaves Ithaca for the horizon. . . . He turns first to Helen, in the gradual weaning of himself from the familial. She will tie a less dangerously holding bond to him than his family once did. (p. 61)

Helen has kept her flame alive, however, and love instantly flares up. It is important to see, though, that Kazantzakis does *not* stress the sexual relation between Helen and Odysseus. This neglect brought inevitable criticism against the author. But it was intentional and appropriate neglect. Odysseus has passed the stage of sentimental eroticism. Furthermore, the intimacy of a sexual bond would have drawn his nature too strongly back toward "society." . . . [He rejoices] in Helen's rediscovered power to represent the eternally loveworthy woman. Her warmth radiates to him. But he is careful not to burn himself.

The looseness of their relationship grows clearer in the following books (IV-VIII). Helen, Odysseus, and Odysseus' men go to Crete. . . . During their long stay in this environment Odysseus and Helen grow progressively farther from one another; they separate. (pp. 61-2)

It is hard for Odysseus to leave Helen. . . . Odysseus has not entirely freed himself from sentimental affection. . . . But he has always been less involved with Helen than with his family. His relation to her has had more of bravura and mere experiment. . . .

The next four books (IX-XII) are an interlude, from the viewpoint of the main argument. Those books involve the adventures of Odysseus and his men in Egypt. . . . (p. 63)

Two points concern the argument. It is of interest, first, that Odysseus grows increasingly aware of "metaphysical" conditions which bear on his relation to society, to other people. Those conditions are aspects of the true severity of the world, especially of the world of inanimate nature. . . . [Calling] on art to express his growing sense of the austerity of existence, Odysseus fashions an image of his God. . . . He is frustrated at first by his tendency to represent himself, in various guises; naively to represent the human, and to worship it as transcendent. . . . [Ultimately] the "great God of Vengeful Wrath!" . . . is his final product.

In view of these metaphysical-aesthetic experiments it hardly surprises us to find Odysseus, in the corresponding books (IX-XII), still further cutting his sentimental ties to other people. Apart from relationships to various revolutionary Egyptians, with whom he contracts no friendship, but only a kind of abstract sympathy, the original comrades are his entire social context. They do still smack to Odysseus of Ithaca, of mutual experiences, of crises surmounted, and of a once congenial Weltanschauung. But this is little more than an aura surrounding the men, and Kazantzakis carefully confines it to that. The men themselves—with their symbolic names, and their abstractly representative personalities—provide little warmth for Odysseus, much less than Helen did. They are echoes from a society of which Odysseus was once a part. They too are casting off from society, but their sense of mission is much less articulate than his; he cannot commune with them. As a result, Odysseus comes simultaneously to realize the true inhumanity of existence, and the impossibility, in a wider sphere than he had before known it to apply, of his contracting close human relationships.

From here on, all familiar social contacts begin to weaken and grow meaningless to Odysseus. He is still followed by his companions, as he travels farther into Africa. . . . [Most] of the original group are with their leader when he reaches the lake-source of the Nile (end of Book XIII). But Odysseus' vital relation is no longer with these men; it is with the band of riff-raff who have followed him out of Egypt. His relation to them is creative and mastering, in one sense; it is also the most abstract, principle-based relation that we have seen Odysseus adopt toward others. (pp. 63-5)

They are also following Odysseus' vision of a place [with a prosperous new social order]. . . . This is a positive Odysseus. We suspect, though, that this new experiment in social organization will be less beneficent than is implied. The benevolent social motive will be a cloak.

After an enormously difficult trek, during which Hunger and Terror, dramatizations of Odysseus' god, make themselves continually felt, Odysseus and his band reach their destination. There Odysseus, seeking the vision on which to found his new city, climbs to a high mountain (Book XIV) and communes with the "nature of reality," in the hope of founding his city upon it. But what Odysseus discovers there does not soften his relations to society. He finds that reality is a stumbling but bloody and inexorable ascent of god through matter toward spirit. This is no longer the maleficent god of Book XI, who hated mankind. But it is a god who is totally indifferent to the individual, who tolerates humanity only as an artery of his own pounding force. It is this god that Odysseus plans to serve, as he descends from the mountain.

Back in his new community he begins slowly to indoctrinate citizens, and the spirit of the state as a whole, with his severe evolutionary metaphysics. He approaches his "people" as a crafty master. They are divided into three groups—craftsmen, warriors, and intellectuals—whose interrelations are fundamentally communistic: children are to be educated in common, older people allowed to die. . . . And then, when it is time to inaugurate the city, nature intervenes, to *prove* the truth of the leader's philosophy. A tremendous earthquake wipes out Odysseus' embodied vision, at the same time confirming his disembodied conviction that even bloody and aborted struggle toward "spirit" is a manifestation of God.

What we see to this point is a slow alienation of Odysseus from warm, familial, social contexts. That alienation is slow, not briskly shown. Yet when we consider the various "social" scenes against which Odysseus plays his character in the first fifteen books—against the backgrounds of family, Helen, his men, and a section of society, in that order—we are impressed by two lines of development: of movement away from the warm, personal, intimate; of movement toward relationships which are increasingly abstract, promoted by the hero's principles. Both of these movements accelerate after Book XV.

From that point on, the only true relation accessible to Odysseus is an inward one, or rather an inward-cosmic one, a relation to the cosmic attained within himself. He will meet many more people, but will fail to encounter them closely; he will seem almost to pass them by, as if in a separate existential compartment. After the destruction of his city he will be mainly concerned to be true to himself—as an ascetic mediator—and, through himself, to the ultimate character of reality. Here is the secret of his successful transcendence of the ego, his ascension to a more than personal level.

The first stage of his spiritual trajectory, "in beyond" other people, away from the social altogether, can be delimited by the period between his first true practice of asceticism (Book XVI) and his encounter with the Negro fisher (Book XXI). (pp. 65-7)

In becoming an ascetic, after his experiment with city-planning, Odysseus does not revolt in disgust against a former way of life and thought. Both the content of his thought and the attitude he adopts are continuous with the old. In thought he enlarges his dreadful former evolutionism with a more loving pantheism: this recourse saves him, enabling him to savor the good in nature, even in the midst of destructiveness. . . . In the attitude—especially toward the human world—which accompanies this change of thought, Odysseus isolates himself more than before. Growing closer to non-human nature, he draws away from the human. Even in his negotiation with the one inescapable feature of the human, himself, he expresses himself as though concerned with a part of outer nature. We see this in his peroration to his five senses. . . . He praises each sense as partially himself, partially the natural outer world with which that sense coincided. (pp. 67-8)

The convictions into which Odysseus is growing are tried out on a number of exemplary characters, characters who are almost allegorical. Of most importance are a prince (Buddha?), a world-famous prostitute, an impractical idealist (Don Quixote?), a hedonist, and a Negro fisher-boy (Christ?).

No longer does Odysseus transact seriously with the human. He no longer looks for, or wants, love. He has no intention, or real hope, of converting or of constructing. He has, as he

remarks after the destruction of his city, passed beyond "all sorrow, joy, or love." He enters into dialectic with his allegorical opponents: he reproves the prince for passivity, the hedonist for indifference, and the impractical idealist for idealism; he even reproves the Negro fisher-boy, who alone makes a significant impression on him. It is only in this encounter that Odysseus feels himself confronted by another philosophy of vital power. This meeting is well conceived. It culminates in Odysseus' test of the boy's philosophy. . . . With the exception of [that] scene, however, there is almost no felt dialogue between Odysseus and the representative figures who cross his path in these last days of his existence among mortals. (pp. 68-9)

In the final three books we see him almost entirely isolated from other beings, sailing toward the South Pole. He is no longer thinking and expressing the pantheism which had calmed him after the destruction of his city. To a great degree he now *is* the nature which he had before imagined himself part of. Even the distance of thought has vanished. . . . The essential vision of the last three books is of man's inextricable, progressive return into the elemental source.

This hero's last meeting with humanity has less than ever of the human, and indeed ends in natural disaster. Having crashed into an iceberg, Odysseus is thrown onto land, and makes his way—with great difficulty—to an eskimo settlement. There he remains for some time, in the igloo of the witch doctor. . . . [When the eskimo community perishes in an ice crevice,] he is horrified, tempted to damn God. His last feeling, though, is praise. (pp. 69-70)

Such general praise, directed at the general, futile character of the human drama, is the last note of the epic. Odysseus has finally been thrown from his boat, and is dying, trying to hold with bloody hands to the face of an ice cliff. Through his mind—and this is the theme of the last book—pour pell-mell all of his former comrades and friends. All his memories of people fill him. Yet the reunion is unsentimental: it has the supreme calm and distance of an epic summation. All that humanity from whose warmth Odysseus has been gradually separating himself—in favor of closeness to nature—is called up in a fictive last vision, which finds the man for a removed, desperate instant again hospitable to the human.

Spiritual movement and change are central to Kazantzakis' creation. I have allowed, already, for the limitations of this point. The Odysseus of Book I, who meets Telemachus and Penelope, is recognizably the same character who sails to death at the South Pole. In one sense, Odysseus is "unified": his questingness, vitality, and energy are constant. To this degree he resembles Homer's character. Yet within this unity a modern restlessness is held. Odysseus is determined to revise himself, to seek, ceaselessly, and to do so with an alert consciousness of his own directions. Here is the paradox of the literary character who is pre-eminently a quester. His "traits" forever exist in tension, threaten to be displaced. "Character" threatens to dissolve itself.

Homer's Odysseus lacks this kind of inner tension. Organically vigorous, he nevertheless remains essentially static. (pp. 70-1)

This general difference in character may be hastily summarized as that between the "vertical" character (Kazantzakis' Odysseus) and the "horizontal" character (Homer's Odysseus). The vertical character is one whose movement as mind and spirit, though not necessarily as moral being, is "upward." He changes, but, like Kazantzakis' own Odysseus, he does not simply change. For as the plot which involves him develops, growing at every stage more complex, because it subsumes the stages which have preceded it, so the character himself develops, subsumes, and grows more complex. "Change," here, takes on evolutionary significance: it involves the preservation, at each new stage of the character's growth, of all the preceding stages. The "horizontal" character, by contrast, not only remains the same . . . but he does not grow more complex with the development of his plot. It will be seen, of course, that the application of this point to a character like Homer's Odysseus needs qualification. Still it holds. (pp. 71-2)

This distinction, of course, still leaves us well outside Kazantzakis' craft and vision, in his *Odyssey.* I have not made it clear—if that can be done—just *how* Kazantzakis has managed to remake the Homeric Odysseus into a "vertical" character, just *how* he has been able to dynamize the myth in his way. That question, which leads toward the center of Kazantzakis' re-experience of an ancient theme, is not a preliminary one. We cannot speak of some "handling from the inside" in Kazantzakis, as though Homer had been less adroit at that. Homer was a master of brief speech and significant action which seemed to grow from the essential nature of his characters. We must speak, rather, of a distinctive view and grasp of character in literature, which led Kazantzakis to reconstruct his myth as he did. We may imagine Kazantzakis to have dealt, at the initiatory stages of the work on his *Odyssey,* not with a theme which was public property and which could properly be perfected as such, but—given the mind of our age and the long seasoning of the myth—with a gradually shaping inner vision full of "intentions" and "implications" meaningful to him. These intentions—senses of the clash between spirit and matter, of some kind of transcendence through spirit, of the superiority of quest over discovery, and so forth—found their way into a whole verbal product, a verbal unity of feeling, Odysseus. We will not imagine that any doctrinaire view of the literary character led Kazantzakis to this kind of creation. It will have been the case, simply, that certain potentialities, above all certain preoccupations with transcendence and growth, in his own character, translated themselves into Odysseus. Homer's Odysseus could hardly have been re-encountered on a deeper subjective level. (pp. 72-3)

> *Frederic Will, ''Kazantzakis' 'Odyssey','' in* Hereditas: Seven Essays on the Modern Experience of the Classical, *edited by Frederic Will (copyright © 1964 by the University of Texas Press), University of Texas Press, 1964, pp. 57-73.*

F. A. REED   (essay date 1965)

[Kazantzakis singles] out Homer, Bergson, Nietzsche and Zorba as those mortals whose influence has been most vital to his life and work. (p. 178)

Kazantzakis' great cohorts, the "bodyguards of the Odyssey" as he called them, along with a host of secondary, though by no means inferior figures, Christ, Lenin, Dante, Buddha, Greco, Psycharis and others, whom he enshrined in a series of *terza rima* cantos, helped enrich him with the formal means, the discipline, the example—he also called them his "models and guides"—for the technical consummation of his creation. But from his dreams and travels he drew the raw material of his work—the interplay and echo of ancestral cries in his own double-born soul; the meeting and mingling of European, African and Asian in his Cretan blood; the temperament at once withdrawing and passionate. . . . (pp. 178-79)

Dream images abound in Kazantzakis' works—dreams provided him with a fruitful point of contact with subconscious currents which he might never have touched in his waking hours. Such images figure prominently in the superstructure of his *Odyssey,* as well as in innumerable more detailed incidents woven into its general fabric. And the entire closing section of *The Last Temptation of Christ* occurs in that dream state of suspended time which is one of Kazantzakis' favorite devices. In his dreams, logical fragments, components of thought as yet unorganized, would be caught up in the vortex of his subconscious and be given form at last, would ascend to knowledge's highest peak: to become vision.

Through dreams he maintained close contact with an entire world of childhood memory: the highly-charged atmosphere of Cretan freedom struggles; the forms of his parents, grandparents, ancestors; the soil and air of Crete itself. (p. 179)

Travel was, on the conscious level, what dreams were in his hours of sleep. Travel for Kazantzakis was far more than a mere changing of location, or a relief for heart and eye, a diversion. Travel is an agonizing quest, charged with hope and fear—all else in our age would be self-deceit and cowardice. He was to find in his travels the image that best expressed his soul, and hence his conception of the soul of contemporary man: Odyssey.

His own wanderings, in themselves a bewildering though not incoherent Odyssey, served a twofold purpose. First, as an occasion to make contact with the mercurial kaleidoscopic surface of the world, . . . and then to grasp beneath the ephemeral surface, . . . the timeless manifestations of landscape, of man, of history petrified in marble. (p. 180)

He came to realize that the "eternity" which he sought in his vision was not a concept of quantity, either spatial or temporal, but rather of quality.

Second, travel was his greatest source, a rich font of impression, color, odor, sound and detail, all of which was stored away, catalogued, reworked and then brought back to find a place in his creation. Each journey became a search for material for his *Odyssey.* (pp. 180-81)

From these two opposing tendencies the extraordinary pulse of Kazantzakis' travel books draws its strength. The confrontation of a soul which craves for an instant of touch and for the warmth of real flesh with the ascetic-artist who has set out to gather the multicolored booty of the sensible world and force it into submission beneath the patterns of his vision.

This conflict finds expression in the language and structure of the works themselves. Though written in a thoroughly "demotic" Greek, with a generous sprinkling of uncommon words, the books still very much reveal the desk-bound scholar; here we find a line or two from an obscure document, from an unknown poet, there a metaphor or proverb drawn from a Muslim philosopher or a Byzantine mystic. (p. 181)

Perhaps more than any other of Kazantzakis' travel books, *Journey to the Morea* escapes the limitations of a single voyage. He visited the Peloponnesos, for varying lengths of time, on five distinct occasions, and from the wealth of memory and incident inherent in this total, he was able to invest the *Journey* with unusual depth. (pp. 181-82)

Each of Kazantzakis' works should be viewed as the repetition, elaboration or elucidation of a concept or image from the *Odyssey*. The novels, the *Greek Passion, Freedom or Death,* the *Last Temptation* all embody one of the many germs of the Odyssean conception; the travel books to a lesser extent, without the same concentration. Here it is essential to clarify the often overlooked fact that Kazantzakis was a writer (and a man) of one single, all encompassing vision: Within the *Odyssey* can be found the points of departure for all his later novels. Through the novels Kazantzakis sought a level from which he might successfully address himself to a much broader readership than his poetry would have ever permitted—in their sum they do not exceed or unexpectedly alter the vision of the great work of his "acme" (as the ancient Greeks would have said). The travel books are of a different category: They do not elaborate, they prefigure.

Journey to the Morea abounds with these prefigurings of the *Odyssey*. As an example . . . : Two representatives of strife-torn pre-Classic Greece journey to far-off India, seeking the Word that will help them bring order to their chaotic civilization. The sage who greets them so ironically on the bank of the Ganges is none other than Prince Motherth, the Buddha figure of the *Odyssey*. In the face of his exhortations to nirvanic nothingness, the Greeks plant firm in earth their image of Helen. . . . (pp. 183-84)

Kazantzakis plays upon the eternal antithesis of Greek thought, anthropomorphic and Apollonian, with the formless abyss of the Orient. In the *Odyssey* the younger of the Greeks is about to be ensnared by Motherth's radiant, obliterating smile when the death call of the dying Odysseus rends the air and an eagle swoops down to carry the sage away. (p. 184)

But in the *Journey* the Greeks' retort refutes the enticing sage and with assurance they answer: "'Helen,' ascetic, means to do battle for Helen."

The reader senses Kazantzakis in the grip of an Odyssean predilection. (p. 185)

Within the frugal confines of the *Journey* the reader will discover as well the foreshadowing of other familiar characters, tropes and images. The figure of the blind old Cretan, Perdikokostandi, appears, with slight modification, again and again in Kazantzakis' mature prose: [as Zorba's grandfather; as the regal, sensuous old monarch in *Mélissa;* as the figure of old Sifakas in *Freedom or Death*]. . . . These few indications should help illustrate to what extent Kazantzakis' method and vision is rooted in the soil of his dreams and travels, in the soil of Greece, and more, of Crete. (pp. 185-86)

Journey to the Morea will perhaps serve to help clarify Kazantzakis' relation to his native land. While certain sections of it find a place, albeit highly revised, in *Report to Greco,* there they lack the same systematic context. Furthermore it should be stressed that the *Report* makes no claim to chronological exactitude—events and images are given free play, virtually ideal form. In the *Journey,* partially due to the scrupulously observed external format, Kazantzakis' feelings and judgments about Greece are more objectively accessible; thus they can be readily, and no less truthfully, evaluated.

That which in the end will most certainly impress the reader of the *Journey* is its remarkable faculty for grasping the broad span of history—not coldly, with a scholarly, measured stride, but with a single fiery, engaged and penetrating glance, a glance rooted always in the uneasiness of the present. . . . This he requires of modern Greece: correspondence of man and landscape, and further, realization of the path that Greece must follow, midway between the treacherous influences of East and West—synthesis or abject submission to a fate untrue to its nature.

Travel in the Peloponnesos reveals to him with frightening intensity the pitiful plight of his race. With the same eye that has feasted on the riches of the Orient and gazed at Russia's interminable snowy expanse, he now searches about him trying to discover Greece's true face. . . . (pp. 186-87)

Kazantzakis traveled through Greece seeking those souls, those landscapes, that would inspire him with courage and confidence in his homeland. Sensing profoundly the currents of his age (the reader of today will find Kazantzakis' *Odyssey* pertinent as never before), he wandered much of the turmoil-ridden world. In Greece he was not fated to see the wild conflict of contemporary man's soul, as he did in Spain; but rather to feel anguish, and isolation. He sought there fulfillment of the Greek ideal, and behind that, we sense as well, the paradox-rich lucidity of the Cretan Glance. Only once or twice in his journey could he exclaim: "Suddenly a soul leaps up before you which has reached the peak of the Greek mission—to unite boldness with knowledge, passion with the game." (pp. 188-89)

> *F. A. Reed, "Translator's Note," in* Journey to the Morea *by Nikos Kazantzakis, translated by F. A. Reed (copyright © 1965, by Simon and Schuster, Inc.; reprinted by permission of Simon and Schuster, a Division of Gulf & Western Corporation), Simon & Schuster, 1965, pp. 178-89.*

PETER BIEN (essay date 1977)

[*Buddha*] presents the reactions of a man torn between the need to remain Buddhistically aloof from events and the opposite need to participate in the world's ephemeral shadow-dance—to indulge in the supreme folly of trying to act as though the phenomenal world were real. But these contrary reactions are held at arm's length, as it were, and are unified by the magic of the poetic imagination. (pp. 252-53)

[The plot is] the realistic part of the play. Added to this, and giving the work its uniqueness and distinction, is vision—maybe even "delirium." Technically, this is conveyed in an extremely skillful way by the three pageants which are interwoven into the realistic plot, one in each act, and which depict the life, temptations and salvation of Buddha. These are the work of the Magician, who in turn is the functionary of the Poet who appears as Prologue and who makes us realize that everything we witness—Yangtze, suicides, passions, Buddha, heroism and resignation, the entire spectrum of life and death—is a plaything of the aesthetic imagination: a dream. The realistic action is framed by art at the beginning and by metaphysics (Buddha, obliteration, Nada) at the end. All that we think is life, Kazantzakis is telling us, is a dream ending in Nothing.

But the play's greatest surprise is that this seeming nihilism is not the last word. The last word is imagination. . . . This work is crucial in Kazantzakis' own development because it is the first major drama in which he dealt openly with the aestheticism which he all too often tried to suppress. Here, art is clearly presented and accepted as a salvation subsuming the paths of activism and of renunciation without denigrating either. The play possesses genuineness, authenticity, control, and also serenity, because Kazantzakis was no longer struggling to be what he was not. Since in this work he accepted the fate which had designated art as his definitive path, he was for once working not against himself but instead in full cooperation with his most natural gifts and drives.

The play's priorities determine its form. The work [unfolds on two levels]. . . . Realism and vision. But these two components of the full icon—the totality of existence—are both established as playthings of the mind. The drama opens with a prologue in which the Poet, in a splendid soliloquy, first invokes the mind, then proceeds to traverse the full arc of existence, ascending from inert matter upward to animation and vitality, then descending through pain, longing and distress to Buddhistic annihilation. Finally, he reminds us once again that both life and death—the sweet mask and the abominable face behind, the lower and upper levels of the icon—are dreams engendered by the mind. (pp. 253-55)

It is important for us to appreciate the triune structure—the mystic triangle—that gives the work its shape. If the characters with their earthly joys and cares are Christ, if the void to which they shall return is the Holy Spirit, then the Poet is God the Father, incorporating the two other hypostases, synthesizing them, yet remaining at the same time separate. The poetic imagination is not the upper half of the icon; it is the creator and destroyer of the entire icon: lower and upper halves, earth and heaven. . . . It is also important for us to appreciate that the Mind invoked in this play is neither the mind which wallows in "big ideas," nor that which throughout Kazantzakis' works is seen as inhuman, cruel, and opposed to the compassionating heart. This is the logical, intellectual faculty, which analyzes. The mind invoked in *Yangtze* [*Buddha*] is of course the great foil to this analyzing mind; it is the intuitive faculty, which synthesizes. Far from being inhuman, it is the highest, ultimate manifestation of our humanity: for it is the power of self-consciousness and of spiritual creativity. Kazantzakis goes out of his way to distinguish this intuitive mind from the theoretical, intellectualizing mind by incarnating the latter in the figure of the Mandarin, who is then presented in an entirely negative light as the Magician's foil and enemy. . . . Wisdom and her "hundred-year-old infant," the analytical mind, are incapable of exorcising Buddha (death), who is beyond wisdom and reason. . . . This power is reserved for the imagination and is manifested by the Magician, who, of all the characters, is best able to respond with dignity to the human condition: the inevitability of extinction. Unlike the Mandarin, he conquers both hope and fear. And he knows that once we have looked the abyss in the face without cringing, all we have left is Imagination. . . . So his response is to play: to abolish the world of pain by leading the sufferer into the country of myth. He cannot of course stop the Yangtze, cannot conquer fate in any "realistic" way, yet he possesses a great power, bequeathed to him by Imagination. . . . (pp. 255-56)

Now all this may seem childish and evasive, hardly the noble, profound response to fate that Kazantzakis intends it to be. But Kazantzakis is trying with utmost seriousness to give us his conception of that which exists apart from the subjectivity of human knowledge. By making the Magician call life a game and state audaciously that he can escape fate by changing the eyes with which he views the world, Kazantzakis is attempting to remind us that our normal, commonsensical con-

ception of reality is outrageously incorrect, so incorrect that we come closer to truth with "play" instead of seriousness, "evasion" instead of confrontation. Where we go wrong in our commonsensical approach is to think that the multiplicity we see before us is real. We cannot see through this multiplicity to the One behind it; thus we think that individual beings are truly separate from one another, and we think as well that life is separate from death. But the Magician stands outside this commonsensical approach. He plays with the illusion of multiplicity, as well as with the illusion of youth's (life's) separation from old age (death), by donning successive masks. . . . By means of play and magic—which, Kazantzakis is telling us, are truer than truth—the Magician shows us the Oneness behind youth, maturity and age, for he has an additional mask, a yellow, perfectly round one—Spirit, his true face—which he dons before conjuring up out of thin air the three pageants: those fairytales within the Fairytale. . . . (pp. 256-57)

This, I believe, is what is really meant when the Magician says that he changes the eyes with which he sees the world. What is meant is a drawing aside or away or back, so that we may see better: may penetrate the multiplicity to the Oneness beyond. But here we also have a definition of art; it too is a stepping away or back, the nearest that man can come in this life to approximating the literal drawing aside—death—which reintegrates the divided One. So the Magician, being above and beyond the multiplicity, "directs" with the insouciance of a saved man, a god. He is the Artist, and as artist he is the One whence spring all the various characters, passions, births, deaths, hopes and fears of the deceptive multiplicity. This of course happens implicitly in every work of art, but Kazantzakis, in introducing the Magician and employing the frame situation, makes it explicit—lest we, the audience, forget when viewing the play, just as we tend to forget when viewing that other Play which we call life. The characters are presented not only as puppets responding to his direction and dependent upon his mind for animation, but as facets of his oneness: they too are his many masks. Kazantzakis does here, but with infinitely more skill, what he had attempted earlier in *Toda Raba,* though only by sterile and unconvincing statement, as opposed to what Henry James called "rendering." There, the various characters were presented as "merely different facets of a single consciousness"—or so we are told in the headnote. Here, we actually see the Magician divide himself (for only thus can he entertain us) into the full spectrum of human types; we actually experience this primal act of creation whereby the One becomes the Many. Thus, although we see the various actors and share their problems, we remain aware of the integral artistic energy behind them—an energy which Kazantzakis presents to us as man's purest expression, and as that part of him which, like the canary in the play, is the very last to be engulfed by the inevitable destruction of all things material. And even after the material basis of "song" is destroyed, the song itself lingers on, like the light from an exploded star. (pp. 257-58)

We now move inside the frame to the icon itself, with its two levels. Though the upper level is heaven and the lower earth, though the upper is Buddha and the lower Epaphos, the God of Touch, the division does not act to separate death from life. What Kazantzakis (the Poet? the Magician?) does is to present on each level the full spectrum of infra-Epaphos to ultra-Buddha, life to death, conceived as a totality. On each level we mount one leg of the parabola and descend again on the other leg. The upper level, that of vision, is presented in the three Buddhistic pageants. Here we follow Buddha's life, and have conjured up for us the attraction of women and earth, the temptations of activism, pride, anger, family cares, patriotic duty—in short, the enticing multiplicity of Epaphos. Indeed, these Buddhistic sections contain some of Kazantzakis' most delicious and effective evocations of the sensual life. (pp. 258-59)

On the icon's upper level we are offered the full spectrum of life and death. But Buddha himself is the sweet call of death; he is the inhuman law of nature which we must learn to accept. Buddha is fate, the equivalent—in the realm of vision—of the Yangtze in the realm of matter. Buddha is the Yangtze, the Yangtze is Buddha. The two realms do not differ; they are merely aspects of the same oneness.

Similarly, on the lower level, we are offered another full spectrum of life and death. We mount the parabola on one leg and then descend its other leg until we reach the Yangtze. At the very end, as the river is about to wash away all the people, passions, buildings, etc., of the preceding multiplicity, Old Chang, guided by the Magician, realizes who the Yangtze is. Crossing his arms and bowing to the rising river, he cries "Welcome" to Buddha—and the lower level is united with the upper.

The passage from life to acceptance of death, shown on the upper level through the history of Buddha, is shown on the lower level chiefly through the characters Old Chang and Mei-Ling. (p. 260)

[The] great challenge which [Kazantzakis] set himself in writing this play was to keep Buddha from swallowing up Epaphos. By means of plot, characterization and diction, he attempted a "magic act" designed to cause us to mistake the puppets [the characters] for living beings so that we too, at least for a moment, might fall into the error of valuing the mask for its own sake.... On the upper level he presents the sweet mask by means of declamation, narration, and allegorical encounter. The pageants resemble a seventeenth-century masque such as John Milton's *Comus;* basically static, they depend for their effect on the evocativeness of language and the ingenuity of *mise en scène*. On the lower level, however, Kazantzakis necessarily treats the same themes in a completely different way, avoiding allegory, high diction and declamation. Most importantly, he creates real people with real problems and real conflicts, at least to a significant degree.

On this lower level Kazantzakis assembles diverse personages and lets them react in differing ways to the human condition. (pp. 260-61)

Each of the two major characters ... achieves freedom and salvation, and each does so in a different way. Mei-Ling, sister and accomplice of the revolutionary Young Chang, reminds us of Siu-lan, sister and accomplice of the revolutionary Li-Te in *Le Jardin des rochers*. (p. 262)

The secret that Mei-Ling knows is this: The ultimate good deed is to sacrifice oneself futilely in a lost cause. Futilely, that is, on the realistic level of results, tangible honor, and political efficacy. Though Mei-Ling throws herself into the river, no temple or plaque will be erected in her honor, the river will not be placated, the populace will not be saved— and yet a "cry" will remain, affirming human solidarity and man's ability to confront fate with dignity. Like everyone

else, Mei-Ling mounts one leg of the parabola and then descends the other. Europeanized and pragmatic like her brother, she ridicules the god Yangtze (the scientific spirit ridiculing fate), calls for stones, cement and iron to subject death itself to man's service, indoctrinates the villagers, tries to awaken her entire country to a spirit of self-improvement, etc. But, as we have seen, the brother is killed, the dams break, the indoctrinated peasants are drowned. Mei-Ling is left with nothing except her individual dignity. All her political endeavor has proved futile, and indeed she realizes the blindness and even cruelty that characterized her committed, political life. . . . But Mei-Ling's suicide isn't just a personal exit, it is the definitive political act, a futile good deed that nevertheless affirms human solidarity. Here, Kazantzakis comes very close to André Malraux's ending of *La Condition humaine,* where Katow dies well both existentially (as an isolated individual in an inexorably hostile universe) and Aristotelianly (as a *zōon politikon*) when he relinquishes his cyanide to men less stalwart than himself. Mei-Ling responds to the people's demand that the river be placated with a second sacrifice, though she knows that this is futile. In giving herself, however, she simultaneously bequeaths a final hope to those less stalwart than she, those unable to surpass hope or despair and therefore unable to conquer fate with dignity. Her own individual need for marriage with the abyss coincides with a wider social need, and thus she dies affirmatively in both spheres, conquering the inhuman fate that wishes to humiliate her. (pp. 263-64)

Mei-Ling's complementary opposite, Old Chang, reaches his salvation in an entirely different way—not through the Quixotic activism of youth, but through meditation and inner struggle. From the very start of the play, he has understood the vanity of all endeavor, though perhaps not existentially. His problem as the action unfolds and as the inhuman universe does its worst, is to struggle with what might be called his human weaknesses but what are more properly the very core of his biological humanity: of the life force which makes him naturally shrink from the metaphysical truths his mind has understood. Once again, therefore, we see the full spectrum of Epaphos-Buddha. Old Chang is a complete man; his passivity and renunciation at the end have validity because he has arrived at this Buddhistic acceptance of death by way of caring for life. . . . Though nominally Old Chang is the leader of a flock, he is treated in the play as the pure, unaccommodated, existential man: an isolated individual confronting the universe. Indeed, as the action progresses, he is stripped of everything that is meaningful to him in life, until he is left completely alone—with the Yangtze. (p. 265)

[He] does not will his destruction from the very start or singlemindedly crave this "exit," as does for example Kazantzakis' character Julian the Apostate in the eponymous play. Though passive as compared to Young Chang or Mei-Ling, he does act in accordance with his culture, advanced age and lordly station, ordering his grandson and heir to be carried to safety. He embraces death only after clinging to life, and consequently is a believable figure. In any case, Kazantzakis is able to relieve him of fear and hope, the two greatest impediments to salvation and freedom. The stripping away of the context of past, present and future which previously gave meaning to the old man's life is accomplished with exemplary plotting and with the inevitability and acceleration characteristic of high tragedy. Deprived of his cultural and human supports, without ancestors, son, daughter-in-law, grandson, daughter or kingdom, Old Chang remains in the pure existential situation: an aloneness which, together with the victory over fear and hope, constitutes the gateway to salvation. The question now becomes: How should a man react at this point? What form of energy must be applied to the wheel of self to push it past this dead center and therefore through the gateway that leads to salvation? Kazantzakis' answer, exemplified in Old Chang, is very clear. It is dignified acceptance.... By the time we have come this far, passing through all the vicissitudes and all the genuinely human responses to them (i.e., responses of fear and hope), this "freedom" is not just rhetoric, not just an abstract, sterile philosophical concept, as in certain of Kazantzakis' other works. It is a true and convincing dignity, a quietude that has been refined out of true and convincing struggles.... Every man, [Chang] tells us, begins by forgetting his inevitable end; he thinks there is a small open door, very small, but big enough for him, at least, to pass through. And he presses forward in this attempt to save himself.

The play implies that this is proper—at a certain stage in life. We must mount one leg of the parabola before we can descend the other. But eventually this hope for survival, because so contrary to the cruel facts of existence, becomes humiliating. At one point—preferably after intense love of life, intense self-deceiving efforts to achieve permanence—we must accept the truth and act accordingly.... Chang's salvation come by virtue of his metaphysical position: his Buddhistic realization that all is vanity, that all of life's cares and vicissitudes that we take so seriously are—beneath their deceptive multiplicity—a unified stream which is going where the waterfall is going: over the brink. The Yangtze not only has the power to wash away man's hopes; the river is the thing-in-itself, the rest being just a deceptive (but ever-so-alluring) mask supplied by the subjectivity of human observation and (defective) knowledge. When Chang opens his arms to welcome the river as the final curtain falls, he is also welcoming Buddha. He knew at the very start of the play that life was a "fairytale," but what he has done in the course of his internal struggles is to transform this inherited, automatic metaphysical position into one which has existential validity because he has arrived at it all over again from the beginning, on his own. He has created his own essence, and this feat of human consciousness gives him a pride and dignity that remain in the air as a cry after the universe has annihilated him. Thus his Buddhism seems strangely affirmative, a valid and noble reaction to the fact of death, neither a cringing nor a flight, and least of all an intellectual stunt whereby the responsibilities of manhood are evaded by being passed through the sieve of metaphysics.

The play *Buddha* lives up to Kazantzakis' claims for it. Though it might strike some as nihilistic, a more accurate label would be "tragic," for it affirms man's nobility at the same time that it shows the omnipotence of what Paul Tillich calls the forces of nonbeing. It is not a pessimistic work nor even a sombre one, despite its subject matter. Instead, because of the comprehensiveness of what it attempts and the unfailing energy and remarkable powers of synthesis that Kazantzakis brought to the task he had set himself, the work as a whole gives one a feeling of magnificence. It is uplifting, not depressing—a hymn to the pride and dignity not only of its characters but of its author. Indeed, what I said about Old Chang can be said about Kazantzakis as well: his resignation seems acceptable because it is earned, experiential. The play is the product not of a man who was attempting to evade experience by passing it through the sieve of metaphysics,

but of one who had been pushed by experience to question his assumptions all over again from the beginning and to emerge with a fresh consciousness of his relation to everything around him, of the very rationale for his existence. In other words, it is the product of a man who had been pushed by experience to renewed and expanded self-consciousness. Kazantzakis would claim that human nobility lies precisely in this capability for self-awareness and furthermore that awareness is the non-material goal of material evolution. The play gives artistic flesh and blood to these claims, making them seem true in the fictional world of the characters and also in the real world of the author. To my mind, at least, it affirms Kazantzakis' nobility as well as Old Chang's.

I have tried to show the comprehensiveness of this play, drawing attention to the Poet and Magician who serve as frame, to the icon itself with its upper and lower levels of Buddha and Epaphos respectively, and to how in each of these areas we are given the full spectrum of life and death, the full parabola. (pp. 266-68)

In writing the play *Buddha,* Kazantzakis attempted once more to synthesize the disparate aspects of himself, and to emerge with a coherent, unified—though not uniform—whole. It was an exercise, as I have said, in self-consciousness, much like the *Odyssey* but surpassing that work in genuineness because of the immediacy of Kazantzakis' experiences. I do not pretend that the answers Kazantzakis discovered for himself were radically different from answers he had discovered previously. They were not. In both works irreconcilables are reconciled because Kazantzakis (good Bergsonian that he was) placed all contraries in a stream of evolving time. "Process" is the key word. Regarding the Buddhistic sense of the futility of all action, he does not simply present this to us as a truth; he makes us arrive at it by undergoing a process. What process? That of acting, of attempting the game, trying to cheat fate. In short, he insists that our passivity and resignation be earned, that we cross our arms and calmly approach the waterfall only after we have rowed energetically in the stream of life. Activism and futility are reconciled because activism is seen to be the precondition of the genuineness of the Buddhistic position. How can we truly sense the abominable abyss behind the sweet mask, Kazantzakis asks us, if we have not first worn, and loved, that mask? How can we conquer desire if the desire has never been felt? In this way, Kazantzakis justifies the Quixotic attempt of human beings to make their world a better place, and yet at the same time insists that we must not justify this striving in terms of the material results it produces, since such results are so hopelessly deceptive and ephemeral. Activism is justified immediately because it places a crown of heroic dignity upon those who strive with open eyes, and ultimately because it leads to the non-material "result" of self-consciousness.

The reconciliation between art and politics is parallel to the above. This too depends upon process, though here the process itself is not shown; instead, the artistic position is presented from the very start, as already attained.... Art is presented as an exit, indeed the supreme exit, from fear, hope and despair. Yet just as the metaphysical exit must come only at the end of the journey of active participation, so must the aesthetic. In *Buddha* we do not see the evolution of the artist, but we do see the consequences of this evolution, which are these: (1) The proper subject matter of art is the full spectrum of existence—Epaphos through Buddha. (2)

This spectrum must be known experientially by the artist. The aesthetic and the political are reconciled because active participation in life is the only path whereby imagination earns the right to step back from life and treat it with engaged aloofness. The artist accepts the unaesthetic as a precondition of saving himself through the aesthetic.

These were the answers Kazantzakis arrived at in his renewed attempt, under the pressure of the events of 1940-1941, to synthesize the disparate aspects of himself and emerge with a coherent whole. As I have said, the answers were not new. As always in Kazantzakis, they lay within a continuum, and thus reached back to the *Odyssey* and other previous works, and were to reach forward to *Zorba* and other subsequent works. But of all Kazantzakis' immense output, the play *Buddha*, I believe, is the clearest, most genuine and comprehensive exposition of his mature position, because it both isolates and amalgamates the disparates so deftly, and also because it so openly and unapologetically treats the aesthetic as the primary way to salvation. (pp. 269-70)

Finally *Buddha* is successful as a work of art. Certainly it is one of Kazantzakis' most important achievements, and one which will fare better I believe than the *Odyssey* if the two works are judged by aesthetic criteria. There are of course defects one could cite. The play is longer than it ought to be; several parts of the pageants are so completely undramatic that they become tedious, and at one point at least the plotting is too artificially neat. But these are quibbles when considered next to the play's virtues. *Buddha* makes me think of Bertolt Brecht's *The Caucasian Chalk Circle* (1949). Both plays employ some of the same devices, both are "total theatre" and "epic theatre," both walk the tightrope betyween allegory and realistic immediacy, both are fiercely intellectual without being didactic. *Buddha* is splendidly theatrical—full of color, pageantry, fantasy, music, as well as convincing characterization. This is to say nothing of the language, which is juicy, sonorous, daring and beautiful, without being ostentatious or verbose. As for other virtues . . . : the successful combining of immediacy and vision, realism and delirium; a form which is truly an expressive form; a stylization which drains off and neutralizes certain artificialities that invade the realistic portions; ideas incarnated in characters whose conflicts are those of human with human, not only of idea with idea; epic and mythic scope, yet a sense of the events being anchored in the particular and the local; a genuine sense of Epaphos; finally, a balance between distance and involvement—the author being above and beyond his characters, full of a quietude they do not possess, yet this distance never becoming a callousness or Olympian indifference. How curious that of all Kazantzakis' major works, *Buddha* has been the most neglected! (pp. 270-71)

Peter Bien, "'Buddha,' Kazantzakis' Most Ambitious and Most Neglected Play," in Comparative Drama *(© copyright 1977, by the Editors of* Comparative Drama*), Vol. II, No. 3, Fall, 1977, pp. 252-72.*

PETER MACKRIDGE (essay date 1980)

[*Serpent and Lily*] is a curiosity. It consists of the first two works—a novella and an essay—which Kazantzakis published (in 1906, when he was twenty-three). They are undoubtedly juvenilia.

The essay, **"The Sickness of the Age"**, which is appended to the novella here certainly helps the reader to appreciate what Kazantzakis was intending to do in his first work of fiction and also points to some of the ideas which were to absorb him throughout his career. In it he presents a highly personal version of the history of Western civilization. According to him, the classical age was the childhood of man, in which simplicity and instinct were supreme; ancient man lived a life of untrammeled joy, which was reflected in the uninhibited antics of the ancient gods. This joy was destroyed by "the pale Nazarene" who through his suffering and his emphasis on the life to come distracted men's attention from the good things of life, directing them instead towards a non-existent Heaven. Finally, in the modern age, science has proved that this Heaven is indeed false, so that now we have absolutely nothing to believe in. Excessive self-knowledge and knowledge of the outside world have destroyed all mystery and with it all our convictions and all the basis of our morality. . . .

The plot of *Serpent and Lily* is perhaps meant to be an example of what might happen to a hypersensitive soul not strong enough to find its own way amid the sickness of the age. (Kazantzakis himself presumably felt himself to be a Nietzschean *Übermensch* who was better equipped to cope with contemporary problems.) It is a lyrical, melodramatic tale heavily influenced by symbolism, aestheticism and "decadence". There are clear parallels with the work of D'Annunzio, which like that of Kazantzakis also bears witness to the influence of contact between a young provincial's impressionable nature and the sophisticated life of the modern city.

Serpent and Lily is suffused with what the Greeks call *archaiolatreia* (love of the ancient) and *oraiolatreia* (love of the beautiful). The painter who narrates the story in his journal idealizes his beloved as Athena and wants his love for the girl, which provides the nucleus of the story, to be chaste (inspired not by Aphrodite Pandemos but by Aphrodite Ourania). But this cannot be: the Lily (innocent, ideal love) is always intertwined with the Serpent (which seems to symbolize at times knowledge or lasciviousness, at others death or the flesh). Thus love is constantly jeopardized by both the mortality and the fleshly desire it necessarily contains within it. . . .

We should not assume that the novella is only a cautionary tale: there is certainly much of Kazantzakis in the narrator. The morbid wallowing in sexual detail coupled with a repulsion towards sexual activity itself, the egocentricity, the sadistic tendencies and the novella's obsessive symbolism may perhaps delight aficionados of Kazantzakis's work, but it is difficult to see its importance to world literature. Perhaps the most fascinating aspect of the book is its total lack of contact with the social situation in Greece in the first decade of this century. But in this respect Kazantzakis was only one of many Greek writers about whose work one could say the same.

Peter Mackridge, "A Bed of Roses," in The Times Literary Supplement *(© Times Newspapers Ltd. (London) 1980; reproduced from* The Times Literary Supplement *by permission), No. 4032, July 4, 1980, p. 749.*

ADDITIONAL BIBLIOGRAPHY

Bien, Peter. "The Mellowed Nationalism of Kazantzakis' *Zorba the Greek*." *Review of National Literatures* 5, No. 2 (Fall 1974): 113-36.

Discusses *Zorba* as representative of Kazantzakis's political experiences during World War II in Greece.

Durant, Will, and Durant, Ariel. "Nikos Kazantzakis." In their *Interpretation of Life: A Survey of Contemporary Literature*, pp. 269-98. New York: Simon and Schuster, 1970.
    A chronicle of Kazantzakis's life and the evolution of his personal philosophy.

Poulakidas, Andreas K. "Kazantzakis and Bergson: Metaphysic Aestheticians." *Journal of Modern Literature: Nikos Kazantzakis Special Number* 2, No. 2 (1971-72): 267-83.
    Illustrates how Kazantzakis took Bergson's abstract concepts, such as time, memory, and creative evolution, and presented them in literary language and in concrete imagery.

Alexander (Lange) Kielland

1849-1906

Norwegian novelist, short story writer, and dramatist.

Kielland's works were inspired by his indignation at the social inequities of his day. While critics have praised his elegant language, wit, and style, his attacks on the hypocrisy of the clergy and the governing bureaucracy prompted cries of protest from many in Norway. Kielland is best known for his masterpiece *Garman og Worse (Garman and Worse)*, in which his disillusionment is tempered by rich descriptions of his cultivated ancestral home in Stavanger. His dramas, for which he is less known, satirize contemporary issues such as the "new woman."

Kielland was born in Stavanger, a milieu which served as the prototype for his most successful works. His mother's family included many government officials, and provided the background for his later attacks on the bureaucracy. Despite a strong interest in literature, Kielland earned a degree in law and then went into business as the owner of a brick-works for nine years. During this time he studied writers such as Mill, Kierkegaard, and Heine, whose ideas he later incorporated into his own work. Determined to write, Kielland finally left the brick-works for Paris and, at the age of thirty, began his literary career. While in Paris, Kielland met the Norwegian writer Bjørnsterne Bjørnson who, impressed with Kielland's talent, encouraged him to write.

Kielland's first collection of short stories, *Novelletter*, quickly established him as an accomplished writer of unusual clarity and wit. Reflecting the stylistic influence of French literature, these stories combine a subtle ironic tone with hints of romanticism. Kielland's social concerns are already evident in these early stories, however, which touch on some of the predominant themes of his later works.

Critics agree that in *Garman and Worse* and *Skipper Worse* Kielland most successfully combined his plea for social reform with his supple style and elegant language. Working with childhood memories and basing his characters on family members, Kielland vividly portrays his native Stavanger. *Garman and Worse* integrates exquisite description, astute characterization, and incisive criticism of social hypocrisy and injustice. *Arbeidsfolk*, published the following year, attacks the bureaucracy, and while this novel contains some brilliant passages, Kielland's indignation overwhelms his style. In *Skipper Worse* Kielland returns to the familiarity of his homeland for his subject and once again achieves the fine elemental blend evident in *Garman and Worse*. Based on the pietistic movement in Norway, *Skipper Worse* is noted for its deft portraiture, precise construction, and beautiful evocation of Norwegian seascapes.

Pessimistic in mood, Kielland's last novel, *Jacob*, suggests disillusionment with his ability to effect social reform. Following the publication of *Jacob*, Kielland ceased writing. While some critics feel that he was discontented with the extremes of both the bohemian writers and the romantic revival of the 1890s, the exact reasons for Kielland's abrupt exit from the literary scene are unknown. Although he is no longer widely read outside of Norway, Kielland is remembered in Norwegian lit-

erature for his cosmopolitan sophistication, grace, and beautiful use of the language that is distinctly different from the provincial styles of his contemporaries Bjørnson and Jonas Lie.

PRINCIPAL WORKS

Novelletter (short stories) 1879
Garman og Worse (novel) 1880
  [*Garman and Worse*, 1885]
Nye novelletter (short stories) 1880
Arbeidsfolk (novel) 1881
Else (novel) 1881
  [*Elsie*, 1894]
Skipper Worse (novel) 1882
  [*Skipper Worse*, 1885]
Sne (novel) 1886
  [*Snow*, 1887]
Tre par (drama) 1886
  [*Three Couples*, 1917]
Jacob (novel) 1891
Tales of Two Countries (short stories) 1891
Norse Tales and Sketches (short stories) 1896

*This is the date of first publication rather than first performance.

H. H. BOYESEN (essay date 1882)

To my mind, there have appeared no novels in Norwegian literature which in artistic finish equal those of Alexander Kielland. The first collection of novelettes ["**Novelletter**"] ... was a mere *jeu d'esprit,* although two of the sketches, '**Balstemning**' and '**En Middag**,' struck distinctly the note which has vibrated through the author's later and more comprehensive works. The wit was there, too, and it was this which made the sudden success of the book; for wit is a very rare gift, and in Norway rarer than in any other country except Germany. People were content to laugh, and to disregard the vague warning which the book contained. But the second work, the novel, '**Garman and Worse**' ..., struck the same note again, and with increased force; and the guardians of the Norse throne and altar became indignant, and some of them, perhaps, a little alarmed. The picture given in this book of the Lutheran clergy is so striking, so convincing, and so exquisitely finished that it is hardly to be wondered at that it excited indignation among those who had thus involuntarily sat for their portraits. ...

The central theme in the novel '**Garman and Worse**' is not, however, the description of clerical but of commercial affairs. It is again the struggle between the old tradition and the spirit of the time that chiefly engages the author's attention, although he never preaches in *propria persona,* preferring to let the action and the logic of events preach for him. He is, in fact, so conscientious an artist that he never, like Thackeray and George Eliot, plays chorus to his own drama, rarely admits a single comment not included within the frame of the action. The mercantile magnates on the western coast of Norway ... are characterized with a precision which only intimate knowledge could afford. Mr. Kielland himself has sprung from one of these great commercial families, and one cannot help suspecting that he must have made his studies for the characters of Consul Garman and his brother among the surroundings of his childhood. The bureaucratic world, with its small intrigues, its punctilious formality, and its purblind conservatism, is also illustrated in '**Garman and Worse**' by some vividly conceived types; and the book as a whole, gives a picture of life on the western coast of Norway such as can nowhere else be obtained. ...

Of Mr. Kielland's second novel '**Arbeidsfolk**' (Working People) it is difficult to speak except in hyperbolical terms. It will either be extravagantly praised or extravagantly condemned. It is a novel with a strong tendency, and those who disapprove of the tendency will, naturally enough, also disapprove of the book, It is ferocious, at times, in its realism; and it deals with some 'forbidden' topics; but it is not, for all that, in the least coarse. ... [After] having read the book twice, carefully, I have been unable to detect in it the slightest disrespect for religion *per se,* still less anything destructive of social order. If, however, social order is not conceivable except under an unpopular and reactionary monarchical government, then I can well understand how '**Working People**' should be looked upon as a revolutionary manifesto. (p. 159)

In Mr. Kielland's third novel, '**Elsa**' ..., which he styles 'a Christmas tale,' he deals with the responsibility of society for its outcasts. This story, which, in point of execution, is a veritable little masterpiece, reminds one remotely of Dickens's Christmas tales (notably 'A Christmas Carol' and 'The Cricket on the Hearth'), with the sentimental and the fantastic element left out.... Where the responsibility belongs for such a character as Elsa, surnamed 'the Flea,' is made very evident in this tale; and the conclusion is irresistible that we are all responsible for her.... The crying injustice of 'the Flea's' fate, as compared with that of her destroyer, is a thing which we daily witness and pass by callously and without wonder. The glaring contrast between the lives of the respectable and the disreputable, and the former's demoralizing effect upon the latter, are demonstrated in this tale with a convincing clearness and vigor which would be startling to those who have not thought the subject worth considering. (pp. 159-60)

H. H. Boyesen, "A New Norwegian Novelist," in The Critic (© The Critic 1882), Vol. II, No. 38, June 17, 1882, pp. 159-60.

THE NATION (essay date 1891)

The half-score of studies in imaginative prose which ... [comprise Alexander Kielland's *Tales of Two Countries* are] the work of the Norwegian author's 'prentice hand. But it was none the less a hand which had already gained the skill to draw with firm and broad strokes. Tentative as they are, both in subject and treatment, no signs of hesitation appear in the execution of these small but boldly outlined sketches. What first strikes the reader after turning them over, one by one, is the range and variety of the themes on which they touch. The most unlike among them differ almost as widely in form and thought as a poem may from a prose tale. Before the collection was finished, the author had already made himself as familiar with the outward aspect, and with at least some phases of the life, of the Parisian boulevard as he was with the wild natural scenery of the peat-moor and heath and the paralyzing monotony of existence in a "stagnant little town" in his own country. "**Romance and Reality,**" a brief history of matrimonial shipwreck, shows the dreary details of this provincial stagnation. Though told with humor and feeling, it is a trifle didactic in tone, and is, perhaps for this reason, less successful in general effect than its companion pieces. In "**Pharaoh,**" a little spiritual drama, as strong as it is brief, the voice of the Parisian mob is heard, though only in a "long, withdrawing roar." A high order of talent was needed to produce within the compass of so few pages and by means so simple as the chance visit of a commonplace young couple from Lyons to the fête of Saint-Germain, so large a perspective of life as is disclosed in the little episode called "**At the Fair.**" ... However slight in motive they may seem individually, these novelettes, as they were called in the original, have the qualities that put them in the ranks of the literature that has more than a day to live.

"Four Novels," in The Nation (copyright 1891 The Nation magazine, The Nation Associates, Inc.), Vol. 53, No. 1363, August 13, 1891, p. 125.

HJALMAR HJORTH BOYESEN (essay date 1891)

["**Novelettes**"] was, to all appearances, a light performance, but it revealed a sense of style which made it, nevertheless, notable. No man had ever written the Norwegian language as this man wrote it. There was a lightness of touch, a perspicacity, an epigrammatic sparkle, and occasional flashes of wit which seemed altogether un-Norwegian. It was obvious that this author was familiar with the best French writers, and had acquired through them that clear and crisp incisiveness of utterance which was supposed, hitherto, to be untransferable to any other tongue.

As regards the themes of these **"Novelettes,"** it was remarked at the time of their first appearance that they hinted at a more serious purpose than their style seemed to imply. Who can read, for instance, **"Pharaoh"** (which in the original is entitled **"A Ball Mood"**) without detecting the revolutionary note that trembles quite audibly through the calm and unimpassioned language? There is, by the way, a little touch of melodrama in this tale which is very unusual with Kielland. **"Romance and Reality,"** too, is glaringly at variance with conventional romanticism in its satirical contrasting of the prematrimonial and the postmatrimonial view of love and marriage. The same persistent tendency to present the wrong side as well as the right side—and not, as literary good manners are supposed to prescribe, ignore the former—is obvious in the charming tale, **"At the Fair,"** where a little spice of wholesome truth spoils the thoughtlessly festive mood; and the squalor, the want, the envy, hate, and greed which prudence and a regard for business compel the performers to disguise to the public, become the more cruelly visible to the visitors of the little alley-way at the rear of the tents. In **"A Good Conscience"** the satirical note has a still more serious ring; but the same admirable self-restraint which, next to the power of thought and expression, is the happiest gift an author's fairy godmother can bestow upon him, saves Kielland from saying too much—from enforcing his lesson by marginal comments, *à la* George Eliot. (pp. 108-09)

Kielland lightly touched in these **"Novelettes"** the themes which in his later works he has struck with a fuller volume and power. What he gave in this little book was a light sketch of his mental physiognomy, from which, perhaps, his horoscope might be cast and his literary future predicted.

Though a patrician by birth and training, he revealed a strong sympathy with the toiling masses. But it was a democracy of the brain, I should fancy, rather than of the heart. . . . I found it difficult to believe that he was in earnest. The book seemed to me to betray the whimsical *sans-culottism* of a man of pleasure who, when the ball is at an end, sits down with his gloves on, and philosophizes on the artificiality of civilization and the wholesomeness of honest toil. . . . He loves the people at a distance, can talk prettily about the sturdy son of the soil, who is the core and marrow of the nation, etc.; but he avoids contact with him, and, if chance brings them into contact, he loves him with his handkerchief to his nose. (pp. 110-11)

In his next book, the admirable novel **"Garman and Worse,"** he showed that his democratic proclivities were something more than a mood. . . . The tendency which had only flashed forth here and there in the **"Novelettes"** now revealed its whole countenance. The author's theme was the life of the prosperous *bourgeoisie* in the western coast towns; and he drew their types with a hand that gave evidence of intimate knowledge. . . . The same Gallic perspicacity of style which had charmed in his first book was here in a heightened degree; and there was, besides, the same underlying sympathy with progress and what is called the ideas of the age. What mastery of description what rich and vigorons colors, Kielland had at his disposal was demonstrated in such scenes as the funeral of Consul Garman and the burning of the ship. There was, moreover, a delightful autobiographical note in the book, particularly in the boyish experiences of Gabriel Garman. Such things no man invents, however clever; such material no imagination supplies, however fertile. Except Fritz Reuter's Stavenhagen, I know no small town in fiction which is so vividly and completely individualized, and populated with such living and credible characters. . . . [If these portraits] have a dash of satire (which I will not undertake to deny), it is such delicate and well-bred satire that no one, except the originals, would think of taking offence. . . . The members of the provincial bureaucracy are drawn with the same firm but delicate touch, and everything has that beautiful air of reality which proves the world akin.

It was by no means a departure from his previous style and tendency which Kielland signalized in his next novel, **"Laboring People."** . . . He only emphasizes, as it were, the heavy, serious bass chords in the composite theme which expresses his complex personality, and allows the lighter treble notes to be momentarily drowned. His theme is the corrupting influence of the upper upon the lower class. He has in this book made some appalling, soul-searching studies in the pathology as well as the psychology of vice.

Kielland's third novel, **"Skipper Worse,"** marked a distinct step in his development. It was less of a social satire and more of a social study. It was not merely a series of brilliant, exquisitely finished scenes, loosely strung together on a slender thread of narrative, but was a concise and well-constructed story, full of beautiful scenes and admirable portraits. The theme is akin to that of Daudet's "L'Évangéliste;" but Kielland, as it appears to me, has in this instance outdone his French *confrére*, as regards insight into the peculiar character and poetry of the pietistic movement. He has dealt with it as a psychological and not primarily as a pathological phenomenon. A comparison with Daudet suggests itself constantly in reading Kielland. Their methods of workmanship and their attitude toward life have many points in common. The charm of style, the delicacy of touch, and felicity of phrase, are in both cases pre-eminent. (pp. 111-13)

Kielland has to produce his effects of style in a poorer and less pliable language, which often pants and groans in its efforts to render a subtle thought. To have polished this tongue and sharpened its capacity for refined and incisive utterance, is one—and not the least—of his merits.

Though he has by nature no more sympathy with the pietistic movement than Daudet, Kielland yet manages to get psychologically closer to his problem. His pietists are more humanly interesting than those of Daudet, and the little drama which they set in motion is more genuinely pathetic. Two superb figures—the lay preacher Hans Nilsen and Skipper Worse—surpass all that the author had hitherto produced in depth of conception and brilliancy of execution. The marriage of that delightful, profane old sea-dog Jacob Worse with the pious Sara Torvestad, and the attempts of his mother-in-law to convert him, are described not with the merely superficial drollery to which the subject invites, but with a sweet and delicate humor which trembles on the verge of pathos. In the Christmas tale, **"Elsie,"** Kielland has produced a little classic of almost flawless perfection. With what exquisite art he paints the life of a small Norwegian coast-town in all its vivid details! . . . [Here Kielland] portrays a heroine with no corrupt predisposition, destroyed by a corrupting environment. . . . In the end, there is scarcely one who, having read the book, will have the heart to condemn her.

Incomparably clever is ["**The Society for the Redemption of the Abandoned Women of St. Peter's Parish's**," a] satire on the benevolent societies which exist to furnish a kind of officious sense of virtue to their aristocratic members. . . . St. Peter's parish is aristocratic, exclusive, and keeps its wickedness discreetly veiled. The horror of the secretary of the society, when she hears that "the abandoned woman" who calls upon her for aid, has a child without being married, is both comic and pathetic. In fact, there is not a scene in the book which is not instinct with life and admirably characteristic. (pp. 114-15)

[Kielland's last book, "**Jacob**," is] written in anything but a hopeful mood. It is rather a protest against that optimism which in fiction we call poetic justice. The harsh and unsentimental logic of reality is emphasized with a ruthless disregard of rose-colored traditions.

From the pedagogic point of view, I have no doubt that "**Jacob**" would be classed as an immoral book. But the question of its morality is of less consequence than the question of its truth. The most modern literature, which is interpenetrated with the spirit of the age, has a way of asking dangerous questions—questions before which the reader, when he perceives their full scope, stands aghast. . . . What the thinking part of humanity is now largely engaged in doing is readjusting itself toward the world and the world toward it. Success is but adaptation to environment, and success is the supreme aim of the modern man. The authors who, by their fearless thinking and speaking, help us toward this readjustment should, in my opinion, whether we choose to accept their conclusions or not, be hailed as benefactors. It is in the ranks of these that Alexander Kielland has taken his place, and occupies a conspicuous position. (pp. 116-17)

> *Hjalmar Hjorth Boyesen, in his introduction to* Tales of Two Countries *by Alexander Kielland, edited by William Archer (copyright, 1891, by Harper & Brothers), Harper and Brothers, Publishers, 1891 (and reprinted as "Alexander Kielland," in* Essays on Scandinavian Literature *by Hjalmar Hjorth Boyesen, Charles Scribner's sons, 1911, pp. 107-120).*

THE ATHENAEUM (essay date 1892)

Kielland excels in vividness of presentment and keen appreciation of nature [in *Tales of Two Countries*]. . . . He can be sympathetic, but he is seldom genial; his prevailing bent is towards pessimism, and his satire is uniformly mordant. A story is generally supposed to have a beginning and an end; but there is no rounding off or winding up in Kielland's work. These "tales" are rather episodes or transcripts of a fragment of life, and in spite of their poetical feeling and pathos the resultant impression left by their perusal is singularly tantalizing and unsatisfying. (p. 178)

> *"Novels of the Week: 'Tales of Two Countries',"*
> *in* The Athenaeum, *No. 3354, February 6, 1892, pp. 176-78.**

WILLIAM H. CARPENTER (essay date 1896)

Alexander Kielland is the least Norwegian of all the Norwegian writers. . . . [His] attitude towards his material . . .

is new to Norwegian literature. For the first time in his pages, among both his forbears and his contemporaries, we meet with the point of view of a man of the world. Björnson and Jonas Lie have always a sort of homely provincialism, inherent and characteristic, that is part and parcel of their literary personality, whose absence would be felt under the circumstances as a lack of necessary vigour. Kielland, on the contrary, as inherently, has throughout unmistakably an air of *savoir vivre*, in the long run much surer in its appeal to us outside of Norway because of its more general intelligibility. Björnson and Jonas Lie in this way have secured places in literature in no small part because of their characteristic Norwegianism; Kielland to some little extent has secured his place because of the want of it. Ibsen is here left out of the discussion. He is quite *sui generis*, and apart from the mere choice of environment for his work could belong anywhere.

If it is sought still further to distinguish the grounds of difference between Kielland and the other Norwegians, it will be found that besides this always inherent dissimilarity of attitude there is also in his writings a strikingly different use of language. . . . Kielland writes Norwegian, heavy and plodding, and withal, let it be added, honest, as it is in the other writers of Norway past and present, as nobody else has been able to write it. There is an epigrammatic capacity in it that has otherwise been left to lie fallow, a sparkle hitherto unsuspected beneath its sombre surface. It is all done by fair means. Just where he has caught the trick it is impossible to say, but the staid Northern tongue is all at once filled with the vivacity of the South, and its new airs and graces, moreover, are felt to become it. His use of Norwegian reminds one of Henry James's use of English at his happiest, only there is the difference that Kielland is a pioneer in this respect in his literature, while Henry James is, after all, but one of many. (pp. 229-30)

Kielland's novels are one and all novels of tendency. . . . They are strong, liberal, and modern; so much so that many of them have evoked a loud spirit of protest in Norway, where leaven of this sort is still striven against in many quarters. . . .

[From Kierkegaard] he has his ethical standards. . . . From John Stuart Mill has come his type of women. There are traces of Dickens in his humour and his love for character description from the lower ranks of life, and on our own account be it said, in his frequent exaggerations. Last, but not least, there is the undoubted influence of the modern Frenchmen, like Balzac and Zola. (p. 230)

[Kielland's first novel, *Garman and Worse*,] is full of clever characterisation and of portraiture of undoubted truthfulness, even if, as one of his critics says, he is more of a physiognomist than a psychologist. In *Laboring People* he strikes a much deeper note of feeling. The book treats of the sociological problem of the classes, and in particular of the adverse influence of the higher upon the lower, and the same theme is again the subject of *Else*. Kielland attains possibly his highest development in his third novel, *Skipper Worse*, whose theme is the pietistic movement in Norway. There is in this book a sureness of touch, a dignity and a conscious power that entitle its author, more than does any other single one of his works, to the place that has been conceded him well up in the front rank of contemporary novelists. (pp. 230-31)

> *William H. Carpenter, "Alexander Kielland," in*
> The Bookman, *New York (copyright, 1896, by*

George H. Doran Company), Vol. IV, No. 3, November, 1896, pp. 229-31.

THE ATHENAEUM (essay date 1897)

Of all the novelists of Scandinavia, perhaps Alexander Kielland most resembles Guy de Maupassant. His art, at any rate, is much more Gallic than Norse, especially in his shorter stories. At its best his style possesses all the elegance, refinement, and pregnant conciseness which distinguish the work of the author of 'Pierre et Jean,' and he has the same skill in treating risky and ambiguous subjects with mingled piquancy and discretion. But the Norwegian is more humane and sympathetic than the Frenchman, and, an aristocrat by nature, has, nevertheless, always championed the cause of the downtrodden lower classes with a perfervid indignation which wins our respect despite its exaggeration. Of the ten stories which make up [*Norse Sketches and Tales*] only two, **'Trofast'** and **'Karen,'** are fairly representative of the author's peculiar genius. . . . There can, indeed, be no doubt that the satire sometimes goes too far. Thus the comparison [in **'Trofast'**] of the loyalty of Danish subjects to the cringing subserviency of the Danish boarhound to its master might well have been omitted; but as a whole, the story is a little masterpiece of sardonic humour. **'Karen,'** a pathetic tale of seduction and suicide, is a model of artistic restraint and suggestiveness. There is not a word too much in it, and every word tells.

"Scandinavian Novels: 'Norse Sketches and Tales'," in The Athenaeum, No. 3637, July 10, 1897, p. 62.

ALBERT MOREY STURTEVANT (essay date 1933)

One outstanding characteristic of Kielland's novels . . . is the fact that they preserve a series of identical characters. His novels constitute a continuous picture of Stavanger life and in this picture these characters reappear with great frequency from novel to novel. Nowhere else in Norwegian literature do we find this repetition of characters to such a marked degree as in Kielland—because of the fact that his novels are serial in character.

But in none of Kielland's novels do we find any inconsistency in the portrayal of a character which appears in another novel. The Garmans, the Worses, Provsten Sparre, Adjunkt Aalbom, Konsul With, Georg Delphin, the Løvdahls, Bankchef Christiansen, the Kruses all reappear in various novels, but always as the same personalities with the very same characteristics except for the change which time and circumstances may necessitate. (p. 101)

Kielland was as consistent in the matter of chronology of events as in the portrayal of his characters; the chronology of events in one story does not, so far as can be determined, conflict with that of any other story. This fact serves as additional testimony to the real worth of Kielland's art. Through the maze of the numerous characters and events he weaves a consistent story of Stavanger life in spite of the various social themes involved.

The chronology of milieu in Kielland's novels does not by any means correspond to the order in which they were written. One outstanding example is *Skipper Worse* . . . which treats of events that happened two generations earlier than those in *Garman & Worse* . . . with which the former is so closely associated. (pp. 101-02)

In the composition of his novels the various events did not, of course, shape themselves in Kielland's mind as *one* story but as a *series* of stories some of which, though written later than others, take place at an earlier time. This is in itself an interesting theme aside from the question of literary art. (p. 102)

Kielland has in *Skipper Worse* reversed the chronology of events as related in *Garman & Worse*. . . . [This] reversal of chronology was due to the fact that the new theme, the Haugianer religious movement, did not occupy the author's attention until after *Garman & Worse* was written. . . .

Kielland himself said that he found two faults in *Skipper Worse;* the first, in that he had not made enough out of the character of Henrietta, and the second—no one any longer knows.

In regard to the first alleged fault, it is difficult to see how the author could have improved on his delineation of Henrietta's character. His brevity and clarity of treatment, both as regards her character and her tragic death, reveal Kielland at his best; at least this treatment can not possibly be construed as faulty. . . .

But what could the second alleged fault have been? Could Kielland have felt that *Skipper Worse* ought to have been written before *Garman & Worse* in order that the two stories might follow each other in chronological sequence of events? (p. 107)

[If] *Skipper Worse* had been written before *Garman & Worse*, the reader would have experienced less difficulty in distinguishing the two generations of Garmans and Worses from each other. As it is, the story of the grandfathers (Morten W. Garman and Jacob Worse) in *Skipper Worse* follows the story of the grandsons of the same name (Morten W. Garman and Jacob Worse) in *Garman & Worse*. This is confusing to the reader who naturally expects in *Skipper Worse* a continuance of, not a retrogression in, the story of these two families. (pp. 107-08)

If we read the two novels carefully in conjunction with each other we find no discrepancy either in the chronology of events or in the delineation of the characters. When one is fully acquainted with the events in both novels the reversal of chronology is not disturbing. But this acquaintance requires very close study—a fact which is confirmed by my own personal experience—and such close study should not be necessary in order to avoid confusion. Perhaps then Kielland felt that greater clarity and interest could have been gained if he had written *Skipper Worse* before *Garman & Worse*, i.e., in the order of the sequence of events. (p. 108)

No author in all Norwegian literature shows such a thoroughgoing acquaintance with his own characters as does Kielland, with the possible exception of Henrik Ibsen.

But there is this difference between the two authors in this regard.

Ibsen, the dramatist, *analyses* his characters, whereas Kielland, the novelist, *portrays* them.

Ibsen's analysis is fundamentally based on study and imagination; he infuses into his characters his profound knowledge of human nature.

Kielland, on the other hand, reflects his own personal acquaintance with living characters; they appear as he knew them, natural and simple as they were, without the infusion of psychological analysis.

Ibsen's characters seldom reoccur; Kielland's characters reappear continuously but being the reflection of the author's own life in Stavanger they remain consistent in every detail. . . .

[To] Kielland's universally acknowledged clarity of style we should add *clarity of exposition*, in which *consistency* is one of the chief features. (p. 109)

> *Albert Morey Sturtevant, "Regarding the Chronology of Events in Kielland's Novels," in* Scandinavian Studies and Notes, *Vol. XII, No. 8, November, 1933, pp. 101-09.*

HARALD BEYER (essay date 1952)

[In *Novelettes (Novelletter)*, Kielland's] form combined an ironic and jesting tone with an almost romantic sensibility. Yet a purpose was evident even in these early stories. He was out to break a lance against the injustices of the world. His opinions were democratic and liberal, though his personality and way of life were those of an aristocrat. His later books brought out his purpose even more clearly. He prided himself on making his books socially useful, not just entertaining. . . .

Kielland tried in his writing to combine thinkers who were as different as Kierkegaard and Mill. Kierkegaard's demand for personal participation led Kielland to attack all forms of hypocrisy and dishonesty. Among his favorite targets were the state church and its pastors, but never Christianity itself. On the contrary, he liked to contrast the lofty ideals of Christianity with the term-serving, worldly parsons of the state church. He contended that in so doing he was acting in behalf of true Christianity. . . .(p. 234)

Kielland often expressed his scorn for "psychologizing" literature, and he cared little for the praise of aestheticians. But he loved his own weapons, his cool and supple style, his elegant language and his eye for composition. He was aware that his purpose would remain unfulfilled if it were not borne by an artistic form and a convincing psychology. But he also digressed from his purposes and created purely lyrical moods, in his short stories as well as in his novels. (pp. 234-35)

[In the novel *Garman and Worse (Garman & Worse)*] he portrayed the life of his native Stavanger. The story combines vivid descriptions of nature with an ironic view of his fellow men. Two worlds are here contrasted: the merchant aristocracy and the common people. Between them stand the ministers, who use their "patent felt" to prevent all conflicts between idealism and reality, whose task it is "to smooth out all doubts and to put the damper on all vigorous life of the individual." (p. 235)

Kielland felt that his novel was too tame, and after some more short stories and plays, he published his most argumentative novel, *Working People (Arbeidsfolk . . .)*, an unrestrained attack on the bureaucracy, especially the lawyers in government offices. Although there are brilliant passages, the purpose overwhelms the artistry; and besides, Kielland was out of his depth in describing the Oslo scene. Much more effective was the little "Christmas story" *Else . . .* in which

he ridiculed a hypocritical charity and gave a naturalistic portrayal of social misery. In his second masterpiece, *Skipper Worse . . .*, he returned to the familiar scene of his own environment, but this time projected back to the generation of 1840. . . . He has given a masterly description of the gradual decay of his bold and merry skipper. Through the whole novel blows a fresh wind, even in the stuffy meeting houses, with a salty tang of sea and herring.

The novels [*Poison (Gift)* and *Fortuna*] . . . reflect Kielland's conception of his contemporaries. Primarily they are sharp attacks on antiquated educational methods and social hypocrisy, which he described as a poison instilled into the young. . . . In the novel *Snow (Sne . . .)* the author attacked the fusion of Christianity and conservative politics, much in the vein of Bjørnson's *Dust.* (pp. 235-36)

[*St. John's Festival (Sankt Hans Fest)* is] Kielland's sharpest and most satirical book. Here he made hypocrisy the leading theme. . . . Much lighter was the satire with which Kielland amused himself in such plays as [*Three Couples (Tre Par)*, *Betty's Guardian (Betty's Formynder)*, and *The Professor (Professoren)*,] . . . in which he poked fun at some of the topics commonly discussed in his day. (p. 236)

> *Harald Beyer, "Novelists of Realism" (1952), in his* A History of Norwegian Literature, *edited and translated by Einar Haugen (reprinted by permission of New York University Press; copyright © 1956 by The American-Scandinavian Foundation), New York University Press, 1956, pp. 228-50.**

KJETIL A. FLATIN (essay date 1979)

[Alexander Kielland] was *the* letter writer among the "big four" of nineteenth-century Norwegian literature. He cultivated letters as a literary genre and in later years had plans [which he abandoned] to have them published in a series of volumes. . . . [A] complete presentation would not always enhance the image the public had of him as a fearless fighter for social justice. There are examples of expediency in his early letters, not least when he addresses his publishers or the powerful Brandes brothers. (pp. 304-05)

The letters [of *Brev 1869-1906. I: 1869-1883*] demonstrate the intellectual awakening and the growth of the writer Kielland. He remained a representative of the upper class throughout his life—his witty, ironic, elegant style is in itself a testimony to this fact—but he was nevertheless filled with a zealous desire to create social justice. He was not always successful, and he became occasionally exasperated at the reception his books received. (p. 305)

> *Kjetil A. Flatin, "World Literature in Review: 'Brev 1869-1906. I: 1869-1883'," in* World Literature Today *(copyright 1979 by the University of Oklahoma Press), Vol. 53, No. 2, Spring, 1979, pp. 304-05.*

K. A. FLATIN (essay date 1979)

The second volume of Alexander Kielland's correspondence with family and friends [*Brev 1869-1906. II: 1884-1889*] contains about 350 letters. . . . The years 1884-89 were the beginning of the end of Kielland's literary life. After the first years of explosive productivity his wells were beginning to run dry, and as the years passed by the struggle to keep up with expectations became increasingly painful to himself and to family and friends. It became doubly painful because of the resulting financial woes which forced him to leave his patrician lifestyle and even seriously to consider moving to America "as a common immigrant." . . .

The letters are, despite Kielland's desperate situation, delightful reading. With his incomparable wit he showers politics, sex, public morality and the leading personalities of the day with irony and sarcasm. The letters offer the reader a way to understand the 1880s in Scandinavia that no work of fiction or literary history can match.

K. A. Flatin, "World Literature in Review: 'Brev 1869-1906. II: 1884-1889'," in World Literature Today *(copyright 1979 by the University of Oklahoma Press), Vol. 53, No. 4, Autumn, 1979, p. 697.*

ADDITIONAL BIBLIOGRAPHY

Harper's New Monthly Magazine 83, Supp. 3 (September 1891): 648.
　　Contemporary review of *Tales of Two Countries*.

Karl Kraus

1874-1936

Austrian critic, dramatist, essayist, aphorist, poet, journalist, and translator.

Kraus is chiefly known as a satirist whose favorite target was the bombast of the Viennese press. The dominant concern in all his work is the misuse of the German language, which he believed symbolized the disintegration of European culture and the inevitability of worldwide destruction. He regarded German as the "universal whore whom I have to make into a virgin," and saw himself as one of the few rightful arbiters of the language's correct use.

The son of a Jewish paper manufacturer, Kraus showed little interest in the family business. Having had a brief, unsuccessful acting career, he turned to journalism and began to contribute articles to the respected Viennese *Neue Freie Presse*, a newspaper he was later to castigate vehemently. His criticism of journalism centered around its tendency toward glib superficiality, cliché, and sensational gossipmongering. In 1899 he founded the polemical journal, *Die Fackel (The Torch)*. From 1911 until 1936 Kraus was the sole contributor to *The Torch*, which, until his death played a vital and controversial role in the Viennese cultural and literary scene.

Kraus believed that there is a direct relationship between meaning and form; the purpose of his work is to show the ramifications of a breach in this relationship. One of his techniques in *The Torch*, for example, is to quote a seemingly inconsequential item in a rival newspaper, and, by criticizing its word usage and grammar, argue that sloppy writing betrays faulty reasoning and lack of imagination, which, in turn, make possible social intolerance and war. His collections of essays and aphorisms, most of which contain material first published in *The Torch*, established his reputation as a writer with an almost religious reverence for the purity of language. Many critics agree that the characteristics of Kraus's style—verbal precision, witty punning, and mordant satire—are best seen in his collections of aphorisms.

Disgust for the carnage of the First World War provoked Kraus to compose his most powerful protest against the press: the pacifist drama *Die letzten Tage der Menschheit (The Last Days of Mankind)*, in which he accuses the press of instigating and perpetuating the war. In this monumental work Kraus presents his vision of imminent apocalyptic doom. Although the length of the play—it has over two hundred scenes—has prevented production in its entirety, *The Last Days of Mankind* is considered by many the most effective antiwar drama ever written.

The many poems Kraus wrote throughout his career reveal the same concern for the careful use of language evident in his prose. His poems are criticized for their lack of originality, yet at times they display great lyric beauty. A master of the German language, Kraus was also a well-known interpreter of other's works. His appreciation of Shakespeare, Goethe, Offenbach, and others led him to start a *Theater der Dichtung (Theater of Poetry)*, which enjoyed great popular success. Alone on stage, Kraus would recite whole plays by Shakespeare, poems, and entire operettas in order to emphasize the pure poetry in the works of the great masters.

By personal permission of Frederick Ungar

Although during his lifetime Kraus's influence was restricted to Vienna, several new editions of his work attest to an interest in the English-speaking world. Almost alone in his opposition to the war and pseudopatriotic rant, Kraus so skillfully combined linguistic mastery with prophetic foresight that Erich Heller refers to him as "the first European satirist since Swift."

PRINCIPAL WORKS

Die demolirte Literatur (essays) 1897
Sittlichkeit und Kriminalität (essays) 1908
Sprüche und Widersprüche (aphorisms) 1909
Die chinesische Mauer (essays) 1910
Pro domo et mundo (aphorisms) 1912
Worte in Versen. 9 vols. (poetry) 1916-30
  [*Poems*, 1930]
Nachts (aphorisms) 1918
Die letzten Tage der Menschheit (drama) 1922
  [*The Last Days of Mankind* (abridged version), 1974]
Traumstück (drama) 1923
Wolkenkuckucksheim (drama) 1923
Traumtheater (drama) 1924
Die Sprache (essays) 1937

Die dritte Walpurgisnacht (essays) 1952
Half-Truths and One-and-a-Half Truths (aphorisms)
  1976
In These Great Times (essays, poetry, and drama) 1976
No Compromise (essays, letters, drama, aphorisms, and
  poetry) 1977

*This is the date of first publication rather than first performance.

DONALD G. DAVIAU (essay date 1961)

Kraus's grandiose, apocalyptic tragedy, *Die letzten Tage der Menschheit,* chronicles with historical accuracy the events in Austria during the war years 1914-1918 and depicts the cultural and ethical decline which had undermined the stability of the country. . . . His purpose is to portray in detail the calamitous state of mankind because of its lapse into a system of relative morality, which has brought with it sacrifice of integrity and honesty. His message affirmed the need for an absolute system of morality, for a revival of truthfulness in all phases of life. In an age which had neglected its cultural heritage and ignored its humanitarian tradition, Kraus emerged as a prophet, who saw clearly and proclaimed fearlessly, if not the way to the promised land of the future, at least the way to avoid self-destruction. (p. 47)

Die letzten Tage der Menschheit is not intended as a drama of character or action, but as a portrayal of the meaninglessness of language in Austria and its ensuing repercussions. Kraus did not attempt to create external aspects of beings or rounded personalities, but to convey the essence, the very soul, of his characters. He purposely left his figures shadowy and masklike to highlight their lack of depth and integrity. He wanted to make audible this tragic loss, to preserve in his drama, as a testament for the ages, a knowledge of the essential degradation of his time. (p. 48)

Kraus did not need to characterize his people in stage directions, for their language alone affords an accurate and unmistakable portrait which can be fleshed out in the reader's mind. Thus, not only is what is said important, but so too is the manner of expression. Sentence construction, vocabulary, and pronunciation, which Kraus approximates in dialectical renditions, become indicative of the type of mentality being portrayed. Language thus becomes not merely a means of identification, but ultimately and most importantly the basis by which these people must be judged.

Kraus, the fanatic of truth, was logically a fanatic of language, the universally accepted means of communicating truth among men; for he believed that language served as an index to the state of morality of any given culture. The closer language, thought, and deed coincided, the closer the individual or society approached moral perfection. In this sense Kraus, the *Aufklärer,* believed in the perfectibility of man. His tragedy shows the result of the breakdown of language, when words no longer represent actions or thoughts. . . . The inevitable concomitant of the breakdown in the communicativeness of language, as Kraus demonstrates, is the loss of ethical standards, which leads to the decline of society, and, if carried to its logical extreme, to the destruction of humanity itself. (pp. 48-9)

Kraus's method in this drama—satire—is directed exclusively at revealing the discrepancy between word and deed with the ultimate aim of restoring meaning to language. . . .

Kraus shows how words in his society have lost their significance by portraying scenes in which phrases are parroted mechanically, demonstrating that the speaker has not thought about their meanings. Slogans such as "jetzt ist Krieg," "Krieg ist Krieg," "durchhalten," "Heldentod fürs Vaterland". . . , recur constantly in the most inane and ludicrous contexts. These catchwords are frequently uttered in situations where they sound paradoxical and even grotesque. Not only are these words misused, but with equal glibness they are mangled and mispronounced by the lower classes, who try to echo newspaper phraseology. . . . (p. 49)

By examining the phraseology of war, Kraus attempts to expose the rottenness and corruption concealed behind the patriotic clichés. He points out the illogic of calling soldiers "Einrückende," when they have no free choice in the decision. More accurately, they should be termed "einrückend gemachte." He reveals the sham glory of the concept "Er starb den Heldentod fürs Vaterland" by juxtaposing a government declaration, in which workers are threatened with being sent to the front as punishment for complaining about working conditions. . . . (p. 50)

The responsibility for the breakdown of language Kraus attributes mainly to the press, and particularly to Moritz Benedikt's *Die Neue Freie Presse,* the most influential newspaper in Vienna. He devoted the largest portion not only of this drama, but of all his works, to denouncing the evils of journalism, which he held directly accountable for the moral irresponsibility that made war possible. The press, in Kraus's opinion, introduced chaos into the world by ignoring the question of right and wrong and by twisting events to suit its own purposes. Reporters did not report what was true, but what they wanted their readers to believe. . . .

One of Kraus's favorite terms for journalists is *Hyänen,* and their activity he describes as "Walzer der Hyänen um die Leichen". . . , for he feels that they gleefully pick over the bones of the dead for a story. The full measure of his hatred and contempt is reserved for Benedikt, who, he claims, has triumphed over all the moral and spiritual values of his time. . . . In the epilogue Kraus portrays Benedikt as Antichrist, rejoicing in his victory over the power of good. . . .

By substituting empty phraseology for factual reporting, the press created a situation in which the word no longer represented the deed, but existed independently of reality. The effect of this dishonesty was to produce a society incapable of judging truth. . . . (p. 51)

Equally culpable with the press are the military high command and the system of bureaucracy, which suppress truth to conceal bungling and inefficiency. Kraus believes that if the public knew the truth about war and its conduct, the war could not continue. Conversely, evil flourishes best when it can be concealed behind an ideal, as in this instance war behind patriotism. According to Kraus, the military, which should be a tool of society, has become an autonomous body fighting to protect and expand its own interests and sphere of authority rather than to serve humanity. . . . They protect themselves from criticism by using gibberish and official gobbledygook. . . , and by exercising their unchallengeable authority. . . . The retention by the military of the vocabulary of knighthood in an age of modern warfare produces that gap betwen language and reality which Kraus is attacking. (p. 52)

The aspect of the war that caused Kraus the profoundest suffering was that those most guilty were spared from the consequences of their actions, while innocents died in their stead. Once he had become resigned to the fact of war, he had accepted it as a means of scourging the earth of its destroyers. However, in this he was disappointed. *Die letzten Tage der Menschheit* is his testimonial for the ages on behalf of the vain sacrifices of war. In addition, it is his attempt to redeem his own spirit from having been witness to this crime against humanity. . . .

The term *Erlösung* is of fundamental importance, for Kraus's personal salvation, his hope for the future of humanity, stems from a profound religiosity. Significantly, the play concludes with the voice of God intoning the words attributed to Emperor Wilhelm II, "Ich habe es nicht gewollt." This final statement counterbalances the apparent negativeness of the entire work. Kraus indicates here his belief that God does not intend His world to exist in chaos nor to end in apocalypse. Man controls his own fate, and it is his hope that humanity will work in a positive direction toward achieving that ideal state which formed Kraus's vision.

The means to salvation, according to Kraus, lie in man's relation to his language. In *Die letzten Tage der Menschheit,* he demonstrated the major dilemma of the modern world— the rootlessness of language, the divorce of language from meaning. (p. 54)

> *Donald G. Daviau, "Language and Morality in Karl Kraus's 'Die letzten Tage der Menschheit'," in* Modern Language Quarterly *(© 1961 University of Washington), Vol. XXII, No. 1, March, 1961, pp. 46-54.*

MAX SPALTER (essay date 1967)

[Reverence] for the written and spoken word inspired Kraus to polemics in which he saw himself as the vengeful guardian of the living word against all defilers; it inspired him also to write *The Last Days of Mankind* . . . , a panoramic episodic play about World War I that is as much a satire prompted by the pettiness of those who made the war possible as it is a tragedy of European man rushing suicidally into oblivion. It is a play of such epic dimensions and astonishing linguistic brilliance that no critic of its contents can begin his work unapologetically. (p. 138)

The first act makes it laughably obvious that a steady diet of sweet fictions has spoiled the Viennese appetite for cold, hard truth: the very sparks which ignite World War I warm the cockles of superpatriotic hearts, which beat never so wildly as when the death of peace is assured. The refrain, *Serbien muss sterbien,* sums up how the average Austrian feels about his Slavic neighbors. The commencement of the "Great War" is an occasion for rejoicing, whether it be on the part of mobs drifting though Vienna's streets to the rhythms of jingoistic slogans or of sedate citizens who approve wholeheartedly of violence on behalf of the "civilized" Austrian Empire. In this atmosphere a historian sees in the hoodlums out to maul the Jews the very finest qualities that times of stress call for; after all, hooliganism reflects alertness to enemy infiltration.

Kraus handles the dynamics of crowd action with an eye for grotesque comedy that is bound to recall Shakespeare. The crowd is stimulated by a phrase or slogan, echoes it with childish glee, then proceeds to embroider its own set of ridiculous variations. The result is quite comic. . . . (p. 139)

Although Kraus could not be more explicit about his distaste for street-corner chauvinism and inflammatory journalism than in the scenes where he lets events speak for themselves, he devotes a good share of the first act to explanatory comment. The explaining is done by a character called The Carper, who engages in a kind of moral debate with his emotional antitype, The Optimist. (p. 140)

The more The Carper speaks, the easier it is to recognize his views as those of Kraus, who, like The Carper, laid the blame for what is wrong with the modern world on universal materialism; castigated the Germanic world for failing to live up to its reputation for *Geist* and *Kultur;* found in the debased quality of modern German speech the surest signs of a degenerate culture; derided the individual German for making organization and efficiency ends in themselves, to the exclusion of any real human values; and predicted that no matter how terrible the present, the future would be a hundred times worse. Kraus, like The Carper, saw no escape for men who had bound themselves to a civilization of machinery and had informed themselves by means of a press that was anti-thought. . . .

[The war is a lark] for Kraus's favorite target, the press. The art of misquotation is carried to new heights; journalists devote their talents to the exaltation of the barbaric; they see, hear, and speak no evil that will define war as a dirty business. One such journalist visits Belgrade, and the city strikes her as ugly enough to have deserved its bombing: unfortunately, its rubble is not photogenic enough for her paper. (p. 141)

Though experts are prepared to stress that Germany is an innocent country fighting a defensive war, and though the Protestant clergy sanctions the war as a moral necessity, The Carper sings a different tune. He will not allow The Optimist to diminish in any way the terrible guilt for the war which all Germans share. (p. 142)

The fourth act takes us to that stage of the war in which the slogans that once came from the heart serve to rationalize what cannot be faced. To a child craving food a father can give only the reassurance that the Russians must be starving. And if sheer hunger drives a young woman into the world's oldest profession, she still is not entitled to the sympathy of those who bring her to justice. In the eyes of justice she is a "syphilitic slut." (p. 143)

As horrible as the content of the fourth act is, its final image of joy at the senseless killing of innocent animal life sickens as nothing before.

Those who refuse to acknowledge such horror remain worlds apart from those who must acknowledge it at the price of every illusion that man is a civilized creature. (p. 145)

The Carper's tone is more apocalyptic than ever. The war, he explains, is like no other of history. It has eaten its way into the fabric of all civilized life, damaging irrevocably modern society's potential for sanity, threatening for all time the future of the human race. (p. 146)

In a rhymed epilogue, Kraus recapitulates the motifs of his epic play in images and comments explicitly designed to shock. There are recitations by Masculine Gasmasks and Feminine Gasmasks; by hyenas with human faces; by all sorts of human deformities going about the business of milking the war for all it is worth. . . .

In the Epilogue, Kraus crystallizes his indictment in operatically ingenuous fashion. Those to be condemned simply condemn themselves by monologues and comments devoid of humanitarian resonance. The impression of unmitigated monstrosity is reinforced by such gestural imagery as the dancing of hyenas around corpses. The only real tension of the Epilogue derives from the confrontation of Voices from Above and Voices from Below, in which the higher voices speak truth while the lower voices cling to the very falsehoods about to blow up in their faces. Finally, truth manifests itself in a fashion that cannot be denied: a rain of meteors descends upon the earth; rotten mankind is incinerated; the noise of the human beast has finally been stilled. "This was not my wish" is God's only comment, but it makes us realize that Kraus's God is not the sadistic God of Büchner and Grabbe. He is, in fact, the Judaeo-Christian God and can only weep at what man has brought on himself. (p. 148)

Like Büchner, Kraus implies that those who twist language to their own purposes are just as ready to do violence to civilization for their own purposes. In Kraus is culminated the tradition of drama in which speech serves not to further plot but to reveal in an instant the forces whose pressure moves the world. No one before Kraus made of the word so irrefutable a revelation; no one possessed the encyclopedic linguistic knowledge which allows Kraus to employ speech patterns that are as diverse as they are authentic; it is hard to imagine anyone going further to show that drama is possible with the most chaotic interplay of dialects. The linguistic revolution begun by [J.M.R.] Lenz could not be more complete. . . .

A great deal of Kraus's drama is plainly monological: characters get started on some obsessive idea and simply talk themselves blue in the face. And all too often, when there is dialogue, it could just as well be monologue, for the whole point of a conversational exchange is that no one really listens to anyone else, even when to listen means the difference between sanity and insanity. (p. 149)

Kraus's prose encompasses extremes of barely articulate vulgarity and highly eloquent moral consciousness. Not the least of his achievements, however, are the versified renditions he puts into the mouths of characters devoid of civilized awareness. After a battle, officers and journalists cannot resist celebrating the slaughter of thousands with poetry whose brutish overtones would prove distasteful in any context. On and on they vocalize their glee at the mangled corpses which cover the countryside, comparing the piles of dead to a good catch of fish. As if this were not enough, Kraus indicates that the singers in question should underline their moral cretinism by illustrative gestures. His predilection for theater which lays great stress on physical expressiveness may well have originated in Kraus's youth, when he witnessed performances at Vienna's old *Burgtheater*. Like Brecht, he favored a highly theatrical style of acting.

This is by no means a minor point. If epic theater in its earlier phases can be related to interest in puppetry as a metaphor for the human condition, epic theater in its latest phases is equally gesture oriented. Brecht would intellectualize this as none of his anticipators did, but one need only skim through

Kraus's play to appreciate how meticulously he suggests physical gesture. Speech after speech is rendered in such idiosyncratically vivid language, and with such attention to rhythm, intonation, and articulation, that we cannot help imagining a living speaker to the faintest twitch of his face. In Kraus culminates the mimetic approach to dialogue which . . . goes back to Lenz, an approach based on the idea that characters speak and move in a way that betrays the forces that are pulling them along. (pp. 151-52)

Every act of Kraus's play begins in the same way, with the shouting of headlines and the desultory conversation of groups moving along in the open air. This technique of capturing the emotional climate of a society from random observations of strollers caught off guard, Kraus may well have learned from [Christian Dietrich] Grabbe, who, in *Napoleon*, worked just this way. Like Grabbe, who indicated in his title that *Napoleon* was as much concerned with the final hundred days of the Emperor's reign as with the Emperor himself, Kraus is out to depict the spirit of an era; like Grabbe, he does this by shifting across every level of society, reproducing the texture of a historical period as much through the views of the man in the street as through the views of the high and mighty. Most important, like Grabbe, Kraus shows how totally antithetic to any kind of greatness the very substance of a time can be, though he would hardly share Grabbe's feeling that time itself is the ultimate villain. For Kraus, man sins against the time and not vice versa.

What Kraus achieved with episodic drama is monumental enough to put him in a class all his own; nonetheless, the major features of his truly epic play connect him with the Lenz-Brecht tradition. In a breakdown of his style we find that Kraus's individual scenes are autonomous units of meaning and that they have no prescribed length; he is as prone to mix comic and tragic effects as he is to mix the lyrical and prosaic; he subordinates action to commentary and characterization to satire; he makes of language an ultimate key to the nature of human life: the speech of his characters comments on what they are in more or less the same way that the dialogue of Lenz, Büchner, and Wedekind acts as such a commentary; even the use of visual aids to add a dimension of explicitness to drama, considered by many to be a purely Brechtian technique, is to be found in *The Last Days of Mankind*. (pp. 152-53)

In *The Last Days of Mankind*, characters are not individualized by the criteria of meticulous psychological realism; they are blatantly caricatured into types that embody the very qualities which their creator detests and which he sees to be the dominant qualities of an impossibly heartless society. Kraus's gallery of characters who exist to be indicted includes such constructions as The Patriot and The Subscriber, whose entire psychology is predictable on the basis of the latest editorial in war-glorifying newspapers; their functional names sum up all that they stand for in the play. . . .

This brings us to the realization that *The Last Days of Mankind* is an astonishing blend of naturalism and antinaturalism. In spite of the fact that a great portion of the play consists of material lifted straight from life, the effect is unnaturalistic; if anything, the effect is grotesque. Like Büchner in *Danton's Death*, and like Grabbe in *Napoleon*, Kraus can make truth seem more weird than fiction, can show a world of fact to be inhabited by ludicrous marionettes. It is precisely this ability to put on stage a world that is recognizably real but at the same time frighteningly laughable that distinguishes the tradition of anti-idealistic drama begun in Germany by J. M. R. Lenz. (p. 154)

Kraus exploits to the limit . . . episodic structure to reinforce a sense of futility, even if he sees at work no particular suprahuman demons with a taste for human flesh. For Kraus, the very worst demon of all is mankind's vast stupidity, and he makes its presence felt on every page of *The Last Days of Mankind*. . . .

Lenz and Kraus, for all their differences, spoke a common language of the theater, found in *characters speaking* more real drama than in characters interrelating. Both realized that action does not speak louder than words when action is merely the consequence of what words imply. It is true that Lenz concluded his plays with messages of sanity while Kraus's *Walpurgisnacht* of a play ends in the most awful chaos; but this difference is really not one of dramaturgy; rather, it reflects Kraus's conviction that he was, indeed, living in mankind's final period, and that his play would achieve the recognition it deserved only on another planet. (p. 155)

> Max Spalter, "Karl Kraus," in his Brecht's Tra-
> dition *(copyright © 1967 by The Johns Hopkins*
> *Press), The Johns Hopkins University Press, 1967,*

WILMA ABELES IGGERS   (essay date 1967)

Quantitatively the largest part of Kraus's work dealt directly with his place in the world, and most of the remainder did so indirectly. This tendency to center his attention on himself must be thought of as extending over the whole period of Kraus's literary activity in such a way that *Die Fackel* in its first year of publication presented itself to the reader merely as a generally cultural and political periodical with a strong personal and ethical note, but later became more and more of a subjective diary of Kraus. In it he constantly held the world to account for its attitude toward him. His themes often seemed to be opportunities for repeating that his writings were his own business, and yet he again and again belied his own words by attempting to justify himself, and by trying to influence his readers. In fact, his interest in having his "diary" read, so that he might influence his readers by it, was great enough to make him collect articles from *Die Fackel* and publish them as books according to general themes. There were seven volumes of them, written for the most part in the first decades of the twentieth century and published under the following titles: [*Sittlichkeit und Kriminalität* (Morality and Criminality), *Die Chinesische Mauer* (The Chinese Wall), *Weltgericht* (The Last Judgment), *Untergang der Welt durch die schwarze Magic* (The End of the World through Black Magic), *Literatur und Lüge* (Literature and Lie) and Die Sprache (Language)]. (pp. 11-12)

Kraus was only rarely a poet. Much of his "poetry" [in the nine volumes of *Worte in Versen*] was parody; *"Volkshymne"* modeled on "Gott erhalte", (the Austrian imperial anthem) is an example. Many more of Kraus's poems were political satires, denunciatory of the emperor, of various disputing nationalities of the empire, of self-styled Christians who mistreated illegitimate children, and of contemporary poets and their work.

If one of the criteria for poetry is permanent value, most of Volume VII of *Worte in Versen* (and many other individual poems) must be discounted, because it deals for the most

part with details of contemporary politics. Many of Kraus's poems were of doubtful poetic value merely because of their highly moralistic tone; thus, for instance, *An den Bürger* (To the Citizen), somewhat like [Hugo van] Hofmannsthal's great poem *Manche freilich* (Some of course), was an appeal to middle-class people not to forget about those who toil in the mines and do similar hard, unpleasant work for them, very reminiscent of some poems found in old German elementary-school readers. Poems dealing with Kraus's working habits, language, and rhyme were rather frequent.

Even what might be called Kraus's lyric poetry proper is very uneven, in content and form rarely deviating from the pattern of the nineteenth-century *Epigonentum* (epigones). These poems deal with love, hatred, childhood memories, dream visions, waterfalls, winter, spring, death, the green at the roadside, the eyes of an old beggar woman, the loyalty of a dog, the death of a butterfly, or the mood expressed by his surroundings on a certain day. During the reading of these poems, one too often has the feeling that whatever Kraus genuinely felt about these things is hidden by his too consciously-willed expression. He was no doubt aware of the effective contrast between the usual grouchy Kraus and his childlike, naive self. . . . In *Schnellzug* (Express train) he employed a technique which had appealed to generations of sentimental readers before him. Only when he freed himself from entirely conventional topics, as well as from his lifelong annoyances, did Kraus's poetry come close to being truly lyrical. This is true in some verses dealing with his fear of death, *Todesfurcht* (Fear of Death) being an example, and also to some extent in his poems of escape, such as *Jugend* (Youth) and *"Vallorbe."* . . . There are also some individual poems from [his drama] *Die letzten Tage der Menschheit* in which his horror and bitterness over what was happening let him forget all about how poetry was conventionally written. *Der tote Wald* (The Dead Forest) is an example. . . . It is hardly possible, nevertheless, to be deeply moved by Kraus's poetry. It leaves no images behind, and strong feelings are rarely transmitted by it. Kraus irritates his readers by obviously anticipating their judgments. Instead of seeing, as *he* did, his usual satire as the reverse of lyric poetry, one is likely to consider his lyric poetry merely the reverse side of his usual coin: one senses that the usually pessimistic and mistrustful Kraus only momentarily pretended to be full of the milk of human kindness.

Because, however, he always emphasized ethical value judgments, it is impossible to judge his poetry solely from the aesthetic point of view. With Kraus, nothing was entirely a matter of aesthetics; it was only a frequent, very welcome aid to the ultimate, ethical purpose.

Much of his verse is really on the level of jingles where the form of verse was chosen only for more effective expression. Often the point lies in the mere coincidence of similarity of sound, used in the service of ridicule of his fellow-writers, which was one of his perennial themes. . . . In order to be fair to Kraus, however, we must realize that, in view of his own theory of the relation of satire and poetry, he *could* hardly be a poet. He definitely considered himself a satirist who could only exist in an age of decay, just as a poet could only exist in a more hopeful age. Thus while the poet re-created the positive, he, the satirist, had the more menial task of wiping out and burning out the negative. (pp. 12-15)

Die letzten Tage der Menschheit is Kraus's first drama, and perhaps the greatest work that came out of World War I. . . .

The play is unquestionably the most valuable one of Kraus's works, although it is no more of a drama in the conventional sense than his other plays. What gives it a great quality of genuineness is the fact that it is merely a condensation of several volumes of *Die Fackel*, centered thematically around the First World War. (p. 15)

Kraus's other dramas followed during the twenties.... [*Literatur, oder man wird doch da sehn* (**Literature, or We'll See about That**)] is the most permanent expression of Kraus's hatred for his own Jewish businessman's background. [Franz Werfel, an expressionist poet, novelist and dramatist], whose background was so strikingly like Kraus's, is the central character. The play portrayed faithfully, with only slight caricature, a Central-European Jewish family just at the point of switching its occupation from commerce to literature. The proper local color and linguistic habits are supplied by the Jewish family, consisting of at least two generations of men and a few intellectual, and hence, to Kraus, repulsive women. The younger generation conducts the conversation in frequently Freudian language, speaking of their libidos and inhibitions. They make pretentious remarks about fashionable topics, thus usually revealing their basic lack of understanding. In a very casual tone they discuss the Manns, Rolland, Stefan Zweig, Neo-Catholicism, and Zionism, interpolating typical Jewish business phrases at the most inopportune places.

Two themes, however, continue throughout the play: first, Werfel's preoccupation with Goethe and with his own Goethean qualities, expressed in language spiced with quotations from Faust. The second theme is everybody's constant awareness of the existence of Kraus. Kraus seemed to care much more for occupying a prominent place in the public consciousness than about whether he was loved or hated. The place he occupied, as he has depicted it, was extremely important; everybody seemed to be aware of his existence. The climax of the play is a press representative's speech, designed to encourage the young men present to become journalists. (p. 16)

In *Literatur, oder man wird doch da sehn*, one gains the impression that Kraus has divided all his people into three groups. The first consists of those who hate or at any rate very severely criticize him, speaking of his Jewish self-hatred and father-complex and saying that he has no character and has exhausted his talent long ago. Another group in the play considers Kraus foolish for merely making himself enemies and thinks he could have done much better if he had not insisted on going his own way. At this point, a voice interjects the rumor that Kraus, having earned enough money, will now retire to the stock exchange. The third kind of attitude is taken by Werfel himself; torn between love and hatred, he finally realizes how much he owes Kraus. Kraus believes to have revealed Werfel's basic insincerity when he has Werfel's father remind him of his conscious imitation of Goethe.... (pp. 16-17)

[*Traumtheater* (**Dream Theater**) and *Traumstück* (**Dream Play**)] are brief lyric sketches containing some of the most important themes of Kraus's work. Presented in poetic language and form, they generalize on the poet's dream or semi-dream experiences in such a way as to increase the suggestion of the more than specific truth of what is being said. In *Traumtheater* Kraus sees a dream vision of the beloved in another man's arms. Characteristically she is an actress, for to him the actress is always the heightened woman. He feels what

he has not permitted himself to feel when awake: the woman only gained by the new relationship, appearing even purer afterwards. In *Traumstück* he, the poet, taking a breathing spell after a section of his life's work, suspects that it has been in vain and will dissolve in nothingness. Half desperate, he falls asleep and sees first horrible creatures, symbolizing the war profiteers, psychoanalysts and other characters distasteful to him; then he sees a landscape and a butterfly. These, together with beautiful music and the voice of the eternally feminine, stir him again into going on with his work, for he knows that he has a mission which he must fulfill no matter how much he momentarily envies people satisfied just to vegetate. Clearly suggesting the close relation of artistic creation to dreams, both plays were also examples of the absurd theater more than a generation before the term even existed. (p. 17)

[Theodor] Lessing called Kraus the most shining example of Jewish self-hate. At any rate, the Jews and their problems were among the most constant themes of Kraus's publicistic activity. His first independent pamphlet, *Die demolierte Literatur* ..., dealt with a largely Jewish group, the literary clique which used to congregate at the *Café Griensteidl*. His second brochure, *Eine Krone für Zion* ..., ridiculed Herzl's Zionist movement. In all the thirty-seven years of *Die Fackel* there was hardly an issue which did not contain a gloss poking fun at a Jewish journalist's language.... Parallel with the rest of Kraus's development, his discussion of his own position became more and more general, expressed in more and more veiled language until, toward the end, there were only cryptic hints from which one could conjecture. In the course of time, his attitude towards the Jews also changed to some extent. In the thirties he was even willing to mediate donations for Palestine in *Die Fackel*. He was probably never quite sure what to think of the racial problem. (pp. 174-75)

Because he was not antisemitic on principle, he was able to approve of and even to admire such individual Jews as Peter Altenberg, Else Lasker-Schüler, and Adolph Loos. Again, the explanation is simple: Kraus did not find in them the traits which he considered Jewish. To him Jewish traits included Central-European Jewish mannerisms and expressions, a strong interest in business, membership in a Jewish literary clique, and some related traits.... Kraus never analyzed; he only expressed intuitive flashes of insight, their syntheses, and individual witty comments. His writings about Jews are especially subjective. Since most of those whom he considered typically Jewish were distasteful to him, he had no pity for their sufferings and therefore, in spite of different motives and intentions, many of Kraus's views concurred with those of the most vicious antisemites until he was awakened by the horror of Hitler's concentration camps. And even then his attitude was not one of clear protest. (p. 177)

One would entirely misunderstand Kraus's significance if one were to try to analyze his views in a purely intellectual manner, to try to define his concepts, and to arrive at theories. It was only rarely and in a very fragmentary way that Kraus dealt at all systematically or even connectedly with any of the phenomena which occupied him. When he did so, it was under the impact of intense, often violent, emotion. The reader felt the sincerity of these outbursts, and experienced something of the author's intensity in the rapid alternation of despair, hysterical laughter, and lyric beauty. Underlying such passages, one sometimes senses scraps of attitudes which may be pieced together into a basic attitude toward the world. One is closest to the "core" of Kraus in those writings which by their very form suggest freedom from convention, such as small *Notizen, Glossen* (notes, glosses), and comments on the latter, and most of all between the lines of passages reprinted from contemporary newspapers and books.

At first, Kraus's work presents a picturesque manifold of themes, styles, literary media and opinions. (p. 192)

What is the underlying unity?

The difficulty in finding it is increased by Kraus's often intentionally involved style, especially by the paradoxical form of his witticisms. However, ultimately the key to his unity emerges clearly: it is his sensitivity to all phenomena around him which he felt to be good or bad. He reacted to them violently, often constructing a minor work of art out of a (usually negative) reaction, and forgetting in his creative zeal that he had, in order to strengthen his argument of the moment, permitted the pendulum to swing too far in the opposite direction, and thus himself to appear as the advocate of something which he would probably expressly reject tomorrow. (pp. 192-93)

Kraus, a cultural and social critic who either despised or ignored all comparable critics, was able to view each particular case with a more penetrating mind than others, unrestricted by cumbersome scientific method. But he never went beyond pointing a finger at immediate evils and immediate responsibility to a deeper analysis of social causation and social dynamics, or even proposing alternate courses of action. This kind of thinking would have much too taming an effect on his polemics. It is useless to speculate whether Kraus would have meant more to the world if he had been a critic with a consistent philosophy of science and literature which would have filled the gap between his basic values and concrete cases. (p. 193)

Kraus's greatness lay in pointing out the basic shallowness of an era of commercialization which rested on a false conception of the rationality and goodness of man who had been reared since the Renaissance on the belief in his own potential omnipotence. Kraus showed that man was not all-powerful, but essentially a puny creature, made even more puny by his faith in his increasing power. Modern man, in the age [of] technology, had to realize that living was the prime purpose of life and that wealth constituted merely an instrument for living which was completely irrelevant when man was not aware of the basic meaning of life. The limitations of Kraus's thought lay partly in the very negative character of his work. Kraus did not help his followers to find a meaning in life. He exposed an age which had lost all faith in absolute values and reminded his readers of ages in which life had not been totally subjugated to commercial purposes, but he did not attempt to show how man could introduce meaning into the modern world. Kraus's message was essentially one of despair. According to him, the world was facing its end.

A criticism of Kraus which goes deeper is that he, too, much a part of his age, did not entirely understand it. Kraus was fighting in part against ideas and institutions which no longer played a dominant role. Among these were philosophic rationalism and scientism, a liberal political party, and a middle class from whose hands economic power had passed into those of giant corporations.

Kraus did not offer a recipe, philosophic or otherwise, by which to live; he had none himself. He wanted to instill in others the habit of thinking responsibly on the basis of the same fundamental values which were his and, as he believed, ought to be mankind's. The regression to ultimate values itself was a corollary of the emotion by which he expressed them. Together with his witticisms, his style therefore gives the impression of something irrational. In fact, however, the few decisive fundamental values in which he is consistent are rationally formulated and understandable, although they are always wrapped in the passionate faith by which he clung to them.

The essential merit of Kraus, however, was not a system which he might have left behind but a spirit of absolute earnestness and sincerity and integrity with which he sought to guide his contemporaries to the most intensive possible use of their faculties. In a very localized way he succeeded in giving a feeling of purpose to lives which no religion could have provided for them at that particular stage of development and in that locality.

Many of the problems which faced Kraus still face us today, and only the extent to which they are in the limelight has changed. . . . He was still greatly surprised by the evils which we have come to take for granted and he arouses us out of our lethargy by calling phenomena by such lay words as "good" and "evil," unusual in men as complex, and as "modern" as Kraus. (pp. 228-29)

> *Wilma Abeles Iggers, in her* Karl Kraus: A Viennese Critic of the Twentieth Century *(copyright 1967 by Martinus Nijhoff; reprinted by permission of Martinus Nijhoff), Martinus Nijhoff, 1967, 250 p.*

RICHARD HANSER   (essay date 1968)

In our day of team journalism and massive publishing combines, [Karl Kraus's] career seems hardly credible. For something like forty years he singlehandedly produced a magazine which caused more comment, stirred more controversy, was more eagerly followed and more passionately hated than any comparable publication of its era. *Die Fackel* ("The Torch"), as he called it, needed neither an expensive editorial staff nor a pool of celebrated contributors to become a phenomenon of European journalism. It needed only Karl Kraus. After the first few issues, he wrote the entire contents by himself. What made it a fermenting force through the years was the inexhaustible brilliance and penetration of his mind, the power of his pen, the impact of his satiric wit. . . .

Though he drew his material, as the commerical press did, from day-to-day events, he had no interest in reporting news in the usual sense; his passion was for sub-surface significance, interpretaion. In a seemingly trivial occurence on a Viennese street corner, in a snatch of coffee-house conversation, in a twist of phrase on the back page of the morning newspaper, he could find signs and portents far more indicative of the state of society than all the pronouncements of the politicians or the effusions of editorial writers. For him, the newspapers revealed infinitely more unconsciously and unwittingly than they ever said intentionally.

It was chiefly in the *language* of the press that Karl Kraus uncovered the clues which told him what was sick, perverse and wrong in the world around him. He believed that there was a profound, a mystical, relationship between word and deed, between language and action, and that the two inter-acted on each other according to a natural law by which debasement of one inevitably led to the corruption of the other. . . .

When Karl Kraus railed at the press, as he constantly did, for its grammatical errors, its misuse of words, and its abom-inations of style and usage, he was no mere school-marmish quibbler. He was, by his own lights, a defender of civilization against the encroachments of barbarism. (p. 24)

[Grammar] was an obsession, but a fertile and productive one. He produced precise, didactic essays on grammar—on the subtle differences between *nur noch* and *nur mehr,* and between the use of *als* and *wie.* In his unremitting attacks on what he called *Zeitungsdeutsch,* newspaper German, he urged a penal code against the "public prostitution of the language", and he hoped for a law that would inflict physical punishment for misusing conjunctions. . . .

He was essentially a moralist, driven by his nature to protest, denounce, excoriate, condemn and satirize the hypocrisies and injustices of his time. He was ferocious in his polemics, attacking what we now call The Establishment without fear, and abusing his numerous enemies without mercy. He was not free of personal animosity, and he was not always just. (p. 26)

Karl Kraus, whatever his failing and defects, deserves an honored place in the ranks of those who, through the cen-turies, have lifted a torch, a *Fackel,* against the gathering dark. (p. 27)

> Richard Hanser, "Karl Kraus: A Torch-Bearer for His Time," in American German Review *(copyright 1968 by National Carl Schurz Association, Inc.), Vol XXXIV, No. 5, August/September, 1968, pp. 24, 26-7.*

ERICH HELLER (essay date 1971)

Karl Kraus's satire is more deeply rooted in its own medium than the work of any other recent writer of German prose. 'The German language,' he said, 'is the profoundest of all languages, but German speech is the shallowest.' The genius of Karl Kraus could not have arisen from the ground of another language; for the inspiration of his satirical work is the contrast between his faith in words and the speech of the faithless: and it is German that offers the biggest scope for this faith as well as its blasphemers. (p. 237)

[Karl Kraus's] work does not convey through the written word something which, if needs be, could be conveyed in another medium; he merely confronts with the uncorrupted spirit of language the representative idiom of his society; and at the approach of his words the language-scene of the age is uncannily illuminated, showing souls and minds corrupted by untruth and self-deception.

In 922 numbers of his journal *Die Fackel* there is not one polemical essay which does not begin and end with an op-position of this kind. His campaigns are not aimed at hostile opinions or ideologies. In every single case his field of action is the ever-widening no-man's-land between appearance and reality, expression and substance, word-gesture and person-ality. The tirades of rhetoricians, the pamphlets of politicians, the *feuilletons* of renowned authors are passed through the filter of language, leaving behind mere dregs of folly and residues of false pretence. The dead word is resurrected and

comes back as a spirit of destruction. Men, having tried to live on empty phrases, die of their own clichés. The triumphs of medical science are undone by the products of the printing-press, and the effect of the ink used by journalists is seen to be as deadly as the Black Death.

For Karl Kraus the word has personal life. Language, passion and thought are one and the same for him. Language is the name of the activity of his passionate thinking; his passion and his thought are identical with their articulation. This is as much as to say that the objects of his thinking and writing are not concepts, but ideas; and not ideas which he 'holds,' but ideas by which he is held. 'Poetry and passionate speech,' said Goethe, 'are the sources of the life of every language.' In this sense every word which Karl Kraus wrote is alive with the life of language, every sentence the result not of construction, but of creation and growth. (pp. 237-38)

[Newspapers] were Karl Kraus's main theme; and the men who wrote them, and the things about which they wrote: society, law-courts, sex and morality, literature, theater, war, commerce and merchandise, in brief, the whole world that is called into being by a headline, organized by a leading article and sold by an advertisement. But his contrast-theme was the words that make up a drama by Shakespeare or a poem by Goethe. Thus his theme behind the themes was the culture of Europe, its glory, its betrayal and its doom. Ex-ploring the labyrinths of contemporary verbiage, Karl Kraus never lost the thread. His purpose was 'to show the very age and body of the time his form and pressure.'

When in 1899 he founded *Die Fackel,* his subjects seemed of little more than local interest; but as the locality was Vienna, it was the heart of a European empire that was examined, and its beat was found defective. His Vienna was easily recognized as the cherished city of the world's tourists, but under his gaze the waltz was performed under the threat of the Day of Judgement. (p. 241)

In Karl Kraus's satirical work [the dissolute scene of Vienna is] confronted with the integrity of a tradition and culture which in him had preserved itself and retained an amazing vigor. He had an unfailing ear for two kinds of sound: the common talk of the town which he reproduced with flawless precison, and the language of prophecy which he discerned as the whispered accompaniment of the degraded vernacular, suddenly forcing it into a key of ultimate significance. Op-pressed by the confusing chorus of apparent triviality, his ear was tuned to the pitch of the Absolute. People gossiped about the war; he heard them lament the loss of their souls. At every street-corner acts of high treason were committed. The shouts of newspaper-boys announcing in mysterious vowels latest editions, became monstrous threats to man's spiritual safety or shrieks of anguish from the lowest deep.

This metamorphosis of the commonplace will for ever remain one of the greatest achievements in the German language. For the technique of Karl Kraus, if indeed it was technique, was literal quotation. He took the material of experience as it was: the coffee-house conversation of the journalists, the stock exchange rendezvous of the racketeers, the fragments of talk that reached his ear in the streets of Vienna, the judgments of the law courts, the leading articles of the news-papers and the chatter of thier readers—in fact, all that looks like the triviality of daily life—and endowed it with a soul: an anti-soul, as it were. (pp. 243-44)

Leaving the material of actuality intact, he yet gave it the deeper significance of satire, drama, and tragedy—by creating another context for it. He took the frivolous seriously, and discovered that the situation was desperate. Thus he did 'invent' after all; but his invention was of the simplest kind. It consisted in assuming the existence of natural states of culture and of self-evidently correct norms of human conduct; for instance, that modesty befits the mediocre—and instantly mediocrity was seen to have risen to demonic heights from which it ruled the world. Or he assumed that the prominent German writers and journalists of his time wrote in the German tongue—and the German tongue answered back, saying that they were illiterates. He dealt with the practice of the law courts as though it were based upon justice; with the theatre as though it were concerned with the art of drama; with journals as though they intended to supply correct information; with politicians as though they desired the promotion of communal prosperity, and with philosophers as though they were seekers after truth. The satirical effect of these inventions was annihilating. (pp. 244-45)

The Last Days of Mankind is not a drama in any accepted sense of the word. . . . It has no hero, no unity of space, time or action. In time it stretches from 1914 to 1919. It takes place on the battlefields of Europe, in stock exchanges and hospitals, the offices of journals, the lecture-rooms of universities, the headquarters of armies, and again and again in the streets of Vienna. (p. 246)

We have not yet grasped the demonic possibilities of mediocrity, believing as we do that the only appropriate partner for Mephisto is a Faustian genius. It was Karl Kraus who discovered to what satanic heights inferiority may rise. He anticipated Hitler long before anyone knew his name. (p. 247)

In our uncanny and enlightened epoch [reality] is merely the result of a conspiracy of sobriety, scientific planning, mediocrity and human insignificance. The demonstration of the terrifying incongruity fills the pages of *The Last Days of Mankind*. Its heroes are troglodytes living in the skyscrapers of history, barbarians having at their disposal all the amenities and high explosives of technical progress, fishmongers acting the role of Nelson, ammunition salesmen crossing Rubicons, and hired scribblers tapping out the heroic phrases of the bards. And there are, on the more passive and pathetic side, their victims on active service: farm laborers with a few weeks of battle training, honest-to-goodness little people with pensionable salaries and paid holidays, decent folk whose imagination is unable to grasp even a fragment of the horror which they are commanded to inflict upon the world by faithfully serving machines, pulling levers and pressing buttons. And the effects are registered by men whose imagination is blunted and whose moral judgment is corrupted by the insidious poison of journalistic language which has emptied the word of all its reality and meaning.

This is Karl Kraus's thesis: If our imagination sufficed to visualize the reality behind the news column of one morning paper, this reality would not and could not exist. And if one man's imagination were inspired by it and gave expression to it, all the tragedies of ancient Greece would dwindle into idyllic sentimentalities before such a drama of human corruption and human agony. But such an imagination does not exist, and therefore there exists such a reality; there exists such a reality, and therefore no such imagination. (pp. 247-48)

Vacuous spirits and enfeebled souls, living in a world replete and luxuriant with the riches of Hell—and (most perverse

of miracles!) in a world of their own making; minds as hopelessly muddled and impoverished as the language of their psychology, and as diabolically exact as the formulae of their missile engineering; intelligence defeated by the task of writing a correct sentence but triumphantly equal to the commission to destroy the world: such is the occasion of Karl Kraus's prophecy. (p. 249)

In the moral sphere where most contemporary writers would lose their way in a tangle of problems he would see none; but he would prove to all of them that they had given too little thought to the sound of their words and to the rhythm and syntax of their sentences. And what, above all, he taught those who were able to hear him was the meaning and extent of moral responsibility. His unfailing and instinctive response to what are 'strictly moral' questions was the result of his having pondered over them endlessly in 'strictly amoral' fields: in the sphere of aesthetics and language. *Language*—the collection of his essays on this subject—is probably the profoundest book that exists on style and the use of German. It is the work of an artist and moralist, not of a pedant and grammarian. There it becomes clear that the ruthlessness of his moral judgment sprang from the delicate tact and care which he showed in his dealings with the 'crystallized tradition of the spirit of man.' To his impatience with the wrong-doers corresponded his infinite patience with language, and to his relentless ethical determination his compassion for the maltreated word. (pp. 250-51)

If there could be any doubt left about the authenticity of Karl Kraus's satire, it would be removed by his lyrical poetry. Although some of his verse is part and parcel of his satirical campaigns, most of his poems are untouched by the spirit of satire, meeting it only at the source of their common inspiration: language. A first and superficial judgment may class this poetry as *'Epigonendichtung'*; and this is what, in a particular sense, he called it himself. Its forms, metres, rhythms and rhymes are traditional. It is determined by the history of German poetry from Goethe to Liliencron. . . . (pp. 252-53)

The unity of thing and word, of feeling and its articulation, which is the essence of poetry, has in Karl Kraus's verse a distinctly erotic character. He was in love with language, but not in the manner of those promiscuous affairs with sounds so liberally encouraged in the society of Symbolists. His passion aimed at a more real possession—the body and soul of words. The subject of his poems is often language itself, and like a true lover he believed in the purifying effect of his love. (p. 254)

In the poetic dialogue *'Eros and the Poet,'* in which the poet boasts of having defeated the distracting god by a final escape into work, Eros yet overtakes and conquers him by rising from the words themselves, even though there is 'no trace of woman.' . . .

The lyrical thought of Karl Kraus is as concrete and sensuous as any 'object' that has ever been received into poetic diction. With him both trees and thoughts grow in precise articulation from the soil of language, and both thoughts and fountains rise and fall with the exact rhythm of Nature breathing through the mouth of Art. And it is surely not only against the background of the thinker's thought and the satirist's Herculean labor that those moments when his poetry relaxes in the purest lyrical concentration are so deeply moving. On the contrary, they are in themselves enhanced by the energy set free through the release from the arduous task. There is indeed enough even of such purely lyrical poems to build up for their maker a poetic reputation of high order, poems in which the world is irradiated with the peace that is in the perfect concord of man, things, sounds and rhythms, leaving us with nothing else to be desired. . . . (p. 255)

The *satirist* Karl Kraus brought to life a world whose every breath was a denial of God's designs, and was the chaos that decided that His will should not be done. The *poet* Karl Kraus praised the order of a universe in which all is well if only He wills it so. The *silent* Karl Kraus bore witness to an unspoken faith that lies on the other side of speechless despair. It is a faith inaccessible to those who are never at a loss for words. . . . (p. 260)

> Erich Heller, "Karl Kraus: Satirist in the Modern World," in his The Disinherited Mind: Essays in Modern German Literature and Thought *(copyright 1971; by permission of Barnes & Noble Books, a Division of Littlefield, Adams & Co., Inc.), third edition, Barnes & Noble, 1971, pp. 235-60.*

HARRY ZOHN (essay date 1971)

The thirty-seven volumes of Kraus's periodical *Die Fackel (The Torch)* contain the major part of his literary output. In its impressive totality, *Die Fackel,* far from being a mere pillory, is not only a running autobiography but constitutes a unique history of Austrian culture and politics as well. It is also the source of most of Kraus's books. (p. 25)

The early Kraus was a casuist, that is, he applied broad ethical concepts, precepts, and standards to specific situations and supplied massive evidence of the corruption rampant in Austrian public life. But gradually he strove to transcend specific cases and occasions and to develop a more universally valid cultural criticism.

In *Sittlichkeit und Kriminalität,* a book which [contains forty-one articles from *Die Fackel*] . . . Kraus was concerned with morality as it was manifested in Austria's courtrooms and newspapers in the early years of this century; and yet its accurate description of human nature makes it a timeless document. The title, translated literally as "Morality and Criminality," really means "Morality and Criminal Justice" or "Court Justice," since Kraus was intent upon laying bare the contrast between private and public morality and showing the hypocrisy inherent in the administration of Austrian justice. . . .

With these sharp satirical pieces Kraus mounts an attack on the hypocrisy of a male society which condemns by day what it enjoys by night. Kraus lashes out at the narrowness of hidebound judges who are out of touch with reality and of jurors of substandard intelligence and a business mentality. Again and again he castigates the distorted, sensational newspaper reports which, to his mind, are more immoral than the crime itself. (p. 42)

In Kraus's development, this collection marked a progression from journalist to polemicist to moralist and the transformation of a critic of society into a critic of culture. The first five volumes of the *Fackel* had been relatively tame, but now there appeared a new polemical vehemence, yet one coupled with great compassion and chivalry, and a new sense of ethical mission directed at the universal—even though, characteristically, the events, circumstances, and persons trig-

gering the satire were local, either Viennese or Austrian. (pp. 42-3)

A number of the cases detailed in *Sittlichkeit und Kriminalität* involve prostitution, and since the physical prostitution of women seemed far less deleterious to Kraus than the intellectual prostitution of men, this gave him an opportunity to comment on the keyhole peeping and the self-righteous hypocrisy of Austrian society. (p. 46)

Die chinesische Mauer (The Great Wall of China) was, next to *Die letzten Tage der Menschheit,* Kraus's most successful book in his lifetime. . . . The indignation of the social satirist in *Sittlichkeit und Kriminalität,* the gloomy and bitter wit of the earlier collection now give way to lighter humor, even though the satire is just as aggressive. To use Friedrich Schiller's categorization of satire, now we get jesting satire in addition to the pathos-filled and punishing kind. The collection contains in brief compass most aspects of Kraus's later concerns, excepting, of course, the horrors of World War I and Hitlerism. (p. 48)

The juxtaposition of two or more newspaper items without comment, one of Kraus's most frequent and most effective techniques, may be noted in two pieces contained in this collection. in **"Die weisse Kultur, oder warum in die Ferne schweifen? Aus einer Berliner Zeitung"** ("White Culture, or Why Roam Far? From a Berlin Newspaper"), the left-hand column carries an item from a newspaper deploring the correspondence between German girls wishing to add to their stamp collections and natives of German colonies in Africa to whom they send photos and other mementoes. The right-hand column contains a number of marriage ads from the same paper, all from men desirous of dowries or of marrying into a business. *"Die Mütter"* ("The Mothers") presents, on the left, a chilling story about a woman who killed her illegitimate child after she had vainly appealed to the authorities and people had refused to help her, and on the right, an article on methods of baptizing an unborn child by inserting a needle with baptismal water into the mother's abdomen. (pp. 51-2)

It is all but impossible to convey in English an idea of Karl Kraus's style, the most brilliant in modern German literature, a style that attempted to make a diagnosis of the linguistic and moral sickness of what Kraus regarded as a language-forsaken age. The allusiveness of this style, its attention to associations among words, and its artful plays upon words make the reading of Kraus's works an intellectual delight of a high order; yet very little of this stylistic brilliance can be transferred to another language. Kraus regarded it as desirable that his writings be read at least twice, for while the contents might be absorbed at first reading, the stylistic artistry would become apparent only after closer attention. He said that a sentence should not be there for people to rinse their mouths with and contrasted his art with the writers of feuilletons who attract at the first glance and disappoint at the second.

Kraus was not only a master of the art of punning, with a deep seriousness underlying his verbal wit, but a skillful practitioner of amphibology, the ambiguity of speech that stems from the uncertainty of grammatical construction rather than the meaning of words, with a phrase or sentence capable of being construed in more than one way. Because of its great intensity and economy of verbal means, Kraus's prose invites close attention. One finite verb can resolve several phrases; the links between nouns and pronouns are not always readily apparent, conjunctions are often dispensed with; and the style is generally elliptical. (p. 63)

Kraus was not only a prose writer *par excellence,* but also a poet. The aphorism is a prose form which occupies an important place in his work. Aphoristic thoughts are apt to appear in Kraus's writings in various guises: Some aphorisms were distilled from a longer text in prose or poetry; in other cases they were lyrically expanded into an epigram or served as the nucleus of a prose piece. Three volumes of aphorisms, drawn from the *Fackel,* appeared in Kraus's lifetime: [*Sprüche und Widersprüche (Dicta and Contradictions); Pro domo et mundo*; and *Nachts (At Night)*]. . . . Some of Kraus's aphoristic statements about that literary form are in themselves notable and revealing: "One cannot dictate an aphorism to a typist. It would take too long." (This could be taken to mean that even the fastest typist could not handle the flash of inspiration, or that the cerebral process producing an aphorism is endless and that no typist could wait long enough. (p. 65)

In his verse [*Worte in Versen (Words in Verse)*] Kraus admittedly is an epigone rather than an innovator; the poet is indebted to Goethe and Shakespeare. He was "unoriginal" in that he needed some occasion to trigger his art, the way an oyster needs the irritation of a grain of sand to produce a pearl. His poems are seldom "romantic" in the sense that they are products of poetic rapture or intoxication; rather, they spring from the rapture of language and logic.

Kraus made little distinction between lyrical or pathetic prose satire and the poetic language of his verse. Some of his poems are versified glosses and polemics, autobiographic excursions, lyrical versions of *Fackel* texts, or satiric ideas given purified form. Their abstractness and concision often presuppose familiarity with Kraus's other works, his life, and his personality. . . . To a certain extent Kraus's poetry is *Gedankenlyrik* in Schiller's sense—poetry with a cargo of thought, reflecting a tradition coming to an end. Yet it also represents a sort of satirist's holiday in the sense that Kraus is here free to reveal himself fully and unabashedly in his love of mankind, the human spirit, nature, and animals. Poetry, to him, was like a freer, purer world, one harking back to the German classical tradition, in which the poet, freed from the goads of the satiric occasion and an ever wakeful moral conscience, was able to reflect on love, nature, fear, and wonderment.

In his poetry Kraus was guided by his conviction that the quality of a poem depended on the moral quality of the poet. ("A poem is good until one knows by whom it is.") In his view, a satirist was only a deeply hurt lyricist, the artist wounded by the ugliness of the world. In the *Worte in Versen,* rhyme and meaning are inseparably fused. (p. 66)

Kraus's poetry was never fully appreciated in his lifetime; it was decried as too unoriginal, intellectual, and not elemental enough. Yet when one realizes that much of Kraus's prose is lyrical, it is easy to see the poetry as only a special coinage from the same mint.

In his orphic epigram **"Zwei Läufer,"** . . . Kraus describes two runners sprinting along the track of time; one is bold; the other, worried. The one coming from "nowhere" reaches his goal; the one from the "origin" falls by the wayside. Yet the runner who has reached his goal makes way for his worried competitor who, however, always reaches the origin. Kraus here depicts two antithetical forces alive in the human

spirit—one that he loves and one that he hates. The world is seen as a circuitous route back to the source; intellectuality may be the wrong road, yet it does lead back to immediacy; satire is a roundabout way to poetry, and poetry, to Kraus, is a philological or linguistic detour on the way to a lost paradise.

Karl Kraus placed himself midway between *Ursprung* and *Untergang,* the origin or source of all things and the end of the world as conjured up by his satiric vision; and he saw language as the only means of going back to the origin—the origin that was forever the goal. Kraus was well aware of the difficulties as well as the rewards of his mission. "The closer the look one takes at a word, the greater the distance from which it looks back," he wrote, expressing the profundity and endlessness of his preoccupation with language and his desire to plumb fathomless depths. Both the triumph and the tragedy of his lonely linguistic quest are summed up in his insight that "only he is an artist who can make a riddle out of a solution." (pp. 66-7)

Harry Zohn, in his Karl Kraus *(copyright © 1971 by Twayne Publishers, Inc.; reprinted with the permission of Twayne Publishers, a Division of G. K. Hall & Co., Boston), Twayne, 1971, 178 p.*

EDWARD TIMMS (essay date 1974)

[Kraus's] writings, remarkable for their verbal wit and stylistic intensity, are a fusion of ethical and artistic impulses. Attacks on contemporary abuses are so framed that the individual target becomes a paradigm of human folly. Timely polemic is thus fused with timeless satire. . . . His monologue consists of variations on a single voice—that of Kraus himself, the satirist.

In his writings the word "satirist" acquires a special meaning; it is the mask adopted by the author in his own work. . . . Kraus defines his position as that of the great antagonist of the society to which (in reality) he inescapably belonged.

At first, the persona he cultivates is that of the "artist", whose intellectual vitality, imagination and sensuous awareness challenge the lethargy of bourgeois existence. In this there are echoes of Wilde's *The Soul of Man under Socialism.* . . . Gradually, however, in the threatening climate of the years immediately preceding 1914, Kraus's literary persona hardens into what Nietzsche calls a "second mask". It is the mask of a visionary satirist denouncing the values of a civilization. The element of self-dramatization in Kraus's satiric monologue becomes particularly clear at this point. . . .

Kraus sustained this exacting role throughout his life. Where Bernard Shaw's "G.B.S." was a rhetorical device that could be discarded at will, Kraus's adoptive persona as satirist became an existential commitment. But this should not deceive us (as it often did his contemporary audience) into overlooking the element of the histrionic. The satirist of **Die Fackel** is a self-stylization, a strategy rich in dramatic possibility. As Walter Benjamin shrewdly observed: "Here we see the true face, or rather the true mask of the satirist. It is the mask of Timon, the misanthrope."

Kraus's monologue is nourished (as Benjamin indicates) by literary sources. His histrionic imagination assimilates the moral pathos of the German classical theatre. Even more integral are the plays of Shakespeare. The satirist's initial stance is that of the Duke in *Measure for Measure:* "a looker-on here in Vienna, / Where I have seen corruption boil and bubble, / Till it o'er-run the stew. . . ." Later Kraus identifies with more tragic roles, from Lear and Hamlet through to Macbeth and Timon. The Bible too, especially Revelations, is called on to underwrite his more prophetic pronouncements. This blending of heroic diction with a vigorous vernacular gives Kraus's satire a disconcerting force. His monologue is not simply the voice of individual protest, but becomes the revitalization of a whole literary and moral tradition.

But the "true mask" of the satirist remains a mask, distinct both from Kraus's social identity and from his private self. And, when we turn to this private self, we encounter a further paradox. . . .

Kraus first met Sidonie Nadherny, a member of an aristocratic family, . . . in September, 1913. There followed a tempestuous relationship which survived several periods of estrangement and endured until the end of Kraus's life. . . .

[His letters to Sidonie collected in *Briefe an Sidonie Náderny von Borutin: 1913-1936* illustrate] one of the paradoxes of satire: that of the satirist in love. The problem is a literary one, not merely a matter of biographical curiosity. How can an author dedicated to satire publicly acknowledge the primacy of love?

No reader of issues of **Die Fackel** after September 1913 would ever guess that their author was privately in love. The stance of misanthropic isolation is maintained: the experience of love does not mitigate the harshness of the satirical vision. Kraus had earlier described himself as "an author who edits his diary in the form of a periodical". From 1913 onwards we see this confessional element being systematically edited out of his published writings. (p. 1393)

In the totally corrupted world seen in his satirical imagination there is no place for an acknowledgement that love and beauty may still flourish among mankind. Even in his poetry the experience of love is carefully disguised.

Kraus's first lyrical poems began to appear in **Die Fackel** in 1913. And it has sometimes been argued that his lyrical affirmations of tenderness and affection provide a positive counterpoint to the harshness of his satire. The situation is more complex. Many of Kraus's poems may have originated in affirmations of love; but he was at great pains . . . to conceal the experience in a form other than that of lyrical affirmation.

The most directly personal poems addressed to Sidonie were simply kept as private manuscripts (they are now printed in the notes to the *Briefe*). Others were radically revised or had their original titles altered. Dedications were stylized or omitted, personal references were reduced to discreet acrostics. Indeed, his love experience was so disguised that the poetry acquires what Kraus called a "double value": an exoteric meaning which conceals its inner point of reference.

The consequences of this strategy are far-reaching. It not only effectively conceals Sidonie's identity, but brings about a paradoxical transposition of the experience of love. Where we might expect lyrical affirmation, we find instead a poetry of elegiac lament.

Two poems published in **Die Fackel** in December 1915 exemplify this poetic procedure. The first, **"Wiese im Park"** . . . , originated in the park at Janowitz. But no reader would guess from the text of the poem that it portrays the scene of Kraus's infatuation. It is not simply that he drops the original reference to Schloss Janowitz from the title of the poem; the poem itself excludes any hint of passion. The poet pictures himself in complete solitude. The mutuality of human relationships is displaced by the nostalgically tinged evocation of an idyllic landscape.

An equally striking transposition takes place in **"Abschied und Wiederkehr"**. This poem was written after one of Sidonie's visits to Vienna. Kraus had seen her off at the railway station. The sadness of this separation was relieved for him by an encounter with a little dog, whose features reminded him of her. Out of this Kraus makes a poem of great pathos. The "parting" is represented as a death, a final and irretrievable loss; the "return" takes the form of a kind of transmigration of souls. Nothing remains of the "inexpressibly beautiful" quality of the actual love relationship. . . .

In short, the experience of love is subordinated in Kraus's writings to the overriding strategy of his satire. For the satirist, the positive point of reference characteristically lies not in the present world and the sphere of human relations, but in the purity of nature and in a past golden age. The poetic correlatives of satire (as Schiller pointed out) are not lyrical affirmation, but idyllic nostalgia and elegiac lament. In his poetic transpositions Kraus is guided by the logic of satire, celebrating the beauty of nature and *temporis acti*, not of an actual experience of love. (pp. 1393-94)

> *Edward Timms, "When the Satirist Falls in Love,"*
> in The Times Literary Supplement (© *Times Newspapers Ltd. (London) 1974; reproduced from* The
> Times Literary Supplement *by permission), No.
> 3796, December 6, 1974, pp. 1393-94.*

FRANZ H. MAUTNER   (essay date 1974)

The Last Days of Mankind is a unique phenomenon in the history of the drama. This satiric tragedy is almost eight hundred pages long, and its list of characters includes approximately five hundred figures. It has half of Europe as its stage. Organized in a prologue, five acts, and an epilogue, it begins with the voice of a newsboy and ends with that of God. The cry of the newsboy resounds in Vienna in June, 1914; the voice of God rings out over a battlefield at the end of World War I, at which point the drama has been transformed into a modern Walpurgis Night. (p. 239)

In a dozen dialects [the] characters speak everyday German; the voice of the heart, as well as that of the journals, is heard; dashing contemporaries introduce themselves in music-hall ditties; Emperor Franz Josef chants the litany of his life. More and more often, as the drama approaches its end, the voice of its author and the lament of nature, profaned by the war, come to the fore. Wordless apparitions, more eloquent than any words, are among the most heartrending episodes of the work; loquacious scribblers betray their own nothingness through the vanity of their own words.

This drama full of sanguinary jokes has no plot, only a sequence of scenes that become ever more threatening, more farcical, and more terrifying. Its protagonist is European mankind, above all the Germans and Austrians, from 1914 to 1918. (p. 240)

Kraus saw in the suffering and the atrocities of those four years the evils that had always been prevalent; during the war they had only become distinctly and fatefully obvious. It appeared to him that the responsibility for this state of affairs lay with a society that, motivated by its craving for prestige and profit, idolized power and the machine, a society for which life's means had become life's goal. To Kraus, the substance of true humanity—heart, soul, and spirit—appeared to be threatened by a morally insensitive intellectualism, a pseudoliberalism that he believed was particularly embodied in the Austrian Jews of this time. "Enlightenment," together with the economic drive for expansion, seemed to have destroyed respect for nature, for every mystery, for the femininity of woman, and for the dignity of man. Other symptoms of degeneration were general, associated with no specific group or world view: a hypocritical sexual morality, dominated by the drive itself, but finding it either despicable or amusing, was coupled with an equally hypocritical sentimentality. Kitschy decorate-your-home art in Germany and an equally calloused *Gemütlichkeit* in Austria were disguises for falsehood and a lack of substance.

The incarnation of all these evils was the press, through its nature, through its power—for it generated public opinion, and with it, values. Corrupt in its commercial interests, in its morals, and in its language, it did not present the essence of things but instead accentuated the sensational; it neglected rational substance in favor of social prestige. (p. 242)

As a consequence of the war, the role of the press and of the essentially "journalistic" world view that it fostered became more important and more disastrous in its effect. Journalism had its share in unleashing and prolonging the war; it intruded itself between the reader and the fighting, suffering, and dying at the front; in this activity it carried over the irreverence, the practices, and the style embellished with the metaphors of a long-vanished chivalric and heroic past, metaphors that were vacuous and hypocritical in the war of machines. What was annoyance became ignominy; what was an inconvenience to private life endangered life itself. Journalism re-created the war in its own image, and the war adapted itself to journalism's forms and needs. (p. 243)

The first three acts [of *The Last Days of Mankind*] take place almost totally in Austria (the first almost exclusively in and near Vienna) and are peopled by Austrian characters. The fourth and fifth acts include German territory, German types, and German degeneration of the spirit as objects of satire that is equally as merciless as that already bestowed upon the Austrians. Just as in the Prologue, the first scene of each act, on Sirk Corner, presents the almost identical dialogue of the quartet of brainless, loose-living home-front officers, whose thoughts circle about moderate drinking and whoring. Nevertheless, references to events of the time, expressed in their conversations and in those of other characters and in the cries of the newsboys, are enough to allow a sort of historical chronology to evolve: each act roughly corresponds to the occurrences of one of the four and a half years of the war. (p. 247)

[In] the fifth act the major motifs of all the preceding acts are brought forward in ever new variations. Once more they are debated dialectically in eight dialogues between the Grumbler and the Optimist and in the Grumbler's desperate monologue at his desk (scene 54). The accusation against Germany and Austria is enlarged to include accusations against monarchy and war. The monologue closes with an explanation and a justification for the drama *The Last Days of Mankind*. (p. 254)

The last voice of living figures in the drama falls silent. There follows a harrowing series of apparitions on the wall of the dining hall in the place where a kitschy tableau "The Time of Greatness" had hung. These apparitions bring before the eye the lamentation of creatures in the war and the wickedness of so many who took part in it. . . . [The] apparitions take on a completely unreal dimension. Choirs of battlefield ravens, indulging in horrible word plays, point with satisfaction back at all the annihilated life; the verses of the syphilitic female auxiliaries point forward to the yet-unborn life of the future. The Unborn Son himself turns to the spectators with the request that they never let him come into this world. Darkness and death cries conclude the fifth act.

The Epilogue. "The Last Night". . . , completely in rhymed verse, follows immediately. It takes place during a starless night on the battlefield, in the middle of all the terror of destruction. The transition of the figures from individual to typical and from typical to symbolic is imperceptible. A gas mask representing a female war correspondent—robbed of her individuality and sexless in appearance—her colleagues photographing a dying soldier, and the hussar from the Hohenzollern skull-and-cross-bones regiment all embody again, in the rhythm and phraseology of their speech, the evil powers that have been quoted, mocked, and damned throughout the drama. (pp. 254-55)

Setting aside the Prologue, the Epilogue, and the dialogues between the Grumbler and the Optimist, one can venture the rough estimate that the text of about half the drama consists of newspaper reports and documents of all kinds, such as reports from the front, editorials, edicts, court judgments, business advertisements, and letters.

By what means did Kraus form scenes out of documents, a drama out of a plethora of scenes? In addition, what means, be they touching or outrageous, did he employ to imbue the scenes with satire? First of all, he assumed a presentation that conforms outwardly to the dramatic genre. Material quoted from numerous printed sources was assigned to a speaker, usually its author. Through the stage directions it is placed in a specific milieu and thereby into a specific atmosphere. By the fact that the speaker voices his own words in such an atmosphere, he unwittingly becomes an object of satire. The rest of the text is freely invented, but is full of quotations and phrases current in those years. The intertwining of documents, quotations, and phrases with ordinary, freely invented action serves to confirm the factual authenticity of the events.

Here, as in all Kraus's works, language has a religious dimension. It is not only the means of representation, but also the object of representation, the focal point of attention, evidence itself. He believed in a mystical unity between word and sense, between word and essence, resulting in an unconscious revelation of spiritual and moral abuses through corrupted word usage. Language in daily usage appeared to him to be just as mishandled and tarnished as all other cultural possessions. Certain wartime phrases surface again and again in the drama in order to reflect the social or spiritual situation.

Whatever abuses Kraus found he reproduced, and he created linguistic misdeeds, serious and humorous, just as a dramatist lets his characters commit real misdeeds. Particularly he employed word play in order to uncover hidden connections. Accurate reading of Kraus's prose and verse brings to light an inexhaustible abundance of word plays of all varieties.

These range from a very few that are inexcusably silly, that derive from the pure joy of the game, through instances that appear less silly at the second glance than at the first, on to those that are very witty and full of emotion, as profoundly penetrating as those in Greek tragedy. (pp. 257-58)

One touches the nerve of the drama in observing that an endless variety of incongruities and contrasts, presented in structured form, runs through the drama, constituting the most prevalent stylistic device and means of creating impact. Incongruities are the rule: satire, after all, is in its essence the visual rendering of reality's apostasy from the ideal, the making visible of the contrast between truth and pretension. An example of this is the scorn that Kraus poured forth on a body of metaphors taken from teutonic tradition, metaphors of chivalry and single-handed combat, the phrases of knightly warfare with its banners and swords. All of this was depleted of imagination in an age of tanks and of gas and air attacks, an age in which the goal of war is the creation of new markets.

As the end approaches, the style of the drama distances itself from the realism of the majority of the scenes, a process that becomes more and more frequent with the progression of the tragic events, until, in the transition from the final scene to the surrealistic Epilogue, all semblance of reality disappears. This path is marked by an increased number of the Grumbler's pathos-laden and lyrical verse monologues, the gradual change in the stage directions, and in the giving of names. Even among the names of characters for a given scene realism and expressionistic caricature exist side by side. (p. 260)

The previous characterization of the peculiarity of the drama as "cyclopean formlessness" is then relevant only for the first impression. It is structured through and through. Repetition—both unchanged and varied—of specific phrases, motifs, and episodes contributes to holding the endless succession of scenes together, to pointing both forward and backward as a structural element and a carrier of meaning. If a phrase such as "to draft" governs a scene that has as its theme the destruction of human dignity and then reappears countless other times, then that theme is echoed whenever the phrase is repeated. The unchanged similarity of the comments of the four home-front officers in the first scene of each act shows their nature to be unchanged by the war, but the subtly changed content of their comments indicates the darkening of conditions from year to year. Some motifs share in the gradual internal and external transformation of the tragedy. Quite a number of episodes come up at least three times: as an event, as an apparition in the last scene of the fifth act, and as a subject of conversation between the Grumbler and the Optimist. (p. 261)

The attempts, renewed again and again from act to act, to reinforce the theme of *The Last Days*—mankind's fall and end—flow together into the Epilogue. It is the obvious concentration of the entire drama, climaxing in the listing of the sins of the questionable heroes, recited by a voice from above. After a short, insolent, bombastic, yet unsuccessful resistance, the exact nature of which is left to the imagination, there follows the word of God: "I did not will it so."

As a whole, in its mingling of tragedy and wit, of dialectic and low humor, in its monumentality, in its technique of making a document into a dramatic character, in its multiplicity of style and forms, the drama is comparable to nothing else. (pp. 262-63)

In summary, *The Last Days of Mankind* is a unique work of art: unique in the magnitude of its subject matter, which develops out of one idea—that of man's destiny—and in the combination of the gigantic nature of the design with the most subtle art of linguistic detail. This drama is, in many respects, bound to a specific time and place—not in its subject, but in the extent to which the local references can be understood. Perhaps here and there it is not free from errors in taste. Nevertheless, we know of no satiric drama that can approach its greatness. (p. 263)

Franz H. Mautner, "Critical Analysis," translated by Sue Ellen Wright, in The Last Days of Mankind: A Tragedy in Five Acts by Karl Kraus, edited by Frederick Ungar, translated by Alexander Gode and Sue Ellen Wright (copyright © 1974 by Frederick Ungar Publishing Co., Inc.), Ungar, 1974, pp. 239-63.

ADDITIONAL BIBLIOGRAPHY

Bloch, Albert. "Karl Kraus' Shakespeare." *Books Abroad* 2, No. 1 (Winter 1937): 21-4.
Praises Kraus's translations of Shakespeare's plays and sonnets.

Daviau, Donald G. "The Heritage of Karl Kraus." *Books Abroad* 38, No. 3 (Summer 1964): 248-56.
Summarizes critical reaction to Kraus's work. Daviau argues that Kraus deserves more recognition and study, calling him "one of the great creative writers of the twentieth century."

Daviau, Donald [G]. "Karl Kraus in English Translation." *The Psychoanalytic Review* 65, No. 1 (Spring 1978): 95-108.
Valuable critique of the merits and demerits of the five anthologies of Kraus's work that are available in English translation.

Menczer, Béla. "Karl Kraus and the Struggle against the Modern Gnostics." *The Dublin Review* 224, No. 450 (1950): 32-52.
Analyzes Kraus's religious views, in particular his objections to gnosticism.

Simons, Thomas W., Jr. "After Karl Kraus." *Salmagundi*, Nos. 10-11 (Fall 1969-Winter 1970): 154-73.
Historical retrospect of Kraus's contribution to the Viennese literary scene.

Stern, J. P. "Karl Kraus's Vision of Language." *Modern Language Review* LXI, No. 1 (January 1966): 71-84.
Examination of Kraus's belief that linguistic abuse leads to inhumanity and moral depravity. This article is closely argued, citing many examples of the importance Kraus attached to the meaning of each syllable and punctuation mark.

Zohn, Harry. Introduction to *Half-Truths & One-and-a-Half Truths: Selected Aphorisms, Karl Kraus,* by Karl Kraus, edited by Harry Zohn, pp. 1-27. Montreal: Engendra Press, 1976.
Excellent introduction to Kraus's life and works.

Aleksandr (Ivanovich) Kuprin

1870-1938

(Also transliterated as Aleksandr, Alexandr, or Alexandre) Russian short story writer and novelist.

Kuprin is remembered primarily as a distinguished Russian realist of the early twentieth century. A prolific and versatile writer, he is noted for his narrative simplicity, clarity, and unusual range of subjects.

Kuprin began publishing his short stories while attending the Russian Military Academy. Publication of his work enraged his superior officers, however, and they punished him repeatedly. He drew upon these experiences in his later works, particularly in *Poedinok (The Duel)* and "Shtabs-Kapitan Rybnikov" ("Staff Captain Rybnikov"). After leaving the military, Kuprin traveled throughout Russia, familiarizing himself with various ways of life and numerous occupations. This desire to understand the diversity of life and human nature is reflected in Kuprin's wide range of subjects and themes. *Kievskie tipy*, his first collection of sketches, presents a gallery of working-class people and evidences Kuprin's already well-developed talent for observation and graphic depiction.

In the early 1900s Kuprin settled in St. Petersburg and formed several friendships vital to his literary development. Most important was his association with Gorky, who recognized Kuprin's talent and published many of his early stories in the journal *Znanie*. Tolstoy was also fond of Kuprin's work and read his short stories at literary meetings. Kuprin came to regard Chekhov as his master, however, and though their friendship was brief, Chekhov offered invaluable criticism; his works became the stylistic models for Kuprin's own. Because Kuprin's subject matter was drawn from his varied background, he scorned the insular world of the urban literati. However, he eventually joined the Moscow literary society *Sreda*, which included other young realist writers such as Ivan Bunin, and Leonid Andreyev.

Although Kuprin's first major work was *Moloch*, a sketch about the industrial working class, it was *The Duel*, his sordid depiction of the Russian military, that made him famous. Kuprin spent more than a decade writing this novel, and it contains some of his richest language and most convincing realism. *The Duel*'s tremendous impact in Russia resulted, however, from its imagined political implications rather than its literary merits. This ruthless portrayal of the officer caste system appeared during the Russo-Japanese war, and though Kuprin intended the work to be an objective account of repressive military life, the enraged Russian public welcomed *The Duel* as a timely indictment of their government's mismanagement of the Manchurian campaign. Although Kuprin protested this misinterpretation, his reputation was thenceforward assured.

Kuprin's controversial study of prostitution, *Yama (Yama: The Pit)*, prompted accusations of pornography, though many of his contemporaries praised its realism and objectivity. Most critics found *Yama* to be disjointed and structurally deficient, which was perhaps due to its method of composition; the book was written over a period of seven years and published in three parts. As an effort to combine documentary with fiction, *Yama* is considered inferior to *The Duel*.

Disillusioned by the October Revolution of 1917, Kuprin emigrated two years later to France. Although he produced more than sixty short stories during his seventeen years in Paris, they constitute no significant development in his art. The best works of this period are permeated by his loneliness and yearning for Russia, yet this long exile impaired his creativity. Sick and dispirited, he returned to Russia in 1937. Though he intended to resume writing, illness prevented any further work. Kuprin died the following year.

Although his corpus is uneven and he never earned the stature of such contemporaries as Chekhov and Gorky, Kuprin's best works display a vigorous style and a great talent for storytelling.

PRINCIPAL WORKS

Kievskie tipy (sketches) 1896
Moloch (novella) 1896; published in journal *Russkoe bogatstvo*
Miniatury (short stories) 1897
Olesya (novel) 1898; published in journal *Kievlianin* [*Olessia*, 1909]

Poedinok (novel) 1905
   [*In Honour's Name* (abridged version), 1907; also
      published as *The Duel*, 1916]
Sulamif (novel) 1908
   [*Sulamith*, 1923]
Yama. 3 vols. (novel) 1909-15
   [*Yama: The Pit*, 1922]
Listrigony (sketches) 1912
The River of Life, and Other Stories (short stories) 1916
A Slav Soul, and Other Stories (short stories) 1916
The Bracelet of Garnets, and Other Stories (short
      stories) 1919
Sasha (short stories) 1920
Domashnii Parizh (sketches) 1927
Mys Guron (sketches) 1929
Zhaneta (novel) 1933
The Duel and Selected Stories (short stories) 1961

WILLIAM LYON PHELPS (essay date 1911)

As Tolstoi, Garshin, and Andreev have shown the horrors
of war, so Kuprin has shown the utter degradation and sordid
misery of garrison life. If Russian army posts in time of peace
bear even a remote resemblance to the picture given in Kuprin's powerful novel *In Honour's Name,* one would think
that the soldiers there entombed would heartily rejoice at the
outbreak of war—would indeed welcome any catastrophe,
provided it released them from such an Inferno. . . . The
officers are a collection of hideously selfish, brutal, drunken,
licentious beasts; their mental horizon is almost inconceiv-
ably narrow, far narrower than that of mediæval monks in
a monastery. The soldiers are in worse plight than prisoners,
being absolutely at the mercy of the alcoholic caprices of
their superiors. (pp. 278-79)

If Kuprin's story be true, one does not need to look far for
the utter failure of the Russian troops in the Japanese war;
the soldiers are here represented as densely ignorant, drilling
in abject terror of their officers' fists and boots, and knowing
nothing whatever of true formations in attack or defence. As
for the officers, they are much worse than the soldiers: their
mess is nothing but an indescribably foul alcoholic den, where
sodden drunkenness and filthy talk are the steady routine.
(p. 279)

Apart from the terrible indictment of army life and military
organisation that Kuprin has given, the novel *In Honour's
Name* is an interesting story with living characters. There is
not a single good woman in the book. . . . Surely no novelists
outside of Russia have drawn such evil women. The hero,
Romashov, is once more the typical Russian whom we have
met in every Russian novelist. . . . He spends all his time in
aspirations, sighs, and tears—and never by any chance accomplishes anything. (p. 282)

> *William Lyon Phelps, "Kuprin's Picture of Garri-*
> *son Life," in his* Essays on Russian Novelists *(re-*
> *printed with permission of Macmillan Publishing*
> *Co., Inc.; copyright 1911 by Macmillan Publishing*
> *Co., Inc.; renewed 1939 by William Lyon Phelps),*
> *Macmillan, 1911, pp. 278-84.*

J. M. MURRY (essay date 1916)

[The] interest of Kuprin's talent is independent of the accidents of his material. He is an artist who has found life wide
and rich and inexhaustible. He has been fascinated by the
reality itself rather than by the problems with which it confronts a differently sensitive mind. Therefore he has not held
himself aloof, but plunged into the riotous waters of the River
of Life. He has swum with the stream and battled against it
as the mood turned in him; and he has emerged with stories
of the joy he has found in his own eager acceptance. Thus
Kuprin is alive as none of his contemporaries is alive, and
his stories are stories told for the delight of the telling and
of the tale. They may not be profound with the secrets of the
universe; but they are, within their compass, shaped by the
perfect art of one to whom the telling of a story of life is an
exercise of his whole being in complete harmony with the
act of life itself. (pp. v-vi)

> *J. M. Murry, "Introduction" (Canadian rights by*
> *permission of The Society of Authors, as literary*
> *representative of the Estate of John Middleton*
> *Murry), in* The River of Life and Other Stories *by*
> *Alexander Kuprin, translated by S. Koteliansky and*
> *J. M. Murray, J. W. Luce and Company, 1916 (and*
> *reprinted by George Allen & Unwin Ltd, 1942, pp.*
> *v-vi).*

STEPHEN GRAHAM (essay date 1916)

It is impossible not to admire [Kuprin's] natural torrent of
Russian thoughts and words and sentiments. His lively pages
are a reflection of Russia herself, and without having been
once in the country it would be possible to get a fair notion
of its surface life by reading these tales in [*A Slav Soul*].
Perhaps the greatest of living Russian novelists is Kuprin—
exalted, hysterical, sentimental, Rabelaisian Kuprin. . . . His
is a rank verbiage—he gives birth to words, ideas, examples
in tens where other writers go by units and threes.

He is occasionally coarse, occasionally sentimental, but he
gives great delight to his readers; his are rough-hewn lumps
of conversation and life. With him everything is taken from
life. He seems to be a master of detail, and the characteristic
of his style is a tendency to give the most diverting lists.
Often paragraph after paragraph, if you look into the style,
would be found to be lists of delicious details reported in a
conversational manner. . . . Every one of Kuprin's stories
has the necessary Attic salt. He is like our English Kipling,
whom he greatly admires, and about whom he has written
in one of his books an appreciative essay. He is also something like the American O. Henry, especially in the matter
of his lists of details and his apt metaphors, but he has not
the artifice nor the everlasting American smile. Kuprin,
moreover, takes his matter from life and writes with great
ease and carelessness; O. Henry put together from life and
re-wrote twelve times.

Above all things Kuprin is a sentimental author, preferring
an impulse to a reason, and abandoning logic whenever his
feelings are touched. He likes to feel the reader with the tears
in his eyes and then to go forward with him in the unity of
emotional friendship. There is, however, under this excitement a rather self-centred cynic despising the things he does
not love, a satirical genius. His humour is nearly always at
the expense of some person, institution or class of society.
(pp. vii-ix)

As compared with [Fëdor] Sologub, whose volume of beautiful tales, "The Sweet-scented Name," has found so many friends in England, Kuprin may be said to be nearer to the earth, less in the clouds. He is a satirical realist, whereas Sologub is a fantastic realist. Sologub discloses the devils and the angels in men and women, but Kuprin is cheerfully human. Both have a certain satirical genius, but Kuprin is read by everyone, whereas it would be hardly one in ten that could follow Sologub. In comparison with Chekhof I should say Kuprin was a little more inventive, and as regards a picture of life Kuprin is nearer to the present moment. (pp. x-xi)

He has written a great deal about the relationship of men and women. His weakness is the subject of women. Whenever they come into question he becomes self-conscious and awkward, putting his subject in the wrong light, protesting too much, and finally writing that which is not fitting just because "all is permitted" and "why shouldn't we?" His poorest work is his coarse work. (p. xi)

> Stephen Graham, "Introduction: Alexander Kuprin," in A Slav Soul and Other Stories by Alexander Kuprin, Constable & Company Ltd, 1916, pp. vii-xii.

THE BOOKMAN (LONDON) (essay date 1920)

It is difficult to place Kuprin if one has to judge him by the volume of short stories ["Sasha."] . . . In "The Murderer" he describes sympathetically a Russian landowner who does to death a kitten under the influence of blood-mania; and he makes one's gorge rise against an author who can treat such a sadic orgy as a story to be recollected and to be told afresh. . . . In "Sasha," the tale of a Jewish fiddler who is the great attraction of an underground beer-garden, Kuprin discovers the "soul of goodness in things evil" in a fashion that reminds one of the De Maupassant of "Boule de Suit" and "Maison Tellier"; and the result is a really great short story told with a large measure of the Olympian aloofness and consequent divine charity so characteristic of the great French master. Smacking of De Maupassant's manner, too, are three or four records of musings over old love affairs which can be consulted in this volume; while the pictures of Ukrainian and of Russian scenery which are presented are suffused with that tender melancholy which draws one so irresistibly to the stories of Turgenev and of Tchehov. But the abiding impression which one gets from these latest sketches of Muscovite life is the old impression of savagery: "Scratch a Russian; and you find a Tartar."

> 'Sasha' in The Bookman, London, Vol. LVIII, No. 343, Spring, 1920, p. 47.

MOISSAYE J. OLGIN (essay date 1920)

Kuprin's works, all of a realistic character, reveal the author as a man of spiritual balance and health. Kuprin is interested in life, in all its manifestations. The Stream of Life he called one of his stories, and the stream of life he is eager to reflect in his artistic productions. (p. 245)

Kuprin is actuated by an insatiable artistic curiosity. He would not shut himself in one corner of the world. There is not one thing that looms up before his eyes to the exclusion of the rest. The problem of God or the life beyond is only one wave in the stream of life; revolution is a ripple; death is an episode; sex is one among many emotions. Joy and sadness are twin brothers wandering through the hearts of men. What remains for the artist is to go through life, to fix his gaze on people, characters, quaint constellations, amusing or touching or shocking happenings.

This Kuprin does with joy and force. His works are all alive with gay designs, brimful of powerful emotions, astir with movement and packed with meaning, swept by strong winds, and pierced through by arrows of light. Kuprin loves everything, and the number of his friends is amazing . . .—all find room in his stories, and to all of them he gives in turn his loving attention. He makes no effort in calling his figures into existence. They come to him with ease and grace. His only task is to choose, to concentrate for a while on a definite point in the everlasting current. This concentration is done with unusual energy. Kuprin takes in every shade, every line, ever detail. His characters are typical. His slang is magnificent. His dialogues are reality itself. His descriptions are a result of numerous and careful observations. Altogether his works unfold before the reader a broad and varied panorama of everyday Russian life at the beginning of the twentieth century. At the same time, there is a touch of sadness in most of Kuprin's writings, as if a man were bashfully yearning for something vague and beautiful which will never be attained. (pp. 245-46)

Kuprin is a direct descendant of the classics. Yet there is a difference between him and the traditional Russian writer. Kuprin lacks a central idea. His works do not revolve around one axis. . . . Kuprin, as seen in his works, loves strength, motion, sharp reliefs, bright colors, and he is more interested in the psychology of men than in universal ideas. Often he is witty, and his humor is refreshing. Sometimes he chooses to become very simple, and then he writes delightful stories for children. (p. 247)

The tragedies of the heroes [in The Duel] are of a more universal than local character. Yet great attention is given to the environment, to the psychology of the plain soldiers, the drilling, the senseless subordination, the inefficiency of the commander. The types of the officers are drawn with a skilful hand. (p. 248)

Oriental nature, oriental tone, and oriental temperament are reproduced in [Sulamith] with much love and artistic finish. One of the best exotic stories in the Russian language.

The scene of action [in The Pit] is a house of ill-repute in a southern Russian town. . . . The work is a gallery of the actual types which could be met in any intellectual circle in Russia. The place where the author finds his men, gives him an opportunity to look deeper into their real selves. Kuprin does not shun details of sex-life, yet he always remains the artist whose frankness is the presentation of truth. He never revels in an artistically superfluous scrutiny of vulgar things. There is almost an unique simplicity in his writings on sex relations. The psychological analysis is very keen. (p. 249)

[Leastrygonians provides one] of the most charming descriptions of the Black Sea coast and its fisherfolk. Kuprin's eye for nature's beauty and his love for the primitive appear at their best in these sketches. Refinement, humor, imagination, make these simple pages almost a hymn to the eternal forces of life. (pp. 249-50)

> Moissaye J. Olgin, "A. Kuprin," in his A Guide to Russian Literature (1820-1917), Harcourt, Brace and Howe, 1920, pp. 245-50.

D. S. MIRSKY (essay date 1926)

Army life is the principal subject of [Kuprin's] early stories. He treats it in the orthodox "oppositional" manner, representing the wretched soldier, oppressed by stupid and mechanical sergeant-majors and brutal officers. The central figure is always a young officer who is himself oppressed by the gloomy reality round him and broods on the meaning of his life and life in general. (p. 122)

The Duel is not really a revolutionary work. Its point of view is rather that of the typical "Chekhovian intelligent.". . . . *The Duel* is very "passive" and "morbid," but within its limitations it is a good novel. The character-drawing is excellent and the gallery of types of infantry officers is convincing and varied. The heroine, Shurochka, the wife of a lieutenant, is one of the best feminine portraits in recent Russian fiction. (pp. 122-23)

Kuprin had in him a valuable germ which remained almost undeveloped: he was attracted towards the "Western" type of story, which unlike the Russian story is a story of action and strong situations, which loves intrigue, and does not shun sensationalism. . . . [Two] or three times he attained something that was not attained by any one of his contemporaries in Russian literature: he wrote several good stories of vigorous and sensational situation with a romantic and heroical keynote. One of the best is *Lieutenant-Captain Rybnikov*. . . . [Another good story] is *The Bracelet of Garnets* . . . , the romantic and melodramatic story of the love of a poor clerk for a society lady. For sheet narrative construction it is one of the best stories of its time. (pp. 123-24)

> D. S. Mirsky, "Kuprin," in his Contemporary Russian Literature: 1881-1925 (copyright 1926 by Alfred A. Knopf, Inc.; Canadian rights by permission of Alfred A. Knopf, Inc.), Knopf, 1926, G. Routledge & Sons, 1926, pp. 122-24.

IVAN BUNIN (essay date 1951)

The fact that [Kuprin's] books (not only of the early but even of the middle period) bristle with cheap banalities is only of secondary importance. . . . The main trouble was that Kuprin's gifts comprised an unfortunate capacity to absorb and use not only small, external clichés but also big, internal ones. So this is how it went: The little Kiev newspaper wants something suitable? All right, I'll do it in five minutes, and I'm not squeamish; if need be I can dash off such phrases as "the setting sun lit up the treetops with its slanting rays." You want a story for *Russian Wealth*? Delighted to oblige! Here's "Moloch": "The factory siren emitted a long-drawn-out wail announcing the beginning of the working day. The thick, hoarse sound, it seemed, was coming from under the earth and spreading low upon its surface."

Is not that an effective, quite a professional beginning? Everything is in its place, including the cheap rhythm of the two sentences, quite worthy of the rhythm of the phrase about the setting sun with its slanting rays. Everything is *as it should be* in the story as a whole, as well; everything in it *conforms to the accepted models of the time;* it contains all that could be expected of a tale about the Moloch. . . . (pp. 105-06)

I have always been aware of the many good points of "The Horsethieves," "The Swamp," "At Rest," "In the Deep of the Forest," "The Coward," "Captain Rybnikov," "Sasha";

of the wonderful tales about the Balaklava fishermen, and even of *The Duel;* and of the beginning of "A Ditch." Yet even these stories contained many things that jarred upon me. . . . [For example,] the last letter of the student who shoots himself at the Hotel Serbia in "The River of Life": "I am not the only one to perish of this moral infection. . . . All the past generation grew up in the spirit of devout silence, of compulsory respect for their elders. They had no personality and no voice. Accursed be that foul time, the time of silence and poverty, that smug, peaceful existence under the shelter of pious reaction." If this is not "literature," what is it? For a long time after [rereading "The River of Life"] I did not read him any more, and when I decided to do so again, I felt distressed at once. (p. 107)

Truly it would have been difficult not to notice Kuprin's hackneyed phrases, used and reused a thousand times. . . . (p. 109)

"Solitude," "Sacred Love," and "Night Lodgings" again turned out to be rather feeble both in plot and in execution; they were written in a manner imitative of Maupassant and Chekhov, and again they were too neat and smooth and "competent.". . . [Every] word is cheap. But the stories of army life were very different, and as I read them I kept exclaiming to myself, "That's excellent!" Here, too, one saw excessive neatness, smoothness, and skillfulness, but it all reached the level of genuine craftsmanship, it was all of a completely different standard; "The Wedding" in particular, which, contrary to the other stories, never made you think, "Oh dear, how much there is in this of Chekhov or of Tolstoy"—a very cruel story, with a flavor of virulent caricature, but truly brilliant. And when I reached the stories written at the peak of his career ("The Horsethieves," "The Swamp," and some others) I simply took no notice of their defects, even though some of them were serious: sometimes it was a cheap idealism, the visible desire to keep up with the spirit of the time; in other instances, a very obvious effort to impress the reader with a dramatic plot or with brutal realism. But I did not think of the flaws and wholeheartedly enjoyed the various qualities which were preponderant in these short stories; the freedom, vigor, and vividness of the narrative, and the excellent style, sharp, rich but never excessively lavish. (pp. 111-12)

> Ivan Bunin, "Kuprin," in his Memories and Portraits (copyright 1951 by Ivan Bunin; Canadian rights by permission of Doubleday & Company, Inc.), Doubleday, 1951, pp. 95-113.

ROBERT LOUIS JACKSON (essay date 1958)

Like the Underground Man [in Dostoevsky's *Notes from the Underground*], the hero of "River of Life" is tormented by [his] very consciousness of disfigurement, by the realization that he cannot change; he knows that he cannot free himself from all the slavishness he despises. In this he resembles those half-heroes of the "underground", Glazkov [in M. N. Albov's "Day of Reckoning"] and Aleksey Petrovich [in V. M. Garshin's "Night"], men with dreams, but shattered personalities. Everywhere in the student's suicide-letter one senses a malice of impotence, a moral self-disgust that is finally expressed in suicide. . . .

[His] terrible words bring to mind not only Glazkov and Aleksey Petrovich, but also the Underground Man and Arkady Dolgoruki [in Dostoevsky's *Raw Youth*]. These "underground'' men impotently rebel against the consciousness of slavery.

In the hero of **"River of Life"** one recognizes that ''antithesis of the normal man'' about whom the Underground Man speaks. . . . Kuprin's hero is not afraid to die, but he fears people. (p. 109)

In the hero of **"River of Life"** ''underground'' hatred of the vulgar, self-confident man of action (here given a certain anti-rationalistic turn) serves to formulate his hatred of a stupid, banal, brutal and faceless society—a society that is for him everything that the army is to Romashev in Kuprin's *The Duel*. . . . Like Glazkov and Aleksey Petrovich, the hero of **"River of Life"** feels estranged from society, despises himself because of his fear of it, and destroys himself in self-disgust.

The hero of **"River of Life"** is spiritually crippled by poverty and begging; his mind is filled with humiliating recollections of the abasement and exploitation of his personality as a child in the service of ''benefactors'' who looked upon him as upon an inanimate object. Even more was he morally corrupted by seven to ten years in a state school—years filled with spying, thievery, onanism, vodka, prostitutes, and venereal disease. In this, in particular, the hero of **"River of Life"** recalls the Underground Man and Arkady Dolgoruki, two heroes of the ''underground'' whose pathology of humiliation developed in school years. (pp. 110-11)

Kuprin's hero has this passive hatred and ''underground'' malice. But the ''underground'' theme of humiliation in **"River of Life"** does not serve as a focus of interest in itself, as it does in large part in *Notes from the Underground*. Kuprin is not interested in developing a psychology of the ''underground'', a philosophy of the irrational. Kuprin . . . is interested in the ''underground'' only in its social context, only as an expression of the individual's alienation from society. It is the fact of protest, rather than the manner of protest, that primarily interests Kuprin.

What is significant, however, is that Kuprin approaches the psychological aspects of the plight of the lonely intellectual in the context of the Dostoevskian ''tragedy of the underground''. Kuprin's hero is a typical man of ''heightened consciousness'' who, together with Glazkov and Aleksey Petrovich, illustrates the contention of the Underground Man that ''every decent person of our time is and must be a coward and a slave''.

The ''River of Life'' will wash away the vulgar, the stupid, the philistine and cruel. This is the dream of the hero of ''**River of Life**''. (p. 111)

> *Robert Louis Jackson, "A. I. Kuprin's 'River of Life'," in his* Dostoevsky's Underground Man in Russian Literature *(© Mouton & Co, Publishers; reprinted by permission of the author), Mouton Publishers, The Hague, 1958, pp. 108-12.*

ANDREW R. MacANDREW (essay date 1961)

[When Kuprin] was appointed second lieutenant in an inelegant infantry regiment stationed in a small garrison town, his only ambition and hope was to escape the surrounding sordidness through self-improvement, by getting ahead in his career. These early aspirations are described in **"The Duel."** . . . Like his hero Romashov, instead of achieving anything, he only found himself enmeshed in the indifferent machine and tossed around passively. As Romashov does, Kuprin

became a heavy drinker and followed the senseless routine of the officers he despised. Probably, like Romashov, he escaped into romantic daydreams (this habit recurs in many of his other stories) only to have these flimsy constructions mercilessly obliterated by reality.

Kuprin's view appears to be a pessimistic one, except, perhaps, for the slight hope that a sensitive human being might find and preserve unbroken a thread of love, which would lead him out of the grinding wheels and cogs of the social machine—whether it be school, the army, or society in general. At one point in **"The Duel"** Romashov is almost saved at the moment of his greatest despair when he discovers another whose sufferings are similar to his but infinitely worse; only when he is able to feel a sympathy for the lowest, the most miserable specimen among the common soldiers does Romashov come close to finding internal peace. But it is the institution that triumphs. Romashov is sucked back into the mainstream of the regiment's existence—a rising wave of events, culminating in his fight with Nikolaev, sweeps him and the others along quite helplessly.

Again, one has the feeling that all would not have been lost had anyone really loved Romashov. But his friend Nazansky, who understands him, is an alcoholic, desperately in need of sympathy himself and unable to give it to another. All he can do is philosophize. Although he persuades Romashov to leave the army, his reasoning is no match for Romashov's helpless passion for Alexandra and her selfish and strikingly futile ambitions. Despite her affection for Romashov, she asks him to expose himself passively to Nikolaev's pistol in a duel in which he must *at least*, be seriously wounded. And so Romashov dies, killed by the impersonal machine that has paralyzed him and robbed him of his most precious instinct— the instinct to live.

It was Kuprin's strong feeling for Greek-like fatality that made him finish this novel (he had intended it originally to follow the actual pattern of his own life) with the symbolic climax of death in a senseless duel. (p. 252)

But, although in most of the writings which reflect these experiences man is generally tossed helplessly around in the stream of life, Kuprin himself found an impelling motive for life. Obviously he himself is speaking through the central character of his novel *The Pit*, which he wrote after he had spent many months living ''behind the scenes'' of a brothel:

> I swear, I'd give anything to become a horse,
> a vegetable or a fish for a few days. . . . I'd
> like to be able to look at the world through
> the eyes of everyone I come across. . . .

And this seems to have been Kuprin's way throughout his life: to come as close as possible to various creatures, to live with them, to feel himself as they felt, and then to describe them with understanding, love, and humble compassion.

This compassion did not lend itself to any political or metaphysical system. This fact caused the religiously inclined as well as the Communists to accuse him of a lack of depth and constructiveness. The Communists have labeled him as, at his best, a brilliant representative of ''critical realism''—as opposed to ''socialist realism,'' which is supposed to have an ''affirmative'' message.

However, the fact that Kuprin's stories and novels are based on his own minute, personal observation of life . . . does not mean that they lack overtones of the great tragedy of human destiny, here and there lightened by hope, love, and a deep understanding of values. They all have an element of symbolism and may provide ample food for thought on such matters as life, human destiny, love, goodness, although Kuprin does indeed fail "to give an answer based on the only scientific philosophy—that of Marxism-Leninism" (according to the Soviet literary critic A. Miasnikov) or to explain away the cruelty of life in terms of some ultimate mission entrusted by God to the Russian people, as Dostoevski does.

The world in Kuprin's stories is complex, and his characters are never mere props to bring home the tragedy and isolation of human life without love. It is difficult to imagine four people who differ more than do Romashov, Arbuzov, Vasil, and Olympus, the central figures of ["**The Duel**," "**The Horse Thieves**," "**Anathema**," and "**The Circus Wrestlers**."] . . . In character, degree of intelligence, station in life, age, in everything, they differ—but they all possess sensitivity and imagination and the ability to love. These elements, shared by all four characters, make each of them a human being of a high order, but leave them hopelessly vulnerable in a world less sensitive than they.

Kuprin's minor characters, however, do not consist of uniformly evil or brutish characters. They are, for the most part, simply limited in their capacity to love. It is not so much that man is a wolf to man; it is that one man is just a lump of wood to another. Alexandra loves Romashov as much as she is capable of loving. In their last meeting, after she has asked him for more than could be demanded from anyone, she becomes his mistress out of genuine passionate tenderness—it is in no way the cynical clinching of a bargain. And most of the officers, the cogs of the infernal machine that leads Romashov to his death, are most tired, limited, defeated men, from the regimental commander on down: Colonel Shulgovich's roaring is a mask assumed by a fatherly but childless family man. In "**The Horse Thieves**" Kozel loves his grandson as much as it is possible for a man so abused by life to love anyone. In "**Anathema**" Olympus's wife simply does not understand what torments him. And in "**The Circus Wrestlers**" Doctor Lukhovitsin fails to grasp Arbuzov's personal tragedy because he sees in him simply the generic picture of the "strong man."

But in addition to these mere cogs, Kuprin also creates characters who carry within them elements of evil. Such are Captain Osadchy with his strange, animal rages, his cruelty, his superhuman voice. Such is the manager of the circus who demands that Arbuzov go through with the bout. Such are the German settler and the lynch mob in "**The Horse Thieves**."

Kuprin makes great use of subconscious elements and symbols to present the tragedy of his protagonists. And in his writing, the dreams and daydreams, the hypnotic effects of oft-repeated words, the connections between childhood and adult experience, neurotic worrying which cannot be shaken off until its cause is found, are very different from the textbook illustrations of psychological phenomena that are artificially woven into so many "psychological novels." In Kuprin, these divagations are as alive and real as are the characters in whom they occur, and they are, consequently, integrated into the harmonious composition of the story.

These divagations are of different degrees. In Romashov, we see the desperate escape mechanism (the daydreams), the way it copes with reality and the way it is shattered against

it. Vasil's dreams, his imaginings as he watches the sunset and the windswept trees, and his heroic picture of the double-ribbed, double-spined Buzyga, serve to make us aware of his sensitivity and the range of his childish imagination. In "**Anathema**," Father Olympus does not actually dream at all. In fact, he spends a sleepless night, but it is the dreamlike state into which Tolstoy's story has plunged him, the magic world that it has opened up for him, that brings about his final revolt. Of course, in "**The Circus Wrestlers**," Arbuzov's dream is the central clue to the whole story—a remarkable piece of insight if one remembers that it was written in 1905 and that Kuprin had probably never heard of Freud. The blocks that the wrestler builds up in this dream—pink and hard as marble and as soft to the touch as cotton—are, of course, his carefully, strenuously developed body. He piles up these heavy pink blocks, and they collapse on him. This is his illness. He builds them up again, and again they crumble, and he is left holding onto life by a thin, taut wire with nothing between him and the depths but a sheet as flimsy as the surface of water. And the vital word he cannot remember, the vital word that explains everything, is *boomerang*—for it is just because he has lived the way he has, because he has developed his body and made it externally so strong and hard, that his heart is failing and he is doomed. (pp. 253-55)

> Andrew R. MacAndrew, *in his afterword to* The Duel and Selected Stories *by Alexander Kuprin, translated by Andrew R. MacAndrew (copyright © 1961 by Andrew R. MacAndrew; reprinted by arrangement with the New American Library, Inc., New York, New York), The New American Library, 1961, pp. 250-56.*

A. B. McMILLIN (essay date 1968)

In [Kuprin's] laconic, undemonstrative style, relying on effective use of detail, in his ironic but sympathetic approach to people, and above all in his apolitical, pragmatic, but generally optimistic attitude to human affairs one can perceive the inheritance of Chekhov's moral outlook. But despite [the] close ties with his contemporaries, Kuprin is an original, versatile and highly readable writer. . . . (pp. ix-x)

An uneven writer, not entirely free from lapses into banality and melodrama, Kuprin makes up in zest and enthusiasm for what he lacks in taste and literary judgement. His best stories are informed with a genuine awareness of the poetry of life whilst the truly infectious vitality and love of humanity emanating from his work ensure his continuing popularity with modern readers. Notably free from the morbid introspection of Dostoevsky and Andreyev, the moralising of Tolstoy and Gorky and Chekhov's almost excessive abhorrence of excitement and sensationalism, Kuprin, in his best work is able to strike some new and stimulating notes. The stories in [*Tales*], taken from the most productive decade of his life, 1897-1907, reflect many of his best and most typical qualities, and in their variety afford us considerable insight into a most interesting man and the depressing but nonetheless fascinating period in which he lived. (pp. xii-xiii)

[*Allez!*'s] theme of unrequited love, together with love in the face of social inequality, is one that recurs often with this writer, notably in *The Army Ensign*. . . . *The Army Ensign* is one of Kuprin's best stories, with a difficult form sustained, and the reader's interest and conviction maintained to the end; it compares favourably with the much better known *The Garnet Bracelet* . . . , where elements of melodrama and a generally sentimental atmosphere banish much of the poetry. With a small number of carefully chosen strokes and a laconic manner worthy of Chekhov himself, Kuprin conveys with truly masterly skill the atmosphere of army life as seen through the haze of the young officer's social and romantic day-dreams. . . . [*From Women's Letters, Autumn Flowers* and *A Sentimental Romance*] also deal with the theme of love— as, indeed, do the majority of Kuprin's stories. Although skilfully written they belong to the world of women's magazines rather than great literature, for only an artist of Chekhov's stature could treat these stories without sentimentality; nonetheless we are forced to admire the writer's skill as a robust young man entering the mind and feelings of an emotional, tear-laden 'hospital flower'. The discrepancy between author and subject in these stories is emphasised by *Black Fog* . . . , in which Kuprin's love of the open-air, natural life is embodied in the Ukrainian Boris at the centre of the story; the purely physical significance of the sunny, healthy Ukraine is contrasted with the murk, both physical and spiritual, of the north, and the hatefulness of artificiality is brought well home in this simple, parable-like 'Petersburg happening'. (pp. xiii-xiv)

[*The Jewess*] is remarkable both for the very clear scene that is evoked by apparently haphazard, Chekhovian means and also for its subject matter: it was, and to a large extent still is highly untypical for a gentile living in the south of Russia to feel anything but scorn and hate for the Jews. . . . The type of fanatical nationalist flourishing and, indeed, officially encouraged at this unappetizing period of Russian history is most convincingly, albeit satirically portrayed in *Measles*. . . . Kuprin avoids mere parody or proselytising by making all the characters into rounded, human beings, with physical passions as well as abstract ideas. Once again the exact smell and flavour of the scene are excellently caught. In *The Murderer* . . . , Kuprin presents the phenomenon of man's lust to kill by the characteristic device of a story within a story; but although this grisly anecdote seems purely concerned with an abstract idea, its real significance lies in the background of political terror and reprisals following the suppression of the 1905 uprising. Set, appropriately, in the claustrophobic atmosphere of a shadowy room, the story stands in strong contrast to the feeling of lightness and spaciousness in most of Kuprin's work. (p. xiv)

As in Pushkin's *The Captain's Daughter*, and Tolstoy's *War and Peace*, [in *Gambrinous*] the great historical events are reflected in the lives of the ordinary people they affect, but the purpose of the story is not so much to portray the trends and movements of history as to show the strength and variety of the human spirit. Compared with the subtlety and quiet restraint of Chekhov's best stories the language here seems bright and sometimes over-saturated, but this, like the frequent enumerations and strong, direct epithets and images, is in keeping with the setting and characters in the tale, for in this story as clearly as in any other we see Kuprin's love of robust, red-blooded men, the open air and broad, heroic natures. The assertion at the end that 'you may maim a man, but art will endure all and conquer all' is not made with a moralist's fervour but with the firm conviction of a stout-hearted optimist. . . .

The positive elements in his writing have no doubt helped to secure his popularity in Russia, but his range is a genuinely wide one. . . . (p. xv)

> *A. B. McMillin, "Introduction" (1968; © 1969 Edito-Service S.A.), in* Tales by Alexander Kuprin,

> *translated by Douglas Ashby, Heron Books, 1969, pp. ix-xvii.*

CARL R. PROFFER (essay date 1969)

While [Kuprin] has many stories marked by complex plots and sensationalism, he also has a lyrical, sentimental strain exemplified by stories such as **"Olesya"** [and **"The Garnet Bracelet"**]. . . .

"The Garnet Bracelet" seems a very old-fashioned story now, especially when we consider that the innovations of modernists like Andreev and symbolists like Bely antedate its writing. Straightforward chronology and unity of setting help make the story a neatly-constructed one, but the only real example of technical aplomb is the way the *Vorgeschichte* of Vera's relation to Zheltkov is introduced—as a joking story by Vasily Lvovich. (p. 43)

In general the characters are convincingly drawn, particularly Anosov, the conventional, faithful army officer who has many literary forebears, beginning with Pushkin's Captain Mironov. The juxtaposition of Vera and Anna is successful in bringing out their differences in character. Like all of Kuprin's tools for characterization, this one was a standard device of Russian realism.

At its best Kuprin's style is commonplace. His nature descriptions are ponderous, and even where they are supposed to be portentous they seem irrelevant. The physical portraits he gives of the main characters also seem clumsy—weighted down by strings of adjectives wrapped around strings of participles. As for Kuprin's metaphor, an example will suffice: "The other flowers, whose season of luxurious love and overfruitful maternity was over, were quietly dropping innumerable seeds of future life." One of the main faults of the story is this kind of verbosity. (pp. 43-4)

It takes some talent to adapt an inherently tragic story from real life and make it seem so falsely sentimental. Kuprin succeeds in this. His clumsy lyricism and the pitiful way he presents Zheltkov result only in what might be called a "pathegedy." Nevertheless, the story stands as a fair example of Kuprin's work and the doldrums of conventional Russian prose fiction during the first years of this century. (p. 44)

> *Carl R. Proffer, "Practical Criticism for Students: 'The Garnet Bracelet'," in* From Karamzin to Bunin: An Anthology of Russian Short Stories, *edited by Carl R. Proffer (copyright © 1969 by Indiana University Press), Indiana University Press, 1969, pp. 43-4.*

PETER H. BONNELL (essay date 1974)

All Russian books of reference seem to stress in their definition of the *očerk* [sketch] the reproduction of reality and, consequently, the need on the part of the *očerkist* for accurate observation. (p. 23)

This type of narrative form is frequently adopted where widely different facts, attitudes, or habits are observed by the narrator. It is true that the *očerk* does not depend for its artistic merit on objectivity on the part of the narrator, but too great a degree of subjectivity and, especially, the introduction of a pronounced social or political bias, spoils the *očerk* as a work of art. (pp. 23-4)

The *očerk* has a tendency toward a weak *sjužet* [narrative structure] and a "plotless" construction. It must, of course, be borne in mind that "plotless" is a relative term: thus, a short story that is said to be "plotless" is so only relative to another short story that Russian Formalists would consider to be a . . . short story of action, that is one based on plot. (p. 24)

[In] its best works the *očerk* is more than just a "document." However, the *očerk*'s link to journalism should always be borne in mind. It is indeed closely related to so-called reportage. . . .

Kuprin came to literature in general and the *očerk* genre in particular via journalism, which . . . is closely related to this narrative form. . . .

The first point that strikes us in the introduction [to Kuprin's collection of *očerki*, *Kievskie tipy*,] is the emphasis on the description of the *collective features* of groups of individuals. In other words, the characters are considered to be types without any specifically individual traits. The traits they possess are those of the group to which they belong. (p. 25)

In addition, though Kuprin intends to copy carefully from nature, there will not be any photography. We must assume that what he meant was that, though he would observe closely, he would only describe the traits common to the group, whereas photography would bring out individual features. What he planned was, therefore, a kind of "distorted" photography with certain traits blown up and others ignored. (pp. 25-6)

To stress the typicalness of the character of the heroes even more, they are given no names, but simply generic designations. . . . These serve also as the titles of the *očerki* and as rigid frames in regard to subject-matter.

At this earliest stage in Kuprin's literary career it is already evident that he chooses his heroes from the greatest possible variety of social, professional and ethnic groups, and invariably knows the subject-matter intimately. In *Kievskie tipy* we find the "jeunesse dorée" next to the vagabonds, the doctors side by side with the thieves, the false witnesses alongside the choristers, the commission agents opposite the firemen. . . .

The cycle may be said to have been an experimental work of the young Kuprin. In it he revealed his ability to observe and listen closely, and to reproduce visual and accoustic impressions accurately and realistically. . . . (p. 26)

If in *Kievskie tipy* character assumes the governing role in the structure of the *očerki*, subordinating the other motivating forces (setting and whatever loose plot there is), in the next cycle, consisting of three *očerki*, it is the setting that assumes the dominant structural role, whereas the character element is almost as totally absent as the plot. The three *očerki* were the result of Kuprin's interest in the rapidly expanding industrial area of the Donbass toward the turn of the century. Chronologically, they are *Juzovskij zavod*, *V glavnoj šachte*, and *V ogne*.

In all three works the narrator-traveler is the principal character, even though he has a traveling companion (a different one in each of the three *očerki*), since the latter is only sketchily drawn and does not participate actively in the narrative. (pp. 26-7)

All three *očerki* are held together by the narrator and the related subject-matter. They are about equal in length, much longer than the longest *očerk* in *Kievskie tipy*.

Kuprin's greatest work in the *očerk* genre, written at the peak of his literary career, is undoubtedly the cycle *Listrigony*, which has as its central subject the Greek fishermen of Balaklava in the Crimea.

Kuprin lived and worked with these simple fishermen and got to know them well. This brings out an important point in Kuprin's technique as a writer: he had to be autobiographical to be good. It was not enough for him to see and hear, he had to actually participate in the activities he described, live close to the people he portrayed. . . . [The] autobiographic nature of his works emphasizes not introspection and self-analysis, but the close observation of mores and customs of a wide diversity of people with whom he had intimate personal associations. The "dialectics of the soul," internal monologues and dialogues, play an insignificant part in Kuprin's work. Not his own thinking about outside phenomena forms the nucleus of the autobiographic nature of his works, but his own visual and accoustic sensations of them.

Aside from the autobiographic nature of almost all his works, Kuprin was undoubtedly greatly influenced by Tolstoj in the choice of one of his principal themes, running in one form or another through many of his works: the antithesis between sophisticated and "natural" man. Whereas in many later works this theme is fitted closely to the plot, in *Listrigony*, on the whole "plotless" as all *očerki*, it does not form a dynamic nucleus. Nevertheless, the central theme of the Balaklava fishermen, the "listrigony," is set off against the background of the subsidiary theme of the antithesis between sophisticated and "natural" man. This antithesis holds the work in a kind of brace which limits the reader's view, prevents him from spreading his immediate interest beyond the scope of the events and facts described in the cycle. (pp. 27-8)

In *Listrigony* we have the unique situation that setting and character are structural elements of equal significance. The reason for this is not hard to find: Kuprin's object was not just to describe the atmosphere of Balaklava in autumn and winter but to show the fishermen's *byt* [mode of life] in all its diversity. While it was possible to lead the reader through mines and factories of the Donbass, merely indicating the conditions and lay-out without describing any workers, in the case of fishing, exclusively a manual toil, *byt* could be shown only through a variety of activities; this in turn involved the need for a number of portraits of the "listrigony." Thus, Kuprin chose a limited number of fishermen, some of them reappearing in several *očerki*, and in these few fishermen he highlighted certain character traits that are typical for the "listrigony" as a whole. There is, therefore, in the matter of these character sketches a certain similarity with the *Kievskie tipy*, except that the fishermen are named and more individualized, and that the scenes, illustrative of various traits, are described in greater detail. These scenes portray vividly the fishermen's *byt* both at work and at leisure.

As a result, the picture that crystallizes in our mind is that of unconscious, unsophisticated, "natural" men who live unedifying lives but are noble even in their vices. Like Tolstoj's Cossacks, they are far more attractive than civilized men who are spoilt and degenerate from an overdose of culture.

Characterization of those fishermen, who are individually portrayed, is mainly indirect, through dialogue, action, narration, and the attitude of others toward them. Direct characterization and biographic data are used only sparingly. Where direct description of character supplements indirect characterization, traits are merely enumerated, leaving analysis of character to the indirect method.

Dialogue is, as always in Kuprin, highly individualized and set off against the author-narrator's own factual, unadorned language. Such dialogue is sometimes very simple, but the very simplicity reflects the atmosphere, the "local color." (pp. 30-1)

[This] so-called "local color" is often reproduced by means of mass scenes which Kuprin handles skilfully. He often renders crowd reactions with a few crisp sentences which synthesize many voices in one, not unlike an opera choir.

Kuprin sometimes uses devices to enable the reader to identify more closely with the narrator. This increases the realism of the description, animates the narrative, and sharpens the reader's attention. . . .

Kuprin almost invariably chooses indirect characterization. He is indeed a master in the handling of dialogue, prefers the narrative over the descriptive tone, and knows how to pack action into a narrative—qualities more typical of a short story writer than of an *očerkist*. That is why in *Listrigony* where "plotless" action, dialogue, and narration can be blended into a vivid narrative, the short story writer in Kuprin sometimes gets the upper hand over the *očerkist*. (p. 31)

Perhaps no other trait is more characteristic of Kuprin than his pagan, hedonistic *joie de vivre*, so different from Andreev's morbid pessimism. That is no doubt one of the reasons why Kuprin had such appeal for Tolstoj, who often praised his works. This trait is vividly reflected in the last *očerk* of the cycle, *Bešenoe vino*. . . . (p. 32)

As in *Listrigony*, [in his cycle *Lazurnye berega*] Kuprin is only interested in the off-season when Nice is taken over by the workers and employees who have the time of their lives. The author no longer finds the city so distasteful and describes its endless festivities in minute detail. He draws his circles of observation wider and wider: first, he paints the atmosphere and the people dancing in the canvas tents, then he depicts in sharp outline the genre-picture outside the tents in all its variety and picturesqueness. Invariably Kuprin's sharp observation, his ability to select striking detail, his plain and unadorned language make these *očerki* delightfully attractive. Sometimes he succeeds in capturing vivid scenes with a few laconic yet colorful brush strokes. Among such scenes are especially those where many people are simultaneously engaged in a variety of activities, so that the selection of significant detail is of prime importance. . . .

What makes this cycle different from Kuprin's other *očerki*, even *Listrigony* is the light humor and jesting tone that pervade the whole cycle, except for *Nicca*, an *očerk* written in a satiric vein. In general Kuprin's works lack humor, but he handled it well when he did use it. . . .

[Kuprin's later *očerki*] are filled with sadness and melancholy, quite unrelieved by any humor. Kuprin's lust for life, which had marked his previous works, had given way in these later *očerki* to resignation and even despair. More than any other Russian writer condemned to live away from his homeland, he felt the adverse effect of the loss of his native

soil. . . . In the rare instances when he used French subject-matters, mostly confined to *očerki*, he constantly compared streets, cities, people, conditions with those in Russia. The result was the nostalgic mood which runs through most of his later *očerki*. (p. 37)

This tendency to be forever reminded of Russia is particularly evident in *Jug blagoslovennyj*, a cycle of four . . . *očerki* devoted to the Gascogne. . . .

[In] the cycle *Mys Guron*, consisting of four *očerki*, in which the author depicts the fishermen of Provence, his melancholy almost turns to despair, for they remind him forever of his beloved "listrigony." And yet, for all the despair of a broken man, even at that time the real Kuprin breaks through on occasions with his lust for life, his vitality, his glorification of strong, "natural" men in pursuit of heroic deeds. This is the case in *Puncovaja krov'*, . . . [an] *očerk* that is devoted to the description of bull-fighting in Bayonne. It belongs to one of Kuprin's most colorful *očerki*, replete with the picturesque variegation characteristic of this ancient pageantry. In the sharpness of the lines, the brilliance of the colors, and the flexibility of the language this work marks one of the highpoints in Kuprin's output as *očerkist*. . . .

Kuprin [was] in his best *očerki*, one of the leading representatives of this genre. What catches our eye . . . is his exceptional power of observation and his excellent visual memory. . . . [His] *očerki* contain many passages that reveal an extreme succinctness in their descriptions, syntactically highly fragmented sentences, often just word scraps which result in a surprisingly poetic language. (p. 38)

> *Peter H. Bonnell, "Kuprin and the Očerk," in* Mnemozina: Studia litteraria russica in honorem Vsevolod Setchkarev, *edited by Joachim T. Baer and Norman W. Ingham (© 1974 Wilhelm Fink Verlag), Fink, 1974, pp. 23-40.*

NICHOLAS LUKER (essay date 1978)

Kuprin's first tale ["**Poslednii deb i st**" ("**The Last Debut**")] with its unfelicitous title, has several defects that he later acknowledged. In particular, the sharp contrast between hero and heroine is a time-honored romantic cliché: he the cynical seducer, she the pure beauty destroyed by her selfless love for him. The contrast is made more blatant by the hackneyed description of their faces. His is typically demonic . . . , and hers has earned her the name of goddess. . . . The convention is reinforced by the excessively pompous style used by both narrator and characters. . . . (p. 23)

Despite its stilted language and stereotyped characters, "**The Last Debut**" has the narrative dynamism typical of the later Kuprin. At the same time, though beset by literary clichés, its treatment of love and the pain it can bring is deeply sensitive, a quality that would be the hallmark of his best works. (p. 24)

While Kuprin's first large prose work [titled "**V potmakh**" ("**In the Dark**")] shares many flaws of "**The Last Debut**"—melodramatic passages, unnatural situations, and bombastic language—it demonstrates his ability to handle successfully a complex plot with its major and minor characters, varied settings, and dialogues.

["**Doznanie**" ("**The Enquiry**")] was Kuprin's first army story and the most important work of his years as a soldier. It was also the first in a long series of tales about the military that culminated ten years later in *The Duel*. (p. 26)

"The Enquiry" is central to Kuprin's development because in Kozlovsky it presents the first in a succession of sensitive young officers at odds with their fellows and painfully aware of the injustice prevalent in the army. That type is continued in figures like Yakhontov of "Pokhod ("The March" . . .), and exemplified by Romashov of *The Duel*. (p. 27)

Kuprin's sketches [*ocherki*] are investigations of particular environments, such as a factory or mine, or portraits of people typical of specific social classes, occupations, or circumstances. Description and documentation are paramount, and there is no hint of a story line. . . .

Kuprin's contributions to the genre fall into two distinct groups. The first consists of four industrial sketches that serve as preliminary drafts for the setting of *Moloch*. The second group—collectively entitled *Kievskie tipy (Kiev Types)*—are sixteen in number, and are descriptive portraits of types of people observed by Kuprin in the city. (p. 31)

[However] revealing his treatment [in *Kiev Types*], it is broad rather than deep, and involves no exploration of individual psychology. Nevertheless, valuable in the documentary sense as firsthand pictures of figures central to Kiev life, the sketches are remarkable for their color, clarity, and scrupulous attention to detail. Moreover, they claimed a place in Kuprin's mental treasure house of vivid impressions. Thus several *Types* served as preliminary sketches for later fictional works. . . . (p. 33)

All his sketches, whether of city people or industrial plants, reveal Kuprin's burning curiosity about life around him. At the same time, many of them show concern for the plight of the poor or exploited in a hierarchical society, a fact that gives the lie to the opinion, current early in his career, that he was indifferent to social issues. That concern emerged in more elaborate form in *Moloch*, which exposes the injustice inherent in a society where the rouble is king. (p. 38)

Though [*Moloch*] offered rich possibilities for social comment, Kuprin chose instead to focus on the feelings of an individual locked in a personal struggle with an industrial Leviathan that he sees as destructive of human life. It is on the contrast between these forces, one pitifully weak in its isolation, the other boundlessly strong in its power, that the dramatic effect of *Moloch* relies. (p. 39)

For all that *Moloch* deals with the damaging effects of industrial progress, Kuprin devotes very little space to the factory's workers. Though their plight is revealed convincingly enough in statistical terms . . . , nowhere in the work are they more than a faceless mass drifting uncertainly on the periphery of the action. In the rare instances when they are shown in any detail, it is in crowd scenes witnessed through the hero's eyes. While there are hints of the workers' strength and skill, these qualities are not developed; instead, their dominant characteristics are submissiveness and resignation. (p. 45)

The defects of *Moloch* are several. The melodrama of works like "In the Dark" emerges again, especially in the Bobrov-Nina-Kvashnin triangle, which bears some resemblance to the earlier Alarin-Zinaida-Kashperov pattern. . . . Perhaps the major deficiency of the tale, however, is its lack of consistent pace and polish. An excess of technical detail in the sketch-like sections . . . retards the narrative and diverts attention from the work's primary concern. . . . In his attempt to convey the rapid sequence of events after the revolt is announced, Kuprin creates an impressionistic series of swiftly flitting scenes that culminate in an unsatisfying and hurried ending. (p. 46)

Moloch's originality lies in the clarity with which its central image reveals the price of industrial progress. The argument between Goldberg and Bobrov that gives rise to that image is pivotal to the work, and examines problems that concerned Kuprin himself. While it is hard to see how Kuprin could agree altogether with his hero's rejection of technological progress, Bobrov's view would seem to be one the author broadly shares. . . .

Nevertheless, the prime aim of *Moloch* is not to advocate revolutionary industrial agitation of the kind shown later in Gorky's novel *The Mother*. . . . Concerned primarily with the feelings vis-à-vis capitalist industry of an intellectual who takes no active steps to improve the workers' lot, *Moloch* is, as [Russian critic P. N.] Berkov neatly puts it, a "socio-psychological" rather than a "socio-political" work. (p. 47)

The Polesye tales depend on the contrast between town and country. The hypocrisy and corruption of the urban environment stand out in ugly relief against the natural beauty of the countryside and the spiritual purity of its people. Intended as the opening tale of the cycle, "The Backwoods" is a sketchlike ethnographical piece designed to depict the human beings who inhabit this pristine environment. In its distanced, rather documentary revelation of peasant types, it recalls Turgenev's *Sketches from a Hunter's Album* of half a century before. (p. 49)

Olesya is the most charming of Kuprin's rural tales. Though meant at first to be only part of the Polesye cycle, this poetic story of the love between an urban intellectual and a beautiful country girl expanded into a full novelette of a significance far surpassing that of the other regional tales. (p. 50)

Framed by the quietly evocative beauty of Polesye, his miraculous heroine [Olesya] stands out in brilliant relief against the somber hostility around her. The narrator's memory of her "tender, generous love" became an abiding motif in Kuprin's later work, rising to its crescendo in the gorgeously lyrical *Sulamif (Sulamith . . .)*, then fading softly through the sadly elegiac "Granatovyi braslet" ("The Bracelet of Garnets" . . .) into the poignant resignation of *Koleso vremeni (The Wheel of Time . . .)*. (p. 53)

Kuprin wrote less between 1902 and 1905. . . . But if the quantity of his writing was reduced—some twenty tales in all—its quality was incomparably higher. Gone were the melodramatic elements of his earlier tales, with their penchant for the abnormal. More conscious now of the blatant contrasts prevalent in Russian society, he turned his attention to the plight of the "little man," thus following the best traditions of Russian literature. (pp. 56-7)

"At the Circus" was clear poof of Kuprin's literary maturity. Successful among readers and critics alike, it brought high praise from both Chekhov and Tolstoy. . . . Chekhov described the tale as "a free, ingenuous, talented piece written . . . by . . . an expert." (p. 57)

[The protagonist] Arbuzov is the victim of the circus system, which revolves round money and takes no account of individuals in its service. But, on a higher level, for circus we may read any rigid system based on money that ignores the little man. Kuprin's criticism is levelled at the circus director's ruthless indifference to his artists' needs: since he knows that cancellation of the bout will reduce his takings, he refuses to put it off. (p. 58)

What gives **"At the Circus"** such power is the skill with which Kuprin conveys Arbuzov's feelings as they rise from vague disquiet in the opening chapter, through feverish sickness in his room, to a crescendo of impotent horror just before the bout. Conveyed in taut language that becomes more charged as the tale progresses, his suffering is set delicately into the more relaxed frame of circus acitivity with its varied characters engaged in their rehearsals. . . . The story's wealth of semidocumentary material about circus life lends it verisimilitude. . . . In the Chekhov manner, the narrative is compressed, shorn of detail that would contribute little either to Arbuzov's spiritual condition or to the background against which it belongs.

Realism and humane concern lie at the heart of **"At the Circus."** Drawn from lived life and peopled with real types with whom Kuprin was closely familiar, it pointed the direction his best work would take in the years ahead. (pp. 58-9)

The Duel tells of its [hero Romashov's] growing distaste for army life and his gradual realization that he is a uniquely individual human being. . . .

The first chapter of *The Duel* is a prologue designed to outline many issues central to the work as a whole. Furthermore, it offers a glimpse of the hero's position vis-à-vis army life and its traditional preoccupations, dwelling in particular on his attitude to injustice and violence. . . .

With his very first sentence Kuprin plunges us into the thick of army life, as the evening exercises in guard duty draw to a close. The dismal generality of the scene is reinforced by a deliberate neglect of locational detail. (p. 75)

[Kuprin examines the officers in] detail. He sketches their appearance or temperament in swift, broad strokes, dwelling on characteristics that particularize them throughout the novel. (p. 76)

[Not] all the officers incur Kuprin's censure; a handful of them are portrayed with sympathy as embodying qualities that distinguish them from their unsavory fellows. The most interesting is Second Lieutenant Mikhin, a small, timid man whom Romashov likes. An episodic figure, he is the only officer who resembles the hero in temperament. (pp. 80-1)

If tedium and sterility are the pervasive essence of army life, then violence is the inevitable result of the frustration they bring. Might is right in this world of the fist, and the officers rule their men by as much brutality as is necessary to reduce the common soldier to a petrified animal. Physical force and the verbal abuse that accompanies it are a relentless refrain through *The Duel* and become the most repulsive distinguishing mark of the officer type. . . . Its senseless violence was what sickened Kuprin most about army life. The spectre of sanctioned brutality stalks the pages of *The Duel* from beginning to end as Kuprin writes out his pain and horror. Romashov's growing loathing for the violence he sees daily around him accelerates his alienation from the officer caste. (pp. 82-3)

The meaning of the novel's title reaches far beyond the collision between Nikolaev and Romashov that concludes it. It embraces not only the hero's inner conflict with himself, good against evil, conviction against officer's duty, but also the wider confrontation between the sensitive individual and the whole of army life. In his unequal struggle against the brutality and philistinism rampant around him, that individual could expect nothing less than annihilation.

Like *Moloch*, *The Duel* sets its hero at center stage, focusing on his feelings and experiences. But unlike Bobrov, whom we find formed *a priori* when that work begins, Romashov develops significantly as the novel progresses. He is the compositional core of the work and from no chapter is he absent. . . . The timid lieutenant of the opening chapter is transformed into a thinking human being acutely aware of the inhumanity of army life and deeply troubled by his own role in it. Kuprin's revelation of his hero's psychology and his damning portrayal of the military are closely dependent on each other. Romashov's moral stature grows in direct proportion to his increasing distate for the army.

Kuprin's exploration of his hero begins in earnest in Chapter II. However, he makes no attempt to throw light on Romashov's character by offering a detailed biography. Instead, he prefers to reveal facets of his hero's character gradually, through situations and contact with other figures in the novel rather than through direct authorial intrusion.

Romashov's dejection is the inevitable result of provincial army life, its inescapable monotony and squalid boredom symbolized by the clinging mud that squelches underfoot in the remote border town. This first portrait of the hero reveals an inveterate dreamer who takes refuge from reality in romantic fantasies. (pp. 84-5)

Yet however persistent his dreamings, they do not save him from being degraded by the philistinism of army life. . . . He is drinking heavily at the club, is involved in a sordid affair with another officer's wife, has taken to gambling, and grows increasingly tired of the service. Worst of all, he has almost ceased to think. . . . However, unlike his colleagues, he is aware of his degeneration, and though still too weak to halt it, knows it should stop. In his dreams he visualizes the damage being done him by army life. If his waking fantasies evoke the untainted world of childhood, his sleeping dreams show that his adult self is being destroyed. The process is neatly represented by his vision of a split within him between his younger and older self: the embodiment of purity, the younger Romashov weeps as his older "double" drifts off into the sinister darkness. (pp. 86-7)

Chapters X and XI show Romashov's increasingly vocal opposition to brutality inflicted on the ranks. His strengthening convictions are expressed in sure, steady words, so unlike his earlier faltering phrases. . . . Again, but now more urgently, he thinks of leaving the army.

The skillfully maintained tension between Romashov's romantic notions of himself as a glorious officer and the grim reality of army life reaches its climax in Chapter XV, when it finally snaps. As the parade begins, all thoughts of his ego vanish and his feeling is one of pride at his participation in this stirring spectacle. . . . But during the marchpast disaster strikes. Intoxicated by dreams of martial distinction, he loses his alignment and throws the men marching behind him into confusion. The chaos of the moment is exemplified in the pathetic figure of Khlebnikov, struggling along twenty paces behind and covered with dust. . . . Feeling disgraced forever, he resolves to shoot himself.

His shame at his public disgrace turns Romashov's growing spiritual alienation from his fellow officers into actual physical isolation. . . . But his shame sharpens his self-awareness by showing him the similarity between his own experience and that of the common soldier, Khlebnikov. In their own ways, both are victims of an inhuman system. Now Kuprin fuses hitherto separate elements of his plot: the officer's growing self-awareness and the private's unrelieved suffering. . . . Romashov's identification of himself with the common soldier Khlebnikov is eloquent proof of his alienation from the officer caste.

To cement their spiritual kinship, Kuprin brings Romashov and Khlebnikov physically together in Chapter XVI. . . . [They] have shared the day's disgrace and are equally unhappy. It is now that the motif of human concern reaches its moving crescendo. Filled with compassion, Romashov embraces the sobbing soldier and comforts him. . . . The identification of officer with soldier, man with man, is complete, as both stand bewildered before the senseless savagery of their life. (pp. 89-91)

However little it does for Khlebnikov, Romashov's conversation with the soldier acts as a catalyst on the confusion of his feelings and brings him maturity overnight. . . . Romashov withdraws from the society of his fellow officers, and now regards people and events around him with sad calm. He has thus been purged of the army in body and soul by his conversation with Khlebnikov, a process suggested by his thoughts of *lustrum,* the ancient Roman purificatory sacrifice. (pp. 91-2)

Romashov's duel with Nikolaev represents the culmination of his estrangement from his fellow officers. In holding views contrary to theirs, he puts himself beyond the pale of the officer caste. . . . Paradoxically, it is the army that makes of Romashov the thinking individual he becomes. But as he prepares to enter a new life, he is obliged to settle accounts with the old. Whatever his hopes for the future, the army demands retribution in the present, and the gathering gloom of the closing chapters is a reminder that Romashov is doomed. Nemesis stalks *The Duel* from its earliest pages, drawing closer to Romashov with ever more rapid strides. Nikolaev is its embodiment, and his bullet its sentence.

Nazansky is the most intriguing yet most unsatisfying character in *The Duel*. (pp. 94-5)

Though we see Romashov and Nazansky together only twice, they belong indivisibly at the philosophical center of *The Duel*. Indeed, it is Nazansky, not Romashov, who enunciates Kuprin's philosophical views in their developed form. . . .

Nazansky's second appearance, in Chapter XXI, provides the key to Kuprin's philosophy in *The Duel*. Here his monologue demonstrates his ideological kinship with Romashov, developing the individualist anarchist views Romashov first formulated while under arrest in Chapter VI. If there Romashov groped toward a realization that his own self is the only true reality, from Nazansky he now receives eloquent, if rather confused, confirmation. . . . Thus, on the eve of Romashov's duel, Kuprin has Nazansky develop his hero's views as the maturing Romashov would eventually have done had he not been killed. Indirectly, Nazansky's philosophizing, frequently punctuated as it is by Romashov's rapturous words of agreement, underlines the tragedy of the hero's death on the brink of a new life. (p. 97)

If anyone puts Nazansky's philosophy of aggressive individualism into practice, it is Shurochka Nikolaeva, whose egoism actually destroys her fellow man. As the woman Romashov loves, she is the linchpin in the confrontation between her husband and the hero, and her ambition sends Romashov to his death. (p. 101)

The balance in Shurochka between feminine goodness and evil pride shifts toward the latter as the novel develops, and pitiless egoism emerges as the dominant, though skillfully masked, trait of her character. Kuprin shows the process subtly through Romashov's eyes. Her attitude toward dueling provides the first clue to her ambition and the callousness that accompanies it. . . . In the penultimate chapter, when she comes secretly to Romashov at night to persuade him to fight the duel, the baseness of her egoism is revealed in full measure. (p. 102)

Though he sees the selfish motives behind Shurochka's request, Romashov apparently fights the duel because he believes Nikolaev has come to some agreement with his wife. Since the hero is now aware of Shurochka's baseness, no other reason would seem sufficient to make him face Nikolaev's fire now he has decided to retire from the army. Like his concern for Khlebnikov, his behavior in Shurochka's best interests demonstrates that Romashov cannot follow Nazansky's philosophy to the letter. Yet the final chapter seems to prove that Nazansky is right. By acceding to Shurochka's request, Romashov denies the primacy of his own self, and sacrifices it on the altar of her ego. (p. 103)

Kuprin's language in the novel is unprecedentedly rich and flexible. Each character is individualized by his speech or the language of his thoughts, and the work's abundance of dialogue enables us to hear each person's voice. But however much those voices vary, the hall-marks of Kuprin's prose remain invariably simplicity, clarity, and versatility. (pp. 103-04)

While Nazansky is revealed primarily through his speech, Romashov is shown chiefly through his inner monologues of varying length and intensity, in which Kuprin elaborates his hero's thoughts and demonstrates his penchant for romantic fantasy. . . . [Apart] from his biting remarks to Raisa in Chapter IX and his angry outburst to Nikolaev toward the close, Romashov's speech is as undistinguished as his personal appearance.

In accordance with the neutral quality of most of Kuprin's language, his descriptions are neither extensive nor elaborate, and his restrained prose contains few metaphors or similes. (p. 106)

In his strongly autobiographical tale "Lenochka" . . . , Kuprin turned to the love of ordinary mortals in an everyday world where time takes its relentless toll. With Chekhovian restraint he tells of the love of two young people, recalled in the twilight of middle age. . . .

Pervaded though it is by wistful melancholy, the tale is quietly optimistic, for it affirms the continuity of life. All things change in a world where life is followed by death, but all our lives are interwoven because life itself never dies. . . .

To Kuprin sadness and tragedy are as much a part of love as the joy and ecstasy it brings to fortunate human beings. The theme of suffering and disappointment in love, already apparent in *Moloch* and *The Duel*, reaches a profoundly moving crescendo in his shorter works of these years. (p. 126)

[In the famous story **"The Bracelet of Garnets,"**] hopeless love finds its quietly tragic apotheosis. [It] develops the theme of unsuccessful love . . . [and pivots on two ideas]: that love is as powerful as death, and that real love comes only once in a thousand years. . . . Precisely because it is so hopeless, Zheltkov's love lacks . . . urgent sensuality. . . . Instead it is an emotion of boundless nobility and pure selflessness, the highest spiritual experience attainable by man. (pp. 126-27)

Zheltkov's tragedy is that of a man wholly committed to a single ideal. . . . But neither Zheltkov's living nor his passing are in vain, for his love has found its way into his beloved's heart and brings about her spiritual resurrection. . . . In a finale unequalled in his writing for its poetic power, Kuprin shows the rebirth of his heroine as she becomes one in spirit with him who loved her more than life itself. (p. 128)

Kuprin's novelistic study of prostitution, *The Pit,* was the longest and most ambitious work of his career. (p. 133)

Many weaknesses of the novel stem from the fact that it took seven years to write and that Kuprin became tired of it, finding the completion of Parts II and III difficult and even loathsome. . . . Kuprin's sporadic work on the novel is reflected in its structure. Its three parts are linked by the flimsiest of transitions. . . . While some symmetry is achieved by the rise and fall of the Yama red light district with which the work opens and closes, its action is set artificially in a three month period between those processes and relies on a series of loosely connected episodes . . . that bear little relation to the theme of prostitution. Moreover, such plot as the novel possesses lacks a clear thread, and too often wanders into digression and superfluous detail. Consequently the work is long and cumbersome, and fails to show Kuprin's purpose clearly. The reader feels that *The Pit* outgrew its author's initial intentions and swamped them. From a necessary, topical study of prostitution it swelled into a vast, disordered canvas depicting the social and moral issues of its age, many of which are only tenuously linked with the problem of vice. . . .

Kuprin could not decide whether his novel should be documentary reportage or pure fiction, and either oscillates between the two or attempts to combine them in an artificial way. But he is more successful when in documentary vein, and so Part I, with its details of life in the brothel, is by far the best. . . . But Kuprin's documentation of brothel life is not infrequently overdone, and burdens his narrative. (p. 134)

Kuprin is interested not so much in the psychology of individual characters as in the life of a particular social group—his prostitutes and those associated with them. This lack of personal focus makes *The Pit* very unsatisfying artistically, however convincing it may be as a social document. What human interest the work possesses is either blanketed by Kuprin's plethora of subsidiary themes or submerged by his documentary preoccupations.

Platonov is Kuprin's mouthpiece in the novel. A wooden figure who plays no essential part in the work, he is a *raisonneur* who stands on the periphery of the action, obediently commenting on it for Kuprin. His position as an intimate observer of brothel life is oddly equivocal, and his relationship with the various prostitutes curiously avuncular. After helping his author explain the bases, workings, and effects of prostitution, he drifts out of the novel as mysteriously as he first appeared, a lifeless assemblage of weighty words. The core of his tiresome philosophizing is that the horror of prostitution lies precisely in the fact that those engaged in it see nothing horrible about it. (p. 135)

The Pit is not one of Kuprin's best works, as he himself admitted. . . . Not only did he lack a clear objective in writing the novel, but also had no solution for the problem of prostitution it examined. . . . As a study of prostitution *The Pit* is unique, but as literature it leaves much to be desired. It was to be Kuprin's last major work, and to many it signaled the decline of his creativity. (p. 136)

With his contemporaries Chekhov, Gorky, and Bunin, [Kuprin] brought the genre of the short story to an efflorescence without parallel in Russian letters. What he conceded in restraint to Chekhov, conviction to Gorky, and subtlety to Bunin, Kuprin made up for in narrative pace, construction of plot, and richness of theme. These latter qualities, coupled with his abiding interest in the human soul, make him still very readable today. (p. 154)

Kuprin cannot correctly be viewed as belonging totally to any literary grouping of his time. Instead, he might best be described simply as one of the most distinguished Russian realistic prose writers of the early 1900s. As in his immensely varied life, so in his writing, he traveled his own road.

Kuprin's talent is essentially optimistic, assertive of life in all its manifestations. Despite the gloom of his declining years, his career was devoted to the exaltation of man and the beauty of natural things. . . . As generous and all-embracing as the life it extols, Kuprin's giant spirit strides the pages of his works with a vigor time cannot diminish. (p. 155)

Nicholas Luker, in his Alexander Kuprin *(copyright © 1978 by Twayne Publishers, Inc.; reprinted with the permission of Twayne Publishers, a Division of G. K. Hall & Co., Boston), Twayne, 1978, 171 p.*

ADDITIONAL BIBLIOGRAPHY

Berkenblit, S. E. "General and Biographical Notes." In *Sentimental Romance and Other Stories,* by Alexander I. Kuprin, translated by S. E. Berkenblit, pp. 1-11. New York: Pageant Press, 1969.
    Biographical sketch.

Guerney, Bernard Guilbert. Introduction to *Yama: The Pit,* by Alexandre Kuprin, translated by Bernard Guilbert Guerney, pp. xi-xvii. New York: The Modern Library, 1932.
    Critique of *Yama: The Pit* including a brief survey of Kuprin's life and career.

Persky, Serge. "Alexander Kuprin." In his *Contemporary Russian Novelists,* translated by Frederick Eisemann, pp. 274-88. Boston: J. W. Luce, 1913.
    Discusses Kuprin's genius as a storyteller "who imposes neither thesis nor moral upon his reader, but paints life as it appears to him."

Vernon Lee

1856-1935

(Pseudonym of Violet Paget) English essayist, critic, novelist, travel writer, biographer, short story writer, and dramatist.

Vernon Lee's contribution was primarily to culture in its broadest sense rather than to literature in particular. Her novels and short stories were not very successful in their time, nor have they since gained more than modest recognition. The field in which she excelled was that of aesthetic and intellectual commentary. Like her contemporary Walter Pater, Lee was a highly sensitive student of the art and ideas of the past, and the learning she acquired led to insightful studies in the psychology of aesthetics.

Lee was born in France to British parents. Throughout her childhood her family traveled around Europe; thus she became intimate with various languages and cultures. For the rest of her life she was the ideal cosmopolitan and abhorred the notion of allegiance to a single nationality. Eventually the family settled in Florence, and Lee began applying the precocious learning of her adolescence to the study of Italian art, resulting in her *Studies of the Eighteenth Century in Italy*. Commentators of the time considered these essays an amazing performance in scholarship and critical thought that revealed a neglected era in artistic history. Lee's background in this period subsequently yielded the novel *Ottilie*, the biography *The Countess of Albany*, and *Belcaro*, a work concerned with the philosophy of art. *Belcaro* introduces Lee's belief that music and the visual arts should be appreciated for their form alone and not be made to serve any intellectual or didactic function, a role she reserved for literature. The dialogues of *Baldwin* stress the ethical nature of literature, as well as articulating her agnosticism and her views on the importance of the individual in society.

In 1881 Lee visited London and began to establish herself in the English literary milieu. She came to know many of its prominent figures—Dante Gabriel Rossetti, Oscar Wilde, Walter Pater, William Morris, Edward Burne-Jones—and her novel *Miss Brown* satirizes the aesthetic movement with which they were associated. Interest in this novel is for the most part limited to students of literary history. More enduring among Lee's works of fiction are the supernatural tales collected in *Hauntings*, which examine the intrusion of the past upon the present. The detailed historical background displayed in these stories gives them that sense of distance from contemporary life which their author believed essential to works of supernatural fantasy. Lee's keen sense of the past was a counterpart to her feeling for the "spirit of the place" or *genius loci*. This imaginative intuition informs her numerous collections of travel essays, which are among the most popular of her works.

Having begun her career as a Victorian author, Lee continued to publish well into the twentieth century, examining changing intellectual trends in such works as *Vital Lies* and extending her interest in aesthetic theory with *The Handling of Words*. During the First World War she was a committed pacifist. Her polemic on the war, *Satan the Waster*, inspired George Bernard Shaw to praise her intelligence and sanity in a time of world chaos. Though no longer widely read, Lee is recalled in mem-

oirs and biographies as one of the best minds of her day, a brilliant conversationalist, and the nineteenth-century "new woman" par excellence.

PRINCIPAL WORKS

Studies of the Eighteenth Century in Italy (essays) 1880
Belcaro (essays) 1881
Ottilie (novel) 1883
The Countess of Albany (biography) 1884
Euphorion (essays) 1884
Miss Brown (novel) 1884
Baldwin (prose dialogues) 1886
Juvenilia (essays) 1887
Hauntings (short stories) 1892
Renaissance Fancies and Studies (essays) 1895
Limbo, and Other Essays (essays) 1897
Genius Loci (travel essays) 1899
Ariadne in Mantua (drama) 1903
Penelope Brandling (novel) 1903
The Enchanted Woods (travel essays) 1905
Gospels of Anarchy (essays) 1908
The Sentimental Traveller (travel essays) 1908

Vital Lies (essays) 1912
Louis Norbert (novel) 1914
The Tower of Mirrors (travel essays) 1914
Satan the Waster (prose dialogue) 1920
The Handling of Words (essays) 1923
The Golden Keys (travel essays) 1925
Music and Its Lovers (essays) 1932
The Snake Lady, and Other Stories (short stories) 1954

JOHN ADDINGTON SYMONDS (essay date 1880)

I want to thank you for your book, [*Studies in the Eighteenth Century in Italy*]. (p. 635)

I found it charming. Whether it would charm equally a man who loved Italy less, who believed in the Italian opera less, who had less previous feeling for your century, & who less sympathized with your point of view about the superiority of living art to culture, is a different question. I mean that I am no fair sample of the public.

As an older craftsman, may I speak to you, a younger craftsman, frankly? I think you have a real literary gift. You have the main thing—Love; [which] in art of all kinds takes the same place as Charity among the Virtues. You love your subject simply, & you bring to the treatment of it rare qualities—almost too exuberant in their unpruned vigour.

I should like you to write the phrase of Sacchini over your desk—"Chiarezza, bellezza, buona modulazione" [clarity, beauty, good modulation]. On the point of clearness, I feel that each of your chapters (except perhaps the "Musical Life") suffers from want of previous thinking out. They lack a leading motive, an organic *gliederung* [articulation]. There is a kind of allusiveness & outpouring in your way of dealing with material, which cannot fail to confuse people for whom the whole set of musicians & literary people are unknown.

When the subject itself is simple, as in the case of Metastasio, you go right. Some of the analyses of his plays leave nothing to be desired, & you have your point about the reality of the opera.

On the point of beauty, you must abandon superfluous adjectives, repetitions, & incoherent strings of clauses with a dash to save all at the close. Relentless compression would add infinitely to the grace of your style.

As for good modulation, what I feel you lack upon this point is that your transitions are often violent and not well *motivist*. This criticism really resolves itself into the same as I ventured to make under the head of clearness. An uninstructed reader might feel himself in a thick luxuriant wood, & long for a little more definiteness. . . whereby he should guide himself through your animated allusions. (pp. 635-36)

> *John Addington Symonds, in his letter to Vernon Lee on May 23, 1880, in* The Letters of John Addington Symonds: 1869-1884, *Vol. II, edited by Herbert M. Schueller and Robert L. Peters (reprinted by permission of the Wayne State University Press; copyright 1968 by Herbert M. Schueller and Robert L. Peters), Wayne State University Press, 1968, pp. 635-36.*

COSMO MONKHOUSE (essay date 1885)

Miss Brown is not only a vivid picture of human life, but also both a severe satire and a tragedy. The subject of the satire is the falseness of the aesthetic ideal, and the tendency of its worshippers to gravitate towards the grossest immorality, while that of the tragedy is the sacrifice, to put it shortly, of a noble character on the altar of gratitude. These difficult themes are treated with great brilliance and originality, and with a literary and imaginative force which demand recognition. It is only to be regretted that both tragedy and satire are extremely and needlessly painful and unpleasant. (p. 6)

Miss Brown herself is a creation of which the author may be proud. . . . [She is] a character conceived with great force, and carried out with greater consistency almost to the end. But the end, besides being unutterably sad and extremely repulsive, seems to me false. Although Miss Brown throughout has a natural tendency to self-sacrifice, she has too much rectitude to enter deliberately into a life which would be a ceaseless lie, and too much common sense not to see that the sacrifice would be vain.

Nor can I entirely approve of the method, clever though it be, which Vernon Lee has adopted to satirise a small but well-known section of society. Vernon Lee has dealt with it much in the same fashion as the Oriental robber, who, after plundering a caravan, stripped all his victims naked, threw all their clothes into a heap, and then amused himself with watching them struggle for shoes and turbans, shawls and burnouses. By first separating and then mixing haphazard the christian and surnames, the places of residence, the elements of character, and domestic conditions, appertaining to a number of more or less known persons, the author has, indeed, effectually confused their identities, but has nevertheless ridiculed them individually as well as collectively.

Moreover, Vernon Lee has forgotten that to trick up an imaginary character in the clothes of a well-known person, though it will not prejudice that person in the eyes of those who know him, may well do so in the eyes of those who only know his clothes. If Mr. Jeremiah Brown, a perfectly harmless and worthy person, but well known to the public as a writer of verses, has a villa at Fulham, and a novelist introduces a poet of the name of Jeremiah Smith, with a villa at Fulham, where he keeps a harem, persons who do not personally know Mr. Jeremiah Brown will jump to the conclusion that he keeps a harem. This is a serious and by no means imaginary objection to the satiric method of Vernon Lee.

Altogether it is extremely difficult to form an impartial opinion of this remarkable novel, distinguished as it is by both faults and virtues of no common kind. (pp. 6-7)

> *Cosmo Monkhouse, "Literature: 'Miss Brown: A Novel'," in* The Academy, *No. 661, January 3, 1885, pp. 6-7.*

HARRIET WATERS PRESTON (essay date 1885)

In [*Studies of the Eighteenth Century in Italy*, Vernon Lee] gives herself great scope, and is able to embrace, in her extensive outlook over the last century, both literature and music; being, as she goes on to say, still with magnificent modesty, "neither a literary historian nor a musical critic, but an æsthetician," and finding both literature and music within the "æsthetician's" domain.

The truth is that she has qualifications of no mean order for both the offices which she disclaims. There is a deal of curious learning, not ungracefully employed, in the picturesque *résumé,* with which her volume opens, of the history of the Arcadian Academy at Rome; that musty and shadowy institution, whose annals are so obscure and its local habitation so problematical that it would puzzle some of its own honored members, we fancy, to give a clear account of it without the help of Vernon Lee. The great days of the Academy live again under this vivacious pen. . . . [The] busy and buoyant imagination of the writer sees not merely the world of Italy around each successive figure, but the world of Europe around that; and she is incessantly trying, by means of episodes and excursions, to make her reader share the extent and the completeness of her own view. There is a sketch . . . of the general social condition and life of Italy, in the last century, outside the four great cities of Rome, Florence, Naples, and Venice, visited by the ordinary traveler, which is a perfect marvel of lively realization and telling detail. It is a great deal too long to quote; and the fact that it is so points to one of the faults of Vernon Lee's style,—a sort of riotous verbiage and eager habit of iteration and reiteration. . . . (pp. 220-21)

Taking the book as a whole, its matter and its workmanship, let us cordially admit that it is a great feat to have been performed by a girl in her earliest twenties. The critical faculty is lower than the creative, and usually, although not always, of later development, and there are hundreds of bright scholars and bright talkers for one born maker; but the thing which this young woman has accomplished would have been creditable to a mature man who had spent his life in the same line of research, and it is relatively as remarkable, in its lesser way, as the renowned precocities of production of Mozart, Mendelssohn, and Keats.

How can such promise be sustained, how has it been sustained, by Vernon Lee; or is this sort of pre-maturity really promising at all? We must confess that in our own case a sense, which we believe to be wholesome, of something very like relief blends with the disappointment with which we find her second volume of essays, bearing the fanciful title of *Belcaro,* very much more youthful and less weighty than her first. It is more youthful, and it is much more feminine, intensely subjective, and at the same time gloriously lawless. It is all about herself and her emotions and her speculations. . . . *Belcaro,* like its predecessor, treats of things "æsthetical," but in a looser and more general way; with painting and sculpture chiefly, in place of musical and dramatic art. The book does not assume to be technical, but it is full of artistic intelligence and a cultivated susceptibility to beauty. It is redolent of Italy, also, in a charming way, each paper having its separate framework of delicately wrought Italian scenery; for the writer has learned, and learned well, from the illustrious art-critic whom she professes, in the essay on Ruskinism, to have so far outgrown, the art of landscape painting in words. There is a certain fervor and honesty of purpose, also, discernible amid its rather scatter-brained declamation,—a desire to shake herself free of artistic affectations and conventionalisms, and to enter into the heart, and fathom for herself the sublime secret of those great antiques which she so truly loves to contemplate and to talk about. But still this book is not intrinsically important, like the first. It is all compact, as we have said, of imagination, emotion, and theory, with flashes of keen discernment here and there, and some few fresh and happy

suggestions in the way of specific criticism (particularly in the chapter entitled "In Umbria," which deals with the man Perugino and his work), but with much also that is tumid, and much that is, we fear, preposterous. The author indeed insists with vehemence, both in the "Preface" and in the "Apology or Postscript" to *Belcaro,* that she has had a fixed purpose, running straight amid all the anomalies of her book, and unifying all its vagaries; and we are, in fact, enabled to conclude from the whole that just at present she believes in art for art's sake, its own "excuse for being" and its own exceeding great reward. . . . (pp. 223-25)

Our private notion is that Vernon Lee took what may be called her intellectual "fling" in *Belcaro,* and that the preternatural weight and wisdom of her first publication not only entitled her to such a fling, but rendered it almost inevitable. Antics are ever a proof of strength, and it is a great deal easier to reduce an excess than to supply a lack. . . . The rampant verbiage of Vernon Lee's style, for example, implies at least a marvelously rich vocabulary; and what so natural as that she should be prone, coming so early into such a heritage, to fling her wealth about a little wildly and wastefully? . . .

Since the appearance of *Belcaro* she has published a novelette entitled *Ottilia, A Life of the Countess of Albany,* and *Euphorion. Ottilia* is a simple story, simply told, careful and even subtle in its delineation of character, humorous and humane. It is not very strong, but it is very symmetrical, and free, even singularly free, from extravagance, whether of sentiment or style. (p. 225)

The little story of *Ottilia,* already briefly mentioned, simple as it is, and so much less dramatic than the real life of the Countess of Albany, derives, no less than the latter, a wonderful charm from its author's perfect acquaintance with the period in which the scene is laid. All the dry research which had to precede the essays on the *Musical Life* and the *Venetian Comedy* helps to enrich the background of this quiet tale, giving depth to its landscape, body to its color, and reality to its quaint figures. One might smile at the ambitious nature of Vernon Lee's initial enterprise, if one were not constrained thoroughly to respect in her the serious and patient courage which, earlier yet, had attacked and gone triumphantly through such a world of preliminary toil. The charge of self-conceit cannot lie heavily against one who is even more eager to learn than she is impatient to teach; and however bold in announcing her own conclusions, she is keenly attentive to the conclusions of others. (p. 227)

Harriet Waters Preston, "Vernon Lee," in The Atlantic Monthly *(copyright © 1885, by The Atlantic Monthly Company, Boston, Mass.), Vol. 55, No. 328, February, 1885, pp. 219-27.*

THE SPECTATOR (essay date 1905)

Something in their past history, we imagine, may account for the one fault of these fascinating essays [in *The Enchanted Woods*]—their shortness. They are all much of the same length: sometimes it seems right and enough; sometimes, and much oftener, one resents it and begs for more; it seems as if there must be more to be said on this subject or the other, in the writer's charming way. . . .

One of the best features of "Vernon Lee's" mind and work is her cosmopolitan wideness of sympathy. Knowing Italy far better than many people who write about it with greater airs of intimacy, she is yet able to find her enchanted woods, her cities of romance, her nymph-haunted springs and streams, in many another country. She has, in fact, a poet's mind. We find in her—and it is a rare discovery—something of the spirit of Keats. . . . (p. 330)

"'The Enchanted Woods'," in The Spectator *(© 1905 by* The Spectator; *reprinted by permission of* The Spectator), *No. 4001, Mar. 4, 1905, pp. 330-31.*

VAN WYCK BROOKS (essay date 1911)

Two points connect Vernon Lee immediately with both [Walter] Pater and [J. A.] Symonds. She was at first, as they were always, occupied with pure æsthetics. Her equipment in facts too was much the same as theirs, although in her study of the Renaissance the emphasis fell rather upon its aftermath. In her early books one observes that the eighteenth century obsessed her less for its lookings-forward than as the last age in which the Renaissance mood remained authentic,—remaining so remote from its original springs that its manifestations were highly tenuous, complex and subtle. From the first she wrote with authority. Her impulse came from the study of facts, facts accepted and half-forgotten and fertilized with fresh facts until her mind was unable to generate a barren or a superficial thought or a thought not hung about and garlanded with associations. With her the process gave birth not to opinions but to radiations, sudden risings to the surface and the sunlight of strange fragments of human experience bearing with them odors and evanescent hues and curious forms that belong to the depths whence they have come: fragments really of those wraithlike existences we call race, history, tradition, which in the hands of art become nations and periods. For without art there is no such thing as a nation or a period: without art the past is as formless, as essentially non-existing, as the future.

Vernon Lee gave herself at first entirely to the creating of nations and periods. And one of the charming examples of her early gifts, interests, and theories is *The Prince of the Hundred Soups* . . . , a "puppet-show in narrative," in which the traditional Italian mask comedy with all its type characters is written out into a tale as delicate and whimsical as *The Rose and the Ring.* (pp. 449-50)

In 1883 Vernon Lee published a novel, *Miss Brown,* which is I suppose the most colossal piece of amateurishness that can still rightly be claimed for literature. (As a detail, one feels in reading this novel that the writer is never quite certain whether a character should be made to *remark* or *observe.*) Now the only figure in this book that entirely fails to exist is Miss Brown's brother, Richard Brown, who is offered as a great labor-leader, formerly a miner. Inadvertently he is made to quote Pater and to be familiar with far too many other unlaborlike things to serve in true fiction. (In Vernon Lee one sees that the trappings of the mind are not always portable baggage for a traveling spirit.) But this laborman *does* throw a black shadow over the languorous twilight of those very small pre-Raphaelite satellites of his sister: and she, like a great slumbering Titan, awfully pure, stirs in her dream. She has all noble traits except receptiveness, all effectual traits except adaptiveness. She opens her eyes upon two worlds: on the one side her husband, the Priors, old Saunders,—the world, for better or worse, of art; and on the

other Richard Brown. . . . Three facts in the story are significant. These are: the character of Miss Brown, the failure of Richard Brown to assume a form approaching in coherence the figures who stand for the world of art, and the fact that Richard Brown, inchoate as he is, forms a disquieting element in the story.

In perspective one sees that this novel is a symbolical expression of Vernon Lee's transitional period.

In the opening of *Juvenilia* . . . , she tells of a kind of conversion through which she has been led to put away childish things:

> For do what we will, devote ourselves exclusively to the pleasant and certain things of this life, shut our eyes and ears resolutely to the unpleasant and uncertain, we shall be made, none the less, to take part in the movement that alters the world. . . . The question therefore is, in which direction our grain of dust's weight shall be thrown?

This new light shines upon two collections of dialogues, which deal as their sub-titles say with "duties and aspirations." These books are *Baldwin* . . . and *Althea.* . . . In these dialogues a number of shadowy, half-allegorical but modern men and women take part, wandering in lovely scenes at sunset or after dawn: little pictures of the world about them are set here and there as a kind of refrain, as if nature in the arrangement of some cloud-group or the uncertain waving of an ilex-tree were glad to give a universal application to each of these conflicting turns of the human mind.

In *Baldwin* we observe an effort to throw the grain of dust's weight decisively in a certain direction. Baldwin is intended to picture the perfect positivist, cheerful, sane, well-organized, convinced of the self-sufficiency of the world. His mission is to clear the ground, to rid his friends of sentiment, superstition, or faith in any but the useful issues of morality. . . . We discover that he is however but a cloudy symbol. . . . He himself offers a doubt as to whether science, in its ultimate elimination of pain, will not thus take away part of the steel upon which character sharpens itself. Thus in the end he becomes non-committal.

We are told that Althea is naturally the pupil of Baldwin. From him certainly she has learned that there is a certain futility in attempting to cast one's grain of dust's weight in any rigid direction. Althea is described as "one of those rare natures so strangely balanced that they recognize truth as soon as they see it . . . natures which know spontaneously what the rest of us learn by experience and reflection; fortunate samples of what we may perhaps all become but, for that very reason, incapable of serving as guides in the difficult way of becoming." . . . Here at last assertion is thrown to the winds and we have a personality (Miss Brown again really) so entirely in solution, so inherently intelligent and pure, that we recognize in her the achieved human soul, in whom the serenity of perfect intuition has succeeded the battles of thought and in whom progress has arrived at its destination. . . . In Althea we contemplate the ideal of a future in which character will have taken the place of thought.

Althea urges nothing, but she offers above all, as the wind and the stars offer it, a silent reproof to all propaganda. And the more we come to identify her with Vernon Lee's view of life, evolving but always essentially the same, we discover a reason for the failure of Baldwin to justify his apparent assertiveness and for the incoherency of the propagandist Brown amid a group of clearly-conceived artists who in all their insignificance are at least passive.

It is Althea who speaks in the collection of essays, *Gospels of Anarchy* . . . , which are devoted to Tolstoy and Nietzsche, Emerson, Whitman, and Ruskin, Professor James and H. G. Wells. Here we find that Vernon Lee has passed into a fully developed quietism in which however the world has taken the place of heaven. You may if you like—I understand her to say—expect the world to live after a pattern that seems to you the best; but the fact is that the individual has no more than enough energy to get through the day all by himself. Man really has no gift for organization, no room for the vicarious experience of other men's ideas. Therefore why be urgent? Why plan out elaborate utopias that have no power to illuminate each passing hour in the solitary growth of a human life? . . . But I should like to give what seems to me the central passage in this book:

> To be able to face *fact* as *fact*, as something transcending all momentary convenience and pleasantness; yet at the same time to preserve our human preferences, to exercise our human selection all the more rigidly because we know that it is *our* selection, reality offering more but we accepting what we choose; such a double attitude would surely be the best. . . .
>
> (pp. 451-54)

The conception of this perfect apprehension of fact in a state which implies also the full expression of personality is the conception of a perfect intuition. And it is Vernon Lee's conception of the future. It is a kind of quietism that has got rid of heaven and become sublunized. Now the reason we got rid of heaven was because we discovered that we could have all the really good things of heaven without waiting so long for them. (p. 454)

Althea represents quite literally the idea of heaven expressing itself in human society. And in this society the artist having regained his normality would cease to exist, while art, exactly as in some celestial scene of Fra Angelico's, springing up everywhere as a kind of exultation would

> Float and run
> Like an unbodied joy, whose race is just begun.
>
> (p. 455)

Now certain it is that the books which tell us the most about Vernon Lee are those of hers that are least known. As a figure, as one who has attained to a distinguished view of life, she has never assumed popularly a clear-cut form. I can think of three reasons for this. For one, she has kept herself as a human being sedulously unknown. For another, her views are so free from the stress and prejudice of propaganda that they have never lent themselves to combat, refutation, discipleship, or that exaggeration which implants an idea in the popular mind. But a third reason is, I think, the most responsible. She has won a reputation, too considerable to be called secondary, as an occasional writer. Almost every pleasant thing in the lives of cultivated men and women she has touched with a happy phrase. Her gift has been so gracious that she seems not to have asked for austere consideration. (p. 456)

Van Wyck Brooks, "Notes on Vernon Lee," in The Forum *(copyright, 1911, by The Forum Publishing Company), Vol. XLV, No. 4, April, 1911, pp. 447-56.*

DESMOND MacCARTHY   (essay date 1931)

In her travel sketches [Vernon Lee] has hunted and captured the *genius loci*. In the art of weaving a delicate net of words in which to catch "the spirit of place," not even Henry James is more skilled. This can only be done by one who has an imaginative sense of the past, and an analytic interest in immediate impressions. Vernon Lee is gifted in both these respects; and also in her later essays, **"The Spirit of Rome," "The Sentimental Traveller," "The Haunted Woods," "The Tower of the Mirrors," "Genius Loci,"** she found a style peculiarly adapted to this end. At first she wrote with Ruskinian fervour and Pateresque deliberation, but her later manner has something of the looseness of talk—let us call it an epistolary style. . . . On abstract subjects too she "talks" with her pen, though her thinking is precise. In **"Vital Lies,"** in which she examines current philosophies of life, her style is often redundant, but it conveys the excitement of impromptu discussion. (p. 21)

If there has been a development in her work it has been in the direction of becoming more psychological. "We live in a historical age," nineteenth-century critics used to say, conscious of their preoccupation with the past. Vernon Lee has written her later books during a period which, at any rate with equal accuracy, can be described as a psychological one. The two main characteristics of her books are that they are those of a writer at once sensitively receptive and passionately curious. It is the blend in them of the restless intellectual analyst and the aboundingly grateful æsthetic observer which makes them so fascinating. Her curiosity has of course made her susceptible to the influence of contemporary theory and investigation. No science is changing more rapidly, or is really at bottom in a greater state of confusion, than psychology, and some of her work, based upon what was once the latest theory, has been undercut by later investigations. To a certain extent some of the notes and disquisitions in which the comparatively brief **"Ballet of the Nations"** in **"Satan the Waster"** is embedded, have suffered from being undercut by recent explanations of the unconscious. But the book remains the most thorough literary analysis of War neurosis. It is an armoury stuffed with sharp pacifist weapons, a classic among anti-war books; a work of ardent reasoning, eloquent and shrewd.

It was inevitable that Vernon Lee should be one of the older writers most affected by the War. She hammers the enemies of Culture, in defence of that disinterested interest in men and times, in customs and ideas, which are different from those contemporary and national, and of that faith which lies at the root of all Culture; that appreciation and learning are ends in themselves. The object of **"Satan the Waster"** is to show by allegory and discourse how easy it is to enlist the virtues themselves on the side of the powers of destruction. One impression it cannot fail to leave behind: an uneasy distrust of, possibly a downright contempt for, that glowing and dangerous emotion—moral indignation. (pp. 21-2)

Desmond MacCarthy, "Vernon Lee" (reprinted by permission of the Estate of Desmond MacCarthy), in The Bookman, *London, Vol. LXXI, No. 481, October, 1931, pp. 21-2.*

RICHARD CARY (essay date 1960)

The essays in [*Limbo and Other Essays; Genius Loci; The Enchanted Woods; The Spirit of Rome; The Sentimental Traveller; The Tower of the Mirrors;* and *The Golden Keys*] were largely extracted from [Vernon Lee's] steady contributions to the *Westminster Gazette*. In style, tone and depth they are far superior to what one expects from newspaper illuminati. Here is evidenced a taut but delicate intelligence, raising scores of prose vignettes above platitude with illusive poetic charm. The language is apt, the allusions from art and literature abundant, the philosophy forceful but not disagreeable. . . .

Her hypothetical *genius loci* did not spring full-blown from the fore edge of her first book on travel. *Limbo* . . . reveals only casually the substantial image which evolves Proteus-like in succeeding volumes. **"The Lie of the Land"** merely suggests qualities which will figure importantly in Lee's later individuation of the idea. (p. 132)

Direct references to the *genius loci* or its several aliases are most frequent in **The Enchanted Woods**. . . . One is apt to find generalizations about the elusive divinity in the initial and terminal sections, while in between lies an enticement of details. She laments the "stupid wicked carnival sacrilege" which ignores the organic habit and reason of places (climate, soil, vegetation, lie of land, history) and makes them "into living creatures, charming friends, or venerable divinities." She decrees the impersonality of the spirit, yet in the next breath conjures it as "a human voice and human eyes . . . personified in kindly living creatures." She asserts that "whole districts have meant friends," and tarries hopefully "at unknown gates in alien places" for a glimpse of the fugitive. She concedes that it plays questionable tricks of recall and identity on dedicated travelers, but assigns it the very human traits of friendliness and humility. In Gascony she concludes that "The Genius Loci of these parts must be, and is, a human soul." (p. 134)

[*The Spirit of Rome*] has, conversely, precious little to say about the deity as such. Lee states plainly in the opening pages that she intends to confine herself to the city's physical character. There are a couple of phrasal curtsies to the *genius loci* but no dilate descriptions or discussions. The spirit is implicit here. One derives as one may, with no assist from the author. This is less tasking than it might seem, for these are brief "left-over" notes and no significant unorthodoxies intrude. (p. 135)

In *The Sentimental Traveller* Lee re-emphasizes the god's tendency to caprice: he refuses his presence, sometimes coyly, assuming odd disguises "when indiscreetly invited to prophesy;" and sometimes obstinately, when "scared by elaborate ritual." Not infrequently, as she hinted in *The Enchanted Woods*, caprice can turn to Calvinistic vehemence. The *genius* exhibits elements of Jehovah's jealous wrath in "smiting and humbling," "delighting to flout self-righteous worshippers." Here, Lee also decries the dilettantism of such as Pater, Stevenson and Ruskin, who profane the cult through their eulogies of picturesque squalor and decay. "The Genius of Places," she declares huffily, "is no immoral divinity." Salient, however, is her extension of the *genius'* function to "reveal our real self to ourselves." We carry this ineffable spirit within, "to be brooded over in quiet and void." As in all mystic communion, there occur moments of "aridity," during which we are prone to regard certain well-traveled districts as hackneyed. But this is the fault of "our own eyes

and soul, because we see their commonplace side and the rubbish of everyday detail which we bring with us." In compensation, the power which the *genius* grants us—of seeing things in the shape of our hearts' dream—endues drabness with the stuff of Eden, Arden, and the Hesperides.

Six years later, *The Tower of the Mirrors* . . . repeated the incommunicable, untranslatable message which the god of places poured into Lee's innermost soul, compounded the inconsistency that the *genius* was "after all, largely the spirit of a region's inhabitants," and once more endorsed the spirit's ability to recall similar loved places "like views in opposite mirrors." But no new notions cropped up. . . .

[In *The Golden Keys*], the image of *genius loci* was virtually complete. . . . She unfurls another catalogue of its luminous properties: the philosophy, poetry, music of a nation; the shape of its buildings; the kindly, gracious, childish habits of its people; the winter boxes for birds; the wheels for storks; the be-ribboned Christmas trees; the green garlands over church doors; the dionysiac bunches of grapes on sanctified statues. And she rejoices over its evocative propensities. (pp. 135-36)

In the last sad chapter, Lee mourns the war's devastation of the *genius* cult. "Sacked, burnt, defiled ten thousand times over by millions of indignant wills and by imaginations thirsty for reprisals," the spiritual as well as material aspects of places are beyond revival. "The plough and the salt of oblivion" have transfigured them irrevocably. But her god died hard. (p. 137)

Richard Cary, "Aldous Huxley, Vernon Lee and the 'Genius Loci'," in Colby Library Quarterly, *Series V, No. 6, June, 1960, pp. 128-40.**

PETER GUNN (essay date 1964)

[In *Studies of the Eighteenth Century in Italy*] Vernon Lee treats her subject in a way which is both informative and lively, her attitude appearing to be one of amused tolerance at the antics and foibles of [The Academy of] Arcadians and others; but her understanding of the social conditions, in which, for example, the popular *commedia dell'arte* developed into the easy naturalism of Goldoni's comedies, shows the width of her knowledge and sympathies. (p. 68)

The *Studies of the Eighteenth Century in Italy* is a remarkable book on any count. . . . [The value of the work depends] on the unerring critical insight which led [Vernon Lee] to assess the importance of the various strands that went to constitute the cultural pattern of the eighteenth century in Italy. (p. 74)

The style of the *Eighteenth-Century Studies* varies very much. . . . The language is vigorous, fluent and lively; the ideas expand and overflow into a robust discursiveness. [Vernon Lee's] descriptions of the characters and lives of the musicians and singers, and of the society in which they moved, and which formed their audiences and their inspiration, have a quality often picaresque in its exuberant vitality. Her vocabulary is already extensive, and she shows her delight in the choice of words and the building up of pictorial linguistic effects. . . . We are reminded at times of Carlyle, when, for example, she uses racy staccato mock-heroic sentences to convey the vividness of actuality to her account of historical events. She was not afraid to make powerful generalizing sweeps, sometimes sorely in need of qualification. She was also shamelessly partisan, and as such she was not invariably right or even fair. . . . But the *Eighteenth-Century Studies* is a thoroughly engaging work, expansive, learned, sympathetic; full of intellectual vigour and aesthetic enthusiasm—it has many of the abiding qualities of a minor classic. (pp. 74-5)

Ottilie is the outcome of [Vernon Lee's] researches in the eighteenth-century civilization in Italy; with *The Countess of Albany, The Prince of the Hundred Soups, Winthrop's Adventure* and *Belcaro*, it forms an appendage to her *Eighteenth-Century Studies*. As she explains in her preface, she had responded to the historical essayist's desire to resuscitate in imagination something of the intimacy of the lives of men and women of former times, about whom the historian must be silent by reason of his ignorance of their true thoughts and feelings. And in this instance her desire was to recreate the Germany she knew in her childhood, illuminated now by the knowledge she had gained in her Italian studies. Her use of 'idyll' in the additional title of the book is gently ironic. (pp. 82-3)

[Through a somewhat meagre plot,] Vernon Lee has conveyed a vivid sense of the restless stirrings of the time, when the brittle surface of French culture among the upper classes in Germany was broken into fragments by impulses loosed with the discoveries of Winckelmann and the writings of Lessing, Herder, Schiller, and Goethe. The characters of the brother and sister are drawn with great economy and psychological subtlety. By the choice of such undistinguished persons, set in this little Franconian backwater, Vernon Lee succeeds in revealing immediately and intimately to the reader the reactions of specific men and women to great historical events. Not that Ottilie was conscious of the intellectual and spiritual ferment of the *Sturm-und-Drang* period; her life was too simple and remote for that; and if her brother was indeed aware of it, his character was so formed that some such *dénouement* as befell him was inevitable, irrespective of the events of the time. Yet, in and through the domestic tragedy of this humdrum couple there is borne in on us what it meant to be German living in that revolutionary but ambiguous age, which we see reflected in such literary works as *Laocoon, Werther,* and *Hermann and Dorothea*. *Ottilie* is one of the most subtle and successful of Vernon Lee's stories. (pp. 83-4)

The essays which were gathered together in *Euphorion* were written over a number of years. . . . The reader is immediately struck by the force of the language [Vernon Lee] uses. The 'exuberance', which [John Addington] Symonds noticed in the *Eighteenth-Century Studies,* has changed from what might then have been nothing more than a youthful display of high-spirited rhetoric into something ill-balanced, even morbid. It is not simply a question here of her conscious reaction against the 'pure mindedness' of [John] Ruskin or the over-fastidiousness of [Walter] Pater, though this revolt might constitute an element in her attitude and in the forcefulness of her language. She always delighted in calling a spade a spade, in shocking her contemporaries by giving the name to what many dared not express. In the introductory chapter to *Euphorion* she refers to the 'imperious necessity we sometimes feel to see again and examine, seemingly uselessly, some horrible evil'. Her choice of words, however, reveals a state of mind far different from that of a detached observer. She speaks of 'carnival songs of ribald dirtiness' and 'stories of filthy intrigue and lewd jest'. (pp. 91-2)

Examples can be multiplied . . . but we have here sufficient evidence to mark the significant change in the focus of attention from the Vernon Lee of the *Eighteenth-Century Studies* to the young woman of twenty-eight who brought out *Euphorion* and *Miss Brown*. . . . And in the most profound of the *Euphorion* essays, that on Medieval Love, we find an analysis of human love which reveals much of Vernon Lee's own mind at this time when she first became acknowledged as a writer of international reputation. Her intention in this essay is to show how Dante's passion for Beatrice grew out of the 'passionate but unchaste' love of the middle ages, 'leaving behind the noisesome ashes and soul-enervating vapours of earthly lust'.

As usual, she does not beat about the bush; we are told that the courtly poetry of Provence and Languedoc, the troubadour songs of *Parage* and *la tradition courtoise,* arose from the feudal, barrack-like existence of great ladies surrounded by indigent, womanless youths. . . . In stressing the possibility of these Provençal love-poems being addressed to a real lady . . . , and in diminishing the importance of the mystical, symbolic element which was in the poems from the beginning, Vernon Lee markedly fails to make clear how the expression of passionate love became refined into the language and thought of Dante's *Vita Nuova*. (pp. 92-3)

The most brilliant of the *Euphorion* essays (for to point to defects is not to deny their brilliance) is an attempt to account for the extraordinary discrepancy between the Italy of the late renaissance as envisaged in fascinated horror by the Elizabethan dramatists (with the notable exception of Shakespeare) and the Italy as portrayed by the generality of its own painters, poets and prose writers. (pp. 93-4)

[If] the Elizabethans, with their psychological concern and strongly marked ambivalence towards horror, saw the evils of renaissance Italy, many of the Victorians (forgetful of Shelley) refused to lift their eyes to look that way. To Vernon Lee, then, must be conceded the merit of redirecting her contemporaries' attention. (p. 94)

[In *Miss Brown*] Vernon Lee had set out to write a satire that would expose the 'sins', shams, insipidity and ridiculous artificialities of the so-called 'fleshly school'. What she in fact wrote was a very bad novel. The truth was that she was too emotionally involved to maintain the satire, which becomes confused with observations of her own, often, to our eyes, quite as absurd as that which she is satirizing. She describes one of [Walter] Hamlin's paintings: 'A beautiful naked youth was clutched by a huge, haggard woman, her torn dress licking his body like flames, her lips greedily advancing to his delicate face, which shrank back, like a flower withering in the heat of a furnace.' . . . The writing is so extravagant that passages equally ludicrous abound; all that controlled accuracy of description and feeling, which her best work shows, is melted in the white-hot fury of her scorn and revulsion. The novel is ill-constructed, being dramatically loose, wordy, far too long; it fails as a satire, and as a realistic novel of the development and play of character it does little better. Psychologically Miss Brown may be just possible, but the reader does not come to regard her as a possible human type so much as a lay-figure for Vernon Lee to clothe with her own emotional, moral and sociological preoccupations and prejudices. Hamlin, who is described as a genius, is a wraith-like figure, quite unconvincing. Others of the minor characters are satirically or sympathetically drawn, and are more successful. But the reader feels all the time that Vernon Lee has not called on her imagination to create these characters, but has relied on her observations of members of those circles whom she had met in London, and still more on her own untransmuted background. (pp. 101-02)

[*The Countess of Albany*] is quite excellent; it is a study in disillusionment, with a profound feeling for the period and sureness of psychological touch. . . . *The Countess of Albany* reads like a novel; the story, on the surface, has all that romance requires. The beautiful and intellectual Princess Louise of Stolberg is married for political reasons at the age of nineteen to the morose, besotten, middle-aged Count of Albany, as the Young Pretender was then known. Gone was every trace of the 'so sweet a prince', the Charles Edward Stuart who led the clans to Culloden, and in its place was the harsh, disreputable reality—a drunken, jealous, bullying wreck of a man. Louise d'Albany was rescued from the violence of her husband by the proud, pedantic Count Vittorio Alfieri. . . . Mme d'Albany's later life together with Alfieri was endurable, but it was little more. . . . 'The Countess of Albany, who had been so horribly unhappy with her legitimate husband, must have been rather dreary of soul with her world authorised lover.' Expressed in this way it may seem that Vernon Lee has written a cautionary tale. The truth is otherwise; she has not romanticized where romance no longer existed; the leading characters of her book were precisely such as to lend themselves to this penetrating study in misanthropy. (pp. 110-11)

[The essays on aesthetical questions which make up the two small volumes of *Juvenilia*] reveal a significant change in the orientation of [Vernon Lee's] interests. The attitude to society, and to the place of art in social life, which she came increasingly to adopt, has some resemblance to that held by Tolstoy about the same time, or a little later. 'Art, music, beautiful nature, poetry . . . all this has in reality but one fault: that it is unequally distributed. The pity of it is that we, a small class, monopolize all such consoling things. . . .' Works of art, she maintains, should bring light, understanding and pleasure to those who need them most, the disinherited poor. There was, then, an element of disparagement in her calling these miscellaneous essays on music, literature, and personal recollections '*Juvenilia*'. The sense of the beauty of the natural world and of art, and the wonder which accompanies our appreciation of it, develop with our adolescence. The awareness that all is not well with the world normally comes later, with maturity. But her title is not one entirely of disparagement, for the youthfulness which perceives the beauty, and the maturity on which depends our choice of action in relation to the evil, are in some sense complementary; and as such they should remain throughout our lives, the youthfulness re-appearing in an openmindedness to new impressions and in a perpetual freshness of appreciative outlook. Yet art, if it brings some persons pleasure and enlarges their understanding and sympathy, hardly touches the lives of the vast majority, whose work allows the minority their freedom to enjoy art. This, of course, is (or rather was) one of Tolstoy's most telling points. (p. 111)

At the time of writing *Miss Brown* the moral problems of the relation of the artist to society were in the forefront of [Vernon Lee's] mind. But it was in the two volumes: *Baldwin: being Dialogues on Views and Aspirations* . . . and *Althea: a Second Book of Dialogues on Aspirations and Duties* . . . that we find a steady elaboration of her ideas on the place of the individual in society. The character Baldwin appears in the two sets of dialogues (though far more prominently in the earlier one which goes by his name), and is clearly to be

identified with Vernon Lee herself, in spite of the somewhat elaborate play of semi-mystification of the book's introduction. (p. 112)

Baldwin is not easy reading; it has more than its share of the high seriousness of the period, at times suggesting to the reader the moral purpose of an evangelical tract. The dialogue form allows for the natural shift of thought, but has the disadvantage of leaving many strings untied and many contradictions unsolved. Vernon Lee was not unaware of this, or of her dogmatical tone. A more connected form of exposition might have improved the logic and avoided the gaps and contradictions, but it might not have succeeded better in bringing her views before the educated general-reading public, which was clearly her intention in both *Baldwin* and *Althea*. (p. 116)

One cannot share Vernon Lee's opinion that *Althea* is an immeasurably superior book to *Baldwin*. . . . *Althea* is a further carrying out of the ideas already stated or implicit in *Baldwin*, but without the force, (though perhaps in places with some small addition to the clarity) of the earlier dialogues. At times the language becomes flaccid, and degenerates into something very like the generalities of pious exhortation. (pp. 120-21)

[Vernon Lee's] treatment of art in [*Renaissance Fancies and Studies*] was still what she would have regarded as 'literary', but scattered through them there are suggestions of the turn her mind was taking at the time towards a more restrictedly psychological view of our response to works of art; these essays mark the transition.

The first study, **'The Love of the Saints'**, shows the brilliance of her historical intuition. If throughout her life she ran foul of academic persons—the 'experts'—here, in this account of the change brought about in European thought and feeling, and in the arts expressing them, by the Franciscan movement of the early thirteenth century, we have an example of the advantages gained from the untrammelled play of an imagination such as hers on the more recondite connexions of history. She would have been hard put . . . to *prove* some of her contentions; but the sweep and fertility of ideas, the suggestiveness, of this essay are most remarkable. (p. 142)

It was with her *Genius Loci* type of travel essay that Vernon Lee reached her widest public. . . . [These] little personal essays on various subjects are in the tradition of Hazlitt and Charles Lamb. They are addressed to cultivated, travelled people with time on their hands: nothing separates us from this period so much as the realization that few of us today have the leisure or the type of cultivated, discriminating taste which would allow us fully to catch their particular savour. (pp. 180-81)

Penelope Brandling is a tale, set in the eighteenth century, of a young woman who marries unwittingly into a family of wreckers, living in a lonely house on the Welsh coast. From a psychological point of view this story is more straightforward than is customary with Vernon Lee; it is simply told, and, once it gets going, moves quickly. It has more the quality of an adventure story, with touches of suspense and romance. (p. 187)

[Vernon Lee] was a critic rather than an original thinker; and [the essays in *Gospels of Anarchy*] should be seen as attempts to clarify and evaluate certain ideas which were current in her day: she was a journalist (in no pejorative sense), writing on topics which were occupying the minds of well-read and cultivated contemporaries. With the years, she had modified some of the ideas of *Baldwin* and *Althea*. . . . (p. 188)

Vernon Lee, by the choice of her title, *Gospels of Anarchy*, intends that the essays should be regarded as an examination of some of the works of men whom she classes (somewhat indiscriminately) as anarchists—men, that is, who would not be simply considered as reformers, but rather as disturbing innovators, and more often than not, iconoclasts. She deals with such writers, thinkers and scientists as Stirner, Nordau, Lombroso, Nietzsche, Ruskin, Emerson, Tolstoy, Ibsen, William James, and H. G. Wells. These essays differ from those in the volumes which followed them, *Vital Lies . . .* , in being immensely readable. *Gospels of Anarchy . . .* abounds in pithy and pregnant observations. . . . (p. 189)

Vital Lies is a much inferior book to *Gospels of Anarchy;* it is not surprising that it largely fell on deaf ears. It is repetitive, tendentious, at times grossly unfair; it falls between two stools, being inadequate in logical rigour to what would be required by philosophers, and yet unlikely (from its lack of clarity and constructive development) to appeal to the ordinary educated reader. In parts it consists of roughly thrown together notes and somewhat coy comment—only too often her intellectual roguishness, her verbal sallies *ad hominem,* get out of hand and become most painfully arch. (p. 197)

In [*Satan the Waster*] Vernon Lee gave perhaps the most complete expression of the many sides of her complex personality. *Satan the Waster* is polemical writing at its best. Gone are all the one-sidedness, arrogance and particularity of her earliest pacifist writings, and in their place there now appears a universality, born of her understanding and her compassion; it is a view which combines humanity, sympathy, simplicity and humility in an eloquent persuasiveness. (p. 208)

To readers of a certain type of mind—those who find pleasure in the psychological revivescence of the feelings and emotions of people in other places and other times—the short stories of Vernon Lee will always appeal. This extraordinary ability of hers to 'feel herself into' (*empathetically*) a remote historical period, with an intensity of realization of the sentiments and passions of those then living, had been characteristic of her from childhood. It seemed that the *actuality* of the past was often, with her, more potent than that of the present. Henry James had commented on her uncanny power of evoking the very warmth and scents of life as it went on in Italian towns and countryside. Her imagination was of the sensuous kind: the colours (even the changing temperatures) of the landscape, the architectural shapes and textures, the sound of the movement of silken dresses, the peculiar pitch and timbre of voices—her writing conveys all these qualities. And her understanding of the thoughts, moods, and ephemeral feelings of people in past times was no less precisely revived. (p. 225)

Music and its Lovers [is] the last of Vernon Lee's major works. . . . It is not so much a study of music as of the effects which music has on its lovers—'the emotional and imaginative responses to music'. Her observations led her to make a fundamental distinction between two main categories of responses; those of the persons whom she called '*Listeners*', as opposed to those she referred to as '*Hearers*'. 'The conclusion became obvious that there existed two different modes of responding to music, each of which was claimed

to be the only one by those in whom it was habitual. One may be called *listening* to music; the other *hearing*, with lapses into *over-hearing* it. Listening implied the most active attention, moving along every detail of composition and performance. . . . On the other hand, '*hearing* music . . . is not simply a lesser degree of the same mental activity, but one whose comparative poverty from the musical side is eked out and compensated by other elements. . . .' (pp. 228-29)

Music and its Lovers is an immensely valuable book. . . . (p. 229)

> *Peter Gunn, in his* Vernon Lee: Violet Paget, 1856-1935 *(© Oxford University Press 1964; reprinted by permission of Oxford University Press), Oxford University Press, London, 1964, 244 p.*

VINETA COLBY (essay date 1970)

[Vernon Lee's] only fiction of any enduring value is a small group of short stories, mainly fantasies and ghost stories. . . . During her lifetime her fame—more accurately her reputation, because she never achieved any really popular success—rested on travel writing, essays, and studies of eighteenth-century Italian literature and music. Yet in a sense almost everything that Vernon Lee wrote bore the stamp of fiction. She did not write narrative often, but she made history, biography, and aesthetics accessible to her readers by using the techniques of prose fiction. Her failure to reach. . . [a wide public] is easily explained. She was too far removed. . . intellectually from the public. She was unaware of the precise nature of their tastes and needs. But she worked tirelessly to educate and to enlighten. . . . [Vernon Lee] approached the novel as an art form rather than as a medium for public expression and communication. Paradoxically, she was at once a puritan preaching a strict morality and an aesthete reveling in the absolute moral detachment of pure art. (pp. 235-36)

Vernon Lee indeed was more thoroughly committed to art than was any other woman of her generation. She practiced aesthetics consciously and professionally. Everything that she studied (and whatever she studied she tackled with seriousness and professional competence—art, music, literature, history, philosophy, and psychology) became the material of her aesthetics. Not surprisingly, therefore, she viewed the novel as an art form in an age in which formal criticism of it was only just beginning to emerge. Along with her friend and mentor Henry James, she was one of the first to write criticism (rather than reviews) of fiction, to analyze technique, to examine the psychology not only of the writer and his characters but of the reader who responds to the novel. Though her own novels are negligible, what she thought and wrote *about* the novel is today recognized as sound and significant. (p. 237)

[Lee] had from the outset a reverence for art that was nothing short of religious in its intensity. But simultaneously, and for reasons so deeply rooted in her character that it is difficult to do more than merely speculate about them, she also had a bristling distrust of "pure" aesthetics and a downright distaste for aestheticism and "art for art's sake." Operating always within her was a kind of puritanical vigilance far more subtle and refined, thanks to her European background, than that of the English philistine—but persistent and persuasive. Art is good, not because it is good in itself (though she believed this) but because its effects on us are good. It arouses our better instincts, exhilarates and stimulates us to loftier thought and nobler action. Vernon Lee pondered long and deeply on the subject. Over the years, although she altered many of her views, she never abandoned this fundamental position.

Her puritanism betrays itself the instant she raises the question of the purpose and value of art, and that question is the essence of everything that she writes about art. "The contemplation of beautiful shape is . . . favoured by its pleasurableness, and such contemplation . . . lifts our perceptive and empathic activities, that is to say a large part of our intellectual and moral life, on to a level which can only be spiritually, organically, and in so far, morally beneficial." Art is therefore socially useful, producing happiness, spiritual refreshment, and tending "to inhibit most of the instincts whose superabundance can jeopardise individual and social existence." (p. 238)

[In emphasizing] the constructive, affirmative purposes of art, Vernon Lee in no way dilutes its purer values. Commenting on the spiritual evolution of her friend Walter Pater, she noted precisely the course on which she too was embarked:

> He began as an aesthete and ended as a moralist. By faithful and self-restraining cultivation of the sense of harmony, he appears to have risen from the perception of visible beauty to the knowledge of beauty of the spiritual kind, both being expressions of the same perfect fittingness to an ever more intense and various and congruous life.

If, however, the evolution from aesthete to moralist produced a narrowing of sensibility or any restriction or limitation upon the province of art itself, Vernon Lee would have deplored it. But as she traced its course, and demonstrated it in her own development, this heightened moral sense actually extended one's appreciation. (p. 239)

There is no element of compromise in the thinking of Vernon Lee. She was often superbly wrong-headed and unyielding. But her puritan aesthetic was a logically based position, not the result of any timid yearning to make art useful and respectable. She clearly affirmed the independence of the "Beautiful" from mere codes of right and wrong, rejecting, for example, Tolstoy's condemnation in *What Is Art?* of all art that does not serve an immediate moral purpose, with the argument that art "like science itself, like philosophy, like every great healthy human activity, has a right to live and a duty to fulfill, quite apart from any help it may contribute to the enforcement of a moralist's teachings." The question of moral good or bad is irrelevant. Beauty, she wrote, is "aesthetically good . . . pure, complete, egotistic; it has no other value than its being beautiful."

So firm is Vernon Lee's faith in art that she holds it essentially incorruptible and, therefore, divine. "For even if beauty is united to perverse fashions, and art (as with Baudelaire and the decadents) employed to adorn sentiments of maniacs and gaolbirds, the beauty and the art remain sound." Her fundamental optimism is the fruit of faith: "Art is a much greater and more cosmic thing than the mere expression of man's thoughts or opinions on any one subject. . . . Art is the expression of man's life, of his mode of being, of his relations with the universe, since it is, in fact, man's inarticulate answer to the universe's unspoken message." (pp. 240-41)

With art conceived in such lofty terms as these, inevitably Vernon Lee met practical difficulties when she confronted the problems of writing criticism of the novel. The art form that she conceives as almost a way of life and of faith is painting, followed closely by architecture, sculpture, and music—all in the grand classic sense, though not necessarily in the classic style. The chief problem was the always elusive aesthetic question of the nature of beauty. The aim of art, she insists, is to produce the beautiful. The more "abstract" arts of architecture and music (i.e., those not primarily concerned with imitating reality) are those which most directly produce the desired effects of beauty. . . . Literature lacks the purity, the precision, the definiteness, the "massive certainty" of the other arts. It is, she once declared, "a mode of merely imparting opinion or stirring up emotion, the instrument not merely of the artist but of the thinker, the historian, the preacher, and the pleader."

Such dogmatic pronouncements are characteristic of Vernon Lee, but they represent only one side of the coin. Read in context they reflect no disparagement of literature, only a kind of dogged determination to define precisely the boundaries of the arts. In removing literature, specifically the novel, from the realm of the aesthetic, she was not excluding it from the realm of art but simply from the Beautiful. . . . At one point, writing of literature as "infinitely less aesthetic" than the other arts, she conscientiously adds a footnote: "By *aesthetic* I do not mean *artistic*. I mean . . . that which relates to the contemplation of such aspects as we call 'beautiful' whether in art or in nature." The novel is only slightly less artistic than the other arts, and if a value must be placed upon it, one must also acknowledge its ethical function. There is more than a hint of puritan conscience in her remark: "The novel has less value in art, but more importance in life. . . . Hence, I say, that although the novel . . . is not as artistic, or valuable as painting, or sculpture, or music, it is practically more important and more noble."

The novel, then, needs no excuse or apology. Vernon Lee shared the outrage of her contemporaries at the "excesses" of the French novel. . . . What she mainly objects to in Balzac, for example, is is not questionable morality but a tendency she detects in many other French novelists as well to probe character too clinically and microscopically, to concentrate on merely one aspect of character or of society rather than on the flux and complexity of life. Thus Balzac isolates one peculiarity in Père Goriot, "the Bump of Philoprogenitiveness. The rest of the brain, one might say, has been cut away.". . . It is the novelists whom we grasp intuitively, for their compassion, their total identification with their characters—Tolstoy, Stendhal, Thackeray—that Vernon Lee most admires. "The novel of this school seems not written but lived." The analytic novel may be more precise and perfect in art because the novelist has almost scientific control over his subject. But the "synthetic" novel (in the sense of bringing together feeling *and* form) gives us the real sense of life.

This is the subjective approach to the novel. Yet Vernon Lee's criticism is as minutely analytical as the type of Balzacian characterization which she disliked. But here she was dealing with technique rather than with character. Her essays on the writing of fiction, published over some forty years and collected . . . in *The Handling of Words*, are today read with appreciation by students of the novel because they are pioneer attempts in the close literary analysis of selected texts.

A great deal of the book, to be sure, is dogmatic and wrong-headed. She writes as if the craft of fiction were a game, with rules and percentage points to be awarded for ''good'' or ''bad'' technique. (pp. 241-44)

Although Vernon Lee objected to minute analysis as a technique of art, she favored it as a technique of criticism, a tool for the study of art itself. All her aesthetics is based on exhaustive study of the psychological reactions of the viewer to art, the listener to music, the reader to literature. . . .

The essays in *The Handling of Words* examine the specific techniques by which the novelist manipulates the mind of his reader—techniques of construction (point of view, for example) and language (quite literally the choice of words, hence the title of the book). Because the writer, unlike the painter, sculptor, or musician, must work with only the fragments of consciousness—memory, association, moods—he must carefully select among those fragments so as best to play upon the mind of his reader. (p. 245)

The most interesting sections of *The Handling of Words* are those in which she demonstrates her critical principles by analyzing specific passages (of about 500 words each) chosen at random from a variety of types of narrative. Long before the formal study of semantics and the ''communication arts'' Vernon Lee was exploring questions of connotative meanings, patterns of association, the effects of sentence length and prose rhythms. Her studies reflect a certain amount of pedantry, mere adjective counting, but in the main they are surprisingly suggestive. (p. 246)

Vernon Lee's critical judgments are never tainted with humility or false modesty. She found lazy writing in Hardy (though she concludes her analysis of this passage by conceding its appropriateness to the overall effect of dreamy, sensual life in nature that he was striving for), carelessness and fatuousness in Landor, deficient logic and haste in Kipling. She even dared to improve upon the writer whom she most admired and imitated, Walter Pater. . . . But Vernon Lee's tendency to carp, her abrasiveness of expression, her dogmatism, and an irritating habit of repetition weaken the really perceptive observations in *The Handling of Words*. One is tempted to see in her strictures on other and far better writers all her own manifold weaknesses. (pp. 247-48)

[An uncompromising oracular pose] dominates the unfortunate *Miss Brown*. Having surveyed the arts in London for two or three seasons, Vernon Lee felt entirely competent to judge them decadent and to warn of ominous things to come. The novel is a remarkable demonstration of her ambivalence: the aesthete writing knowledgeably about pure art, the puritan sternly judging the moral implications of certain types of art. . . . *Miss Brown* might be a typical Victorian novel—a beautiful but poor heroine rescued from the misery of servant-life by a well-to-do poet and artist who educates and ultimately marries her. There is a sinister villainess who lures the hero away temporarily and a stalwart rival suitor for the heroine, but the intrigue, having padded out the requisite number of volumes, is evaporated by the inevitable happy ending. This, however, is merely the barest outline of the plot. The readers who picked up the somber-looking volumes were soon plunged into a scene of absurdity and affectation, of posturing poets and painters, and of more sinister things—a sensual adultress, drug addiction, alcoholism, and various unnamed and unnamable debaucheries. The fact that the scene was London, the time immediately contemporary, and

most of the characters readily identifiable as members of the very circles in which Vernon Lee was moving, added shock and sensation. (pp. 254-55)

There seems little doubt of the high-mindedness of Vernon Lee's intention. She did not mean to offend; she meant only to castigate what she termed ''the cheap-and-shop shoddy aestheticism'' of pre-Raphaelitism. . . . Her criticism of the pre-Raphaelites, however, is based not on . . . merely superficial mannerisms, but on their fundamental philosophy of ''art for art's sake,'' their ''moral indifference'' to society and its problems. Early in the novel the conflict is anticipated when the hero, Walter Hamlin, an Oxford educated aesthete-poet-painter, tells the heroine, Anne Brown: ''The world is getting uglier and uglier outside us; we must, out of the material bequeathed to us by former generations, build for ourselves a little world within the world, a world of beauty, where we may live with our friends and keep alive whatever small sense of beauty and nobility still remains to us.'' Miss Brown, at first under his influence, gradually begins to think independently. She criticizes his poetry for its affectation: ''. . . the poetry of pure beauty sickened her.'' When she calls his attention to the poverty and misery of the cottagers on his country estate and urges him to build a factory to give them work, he objects on aesthetic grounds and reaffirms his decadent philosophy of the ugliness and hopelessness of everyday life.

Through this puritanical zeal of the plainly named Miss Brown and her radical M. P. cousin Richard Brown, Vernon Lee herself speaks, wagging her finger and banging her fist, preaching her own brand of idealistic socialism. If art were properly used, it would serve society, not scorn it. (pp. 256-57)

Vineta Colby, ''The Puritan Aesthete: Vernon Lee,'' in her The Singular Anomaly: Women Novelists of the Nineteenth Century *(reprinted by permission of New York University Press; copyright © 1970 by New York University), New York University Press, 1970, pp. 235-304.**

HORACE GREGORY (essay date 1971)

When I began my reading of Vernon Lee I vaguely felt an affinity, difficult to define, between her writings and those of Virginia Woolf's. (p. 103)

We must approach the question of affinity between these two writers by an unfamiliar path, and admit before we start that they had different, and, at times, contrasting minds and sensibilities. Virginia Woolf deliberately employed common sense whenever she spoke of ghosts, and as she did so a matter-of-fact, stiff-backed manner commands her prose as though she had been on the point of saying ''nonsense'' loudly to her hearers. She had no patience with, no time for wayward flights of superstition. As the reader of her stories will soon discover, ghosts are boldly listed in Vernon Lee's dramatis personae. They are the instruments of fate, of the furies that cross the careers of her characters. They are among the signs of evil—and active evil—that possess the unwary; they haunt the scene; they invade the body and half-innocent imaginations of guilty souls. Here is ground where the two writers seem to part decisively: yet the moment one admits this difference, what of Virginia Woolf's *Orlando*? The line of difference persists but the theme of possession remains; there *is* an affinity in imaginative quality between the two writers as though their agreement not to meet had been one of making a separate invasion of a like territory of fiction.

This invasion of the same terrain by Virginia Woolf and Vernon Lee comes to light in her essay on *Limbo*; a masterly little essay it is, yet it is, like many of her occasional pieces, too short a ledge on which to rest the weight of a posthumous reputation. Her essay reflects among other things her thoughts on the nature of genius which was a subject that often attracted the critical sensibility of Virginia Woolf. (pp. 103-04)

[Vernon Lee] had decided that genius was organic and had nothing to do with machinery, that it was a living organism, that genius itself was immortal but men of genius were mortal—which was a sensible though brilliant middle step in her inquiry. Within her view of genius Vernon Lee placed the element of charm, which is not the whole of genius by any means, but is one of those elements too frequently forgotten by the majority of twentieth-century critics. She had no sentimental regard for the mute inglorious Miltons of Thomas Gray; to her they were mute and inglorious because they lack the charm, the spell-invoking quality that has always been an enduring element of poetic genius, and following her lead through Dante's mention of Unchristianed Babies she found a way of considering the charm of youth. (p. 104)

The difference is that Vernon Lee never stressed (while Virginia Woolf employed) the techniques and sensibility of symbolism; in this difference the line of distinction between the two writers is clear enough for anyone to read, to understand. In passages of prose where Virginia Woolf has diffused her brilliance and does not arrive at a logical decision, parallel passages in Vernon Lee's prose show the elder woman exerting a conscious will to make up her mind. At worst Vernon Lee's style was florid in the manner of the late Victorians who with less wisdom than intuition followed in the esthetic footsteps of Walter Pater, yet Vernon Lee never lost her way in these dubious pastures for more than the briefest of holiday excursions. . . . (p. 105)

Within the twenty-five years after [the publication of] *Studies of the Eighteenth Century in Italy*, a number of short novels and stories appeared under the pen name of Vernon Lee. The first was a by-product of her *Studies, The Prince of a 100 Soups*, a narrative inspired by her readings in Carlo Gozzi, the tales of E.T.A. Hoffmann, and the Italian comedy of masks. . . . Today this little extravaganza reveals no more than a glittering flow of narration and girlish, high-spirited facility; Vernon Lee had no gift for the writing of fantastic comedy; her wit, her gifts were of another kind; nor could she present her modern "problem novel," her *Miss Brown* in enduring prose. These early books were fluttering demonstrations of a talent for writing; they are of interest only to the biographer who may wish to pierce the veil of Vernon Lee's personality by way of reading her early ventures into fiction. Yet among these first attempts. . .she did succeed in drawing upon the true sources of her gifts. But if genius can find a definition within writing of less than monumental scope, genius was hers, and something more than the flicker of its presence came into being in a short novel *Ottilie*, and a biography *The Countess of Albany*.

Ottilie has for its subtitle "An Eighteenth Century Idyl." There was probably a slight hint of irony in Vernon Lee's choice of "Idyl" to describe the nature of her provincial

romance set within an imaginary Franconia a hundred years before *Ottilie* was written. It would be easy to say that its young author was all too obviously an enthusiastic reader of the *Tales of Hoffmann*, the *Sorrows of Werther*, and of *Adolphe* by Benjamin Constant. That she was, and her romance does not disguise its literary heritage. But it was also written as though its author had never read an English novel; the romance could have been presented as a rarely felicitous translation from French, Italian, or German and few critics would have suspected a hoax. In her preface of 1883 Vernon Lee laid claim only to being an essayist, not a writer of romantic tales or novels; she confessed to being haunted by the spirits of men and women whose names she had read in historical researches and could not dispel their presence in her imagination; this she insisted was the *raison d'être* of *Ottilie*.

So much for the prudence and candor with which Vernon Lee submitted her romance of *Ottilie* to the public. As to why it can be reread today with pleasure, interest, and a sense of rediscovery is another matter. Up to the moment that she wrote her idyl no writer in English of the nineteenth century with the exceptions of three Americans, Edgar Allan Poe, Fitz-James O'Brien and Herman Melville and one Anglo-Irishman, Sheridan Le Fanu, had entered so deeply into the psychology of incestuous human relationships as Vernon Lee. *Ottilie*, in its external calmness of confessing a brotherly-sisterly relationship of guilt and love is scarcely a Gothic novel; her manner of presenting the theme of possession, of one psyche haunted by another, is too serene to reflect the fires of hell which burn so violently in the pages of Hoffmann and of Poe. . . . The three figures in the romance are possessed by forces greater than themselves; none escapes the working of destiny. Within its genre we have had few examples in twentieth-century fiction to equal *Ottilie*: to find them we must turn to *The Blood of the Walsungs* of Thomas Mann, to *Les Enfants Terribles* of Jean Cocteau. (pp. 108-09)

Not the least of [Vernon Lee's] stories is *Prince Alberic and the Snake Lady*, a story within a story and which has at its center a legend that echoes the tales brought from the East into southern Europe by the Crusaders to the Holy Land. The snake in the legend is of an origin which is of the East and is not to be confused unwittingly with the serpent of Eden's garden. This snake descends from the benevolent dragons of the East and is the heiress of Good, now transformed in the Christian world to Evil. It is this mutation of the snake lady and her magic qualities, compounded of both Good and Evil which endows Vernon Lee's version of the legend with its undercurrents of inherited fears and ecstasies. Beneath the charms of what seem to be no more than a Gothic fairy tale, deeper realities exist, and behind their psychological revelations, lies the conflict of Western taboos against the religions of the East. No one has told the story of the snake-dragon with more persuasion than Vernon Lee.

A foil to the legend of Prince Alberic is a fifteenth-century story, *A Wedding Chest*. . . . This sanguinary little romance is filled with the bloodstained shadows of fifteenth-century Italian courtship and revenge; and lively ghosts they are, breathing the passions of holy and profane love with the violence of John Webster's tragedies. . . . Vernon Lee's tales and romances are possessed by genii of time and place as well as the personality of their author. It is through her eyes that a present generation of readers at home or abroad may set their blue guidebooks aside to rediscover Europe. And if the Italy they find is unlike any other Italy in English fiction, it is because no English writer since Vernon Lee (and I am aware of the Italys of Henry James, E. M. Forster, Norman Douglas, and D. H. Lawrence, all excellent of their various kinds) has peopled Italy with such enduring ghosts and shades. One sees them glimmering in Rome's fountains, one sees them pace the waters of the Arno, and hears echoes of their voices across the Grand Canal; they are moonlit visitors. (pp. 110-12)

Horace Gregory, "The Romantic Inventions of Vernon Lee" (1971), in his Spirit of Time and Place: Collected Essays of Horace Gregory *(reprinted with the permission of W. W. Norton & Company, Inc.; copyright © 1973 by Horace Gregory), Norton, 1973, pp. 100-12.*

JULIA BRIGGS   (essay date 1977)

Vernon Lee's fame as a writer of ghost stories rests on a single volume, *Hauntings*. . . . The first tale, **'Amour Dure'**, gives characteristic expression to her romantic passion for the high Renaissance. It is almost [Robert Browning's] 'My Last Duchess' in reverse. Begun as a historical novel entitled **'Medea da Carpi'**, the story concerns a coldly ambitious woman whom men found irresistible, a version of Lucrezia Borgia or Vittoria Corambona. . . . [Vernon Lee] ingeniously rewrote it in the form of a diary of one Spiridion Trepka, a Polish historian who takes his place as the last lover over whom the duchess, now three hundred years dead, exerts her fatal fascination. The story is neatly constructed, and the device of the diary works well, allowing the reader to remain one step ahead of the narrator. The weakest moment is the melodramatic climax in which the Pole is warned of his danger by Medea's earlier betrayed lovers. Although the experience is inevitably romanticized, the sensation of being deeply attracted to a portrait or piece of writing of another age is common enough to endow a certain conviction. (pp. 119-20)

'A Wicked Voice' effectively begins with the examination of an engraving of an eighteenth-century singer, Zaffirino. If **'Amour Dure'** belongs to the world of Browning's 'My Last Duchess' or *The Ring and the Book,* this tale portrays the society of 'A Toccata of Galuppi's'. . . .

The tale of a musician's pact with the Devil is traditionally told of violinists rather than singers and, as if to meet this objection, the second paragraph of **'A Wicked Voice'** begins 'O cursed human voice, violin of flesh and blood'. In conception this story may owe something to E.T.A. Hoffmann's elaborate 'Rath Krespel', where the heroine's uniquely beautiful voice is mystically linked with the tones of a wonderful violin. (p. 120)

Zaffirino's sapphire confers on him supernatural powers, of a sexual, as well as a musical nature, so that 'the first song could make any woman turn pale. . .the second make her madly in love, while the third song could kill her off on the spot, kill her for love, there under his eyes, if he only felt so inclined'. Zaffirino is in fact a male version of Medea, possessing the same cruel and sadistic attitude to the opposite sex. The scene in which he watches the Procuratessa die during the course of his last song (described twice, since it is seen first in a dream, and later re-enacted in a haunted house) is similar in its self-indulgent lingering to the scene where Medea watches the Prinzivalle tortured to death. Fur-

ther points of comparison with **'Amour Dure'** become apparent when it is remembered that the male narrator's passion for a voice in **'A Wicked Voice'** would more logically attach itself to a woman's. If Zaffirino is regarded as an essentially female rôle, it becomes clear that three of the four stories in *Hauntings* are narrated in the first person by a creative male attracted to a cold and sadistic female who is unobtainable, either because she is dead, or in love with the dead. The fascination exerted by the seductive beauty of the dead is one of the obsessive elements in Vernon Lee's fantasies. (pp. 120-21)

If the compulsive elements in her writing are in some ways a weakness, they are in other respects a source of strength. The cruel lady may represent a fascinating if forbidden ideal, but the imaginative narrator usually shares his creator's vitality. In **'A Wicked Voice'**, the story is told by a Wagnerian composer who had been working on an opera of 'Ogier the Dane', but is now doomed to compose trite eighteenth-century melodies—a genuinely comic invention in an otherwise melodramatic story. In **'Oke of Okehurst'** (originally entitled **'A Phantom Lover'**) the narrator is an artist whose personality is partly based on that of the portrait painter, John Sargent, her life-long friend. What remains in the memory even after the cold heroine and her murdered cavalier poet, Lovelock, have been forgotten, are the fine evocations of the Jacobean house in its rainswept Kentish setting, a scene that might well have appealed to a landscape painter. The tale has an extra twist in that the narrator refuses to accept a supernatural explanation. He himself has seen nothing, and is doubtful whether anyone else has, though his account does ample justice to the sinister atmosphere of Okehurst. Technically speaking, therefore, the story conforms to the 'psychological' prototype, that is, the reader is left uncertain whether to accept a rational explanation or to believe that the events had a supernatural origin. The narrative unfolds at a leisurely pace, with a wealth of small incidents that emphasize the similarities between the present-day Alice Oke, and her seventeenth-century ancestress whose portrait, a treasured heirloom, somehow challenges the painter-narrator to surpass it. Vernon Lee treats the concept of the 'phantom lover' with delicacy, and the implausible denouement with sufficient speed to make this the best of her ghost stories.

Running through *Hauntings* is the theme of the fascination that the dead exert over the living, the power that past beauty, whether of face or voice, can command, even after its own decay. Henry James's early story, 'The Last of the Valerii', enacts a similar infatuation with the antique world, but his conception of the ghost story was in general much less narrow than Vernon Lee's. A small group of his stories represent his sense of self-discovery as a European in terms of a not unwelcome confrontation with a ghostly past, but these are only aspects of a much wider-ranging achievement in the genre. . . . Vernon Lee, on the other hand, used this medium primarily as an expression of her response to the past, where she found release from the behavioural constraints that her own times imposed upon women who, like herself, were over-endowed with masculine traits, longed for emancipation and preferred their own sex to men. Once through the magic doors, she could imagine herself as a man, or at least a woman as coldly and dangerously beautiful as Medea or Alice Oke.

In the preface to *Hauntings* she admitted that she had little interest in the ghost story when it was set in the drearily familiar world, 'for what use has it got if it land us in Islington or Shepherd's Bush?' She rejected modern urban life in favour of a mode closer to romantic historical fiction. . . . Her ghost stories reflect the attractions of such a past, washed clean of its trivializing prosiness. If much of her work was escapist in tendency, its strength lay in her recognition of the power of the escapist impulse, and with it, the power of history to obsess, even to possess the writer, so that confrontation with the dead becomes the desired, the logical outcome of his research. For such a dedicated historian the ghost story might express not only a sense of the continuing vitality of the past, but his profound desire to experience it personally, at first hand. Thus normal caution is overcome and. . .the haunted pursues the haunter. (pp. 121-23)

> *Julia Briggs, "A Sense of the Past: Henry James and Vernon Lee," in her* Night Visitors: The Rise and Fall of the English Ghost Story *(© 1977 by Julia Briggs; reprinted by permission of Faber and Faber Ltd.), Faber and Faber, 1977, pp. 111-23.**

ADDITIONAL BIBLIOGRAPHY

"Music and Comedy in Eighteenth Century Italy." *The Dial* XLV, No. 539 (1 December 1908): 401-04.
    Review of later edition of *Studies of the Eighteenth Century in Italy* containing a preface by Vernon Lee, giving much background on art and music of the period.

Fremantle, Anne. "Vernon Lee, a Lonely Lady." *Commonweal* LX, No. 12 (25 June 1954): 297-99.
    Biographical sketch and brief review of *The Snake Lady.*

Lewis, Wyndham. "A Lady's Response to Machiavelli." In his *The Lion and the Fox; The Role of the Hero in the Plays of Shakespeare,* pp. 111-14. London: G. Richards, 1927.
    Examines Vernon Lee's attitude in *Euphorion* toward Renaissance figures in Italy and England.

"Anthropomorphic Aesthetics." *The Nation* 95, No. 2455 (18 July 1912): 66-7.
    Review of *Beauty and Ugliness* that compares the aesthetic theories of Lee with those of Bernard Berenson, Karl Groos, and Theodor Lipps.

Ormond, Leonee. "Vernon Lee As a Critic of Aestheticism in *Miss Brown.*" *Colby Library Quarterly* IX, No. 3 (September 1970): 131-54.
    Background on the aesthetic movement in English literature satirized in *Miss Brown,* and an examination of this work as a roman à clef.

"The Handling of Words." *The Times Literary Supplement,* No. 1105 (22 March 1923): 185-86.
    Considers "curious and perverse" Vernon Lee's idea that literary art consists of "the manipulation of the mind of the reader," while approving of her stylistic analysis of the specific authors she examines.

Wharton, Edith. "Life and Letters." In her *A Backward Glance,* pp. 112-42. New York, London: D. Appleton-Century Co., 1934.*
    Reminiscence calling Vernon Lee a "highly cultivated and brilliant woman."

Jonas (Lauritz Idemil) Lie

1833-1908

Norwegian novelist, dramatist, poet, and journalist.

Lie is as important to the development of the Norwegian novel as Ibsen is to the Norwegian drama. A prolific novelist, Lie introduced many of the developments of European literature to Norway. Although he achieved early success as a novelist of the sea, his later work is more specifically concerned with the problems of marriage and family life, and the psychology of human behavior.

Lie spent much of his childhood in the northern coastal city of Tromø, where months of continuous daylight alternate with months of unrelieved darkness. This mysterious atmosphere and the superstitious folklore of the region permeate the mood of much of Lie's fiction and affect the consciousness of many of his characters. After several years in his family's traditional profession of law, disastrous financial speculation and subsequent bankruptcy caused Lie to turn to writing for his livelihood.

Encouraged by his friend, the novelist Bjørnstjerne Bjørnson, and aided by the indispensable editorial advice of his wife, Thomasine, Lie published his critically praised first novel, *Den fremsynte* (*The Visionary; or, Pictures from Nordland*). This work, which has many romantic elements, such as a fey hero tortured by clairvoyant visions, the exotic setting of northern Norway, and an idealistic belief in the essential goodness of people, was hailed as a refreshing change from the prevailing realism of contemporary Norwegian literature. Thomasine had an important influence on Lie's literary career: by cutting excessive digression and curbing unwieldy story lines she helped to bring form and structure to Lie's work.

With the enthusiastic reception of *Lodsen og hans hustru* (*The Pilot and His Wife*), a simple sea tale underscoring his belief in the necessity of trust and honesty in marriage, Lie was granted a government pension for life. Thereafter he lived abroad, mostly in Paris, and rarely returned to his homeland. During his career Lie experimented with the techniques of several literary schools, such as romanticism, naturalism, and symbolism; however, his mature artistic method culminated in a highly sophisticated impressionistic style. Intrigued by the impressionist movement in art, Lie began to apply its methods to his prose, achieving what Alrik Gustafson has called "impressionistic realism."

His developing style was complemented by new interests in subject matter. Influenced by the naturalistic precepts of Zola, Lie abandoned the romantic, rather sentimental presentation of Norwegian life in his early novels for realistic examinations of the stifling provincialism of the middle classes. *Familjen paa Gilje* (*The Family at Gilje*), considered by many to be his masterpiece, is notable for its recreation of bourgeois family life in the nineteenth century, and for its psychological portraits. The social and political concerns of his countrymen Ibsen and Bjørnson heightened Lie's awareness of the disenfranchised in society, yet he refused to become embroiled in the popular causes of the day. While many of his portrayals of marriage and family life are critical of rigid conventionality, Lie is essentially conservative.

An interest in the experiments of the symbolists inspired Lie's return to the supernatural concerns of *The Visionary*. However, a new understanding of what he called "the troll in man" replaced his former idealistic view of human nature. In *Trold* (*Weird Tales from Northern Seas*), fantastic creatures and supernatural phenomena symbolize repressed desires, unrestrained instinct, and existential dread in the psyches of men and women.

Although Lie is not widely read outside Norway, and his resistance to the dictates of any single literary school or political doctrine dismays many critics, his various experiments did much to vitalize the Norwegian novel.

PRINCIPAL WORKS

Den fremsynte (novel) 1870
   [*The Visionary; or, Pictures from Nordland*, 1894]
Tremasteren "Fremtiden" eller liv nordpaa (novel)
   1872
   [*The Barque "Future"; or, Life in the Far North*, 1879]
Lodsen og hans hustru (novel) 1874
   [*The Pilot and His Wife*, 1876]

Thomas Ross (novel) 1878
Adam Schrader (novel) 1879
Rutland (novel) 1880
Gaa paa! (novel) 1882
Familjen paa Gilje (novel) 1883
　[*The Family at Gilje*, 1920]
Livsslaven (novel) 1883
　[*One of Life's Slaves*, 1895]
Kommandørens døtre (novel) 1886
　[*The Commodore's Daughters*, 1892]
Onde magter (novel) 1890
Trold (short stories) 1891-92
　[*Weird Tales from Northern Seas*, 1893]
Niobe (novel) 1893
　[*Niobe*, 1897]
Dyre Rein (novel) 1896
Ostenfor sol, vestenfor maane og bagom Babylons taarn!
　(novel) 1905

THE SPECTATOR (essay date 1874)

Den Fremsynte was a very powerful little book; it introduced one to the streets of Christiania, during a violent winter storm. . . . [We] are taken up to the Arctic coast of Norway, into the neighborhood of the Lofoden Islands, where the hero, a nervous, morbid youth, afflicted with second-sight, and the only son of an insane mother, is brought up, under influences the most sinister and dreary possible. The character of this youth is worked out in a manner so masterly, that the sketch has a positive psychological and physiological value. . . . The descriptions of the wild and unfamiliar life in the fjords, the traces of superstition still remaining among the inhabitants, the desolate and even appalling character of the scenery, all is made use of to increase the impressiveness of what is truly a very nobly-written study of human life in one of its more anomalous forms.

The next important work of Jonas Lie was a much larger novel, *Tremasteren "Fremtid," "The Three-master 'Future'; or, Life in High Latitudes,"* an excellently studied story of seafaring life. . . . [However] a still longer book has appeared, in which no external influence is noticeable, a book which stamps Jonas Lie finally as a man of independent genius. It is, as its predecessors were, a story of "sorrow on the sea."

Lodsen og hans Hustru; or, *"The Pilot and his Wife,"* begins in the reflective manner peculiar to Lie. He loves to show you at the outset the condition into which the characters he is about to develop found themselves late in their story. Then, having imprinted a single photographic picture on the memory, he returns to the beginning, and shows by what processes they entered upon the state in which you have seen them. Finally, he tells you what followed that state also. (p. 1370)

The analysis of character in this book is of a remarkably subtle kind. The three principal persons, each noble in a certain way, but so differently constituted, are incessantly throwing one another into relief, and the little touches that adorn the web and woof of the story are exquisite beyond all praise. The vivacity of the plot, now laid in Norway, now in Brazil, now in New Orleans, now in Amsterdam, and the originality of treatment throughout, give the story a kind of cosmopolitan character that is new and very fascinating,

while the pictures of life on board ship, sometimes startlingly realistic, and always drawn without a suspicion of that sentimentality that gives English marine romance so often an air of doubtful accuracy, are grouped with an astonishing variety and vigour. English stories of the sea are mainly books for boys; this is a book for men, in the sense that George Eliot's novels are. (p. 1371)

> *"Jonas Lie," in* The Spectator (© *1874 by* The Spectator), *Vol. 47, No. 2418, October 31, 1874, pp. 1370-71.*

EDMUND GOSSE (essay date 1892)

In 1870 appeared [Jonas Lie's] first story, *Den Fremsynte* (**"The Man with the Second Sight"**), a melancholy little romance of life in the Arctic part of Norway, the world of brief lustrous summers and age-long winters. This tale was written in the manner which Björnson had brought into fashion, but it showed original features of its own, both in treatment and in location. (p. vii)

[The] true importance of Jonas Lie as a student of human nature, and as the constructor of a strong and original plot, was first exhibited by his powerful novel called *Livsslaven* (**"The Slave for Life"**) . . . , which dealt with the toils and pleasures of artisans in the Norwegian capital; this is a gloomy and pessimistic story of a smith's apprentice, with his struggles for existence and his ultimate final failure owing to the irresistible indulgence of a passionate physical instinct. *Livsslaven* achieved a very great success; it was realistic, and modern in a certain sense and to a discreet degree, and it appealed, as scarcely any Norwegian novel had done before, to all classes of Scandinavian society. It was followed within a few months by *Familjen paa Gilje* (**"The Family at Gilje"**), another study of the sinister side of modern life, illuminated, however, by a genuine humour, an element which here made its appearance in Lie's works for the first time. (p. x)

Like so many of the leading writers of Norway, Jonas Lie has been mainly a voluntary exile from his fatherland. . . . This prolonged absence from home is the more remarkable because his books deal almost exclusively with local types and local manners—are not merely Norwegian, but provincially Norwegian. It is the characteristic of the later and greater works of Jonas Lie that in them he has presented to us clearer and simpler aspects of Norse life than any other author. Without reaching the intellectual passion of Ibsen or the romantic tenderness of Björnson, Lie comes really closer than either of these more inspired poets to the genuine life of the Norwegians of to-day. . . . He stands, as a novelist, with those minute and unobtrusive painters of contemporary manners who defy arrangement in this or that school. . . . It would be a mistake to call him a great creative artist. He has slowly discovered his vocation, and late in life has secured an audience. His truthfulness, his simple pathos, his deep moral sincerity, have gradually conquered for him a place in the hearts of his countrymen and countrywomen which no one can dispute with him. [His style] is colloquial almost to a fault. . . . (pp. xi-xii)

> *Edmund Gosse, in his introduction to* The Commodore's Daughters *by Jonas Lie, translated by H. L. Braekstad and Gertrude Hughes, William Heinemann, 1892, pp. v-xii.*

HJALMAR HJORTH BOYESEN (essay date 1895)

[Jonas Lie's] career represents at its two poles a progression from the adventurous romanticism of his maternal heritage to the severe, wide-awake realism of the paternal—the emancipation of the Norseman from the Finn. (p. 123)

All that lay beyond the range of the senses drew him with an irresistible, half-shuddering attraction; and he resented all attempts to explain it by ordinary mundane laws. As his first novel ["**The Visionary**" *(Den Fremsynte)*] abundantly proves, he possesses in a marked degree the "sixth sense" that gropes eagerly and with a half-terrified fascination in the dusk that lies beyond the daylight of the other five. (p. 131)

It was evidently himself, or rather the Finnish part of himself, the author was exploring [in "**The Visionary**"]; it was in the mine of his own experience he was delving; it was his own heart he was coining. That may, in a sense, be true of every book of any consequence; but it was most emphatically true of "**The Visionary.**" It is not to the use of the first person that this autobiographical note is primarily due; but to a certain beautiful intimacy in the narrative, and a *naïve* confidence which charms the reader and takes him captive. With a lavish hand Lie has drawn upon the memories of his boyhood in the arctic North; and it was the newness of the nature which he revealed, no less than the picturesque force of his language, which contributed in no small degree to the success of his book. But, above all, it was the sweetness and pathos of the exquisite love story. Susanna, though as to talents not much above the commonplace, is ravishing. To have breathed the breath of such warm and living life into a character of fiction is no small achievement. It is the loveliness of love, the sweetness of womanhood, the glorious ferment of the blood in the human springtide which are celebrated in "**The Visionary.**" The thing is beautifully done. I do not know where young love has been more touchingly portrayed, unless it be in some of the Russian tales of [Ivan] Tourguéneff. The second-sight with which the hero, David Holst, is afflicted, introduces an undertone of sadness—a pensive minor key—and seems to necessitate the tragic *dénouement*. (pp. 138-39)

[By] "**The Visionary**" Jonas Lie was bound to be judged, whether he liked it or not. That is the penalty of having produced a masterpiece, that one is never permitted to follow the example of *bonus Homerus,* who, as every one knows, sometimes nods. Jonas Lie was far from nodding in ["**The Barque Future**" *(Tremasteren 'Fremtiden' eller Live Nordpaa)*]. . . . There was an abundance of interest in the material, and a delightful picturesque vigor in the descriptions of nature. But of romantic interest of the kind which the ordinary novel-reader craves, there was very little. (p. 141)

["**The Pilot and his Wife**" *(Lodsen og hans Husfru)*] is an every-day story in the best sense of the word, the history of a marriage among common folk. And yet so true is it, so permeated with a warm and rich humanity, that it holds the reader's attention from beginning to end. Then, to add to its interest, it has some bearing upon the woman question. Lie maintains that no true marriage can exist where the wife sacrifices her personality, and submits without a protest to neglect and ill-treatment. (p. 143)

[There is] a certain air of effort about ["**The Pilot and his Wife**"] of a strenuous seriousness, which is, I fancy, the temperamental note of this author.

"**The Pilot and his Wife**" besides reviving Lie's popularity also served to define his position in Norwegian literature. He

had at first been assigned a definite corner as the "poet of Nordland," but his ambition was not satisfied with so narrow a province. In all his tales, so far, he has surpassed all predecessors in his descriptions of the sea: and the critics, when favorably disposed, fell into the habit of referring to him as "the novelist of the sea," "the poet of the ocean," etc. (pp. 143-44)

In 1875 [Lie] published a versified tale, "**Faustina Strozzi,**" dealing with the struggle for Italian liberty. In spite of many excellences it fell rather flat. . . . Even a worse fate befell its successor, "**Thomas Ross**" . . . , a novel of contemporary life in the Norwegian capital. It is a pale, and rather labored story, in which a young girl . . . is held up to scorn, and the atrocity of flirtation is demonstrated by the most tragic consequences. There is likewise an air of triviality about "**Adam Schrader**" . . . ; and Lie became seriously alarmed about himself when he had to register a third failure. Like its predecessor, this book is full of keen observations, and the sketches of the social futilities and the typical characters at a summer watering-place are surely good enough to pass muster. But, somehow, the material fails to combine into a sufficiently coherent and impressive picture; and the total effect remains rather feeble. (p. 145)

Jonas Lie reconquered at one stroke all that he had lost, by the delightful sea-novel "**Rutland**" . . . , and reinstated himself still more securely in the hearts of an admiring public by the breezy tale, ["**Press On**" *(Gaa Paa)*]. . . . But after so protracted a sea-voyage he began to long for the shore, where, up to date he had suffered all his reverses. It could not be that he who had lived all his life on *terra firma,* and was so profoundly interested in the problems of modern society, should be banished forever, like "The Man Without a Country," to the briny deep, and be debarred from describing the things which he had most at heart. One more attempt he was bound to make, even at the risk of another failure. Accordingly [he wrote] . . . "**The Life Prisoner**" *(Livsslaven),* which deserved a better fate than befell it. The critics found it depressing, compared it to Zola, and at the same time scolded the author because he lacked indignation and neglected to denounce the terrible conditions which he described. . . . ["**The Life Prisoner**" *(Livsslaven)*] is a dismal tale. It was, in fact, the irruption of modern naturalism into Norwegian literature. It reminds one in its tone more of Dostoyevski's "Crime and Punishment" than of [Zola's] "L'Assommoir." For my mind Dostoyevski is a greater exponent of naturalism than Zola. . . . The pleasing and well-bred truths or lies, to the expounding of which *belles lettres* had hitherto been confined, were here discarded or ignored. The author had taken a plunge into the great dumb deep of the nethermost social strata, which he has explored with admirable conscientiousness and artistic perception. Few men of letters would object to being the father of so creditable a failure. (pp. 146-47)

[The victory came when he published] what, to my mind, is the most charming of all his novels, ["**The Family at Gilje**" *(Familjen paa Gilje)*]. . . . That is a book which is taken, warm and quivering, out of the very heart of Norway. The humor which had been cropping out tentatively in Lie's earlier tales comes here to its full right, and his shy, beautiful pathos gleams like hidden tears behind his genial smile. It is close wrought cloth of gold. No loosely woven spots—no shoddy woof of cheaper material. . . . [The] whole company of sober, everyday mortals that come trooping through its chapters are so delightfully human that you feel the blood pulse under their skin at the first touch. It is a triumph indeed, to have written a book like "**The Family at Gilje.**"

From this time forth Jonas Lie's career presents an unbroken series of successes. ["**A Maelstrom**" *(En Malstrom)*, "**Eight Stories,**" "**Married Life**" *(Et Samliv)*, "**Maisa Jons,**" "**The Commodore's Daughters**" *(Kommandorens Dotre)* and "**Evil Powers**" *(Onde Magter)*] . . . which deal with interesting phases of contemporary life, are all extremely modern in feeling and show the same effort to discard all tinsel and sham and get at the very heart of reality.

He had by this series of novels established his reputation as a relentless realist, when . . . he surprised his admirers by the publication of two volumes of the most wildly fantastic tales, entitled "**Trold.**" It was as if a volcano, with writhing torrents of flame and smoke, had burst forth from under a sidewalk in Broadway. It was the suppressed Finn who, for once, was going to have his fling, even though he were doomed henceforth to silence. It was the "queer thoughts" (which had accumulated in the author and which he had scrupulously imprisoned) returning to take vengeance upon him unless he released them. The most grotesque, weird, and uncanny imaginings (such as Stevenson would delight in) are crowded together in these tales, some of which are derived from folk-lore and legends, while others are free fantasies.

Before taking leave of Jonas Lie, a word about his style is in order. Style, as such, counts for very little with him. Yet he has a distinctly individual and vigorous manner of utterance, though a trifle rough, perhaps, abrupt, elliptic, and conversational. Mere decorative adjectives and clever felicities of phrase he scorns. All scientific and social phenomena—all that we include under the term modern progress—command his most intense and absorbed attention. Having since 1882 been a resident of Paris . . . he has had the advantage of seeing the society which he describes at that distance which, if it does not lend enchantment, at all events unifies the scattered impressions, and furnishes a convenient critical outpost. He does not permit himself, however, like so many foreigners in the French capital, to lapse into that supercilious cosmopolitanism which deprives a man of his own country without giving him any other in exchange. No; Jonas Lie is and remains a Norseman. . . . (pp. 148-50)

> *Hjalmar Hjorth Boyesen, "Jonas Lie," in his Es-*
> *says on Scandinavian Literature (abridged by per-*
> *mission of Charles Scribner's Sons; copyright ©*
> *1895 Charles Scribner's Sons), Scribner's, 1895*
> *(and reprinted by Scribner's, 1911), pp. 121-51.*

BJÖRNSTJERNE BJÖRNSON (essay date 1896)

Jonas Lie's art has no side-shows. It is concentrated with strong directness on the task in hand. In such a case one should expect to find the plot very elaborate; but it is not so. Large prominent pictures of strongly concentrated scenes are also rare. The narrative moves along smoothly through minor details of characterization, often exquisitely fine, through every-day events, more or less plastically represented, and by the aid of connecting remarks, always from the lips of one of the characters. Often we meet with a droll but nevertheless winning inaptitude; we see at once the line sought for and the means applied to find it. But those difficulties never appear at points where even a master might feel embarrassed, but on the contrary just at points over which

the bungler skips easily. The greater the difficulty, the easier to him; he is embarrassed only when handling that which is easy. Nor does the language flow redundantly from his pen, though it is always sufficient for the demand. When the narrative begins to gather around the decision, the reader notices with admiration how much has been quietly prepared and how free and clear the characters stand in the perspective. This is to some degree the result of his method of narrating,—always placing the objects in the calm light of a shaded lamp. He may stand by and look down between the lines with a roguish smile; but the lines themselves are not allowed to laugh. His soul may be trembling with indignation or exultation, but the moment the feeling begins to make the picture unsteady, some indifferent words are dropped in, and everything is smooth again. The heat is there, but mildly disturbed through the whole. (p. 400)

> *Björnstjerne Björnson, "Modern Norwegian Lit-*
> *erature—II," in The Forum (copyright, 1896, by*
> *The Forum Publishing Company), Vol. XXI, June,*
> *1896, pp. 398-413.*

OLA RAKNES (essay date 1923)

The Family at Gilje is by many considered Jonas Lie's best work. It is the first where he has obtained complete mastery of his peculiar style, the object of which is to make us assist with all our senses at every scene we are introduced to, instead of having to reconstruct the scenes ourselves from the material given by the novelist. This object is attained, not by giving as complete details as possible of every place or event, but by fixing our attention on some characteristic, though perhaps unimportant, detail that will evoke in us similar things from our own experience. The detail in question may be a smell, a sound, a peculiar position of some object, or even a sensation of some rather indefinite kind. The method may have its disadvantages in some kinds of narrative, but when the object is to rouse the reader's sympathetic interest in things he already knows but has slighted because he did not see their significance, then this manner may be without a rival. It may, of course, like any other literary manner, degenerate into mannerism, and some of Jonas Lie's critics have accused him of such degeneration in some of his later works. (pp. 226-27)

The aim which Jonas Lie set to his literary activity was . . . to give to the Norwegian people a poetic reflection of its own life. This, of course, cannot be the work of a single author, and Jonas Lie never imagined it to be. But he has probably contributed more to it than any other man. By the intensity of his vision, by his passionate love of truth, which would not be swerved from the straight path even by his equally passionate patriotism, and by the depth and warmth of his sympathy with everything living, he will always stand as one of the great men of [Norwegian] literature. (p. 231)

> *Ola Raknes, "Jonas Lie," in Chapters in Norwe-*
> *gian Literature by Illit Grondahl and Ola Raknes,*
> *Gyldendal, 1923 (and reprinted by Books for Li-*
> *braries Press, 1969; distributed by Arno Press,*
> *Inc.), pp. 216-31.*

ALRIK GUSTAFSON (essay date 1940)

Of the literary generation in Norway that produced Ibsen and Björnson only one author, besides these two masters, was able to attract international attention. Jonas Lie, the first really important Scandinavian novelist, has this distinction. (p. 25)

Ibsen and Bjørnson had with the years gradually come to take on the stature of literary giants among their contemporaries; and in consequence they had aroused both tremendous enthusiasms and bitterly uncompromising antipathies among Scandinavian readers during the three decades previous to 1890. Lie's less aggressive personality and more quiet artistry had, on the other hand, by the '90's captured the abiding sympathy of nearly all Norwegian readers, the discriminating as well as the popular; and since that time he has become by common consent one with Ibsen and Bjørnson—the three comprising "the great triumvirate" of late nineteenth century Norwegian authors. (p. 26)

[No] Norwegian novelist has written more close to the pulsing soul of Norway than has Jonas Lie. He could do so, of course, only because he had a rare facility at preserving his artistic and intellectual balance in the midst of a thousand foreign impressions. This Ibsen could seldom do; nor could Bjørnson even, for the most part. (p. 28)

It must be admitted in passing, however, that the peculiarly Norwegian quality of Lie's genius is not without its drawbacks. There is to be found in his work, for example, an occasional cropping out of a kind of provincialism that is somewhat distasteful to the non-Norwegian reader. Particularly is this apparent—to take a couple of instances almost at random—in the strongly unfavorable contrast between Norwegian seafaring men and those of other nations in . . . [*The Pilot and His Wife*], or in the equally smug contrast between the Norwegian girl Katharina Linstow and a Miss Wilkins, with her English ways, in *Thomas Ross*. . . . In Lie's more mature novels, however, such as *The Family at Gilje* and [*The Commodore's Daughters*] . . . , he has outgrown such crude provincially motivated methods of contrast. These later novels treat purely Norwegian characters in purely Norwegian milieus, with no naïve admixture of popular, provincially motivated contrasts. (pp. 28-9)

The Visionary, Lie's earliest effort at fiction, was an unqualified popular success with the general Norwegian public, chiefly perhaps because of the sentimentally melancholy love story which provides a kind of structural unity to the otherwise rather diverse mass of Nordland reminiscence and folklore which is more apt to impress the discerning reader. Norwegian critics hailed *The Visionary* as a debut work which revealed great promise despite its idealizing sentimentalities and its crudely contrived narrative pattern. They found Lie's description of the Far North unmatched in Norwegian literature up to this time, and they were deeply impressed by the inclusion of bits of Nordland legend and superstition in this first novel. (p. 37)

Some of his novels that follow in the next couple of decades have touches of this material, but only casually and by the way. . . .

[Lie's second novel, *The Barque "Future,"*] was an improvement on *The Visionary* in some respects, particularly in that it was more robust in tone, avoiding most of the mere sentimentalities of Lie's first novel. And yet *The Barque "Future"* is certainly not a great novel: its treatment of character is superficial and uncertain, and the story itself is based upon a wire-drawn plot that reminds one too much of the traditional mystery story. . . .

In *The Pilot and His Wife* Lie combined a story of domestic life with the romance of the sea, the former element predominating, the latter being used largely as effective background. In careful and penetrating analysis of character this novel is a great advance over Lie's previous stories. He had learned by his earlier partial artistic failures to be more selective in his technique, to centre his attention upon character rather than upon background, and to create freely rather than lose himself in the mere photographic reproduction of outward detail. (p. 38)

[The two novels which followed from Lie's pen in the late '70's—*Thomas Ross* and *Adam Schrader*] reveal a tentative falling off in quality. Somehow they do not seem to move and live as had his earlier novels on sailor folk and the sea, chiefly perhaps because Lie was trying a bit too hard in an entirely new manner and subject matter—soberly realistic fictional treatment of a comparatively diversified urban life. (p. 39)

[In *The Family at Gilje*] it is clear that Lie had finally found the type of story best suited to his genius. In it he escapes entirely from the rather broad, loose canvases of most of his early work—both from the exotic romanticism of his sea tales and from the awkwardly uncertain realism of the novels dealing with contemporary urban life. In his new novel Lie limits himself rigidly in both plot and scene. The story is concerned almost exclusively with the narrow circumstances and the humdrum existence of Norwegian provincial officialdom in the '40's of the nineteenth century. The scene is as restricted as is the narrative groundwork of the story. Gilje is neither a small town nor a sprawling provincial village; it is but the isolated official residence, located "nine days by sleigh from Christiania," of a Norwegian army officer of the mid-nineteenth century. No subject would seem to hold less promise for an interesting tale: even an American Main Street might seem to offer the romance of diversity by comparison. And yet Lie makes Gilje *live*—vividly, intimately, from the first page to the last. Out of the unpromising daily commonplaces of an isolated provincial official's residence of the '40's, Lie manages somehow to spin an intimate domestic tale which is rapid in its movement, penetrating in its character portrayal, rich in a warmly scintillating humor, and instinct with a profoundly real human problem. Lie had finally found in *The Family at Gilje* a genre peculiarly fitted to his genius. He came to find with the years that it is with interiors that he succeeds best—intimately realistic fictional studies in the life of the home, studies which may be said to have a certain broad kinship to Jane Austen's novels from the early nineteenth century in England. Lie's strength as a novelist lies in depth of imaginative insight rather than in bold breadth of coloring. His real triumphs . . . occur in those novels in which he concentrates on character, using a carefully selected detail realism of scene merely to invest his characters with a sense of immediate reality. In *The Family at Gilje,* his first effort in this rigidly limited type of fiction, we find his greatest triumph as a novelist, though in *The Commodore's Daughters* . . . he is almost equally successful.

Lie manages to attain a vivid unity of effect in *The Family at Gilje* by limiting all the directly narrated action of the story to the Gilje farm or to the immediately contiguous countryside. We do not, however, feel particularly oppressed by such a rigid limitation of scene, because Lie constantly keeps us aware of a larger world outside by various skillfully handled indirect methods of narration. We catch numerous glimpses of Christiania life, and even of a larger world than this at times, through vivid letters from the capital—chiefly those of Inger-Johanna, the eldest daughter of the Gilje family and the character about whom the action of the story in one sense centres. It is a part also of Lie's deft narrative technique in this novel that the larger outer world is constantly viewed through Gilje eyes; for Inger-Johanna, though momentarily impressed by the *beaux monde* into which she is suddenly thrown in Christiania, never quite succumbs to this world—she sees fundamentally with Gilje eyes in the end, and to Gilje she therefore ultimately returns.

Vivid as is the reader's impression of the Gilje farm and the surrounding countryside as he moves through the pages of *The Family at Gilje*, it is not easy to define precisely Lie's general method in attaining this effect. . . . Though Lie did in certain respects admire Zola, the great master of naturalism on the Continent, he was never willing to accept the basic doctrine of naturalism: that literature was merely an objective photograph of actual life. (pp. 40-2)

Lie is essentially an impressionist in his realistic technique, i.e. he insists upon using the materials of actual life as the basis of his novels; but he is equally insistent that the author, instead of being tied down to any particular body of "accidental reality," should be free to select those aspects of reality which most adequately fulfill the demands of his own creative insight in any given case. . . . Jonas Lie, as Guy de Maupassant, belongs essentially among those artists, in painting and in literature, who in the late nineteenth century called themselves "impressionists"—artists who did not wish to deny the aesthetic validity of actuality (as the symbolists tended to do), but wished to subject the materials of actuality to the selective processes of individual artistic creation. (p. 43)

The true impressionist in fiction handles all the detail of his art—scene, episode, characterization, and even "the problem," if there is one—with an absolute reverence for the central artistic principle of selection. *The Family at Gilje* is perhaps the most remarkable example in Norwegian literature of scrupulous fidelity to this principle.

Lie's novel, we have said, limits its scene rigidly to the isolated Gilje residence of Captain Jaeger and to the immediately adjacent countryside. It is therefore with a rural scene in the strictest sense of the term that we have to deal. With the subtle instinct of the born impressionist, Lie sees the necessity in a domestic tale such as *The Family at Gilje* of concentrating primarily upon the interior of the Jaeger home. Yet he does not neglect the possibility of increasing the effectiveness of his realism by including on occasion snatches of the less confined phases of the rural scene: the farm itself, its busy barnyard, its broad stretches of field and meadow; and beyond these the rich sweep of natural landscape stretching on to the point where field meets sky in the magnificent irregularities of mountain horizon to be seen from the Gilje lands.

The reader feels that he knows every physical detail of the Jaeger household—all that this home presents to the eye, the ear, the nose, and to the tactual and gustatory sensations. And yet in Lie's art there is almost an irreducible minimum of mere "description"—such long inventories of household detail as would inevitably be indulged in under similar circumstances by a Balzac or a Zola. Lie never pauses merely "to describe"; his primary concern is at every point his story,

and descriptive detail is offered, in consequence, only in deft, vivid bits, in striking fragments—by the way as it were. (p. 44)

It is by a subtle accumulation of incidental bits of realistic detail rather than by labored composition of long descriptive passages that Lie makes us so vividly conscious of the scene in *The Family at Gilje*. Usually he gives to such incidental bits of realistic detail only a short paragraph, sometimes even less—a sentence, a telling phrase, even a single provocative word—before he again plunges into the rapid onward movement of the story itself.

In his handling of episode he is equally selective in his use of detail, similarly impressionistic in his general method. Despite the dull daily commonplaces often associated with such rural isolation as one comes upon in *The Family at Gilje*, Lie manages to select and develop his episodes in such a way as to gain the impression of a constantly moving, vividly rapid action. The discriminating reader is struck, first of all, by the care which Lie has exercised in choosing episodes central to the purposes of his story. From the opening episode, in which we are introduced to nearly all of the central elements in the story which is to follow, down to the final episode, which sketches with deft, telling strokes the final tragedy of Student Grip and the high resolve of Inger-Johanna, the story moves rapidly, with no let-down of interest on the part of the reader. Each episode is necessary to the conduct of the story as a whole; no episode is irrelevant.

It is in the development of each episode within itself, however, that Lie's impressionistic technique attains its most characteristic quality—a certain vivid, full-bodied, tensely animated movement. The opening episode of the novel, for example, is a masterpiece of the story teller's art. The narrative movement of the episode is swift—it never flags; and yet Lie manages to pack into the episode very much more than merely the beginning of a purely narrative thread which he proposes to unravel as the materials of the Gilje story. In it we are introduced intimately to the Gilje scene. In it nearly all of the major characters in the novel are introduced, and definitely characterized. . . . (pp. 47-8)

In this episode also the core of the Gilje "problem"—the future of the children, so precarious because of the family's straitened financial circumstances—is brought into due prominence by means of deft narrative devices. (p. 48)

Though Lie attains his illusion of reality in the development of episode largely by means of a highly selective impressionistic technique, the whole secret of his success in the handling of episode is not to be found in a mere selection of effective narrative detail. A careful examination of his method will reveal that he skillfully combines with his technique of selective detail at least two more particular technical devices: first, he exercises great care in the way in which he opens his episodes; and secondly, he tends to use throughout his development of any particular episode the most strongly *active* kinds of words—especially verbs. And in addition to these two particular techniques, he employs quite frequently a delicately genial play of humor, which, among other effects tends to give further animation and sense of movement to Lie's handling of narrative episode.

Lie usually opens his episode in the midst of an action, oftentimes with a precipitate, almost explosive force, which goes far to insure the reader's rapt attention throughout the development of the episode that is to follow. (p. 51)

Though Lie, unlike his French contemporaries Flaubert and Guy de Maupassant, never developed in theory a carefully defined doctrine of *le mot juste,* in practice he seems to have taken almost the same care with his word choice as did these two representatives of a precisely disciplined French realism. Lie's style is marked by a marvelous economy of words; every word strikes home. Particularly does Lie's style suggest that he sensed the unique value of the verb as a means toward a forceful, animated immediacy of expression. Everywhere in the pages of *The Family at Gilje* does one come upon examples of the effective use of the verb. (pp. 52-3)

Much of the sense of *movement* so peculiar to Lie's development of scene and episode is to be explained in terms of the prominence in Lie's style of verbs and other words deriving directly from verb forms. The original Norwegian is even more characterized by such forms than in the translation; in the Norwegian the sum total aliveness of stylistic effect is intensified by the flavor of racy colloquial turns of speech which defy the most careful art of the translator.

Skillful, however, as Lie is in his handling of every detail in the development of scene and episode in *The Family at Gilje,* it is perhaps in the revelation of character that his art is most completely satisfying in this novel.... The reader inevitably becomes engrossed in the author's central preoccupation with his characters.... So engrossed, in fact, do we become in this living, very human world of characters that the larger implications of the novel, its moral significance as a vivid social document, are for the moment forced into the background of our consciousness. Only after we have completed our reading of the novel do we become conscious of the fact that the fortunes of these characters are really inextricably bound up with a very real human "problem"—a problem, indeed, which stretches far beyond the narrow confines of the isolated mountain residence at Gilje into the whole scheme of Norwegian social and political organization in the middle of the nineteenth century. The novel is really in the last analysis an indictment—nonetheless significant for being indirect—of Norway's system of provincial officialdom in the nineteenth century.

Very subtle is Lie's art here—an art which implies rather than obtrusively states this larger problem of a bureaucratic national organism which finds in Lie's novel its homely, immediate manifestation within the narrow domestic phenomena of Gilje life. So subtle was it, indeed, that Lie's contemporaries, delighted with the story as such, did not always see the implied "message" which the novel really contained. (pp. 54-5)

It is clear to us now ... that Lie really never evaded the immediate social issues of his time. He simply refused to be swept off his feet by the popular catch-words of his generation; and most important of all to discerning readers of a later generation than his own, he insisted on retaining at all costs a rigid intellectual and artistic independence. (p. 56)

It is this conviction which more than anything else gives an almost unique quality to Lie's unobtrusive but telling criticism of life in the midst of so much of the Scandinavian literature from his generation which has "had its day and ceased to be." (p. 57)

Such literary performances as *The Family at Gilje* ... continue to delight, and even to influence, a constantly increasing number of readers—and this primarily because the "problem" that Lie presents in it is so finely subordinated to his

primary artistic concern with certain fundamental laws of human nature as revealed in his vividly sketched characters.

The "problem" of Gilje centres most obviously upon the age-old question of the relation between parents and children; but in a larger sense the novel contains an indirect criticism of the whole social and political structure of mid-nineteenth century Norway which made the immediate domestic problems of Gilje inevitable. In their efforts to get Inger-Johanna and Thinka married to the best advantage, and Jorgen well situated in life, the Captain at Gilje and his wife (always referred to by the author in a tone of genial irony as "Ma") tended to do violence to the usual modern conception of the relation between parents and children. And yet the parents at Gilje are unfair to their children through no inherent viciousness on their part. They themselves are, in fact, no less the victims of a set of circumstances than are their children; and it is this set of circumstances which, in the last analysis, determines the procedure which they adopt with regard to their children.

The core of the Gilje problem is really a financial one; the Captain has to exist, and raise a family, on a salary so small that in the course of the years he has been transformed from what must have been at one time a large, amiable, sanguine spirit, essentially good at heart, into a man whose domestic activities, distorted by provincial isolation and straitened financial circumstances, are often petty, blustering, and dictatorial. And Ma, a more practical nature from the outset perhaps, is even more pathetically a victim of narrow provincial isolation and immediate economic stress. Her constant concern for the household, and especially for "the children," has reduced her in the course of the years almost to the status of a domestic automaton.

Though it is around Inger-Johanna's fate that the plot of the Gilje story tends to centre, the most convincingly drawn characters in the novel are undoubtedly those of Inger-Johanna's parents—the Captain, with "his plethoric, vociferous, somewhat confused nature," and Ma, the Captain's self-effacing, hardworking, externally cautious wife, under whose severely plain exterior lurked both a vigorous practical intelligence and a sensitive woman's soul. It is in Ma, in fact, that we find Lie's greatest attainment in the art of characterization in *The Family at Gilje.* The Captain *seems* merely to loom larger in the story because of his domineering manner and his vociferous methods of procedure. It is really Ma, with her quiet, self-effacing manner, who always finally determines family policies after the heavy artillery of the Captain has spent itself in violently explosive inconsequences. In episode after episode, deftly, and usually by scarcely perceptible indirections, Lie makes us conscious of Ma's real power at Gilje. In her unassuming manner she comes by degrees to command our admiration and respect, and to appeal to our deepest sympathies; while the Captain, in his blustering way, too often invites the reader to a reaction scarcely so serious and dignified. It is only toward the end of the novel, when the Captain, a sick and worn-out hulk of a man, becomes finally resigned to Inger-Johanna's decision not to marry into "high society," that we come upon any real mark of essential nobility in Captain Jaeger's character. And by this time, perhaps, we are not so much impressed by the Captain's tragedy; for a weakly pathetic, half-resigned spirit in a sick, completely broken body is not usually taken to be the human symbol of high tragedy. (pp. 57-9)

Perhaps the most remarkable feature of Lie's creation of the character of Ma is that he avoids all false pathos in it, retaining toward her throughout his novel an attitude of sympathetic understanding which is remarkably objective in its quality. Lie strikes a happy medium here, avoiding both the cold, scientific objectivity of a Flaubert on the one hand and the excessively sentimental subjectivity of a Dickens on the other. Lie's subject for characterization—a mother whose spirit has been all but crushed by narrow, petty circumstances—is surcharged with sentimental potentialities; and yet Lie never yields to the temptation which a lesser, or a careless author would inevitably fall into here. Though his attitude toward Ma is sympathetic, it is neither excessively nor obtrusively so. Lie's sympathy for this character is insinuated into the text in his best impressionistic manner—by skillful indirection, yet with the delicate persistence of constantly recurring, cumulative detail. (p. 59)

The novels and tales which [Lie] wrote after *The Family at Gilje* . . . reveal a partial shift in both his point of view and his technique, though he continues—with one remarkable exception—to centre his attention on domestic interiors. In the matter of technique Lie's later novels seem gradually to take on a sharper, more stylized impressionistic manner, characterized chiefly by an even more scrupulously conscious word choice and by a new emphasis on the basic importance of individual episode. In point of view Lie's later novels seem to lose some of the easy and familiar geniality of his earlier work. Only with increasing difficulty is Lie able in his later novels to view human existence with his former happy vigor and basic amiability. It was perhaps his growing concern with the intricacies of human psychology, and the actions often determined by this psychology, that led his honest, searching mind to a more sober view of the problems of human existence, a view which had little commerce with the relatively facile optimism of some of his early work. (pp. 62-3)

[*The Life Convict*] contains little trace of the ingratiating geniality of his great Gilje novel. *The Life Convict* is in substance a sombrely realistic study in the development of a criminal type; and though its manner of handling the material is relatively objective throughout, it does not seem to have been written without a certain definitely implied *Tendenz*. It at least raises the question—if it does not actually point an accusing finger—of society's responsibility in the creation of the criminal type. *The Life Convict* is not in itself among Lie's great works; but it is of definite importance in any study of Lie's development as a novelist, for it serves to point the way toward a new phase in his development. It should be emphasized, more than previous critics have been willing to do, that in no work after *The Family at Gilje* does Lie reveal with any steady consistency that quietly pervasive geniality of spirit which is so centrally characteristic of his great Gilje novel. Rather do his novels after 1883 reveal a Lie who is becoming slowly enveloped in shadows. Not that his essential amiability of temper ever departs completely from him, nor that he finally develops into a basically tragic author. In his late novels he still retains something of the Lie that we learn to know so intimately in the pages of *The Family at Gilje;* but this Lie has become by degrees more deeply aware of life's darker undercurrents, of those evil powers, lurking seductively on every hand, which distort character and destroy ideal human values—and he does not hesitate to pose as central themes in his later novels some of the characteristic forms which these powers of disintegration take in the life of man. (p. 63)

Lie's two important works from this period—*The Commodore's Daughters* and the two volumes of *Trolls*—provide further evidence of the same kind. The former of these is a contemporary domestic interior, which concentrates on the double tragedy of two vivacious, promising young ladies, each of whose lives is made a sacrifice to narrow parental conceptions of proper social procedures. *Trolls*—perhaps the most remarkable work that Lie has ever written—is a marvelously diversified medley of ancient legends and superstitions, some of them told in the straightforward, unadorned narrative manner of the original folk tale, others conceived in the profoundly lyric vein of the best of romantic nature mysticism, and still others written with an obvious and immediate moral purpose.

The two volumes of *Trolls* are, in a word, different. Not only do they differ from anything Lie had previously written (with the exception of parts of *The Visionary,* and a few other fragments), but they are in a sense unique in the whole of Scandinavian literature in the nineteenth century. This uniqueness is to be found in the fact that Lie handles his folk materials in a way peculiar to himself—in general conception and in composition *they bear the Lie stamp.* . . . [The] years of maturity which had taught Lie something of that distinction which man tries to draw between fiction and fact had never *quite* convinced him that there was not more than a little truth in the old world of legend and superstition. It was therefore, no doubt, that Lie could preserve the old legends . . . with so little loss of the original flavor and spirit of these legends; and it was therefore that he could also on occasion apply the materials of these old tales to problems of so-called "modern import" in a way that marks the two volumes of *Trolls* as one of the most original books ever to come out of Norway.

Much well-deserved praise has been showered by Norwegian critics upon those tales in *Trolls* which preserve the true spirit and manner of the originals—a spirit and manner objective and unadorned, scrupulously avoiding such "modern additions" as a romantic lyric vein or a tendency to "point a moral." Unquestionably the tales which attain this fresh, primitive narrative ideal are artistically the most satisfactory ones in Lie—the ones that rank Lie together with Selma Lagerlöf just below the great master Hans Christian Andersen in the modern literary creation of the Scandinavian fairy tale. And yet it must be remembered—at least by the literary historian—that such happily conceived tales are in the minority in *Trolls.* Moreover, it must not be forgotten that even those tales which have no apparent "purpose," aside from the mere desire to tell a tale, were included in a work to which an Introduction was written that definitely points a broad but profound parallel (which amounts, in a sense, to an identification) between the "evil powers" of an ancient world of folk legend and those "evil powers" which some hold still live on in a so-called "civilized modern life." (pp. 65-7)

It is clear from . . . the Introduction to *Trolls* that Lie is prepared in the tales included in these volumes to use the word "Trolls" in a far more inclusive sense than the usual historical one. He conceives of "Trolls" as not only existing in the minds of the uncultured peasant and fisherfolk of an ancient pagan North, but also as having a kind of very real existence in the life of a modern world. In consequence he uses the word "Trolls" as broadly symbolizing those mysterious, often tragic undercurrents of human life which a modern psychology knows under the names of "the unconscious" or "the irrational." (p. 68)

The brilliant originality of *Trolls*, both in conception and execution, suggests that Lie had large reserves of narrative power which might rank him even higher than he is now placed among Norwegian novelists had these unique reserves been more freely drawn upon. They flash out uncertainly, yet with intriguing promise, in Lie's first novel, *The Visionary;* and they burn with a marvelously varied and intense glow in the two volumes of *Trolls* very late in Lie's career. Otherwise we can but guess at their existence in the far reaches of Lie's consciousness during those years of his life when he chose to concentrate largely upon robustly bracing sea tales and on soberly realistic portrayals of the contemporary scene. (pp. 69-70)

And yet his mastery of the novel of contemporary scene was no mean attainment in itself, and the significance which this attainment has had in the general development of the Norwegian novel since Lie's day is incalculable. It might be said that Lie really created the Norwegian novel, as Ibsen created the Norwegian drama. And Lie's creation—solid and honest at every point—served to give a much needed firmness of form and substance to Norwegian fiction at the very beginning of its development. (p. 70)

> *Alrik Gustafson, "Impressionistic Realism: Jonas Lie," in his* Six Scandinavian Novelists *(copyright © 1940 by The American-Scandinavian Foundation), American-Scandinavian Foundation, 1940, pp. 25-72.*

JAMES WALTER McFARLANE   (essay date 1960)

[*The Visionary*] is fumblingly and self-consciously organized. But its qualities of genuine vitality and freshness of vision are at once evident, even though only intermittently so, and there is no doubt that for such reasons alone it ranks high among Lie's novels. Structurally, it is too elaborate for its touchingly simple theme of the love of a mentally unstable boy, gifted with second sight, for his childhood sweetheart; it is a novice's eagerness that attempts to incorporate within its eighty pages or so a fictional narrator who disappears after the first section, two separate sets of posthumous papers, some flash-back reminiscences, a digression on the character of Nordland and its inhabitants, and a number of interpolated folk tales. The manner of address is on occasion distressingly arch: 'I gave myself up to my memories,' says the fictional narrator whilst his childhood friend, newly met after many years, is out of the room, 'which I will report here, even at the danger that the reader might suppose my friend is staying out rather a long time preparing the punch.' Nor is there, except for the hero's bare assertion at the end of his story that Susanne's love for him has saved his sanity, any real justification for Lie's claiming the point of the story to be that of showing 'love's power of healing the sick mind.' There is magic in this book, but it is in the creation of atmosphere and not in the organization of its parts.

By contrast, the novels that immediately followed seem almost too well architected, their complicated outlines flowing almost too smoothly; and with the disappearance of the earlier crudeness there went also much of the poetic urgency. It is in these novels, especially *The Barque 'Future' (Tremasteren 'Fremtiden' . . .)* and *The Pilot and his Wife (Lodsen og hans hustru . . .)* that Lie developed his eye for detail, his

sense of the insinuative effect of highly-charged triviality that has caused some to call his realism 'impressionistic' and which reaches perfection in such novels as [*Rutland, Go Ahead! (Gaa Paa!)* and *The Family at Gilje (Familjen paa Gilje)*]. . . . These novels are the work of inspired craftsmanship, but not of intuitive artistry; for all their brilliance, it is as though their author's naturally wayward imagination is too tightly reined. When he writes in this vein, his novels often seem to commend themselves as exercises in description and portraiture, an impression that much of his subtitling—'Pictures from Nordland', 'Life up north', 'An Interior from the Forties'—often seems to reinforce: nor does one forget that a good deal of his popularity as a novelist derived from his skill as a seascape artist. (pp. 99-101)

> *James Walter McFarlane, "Jonas Lie," in his* Ibsen and the Temper of Norwegian Literature *(© Oxford University Press 1960; reprinted by permission of Oxford University Press), Oxford University Press, London, 1960, pp. 97-103.*

SVERRE LYNGSTAD   (essay date 1977)

[*The Visionary*] is structured as a frame story with two parts: (1) the last days of David Holst as reported by his friend, a doctor, and (2) David's memoirs. . . . In Part I the doctor finds David forlorn and consumptive in a Kristiania garret. The angle of vision adopted . . . , that of the Nordlander who feels constricted by the city, effects a critique of civilization through primitivism, subsequently a leading preoccupation of Lie as well as of another Norwegian with roots in Nordland, Knut Hamsun. . . .

Both the frame technique and the primitive perspective—stock Romantic devices—are tactfully handled, with the result that they recede in favor of the persona, the doctor. (p. 26)

The first section of "David Holst's Memoirs," entitled "Nordland and the Nordlander," exemplifies an early realistic form, the ethnographical sketch, here enlivened by the relatively new, arctic subject. However—aside from certain passages where Jonas Lie rather than David Holst is speaking—it transcends its genre quality and becomes an integral part of David's experience (pp. 26-7)

Formally an initiation story similar to [Björnstjerne] Björnson's peasant tales, David's account of his life deviates from the genre in several ways. Most of the former . . . end happily with an engagement or a wedding. *A Visionary* does not, nor is the time span limited to the period of initiation. Moreover, being a confession by an exceptional figure, its psychology is incomparably more complex and profound.

Specifically, along with the supernatural, Jonas Lie stresses the power of unconscious forces in behavior, not only in David's story but in the entire work. In the opening chapter the reader has a sense of being on a voyage of discovery, an "inward journey," though Lie uses more homely images, such as doors or gates being unlocked to hitherto unknown chambers of the mind or unfamiliar realms of being. (p. 28)

An important unifying element in *The Visionary* is the symbol structure, polarized like the rest of the story toward extremes of delight and suffering, love and death. Some symbols like rose, ring, cross, and boat, are traditional; others such as fisherman's gaff and its cognates are Lie's own. The first cluster tend to be handled conventionally, though not without subtlety. (p. 30)

[*The Visionary*] is a compact work with far-reaching meanings on many levels. Despite an allegedly old-fashioned technique, it seems curiously modern in form as well as content. The framed narrative served Lie well, helping him to anticipate his impressionistic method. . . .

In its peculiar blend of narrative techniques, styles, and forms, *The Visionary* is a work *sui generis*. It has several obviously romantic elements—the fey hero, the supernatural, the primitive—but they are not romantically treated. On the other hand, realism does not describe the book either, despite the strong sense of everydayness in the midst of the terror of hidden powers. The story is classical in the sense that the sequence of events, unusual as they may be, expresses man's fundamental existential condition. In certain parts it rises to a mythic vision, conveyed, as in the story of Elias, in the style of folk legend. (p. 32)

[*When the Iron Curtain Falls* and *Dyre Rein*] are more akin to *The Visionary* than most of the intervening novels. For though published in 1870, in its atmosphere *The Visionary* is more akin to the 1890s, full of mysticism and nervous anxiety. . . . Thus, the spirit of Jonas Lie's first novel was far ahead of its time. (p. 33)

[*The Pilot and His Wife*] shows great progress both in composition and character portrayal. Though in large part a tale of the sea, its structure is determined by the vicissitudes of marriage rather than nautical adventure. . . .

The book's narrative focus reflects Lie's endeavor to reduce his previous emphasis on nature and popular life in favor of the study of character. . . . From the very first page with its description of the moody, dark-bearded pilot, a man around forty, Salve [Kristiansen] is, with minor interruptions, always at the center of attention. (p. 40)

A structural weakness results from the detailed account—however excellent as such—of Salve's nautical adventures. Incapable of fulfilling their intended function of *explaining* his predicament, they are felt as mere episodes. Moreover, the nautical sections are tendentious, imbued with a myth of Nordic superiority. With his slight build and moderately tall figure, young Salve is heroically invincible; other sailors—Irishmen, Americans, Spaniards, and so forth—are morally and physically inferior. Similarly, Nordic women appear to be more feminine and virtuous than southern ones. . . . Altogether, Lie's sexual and moral chauvinism results in a naive contrast between foreign immorality and Nordic valor and purity. . . . Lie's awareness of the less attractive sides of Norwegian life is still overshadowed by his National Romanticism, his implicit trust in some near-mystic virtue of the Nordic soul.

However, some of the best aspects of Lie's art also have their source in Romanticism. In particular, the Romantic tradition lends power and depth to such figures as are drawn from his own observation and memory. Salve Kristiansen, the pilot, is a case in point. . . . Here was a truly national character type with a legendary aura, due partly to traditional lore of daring exploits at sea, partly to Romantic literary representation. In a country with a coastline as long as Norway's, the pilot was a sort of folk hero, a status Lie's novel exploited as well as enhanced. Add to this a veritably Byronic misanthropy and a secret grief, and there emerge the outlines

of a truly impressive figure, one capable of dominating an entire work. (pp. 42-3)

With all its strengths, *The Pilot* suffers from the lack of a consistent literary method. While Lie has discarded the artificial schema of an externally suspenseful plot, his manipulation of events and characters is evident in the weak denouement and elsewhere. Despite the unquestioned "truth and delicacy" of its characterization, Lie's psychological portrayal is sometimes vitiated by ulterior ends: to help the plot or point a moral. (p. 45)

Lie's recognition of the need for a psychological outlet to frustration is the key to the . . . deeper meaning [of *The Commodore's Daughters*], namely, a vision of the matriarchal family as a dangerous surrogate for meaningful women's roles in society. The dominant figure and the motive force of the novel is Mrs. With, the Commodore's wife, who rules her family with a iron hand. Desiring to maintain her social leadership, she speculates in marriage prospects for her son and her two daughters. The mother *par excellence,* she carries that role so far as paradoxically to ruin every one of her children. . . . And, contrary to Lie's hint, the reason for her destructiveness is not simply that she married a much older man—the Commodore is her senior by fifteen years—but that she is a gifted person, who, for want of anything else, puts her talents into running her children's lives. The novel shows how woman's self-image is being shattered by contradictions: though her role is still defined by motherhood, the old submissive mother has grown into a tyrant, who castrates her husband and devours her offspring. This marks a significant stage in woman's groping toward emancipation. (pp. 91-2)

Jonas Lie seems to identify with Cecilie [the daughter] in her rebellion against these conditions. Yet, he also appears to assume, like most of his characters, that women can attain happiness only as wives and mothers: in the end Cecilie finds meaning in life through being a mother to [her sister's] boy. Moreover, though the Commodore represents an antiquated social order, he is portrayed sympathetically, as though Lie recommends a return to his simple patriarchal values. In contrast to Ibsen who, despite his bourgeois way of life, explored the most unconventional possibilities of experience in his plays, Jonas Lie seldom strays far from the path of accepted ideas. That accounts, in large part, for his limitations as a novelist of social concern. (p. 93)

Though Lie's stock of characters [throughout his work] tend to be variations on a limited number of basic types, he rarely produces a sense of repetition. Because his novels are organic structures, his people are inseparable from the total rhythm of life—landscape, milieu, interiors, family setup, etc.—and therefore are not interchangeable. Partly for the same reason, partly because he focuses on human relations and on group behavior, few stand out as great imaginative creations. (p. 185)

Lie's fiction has no Père Goriot, Becky Sharp, or Oblomov—and no Ivan Karamazov. Captain Jaeger is his closest approximation to the former group of near-archetypal figures; none of his intellectuals even remotely approaches Ivan. A writer who, like Lie, was more concerned about *how* people think—as a clue to their being—than in "*what* they think" could not be greatly interested in portraying intellectuals as such. Yet, his character portrayal lacks neither breadth nor depth, and his figures are anything but marginal or trivial. (pp. 185-86)

While Lie used several methods of portrayal, he early abandoned the formal portrait, utilizing instead recurring motifs and incremental characterization through a succession of glimpses. Already *The Visionary* demonstrates his superior handling of this method: the formal portrait of David . . . is conventionally Romantic and mediocre; the doctor's subsequent observations as David's head is illuminated by the lamplight are sharp, detailed, and suggestive. . . . From [*Adam Schrader*] on, portrayal is nearly entirely indirect, accomplished through dialogue, others' opinions, rumor; or the figures define themselves in the process of observing or relating events. Expressive or symbolic action, exemplified by Sidney's furious lashing of the horses in [*Thomas Ross*] . . . , is effectively used.

These methods are limited insofar as they exclude a direct examination of motive. Lie does not open up his characters to inspection or expose their innermost secrets to the reader; they are not literary specimens to be analyzed, but fellow human beings with whose moods and feelings we can empathize even when we observe them mainly from without. . . . Because he did not pretend to know the cause and effect relationships operative in behavior, he could not analyze the psychic process but only present what was observable, hinting at what lay underneath the surface through intuitive glimpses whose meaning may not have been fully realized even by himself.

These suggestive psychological lacunae have a counterpart in narrative discontinuity: Lie follows his characters in jumps, not in gradual development. He renders the multiplicity of the successive moments and the movement within the scenes presented, thus giving a "firm shape to every stage of development"; but transitions are "obscured." This feature is a direct consequence of Lie's refusal to be anything but concrete. Unlike other Nordic writers, who in his view allowed "reason" to show its "ribs" too clearly in literature, he would not "talk anatomy instead of giving a human being" . . . ; he shows life and people in the sensory immediacy and fullness of the actual present. (pp. 186-87)

Skillful handling of dialogue and the stream of thought, the principal formal components of Lie's mature fiction, is of the utmost value to his character portrayal. (p. 189)

What he lacks because of his limited stock of characters and his circumscribed milieu—with its, admittedly, "small social frame for personality" . . . is redeemed by his thematic range, formal variety, and poetic feeling. Not content with reshaping the realistic novel through impressionism, he went on to create a new abstract fictional form that conveys an image of existence itself. Beyond such formal triumphs, his work contains a wealth of observation and interpretation of life, uncanny visionary insights into the psyche, and a deep humanity—qualities found only in great art. Because Jonas Lie possessed the gift of the poet to "vibrate in unison with all," we are moved by him; he exercises a "strange and disturbing enchantment." (p. 192)

> *Sverre Lyngstad in his* Jonas Lie *(copyright © 1977 by Twayne Publishers, Inc.; reprinted with the permission of Twayne Publishers, a Division of G. K. Hall & Co., Boston), Twayne, 1977, 223 p.*

ADDITIONAL BIBLIOGRAPHY

Larsen, Hanna Astrup. "Jonas Lie." *The American Scandinavian Review* XXI, No. 10 (December 1933): 461-71.
  Survey of Lie's major novels.

Lyngstad, Sverre. "The Vortex and Related Imagery in Jonas Lie's Fiction." *Scandinavian Studies* 51, No. 3 (Summer 1979): 211-48.
  Detailed examination of dominant images in Lie's fiction, such as the vortex, the eye, and the sun.

Wergeland, Agnes Mathilde. "'Second Sight' in Norse Literature." In her *Leaders in Norway and Other Essays,* edited by Katharine Merrill, pp. 139-45. 1916. Reprint. Freeport, N.Y.: Books for Libraries Press, 1966.*
  Claims that Lie's interest in clairvoyance and other supernatural events is endemic to the Norwegian national consciousness.

Wiehr, Joseph. "The Women Characters of Jonas Lie: Parts I and II." *The Journal of English and Germanic Philology* XXVIII, Nos. 1, 2 (1929): 41-71, 244-62.
  Analysis of Lie's women characters, who, in the critic's view, are generally superior to the men. Wiehr concludes that Lie's wife, Thomasine, influenced his sympathetic portrayal of women.

Gabriel (Francisco Víctor) Miró (Ferrer)

1879-1930

Spanish novelist, short story writer, and essayist.

The finely crafted, poetic quality of his prose, and a masterful use of irony and humor distinguish Miró's work. Long thought by many critics a mere *estilista*, adept at the mechanics of writing but with little substance to his work, Miró has been deemed by others a master at blending form and content.

The separation of people from each other and from God because of prejudice, fear, and pride, and the importance of nature and natural instincts are Miró's concerns throughout his canon. His settings are often the gardens and countryside of Spain's Mediterranean coastlands, which, evidencing his early interest in painting, are sensuously and romantically described. Such is the background of his strongest novels, *Nuestro padre San Daniel (Our Father San Daniel)* and *El obispo leproso*, novels of political, social, and religious struggle in the town of Oleza. Together they form a parable of the triumph of freethinking and modern ways over Spain's legacy of tradition and insularity.

Miró grew up in the province of Alicante on the Mediterranean, attending a Jesuit school in Orihuela, which became the model for Oleza. After studying law, he served in minor government positions in Barcelona. Miró began writing because of financial need, but his first novels and short stories met with little success, and not until the appearance of *Nómada* and *La palma rota* did he attract a sizeable readership. The early novel *Del vivir*, however, is notable for Miró's introduction of his alter ego, the wandering, contemplative Sigüenza, who while interacting with the people of Southern Spain, illuminates his creator's beliefs. Sigüenza later appears in *Libro de Sigüenza* and *Años y leguas*, which, along with *Figuras de la pasion del Señor (Figures of the Passion of Our Lord)*, *Our Father San Daniel*, and *El obispo leproso*, are his strongest work.

Miró aroused controversy in his country with the publication of *Figures of the Passion of Our Lord* and *Our Father San Daniel*. Although the books were generally well received, charges that he portrayed Jesus blasphemously in the former and attacked the Roman Catholic church in the latter led to a critical vendetta, instrumental in denying Miró literary awards and greater recognition in his own country. Of all his major works, only these two have been translated into English, perhaps because, as Edmund L. King has observed, he is one of Spain's most untranslatable writers. As a result of this limited exposure in the English-speaking world, Miró is usually perceived as a writer of slow-paced religious works. Many Spanish and English critics have noted Miró's careful descriptions and Flaubertian craftmanship, while but a few have come to appreciate his underlying humanitarian concerns and his technical innovations, such as the manipulation of narrative chronology, which give his stories an aura of timelessness.

Critics have said that Miró's writings defy easy classification; such a work as *Figures of the Passion of Our Lord* cannot be defined by a conventional genre. In form and subject his work stands between the traditions of the introspective Generation of 1898 and the aesthetic Generation of 1925. Miró's sense of

the power of words and his impressionistic use of them produced a rich prose that was widely appreciated only after his death.

PRINCIPAL WORKS

La mujer de Ojeda   (novel)   1901
Del vivir   (novel)   1904
Nómada   (novel)   1908
La palma rota   (novel)   1909
La cerezas del cementerio   (novel)   1910
El abuelo del rey   (novel)   1915
Figuras de la pasion del Señor. 2 vols.   (sketches)
    1916-17
    [*Figures of the Passion of Our Lord*, 1924]
Libro de Sigüenza   (sketches)   1917
El humo dormido   (sketches)   1919
El ángel, el molino, y el caracol del faro   (novel)   1921
Nuestro padre San Daniel   (novel)   1921
    [*Our Father San Daniel*, 1930]
El obispo leproso   (novel)   1926
Años y leguas   (novel)   1928

Obras completas. 12 vols.   (novels and sketches)
1932-49

SALVADOR de MADARIAGA (essay date 1923)

Spain is not a simple, but a complex unity, a trinity composed of a Western, a Central, and an Eastern modality, the norms of which respectively are Portugal, Castile, and Catalonia. Three languages (or groups of languages) embody these three spiritual modalities of the Spanish race. In the West, the Atlantic modality finds its expression in the Portuguese, of Latin languages the most tender and melodious. In the Centre, the Continental modality inspires that stately Castilian in which strength and grace are as harmoniously combined as tragedy and comedy in good drama. To the East, the Mediterranean modality shapes Catalan and its dialects, languages as supple and soft as clay, as vivid as painters' palettes, as receptive as the still waters of the clean sea which bathes the shores where they are spoken. (pp. 148-49)

There is to the south of Valencia a land historically within the kingdom, but spiritually a thing apart. It is the province of Alicante. . . . Alicante is the transition between dramatic Castile and the plastic East. Here, the spirit of the Centre touches the spirit of the East, Castile looks on the Mediterranean. The dramatic feeling of man emerges from its depths of concentration and meets on the surface the plastic sense of things. This delicately poised zone of the Spanish spirit is represented in Spanish letters by two contemporary authors: Azorín and Gabriel Miró.

Both these authors are East-Spaniards in their plastic outlook. Both look at life with the eyes of painters; not of painters like the Grecos of old and the Zuloagas of our day, who allow their inner ghost to guide their brush away from the primary aspects of reality, but of accurate and faithful observers of the surface of things. In both of them, we are struck by the vigour of that feeling for matter which is the typical feature of plastic Spain as of all plastic characters. Colour, texture, sound, inclination, reverberation, all effects on eyes, ears, skin, are most minutely observed, most felicitously rendered by both. . . . Miró, while relating a casual conversation, will seize and express this most trivial detail with exquisite accuracy; 'Don Magín lighted a cigarette and, his palate covered with a wool of smoke which made his voice sound graver, proceeded. . . .' This pictorial character of their art is emphasized by the use of the present tense. Both Azorín and Miró evince a significant leaning towards putting their verbs in the present, a tense which is essentially pictorial and *presents* events as scenes before the reader's eyes. Their narrative work is thus generally composed of a series of pictures, not moving as in the theatre or the cinema, but passing one after the other before our eyes as in a picture gallery. These pictures are usually understood in the manner of brilliant sketches, accurate yet not photographic, for their accuracy is due to the skilful selection of important and telling details, their brilliance to the illumination of these details by a style always clear. Both seem to paint with a sunbeam for a brush.

And then, they are not mere painters. Both approach life from its surface, but have also a feeling for the world of spirit underneath, a kind of uneasiness which does not allow them merely to rest on the surface and gives a human value, and

incidentally distinction, to their pictorial work. In them the plastic movement from the surface inwards is met by a spiritual movement from the depths outwards, a kind of human emotion which reveals the Castilian element in their nature. And it is in the eddies of these two æsthetic waves meeting that their inspiration takes its rise. Hence, these two artists— for they are artists, being of the East—while loving the surface of things with the sensuous love of the plastic Spaniard, give to their treatment of it a tremulous quality which makes it alive and is to their art like the bloom of fresh-gathered fruit. (pp. 152-54)

Gabriel Miró is nearer to the Castilian spirit than Azorín. He certainly is an Easterner. His vision is full of the light of the Mediterranean sea. 'In my town,' he says himself, 'from the moment we are born, our eyes are filled with the blueness of the waters.' And this luminosity is still the prevailing quality of his art. His approach to nature is still through the surface, and his tendency is plastic, as if to seize and mould what his senses, and particularly his eyes, perceive. He has the powers of minute observation which go with the plastic attitude, those powers which seem to consist in a mere capacity for stating what is there, before everybody's eyes, and yet are ever so much deeper, rooted in the recesses of sensibility. He has also, of the Easterner the deliberate attitude. He looks in order to see. We miss with him that casual air of the Castilian who seems to see without deliberately looking. Gabriel Miró is an active observer and a conscious artist.

He is, however, as an artist, both inferior to and more spontaneous than Azorín. The material in him is not so finely worked out by the skilful plastic mind. Now and then we feel an awkward sentence, a word out of place, a turn of idiom which is not quite pleasing or adequate. They are, to be sure, small faults, such faults as we would never notice in other writers, but which, here, leap to the eye, as scratches on the surface of burnished gold. Moreover, the matter with which Gabriel Miró deals is of a heavier, denser nature than that of Azorín. While Azorín prefers to seek his æsthetic emotion in the atmosphere which surrounds the objects of his observation, Miró seems on the contrary to seek emotion in the springs of life that lie hidden within the objects themselves. A more solid mind, he gives things more solidity. A graver mind, he gives them more weight. Hence often the impression that the material which he shapes is more rebellious to the hand than the light and air with which Azorín paints his little pictures.

For Miró is more profoundly affected than Azorín by the spirit of Castile. His material is more densely laden, more intimately amalgamated with human substance. The reader is often arrested by striking images in which a purely plastic form appears filled with a sense which is almost immaterial.

> Silence flowed densely from their mouths as
> dumb water from a gloomy rock.

Examples such as this could be found in practically every page of his works. They reveal a tendency to dwell in that zone of the mind where nature and man are seen, not exactly as one thing, but as two faces of one thing, so that our imagination naturally expresses the one in terms of the other. It is a region in which high poetry is conceived, and, given the power, created. Through his plastic road of access, Miró has penetrated farther than his countryman into the soul of poetry, for, though not so good an artist, he has a deeper sense of nature and man. Not that Azorín is lacking in this quality. He would not be an artist at all if he were. But while, in him, the poetical quality seems to be adjectival to his plastic tendency and merely to enhance and render more exquisite his pictorial ability, in Miró it is vital and strongly felt, it is in fact as central as his plastic tendency, and it sharpens and prolongs his penetration.

This poetic virtue is in Miró so natural and pure that he can, without effort, without almost meaning it, write limpid poetry in three or four simple words of prose that do not change the tone of the whole. Thus, speaking of a pool of clear water:

> And the foliage, the trunks, the rock, the cloud, the blue, the bird, all is seen within; and many a time we know that all this is beautiful because the water says it.

Because the water says it. This is more than mere simplicity. It is limpidity. And it is more than art. It is a clean spring of poetry born of a clear, luminous mind. (pp. 160-62)

We feel here the superiority of Miró over Azorín. His mind is deeper and more capable of a synthetic emotion of the world. This reveals itself primarily in superior powers of creation. I believe that Miró has been misled by his sheer plastic imagination into writing his two volumes of *Figuras de la Pasión*. They no doubt represent a fine effort to re-create several episodes directly or indirectly connected with the life and death of Christ. Often, as in his episode of Herodes Antipas, the ingenious turn given to the story adds a special merit of its own to what would otherwise have been a mere historical *pastiche*. But the style, in its effort to render the splendour of Jewish, Roman, and Assyrian life, is apt to take on that hard-driven gait which makes *Salammbô* such a painful book to read. Certainly, admirers of Flaubert's plastic efforts should find themselves at home in Miró's *Figuras de la Pasión*. But the true business of a Spanish artist is to make poetry with the here and now. And it is in this work that the best of Miró must be looked for. He has written several novels and books of sketches. The best—a good sign—are the latest. Many a fine page may be found in his *El Humo Dormido*, reminiscences of childhood written in a manner not unlike that of Marcel Proust, though fortunately with a more adequate idea of the right proportions between length and depth as well as of the time available for reading in the modern world. In *Nuestro Padre San Daniel*, 'a novel of chaplains and devout people', Miró has written a work which reveals the earnestness of his human preoccupation. There is in him an undercurrent of tenderness which gives his work a slightly melancholy tone. He is never rancorous, like Baroja, nor an ethical dilettante, like Valle Inclán, nor depressing like—but Spaniards are never depressing. He is just a little sad, as if he deplored that nature could be so beautiful and yet men so unworthy of it. Then, on the brink of coming to this conclusion, he repents. This attitude is admirably expressed in one of the most interesting stories in his best book [*El Ángel, El Molino, El Carocol del Faro*]. It is a story of an angel who settles down on Earth. A cherub comes to fetch him back. His wings have fallen, he has grown a beard and has become used to the ways of men. He gives the cherub a most pessimistic view of man's nature. The cherub then says: 'Well, I came to fetch you. Rise and come up.' But the angel says 'No'. And the exquisite page in which he explains why he wants to stay on earth can be summed up in this line of his, which is perhaps the kernel of Miró's philosophy: 'How sweet it is to feel near Heaven on Earth!'

This little book is full of such jewels, written with an eye that searches nature to its minutest details, but also with such an intensity of human feeling that we hardly know where man ends and nature begins in the delicate blend. The danger of such an art is that it may—it sometimes does—degenerate into fancy. As a rule, however, it is the creation of a bright, penetrating, and sensitive imagination, sustained by a poetic feeling of such simplicity and truth that it can elevate the statement of commonplaces to heights of limpid beauty as in this sentence, the serenity of which must not be troubled by translation: 'El alma del agua sólo reside en la tranquila plenitud de su origen.' (pp. 162-64)

> *Salvador de Madariaga, "Azorin: Gabriel Miró," in his* The Genius of Spain and Other Essays on Spanish Contemporary Literature *(© Oxford University Press, 1923; reprinted by permission of Oxford University Press), Oxford University Press, Oxford, 1923, pp. 148-64.**

THE NEW YORK TIMES BOOK REVIEW (essay date 1925)

One of the most unusual of books to issue from the press, not only in recent years, but at any time, is **"Figures of the Passion of Out Lord"** (**"Figuras de la Pasión del Señor"**) by the Spanish writer, Gabriel Miró. It is a book especially difficult to judge against the background of America; its correct setting is Miró's native land of Spain, with its religious fervor and its religious tradition. In this country the appeal of the book will be a group appeal; powerful, one would say, in many quarters less powerful in others. For those strong in what Edmund Burke called "the dissidence of dissent," it will be necessary to reconstruct for the **"Figures"** such a medieval setting as one constructs imaginatively to bring into perspective the religious painting of the older masters. This done, then Miró's portraits stand out upon the canvas in all their splendor of coloring, and with all their profound significance.

To say that a book is unusual is something of a generality, and it is essential that one become specific at once. And the book is not unusual in its selection of theme. The "Passion" of the Lord—His progress to judgment and death—has been (and naturally) as favorite a theme with religious writers down through the centuries as the various phases of that progress have been favorite subjects with the religious painters. The uniqueness of Señor Miró's contribution lies in its peculiar method of approach, and the effect resulting therefrom. The Spanish author has not written a historical novel—although the book is narrative; and he has not built up a drama—although the effect is that of drama. Miró has taken each one of the principal characters of the Passion, has reconstructed that character's past, and has drawn him in the light of that past, playing his part in the final tragedy—has projected him out of that past into the tragedy. Thus the whole becomes a continuous narrative, moving to its tragic end; at the same time the book is drama—of an amorphous sort—with its characters continually coming on and going off the stage. Also, and at the same time. **"Figures of the Passion"** is such a series of painting as, it would seem, only a medievalist could have conceived and executed. . . .

Miró is capable of every dramatic trick, and he uses every one to telling advantage. Jesus is more in the background than in the foreground until the trial scene before Pontius Pilate, when the dramatist places the two in tense and unforgettable contrast. From this point on, the movement on through the crucifixion is hurried and terrible.

Senor Miró has built up his *mise en scéne* with the greatest care; and this is fortunate, for if relief were not needed from the dramatic horror (as it is) relief would more than be needed to counterbalance the many physical horrors with which the Spanish author loads his pages; a matter which will be referred to again. Perhaps the author has carried the results of his archaeological studies too far, or, at least, gives them undue prominence now and again, an in his descriptions of the temple, and the palace of Pilate, which seem over-technical; but his descriptions of nature are sharp and distinct. (p. 6)

It is hardly to be supposed that **"Figures of the Passion"** was conceived in any way as a defense of the crucifixion, and yet, with the historical ramifications of the book; the care with which the author brings to life the customs of the time and the place and the people, subject to Rome and set off against Rome; Herod's jealousy of Pilate, and Pilate's fear of Rome, and, above all, the fanatical jealousy with which the Sanhedrin guarded its immemorial rights—in view of all these, as brought out by Miró (assuming his correctness) the book becomes, if not a defense, at least an explanation of the putting to death of Jesus.

The least pleasing feature of the book—a feature which will be obnoxious to all but certain readers—is the minuteness with which the author goes into the agonizing details of the later phases of the narrative, and unless this is understood the book will, as hinted at earlier, most probably be cast aside. And the explanation, one only can suppose, is the theory that in the mental torture thus engendered does the reader come to a state in which the martyrdom of Jesus is in some degree his own. . . . [The] final passage of the crucifixion scene [is an example]. . . . (pp. 6, 16)

[This scene] was assuredly not written by the author with the mere attempt at objective realism; that it comes of that same religious fervor which welcomes mortification of the flesh and self-imposed suffering in the quest for humility it is necessary to believe. To take any other view is to find in the book banality and a falseness tantamount to literary insincerity.

Most of those who take up **"Figures of the Passion"** will come to the conclusion that it is a mistake to read it through with anything like the continuous application given a novel. Rather, one should move from picture to picture with the deliberateness in which one moves from picture to picture in a gallery. And one should move also reverently, for, truly, these pictures by Gabriel Miró are stations of the cross, stations conceived by a modern attempting with faith to revisualize and to revitalize the most cherished moments of a religious past. (p. 16)

"Tragic Drama of the Crucifixion: 'Figures of the Passion of Our Lord', a Strange Reconstruction of the Medieval Setting," in The New York Times Book Review *(© 1925 by The New York Times Company; copyright renewed © 1953 by The New York Times Company; reprinted by permission), March 15, 1925, pp. 6, 16.*

NEW STATESMAN (essay date 1925)

[*Figures of the Passion of Our Lord*] is a book one cannot ignore. Its design, as the title suggests, is an elaborate reconstruction of a story which to most readers is intimately familiar; it is long, and packed and pressed down with an almost bewildering detail; the air of it is brooding and sultry like a night of successive thunderstorms; and in its insistence on harshness and cruelty and bodily pain, that mobs will jeer at its victims in agony, that torture is something undergone in a terrible solitude of spirit, the narrative of the Passion as related by Sr. Miró is remorseless.

Nowhere, in all his fifteen crowded cartoons of the Passion of Christ, has the Spanish writer sought to lay any specious balm on the feelings of his readers by extracting the mellifluous lessons of "tenderness" or "comfort" from the gall and wormwood of Calvary. Rather has he turned back, with a passionate conviction that cries out over and over again, to a vision of the Crucifixion older, simpler, ruder than those interpretations and refinements to which the great mass of modern Christians have grown complacently accustomed. On this vision there is no gloss of sermons and homilies; the facts of the Betrayal, Trial, and Crucifixion are presented with the lavish prolixity of a powerful historical imagination, and without the timid reticences that have grown up around the physical sufferings of Christ, but with no loss of dignity, and with no attempt to boom out the implicit spiritual overtones. How strangely it compares with those volumes which annually at this season are "recommended" by the several Bishops "for Lenten reading." . . . Beside such books, the Spanish writer's intense realisation of the sequence of Easter is startling.

The purpose, it must be admitted, is different. The "figures" of the title is a word not without its significance. For the book is a painter's rather than a theologian's creation. It is, first and last, visual. It is a narrative followed by the eyes, a recounting of things seen in the fierce light of the South, with the shadows as sharp as the edges of blades, not rounded and softened by meditation and deduction. (p. 17)

[Miró's position was one of] mystical realism; it is back to this that Miró would seem to be reaching. . . .

In the plastic arts, of course, there has often been expression of this. In letters, seldom. It is curious that the conventional criticism of such work as Miró's should amount to little more than that the story of the Passion has been told, once and for all, in the Gospels. Well and good. But could it be urged that in paint there must only be one version of the Last Supper? Again, it might be urged that the violently realistic portrayal of the physical sufferings of Christ is objectionable, somehow an exhibition of "bad form," something which is glibly put down as "Latin," not to say morbid. But this is no innovation in taste. Faced frankly, the act of crucifying *is* peculiarly beastly. Generations who lived nearer to pain and violence that we do, recognised this more sharply than is now customary. . . .

It is hard to think of any comparable contemporary work more moving than this broad canvas from modern Spain. Anatole France and Mr. George Moore remain unscathed, but beside it they are—what? An etching, and a wash drawing. And certainly [Giovanni] Papini is left looking very excited and uncouth: the dignity and significance of Miró's narrative must be obvious at once after the hurrying throbs of the Florentine's voice. (p. 18)

"Gabriel Miró," in New Statesman *(© 1925 The Statesman Publishing Co. Ltd.), Vol. XXV, No. 625, April 18, 1925, pp. 17-18.*

FRANCES DOUGLAS (essay date 1927)

Spanish fiction of the day is perhaps more distinguished for beauty of style than for action and complication of plot. . . . [The modern writers] excel in description of character, in charming word-pictures of landscape and in the presentation of intimate vistas of life in the Spanish cities and in the rural pueblos. Each region is represented by its particular group of novelists, as, to mention only a few, Pio Baroja and Félix Urabayen, illustrious Basques, . . . and Gabriel Miró of the maritime province of Alicante, of which he is an honored son.

Miró is much in the limelight at the moment because of his new novel, **"El Obispo Leproso" (The Leper Bishop).** Miró's work is known to readers of English through his amazing book, **"Figures of the Passion of Our Lord."** . . . Miró possesses the gift of presenting his characters with a vividness that startles, as do the realistic representations of Christ and the saints on the altars of the dark Spanish churches. This may be in part because he was educated in a Jesuit college and has spent his life in a deeply religious atmosphere.

Oleza, the archaic town which he depicts in **"The Leper Bishop,"** is so pious that there was not a single enemy of the faith within its precincts, and the coming of the railroad, with the worldly, hurrying engineers who built it, gives occasion for bitter protest. A marvelously vivid picture of the town and its sanctimonious inhabitants is presented. So unerring is the prose of the author that the book seems to emit the light, to glow with the color and to give off the odor of this Mediterranean district that is so famous for its raisins, its dates, wines and oil. Through reading Miró, so dependable is his psychology, a better understanding of Spain and Spanish character is obtained.

> *Frances Douglas, "Style Is Today Supreme in Spanish Fiction," in* The New York Times Book Review *(© 1927 by The New York Times Company; copyright renewed © 1955 by The New York Times Company; reprinted by permission), July 3, 1927, p. 14.*

TIME AND TIDE (essay date 1930)

[*Our Father San Daniel* is a] crowded, coloured, rather bewildering chronicle of nineteenth-century Spain. Its priests and Carlists, hidalgos, horrors and intrigues make the town of Oleza seem far remote in both time and space than it is really. In his introduction, Mr. Arthur Machen compares Miro to Dickens; the crowded canvas, the lively characterization and exaggerated gusto of Dickens are here, but these colours are darker and softer; these episodes never assume the unity of a Dickens story.

> *"Critic's Commentary: 'Our Father San Daniel'," in* Time & Tide, *Vol. 11, No. 28, July 12, 1930, p. 905.*

SUSAN O'SULLIVAN (essay date 1967)

The richness and the originality of the imagery in the prose of Gabriel Miró have always fascinated his literary critics, whether admirers or detractors of his work. . . . [Very few, however,] have analysed in depth the underlying significance of Miró's imagery. One of the most important studies in this field is L. J. Woodward's article, 'Les Images et leur fonction dans *Nuestro Padre San Daniel* de Gabriel Miró.' (p. 107)

Woodward shows how the characters in *Nuestro Padre San Daniel* are roughly divided into two antagonistic groups—'les vivants et les nonvivants'—and how these two groups are subtly distinguished by Miró through a symbolic use of images of light and darkness. Apart from the main distinction, Woodward indicates how the two groups of characters are further distinguished by sets of opposed images, all dependent on the basic contrast symbolized by the polarities light/dark, warmth/cold, fertility/sterility. It is my intention in this article to attempt a brief analysis of three of these images—the watch, the lemon, and the pair of spectacles from the early work of Miró onwards and to show how the novelist arrived at the particular value which he attaches to them in his later, major novels.

In his study Woodward draws particular attention to Miró's treatment of eyes. . . . Cararajada and Elvira share [the] trait of gleaming, phosphorescent eyes. Even Don Daniel on his death-bed has glazed eyes. Throughout his work, Miró reveals a particular interest in eyes and it is not surprising, therefore, to find that in this and other novels, he extends this image with reference to spectacles, which by their very nature tend to give the wearer a glazed look and form a barrier between him and the world. In the following examples I hope to demonstrate that it is possible to trace the development of the image from a mere detail of physical description to its emergence as a symbol.

In view of Miró's tendency to relate this image to characters whom he portrays as far from sympathetic, it is interesting to find that the earliest occurrence of the image is as a simple visual detail concerning his brother, Juan [in the short, autobiographical article entitled *El Rápido Paris-Orán*]. . . . (pp. 107-08)

However, in the short story, *Corpus* . . . , spectacles are no longer a simple, physical distinguishing mark, but have acquired a stronger—and unpleasant—emotive overtone. The wearer is the Rector, so much admired by Ramonete's devout aunt who only stops scolding Ramonete in church when the Rector enters the pulpit. . . . (p. 108)

The suggestion that the Rector is cold and harsh comes not only from the direct comparison [of the Rector] with the cliché of the bad-tempered schoolmaster, but also from the admiration of Ramonete's aunt, because she strikes the dominant note of indifference and hostility to Ramonete which is echoed by every other figure who appears in the story.

That spectacles, or glass, can paradoxically become an impediment to the vision that they are designed to improve is emphasized in [an] exchange between Ramonete and his aunt [concerning the presence of the host within the monstrance]. . . . (pp. 108-09)

This use of the image to emphasize a specific and unpleasant trait of character continues in *La palma rota* . . . , where the image is attached to a minor figure, the *abogado* whose cultural pretensions are shown to be based on false values and an incapacity for any true emotional response. In the opening chapter the old musician, Gráez, is moved to tears by the novel written by the young hero, Aurelio Guzmán, and is mocked by the [bespectacled] lawyer. . . .

The character of the lawyer here is insignificant but what is interesting is that Miró, when describing a person who represents one facet of the bourgeois society that he, like Aurelio, so much despised, should choose this image alone to characterize that person, as though the image had already acquired a symbolic significance. (p. 110)

[In *Nuestro Padre San Daniel* and *El obispo leproso*] Miró develops this use of his image to such an extent that the image is more important than the minor character it describes. . . . This character, the Bishop's secretary, appears in the narrative only in relation to the Bishop and his rôle is that of a protective barrier between the Bishop and the curious, often hostile society of Oleza. Thus he acts as a pair of spectacles for the Bishop, colourless, cold and impenetrable. (pp. 110-11)

[In] the very introduction of this character to the reader and to Oleza, the man [begins] to disappear, like the Cheshire Cat, behind the defensive screen of his spectacles. Subsequently the secretary's presence is often indicated by the glint of his glasses alone. . . . (p. 111)

The use of the image as a symbol of a barrier between the wearer and others also extends in *Nuestro Padre San Daniel* and *El obispo leproso* to the character of Don Vicente Grifol. This kindly and perceptive doctor is so easily forgotten even by his friends that it seems as though, in his case, his spectacles provide protective colouring, rendering him invisible to the outside world in which, nonetheless, he plays his unobtrusive part. (p. 112)

[It is] significant that, in contrast with all the previous examples given where spectacles gleam or glint suggesting unpleasant characteristics, his should be constantly misted over, for here they are the outward and visible signs of an inner and spiritual grace.

Don Vicente Grifol also provides a clue to the underlying symbolism of the imagery of the lemon tree in *Nuestro Padre San Daniel* and *El obispo leproso*. The association of this image with María Fulgencia . . . [has] become a critical commonplace, but it seems likely that the image has a wider application. (p. 113)

The Bishop is destined to be the sacrificial victim of Oleza and his skin disease is ['the mandate and token of another hidden evil, of an unmentionable etiology']; but contrasted with this physical corruption in his purity of heart which seems to be symbolized by the lemon. On the days when he is well, the Bishop [feeds the pigeons, while sitting, reading, and enjoying the scent of the nearby lemon boughs]. (p. 114)

The lemon is also a symbol, not so much of María Fulgencia, as of the essential innocence and purity of the relationship between her and Pablo. . . . The childlike innocence of this relationship is emphasized . . . throughout. [An example is] the much-commented scene [in which] María Fulgencia cleans Pablo's lapel with ['a lemon like a fragrant ball of light']. (p. 115)

These examples of the use of the lemon image help to reveal the underlying significance of an earlier occurrence, in *Nuestro Padre San Daniel*. The scene is the departure to Madrid of the delegation supporting Don Cruz's candidacy for the Bishopric, which is led by Don Amancio Espuch, alias *Alba Longa*, and which represents the climax of a long and ardent campaign on the part of the conservative and obscurantist element of Oleza. *Alba Longa*, who carries 'un hermoso limón para repararse con su aroma de las bascas del camino', is taking an effusive farewell of Don Cruz when the fateful news arrives that the new Bishop has already been appointed. (p. 116)

It is significant that it [is] Alba Longa who drops the lemon, symbol of innocence and of a love of life that he and his friends cannot share, because he later marries María Fulgencia, and thus provides yet another example of an unsuccessful attempt to unite, or graft, the two opposing factions of Oleza. In the context, therefore, this action of dropping the lemon, combining the suggestion of throwing down the gauntlet with a reminiscence of the golden apple of discord, represents the dichotomy of the society of Oleza, the consequence of which form much of the substance of the two novels.

If the lemon symbolizes 'Inocencia y sensualidad . . .', values of another kind, if not of an opposite type, are often symbolized by a watch. Perhaps the best known example is Monera's watch in *Nuestro Padre San Daniel*. . . . (pp. 116-17)

Monera's habit of consulting his watch unnecessarily reveals his nervous lack of self-confidence and Miró uses this detail to trace Monera's rise and fall in the esteem of his companions. (p. 117)

This gesture is characteristic of Monera but it occurs elsewhere indicating a similar unease. The earliest example concerns Ignacio, the protagonist of *El hijo santo* . . . , who gives all the money in his pockets to the beggars he meets, and who is so embarrassed when he is importuned by more beggars that he smiles timidly and takes out his watch. . . . [In the case of Don César in *El abuelo del rey*,] the gesture suggests not so much unease as a pedantic fussiness. (pp. 117-18)

The watch, which is practical and efficient yet incapable of measuring the inner tempo of one's life—the *tiempo vital* of Antonio Machado—often seems to represent those characteristics of provincial society which Miró most dislike and which were so alien to his own temperament. . . .

Don César in *El abuelo del rey*, is pompous and petty, full of an arid learning that serves no useful purpose except that of inflating his own self-esteem. Monera, in *Nuestro Padre San Daniel* and *El obispo leproso*, is a social climber, servile and resentful, sterile both physically and spiritually.

With Bardells, in *Años y leguas* . . . , the emphasis changes slightly. Bardells is a self-made man, a peasant who by his drive and ruthlessness has achieved the prosperity and status of the middle class, and has long abandoned his youthful ideals and ambitions, just as he broke his engagement with the girl he loved when he discovered that she was incurably ill. Yet he has not completely buried the idealistic, unselfish aspect of his character under the material ambition which is the motive force of his life. The glass of his watch is cracked and he has never had it repaired. . . . The secret of his watch and its significance lies in the story of how the glass came to be cracked. Bardells' fiancée suffered from a heart disease. . . . For six years Bardells waits hoping that the girl will recover. Finally [he breaks the watch in despair]. (p. 119)

Bardells, whose watch still works though the glass is cracked, provides a link with Arcadio and Agustín in *El abuelo del rey*, whose watch is broken and never goes. When Agustín passes his *bachillerato*, his grandfather presents him with 'un relojito de plata empañada' which Augustín quickly discovers is broken and, in his opinion, useless. . . .

[But] in later years when he is far from home and family and embittered by the failure of his illusions, he understands at last its true value. (p. 120)

The broken watch is a symbol of an imagination and of a conception of life that are not confined within the conventions of a materialistic society but which reaffirm the supremacy of spiritual values. Its importance lies not only in the light it sheds on the character of Arcadio in *El abuelo del rey*, but also in the fact that this affirmation is one of the most important themes running through the whole of Miró's work.

Of the three images studied in this article only the lemon image can be considered as fully symbolical. Its use is confined to *Nuestro Padre San Daniel* and *El obispo leproso* where it is given an abstract value which is revealed through a study of its application to the Bishop and to Pablo and María Fulgencia, and which in turn illumines their characters.

The image of the watch which works, however, like the image of glinting spectacles, is often no more than a descriptive technique, although both images are deliberately employed by Miró to convey certain characteristics about the person to whom they are applied. It is only in the later works that these images acquire symbolic significance:—

spectacles: The Bishop's secretary and Vicente Grifol in *Nuestro Padre San Daniel* and *El obispo leproso*

the broken watch: Arcadio and Agustín in *El abuelo del rey*

the cracked watch: Bardells in *Años y leguas.*

Yet even when the image is not a symbol in itself, it can reinforce the symbolism of other, germane images. (pp. 120-21)

The images in Miró's work are not merely structural, but so closely interwoven and inter-related that to attempt to unravel the significance of any one image inevitably leads to the consideration of others. A full-length study is needed to do justice to the complexity of this subject which must be explored if one is to understand fully Miró's attitude—so often misinterpreted—to the themes which recur throughout his work, and to appreciate the way in which the author uses his style as the tool of his psychological perception and subtle intelligence. (p. 121)

> Susan O'Sullivan, "Watches, Lemons and Spectacles: Recurrent Images in the Works of Gabriel Miró," in Bulletin of Hispanic Studies (© copyright 1967 Liverpool University Press), Vol. XLIV, No. 2, 1967, pp. 107-21.

G. G. BROWN (essay date 1975)

In Spanish literature, the tradition of embroidering original works of art, for whatever purpose, with allusions to familiar myth, legend and older literature, gained a new lease of life in the first decades of the twentieth century, when many of the best writers were addressing themselves to a cultured minority of readers in order to affirm, as a reaction against the professed aims of nineteenth-century realism, the difference between art and life. Gabriel Miró is certainly one of the writers who made use of such devices. Nobody is likely to dispute, for example, that the Cervantine elements of *Las cerezas del cemeterio* constitute an important guide to our interpretation of Miró's attitudes to the novel's protagonist. It would seem certain that the biblical allusions in the Oleza novels fulfil a similar purpose to some degree and in some

sense. Calculation of the degree and analysis of the sense are, however, not easy matters. . . . The second question—in what sense—presents a particularly awkward problem in this case. Miró's Oleza novels, *Nuestro Padre San Daniel* and *El obispo leproso*, deal with a particular moment in the social history of a Spanish provincial town. The changes which were taking the place at that moment were of great personal importance to Miró, because they demolished the world in which he had grown up. They were, moreover, changes to which he responded in retrospect in a profoundly ambivalent manner, and always an extremely personal one. He is writing about a real, observed society, writing with a marked sense of personal involvement, probably including more factual and even autobiographical material than it is now possible to verify. . . . Yet, as I hope to show, Miró's purpose goes very much further than that of giving an account of how Orihuela changed during the years of his childhood. From beginning to end, the events he narrates are purposefully associated with stories told in his own favourite book, the Bible. My suggestion is that a proper understanding of these fine, subtle novels depends to a large extent on our being aware of the use Miró makes of biblical parallels.

Every student of Miró's writings will have noticed that his knowledge of the Bible and of biblical scholarship was astonishingly thorough for a Catholic-educated Spaniard of this period. It is also beyond doubt that *Nuestro Padre San Daniel* is in some way related to the Book of the Prophet Daniel. From early on in the novel, Miró takes some trouble to assure us that, in spite of Don Jeromillo's doubts, the wooden image of San Daniel is indeed the image of the Old Testament prophet. (pp. 786-87)

The Prophet Daniel was a Prince of Judah who, during the Babylonian captivity, worked tirelessly, by means of exhortation, prophetic threats and spectacular miracles, to prevent his people—captive Judah—from succumbing to the temptations offered by sensual, luxury-loving, polytheistic Babylon. In Miró's novel, the allusive link is firmly forged by Don Amancio's article in *El Clamor de la Verdad* after the old Bishop's death, when he describes Oleza (his Oleza) as a 'nueva sierva de Babilonia,' . . . and by the subsequent arrival of Álvaro, a putative prince of 'la buena causa' (in this case Carlism), to restore Babylon-Oleza to the paths of righteousness.

So far we are still indisputably on firm ground. Miró has asserted that Oleza's San Daniel is the Old Testament prophet, and explicitly associates the attitudes of the San Daniel faction in Olzea with the outlook and character of the biblical Daniel. It quickly becomes clear how Miró, reading his Bible, must have detested the prophet—arrogant, ascetic, vindictive, obsessed by a sense of sin, the veritable incarnation of the forces of darkness in Oleza. Some quite specific associations between the Old Testament narrative and the behavior of the San Daniel faction help to bear this out. For example, in the story of Bel and the Dragon, Daniel kills the dragon, which the Babylonians are worshipping as a god (but which he knows to be a devil), by feeding it balls of pitch, fat, and hair, which, in the words of the Authorized Version, cause it to 'swell up and burst in sunder.' . . . In *Nuestro Padre*, this becomes one of the sadistic tricks which P. Bellod, like so many characters in Miró's novels, habitually plays on small, defenceless animals. Bellod is uneasy about a cat which is following him about and distracting him from his prayers, and which he suspects of being an agent of the devil.

He gets rid of it by inducing it to swallow a dry sponge, then making it drink water until it swells up and similarly bursts in sunder.

Other associations of the kind are made with the enemies of the Prophet Daniel. In the Old Testament these are principally the so-called Chaldeans, the pagan, polytheistic court astrologers who are the chief counsellors of the Babylonian kings. In Miró's novel, the principal and most effective champion in the struggle against the San Daniel faction is Don Magin, who happens to be learned in the subject of Babylonian and Assyrian history, and warmly eloquent about it. . . . He also has a scholarly or antiquarian tendency to speak of 'los dioses,' . . . which seems to alarm the naive Don Jeromillo, presumably because he thinks that a Christian priest ought to use the singular. The Bishop, Magin's friend, is also learned in such matters. . . . (pp. 787-88)

[Miró's] sympathies lie with Magín and the Bishop, and not with the Álvaro and his sort. But it may be legitimate to pursue the associations considerably further. The Prophet Daniel is famous, of course, for more than slaying dragons and taming lions. Generations of biblical exegetes have been much more interested in his intricate, esoteric prophecies. . . . In view of this pointed allusion, it may be worth while looking at some of the best known prophecies. (p. 789)

[One] evocation of the Book of Daniel which hardly seems likely to be accidental is the business of the rebuilding of the Sanctuary. The ninth chapter of Daniel begins with a torrent of recrimination from the Prophet about the sinfulness of his people and their need for severe punishment. A metaphor of sinfulness which has been used in earlier chapters is repeated. The Sanctuary of the Lord is desolate. . . . In *Nuestro Padre* this must have something to do with the otherwise enigmatic topic of the desolation of San Daniel's chapel. The San Daniel faction believes that it is the Bishop's doing. Bellod is furious, and he and his friends are convinced that the Bishop has instructed the architect to keep the [flood-damaged] chapel closed and a shambles for as long as possible. Much play is made of the fact that the architect himself is suspected of sexual immorality—another suggestion that the 'nueva sierva de Babilonia' is being castigated for condoning indulgence in Babylonian sensuality. The result of the desolation is that traditional supplication to the Saint, now removed to tempoary lodgings, is felt to be inauthentic and inefficacious. But, after the flood, the Bishop seems to relent, and does actually have the Sanctuary restored at last.

This change of heart is related to what may be the most remarkable parallel of all, for it would seem that the time-structure of *Nuestro Padre* is none other than that of Daniel's great prophecy of the Seventy Weeks, traditionally regarded as one of the most important prophecies in the Old Testament. . . . (p. 790)

In Miró's novel the flood takes place on 20 July. Counting back sixty-nine weeks we arrive at the beginning of the action of the novel. 'Present' events in the novel, as distinct from information and anecdotes about the past, begin with the appointment of Bellod as vicar of the parish of San Daniel. No precise date is given for this event, but just after it we are told that 'comenzaba abril.' . . . That is to say that about sixty-nine weeks before 'la riada' (which brings us to 23 March), Bellod is appointed, and the story starts. If this is at all significant, we must naturally look to see if anything happens to mark the end of the first of the three periods of

the prophecy, which would be seven weeks after Bellod's appointment. Again, Miró gives no precise date, but it is plain that it was some seven weeks after 23 March—11 May or thereabouts—when the telegram arrived announcing the appointment of the new bishop. Although he does not actually arrive until 7 June, it is the news of the appointment, inaugurating a sixty-two-week period of strife in Oleza, which sends Don Amancio's lemon, ridiculously transformed into the apple of discord of the Judgement of Paris, rolling across the streets of Oleza. Then, at the end of the sixty-two-week period, the prince who has been threatening the city 'afirmará su alianza con muchos en una semana' (Daniel 9. 27). In the novel, soon after the flood, the Bishop gets the repairs to the Sanctuary finished at last . . . , and, in the chapter entitled 'Hasta los males pasan', there is a notable atmosphere of peace and reconciliation after the crisis. This is also when Pablo is born. (pp. 790-91)

One matter that is . . . certainly related to the Bible is that of the Bishop's leprosy. The subject deserves a study of its own, but for present purposes offers a further illustration of the interesting light which can be thrown on Miró's novel if one investigates its biblical sources. When the Bishop discusses his affliction with Dr. Grifol in the fourth chapter of *El obispo leproso*, their conversation refers to Leviticus 13, where the Mosaic laws for the diagnosis of leprosy are laid down. Their talk makes it clear that Miró was familiar with this relatively obscure part of the Bible. This is not altogether surprising, since leprosy was still endemic in the part of Spain in which Miró had grown up. One of his earliest books, *Del vivir*, written when he was only twenty-three, takes Miró's *alter ego*, Sigüenza, into the leprous villages of Parcent, where at times he ponders on the Old Testament convention of regarding leprosy as a divine punishment for sinful behavior. More interesting, though, is the use which Miró makes, in *El obispo leproso*, of Leviticus 14. This part of the Law goes on to codify the even more abstruse subject of the ritual purification of leprosy. One important ritual involves taking a pair of doves, one of which has to be sacrificed. For the reader of Miró, the allusion is inescapably clear. María Fulgencia was deeply concerned about the Bishop's affliction. During the time she spent as a novice in the convent of La Visitación she kept two doves as pets. The sinister Madre Clavaria, who sees the spectre of sin in every manifestation of María Fulgencia's spontaneous love of joy and beauty, kills *one* of the pair. Whereupon María Fulgencia leaves the convent and impulsively marries Don Amancio: in ordinary human terms a very bad match, but in the terms of Miró's narrative, a decisive link in the chain of events which leads directly from the killing of the pigeon to the destruction of the San Daniel faction.

If such curiously detailed allusions are deliberately intended by Miró, as they must be, the question remains: to what end? It is hardly likely that he made them as a writer like Pérez de Ayala often did, in a spirit of playful pedantry, the spirit of the setter of a crossword puzzle. What Miró seems to wish to do is to graft his reading of his beloved Bible—whose stories he treasures but does not believe—on to his memories of old Orihuela, whose passing he does not regret, but whose memories afford him an acutely pleasant nostalgia. . . . [It] does not seem unreasonable to relate the two parts of Miró's story, *Nuestro Padre San Daniel* and *El obispo leproso*, to the Old and New Testaments respectively. The broad parallel at least makes sense. Old Testament Judaism, of the kind championed by the Prophet Daniel, exclusivist, puritanical, legalistic, arrogant, gave way, after Christ's coming, to the broader, more humane ideals of Christianity, a faith for Gentiles. Miró certainly regarded his historical development with sympathy and approval, the same sort of approval with which he welcomed the new Oleza/Orihuela, brought into being about the turn of the century, largely because the railway (in the novel, the Bishop's achievement) now linked the old town to the modern world outside, and put an end to the unhealthy, claustrophobic influence of the guilt-ridden, clerical-Carlist influence in Oleza.

Miró belonged to the school of thought which considers the fundamental changes from Old Testament to New Testament thinking to have been effected much more by St. Paul than by Christ himself or by the Evangelists. His most explicit statement to this effect is the piece of *El humo dormido* entitled 'San Juan, San Pedro y San Pablo' . . . , where he shows himself to be an ardent admirer of Paul because of his success in providing the early Christian faith with a doctrine—'Pablo es el primer intelectual del Christianismo' . . . —and because of his tireless work, his journeys and his epistles, in the cause of converting people to the new faith. . . . In the Oleza novels, the choice of Pablo's name is not accidental. Don Amancio notes the allusion . . . , and perhaps significantly, prefers to think of Pablo as Saul. St. Paul's conversion was the outcome of a clash between the Judaic faith of his fathers and the call of the new religion of the spirit. He was converted on the road to Damascus by a ray of light which temporarily blinded him. In Miró's novel Pablo is caught uncomfortably between the stern, life-denying world of his traditionalist father—Miró is careful to remind us on several occasions that Pablo is the son of his father as well as of his mother—and that of the impulsive, life-loving Paulina. Pablo breaks free from the dark and narrow world of his father's friends and is pushed towards maturity as a result of his affair with a girl called, surely not accidentally, María Fulgencia. In Miró's essay on St. Paul there are sufficient parallels with *El obispo elproso* to rule out accident; among them, Miró's description, in the essay, of Paul's conversion as *fulminate,* and, in the novel, the unmistakable echo of Acts 9. 4 ('Saulo, Saulo, ¿por qué me persigues?') in María Fulgenica's 'Pablo, Pablo: usted entre ellos.' . . . The association does not stop there. As we see from the essay, Miró's esteem for St. Paul also derives from the Saint's impatience with the hair-splitting dogmatism of Mosaic law in respect of such trivial matters as unclean meats, which are repeatedly swept aside in the Epistles as archaic taboos, irrelevant to the true religious experience of having Christ 'dwell in your heart, rooted and grounded in love'. In this connexion, another curious parallel appears: the matter of María Fulgencia's oddly obsessive search for her Angel, identified at first with the wooden image of the sexless Angel of Salcillo, then with her cousin Mauricio, and finally with Pablo himself. Among a number of suggestive references to angels in Paul's Epistles, the most directly relevant is in Colossians 2. 18, where Paul warns the faithful of Colossae, in the same sentence, against the dangers of self-mortification on the one hand and the worship of angels on the other. No reader of Miró needs reminding of his disapproval of pious self-mortification. But as regards the worship of angels, it is interesting to see that María Fulgencia, the angel-worshipper of Miró's novel, is rather cruelly punished for her folly at the end of *El obispo leproso.* After the scandal, she is removed to Murcia, where she spends her time watching the trains leaving Murcia for Oleza, thinking that her Angel, Pablo, might be indulging in a similar sentimentality at his end of the line. The cruelty lies in the way

Miró goes on to tell us that in fact Pablo does habitually go up to a high window in his house to watch the trains, but that the trains in which he is interested are not the ones which link him to María Fulgencia. The trains he watches are those that run thanks to the Bishop's initiative, connecting Oleza with the wide world outside the province, the trains . . . carrying the beautiful flowers and fruit of the region which can now be exported to the outside world. If there is a thematic association between Pablo and St. Paul, this looks very like an allusion to Paul's missionary journeys, recalled with such admiration by Miró in *El humo dormido*.

It seems impossible to doubt that connexions of this kind were present in Miró's mind. The last chapter of *El obispo leproso* suggests, in a delicate and poignant way, the personal feelings which may have caused him to make the association. The chapter is about the railway, as its title indicates, and all that is now made possible by the railway naturally meets with Miró's approval. This last chapter could well have been influenced by a last backward look at Chapter 12 of the [Book of Daniel, which speaks of an increase in the people's wisdom, related to an increase in travel]. . . . The Bishop [of *El obispo leproso*], who brought the railway on which many will now run to and fro, has led the wise towards maturity, towards an understanding that hierarchs are unnecessary, that the time has come for the people of Oleza to grow up, and stop looking to some father-figure for authority. That, surely, is the point of his weary indifference, from the very start of the novel, to the fractiousness of the Olezans and the importance they attach to his office. It is also the point of his failure (because he is dying) to fulfil his promise to help Paulina when she knocks on his door. Also, perhaps, the point of having him suffer from a disease characterized by a progressive epidermal insensitivity which is the paradoxical outward symptom of a critical nervous condition under the flesh—a fact recognized by the wise Grifol. . . . It is certainly the point of Miró's careful statement to the effect that when the leprous Bishop dies, in marked contrast to the period that followed the death of the last Bishop, when Oleza felt itself orphaned and anguished, this time months pass without the new appointment being announced, and nobody cares. . . . Miró plainly sees this as a welcome state of affairs. In fact the novel closes on an almost identical note to that of the ending of his earlier book, *El abuelo del rey.* . . . Both books end by affirming that the changes occurring in Spanish provincial life towards the end of the 1890s were to be welcomed. But the changes marked the end of Miró's own childhood, and of a world whose quaint and often comic charm he evokes with tenderness. In both books he is applying his maxim that there is pleasurable emotion to be had from recalling unpleasant experiences, provided that a sufficient distance in time has been able to play its necessary part. In a sense, this sort of nostalgic evocation is crystallized in Miró's treatment of Don Magín, the representative of all that was best in old Oleza, but in the new Oleza of the last chapter, a sad anachronism, dwindling into insignificance on the station platform while the reader, who is on the train, speeds away to new horizons.

The biblical parallels and allusion would therefore appear to spring from Miró's personal, emotional responses to his childhood memories. As such they become a kind of metaphor of his state of mind, deriving from the awareness that he could best express his feelings about the passing of his childhood in terms of his feelings about the Old and New Testaments. It has often been noted how Miró, throughout his writings, draws comparisons between his native region and the Palestine of biblical times. The purpose of such comparisons is usually of a broadly aesthetic kind. But it would seem that in the Oleza novels, Miró found it psychologically satisfying and figuratively apt to pursue the parallels in a historical sense. (pp. 791-94)

G. G. Brown "The Biblical Allusions in Gabriel Miró's Oleza Novels," in The Modern Language Review (© Modern Humanities Research Association 1975), Vol. 70, No. 4, October, 1975, pp. 786-94.

IAN R. MACDONALD (essay date 1975)

[Miró] made great use of material quarried from books in the composition of his work. But a glance at *Del vivir* completes this observation, puts it back into balance, for it is equally clear how much Miró depends directly on the observation of reality. So much so, that the reader is constantly uneasy as to whether he is in the field of fiction or that of travel and autobiography. The reader constantly puzzles as to whether a fact or an anecdote is true, in the sense of not being fiction. There is a feeling that an imagined 'fact' would be a betrayal of the reader's trust, and a consequent slipping into the acceptance of *Del vivir* as a record of a journey, even though Miró uses narrative conventions from fiction and Sigüenza behaves as a fictional character. But when, for instance, Sigüenza is shown a book about leprosy in the district he is visiting, the sense of unease reappears. Surely Miró must have seen this book, surely the book exists—we refer constantly to the author, not just to the 'yo' of the narration, but to Gabriel Miró, the man behind it all. Even in a typical realist novel the reader does not make this demand, for the writer is allowed to describe the detail of a room that he has imaginatively reconstructed from many rooms: a novelistic room that is more of a room than any real room (to borrow from Ortega). But *Del vivir* evidently does not allow for even so limited a use of the imagination. Miró uses reality . . . in a peculiarly direct way. *Del vivir* makes this very obvious, but it is present in the construction of all Miró's fiction: the characters, places and anecdotes of the Oleza novels are examples. Miró takes chunks of the real world and reorders them into a whole that imposes his vision on them. But this is not to say that he is more realist than the realists. For the realist the operation of imaginatively transforming real rooms into a new room that captures the essence of the real rooms is his object in writing. For Miró the fact that he uses his material directly indicates that it is the ordering of it that is important.

Naturally, the record of Miró's experience of reality that forms the raw material of his work is valuable in itself. The details of the valley around Parcent and the village itself are often magnificently conveyed. . . . Miró's intense faithfulness to the evidence of all his senses and his insight into spiritual reality are constantly apparent. (pp. 184-85)

But though the experience of visiting Parcent provided Miró with the basic material for *Del vivir,* his reading remains an important source, and it is made very plain in the course of the book. In the main body of the text are more than a dozen quotations, while the 1904 footnote includes a further six. Altogether two dozen different writers are quoted or referred to. (p. 185)

Just as Miró uses reality very directly, so he initially used quotations from other writers as if they were nuggets inserted into his own text. The positioning, the context of these quotations often makes them useful within the work, but they inevitably introduce a certain rigidity. It is as if Miró were not certain that he had achieved the effect he wanted, and therefore added a quotation to make all clear. A resonance of authority is added at the cost of Miró's own subtlety. In the later revisions he several times removed sentences and phrases that were over-explanatory—this suggests the same unsureness as a young writer that led to the excessive use of quotation. Though Miró had mastered the technique of recording what his senses told him, he had still not managed to deal in a fully novelistic way with the moral ideas that fascinated him.

If Miró in *Del vivir* records, orders, and speculates, the title reflects these aspects of the work. It is 'from life': its scenes are taken directly from the living reality that Miró has observed. It is 'from the life' (there is an echo of the artist's expression 'Del natural', earlier used as a title by Miró): that is, it is an artistic ordering of what is observed—Miró's time spent in his uncle's studio is evident in this. And it is 'about life', or rather 'about living'; it deals with the problems of pain and suffering and the 'falta de amor'. (p. 186)

What sort of a book, then, is *Del vivir?* In the first place, clearly, it is about the suffering of the lepers of this area of Alicante, and, above all, about their mental suffering. (p. 189)

The suffering of the lepers is but a special case, an extreme case of the suffering of the universe that afflicts all men. The quotation from the Book of Job that stands at the head of *Del vivir* is faithfully quoted from Felipe Scio's translation of the Bible. But one word is added: 'Humanidad'. Job, instead of crying out to God, cries out to humanity. . . . Job presides over *Del vivir,* for Satan 'smote Job with sore boils from the sole of his foot unto his crown' (Job ii. 7), and in Miró's version a note by Scio suggests that some interpreters believe this to be leprosy. . . . The whole of Job xix is an excellent example of the parallel between the plight of Job and the plight of the lepers—solitude, rejection by all, and the hatred even of servants and relatives are their common lot: 'I am an alien in their sight' (Job xix. 15). (p. 193)

Del vivir is not a masterpiece. It is Miró's first work in his own manner, and the extraordinary skill and assurance of parts are marred by an overemphatic narrative method that narrows the range of the events recounted and sometimes pushes them into sentimentality. Yet the typical excellences are there, and the very over-emphasis makes it easier to see what Miró was attempting, so that the book, especially in its unrevised version, offers considerable insight into what was more subtly achieved in the masterpieces that were to come. (p. 204)

Ian R. Macdonald, in his Gabriel Miró: His Private Library and His Literary Background (copyright © by Ian R. Macdonald; reprinted by permission of the author), Tamesis Books Limited, 1975, 250 p.

ROBERTA JOHNSON (essay date 1979)

[*Años y leguas*] the third volume in the "Sigüenza" trilogy and the last of Miró's works to be published in his lifetime, represents his densest writing. It synthesizes and refines all the thematic concerns, images and stylistic tendencies of his earlier works: the nature of perception and its expression in words, time and space in perception, memory, and history, classical motifs and imagery, biblical motifs and imagery, and it adds [an] antological dimension to the figure of Sigüenza. (p. 42)

The structure of the book is episodic. Sigüenza travels about the Levantine countryside engaging in conversations with the local inhabitants and experiencing a variety of reactions to different aspects of the landscape. But there is an underlying unity to the work. Part of the complexity as well as the unity of *Años y leguas* derives from the juxtaposition within the perceiving consciousness of Sigüenza of immediate sensory perception and the perspective of memory. Through this experience he attempts to define himself, and he discovers that he is "himself and his circumstance," to borrow Ortega's famous phrase.

While the ontological preoccupation is a motivating force that propels the book along, as Sigüenza's encounters multiply, his relationship to the rest of humanity is concurrently revealed, primarily through biblical associations. The search for self is related to the quest for the Promised Land. . . . As Sigüenza progresses through his Levantine encounters in *Años y leguas*, he revives and beholds the story of Genesis: the creation (eternal time in the perennial garden) followed by the fall into time and toil. Personal history . . . fuses with social history. . . . [Finally] the two dissolve into universal human history. Like concentric circles generated by the impact of a pebble on the surface of a still body of water, Sigüenza's search for his identity in a specific time and place reverberates in the eternal cycle of man in nature.

The means by which Miró welds the epistemological, ontological, historical, and biblical material in *Años y leguas* is to rely for much of his imagery on the four basic elements of classical and medieval chemistry: earth, air, fire, and water. Miró seems to believe, like Bachelard, that the four elements are fundamental to perception and the creative imagination; they are readily evoked in the Alicantine landscape and seascape of Sigüenza's perceptions, and they are powerful allies to the biblical motifs. For example, Miró once likened the chemistry of water to the attraction of one's native land, a kind of Promised Land. . . . (pp. 42-3)

Miró divided the book into forty-one sections, seventeen primary divisions and twenty-four secondary headings, but the imagistic and tonal clustering suggests two major movements of nearly equal length (sixtyone and sixty-four pages respectively in the *Obras completas* edition here cited) and a short coda of four pages. Although all four elements are present in each section, the first part is governed by water (springs, wells, streams, mills and the sea), coupled with the themes of creation and eternity. The second half is dominated by references to earth: specific geographical places, cultivation activities, spatial limitations, and chronological time. Fire and destruction are the themes of the epilogue or coda. Air (wind, movement of trees and ships) is present to an equal degree in all the sections. The composition of *Años y leguas* might be compared to a Chagall painting in which images whirl in space and repeat themselves in a seemingly chaotic fashion, but upon closer examination, one finds organization in subtle concentrations and movement of material.

In the opening passage, Sigüenza returning to his native countryside remembers a park in Madrid, where he occasionally takes refuge, thus introducing the sheltered garden motif. All four elements are mentioned in his description of Sigüenza's version of Paradise. . . . But almost immediately the water motif asserts itself, and, as is usual in the progression of Miró's imagery, the first experience of the element is through the senses; here the sense of taste. Sigüenza's ritual return to his native land is sanctified by the drinking of its waters. . . . Water is an economic necessity for the farmer, but for Sigüenza it facilitates his conscious grasp of the world; it brings to him, through its taste, a suggestion of his location, "el matiz de la naturaleza." Water has a "refocilo de creación" that is symbolic of the positive, creative prospect Sigüenza entertains for his self-discovery; water's creative properties are also reminiscent of the threshold of the world itself for a short time after God made it. (pp. 44-5)

According to the creation story God made water first, and it remains the primordial life force. Water and the creative process are consistently linked in the imagery of *Años y leguas*. . . .

Water also represents man's desire to create himself, to be aware of his own identity, his own personal life continuity. . . . The water image is developed in the second subsection "Pueblo. Parral. Perfección" in an elaborated metaphor of the village as a shelf laden with water jugs. . . . (p. 45)

Other sections of the first part, "Doña Elisa y la eternidad," "Gitanos," "El señor Vicario y Manihuel," stress eternity, life over death, and the continued production of fruit and plenty. Doña Elisa will soon die, but her property will pass to her heirs, who will continue to cultivate her lands, [and] the gypsies need straw to bed a woman who is giving birth— creating new life. . . . The Mediterranean pervades "Benidorm. Un extranjero. Callosa." One is ever aware of the eternal vastness of the sea in the towns of the Levante; the combined power of the land-seascape overcomes even the academic ardor of a British scholar, who is caught napping in the midday sun. The only place Sigüenza finds time immobilized upon returning to Levante after twenty years is in the water. . . .

Eternal abundance is an important part of the garden-like setting to which Sigüenza comes to comprehend his being-in-the-world and his being-in-time. . . . [The] entire first sixty pages are saturated with plenitude: the grapes are ripe, and a fat pig is slaughtered in "Pueblo. Parral. Perfección." Even a visit to the cemetery, significantly titled "Huerto de cruces," emphasizes life more than death. In the graveyard, Sigüenza's attention is drawn to the crows gorging themselves on ripe figs, and a requiem ceremony degenerates into a picnic. The grave-tender complains that no one thinks about death, that no one comes to the cemetery. Human disappointment and failure are minimized, and satisfaction and happiness are achieved by mere contemplation of the natural surroundings. . . . (p. 46)

In the next to the last section of what I call the first part, Sigüenza reads excerpts from a book of official correspondence. He is particularly fascinated by references to historical figures executed for alchemy—man's futile attempt to reproduce basic chemical elements perhaps included here as a contrast to the success of nature in fusing earth, air, fire, and water in the production of the earthly fruits.

A section entitled "Agua de pueblo" closes the sixty-one pages in which the biblical creation motif is developed and water imagery is prominent. The relation of water to the other elements is here recapitulated . . . and a dissonant tone emerges that presages the fall from Paradise. Sigüenza believes the townspeople are urging him to drink from their well, but in a poignant scene he learns that they are outraged at his trespassing on their water supply. This is no longer the water of eternal creation, but specific water defined in space and time by the people who claim it. . . . (p. 47)

In the next sixty-four pages earth images and motifs emerge in the sections "Caminos y lugares," "El lugar hallado," "Una familia de luto," "Bardells y la familia de luto," "Agustina y Tabalet," and "Imágenes de Aitana" (except for the last subsection of "Imágenes" in which fire dominates). . . . [Man's] fall into space and time is introduced with images of water in its role as co-author with the earth of its fruits, signaling the emphasis in this part on geographical locations, tilling, and cultivation. (pp. 47-8)

According to Genesis man was expelled from his earthly Paradise to suffer the toils of earning his own living, the evils of inter-human competition, and finally corporeal death. Consequently, the themes of cultivation, shepherding, and food gathering and processing emerge in the second half of the book. Sigüenza encounters a variety of men and women who work the land and extract a living from it. (p. 48)

The same abundance and plenty that characterized the first part are present here, but the emphasis is on man's role in the production of the fruits of the earth. . . .

In the section "La besana" (a Catalan word for furrow), Sigüenza cannot resist the urge to take the plow into his own hands. . . . This intimate contact with the life-giving soil penetrates the depths of his being. . . . But Sigüenza finds that he tires quickly at the plow and soon returns it to the farmer. As in his earlier experience with water, his relationship to the earth is perceptual, not practical. For him the soil is a part of the world that aids him in his quest for the meaning of existence.

What Sigüenza eventually learns from his contact with the earth, especially earthly places, is the nature of his self in time. In the second part, time is juxtaposed to eternity. Man is tied to the cycle of the seasons and their effect on the earth upon which he depends for a living. Man's expulsion from Paradise signaled not only his dependence on the soil, time, and work, but it introduces him to pain and suffering. Miró includes in this part, extended sections on the travails of two different families. (p. 49)

Años y leguas begins during the most intense growing season and ends as the harvest is taking place. Sigüenza, like the men who till the soil, lives in and experiences temporal movement, rather than analyzing it intellectually. . . . As the summer progresses, Sigüenza intuitively grasps the minute changes in the landscape that finally reveal fall and the harvest season. We are first warned that the productive, fertile period is ending when Sigüenza discovers that, although the warmth and sunlight of summer persist, the tourists have gone. . . .

[When September arrives and the harvest begins] the sense of time is more acute; the harvested fruits are projected as the manufactured products they will become. . . . Man's relation to time is expressed in a variety of ways in this second section of *Años y leguas*. Sigüenza witnesses the planting activities of an old man who will not be alive to harvest the fruit of his trees, nor does he have any heirs to continue or

enjoy his labors when he is gone. Man's work on earth is in a sense a necessary futility; only God's creation is eternal. . . . (p. 50)

Air, more than any of the other elements, is related to the ethereal and the eternal aspects of time and the world. As a part of the practical world in which man lives, it is essential to the food-making process. . . . And it is often a bridge between the other elements; it circulates and touches the earth and the sea, bearing and combining with the life-giving sun. In the section "La tarde," which introduces the fall harvest season, the life-forming elements are summarized: the land and the sea, earth and water, provide the material and stimulus to growth, while at the perceptual level the sea breezes bring a sensation of sea-side space to the rural landscape. . . .

Air symbolizes the aspects of life that are not tied absolutely to the soil, and man's (perhaps useless) attempt to transcend his earthly dwelling. Air lifts Sigüenza's thoughts from the mundane to the ethereal. . . . (p. 51)

The auto-confrontation and self-search are much more intense in the earth section than in the first part. The fall into time coincides with man's need to understand his existence. Sigüenza's renewed contact with specific places was conceived for that purpose. He struggles with the seemingly impossible desire to experience himself in time, especially before Aitana and at the Peñón de Ifach. Twenty years ago Aitana was a virgin perception, . . . but now he must contend with the present vision *and* the memory. . . . This dual aspect of the visual experience suggests to him the difficulty, perhaps the impossibility, of achieving a sense of a continuous self. . . .

Sigüenza's final failure to recapture himself in time and space is represented in visits to two geographical locations: *el lugar hallado* and the Peñón de Ifach. In "El lugar hallado" Sigüenza believes he is having a pristine experience, that he has never been in that particular place before, but the grounds-keeper arrives to remind him of his visit there twenty years earlier. Memory has utterly failed him; his own consciousness has not persisted in time. At Ifach he understands that in order to be himself, he must abandon himself to the moment. Only by relinquishing the past can he possess this great rock as a part of himself, as an experience. . . . (p. 52)

Biblical references, especially Paradise—the favored place, symbolic of the perdurable self—resurface with the intensification of the ontological quest. In "Sigüenza y el Paraíso" Paradise is a kind of tree, *el árbol del Paraíso;* one of these trees died outside the door of *Bonhom's* daughter, presaging the daughter's own death. And Sigüenza attempts to discover the precise location of the earthly Paradise of the first parents by reading every article and book he can find on the subject. Thus the notion of Paradise, the eternal garden, has been reduced to a perishable tree and a topic for scholarly investigation.

The final section, dominated by fire imagery, "Sigüenza, incendio y término" concludes the destruction of Sigüenza's hopes for a continuous, perdurable self. Sigüenza accidentally sets a brush fire with his cigarette, a cathartic experience and an atonement for his egotistical desire to be something concrete and eternal, to persist in time. Even here, his first wish is to have it known that *he* set the fire, but a guard informs him that the smoke he sees on the hillside is not from his own fire, which had extinguished itself, but from the stacks of the charcoal burners. Neither his self-identity nor his deeds will withstand time. Throughout the book, fire, especially that of the sun, has been a positive element, combining with the others in the chemistry of creation and growing (e.g., "Huerto luminoso y caliente," or "Los montones de la fruta eran como colonias de sol"). (p. 53)

But fire, unlike the other elements, has two sides: a creative aspect and a destructive potential.... Perhaps reflecting God's employ of time (for example, he created water, earth, and life in six days, but destroyed Sodom and Gomorrah by fire in a few minutes), Miró dedicates the lengthiest sections of *Años y leguas* to water and earth, and significantly places the very reign of fire, at least as a destructive force, at the end.

Thus Miró juxtaposes time and eternity through personal experiences that echo biblical and universal ones, all welded by the powerful imagery of the four basic elements. First we have Sigüenza's sensory perceptions of his surroundings, his seeing, touching, tasting, hearing, and smelling the elements that compose his world. Those elements are both eternal and fleeting.... Equally elusive is his quest to achieve a sense of self in time and space.

The elements water, earth, fire, and air combined with the biblical material subtly move us through Sigüenza's early hope for self-discovery, his confrontations with disappointment, failure, hostility, and finally to his acceptance of his own transient reality. (pp. 53-4)

If Sigüenza has not *found* himself in time, he has *experienced* himself in space and time through the elements earth, air, fire and water, and that endows *Años y leguas* with its most important quality—a recreation in words of perceptual cognition.... His conclusion about the nature of his being is that it is his consciousness of the world, his dialectical perceptual relationship to the things that surround him. (pp. 54-5)

> Roberta Johnson, "Time and the Elements Earth, Air, Fire and Water in 'Años y leguas'," in Critical Essays on Gabriel Miro, *edited by Ricardo Landeira (copyright © 1979 Society of Spanish and Spanish-American Studies), Society of Spanish and Spanish-American Studies, 1979, pp. 42-56.*

EDMUND L. KING (essay date 1979)

Miró once told Oscar Esplá ... that a human life is the traversal of a lighted space between two tunnels. Whether the particular image was original with Miró I do not know. Certainly others, from the Venerable Bede to Rubén Darío, have expressed similar ideas. It is significant, though, that Miró emphasizes not the dark tunnels but the light between them. Still, his works are replete with figures of orphans or orphanoids—men and women cut off from their neighbors, their origins, the Absolute (whatever it may be if it exists), and braving their way through life with such props and supports in beliefs and rituals as they can get hold of. I will point to only two of the numerous affecting expressions of this human pathos, one on what can simply be called the literal level, the story "**Corpus**," in which the literal orphan Ramonete cannot see God in the transubstantiated host because he is blinded by the glittering monstrance in which the host is encased. The other, the meditation on Ascension Day, in *El humo dormido*, which closes with a chilling accusation directed at God through Fray Luis de León's famous text

describing the cloud that bears Christ (God the Son, the mediator) back to God (the Father).... [God has] left man alone, poor and helpless in the world, an abandoned child, an orphan.

Life, for man the orphan, Miró says repeatedly, is existentially a place of unremitting uncertainty and fear, ending in inscrutable death. Why is this so and how is it related to our theme? Because life goes on in time. All man's efforts are directed towards thwarting the inexorable enemy, time: most elaborately, the Church and its rituals and myths; most elementally, eating to keep alive, even though one knows that time will win in the end. There is only one heroism: to see the world (life in time, or, better, time in life) as it is, certain to triumph over us in the end, and to love it (cling to lifetime) even so. Thus, the gravedigger's daughter [in "**El Sepulturero**"], who has just barely survived an attack of malaria, looks certain death in the face and eats away to keep alive and even nibbles on the sausage slowly, so that the defiance of time will go on as long as possible. She is trying to beat time at its own game, the game of duration, in spite of the evidence she has before her [—a bloated corpse floating in a flooded open tomb].

Miró hints at many of the conventional aspects of the tempus topos—the *lacrimae rerum, el dolorido sentir*, time as the thief of beauty, Bergson's *durée*, Proust's *recherche du temps perdu*, no doubt others. He writes, though, not to repeat but to transcend.

If the confinement of man in time is the fundamental matrix of human pathos—the tragic sense of life—in general, it is doubly painful and challenging to the verbal artist, the writer, the poet. This observation takes us back to the famous chapter XVI of the *Laokoon*, in which Lessing, for the first time since Aristotle, has something new to say about "poetry." ... (pp. 116-17)

In sum, Lessing argues triumphantly that literature is a temporal medium and should accept the sequential, non-spatial character of temporality.... Even those descriptive poets whom the great German was inveighing against no doubt saw the merit of his argument. They were, in any case, something of an aberration in their abject submission to Horace's famous dictum. Surely it is no more possible to write (or of course to speak) without reference to both time and space than it is to exist outside of time and space. Indeed, while many, perhaps most, writers most of the time take for granted these ineluctable dimensions of reality and do not dwell upon them as such but rather accept them the way a fish accepts water, at some moments in history an exacerbated awareness of them becomes a prominent if not obsessive motive and motif of some, and perhaps most, writers.... Miró himself, evoking, I presume, this more than venerable tradition, in a letter to Andrés González Blanco ca. 10 March 1906, made a remark which merits much more attention than it has received. Speaking of the days he spent in the infirmary of his Jesuit boarding school, he says, "He sentido las primeras tristezas estéticas, viendo en los crepúsculos, los valles apagados y las cumbres aún encendidas de sol." The transitoriness of beauty is not the point for Miró; rather, the inescapable melancholy with which he experiences that transitoriness—we seem to need the word *fugacity* in English—is the fundamental aesthetic experience—*tristeza estética*—the experience of which his art is, to be sure, often the expression but also the experience to which his art is a response. What Lessing had seen as a practical matter, a fact of the verbal artist's life to which the artist should adapt himself, is seen by Miró to be a matter of life and death. Thou shalt *not* pass, he seems to be saying, as he pits his words against time, by representing actions iconically. The actions may be exemplary, like the game of the children in "**El sepulturero**," by definition not caught up in the chronology of the story and thus more or less iconic, or they may be episodes in the narrative dislodged from their proper place in the chronology, portions of time temporarily deprived of flux, subjected to the artist's will, and turned into icons much as the episodes of sacred history are spatialized in the stained glass windows of churches. It would be tautological to argue the particular effectiveness of the disposition of each segment in Miró's narrative. The sum total of the arrangement has whatever effect it has, and that effect is partially and in significant degree attributable to the spatialization of time, the detemporalization of episodes. . . .

It is important to notice, however, that while Miró is crafty, he is not tricky. There is no magical realism here, no phantasy, not even any illusionism. Time *is* real. Time *will* pass, regardless of man's wishes. If man knows this, is there not only pathos in such awareness but a certain comedy in resisting time's passage, only nibbling on the sausage so it will last longer? The touches of witty irony and paradox throughout the story surely encourage this interpretation. (pp. 118-19)

Edmund L. King, "Life and Death, Space and Time: 'El sepulturero'," in Critical Essays on Gabriel Miro, *edited by Ricardo Landeira (copyright © 1979 Society of Spanish and Spanish-American Studies), Society of Spanish and Spanish-American Studies, 1979, pp. 107-20.*

ADDITIONAL BIBLIOGRAPHY

Coope, Marian G. R. "Gabriel Miró's Image of the Garden as 'Hortus Conclusus' and 'Paraiso Terrenal'." *Modern Language Review* 68, No. 1 (January 1973): 94-104.
    An examination of Miró's imagery of the garden as an Edenic setting and as a bower in which love is nurtured.

Coope, [Marian] G. R. "The Critics' View of *Nuestro padre San Daniel* and *El obispo leproso* by Gabriel Miró." In *University of British Columbia Hispanic Studies,* edited by Harold Livermore, pp. 51-60. London: Tamesis Books, 1974.
    An overview of the critical response to Miró's Oleza novels.

Landeira, Ricardo, ed. *Critical Essays on Gabriel Miró.* Manhattan, Kans.: Society of Spanish and Spanish-American Studies, 1979, 150 p.
    A collection of scholarly essays on various aspects of Miró's work. Essayists include Ricardo Landeira, Yvette E. Miller, Roberta Johnson, and many others.

"Gabriel Miro." *The Times Literary Supplement,* No. 1209 (9 March 1925): 184.
    A review of *Figures of the Passion of Our Lord.* The critic sees in the narrative an improvement over the lackluster translation of the Passion found in Spain's New Testament.

Standish (James) O'Grady

1846-1928

(Also wrote under pseudonyms of Arthur Clive and Luke Netterville) Irish historian, novelist, folklorist, journalist, and poet.

A pioneer of the Celtic Revival in Ireland, O'Grady is generally considered the father of the Irish Literary Renaissance. His most important works were compilations and retellings of ancient Irish legends suppressed by centuries of British influence. With these works O'Grady stimulated interest in Irish traditions that led to the development of a new national literature. Yeats and A. E., in particular, credit O'Grady with kindling their interest in the legendary Irish past.

O'Grady was born in County Cork, the son of a Protestant clergyman. After studying at Trinity College, he practiced law briefly. Inspired by a chance reading of O'Halloran's *History of Ireland*, O'Grady decided to bring the legends of Ireland to the modern reader before they were lost forever, as he found in them a sense of the immortal Irish spirit.

The publication of his first work, *History of Ireland*, is often associated with the start of the Literary Renaissance. These two volumes, *The Heroic Period* and *Cuculain and His Contemporaries*, are viewed by some critics as an imaginative epic rather than as a scholarly presentation of legendary history. In them, O'Grady collated legends from several Gaelic sources, added and deleted material for unity of plot and characterization, and imposed several epic devices and motifs upon the stories. He also censored the graphic sexual situations found in the ancient texts. Critics have attacked O'Grady's failure to be faithful to the original Gaelic texts, but O'Grady was more concerned with the legends as living traditions than with scholarly purity. Although the history had a tremendous impact on several important writers, it was not a commercial success.

In addition to his *History*, O'Grady also wrote prose romances based on many of the same Irish legends. These historical novels fall into two groups, those of the heroic age and those of Elizabethan Ireland. *Finn and His Companions*, which Yeats considered to be O'Grady's masterpiece, is a representative novel of the heroic period. *The Flight of the Eagle* has won critical praise as his best work outside the heroic period. The novel deals with Red Hugh O'Donnell, an Irish chieftain from the Elizabethan period whom O'Grady considered important as an exemplar of Irish nationalism at the time of the incorporation of Gaelic Ireland with England.

Besides his dedication to Irish history, O'Grady maintained an interest in contemporary politics throughout his career. As editor of the *All-Ireland Review* he advocated the unionist cause and promoted the development of native Irish art forms. In *Toryism and the Tory Democracy*, his most important political work, he urged the landowning and peasant classes to form a coalition to revive Ireland's economy. The failure of these proposals led to his gradual withdrawal from political journalism.

O'Grady's popularization of Irish legend, however, was more important than his political writings. Because he called attention to Ireland's mythic past at a time when Irish nationalists

were seeking an Irish identity, his work was an important influence on both the artistic and political development of the Irish Republic.

PRINCIPAL WORKS

History of Ireland: The Heroic Period (history) 1878
Early Bardic Literature of Ireland (history) 1879
History of Ireland: Cuculain and His Contemporaries
   (history) 1880
History of Ireland: Critical and Philosophical (history)
   1881
Toryism and the Tory Democracy (political essay) 1886
Finn and His Companions (novel) 1892
The Bog of Stars (short stories) 1893
The Coming of Cuculain (novel) 1894
The Chain of Gold (novel) 1895
The Flight of the Eagle (novel) 1897
In the Gates of the North (novel) 1901
The Triumph and Passing of Cuculain (novel) 1920

W. B. YEATS (essay date 1895)

[Mr. Standish O'Grady's] **'History of Ireland, Heroic Period,'** published in 1878, was the starting point of what may yet prove a new influence in the literature of the world. A couple of years ago, after a long devotion to mediæval Ireland, he returned to his old studies, and wrote his delightful **'Finn and his Companions,'** and now he has just issued **'The Coming of Cuchullin,'** the memorable first part of a kind of prose epic. It is probable that no Englishman can love these books as they are loved by the many Irishmen who date their first interest in Irish legends and literature from the **'History.'** There is perhaps, too, something in their tumultuous vehemence, in their delight in sheer immensity, in their commingling of the spirit of man with the spirit of the elements, which belongs to the wild Celtic idealism rather than to the careful, practical ways of the Saxon. The heroes of [Tennyson's] 'The Idylls of the King' are always merely brave and excellent men, calculable and measurable in every way; but the powers of Cuchullin are as incalculable and immeasurable as the powers of nature. . . .

Mr. O'Grady does not attempt to give the old stories in the form they have come down to us, but passes them through his own imagination. Yet so familiar is he with the old legends, so profound a sympathy has he with their spirit, that he has made the ancient gods and heroes live over again their simple and passionate lives. The Red Branch feasting with Cullan the smith, Cuchullin taming the weird horses, Cuchullin hunting down in his chariot the herd of enchanted deer, whose horns and hoofs are of iron, belong in nothing to our labouring noontide, but wholly to the shadowy morning twilight of time.

> W. B. Yeats, "Battles Long Ago" (reprinted by permission of A. P. Watt Ltd., as literary agents of the Estate of W. B. Yeats), in The Bookman, London, Vol. VII, No. 41, February, 1895, p. 153.

A. E.   (essay date 1904)

We have yet much to learn of the past, and there is an ample field for the poet, dramatist, and historian; but because nature never gifts two writers with the same qualities, it is vain to hope that any later writer will recreate for us the Champion of the Red Branch as O'Grady has done, or make the warrior seem almost a divine type, or remove from battle the lust of blood, as he has, until these conflicts of warriors seem not a warring upon flesh and blood, but the everlasting battle where the Clan Cailitan are the dark powers and Cuculain the spirit of redeeming light. We feel in the unendurable pathos of the story as O'Grady tells it, that Cuculain was in a dark age to the Celt what a greater spirit has been to humanity. He was the incarnation of their ideal, and if we analyze the lavish tenderness of the old bards to their hero, a tenderness which O'Grady has perfectly retained, it will be found at its root to have a purely spiritual quality akin to that we feel to Him who took the burden of the sins of the world upon Him, and came without the scepter and crown of divinity to a people who dwelt in darkness and who knew Him not.

It is this symbolism, which is, I think, the product of an unconsciously spiritual imagination, and not the result of a conscious art, that makes O'Grady apart from and above the English writers who have written of the legendary past. They are too much concerned with the adventures of the body, but with O'Grady every action of his hero, even when advancing to the battle, seems to be an adventure of the soul, and we are stirred as if we followed some noble conquest of darkness rather than the triumphs of man over man. Tennyson indeed has made his Arthur a symbol, but has done it so consciously that we wish for an actual person to speak, and the too evident allegory a little wearies us. O'Grady's Cuculain, more nobly conceived, and in a more epical spirit, as I think, is always a distinct human being, a demigod perhaps, but with a distinct personality, and with something too which, while never offending us with modernity, seems to show that the new religion, which overturned the pagan world, has through O'Grady thrown back a reflected light on the greatest hero of pre-Christian days. O'Grady's finest achievement has been to rescue for us the great pagan virtues and to bring them with a living force into modern Ireland. (pp. 2738-39)

These dreams, antiquities, traditions, once actual, living, and historical, have passed from the world of sense into the world of the soul in O'Grady's rendering of them, and time has taken away nothing from their power, nor made them more remote from sympathy, but has rather purified them by removing them from earth to heaven; from things which the eye can see and the ear can hear, they have become what the heart ponders over; and we have in O'Grady's tales of Cuculain the spiritual and heroic residue, the primitive grossness left out, the strength retained.

O'Grady is the direct representative to-day of the bards who delighted in the heroic life, while in W. B. Yeats is incarnated the spirit of those who sought for beauty and followed Niam across the mystic waters to the World of Immortal Youth. The latter writer with a greater art has not the epical spirit which informs O'Grady's best work, or the incomparable fire and energy which makes the sounding sentences of the epic of Cuculain rear themselves like giants from the page. Through this energy of conception O'Grady is frequently led into hasty writing and exaggerated metaphors, but, at its best, his style is beautiful in its simplicity. (p. 2739)

While it is by his renderings of the ancient stories that O'Grady will be rightly remembered, his books dealing with the Elizabethan period of Irish history should not be overlooked. The period hardly lends itself so well to his somewhat giantesque imagination as the older tales, but in one book, **'The Flight of the Eagle,'** he has written the history of the captivity of Red Hugh with a singular intensity. His narrative, following history closely, is always vivid and is illuminated, like everything he writes, with flashes of poetic beauty. . . .

O'Grady is a writer whose power over the imagination of his countrymen must grow. His best books are out of print, and he has been singularly unfortunate in most of his publishing, but nothing so fine in literature, with all its faults, as his best work can be allowed to die, and it is probably the next generation who will appreciate to the full the work of the man who above all others in Ireland has the true instinct of the heroic in life and in literature. (pp. 2739-40)

> A. E., "Standish O'Grady" (Canadian rights by permission of Russell & Volkening, Inc.), in Irish

Literature, *Vol. VII, Justin McCarthy, Editor in Chief, John D. Morris, 1904, pp. 2737-40.*

A. E. (essay date 1920)

When I close my eyes, and brood in memory over the books which most profoundly affected me, I find none excited my imagination more than Standish O'Grady's epical narrative of Cuculain. Whitman said of his *Leaves of Grass,* "Camerado, this is no book: who touches this touches a man" and O'Grady might have boasted of his **Bardic History of Ireland,** written with his whole being, that there was more than a man in it, there was the soul of a people, its noblest and most exalted life symbolised in the story of one heroic character.

With reference to Ireland, I was at the time I read like many others who were bereaved of the history of their race. I was as a man who, through some accident, had lost memory of his past, who could recall no more than a few months of new life, and could not say to what songs his cradle had been rocked, what mother had nursed him, who were the playmates of childhood or by what woods and streams he had wandered. When I read O'Grady I was as such a man who suddenly feels ancient memories rushing at him, and knows he was born in a royal house, that he had mixed with the mighty of heaven and earth and had the very noblest for his companions. It was the memory of race which rose up within me as I read, and I felt exalted as one who learns he is among the children of kings. That is what O'Grady did for me and for others who were my contemporaries. . . . In O'Grady's writings the submerged river of national culture rose up again, a shining torrent, and I realised as I bathed in that stream, that the greatest spiritual evil one nation could inflict on another was to cut off from it the story of the national soul. . . . But there was essential greatness in that neglected bardic literature which O'Grady was the first to reveal in a noble manner. He had the spirit of an ancient epic poet. He is a comrade of Homer. . . . He has created for us or rediscovered one figure which looms in the imagination as a high comrade of Hector, Achilles, Ulysses, Rama or Yudisthira, as great in spirit as any. Who could extol enough his Cuculain, that incarnation of Gaelic chivalry, the fire and gentleness, the beauty and heroic ardour or the imaginative splendour of the episodes in his retelling of the ancient story. . . . Standish O'Grady had in his best moments that epic wholeness and simplicity, and the figure of Cuculain amid his companions of the Red Branch which he discovered and refashioned for us is I think the greatest spiritual gift any Irishman for centuries has given to Ireland. (pp. ix-xiv)

O'Grady in his stories of the Red Branch rescued from the past what was contemporary to the best in us to-day, and he was equal in his gifts as a writer to the greatest of his bardic predecessors in Ireland. His sentences are charged with a heroic energy, and, when he is telling a great tale, their rise and fall are like the flashing and falling of the bright sword of some great champion in battle, or the onset and withdrawal of Atlantic surges. He can at need be beautifully tender and quiet. (pp. xv-xvi)

There are critics repelled by the abounding energy in O'Grady's sentences. It is easy to point to faults due to excess and abundance, but how rare in literature is that heroic energy and power. There is something arcane and elemental in it, a quality that the most careful stylist cannot attain, however

he uses the file, however subtle he is. O'Grady has noticed this power in the ancient bards and we find it in his own writing. It ran all through the **Bardic History,** the **Critical and Philosophical History,** and through the political books, **"The Tory Democracy"** and **"All Ireland."** There is this imaginative energy in the tale of Cuculain, in all its episodes. . . . In the later tale of Red Hugh which he calls **"The Flight of the Eagle"** there is the same quality of power joined with a shining simplicity in the narrative. . . . We might say of Red Hugh and indeed of all O'Grady's heroes that they are the spiritual progeny of Cuculain. From Red Hugh down to the boys who have such enchanting adventures in **"Lost on Du Corrig"** and **"The Chain of Gold"** they have all a natural and hardy purity of mind, a beautiful simplicity of character, and one can imagine them all in an hour of need, being faithful to any trust like the darling of the Red Branch. These shining lads never grew up amid books. They are as much children of nature as the Lucy of Wordsworth's poetry. (pp. xvi-xviii)

How pallid, beside the ruddy chivalry who pass huge and fleet and bright through O'Grady's pages, appear Tennyson's bloodless Knights of the Round Table, fabricated in the study to be read in the drawing-room, as anœmic as Burne Jones' lifeless men in armour. The heroes of ancient Irish legend reincarnated in the mind of a man who could breathe into them the fire of life, caught from sun and wind, their ancient deities, and send them forth to the world to do greater deeds, to act through many men and speak through many voices. . . . For my own part I can only point back to him and say whatever is Irish in me he kindled to life, and I am humble when I read his epic tale, feeling how much greater a thing it is for the soul of a writer to have been the habitation of a demigod than to have had the subtlest intellections. (pp. xix-xx)

[O'Grady] was the last champion of the Irish aristocracy and still more the voice of conscience for them, and he spoke to them of their duty to the nation as one might imagine some fearless prophet speaking to a council of degenerate princes. When the aristocracy failed Ireland he bade them farewell, and wrote the epitaph of their class in words whose scorn we almost forget because of their sounding melody and beauty. He turned his mind to the problems of democracy and more especially of those workers who are trapped in the city, and he pointed out for them the way of escape and how they might renew life in the green fields close to Earth, their ancient mother and nurse. He used too exalted a language for those to whom he spoke to understand, and it might seem that all these vehement appeals had failed but that we know that what is fine never really fails. When a man is in advance of his age, a generation unborn when he speaks, is born in due time and finds in him its inspiration. O'Grady may have failed in his appeal to the aristocracy of his own time but he may yet create an aristocracy of character and intellect in Ireland. The political and social writings will remain to uplift and inspire and to remind us that the man who wrote the stories of heroes had a bravery of his own and a wisdom of his own. (pp. xxi-xxii)

A. E., "Introduction" (Canadian rights by permission of Russell & Volkening, Inc.), in The Coming of Cuculain *by Standish O'Grady, Frederick A. Stokes Company, 1920, pp. ix-xxiii.*

ERNEST BOYD (essay date 1922)

What the older poets were unable to achieve in verse was accomplished by the prose of Standish O'Grady. This poet, disguised in the mantle of an historian, infused the new spirit which was to revitalise Irish literature.

Nothing further from the ordinary conception of historical writing can be imagined than [the] two volumes relating the history of Ireland's heroic age [*The History of Ireland: The Heroic Period* and *Cuculain and his Companions*]. That they should differ from the manner of . . . other orthodox historians, was necessary and inevitable, if we view them in the light of their ultimate destiny, for how otherwise could a young and comparatively unknown barrister achieve such extraordinary results in a field already laboured by recognised authorities? But it did not require the confirmation of subsequent events to emphasise the fact that with Standish O'Grady a new method of treating Irish history was inaugurated. . . . Nowhere more than in Ireland had the historian of antiquity been content to accumulate names and dates, and to tabulate events, solely with a view to presenting as exhaustive a mass of antiquarian research as possible. The ignorance of Irish laws, customs and traditions, resulting from the desuetude into which the language had fallen, explains to some extent the character of Irish history. So many facts had become obscured, so much literature was threatened with oblivion by the spread of Anglicisation, that the work of translation and excavation seemed at once the most imperative and the most important. But, as Standish O'Grady pointed out, a generation of workers had laboured patiently at this task, the bardic writings had been largely translated, the remains of ancient Ireland had been investigated, and a large quantity of material now lay within easy reach of the true historian. At the same time, a precedent had unfortunately been created, with the result, as he says, that "the province of archaeology has so extended its frontiers as to have swallowed up the dominion of pure history altogether." The antiquarians have unearthed "mounds of ore," to be smelted and converted into current coin of the realm, but they stand "in their gaunt uselessness," awaiting literary exploitation.

It was O'Grady who came with the fire of imagination which transmuted this ore into gold. Leaving aside all the preoccupations of archaeology, the inquiries and investigations, the balancing of statements and probabilities, he undertakes "the reconstruction by imaginative processes of the life led by our ancestors in this country." Taking the material furnished by the antiquarians, he remoulds and absorbs it, reducing to its artistic elements the entire history of the heroic period as revealed in bardic literature. . . . He so immerses himself in the past that he identifies himself with his heroes and heroines, they cease to be legendary and become for him living men like himself, moving about the same country, treading the same earth—his ancestors, as they are the ancestors of every Irishman. As he ponders over the bardic tales he catches their note of epic grandeur, and the spaciousness of diction which characterised the bards of old is reflected in his own style. Thus he describes heroic Ireland as he sees it in the dazzling light of the bardic imagination. . . . (pp. 28-30)

As befits a work destined to be the source of a literature, O'Grady's *History* has a certain primitive energy, a naïve amplitude such as we expect in epic narrative. Not content with the vast uncharted territory before him, in which the annals of the bards are but stepping stones "set at long distances in some quaking Cimmerian waste," he must begin with the Pleistocene epoch, and briefly trace the transfor-

mations which preceded the inhabitation of Ireland by the human species! One feels that he is attracted to these periods by the immensity of the events which they cover and by the gigantic creatures to which they gave birth. We see him linger with the delight of Homeric simplicity over mastodon and megatherium, pleiseosauros and trogatherium, the size of these monsters fills him with the same satisfaction as he experiences when describing Ireland, sinking beneath the slowly descending glaciers that covered Europe, or submerged by the waters of the ocean, "as with a vast millennial suspiration, the earth's bosom fell." But these chapters are merely the preliminary exercises of a mind enamoured of greatness, whether material or spiritual. They hardly bear more relation to scientific accuracy, than the geology and geography of the *Iliad*. (pp. 31-2)

Standish O'Grady sees the gods and demigods, the heroes and kings of Irish history, with the eyes of an epic imagination. He is not concerned with deciding the exact point at which the legends merge into history, but embraces the whole epoch, assimilating all that is best and most lordly in the bardic compositions with the knowledge gleaned from all manner of sources, contemporary documents and recent commentaries. The result is an astonishingly vigorous narrative, which rolls along with a mighty sweep, carrying the reader into the very midst of the great life of the heroic period. The past lives again in these pages, lit up by the brilliance of a mind stored with a wealth of romantic vision. (p. 32)

[*The History*'s] real distinction lies in the wonderful series of graphic pictures which the author has drawn of the great spoil. This, the chief of the epic romances of Irish literature, is conceived in truly epical spirit. The protagonists, Maeve, Fergus, Ferdia, on the one side, Conchobar, Laeg and, above all Cuculain, on the other—these stand out in fine relief. We move between the camps of the contending hosts, we attend their councils of war, we hear their cries of joy and grief, we sit amid their feasts. As he narrates the events of this struggle between Maeve and the Red Branch, Standish O'Grady attains to something of the style of the Greek historians. His manner of rendering the speeches of the chieftains and warriors reminds us, sometimes of the simplicity—so penetrating and effective—of Herodotus, sometimes of the terse wordpainting of Thucydides. When he leaves the main course of events to evoke some picture of contemporary manners, the feasting of the heroes, the domestic employments of the women, the games of the children, the contests of the youths, he achieves, at his best, the *naïveté* and simple grandeur of Homer. He has the truly Celtic love of the sonorous phrase, but his style bears traces of his classical scholarship.

The finest qualities of the historian are revealed by his treatment of the story of Cuculain. Step by step this heroic and lordly nature is unfolded before us with the skill and sympathy which come of deep understanding coupled with a power of vision and expression. We feel that there is a harmony between the author and his subject to which we owe this great and spirited re-creation. (pp. 33-4)

With consummate insight Standish O'Grady contrives to give the necessary light and shade to the portrayal of this heroic being. While bringing into prominence the terrible strength, the extraordinary skill and endurance of Cuculain, he never fails to illustrate his contrasting qualities of gentleness and kindness which excite the love and admiration of his enemies. (p. 36)

[The] interesting essay on Early Bardic Literature,... provided an instructive exegesis on the entire *History,* and was subsequently reprinted as an Introduction to the concluding volume. Here Standish O'Grady makes an eloquent plea on behalf of the bardic remains of Ireland, pointing out their value as historical documents, and vindicating them against the neglect of the English-speaking literary world. ... [The] wonderful epic cycles of Ireland are unknown or ignored. In thus asserting the claims of bardic literature, [O'Grady] is obviously proclaiming the intention of his own work and, as we know, his appeal was not in vain, so far as his own countrymen are concerned. Circumstances have since rendered most of his arguments inapplicable to present conditions, but without under-estimating labours of recent writers in the same field, we cannot but recognise in Standish O'Grady the pioneer. By an unusual combination of scholarly precept with literary practice he succeeded in dispersing the clouds of prejudice and ignorance that obscured a glittering source of inspiration from the eyes of the poets.

Valuable as this essay is as the preliminary manifesto of the Literary Revival, and as a succinct statement of the main facts relating to the ancient literature of Ireland, it derives an incidental interest as a sort of apologia for the author's conception of history as revealed in his first book. This latter, it goes without saying, possessed none of the charms of the usual, and the critics, with one or two exceptions, accorded it the traditional reception extended to innovators. (pp. 38-9)

Standish O'Grady's method of writing history drew upon him the adverse criticism of those who held to the orthodox conception of historiography, so much so, in fact, that in his second volume he felt called upon to make certain concessions to such critics and to enter a defence of his own style. Not content with this, he published in 1881 the first volume of a *Critical and Philosophical History,* which was by way of redeeming his former errors, and offering to the public a more conventional study of the same period traversed by his earlier work. This History, however, was never completed, and now serves only to bear witness to the soundness of the instinct which prompted the author to abandon himself in the first instance to the visualisation of a naturally epic imagination. Perhaps it may be profitably regarded as a commentary or appendix to the *Bardic History.* O'Grady strives earnestly to conform to the traditional manner, quoting dates, citing authorities, and explaining legends, but beneath the array of facts is felt the throb of romance and of poetry. At times this restraint is relaxed and the bardic note is heard again. Sometimes he interpolates passages from the earlier history, and even elaborates them, as in the famous dialogue between Ossian and St. Patrick, sometimes he simply follows the bent of his mind, forgetting the critics he would placate, and once more the material of heroic Ireland glows with the life breathed into it by the epic spirit. ... The imaginative element is too strong to be long held in check, and in the pages of this volume it frequently preponderates at the expense of the critical and philosophical intentions of the author. Unfortunately such passages derive an inevitable incongruity from their juxtaposition with matter of a purely prosaic and historic nature, and seem curiously out of place in a work of this kind. It is easy, therefore, to understand why the second volume was never published. The first remains, odd and inconclusive, to emphasise the essentially epical and poetic quality of Standish O'Grady's genius and to illustrate his inability to break the mould of his mind.

Unable or unwilling to adopt the conventional historical methods, O'Grady was forced to find some other medium by which to give expression to his peculiar talent for historic reconstruction. Given the preponderance of the romantic and imaginative in his work, it was clear that the most obvious path must lead him to the novel. Henceforward we shall find him employing his activities, almost exclusively in the field of romance. It is true that he did not altogether forsake pure history. ... Similarly, his political writings, [*The Crisis in Ireland, Toryism and the Tory Democracy,* and *All Ireland*] ... need only be mentioned in passing. They all possess unusual qualities and have more claim to be considered as literature than might be anticipated from their original scope and purpose. *Toryism and the Tory Democracy,* in particular, is an interesting instance of the application of O'Grady's method to history somewhat less remote than that of heroic Ireland, to the period preceding and covering the first years of the union of the English and Irish Parliaments. Most remarkable is the section *Ireland and the Hour,* in which, continuing *The Crisis in Ireland,* the author addresses the Irish landowners. This eloquent indictment of a worthless aristocracy, lost to all sense of its duties, clinging fearfully to the protection of England, and devoid of those intellectual and spiritual qualities which alone could justify its privileges or excuse its insolence—this indictment is one of the finest pieces of political writing in Irish literature. The pen that wrote the *Bardic History* is easily recognisable, whether it be in the passages that so remorselessly sum up the continued years of incompetence and neglect, or those in which the glories of the great Irish aristocracies of the past are evoked in forcible contrast. It is surely the mark of genius that a work written for the moment should endure by its intrinsic worth. Like the pamphlets of Swift, O'Grady's *Tory Democracy* possesses those qualities of style and emotion which enable such writings to retain their interest when their object has long since been accomplished, or has ceased to engage public attention. (pp. 44-6)

The series of historical romances which followed the publication of the histories fall into two groups, the one dealing with heroic age, the other with the Elizabethan Ireland. Contrary to what might be expected, it was not from the bardic material that O'Grady's first novel was fashioned, fresh as this material must have been in his mind. Perhaps, indeed, the comprehensive studies he had already given of heroic Ireland, induced him to break new ground by turning to the Elizabethan period, and to come forward as a novelist ... with *Red Hugh's Captivity.* In describing this work as a novel, advantage has been taken of the proverbial amorphousness of the *genre.* *Red Hugh's Captivity* hesitates between the history and the novel, and might almost indifferently be attributed to either, particularly in view of the author's conception of history. From the Introduction it is evident that O'Grady intends to do for Irish history in the sixteenth century what he had previously done for the heroic period. (p. 47)

This century is one of vital interest to Irishmen, for it witnessed the struggle of Gaelic Ireland against her assimilation by England, resulting in the incorporation of the Irish with the English-speaking race. The age was crowded with remarkable personalities, the Irish chiefs and petty kings whose resistance to England constituted the last stand of the old Gaelic and feudal order against English civilisation. Naturally, however, the more general histories of the time could not do justice to these figures, and the events in which they were concerned, so, as a rule, they were hastily sketched in as very minor detail in a large picture. While recognising this as inevitable in the circumstances, Standish O'Grady determined to devote a series of smaller pictures to filling in precisely this detail, so important to Irishmen, and so neglected in the comprehensive studies of the professional historians. Shane O'Neill, Feagh mac-Hugh O'Byrne, Red Hugh O'Donnell—all the great chieftains are rescued from what he describes so aptly as "the sombre immortality of the bookshelf." They and their followers are presented in the setting of their own stirring times, a background filled with patiently elaborated sketches of feudal life and customs.

In *Red Hugh's Captivity*, as has been suggested, O'Grady does not seem quite sure of his style, which oscillates between pure history and romance. The narrative is too frequently obscured or interrupted by the clumsy interposition of historical data, as though the author were overburdened with the results of his researches in the archives. Conscious, apparently, of the ineffectiveness of his attempt, he returned . . . to the same story of Red Hugh's escape from Dublin Castle, and in *The Flight of the Eagle* gave to Irish literature one of its most spirited and beautifully written romances. Here the skeleton of history is concealed by a vesture of fine prose, the spoils of the Record Office no longer obtrude themselves, but are discreetly added for reference in an appendix, and the whole episode is welded into a harmonious narrative. The episode of Red Hugh's capture and flight is the most famous and significant of the dramas enacted in Elizabethan Ireland, marking, as it did, the beginning of the Nine Years' War which proved to be the greatest obstacle to the establishment of English rule, and might have changed the destiny of the Irish people. *The Flight of the Eagle* is a fascinating picture of the social and political life of the time, and is probably the only work at all worthy of the picturesque and daring young rebel whose story is related. Its many beautiful passages entitle it to rank with the *Bardic History*. (pp. 48-9)

If *The Flight of the Eagle* represents such an advance upon *Red Hugh's Captivity*, and is the finest work O'Grady has done outside of the heroic period, it is doubtless because the years intervening between the two had seen the publication of almost all his work in the field of historic romance. The charming volume of Elizabethan stories, *The Bog of Stars*, . . . enabled him to add to his saga of Red Hugh by the addition of incidents in the life of the hero and his associates, not directly part of the events with which the two main narratives are concerned. At the same time he extended the scope of his historic reconstructions by the elaboration of various important phases of the struggle against the Tudor dynasty. The appearance of *Ulrick the Ready* . . . marked the last stage of his advance in the art of narration. The manner in which he handles his historical material has lost all the clumsiness of his first effort at long narrative, the odour of the archives no longer hangs about his pages, and the ease and fluency of the story indicates a complete mastery of detail. Indeed he is now threatened with the dangers of this facility and succumbs to the extent of writing *In the Wake of King James*. Here he reveals all the faults of a certain type of popular pseudo-historical novel, in which an historical setting is exploited as a pretext for the telling of some banal tale of love and adventure. Fortunately, instead of continuing in this direction O'Grady bethought himself of his first work, and returned to the half-accomplished task of *Red Hugh's Captivity* with the fortunate results already described.

In considering the group of stories based upon bardic literature little can be added to what has been said of the history of the heroic period. With the exception of *Finn and His Companions* . . ., a simple retelling of some of the principal incidents of the Ossianic cycle addressed to children, the remaining works are adaptations from the histories. *The Coming of Cuculain* . . . consisted almost entirely of a literal transcription of the earlier chapter relating to the childhood and youth of Cuculain, in the first volume of the *History of Ireland*. At that date, as we have seen, O'Grady was practising his skill as a novelist, and this book may be regarded as an exercise, for he has taken his earlier material and elaborated and rearranged it to form a continuous narrative. Some years later, . . . he remodelled similarly the concluding chapters of the same volume, and *In the Gates of the North* presented the story of Cuculain's manhood, concluding with the hero's splendid defence of Ulster, single-handed, against the champions of Maeve. These accounts of Cuculain thus presented in the form of historic romance lose nothing in the process, and are, therefore, significant as indicating the essentially imaginative, romantic quality of O'Grady's mind. In this form, moreover, they must have reached a public not likely to be attracted to a work ostensibly of pure history, and consequently they have helped materially to attain the chief end their author had in view: to rehabilitate the bardic literature of Ireland and to place the Irish people in possession of their lost national heritage.

It is, however, as an historian that Standish O'Grady exercised the greatest influence upon the Literary Revival. With a fine sense of what was needed to give nerve and backbone to Irish literature he turned in succession to the two epochs in the history of Ireland when the national spirit was most strongly and truly defined; the heroic age, when the Celtic soul had reached its plenitude, the Elizabethan age, when the last sunset glow of the old ideals flared up to show the final rally and dispersion of Gaelic civilisation. His *History of Ireland* offends against most of the accepted canons of historical writing, his novels are marred by faults of construction at which the most commonplace "circulationist" would smile, but all these faults are redeemed by the inner quality which they derive from burning idealism and epic grandeur of the mind that conceived these works. The *Bardic History*, in particular, was a veritable revelation. Here at last was heard the authentic voice of pagan and heroic Ireland; in the story of Cuculain, modern Irish literature had at length found its epic. (pp. 50-2)

There is not an important writer of the Revival but has acknowledged his debt to Standish O'Grady, more particularly the generation just springing up when his best work appeared. . . . Historian, dramatist, novelist, editor, publisher, poet and even economist, Standish O'Grady was, above all, and always, an idealist, and in every phase of his activities he has never failed to champion the great ideals which first attracted him to the noblest period in the story of his race. As a personality he has exerted a profound influence upon the literary generation whose ardour he had already kindled by his re-creation of heroic Ireland. As he was the first to reveal a truly noble tradition, it was fitting that he should create, and for a time watch over, the medium through which so much was expressed that was the direct outcome of his own teaching and example, and that he should finally become sponsor for some of the children of his own literary offspring. It is with a peculiar sense of appropriateness, therefore, that we may salute in Standish James O'Grady the father of the Literary Revival in Ireland. (pp. 53-4)

Ernest Boyd, "Sources: The Father of the Revival, Standish James O'Grady," in his Ireland's Literary Renaissance *(by permission of Barnes & Noble Books, a Division of Littlefield, Adams & Co., Inc.), revised edition, Barnes & Noble, 1922 (and reprinted by Barnes & Noble, 1968, pp. 26-54.)*

NORREYS JEPSON O'CONOR (essay date 1924)

One of the earliest of Gaelic poems is addressed to "Aed, great in kindling splendor." The phrase might well be applied to Standish O'Grady, whose three books, *The Coming of Cuculain, In the Gates of the North,* and *The Triumph and Passing of Cuculain,* have recently been published in this country, thus giving American readers easy access to writing which had a marked influence upon the earlier years of the so-called Celtic renaissance. Since Mr. Yeats and others have acknowledged their debt to Mr. O'Grady, it seems strange that many of the critics who have written of the Celtic revival should show little or no first-hand acquaintance with the work of the author of *Irish History: Heroic Period, Early Bardic Literature,* and *Irish History: Cuculain and his Contemporaries.* (p. 179)

As their titles indicate, the new books deal with Cuchulain (a more usual spelling of the name), the hero of the oldest Irish saga cycle, the champion who, single-handed, defended Ulster against invasion. Mr. O'Grady has relied for his facts chiefly upon the epic tale, "The Cattle Raid of Cooley," although, in order that the picture of the hero's life may be more fully delineated, he has, properly, drawn upon other texts. No one who reads the books will fail to understand the spell they have laid upon Irishmen; the author's writing has the power mentioned in the old poem about Aed. Not only does Mr. O'Grady kindle the splendor of Ireland's heroic past, but he stirs the reader's enthusiasm for it; the narrative has vividness, color, sound, movement. Of course much of this is due to the wealth of detail—unusual in other early literatures—which distinguishes Irish, but much also is to be attributed to the modern author. He makes abundant use of a device thoroughly appropriate to epic narrative—simile; and his figures are happily chosen, since nearly all depend for their effect upon Nature, and, therefore, do not have an exclusively modern flavor; the atmosphere of antiquity is well sustained. (p. 180)

However, Mr. O'Grady's great achievement is that from the obscure, confused, incoherent narrative of most of the early Irish texts he has made a connected story with a beginning, a middle, and an end. The extent of his accomplishment is seen by comparing his rendition with a literal translation of the original. (p. 181)

Not only has Mr. O'Grady made his story clear, but he has thoroughly steeped himself in the history, social customs, and literature of the Irish past, so that, in retelling the Gaelic narratives, he is able to make additions and changes which are in the spirit of the originals; above all, he has the gift of arranging his material for dramatic effect; each one of the many combats of Cuchulain piques the attention, and the pitfall of monotony is almost entirely avoided. He fully understands the value of suspense.

The author's style has the sweep appropriate to an epic; but his books suffer from defects which may be attributed partly

to their sources and partly to the time in which they were written. Monotony lurks dangerously in the background; there is also a tendency toward over-elaboration, which is not merely a Gaelic heritage, but an earmark of the writing of the eighteen-nineties. Likewise, the stories are marred by unfortunate attempts to orientate the morality of pagan Ireland with that of the reign of Queen Victoria. Greater accuracy would have ensured the preservation of fine passages which have been sacrificed, notably in the Deirdre story, and that striking bit from the story of Cuchulain's death where the hero goes to his last fight while the queens put up a cry of wailing and lamentation because they know the hero will not come again. There is also much carelessness in regard to details of good English: clauses out of place interfere with essential clearness, as do pronouns vague in reference. Nevertheless, these books are a successful working-over of early Irish; they possess a vitality not shared by many later and supposedly more faithful accounts. (pp. 184-85)

Norreys Jepson O'Conor, "The Father of the Celtic Renaissance," in his Changing Ireland: Literary Backgrounds of the Irish Free State, 1889-1922 *(copyright 1924 by The President and Fellows of Harvard College), Cambridge, Mass.: Harvard University Press, 1924, pp. 179-85.*

VIVIAN MERCIER (essay date 1958)

In order to justify [my high opinion of O'Grady's abilities] I shall have to consider at least four aspects of his many-sided personality: the historian, the storyteller, the politician, and the journalist. I do so reluctantly, for a severe critic of O'Grady might claim that his versatility was his greatest weakness, and that he failed at everything because he concentrated on nothing. "At best," such a critic would say, "he never got beyond the standing of a talented amateur in any of those four fields." Perhaps, but the whole Irish Literary Revival, like the Abbey Theatre, the Gaelic League, and the entire political and military leadership of the Irish Revolution, was the work of rank amateurs.

Although O'Grady attempted far too much, he employed his many means always to the same end—that of ensuring continuity between Ireland's past and her future. As a historian and historical novelist, he sought to fire the imaginations of his Irish readers by his portrayal of a bygone Ireland; as a politician and journalist, he strove to preserve those qualities of truth, courage, and generosity which he found in aristocratic Anglo-Ireland and to transmit them intact to the democratic Ireland that he was approaching. Moreover, he succeeded. (pp. 285-86)

Having called O'Grady a historian, I must hasten to add that he was unlike any other historian who ever lived, with the possible exception of Herodotus. He wrote history simply because the professional historians would not or could not write the kind of epic narrative he wanted to read. His first (and most important) original work bore the title *History of Ireland* . . . : it must be regarded as the fuse which exploded the long-awaited Literary Revival. This "history," however, consisted mainly of a retelling of the Early Irish sagas—legends which were then virtually unknown to all but a few specialists. O'Grady defended his decision to allot so much space to heroic history, instead of passing on at once to authenticated fact, by calling attention to a profound truth—one which Yeats also loved to assert: "A nation's history is made for it by circumstances, and the irresistible progress of events, but their legends they make for themselves.... The legends represent the imagination of the country; they are that kind of history which a nation desires to possess. They betray the ambitions and ideals of the people, and, in this respect, have a value far beyond the tale of actual events."

For a while, unfortunately, O'Grady became convinced of the essential historicity of the legends, but he soon reverted to a soberer view and ... published Volume I of a *History of Ireland: Critical and Philosophical* in which he treated the bardic history of the country with great skepticism. This work was so neglected by the public that no further volumes appeared. I believe, however, that it will one day be shown to contain some very shrewd guesses, the offspring of an original and intuitive mind.

O'Grady's last attempt at a history of Ireland, modestly entitled *The Story of Ireland,* was an infuriating and unpopular little book. Under Carlyle's influence, he praised Oliver Cromwell and maintained that the Irish people had, on the whole, welcomed the overthrow of their feudal lords by Elizabeth. An unpopular opinion need not be erroneous, of course, but his view of Cromwell, unlike his view of Elizabeth, seems to have been based on little or no independent research.

O'Grady the story-teller chose for the subject of his first book an episode from the Elizabethan conquest of Ireland. He must have been dissatisfied with *Red Hugh's Captivity* ..., for he rehandles the narrative of Hugh Roe O'Donnell's capture and two escapes in *The Flight of the Eagle* eight years later. The latter is one of O'Grady's most satisfying works. In it he once again proves himself able to strike and sustain the epic note. His "saga" of Red Hugh is worthy of its hero, that Homeric figure from real life.

The Bog of Stars, a series of shorter narratives and sketches from Elizabethan Irish history, has probably had more Irish readers than any other of O'Grady's books. The title story and the account of the Battle of the Curlew Mountains rank among his best work.

If *The Flight of the Eagle* and *The Bog of Stars* read like fiction rather than history, *Ulrick the Ready* resembles history rather than fiction. In it, O'Grady misses chance after chance as a novelist, dismissing his hero's part in the Battle of Kinsale with a single sentence.

During the 1890's O'Grady wrote several books quite frankly for boys. Two of these, *Lost on Du-Corrig* and *The Chain of Gold,* were the only works which ever earned him significant amounts of money. They are rather similar tales of mystery and adventure.

O'Grady the politician was a man whose views were profoundly influenced by his interpretation of history. Like Carlyle, who probably derived his theory from Hegel, Standish O'Grady saw history as an evolutionary process, in which one class or social system would succeed another as the chosen instrument of the *Zeitgeist* or "Genius of the age." He pointed out that "Rural Ireland was once held under the Clan system. It fell before Feudalism.... Feudalism, with its great Lords and Captains, flourished long, and fell before the modern Landlord.... And the Landlord has got to go, too, following, in his turn, the Clans and the great Captains."

Yes, the landlord had to go; O'Grady's whole activity as a politician aimed at enabling him to go in peace and, if possible, with dignity. (pp. 286-88)

[He] founded, (in January 1900) the weekly *All Ireland Review,* which ran until April 1906. All six of its volumes are still worth reading for their humor, their passion and their humanity. In this one-man magazine O'Grady's unique personality found its fullest expression.

I must not end this brief account of Standish O'Grady without trying to answer the question: What did he do to deserve the title of "Father of the Irish Literary Revival"? I would give a twofold answer. First, in his volumes of legendary history he used the Irish legends for a primarily *artistic* purpose and so paved the way for W. B. Yeats. Secondly, he differed from that other pioneer of the Revival, Sir Samuel Ferguson, in refusing to regret that the heros of Irish legend were not Victorian gentlemen. Like Carlyle, Standish O'Grady suspected that the Victorian era might represent a depression rather than a peak in human development; therefore, in spite of all his bowdlerizing and didacticism, he was prepared to glory in certain aspects of ancient Ireland *for their own sake.* (pp. 289-90.)

Vivian Mercier, "Standish James O'Grady," in Colby Library Quarterly, Series IV, No. 16, November, 1958, pp. 285-90.

PHILLIP L. MARCUS (essay date 1970)

While staying at a country house in the West of Ireland [O'Grady] was forced by bad weather to remain indoors, and in the library of the house happened upon a three-volume history of Ireland by Sylvester O'Halloran—the first history of his country into which he had ever looked.... Determined to learn more, he went upon his return to Dublin to the Royal Irish Academy, and soon he was deep in research. His most important discovery was the works of the great Gaelic scholar Eugene O'Curry, in whose encyclopedic compilations *Lectures on the Manuscript Materials of Ancient Irish History* and *Manners and Customs of the Ancient Irish* he met for the first time Ireland's rich store of heroic literature. That literature became the greatest formative influence upon his personal world-view and the books he himself was to write. He suddenly saw that he had been the victim of a grievous illusion: his country not only had an indigenous tradition, but a tradition that one could be proud of and inspired by. In fact, no country in Europe had a more glamorous and impressive body of epic materials, and only in Greece was there anything even comparable. Determined that others would not remain in the same state of ignorance that he had endured, he began to write his own history of Ireland *(History of Ireland,* **Volume One,** *The Heroic Period;* **Volume Two,** *Cuculain and His Contemporaries);* he completed it between 1878 and 1880 and published it at his own expense, as there was no contemporary market for such subjects. This unimpressive looking work, which fell from the presses almost stillborn, was soon to be diligently sought and reverently studied and quoted by the young men and women who collectively constituted the "Irish Renaissance."

The material with which O'Grady was working falls into three major categories. In the first of these are all legends involving the Tuatha Dé Danann (Tribes of the Goddess Danu), thought to have been the gods of the ancient Irish, and other early groups supposed to have invaded Ireland. The second category, often called the Red Branch Cycle, deals with heroes treated as having lived in what is now Ulster at about the beginning of the Christian Era. Chief figures in this cycle include Conchobor, King of the Ulidians; Fergus MacRóig, who had been king until ousted by Conchobor; and above all Cú Chulainn, the greatest warrior of the Red Branch. The most important event in this cycle is the Cattle-drive of Cualnge, in which the northern province is attacked and pillaged by forces from all the other provinces of Ireland under the leadership of Medb, Queen of Connaught and Fergus MacRóig, who has defected from the Ulster side. At the time of the invasion all of the Red Branch heroes except Cú Chulainn are overcome by a mysterious malady that deprives them of their faculties, and thus he has to defend the province alone. He does so successfully, though in the process he has to kill his boyhood friend Fer Diad and is very seriously wounded himself. Another portion of this cycle is the famous tale of Deirdre (the Irish Helen of Troy) and the Sons of Usnach. The central concern of the third category is the exploits of the Fianna, a kind of Irish militia, and of its leader, Fionn MacCumhaill. The events of this cycle are traditionally placed in the third century, during the reign of the historical monarch Cormac MacArt. (The degree of historicity in all three of these groups of legends is a subject of continuing debate.) O'Grady's imagination was moved most powerfully by the Cú Chulainn story, and it was this which comprised the central concern of the *History;* he was, however, strongly interested in the other two groups as well and eventually gave them fuller treatment, the gods in his *History of Ireland: Critical and Philosophical* and the Fianna in *Finn and His Companions.*

O'Grady's task in trying to make these legends better known was a more difficult one than the above scheme might suggest, for they did not come to him in any such neat arrangement. The old stories in fact survived not in a single, unified fabric, but rather in a myriad of fragments. Many of the individual stories were incomplete and often there might be several variant versions of a single tale. Further confusion came from textual corruption and from modifications intentionally introduced by clerical copyists, who brought in anachronistic Christian elements and sought to obliterate evidence of "paganism" by euhemerizing the old Irish gods. Nor was there any formal harmony in the old texts, which were a jumble of prose and verse, epics, lyrics, pseudo-histories, genealogies and other miscellaneous kinds of writing. Finally there was the language problem: the stories were preserved primarily in Middle Irish, and even by the second half of the nineteenth century English translations were relatively few and difficult to obtain. There was not even a single published rendering of the entire story of the Cattle-drive of Cualnge (the *Táin Bó Cúalnge*) and thus O'Grady, who could not read Irish, had to rely primarily upon a manuscript translation which a later and more accomplished Gaelic scholar has termed "wretched." (pp. 14-18)

These extremely difficult conditions raised the further issue of precisely how faithful to the received materials one must be in presenting them to modern audiences. One possible alternative was the absolute faithfulness of the scholar, which had the obvious disadvantage of sacrificing appeal to many general readers. A second course might involve turning into verse or "literary" prose the literal rendering of a scholarly translation, but the blurring of aesthetic virtues in the form and organization of most of the surviving tales constituted a serious drawback to this approach. A method yet more likely to appeal to a broad audience while even less faithful to the sources would be to use a literary medium and also to impose an aesthetically satisfactory form. To make the subject matter into a "good story" might involve altering the genre of the original, changing the plot by combining different versions and omitting or even adding elements, and elaborating and making consistent the characterizations. The author using this approach would have to stress his concern with faithfulness to the "spirit" of his sources. While a few other writers (notably Ferguson) had used the legendary materials before O'Grady, no one approach had been clearly validated; consequently he had to solve this problem himself, and he found himself attracted by the polar extremes of scholarly respect and imaginative improvement. (pp. 18-19)

The approach which O'Grady used in the imaginative portions of the *History* to reduce the corpus of legendary materials to its "artistic elements" was itself influenced by a combination of motives. Chief among these was his desire to present a glamorous and appealing image of the Irish heroic age, which he frankly idealized. (p. 22)

Clearly this idealized vision of the heroic past of their country had much to do with the book's appeal to other Irish writers. . . . However, while O'Grady's approach was effective, it was not really faithful even to the spirit of his originals.

Those originals are no more uniform in world-view than they are in style, and in them the heroic and noble are mixed with the comic, the fantastic, the coarse. Thus in the case of his central character, Cú Chulainn, O'Grady could not accept the descriptions of him as having three-colored hair (thought by some scholars to be a vestige of an original association of him with the sun), seven-colored pupils in each eye, and seven digits on each of his hands and feet, let alone his grotesque "distortions." . . . (p. 23)

In the "archaeological" section of the second volume of the *History* he asserted that "a noble moral tone pervades the whole" of the early literature. But this was plainly untrue, and as he himself admitted many years later, he found things in that literature which he "simply could not write down and print and publish," things reflecting "the very loose morality of the age." At the time of writing the *History* he tried to convince himself that most of the "ignoble" elements were not canonical, and that he was capable in each case of judging. One such element was the sexual liaisons between Fergus and Medb, which he omitted entirely. Cú Chulainn's affairs with the amazon Aoife, who bore him his only son, Connla, and with his concubine Ethne Inguba were similarly unacceptable. In both of these cases O'Grady was not content merely to omit the offending incident: he felt compelled to provide substitutes. Thus he retained Cú Chulainn's son, but made his mother Emer, Cú's actual wife; and he added a scene showing Ethne as a child, fascinated by Cú when he visits the home of her family, and later referred to her as "a very dear friend" of Cú Chulainn.

In both of these latter incidents prudishness and the desire to preserve an idealized vision of the subject-matter are blended with a strong vein of sentimentality. Unable to resist the easy sentiment obtainable in literature from child characters, O'Grady not only fabricated the incident involving the childhood of Ethne, but also invented a younger offspring for Cú Chulainn, an infant named Fionscota, and several episodes involving the parental tenderness of the great warrior. (pp. 24-5)

O'Grady's education had left him with a thorough knowledge of and a deep love for Classical literature, and it is consequently no surprise that when seeking a literary model for the form of his work he should turn to the epic. . . . The choice of models was a good one. It has been suggested by some Celtic scholars that the *Táin* shows the direct influence of the great Classical epics; in any case it contains such features associated with the epic genre as the involvement of deities in the affairs of the heroes (Cú Chulainn is first harrassed, then helped, by the war goddess Mórrigu and has the support of the sun god Lugh, treated in some versions as his real father), the lengthy cataloguing of forces involved, the conference of military leaders, and of course the full-scale battle. All O'Grady had to do, therefore, was to add some traditional stylistic devices, notably an invocation to the Muses and several heroic similes. . . . The Miltonic seriousness with which O'Grady viewed his task was to be justified by the role his book came to play in reviving the worship of these ''sacred influences,'' of modern Ireland's ancient heritage. There are heroic similes scattered throughout both volumes but they are not numerous enough to produce a strongly felt pattern. (pp. 28-9)

In the areas of narrative organization and the depiction of characters, O'Grady made numerous and varied changes in his source material. His personal interests and biases provided the motives for many of these changes, while many others were of course necessitated by the unsatisfactory condition of the surviving texts: as O'Grady himself explained, in order ''to be faithful to the generic conception, one must disregard often the literal statement of the bard. That the whole should be fairly represented, one must do violence to the parts. . . .'' In other words, his first task was to eliminate contradictions and select from among variant accounts those which would be the most genuine, the closest to the ''main idea.'' Here the requirement of faithfulness to the old stories presented no difficulties, as the process was simply one of separating what he considered to be the legitimate from the bogus and omitting the latter. His modifications, however, were not merely selective: he also took the far greater liberty of adding materials, either taken from other contexts or fabricated by himself. (pp. 31-2)

Characterization in the modern sense may very well have been a concern unknown to the makers of the early Irish literature, but it was certainly a central one of O'Grady's. He not only felt free to provide personalities for many minor figures who were in the sources almost uncharacterized, but also undertook major revisions in the treatment of the central characters. Of course Cú Chulainn himself is the prime example, and enough has already been said to make clear the extent to which O'Grady remade his image. Fergus, Laeg, Fer Diad, and Medb are among the others who received close attention. The treatment of Medb was perhaps most at variance with the source materials. O'Grady tried to make her seem more ''feminine,'' to endow her with some of the personality traits traditionally associated with the ''weaker sex,'' and at times the proud amazon of the sources seems more like the delicate fainting heroines of the nineteenth-century novel.

Thus O'Grady's method of turning the old texts into ''good stories'' was not without serious flaws. But despite those flaws the *History* still ''works,'' the intrinsic virtues of the legends and O'Grady's strong enthusiasm for them often compensating for failures in the rendering (there are, too, some notable successes), and—particularly if the scarceness and generally poor quality of other literary treatments of the legendary materials available at the time is considered—it

is easy to see how the book could have been so powerful in its impact upon those who read it.

Those who read it were, however, very few indeed and . . . O'Grady was discouraged. Then he had an experience, reminiscent of his discovery of O'Halloran's *History of Ireland,* which showed him a new course of action. Browsing one day in the library of the University Club he discovered that the club's copy of George Petrie's seminal archaeological study of the round towers of Ireland was uncut; this experience, his son relates, ''opened his eyes to the mistake he had made. The public were not attracted by a sober treatise. Fiction and romance were their intellectual delicacies. Accordingly . . . he rewrote the Celtic legends in the guise of a novel.'' O'Grady's first attempts were not exactly ''sober treatises,'' but clearly neither the ''History'' nor the ''Epic'' rubric would attract the great audience there was for fiction; and so he set to work upon what was to become a trilogy upon the life of Cú Chulainn [*The Coming of Cuculain, In the Gates of the North,* and *The Triumph and Passing of Cuculain*]. (pp. 35-6)

The Coming of Cuculain and *The Gates of the North* covered Cú Chulainn's life to the same point as Volume One of the *History,* while *The Triumph and Passing of Cuculain* rehandled the material originally related in Volume Two. *The Coming of Cuculain* required by far the greatest revisions, for in the *History* O'Grady had dealt only very briefly with Cú's boyhood. In the new version (which he prefaced with a request that the reader ''forget for a while that there is such a thing as scientific history'' and ''give his imagination a holiday'') he had to go back and give substance to the outline of the events of Cú's early life as he had originally described them. Thus the action of the day upon which Cú took arms, which occupied eight pages in the *History,* is given nearly seventy in *The Coming of Cuculain.* In making this expansion, O'Grady continued to take the liberty he had originally allowed himself of inventing copious quantities of details—always, presumably, in the spirit of the original sources. And there was also a thorough revision of the verbal texture of the narrative. (p. 37)

In general the trilogy, though thoroughly rewritten, has the same basic shape as its earlier form, and is not noticeably *better* from an aesthetic point of view. However, it probably would still have achieved something of the greater circulation for which O'Grady had hoped if its publication had not been so long a process. . . . As a result it was primarily the *History,* scarce as it was and full of false starts and hesitations in method, through which his vision of Ireland's heroic past made its impact upon the modern Irish consciousness.

Between the appearance of the *History* and the first volume of the Cú Chulainn trilogy O'Grady published one other literary rendering of the early Irish legendary materials, *Finn and His Companions.* . . . (pp. 41-2)

In contrast to his approach in the *History,* O'Grady did not in *Finn and His Companions* attempt to recreate this entire narrative. Perhaps he lacked sufficient time or felt that such treatment would be inappropriate for these materials. In addition, the book was published in Fisher Unwin's ''Children's Library'' series, and the youthful potential audience meant that any incidents involving sex or showing the main characters in an unfavorable light would have to be cut out. Of course O'Grady had made similar omissions in the *History,* but here the effect was more damaging to the total impact of the book. . . . On the other hand, those episodes O'Grady did use seem to have been chosen primarily for moralistic reasons rather than with aesthetic excellence in mind. . . . [In] the arrangement of those stories the moral scheme is again clear, the artistic blurred. . . . [The] highly selective and chronologically confusing narrative which results from the arrangement of the episodes . . . has little literary appeal and might be difficult even to follow for those having only slight familiarity with the traditional legends. (pp. 43-4)

> *Phillip L. Marcus, in his* Standish O'Grady *(©︎ 1970 by Associated University Presses, Inc.),* Bucknell University Press, *1970, 92 p.*

RICHARD FALLIS (essay date 1977)

In 1878, Standish O'Grady published his *History of Ireland: Heroic Period,* and with that work the Gaelic and Anglo-Irish traditions finally came into fruitful contact. Departing from the conscientiously scholarly style of early versions of the ancient stories, O'Grady attempted, so he said, "the reconstruction by imaginative processes of the life led by our ancestors in this country," hoping "to make this heroic period once again a portion of the imagination of the country, and its chief characters as familiar in the minds of our people as they once were." O'Grady eventually succeeded in both aims, his history becoming one of the most influential books in modern Ireland. (p. 48)

Earlier in the nineteenth century there had been . . . a great deal of attention to the traditional literature of Ireland. The scholars had produced their editions of the ancient tales and translations of Gaelic materials and the popularizers, writing often for Irish emigrants around the world, had published green-bound volume after green-bound volume of quaint tales. Yet the gap between scholarship and popularization long remained unbridged; readers who would put down hard cash for *Tales from Irish Hearths and Homes* had little interest in the scholarly translations and dictionaries of Gaelic, and vice versa. (p. 62)

The publication of Standish O'Grady's *History of Ireland: Heroic Period* . . . demonstrated that it was possible to combine the work of the scholars with the techniques of popularization and so produce a work which would become part of the living Irish imagination. O'Grady believed that Irish history and legend needed to be treated imaginatively, and he was willing to use the work of the scholars as the raw materials, but no more than the raw materials, for his re-creation of ancient Irish life and legend. He was no great prose stylist, but his *History* and the many other books he wrote had a contagious enthusiasm for the life and literature of Gaelic Ireland. He had himself grown up in Cork unaware of the ancient literary heritage of his country, and it was only

in his late twenties that he discovered a history of Ireland which changed his life. His enthusiasm was that of the late convert; if he sometimes overstated his case, as when he claimed that all ancient Gaelic writing was deeply moral, those overstatements were simply an extension of his passionate enthusiasm. Although he made numerous and sometimes prudish changes in his originals, his *History* deserves its place as a modernized Irish epic. His great achievement lay in weaving scores of episodes into a believeable whole so that even if his version of the *Táin* is not really accurate, it makes exciting reading. At the time of its publication, O'Grady's *History* received less attention than it deserved, but by the nineties, it had become almost a bible for young Irish writers and nationalists. They found in it stirring re-tellings of the ancient tales, and they also found in his Cuchulain an exemplar of the Irish spirit, manly, courageous, extravagantly emotional, and genuinely noble.

O'Grady's work provided a model for a way to deal with the Gaelic inheritance of heroic legend, the way of imaginative re-creation. O'Grady's methods had their problems, though (his prose idiom was no more Irish than any other Victorian journalist's, for one thing), and what was a good method for dealing with ancient stories would not do for folklore that was still current in the countryside. (pp. 62-3)

> *Richard Fallis, "Before the Irish Renaissance: Literature in Gaelic and English" and "The Years of the Celtic Twilight: the 1890's" in his* The Irish Renaissance *(copyright ©︎ 1977 by Syracuse University Press, all rights reserved), Syracuse University Press, 1977, pp. 30-54, 55-72.**

ADDITIONAL BIBLIOGRAPHY

Boyd, Ernest A. "'A Fenian Unionist': Standish O'Grady." In his *Appreciations and Depreciations,* pp. 3-22. 1918. Reprint. Freeport, N.Y.: Books for Libraries Press, 1968.
    Discussion of O'Grady's political views.

Clarke, Austin. "Standish James O'Grady." *The Dublin Magazine* XXII, No. 1 (January-March 1947): 36-40.
    Biographical study of O'Grady's life that includes brief critical remarks on his major works.

O'Grady, Hugh Art. *Standish James O'Grady, the Man & the Writer: A Memoir by His Son.* Dublin: The Talbot Press, 1929, 84 p.
    Memoir by O'Grady's son which includes valuable insights into O'Grady's research methods.

Yeats, W. B. "The Trembling of the Veil: Ireland After Parnell" and "Dramatis Personae." In his *Autobiographies,* pp. 197-250, 383-458. London: Macmillan & Co., 1955.*
    Discusses Irish political activities during O'Grady's lifetime and how those events affected his works.

Wilfred (Edward Salter) Owen

1893-1918

English poet.

Owen is considered the best of those poets whose work was inspired by experiences in World War I. His poems are not idealistically patriotic like Rupert Brooke's, nor do they rage desperately against war like Siegfried Sassoon's. Rather, the subject of Owen's poems was the "pity of war"; he exposed with striking compassion the grim realities of war and its effects on the human spirit. Owen's unique voice was complemented by his unusual and experimental technical style; he was the first to use para-rhyme—rhyme achieved by matching the first and last letters of words. This distinctive technique, coupled with a prominent use of assonance and alliteration, influenced the poets of the 1920s and 1930s, notably W. H. Auden and Stephen Spender.

A thoughtful, imaginative youth, Owen developed an interest in poets and poetry, especially in Keats, whose influence can be seen in many of Owen's poems. Owen's delicate health and the harsh English winters prompted him to spend time in France, where he worked as a tutor. There he met Laurent Tailhade, a French symbolist poet, whose chief influence can be seen in the pacifist ideas found in Owen's writing. Upon returning to England, Owen enlisted and fought in France until hospitalized with an injury. Later sent to Edinburgh's Craiglockhart hospital for treatment of shell-shock, he met another poet, Siegfried Sassoon, who became Owen's mentor. Sassoon's respect and encouragement confirmed for Owen his ability as a poet. He wrote most of his critically acclaimed poems after this meeting in the thirteen months prior to his death.

Since he was killed the week before the Armistice, Owen never knew the success of his work. The first collection, *Poems,* was compiled by Siegfried Sassoon, whose colloquial, satirical, and direct style influenced many of Owen's lyrics. Among his best known poems are *"Dulce et Decorum Est,"* "Anthem for Doomed Youth," and "Strange Meeting." Through these poems, Owen spoke for a generation wasted in the First World War. "Strange Meeting" is considered by most critics to be the finest of all the poems of that war. In this elegy Owen's themes are historical, humanistic, and mystical. The narrator of the poem, in a dreamlike vision, encounters a German soldier that he had killed. In the dialogue that ensues, Owen protests the futility of war, considers the conflict between ego and conscience in war, and suggests an analogy between the soldier and Christ, and between the enemy and oneself. "Strange Meeting," one of Owen's last poems, was never completed.

Ironically, because of the war, Owen, fulfilled his poetic destiny. He wrote only a small number of poems, yet their quality assures him a place in the history of English literature.

PRINCIPAL WORKS

Poems (poetry) 1920
The Poems of Wilfred Owen (poetry) 1931
Thirteen Poems (poetry) 1956
The Collected Poems of Wilfred Owen (poetry) 1963
Collected Letters (letters) 1967

Wilfred Owen: War Poems and Others (poetry) 1973

SIEGFRIED SASSOON (essay date 1920)

All that was strongest in Wilfred Owen survives in his poems; any superficial impressions of his personality, any records of his conversation, behaviour, or appearance, would be irrelevant and unseemly. The curiosity which demands such morsels would be incapable of appreciating the richness of his work.

The discussion of his experiments in assonance and dissonance (of which *Strange Meeting* is the finest example) may be left to the professional critics of verse, the majority of whom will be more preoccupied with such technical details than with the profound humanity of the self-revelation manifested in such magnificent lines as those at the end of his *Apologia pro Poemate Meo,* and in that other poem which he named *Greater Love.*

The importance of his contribution to the literature of the War cannot be decided by those who, like myself, both admired him as a poet and valued him as a friend. His conclusions about War are so entirely in accordance with my own that I cannot attempt to judge his work with any critical detachment. I can only affirm that he was a man of absolute integrity of mind. He never wrote his poems (as so many war-poets did) to make the effect of a personal gesture. He pitied others; he did not pity himself. In the last year of his life he attained a clear vision of what he needed to say, and these poems survive him as his true and splendid testament. (p. v)

Siegfried Sassoon, in his introduction to Poems *by Wilfred Owen (Canadian rights by permission of Chatto & Windus), B. W. Huebsch, Inc., 1920, Chatto & Windus, 1921, pp. v-vi.*

J. MIDDLETON MURRY   (essay date 1921)

The name and the genius of Wilfred Owen were first revealed by the publication of his finest poem, **"Strange Meeting,"** in the anthology "Wheels" a year ago. I still remember the incredible shock of that encounter, the sudden, profound stirring by the utterance of a true poet. Since that time other fragments of Owen's work have been made known, and if none so evidently bore the impress of poetic mastery as **"Strange Meeting,"** they were a part of that achievement. We could be sure that when the promised volume of his poetry appeared it would be single, coherent, and unique.

And so it is. Here in thirty-three brief-pages [***Poems***] is the evidence that Wilfred Owen was the greatest poet of the war. There have been war-poets; but he was a poet of another kind. He was not a poet who seized upon the opportunity of war, but one whose being was saturated by a strange experience, who bowed himself to the horror of war until his soul was penetrated by it, and there was no mean or personal element remaining unsubdued in him. In the fragmentary preface which so deeply bears the mark of Owen's purity of purpose, he wrote: "Above all this book is not concerned with Poetry. The subject of it is War, and the Pity of War. The Poetry is in the pity."

"The Poetry is in the pity." Whatever the new generation of poets may think or say, Owen had the secret in those words. The source of all enduring poetry lies in an intense and overwhelming emotion. The emotion must be overwhelming, and suffered as it were to the last limit of the soul's capacity. Complete submission is an essential phase in that process of mastering the emotion with which the poet's creation begins, for the poet himself has to be changed; he plunges into the depths of his emotion to rise mysteriously renewed. Only then will the words he utters bear upon them the strange compulsion of a secret revealed; only then can he put his spell upon us and trouble our depths. For the problem of poetry is not primarily, or even largely, a conscious problem; true poetry begins with an act, a compelled and undeliberate act, of obedience to that centre of our being where all experience is reconciled.

And the further process of poetry is also an instinctive adjustment rather than a conscious seeking. The poet's being, changed by the stress of its overwhelming experience, gropes after a corresponding expression. Learning and the intellect are no better than tentative guides. The correspondence toward which the poet moves is recognized and ratified by other powers than these. And Owen's search after some garment for his new comprehension more closely fitting than the familiar rhyme arose, not from any desire to experiment

for experiment's sake, but from the inward need to say the thing he had to say most exactly and finally. . . . I believe that the reader who comes fresh to [**"Strange Meeting"**] does not immediately observe the assonant endings. At first he feels only that the blank-verse has a mournful, impressive, even oppressive, quality of its own; that the poem has a forged unity, a welded and inexorable massiveness. The emotion with which it is charged cannot be escaped; the meaning of the words and the beat of the sounds have the same indivisible message. The tone is single, low, muffled, subterranean. The reader looks again and discovers the technical secret; but if he regards it then as an amazing technical innovation, he is in danger of falsifying his own reaction to the poem. Those assonant endings are indeed the discovery of genius; but in a truer sense the poet's emotion discovered them for itself. They are a dark and natural flowering of this, and only this, emotion. You cannot imagine them used for any other purpose save Owen's, or by any other hand save his. They are the very modulation of his voice; you are in the presence of that rare achievement, a true poetic style.

Throughout the poems in this book we can watch Owen working towards this perfection of his own utterance, and at the same time working away from realisitc description of the horrors of war towards an imaginative projection of emotion. The technical refinement works parallel with the imaginative sublimation. But even the realistic poems are hard and controlled, and completely free from weakness of emotional dispersion; while on Owen's highest plane no comparison at all between him and the realistic poets is possible. He speaks to the imagination; his poems evoke our reactions, not to a scene of horror played again before our eyes, but to words spoken in silence when all material tumult has died away; they are the expression of that which remains in the soul when the nightmare of the senses is over.

His poems are calm. In spite of the intense passion which is their impulse, they have a haunting serenity. For the poet has, at whatever cost, mastered his experience; his emotion has become tranquil. In these poems there is no more rebellion, but only pity and regret, and the peace of acquiescence. It is not a comfortable peace, this joyless yet serene resignation; but it is a victory of the human spirit. We receive from it that exalted pleasure, that sense of being lifted above the sphere of anger and despair which the poetic imagination alone can give. . . . [In **"Anthem for Doomed Youth"**] the calm is unmistakable, and indeed so evident that one might describe the sonnet as being in the familiar sense beautiful. Beauty of this kind is not to be found in the ghastly poem called **"The Show"**; but a still deeper calm is there. The poem is in Owen's later style, though the complex scheme of assonances is somewhat obscured by the arbitrary manner in which it has been printed. (pp. 705-06)

It may be true, as Mr. Sassoon suggests in his introduction, that the majority of war poets wrote for the sake of the effect of a personal gesture, and that Owen did not. But the important difference between Owen and the rest is a difference in the power and quality of the imagination, which seems to arise in a difference in the power and quality of the kindling experience. So profound is this that we can hardly refrain from calling Owen a great poet. He had, more surely than any other poet of his generation, the potentiality of greatness; and he actually wrote one great poem. **"Strange Meeting"** is complete, achieved, unfaltering, and it is not solitary, for although Owen wrote no other poem which is wholly on this secure imaginative level, we cannot but regard it as the culmination of poems hardly less achieved. **"Exposure"** is charged with the same sombre mystery, and the unity of technique and emotional intention is almost as close. **"Greater Love,"** which seems to have been written before Owen's final period had begun, will reveal the purity of the poet's emotion to those who may be disconcerted by his later work. . . .

But it is not this poem, beautiful and poignant though it is, which will vindicate the claim that Owen is the greatest poet of the war; it is **"Strange Meeting"** and certain fragments of other poems which are lifted up by a poetic imagination of the highest and rarest kind. . . . (p. 706)

[Even] if we admit that Owen was a poet of unusual imaginative power, why is he the only poet of the war? Other poets—true poets some of them—have written of the war. Why are they less than he? For this single reason. The war was a terrible and unique experience in the history of mankind; its poetry had likewise to be unique and terrible; it had to record not the high hopes that animated English youth at the outset, but the slow destruction of that youth in the sequel; more than this, it had to record not what the war did to men's bodies and senses, but what it did to their souls. Owen's poetry is unique and terrible because it records imperishably the devastation and the victory of a soul. (p. 707)

> *J. Middleton Murry, "The Poet of the War," in* The Nation and The Athenaeum, *Vol. XXVIII, No. 21, February 19, 1921, pp. 705-07.*

EDMUND BLUNDEN   (essay date 1931)

Much of [this collection, *The Poems of Wilfred Owen*,] represents the early period of his enthusiasm for poetry, when he was finding his own way to the secrets of style, and discovering the forms of verse on which he would build up his own House Beautiful. These papers are chiefly remarkable as picturing the isolation in which a poet discerns that he is a poet, the delight and difficulty of the high calling to which he finds himself born, and the fruitful uses of practice in thought and its richest verbal presentation. In them, the young Owen is, without knowing it, the guarantor of the eventual poet who, plunged into the abysses of the breaking of nations, has skill to speak. Their fancies, devices, luxuries, concords enabled him to meet the shocks and amazements of immense suffering with the courage of a masterly artist. (pp. 3-4)

The problem of dating most of Owen's papers is such that one cannot be sure when he thought out the use of assonances, instead of rhymes, which he perfected. He was an unwearied worker in the laboratory of word, rhythm, and music of language, partly by nature and partly from his close acquaintance with French poetry and its exacting technical subtleties. . . . At all events, having discovered and practised this para-rhyme, Owen became aware that it would serve him infinitely in the voicing of emotion and imagination. What he made of it is felt at its fullest, perhaps, in the solemn music of **"Strange Meeting"**, but again and again by means of it he creates remoteness, darkness, emptiness, shock, echo, the last word. So complete and characteristic is his deployment of this technical resource that imitators have been few; but, indeed, there is another cause why they have been so. Only an innate, unconventional command over language, and a

rich and living vocabulary—in short, only a genius for poetry could for long work in that uncommon medium. (pp. 28-9)

In July 1914 Owen, like most of his contemporaries, was intent upon the brighter side of experience. . . . That note was soon to be changed, and the "Endymion" phase of Owen's poetical life was at a close. Thenceforward he moved into the sphere of the later "Hyperion", to the lofty sorrow and threnody of which the latest of his writings must be likened; moreover, when he was to be moved by lighter forces of life, they were to be those of a ghost-like secrecy and dimness. In understanding and expressing those mysterious backwaters of a European war's great current, Owen had the advantage of being attuned to the sadness of the French poets; he is, at moments, an English Verlaine. It did not take him long, after the sudden dismissal of peace, to feel and utter the solemn death of a period, and in himself the transition from a youth of maying to an agedness of mood. (pp. 9-10)

He was, apart from Mr. Sassoon, the greatest of the English war poets. But the term "war poets" is rather convenient than accurate. Wilfred Owen was a poet without classifications of war and peace. Had he lived, his humanity would have continued to encounter great and moving themes, the painful sometimes, sometimes the beautiful, and his art would have matched his vision. He was one of those destined beings who, without pride of self (the words of Shelley will never be excelled), "see, as from a tower, the end of all". Outwardly, he was quiet, unobtrusive, full of good sense; inwardly, he could not help regarding the world with the dignity of a seer.

Owen was preparing himself to the last moment in experience, observation, and composition for a volume of poems, to strike at the conscience of England in regard to the continuance of the war. This volume had begun to take a definite form in his mind, which may be traced in the hastily written and obscurely amended Preface and Contents found among his papers. That they and his later poems exist at all in writing is, to all who knew, or realize, the fierce demands made on company officers in the front line and in its vicinity, a wonderful proof of his intellectual determination. (pp. 39-40)

> *Edmund Blunden, "Memoir" (reprinted by permission of A D Peters & Co Ltd), in* The Poems of Wilfred Owen *by Wilfred Owen, edited by Edmund Blunden, Chatto & Windus, 1931 (and reprinted by Chatto & Windus, 1967), pp. 3-44.*

FRANK SWINNERTON   (essay date 1934)

With Wilfred Owen, we reach the height of what may be termed strictly War Poetry. In his work, which was first published posthumously under the editorship of Siegfried Sassoon, and which has now been finally collected and introduced by Edmund Blunden, there is no effort to render the delights of War, or the noises of guns and other instruments of death. We have, instead of impressionism, a peculiar reflective hatred of war from which hysteria is entirely absent; an attempt to give in poetry, not the "wukka-wukka" (as [Ford Madox] Hueffer) or "toc-toc-toc" (as [Robert] Nichols) of the machine-guns, but the silent thoughts of men, the deadliness of trench warfare, the deep indignation of the soldier at civilian barbarism. (p. 325)

He had, of course, written poetry before the War—some of it ingeniously experimental, as an example printed among his

other poems clearly shows;—but it was the War which produced his rapid maturity. And even then it was during his
stay in a War Hospital near Edinburgh, when Siegfried Sassoon was a fellow-patient, that he made the greatest progress.
(pp. 325-26)

His poetic instinct was so sure that he would sooner or later
have discovered for himself all that could be taught. Since,
however, time proved so brief, it is to Sassoon that we must
give thanks for a friendship and influence which aided the
production of Owen's best poems. If Owen had lived, he
might have carried into the post-War period an even stronger
power, as one infers from the magnificent fragment, *Strange
Meeting*. As it is, the poems that we have deal chiefly with
War conditions and War reflections; and of all the men active
at that time he is the one most accurately described as a poet
of the War. How far we are from former picturesque renderings of sight and sound in the terrible stanzas of *Exposure*. . . . (p. 326)

[This poem] is, as it seems to me, a point of progress between
the mellifluous lyricism of pre-War days (and first consequent
impressionisms of the War) and the righteous anger passionately felt and expressed in other moods by Owen or with
characteristic irony by Sassoon. Such points hint only at a
development which somebody more competent than myself
should trace simply for the understanding of common people;
for the disillusion of the War poets has been appropriated
by a later generation as if that later generation, too, had
suffered; whereas it has merely not been able to climb out
of a bitter convention and remains self-righteous. Owen could
not have remained a pessimist: he must have constituted
himself a positive voice in a day of negations. One cannot
read his poems without realizing his natural bravery. He had
very exceptional talent, unusual skill and intelligence and
enterprise in versification, the imaginative power to identify
himself with other men and yet retain his own character
unimpaired, and a breadth of sympathy unsurpassed by any
of his contemporaries. For these qualities, in my opinion, he
stands first among his peers. (p. 327)

> *Frank Swinnerton, "The War-Time Afflatus," in
> his* The Georgian Scene: A Literary Panorama
> *(copyright 1934, © 1962 by Frank Swinnerton; re-
> printed by permission of Holt, Rinehart and Win-
> ston, Publishers), Farrar & Rinehart, 1934, pp. 317-
> 36.* *

STEPHEN SPENDER (essay date 1935)

Wilfred Owen, in the Preface to his Poems, makes his attitude—which in any case is clear in his poetry—doubly clear
by a straightforward statement:

> 'My subject is War, and the pity of War.
> 'The poetry is in the pity.

> 'Yet these elegies are to this generation in no sense con-
> solatory. They may be to the next. All a poet can do to-day
> is to warn. That is why the true Poets must be truthful.'

In other words, an attitude of pity—a pity which is fierce and
in no sense consolatory—is the only attitude possible for him
to adopt towards the War. But he fully realizes that to another
generation, a post-war generation, pity would not suffice as
the inspiration of poetry. The poetry is only in the pity when
the motive for pity is quite overwhelming. An immense and
terrifying pity is the extreme unction of tragedy, the poetry

in the pity of the last act of *King Lear*, or in Greek tragedy.
This kind of pity was forced on to Owen, by his sense that
the War was quite beyond his control. The external circumstances of his suffering were forced on to him, and it was his
job to create a synthesis by which he could accept them: he
could not do more than accept them. (pp. 217-18)

In one of Owen's last and most beautiful poems, *Miners*, his
feeling of pity seems to have reached a stage one step beyond
which would lead him to a subjective world. . . . (p. 218)

Beautiful as these lines are, one sees that the poet is conjuring
up an emotion of pity in order to achieve them: he is not
writing because he believes that the lives of the men who dig
coal and who die in wars could in any way be altered, or,
on the other hand, are in any way justified. His one emotion
is a passive grief for the men and boys. The difficulty is, that
poetry inspired by pity is dependent on that repeated stimulus
for its inspiration. If Owen had survived the War, he would
presumably have been compelled either to become a writer
with some political philosophy, or else he must have harked
back constantly to his war memories for inspiration. That
has happened to other war writers, who go back to the War
in search of ghosts and horrors, not in search of any explanations.

Owen may indeed have been a far greater loss than any of
us know; because he evidently realized that his war poetry
could only represent a *transitional* attitude, when he wrote
'All a poet can do to-day is to warn.' He meant that the next
generation must occupy itself with different problems.

In his few poems Owen did not merely make a record of his
experience; he made an architecture. He is not dictated to,
even by suffering. A great deal has been written about his
poetry, but I do not think that anyone has pointed out how
very different all his poems are from each other. Each poem
takes an entirely different aspect of the War, centred always
in some incident, and builds round it. In the few notes which
he left for the plan of his book, one sees that each of these
poems was meant to contribute to a whole edifice: he had
planned a book of true poetry about the War, not a series
of poems about the War.

There are, of course, artists who live in the spirit of Owen's
preface. (pp. 219-20)

Owen is an impersonal artist in a sense that James, Joyce,
Yeats and Eliot are scarcely ever impersonal. He is not ob-
jectifying his private mental experience, and 'thus escaping
from personality.' The pressure of meaning in his poetry is
not the pressure of self-expression, of his private utterance,
but the pressure of a whole world of everything that is not
himself, of war, of an actuality that is scarcely even interpreted in his poetry, but which is re-created through it. In
his art he is not creating his own world, he is re-creating the
external world.

For this reason his technique, although it is striking and
original, is subsidiary to his meaning. Although his use of
assonance is a completely successful way of expressing what
he has to say, one can quite well imagine his war poetry
written in a different medium: in a very individual free verse,
or dramatically, or in a use of conventional forms as original
and concentrated as, for example, the sonnets of Gerard
Manley Hopkins. His style is not, in fact, indistinguishable
from its content, it is simply a very effectively invented means
of conveying it. Nor is it limited to a particular use: it has

been adapted by young writers far more effectively than the styles of either Eliot or Hopkins. I think it is true to say that Owen is the most useful influence in modern verse, although he is a lesser poet than Hopkins or Eliot. (p. 220)

[Owen's poetry] exists by its reference to some external object: if it had not been the War, it might have been the industrial towns, and the distressed areas. (p. 221)

> Stephen Spender, "Poetry and Pity," in his The Destructive Element: A Study of Modern Writers and Beliefs, Jonathan Cape Ltd., 1935, (and reprinted by Jonathan Cape, 1938), pp. 217-21.*

W. B. YEATS   (essay date 1936)

My Anthology [The Oxford Book of Modern Verse] continues to sell & the critics get more & more angry. When I excluded Wilfred Owen, whom I consider unworthy of the poets' corner of a country newspaper, I did not know I was excluding a revered sandwich-board Man of the revolution & that somebody has put his worst & most famous poem in a glass-case in the British Museum—however if I had known it I would have excluded him just the same. He is all blood, dirt & sucked sugar stick (look at the selection in Faber's Anthology—he calls poets 'bards', a girl a 'maid' & talks about 'Titanic wars'). There is every excuse for him but none for those who like him. (p. 113)

> W. B. Yeats, in his letter to Dorothy Wellesley on December 21, 1936, in Letters on Poetry from W. B. Yeats to Dorothy Wellesley, edited by Dorothy Wellesley (reprinted by permission of Michael Yeats and Anne Yeats), Oxford University Press, London, 1940 (and reprinted by Oxford University Press, London, 1964), pp. 112-14.

DAVID DAICHES   (essay date 1936)

It seems presumption for one who did not grow up till after the war was over to write of the poetry of Wilfred Owen; yet it is not really so. Really it is a tribute to the greatness of his work that it can be critically discussed by a generation that was too young to appreciate the realities of war. Unlike most war poetry, Owen's does not belong to a single period, it does not derive its value solely from the background of special emotion against which it was originally set. His genius had not only a universalising quality, but a quality of insight and penetration that enabled him to pierce to the heart of phenomena by stating them, recording them. His mood was foreign alike to purposeless bitterness and uncontrolled sentimentality. He had something to say, and he said it effectively, poetically, so that eighteen years after the end of the war ... his reputation is greater than ever, and the power and cogency of what he has written remains, as it will always remain.

Like so many young poets, Owen began in the Keats tradition. He loved language and played excitedly with its riches. There is more than a superficial parallel between the pre-war Owen and the immature Keats, while the change wrought in Owen by the war can be compared to the change that took place in Keats with the consciousness that he had only a limited time to live. Keats' development is illustrated most clearly in his letters, but the wisdom and maturity that came to Owen with the war is patent in his poems. What Mr Blunden has called "the 'Endymion' phase of Owen's poetical

life" [see excerpt above] came abruptly to a close; the early Keats and the more superficial side of Tennyson vanished from his work . . . [and] gave place to a clear-eyed awareness and a sense of reality (reality of fact and also reality of values) that sometimes startle us, as the greatest touches of the greatest poets startle us by their truth. (pp. 52-4)

[The] early Owen, writing in an already worn tradition, . . . [is] kept vital by his poetical curiosity and his experiments in verbal technique. His war poetry shows an amazing advance in expression as well as content. (p. 54)

He was not concerned to decorate fact, to poetise experience for the sake of poetry, to make life an excuse for a theme. He wrote poetry for the sake of life, in order to reach out through the facts of war to fundamental aspects of human thought and emotion. He taught as he learnt. . . . (pp. 54-5)

It is this ability to accept the lesson and convey it simply (yet with great art) that distinguishes Owen from most other war poets. He kept himself in control, kept his vision undistorted by blind anger or unreasoning despair. . . . Owen sees into things with more genuine vision. His sense of the futility of war is no less than [Siegfried] Sassoon's, but he expresses it with greater restraint and, therefore, more effectively. In his short poem *Futility* he is talking of a smashed-up soldier. . . . This is real pathos, genuine emotion with the facts undistorted. It can be put beside other of his lines . . . to show what Owen meant when he wrote: "All a poet can do to-day is to warn. That is why the true Poets must be truthful." He did not sacrifice truth to indignation. Even in that terrible poem *Disabled* there is no distortion. . . . It is by effective juxtaposition and arrangement that Owen gives greatness to his poems, not by wresting and elaborating the single fact out of all relation to truth under the impulse of an uncontrollable emotion. . . . There is enough real irony in war to make such subterfuges unneccessary, though it is much more difficult—the line of *most* resistance—to make poetry out of the genuine fact. Owen does it in *Dulce et Decorum Est* and *Mental Cases* and half-a-dozen other poems.

"All a poet can do to-day is warn. That is why the true Poets must be truthful." But there are many kinds of truth. Obvious truth of fact—truth to what he *saw*—is not the easiest to tell, but Owen told it, holding it in his hand, as it were, unbroken, and displaying it to all who wished to see. He captured, too, another kind of truth—truth to what he *felt*. That this was worth recording was due to the fineness of Owen's own character, which guaranteed a value to his sense of things greater than that which belonged to the things themselves. Here was no distortion to meet emotion, but interpretation to explain an urgent sense of significance. *Strange Meeting* is a poem of this kind. He tells how in a vision he escaped out of battle "down some profound dull tunnel" to meet a strange face. . . . This is interpretation and commentary at its highest. All petty and transient emotion, irony, have passed away, giving place to an insight unparalleled in this kind of poetry. (pp. 55-9)

We may well ask what a poet can do in the face of such a devastating experience as modern warfare. What, at least, should he try to do? Is it his duty to denounce war in stirring rhetoric, or to glorify his cause and his country, or to describe what he sees, or to preach a point of view? There have been poets who have done all these things. But Wilfred Owen did very much more. He came to the war with an intense poetic sensibility, a generous and understanding nature, and an ability to penetrate to the inner reality of the experience in the midst of which he found himself. "Inner reality" is a vague term, but its definition is implied in Owen's poetry. It refers to an ability to relate these particular facts to the rest of human experience, to the life of men and women in cities and fields, to see war in its relation to all this, to appreciate just what this activity meant—what it meant as a whole and what particular aspects of it meant—in a world which was already old before the war, where happiness and suffering were no new phenomena, where men had lived diversely and foolishly and richly and gone about their occupations and were to do so again when all this was over. Owen never forgot what normal human activity was like, and always had a clear sense of its relation to the abnormal activity of war. His own table of contents gives the motive of his poem *Miners* as "How the future will forget the dead in war." . . . This is relevant comment, with no irrelevant bias. A sense of the relation of the conditions he was describing to past and future human activity is strong in Owen's poetry and helps to give it meaning and importance for the post-war generation.

Owen was no sentimentalist, but on the other hand he did not shrink from expressing the great emotional values brought out in the war. There is a world of profound feeling in his *Greater Love.* . . . "Full like hearts made great with shot"— the profound irony of the phrase is above bitterness; and there is more than irony, there is all the suggestion of the nature of the sacrifice of youth and the pity of war without any exaggeration or hysteria. There is nothing here but the truth, the truth presented in all of its many-sided aspects simultaneously. In so much other war poetry personal irritation forces the note and twists the fact: Owen remains calm and clear-eyed and therefore all the more intense.

Even the personal note is restrained in Owen, disciplined to subjection to what must be said, what must be communicated at all costs. . . . Owen's point of view is essentially *epic* in its scope and manner of treatment. It is a Homeric dirge on the dead warrior and the living soldier. (pp. 60-3)

This clarity of vision which enables him to see and express so much at once is responsible for some of those short verses or even phrases which are not exhausted of meaning at the second or third reading—passages which have an all-embracing quality and a depth that proclaim at once the true poet. . . . There is in Owen none of that impatience which Sassoon often shows—impatience with those who have been spared the consciousness of war's horrors and its perpetual presence with them. . . . [*The Kind Ghosts*] is symbolic in its significance; its application is almost unlimited in scope. The mood is intense, with a hint of serenity. Its opposite is a poem like *Arms and the Boy* where the intensity is that of a deep and sad irony. The motive of the poem is briefly given in his table of contents as "The unnaturalness of weapons." It is always a simple but profound truth like this that lies at the heart of Owen's poetry.

Owen is claimed by some modern poets as an important influence on their poetry, but it is difficult to see how Owen's poetry can influence those who have so much less to say. The poet of to-day cannot have anything as important to say as Owen had, because his experience is more dissipated and his view of reality generally more superficial. We are not to-day brought suddenly face to face with fundamental values; values are muddled and deceptive and our activity altogether less intense. So, although we can appreciate Owen's poetry to the full, we can learn little that will be of any help in the practice of poetry in the present age. And in fact the *content* of Owen's poetry has not influenced modern poets at all in their search for new poetic matter. The only influence at all discernible lies in the copying of that peculiar half-rhyme which Owen used so much by poets like W. H. Auden. . . . But the device is isolated and used in completely different contexts—different in manner as well as matter.

These half-rhymes of Owen are only one sign of his constant experimenting with technique and his interest in language for itself. His very earliest poems show him fascinated by the manipulation of words . . . and had not the war turned his attention to other aspects of poetry there can be little doubt that he would have taken his place among those who were to help in the forging of a new poetic medium. That task is still uncompleted, a fact which gives us one more reason for wishing that Owen's career had not been cut short as it was.

What Owen's place in the development of English poetry might have been can only be a matter of conjecture, and conjecture of this kind is never very profitable. But it is enough to judge him by what he did accomplish, leaving aside all hypothetical questions of what he might have done. His achievement was very real. Out of his experiences in the war he fashioned poetry which expresses in rich and cogent English some of the most fundamental aspects of human thought and emotion. Amid all the horror that he encountered he preserved unscathed his sense of values and his power of intense observation and penetration, never allowing his judgment to be warped by personal bitterness or his powers of expression to be weakened through fear or prejudice. His poetry serves a double function. It stands as a lasting exposure of the pity and futility of war, and at the same time it illumines significant channels of human experience that belong to no one time and place. . . . It is because he kept those terribly clear eyes of his constantly on the object that, in writing of war, he wrote at the same time a commentary on much more than war. By limiting his aim, with an honesty of purpose rare among poets, he enlarged his achievement. (pp. 63-7)

The poetry of Wilfred Owen, slight though it is in bulk, is a rich contribution to English literature. The farther back the war years recede into the past the more clearly he stands out above the mass of war poets. Not only has his poetry an eternal plangent appeal . . . but it remains at once a monument—small yet perfectly wrought—to the English language, and an example of how the mind of the true poet works in the face of experiences that divide him into man who suffers and artist who contemplates and understands and welds into lasting verse. He brought his suffering into his poetry sufficiently to make it genuine but not so that it warped his sense of truth. That is perhaps his greatest achievement. (pp. 67-8)

David Daiches, "The Poetry of Wilfred Owen," in his New Literary Values: Studies in Modern Literature *(reprinted by permission of the author), Oliver and Boyd, 1936 (and reprinted by Books for Libraries Press, 1968; distributed by Arno Press, Inc.), pp. 52-68.*

DYLAN THOMAS   (essay date 1946)

[In a volume of his poems, Wilfred Owen] was to show, to England, and the intolerant world, the foolishness, unnaturalness, horror, inhumanity, and insupportability of War, and to expose, so that all could suffer and see, the heroic lies, the willingness of the old to sacrifice the young, indifference, grief, the Souls of Soldiers.

The volume, as Wilfred Owen visualised it in trench and shell hole and hospital, in the lunatic centre of battle, in the collapsed and apprehensive calm of sick-leave, never appeared. But many of the poems that were to have been included in the volume remain, their anguish unabated, their beauty for ever, their truth manifest, their warning unheeded. (pp. 117-18)

[He] was the greatest poet of the first Great War. Perhaps, in the future, if there are men, then, still to read—by which I mean, if there are men at all—he may be regarded as one of the great poets of all wars. But only War itself can resolve the problem of the ultimate truth of his, or of anyone else's poetry: War, or its cessation. (p. 118)

[The] voice of the poetry of Wilfred Owen speaks to us, down the revolving stages of thirty years, with terrible new significance and strength. We had not forgotten his poetry, but perhaps we had allowed ourselves to think of it as the voice of one particular time, one place, one war. Now, at the beginning of what, in the future, may never be known to historians as the "atomic age"—for obvious reasons: there may be no historians—we can see, rereading Owen, that he is a poet of all times, all places, and all wars. There is only one War: that of men against men.

Owen left to us less than sixty poems, many of them complete works of art, some of them fragments, some of them in several versions of revision, the last poem of them all dying away in the middle of a line: "Let us sleep now . . ." I shall not try to follow his short life, from the first imitations of his beloved Keats to the last prodigious whisper of "sleep" down the profound and echoing tunnels of "Strange Meeting." Mr. Edmund Blunden, in the introduction to his probably definitive edition of the poems, has done that with skill and love [see excerpt above]. His collected poems make a little, huge book, working—and always he worked on his poems like fury, or a poet—from a lush ornamentation of language, brilliantly, borrowed melody, and ingenuous sentiment, to dark, grave, assonant rhythms, vocabulary purged and sinewed, wrathful pity and prophetic utterance. (pp. 118-19)

Who wrote ["Exposure"]? A boy of twenty-three or four, comfortably born and educated, serious, "literary," shy, never "exposed" before to anything harsher than a Channel crossing, fond of *Endymion* and the open air, fresh from a tutor's job. Earlier, in letters to his mother, he had written from the Somme, in 1917, in that infernal winter: "There is a fine heroic feeling about being in France, and I am in perfect spirits . . ." Or again, he talked of his companions: "The roughest set of knaves I have ever been herded with." When he heard the guns for the first time, he said: "It was a sound not without a certain sublimity."

It was *this* young man, at first reacting so conventionally to his preconceived ideas of the "glory of battle"—and such ideas he was to slash and scorify a very short time afterwards—who wrote the poem? It was this young man, steel-helmeted, buff-jerkined, gauntleted, rubber-waded, in the freezing rain of the flooded trenches, in the mud that was not mud but an octopus of sucking clay, who wrote ["Anthem for Doomed Youth."] . . . (p. 122)

There is no contradiction here. The studious, healthy young man with a love of poetry, as we see him set against the safe

background of school, university, and tutordom, is precisely the same as the sombre but radiant, selfless, decrying and exalting, infinitely tender, humble, harrowed seer and stater of the "Anthem for Doomed Youth" and for himself. There is no difference. Only, the world has happened to him. And everything, as Yeats once said, happens in a blaze of light.

The world had happened to him. All its suffering moved about and within him. And his intense pity for all human fear, pain, and grief was given trumpet-tongue. He knew, as surely as though the words had been spoken to him aloud, as indeed they had been though they were the words of wounds, the shape of the dead, the colour of blood, he knew he stood alone among men to *plead* for them in their agony, to blast the walls of ignorance, pride, pulpit, and state. He stood like Everyman, in No Man's Land. . . . And out of this, he wrote the poem called ["Greater Love."] . . . (pp. 123-24)

It was impossible for him to avoid the sharing of suffering. He could not record a wound that was not his own. He had so very many deaths to die, and so very short a life within which to endure them all. It's no use trying to imagine what would have happened to Owen had he lived on. Owen, at twenty-six or so, exposed to the hysteria and exploded values of false peace. Owen alive now, at the age of fifty-three, and half the world starving. You cannot generalize about age and poetry. A man's poems, if they are good poems, are always older than himself; and sometimes they are ageless. We know that the shape and the texture of his poems would always be restlessly changing, though the purpose behind them would surely remain unalterable; he would always be experimenting technically, deeper and deeper driving towards the final intensity of language: the words behind words. . . . Owen, had he lived, would never have ceased experiment; and so powerful was the impetus behind his work, and so intricately strange his always growing mastery of words, he would never have ceased to influence the work of his contemporaries. Had he lived, English poetry would not be the same. The course of poetry is dictated by accidents. Even so, he is one of the four most profound influences upon the poets who came after him; the other three being Gerard Manley Hopkins, the later W. B. Yeats, and T. S. Eliot.

But we must go back, from our guesses and generalisations and abstractions, to Owen's poetry itself; to the brief, brave life and the enduring words. In hospital, labelled as a "neurasthenic case," he observed, and experienced, the torments of the living dead, and he has expressed their "philosophy" in the dreadful poem "A Terre". . . . (pp. 125-26)

To see him in his flame-lit perspective, against the background now of the poxed and cratered warscape, shivering in the snow under the slitting wind, marooned on a frozen desert, or crying, in a little oven of mud, that his "senses are charred," is to see a man consigned to articulate immolation. He buries his smashed head with his own singed hands, and is himself the intoning priest over the ceremony, the suicide, the sunset. He is the common touch. He is the bell of the church of the broken body. He writes love letters home for the illiterate dead. Ignorant, uncaring, hapless as the rest of the bloody troops, he is their arguer shell-shocked into diction, though none may understand. He is content to be the unhonoured prophet in death's country: for fame, as he said, was the last infirmity he desired. (pp. 129-30)

There are many aspects of Owen's life and work upon which I haven't touched at all. I have laboured, in these notes

..., only one argument, and that inherent in the poems themselves. Owen's words have shown, for me, and I hope (and know) for you, the position-in-calamity which, without intellectual choice, he chose to take. But remember, he was not a "wise man" in the sense that he had achieved, for himself, a true way of believing. He believed there was no one true way because all ways are by-tracked and rutted and pitfalled with ignorance and injustice and indifference. He was himself diffident and self-distrustful. He had to be wrong, clumsy, affected often, ambiguous, bewildered. Like every man at last, he had to fight the whole war by himself. He lost, and he won. In a letter written towards the end of his life and many deaths, he quoted from Rabindranath Tagore: "When I go hence, let this be my parting word, that what I have seen is unsurpassable." (pp. 130-31)

> *Dylan Thomas, "Wilfred Owen" (1946), in his* Quite Early One Morning *(copyright 1954 by New Directions Publishing Corporation; all rights reserved; reprinted by permission of New Directions, New York; in Canada by David Higham Associates Limited, as literary agents for The Estate of Dylan Thomas), New Directions, 1954, pp. 117-33.*

BABETTE DEUTSCH   (essay date 1952)

A very conscious craftsman, whose name was to be repeatedly invoked by those who came after him, Owen spent pains on form in a manner that was apt to draw attention away from the poem to its technical details. Thus, the onomatopoeia in his **"Anthem for Doomed Youth"** is all too obvious. . . . The listener forgets the significance of the sound in observing its appropriateness. One of Owen's most memorable poems, **"Strange Meeting,"** which remained unfinished, is similarly flawed by the obtrusiveness of the technical devices, as well as by irrelevant archaisms. Nevertheless, the validity of this subtle, painful dream of an encounter between two soldiers from opposing lines has become brutally clear. Owen died before he could give right utterance to "the truth untold." But he foresaw what was to come. . . . One of the weaknesses of this prophetic if imperfect work is that the couplets, accenting as they do the cleverness of the inexact rhymes, seem unsuitable to the material. In **"The Show,"** the technical innovations are more effective. This poem gains strength from the fact that it relies not on statement but on metaphor. "From a vague height," where his soul stands with Death, the poet looks down on "a sad land, weak with sweats of dearth." The flatness of the vowels helps to display the barren fields, pocked and scabbed with plagues that are not named. He describes what he sees crawling over that sad land in terms that actualize the hideousness of trench warfare. The imagery is sustained in all its powerful ugliness to the end. This is one of the most terrible poems of the war. Its force is not lessened by the double meaning of the final line, which suggests, perhaps unintentionally, the treason of the intellectuals, and which makes the victim a partner in the guilt. (pp. 349-50)

In the fragmentary notes that prefaced his posthumous book he wrote that he was not concerned with poetry: "My subject is War, and the pity of War. The Poetry is in the pity." That phrase has become part of the language. . . . Owen, scribbling against the cruel helplessness of the situation he shared with less articulate men, had felt that all he could then do was to warn: "That is why true Poets must be truthful." Perhaps had he lived to revise those notes, he would have seen the

truth more clearly. "Pity spareth so many an evil thing," as Artemis complains in Pound's thirtieth Canto. To make as much of this anemic emotion as Owen did is to run the danger of producing poems that have been described as "all blood, dirt, & sucked sugar stick." The man responsible for that description [W. B. Yeats] insisted that passive suffering was not the theme for poetry. Good poems, including some by Yeats, have been written on that theme, but the pity must come alive in a kindled indignation. And it is without meaning unless the poet controls his material with the sensitive power that the jockey exerts over his horse, the pilot over his ship. Owen, without achieving Keats' imaginative greatness, was given to his youthful lushness. (p. 351)

> *Babette Deutsch, "Wars and Rumors of Wars," in her* Poetry in Our Time *(copyright © 1952 by Henry Holt and Company, Inc.), Holt, 1952, pp. 348-77.**

HOWARD SERGEANT   (essay date 1954)

Wilfred Owen though strongly influenced by Siegfried Sassoon, nevertheless went far beyond that poet in his efforts to comprehend war in all its various aspects and to grasp its real significance to the age in which he lived. It is for this reason, quite apart from his technical interest, that of all the poets who wrote of the First World War, Owen constitutes the strongest link between the poetry of the nineteenth century and that of today. (p. 9)

[Wilfred Owen] went to Bordeaux in 1913 as a tutor, and whilst he was living in France gained the friendship of the poet Laurent Tailhade. There is no evidence of any direct French influence upon his poetry, but it is not unlikely that Tailhade, himself an innovator, encouraged him in his technical experiments and that the two poets discussed Tailhade's pacifist ideas. Certainly Owen's study of French poetry strengthened his own writing, for until this period his major influence had been that of Keats, and the lushness of his earliest verse betrays the fact that it was Keats's appreciation of the sound-values of words rather than the depth of his imagination which appealed so strongly in the first instance to Wilfred Owen. Not that he ever renounced his earliest allegiance. His affinities with Keats are just as pronounced in his later work—particularly in *Strange Meeting*, which many critics consider to be his finest poem—but they are revealed through the individual mastery of language combined with a fully developed outlook. (pp. 9-10)

[When] his tutorial contract had expired, he returned to England to enlist, and, towards the end of the following year was sent to the Front. Like Sassoon he was appalled by the horrors of warfare, and his first reactions were those of bitterness and anger against the conditions which caused so much suffering, and of compassion for his fellow victims; yet even at this stage he seems to have been groping beneath the surface of immediate events to an all-embracing knowledge of the human spirit. His sensitivity is conveyed in one of the earliest of his war poems, *Exposure*. . . .

[Owen and Sassoon] became firm friends, and Owen, given the right encouragement, developed rapidly. (p. 10)

After a few poems in the style of his friend, whose work he approved, Wilfred Owen began to assert his own individuality in an unmistakable manner. In the poems which followed there is both realism and indignation, but these attributes are subordinate to the burning pity which possessed him whenever he contemplated the tragedy of war, and which reached its most perfect expression in *Greater Love*. . . . It is a pity not for the individual alone, but for the whole of humanity, symbolized by the common soldier. . . . (pp. 10-1)

It was because his range of vision extended beyond the bloodshed and the agonies of the Western Front—though he never overlooked personal grief or suffering—and because he was so aware of his own responsibility to future ages, that he was acutely conscious of the human tragedy and all its implications. 'The true Poets must be truthful'—that is, they must concern themselves with transcendent realities as well as the realities of the moment, however distressing. This is admirably brought out in *Strange Meeting*. In this poem Owen describes how he encounters, in a subterranean corridor of Hell 'long since scooped / Through granites which titanic wars had groined', an enemy soldier, obviously the German counterpart of himself, whom for the purposes of the poem he is alleged to have slain on the previous day. 'I am the enemy you killed, my friend,' announces the German. . . .

Not only the immediate unpalatable facts but also the greater long-term truth about war must be told, insists the poet, otherwise 'men will go content with what we spoiled. Or, discontent, boil bloody, and be spilled.' One has but to look back over the last twenty years, to the battlefields of China, Europe, Africa, and Asia, to appreciate the soundness of his prognosis; or to the division of nations under the contemporary pressure of events into armed ideological camps, to realize that when Owen said 'None will break ranks, though nations trek from progress' he visualized clearly the situation which could, and which actually did, arise out of the conflict in which he lost his life. (p. 11)

Despite the conditions in which he wrote and despite his conflict of mind about his own participation in the war, Wilfred Owen was, as Mr. Blunden has observed, 'an unwearied worker in the laboratory of word, rhythm and music of language', and he has had a strong influence upon his successors. His experiments with assonance and dissonance and his preoccupation with sound effects led him to the discovery of a new technique—the use of para-rhyme in place of true end-rhyme; that is, the retention of the consonants with a change of vowel or diphthong in the last words of the lines, which, if the traditional manner had been followed, would have required complementary rhymes as in:

> I am the enemy you killed, my friend,
> I knew you in the dark; for so you *frowned.*

Thus he opened up a wide range of verbal relationships to later poets, who would otherwise have been confined to the limited number of perfect rhymes to any particular word, or compelled to forgo the advantages of rhyme in order to avoid such limitations. Earlier poets had, of course, exercised their licence by using para-rhyme or near-rhyme in isolated cases, but Owen was the first poet to develop it into a method by which he could convey 'remoteness, darkness, emptiness and shock'. Occasionally he introduced variations by retaining only the final consonants or dropping the pitch of the echo-word, and made this even more appealing to the senses by skilful alliteration and internal echoes, and by adapting the rhythm of the lines to the feeling communicated. The method is demonstrated in *Insensibility*. . . .

It was, perhaps, his technique which made the greatest impression upon the poets of the next generation; but as the

significance of his poetry in relation to ensuing events became apparent, Owen's reputation grew rapidly, and today he is generally acknowledged to be the most important of the poets of the First World War. . . .

If he left only a small body of work, it is yet enough for us to form some idea of the loss to English poetry caused by the death of this young poet whose main subject, though he professed to be writing of War and 'the pity of War', was, in fact, humanity itself. (p. 12)

> *Howard Sergeant, "The Importance of Wilfred Owen," in* English, *Vol. X, No. 55, Spring, 1954, pp. 9-12.*

SAMUEL J. HAZO (essay date 1959)

There is something disarmingly categorical in referring to any poet as a war poet. It may imply that his poetry may have certain limitations or possibly a special dignity by virtue of the military circumstances under which it was created. Such implications often make the critical analysis and appraisal of such poetry difficult. In the case of Wilfred Owen, these implications—together with the fact, as C. Day Lewis has reminded us, that Owen, like Gerard Manley Hopkins, has been stylistically imitated by numerous admirers—have tended to obscure rather than clarify Owen's poetic merit.

It is, of course, true that Owen's best poetry was written while he was a soldier in World War I. It is also true that Owen's experiments with assonance and "para-rhyme," as Edmund Blunden has identified it, have been extensively imitated. However, Owen's stature as a poet cannot be made narrowly dependent upon the historical event that provided the subject matter for his poems (and also caused his death) nor on the *post facto* flattery of poetic imitation. (p. 201)

Despite the fact that Owen wrote that his poetry originated in the "pity of War," it is evident to any perspicacious reader of Owen's later or "war" poems that not all spring from pity. Many of them are revelations of acrimony, protest, pessimism, outrage and hatred. Yet Owen did write poetry that originated in the profounder wells of pity. Owen, like Keats, gradually acquired a more dramatic and objective voice in his poetry—a voice potentiated and purified by suffering and capable of expressing less purely personal or autobiographical responses to the war that was the source and cause of that suffering. The sensitive reader does not hear this voice in *"Dulce et Decorum Est"* or **"The Chances,"** but it is at the very core of **"Greater Love," "Anthem for Doomed Youth"** and **"Strange Meeting."**

It has been said that man's life can frequently be understood in retrospect by regarding that life in light of its particular mission. If this has any relevance to the life of man, it may have some relevance also to his art. In retrospect, it would appear that war was Owen's mission and his purgatory. This mission is objectified in the acrimony, protest, pessimism, outrage, hatred and pity of Owen's poetry. Yet Owen's passage from acrimony to pity, from the descriptive to the transfigurative, from the autobiographical to the objective cannot be chronologically traced as readily as events in a man's life. The progression from the indignation of *"Dulce et Decorum Est,"* **"Arms and the Boy"** and **"Smile, Smile, Smile"** to the divine pity of **"Miners," "Greater Love," "Anthem for Doomed Youth"** and **"Strange Meeting"** was possibly suprachronological, emerging in particular poems when Owen's objective correlatives were exact but otherwise remaining latent or vague when Owen's words were merely products of the personal and not the transfigurative or when the germinal idea of a poem was conceived in the heat of his own indignation rather than in his imagination.

A typical poem of indignation is *"Dulce et Decorum Est."* The entire series of images in the poem is oriented toward the Horatian motto which concludes it—"Dulce et decorum est/Pro patria mori." In the severity of the contrast between the imagery and the motto, the poem emerges as a study in irony heightened by rhetoric. Everything in the poem seems to exist only to show the falsity of this motto in modern warfare. By indicating the "old Lie" as directly as it does, the poem becomes persuasively direct rather than imaginatively evocative. A case could possibly be made that it is more didactic than purely rhetorical, but the fact remains that the poem is essentially an outgrowth of indignation. Whatever is poetic in it is subordinated to a rhetorical end. The same could be said of the stark *"S.I.W."* in which Owen comments with journalistic brevity on a soldier who, through cowardice, ends his own life.

And with him they buried the muzzle his teeth had
  kissed,
And truthfully wrote the mother, "Tim died smiling."

This is pessimism and disdain versified. The sequence of four poems that comprise *"S.I.W."* had this couplet as its fourth and concluding part, but all four parts are suffused with the same sense of disdain, which is directed toward those who see war as something it is not. Such people are symbolized in *"S.I.W."* by the suicide's unctuous father who "would sooner see him dead than in disgrace" and by the mother who would "fret" until "he got a nice safe wound to nurse." Not even the understatement and omnipresent irony in the poem can disguise its iconoclastic purpose nor conceal the unmistakable influence of Sassoon.

Similar indignation-spawned poems are those that deal with the wounded. In these poems Owen combines an almost clinical purview with a stoic acceptance of the inevitability of such misfortunes in war. Moreover, Owen frequently seems to be using the poems as an outlet for a Housman-like fatalism (**"Inspection"**) or sardonic glee (**"The Chances"**). The reliance upon rhetoric is still present, and the concluding lines of the Dantesque **"Mental Cases"** reveal Owen's occasional propensity to lapse into a somewhat tempered didacticism. (pp. 201-03)

Yet even in this poem there is an equating of the soldier's suffering with the scourging of Christ—one aspect of a parallel that is at the core of Owen's best poems and which will be considered at greater length later in this essay.

In poems like **"Conscious"** and **"Disabled"** the tone is, though free of didacticism, close to sentimentality. Both poems begin in loneliness—the loneliness of unnamed soldiers alone in hospital wards—and end in dismay—the dismay of men for whom there is no promising future and only a pain-ridden and almost hopeless present. It would be redundant to say that there is an inherent pathos in the circumstances of such men. After reading **"Conscious"** and **"Disabled,"** one cannot help but feel that Owen has slightly battened on this poignancy. In an attempt to dramatize the plight of these wounded men, he has verged on melodrama.

To refer to these few poems as poetic failures is not to disparage much that is good in them such as the interesting experiments with half-rhyme, translucent imagery and the satirical implications of Owen's irony. My point is only to indicate that as organisms these poems do not wholly succeed in dramatizing poetic moments. The fault is not in the subject but in the poet's treatment of it. . . . To find the Owen that [Herbert] Read and [Dylan] Thomas [see excerpt above] have placed in such high regard, it is necessary to consider poems like **"Greater Love," "Anthem for Doomed Youth"** and **"Strange Meeting."**

In my brief treatment of **"Mental Cases,"** I noted that Owen used an image of the Passion of Christ ("scourging") as descriptive of the suffering of soldiers. My reason for entitling the essay as I have is not only to suggest the synonymity of "passion" and "suffering" in the life of Owen considered as soldier, but also because Owen himself frequently alluded to men's suffering in war as a repetition of the drama of Golgotha—an analogue to the Passion of Christ. This analogue is explicitly stated in **"At a Calvary Near the Ancre."** (pp. 203-04)

This "greater love" is, of course, the love described in the fifteenth chapter of the Gospel of St. John: "Greater love than this no man hath, that a man lay down his life for his friends." But while **"At a Cavalry Near the Ancre"** is the versification of this truth in an explicit way, the poem called **"Greater Love"** is the spontaneous unfolding and interpretation of its realization. . . . The "progressive creation" of **"Greater Love"** is structured along two motifs developed in counterpoint and culminating in the image of the Christ of the Passion in the final verse. To stress the superiority of the soldier's act of love, which implies the necessity of sacrificing one's life for one's countrymen, to other forms of love, Owen contrasts it with sexual love. The imagery of love between man and woman, which is utilized similarly in the fifth stanza of *"Apologia Pro Poemate Meo,"* is counterpointed with images of soldiers dead, wounded and disfigured. "Kindness of wooed and wooer" cannot approach the soldiers' "greater love." "Red lips" are less red than the blood-stained stones on which the soldiers have fallen. The beloved's "slender attitude" does not tremble as exquisitely as bayoneted arms and legs. The beloved's voice is not as "dead" as the remembered voices of dead soldiers, nor are her hands as pale as hands that have trailed the "cross through flame and hail." This final image is not only a symbol of suffering but of suffering and death accepted for the sake of others. It establishes an immediate parallel with the Passion and Crucifixion. The soldiers' sacrifice is thus an act of immolation which hallows them and makes remote and paltry the grief of others for them.

This equation of the soldier's lot with Christ's lot during the Passion gives the poem a transcendental significance. The soldier is no longer pathetic in his suffering. He is exalted in his agony and ennobled while he is destroyed. **"Greater Love"** is thus truly elegiac in its stark and fecund simplicity, and the simplicity is the result of Owen's having found the best correlatives to express what the purifying pressures of suffering revealed to him—the "pity of War" and the poetry inherent in the pity. Despite the complexity of war and its havoc, the tone of **"Greater Love"** is not bitter but reverent, not negative but affirmative, not confused but translucent. (p. 204)

In the **"Anthem for Doomed Youth,"** a similar counterpointing of motifs is effected in a contrast of a conventional with a military requiem, of the usual with the actual. (p. 205)

Burial is usually associated with the conventional tributes of "passing-bells," "orisons" and "choirs." But the disorder of war has reversed the conventional. The usual funereal tributes mock dead soldiers for much the same reason that "English poetry," according to Owen in his memorable "Preface," "is not yet fit to speak of them." By implication, there is a certain unworthiness associated with the conventional means of tribute for the military dead. Their "bells" and "orisons" are the sounds of "guns" and rifle fire; their "choirs" are only the "wailing shells." Yet the rifle fire and the sound of shells in trajectory and upon impact are advanced as being more in keeping with the soldiers' sacrifice—the final act of "greater love." The usual or conventional requiem appears in contrast as a mockery, a sham, a burlesque. This irony is mollified in the sestet, but it is the octave's sardonic quality which makes the effect of the sestet more poignant. (pp. 205-06)

Here, as in the octave, there is the contrast of the usual with the actual. The "candles," the "pall," the "flowers," the usual or conventional trappings, are contrasted with worthier forms of remembrance. The acolyte's candle is thus superseded by the glimmer of loss in the acolyte's eye, the "pall" by the "pallor of girls' brows," and the flowers by the "tenderness of silent minds" and the drawn blinds at evening. These worthier forms of remembrance suggest inward grief rather than any outward signs of loss, and this inward grief is implied as being more commensurate with the sacrifice of the "doomed youth."

"Strange Meeting" has been called an unfinished poem by [Edmund] Blunden, and both [David] Daiches and Babette Deutsch consider it as such. Yet to preface a consideration of this poem with such an identification is misleading, in much the same way in which critics have been misled by regarding Coleridge's "Kubla Khan" as a fragment. Blunden does not explain where the poem seems to be unfinished; he merely notes in an appendix to his edition of the poems a number of alternative lines that Owen himself excluded from the poem as he left it.

Yet, if one regards **"Strange Meeting"** as a further elaboration on the theme of "greater love," one can say that the poem is thematically entire. Like **"Greater Love"** and **"Anthem for Doomed Youth,"** **"Strange Meeting"** is a meditative elegy. The analogy is again established between the soldier and Christ. Because **"Strange Meeting"** is a fantasy, the Christ-like figure in the poem exceeds literal verisimilitude. He is a soldier who has been fatally bayoneted. In a "profound dull tunnel" that is reminiscent not only of a Dantesque hell but of a sepulchre, the soldier rises to confront the man who killed him. I cannot refrain from suggesting that there are Christ-like overtones even in the soldier's entombment and resurrection. However, once the scene has been established, a dialogue ensues. In response to his killer's statement that he has "no cause to mourn," the soldier who has been addressed as "Strange friend" not only expresses his regret that he has been deprived the "undone years" but condemns the futility and hopelessness of war. Because of the propensity of men to ignore the "pity of war, the pity war distilled," the soldier prophesies that the loss of his life will probably effect no real good. As in Owen's **"The Next War,"** there is the suggestion advanced that "greater wars" will come. (pp. 206-07)

Coupled with his regret and his prophetic vision is the speaker's wish that his sacrifice could have been other than in the line of a soldier's duty. If he had had a choice, he would have chosen a more ministerial form of service. It is this wish that the analogy between the soldier and Christ is most obvious. The Christ-like character of the soldier is strengthened not only by the associative allusion to the thorn-crowned Christ but in imagery suggestive of ablution and purification. (p. 207)

Without lapsing into an explicit allegory, Owen has created within a soldier's fantasy or dream of a meeting in Hell a scene which has mystical, messianic and apocalyptic overtones. As we become spiritually attuned to the poet's theme, we are gradually prepared to accept these overtones. We recognize that "the figure of the man, the strange friend, has grown to such significance that he is only an allegorical image of 'the enemy' or of the spirit within each soldier that must be killed before battle can take place, the spirit of Pity, but is also the Anti-self, the conscience, the love killed by the lover, the figure of Christ . . .". We are also prepared to accept the suitability of the half-rhymes that Owen has used to realize the poem's interwoven themes of hope and frustration, desire and disappointment. Babette Deutsch's comment that the poem is "flawed by the obtrusiveness of the technical devices, as well as by irrelevant archaisms" [see excerpt above] is made in complete disregard of the fact that the effect of half-rhyme is diatonic and, therefore, uniquely suited to the disharmony and cacophony of war and the interwoven themes of the poem—"the bitter frustration by war of the ecstatic creativity of the human spirit." Finally, we realize that **"Strange Meeting"** develops the mystical aspect of the Christ-soldier analogy. The soldier who speaks in this poem is one who has suffered the Passion out of "greater love" and who has not made but been the sacrifice. He has passed beyond death's dominion. Yet his legacy—even for the man who killed him—is forgiveness. (pp. 207-08)

The voice that one hears in **"Strange Meeting,"** as well as in **"Anthem for Doomed Youth"** and **"Greater Love,"** is the dramatic voice of Wilfred Owen. Freed of the influences of Keats and Sassoon and purified by suffering, Owen was able to articulate "the pity war distilled." Yet to call Owen a war poet, as we must in a historical sense, does not mean that we should ignore or belittle those elements in his best poems that transcend military bounds. The basis for this transcendence is Owen's equation of the soldier's suffering and death with the Passion and death of Christ. Owen, with thousands of others, underwent this Passion. As a soldier, he saw "God through mud" and shared in a twentieth century counterpart of Golgotha the "eternal reciprocity of tears." In his best poems, which are his testament, he has transfigured rather than mirrored this experience, and left a dramatization of the meaning of suffering in war whose transcendental significance is central to a complete understanding of his art. (p. 208)

> *Samuel J. Hazo, "The Passion of Wilfred Owen,"* in Renascence *(© copyright, 1959, Marquette University Press), Vol. XI, No. 4, Summer, 1959, pp. 201-08.*

C. DAY LEWIS (essay date 1963)

Wilfred Owen must remain, in one respect at least, an enigma. His war poems . . . seem to me certainly the finest written by any English poet of the First War and probably the greatest poems about war in our literature. His fame was posthumous—he had only four poems published in his lifetime. The bulk of his best work was written or finished during a period of intense creative activity . . .—a period comparable with the *annus mirabilis* of his admired Keats. The originality and force of their language, the passionate nature of the indignation and pity they express, their blending of harsh realism with a sensuousness unatrophied by the horrors from which they flowered, all these make me feel that Owen's war poems are mature poetry, and that in the best of them—as in a few which he wrote on other subjects—he showed himself a major poet.

The enigma lies in this maturity. Reading through what survives of the unpublished poetry Owen wrote before 1917, I found myself more and more amazed at the suddenness of his development from a very minor poet to something altogether larger. It was as if, during the weeks of his first tour of duty in the trenches, he came of age emotionally and spiritually. His earlier work, though an occasional line or phrase gives us a pre-echo of the run of words or tone of thought in his mature poetry, is for the most part no more promising than any other aspiring adolescent's of that period would have been. It is vague, vaporous, subjective, highly 'poetic' in a pseudo-Keatsian way, with Tennysonian and Ninety-ish echoes here and there: the verse of a youth in love with the *idea* of poetry—and in love with Love.

And then, under conditions so hideous that they might have been expected to maim a poet rather than make him, Owen came into his own. No gradual development brought his work to maturity. It was a forced growth, a revolution in his mind which, blasting its way through all the poetic bric-à-brac, enabled him to see his subject clear—'War, and the pity of War'. The subject made the poet: the poet made poems which radically changed our attitude towards war. The front-line poets who were Owen's contemporaries—[Siegfried Sassoon, Isaac Rosenberg, Robert Graves, Edmund Blunden, Osbert Sitwell]—played a most honorable part, too, in showing us what modern war was really like; but it is Owen, I believe, whose poetry came home deepest to my own generation, so that we could never again think of war as anything but a vile, if necessary, evil. (pp. 11-12)

What Wilfred Owen's future as a poet would have been, had he survived the war, it is impossible to say. War is the subject of nearly all his best poems, and a reference point in others, such as *Miners*. It is true that he wrote a few poems of great merit on other subjects. But when, during the great productive period, he sought to write or finish such poems, we often notice in them a regression to his immature manner. It is interesting to speculate upon what subject might have fired his imagination and possessed his whole mind, as did the war experience. Would the vein of savage indignation prove exhausted, or might Owen have found it renewed in the struggle against social injustice which animated some of his poetic successors? It seems possible; but his honesty, fervour and sensuousness might have been directed elsewhere to produce a Catullan kind of love-poetry. My own conviction is that, whatever poetry he turned to, he would have proved himself in it a poet of a high order. His dedication was complete: he passionately wanted to survive the war, so that he might continue to write poetry.

Certainly, in the writings of his last two years, he showed himself both a serious poet and an increasingly self-critical one. If we follow the successive drafts of the poems over

which he worked longest—*Anthem for Doomed Youth*, for instance—we can see how admirably he kept sharpening the language, focusing ever more clearly his theme. Clumsiness there sometimes is, in these later poems; but nothing facile, and no shallow amateurism. Even his juvenilia, undistinguished though for the most part they are, present one promising feature—a gift for sustaining, in the sonnet form particularly, what musicians call *legato;* for keeping the movement of the verse running unbroken through an elaborate syntactical structure.

The language and rhythms of Owen's mature poetry are unmistakably his own: earlier influences have been absorbed, and we recognize in the style an achieved poetic personality. But it was achieved not solely through the impact of war. . . . (pp. 23-4)

Although his later work was largely cleared of derivativeness and false poeticism, Owen was not a technical innovator except in one respect—his consistent use of consonantal end-rhymes (grained/ground; tall/toil). . . . Consonantal rhyme, and other forms of assonance, are common in Welsh poetry and had been used previously in English by Vaughan, Emily Dickinson and Hopkins. There is no evidence that Owen had read any of the three last; nor could he read Welsh—his parents were both English and he was born in England. The first surviving poem in which he experiments with consonantal rhyme is *From My Diary, July 1914*, while *Has your soul sipped?* . . . may be another early experiment. (p. 25)

Again, it has been noticed how Owen tends to have a lower-pitched vowel following a higher one as its rhyme; and this has been explained as a method of stressing the nightmare quality or the disillusionment of the experience about which he was writing. It may be so. But, lacking a theoretical statement by Owen about his rhyme, we should be cautious in attributing its workings to any *methodical* practice. Poets, when they have such urgent things to say as Owen had, seldom attend so consciously to musical detail; the harmonies of the poem, and its discords, are prompted by the meaning rather than imposed upon it. (p. 26)

By temperament and force of circumstances, Owen had led a solitary life, cut off from any close fraternity with other men, out of touch with the cultural movements of pre-war England. Shy and diffident as he was, this previous isolation must have heightened the sense of comradeship he felt when, in the army, he found himself accepted by his fellows and able to contribute to the life of a working unit. The old solitude was fertilized by the new fraternity, to enlarge his emotional and imaginative scope. Laurent Tailhade's eloquently uttered pacifist beliefs had, no doubt, impressed themselves upon the young Owen; but I can find no evidence that Owen was influenced by his poetry. At the Craiglockhart War Hospital, Owen met a man whose poetry and pacifism appealed to him alike. Siegfried Sassoon brought out, in a way almost embarrassing to him, all the younger poet's capacity for hero-worship: he had been a most gallant Company commander; he had written poems and a prose manifesto condemning the war in an uncompromising manner. No wonder Owen felt at first like a disciple towards him.

It was a sign of Owen's integrity and growing independence as a poet that his work was not radically affected by his admiration for this new friend. In a few satirical or colloquial poems, such as *The Letter, The Chances,* or *The Dead Beat,* we may perceive Sassoon's influence; but Owen must have known that Sassoon's ironic and robust satire was not for him, and he continued in the tragic-elegiac vein which he had started working before he met the other poet. What Sassoon gave him was technical criticism, encouragement, and above all the sense of being recognized as an equal by one whose work he respected: it meant the end of his isolation as an artist. (pp. 26-7)

Wilfred Owen described himself as "a conscientious objector with a very seared conscience". He had come to see the war as absolutely evil in the agonies and senseless waste it caused: on the other hand, only as a combatant could he conscientiously and effectively speak for the men who were suffering from it. This conflict within himself . . . , was a basic motive of the war poems. It is a conflict every honest poet must face under the conditions of modern total war; for, if he refuse to take any part in it, he is opting out of the human condition and thus, while obeying his moral conscience, may well be diminishing himself as a poet. This conflict is seldom overt in Owen's war poetry, which, although it makes use of his personal experiences, is remarkably objective: his 'seared conscience' and his inward responses to that experience provided a motive power, not a subject, of the poetry.

Looking once again at this poetry, thirty-five years after I first read it, I realize how much it has become part of my life and my thinking—so much so that I could hardly attempt dispassionate criticism of it. Now, as then, I find Owen's war poetry most remarkable for its range of feeling and for the striking-power of individual lines. "He's lost his colour very far from here" would stand out even in a play by Shakespeare or Webster: "Was it for this the clay grew tall?" has a Sophoclean magnificence and simplicity. Ranging from the visionary heights of *Strange Meeting* or *The Show* to the brutal, close-up realism of *Mental Cases* or *The Dead Beat,* from the acrid indignation of such poems as *Dulce Et Decorum Est* to the unsentimental pity of *Futility* or *Conscious,* and from the lyricism of *The Send-Off* to the nervous dramatic energy we find in *Spring Offensive,* the war poems reveal Owen as a poet superbly equipped in technique and temperament alike. He was not afraid to be eloquent; and because he was speaking urgently for others, not for self-aggrandisement, his eloquence never ballooned into rhetoric. The war experience purged him of self-pity and poetic nostalgia. During his great productive year, the pressure of his imaginative sympathy was high and constant, creating poems that will remain momentous long after the circumstances that prompted them have become just another war in the history books. They, and the best of his poems not directly concerned with war, are in language and character all of a piece. (pp. 27-8)

C. Day Lewis, in "Introduction" (copyright ©
Chatto & Windus Ltd, 1946, 1963; reprinted by per-
mission of New Directions; in Canada by author
and Chatto & Windus Ltd), to The Collected Poems
of Wilfred Owen, *edited by C. Day Lewis, Chatto*
& Windus, 1963, pp. 11-29.

TED HUGHES (essay date 1964)

Wilfred Owen's 20 or so effective poems [in *The Collected Poems of Wilfred Owen*], all quite short, belong to a brief, abnormal moment in English history, and seem to refer to nothing specific outside it. That moment—the last two years of trench warfare in France, 1916-18—was so privately English (and perhaps German) and such a deeply shocking and formative experience for us that it is easy to see some of the

reasons why Yeats dismissed Owen's verse (largely on principle), and why many discriminating American readers find it hard to account for his reputation, and why with the English his reputation is so high.

The particular pathos and heroism and horror of the fighting in France are not imaginable without a full sense of the deaf-and-blind tyranny of jingoism—the outraged, rhetorical patriotism-to-the-death, the bluster and propaganda of England's unshaken imperial insolence—of those who remained in England. These were the politicians, financiers, businessmen, all who found themselves too old, or too importantly placed, or too deeply embedded in business, or too much of the wrong sex, fastened like a lid over the men who were rubbished with such incredible pointless abandon into the trenches. For these men, Owen, who died in France a week before the Armistice, determined to become the Voice of Protest.

He had all the gifts ready for it. In 1911 he had started a year as pupil and lay assistant to the vicar of Dunsden, Oxfordshire, and there seems to have been an idea of his taking holy orders. This readiness to give his life to Christ was to be important, as was his talent for righteous wrath and quick sympathy for the oppressed that went with it. (p. 4)

He worked within a narrow program—not that his times or situation allowed him much alternative, but he did formulate it deliberately. He wanted to oppose the propagandists in England with a propaganda of a finally more powerful kind. He set himself to present the sufferings of the front line, with the youth and millions of deaths and smashed hopes of his whole generation behind him, as vividly and frighteningly as possible, not because they were piteous—in spite of all his misleading talk about "pity"—but because it was wrong, and the crime of fools who could not see because they would not feel.

The enemy was not Germany. The only German in his poems—in "Strange Meeting"—is one he has been made to kill, who calls him "my friend," and who turns out to be himself. The real enemy is that Public Monster of Warmongering Insensibility at home. For England, the Great War was, in fact, a kind of civil war (still unfinished—which helps to explain its profound meaning for modern England, its hold on our feelings, and why Owen's poetry is still so relevant). His poems had to be weapons. Nothing in them could be vivid enough, or sorrowful enough: words could never be terrible enough, for the work he had to do. He had an idea of helping his cause along with merciless photographs of the trenches that would be displayed in London. Few poets can ever have written with such urgent, defined, practical purpose. And it is this attitude of managing a vital persuasion which perhaps explains his extraordinary detachment from the agony, his objectivity. He is not saying, "Ah, God, how horrible for us!" but "Look what you've done, look," as he glues the reader's eyes to it.

The big thing behind these few short poems that makes them live—as for instance Sassoon's similarly indignant poems do not—is Owen's genius for immersing himself in and somehow absorbing that unprecedented experience of ghastliness, the reality of that huge mass of dumb, disillusioned, trapped, dying men. His every line is saturated with the vastness of it, a hallucinated telescope into the cluttered thick of it—and always, at bottom, the redeeming discovery.

His work is a version of old-style prophecy: apocalyptic scenes of woe and carnage mingled with fulmination against the Godless oppressors, and somewhere at the bottom of the carnage, the Messiah struggling to be born—"Christ is literally in no-man's-land. There men often hear his voice," he wrote. It was the god of love and peace, of "passivity at any price." It was Owen who showed what that war really meant, to us, in immediate suffering and general implication, as nobody else did. (pp. 4, 18)

> Ted Hughes, "The Crime of Fools Exposed," in The New York Times Book Review (© 1964 by The New York Times Company; reprinted by permission), April 12, 1964, pp. 4, 18.

BERNARD BERGONZI (essay date 1965)

Owen's reputation has grown slowly but surely since the first selection of his work appeared under Siegfried Sassoon's editorship in 1920.... He is, by common consent, the greatest poet of the First World War.... In the face of such an assured status, it can do Owen no harm, and may be critically illuminating, to consider one or two unfavorable judgments that were passed on him during the years when his reputation was becoming established. (pp. 121-22)

[It] *is* true that Owen's range is narrow, in some ways 'all on one note': his concern is with suffering, and he directs his energies to rendering it with as much power and fidelity as he can muster. This, of course, is deliberate—'Above all I am not concerned with Poetry.... My subject is War, and the pity of War'—but his conscious restriction of range does, I think, count against him if he is being considered as a claimant for absolute greatness.... Another, more celebrated criticism of Owen was levelled by W. B. Yeats in his last years [see excerpt above].... (p. 124)

The venomous tone of Yeats's remarks is inexcusable, denoting a degree of senile rancour and, perhaps, of jealousy. He was also using Owen as a stick to beat the Leftist 'pylon poets' of the 'thirties, who had lately adopted Owen as a progenitor of their own attitudes. Yet however grotesque Yeats's assertions are as literary criticism, they contain a seed of truth.... In particular, I think, they underline the extreme rapidity of Owen's development, and the unevenness of his finally achieved maturity. It is well to remember that Owen, despite his early interest in poetic experiment and his technical curiosity, began as a manufacturer of sub-Keatsian poetic confectionery, and that traces of mawkishness can be found even in the work produced in the final great creative phase of his Keatsian *annus mirabilis*, 1917-18. This is particularly true in those occasional poems in which Owen's imagination is not involved with its major subject, the war; as, for instance, **'The Kind Ghosts'**.... Owen was brought to a cruelly premature flowering in the hothouse of the Western Front, and his work shows something of the fragility as well as the brilliance of the forced product. Yeats's criticism of Owen's diction does point to the undeniable fact that his language was slower to develop than his sensibility, and wasn't always equal to Owen's demands on it.

Having acknowledged these limitations, one can go on to point to the magnitude of Owen's achievement. Within a few months he gave the poetry of the anti-heroic attitude—prefigured by Byron and Stendhal, and, more immediately, in the verse of Sassoon and the prose of Barbusse—as absolute an expression as the traditional heroic attitude had received in countless epics and dramas of the Western tradition. And

this reflected a basic change in human sensibility.... War was no longer the same; modern technology had seen to that; and Owen ensured that it could no longer be *seen* as the same. In theory, no doubt, to die in agony from a gas attack was no different from dying 'cleanly' by the sword or a bullet in the traditional manner; in practice, however, the discrepancy between ends and means became too great, and the horror of the means discredited the end.... (pp. 125-26)

Owen's first poetic treatment of the war is a sonnet called **'1914'** which is, in Mr. Day Lewis's words, 'of interest both for its resemblances and its unlikeness to the state of mind expressed in Rupert Brooke's *1914*'.... Basically, this sonnet is no more than a rhetorical exercise (the Keatsian strain is evident in the closing lines of the octet), but it is thematically interesting inasmuch as there is a deflection from personal excitement and idealism to the generalized apocalyptic note sounded by a number of European poets in 1914.... (pp. 126-27)

The poems by which Owen will be remembered were written [after his meeting with Siegfried Sassoon].... Meeting Sassoon did not transform Owen's poetry, for he had already embarked on his mature poetic manner ... but the older poet's encouragement and example were of immense help to Owen in confirming him in his path. In Sassoon he found the intellectual stimulus that he had so far lacked.... In a few poems, such as **'The Chances'** and **'The Letter'**, we see Owen attempting Sassoon's bitterly epigrammatic vein, and achieving a modest success; but it is equally evident that his real talents were best expressed in other kinds of writing.

Some idea of the assistance Owen received from Sassoon is evident from the discussion of the various drafts of **'Anthem for Doomed Youth'** in C. Day Lewis's edition. He substituted 'patient minds' in the penultimate line for Edmund Blunden's former reading of 'silent minds', and shows from the manuscript that 'patient' was inserted in the final version at Sassoon's suggestion.

Unlike other war poets, Owen rarely attempts a contrast, nostalgic or ironic, between the trenches and remembered English scenes. His absorption in the concrete realities of the Front is complete, and the only authentic England is in France.... His poetry is also rooted in the despair springing from an awareness that the war might go on for an indefinite number of years, with no possible end in sight.... Owen's dominant theme is the slaughter, or maiming, apparently endless, of young men; and it is marked by a concentration on 'The thousand several doors where men may take their exits': gassing, in **'Dulce Et Decorum Est'**; blinding, in **'The Sentry'** and **'A Terre'**; mutilation, in **'Disabled'**; madness, in **'Mental Cases'** and **'The Chances'**; shell-shock, in **'The Dead-Beat'**; and suicide, in **S.I.W.'**. Owen is distinguished from Rosenberg by his stress on the details of death and mutilation, and by his predominantly realistic manner of description. But in one of his most terrifying poems, **'The Show'**, he moves into symbolism, in a nightmare vision where the battlefield is seen as a mass of writhing caterpillars.... But this kind of obliquity is not Owen's characteristic manner, which usually stays closer to the human end of the spectrum. One of his finest and most typical poems is **'Futility'**.... With considerable economy of means, Owen places the tragedy of an individual death on a plane of cosmic significance; or rather, this death, so futile in its finality, points to an ultimate futility in the whole order of things. The 'sowing' of the first stanza, with the multiple associations of rural activity, of a young man's unrealized potentialities, and of unachieved sexual fulfilment, is transformed in the second to an image of life itself, the germ awakened in the nascent earth by the action of light, leading, ultimately, to the emergence of human life—epitomized in the fine image, 'Was it for this the clay grew tall?' This poem, so satisfactory in its movement and over-all structure, does nevertheless show signs of the fumbling that Owen's inexperience manifested even in his mature phase: the last two lines of the first stanza are rather weak, and the phrase, 'Are limbs, so dear-achieved', though worked over a good deal (as the manuscripts indicate), is still clumsy.

The poem illustrated the constant preoccupation of Owen's major phase: the destruction of youth. The note here is mutedly sensuous; it is more overtly so in other poems. **'Greater Love'** is a key example, in which Owen explores the ultimate sacrifice made by the dead; their devotion both resembles and transcends sexual love. I have already mentioned, in discussing Sassoon, the attitude which rejected women and feminine values, seeing in them manifestations of the uncomprehending civilian ethos; Sassoon gave it angry ·expression in 'Glory of Women'. Owen clearly shared this feeling, stressing the masculine self-sufficiency of the companionship of the trenches, as in **'Apologia Pro Poemate Meo'**. . . . As Day Lewis remarks, 'Owen had no pity to spare for the suffering of bereaved women'; there is, admittedly, the beautiful line in **'Anthem for Doomed Youth'**, 'the pallor of girls' brows shall be their pall', but this is a visual detail rather than a profoundly compassionate note. Male fellowship and self-sacrifice is an absolute value, and Owen celebrates it in a manner that fuses the paternal with the erotic (not that one would overestimate the latter quality, but its implicit presence will surely be apparent to any open-minded reader): Owen's attitude to the 'boys' or 'lads' destined for sacrifice has some affinities with Housman's.

One uses the word sacrifice advisedly: Owen had early on abandoned orthodox Christianity, and marked his abandonment in the poem, **'At a Calvary near the Ancre'**. . . . It is the sense of the war as a ritual sacrifice, in which he was involved as both priest and victim, that gives Owen's finest poems their particular quality, for transcending the simple protest and rebellion of Sassoon (or some of his own less ambitious pieces).

Among Owen's finest poems is **'Strange Meeting'**. (pp. 127-32)

The opening is magnificently dramatic, but later passages seem to me needlessly obscure: Owen has created a powerful myth, but does not seem at all sure what, in detail, he wishes to do with it. . . . **'Strange Meeting'** is, I suggest, a slightly overrated poem, which has many splendid lines but is not entirely thought through. (p. 133)

Owen's poems need to be read together: they mutually illuminate each other and have a cumulative power. In their totality, as I have suggested, they have done more than any other work in English to form a sensibility that can grasp the nature of technological war. If Brooke and Binyon seem irrecoverably anachronistic, then that is largely because of what we have learnt from Owen. And he achieved this change in our perceptions by hammering hard at limited but intense areas of experience: for all his power, his emotional range is restricted. He wished it to be, as his 'Preface' makes clear. . . . I find it hard to imagine how Owen might have developed had he survived: the war was his overwhelming

subject, and the work of his great final year was, in more than one sense, a consummation. It seems to me that a total cessation of creative activity would have been as likely a result of the anti-climax of peace as the vein of Catullan love-poetry that Mr. Day Lewis tentatively suggests he might have gone on to produce. (pp. 134-35)

> *Bernard Bergonzi, "Rosenberg and Owen," in his*
> Heroes' Twilight: A Study of the Literature of the
> Great War (© 1965 by Bernard Bergonzi; reprinted by
> *permission of A D Peters & Co Ltd), Constable and*
> *Company Ltd., 1965, pp. 109-35.**

DOMINIC HIBBERD (essay date 1975)

The criticism is sometimes made of Owen that he was always too much under the domination of the Victorians. It is true that his facility for imitation and his habit of venerating great writers made him an easy prey to the captivating music of Tennyson and Swinburne, but at his best he was able to get the upper hand. Although the influence of other poets is frequently evident in his work, his style in unmistakable and unique; often the trace of another poet in his lines adds to the poem's meaning and is meant to do so, as in the echoes of Keats's *Hyperion* and Shelley's *The Revolt of Islam* in **'Strange Meeting'**. The red roses in **'The Kind Ghosts'** are more terrible than anything Swinburne ever managed in his numerous images of blood and flowers, while **'Futility'** shows what Owen could do with the Tennysonian tradition. . . . This is, in the opinion of many, Owen's most nearly flawless poem. . . . It is far from a damaging criticism in this case to suggest that **'Futility'** is in direct descent from the great stanzas in *In Memoriam*. . . . (pp. 31-2)

Nature in many of Owen's poems is a hostile force, as in the deathly snow of **'Exposure'** or the 'winds' scimitars' in **'Asleep'**, but this hostility is a response to war. In **'Spring Offensive,'** where his understanding of this problem is most fully set out, nature tries to prevent men from going into an attack, launches a violent onslaught against them when they ignore the appeal and becomes peaceful again as soon as the attack is over. His early poems show repeatedly that he believed nature to be a source of blessing to those in harmony with the natural order, and the reader of his letters soon becomes accustomed to his odd elaborations of this belief ('we ate the Vernal Eucharist of Hawthorn leaf-buds'). His poems are consistent with the Romantic tradition in this and other ways; they are not the ironic denial of it that some critics have understood them to be.

Owen is not an easy poet, yet from the details of his technique to the largest statements of his elegies there runs a consistent pattern. A line such as 'Rucked too thick for these men's extrication' (**'Mental Cases'**) shows his characteristic rhyming ('Ruck-/thick/-tric-') and an equally characteristic use of an unexpected but simple word ('Rucked') leading to the more elaborate 'extrication'. This kind of combination can be seen again in, for example, **'Strange Meeting'**, where a single line contains the colloquial 'thumped' and the archaic 'made moan'; or in **'Futility'**, where the startlingly simple familiarity of 'kind of sun' preceds a complex image of clay that is developed from biblical and older origins. Similarly, the tunnel in **'Strange Meeting'** is at once a dug-out and the Underworld, the men in **'Mental Cases'** are inhabitants of a mental hospital and of the Inferno, and the infantry in **'Spring Offensive'** charge both an unseen human enemy and the Romantic landscape itself. Parallel to these ambivalences, which are wholly deliberate, are Owen's frequent allusions to earlier poets, particularly Shelley, Keats and Dante; these, too, are deliberate and they bind his poetry into literary tradition. The echo of Keats's odes in the description of the landscape in 'Spring Offensive' suggests the strange possibility that the landscape *is* that of the odes, a suggestion which, if we follow it, adds much to the significance of the poem; yet it is easy to dismiss the echo as being unintentional, proof only of Owen's inability to get away from nineteenth-century diction. The old view of his poems as products of the war, forced out of an immature and ill-informed mind under the pressure of intense experience, is slow in dying but does not deserve to live; the major poems are the result of long years of training and preparation, finding fruit not in some hasty scribble done on the back of an envelope in the trenches but in the meticulous, protracted labour which went on at Ripon in the spring of 1918.

If memories of the Great War ever fade, much of the verse we associate with it will also be forgotten. Owen's poetry seems more likely to endure than most; it is uneven, incomplete and sometimes of poor quality, but at his best he belongs to English literature and not just to an historical event. (pp. 33-4)

> *Dominic Hibberd, in his* Wilfred Owen, *edited by Ian Scott-Kilvert (© Dominic Hibberd 1975; Longman Group Ltd., for the British Council), British Council, 1975, 44 p.*

DENNIS WELLAND (essay date 1978)

In all Owen's writing no phrase is more revelatory than his description of himself as 'a conscientious objector with a very seared conscience', which occurs in the important letter where he records poignantly his realisation that 'pure Christianity will not fit in with pure patriotism'. Already in his earliest poetry we have seen an uneasiness over religious belief finding expression in a somewhat derivative idiom that detracts from its spontaneity, but of the intensity of the spiritual crisis into which his participation on the war plunged him there can be no doubt. . . . The significance of that elaborate metaphor [in a letter to Osbert Sitwell Owen portrays himself as preparing the Christ-soldier for his suffering and death] lies in the role the writer assigns to himself: he is in every instance betraying the Christ-soldier and thus alienating himself from the mercy of Christ.

Such popularly-accepted phrases as 'the supreme sacrifice' illustrate how readily the soldier came to be thought of in a role similar to that of the crucified Saviour. . . . The basis of this identification is, of course, the scriptural text which Owen quotes in the following form in the letter speaking of his seared conscience, and again at the end of 'At a Calvary' (it also gave him the title for one of his most deeply-felt poems): 'Greater love hath no man than this, that a man lay down his life for a friend'; but the same letter contains the realisation that the soldier who makes this sacrifice may in the course of so doing disobey 'one of Christ's essential commands . . . do not kill'. . . . [The] greatness of 'Strange Meeting' lies, in part, in the success with which it (like 'The Show') develops the *doppelgänger* theme as a perfect symbol of this dichotomy. Since this religious problem underlies so much of Owen's poetry it is not extravagant to see a possible reference to Christ in the sun 'whose bounty these have spurned' in 'Spring Offensive': ignoring the 'essential com-

mandment' is tantamount to spurning the salvation Christianity offers.

This is not to attribute to Owen in these poems a wholly orthodox Christian view. In 'At a Calvary near the Ancre' he is as much at odds with the 'pulpit professionals' as in the letter on pacifism, but in both cases his accusation is that Christ has been betrayed by His Church. . . . In this sentiment Owen was by no means alone. The religious assurance of earlier war poets was dying out by 1917: Christ in Flanders was too much of a paradox to be easily accepted any longer. (pp. 85-6)

Yet it would be unjust to dismiss [the later war poets] as irreverent, godless, and blasphemous. Their agnosticism is the product of their circumstances and often conceals . . . a very real desire to believe. The frequent invocation of Christ . . . suggests something deeper than army blasphemy, and the tendency to draw on Biblical stories for satires is surely an indication of how prominent their old faith was in their minds, even if they found temporary difficulty in reconciling it with their circumstances. Thus the sacrific of Isaac by Abraham provided both Osbert Sitwell and Owen with a theme, while Sassoon draws on the story of Cain and Abel. That these are Old Testament stories is not unconnected with the fact that whereas the 'bardic' poets had usually invoked God in their patriotic poetry, it is to Christ that the later poets more frequently appeal. (p. 87)

God, that is, has been identified with Jahveh, the Old Testament God of battles and of wrath, whose interest in the perpetuation of the war is sharply contrasted with the compassion of Christ who, as Divinity incarnate, can sympathise with the human suffering war involves. In the face of this prolongation of suffering neither victory nor death has any great significance. The war that Jahveh wishes for is death, the death of the spirit, whereas the compassion represented by Christ is life-giving and kind, like the sun in 'Futility' and in 'Spring Offensive' where the antithesis between the sun, 'the friend with whom their love is done', and the 'stark, blank sky' full of incipient menace and hostility may be a reflection of this antithesis between Christ and God.

Questionable as its theology may be, Owen's position here is one to which many must, in varying degrees, have been attracted . . . , and it is one for which the Church was itself partly to blame because of the ardent and uncritical support it appeared to give to the continuance of the war. . . . It is hardly surprising that Owen's poetry should contain such statements as 'God seems not to care' and 'love of God seems dying', though his refusal to word either of them more dogmatically indicated the strength of the religion in which he had been brought up.

Owen's pacifism, however, although usually expressed in Christian terms, is not entirely the outcome of the conflict between his military experience and his religious upbringing. There is another influence behind it, more powerful than is sometimes recognised. During his stay in Bordeaux he had made the acquaintance of the French poet Laurent Tailhade. . . . [Despite] the discrepancy between their ages, a real friendship seems to have developed between them. . . . [But] it is not as a poet that Tailhade most significantly influenced his young English friend. Originally intended for the Church, Tailhad had early in life revolted against Christianity but was none the less a confirmed pacifist who had been in considerable trouble with the authorities for his *Lettre aux*

Conscrits.... This and his address *Pour la Paix*, ... anticipate Owen so markedly in sentiment and even on occasion in turns of expression that it is impossible that Owen should not have known them. The definition of poetry in *Pour la Paix* is very close indeed to the conception of it that underlies Owen's draft preface.... (pp. 87-9)

The only call to which Owen answers is not that of the church but of human suffering. It is human sympathy rather than abstract morality that determines his ethical position.... (p. 90)

The lonely independence . . . becomes increasingly dominant in Owen's poetry in direct proportion to the increase in his dedication to the task of speaking for 'these boys . . . as well as a pleader can'. His sense of comradeship and solidarity leads to no sentimentally Whitmanesque merging of identity with them, but at the same time his awareness of isolation is more firmly grounded and poetically more valuable than the uneasy Romantic pose of the juvenilia to which it is directly related. The ten-stanza poem, of which **'This is the Track'** originally formed the three last (and only revised) verses, develops an image used in a letter to Sassoon in November 1917 ('I was always a mad comet; but you have fixed me'); in the poem he aspires to be a solitary meteor awakening in men premonitions and intimations of eternity. the published stanzas illustrate a similarly purposeful self-sufficiency coupled with an almost messianic belief in the poet's responsibility, the exercise of which may even 'turn aside the very sun', but another and rather better poem of probably similar date puts the other side.

'Six o'clock in Princes St' is just as Tennysonian in origin as is the contemporaneous **'Hospital Barge'** sonnet which he described as "due to a Saturday night revel in **'The Passing of Arthur'**," but it is more critical of that revel than is **'Hospital Barge'**. A half-envious watching of the home-going crowds creates dissatisfaction with his own loneliness.... Certainly the mood is antithetical to that of **'The Fates'**, written less than six months earlier, with its Georgian confidence in beauty and art as an escape from 'the march of lifetime'; and the choice of the verb 'dared' in the last line shows an honesty of self-knowledge anticipatory of those letters of the following summer in which he told at least two of his friends how glad he was to have been recommended for the Military Cross 'for the confidence it will give me in dealing with civilians'. (pp. 93-4)

There is a richness and complexity about **'Miners'** that is quite absent from, for example, so slight a piece as **'The Promisers'** and even from **'Winter Song'**. The burning coal becomes a symbol for, in turn, the remote past, the miners who dug it, and, by a well-managed and apparently easy but none the less effective transition, the war dead. The atmosphere of the opening stanzas with their leaves, frond-forests, ferns, and birds is reminiscent of **'From My Diary'** and the **'Sonnet: to a Child'**, but where **'From My Diary'** contents itself with the creation of that atmosphere and the sonnet associates it pleasantly but conventionally with the ideas of anamnesis and growing old, **'Miners'** contrasts it with the 'sourness' of the sacrificed lives (to use Owen's own word for the poem's quality). Out of the oxymoron of this fusion comes a new strength, while the end of the poem gains in emotive force by the unexpected identification of the poet with the suffering of the lost which he has hitherto described detachedly. (It is of course the same device that he uses so

effectively in **'The Show'**, **'Mental Cases'**, and **'Strange Meeting'**. (pp. 95-6)

Though not specifically war-poems, these, like **'The Kind Ghosts'**, illustrate Owen's range and may offer some indication of how his poetry might have developed had he lived, but they are important also as examples of the positive though indirect influence on his poetry of the compassion and the sense of isolation induced by his 'very seared conscience'. (p. 98)

[There are] two types of poem with which Owen experiments: his poems of dramatic description (such as **'The Chances'**) and the more subjective lyrics of personal response (such as **'Greater Love'** or **'Apologia'**). Both have their advantages and their limitations, but what Owen needed for the full attaining of his purpose was a poetry where the more objective detachment of the one could be harnessed with the emotional intensity of the other. He often achieved this in his poems of imaginative description such as **'Spring Offensive'** but he also accomplished it in what I would call poems of visionary description; of these **'The Show'** is a good example, but **'Strange Meeting'**, the poem that Sassoon once called Owen's passport to immortality, and his elegy to the unknown warriors of all nations', is the best, especially for the way in which it brings together so many strands of his work already discussed. Essentially a poem of trench warfare, realistically based on the First World War, it is a fine statement of Owen's moral idealism as well, but it is also a poem that shows his true relationship to the Romantic tradition as something much more positive and creative than his earlier aestheticism suggests. (pp. 98-9)

From his echoing of it in an unpublished poem, we may be certain that he knew Wilde's line 'Yet each man kills the thing he loves' and this too lies at the back of **'Strange Meeting'**. The point is well made by the enemy's identification of himself with his killer in lines that are in effect Owen's own elegy, the final comment on his spiritual progress from the artificial aestheticism of the early years to the altruistic, splendid pity of these last poems.... The enemy Owen has killed is, he suggests, his poetic self, and 'the undone years, The hopelessness' of which the enemy speaks are in one sense very personal to Owen, while in another sense they are tragically universal. Other poets had mourned the cutting-off of youth before its prime, but usually in terms of the loss to the individuals themselves or to their friends; if they envisaged the world becoming poorer they did not envisage it becoming actually worse, because tacitly or explicitly they assumed that the progress which the war had interrupted could be resumed by the survivors when it ended. Owen's vision is more penetrating and less comfortable. The war has not merely interrupted the march of mankind; it has changed its whole direction and done incalculable and irreparable damage. It is this terrible prophetic vision of a dying world embodied in this and other poems that gives Owen's work abiding relevance, but what he mourns is not merely the men themselves. Not only 'the old Happiness' but the potentialities offered by the past are unreturning, and there is truly no sadness sadder than the hope of the poet here foreseeing the disintegration of values, the retrogression of humanity, involved in this second Fall.... Only the men who fought in that war had, in Owen's belief, been vouchsafed an insight into the Truth, but it was too late to put that knowledge to any constructive use. If only they could have held themselves apart from the process of disintegration, had they only had the opportunity . . . they might, in the fullness of time, have been empowered to arrest that march and to restore the truth. . . . Here perhaps is the last flourish of that messianic impulse which Christianity and Romanticism had combined to implant in Owen in the dedicated ideal of service to humanity. . . . But the opportunity for such service is gone, and characteristically in one of his simplest but most effective phrases Owen indicts himself as much as anyone else for the destruction of that opportunity: 'I am the enemy you killed, my friend'.

Despite the technical maturity with which this rich complex of ideas is developed, despite the creative genius that evolved so superb a myth for its poetic purpose, it is more than the loss of a poet that one laments after reading **'Strange Meeting'**. The sleep to which the dead enemy invites him is certainly

> less tremulous, less cold,
> Than we who must awake, and waking, say Alas!

for **'Strange Meeting'** carries its own conviction of the irreparable loss to humanity of 'us poor lads/Lost in the ground'—irreparable not for what they were but for what they would have been, not for what they gave but for what they would have given. (pp. 100-03)

> *Dennis Welland, "The Very Seared Conscience,"*
> *in his* Wilfred Owen: A Critical Study *(© Dennis*
> *Welland 1960, 1978), Chatto & Windus, 1978, pp.*
> *84-103.*

ADDITIONAL BIBLIOGRAPHY

Blunden, Edmund. "Mainly Wilfred Owen." In his *War Poets: 1914-1918*, pp. 29-36. Harlow, England: Longman Group, 1958.

Explores the influences of Sassoon and the war on Owen's poetry.

Freeman, Rosemary. "Parody as a Literary Form: George Herbert and Wilfred Owen." *Essays in Criticism* XIII, No. 4 (October 1963): 307-22.*
Discusses Owen's parodic use of love imagery in describing war scenes.

Gose, Elliott B., Jr. "Digging In: An Interpretation of Wilfred Owen's 'Strange Meeting'." *College English* 22, No. 6 (March 1961): 417-19.
In-depth study of the subconscious influences on a person involved in war.

Hibberd, Dominic. Introduction to *Wilfred Owen: War Poems and Others,* by Wilfred Owen, pp. 19-50. London: Chatto & Windus, 1973.
Biographical introduction, critical commentary, and comparisons to Owen's contemporaries.

O'Keefe, Timothy. "Ironic Allusion in the Poetry of Wilfred Owen." *Ariel* 3, No. 4 (October 1972): 72-81.
Examines the ironic allusions in Owen's poetry to other literature and the Bible.

Owen, Harold. *Journey from Obscurity: Wilfred Owen, 1893-1918: Memoirs of the Owen Family.* 3 vols. London: Oxford University Press, 1963-65.
Complete biography of Wilfred Owen and his siblings, by his brother.

Posey, Horace G., Jr. "Muted Satire in 'Anthem for Doomed Youth'." *Essays in Criticism* XXI, No. 3 (July 1971): 377-81.
Explains the satire on the Christ theme in "Anthem for Doomed Youth."

Sitwell, Osbert. "Wilfred Owen." In his *Noble Essences: A Book of Characters*, pp. 101-24. Boston: Little, Brown and Co., 1950.
Discussion of Owen's background with biographical information and with references to specific poems.

White, Gertrude M. *Wilfred Owen.* New York: Twayne Publishers, 1969, 156 p.
Studies Owen and his poetry, and discusses his poetic craftsmanship and the growth of his posthumous critical success.

Kostes Palamas

1859-1943

(Also transliterated as Kostis, Kostes, Kostís, or Costis; also Palamàs, or Palamás) Greek poet, short story writer, critic, and dramatist.

Palamas is considered one of Greece's greatest modern poets. As a central figure in the demotic movement of the 1880s, he opposed the use of Classical Greek for literary expression and in public life, favoring the more vital Modern Greek spoken by the people. His poetry ushered in a new acceptance and appreciation for the demotic speech. Although reviled by many as a traitor to Greece's glorious past, he was a fierce patriot whose poems express his country's aspirations and cultural pride.

Raised in Missolonghi, the scene of Greece's nineteenth-century struggle for independence from the Turks, Palamas was imbued with a feeling for Greece's culture and history. He studied at the University of Athens, and later, as its secretary, became convinced that the demotic speech was more suitable for modern poetic expression than Classical Greek. His contention that Modern Greek should be the country's official language was generally regarded as radical and dangerous. A founder of "the new school of Athens," he wrote poetry in the demotic mode, developing a clean, restrained style, closely allied with contemporary Parnassian and symbolist trends. Angry reactions to Palamas's poetry, and the demotic translations of Homer and the Gospels by his sympathizers, led to riots at the University of Athens, in which several people were killed and Palamas's resignation demanded. Largely through the efforts of Palamas, the demoticists, called "the hairy ones" by their enemies, prevailed over the purists and Modern Greek became Greece's official language.

The subject of Palamas's poetry throughout his career is Greece and the Greek people. His work is usually divided into two periods: the subjective, lyrical poems of his first period, and the long epic compositions of his second. *Tragoúdia tes patrídos mou*, his first collection of poetry, reveals a purer, less embellished style than that of his romantic predecessors. Poems extolling the heroism of Greek revolutionaries, love poems, and nature poems, in robust, demotic language, describe the Greece of Palamas's day, rather than the idealized Greece of ancient times. The poem *Ho dodekálogos tou gýphtou* (*The Twelve Words of the Gypsy*), on the other hand, considered his masterpiece by many critics, is set in the period shortly before and after the fall of Byzantium. This epic presentation of a gypsy's search for spiritual peace and happiness has been variously interpreted as symbolizing the plight of war torn Greece, the emergence of the modern Nietzschean Superman, and the triumph of a highly individualistic romantic hero over the strictures of nature and society. *The Twelve Words of the Gypsy* is said to evince Palamas's most characteristic features—powerful, metaphor-filled language, multifaceted layers of meaning, and erudite knowledge of history and world literature.

Critics disagree on the relative merits of the early lyrics over the later epic works. Some prefer the polished succinctness of the shorter works, criticizing the latter as being too long and philosophically complex. Others prefer the thematic intricacy

P. Fuller

and monumental scale of the epics. There is no doubt among critics, however, concerning Palamas's importance to modern Greek literature. As one of Greece's foremost poets, and as a leading critic and polemicist, Palamas breathed new inspiration into Greek literature at a critical juncture in its development.

PRINCIPAL WORKS

Tragoúdia tes patrídos mou   (poetry)   1886
Ímnos is tin Athenán   (poetry)   1889
Íamboi kai anápaestoi   (poetry)   1897
Ho táfos   (poetry)   1898
   [*The Grave*, 1930]
Thánatos tou palikariú   (short stories)   1901
   [*A Man's Death*, 1934]
Trisévgene   (drama)   1903
   [*Royal Blossom; or, Trisevyene*, 1923]
He asálleute zoé   (poetry)   1904
   [Published in two volumes: *Life Immovable*, 1919; *A Hundred Voices*, 1921]
Ho dodekálogos tou gýphtou   (poetry)   1907
   [*The Twelve Words of the Gypsy*, 1964]

He phlogéra tou basiliá   (poetry)   1910
  [*The King's Flute,* 1967]
I politeía ke i monaxiá   (poetry)   1912
Vomi   (poetry)   1915
I pentasyllavi ke ta pathitika kryfomilimata   (poetry)
  1925
Poems   (poetry)   1925
Thili ke skliri stichi   (poetry)   1928
I nychtes tou Phemiou   (poetry)   1935
Vrathini Fotia   (poetry)   1944
Three Poems   (poetry)   1969

*This is the date of first publication rather than first performance.

KOSTES PALAMAS   (essay date 1906)

Who knows if *The Twelve Words of the Gypsy* was not first planted in my mind by a memory, as vivid as a vision, of some Mayday festival which I had enjoyed as a child in my village; a Mayday animated by the dances of Gypsy women. (p. xxiv)

I felt inside me that I was a Gypsy, although I was ashamed to confess it; a Gypsy with all his vices and his miseries; I was one with that accursed race, however much I might hide it under fine clothes; it was of myself that I was singing. (pp. xxiv-xxv)

The Twelve Words of the Gypsy should be ranked with that series of my poems which I call **"The Great Visions,"** like **"The Ascrean"** and **"The Chains"** in **"Life Immutable."** (In fact **"The Chains"** was, originally, one of *The Twelve Words.* Later on, I saw that it would go better apart, and so I separated them.) In *The Twelve Words,* epic legend is combined with lyrical thought; in it a simple story is unfolded with a less simple meaning. It is fitting here to recall some significant words in Plato's *Phaedo:* "The poet, to be a poet, must use fiction for his verse and not reality." It was fiction that I took for my work. The Gypsy, élite of his race, might have exclaimed with Heraclitus: "To me thousands are one." Yet he is incompatible among his fellows, "set apart among the set apart"; he is deeply conscious of the value of social life, but he cannot adapt himself to companionship; he wants to work like others, but he cannot; he tries every craft and he feels cramped and awkward in all of them; he is cramped and awkward, too, in his love which he had dreamed of as so immense. (pp. xxvii-xxviii)

The epic legend is developed around the Gypsy race when it first appeared in Thrace, about one hundred years before the fall of Constantinople, and pitched its tents outside that city. In the background of the picture there looms, as through the mist of a dream, the great City blessed—at that time cursed—by God; "The land of our desires," as it is called somewhere by Markoras. The concept of a definite period is not found in the poem. The sense of passing time does not seem to have been clearly imaged even by Homer himself. The epic poets do not trouble themselves much with such matters; so let it be pardoned also in my own poem because of the epic and philosophical elements which it contains. I seem to involve my hero in actions and in thoughts which are separated from each other by years and epochs. But I am not telling my story in a smooth and orderly manner; I

am trying somehow, with the art at my command, to clarify what I see like in a dream.

Lyrical thinking shows itself, I think, everywhere in the poem, sometimes distinctly and sometimes blurred, both in the principal parts and in the episodes. But whereas, elsewhere, those parts of a work which are not directly related to the story can be considered as episodes, here it can be said that those episodes are the principal part of the poem and all the rest just a pretext for embellishment. I feel tightly bound to the Gypsy spirit; but my Gypsy life is illuminated by the Word; and Poetry is the highest flowering of the Word. I had no particular desire to take as the principal goal of my poem a pictorial reconstitution of Gypsy life and nature; such a use of Art does not please me. I used the Gypsy as a pretext and an occasion to express through him, through a type congenial to my soul, my intellectual aspirations. I wished to describe in my turn, however weak may be my voice, the emotion of Man in the face of certain problems of life, his submission or his resistance; the feelings of the citizen and the thinker when confronted with certain episodes of the history of his nation. (pp. xxviii-xxix)

The lyrical thinking of *The Twelve Words of the Gypsy* is not placid; it has a tumultuous stride and assumes different aspects ranging from gibes and dirges of bitter denial to the triumphant trumpet call of faith; from doubt and nihilism to the proclamation of energy, progress, virile love and confidence in the beauties of the future.

My hero is successively a destroyer and a creator. He is, perhaps, a clumsy destroyer and an unlucky creator. The poem may be worthless. I do not know quite what to make of it. . . . (pp. xxix-xxx)

The metrical pattern of *The Twelve Words,* in keeping with my hero's character, is also spontaneous and unpremeditated; the verse flows freely according to its fancy, sometimes with rhyme and sometimes without; sometimes seeking to direct its current into the channels of stanzas, sometimes racing ahead in full flood. Yet, in spite of all these fantasies, the verse always remains regulated, always based on the iamb and the trochee. It rarely changes its step; it moves freely and occasionally in a disorderly manner, but it never becomes unmetrical or anarchic.

The quotations placed at the beginning of each Word, which give *The Twelve Words* the aspect of the much ornamented palaces of the Frankish conquerors of Thebes during the Middle Ages, do not always bear a close and direct relation to the poems which they adorn. One might think that the Gypsy's Words were born more or less from the words which appear at their head. This is not so. The truth is that I naturally built my house first and decorated it afterwards. It was an opportunity to hang on my walls some memorials of those great acquaintances who deign to converse with my humble self each time I turn to them and live in their company. My famous friends are many: I did not invite them all because my house could not contain more of them. Do not think that they must all agree with what I say in the verses headed by their names. Some of them might even be displeased if they could see where I have placed them. Forgive me, O august immortals, for having dared to seek your help whether you wished it or not! And if I have given to each section of my poem the name *Logos,* It was not so much to recall the custom of some forgotten Byzantine poets or to suggest some external affinity to works of rhetoric, but rather to shelter my poem beneath the shadow of the creative Word. If you should judge it inferior to the Word, forgive me, O glorious immortals! (pp. xxxiii-xxxiv)

> Kostes Palamas, "Introduction" (1906), in his The Twelve Words of the Gypsy, *translated by Theodore Ph. Stephanides and George C. Katsimbalis (copyright © by Memphis State University Press, 1975), Memphis State University Press, 1975, pp. xxiii-xxxiv.*

ARISTIDES E. PHOUTRIDES (essay date 1919)

Kostes Palamas! A name I hated once with all the sincerity of a young and blind enthusiast as the name of a traitor. This is no exaggeration. I was a student in the third class of an Athenian Gymnasion in 1901, when the Gospel Riots stained with blood the streets of Athens. The cause of the riots was a translation of the *New Testament* into the people's tongue by Alexandros Pallis, one of the great leaders of the literary renaissance of Modern Greece.... The students of the University, animated by the fiery speeches of one of their Professors, George Mistriotes, the bulwark of the unreconcilable Purists, who would model the modern language of Greece after the ancient, regarded this translation as a treacherous profanation both of the sacred text and of the national speech. The demotikists, branded under the name of... "the hairy ones," were thought even by serious people to be national traitors, the creators of a mysterious propaganda seeking to crush the aspirations of the Greek people by showing that their language was not the ancient Greek language and that they were not the heirs of Ancient Greece.

Three names among the "Hairy Ones" were the object of universal detestation: John Psicharis, the well known Greek Professor in Paris, the author of many works and of the first complete Grammar of the people's idiom; Alexandros Pallis, the translator of the *Iliad* and of the *New Testament;* and Kostes Palamas, secretary of the University of Athens, the poet of this "anti-nationalistic" faction. Against them the bitterest invectives were cast. The University students and, with them, masses of people who joined without understanding the issue, paraded uncontrollable through the streets of Athens.... (pp. 5-6)

[The] rioters became so violent that arms had to be used against them, resulting in the death of eight students and the wounding of about sixty others. This was utilized by politicians opposing the government: fiery speeches denouncing the measures adopted were heard in Parliament; the victims were eulogized as great martyrs of a sacred cause; and popular feeling ran so high that the Cabinet had to resign.... (p. 7)

About two years later, I had entered the University of Athens when another riot was started by the students after another fiery speech delivered by our puristic hero, Professor Mistriotes, against the performance of Aeschylus' *Oresteia* ... in a popular translation made by Mr. Soteriades and considered too vulgar for puristic ears. This time, too, the riot was quelled, but not until one innocent passer-by had been killed.... It was the day after the riot that I first saw Palamas himself. He was standing before one of the side entrances to the University building when my companion showed him to me with a hateful sneer.... I paused for a moment to have a full view of this notorious criminal. Rather short and compact in frame, he stood with eyes directed

towards the sunlight streaming on the marble covered ground of the yard. He held a cane with both his hands and seemed to be thinking. Once or twice he glanced at the wall as if he were reading something, but again he turned towards the sunlight with an expression of sorrow on his face. There was nothing conspicuous about him, nothing aggressive. His rather pale face, furrowed brow, and meditative attitude were marks of a quiet, retiring, modest man. Do traitors then look so human? From the end of the colonnade, I watched him carefully until he turned away and entered the building. Then I followed him and walked up to the same entrance; on the wall, an inscription was scratched in heavy pencil strokes:

> Down with Palamas! the bought one! the traitor!

At last my humanity was aroused, and the first rays of sympathy began to dispel my hatred. That remoseless inscription could not be true of this man, I thought, and I hurried to the library to read some of his work for the first time that I might form an opinion about him myself. Unfortunately, the verses on which I happened to come were too deep for my intellect, and I had not the patience to read them twice. I was so absolutely sure of the power of my mind that I ascribed my lack of understanding to the poet. Then his poems were so different from the easy, rhythmic, oratorical verses on which I had been brought up. In Palamas, I missed those pleasant trivialities which attract a boy's mind in poetry. One thing, however, was clear to me even then. Dark and unintelligible though his poems appeared, they were certainly full of a deep, passionate feeling, a feeling that haunted my thoughts long after I had closed his book in despair. (pp. 7-9)

Years went by. I was no more in Greece. I had come to [America], where a new language, a new history, a new literature opened before me. Here, at last, I began to assume a reasonable attitude towards the question of the language of my old country, and here first I could read Palamas with understanding. Gradually, his greatness began to dawn on me.... (p. 9)

I wrote to him for permission to translate some of his works. The answer came laden with the same modesty which is so prominent a characteristic of the man. He is afraid I am exaggerating the value of his work, and he calls himself a mere laborer of the verse. Certainly he has been a faithful laborer for a cause which a generation ago seemed hopeless. But through his faith and power, he has snatched the crown of victory from the hands of Time, and he may now be acclaimed as a new World-Poet.

"The poetic work of Kostes Palamas," says Eugène Clement, a French critic, in a recent article on the poet, "presents itself today with an imposing greatness. Without speaking about his early collections, in which already a talent of singular power is revealed, we may say that the four or five volumes of verse which he has published during the last ten years raise him beyond comparison not only above all poets of Modern Greece but above all poets of contemporary Europe. Though he is not the most famous—owing to his overshadowing modesty and to the language he writes, which is little read beyond the borders of Hellenism—*he is incontestably the greatest.* The breadth of his views on the world and on humanity, on the history and soul of his race, in short, on all problems that agitate modern thought, places him in the first rank among those who have had the gift to clothe the philosophic idea in the sumptuous mantle of poetry. On the other hand, the vigor and richness of his imagination, the penetrating warmth of his feeling, the exquisite perfection of his art, and his gifted style manifest in him a poetic temperament of an exceptional fulness that was bound to give birth to great masterpieces." (pp. 11-12)

To his birth place [Patras, one of the most ancient towns in Greece], the poet dedicates one of his collection of sonnets entitled **"Fatherlands."**. . . (p. 14)

But in Patras, the child did not stay long. His early home seems to have been broken up by the death of his mother, and we find him next in Missolonghi. . . . The town itself is a shrine of patriotism for modern Greeks. For from 1822 to 1826, with its humble walls hardly stronger than fences, it sustained the attacks of very superior forces, and its ground was hallowed by the blood of many national heroes. (pp. 15-16)

Here then, "the spirit's spark" was first kindled, and here, in the city of his ancestors, the poet was born. The swampy meadows overgrown with rushes and surrounded with violet mountains, the city with its narrow crooked streets and low-roofed houses, the lagoon with its still shallow waters and modest islets, the life of townsmen and peasants with their humble occupations, passions, and legends, above all, the picturesque distinctness of this somewhat isolated place, secluded, as it seems, in an atmosphere laden with national lore—these were the incentives which stirred Palamas in his quest of song. They have stamped their image on all his work, but their most distinct reflection is found in *The Lagoon's Regrets*, which is filled with memories of the poet's early life in a world he always remembers with affection. . . . (pp. 17-18)

The poems of this collection are short but exquisitely wrought in verse and language, full of life and of feeling. They are especially marked with Palamas' attachment to the little and humble, which he loves to raise into music and rhythm, and for which he always has sympathy and even admiration.

Missolonghi nurtured the poet in his youth and led him to the threshold of manhood. But when he had graduated from the provincial "gymnasion," he naturally came to Athens. . . . (p. 19)

The spiritual and intellectual currents moving the Greek nation of today start from this city. (p. 25)

Into this world, the poet came to finish his education. In one of his critical essays (*Grammata*, vol. i), he tells us of the literary atmosphere prevailing in Athens at that time, about 1879. That year, Valaorites, the second great poet of the people's language, died, and his death renewed with vigor the controversy that had continued even after the death of Solomos, the earliest great poet of Modern Greece. The passing away of Valaorites left Rangabes, the relentless purist, the monarch of the literary world. He was considered as the master whom every one should aspire to imitate. His language, ultra-puristic, had travelled leagues away from the people without approaching at all the splendor of the ancient speech. But the purists drew great delight from reading his works and clapped their hands with satisfaction on seeing how near Plato and Aeschylus they had managed to come.

Young and susceptible to the popular currents of the literary world, Palamas, too, worshipped the established idol, and offered his frankincense in verses modelled after Rangabean conceptions. In the same essay to which I have just referred, he tells us of the life he led with another young friend, likewise

a literary aspirant, during the years of his attendance at the University. The two lived and worked together. They wrote poems in the puristic language and compared their works in stimulating friendliness. But soon they realized the truth that if poetry is to be eternal, it must express the individual through the voice of the world to which the individual belongs and through the language which the people speak.

This truth took deep roots in the mind of Palamas. His conviction grew into a religion permeated with the warmth, earnestness, and devotion that martyrs only have shown to their cause. Believing that purism was nothing but a blind attempt to drown the living traditions of the people and to conceal its nature under a specious mantle of shallow gorgeousness, he has given his talent and his heart to save his nation from such a calamity. In this great struggle, he has suffered not a little. (pp. 26-8)

As a "soldier of the verse," he himself fights his battles of song in every field. In short story, in drama, in epic poetry, and above all in lyrics, he creates work after work. From the *Songs of my Country*, the *Hymn to Athena*, the *Eyes of my Soul* and the *Iambs and Anapaests*, he rises gradually and steadily to the tragic drama of the *Thrice Noble-One*, to the epic of *The King's Flute*, and to the splendid lyrics of *Life Immovable* and *The Twelve Words of the Gypsy* which are his masterpieces.

Nor does he always meet adversity with songs of resignation. At times, he faces indignantly the hostile world with a satire as stinging as that of Juvenal. He dares attack with Byronic boldness every idol that his enemies worship. Often he strikes at the whole people with Archilochean bitterness and parries blow for blow like Hipponax. At times, he even seems to approach the rancor of Swift. But then he immediately throws away his whip and transcends his satire with a loftier thought, a soothing moral, a note of lyricism, and above all with an unshaken faith in the new day for which he works. (pp. 30-1)

In tracing the great life influences of our poet, we must not pass over the loss of his third child, "the child without a peer," as he says in one of his poems addressed to his wife, "who changed the worldly air about us into divine nectar, a worthy offering to the spotless-white light of Olympus." To this loss, the poet has never reconciled himself. The sorrow finds expression in direct or covert strains in every work he has written. But its lasting monument was created soon after the child's death. A collection of poems, entitled *The Grave*, entirely devoted to his memory, is overflowing with an unique intensity of feeling. The poems are composed in short quatrains of a slowly moving rhythm restrained by frequent pauses and occasional metrical irregularities, and thus they reflect with faithfulness the paternal agony with which they are filled. They belong to the earlier works of the poet, but they disclose great lyric power and are the first deep notes of the poet's genius. (pp. 33-4)

Greece seems to encompass the physical world with which Palamas has come in contact. He does not seem to have travelled beyond its borders, and even within them, he has moved little about. With him scenery must grow with age before it speaks to his heart. Fleeting impressions are of little value, and the appearance of things without the forces of tradition and experience behind it does not attract him. . . . (p. 38)

We must not think, however, that the spirit of Palamas rests within the narrow confines of his native land. On the contrary, it knows no chains and travels freely about the earth. He is a faithful servant of "Melete," the Muse of contemplative study, a service which is very seldom liked by Modern Greeks. . . . There is hardly an important force in the world's thought and expression whether past or present to which Palamas is a stranger. The literatures of Europe, America, or Asia are an open book for him. The pulses of the world's artists, the intellectual battles of the philosophers, the fears and hopes of the social unrest, the religious emancipation of our day, the far reaching conflict of individual and state, in short, all events of importance in the social, political, spiritual, literary, and artistic life are familiar sources of inspiration for him. With all, he shows the lofty spirit of a worshipper of greatness and depth wherever he finds them. (pp. 38-40)

Nor does he lift his voice only for individual or national throbbings. He sings of the great and noble whenever he sees it. One of his best lyric creations is a song of praise to the valor of the champions of Transvaal's freedom, his **"Hymn to the Valiant,"** the first of the collection entitled **"From the Hymns and Wraths."** . . . (p. 40)

From the number of the life influences . . . in Palamas' work we may conclude that he is a true representative of the great world and of the age in which he lives. Loving and true to his immediate surroundings, he does not localize himself in them, nor does he shut his thought within his personal feelings and experiences, but he travels far and wide with the thought and action of the universal man and fills his life with the life of his age.

It is exactly this universalism that makes *The Twelve Words of the Gypsy* his best expression and at the same time the most difficult to understand thoroughly. The poem is reflective both of the growth of the poet himself and of the development of the human spirit throughout the ages with the history and land of Hellas as its natural background. Consequently, its message is both subjective and objective. Although differently treated, the theme is the same as that of the **"Ascrean"** which appears in the latter part of *Life Immovable* and which may be considered as a prelude to *The Twelve Words of the Gypsy*. There is a flood of feeling and a cosmic imagery throughout, but they only form the gorgeous palace within which Thought dwells in full magnificence and mystic dimness. "As the thread of my song," says the poet in his preface, "unrolled itself, I saw that my heart was full of mind, that its pulses were of thought, that my feeling had something musical and difficult to measure, and that I accepted the rapture of contemplation just as a lad accepts his sweetheart's kiss. And then I saw that I am the poet, surely a poet among many—a mere soldier of the verse, but always the poet who desires to close within his verse the longings and questions of the universal man and the cares and fanaticism of the citizen. I may not be a worthy citizen. *But it cannot be that I am the poet of myself alone; I am the poet of my age and of my race; and what I hold within me cannot be divided from the world without.*" (pp. 50-1)

> *Aristides E. Phoutrides, "Kostes Palamas, a New World-Poet" (originally published in a slightly different form in* Poet Lore, *Vol. XXVIII, No. 1, January, 1917), in* Life Immovable, First Part *by Kostes Palamas, translated by Aristides E. Phoutrides (copyright © 1919 by the President and Fellows of Harvard College), Cambridge, Mass.: Harvard University Press, 1919, pp. 3-51.*

FREDERIC WILL (essay date 1963)

[Kostes Palamas] made his debut with lyrics, faded and delicate pieces—as the *Songs of my Fatherland* . . .—in the Greek-Victorian style of Drosines. The influence of Leconte de Lisle and Sully Prudhomme injected more vigor and polish, seen in the *Eyes of my Soul* . . . , and still more in the *Iambs and Anapaests. The Tomb* . . . , written as a memorial to his dead son, is poignant and controlled, and suggests the immensity of disciplined feeling soon to break out of Palamas' epic mind. His [*Twelve Words of the Gypsy* and *The King's Flute*] . . . are the proof of this power. In each, he negotiates thoroughly and deeply with his national-spiritual past.

Like the most articulate of later generations of Greek writers—Seferis, Sikelianos, Kazantzakis—Palamas was deeply and constantly concerned with that past. . . . To its writers [Greece's] past was likely to be crushing, a weight which could neither be carried nor avoided. Palamas was the first skilled carrier. He bore the easier weight, the medieval and not the pre-Christian, but even that was a huge achievement, on behalf of his people. For he not only managed the medieval Hellenic, but he saw the eternally Greek in it.

That visionary power shows itself best in the *Twelve Words of the Gypsy*. There Palamas' supple abilities are employed to best effect; vaguely, mantically, but in terms of a conceivable historical landscape with a few recognizable landmarks. The past is forever yielding glimpses of the eternal.

The poem's physical center is Constantinople, The City, around 1350, about a century before it fell to the Turks. Time is meant vaguely here. Imagination shapes it. . . . What we see of the City's centrality is accented by our perception of what lies beyond it. Thrace and Anatolia are crude and rural; men in those landscapes stream, magnetized, toward the Center. One of those men, the dynamic strand of the epic, is a Gypsy among gypsies, a supreme representative of that turbulent race. He is the one clear figure for our eyes throughout the epic. . . . At one time the Gypsy himself addresses us; at another the narrator conducts us on metaphysical or descriptive excursions into the historical world where the Gypsy exists. The interweaving of Gypsy, variegated City, and metaphysical rumination creates a strangely brilliant tapestry of impressions. It is not a decorative tapestry; it is far too dynamic. So it resembles lived history, multiple action and thought deploying themselves inextricably. (pp. x-xiii)

As a whole, the poem coheres and compels. The blending of the Gypsy with the gypsies with the world of the City is achieved with large synthetic imagination. Many individual scenes build the power: the first coming of the Gypsy; his efforts as lover and sculptor; the old men carrying ancient texts abroad; the Festival of Kakava; the Gypsy's rejection of a homeland for his race; the Emperor's indifference to the Turks; the Gypsy's prophetic speech; the legend of the Tearless One. Much here fulfills major requirements of poetry; it is both sensuous and woven through with experienced thought. Within himself the Gypsy bears meanings which Palamas fully masters and incarnates. Right here, though, is one danger and the border of another. The danger is a vagueness of thought which offends against even the liberality of epic poetry. Palamas has read Nietzsche. He has thought eclectically about the value of freedom and the evil of all restraint. Much of this thought and reading has been projected effectually into the image of the Gypsy. But that image is vague. There is so much mere, unbounded, undefined passion for freedom that in the end we wonder just what it really is that the Gypsy wants. Such philosophical vagueness spreads. There is finally a related vagueness from sentiment. Some of the Words are maudlin, the twelfth especially. Others, especially the tenth, are high-flown and abstract (using words like "Gods," "Fatherland," and "Wisdom" with terrible banality) and corrode the energies of the whole. It is an awful disappointment to find the postscript addressed, as from a Victorian gent, to a darkly anonymous lady. Palamas is too good for that. (pp. xviii-xix)

[The thought of *Twelve Words* occupies a] penumbral situation between profundity and fuzziness. . . . The language of this thought is difficult at its center, just where it turns through impression into implication. It is an accumulative language, piling up adjectives, turning to extravagant imagery, varying line-lengths with a sawtoothing complexity, and rhyming, inwardly and outwardly, with tactful showiness. Touching Palamas' speech where it turns into thought requires much energy. . . . Below this level of difficulty, though, is the level of the dictionary. The words of this making are often obscure, or elusively applied. Like Kazantzakis for his *Odyssey*, Palamas provides a glossary. But that is only a start. (pp. xix-xx)

> Frederic Will, "Kostes Palamas and 'The Twelve Words of the Gypsy'" (1963), in The Twelve Words of the Gypsy *by Kostes Palamas, translated by Frederic Will (reprinted by permission of the University of Nebraska Press; © 1964 by the University of Nebraska Press),* University of Nebraska Press, *1964, pp. ix-xx.*

FREDERIC WILL (essay date 1967)

Kostes Palamas provided the introduction to an introduction when he wrote "*The Twelve Words of the Gypsy* are the propylaea through which we enter into *The King's Flute*." He thereby interrelated his two great epics. (p. ix)

First impressions, admittedly, may seem to contradict this statement. *The King's Flute* is bound, as *The Twelve Words* was not, to historical detail. True, *The Twelve Words* was set in the mid-fourteenth century; but the temporal foci are fuzzy. (p. x)

The King's Flute, by contrast, seems much more bound to historical detail. It does, in fact, concern real people and real events to a degree unknown in *The Twelve Words*. The protagonist is the eleventh-century Byzantine emperor Basil II, the Bulgar-killer. The theme or frame for feeling is Basil's journey through Greece to Athens, to worship the Virgin Mary in her cathedral, the Christianized Parthenon. The epic is a historical narrative.

From the beginning, though, this history has been organically widened out into myth and visionary panorama. The tale has been recounted by a magic flute, found in the mouth of the corpse of Basil. That flute chants the epic, which is thus heightened to a visionary document of Basil's time and experience. (pp. x-xi)

Greek this is, in one sense of that complex word; chiefly Byzantine Greek, to be exact. Where it is Byzantine Greek, however, it manages in a surprising way also to become generally human. Here we touch the mystery of that phase of human spirit which the Rome of the East fostered in the High Middle Ages and to which Palamas was so attuned. Byzantine Greek comes here to connote that high point of

a civilization at which pomp, brutality, and majesty intersect most firmly with the need for divine compassion. Palamas was a master at plotting this intersection. (p. xi)

Basil [is] explicitly grand-style visionary—like the Gypsy as prophet in *The Twelve Words of the Gypsy*—and with him we see the emergences of new, more modern powers: of Mammon, of America, of socialism, and finally, in one of its inevitable rebirths, of that Hellenism which he represents, which is at once Christian and pagan, warlike and compassionate, wherever and in whatever place. . . . (pp. xviii-xix)

Much less is specifically memorable in [*The King's Flute*] than in *The Twelve Words,* but it operates on a more consistent level of poetic coercion. Its digressions—into Basil's past, into the life of the holy monk, into presenting such figures as Augusta Theophano—all prompt the reader to a firmer affective grasp of the "argument." Its projection of thrust—toward Athens, the Parthenon, and Mary—is felt everywhere, furnishing an implicit directional energy it never relinquishes. The City, Constantinople, plays the same axial role in *The Twelve Words,* but there all geography is metaphored far more than in *The King's Flute.* In the earlier work, meaninglessly unlocalized events are always threatening the movement of the whole.

The single episodes of *The King's Flute* cannot be dismissed as unmemorable, even when allowance is made for Palamas' not wanting to create, here, what we might call memorable scenes. Much *does* stay in precision: the meeting of young Basil with the Bulgarian Tzar, the specters moving on Prinkipo Island, the pouring of troops down over the Greek landscape, the speech by Mount Parnassos, the first glimpses of the Parthenon, Basil's description of his relation to Bardas the Hard, and much else. I wonder, though, whether even in these, the hardest and clearest episodes, the ear, and behind it the mind's intuition, are not working far harder than the eye; far harder than is customary, that is, even in an art like poetry, where the eye normally works only as an interior sense.

The special unity and completeness of *The King's Flute* result from its consistent address to the ear-as-mind. A liturgical tone results, and is maintained with unremitting finesse. The work streams ahead, an enormous river of prayer and adoration, continually deflected—though never meandering—into tributaries which invariably, through marsh, stream, or delta, find their way back to the sea of compassion, to [Mary, the Divine] Lady. (pp. xix-xxi)

[Palamas'] Greek archaizes, in several ways. He is consciously rhetorical, often unashamedly—though complexly—grand; and he is addicted to an immensely widespread vocabulary, which draws its richness from ancient and Byzantine as much as from modern strata of the language. (Even to try to match this last dexterity in an English poem, we would need to sprinkle our text with actual, unchanged words from Old and Middle English.) And of course his created mood is as far as possible purely Byzantine. *It* is ancient.

At the same time, Palamas manages to be modern in several of the senses we give that word when it is applied to poetry. He writes shaggy lines, sometimes of variable lengths and variable stress patterns, although his stock line is the fifteen-syllable political verse-line, traditionally Greek. He distorts his syntax, sometimes consciously refuses to complete sentences, maintains acute oral tenseness. Above all, he links sentences, paragraphs, and cantos by chains so delicate, unpredictable, and long that one at times feels almost too much in the poet's hands. (pp. xxii)

> *Frederic Will, in his introduction to* The King's Flute *by Kostes Palamas, translated by Frederic Will (reprinted by permission of University of Nebraska Press; © 1967 by the University of Nebraska Press), University of Nebraska Press, 1967, pp. ix-xxxv.*

ROY ARTHUR SWANSON (essay date 1968)

Palamas's poetry, solidly rooted in Greek traditions and refreshingly stabilized by Parnassian discipline, is also deftly colored and intensified by a lyricism that is kindred to *imagisme* and *symbolisme*. In particular, it is the happy marriage of lyric and epic that gives *The King's Flute* its distinction. The elements of lyric and epic are starkly discernible and at the same time melodiously inseparable in, for example, the concluding line of the prologue: "Darkened all the lights, a song of heroes!" . . . The flute, itself an instrument to accompany lyric song, voices its historico-epic identity by singing of its integration with the muses of history and epic: "Myself the flute, the epic, prophet's reed. A sistered twin to Klio; my tongue Kalliope." . . .

In *The Twelve Words of the Gypsy* the bard-spokesman is the titular wandering minstrel. The poem is a manifesto in invocation of artistic and political freedom; and in the poem the two freedoms are melded in confluence. Pasternak had his wanderer, Zhivago, write poetry and work for political freedom. Palamas's wanderer *is* poetry and political freedom. In *The King's Flute* Palamas confounded those who would catalogue him as an allegorist: he eliminated the musician and let the musician instrument speak. The symbol, then, achieves the dimensions of a character. *The Twelve Words of the Gypsy* may suffer from its contiguity to allegory; but *The King's Flute* cannot. Moreover, the hendecalogue of the flute includes an energetic address to the troops of Emperor Basil II by Mount Parnassus itself. Parnassianism, *imagisme, symbolisme,* epic, history, and lyric are all resolved in this passage, which is the omphalos of the poem, and for which I, dredging my critical vocabulary, can offer in appraisal only the phrase, "a triumph of anagoge." (p. 383)

The epic and lyric elements of *The King's Flute* are individually discernible: we can put our finger on a characteristic of epic here (catalogues, extended similes, dramatic dialogues, and the like) and on a characteristic of lyric there (melody, emotion, ambiguity, and the like); but these elements, in this poem, cannot be divorced—they are inseparable. The epic element informs the historical narrative. The lyric element is, by and large, precatory. The unity of the poem is, in fact, the union of epic and lyric, and, thereby, the union of all that is informed by the epic elements (for example, history) and all that is informed by the lyric elements (for example, prayer). Wtihin this frame of reference, the poem is history and the poem is prayer; or, we can go on to say that this historical epic is a lyric prayer. (p. 384)

> *Roy Arthur Swanson, "Book Reviews: 'The King's Flute'," in* The Modern Language Journal, *Vol. LII, No. 5, June, 1968, pp. 383-84.*

THANASIS MASKALERIS (essay date 1972)

Palamas the poet emerged with the Generation of 1880, a group of writers who shaped the richest period of modern Greek literature. The social, intellectual, and creative efforts of these writers were animated by the conviction that the only idiom capable of creating a significant literature was the demotic *(demotiké),* the spoken tongue of the time. . . . In a wider sense, the Generation of 1880 sought a synthesis of the present with the entire Greek past, the shaping and defining of a new Hellenic culture. In this far-ranging movement of reform and regeneration, Palamas was the leading figure, both as an original poet and as a fighter for the establishment of the demotic. (p. 11)

Songs of My Country is the first collection of Palamas's poems in the demotic. (p. 23)

In the poems of this collection Palamas makes extensive use of rhythms, imagery, and themes of folk songs and chants of lamentation, and he succeeds remarkably in clothing his ideas with the common dress of the folk idiom. . . . With *Songs of My Country* Palamas begins what will become a lifelong task: bringing poetry down to concern itself with the actual conditions of his environment and at the same time elevating the demotic to express the loftiest thoughts and feelings of the poet.

In his next two poetic works, [*The Hymn to Athena* and *The Eyes of My Soul*] . . . , Palamas continued to assimilate the past and relate it to present social needs. This assimilation and reevaluation of the past was an attempt to solve a serious problem: the empty love of his contemporaries for the Greek past. (p. 24)

In *The Hymn to Athena* and *The Eyes of My Soul,* the language of Palamas has become richer and more effective, a more genuine and better controlled demotic. The somber moods and the musical free verse in *The Eyes of My Soul* indicate the influence of Symbolism. In contrast, *Songs of My Country* shows a stronger influence of the Parnassians in both form and themes. (pp. 24-5)

[*Iambs and Anapaests*] is a landmark in Palamas's development. From the standpoint of form, it can be seen as his first mature work. Palamas's heretofore uncontrollable and often rhetorical verse now achieves a conciseness and a rhythmic control that have ranked *Iambs and Anapaests* as a masterpiece. Here, too, as in the earlier work, the imagination sweeps across wide worlds; feeling and thought soar to great heights, but the effect is quite different. The near-epigrammatic expression of this verse at once heightens and controls the lyrical sweep; the rhythm has the impact of magic.

In *Iambs and Anapaests* Palamas, for the first time, gives a Classical balance to the discords of his consciousness. He begins to see poetry as "a symbol of the rhythm of the world" and to feel its divine and redeeming power. But as he is lifted above the world of contradictions, he becomes "a slave of Rhyme, the new Omphale."

In *Iambs and Anapaests* Palamas's vision penetrates simultaneously the realms of nature, history, and science, without losing contact with folk tradition. (p. 25)

Science is envisaged in all its power, but also in its limitations. . . . The poet sees that science, which in his time was proclaimed a savior of humanity, cannot become a new religion. In his attempt to find such a religion, he embraces all of life with passion. (pp. 25-6)

[*The Grave*] has been universally acclaimed as one of Palamas's masterpieces. It is a long elegy written immediately after the death of his youngest son, Alkis. Here in terse musical verses of exquisite tenderness, Palamas expressed both the grief of the father for the death of his child and the metaphysical transport of the poet as he encounters and contemplates death. The emotional element of the poem, however, is overwhelmingly predominant. Lyrical purity, rarely sustained in the long poems of the "thought-ridden poet," is here masterfully achieved. (p. 26)

In its unadorned language, simple melodiousness, and richness of folk materials, *The Grave* is almost a traditional song of lament. . . . (p. 27)

[In *The Greetings to the Sunborn Woman*] the search of Palamas for a new religion centers again on science. In this, as in several subsequent works, science becomes a central theme which finds its fullest expression in *The Dodecalogue of the Gypsy*. For Palamas, science always bathes in beauty and breathes in a metaphysical air. The Sunborn Woman is such a science ideal. She is offspring of the Sun, the source of Truth and Beauty. At the same time, she is a symbol of the new consciousness that was emerging in his times, the new Greek consciousness represented by the demotic revival and the new European consciousness that would rise as the outcome of the battle between metaphysical theocracy and positivism. (pp. 27-8)

Will the new consciousness stop at the idol of science? This is the central question asked in *The Sunborn Woman*. And the poet's answer is a negative one: he and the new art must go beyond science. His faith in a more complete ideal of life expands his horizons and prepares him for a wider vision. A universal humanism is beginning to take shape. (p. 28)

Life Immovable marks the beginning of Palamas's second creative period. . . . It is a large collection, diverse in subject matter and prosodic experiments. Its complex lyrical movements reflect Palamas's struggle to master and express his many conflicts and concerns. . . . The whole collection is a song of all life elevated to the harmony and immutability of poetic sublimation. The poet's life, too, becomes "immovable" in the realization of his lyrical passion beyond and above the turmoils of everyday life. . . . (p. 29)

"Fatherlands" is a group of sonnets about various localities of Greece and other countries. . . . A feeling of cosmopolitanism overflows in Palamas's verse and leads him to an ideal conception of fatherland which goes far beyond his early patriotism. In the following sonnet of this section, the poet's imagination rises to a universal vision of the earth and relates the indestructible elements to man's mortality and to the life of art. . . . (p. 30)

[The poems in the section], "The Return," grew out of the gloomy aftermath of the Greco-Turkish War of 1897. The defeat of the Greeks in this war was a shattering blow to national aspirations, to the hope for recovering large Greek-populated territories from Turkish rule and recapturing the glory of Byzantium. This dream for territorial expansion and regaining old glories, later known as *Megali Idea* (Great Idea), played an important role in the national life for an entire century. . . . Palamas's work reflected and often rekindled this burning ideal. Thus in the opening poem of "The Return," he attempts to soothe his suffering Mother (Greece) and to inspire hope in his discouraged countrymen. The poet becomes, once again, "the greatest patriot." But general hopelessness afflicts the poet's heart as well, and the prevailing tone in "The Return" is one of anguish and pessimism,

a pessimism that moves from social concern to personal confession. . . . (pp. 30-1)

[In "Fragments from the Song of the Sun,"] Palamas once again turns to the gods and heroes of the past, particularly to those of ancient Greece. His imagination raises them into lofty symbols illuminated by a cosmic sun, father and unifier of all. This sun of the "Fragments" is a complex symbol, representing a life-giving source that permeates both the physical universe and the inner world of man. And the poet, one feels, is a humbler counterpart of this mighty sun. (p. 32)

From the point of view of form, "The Palm Tree" is one of Palamas's most perfect works. The idea that form and content must be harmoniously blended, which had strongly influenced Palamas, is perhaps more completely realized in this poem than in any other. Here, in a lyrical monologue of three hundred and twelve lines, Palamas's musical use of the thirteen-syllable line is unsurpassed in modern Greek poetry. It is interesting to note also that Palamas gradually abandons conventional symbolism, which is based primarily on mythology, and creates his own private symbols that rise out of his direct contact with nature. (p. 35)

[*The Dodecalogue of the Gypsy*] is the most complete synthesis of Palamas's poetic consciousness. In the sweeping movement of this epiclyric composition the polyphonous music of the poet's soul is heard in all its tonal and thematic richness. Yet, in spite of its subjective mold, *The Dodecalogue* simultaneously reflects significant evolutionary steps in the life of Hellenism and of mankind, as well as contemporary conflicts. It is a poem of action; here the poet lives his life in the unfolding of the tale, unlike in "The Ascrean" where he reconstructs his past under the guidance of memory. And the active life of the Gypsy reflects the culmination of Palamas's own struggles. (p. 46)

The poem is at the same time personal and objective. The Gypsy is a symbol of the poet's life with all the sufferings and wandering of thought, as well as a symbol of humanity with its aspirations and cultural transformations. . . . Thus *The Dodecalogue* combines all three of Palamas's lyricisms: the individual, the national, and the universal. (pp. 46-7)

The form of *The Dodecalogue* presents certain complications which stem mainly from the combination of several genres in a single work. Its epic, lyrical, and dramatic elements are almost equally strong. Palamas had intended to write an epic with the Gypsy as the hero, but the charge of his lyricism changed the nature of the poem. Under the lyrical requirements its mythical unity is interrupted by forward and reverse jumps in time and by changes in locale. . . . The lack of a definite mythical and temporal order is compensated by the effect of the lyrical sweep which gives a musical unity to the poem. Thus, *The Dodecalogue* can be seen as twelve lyrical movements unified by the poet's psychological unity. (pp. 47-8)

Palamas's Gypsy has many characteristics of the Romantic hero—passionate nature, love of freedom, and excessive individualism. But the Romantic fatalism and sense of final destruction are substituted in the Gypsy by his faith in a final unity with nature and society. The Gypsy as an individual always moves in relation to an objective background of nature or society. The subject constantly strives to relate himself with the objective world, and self-knowledge springs from his conflicts with society. Through a process of destructive and creative action, the Gypsy evolves from the free self that he was in **"The Arrival"** to the free social superman of the last three songs; from an individual instinctively aware of his race to a full conscious and purposeful social being in complete communion with all humanity.

In *The Dodecalogue* Palamas does not rise to the harmony of the ideal esthetic spheres that he sought in *Life Immovable*. Here he lives in the concrete world of human situations, and his verse is constantly charged with the emotions of human involvement on the level of moral and social action. And it is in the unity of self and society that the poet achieves self-realization. (p. 67)

All the essential ideas of Palamas are present in *The Dodecalogue*. His love of country, his Classicism, his science ideal, his poetic ideal, and his pantheism find their climactic formulation in this poem of Heraclitean movement and complexity. Palamas has drawn from many sources; folklore, memories of childhood, philosophical and literary works, science, and history, all contributed to its composition. *The Dodecalogue* is the triumph of the poet and, above all, a symbol of life in all its vitality and richness. (p. 68)

The most significant decade in Palamas's creative life closed with the publication of *The King's Flute* . . . , a long epico-lyric poem comparable, both in magnitude and in scope, to *The Dodecalogue of the Gypsy*. Taken together, the two poems present, in the widest terms, a position of the individual in the universe and a place of Hellenism in history; they reveal the poet's most complete vision of life centering on his perennial concern: Man-Hellenism. . . .

For the creation of the Gypsy, the idealized individual, a decadent world was suitable background, and Palamas depicted crumbling Byzantium for the poem's setting. But in writing *The King's Flute,* in which the national and human fate and ideals are examined, a glorious, triumphant moment in the history of Hellenism was more fitting for his purposes. Thus, he chooses eleventh-century Byzantium and Emperor Basil II, the Bulgar-Slayer, as his hero. Now that his concerns are more strictly social and national, an evocation of the glorious past would be a positive source of inspiration, a motive for action, to the defeated, post-1897 Greeks. (p. 69)

[Palamas's] hero is the great personage of history who shapes the destinies of peoples and determines the course of events; he is a mirror of Byzantine life and culture and, finally, a reflection of the poet's own personality and mission. . . . [The] search into the Byzantine soul and culture, is here the dominant concern. . . . [We] see the Byzantine spirit with all its conflicts and torments; we witness the unceasing battles of worldly and spiritual forces. The great war hero becomes the embodiment of human struggle exemplified by every mode of external and internal conflict. Strife is his very essence; the preservation of the empire and the salvation of his soul are his supreme duties and goals. Mingled with the glitter of imperial power, the intrigues and the bloody battles, we see the monastic yearning, the spiritual flame gasping for the absolute under the guidance of the gentle protectress of Byzantine Christendom he has come to worship. This is a great dramatic moment: to witness the hardened, ruthless, superhuman soul of the mighty warrior transformed into that of a humble worshiper of the Lady of Grace and Compassion; to see pity, love, and humility suddenly blooming in his praying soul. Here, naked before us, is the paradoxical nature of man consumed by the fire of Christian faith. The beast in

him, the greed for power, the madness of materiality and carnality, are incessantly opposed by the yearning for grace, by humility, by the spiritual passion for God. The warrior and the mystic, the killer and the saint live in one heart. One thinks of Dostoevsky and the terrible ambivalence of man. Palamas is torn by this ambivalence, the Passion and the Dream, and here he adds to it the sharpness and power of its Byzantine counterpart. (p. 97)

The first decade of the twentieth century is generally considered the culmination of Palamas's creative life. During this period, when Palamas was in his forties, each side of his personality—the lyricist, the visionary, the social revolutionary—found expression in his greatest works: *Life Immovable, The Dodecalogue of the Gypsy,* and *The King's Flute*. A fourth masterpiece, the play *Trisevgeni*, was also written during this decade. In this powerful drama Palamas captured, perhaps more fully than in any other work, the new spirit of Greece that he represented, the beauty and vitality of the demotic tradition and movement. These four works are at once his best and the most representative of his genius. (p. 105)

Thanasis Maskaleris, in his Kostis Palamas *(copyright © 1972 by Twayne Publishers, Inc.; reprinted with the permission of Twayne Publishers, a Division of G. K. Hall & Co., Boston), Twayne, 1972, 156 p.*

LINOS POLITIS (essay date 1973)

Critics have observed that a dualism exists in [Palamàs's] poetical thought, and that he hovers between two poles, accepting or rejecting both at once: on the one hand energetic action, affirmation, faith, and on the other retirement, denial, disbelief. But all these contradictions revolve round one central point, which we may call 'the meaning of art': the outlook and the volition of the poet. His work moves between two extremes, in a major or in a minor key. There are poems that are more lyrical, where he writes of home, of retirement, of the 'immovable' life (what he called 'lyricism of the Me'), and others ('lyricism of the Us') in which he extends his range into large epic compositions and 'great visions'. In his own day his poetry in the major key was over-estimated; it appears that it is his poetry in the minor key that has better stood the test of time. (pp. 157-58)

[His early volumes] do not yet express his personality; the poet is still struggling to free himself from the conventions and commonplaces of the time, and to set out on his own path.

This, we may say, was first achieved in *Countries*, a series of twelve fine Parnassian sonnets. . . . Then one important stage in his work follows another: [*Iambs and Anapaests* and *The Tomb*]. . . . The former is a small collection of forty poems in similar metres: three quatrains in which iambic and anapaestic verse alternates—a breaking up of the traditional fifteen-syllable line, and at the same time a reminiscence of Kalvos, whose musical verse particularly fascinated Palamàs at this time. We also discern something else in this collection, the first appearance of 'symbolism' in Greek poetry; the vague and the undefined, the extension of the meaning of words that the French *Symbolistes* sought, are here in *Iambs and Anapaests*. (p. 158)

[*The Tomb*] is also a small collection, and the poems are all on one subject, an elegy on the death of his little son. But the next collection, *Life Immovable* . . . , is one of his most important and one of the richest, including poems of the last decade, beginning with *Countries,* to which we made reference above. In compositions such as *The Return* or *Lines to a Well-Known Tune* the poet draws on reminiscences of his childhood and renders sounds 'that awake in him like sighs'. *The Palm-Tree,* a long poem in thirteen-syllable lines, is one of his most lyrical poems and, perhaps for this very reason, one of the most difficult to understand. It was written in 1900, and this year, the turning-point of one century into another, may be called a watershed in his poetry. In the years that followed, his inclination for large compositions, for 'great visions', will be dominant. He will abandon the pure lyricism of *The Palm-Tree.* First among the 'great visions', *The Ascraen* (i.e. Hesiod), a long and inspired poem in the same collection, is an attempt at a synthetic approach to the world, and is influenced by mystic theories and by Orphism.

The most representative of these 'visions' is his great poem, *The Dodecalogue of the Gipsy* . . . , divided into twelve 'words' (parts), and in a variety of rhythms, among which an entirely original free trochaic verse is dominant. The gipsy, the central personage, follows the path of negation, of a complete nihilism with regard to everyone and everything, until finally a violin reconciles him with life. The symbolism could easily become too obvious, but the poet escapes this danger by the wide range of his poem, which is sometimes near to pure epic, and at other moments has happy flashes of genuine lyric inspiration. Moreover the poet situated his action in a historical setting, on the eve of the fall of Constantinople, and this gives a richness of colour to its development; an interesting complication of the action is produced by an account of the flight of the Greek scholars from Constantinople to the West, and the burning of the works of the neo-Platonist Gemistòs-Plethon. In this manner (and it is this that is of most consequence) the ideas and problems of the poem are connected with the anxieties and struggles of the poet's own time. (pp. 159-60)

[*The King's Flute*] is a poetical appraisal of Byzantium at the height of its glory under the Macedonian dynasty and an account of the journey of Basil II into Greece proper as far as Athens (the symbol of the unity of the ancient with the Byzantine world, and of the continuity of modern Greek tradition). Palamàs considered this his most important work, but it may be doubted if poets are the best judges of their own works; the mere breadth of range is often fatiguing, the numerous innovations in the fifteen-syllable line end by destroying its traditional harmony, the manner of the poem is far more bookish than epic. But Palamàs's art is here seen at its full maturity, and in his handling of the language and the verse he introduces in a masterly way reminiscences both of learned and popular Byzantine texts. . . . (p. 160)

Palamàs collected what we might call his left-over lyrical poems in two volumes [*The Sorrows of the Lagoons* and *The City and the Solitude*]. . . . The lagoon is that of Missolonghi, and the poems are lyrical reveries about his life there. (pp. 160-61)

The City and the Solitude—the title is characteristic of what we called Palamàs's dualism—contains poems either on national subjects (the whole last book refers to the 1912 war, which had just broken out), or expressing the 'secret speech' of the soul (the **'Scent of the Rose'** is a minor masterpiece). The collection . . . *The Altars,* is more confined to the major

key, and contains many long compositions. . . . It is a collection of his prime.

After *The City and the Solitude, Untimely Poems* . . . suggest by their title that the poet thought their minor key ill adapted to a world that had just emerged from the First World War. The following volumes already show decline—the poet was over sixty. Often he republished old poems in a new recension or, following his passion for formal perfection, he devoted himself to the cultivation of one or another verse form: *The Fourteen Lines* (sonnets with a great deal of freedom in construction), *The Five-Syllables and the Pathetic Whispers.* . . . The *Timid and Cruel Verses* . . . are, as he wrote in the prologue, 'taken out of the bottom of drawers and out of envelopes belonging to every period of my life'—they make no addition to our general picture of him; we might say the same of *Passings and Greetings* . . . , his penultimate collected volume. On the other hand [*The Cycle of Quatrains* and even more *The Nights of Phemius*] . . . , his last collection, are distinguished by a different point of view. The poet of the great epic compositions, who had so often been blamed for grandiloquence, was now trying his voice in the limited range of the quatrain. His voice, indeed, no longer had its former vigour: it was low and elderly; but its sadness and its nostalgic reverie make it particularly appealing, his voluntary self-limitation to the simple metrical form often increases its expressiveness, and by his elliptical character of expression they acquire an almost dramatic tension. . . . (pp. 161-62)

We may say that Palamàs was, first and foremost, a poet; his personality is fully expressed in his eighteen volumes of poetry. His prose work is not remarkable; of the few short stories that he published between 1884 and 1900 the most important is *A Man's Death* where he exposes a typically Greek view of life and misfortune. His single theatrical work, *Trisevgeni* . . . , is particularly significant: a poetic drama in an age of realism in the theatre. The heroine is clearly drawn: an exceptional, uncompromising character whom other people do not understand, not even those who love her or are loved by her.

Finally, Palamàs wrote a number of articles in newspapers and periodicals. . . . Particular mention should be made of his polemical articles (he was always an advocate of the demotic language, and never wavered, even in difficult times), and also of his articles and essays on modern Greek literature. In a sense he is the first scholar of modern Greek letters; he wrote about all the personalities of modern Greek literature, and he spoke authoritatively and with the sharpness of a critic, the accuracy of a scholar, and the sensibility of a poet. (pp. 162-63)

> *Linos Politis, "The Generation of 1880; The New Athenian School; Kostis Palamàs," in his* A History of Modern Greek Literature *(© Oxford University Press 1973; reprinted by permission of Oxford University Press), Oxford University Press, Oxford, 1973, pp. 150-63.**

CHRISTOPHER ROBINSON (essay date 1974)

[A] cursory glance through the poetry of Costis Palamas . . . shows that Greece in the broadest sense provides him with a wide range of themes and images. (p. 41)

Palamas' writings about his own poetry are by no means free of contradictions and confusions. Yet, his central statement on the subject—*My Poetic* . . . —sets out certain useful guidelines. Palamas sees himself as a synthesist reconciling, both in terms of ideas and of poetic forms, elements normally regarded as incompatible. At the root of his work, he says, lies the struggle between intellect and emotion which typifies much late nineteenth-century European poetry. With this struggle are associated two opposing tendencies: scientific positivism and metaphysical idealism, the former encouraging the poet to absorb and express the facts of the world around him, the latter pressing him not to be satisfied with the limited truth of these physical phenomena. Both tendencies exist in each of the three basic divisions of his work, where he distinguishes *personal*, by which he means "lyricism of the *I*," *temporal*, or "lyricism of the *we*," and *general*, or "lyricism of the *all*." (As these are rather awkward phrases in English, I shall use the terms *self*, *group*, and *totality* to represent them. (p. 42)

In his first published collection, *Songs of my Homeland* . . . , the emphasis is on patriotic verse of the crudest type, particularly in the first and last of the four sections, the eponymous **"Songs of the Homeland"** and the **"War Songs."** . . . The opening poem, **"New Year Presents,"** sets the key for the major trends of the whole work. It is a dialogue between poet and country in which Greece proclaims that all she asks of the poet is the return of her old glories, both politically in the heroic images and culturally in that it is the poet's task to achieve the return of glory. The images themselves join the folksong tradition of the young hero with a body as supple and strong as a lion and the land born of the nereids with the symbol of Byzantium, the double-headed eagle. . . . (p. 46)

Where there is a Byzantine patina to the material, it is designed for propaganda purposes and devoid of genuine exploration of national roots. So **"Skyloyiannis"** is primarily anti-Bulgarian emotionalism: Palamas specifically works in a quite unhistorical picture of all Macedonia as obsessed by its Greekness. . . . Empty chauvinistic rhetoric of the worst sub-Kipling variety! However, among this unprepossessing plethora of Romantic distortions there is, particularly in the two central sections of the collection, poetry of a very different kind. **"Songs of the Lake"** transfer the would-be historical image of Mesolonghi to the private one of the poet's childhood memories of the place. Greece becomes a living geographical entity, if a somewhat idealized one. Artlessly the poet sings in praise of the simple life of the fisherfolk, and a folktale like the "sunborn girl" is used to express purely private emotions. . . . This greater sensitivity to the living Greece is not confined to poems of the "self." There are more objective transcriptions of village life and customs, together with imitation folksongs like the tale **"The mirror of St. John,"** in which the bridegroom whom the beautiful village maiden sees in her mirror is Death come to take her away.

What can be detected in this mélange is an attempted, though as yet unsuccessful, resolution of the portrayal of the self with that of the group. Palamas uses a generalized rustic evocation of Greece with a set pattern of historical reference, mostly to the siege of Mesolonghi, plus a certain amount of medieval and Byzantine material reflecting similar heroic values. . . .

[But] the would-be rustic simplicity of the folk-tale style in which [this patriotic verse] is all dressed, though it is intended to avoid Romantic rhodomontade by giving a greater realism to the abstractions, is too vaguely observed, too traditionally folksy to be convincing. In practice the assumption of rusticity when assimilated to patriotic sentiment has the effect of emphasizing the emotional naivete of both elements at the expense of any true Wordsworthian simplicity.

So far Palamas has toyed with history, contemporary politics, folklore, and has set patriotic and personal material side by side. But there has been no convincing integration of the different levels into a new vision. The second major work, the *Hymn to Athena,* . . . shows a significant advance in this respect. The theme of the poem is an address to the patron goddess of Athens, which starts with her birth on Olympus, progresses through the mythology associated with her as far as the founding of the city, and closes on a great speech by the goddess to her new creation. (pp. 46-8)

In *Hymn* the ideals of classical wisdom and virtue are evoked through mythological symbols for the first time in Palamas' poetry. (p. 48)

Although the *Hymn to Athena* marks a progress in Palamas' attempts to blend different levels of Greek tradition, it is still an immature work. Except for the symbol of the olive tree, the evocation of natural features is descriptive and therefore inadequately linked to the overtly symbolic mythological material, while some of the latter seems to owe its place more to the scholarly imitation of Ovid and the Homeric Hymns than, to any creative function in its context. The patriotic message itself is largely confined to rhetorical generalities, and the overall effect has more than a hint of that very ancestor-worship on which Palamas poured scorn, rather than living up to his ideal that the ancient spirit should provide living symbols for the thoughts and feelings of the modern. (pp. 49-50)

The Eyes of my Soul [is] the work that marks the beginning of [his period] of greatest poetic achievement. . . . The key values of the collection are beauty, bravery, and virtue, symbolized by the three figures on the Cerameicus tombs in the poem of that name. Beauty is the aesthetic perfection of classical art, as in **"Niobe,"** where the emotions aroused by the famous bowl representing the death of the Niobids . . . are recreated. Virtue is the upholding of certain abstract standards, as truth, in the poem of that name, and justice in **"Birth of the Lily."** Bravery is the willingness to defend a cause and die for it, as in the opening stanzas of the Hydriot proclamation. . . . (p. 50)

The various values are made to interrelate, both among themselves, with bravery and virtue becoming functions of beauty, and with outside forces, notably nature. Thus in **"The Cerameicus Tombs"** the first section **"Hymn to Life,"** an exultant hymn to the beauty of the natural surroundings, is juxtaposed with **"O Graves,"** which develops the idea of the past living on through the art of the grave carvings. In the main body of the poem the three graves, Dexileos the young hero, the wife of Agathon, and Hegeso the fair maid, stand respectively for Bravery, Virtue and Beauty, but they share the refrain: "O joy, O victory of life, unheard of happiness in the marble Elysium, Elysium of Art." Art gives each of these archaic voices the power to speak to those sensitive to their "secret tones," and thus to convey the eternal truths which they embody. (p. 51)

In the **"Cerameicus Tombs"** the poet had presented himself as the interpreter of the "secret voices" of the classical past. Now he extends the role to that of the man who by his art will give back life to the dumb heritage of the past by rekindling its symbolic power. Already we are approaching a synthetic vision of the meaning of Greece within the modern world.... If the poetry is still inclined to angular rhetoric and infelicitous images, it is technical command that the poet lacks rather than a clear understanding of his own vision. (pp. 52-3)

What Palamas achieves for the first time in *Homelands* is the resolution of the different aspects of Greece into a harmonious and expressive force within the *self*. These are intensely personal poems in which the poet explores the roots of his own creative impulse.... The sense of time as a barrier is eradicated by the interplay of physical, cultural and religious references from different periods. The space-time continuum is complete.... The relevance of past to present, not merely for the poet's self but for the group in which he functions, has found an expression which combines the artistic control of imagery developed in *Homelands* with the ideas tentatively and gauchely projected in *The Eyes of my Soul*. The combination of public and private affliction caused by the 1897 Greco-Turkish debacle and the death in 1898 of the poet's much loved little son Alkis delayed the further exploitation of this newly synthesized sense of nationality. Palamas concentrated on personal poetry which, where it used essentially Greek material, tended to prefer the limited range offered by Greek myth and folklore, as in the poem-cycle *The Tomb* written in remembrance of Alkis.... When, with "The Palm Tree" ... he returns to a concern with man's place in a wider scheme of things, it is the *totality* that concerns him rather that the group. The poem is not of direct interest here because its imagery is drawn almost exclusively from nature, centering on a palm tree familiar to the poet and on some small blue flowers that habitually grew in its shade. Out of this simple material grows an enquiry into the nature of creator and creation.... "The Palm Tree" also introduces the theme of the Orphic life-cycle, the necessary process of corruption and decay before new growth can occur, an idea whose application to the rotten state of Greece was to provide the stimulus the poet needed for a return to a positive and optimistic exploration of national material....

It is *The Ascraen* ... that for the first time brings together this faith in the symbolic power of the Greek past, the evocation of nature and the belief in the importance of the poet to the *group*. There is hardly one of Palamas' major symbols that is not employed in the work. As in the later *Dodecalogue of the Gipsy* and *The King's Flute* the symbolism is often at two levels, firstly the strictly personal, which is not always clearly formulated even in the mind of the poet himself, and secondly the universal. The outline of the poem, of which the first half closely follows Hesiod's *Works and Days*, represents approximately the reappearance of the poet Hesiod on earth, his account of his life, his vision of the Muses, his destruction at the hands of woman, subsequent experience in Hades, and his return to meet Palamas, to whom he imparts his spirit, thus making him his cultural heir. The dominant theme is therefore that of poetic immortality, the modern writer inheriting the poetic secrets of the world from the ancient one.... (pp. 54-6)

What is notable about *The Ascraean* is that, though it represents an expansion in the use of the "Greece as space-time continuum" theme from a purely personal to a partially metaphysical function and though it is one of the first examples of Palamas' fascination with Orphism and its application to the predicament of modern man, it shows, in limiting itself

to myth and literary allusion drawn from exclusively classical sources, a reduction in the richness of Greek material found in *Homelands* and *Iambs and Anapaests*. This richness is restored in the *Dodecalogue of the Gipsy*.... This epico-lyric poem embodies, for the purposes of the present study, a seeming paradox. The theme is of the gipsy (the poet) who, seeking to contribute to society and to embrace its beliefs, is rebuffed by his fellows and repelled by the inadequacies of their creeds. Eventually, after the final collapse of civilization, he finds his true rôle as a creative artist who will be the voice of the new Nietzschean world that rises from the ashes of the old. Now, both the choice of the isolated gipsy figure and the theme of the necessary degeneracy of society before its rebirth involve a rejection of *homelands*.... Yet, nine of the twelve cantos are built up on Greek themes, not only in the pictures of the decline of Byzantium which form the basic symbols for the cycle of decay, but also in the Orpheus myth of the final canto, where the gipsy achieves his true status. The use of these themes cannot be dismissed as the mere illustration of abstractions, which could be exchanged equally well with other non-Greek images. They have an essential part in the sequence of juxtaposed images of which the poem is composed and whose non-rational succession is calculated to create a related series of emotional responses in the reader. Their Greekness, therefore, is one of the elements that must engage the reader's sympathy as much as contribute to his revulsion with a particular facet of society. In fact, considered more closely, our original paradox resolves itself. Palamas' by now familiar distinction between creative and non-creative use of the Greek past is here expanded into a distinction between creative and non-creative response to the total concept of *homeland*. (pp. 57-8)

Palamas castigates the non-creative response to the past in those around him. He tries to exemplify the creative response in himself. The destruction-rebirth cycle which is to symbolize past, present and future of the Greek nation is new in the sense that it incorporates many ideas taken from Nietzsche's *Thus spake Zarathustra*, but the symbols which give life to these ideas also depend on a close identification with the elements of the Orphic cycle.... In the *Dodecalogue* the decline symbolized by the collapse of Byzantium over the first seven cantos, the moment of annihilation in canto 8, and the consequent birth of a new and purified world in the following three cantos, forms one complete cycle. To complete the symbolism, having used Orphic beliefs as fundamental images of the human condition, Palamas identifies his own creative powers, in the last canto (as at the end of the *Ascraean*), with those of Orpheus himself, whose lyre, like the poet-gipsy's violin, gave him the power to move nature. So the poem uses the Orphic cycle to express all three levels of *lyricism*, Palamas' private need for regeneration as an artist, the way in which the pessimistic Greek society of the post-1897 debacle period should begin to move toward a new national identity, and the philosophical conviction that a cyclic pattern should be seen as an inevitability in cultural and political history alike. (pp. 59-60)

[In *The King's Flute*], for the first time the full synthesis of Greek themes achieves entirely positive expression. The twelve cantos of the poem develop a single historical theme, the glories of Basil II the Bulgar-slayer and his great march to pay homage to the Virgin Mary in the Parthenon.... What the poem conveys is, in fact, an intensely emotional definition of Greek consciousness, an aggressive Romantic call to patriotic revival completely at odds with the contemporary realist affection for a declining civilization expressed by Cavafy in a poem like "Demetrius Soter." (p. 61)

Although he wrote much poetry after *The King's Flute,* little is added—as far as Greek themes and images go—to the picture already composed. Greek victories in the Balkan Wars took much of the steam out of political patriotism, and though *Altars* . . . maintains the theme of moral, political and cultual regeneration, it merely continues to exploit the same, albeit matured, vision of Greece as space-time continuum. . . . *The Wolves* . . . betrays a raw nationalism that, in all but technical command, is a reversion to the hate-inspired allegories of *Songs of my Homeland.* (pp. 63-4)

Greece in the poetry of Palamas is . . . an entity that develops gradually from the bald Romantic nationalism of the early works to a new kind of creative patriotic vision in *The King's Flute.* Myth and folk legend, classical philosophy and Orthodox religion, ancient aesthetics and mediaeval iconography, the heroes of Athens, Byzantium and the War of Independence, all are brought together into a view of Greece where the values of the past are organically subsumed into the forms and ideas of the present and future. Similarly, what comes to the poet from outside Greece through his reading of Taine, Hegel, Nietzsche and Ibsen is reexpressed in native symbols, the new finding communication in the old. By drawing on the unseen but everpresent Greek essence, Palamas feels he can best express both what is essential to him as individual and what is common to the world around him. Greece is the symbol of the totality, and in it the *I* and the *We* find their meaning. Though history proved Palamas wrong on a political plane, nothing can undermine the emotional validity of the lyric poetry in which he clothed his vision. (p. 64)

Christopher Robinson, "Greece in the Poetry of Costis Palamas," in Review of National Literatures *(copyright © 1974 by St. John's University), Vol. V, No. 2, Fall, 1974, pp. 41-65.*

ADDITIONAL BIBLIOGRAPHY

Dimaris, C. Th. "Palamas: The New Synthesis." In his *A History of Modern Greek Literature,* translated by Mary P. Gianos, pp. 394-421. Albany: State University of New York Press, 1972.*
    Analysis of the literary and historical influences on the work of Palamas and his contemporaries.

Phoutrides, Aristides E. *"Life Immovable."* In *Life Immovable,* by Kostes Palamas, translated by Aristides E. Phoutrides, pp. 55-67. Cambridge: Harvard University Press, 1919.
    A survey of the poems that appear in Palamas's collection entitled *Life Immovable.*

Phoutrides, Aristides E. "Hesiodic Reminiscences in the 'Ascraean' of Kostes Palamas." In *"A Hundred Voices" and Other Poems from the Second Part of "Life Immovable",* by Kostes Palamas, translated by Aristides E. Phoutrides, pp. 21-38. Cambridge: Harvard University Press, 1921.
    Comparison of Palamas's poem "Ascraean" with the Hesiod's *Works and Days.*

Thomson, George. Introduction to *The Twelve Lays of the Gypsy,* by Kostis Palamas, pp. 1-24. London: Lawrence & Wishart, 1969.
    Study of the political and philosophical influences affecting Palamas's life and work. The critic employs a socialist perspective to analyze the structure and themes of *Twelve Lays.*

Władysław Stanisław Reymont

1867-1925

(Born Stanisław Władysław Rejment) Polish novelist, short story writer, and journalist.

Reymont was a major figure in Polish literature in the first quarter of the twentieth century. He opposed the proindustrial positivist movement in order to depict realistically the lives of peasants and the urban proletariat. His literary reputation rests on the tetralogy *Chłopi (The Peasants)*, which critics praise for its sweeping, epical quality, finely drawn characterizations, and skillful rendering of the peasant idiom.

The son of a poor village couple, Reymont grew up near the industrial town of Lodz. Having had little formal education, he pursued a number of occupations—actor, novice monk, tailor, and railway clerk—before devoting himself entirely to literature. He began his literary career by contributing short stories and journalistic pieces to various Polish newspapers and journals. *Pielgrzymka do Jasnej Gory*, a fictional account of the traditional religious journey to the holy shrine in Czestochowa, first brought him to the attention of literary critics. The hallmarks of his mature style, such as keen observation of people and their behavior, and poetic description of the Polish countryside, are already apparent in this early short story. Severely injured in a railroad accident, Reymont was awarded a settlement large enough to allow him to travel and undertake large literary projects.

Reymont's style and methods were greatly influenced by the schools of literary thought developing in Europe: critics discern the characteristics of naturalism, realism, and symbolism in his writing. He tended to work in thematic cycles derived from his varied and colorful background. A recurring subject of his work was the theater; his first novel, *Komediantka (The Comedienne)*, is a naturalistic study of a young actress's experiences traveling with a seedy theatrical company. He soon repudiated the tenets of naturalism, however, believing the style to be contrived, and attempted an objective, realistic portrait of the rapidly industrializing Lodz. The resulting novel, *Ziemia obiecana (The Promised Land)*, is both an exposé of the town's ruthless industrial magnates, and sociological and psychological analysis of its ethnic groups and social classes.

Disgusted with the corruption and squalor wreaked by uncontrolled industrialization, Reymont turned his attention to depicting the rural village life he knew as a youth. The resulting work, *The Peasants*, is considered by many critics to be as masterful a portrait of peasantry as those of Hardy, Zola, or Verga. In this novel Reymont infuses realistic portrayal with symbolism and myth. Using highly lyrical, subjective language, he tells the story of a father and son in love with the same woman, Yagna, whom critics have called "the Polish Tess." The classical theme of incest, the conflict between collective morality and individual passion, and a four-part structure based on the recurring cycle of the seasons, all contribute to the novel's timelessness and epic grandeur. *The Peasants* marks the zenith of Reymont's career. In 1924 he was awarded the Nobel Prize in literature.

Although Reymont later published historical fiction and works dealing with spiritualism and the occult, he did not again enjoy

the critical and popular success generated by *The Peasants*. Critical reception of his work has not always been positive: faults commonly cited by critics are exaggeration, melodrama, and a tendency toward prolixity. But if Reymont's popularity has waned, he is nevertheless credited with producing a monumental novel of enduring worth and interest.

PRINCIPAL WORKS

Pielgrzymka do Jasnej Gory (travel essay) 1894; published in journal *Prawda*
Komediantka (novel) 1896
  [*The Comedienne,* 1920]
Fermenty (novel) 1897
Ziemia obiecana (novel) 1899
  [*The Promised Land,* 1927]
*Jesien (novel) 1904
*Zima (novel) 1904
*Wiosna (novel) 1906
*Lato (novel) 1909
**Ostatni Sejm Rzeczypospolitej (historical novel) 1911
**Nil desperandum (historical novel) 1916
**Insurekcya (historical novel) 1918

389

Chłopi (novel) 1921
  [*The Peasants,* 1924-25]

*These volumes were collected under the title *Chłopi* in 1921.
**These volumes were collected under the title *Rok 1794* in 1946.

ADOLPH STENDER-PETERSEN   (essay date 1925)

[Wladislaw Stanislaw] Reymont knows his country as few other writers. . . . The scenes he had witnessed, the misery and the beauty among which he had lived, the confusion and the calm, whether found in country or city, became material for novels, long or short, diffuse or concise, but always well told, and produced with the same natural regularity as that with which the apple ripens on the tree, deepens in color, and then drops into the greedy hands of men.

From his pious journey to Czenstochowa dates his *Pilgrimage to Jasna Gora,* one of his first novels. To the tragic features of the barnstormers' life the novels . . . [*Lilli* and *The Comedienne*] bear witness. About the life of the railroad men we read in *Ferments* and *The Dreamer.* The sufferings of the Polish peasants during the war he describes in his masterly sketches *Behind the Front.* . . . (pp. 167-68)

On a single occasion he tried his hand as an historical writer, in the novel *The Year 1794,* and though that year signifies Poland's greatest degradation, it is characteristic of Reymont's unshakable faith in his people that the novel does not describe how the country fell, but how it carried within itself, even then, the seeds of a resurrection, power for new historic deeds. . . . It is the heroic figure of Kosciuszko which rises before the reader; it is the proud motto of Kollontaj, '*Nil Desperandum,*' which is made the slogan of the whole nation.

Only once has Reymont tried to describe life in a big city, in the novel *The Promised Land,* and here, with a realistic power, strongly influenced by Zola, he made a soulless and shapeless conglomeration of the industrial city of Lodz,— the object of his colorful description,—without hiding or softening the immorality which is so characteristic of factory towns. But it was not his natural field; he soon returned to his original element, the Polish peasants. . . .

In [*Chłopi (The Peasants),* a] big and yet perfectly balanced work, he has found a new expression for his poetic individuality without surrendering his original characteristics. In it he has been able to unite his objective realism in the reproduction of concrete facts with a passionate and yet externally perfectly controlled personal interpretation of the mystery of nature, of life, and of the human soul; and he has created a synthesis of his own self.

In its union of a finely chiseled plasticism with a heavy, musical, fundamental pathos, in its deep, strong, swelling lyricism, in its mood and its attitude toward the world, lies the real charm of this 'neo-naturalism.' (p. 168)

In four big panoramas he unfolds the peasant's simple, patriarchical, and at times disturbed, circle of life. Autumn, winter, spring, and summer, the zenith of life, pass slowly by the reader. Leisurely we progress with the peasant through the seasons, attend his festivals, participate in his toil, suffer with him in his sorrows, and rejoice with him in his joy. Like him we bend before Nature's great laws, trailing along the

eternal *Circulus vitiosus,* from life to death, and back to life again. Like threads of silver, fine symbolic traits shine through the even surface of the narrative, and a poetic brilliancy and an almost Homeric pathos, the arch-Polish *abundantia rerum,* pervade the entire work, appearing strongest in the rhythm of the language, which rises and falls, but never rests.

Its characters, placed against the background of Polish scenery, are plastic and tangible, but they never emerge from the context as independently living figures. They form a unit with nature, the forest, the land, the mud. They exist only in so far as they are part of this environment, part of this peasant race. (pp. 168-69)

The Peasants is the final summing up of Reymont's fruitful life, in comparison with which everything he had written before or has produced since pales into insignificance. In the annals of Polish literature *The Peasants* will be noted as the masterpiece of a master, and in 'world literature' it will take rank as a classic. (p. 169)

> Adolph Stender-Petersen, "Reymont, Winner of the Nobel Prize," in The Living Age *(copyright 1925, by the Living Age Co.), Vol. CCCXXIV, No. 4202, January 17, 1925, pp. 165-69.*

JOSEPH WOOD KRUTCH   (essay date 1925)

If one may judge from the two volumes already published ["**Autumn**" and "**Winter**"], "**The Peasants**" is a work which will be read with growing respect. It is obviously intended to present a complete panorama of the life of the Polish peasant, and it gathers force somewhat slowly because it is planned upon a truly gigantic scale; but the interest mounts steadily, and one finishes the instalments already published with the feeling that from the first page to the last there has been slowly built up a structure which becomes more and more impressive as it is seen more and more as a whole. Seldom has a book been written with an air of more calm or unhurried confidence. The author seems to have unlimited time at his disposal and (what is a good deal more important) to know exactly what he intends to do with it. At first he seems to begin almost at random, so that the imagination of the reader hardly knows what to do with the profusion of material which is given it. Gradually, however, the innumerable details relate themselves one to another. The village and its life take on a solid substantiality; one is in the presence of a microcosm of whose definite existence there can be no doubt.

Whatever greatness or defects the finished work may reveal, one thing is sure: the novel is an amazing piece of literary architecture. It is not always possible to see the relations of the parts to one another, because the framework upon which they are organized is not always evident to the mind; but what the reader does not see he feels. The author has conceived and held in his mind some plan of articulation as effective as it is complicated. The various activities of the village—its feasts, its ceremonies, its labors, and its tragedies—seem to belong to some living whole, and it is this community existence which the author has managed to dramatize. The novel has its central characters, but in actuality it is not about them that the interest centers. The whole of which they are a part is the real subject of the book. They are merely one of the means by which this whole is typified.

It is peasant life, not the life of any particular peasant, which Reymont is treating. . . .

That the four volumes are given the names of the four seasons is no accident or affectation. Throughout the entire action the movements of nature—the recurrent seasons and their appropriate phenomena—are integrated with the activities of man. The recurrent pains and pleasures of the peasants keep step with the mighty rhythm of the earth. Reymont sees his people as something at once less and more than individuals; he sees them as natural phenomena, parts of the great whole in which the mighty swing of the earth about the sun is linked in inseparable union with the bursting of the smallest bud upon the tiniest herb. Essentially Christian though his ethical scheme seems to be, there is something pantheistic in his feeling for the oneness of all nature. No ancient could have conceived a work of art composed of such an infinitude of details, though when Theocritus described his shepherds or Lucretius addressed his prayer to the mighty mother of all things each was moved, I think, by a sense of the unity of the universe not essentially different from that which has animated the author of **"The Peasants."**

There are signs to indicate that the story, properly so called, of the central characters is to occupy a place of increasing importance. Perhaps it will come in the end to seem the center of the reader's interest, but the total impression of the book will remain, I think, the one just described; and it will be great, less as a novel in the ordinary sense than as a remarkably sustained development of an essentially poetic, almost religious, idea.

> *Joseph Wood Krutch, "Earth's Diurnal Course,"* in The Nation *(copyright 1925 The Nation magazine, The Nation Associates, Inc.), Vol. 120, No. 3107, January 21, 1925, p. 73.*

EDWIN BJORKMAN   (essay date 1925)

Viewed in retrospect through the more vivid pages of ["Winter,"] "Autumn" appears already in a new perspective. Even then that earlier part must be held too deliberate in its movement, too long drawn out, too overburdened with details having but a slight connection with the human dramas furnishing the backbone of the whole series. But as a mere prelude to a story growing in tenseness and significance with each new episode it commands a patience and suspension of judgement hard to grant it when seen starkly by itself.

"Winter" marks unquestionably a great improvement in several respects. The action gathers speed and suspense. The characters are no longer stagnant. There are several scenes of compelling power. . . .

What [M. Reymont] wishes to bring home to us is not the life of this or that individual, whether good or bad, great or small, but the life of a people, of a whole human group of a certain class, living on a certain plane and in a given environment. His ultimate hero is not Borynn or Antek, saintlike Roch or the basely scheming Matthew, but the Polish peasant as a collective being. In this sense his conception is truly epic, and as such it must be viewed with profound respect. . . .

[Some] reservations nevertheless remain with me, even at this time, concerning M. Reymont's execution of his impressive design. I continue, though more regretfully than before, to regard his work as too top-heavy with details

which, however interesting they may be ethnographically, yet tend to distract the attention from what, after all, should be a dramatic presentation of human joys and sorrows and envies and hardships and triumphs.

There are too many words for the thing to be told; too many exaggerations vainly used to sweep our emotions along with the force of a wintery blast from those immense plains; too many artificially colored enumerations deliberately reminiscent of greater epics, written when man's every-day life still made that the most natural mood for his poetic self-expression. . . .

As a vivid and faithful record of human life seen collectively and comprehensively at a given time and place, ["**The Peasants**"] deserves high praise and is well worth reading. Judged as a piece of art pure and simple, as a masterpiece worthy of the world's highest literary distinction, it is to me not without grave flaw.

> *Edwin Bjorkman, "More Reymont," in* The Literary Review *(copyright, 1925, by N.Y. Evening Post, Inc.), January 24, 1925, p. 3.*

ANNIE RUSSELL MARBLE   (essay date 1925)

[In *The Peasants*], Reymont became the "mouthpiece of the peasant and rural elements." Combined with Reymont's devotion to the peasant village as "protagonist," is his passion for Nature in her varied aspects; hence he made his divisions of the book to show the four seasons. Like Thomas Hardy and George Meredith he uses Nature as a vital personality in his story, aiding or restraining the development of his leading characters, especially Yagna, who has been called "a Polish Tess." The English author is superior in condensation and dramatic sympathy. (p. 272)

In *The Peasants*, the slow movement is varied by scenes of intense emotion, like the marriage festival in *Autumn*, or the death of Kuba. . . . In addition to specific, haunting situations, there are interwoven customs and legends and a wonderful collection of Polish proverbs (a mine of literature!). Passions of love and hate and revenge, the constant excess of vodka and clouded minds, fear of landlord and slumbering revolt against the loss of forest lands and oncoming industrial domination—such are significant factors in this panoramic novel. In the background is the dull color of the soil, the rank smells and fragrant odors of farmyards and woods, sunsets of splendor, and terrifying storms. (pp. 272-73)

Many passages in this novel are repugnant to Anglo-Saxon aesthetic tastes, if one is unable to assimilate the raw sordidness of many modern stories of the soil, with the passages of emotional vigor and poetic beauties. Reymont has revealed, in panoramic form, the life of the Polish peasant, typified in the family and associates of Boryna; he has treated his big theme with psychological insight, realistic photography, and robust idealism. The first and second volumes seem more spontaneous and dramatic than the later. (pp. 273-74)

[Despite] his faults of diffuseness and unevenness of structure, Reymont is gifted in depicting the small and large interests of the Polish peasant, in revealing their aspirations and dormant passion for freedom.

As an example of "the novel of the soil," so close to earth that the reader often finds his senses are keen and that other faculties are almost dormant, [*The Peasants*] by Reymont proclaims him a masterful interpreter of peasant life. In every volume there are lapses of interest and diffuseness. In retrospect, however, the many monotonous pages will be forgotten and the outstanding scenes of passionate love, hatred, suffering, and primitive ecstasy will remain in memory as tributes to this . . . Polish novelist who is listed among the Nobel prize winners in literature. (pp. 275-76)

> *Annie Russell Marble, "Honors to Polish Fiction,"*
> *in her* The Nobel Prize Winners in Literature, *D.*
> *Appleton and Company, 1925 (and reprinted by*
> *Appleton, 1927), pp. 264-76.**

ERNEST BOYD (essay date 1925)

[*The Promised Land*] is a book which will remind readers of Zola's *Germinal* as the vast, turbulent, swarming picture itself is completely influenced by the Naturalist technic. Its weakness lies in the author's failure to develop effectively the contrast between the exploiters and the exploited, a contrast which is discreetly suggested in deference, obviously, to the susceptibilities of the censorship. His analysis is in parts excellent, but his synthesis is weak; he is without fundamental ideas, and the book best serves as a mirror of external circumstances. (p. 285)

The Promised Land was an earnest of what [Reymont] was finally to accomplish in *The Peasants*. With such minor efforts as the two thrillers, *The Vampire* and *Opium Smokers*, we need not delay. A lengthy historical novel, *The Year 1794*, marks his failure to do the inevitable three-volume romance, in the Sienkiewicz manner, of the former grandeur of Poland, this time at Grodno, during the last year of the independent Polish parliament. His theme is the contrast between the refined world in the whirl of its enjoyments and the masses whose patriotic remnant saved the ark of nationalism in the flood which overwhelmed and destroyed old Poland, when Kosciusko fell. Reymont has not . . . the picturesque facility of a Sienkiewicz, and when he does not entirely possess and dominate his material there is no compensation in the shape of mere narrative entertainment as Dumas understood it. This novel is one of the least successful of Reymont's works.

His most successful is *The Peasants*, which is not so much a novel as a prose epic, elemental, undidactic, and primitive, full of a natural poetry, narrating the life and adventures of a village rather than telling the story of a hero and heroine. The very order of the volumes is significant, for the rural year begins in autumn, and ends in summer with the harvesting which is the final splendid picture upon which Reymont closes. His four parts are not dictated by artistic considerations; they are not four acts of a drama, for there is no culminating point in the third volume, *Spring*, which is actually the most monotonous and ineffectual of them all. They are simply the four stages of life as lived by and for the soil. The woman of destiny, the mystic Helen, who is the human pivot about which the village epic revolves, is the traditional figure since Homer, the woman for whom men destroy themselves, the temptress who is herself the victim of love. Yagna comes between father and son, she becomes the scourge of virtue, and is dramatically humiliated and punished in the end. The rivalry of Antek and his father supplies the slender thread of what must be accepted in lieu of a plot, but their story is but an incident in a vast panorama of events.

To compare Yagna to Tess of the d'Urbervilles is misleading, for her tragedy is incidental and almost impersonal, in the sense that the woman herself is never individualized, but simply fulfils her rôle as the element of sex in this ambitious unfolding of every aspect of rural existence in Poland. Reymont is a chronicler, amazingly sensitive to direct impressions, utterly unconcerned with rationalization and analysis. We witness the peasant at every hour of his day, through the four seasons of his year, as he ploughs, sows, and harvests; as he tends his cattle, feeds his family, and transacts his business at the fairs. The eternal acts of all who have tilled the soil from the beginning of time are here, together with all the wealth of local and picturesque detail which fixes these scenes in Poland particularly: marriage ceremonies and quaint superstitions, religious fervor and brutal merrymaking, the revolt of the farmer against the landed gentleman, the revolt of the Pole against the foreign oppressor. At each season the setting, atmosphere, and gestures merge into a harmonious whole, so intimate and inevitable is the bond holding these peasants to the soil and identifying their every movement with the rhythms of nature. The relative flatness of the third part, *Spring*, may even be explained by the fact that in Poland the awakening of spring is not the joyous bursting forth of life, but a moment of crisis, of painful adjustments amongst a peasantry whose labors have not carried them on easily from one harvest to another. It is a transition period of privation.

Even in English it is possible to discern the natural charm and poetry of Reymont's writing, which has been highly praised by Polish critics. His descriptions are marvels of vividness and accuracy, smacking of the soil and revealing direct observation rather than literary cunning. (pp. 285-87)

The position of Wladyslaw Reymont in the literature of Young Poland is a peculiar one, for, apart from his style and his preoccupation with the minor bourgeoisie and peasants, he belongs to the tradition of [Henryk] Sienkiewicz. . . . Reymont's connection with this literature was accidental, as all the circumstances of his life were remote from literary movements and the play of ideas. He is not an intellectual, but perhaps for that reason he could better catch the qualities of rural life which he has transferred to *The Peasants*, in a manner which renders that saga of nature a unique, if not an absolutely first-rate work of modern literature. (pp. 288-89)

> *Ernest Boyd, "Wladyslaw Reymont," in his* Studies
> from Ten Literatures *(copyright © 1925 by Charles*
> *Scribner's Sons), Scribner's, 1925, pp. 281-93.*

R. DYBOSKI (essay date 1926)

It was in [his first works, *The Comedienne* and *Ferments*, novels about the lives of travelling actors,] that Reymont, regardless of the clamour of conflict between the literary schools of Poland at the time, resolutely and independently chose his path as a literary artist—a path identical with that of the greatest modern French masters of the novel—the path of realism pure and simple. Unafraid of the charges of banality and of want of moral discrimination, he henceforward remains faithful to this creed throughout his literary practice.

This principle of unflinching realism leads Reymont to his first great success in *The Promised Land*, a fascinating picture of industrial life in the town of Łódź, the Polish Manchester; with its swarms of German, Jewish, and Polish business men and mere adventurers. The description of *milieu*—the strong side of Zola and his school—is already here carried through with the hand of a mature master: the reader seems to pass bodily from the tastelessly furnished drawing-rooms of millionaires to their squalid factories, from the theatre to the church, from the public-house to the street, and from the town into the country around.

But no less a gift than that of accurately recording and expressively presenting a *milieu*, consists in the teeming vitality of Reymont's imagination, which continually pours forth a stream of varied human figures. (pp. 557-58)

[*The Peasants*] was at first conceived, like Reymont's former novels, as a *roman naturaliste* in the fashion of, say, Zola's *La Terre*. But, outgrowing this design, it became that seemingly impossible thing—a modern prose epic. For it is, in its complete majesty, not a novel at all. In four volumes, called after the four seasons, it presents scenes from the immemorial yearly round of life in a small, out-of-the-way village of Russian Poland. The really outstanding events of the story are connected with the periodical events in the realm of nature: seed-time and harvest, autumn rains and winter snows are the framework; peasant customs and traditions connected with them furnish the colouring; and the elemental passions of a family drama—love and greed—rage with a force drawn from daily communion with the pitiless laws of animal and vegetable life. . . . The central figures—the old man, and his young wife who becomes the mistress of his son—stand out against the eternal background of the country in the stark grandeur of a tragic pathos bare of all trappings of social circumstance, race, and creed. The woman—the *grande amoureuse* of the village—turns almost into a symbol of the ruthless force of love in nature—a Lucretian *Venus genetrix* in Polish peasant garb; and symbolism of the peasant's hereditary instinct for struggle with the Earth for her fruits is present in the death-scene of her husband, who drops down in the moonlit furrows, pretending to sow in his delirium. Men and the soil are one in the work: landscape is hardly ever painted for its own sake, but always as interwoven with the unending bustle of the human puppets which the Earth beholds with the same "terrible composure" as Hardy's Egdon Heath looking on their tragedies. (pp. 558-59)

After having accomplished the great creative effort of his life, Reymont looked back, as if in relaxation, on the beginnings of his career, and returned, in **The Dreamer,** a largely autobiographical novel, to the scenes of his early days as a railway clerk. In another story of this later period, called **The Vampire,** we are taken into the mysterious under-world of London; and the belief in occult phenomena, which possessed Reymont in his last years, is made manifest for the first time.

After such diversions, Reymont braced himself for another large task, and entered the field of the historical novel, illuminated by the genius of [Henryk] Sienkiewicz. To Sienkiewicz's memorable *Trilogy* on the wars of Poland in the 17th century he produced a rival in a trilogy of novels of Kościuszko's insurrection and the last partitions of Poland [called **The Year 1794**]. . . . But in its execution, the ambitious design equals neither Sienkiewicz's great work nor Reymont's own **Peasants.** The master's method of realism here turns against him; the canvas becomes too crowded with detail often irrelevant or futile; epic calm degenerates into dryness; and emotional appeal, when attempted, cannot rival the strength with which history itself speaks to the Pole on these matters.

Reymont, indeed, was not destined to create a second work like **The Peasants.** His original intention of presenting, in imitation of cycles like Balzac's *Comedie humaine* or Zola's *Les Rougon-Macquart,* all classes of Polish society in successive works, never matured; his short war-time stories, poignant as some of them are, have too much of the passing moment in them for literary permanence. . . . (pp. 559-60)

It is, after all, with the fame of **The Peasants** that Reymont's estimation in the history of Polish and of universal literature will stand or fall. And it is the firm belief not of Poles only that the creator of **The Peasants,** now dead, has entered the ranks of the immortals and will never cease to be regarded as one of the greatest writers of this age. (p. 561)

R. Dyboski, "Żeromski and Reymont," in The Slavonic Review *(reprinted by permission of the University of London), Vol. 4, No. 12, March, 1926, pp. 552-61.**

MANFRED KRIDL (essay date 1956)

[In Reymont's first collection of short stories, *Spotkanie* (**The Meeting**),] we note the naturalistic treatment of peasant life, as in *Tomek Baran, Suka* (**The Bitch**), a contrast between a beastly woman who tortures her child and a humane bitch who saves her puppies; *Death* is the grim story of a peasant who, during his life, gave his land too readily to his daughter who then chased him out of his home; he went to his second daughter who dragged him into the pigsty even as he was dying, and robbed him when he was dead. These scenes are described in the manner . . . [of Zola,] with an objective, 'scientific' detachment, and in an expressive, hard language which relates exactly and in detail. His first two novels [*Komedjantka* (**The Comedian**) and *Fermenty* (**Ferments**)] . . . describe the life of Janka Orlowska. . . . Of the two novels, *The Comedian* is the more interesting and lively. It portrays well the world of provincial actors: a mixture of barn-storming bohemianism and of a sort of devotion to art, lack of moral scruples and a feeling of superiority toward the philistines. It is a world full of intrigue, jealousy, and quarrels, sometimes even of criminal instincts—and all this is presented very vividly. The technique is 'impressionistic,' one which operates with small touches of color and light, which in this case consist of a multitude of large and small scenes, genre sketches, dialogues, theatrical rehearsals and performances, the private lives of actors, their attitude to the 'bourgeois' environment, etc. These touches, expressive in themselves, blend into a general picture which is somewhat glaring, deprived of subtle nuance. The eye of the impressionist artist seizes on the phenomena of life, as it were, 'in the act,' fixes them quickly, as with a camera, but often without developing them sufficiently from an artistic point of view. Intoxicated by this mass of phenomena on all sides, Reymont's imagination cannot always discriminate and transform it into artistic material, and much 'raw' material lies bulkily about his work.

The characteristic traits of both novels, and particularly of the first, are found again in more pronounced form in *Ziemia obiecana* (**The Promised Land** . . .). The 'promised land' is Łódź, Poland's biggest industrial center, which at that time reached the peak of its development. In this novel there reigns a positive orgy of colorful impressions, full of vivid light and, in this case also, of sound. We see a huge conglomeration of people of different classes and nationalities:

there are millionaire businessmen and industrialists, the middle class, and the workers; Poles, Germans, and Jews; a variety of psychological types which embody various aspects of the mentality of the so-called 'Lodzermensch' (a man of Łódź), that is the speculator on a large or small scale, who tries to make money in all possible ways. . . . It is Sodom and Gomorrah rather than the promised land, with a wide gap between the life of the rich and the misery of the exploited workers and craftsmen. Between these poles rages a chaos, forever erupting with new sensations in industrial, commercial or private life, across which the author tries to spin a thread of novelistic plot, centered around Karol Borowiecki and his partners, the Jew, Moryc Welt, and the German, Max Baum. But here he fails, for his technique of building over and over expressive, often glaring, scenes from the life of Łódź obscures the slight plot and does not allow it to become a structural center. This situation is aggravated by another trait of Reymont's technique: the presentation of phenomena always at the highest possible point of intensity and tension; almost every scene is depicted in a language, full of hyperbolization and amplification, in which synonyms are piled one upon the other. In order to describe a single trait, a gesture, a motion, an urban landscape or whatever, Reymont is not satisfied with one or two forceful expressions; he gathers several or a dozen of them, thus drawing out and lengthening the description, not always in the interest of clarity. Naturally, this way of writing contributes even more to the 'autonomy' of the individual fragments, and impairs the transparency of the whole picture. This picture is, nevertheless, impressive in its scope and in the wealth of reactions which spring from Reymont's creative imagination, his extraordinary sensitivity to all aspects of the material world, and ability to capture and fix them as on a film. (pp. 435-37)

[*The Peasants* possesses] a specifically Polish character, which [is] at the same time a universal one; it presents on Polish soil problems of universal significance. In Reymont's novel this 'universality' is limited only to one social class, the peasantry, but this class exists the world over, forming the majority in many countries and in others constituting at least an important fraction of the population. And almost everywhere the peasantry has been considered as 'the salt of the earth,' the nourisher of nations, a class which preserves the oldest traditions and represents the purest physical and spiritual type of its nation. (pp. 437-38)

Reymont's peasants are endowed with those general peasant traits. We may add still a particular greediness for land, before which all scruples of kinship or attachment disappear. Furthermore, there is a characteristic caste spirit among them which makes itself felt in the sharp differentiation in significance, influence, and social rank between the rich and the poor peasants, those settled on their land and those deprived of it, between the farmer and the ploughboy. Within this framework there is, of course, room for a wealth and variety of individual traits, physical and psychological types. (p. 438)

As in *The Promised Land* the fictional plot plays no major structural part. . . . [The main task of the author] is to give the fullest and most universal portrayal of life in a Polish village. In this respect we feel that we really get to know Lipce thoroughly, in all the details of private, family, economic, emotional, and intellectual life. That whole life, with its chores, occupations, customs, traditions, rituals, parties, holidays, etc., is described with exactitude and a truly epic respect for the particular instance and the concrete detail.

This is no longer the impressionistic technique of *The Promised Land*, blurring into a glaring and hurried picture, but a quiet, sedate epic narrative sustained in tone and tempo, sometimes even excessively broad and expansive, as though in love with itself or as if the author regretted parting with a given scene, phenomenon, or description and feared that he might omit something. No more snapshots, synthetic short-cuts and condensations of the kind used by Reymont in his earlier novels; on the contrary, what we usually call episodes grow in *The Peasants* into extensive and integral parts of the narrative, constituting, as it were, separate structural centers which are justified by the general character of the whole.

One significant trait may be observed in Reymont's way of handling that tremendous wealth of motifs, namely a tendency toward stylization. A Polish critic, Stanisław Brzozowski, correctly stated that Reymont stylizes the peasants 'as peasants'; one may add that he stylizes not only the peasants but the whole of peasant life. Stylization in literature is revealed in a portrayal of characters and scenes in such a way as to bring out most expressively only some distinguishing characteristic traits and to make them designate a given phenomenon by themselves. Reymont's peasant exhibits . . . a certain dignity, seriousness, and even some solemnity in behavior, in his attitude toward people and in his work; he solemnly celebrates the tilling and sowing of the land, the customary rites of baptism, marriage, or funeral, the distribution of food, the process of eating and drinking, invitation to the table, as well as dancing and entertainment. The most representative characters in *The Peasants* carry out these ritualistic tendencies. The old Boryna and a number of other 'notables' of the village may serve as examples. In connection with stylized characters, their environment and the events in which they take place are also stylized. In this way the author creates fabulously colorful pictures of nature, harvest, harvest-home parties, dances, weddings, funerals, and processions in the traditional . . . style, which is at once highly decorative and, as it were, rooted in hierarchy. The picturesque and colorful quality is, after their stylization, the main feature of these scenes, as of nearly all that life in Reymont's interpretation. This is an art of a special kind, full of gusto and color, but at the same time slightly conventionalized with the concentration falling on one kind of traits while others are eliminated—one of the basic features of any stylization.

The language of *The Peasants*, which creates the epic quality of the novel, possesses certain significant characteristics. First of all, the peasant language is used not only in the dialogues, but also in descriptions and accounts given by the author. This lends the novel a uniform linguistic tone which strongly assists the organic unity of the whole. This language is closest to that variation of the Mazur (Masovian) dialect which is spoken in the Łowicz region. The author uses it masterfully and enriches it with his own linguistic intuition. This dialect must also reflect his own style, especially in the passages where he speaks as author. Here we find perhaps to an even greater extent the same tendencies of amplification and hyperbolization as in *The Promised Land*. The tendency to amplify generally helps the broad epic sweep of the narrative, while hyperbole is in keeping with the other trend of stylization. Both appear with particular clarity in descriptions of nature. (pp. 438-41)

Generally speaking, *The Peasants* is undoubtedly Reymont's masterpiece and one of the finest Polish novels of all time.

His later works, a historical novel, *Rok 1794* **(The Year 1794)**, and some others, achieved no greater significance either in the development of his production or in that of the novel in Poland. (p. 443)

> *Manfred Kridl, "Young Poland," in his* A Survey of Polish Literature and Culture, *translated by Olga Scherer-Virski (reprinted by permission of the publisher; originally published as* Literatura polska na tle rozwoju Kultury, *Roy Publishers, 1945), Columbia University Press, 1956, pp. 403-71.**

JERZY R. KRZYZANOWSKI   (essay date 1972)

[Reymont's work] is deeply rooted in Polish literary tradition, reflecting its various literary fashions and trends, yet it bears the unmistakable mark of his personal style. Almost every period of Polish literary history, from the late Realism of the 1890's through the short-lived Naturalism, and symbolic Neo-Romanticism, up to the new forms in fiction in the 1920's left its mark in Reymont's short stories and novels. Many of his works also reflect various political developments and deal with contemporary issues, while his historical novels revive the best traditions established by his predecessors. But some of his novels transgress the limits of a purely national literature and achieve a universal appeal. It is, perhaps, the combination of those elements of national character and universalism which makes Reymont a novelist of major importance. (pp. 17-18)

The main theme of [Reymont's first novel, *Komediantka* **(The Comedienne)**], the struggle of its heroine, Janka Orlowska, against a hostile world, is . . . presented in a rather shapeless structure. Instead of a traditional plot characterizing a romance—a dramatic action usually involving two characters—Reymont follows the story of Janka as she rejects her social position and her home in order to pursue her dream of an artistic career in theater. The novel concentrates heavily on a panorama of theatrical life—its people, conflicts, and the actors' bitter struggle for survival against the most pedestrian odds and basic material needs, with Janka serving as an example of a young person deceived by the external glitter of the seemingly carefree career. The theater which for her represented "a Greek temple" proves to be a lie, although she remains blind to the most obvious facts of that reality. To emphasize that contrast Reymont introduces Janka dramatically to the strange world of illusion. Having arrived in Warsaw from a provincial railroad station—a familiar setting in many of the author's works—she witnesses a vulgar quarrel over money among the actors. The shabbiness of the surroundings and the pitiful situation of the actors is obvious to the reader, but for Janka the theatrical world still is as enchanting as she had dreamed. (pp. 28-9)

Judged by the standards of a psychological novel, *The Comedienne* is not convincing. It possesses, though, many virtues as a sociological study of the theatrical world. Reymont vividly portrays the social standing of the actors, their problems and difficulties, from their most mundane hardships to their theoretical discussions on art. (p. 29)

While the basic tone of *The Comedienne* is strictly Realistic, scenes such as the death of an old woman, or Janka's ordeal in the last chapters of the novel, clearly exemplify the characteristic features of Naturalism. All details are presented with scientific exactness. But Reymont, unlike Zola, was not consciously working out a literary concept here. Because he lacked a solid philosophical and theoretical background, he relied more on haphazard reading than on any sound theoretical knowledge. Most of all he relished "real life," those facts, people, and situations he could visualize and link with his own experience. (pp. 30-1)

His first novel, in spite of its shortcomings in style and structure, its superficial character design notwithstanding, is a considerable achievement for a first attempt in long form of fiction. It laid solid foundations for the further development of Reymont's art. Authentic, passionate, and permeated with the author's own experiences, it made a good point of departure for the social novels he was to create, even though it was often badly written, contrived, and psychologically shallow. It affords important insight into the career of the novelist just learning his new trade, for it contains the germs of both his artistic strengths and weaknesses. (p. 31)

Basically, Reymont's creative method remains unchanged in [*Fermenty* **(The Ferments)**], although this is better constructed, more logically executed, and richer in problems than was *The Comedienne*. Surrounding the central characters there appear a multitude of minor figures, often superficially drawn, always possessing some bizarre features—they are either drunkards, or emotionally disturbed, or social misfits—characters who add to the local color but also belong organically to the story. Since many of them are truly pathological, often bordering on sheer madness, the novel develops an additional tension by constantly exposing Janka to their presence. (p. 32)

The richness and variety of the characterization in *The Ferments*, which mark a definite advance in Reymont's artistic ability to handle complexity, are enhanced by his shift in setting. In direct contrast to the ugliness and poverty of the city, which sets the scene in *The Comedienne*, in *The Ferments* Reymont takes Janka back to the countryside, to nature, which serves a double purpose in the novel. The landscapes and open horizons, depicted with the skill of a painter, represent natural beauty, but they also perform the symbolic function of underscoring human emotions and yearning. In the scene of Janka's first walk in the woods the beauty of nature is described in almost as masterly a fashion as Reymont later achieves in *The Peasants*, and the power of Nature to heal Janka's spiritual wounds also foreshadows the calmness she will enjoy after deciding to marry Grzesikiewicz and to abandon her folly at last. In another scene when wild crows attack Janka, the birds represent all the tensions and terror of her mind in her growing awareness of her loneliness in the world.

Material objects, too, become charged with symbolic value in *The Ferments*. The railroad station in which Janka recovers is also a symbol of the heroine's hopeless situation after her efforts to escape it proved futile. Janka fully realizes her plight through the monotonous sequence of arrivals and departures of trains; even a simple image of a train passing at night by her window mimics her state of mind.

Such use of symbols occurs frequently in *The Ferments*. Although they are at times rather obvious, they are nevertheless impressive, and mark a significant advance in Reymont's skill from his first novel, where symbols either do not exist at all or were crudely and simplistically detached from the simple descriptions and tone of *The Comedienne*. (pp. 35-6)

The peasants are introduced in this novel with a special care. . . . [The group] is not presented *en masse* but consists of individual characters and silhouettes, some sketched with just a few strokes of the pen, some marked with only a few characteristics, but all are presented plastically, three-dimensionally. The ability to capture the characters of the peasants individually in minute detail while also rendering them typical of a group represents another success of Reymont's in *The Ferments.*

The novel is not perfect, to be sure. It contains many superfluous rhetorical digressions, and its style in some parts is as careless as in *The Comedienne,* but taken as a whole, the second novel represents an important step forward both philosophically and technically. Furthermore, it clearly suggests the direction of Reymont's developing art in its emphasis on human groups as well as on individuals who form such a group, a group bound together with multiple ties, different but uniform as a community of people and, consequently, the whole nation. (p. 38)

Apparently having exhausted the theatrical theme in his first two novels and early short stories, Reymont confronted the industrial city, fascinated by the multitude of possibilities suggested by its social and psychological complexity. The instinct of a novelist must have told him that the topic would prove fruitful, and *Ziemia obiecana (The Promised Land),* the resulting novel, has few equals in literature even now. (p. 45)

Reymont centered his interest on the Polish, German, and Jewish inhabitants of the city. Different in their ways of life, education, experience, and even language, the Poles, Germans, and Jews came together only in the common pursuit of business and created contrasts seldom encountered before in Poland or the rest of Europe. (pp. 45-6)

To deal with a multitude of problems among the three groups, Reymont uses a device foreign to the standard Realistic novel and expands the traditional limitation of fiction to individual characters by encompassing national groups. He wrote a "novel without a hero" by concentrating almost equally upon three characters, each representative of his nationality: Karol Borowiecki, a Polish engineer; Max Baum, a German technician, and Moryc Welt, a Jewish businessman. Borowiecki emerges as the strongest character and becomes by the end the protagonist, but initially that role is shared by all three. Throughout, Reymont works to present each character's virtues and vices objectively. (p. 46)

Their potential factory soon recedes into the background, . . . as Reymont emphasizes the entire industrial jungle. He begins to shift characters and scenery, starts and drops new plots, flashes vignettes and scenes with staggering speed, using as it were, a movie technique in fiction. The novelist proves to be a diligent director of his imaginary film; there is order in the kaleidoscopic presentation of Lodz, and he never loses control over his characters and their fates. Subplots, crossing and interweaving with one another, move the action forward, and the panorama of the city comes to life as the action progresses. (pp. 46-7)

By its very nature, the novel focuses not on family relationships, but rather on uprooted characters coping with a new environment. Thus Reymont departed from the European traditions of Realism and Naturalism, which attempted an all-embracing epic presentation, and fashioned family sagas that explored the interrelationships and conflicts among a group of kinsmen. In this respect *The Promised Land* is much closer to American naturalistic novels such as [Theodore]

Dreiser's and [Stephen] Crane's than to Reymont's European predecessors. (pp. 47-8)

[In] *The Promised Land,* Reymont emerged as a mature novelist, in full control of his technique and able to employ it in a major novel of ambitious scope. This novel contains all the characteristics of his later style, brought to a more perfect and sophisticated level in *The Peasants.*

One mark of Reymont's style, accurate depiction of detail, is rooted in his unusual ability to perceive the world around him and to retain whatever he encountered. (p. 54)

Reymont's highly metaphorical language often is drawn from the vocabulary of the biological sciences, particularly zoology and entomology. Factories are referred to as beasts, monsters, octopuses, spiders, and the like, in order to reveal their inhuman and apocalyptic qualities, especially when the machines have become a threat to the fate of men. (p. 56)

[Another] quality of Reymont's style [is] highly emotional diction. He "enlarged his gestures" in literature as well as in life. He often replaces denotative terms with synonyms of a higher connotative intensity, which are, unfortunately, often untranslatable because of the way in which Reymont uses the possibilities of inflection in Polish to create new, more emotional forms of words. . . . Such characteristics of imagery and diction play an ever-increasing role in Reymont's work; in *The Promised Land* they are introduced for the first time as an outstanding stylistic feature and their presence is part of the reason for the significance of that novel in Reymont's creative development. (p. 57)

The Promised Land played a crucial role in Reymont's creative development as well as in the history of Polish literature. (p. 60)

Accurate description, powerful imagery, and vivid dialogue contribute to the richness without weakening the novel's sociological, almost documentary, character. . . . [The] artistic technique suits the modern subject. With this novel Reymont introduced a new type of fiction, which was to develop further in the twentieth century. (p. 61)

Most critics who devote considerable attention to the universal meaning of *The Peasants* have failed to recognize how Reymont's masterly creation of living characters makes it a work of modern fiction instead of a poetic treatise on the countryside. United by a common heritage and acting as part of the community, his characters are a true embodiment of both poetry and national character. . . . (p. 79)

Traditionally, most critical attention goes to Boryna, who, with his eternal love for his land and sense of duty to it, is generally considered as the symbolic peasant. Indeed, the scene of his last sowing symbolizes the ultimate union of a peasant with his land, with Mother Earth. (pp. 79-80)

Above all a man of action and violent passions, Maciej Boryna is introduced at the beginning of the novel in a series of scenes which stress these qualities. (p. 80)

The images of blood and violence which mark Boryna throughout the novel occur even at the reconciliation of father and son. . . .

Another image which recurs throughout Reymont's entire work is the destructive power of fire and finally, in *The Peasants,* fire becomes fully symbolic. (p. 81)

Reymont seems to have used symbols as stylistic devices to underscore the psychology of his characters. They are, above all, real people who live, love, hate, enjoy themselves and suffer with all-too-human intensity. They can be interpreted as universal symbols but they are also endowed with psychological validity. The novelist's primary goal in *The Peasants* was to depict as faithfully as possible the multiplicity of village life, to create characters and conflicts which might have existed under real conditions. When Reymont succeeded in charging his novel with universal meaning through the conscious use of symbols, he enriched its structure without changing its basic Realistic concept. (p. 83)

Reymont depicted his Lipce [the setting of *The Peasants*] with all the folklore linguistic details particular to that specific village; by making it individual, he succeeded in making it typical, a goal achieved only by a few masters of fiction. The symbolic images further enhanced the setting, charging it with universal meaning far beyond the actual village of Lipce, beyond any local or even national boundaries. Even so, *The Peasants* contains almost documentary details which make the novel a contribution to the history of the cultural and social development of Poland, as Balzac's and Zola's works contribute to the social history of France. (p. 86)

The relationship between the main characters and the community, on the one hand, and the balance between action and description on the other, structure the novel. An analysis of the relationship between these two factors explains many facets of Reymont's art. The main plot, the incest in the Boryna family, concerns the community, too; eventually, Jagna is violently expelled by the villagers. Her personal drama becomes a core of the action which unites all the characters and the community as a whole in the climax of the novel. The subplots have previously been resolved, their climaxes placed strategically at the end of each volume. Such a climax occurs, for example, at the end of *Winter* when the villagers, hitherto separate and socially stratified, learn that the forest which traditionally belongs to Lipce has been sold by the squire, they unite there and fight for their rights. The battle, described in the best tradition of [Henryk] Sienkiewicz's historical novels, results in a victory attained at a heavy cost. Boryna is fatally wounded, and he is subsequently replaced by Antek, who will become the leader of the community. In the next volumes of the novel, when the Russian authorities press for a new school with instruction in Russian, Antek, released from jail, where he had been kept for killing the forester, organizes a boycott against the vote for the new school. He and his former rival for Jagna's favors, Mateusz, represent the new spirit of the united peasants, the young generation leading their class toward a new, more enlightened way of life. (p. 88)

[Reymont] believed that the peasants played a decisive role in the life of the country, and his novels were among the very few in Polish literature to reflect that belief. The protagonists in the works of Sienkiewicz and [Stefan] Zeromski had been mainly noblemen, and peasants appeared only incidentally, but Reymont emphasized the peasants in the historical process. Unfortunately, he succeeded only in part. While many scenes in *The Year 1794* deal with the peasants as a new social force, the protagonist, Sewer Zareba, in spite of his Jacobin and revolutionary connections, is another nobleman hero of Polish literature. He is much more progressive than his predecessors, but his characterization is still a compromise between Reymont's own convictions and the powerful pressure

of tradition. The choice of that particular period in Poland's history is still, however, in full accord with the author's concept of the historical role of the peasants in the past, and his hopes for the approaching future.

The structure of *The Last Diet of the Republic* [the first volume of the trilogy of historical novels entitled *The Year 1794*] and the other works in the trilogy is very close to that of *The Promised Land*. Made up of a variety of characters, places, scenes, and events, it is linked together by the protagonist who, like Borowiecki in the earlier novel, moves from one environment to another, permitting the author to enter different milieux and to tie them into one plot. As in the other novel, the love story, Zareba's unhappy affair with Iza, is an attempt to introduce romance, but it does not play an important role in the intrinsic structure of the novel. The love plot soon becomes a nuisance, since the real interest focuses on a patriotic conspiracy involving Zareba. Accordingly, the novel focuses on historical events, in particular on the last days of the country's independence and its last diet [a national legislature]. (pp. 99-100)

[The] structure of *The Last Diet* is uneven; many themes are dropped before they have been fully developed, many characters appear without contributing either to the progress of action or in their relationship to the plot. In general, the novel lacks a structural unity, and this made it inferior in comparison with other novels in Polish historical fiction. Nonetheless, *The Last Diet* contains some chapters of high artistic value.

The opening chapter deserves attention because of the mood it evokes. Beside fulfilling the usual expository function, it renders the general tone of regret, sadness, and despair which reigned in the soon-to-perish nation. It sounds like a sad refrain in the famous scene of the grand polonaise danced at the party with its recurring symbolic image of a Polish noblewoman dancing with the Russian envoy. . . .

Such impressive images render the atmosphere of doom awaiting Poland. And although even the bravest endeavors of the patriots could not have averted the course of history, we follow their desperate struggle with the intense feeling that it was not in vain. Reymont's novel, then, fulfills its social and psychological functions in awakening feelings of compassion for the Polish patriots. And that was precisely the author's goal. (p. 102)

The variety of complex subplots introduced in the first volume of the trilogy broadens in the second one entitled *Nil Desperandum (Never Despair)*. In spite of the lamentable conditions in Poland after the second partition in 1793, the conspirators did not, indeed, fall into despair. Through their sacrifices and patriotic endeavors, a Polish army was formed again both in the northern and in the southern provinces, and a leader arose whose name and authority were impressive enough to unite quarreling political factions. He was Thaddeus Kosciuszko, a hero of the American Revolutionary War and the most able and courageous general of the Polish campaign of 1792. (pp. 107-08)

To Reymont, Kosciuszko embodied the truly national spirit of the peasantry. . . . Kosciuszko is mentioned frequently in the first volume, and emerges more realistically as a military leader in the third, against the ambitious and bold panorama of the battle at Raclawice; he appears in *Nil Desperandum* only in a series of brief sketches, more like a savior of the nation than a real person. Accordingly, he is described metaphorically, in terms related to his superhuman task and spiritual ordeal; his historical role and spiritual experiences are emphasized. (p. 108)

Compared to the preceding volumes, [*Insurekcja*] *The Insurrection* reverses basic elements of composition. The plot and fictional characters become secondary, while historical events are depicted with powerful strength. In this bloody period in Polish history, with the country's fate at stake, decisions were made on the battlefields rather than in diplomatic negotiations, and so Reymont also changed the setting, and decided to try creating battle pieces according to the best tradition in Polish fiction. . . . Among the fight scenes the presentation of the battle at Raclawice is the most impressive, followed by numerous scenes of street fighting in Warsaw. Reymont had waited until this third volume and proved his creative power in the field so far occupied only by his famous predecessors. (pp. 113-14)

In vivid colloquial conversations among the soldiers, Reymont depicts the spirit of those on whose shoulders the success of the uprising heavily rests. Comparison with a French crowd of revolutionaries in *Nil Desperandum* reveals the Frenchmen as a violent and uncontrollable force, bloodthirsty and uncouth, and the Polish volunteers as soldiers, honest, aware of their goal, determined to fight for liberty. With a few strokes of the pen each character is individualized: some are funny, some lazy, some simply all-too-human in their desire for food or a pair of shoes. There is not enough food, to be sure, and the military discipline is lax, but even so the volunteers are conscientious freedom fighters, and their spirit is high.

When Kosciuszko takes personal command, he is presented in more realistic terms than in the previous novel, a leader committed to chivalry in warfare. (p. 114)

By [the end of *The Insurrection*, the reader] is more involved in the nation's ultimate struggle than in fictional characters. Thus the fiction has moved into the realm of history, into its

real drama, often more poignant than the story of imaginary characters. And if Reymont's trilogy is a partial failure because of its uneven structure and some minor faults, the author achieved something perhaps more important than literary perfection, an impressive image of bygone days, and created a feeling of classical catharsis of national emotions by evoking the glory of the past. (p. 118)

Although those works of Reymont's which were written in accordance with passing trends must slip quietly into oblivion, the bulk of his work remains alive. His theatrical and social novels in some respects can stand comparison with the indisputable mastery of *The Peasants*. His historical trilogy is at least as good as any major historical novel of its time. . . . Reymont's work does not age but speaks to us with the same strong, human voice as it spoke to many generations, in many languages, in many countries throughout the world. (p. 153)

> *Jerzy R. Krzyzanowski, in his* Wladyslaw Stanislaw Reymont *(copyright © 1972 by Twayne Publishers, Inc.; reprinted with the permission of Twayne Publishers, a Division of G. K. Hall & Co., Boston), Twayne, 1972, 169 p.*

ADDITIONAL BIBLIOGRAPHY

Almedingen, Edith M. "Ladislas Reymont—Peasant and Writer." *The English Review* XLII, No. 1 (January 1926): 119-22.
    Biographical sketch and descriptive survey of Reymont's major works.

Borowy, Wacław. "Reymont." *The Slavonic and East European Review* XVI, No. 47 (1937): 439-48.
    Introduction to Reymont's life and works.

Zielinski, Thaddeus. "The Peasant in Polish Literature (II)." *The Slavonic Review* II, No. 4 (June 1923): 85-100.
    Discusses Reymont's positive contribution to the image of the Polish peasants.

Edwin Arlington Robinson

1869-1935

American poet and dramatist.

Best known for his small-town character types—lonely non-conformists, beggars, drunks, and suicides—Robinson achieved a hard-won prominence in American poetry in the early part of the twentieth century. The characteristic features of his work are terse diction, careful metrical forms, austere style, and philosophical themes. Robinson was not an experimental poet as were his contemporaries the imagists; nevertheless his poetic style signalled an end to the flowery sentimentality of nineteenth-century American romantic poetry. Although Robinson was not a systematic philosopher, his poems, despite their sadly ironic tone and often tragic conclusions, are considered to be life-affirming, revealing a transcendental belief in God and in the value of human existence.

Robinson grew up in Gardiner, Maine, his model for the oppressive Tilbury Town which figures prominently in the poetry of the first half of his career. Fascinated by the sounds and rhythms of words, he began to write poetry at an early age. He studied at Harvard for two years, but a decline in the family's circumstances forced him to return home. Because of his brothers' bad investments, alcoholism, and drug addiction, Robinson was left penniless. He rejected business as a career and decided to write poetry. Unable to help his family financially and dependent on friends for money, Robinson developed a sense of personal failure and guilt which haunted him for the rest of his life. Many critics attribute his preoccupation with portraying losers and suicides, and his opposition to the materialist concept of failure, to his own experiences with poverty and hometown scorn. He published his first book of poetry, *The Torrent and the Night Before*, at his own expense, but although it received a few good reviews, Robinson was generally ignored by both critics and the public. President Theodore Roosevelt, however, was impressed with *The Children of the Night* and praised it extravagantly. He arranged a sinecure for Robinson at the New York City Customs House so that he could write without financial worry. Robinson was, nevertheless, financially insecure until the overwhelming popular success of *Tristram*.

Critics divide Robinson's poetry into two types. In his early career, he perfected the poetic form for which he became well known: the dramatic lyric marked by firm stanzaic structure, skillfully crafted rhyming patterns, and simple colloquial speech. The fine psychological portraits in his first volume of poetry, *The Torrent and the Night Before*, and later in *The Children of the Night* and *Captain Craig*, are generally considered his finest achievements. In poems like "Richard Cory," "Luke Havergal," "Mr. Flood's Party," and "Captain Craig," Robinson examines the loneliness and isolation of social misfits. At the source of Robinson's poetry of this period is his belief in the moral superiority of these seemingly worthless characters over their more materially successful neighbors.

In the second phase of his career, Robinson adapted several Arthurian legends into blank verse. *Merlin, Lancelot,* and *Tristram* were well received, but are no longer thought to be as important as the poems of Robinson's first period. Despite

passages of great lyric beauty, the poems are criticized for being too long and monotonous. *Tristram*, however, was a favorite with the public and became a best-seller, a rare distinction for a book of poetry. Robinson also won the Pulitzer Prize three times: for *Collected Poems, The Man Who Died Twice,* and *Tristram*.

Critics disagree on the value of Robinson's work. Ignored until relatively late in his career, Robinson was then fulsomely praised by some critics. Many modern critics, however, find his work intolerably old-fashioned; at a time of great experimentation, Robinson adhered to the metrical rules of his predecessors. His poems are criticized for their lack of striking imagery and for their starkness and gloom. Many think Robinson diffused his talent for dramatic, arresting characterizations, seen in the shorter poems, by attempting to develop the narrative power needed to sustain interest in the long reenactments of Arthurian legends.

Although Robinson's achievement has been somewhat eclipsed by the success of the imagists, he will be remembered for the powerful, dramatic poems of his first period. In these poems he created characters—Captain Craig, Eben Flood, and Richard Cory—who have become classic types in American literature.

PRINCIPAL WORKS

The Torrent and the Night Before (poetry) 1896
The Children of the Night (poetry) 1897
Captain Craig (poetry) 1902
Van Zorn (drama) 1914
The Man against the Sky (poetry) 1916
Merlin (poetry) 1917
Lancelot (poetry) 1920
The Three Taverns (poetry) 1920
Avon's Harvest (poetry) 1921
Collected Poems (poetry) 1921
The Man Who Died Twice (poetry) 1924
Tristram (poetry) 1927
Sonnets 1889-1927 (poetry) 1928
Cavendar's House (poetry) 1929
Collected Poems (poetry) 1929
Matthias at the Door (poetry) 1931
Talifer (poetry) 1933
King Jasper (poetry) 1935

WILLIAM P. TRENT   (essay date 1897)

Mr. Edwin Arlington Robinson, of Gardiner, Maine has sent us a tiny volume of verse [entitled] **"The Torrent and the Night Before."** . . . We wish we could praise . . . the independence shown in the short dedication which runs as follows: "This book is dedicated to any man, woman, or critic who will cut the edges of it—I have done the top." Independence is all very well—but Mr. Robinson's has an unnecessary note of flippancy about it.

We have, however, made ourselves one of his dedicatees, for we have cut the edges of his book and we are glad to have done so. Mr. Robinson has one important quality of the poet—one that is a sufficient excuse for his having published his verses—to-wit, a knowledge of the technique of his art and an obvious love for it. (pp. 243-44)

Mr. Robinson has, of course, a good deal to learn in the coming years. He must learn that if he wishes to write "ballades" he must improve on those given on pages 6 and 10 of his book. He must learn that the impressionist effect produced in **"The House on the Hill"** is not worth striving after, and that the chaotic effect produced in **"A Poem for Max Nordau"** is distinctly to be avoided. He must learn to put a little more concreteness into such poems as **"Her Eyes,"** and **"An Old Story,"** if he wishes to be loved and "understood" of the people. . . .

We think that he handles the sonnet very well indeed—especially when he writes of his favorite authors. (p. 244)

There are other things to praise in Mr. Robinson's book, the Browning-like verve of the last poem, the felicity of the **"Horace to Leuconoë"** (though surely Mr. Robinson must feel that the sonnet form is a lame one in which to render Horace in spite of the example of a distinguished living poet), the homely patriotism of the sonnet in praise of Boston. There are also other things to condemn such as the lack of restraint in the poem entitled **"The Wilderness."** (p. 246)

William P. Trent, "A New Poetic Venture," in The Sewanee Review *(© 1897 by The University of the South), Vol. V, No. 2, April, 1897, pp. 243-46.*

MAY SINCLAIR   (essay date 1906)

[Mr. Robinson's poems in *Captain Craig*] fall into three groups: lyrics, including ballads and old ballade forms; character sketches and psychological dramas; poems dramatic in everything except form. It is, in fact, difficult to name these dramas that cannot be played, these songs that cannot possibly be sung. But the point of view is dramatic, the emotion lyric. In his songs (since songs they must be called) he has reduced simplicity to its last expression. (p. 429)

In some of his shorter poems (*Sainte-Nitouche* and *As a World would have it*) he has pressed allusiveness and simplicity to the verge of vagueness. In his longer psychological dramas (for they are dramas in all save form) he is a little too analytically diffuse. In all he has rendered human thought and human emotion with a force and delicacy which proves him a master of this form. For imaginative insight, subtlety, and emotional volume, *The Night Before* may stand beside Browning's *Soul's Tragedy* and Meredith's *Modern Love;* and *The Book of Annandale* will stand alone, though in a lower plane, in its burning analysis of the conflict between scruple and desire. Quotation would give no idea of the spirit of this poem. It is woven all of one piece, and its strength lies in its profound human quality rather than in the force of single passages. Mr. Robinson has few purple patches; he works solidly and soberly, often in grey on grey.

Above all, he has the great gift of spiritual imagination and an unerring skill in disentangling the slender threads of thought and motive and emotion.

All these qualities are conspicuous in the long blank verse poem, *Captain Craig*, which gives its title to Mr. Robinson's first volume. . . . At a first glance there is little charm about this severely undecorated poem, written in unmusical and often monotonous blank verse, shot with darts of intellectual brilliance, but unrelieved by any sensuous colouring. The charm grows in the reading. *Captain Craig* is a philosophy of life, taught through the humorous lips of a social derelict, a beggared Socrates, disreputable as the world counts reputation. It is a drama of the Unapparent, revealing the divine soul hidden in the starved body of that "sequestered parasite"; a soul that had the courage to be itself, abiding in its dream, facing the world as a superb failure. (pp. 431-32)

The Captain's religion is a protest against the sin of *accidia*. He, ragged, old, and starved, challenges his friends to have courage and to rejoice in the sun. . . . (p. 432)

The message of this poet is: Be true to the truth that lies nearest to you; true to God, if you have found Him; true to man; true to yourself; true, if you know no better truth, to your primal instincts; but at any cost be true. *Captain Craig* is one prolonged and glorious wantoning and wallowing in truth. (p. 433)

Mr. Robinson's genius has no sense of action, brutal and direct, but he has it in him to write a great human drama, a drama of the soul from which all action proceeds and to which its results return. (pp. 433-34)

May Sinclair, "Three American Poets of To-day," in The Fortnightly Review *(reprinted by permission* *of Contemporary Review Company Limited), n.s. September 1, 1906, pp. 421-37.**

AMY LOWELL (essay date 1917)

We must never forget that all inherited prejudice and training pulls one way . . . ; the probing, active mind pulls another. The result is a profound melancholy, tinged with cynicism. Self-analysis has sapped joy, and the impossibility of constructing an ethical system in accordance both with desire and with tradition has twisted the mental vision out of all true proportion. It takes the lifetime of more than one individual to throw off a superstition, and the effort to do so is not made without sacrifice.

Unless one understands this fact, one cannot comprehend the difficult and beautiful poetry of Edwin Arlington Robinson. (p. 10)

That Mr. Robinson is conscious of the chief cause of his melancholy, I think extremely doubtful. His temper is too unscientific to lead him to a minute self-examination, with the test-tube of atavism for a guide. There is evidence of a greater peace of mind in his later work, as we shall see, but even there, "peace" is hardly the word, it is rather that his recent poems are less mordant. He has raised for himself a banner, and it bears upon it a single word: "Courage." (p. 24)

[No] one, even picking it up at a time when the poet's name was quite unknown, could have failed to have been struck by [the] sincerity and strength [of **"Children of the Night."**] There is no hint here of the artificial melancholy which has become so much the fashion among youthful aspirants to poetry. The poet is fighting his sorrow, and that it masters him is due to no lack of personal virility. Mr. Robinson himself is a strong man, his weakness is his inheritance, that outworn Puritan inheritance, no longer a tonic, but a poison, sapping the springs of life at their source. His existence is one long battle between individual bravery and paralyzing atavism. So the sentiments he voices are cynical, but the manner of them is sure and strong.

The first poem in the book shows the breaking down of the old belief, and the endeavour to feed his life without it. (p. 26)

As a poem, ["**The Children of the Night**"] is far less important than others in the volume, but as a psychological note, it is invaluable.

The true vigour of the book, however, the dominant chord, is chiefly to be found in the objective sketches of personalities which it contains.

Mr. Robinson preceded Mr. [Edgar Lee] Masters in short pictures of men's lives. The unconscious cynicism I have spoken of is in them, but sometimes (unlike Mr. Masters) something more. (p. 29)

[In "**John Evereldown**"], Mr. Robinson has recourse to the ballad technique. . . . The simplicity of the ballad manner covering an acute psychological analysis is one of Mr. Robinson's favourite turns, and it certainly heightens the force of the criticism, growing as it does out of quaintness. It gives a grotesque quality to the work, and sharpens the edge of tragedy. (p. 30)

In reading Mr. Robinson, it is always necessary to note the almost unapproachable technique with which his poems are wrought. He employs the most complete reticence, he per-

mits himself no lapses from straightforward speech to force a glittering effect. But the effect is never commonplace, never even unpoetic. It is indeed art concealing art. So admirable is his technique, that not only do we get the essence of poetry in these astringent poems, we get drama. . . . They appear simple, these poems; and they are really so immensely difficult. Mr. Robinson has carefully studied that primary condition of all poetry: brevity; and his best effects are those gained with the utmost economy of means.

A moment ago, I referred to the grotesque note in these poems, and grotesque they often are. Weird—dour—a harsh, ghostly reverberation struck by a line. (pp. 31-2)

So slight, yet so sharp, are these touches, it never seems as though the poet were conscious of them. He knows how to inject them into the context, by accident, as it were. This creating an atmosphere with a back-hand stroke is one of the most personal and peculiar traits of Mr. Robinson's style. Such passages blow across his pages like mists from the grey valley of the Styx.

I have spoken of Mr. Robinson's "unconscious cynicism." It is unconscious because he never dwells upon it as such, never delights in it, nor wraps it comfortably about him. It is hardly more than the reverse of the shield of pain, and in his later work, it gives place to a great, pitying tenderness. (p. 33)

"Success through failure," that is the motto on the other side of his banner of "Courage." It is true that he carries the doctrine almost too far. So far that it nearly lapses into Nirvana. But one must never forget that to him it is a symbol of a protest against brutal, unfeeling materialism.

The stark sincerity and simplicity of this book must have had the effect of a galvanic shock upon the small company of readers who stumbled upon it. But the times were not yet ripe for such poetry, and it was to be years yet before Mr. Robinson received his due. (p. 34)

So five years passed before the next volume of poems was issued, "**Captain Craig**." . . .

It is quite evident, in examining this book, that the five years of silence had not been without fruit. Already, there is a surer touch and a deeper-probing psychology. The excessive subjectivity of "**The Children of the Night**" is making way for an interest in the world outside of the poet. Although the first book contained many sketches of character, we feel that the interpretation of these characters is very much tinged by the author's personality. To the end, Mr. Robinson never succeeds in completely omitting the writer from the thing written, even in intentionally objective and dramatic pieces, but each volume of poems is an advance in this respect. (p. 35)

The most important poem in "**Captain Craig**" is not, to my mind, the title poem, but "**Isaac and Archibald**." . . . "**Captain Craig**" is a dreary, philosophical ramble . . . , which, in spite of the excellent manipulation of its blank verse, reveals a fault which the earlier volume was conspicuously without, namely, verbosity. The one fault which has grown upon Mr. Robinson with the years is a tendency to long-windedness. There is an interminable amount of talking in "**Captain Craig**," and one must admit that the talking is both involved and dull.

The poem is built upon that favourite theory of the poet's: the success of failure. But here it is pushed too far, to the verge of the ridiculous, in fact. (p. 37)

Other authors have painted derelicts who have gained wisdom through much contemplation, real wisdom which we acknowledge to be sound, but in **"Captain Craig"** Mr. Robinson's craft has played him false. His technique is here, beautiful as always, but his content is neither convincing, dramatic, nor interesting. (p. 39)

[Mr. Robinson's third book of poetry, **"The Town Down the River,"**] contains, beside the title poem (a misty lyric of future and change, with a slight optimistic note which is absent in his earlier work), three studies of public characters: Lincoln, Napoleon, and Theodore Roosevelt. Of these, the Lincoln is the most successful. The truth is that Mr. Robinson is too individual a man, too wrapt up in his own reactions, to be a good mouthpiece for other individual men not of his creating. His Napoleon poem bears the title, **"An Island,"** and is a monologue placed in the mouth of the dying Emperor. But the man who speaks is not in the least like Napoleon, these are not Napoleon's thought-processes. This is no character study; perhaps it was not an attempt at one. Call it a poem upon an imaginative theme, and it has some fine passages. . . . (p. 41)

One of the most characteristic sections of the book is a group of poems entitled **"Calverley's,"** and here again we have the short character vignettes which gave so much distinction to **"The Children of the Night."** Calverley's is a tavern, and the host and its principal frequenters are drawn with Mr. Robinson's sympathetic, clear understanding. (p. 45)

There is one curious mannerism in Mr. Robinson's work, and one which is the absolute opposite of the ballad quality of which he is at times so fond. This mannerism consists in the obscuring of a thing under an epithet, more or less artificial and difficult of comprehension. . . . The most extravagant case of this sort . . . is in **"How Annandale Went Out,"** where he speaks of the hypodermic syringe as "a slight kind of engine."

In less skilful hands, such a mannerism would be unbearable, but Mr. Robinson often manages to convey with it a subtle symbolism, to underlay the fact of his poem with a cogent meaning, tragic, ironic, cynical, what he pleases. Doubtless the method contains hidden germs of danger; it may easily degenerate into artificiality. But, so far, Mr. Robinson has not allowed it to degenerate, and employed as he employs it, it is valuable.

Fine though much of this book is, it seems more a maintaining of a position than a definite advance. The leap forward was not to come until six years later, with **"The Man Against the Sky."**

In the interval, Mr. Robinson turned his attention to plays, [**"Van Zorn"** and **"The Porcupine."**] . . .

It is always a dreary task to record the lapses of genius, and it is as lapses from his usual high achievement that Mr. Robinson's plays must be considered. In another man, they would merit praise for their sincerity and effort, but they fall much below the level of accomplishment of the poet's other work, and, coming from his pen, they must be considered as failures.

To be sure, **"Van Zorn"** is quite unlike any other play, and in these days of facile playwriting, that alone is a distinction. But a play certainly should be dramatic above all other things, and dramatic **"Van Zorn"** is not. The play depends rather upon hints of a drama carried on in the actor's minds than upon anything the audience actually sees or hears. The dialogue is pleasant, easy, colloquial, rather than brilliant; it stays on the same agreeable level, neither mounting nor sinking. So far as it and the action are concerned, the play is one of half tones. The swift vigour of the author's character poems is completely lacking. Those brief, virile dramas scattered throughout his books have lent no cutting edge to this long play. It is diluted, thinned to a mere essence, and strangely enough, realism has also fled, for neither plot nor characters bear the stamp of life. (pp. 47-9)

The second play, **"The Porcupine,"** has even less to recommend it. The slightly supernatural light which dimmed the crudities of **"Van Zorn"** and lent it a suggestion of unseen possibilities, is absent here. **"The Porcupine"** reads like the work of a youth, unversed in the technique of the world and also of the theatre. The plot is confused and extraordinarily unlikely. (p. 50)

The play is a bookish production, compounded of reactions from Russian and German dramatists, but it lacks the stark reality which brings those authors to success. The strangest thing about it is its immaturity, and one asks whether it is, after all, merely an old work resurrected.

Whatever Mr. Robinson's accomplishment in his preceding books, there can be no doubt of the high position he holds in American poetry when we examine **"The Man Against the Sky."** . . . It would seem as though his previous books were merely working up to this achievement, so far beyond them is this volume. A little book . . . , and yet, in reading it, one experiences a sensation akin to that of the man who opens a jar of compressed air. It is a profound wonder that so much can have been forced into so small a space. For **"The Man Against the Sky"** is dynamic with experience and knowledge of life.

In the twenty years which have elapsed since the publication of **"The Children of the Night,"** we have seen Mr. Robinson's entire production to consist of four volumes of verse and two plays. Each volume is slim and reticent, and yet small as is the bulk of the work to make up the quota of the best years of a man's life, in it the poet has achieved the result of putting before us a personality of original thought, of original expression, and quietly and unobtrusively making that personality a force in present-day literature.

If we take the poetic currents in evidence in America to-day, we shall find certain distinct streams which, although commingling, keep on the whole very much to themselves. The strange thing about Mr. Robinson's work is that it seems to belong to none of these streams. And yet no one reading these poems would feel justified in calling him not modern. The truth is that they are modern because they are universal. The scenes, the conversations, are modern; were the poet writing in the fifteenth century, these accessories would differ, but the content would be as modern in one age as another, because the essential quality of humanity does not change; men clothe their philosophy in different terms, the philosophies even may vary, but human nature does not vary, and Mr. Robinson deals with something which may fitly be called raw human nature—not crude human nature, but human nature simple, direct, and as it is.

Those last three words contain the gist of the matter. In them lies Mr. Robinson's gift to the "new poetry": Simple, direct, and as it is. Mr. Robinson's modernity is unconcerned with forms, he has been tempted by no metrical experiments. It is in keeping with his serious outlook upon life that he is content to forge his stern poems out of existing material. (pp. 51-2)

"**The Man Against the Sky**" (a symbolic title of great beauty) is curiously named from the last poem in the book. Why it is the last is evident, for it is a serious argument against a materialistic explanation of the universe, and bears with it a sense of finality which forbids its being followed by any other poems. (p. 53)

The volume opens with "**Flammonde**," and here the change from the poet's early work is very evident. There is a mellowness of soul, a gentle commiseration for the follies of the world, which has banished the acrid denunciation of such poems as "**John Evereldown**" or "**Richard Cory**." (p. 55)

Perhaps no poem which Mr. Robinson has written serves so well as ["**Flammonde**"] to illustrate certain qualities of the poet's style. Here we have one of the simple, direct stanza forms in which he delights. There is no very haunting lilt in this rhythm; there are no tricks, no advised and conscious expertness of rhyme schemes; no pleasure in new inventions; no uneven lines falling into an original pattern. It is all straight, severe, and quiet. It is also admirable. The poet never compromises with his metre; he allows himself no false accents nor over-long lines. In fact, the charm of the form is just here: in the apparent ease with which this fitting of words and metre is accomplished. They seem to be absolutely one and inevitable. (p. 59)

"**Flammonde**" reveals characteristics of style besides those of rhythm. Nowhere else can we find better illustrated the poet's extraordinary powers of condensation made possible by a rarely imaginative use of epithet. (pp. 59-60)

Tenderness is one of the finer qualities of Mr. Robinson's later poetry. The swift, caustic etching of his early poems has mellowed into a gentle, extenuating understanding. Youth condemns; maturity condones. And where maturity has lost nothing of the vitality of youth, the result is great poetry. (p. 60)

I have spoken several times of Mr. Robinson's obscure, sometimes positively cryptic, method of expressing an idea. In "**Captain Craig**," this method degenerated into a confusion so intense that the reader wearied in tracking the poet's meaning. In fact, it may very fairly be said to have ruined the poem.

Mr. Robinson never entirely shakes off this mannerism, but in "**Flammonde**," it is held in leash, with the result that instead of confusion, we get a sense of haunting mystery. . . . (pp. 60-1)

The most recent poem which Mr. Robinson has written [is] "**Merlin**." . . . This is, as its name implies, a re-telling of the Arthurian legend, and one cannot help a slight feeling of disappointment that this re-telling is neither so new nor so different as one might have expected. For some reason, the author seems here to have abandoned his peculiar and personal style. Instead of a vivid, modern reading of an old theme, instead of the brilliant psychological analysis applied to history and legend which made "**Ben Jonson Entertains a Man from Stratford**" so memorable, we find in this book only a rather feeble and emasculated picture, tricked out with charming lyrical figures, it is true, but lifeless and unconvincing. Merlin is no great wizard, swept into Vivian's toils by a fascination which no man, not even he, can resist; he

is a vain, weak old man, playing at a pastoral. Even when conflicting emotions are supposed to tear him, they do not tear, in spite of the author's assurances. . . . (pp. 63-4)

To be sure, Merlin is a broken man; but nothing in the poem carries a conviction that he was ever very much otherwise.

It is a long, meandering tale of some thirteen hundred blank verse lines. But the fault is not in its length, it is in the manner in which the poet has composed his story. Now the poet who would be a story-teller must concern himself with something beside poetry, beside psychology; he must learn the manipulation of plot. It is just in this matter of plot that Mr. Robinson's work reveals its less able side. When a tale is to be told in a single scene, Mr. Robinson is sure, swift, and adequate. String it out to a series of episodes, and it becomes, not only diluted, but involved to the point where it loses that sharp stroke of drama which makes the glory of his shorter pieces. (pp. 64-5)

In reading ["**Merlin**"], we feel that Mr. Robinson was hampered by the weight of tradition hanging about his subject. He could not quite get to its kernel, absorb it as his own, and, forgetting the necessity of doing something remarkable with it, make it remarkable because remoulded in the fires of his own brain. It is good work, creditable work, but it is not great work, and the poet's peculiar excellencies are often lacking. There is too much of the fustian of the antiquary; too little of the creative vision of the poet. (pp. 65-6)

Mr. Robinson is constantly desiring a larger canvas than his fugitive poems permit. He has tried plays, now he essays a narrative poem. Yet, for some reason, he seems never to have realized the different technique necessary for these more sustained efforts. He still remains the poet of the fleeting instant. (p. 66)

Certainly, no one will ever go to Mr. Robinson's books to make a gay mood more gay, to fill himself with the zest and sparkle of life. These things Mr. Robinson has not to give. His poems do not invigorate; they mellow and subdue. But in our material day, the spirituality of Mr. Robinson's work is tonic and uplifting.

The cryptic expression of much of his poetry can hardly be considered other than a flaw, as it often is in Browning, and why the failure in atmospheric sense which permits such names as "**Flammonde**" and "**Bokardo**" to connote New England types, is a question difficult to answer. Mr. Robinson is a painstaking poet, a poet of many revisions. He prunes every tendency to luxuriance from his style. He aims at the starkness of absolute truth, and granted that what he sees be the truth, he usually attains it.

This poetry is "cribbed, cabin'd and confined" to a remarkable degree, but it is undeniably, magnificently noble. (pp. 74-5)

Amy Lowell, "Edwin Arlington Robinson," in her Tendencies in Modern American Poetry *(© 1917 by Macmillan Company), The Macmillan Company, 1917 (and reprinted by Haskell House Publishers, Ltd., 1970), pp. 3-78.*

CONRAD AIKEN (essay date 1921)

[There] is perhaps no other poet, with the exception of Mr. Thomas Hardy, who so persistently and recognizably saturates every poem with his personality [as does Mr. Robinson. . . . His ballads are often] told by the retrospective friend of the protagonist—apologetic, humorous, tartly sympathetic, maintaining from beginning to end a note about midway between the elegiac and the ironic. This is the angle of approach which has been made familiar to us in how many of the short ballad-like narratives of Mr. Robinson. . . . What we see here, in short, is an instinctive and strong preference for that approach which will most enable the poet to adopt, toward his *personae,* an informal and colloquial tone, a tone which easily permits, even invites, that happy postulation of intimacy which at the very outset carries to the reader a conviction that the particular *persona* under dissection is a person seen and known. The note, we should keep in mind, is the ballad note—best when it is swiftest and most concise. . . . The action is indeed, in the vast majority of cases, an off-stage affair, the precise shape and speed of which we are permitted only to know in dark hints and sinister gleams.

The dark hint and sinister gleam have by many critics been considered the chief characteristics of this poet's style; and it is useful to keep them in mind as we consider, in a workshop light, his technique and mode of thought. (pp. 335-37)

If we examine Mr. Robinson's early work, in *The Children of the Night* or *The Town Down the River,* in search of the prototype of the "hint" and "gleam" which he has made—or found—so characteristic of himself, we discover them as already conspicuous enough. But it is interesting to observe that at this stage of his growth as an artist this characteristic revealed itself as a technical neatness more precisely than as a neatness of thought, and might thus have been considered as giving warning of a slow increase in subservience of thought to form. The "subtlety"—inevitable term in discussing the gleaming terseness of this style—was not infrequently to be suspected of speciousness. In **"Atherton's Gambit,"** and other poems, we cannot help feeling that the gleam is rather one of manner than of matter: what we suspect is that a poet of immense technical dexterity, dexterity of a dry, laconic kind, is altering and directing his theme, even inviting it, to suit his convictions in regard to style. Shall we presume to term this padding? Padding of a sort it certainly is; but Mr. Robinson's padding was peculiar to himself, and it is remarkable that precisely out of this peculiar method of padding was to grow a most characteristic excellence of his mature manner. For this padding (the word is far too severe) took shape at the outset as the employment, when rhyme-pattern or stanza dictated, of the "vague phrase," the phrase which gave, to the idea conveyed, an odd and somewhat pleasing abstractness. Here began Mr. Robinson's preference, at such moments, for the Latin as against the English word, since the Latin, with its roots in a remoter tongue, and its original tactilism therefore less apparent, permits a larger and looser comprehensiveness; and for such English words as have, for us, the dimmest of contacts with sensory reality. However, it must be remarked that, for the most part, in the first three volumes, the terse "comprehensiveness" thus repeatedly indulged in was often more apparent than real: one suspects that behind the veil of dimness, thus again and again flourished before us by the engaging magician, there is comparatively little for analysis to fasten upon. The round and unctuous neatness of the poems in these volumes has about it just that superfluity which inevitably suggests the hollow. This is not to imply that there are not exceptions, and brilliant ones—**"Isaac and Archibald"** is a wholly satisfying piece of portraiture, and **"Captain Craig"** has surely its fine moments. But for the development of this characteristic into something

definitely good one must turn to the volume called *The Man Against the Sky* and to the others that followed it. Here we see the employment of the "vague phrase" made, indeed, the keynote of the style—the "vague phrase," no longer specious, but genuinely suggestive, and accurately indicative of a background left dim not because the author is only dimly aware of it, but because dimness serves to make it seem the more gigantic. That, if true of the background, a strange, bare, stark world, flowerless, odorless, and colorless, perpetually under a threat of storm, is no less true of the protagonists. These, if their world is colorless, are themselves bodiless: we see them again and again as nothing on earth but haunted souls, stripped, as it were, of everything but one most characteristic gesture. If they are shadowy they seem larger for it, since what shadow they have is of the right shape to "lead" the eye; if their habiliments of flesh, gesture and facial expression are few, we see them the more clearly for it and remember them the better. This is the style at its best, but if we move on once more to the last volume, *The Three Taverns,* and *Avon's Harvest,* even perhaps to some things in *Lancelot* (though here there are other inimical factors to be considered), we shall see a deterioration of this style, and in a way which, had we been intelligent, we might have expected. For here the "vague phrase" has become a habitual gesture, otiose precisely in proportion as it has become habitual. The "vague phrase" has lost its fine precision of vagueness, the background has lost its reality in a dimness which is the dimness, too often, of the author's conception, and the one gesture of the protagonist is apt to be inconsiderable and unconvincing. We savor here a barren technical neatness. The conjuror more than ever cultivates a fine air of mystery; but nothing answers the too-determined wand.

In connection with this characteristic vague phrase, with its freight of hint and gleam, it is useful to notice, as an additional source of light, Mr. Robinson's vocabulary. We can not move in it for long without feeling that it indicates either a comparative poverty of "sensibility" or something closely akin to it; either a lack of sensibility, in the tactile sense, or a fear of surrendering to it. We have already noted, in another guise, the lack of color; we must note also the lack of sense of texture, sense of shape. As concerns his meter these lacks manifest themselves in a tendency to monotony of rhythm, to a "tumbling" sort of verse frequently out of key with the thought. . . . We must be careful not to impute to him a total lack of sensory responsiveness, for, as we shall see in *The Man Against the Sky* and *Merlin,* this element in his style reaches its proportional maximum and betrays a latent Mr. Robinson, a romanticist, who, if he uses color sparingly, uses it with exquisite effect.

In general, however, Mr. Robinson's eye is rather that of the dramatist than of the poet—it is perceptive not so much of the beautiful as of significant actions; and the beautiful, when it figures here at all, figures merely as something appropriate to the action. In this regard he is more akin to Browning than any other modern poet has been, if we except Mr. Thomas Hardy. Like Browning, he is a comparative failure when he is an out-and-out playwright; but he is at his most characteristic best when he has, for his poetic framework, a "situation" to present, a situation out of which, from moment to moment, the specifically poetic may flower. This flowering, we are inclined to think, is more conspicuous and more fragrant in *The Man Against the Sky* and *Merlin* than elsewhere, most fragrant of all in *Merlin.* Differences there are to be noted—**"Ben Jonson Entertains a Man from Stratford"** represents the perfection of Mr. Robinson's sense of scene and portraiture, sees and renders the actual, the human, with extraordinary richness. In *Merlin,* however, where Mr. Robinson's romantic *alter ego,* so long frustrated, at last speaks out, we cannot for long doubt that he reaches his zenith as a poet. The sense of scene and portraiture are as acute here, certainly, but the fine actuality with which they are rendered is, as in the best poetry, synonymous with the beautiful; and the poem, though long, is admirably, and beyond any other American narrative poem, sustained. The "vague phrase" here swims with color, or yields to the precise; the irony (Mr. Robinson's habitual mode of "heightening," so characteristically by means of ornate understatement) is in tone elusively lyrical. Merlin and Vivien move before us exquisitely known and seen, as none of the people whom Tennyson took from Malory ever did. It is one of the finest love stories in English verse. (pp. 337-40)

> *Conrad Aiken, "Robinson, Edwin Arlington (1921)" (originally published in* The Freeman, *September 21, 1921), in his* Collected Criticism *(copyright © 1935, 1939, 1940, 1942, 1951, 1958 by Conrad Aiken; reprinted by permission of Brandt & Brandt Literary Agents, Inc.), Oxford University Press, New York, 1968, pp. 333-40.*

HARRIET MONROE   (essay date 1926)

Robinson was chiefly interested in some of the less obvious aspects of human psychology—one might almost say the psychology of failure; and . . . he brought to bear upon this fascinating study a keenly sympathetic mind moved by wonder and awe, and lit by a somewhat acrid humor. The heart-motive was there also, but emotion was held in stern control—the intellect had to authenticate it. (p. 3)

If the psychology of failure, or of that uncertain middle ground between spiritual success and failure, is Robinson's recurrent motive, it may be interesting to study his attitude and his methods in presenting that motive in art. It is heroic, not ignoble, struggle that engages him, or if not heroic, at least the struggle of highly strung sensitive souls to fulfil their manifest destiny; ending either in acceptance of compromise, or in tragic spiritual revolt that induces some kind of dark eclipse. The form is usually narrative, with the poet as the narrator, under some assumption of friendship or at least neighborliness; but in the longer poems we have, as a rule, monologue and dialogue, the characters unfolding their perplexities, or recording their action upon each other, in long speeches which are not talk, as talk actually ever was or could be, but which are talk intensified into an extra-luminous self-revelation; as if an X-ray, turned into the suffering soul, made clear its hidden structural mysteries.

Robinson's method is thus akin to that of the psychoanalyst who encourages confessional monologue, or uses dialogue, as a probe to strike through the poison of lies and appearances and reveal the truth. (pp. 4-5)

> *Harriet Monroe, "Edward Arlington Robinson" in her* Poets & Their Art *(originally published in a slightly different form in* Poetry, *Vol. XXV, No. 4, January, 1925), © 1926 by The Macmillan Company), Macmillan, 1926, pp. 1-11.*

LLOYD MORRIS   (essay date 1927)

It may be said not only that **"Tristram"** is the finest of Mr. Robinson's narrative poems, but that it is among the very few fine modern narrative poems in English. In the total development of Mr. Robinson's art it occupies a special position. For in **"Tristram"** certain capacities hitherto only intimated are completely fulfilled; to many of Mr. Robinson's admirers who have not perceived the intimations in his previous work, this fulfilment may even seem surprising. To me it seems an inevitable development, and for me the poem takes its place as the most complete and most characteristic expression of his genius.

Hitherto Mr. Robinson has chosen to study passion rather in its consequences than in its career. He has been chiefly concerned with the ultimate effect of life upon the soul, and only infrequently has he been preoccupied by the ebb and flow of immediate experience. Many of his shorter poems suggest a story without telling it, or interpret a situation without reproducing it; **"Eros Turannos,"** which is perhaps the most notable of his poems about love, is actually a poem about the effect of having loved. In **"Merlin"** and again in **"Lancelot,"** however, Mr. Robinson indicated his capacity for the direct expression of immediate experience; in them a careful reader might have found the prophecy of a great poem having as its subject the career of passion in human destiny. It is this poem that Mr. Robinson has given us in **"Tristram."**

Like all legends which fix some of the eternal attitudes of the human spirit, that of Tristram and the two Isolts is susceptible of various interpretations. . . . It is of this fact that Mr. Robinson's superb treatment of the legend reminds us, for his poem, as I read it, is singularly free of ethical implications. This, he seems to say, is what happened; the events and not their interpretation form the subject. Life itself is the source of the tragedy in his version; and art is the celebration, not the indictment, of life.

In its dramatic structure **"Tristram"** has a classical austerity and inevitability, for all of Mr. Robinson's aptitude for restraint is, in this poem, directed upon the elements of form and design. What makes the poem notable, what makes it specifically distinguished in the roll of his works, is the intensity of its emotion; passion sweeps through it with a vigor and beauty that are new, in this full resonance, to Mr. Robinson's art. The old familiar intellectual magic that he has exercised is there, but it is subdued by the glamor of this new spell. For in **"Tristram"** Mr. Robinson has recreated, in its noblest guise, the ecstasy of passion.

> *Lloyd Morris, "The Career of Passion," in* The Nation *(copyright 1927 The Nation magazine, The Nation Associates, Inc.), Vol. CXXIV, No. 3229, May 25, 1927, p. 586.*

ALLEN TATE   (essay date 1933)

Edwin Arlington Robinson [is the] most famous of living American poets. . . . In his early years [Mr. Robinson] wrote some of the finest lyrics of modern times: these are likely to be his permanent claim to fame.

Able critics have thought otherwise. Not only, they say, are Mr. Robinson's long narrative poems his best work; they are the perfect realization of a "tragic vision." . . . [However,] Mr. Robinson writes, I believe, less from the tragic vision than from the tragic sentiment; and the result is the pathetic tale of obscure ambition or thwarted passion; not tragedy. (pp. 358-59)

[Is] Mr. Robinson a true tragic poet, or is he a modern poet like other modern poets, whose distinguished gifts are not enough to give him more than the romantic ego with which to work?

Talifer is a psychological narrative of the order of *The Man Against the Sky*. It is the eighth or ninth specimen of this kind of poem that Mr. Robinson has given us. Because the type has grown thinner with each example, the new narrative being, I believe, the least satisfactory of them all, it is the occasion of some inquiry into the causes of Mr. Robinson's preference for this particular form. It is a form that includes the three Arthurian poems, *Merlin, Lancelot,* and *Tristram.* . . .

Mr. Robinson's style in the new poem [*Talifer*] is uniform with the style of its predecessors; it is neither better nor worse than the style of *The Glory of the Nightingales* or of *Cavender's House*. It requires constant reviewing by Mr. Robinson's admirers to keep these poems distinct; at a distance they lose outline; blur into one another. They constitute a single complete poem that the poet has not succeeded in writing, a poem around which these indistinct narratives have been written.

We get, in them all, a character doomed to defeat, or a character who, when the tale opens, is a failure in the eyes of his town, but who wins a secret moral victory, as in *The Man Who Died Twice*. But Talifer, whose ego betrays him into an emotional life that he cannot understand, is not quite defeated. The tragic solution of his problem being thus rejected by Mr. Robinson, and replaced by a somewhat awkward bit of domestic irony, Talifer at first sight appears to be a new kind of Robinsonian character. Yet the novelty, I think, lies in the appearance. For Talifer is the standard Robinsonian character grown weary of the tragic sentiment, accepting at last the fact that his tilt at fate had less intensity than he supposed. . . . (pp. 360-61)

[The] character of Karen is vaguely conceived, with the result that Talifer's relation to her is incomprehensible. . . . The plot, in brief, lacks internal necessity. And the domestic peace of the conclusion remains arbitrary, in spite of Mr. Robinson's efforts through his mouthpiece, Doctor Quick, to point it up with some sly irony at the end. The irony is external—as if Mr. Robinson had not been able to tell the story for what it was, and had to say: This is what life is really like, a simple wife and a child—while ring those bells of peace that would be romantically tiresome if one had tragic dignity.

Mr. Robinson's genius is primarily lyrical; that is to say, he seldom achieves a success in a poem where the idea exceeds the span of a single emotion. It is, I think, significant that in his magnificent "The Mill" the tragic reference sustains the emotion of the poem: his narrative verse yields but a few moments of drama that are swiftly dispersed by the dry casuistry of the commentary. The early "Richard Cory" is a perfect specimen of Mr. Robinson's dramatic powers—when those powers are lyrically expressed. . . . (pp. 361-62)

It is probable that the explanation of the popular success of *Tristram*, and of most of Mr. Robinson's narratives, lies in our loss of the dramatic instinct. It is a loss increasingly great since the rise of middle-class comedy in the eighteenth century. Since then, in the serious play, instead of the tragic hero whose downfall is deeply involved with his suprahuman relations, we get the romantic, sentimental hero whose problem is chiefly one of adjustment to society, on the one hand,

and, on the other, one of futile self-assertion in the realm of the personal ego. Mr. Robinson's Talifer exhibits both these phases of the modern sensibility. . . . (p. 362)

The dramatic treatment of the situation [in *Tristram*] Mr. Robinson permits himself to neglect; for the dramatic approach would have demanded the possession, by the hero, of a comprehensive moral scheme. He would have rigorously applied the scheme to his total conduct, with the result that it would have broken somewhere and thrown the hero into a tragic dilemma, from which it had been impossible for him to escape. The story as it is told is hardly more than anecdotal; Mr. Robinson turns his plot, at the end, into an easy joke about the deliquescent effects of marriage upon the pretensions of human nature.

It is one of the anomalies of contemporary literature that Mr. Robinson, who has given us a score of great lyrics, should continue to produce these long narrative poems, one after another, until the reader can scarcely tell them apart. We may only guess the reason for this. Our age provides for the poet no epos or myth, no pattern of well-understood behavior, which the poet may examine in the strong light of his own experience. For it is chiefly those times that prefer one kind of conduct to another, times that offer to the poet a seasoned code, which have produced the greatest dramatic literature. (pp. 362-63)

Mr. Robinson has no epos, myth, or code, no suprahuman truth, to tell him what the terminal points of human conduct are, in this age; so he goes over the same ground, again and again, writing a poem that will not be written. . . .

It is to be hoped that Mr. Robinson will again exercise his dramatic genius where it has a chance for success: in lyrics. (p. 364)

> *Allen Tate, "Again, O Ye Laurels," in* The New Republic, *Vol. 76, No. 986, October 25, 1933 (and reprinted as "Edwin Arlington Robinson," in his* On the Limits of Poetry, *William Morrow, 1948, pp. 358-64).*

ROBERT FROST (essay date 1935)

It may come to the notice of posterity (and then again it may not) that this, our age, ran wild in the quest of new ways to be new. . . .

Robinson stayed content with the old-fashioned way to be new. (p. 33)

The latest proposed experiment of the experimentalists is to use poetry as a vehicle of grievances against the un-Utopian state. (p. 34)

But for me, I don't like grievances. I find I gently let them alone wherever published. What I like is griefs and I like them Robinsonianly profound. . . .

Robinson was a prince of heartachers amid countless achers of another part. The sincerity he wrought in was all sad. He asserted the sacred right of poetry to lean its breast to a thorn and sing its dolefullest. Let weasels suck eggs. I know better where to look for melancholy. A few superficial irritable grievances, perhaps, as was only human, but these are forgotten in the depth of griefs to which he plunged us. (p. 35)

[His] much-admired restraint lies wholly in his never having let grief go further than it could in play. So far shall grief go, so far shall philosophy go, so far shall confidences go, and no further. Taste may set the limit. Humor is a surer dependence. (p. 37)

His theme was unhappiness itself, but his skill was as happy as it was playful. There is that comforting thought for those who suffered to see him suffer. Let it be said at the risk of offending the humorless in poetry's train (for there are a few such): his art was more than playful; it was humorous.

The style is the man. Rather say the style is the way the man takes himself; and to be at all charming or even bearable, the way is almost rigidly prescribed. If it is with outer seriousness, it must be with inner humor. If it is with outer humor, it must be with inner seriousness. Neither one alone without the other under it will do. (pp. 37-8)

Robinson has gone to his place in American literature and left his human place among us vacant. We mourn, but with the qualification that, after all, his life was a revel in the felicities of language. (p. 39)

> *Robert Frost, in his introduction to* King Jasper *by Edwin Arlington Robinson (reprinted with permission of Macmillan Publishing Co., Inc.; copyright 1935 by Macmillan Publishing Co., Inc.; renewed 1963 by Macmillan Publishing Co., Inc.), Macmillan, 1935 (and reprinted as "Introduction to 'King Jasper',"* in Edwin Arlington Robinson: A Collection of Critical Essays, *edited by Francis Murphy, Prentice-Hall, Inc., 1970, pp. 33-9).*

YVOR WINTERS (essay date 1946)

[Edwin Arlington] Robinson was not a systematic thinker, and his thought shows conflicting tendencies. I believe that Robinson is essentially a counter-romantic, and yet he resembles other great counter-romantics of the nineteenth and twentieth centuries in the uncritical fashion with which he adopts a few current notions of a romantic nature as if they were axiomatic. (p. 29)

The evidence of a counter-romantic tendency in Robinson's thinking is to be found easily and repeatedly in his best poems, of which one of the most imposing is **"Hillcrest,"** from *The Man Against the Sky*. . . . The first six stanzas [of "Hillcrest"] show less strength than the last seven, but they seem largely successful, both in themselves and as a preparation for what follows. In two lines one sees an indication of one of Robinson's characteristic weaknesses . . . , a tendency to facile and superficial intellectualism, an intellectualism which is clever rather than perceptive, and which reduces his dry rhythm to [jingling parlor verse]. . . . This kind of thing intrudes, or almost intrudes, too often in Robinson's best work. As a statement of principles, the poem represents a pretty explicit negation of the essential ideas of the romantic movement, especially as that movement has been represented by the Emersonian tradition: it tells us that life is a very trying experience, to be endured only with pain and to be understood only with difficulty; that easy solutions are misleading; that all solutions must be scrutinized; and that understanding is necessary. It is a poem on the tragedy of human life and on the value of contemplation; it expresses neither despair nor triumph, but rather recognition and evaluation.

There are many poems of which the subject is the endurance of suffering, endurance unlightened with hope of anything better. These poems commonly deal with the lives of persons other than the poet, and the subjects offer material for the intellectual examination recommended in **"Hillcrest,"** for the moral curiosity of the heir of the Puritans. Such a poem as **"Eros Turannos,"** for example, puts into practice the principles stated in **"Hillcrest";** like **"Hillcrest,"** it is one of Robinson's greatest poems. . . . In such a poem we can see to an extraordinary degree the generalizing power of the poetic method; for this piece has the substance of a short novel or of a tragic drama, yet its brevity has resulted in no poverty—its brevity has resulted, rather, in a concentration of meaning and power. (pp. 30-2)

Three of Robinson's later sonnets seem to me among the greatest of his works: **"Lost Anchors," "Many Are Called,"** and **"The Sheaves."** In fact if one adds to these sonnets and **"The Wandering Jew"** two or three of the blank verse monologues—**"The Three Taverns," "Rembrandt to Rembrandt,"** and perhaps **"John Brown"**—one probably has Robinson at his greatest.

"Lost Anchors" is a commentary on the conversation of an old sailor; the sailor is not of great importance in himself, but he is made a symbol of the immeasurable antiquity of the sea and of its ruins. . . . The poem is wholly admirable, but the skill with which the sailor's illegitimate birth, mentioned, as it is, at the very end, is made to imply the amoral and archaic nature of the sea, is something which can scarcely be too long pondered or too greatly admired.

"Many Are Called" is a sonnet on the rarity of poetic genius and the loneliness of its reward. (pp. 39-40)

"The Sheaves" employs a descriptive technique to symbolize the impenetrable mystery of the physical universe as seen at any moment and the mystery of the fact of change. (pp. 41-2)

There are a good many poems which deal with the subject of God and immortality, but they are not remarkably clear. The most ambitious of these is **"The Man Against the Sky,"** a fairly long contemplative poem, of which the versification is generally similar to that of [Matthew Arnold's] "Dover Beach." The poem opens with a description of a solitary man crossing a hilltop into the sunset. This man is symbolic of man in general approaching death. Robinson says that his symbolic man may have progressed through great anguish to a triumphant death; or that he may have proceeded easily in the light of an uncritical faith; or that he may have been disillusioned, a stoical artist or philosopher, passing indifferently to extinction; or that he may have been disappointed in life and fearfully unreconciled to death; or that he may have been a mechanistic philosopher, proud of an intellectual construction which gave him no personal hope; but in any event that he represents all of us in that he approaches death alone, to face it as he is able. Robinson asks, then, whether we may not have some expectation of a future life, even if we doubt the existence of Heaven and Hell; and why, if we believe in Oblivion, we are guilty of perpetuating the race. He replies that we know, "if we know anything," the existence of a Deity, a Word, which we perceive fragmentarily and imperfectly, and that this knowledge is our sole justification for not ending ourselves and our kind. . . . The nature of this Deity, and the nature of our knowledge, are not defined further than this; the crux of the poem is thus offered briefly and vaguely in a few lines; and the greater part of the concluding section is devoted to describing the desolation which we should experience without this knowledge. Philosophically, the poem is unimpressive; stylistically, it is all quite [weak] . . . ; and structurally, it seems to defeat its purpose—for while it purports to be an expression of faith, it is devoted in all save these same few lines to the expression of despair. (pp. 46-8)

[There] are occasional indications of a romantic attitude in Robinson, an attitude belonging especially to the 1890's, the period of his youth. "**Flammonde**" will do as an example. The poem praises an individual whom one might characterize as the sensitive parasite or as the literary or academic sponge. . . . Now the near-genius of this kind, who represents an especially unfortunate type of failure, and who is frequently, as in the case of Flammonde, a somewhat unpleasant specimen, obsessed Robinson throughout his life for reasons which were largely personal. Frequently the poverty in which he lived threw him into the company of such people, and he may at times have visualized himself as one of them, though he could scarcely have visualized himself as Flammonde. But this obsession is not in itself an explanation of the language which Robinson uses, language which is reminiscent of the worst sentimentalism of the nineties, or even of lachrymose popular balladry. . . . The classicism, the precision, of Robinson's great work is not in this poem; there is nothing here of it but an empty mannerism. The substance as a whole and phrase by phrase is repulsively sentimental. Yet the poem has been repeatedly offered as one of Robinson's great achievements; it perhaps comes as close to the classical as the average critic of our time is able to follow. In "**Richard Cory**," another favorite, we have a superficially neat portrait of the elegant man of mystery; the poem builds up deliberately to a very cheap surprise ending; but all surprise endings are cheap in poetry, if not, indeed, elsewhere, for poetry is written to be read not once but many times. Such poems, however, although there are more like them, are relatively rare. (pp. 51-2)

[Nearly] all of Robinson's best poems appear to deal with particular persons and situations; in these poems his examination is careful and intelligent, his method is analytic, and his style is mainly very distinguished. If we are to risk pushing historical influences for all they are worth, we may say that in such poems Robinson exhibits the New England taste for practical morality, a passionate curiosity about individual dramas, and that in examining them he is guided by the moral and spiritual values of the general Christian tradition as they have come down to him in the form of folk wisdom or common sense, although in the application of these values he shows a penetration and subtlety which are the measure of his genius. In his more generalized, or philosophic, poems, he is almost always careless in his thinking and equally careless in his style, and it is in these poems that one may see—often in the method and sometimes in the form of the thought—the influence of Emersonian romanticism. "**Hillcrest**" is the most notable exception to this last statement.

Robinson is thus a poet whose thought is incomplete and in a measure contradictory; he would have been a greater poet had this not been so, but we should remember that he is no worse in this respect than Wordsworth, Hardy, Arnold or Bridges, if indeed he be as bad. Furthermore, within certain definitely delimited areas during the greater part of his career, his approach to his material is sound; we have seen this approach defined in "**Hillcrest**" and practiced in a number of other poems. The approach is what we may call critical

and rationalistic; and the poetry is reasoning poetry. . . . It is an extremely careful poetry. I do not mean this in any superficial sense; I mean that Robinson not only scrutinizes his thought but also is watchful of his feeling. His New England heritage here is not a defect, even though he chooses occasionally to ridicule it; the feeling which *ought* to be motivated by his comprehension of the matter is what he seeks to express—he is not simply on a tour in search of emotion. And since his matter is often important and his comprehension sometimes profound, this exact adjustment of feeling to motive results on certain occasions in poetry of extremely great value. (pp. 57-9)

Of the three Arthurian poems *Merlin* and *Lancelot* contain the best poetry—in fact, they contain the best poetry to be found in Robinson's longer works, regardless of subject; *Lancelot*, moreover, is the best constructed of Robinson's longer poems and strikes me as one of the most powerfully constructed long poems in English; *Tristram*, though far inferior in both respects, is probably better than nearly any other long poem by Robinson. (p. 61)

[*Merlin*] is the first attempt at what one might call a formal narrative. Merlin himself is conceived not as an aged and mysterious magician such as we find in Malory, not as a senile and incredible stock figure such as we find in Tennyson and find parodied in Mark Twain, but as an extremely intelligent man in middle age, at the height of great mental and physical power, who is adviser to the king not because he is incapable of being a knight but because he is capable of more important work. His prophetic power appears to be mainly the clear foresight of great intelligence, but it is given a supernatural air by the fatalism which is central to the theme. Merlin perceives that, given certain men of great force and limited understanding in certain initial situations, certain disasters are virtually inescapable. The poem deals with two actions, which are only loosely connected: on the one hand Merlin's love affair with Vivian, and on the other the disintegration of Arthur's kingdom. The first of these is handled ingeniously and sometimes charmingly, but it is not in itself extremely impressive; the second is seen as a spectacle, and in its last stages, and it is not seen as a drama, and the chief power of the poem resides in the commentary, largely through the mind of Merlin, on the spectacle. The actions are connected only to this extent, that Merlin's love for Vivian prevents his coming to Arthur's aid until too late, yet the real theme of the poem is that the catastrophe was inevitable and that no help would have availed. There is, then, no real causative relation of the one part to the other, though conversely Merlin's distress over Arthur's situation brings about the end of his relations with Vivian. The situation between Merlin and Vivian is dramatic as far as it goes, but it is of secondary interest in the poem; the main interest for us, as for Robinson, is the spectacle of Arthur's downfall, but this, so far as the structure of the entire poem goes, merely provides a frame for the love story. (pp. 62-4)

The poem shows something of Robinson's style at its worst and at its best. In *Merlin,* as in all the long poems, there is too much conversation, and Robinson shows a taste for a certain kind of conversation of which he is far from being a master—that is, for the playful and whimsical. This kind of conversation occurs most frequently, although not invariably, between men and women; at its best, it is not without a certain charm, but much of the time it displays a pedantic briskness or even pertness which is very hard to endure. . . .

The greatest poetry in *Merlin*, and some of the greatest in Robinson, is to be found in the concluding pages. . . . This appears to me to be great writing and well beyond anything in [Tennyson's] *Idylls of the King*. The dry movement so familiar in Robinson's blank verse has vanished; the language is weighted and sinuous, yet is wholly without ornament.

The power is the final result, however, of the concept back of the poem, the concept of human tragedy as the consequence of a falling away from wisdom, and of the falling away as inevitable. (pp. 67-8)

In the construction of [*Lancelot*] Robinson has avoided the weakness of *Merlin* and the weaknesses of Tennyson. The action is not double, as in *Merlin,* but single; yet the initial act which precipitates the catastrophe, Lancelot's going to Guinevere, does not in itself bear the whole burden of the catastrophe; for Modred is ready and waiting. . . . Arthur, moreover, bears a fair share of the responsibility for his own downfall. Modred, in Robinson as in Malory, is Arthur's illegitimate son, not as in Tennyson and more genteelly, his nephew; Arthur, in begetting Modred, has set his tragedy in motion, and in neglecting Modred to war on Lancelot, even after the return of the Queen, he incurs further responsibility. Lancelot and Guinevere thus have no more than a reasonable share of responsibility for the related tragedies. (pp. 82-3)

[Tennyson] is inferior to Robinson in [this] respect: he never draws his concept into a single related action, as Robinson does in *Lancelot.* Each ''Idyll'' allegorizes a fragmentary aspect of the theme, and the group of *Idylls* is a group of related fragments, with their only unity in the allegorical theme, with no unity in action. . . . But Robinson gives us the fall of Arthur's kingdom in a single unified story; and moreover, he gives us this merely as incidental, though closely related, to his main action, which deals with the effort of the individual to achieve growth out of error, salvation out of tragedy. Lancelot and Guinevere understood their own experiences, in spite of their normal human obtuseness and weakness, and they grow before our eyes; the growth is traced with a good deal of subtlety. Their choice of the conventual life is the outward sign of the later stages of their growth; it is not, as in Malory, a sign of exhaustion and perhaps a mere prelude to purgatory, nor is it, as in Tennyson, merely a pathetic manner of getting themselves off the stage. They have sacrificed the limited life to the greater, passion to wisdom, the personal to the general. The sacrifice is genuine tragedy; that which is purchased by the sacrifice is genuine gain. Robinson's plan has the power to generate and support poetry as great as he can write. . . . Had Robinson been as brilliant in the writing of his poem as he was in the planning, it could easily have had the greatness of a Racinian tragedy; the poem seems to have fallen short of this achievement mainly through Robinson's inability to criticize himself clearly, through a failure to cut and revise where cutting and revision were needed. As it is, the *Lancelot* is one of the few deeply impressive narrative poems written in English in more than two hundred years.

The theme of *Merlin* is fate; the subsidiary theme of *Lancelot* is the tragic theme that human acts have consequences and that imperfect humans act unwisely and arrive at disaster, and the primary theme is the triumph over tragedy through personal renunciation and understanding. It is these themes which give power to the characters and the actions. (pp. 84-6)

''The Three Taverns'' is an address by Paul the Apostle to the Christians who came out to meet him as he approached Rome toward the end of his career. It is partly a summary of his career and mainly an explanation of it. Robinson is dealing in this poem with a single-minded man of great intensity and dignity, whose purpose so far transcends all other aspects of his character as to render them negligible. (p. 134)

In ''The Three Taverns,'' there is no conflict between characters and no occasion for characters to argue, dissect and conceal, as there is in the longer poems; we have a great mind, of whom the records are remarkably full, drawing itself together to meet its end. Robinson handles the material as it should be handled; he does not expand it, but he contracts it to essentials; he exhibits the greatness of the man, not the mannerisms of his speech. The poem is bare of all decoration, and is written in a blank verse which is compact and well organized. It is one of the greatest poems of its kind and length in English. . . . The language offers no superficial enticements, and if read carelessly may seem to have little life; but as one understands it more precisely it gathers force. (p. 136)

''Rembrandt to Rembrandt'' is in the form of a soliloquy by the painter, or rather of an address, presumably a silent one, which he makes in the decline of his popularity to a portrait which he had painted of himself earlier in his career. It is a study in the bitterness of the neglected artist and in his doubts of himself, a subject which Robinson felt as a personal one. It is not the easiest of reading, but such difficulty as it offers is not factitious; it is the result of profound perception and extremely close and careful language. As in ''The Three Taverns'' and the great rimed poem of about the same period, ''The Wandering Jew,'' the language is largely abstract, and its power resides in the great concentration and generality of reference which can be achieved with such language; the great poems of *The Man Against the Sky* are open and obvious, both in plan and in perception, as compared to these three poems. . . . If I were to single out one of Robinson's poems in blank verse as perhaps the greatest, with respect both to scope of subject and to mastery of language, [''**Rembrandt to Rembrandt**''] I believe, would be the poem, in spite of my great admiration for a few others. . . . (pp. 138-39)

> *Yvor Winters, in his* Edwin Arlington Robinson *(copyright 1946 by New Directions; copyright renewed © 1974 by Janet Lewis Winters as widow of the author Yvor Winters; all rights reserved; reprinted by permission), New Directions, 1946, 162 p.*

HYATT HOWE WAGGONER (essay date 1950)

[E. A. Robinson] was, toward the end of his life, ordinarily unable to find the symbols he needed. His poetry gives evidence of the paralysis of the will . . . , though few of his poems express it. The result is, of course, an impoverishment of his work which, were it not for a relatively few poems, would make it impossible to consider him a major poet. The common, the almost unanimous opinion that Robinson's best work was done in the short poems, and especially in the poems of the early and middle periods, seems to me justified; but no good reason for this has ever been suggested. There must have been a number of reasons why the poems to which Robinson devoted the major portion of his poetic energy during the last twenty years or so of his life are generally less satisfactory than his early and his casual poems, but one of the reasons and not the least significant will be found, I think, to be similar to that which prevented Hawthorne from completing, indeed even from satisfactorily starting, his late romances. Robinson's sympathy for Hawthorne was deep, and the parallel between them striking. The thought of each led to an impasse which paralyzed the sensibilities. (pp. 18-19)

Robinson's poetry is that of a man whose mind and heart are at odds, His didactic poems are ordinarily his poorest work, and the more ambitious his effort in this direction the weaker the result. When **"The Man Against the Sky"** again and again breaks down into rhymed prose, the failure is not a "technical" one but the result of a breakdown of thought and feeling, an impasse of the soul. If the philosophic passages in his long narrative poems are frequently thin and verbose, unconvincing and even tedious, it is because they are most often on the theme of ultimate meaning and on this theme Robinson could only think and feel by turns. (pp. 22-3)

It is clear upon even casual inspection that the significance of science for Robinson in the nineties and the earliest years of this century lay in the fact that it was in conflict with "the creeds." Just which religious doctrines were disproved by science, Robinson never made clear in his poetry, nor is it likely that he thought much about it. It simply seemed to him as to others that science had cut the ground out from under any supernaturalist interpretation of life and the world. So the "obsolescent creeds" must go; only the "common creed of common sense," the doing of "his will," could stand in the face of the new knowledge. Yet there must, he thought, be immortality; if there were not another chance, it would be better if we had never been born. One must somehow maintain confidence in "Life's purposeful and all-triumphant sailing." There must be a God, and He must be Love, and just. "It is the faith within the fear That holds us to the life we curse." The chief impression one gets from Robinson's earliest work is that he is whistling in what he customarily wrote as "the Dark."

The faith he longed for and at times thought he had was a sort of Emersonian romantic naturalism. (pp. 24-5)

But Emerson's solution of saving God by identifying Him with the whole course and nature of things seemed less and less like a solution to Robinson, as to the literate public generally, as the years went by. Open skepticism became more prominent in the poems than the desperate hope, which became steadily more desperate and more attentuated. Like Cavender, Robinson knew a need to believe rather than a belief. . . . (p. 26)

"The Man Against the Sky" is Robinson's most ambitious attempt to set forth his thought on ultimate problems. Although modesty and insight made him declare that his ideas were probably the least important part of his poetry, this poem, on which as much as on any other his reputation was founded, is solely concerned with ideas. In it man's destiny is examined in the light of several current outlooks; various popular philosophies and attitudes toward life are discussed and rejected. (p. 29)

The form is very loose. Irregularly rhymed and with lines of varying length, it seems to fall logically into three main parts, but there is no formal relation between its ten verse paragraphs and the logic to its structure. The language is very general, with the abstract diction, suggestive of philosophic or polemic prose, varied here and there by generalized and

frequently traditional figures. Thus the commonly accepted goals, "a kingdom and a power and a Race," are said to end in "ashes and eternal night"; *eternity, death, faith, ambition, light,* and *dark* and their modifiers make up the core of the poem. The texture is thin, the method discursive. It seems to me that only Robinson's honesty and thoughtfulness save the poem from being completely uninteresting, and even these are not sufficient to make it a really distinguished poem, partly for the obvious reason that distinguished poems are not made by honesty and thoughtfulness and partly because even considered as a prose statement the poem is finally unsuccessful. (pp. 30-1)

The poem ends with a passage which is clearer prose than most of the earlier portions, though it is probably weaker poetry. It might perhaps be called a negative affirmation: since none of the five attitudes reviewed in the second part of the poem, nor any of the several "faiths" presented in the third part, can be accepted, and since no one today has "ever heard or ever spelt" the Word without experiencing the "fears and old surrenderings and terrors" that beset us, the conclusion can only be considered negative in fact, despite its apparent intention of affirming some kind of faith. . . . [The] poem leaves one with the clear impression that science has certainly made it clear that there is nothing after now and that all will indeed come to nought. So one is left echoing the question, why live? (pp. 34-5)

[It] is not only the logical structure—or lack of it—which makes the poem a significant revelation of the effect of the cosmic chill. Consider, for example, the ending from the point of view of its language and figures. Three rhyme words are capitalized in the last eleven lines; because they are both rhyme words and capitalized, they receive the chief emphasis in the climax of the poem. They are *Nought, Now,* and *Nothingness.* Generalized diction seems to me appropriate to certain kinds of poetry, but the effect here of the vague abstractions is surely to suggest the collapse of both poetic technique and controlled feeling. Even the *Nothingness* which receives the final emphasis has not been imaginatively felt, it has only been vaguely feared. Its alternative has not even been conceived. (pp. 35-6)

Even those three figures in the last eleven lines which are not wholly abstract are highly generalized; lacking precision, the "dungeons," "cold eternal shores," and "dark tideless floods" can have only a vague emotional import. They are evidences not only that Robinson too often availed himself of worn nineteenth-century language, but also that he did not really quite know, so far as he expressed himself in this poem, what it was he feared and what it was he hoped. Such was the effect of the cosmic chill on a poet who for other reasons and other poems deserves to rank as one of the chief modern American poets. (p. 36)

Hyatt Howe Waggoner, "E. A. Robinson: The Cosmic Chill," in his The Heel of Elohim: Science and Values in Modern American Poetry *(copyright 1950 by the University of Oklahoma Press; copyright renewed © 1977 by Hyatt Howe Waggoner), University of Oklahoma Press, 1950, pp. 18-40.*

LOUISE BOGAN   (essay date 1951)

The Children of the Night is one of the hinges upon which American poetry was able to turn from the sentimentality of the nineties toward modern veracity and psychological truth.

It is filled with portraits of men who are misfits when they are not actual outcasts; and into each is incorporated something of Robinson's own lonely and eccentric nature. The secret dreamer, the lonely old roisterer, the enigmatic dandy, the baffled lover, the cynic and the suicide—all are filled with an acute but ambiguous bitterness, and at the same time are touched in with the utmost delicacy and tenderness of understanding. Robinson, with the sympathy of a brother in misfortune, notes their failures and degradations without losing sight of their peculiar courage. The structure of these early poems is impeccably correct although subtly varied. Their originality lies in their tone, and in their diction. Robinson, from the beginning, was able to twist the clichés of sentimental poetry to a wry originality. His vocabulary and idiom were based squarely on the everyday New England speech of his period; and his rhythms are often exactly the rhythm of that speech. To reproduce these rhythms was in itself a triumph at the time. The native witticisms, which appear so delightfully in **"Mr. Flood's Party"** were themselves formal and fixed; Robinson knew this and treated them with a fitting poetic formality. Robinson never completely lost this peculiar coloring; the dry native strand is woven into even the most nebulous and complicated work of his later period. And if his beliefs, based on a Protestant small-town skepticism, never greatly enlarged, neither did they wear down into insignificance through the abrasion of time and subsequent experience. (pp. 20-1)

Robinson's reaction to events and his conclusions concerning human life and destiny continued to be based on the idealism of his youth, to which was added a simple variety of agnosticism and stoicism. His later long poems, in which he adumbrated rather than described a set of human actions, are, it is evident, profoundly symbolic. . . . [Robinson's symbols] were his obsessions rather than his creations, and they were repetitive obsessions as time went on. His tenuosities of language served to disguise them, so that the poet could bring them up to consciousness; they are never figures of human life, but of fear, bafflement, ambivalence, and despair. (p. 22)

> Louise Bogan, "The Line of Truth and the Line of Feeling," in her Achievement in American Poetry: 1900-1950 *(copyright 1951 Henry Regnery Company), Henry Regnery Company, 1951, pp. 19-27.**

ELLSWORTH BARNARD (essay date 1952)

Though [Edwin Arlington] Robinson's characters are all individuals, they fall roughly into several classes, and among the members of each class one may discover a sort of family resemblance. The group of which the discerning reader perhaps becomes first aware, and which includes some of the poet's most vivid and stirring creations, is composed of persons who are failures in the eyes of the world but not (if the phrase may be used without committing Robinson to a theological dogma) in the eyes of God. For them, whatever wealth or fame or other treasures they may have once laid up on earth have vanished—snatched or worn or thrown away by Fate or Time or themselves. Yet in place of these tangible glories, after moth and rust and unreined passion have done their work, has come a faith that in some sense or other they are "saved," that in the sum of things their lives have counted, and that for them the future, on earth or elsewhere, can hold no terrors.

This is the central theme of *Captain Craig*. . . . (pp. 122-23)

The triumph (as Robinson at least regards it) that is recorded at the end of [*Captain Craig*] is not only over the loss of things conventionally valued but over the still more corrosive sense of having betrayed one's better self. It is a question whether the trial endured by these persons [like Captain Craig] is harder or easier, their triumph greater or less, than that of another group of people that we meet in Robinson's poems: those who, like Job in the great biblical drama, are afflicted though guiltless; who in fact seem singled out to be the pawns in a cosmic contest between Good and Evil. Certainly it is no easy victory that is won by the painter in *Rembrandt to Rembrandt*. And an even higher price (perhaps) is paid by other historical characters, in whose fidelity to a vision Robinson found a theme for poetry. Such are John Brown, Toussaint L'Ouverture, and Lincoln (*The Master*). Their world is far from Rembrandt's; the evil that they defy is more aggressive; the climax of their strife is more dramatic; but in essence their trial and triumph are the same. The three crusaders against Negro slavery die . . . ; but in the long and painful struggle preceding the fatal climax they have been sustained by the vision—which history is slowly justifying—of ultimate victory for their ideals. (pp. 124-25)

A second more or less clearly defined category of characters, again dependent on the basic Robinsonian principle of disparity between appearance and reality, includes those persons whose lives are outwardly illustrious but inwardly empty.

The transition—logical, of course, and not chronological—between this and the previous group may be found in the protagonists of two late long poems: Nightingale in *The Glory of the Nightingales* and Matthias in *Matthias at the Door*. They save their souls in the end, one by dying and one by living. But their previous lives are of a different pattern from those so far considered. Born to greatness or to the easy achievement of it—great possessions and the power that these confer, a name written large for all to know, the honor and admiration of the multitude (not made less pleasant by some admixture of envey and fear)—they have found this outward splendor all but fatal to inward peace, and have been tempted by it to what is for Robinson the cardinal sin: callousness or cruelty toward other human beings. And they are only saved because events deprive them of their satisfaction with what they have had. (pp. 126-27)

In a way, therefore, Nightingale and Matthias are still among the "elect." But there are others among Robinson's characters for whom, from the limbo of mere material wealth and social station, no redemption is destined. The most obvious and perhaps the least interesting (though, like most other characters in the long poems, he improves with repeated acquaintance) is King Jasper, the captain of industry in Robinson's self-styled "treatise on economics," whose kingdom was founded on the betrayal of his friend Hebron, and who finds no way to atone for this betrayal before retribution in the form of his friend's fanatical son strikes him down....

A spiritual cousin of King Jasper is (oddly, it may seem) King Arthur, whose kingdom is built upon a quicksand of dishonor that is fated finally to engulf him. The glamour of his reign hides from all but a few the unconfessed sins of his early manhood; but it cannot avert the ruin to which they eventually give rise. (p. 127)

Arthur and Jasper perhaps deserve what comes to them. At least they seem clearly to have caused it. If destiny was unkind, it was only through having endowed them with power, or the desire for it, without the strength to resist its corrupting influence. But for others the threads of life are tied in a different, and more confusing, though not less fatal knot. For they have wealth and a respected place in the world, without the temptation to evil that kings must face—and without, in fact, being guilty of evil, as far as we can see. And yet they also are destroyed.

One of them is Richard Cory. There is no hint here of hidden guilt. . . . We seem to be confronted here with the dark opposite of the Divine Grace that brings salvation to Captain Craig and Fernando Nash and Lancelot and the rest. Somehow Richard Cory is cursed with the inability to believe that life is worth living. . . . The thing that in most men gives worth to life, even in the midst of suffering, has simply been left out of his makeup. And with only this thing lacking, and nothing to suffer except the lack of it, life becomes intolerable. But why this spiritual vacancy exists remains a mystery.

From another point of view, this lack may sometimes seem to be a gift, although an apparently malign one—the gift of seeing the hollowness, the worthlessness, of what men commonly and conventionally live for, or are at least satisfied with. For most practical purposes, one may infer, no faith is needed; an illusion will do as well. But what of the man, asks Robinson, to whom illusion is forbidden and faith not granted?

He asks it most explicitly in *Tasker Norcross*, a poem that probably only he would ever have thought of writing. . . . Norcross differs from Richard Cory in that he has few gifts (except wealth) and no graces. But he has the same fatal incapacity for illusion, and it destroys him. . . . [He] has no friends—and knows it. He has no religion—and is aware of the vacancy in his life. For him, pictures, symphonies, and architectural triumphs are merely groups of sensations that have nothing to say—yet he perceives the pleasure that they bring to others. Where most persons are able to find meaning and purpose in the world, he finds a vacuum. (pp. 127-29)

From such persons as Tasker Norcross it is only a step to the place reserved for a greater number of Robinson's characters than are to be met with in either of the regions so far explored; a place to whose inhabitants the Fates permit neither outward nor inward success, neither the form nor the substance of security; neither material mansions to protect them as far as may be from the ills that flesh is heir to, nor houses not built with hands where mind and soul may be at peace.

Among these dwellers in the valley of the shadow are those who are paradoxically distinctive and interesting—to the reader—mainly because, as in the case of Norcross, their lives and characters are almost destitute of distinction and interest. . . . It is characteristic that Robinson should have undertaken to call the world's attention to these forgotten men and women. (pp. 130-31)

Obviously an author must not paint such portraits too often. In the nature of things one cannot write too much about dullness without becoming dull. And even Robinson, with his penetrating eye for the spark of kindred humanity alight within the dingiest bodily dwelling, behind the drabbest curtains of spiritual commonplaceness, has relatively few characters of this sort; and most of them are presented posthumously, when "eloquent, just, and mighty Death" has conferred upon them some measure of distinction. (p. 131)

More commonly, Robinson prefers to deal with lives distinguished by some ironic incongruity. And among poems of this sort, few are more appealing than the stories of persons whose dreams outrun accomplishment and become in the end a substitute for it; men and women who are indeed "pensioners of dreams" and "debtors of illusions," but who differ from their kindred in *The Valley of the Shadow* in that their dreams are not the result of opium but are the opiate itself. (p. 132)

Akin to the dreamers in their reluctance to face reality are those who waste their lives in trivial activities. . . .

Under another heading in Robinson's catalogue of failures come the stories of promise unfulfilled or talent misapplied: lives like those of Captain Craig or Fernando Nash, but without the saving grace that they are permitted to know. . . . (p. 133)

At this point it may begin to seem that almost all existence, to Robinson's mind, is a "wrong world" of some sort or other. Yet perhaps still sadder than any of the sufferers so far met are those condemned for no apparent cause to a solitary confinement of the soul. (p. 134)

To be sure, the note is never shrill or strident. Robinson's shuddering abhorrence of anything that might be labeled "sentimentalism" makes him keep the emotion firmly in check—by comic or ironic touches, by stress on seemingly trivial everyday details, by calculated indirection and understatement. Such is the tone, for instance, of *The Long Race* and *Reunion*, two sonnets that dramatize the slow but inevitable and irreparable destruction of human ties by time and separation. . . .

In *Aunt Imogen* it is a person's whole life that is involved. Yet the near tragedy is not thrust upon the reader, who may very well carry away from a casual perusal only an impression of the festal mood of the children—"Aunt Imogen made everybody laugh"—rather than the woman's endurance of the lightning-like assault of terror and despair that comes with the recognition that her passionate longing for motherhood must always be unrealized. . . . (p. 135)

There are in Robinson's poems, nevertheless, men and women to whom destiny is kind: who, if they have the physical well-being and the high station in society that are generally thought to constitute success, do not have to pay for these with moral ruin or a bankrupt faith; or who, if such blessings are denied, do not miss them. Nor for them do peace and inner security, though sometimes painfully bought, come only at the end and at the cost of a lifetime of illness, poverty, loneliness, frustration, disgrace, or sense of guilt. Their ambitions and endowments correspond; for them the possible and the desirable more or less coincide; what they want, on the whole, is what they get, and what they get is all they need.

This harmony and proportion are found most often, in Robinson's view, in lives that are otherwise undistinguished. (pp. 139-40)

Isaac and Archibald, for instance, are "two old men"—that is all, and that is enough. Their happiness is simply in "all the warmth and wonder of the land" around them; in their thankfulness to God "for all things / That He had put on earth for men to drink" and otherwise enjoy; and in their serene and undramatic faith. . . .

Here there is nothing of Wordsworth's sententiousness about "rustic and humble life"; nor is there any intimation that rusticity and humbleness are the cause of virtue and contentment. But there is an assurance no less strong than in the work of the great prophet of English Romanticism that wealth and station are irrelevant to the "good life." (p. 140)

Such cheerful stories, however, can hardly be considered typical of Robinson's work. More often, the cost of happiness, when it comes, is so high that one wonders whether it has been, or ever can be, fully paid. At the end of *Roman Bartholow*, for instance, Bartholow has the world all before him, and does not doubt that the new life will be fair. Yet the question lingers whether the future can be wholly unshadowed by the horror of what has passed—his own long despair, his betrayal by the man who had been his savior, the suicide of the woman whom he had once loved. Is the happiness that he and the others in the group find at last, with or without a painful apprenticeship, *altogether* without alloy? (p. 143)

It will have been evident in the foregoing analysis that the lines of classification are not always sharp, straight, and unyielding; that sometimes the boundary between success and failure is hard to draw, and that often the balance in which happiness and misery are weighed is hard to read. (p. 144)

Ellsworth Barnard, "Characters: A Spiritual Genealogy," in his Edwin Arlington Robinson *(© 1952 by Macmillan Publishing Co., Inc.), Macmillan, 1952, pp. 121-48.*

BABETTE DEUTSCH (essay date 1952)

[Edwin Arlington Robinson] deserves consideration because his best work is finely representative of traditional poetry, because in a few pieces he evoked, as no poet had previously, a landscape with figures familiar to his fellow Americans. . . . [He] might be humorous about very human failings . . . , but he seldom omitted to convey, as a good New Englander, the sense of moral responsibility.

Robinson wrote a number of long narratives in verse, some purporting to deal with his contemporaries, the more famous ones serving up stories from the Arthurian cycle in a less watered fashion than Tennyson's but without the blood and iron of Malory. He had small gift for narrative, and a great temptation to chew a cud of "ifs" and "buts" rolled up into one juiceless ball. Whether his characters move against the drafty, tapestried background of the middle ages or among the furniture of twentieth-century America, they have a habit of talking like their author. Their metaphors, like his, are largely a matter of lights and shadows, of music, discords, and silences. Their diction, like his, is involved and abstract.

[Robinson's] mannered elaborations of sentence structure . . . readily fall into hesitancies and restrictive glosses reminiscent of Henry James. The poet had a less sensitive grasp of language than the novelist and a less profound feeling for symbolism, so that his verse narratives are not as poetic as James' greater prose fictions. Nevertheless the two writers exhibit interesting resemblances. Both rely on a gift for creating atmosphere. Both tend to shove the murders and adulteries offstage, and make the action the subject of endless discussion among the characters. Both are preoccupied with the theme, exemplified in the lives of so many New Eng-

landers and at some period in their own lives, that worldy failure may issue in spiritual triumph, though they recognized how barren even to the victors spiritual victories may sometimes seem.

The Puritan consciousness, the Puritan conscience, are offered repeated, if somewhat obscure, testimonials. Indeed, the pallid gleam of transcendentalism hovers over Robinson's work, from the sonnet called **"Credo"** that he wrote before the turn of the century to the long narrative in verse that he completed just before his death nearly forty years later. (pp. 55-6)

[If] he was not a deeply imaginative poet nor a technical innovator, he was an acute explorer of a small corner of his world, concerning himself particularly with those shabby, frustrated, but fascinating inhabitants of it who command our charity and our amusement, our pity and our shamed admiration. (p. 57)

Robinson's more ambitious dramatic monologues, such as **"Ben Jonson Meets a Man from Stratford"** or **"Rembrandt to Rembrandt,"** do not have the authenticity of his New England portraits. At least one of these, **"Isaac and Archibald,"** . . . anticipated, in its apparent simplicity and its gentle irony, the rural conversation pieces that Robert Frost was to produce more than a decade later. One is made to see with uncommon clarity two old men, from the viewpoint of a little boy who walked one of them to and from the other's farm, went down cellar with him to fetch cider, sat with the ancient pair in the orchard while they played seven-up and made sly innuendoes on the subject of old age, and listened to each in turn lament, not without pride in his own relative vigor, the senescence of the other. The presentation of the two old men through the eyes of the boy is an instance of Henry James' indirect method of revealing character, and the piece has many slighter Jamesian touches, such as the phrase about "a small boy's adhesiveness / To competent old age," or Isaac's "sweet severity" that made him "think of peach-skins and goose-flesh." Yet it remains all recognizably Robinson's own, including the reference to a transcendental "light behind the stars," and his characteristic method of seeking to define by negatives and repetitions. (pp. 58-9)

Robinson was incapable of the savage realism he praised though he reiterated the need to look truth in the face and wrote a few dramatic lyrics, like **"The Mill,"** stern enough to have been penned by Hardy. Technically, his work is of interest insofar as it shows how individual phrasing is an index to style where a man is using the accepted forms of an older day. His preference for blank verse and his monotonous end-stopped lines emphasize the old-fashioned character of his performance. It is honest, serious work, and represents, in the old phrase, "the application of ideas to life." Too often the ideas have reference to a world no longer actual and inadequately realized. Robinson's pedestrian reasonableness generally prevented him from transmuting his ideas into the stuff of poetry. Yet his most severe and delicate sonnets, lyrics, and character studies are memorably wrought "in the old style that lives the while it passes." (p. 60)

Babette Deutsch, "The Glove of a Neighborhood," in her Poetry in Our Time *(copyright © 1952 by Henry Holt and Company, Inc.), Holt, 1952 (and reprinted by Columbia University Press, 1956), pp. 55-78.*

JAMES DICKEY (essay date 1965)

Robinson achieved unusual popularity in his lifetime. When he died . . . , he had won the Pulitzer Prize three times and had gained a distinction rare for a poet—his book-length poem *Tristram* had become a best seller. But in the public mind, Robinson has during recent years been regarded as only his vices of prolixity, irresolution, and occasional dullness would have him. Yet if we could manage to read Robinson as if we did not know him—or at least as if we did not know him quite so well as we had believed—or if we could come to him as if he were worth rereading, not out of duty and obedience to literary history but as a possible experience, we would certainly gain a good deal more than we would lose. (pp. 210-11)

[A first perusal of **"Calverly's,"** for instance, might] lead the perceptive reader to suspect that the poet is more interested in the human personality than he is in, say, nature; that he is interested in people not only for their enigmatic and haunting qualities but also for their mysterious exemplification of some larger entity, some agency that, though it determines both their lives and their deaths, may or may not have any concern for them or knowledge of them. Of these men, the poet cannot say "where their light lives are gone," and because he cannot say—and because there is nothing or no way to tell him—he cannot know, either, what his own fate is, or its meaning; he can know only that he himself was once at Calverly's, that the others who were there are gone, and that he shall follow them in due time. He cannot say what this means or whether, in fact, it means anything. Though he can guess as to what it might mean, all he finally *knows* is what has happened.

This condition of mind is a constant throughout all but a very few of Robinson's poems. It links him in certain curious ways with the Existentialists, but we are aware of such affinities only tangentially, for Robinson's writings, whatever else they may be, are dramas that make use of conjecture rather than overt statements of ideas held and defended. (pp. 213-14)

The unity of the poet's mind is a quality that is certain to make its presence felt very early in the reader's acquaintance with Robinson. One can tell a great deal about him from the reading of a single poem. All the poems partake of a single view and a single personality, and one has no trouble in associating the poems in strict forms with the more irregular ones as the products of the same vision of existence. The sensibility evidenced by the poems is both devious and tenacious, and it lives most intensely when unresolved about questions dealing with the human personality. Robinson is perhaps the greatest master of the speculative or conjectural approach to the writing of poetry. Uncertainty was the air he breathed, and speculation was not so much a device with him—though at its best it is a surpassingly effective technique—as it was a habit of mind, an integral part of the self. (p. 214)

Robinson's tentative point of view was solidly wedded to a style that has exactly the same characteristics as his mind. It makes an artistic virtue, and often a very great one, of arriving at only provisional answers and solutions, of leaving it up to the reader's personality—also fated—to choose from among them the most likely. Thus a salient quality of Robinson's work is the extraordinary roundness and fullness he obtains from such circumlocutions of his subjects, as though he were indeed turning (in William James's phrase) "the cube of reality." One is left with the belief that in any given sit-

uation there are many truths—as many, so to speak, as there are persons involved, as there are witnesses, as there are ways of thinking about it. And encompassing all these is the shadowy probability that none of them is or can be final. What we see in Robinson's work is the unending and obsessional effort to make sense of experience when perhaps there is none to be made. The poet, the reader, all of us are members of humanity in the sense Robinson intended when he characterized the earth as "a kind of vast spiritual kindergarten where millions of people are trying to spell God with the wrong blocks." (p. 215)

Robinson wrote an enormous amount of poetry . . . , but at the center of it and all through it is the Personality, the Mind, conditioned by its accidental placement in time and space—these give the individuations that make drama possible—but also partaking of the hidden universals, the not-to-be-knowns that torment all men. In these poems "The strange and unremembered light / That is in dreams" plays over "The nameless and eternal tragedies / That render hope and hopelessness akin." Like a man speaking under torture—or self-torture—Robinson tells of these things, circling them, painfully shifting from one possible interpretation to another, and the reader circles with him, making, for want of any received, definitive opinion, hesitant, troubling, tentative judgments. The result is an unresolved view, but a view of remarkable richness and suggestibility, opening out in many directions and unsealing many avenues of possibility: a multidimensional view that the reader is left pondering as the poem has pondered, newly aware of his own enigmas, of what he and his own life—its incidents and fatalities—may mean, could mean, and thus he is likely to feel himself linked into the insoluble universal equation, in which nature itself is only a frame of mind, a projection of inwardness, tormenting irresolution, and occasional inexplicable calms. (p. 216)

Robinson's method—which on some fronts has been labeled anti-poetic—would not amount to as much as it does were not the modes of thought presented in such powerful and disturbing dramatic forms. For an "anti-poet," Robinson was an astonishing craftsman. One has only to read a few of his better poems in the classic French repetitive forms, such as **"The House on the Hill,"** to recognize the part that traditional verse patterns play in his work. . . . [It] is true that his verse is oddly bare, that there are few images in it—though, of these, some are very fine indeed—and that most of it is highly cerebral and often written in a scholarly or pseudoscholarly manner that is frequently more than a little pedantic. Many of his poems contain an element of self-parody, and these carry more than their share of bad, flat, stuffy writing. . . . At his worst, Robinson seems to go on writing long after whatever he has had to say about the subject has been exhausted; there is a suspicious look of automatism about his verse instrument. The reader, being made of less stern stuff, will almost always fail before Robinson's blank verse does. (pp. 217-18)

[If] the casual reader skims only a little of a particular poem and finds that nothing much is happening or that event, action, and resolution are taking place only in various persons' minds, he is also likely to shy away. But once *in* the poem, committed to it, with his mind winding among the alternative complexities of Robinson's characters' minds—that is, winding with Robinson's mind—the reader changes slowly, for Robinson hath his will. One is held by the curious dry magic that seems so eminently unmagical, that bears no resemblance to the elfin or purely verbal or native-woodnote magic for which English verse is justly celebrated. It is a magic for which there is very little precedent in all literature. Though external affinities may be asserted and even partially demonstrated with Praed and Browning, though there are occasional distant echoes of Wordsworth, Keats, Hardy, and Rossetti, Robinson is really like none of them in his root qualities; his spell is cast with none of the traditional paraphernalia, but largely through his own reading of character and situation and fate, his adaptation of traditional poetic devices to serve these needs—an adaptation so unexpected, so revolutionary, as to seem not so much adaptation as transformation. (pp. 218-19)

Robinson is equally skilled as a technician in both memorable poems and trivial ones. In the less interesting poems, particularly the longer ones, Robinson's air of portentousness can be tiresome. Reading these, one is tempted to say that Robinson is the most prolific *reticent* poet in history. Though he gives the impression that he is reluctant to write down what he is writing, he often goes on and on, in a kind of intelligent mumbling, a poetical wringing of the hands, until the reader becomes restive and a little irritated. . . . Then there is the gray, austere landscape of the poems, the lack of background definition. One is accustomed to finding the characters in a poem—particularly a narrative poem—in a *place*, a location with objects and a weather of its own, a world which the reader can enter and in which he can, as it were, live with the characters. But there is very little of the environmental in Robinson's work. What few gestures and concessions he makes to the outside world are token ones; all externality is quickly devoured by the tormented introversion of his personages. In Robinson, the mind eats everything and converts it to part of a conflict with self; one could say with some justification that all Robinson's poems are about people who are unable to endure themselves or to resolve their thoughts into some meaningful, cleansing action. So much introversion is not only harrowing; it can also be boring, particularly when carried on to the enormous lengths in which it appears in **"Matthias at the Door"** and **"Avon's Harvest."**

And yet with these strictures, the case against Robinson's poetry has pretty much been stated, and we have on our hands what remains after they have been acknowledged.

No poet ever understood loneliness or separateness better than Robinson or knew the self-consuming furnace that the brain can become in isolation, the suicidal hellishness of it, doomed as it is to feed on itself in answerless frustration, fated to this condition by the accident of human birth, which carries with it the hunger for certainty and the intolerable load of personal recollections. He understood loneliness in all its many forms and depths and was thus less interested in its conventional poetic aspects than he was in the loneliness of the man in the crowd. . . . (pp. 219-20)

The acceptance of the fact that there is no way, that there is nothing to do about the sadness of most human beings when they are alone or speaking to others as if to themselves, that there is nothing to offer them but recognition, sympathy, compassion, deepens Robinson's best poems until we sense in them something other than art. A thing inside us is likely to shift from where it was, and our world view to change, though perhaps only slightly, toward a darker, deeper perspective. . . .

Though Robinson's dramatic sense was powerful and often profound, his narrative sense was not. His narrative devices are few, and they are used again and again. (p. 221)

And yet Robinson's peculiar elliptical vision, even when it is boring, is worth the reader's time. The tone of his voice is so distinctive, his technique so varied and resourceful, and his compassion so intense that something valuable comes through even the most wasteful of his productions. Not nearly enough has been made of Robinson's skill, the chief thing about which is that it is able to create, through an astonishing number of forms and subjects, the tone of a single voice, achieving variety within a tonal unity. And it is largely in this tone, the product of outlook (or, if I may be forgiven, inlook), technique, and personality, that Robinson's particular excellence lies. . . . (p. 222)

Though his mind was not rich in a sensuous way, it was both powerful and hesitant, as though suspended between strong magnets. This gives his work an unparalleled sensitivity in balance; and from this balance, this desperately poised uncertainty, emanates a compassion both very personal and cosmic—a compassion that one might well see as a substitute for the compassion that God failed to supply. It is ironic at times, it is bitter and self-mocking, but it is always compassion unalloyed by sentimentality; it has been earned, as it is the burden of the poems themselves to show. This attitude, this tone, runs from gentle, rueful humor—though based, even so, on stark constants of human fate such as the aging process and death—to the most terrible hopelessness. (pp. 222-23)

At times it appears that Robinson not only did not seek to avoid dullness but courted it and actually used it as a device, setting up his major points by means of it and making them doubly effective by contrast, without in the least violating the unity of tone or the huge, heavy drift of the poem toward its conclusion. He is a slow and patient poet; taking his time to say a thing as he wishes to say it is one of his fundamental qualities. This has worked against him, particularly since his work has survived into an age of anything but slow and patient readers. (p. 225)

The Robinson line is simple in the way that straightforward English prose is simple; the declarative sentence is made to do most of the work. His questions, though comparatively rare, are weighted with the agony of concern, involvement, and uncertainty. It is the thought, rather than the expression of the thought, that makes some of Robinson difficult, for he was almost always at pains to write simply, and his skills were everywhere subservient to this ideal. My personal favorite of Robinson's effects is his extremely subtle use of the line as a means of changing the meaning of the sentence that forms the line, the whole poem changing direction slightly but unmistakably with each such shift.

> What is it in me that you like so much,
> And love so little?

And yet for all his skill, Robinson's technical equipment is never obvious or obtrusive. . . . (p. 226)

Robinson's favorite words, because they embody his favorite way of getting at any subject, are "may" and "might." The whole of the once-celebrated *"The Man Against the Sky,"* for example, is built upon their use. When the poet sees a man climbing Mount Monadnock, it is, for the purposes of his poem, important that he *not* know who the man is or what he is doing there, so that the poem can string together a long series of conjectural possibilities as to who he might be, what might happen to him, and what he might conceivably represent. (p. 227)

This particular poem, which not only uses this approach but virtually hounds it to death, is not successful mainly because Robinson insists on being overtly philosophical and, at the end, on committing himself to a final view. Another shortcoming is that he is not sufficiently close to the man, for his poems are much better when he knows *something* of the circumstances of a human life, tells what he knows, and *then* speculates, for the unresolved quality of his ratiocinations, coupled with the usually terrible *facts*, enables him to make powerful and haunting use of conjecture and of his typical "may have" or "might not have" presentations of alternative possibilities.

It is also true of this poem that it has very little of the leavening of Robinson's irony, and this lack is detrimental to it. This irony has been widely commented upon, but not, I think, quite as accurately as it might have been. Though it infrequently has the appearance of callousness or even cruelty, a closer examination, a more receptive *feeling* of its effect, will usually show that it is neither. It is, rather, a product of a detachment based on helplessness, on the saving grace of humor that is called into play because nothing practical can be done and because the spectator of tragedy must find some way in which to save himself emotionally from the effects of what he has witnessed. . . . [The irony] is not based on showing in what ridiculous and humiliating ways the self-delusion of Leffingwell made of him a parasite and sycophant; it works through and past these things to the much larger proposition that such delusion is necessary to life, that, in fact, it is the condition that enables us to function at all. (pp. 227-28)

[In] Robinson's poems the necessity to lie (and, with luck, sublimely) is connected to the desire to remake the world by remaking that portion of it that is oneself. Robinson shows the relation between such lies and the realities they must struggle to stay alive among, and he shows them with the shrewdness and humor of a man who has told such lies to himself but sadly knows them for what they are. The reader is likely to smile at the absurdity—but also to be left with a new kind of admiration for certain human traits that he had theretofore believed pathetic or contemptible. (p. 229)

It is curious and wonderful that this scholarly, intelligent, childlike, tormented New England stoic, "always hungry for the nameless," always putting in the reader's mouth "some word that hurts your tongue," useless for anything but his art, protected by hardier friends all his life, but enormously courageous and utterly dedicated (he once told Chard Powers Smith at the very end of his life, "I could never have done *anything* but write poetry"), should have brought off what in its quiet, searching, laborious way is one of the most remarkable accomplishments of modern poetry. Far from indulging, as his detractors have maintained, in a kind of poetical know-nothingism, he actually brought to poetry a new kind of approach, making of a refusal to pronounce definitively on his subjects a virtue and of speculation upon possibilities an instrument that allows an unparalleled fullness to his presentations, as well as endowing them with some of the mysteriousness, futility, and proneness to multiple interpretation that incidents and lives possess in the actual world.

Robinson's best poetry is exactly that kind of communication that "tells the more the more it is not told." In creating a body of major poetry with devices usually thought to be unfruitful for the creative act—irresolution, abstraction, conjecture, a dry, nearly imageless mode of address that tends always toward the general without ever supplying the resolving judgment that we expect of generalization—Robinson has done what good poets have always done: by means of his "cumulative silences" as well as by his actual lines, he has forced us to reexamine and finally to redefine what poetry is—or our notion of it—and so has enabled poetry itself to include more, to *be* more, than it was before he wrote. (pp. 229-30)

> *James Dickey, in his introduction to* Selected Poems of Edwin Arlington Robinson *by Edwin Arlington Robinson, edited by Morton Dauwen Zabel (reprinted with permission of Macmillan Publishing Co., Inc.; copyright © 1965 by Macmillan Publishing Co., Inc.), Macmillan, 1965 (and reprinted as "Edwin Arlington Robinson," in his* Babel to Byzantium: Poets & Poetry Now, *Farrar, Straus and Giroux, 1968, pp. 209-30).*

W. R. ROBINSON (essay date 1967)

Probably the most frequent "character" to appear in [Edwin Arlington] Robinson's poetry is Tilbury Town, the fictional community that provides the setting for many of his poems and explicitly links him and his poetry with small-town New England, the repressive, utilitarian social climate customarily designated as the Puritan ethic. For Tilbury Town, more than simply a setting, is an antagonistic moral force in the drama of life as Robinson imagined it. In this capacity it is one pole in another aspect of the dualism he inherited from materialism—the dichotomy between self and society, one more obstacle in the way to being whole.

The first reference to Tilbury Town occurs in **"John Evereldown,"** which appeared in *The Torrent and the Night Before* . . . , Robinson's first volume of poetry. Here, simply a place, it has not yet acquired a dramatic role. In other poems of the same volume, however, the small-town community, though unnamed, does begin to assume such a role, as for instance in **"Richard Cory,"** where the collective "we" speaks as a character. By the time of **"Captain Craig"** . . . Tilbury Town is fully dressed for its part and firmly established as a dramatic persona. Here, from the beginning of the poem, the town is Captain Craig's explicit antagonist. . . . At issue, as the captain sees it, is the quality of life, with the two alternatives being the life-enhancing way of the sun-receptive mind and the life-squandering way of the world. The narrator of the poem, one of the few citizens of the town eventually to look after and listen to the captain, agrees with his views but even more explicitly criticizes the town. . . . Tilbury's prudence callously squanders life—literally, in this instance—but the captain does not blame the town, or some privileged faction of it, for his hard times; he is not interested in criticizing prevailing institutions in order to bring about social reform. . . . For both the captain and the narrator it is social or collective man, whose interests are in getting on well materially rather than in humanity or the quality of life, who is the object of their criticism. (pp. 128-30)

Throughout the poem, much is made of the child's consciousness as the source of spiritual health, or as the saving power, and that consciousness is consistently linked with the imagery of light. Both the child and the light are excluded from Tilbury Town, and this repudiation of spirit is the town's most grievous sin. Its social materialism—its prudence, its righteousness and inhumanity, its "cent per cent" engrossment, its obsession with conventional worldly success—results in indifference to the captain as a suffering individual and to the eccentric, anticonformist ways of art, the soul, and the light for which he speaks. The town's prudence being a spiritual crassness and blindness that makes it an adamant enemy of the captain and what he values, the sun's light and the phoenix' fire are forever locked outside its walls.

Although Tilbury Town is not personified in **"Captain Craig,"** as it is in **"Richard Cory"** and other poems where the collective "we" or a representative member is the speaker of the poem, **"Captain Craig"** provides the town with its biggest role. Never again does it rise to such explicit dramatic prominence. Yet whenever it appears thereafter, no matter how briefly, it bears the stamp of the spiritual crassness and blindness suggested in **"Richard Cory"** and fully and explicitly defined in **"Captain Craig."** (pp. 130-31)

Tilbury Town is the most direct geographical embodiment of Robinson's antagonism toward a materialistic community antipathetic to spirit, and **"Captain Craig"** is his largest dramatic rendering of that antipathy. But his most subtle and profound treatments of it are found in his deservedly well-known medium-length poems on the artist, in, for example, **"Ben Jonson Entertains a Man from Stratford"** and **"Rembrandt to Rembrandt."** Ben Jonson says of Shakespeare, in defining the source of his black depression, that ["there's the Stratford in him; he denies it, / And there's the Shakespeare in him." "Manor-bitten to the bone" and at the same time "Lord Apollo's homesick emissary,"] . . . Shakespeare is torn between the contrary pulls of these two sides of his being. (p. 132)

In Shakespeare the conflict is internalized, as it was personally for Robinson, so that he is the victim of the mutual animosity of both sides. Rembrandt, though he is caught in the same countercurrents, has a better time of it in that he makes the choice of art at the sacrifice of his fame and fortune in Holland and becomes free of the rending antagonisms within himself. (p. 133)

These two poems reveal that even the most concrete representation of the conflict between self and society, which begins with an antagonism between an artist's worldly ambition and his devotion to his art, transcends the psychological and moral issue of art versus materialism and becomes an antipathy inherent in the dualistic nature of life. Two aspects of life, two realities, are pitted in eternal hostility, and when caught between them, a man's vital being is torn apart. When he chooses between them, he must pay the price of either self-betrayal or exclusion from the human community. There are two truths and each abhors the other, so that man is trapped in a dilemma in which every gain automatically entails a loss; every joy, suffering, no matter what choice he makes.

Other poems more explicitly universalize the alienation of self and society. In them the hostility is objectified even more than it is in **"Rembrandt to Rembrandt"**: the antagonists become separate entities that stand over against one another. Both Rembrandt and Shakespeare are instances of inner conflict, which one man resolves and the other does not. But this is not so in the **"Wandering Jew"** . . . , where a mythic figure angrily battles the society in which he finds himself—New York in this case. (pp. 134-35)

[In **"The Wandering Jew"**] myth replaces art as the enemy of society, the two being at heart the same, of course, except that myth is more inclusive. No longer do art and materialism

simply offer a choice of contrasting values, if that is all they ever did; now they are clearly but one form of a much larger conflict. And that conflict extends even beyond myth and society: a still more inclusive form of it, found in such poems as **"Three Taverns"** and **"Nicodemus,"** is the hostility between the religious experience and the social forms of religion—dogma and the church. (p. 135)

The antagonism between the mystical inner reality and society is stated in its most general form by Robinson at the end of **Lancelot**—though the antagonism must be understood to include personal relations (that of lovers, in this case) as well as that of an individual to a group. . . . The Light and the world are not simultaneously available to man; he must choose between them; and what is finally at stake in that choice is life and death. . . . Shakespeare's black depression, the Wandering Jew's anger, Rembrandt's and St. Paul's risking all for the Light . . . all reveal how the man with special knowledge of the spirit's truth reacts to society, to life in death. Inherent in man is a hostility between inner being and external forms and relations, between what Emerson called "the instantaneous instreaming causing power" and the objects that can hinder or misdirect its flowing.

Despite his obvious sympathies with the spirit, Robinson never assumes an immediate or long-run triumph by the self over society in which social forms are "saved." As with every subject, his concern for truth led him to adopt an objective attitude toward the relation between self and society; he simply records from various points of view and with varying results things as they are, the simultaneous presence and irreconcilability of self with society. Rembrandt chooses art and is free; Shakespeare cannot choose and suffers; St. Paul discovers the inner man and is doomed; . . . the Wandering Jew is the truth, but he . . . is impotent. Richard Cory is viewed from the point of view of the town; the town is viewed from the point of view of Eben Flood. The first dies tragically; the second lives comically. . . . But in every poem, regardless of what happens, the initial truth, the given condition of human existence, is the alienation of self from society, a schism between art and social values, the spirit and social forms, the soul and doctrine, the Light and the world. And finally that schism is an irremediable dichotomy in man's being between his personal and his social self. The pressure of creative power against achieved form is never more than momentarily relaxed. (pp. 136-37)

W. R. Robinson, "The Alienated Self," in his Edwin Arlington Robinson: A Poetry of the Act *(copyright 1967 by Western Reserve University; reprinted by permission of the author), The Press of Western Reserve University, 1967 (and reprinted in* Edwin Arlington Robinson: A Collection of Critical Essays, *edited by Francis Murphy, Prentice-Hall, 1970, pp. 128-47).*

WILLIAM H. PRITCHARD (essay date 1978)

To insist, as I am going to, that the life and challenge of Robinson's poetry lies in its way of saying rather than in the truth or relevance or wisdom of the idea communicated (frequently it is difficult to identify what exactly the "idea" amounts to) sounds unadventurous. As with any poet, where else should one look than to the particular sequences of words which somehow constitute a living voice? Yet Robinson's voice is often a consummately dead one, so discussion of the poems is all the more likely to take place with only cursory attention paid to those particular sequences. (pp. 89-90)

[Robinson] is invisible, does not in the main write directly out of his personal experience, does not attempt to dramatize the self, as did Yeats and Hardy in their very different ways.... [Robinson's "invisibility"] means that the words of his poems take on a fascinating, sometimes a maddening life of their own, with the illusion that they are operating somehow independently of their creator's will; and that whatever they are engaged in, it is not merely or mainly to make responsible, sympathetically acute statements about a world which lies beyond them. "His life was a revel in the felicities of language," said Frost in his felicitious tribute to Robinson [see excerpt above]. How strange the word "revel" sounds applied to this soberest and gloomiest of the poets—to the "prince of heartachers," as Frost also called him. Yet it is a profoundly right thing to say, and provides the best way into Robinson's genius. (p. 90)

One of the strangest of Robinson's early poems is titled **"The Book of Annandale,"** a longish affair in two parts, ostensibly presenting the responses of a man (Annandale) and then a woman (Damaris) to the death of their respective spouses. Though Annandale has lived happily with his young wife for a few years, he finds himself after her funeral rather calm, less interested in mourning her than in contemplating the book he's been hard at work on for some time....

It is a curious "poetry" Robinson is effecting here—with its dashes and ellipses and monosyllabic mutterings—that asks to be known "word for word" rather than "For what it meant." Readers of **"The Book of Annandale"** have rightly found the poem obscure.... (p. 91)

The "words" of which Annandale has composed his book do all sorts of impressive things: diffuse a flame of meaning, are choral and triumphant, ring like orisons and feed love's hunger, smite and thrill and cling. This diction is perilously close to the sort of "uplift" tradition of the Beauties of Poetry which Robinson staked his career on avoiding....

Admittedly the Tilbury Town "portrait" poems from *Children of the Night* ... eschew the poetical, aspire to flatness and directness of unembroidered statement. (p. 92)

The griefs which fill these early and attractively desolate poems [such as **"Luke Havergal"** and **"The Pity of the Leaves"**] are nameless, profound, "reverberant through lonely corridors" where one's buried life rises to confront one or where the past shrieks out of ancestral shame. At roughly age thirty-three, the composer of these lyrics was already a thoroughly haunted man, dedicated to celebrating loss in all its shapes and forms, well on his way to becoming the prince of heartachers of Frost's phrase. But to do this memorably Robinson had to avoid at all costs the clearly defined, clearly accounted-for motive; had instead to exploit the possibilities for melancholy, grief, and pain by using words in ways that always hinted there was something beyond them, something deeper, incapable of being at all adequately rendered by language, by "mere" words....

On the basis of the first two volumes, a reader might have thought [Robinson] mainly interested in portraying the aspirations and yearnings of lyric souls embodied in combinations of words with strong musical effects. Yet the writer of **"Richard Cory"** is clearly someone who relished ironic incongruities and was more than eager to exploit the dis-

crepancies between what "we" or society or an observer says about X, and the strange secret truth of X's inner life. With the writing of the long poem *Captain Craig* and the publication ... of **"The Book of Annandale"** and the expertly managed **"Isaac and Archibald,"** Robinson revealed himself as capable of ruminative, humorous verse of a leisured and assured touch. *Captain Craig* is so long that its good moments tend to get buried; but **"Isaac and Archibald"** is exactly the right length. (p. 94)

The volume on which Robinson's achievement can be judged to have deepened and extended itself is *The Man Against the Sky....* After it he published very few short poems ("they just ceased to come") and few readers today are tempted to make an argument that the long poems—whether Arthurian or domestic-psychological—form a solid basis for appreciation. Occasional purple patches, fine lines here and there, but on the whole prolix, fussy, and somehow terribly misguided—the long poems are stone-dead. (pp. 95-6)

There is a habit of comparing Robinson with Henry James, and indeed ... it is superficially plausible if one considers late James generally, say the stories in *The Finer Grain*. But there is an important difference: much energy appears to have gone into the techniques of cultivated attentuation and reader-subversion James was intent on practicing. His narrative renditions of appearances and places are done with sweep and boldness, and there is much comedy in the dialogues among characters, for all their murkiness. Robinson's overall "flat" tone, the monotonous narrative presence at the center of his tales, keeps the cap on everything, allowing no voice to break free of it even momentarily; thus the poems drag their slow lengths along and feel extremely wearied.

In arguing that Robinson's reputation as a significant modern poet depends mainly on a group of lyrics and lyrical narratives from *The Man Against the Sky*, rather than on the later longer narratives, I should also add that the title poem of the ... volume appears to me virtually unreadable.... [Flatulence seems] the quality characterizing the endless maundering which the problem we are supposed to care about (Where was the Man Against the Sky going? What does it all mean anyhow?) is subjected to.... (p. 96)

I myself find Frost both more interesting and "weightier" than Robinson, but am less concerned with arguing that case than with suggesting that three of Robinson's very best poems—**"For a Dead Lady," "Eros Turannos,"** and **"The Gift of God"**—are remarkable for something other than weight or fullness of experience or complexity of moral feeling. In each of them I am struck by the simplicity of their "content" or subject, by contrast with the charming elaborations of their form, the attractiveness they show as tuneful fables about all-too-human situations. With each poem one wonders, just briefly, whether there wasn't a trick in it somewhere, whether the narrating presence is really as calm, as wise, as understanding of life as it appears to be over the compass of the poem. (p. 97)

[The] widely anthologized **"Eros Turannos,"** [is] a poem taken seriously in a way that even admiring readers of Robinson don't quite take **"Luke Havergal"** or **"Miniver Cheevy."** The presumption is that it exhibits psychological, even sociological penetration; and it is a poem for those who see Robinson as having a deep and sensitive understanding of the human heart. (p. 98)

As with other Robinson poems there is the feeling that everything has already happened, some place a long way back, somewhere in myth or pre-history where one struggles with the god and accepts the god's triumph. . . . Robinson is the least "dramatic" of modern poets, if drama means a development in consciousness, a sense that the poem is entertaining choices even as it proceeds to its outcome. Instead the aim of **"Eros Turannos"** is to make the unknown background seem dim, gigantic, intensely suggestive, an object for us to wonder at, rather than penetrate or understand. (pp. 98-9)

Robinson's individuality is not in question, but its nature has not yet been fully defined, nor has it been in these pages. . . .

From [James] Dickey's account [see excerpt above] one might intuit a thoughtful, cautiously skeptical contemplator of experience, intent on not bending it to suit his own temperamental inclinations. The poems which issued from such an imagination would, on that account, feel more truly open, more . . . "exploratory-creative" than I take Robinson's to be—either at their most typical or at their best. At the risk of overstating the case in the other direction, I should call the "speculation upon possibilities," which Dickey finds central to the poems, less a real than an apparent phenomenon. Robinson's reticence, his solipsism even, are real enough gestures of uncertainty, of how-can-we-say-for-sure-since-we-all-know-so-little; yet the poems' rhythms show no such uncertainty, no haltingness of mind and impulse—quite the reverse. The music carries us along, as if by magic. (p. 99)

> *William H. Pritchard, "Edwin Arlington Robinson: The Prince of Heartachers," in* The American Scholar *(copyright © 1979 by the United Chapters of Phi Beta Kappa; reprinted by permission of the publishers), Vol. 48, No. 1, Winter, 1978-79, pp. 89-100.*

ADDITIONAL BIBLIOGRAPHY

Adams, Richard P. "The Failure of Edwin Arlington Robinson." *Tulane Studies in English* XI (1961): 97-151.
> Contends that Robinson's shortcomings as a poet stem from his failure to develop the consistent, romantic philosophy which, according to the critic, most suited his nature.

Anderson, Wallace L. *Edwin Arlington Robinson: A Critical Introduction.* Boston: Houghton Mifflin Co., 1967, 175 p.
> Basic introduction to Robinson's life and works.

Barnard, Ellsworth, ed. *Edwin Arlington Robinson: Centenary Essays.* Athens: University of Georgia Press, 1969, 192 p.
> Collection of critical essays on Robinson's work, including a chronology of Robinson's life and a bibliography of biography and criticism.

Burkhart, Charles. "Robinson's 'Richard Cory'." *Explicator* XIX, No. 1 (October 1960): Item 9.
> Close analysis of the structure and imagery in "Richard Cory."

Cambon, Glauco. "Edwin Arlington Robinson: Knight of the Grail." In his *The Inclusive Flame: Studies in American Poetry,* pp. 53-78. Bloomington: Indiana University Press, 1963.
> Refutes the widely held view that Robinson's Arthurian poems are derivative works by attempting to demonstrate that they are integrally related, in conception and method of characterization, to the more successful poems of the first half of his career.

Cary, Richard, ed. *Appreciation of Edwin Arlington Robinson: Twenty-eight Interpretive Essays.* Waterville, Maine: Colby College Press, 1969, 356 p.
> Collection of critical essays by many of the most important critics of Robinson, such as Yvor Winters, Louis Coxe, and W. R. Robinson.

Cowley, Malcolm. "Edwin Arlington Robinson." In *After the Genteel Tradition: American Writers, 1910-1930,* edited by Malcolm Cowley, pp. 28-36. Carbondale: Southern Illinois University Press, 1937.
> Offers insight on Robinson's struggles to establish himself as a poet.

Coxe, Louis. *Edwin Arlington Robinson: The Life of Poetry.* New York: Pegasus, 1969, 188 p.
> Excellent critical survey of Robinson's poetry. Coxe includes much biographical material and appends a selected bibliography of criticism.

Dauner, Louise. "The Pernicious Rib: E. A. Robinson's Concept of Feminine Character." *American Literature* 15, No. 2 (May 1943): 139-58.
> Argues that Robinson presents essentially two types of womanhood in his poems: the "knowing" type, who ensnares men with her fatal charms; and the "innocent" type, who allows men to dominate her and determine her destiny.

Fussell, Edwin S. *Edwin Arlington Robinson: The Literary Background of a Traditional Poet.* Berkeley, Los Angeles: University of California Press, 1954, 211 p.
> Traces the influence of naturalism as well as classical, biblical, and English literature on Robinson's work.

Gregory, Horace, and Zaturenska, Marya. "La Comedie Humaine of E. A. Robinson." In their *A History of American Poetry: 1900-1940,* pp. 107-32. New York: Harcourt, Brace and Co., 1946.
> Discussion of Robinson's use of subtle humor in his poetry. The critics believe that "not since the eighteenth century had any poet in English employed the arts of poetic wit with greater poise than Robinson."

Kaplan, Estelle. *Philosophy in the Poetry of Edwin Arlington Robinson.* New York: Columbia University Press, 1940, 162 p.
> Study of Robinson's philosophical thought through analysis of several of his poems. Kaplan concludes that Robinson developed no systematic philosophy.

Murphy, Francis E., ed. *Edwin Arlington Robinson: A Collection of Critical Essays.* Englewood Cliffs, N.J.: Prentice-Hall, 1970, 186 p.
> Offers a chronological selection of criticism by such important critics as Conrad Aiken, Josephine Miles, and Morton Zabel.

Neff, Emery. *Edwin Arlington Robinson.* New York: William Sloane Associates, 1948, 286 p.
> Biography, including extracts of many early reviews of Robinson's work.

Scott, Winfield Townley. "To See Robinson." In his *Exiles and Fabrications,* pp. 154-69, Garden City, N.Y.: Doubleday & Co., 1961.
> Reminiscence by an ardent admirer of Robinson.

Van Doren, Mark. *Edwin Arlington Robinson.* New York: The Literary Guild of America, 1927, 93 p.
> Early descriptive survey of Robinson's works through *Tristram.*

Van Norman, C. Elta. "'Captain Craig'." *College English* 2, No. 5 (February 1941): 462-75.
> Analysis of the critical controversy concerning Robinson's "Captain Craig."

Wilson, Edmund. "Mr. E. A. Robinson's Moonlight." In his *The Shores of Light: A Literary Chronicle of the Twenties and Thirties,* pp. 36-8. New York: Farrar, Straus and Young, 1952.
> Appraisal of Robinson's later, long poems, *Roman Bartholow* and *Avon's Harvest.* Wilson finds them too long and dreary.

Bruno Schulz

1892-1942

Polish short story writer, critic, and translator.

With only a small body of extant work Schulz has gained recognition as an important writer in twentieth-century Polish literature. Though his writing displays affinities with a number of authors and artistic movements, he was a literary independent; his work is highly personal and takes the author's inner world as its primary subject. Schulz converted the family life of his younger years and the town of Drohobycz, where he lived his entire life, into a dreamlike and symbol-charged reflection of his own imagination.

Critics most often compare Schulz's work to that of Franz Kafka. Both authors take mysterious and sometimes grotesque liberties with reality in their fiction, transforming banal worlds into alien territory. The uncanny adventures of Joseph K. in Kafka's *The Trial*, which Schulz translated into Polish, have their counterpart in the imaginative life of the Joseph who narrates *Sklepy cynamonowe* (*The Street of Crocodiles*) and *Sanatorium pod klepsydra* (*Sanatorium under the Sign of the Hourglass*). In Joseph's world, for example, his father is metamorphosed from man to crab to a corpse that is not yet aware of its own death.

Throughout his life Schulz led a provincial existence outside contemporary literary and artistic circles. He taught art at his town's high school and was apparently content with his circumstances. For a time he corresponded with Debora Vogel, a writer and editor for the literary journal *Cusztajer*. Vogel suggested that Schulz structure his letters into a book, and the result, *The Street of Crocodiles*, was admired in the Warsaw literary world and won an award from the Polish Academy of Literature. Schulz considered this work an autobiographical novel, and critics have compared it to the work of Proust in the same genre. Like Proust, Schulz devotes much attention in his stories to the narrator's impressions of his past life and to the process of memory itself. Central to Schulz's work is the attempt to define an ideal realm as it is reflected in the imperfect reality of the material world. "An event may be small and insignificant in its origin, and yet . . . it may open in its center an infinite and radiant perspective because a higher order of being is trying to express itself in it and irradiates it violently," Schulz wrote in his story "Księga" ("The Book").

Resisting such labels as symbolism, surrealism, or expressionism, Schulz's work survives as a highly individual if minor achievement in literature stressing the primacy of the imagination. In addition to his story collections, Schulz also wrote one novel, *Mesjaz*, which was lost in the upheaval of the author's life during World War II. Schulz died after being shot by German soldiers occupying his town.

PRINCIPAL WORKS

Sklepy cynamonowe (short stories and novella) 1934
[*The Street of Crocodiles*, 1963; published in England as *Cinnamon Shops, and Other Stories*, 1963]

Sanatorium pod klepsydra (short stories) 1937
[*Sanatorium under the Sign of the Hourglass*, 1978]

ISAAC B. SINGER (essay date 1963)

Schulz cannot be easily classified. He can be called a surrealist, a symbolist, an expressionist, a modernist. Paradoxically, although he was strongly original he was influenced—actually bewitched—by Kafka. . . . [In one of the stories in *The Street of Crocodiles*, Schulz' father] turns into a cockroach. This cannot be plagiarism, because Schulz was too genuine an artist to imitate so brazenly. He wrote sometimes like Kafka, sometimes like Proust, and at times succeeded in reaching depths that neither of them reached.

He possessed, among other qualities, a remarkable sense of humor, and in his work he mocked literature generally and modern literature specifically. His aim may have been to discredit literature, but at the same time he was creating small literary masterpieces in a unique way, mingling realism with fantasy, genuine images with empty abstractions, truth with dream. His use of parody is shown most strongly in **"The Comet."** . . . Here the author burlesques the human mind, astronomy, literature, philosophy, occultism, and the very categories of thought.

In his semi-autobiographical fiction, Schulz tells of a father who was morbidly ambitious, physically broken, estranged from his family, a perfectionist, a tyrant, full of weird caprices, madly curious. . . .

This father of Schulz' stories, who bears an uncanny resemblance to Kafka's father, has a meaning in terms of Freudian nightmares, and is, indeed, almost a Freudian parody.

The best stories [in *The Street of Crocodiles*] are **"Nimrod," "Pan,"** and the title story, **"The Street of Crocodiles."** In **"Nimrod,"** Schulz puts aside his mannerisms and tells with strong realism and genuine love of a little dog which someone abandoned in the house; it is the only story in which Schulz really allows himself to admire a living thing. . . .

If Schulz had identified himself more with his own people, he might not have expended so much energy on imitation, parody, and caricature. As it is, he remains a highly artistic paradox, a literary riddle who, like Kafka, deserves the attention of lovers and critics of literature.

> *Isaac B. Singer, "Burlesquing Life with Father,"* in Book Week—New York Herald Tribune (© 1963, The Washington Post), December 22, 1963, p. 4.

HENRYK BEREZA (essay date 1966)

In [Bruno Schulz's] poetic impressions of life in Drohobycz where the discovery of oil brought an almost patriarchal way of life into collision with modern civilization we can see a reflection of the universal frictions of the contemporary world. The clash between these two cultures is pinned down by Schulz in his descriptions of the old and the new town, of the old inhabitants and the new 'dummies', the old 'cinnamon shops' and the new 'Crocodile Street'. For the fictional character of the Father he drew on his own, a cloth merchant, but—as he himself said—he put into his mouth the philosophy of the Polish catastrophist, Stanisław Ignacy Witkiewicz, portending the annihilation of all the traditional values of humanity in the antheap of modern civilization.

Bruno Schulz is now at last reaping the laurels that are his due as one of the seminal figures of Polish avant-garde prose. (p. 37)

The novelists and dramatists of the Polish avant-garde subscribed to a different philosophy from the poets in the same wing. The latter made no bones of their enthusiasm for modern civilization, for technical progress and for the boundless horizons opened up by science. Their posture was epitomized by Julian Przyboś. Schulz, like the catastrophists, stood at the opposite pole, aghast at the sweeping aside of human identity, the degradation of many by totalitarian systems to the level of a cog in the wheels of the machine, the standardization of ideas and creative endeavour, the decay of moral integrity. Schulz made his own protest at this degeneration, at the atomization and fall of man.

The Father in *Cinnamon Shops* unfolds in his sardonic 'Treatise on Dummies' a vision, Picasso-like in its depiction, Huxleyan in its irony, of the denizens of this brave new world: 'Our creatures will not be the heroes of sagas. Their roles will be short and succinct, their characters without background. Often, for the sake of a single gesture, a single word,

we shall go to the trouble of bringing them to life for this one moment. We admit, frankly, that we shall not bother unduly about the solidity and craftsmanship of our work; our products will be makeshifts, to be thrown away after use. If they are human, we shall give them, for example, only one side of their face, one hand, one leg, only as much as they need for their role. . . . The demiurge liked to work with tasteful, stylish and complicated materials; we give priority to tawdry. We are, quite simply, delighted by the cheap, the tatty, the shoddy. Do you understand, my father would ask, the deep sense of this frailty, this passion for tinsel, papier-mâché, lacquer, string and sawdust'. In gibes like 'we are going to re-create man in the image and likeness of a dummy' Schulz expresses his contempt for the modern world of pretences, mediocrity and rubbish.

But, for us today, the revelation lies not so much in Schulz' ideas as in his technique. In his view of the modern world he was really echoing Witkiewicz, but he forged a perfect idiom for expressing this judgement, creating a vision that was internally consistent, above all in its visual imagery. To an extent equalled by few Polish writers, Schulz was a word painter. Realities were for him a composition of visual forms. His pictures of small-town life suggest again and again the qualities of Chagall or Picasso. From the patriarchal society for which he sees no salvation, he wrings a Chagall-like poetry; the rampant, all-conquering world of the dummies is painted with a Picassoesque distortion. Even for human ideas and emotions he seeks a pictorial equivalent. The influence of Kafka is also in evidence: the final experiences of the Father recall the nightmare in the *Metamorphosis* and many descriptions are touched with the same kind of metaphor. I did not understand what was wrong, but she grew more and more frantic in her rage, becoming one great bundle of gesticulation and abuse. In her paroxysm of fury she seemed about to gesticulate herself to pieces, to fall apart, split, dislocate into a hundred spiders, ramifying on the floor in a black, winking welter of wild, cockroach scuttlings.'

It is this painterly response which is the real eye-opener in his writing. His actual prose style bears none of the hallmarks usually associated with avantgardism. It shows no affinities with [Witold] Gombrowicz with whom he tends to be bracketed. On the contrary, his love of prolixity, purple patches, recondite words link him to the 'Young Poland' movement, to the early work of [Zofia] Nałkowska and [Jarosław] Iwaszkiewicz, among others. This accounts for the studied elegance of his writing, contrasting so markedly with the vagaries of Witkiewicz who in his novel, *Insatiety*, written a little earlier than *Cinnamon Shops*. . . , tried to make a clean break with the language of Young Poland and fell between two stools. Schulz, on the other hand, latched on to this ready-to-hand tradition, but purged it of its overpowering aestheticism.

In Polish literature Schulz will go down as an inspired evoker of a time-honoured world and a Jeremiah of the collapse of the old order of people at one with themselves by the civilization of the dummies. Schulz dissects their downfall beadily and bleakly. He does not idealize the past, like [Adam] Mickiewicz, [Juliusz] Słowacki or [Cyprian] Norwid and he is more scathing about it than Thomas Mann. He was past believing in the hope of salvaging anything. He saw no chance of running away from the harsh truth, either into the past or the future. Foreboding hangs heavily over his vision: the world is falling apart at the seams, assuming monstrous shapes, decaying and dying. . . . It cannot be said that Schulz's dread was all that fanciful; he was fated, after all, to perish in the ghetto as the world which he feared so profoundly spun wildly off its hinges. (pp. 38-9)

Henryk Bereza, "Bruno Schulz," (reprinted by permission of Author's Agency, Warsaw), in Polish Perspectives, *Vol. IX, No. 6, June, 1966, pp. 37-9.*

OLGA LUKASHEVICH (essay date 1968)

[Bruno Schulz] is one of the most original writers of this century. (p. 63)

[His *The Street of Crocodiles*] is no ordinary novel, for it is a collection of thirteen separate stories. Yet, these thirteen stories form together a well-integrated literary unit, all striving to recapture poetically some significant events, feelings and observations of the author's childhood, and to recreate artistically the psychological reality of the author's inner world. Moreover, all thirteen stories have the same purpose and the same motivation, a search into the poetical recollections of the author's childhood for the key to the mystery of his own transformation into an artist; by the same token, the author assigns several of his stories to the elucidation of the failure of his own father to become an artist. Thus, by juxtaposing his father's failure to his relative success in a quest for artistic self-expression, Bruno Schulz investigates the momentous problem of artistic genesis. (pp. 63-4)

[The] purpose of Bruno Schulz's novel was to investigate his own artistic genesis in opposition to his father's failure to become an artist. . . . [The] artist must overcome his feeling of guilt, which is experienced as fear of life and fear of death; . . . sexuality and all its implications increase the artist's fear of death and fear of life. [Finally] the artist must overcome the fear of life, which accrued from fear of death. Bruno Schulz was aware of this double problem of fear of death and fear of life, and of sexuality. For instance, in the story called **"August,"** Bruno Schulz sees the dreaded mortality in the fecundity of Nature and in sexual lust. (p. 73)

This irrational and chaotic natural law which manifests itself in man's body is a deadly force, because it is in direct opposition to man's personality, which is achieved through self-creation and not through birth. To Bruno Schulz Nature is responsible for the sense of mortality because it is a negation of any and all individualism. This is so because Nature, or rather matter, goes constantly through a change of form. This spiritless matter in flux is without personality, and it assumes the most whimsical shapes. For instance, Bruno Schulz imagined in the story **"The Gale"** the potential transformation of his aunt Perasia first into spiders and then into cockroaches. . . .

Moreover, Nature is not a comforter, as the Romantics had thought, but a blind and destructive force as witnessed in the story called, **"Mr. Charles."** Uncle Charles who is struck by cancer and whose body is "like an enormous bowl of dough" is perceived by Schulz as one step closer to the inevitable transformation that would change him into inorganic shapeless matter. . . . (p. 74)

[In the story **"The Comet,"**] Bruno Schulz reconstructs death in life still on another level—this time on the spiritual and psychological level. The symbolic death as the loss of one's individuality is identified by Schulz with science, or rather with modern man's infatuation with science. Thus, Uncle

Edward has only one passion—passion to serve science that eventually transforms him . . . into an electric bell. (pp. 74-5)

Bruno Schulz's fear of the life of actuality is seen also in the two other stories—**"The Street of Crocodiles"** and **"The Night of the Great Season."** This time it is vulgar commercialism and materialism that spell death for Schulz. . . .

[**"The Street of Crocodiles"**] is the street in the center of a new commercial district that sprung in the old patriarchal town of Drohobycz. For Schulz this new district is the symbol of coarseness, cheapness and vulgarity. The reality of this district is constructed on two levels. On the level of the outward appearance, it is "an industrial and commercial district, its soberly utilitarian character glaringly underlined;" on the level of the unseen reality, it is the district where "everything seemed suspect and equivocal, everything promised with secret winks, cynically stressed gestures, raised eyebrows, the fulfillment of impure hopes, everything helped to release the lower instincts from their shackles." A tailor's shop of this district first appears simply as a shop. . . .

But behind the reality of this shop there rises the formidable meaning of the shop as the frightening reality of commercial vulgarity and corruption. (p. 75)

[Death] is identified by Bruno Schulz with practically all manifestations of life; death is seen in birth, sex, fecundity; death is present in the social order and is associated with science and commerce. And it is the life of actuality that spells mortality and decay for Bruno Schulz, the creative artist, and fills him with fear and anxiety. Yet, side by side with these stories which depict death in life, there are stories that reconstruct the author's liberation from fear and apprehension of life. This liberation was made possible by the transformation of this frightening reality into a beautiful world that was experienced by Bruno Schulz in the memories of his childhood. Indeed, such a miraculous change was possible only because Bruno Schulz could recapture the moments of rapture which he had experienced as a child. Thus, the story **"Nimrod"** is a recollection of the author's feelings evoked by the sight of a "splendid little dog" that was given to him as a present when he was a boy. . . . (pp. 76-7)

In the same vein, the story **"Pan"** recreates an episode of Schulz's childhood—his unexpected encounter with a stranger in a garden. . . . (p. 77)

In this story the process of transcending reality is achieved by making the recollected moment a part of mythology. The face [of the stranger] only temporarily belongs to a drunkard or a tramp; only for a split second that it looks human and therefore threatening. Laughter splits the taut features and there is the grinning and triumphant face of the immortal Pan.

The mood of exaltation and spiritual joy is especially evident in the story called, **"Cinnamon Shops."** In it, Bruno Schulz reconstructs his youthful enthusiasm for art, poetry, imagination in a series of dreams in which these elements and life blend into one harmonious vision. Recalling his boyish enthusiasm for art, Schulz creates the dream as a transcendent reality where there is no division between art and life. (pp. 77-8)

The dreams as poetic visions into which Schulz weaves his boyhood reminiscences constitute the reality of Schulz as the creative artist. It is the reality in which life with all its dangers no longer exists, no longer threatens, and in which the moments of existence become immortal and eternally beautiful. (p. 79)

Olga Lukashevich, "Bruno Schulz's 'The Street of Crocodiles': A Study in Creativity and Neurosis," in The Polish Review (© copyright 1968 by the Polish Institute of Arts and Sciences in America, Inc.), Vol. XIII, No. 2, Spring, 1968, pp. 63-79.

COLLEEN M. TAYLOR   (essay date 1969)

There are definite psychological similarities between [Marcel Proust and Bruno Schulz]: both were sickly, neurotic, sexually abnormal . . . , introspective, and shared a fear of "le néant" which they sought to eliminate through art, by, as Sartre said, "creating the feeling that (they) are essential in relation to the world, that is, essential to (their) creation."

Nevertheless, the works of Schulz and Proust are quite different in form, in style, and in their authors' reactions to the past. . . . Proust approaches the past with the powerful, rational intellect of the mature writer; he carefully analyzes his past experiences, reproducing in detail the external world and his past perceptions of it and, on this basis, draws general conclusions about his experience, his personality, and the human condition. Schulz's treatment of the past, on the other hand, is neither analytical, intellectual, nor realistic. Rather, he describes the world as he saw it *during* his childhood in a highly lyrical, emotionally charged prose, without drawing conclusions or offering explanations; he returns in his creative imagination to that time when the dividing line between imagination and external reality has not been drawn and the mind is not yet trapped in what Rimbaud called "the prison of reason." Hence his art is often of a fantastic, surrealistic nature: his father is changed into a crab, a cockroach, and a bird, his aunt becomes a pile of ashes, while rooms fill with strange vegetable growths, fiery bars appear in the air, and even time is speeded up and slowed down. These are among the occurrences in the world of "festivals and miracles" which Schulz describes and which in many respects is the diametric opposite of the world in which Schulz, as a child and as an adult, actually lived. (pp. 456-57)

[Schulz's] childhood was not "realistically" portrayed; rather, Schulz emphasizes its most attractive features, especially in [*Sklepy cynamonowe* (Cinnamon Shops)]. It is as if a spotlight were turned upon certain things while the background remains in darkness. Such an analogy is not out of place here, for one of the distinctive features of Schulz's style is his use of light and color: he literally "paints" with words, which reflects his artistic training.

Colors have strong emotional connotations and perform a symbolic function in Schulz's work. Bright colors are associated with those things that Schulz values and loves. . . .

On the other hand, the most damning epithet in Schulz's lexicon is "grey" or "colorless." He writes of the "grey days of winter, hardened with boredom," the "grey world" of his villain, the Emperor Franz Joseph, who bans the color red from his court **"Wiosna" (Spring).** (p. 459)

[Schulz's] work is dominated by one figure: that of his father, Jakub, the central personage in approximately half of Schulz's stories. (p. 460)

Schulz's attitude toward his father has little in common with that of Kafka, although the importance of the father in their works is often pointed out by critics as proof of the writers' essential kinship. Kafka feared and hated his practical, domineering father, while Schulz felt only love and admiration for his father as an impractical "defender of the lost cause of poetry."

And this admiration took on a special form in his work. In an article entitled **"Mityzacja rzeczywistości" (The Mythologization of Reality)** Schulz states: "All poetry is mythologization and aspires to the restoration of myths about the world. The mythologizing of the world is not yet finished." . . . The figures of Adela, the family maid, the archetype of "woman as destroyer," his aunt, the local half-wit Touya, and other characters in his work can be regarded as attempts to raise the specifics of his private life to the level of the universal.

But the most important example of Schulz's "mythologization of reality" is his elevation of his father to the status of a semi-divine figure: Jakub is compared, among other things, to a Heresiach, an Old Testament Prophet, Atlas, a magus, and St. George. . . . And at the end of the story **"Dead Season"** his father is visited by a mysterious black-bearded man who, "like the angel with Jacob," engages in a deadly struggle with him. "Of what?" asks the narrator. "Of the name of God? Of the Covenant?" No one knew, although from that day on began "seven long years of harvest for the store."

But Schulz's father is identified with another world: with those "doubtful, risky, and equivocal regions which we shall call for short the Regions of the Great Heresy." This is manifested in two ways: in his pagan-like closeness to the animal world and in his theories on Demiurgy by which he seeks to emulate the Creator Himself.

Perhaps what Schulz most admired in his father was his unending battle against the boredom and stagnation of the provincial town and his own household. . . . [In **"Ptaki" (Birds)**] his father imports exotic birds' eggs from all over the world to construct a brilliant aviary, pulsating with life, color, and motion. His father's passionate interest in animals was that of the huntsman and the artist, notes Schulz, but also the result of a "deeper biological sympathy of one creature for another" which was to have "uncanny, complicated, essentially sinful and unnatural" results. For Schulz's father is, in fact, so near to the world of animals that the narrator cannot distinguish them. His father resembles a certain stuffed condor, which even uses his chamber pot, so that after his father's death, the narrator is convinced he has been reincarnated as the stuffed bird. He also suspects that his father has become a cockroach and, later, a crab in **"Ostatnia ucieczka ojca" (The Last Flight of Father).**

However, we must point out that these "metamorphoses" are different from those in the work of Kafka. Gregor Samsa's transformation into an insect in "Metamorphosis" is sudden, apparently without cause, and can be interpreted as an externalization of his feelings of guilt and worthlessness. Kafka narrates the story in a simple, matter-of-fact style, without explanation, and almost from Samsa's point of view, so that the reader accepts the basic premise and the subsequent events of the story as real events. The reader of Schulz's work, however, is not sure whether a metamorphosis did occur—that is, whether Schulz expects us to assume the reality of the event, as does Kafka, or whether he is simply re-creating a child's imaginative processes. That is, the narrator in Schulz's work cannot be regarded as a reliable reporter on external, *objective* reality. Moreover, in Schulz's work a metamorphosis is never a sudden change, but rather the end result of a gradual process, the culmination of the "fermentation of material" for which "ordinary objects were only masks." Spiritual forces in Schulz's world can materialize: the father's resemblance to the condor increased with time because of his sympathy for the noble bird and ends in his reincarnation in his form.... Schulz again is mythologizing by returning to a pagan view of the world in which the line between animals and men is not yet finely drawn, and, as in the old myths, men and gods change into animals, and vice versa.

Schulz's father enters the "Regions of the Great Heresy" in another way: he is also a creator and, in his theories, is the double of Schulz the writer. In **"Traktat o manekinach" (Treatise on Tailors' Dummies),** a series of three lectures made by Jakub to Adela and some sewing girls, Schulz expresses his own views on art and creativity. Jakub says: "We have lived for too long under the terror of the matchless perfection of the Demiurge. For too long the perfection of his creation has paralyzed our own creative instinct.... We wish to be creators in our own, lower sphere; we wish to have the privilege of creation, we want creative delights, we want—in one word—Demiurgy." That is, the artist is an independent creator who constructs in his work a reality distinct from external reality, so that art is no longer a reproduction of existence, but rather an addition, a supplement to it. Art was not to be mimetic or "realistic": Jakub proposes the creation of a "*generatio aequivoca . . . a* species half organic, pseudo-fauna and pseudo-flora, the result of a fantastic fermentation of matter." This concept of art is again close to that of the Expressionists with their slogan "Los von der Natur" and the Surrealists who "saw art as a building process, not an expression or statement of existence as it is." And Schulz's own art exemplifies his theory, for in it he has created a self-contained, independent universe governed by immanent laws. Metamorphoses occur, objects take on lives of their own, while even physical laws are suspended. (pp. 460-63)

Schulz's father was himself a creator. The aviary (**"Birds"**), in which he "conjures up from nothingness these blind bellies, pulsating with life," is one manifestation of his creative power. In the long story **Kometa (The Comet)** he conducts strange scientific experiments, and with a complete disregard for the "principium individuationis," in the spirit of a true demiurge, transforms Uncle Edward into a machine. (p. 464)

In [**"Księga" (The Book)**] the narrator recalls the first book which absorbed his interest: "I call it simply **'The Book,'** without qualifications and epithets, and there is in that abstention and limitation a helpless sigh, a quiet capitulation before the boundlessness of the transcendent, because no word, no allusion is able to shine, smell, flow with that shiver of alarm, that premonition of that thing without name, whose first taste on our tongue exceeds the capacity of our enthusiasm." The book is nothing but an illustrated provincial journal, filled with the banal advertisements of the provinces: Anna Csillag, the "apostle of hairiness," with a cure for baldness, Mr. Bosco from Milan who will reveal his secrets of black magic, Magda Wang with her titillating autobiography *From the Purple Days,* a Polish Dale Carnegie, and so on. Yet the child is unaware of the banality and tawdriness

of these notices; rather, reading them he "passes from ecstasy to ecstasy" and enters a realm of "pure poetry." ... Similarly, in **"Spring"** it is a stamp book which stimulates the boy's dreams.... (p. 467)

[Art,] in the guise of the stamp book, opens the boy's eyes to the relativity of his world, shows him that there do exist other worlds, and reveals "the immeasurability of the world, the endless possibilities of existence." Like Alexander the Great, before he became a demiurge like Franz Joseph, the boy feels the world is his to conquer, and despite the failure in the story of his own private mission, he has nonetheless broken through the form-bound world of Franz Joseph and discovered his own private, beautiful vision of the universe. **"Spring"** ... is a panegyric hymn to the glories of a child's imagination and the subversive power of art. Against the world of boredom, conventions, and form—the Austro-Hungarian Empire, the dreary vulgarity of Drohobycz and the Street of Crocodiles, the school where he taught, the lack of privacy and his own psychological fears and weaknesses—Schulz in his work opposes the world of the artist and the child, the world of his father and the Cinnamon Shops, where reality is not restricted but rather freed through the power of man's imagination. Indeed, when reading Schulz one is convinced of the truth of Baudelaire's famous dictum: "Genius is childhood recaptured at will." (p. 471)

> *Colleen M. Taylor, "Childhood Revisited: The Writings of Bruno Schulz," in* Slavic and East European Journal *(© 1969 by AATSEEL of the U.S., Inc.), Vol. XIII, No. 4, December, 1969, pp. 455-72.*

CYNTHIA OZICK (essay date 1977)

[It] may be misleading to anticipate **"The Street of Crocodiles"** with so "normal" a signal as *novel:* it is a thick string of sights and sinuosities, a cascade of flashes, of extraordinary movements—a succession of what television has taught us to call "film clips," images in magnetic batches, registered storms, each one shooting memories of itself into the lightnings of all the others.

What is being invented in the very drone of our passive literary expectations is Religion—not the taming religion of theology and morality, but the brute splendors of rite, gesture, phantasmagoric transfiguration, sacrifice, elevation, degradation, mortification, repugnance, terror, cult. The religion of animism, in fact, where everything comes alive with an unpredictable and spiteful spirit-force, where even living tissue contains ghosts, where there is no pity. (pp. 4-5)

> *Cynthia Ozick, "With Babel and Singer and Kafka," in* The New York Times Book Review *(© 1977 by The New York Times Company; reprinted by permission), February 13, 1977, pp. 4-5.**

JOANNA ROSTROPOWICZ (essay date 1977)

[When I read *The Street of Crocodiles* for the first time] I was overwhelmed by the feeling of being enclosed in an isolated gallery of movable icons: ageing men with Old Testament faces, small boys with grown-up eyes, provocative and untouchable women....

[*The Street of Crocodiles* is] a very unusual autobiography, a personal bible in which myths materialize into scenes and characters both timeless and realistic.... (p. 377)

When I read Schulz again, a long time after my first enchantment with the poetry of his prose, I was struck by the strength of his morality. Even his perfection of style carried a moral message since he held mediocrity primarily responsible for modern evil. In Schulz's modern morality fable ethics and aesthetics are indistinguishable. The Street of Crocodiles is inhabited by "the cheap human material," by expressionless, hollow, mechanical dummies. This vulgar evil is devoid of the demonic attraction of Gide's Lafcadio or Céline's ragged knights of the night. Schulz would agree with Thomas Mann who wrote in 1938: "The motif of abjectness and degradation plays an essential role in the development of modern Europe. Hitlerism is somehow a Wagnerism for the poor." Only Schulz might go a step further to declare that it is imitation Wagnerism by and for the scum. In Schulz's fable the scum exists at the outskirts of the old town, tempting the normal residents only in their moments of "moral weakness." For the most part the ancient human values of the "cinnamon stores," the powers of creative curiosity and imagination, although wilted and entrusted to the care of a withdrawn old man and a vulnerable child, manage to prevail. (pp. 377-78)

> *Joanna Rostropowicz, "Life's Alchemy," in* The Nation *(copyright 1977* The Nation *magazine, The Nation Associates, Inc.), Vol. 224, No. 12, March 26, 1977, pp. 376-78.*

V. S. PRITCHETT   (essay date 1977)

The ridiculous or preposterous father is a subject irresistible to the comic genius. The fellow is an involuntary god, and the variety of the species extends over the knockabout and the merely whimsical to the full wonder of incipient myth. To this last superior class the fantastic father invented by Bruno Schulz in *The Street of Crocodiles* belongs; the richness of the portrait owes everything to its brushwork and to our private knowledge that the deepest roots of the comic are poetic and even metaphysical. . . .

In his way, the father [depicted in *The Street of Crocodiles*] has the inventive melancholy of Quixote. The delightful thing about him is that he is the embarrassing, scarcely visible nuisance in shop and home. It is hard to know where he is hiding or what he is up to. He is an inquiring poltergeist, coated with human modesty; even his faintly sexual ventures, like studying a seamstress's knee because he is fascinated by the structure of bones, joints, and sinews, are as modest as Uncle Toby's confusion of the fortress of Namur with his own anatomy. A minor character, like Adela the family servant, sets off the old man perfectly. . . .

Like an enquiring child, the father is wide open to belief in metamorphoses as others are prone to illness: for example he has a horror of cockroaches and, finding black spots on his skin, prepares for a tragic transformation into the creature he dreads by lying naked on the floor. But it is in the father's ornithological phase that we see the complexity of Schulz's imagination. The whole idea—it is hinted—may spring from a child's dream after looking at pictures of birds; it is given power by being planted in the father; then it becomes a grotesque nightmare; and finally we may see it as a parable, illustrating the permutations of myths which become either the inherited wastepaper of the mind or its underground. (p. 6)

Schulz's book is a masterpiece of comic writing: grave yet demented, domestically plain yet poetic, exultant and forgiving, marvelously inventive, shy and never raw. There is not a touch of whimsy in it. (p. 8)

> *V. S. Pritchett, "Comic Genius," in* The New York Review of Books *(reprinted with permission from* The New York Review of Books; *copyright © 1977 Nyrev, Inc.), Vol. XXIV, No. 6, April 14, 1977, pp. 6-8.*

JERZY FICOWSKI   (essay date 1977)

[For Bruno Schulz] art was a confession of faith, faith in the demiurgic role of myth. . . .

What is this Schulzian mythopoeia, this mythologizing of reality? On what was his artistic purpose to "mature into childhood" based? Childhood here is understood as the stage when each sensation is accompanied by an inventive act of the imagination, when reality, not yet systematized by experience, "submits" to new associations, assumes the forms suggested to it, and comes to life fecund with dynamic visions; childhood is a stage when etiological myths are born at every step. It is precisely there, in the mythmaking realm, that both the source and the final goal of Bruno Schulz's work reside.

From sublime spheres the Schulzian myth sinks to the depths of ordinary existence; or, if you will, what Schulz gives us is the mythological Ascension of the Everyday. The myth takes on human shape, and simultaneously the reality made mythical becomes more nonhuman than ever before. Conjecture easily changes into certainty, the obvious into illusion; possibilities *materialize*. Myth stalks the streets of Drogobych, turning ragamuffins playing tiddledywinks into enchanted soothsayers who read the future in the cracks of a wall, or transforming a shopkeeper into a prophet or a goblin. Art was to Schulz "a short circuit of sense between words, a sudden regeneration of the primal myths." (pp. 17-18)

Schulz, incorporating mythic archetypes within the confines of his own biography, unites his family to legend. His major work was to have been the lost novel titled *The Messiah*, in which the myth of the coming of the Messiah would symbolize a return to the happy perfection that existed at the beginning—in Schulzian terms, the return to childhood.

Schulzian time—his mythic time—obedient and submissive to man, offers artistic recompense for the profaned time of everyday life, which relentlessly subordinates all things to itself and carries events and people off in a current of evanescence. Schulz introduces a subjective, psychological time and then gives it substance, objectivity, by subjecting the course of occurrences to its laws. The reckoning of time by the calendar is likewise called into question. It can happen, writes Schulz, that "in a run of normal uneventful years that great eccentric, Time, begets sometimes other years, different, prodigal years which—like a sixth, smallest toe—grow a thirteenth freak month." Schulz's fantasies—dazzling, full of the paradoxical and the plausible—are "apocrypha, put secretly between the chapters of the great book of the year." They are Schulz's mythological supplement to the calendar, and when he wishes that the stories about his father, smuggled into the pages of his old calendar, would there grow equal in authority to its true text, he is expressing his own not merely artistic desire to materialize the yearnings of the imagination, to impart to its creations an objective reality, to erase the boundary between fact and dream.

"Should I tell you that my room is walled up? . . . In what way might I leave it?" asks Schulz. "Here is how: Goodwill knows no obstacle; nothing can stand before a deep desire. I have only to imagine a door, a door old and good, like in the kitchen of my childhood, with an iron latch and bolt. There is no room so walled up that it will not open with such a trusty door, if you have but the strength to insinuate it." On one side of that door lies life and its restricted freedom, on the other—art. That *door* leads from the captivity of Bruno, a timid teacher of arts and crafts, to the freedom of Joseph, the hero of *The Street of Crocodiles.*

This is the credo of Bruno Schulz—of the Great Heresiarch who imposed new measurements on time, in this way taking his revenge on life. Yet from behind the mythological faith of the writer there peers, again and again, the mocking grin of reality, revealing the ephemeral nature of the fictions that seek to contend with it.

Many of Schulz's theoretical statements express with precision and accuracy the ideas behind his work, its foundations, and its psychological and philosophical motivations. In response to the questions of the famous Polish writer, philosopher, painter, and playwright Witkiewicz, his friend, Schulz said: "I do not know just how in childhood we arrive at certain images, images of crucial significance to us. They are like filaments in a solution around which the sense of the world crystallizes for us. . . . They are meanings that seem predestined for us, ready and waiting at the very entrance of our life. . . . Such images constitute a program, establish our soul's fixed fund of capital, which is allotted to us very early in the form of inklings and half-conscious feelings. It seems to me that the rest of our life passes in the interpretation of those insights, in the attempt to master them with all the wisdom we acquire, to draw them through all the range of intellect we have in our possession. These early images mark the boundaries of an artist's creativity. His creativity is a deduction from assumptions already made. He cannot now discover anything new; he learns only to understand more and more the secret entrusted to him at the beginning, and his art is a constant exegesis, a commentary on that single verse that was assigned him. But art will never unravel that secret completely. The secret remains insoluble. The knot in which the soul was bound is no trick knot, coming apart with a tug at its end. On the contrary, it grows tighter and tighter. We work at it, untying, tracing the path of the string, seeking the end, and out of this manipulating comes art. . . .

"To what genre does *The Street of Crocodiles* belong? How should it be classified? I consider it an autobiographical novel, not merely because it is written in the first person and one can recognize in it certain events and experiences from the author's own childhood. It is an autobiography—or rather, a genealogy—of the spirit . . . since it reveals the spirit's pedigree back to those depths where it merges with mythology, where it becomes lost in mythological ravings. I have always felt that the roots of the individual mind, if followed far enough down, would lose themselves in some mythic lair. This is the final depth beyond which one can no longer go."

Schulz's work is an expression of rebellion against the kingdom "of the quotidian, that fixing and delimiting of all possibilities, the guarantee of secure borders, within which art

is once and for all time . . . closed off." Though mostly divided up into a series of stories, his writing taken as a whole has the character of a unified, consistent system, similar to systems of belief. His artistry is a unique sacral practice in which myths are accompanied by worship, ritual, and verbal ceremony. Schulz digs down, delving for the taproots, the seeds of our conceptions and imaginings, for, in his words, "the spawning bed of history." He says: "Just beyond our words . . . roar the dark and incommensurable elements. . . . Thus is accomplished within us a complete regression, a retreat to the interior, the return journey to the roots." The meddling with language, with semantics, in these depths, in order to give form to the inexpressible—that is the goal of Schulz's poetic search for definitions. (pp. 18-21)

Jerzy Ficowski, "Introduction" (copyright © Viking Penguin Inc., 1977), translated by Michael Kandel, in The Street of Crocodiles *by Bruno Schulz, translated by Celina Wieniewska, Penguin Books, 1977, pp. 13-22.*

ISAAC BASHEVIS SINGER   (essay date 1978)

Like some other extreme literary modernists before him, Schulz gave himself all the freedoms when he took to his pen—freedom from reality or the order of things, freedom from all literary tradition, methods and genres—sometimes even from logic. On his sheet of paper he was the absolute master, not giving a hoot about what the reader or the critics might think or feel. . . .

Bruno Schulz was and remained a lonely solipsist. His descriptions of nature are highly original, but he saw nature and its wonders mostly through the window of his garret room or from the rotting balcony. He made nature the background of his isolated existence, of his deep depression and melancholy. He was undoubtedly a mystic, but there is no God and there are no angels or demons in his stories. Corpses he has many—corpses who don't realize that they are dead. They eat, drink, even do business. It is hard to know if Schulz ever read the Swedish mystic [Emanuel] Swedenborg, but there is much of Swedenborg's description of hell in Schulz's stories. (p. 34)

Bruno Schulz's second collection of stories [*Sanatorium under the Sign of the Hourglass*] is in many ways richer than the first one and more profound, but poorer in storytelling and in humor. It is a work written by a genius completely submerged in his private gloom. It cannot be read in one sitting. The reader must rest every few pages to awaken from the trance into which he has fallen. But when he returns to his reading he probably will find striking images and metaphors he might have overlooked before because of the denseness of the material. This book is all dream, and possesses the convincing power of dreams. As in dreams, there is no death here, only morbid sickness. The whole book teems with symbols and puzzles that no literary analyst will ever solve. . . . [What Schulz] did in his short life was enough to make him one of the most remarkable writers who ever lived. (pp. 34-5)

Isaac Bashevis Singer, "A Polish Franz Kafka," in The New York Times Book Review *(© 1978 by The New York Times Company; reprinted by permission), July 9, 1978, pp. 1, 34-5.*

JOHN BAYLEY (essay date 1978)

[Schulz] was clearly well acquainted with both Kafka and Freud though there is some uncertainty about when he first read Kafka's work. . . . (p. 35)

Schulz, however, is the kind of writer whose originality is in no way compromised by even such obvious influences. In fact it seems to me probable that his constructions undertake to deflect and transform the kinds of reality inhabited or explored by previous models, a phenomenon familiar in the history of fiction. . . . The hero of Schulz's fabulous world is, unexpectedly, not the son but the father, a figure represented as a symbol of imprisoned consciousness itself, and of the escapes and enfranchisements it can devise. The father in Schulz is in somewhat the same position as the son in Kafka, most specifically the son in *The Metamorphosis*. But all Freud's schematization of the family, the Oedipus complex and the instincts determined by it, are blown away in the invigorating gale of Schulz's creative fantasy.

In one episode of *Cinnamon Shops* . . . it is a real gale, in so far as anything is real in Schulz's world. In his description it takes on a breathtaking paralyzing force which blows out stoves and fills houses with their smoke, and makes the townspeople afraid to go out for fear of being blown into nonexistence. The narrator's father is marooned away from home in his dry-goods store. Belabored by his wife's anxieties, two relatives volunteer to try to get through and bring him home. They put on enormous coats, force the door open against the wind's pressure as if it were the hatch of a submarine. Hours pass and when they suddenly reappear everyone realizes that they have made no attempt to find the father but have been cowering against the wall outside the door, waiting for time to go by. But by now nobody cares. The focus has altered; Aunt Perasia has come "to call." Stimulated by this tiny, vivacious, active personality, household affairs resume their normal course. But her energies, in domestic parallel with the gale outside, assume a more and more frenetic violence. She seems to shrink in size, seizes two splinters of wood from the kindling and uses them as stilts to mount the dresser; is finally oxidized by her own activity into a black petal of ash.

Such things are normal occurrences in Schulz's world, reminding us more of Dickens than of Proust or Kafka, with whom his manner is often compared. But there is nothing macabre in these displays: they give us a happy and wholly free view of "home"—a child's view, which does not seek for explanations or go in for post-mortems. It sounds, from what we know, as if Schulz's father was pretty much like that of the narrator in his books, but the way in which he is, as it were, blessed by matter—an affectionate apotheosis—also seems to be making a tacit challenge to a writer who uses the grotesque for very different purposes.

"Father's Last Escape," the concluding part of *Sanatorium*, makes the reference to Kafka quite explicit. His business liquidated and all his functions and authorities taken over by wife or relatives, Father seems at the end of his tether. . . . Father's only resource is to turn himself first into wallpaper or clothing . . . and then into a big crab-like insect who—unlike Kafka's passive victim—runs nimbly about the house, obstinately and indefatigably looking for something. . . .

[The ending of **"Father's Last Escape"** is] a farewell as epic as in Homer or James Joyce. The father has become the son, has been served at a communion, laid in the tomb of the drawing room, next to the family photographs and a musical cigarette box; has risen again and ascended, or at least vanished.

The palimpsest of myth, both sophisticated and marvelously elemental, is liberated from any specific religious or psychological significance, controlled only by the lyric precision and sobriety of Schulz's art. Such meticulous flights into fancy sometimes remind one of Conrad's explorations of sequence and event in *The Secret Sharer* and *The Secret Agent*. . . .

In [Schulz's] art a kind of potential always seems more important than achievement, in the same way that his imagination makes not only persons but matter itself seem tensed into transition, gravid with new and exciting possibilities of metamorphosis. In practice it seems likely that Schulz achieved exactly what he could do, as Kafka had done in his stories, and that the meditation of a larger work in a more declarative mode contained the presumption of its own unattainability, like Kafka's Castle.

Already in *Sanatorium* there are signs of Schulz losing the simplicity of his original communication and beginning to give a performance on his new literary identity instead of evading what Valéry called "the absurdity of all particular existence." (His books have no real titles: they are labeled arbitrarily from among their own constituents.) When the dog Nimrod, often met with in his pages, learns first to bark, the sound too rapidly becomes no more than itself. "Nimrod kept on barking, but the tone of it had changed imperceptibly, had become a parody of what it had been—an attempt to express the incredible wonder of that capital enterprise, life."

In a no doubt deliberate contrast with the *Angst* of Kafka's, the joy of Schulz's world depends on the way its art seizes the possibilities that preempt realization, or—like the Father—continue to defy it against all the odds. The pleasure it bestows is admirably uncontemporary, though it gives no sense of belonging to the past. It shows what is lost by our narrowing compulsion to define ourselves sexually, socially, or nationally—to "find out who we are"; and how we may lose the sort of imagination Schulz possessed, together with the world of which it could make such divine sense. (p. 36)

> *John Bayley, "Pioneers and Phantoms," in* The New York Review of Books *(reprinted with permission from* The New York Review of Books; *copyright © 1978 Nyrev, Inc.), Vol. XXV, No. 12, July 20, 1978, pp. 35-6.**

GABRIEL JOSIPOVICI (essay date 1979)

It is easy to understand why someone like [Jerzy] Ficowski or Bashevis Singer should feel strongly about Schulz and should speak of him as a Polish Proust or Kafka. Unfortunately, the truth of the matter is that he is not in that class at all. There can be no doubt about his talent or the seriousness of his dedication or the pathos of his end. But this must not blind us to his real worth.

All his work is filled with the richness and wonder of the child's view of reality. Nearly every story deals with childhood in the family home, with his mother, his uncles, Adela the maid, and, above all, his extraordinary, eccentric father. . . . How far this is autobiography and how far it is fiction it is impossible to say, nor is it very important, for Schulz was quite clear that what he wanted to do was to raise the ordinary and humdrum lives of his people and his town to the level of myth. (pp. 362-63)

Schulz has a marvellous gift for evoking the wonder and terror of the most ordinary experiences: a walk through the snow, the smell of a spring night, the empty rooms of a big house. Anything he turns his attention to is at once seen as far more extraordinary and mysterious than we, set in our adult habits, could possibly have imagined.

But, for the reader, page after page of such evocation can grow tedious, however much it means to Schulz himself. And as a writer, too, he sensed that there was a problem: 'It is part of my existence to be the parasite of metaphors, so easily am I carried away by the first simile that comes along,' he writes in one of the stories. 'Having been carried away, I have to find my difficult way back to my senses.' If the imagination has the power to transmute reality at all times and places, what is going to act as a brake on it? The stories all start from the concrete and specific, then grow more and more widely surrealistic as image generates image and the plot, freed from the shackles of verisimilitude, careens wildly in all directions. Inevitably, the climax is death, disintegration, apocalypse.

Schulz attempts to control his fantasy in these stories by a kind of irony. Unfortunately, the irony does not bite very deep; it remains a merely literary device by means of which he tries to keep the balance between imagination and reality. A comparison with Kafka is illuminating here. Kafka, too, started by writing first-person narratives in which the whim of the hero could alter the reality of his surroundings. But he quickly gave that up, and found his true vein in exploring the contradiction between our sense of ourselves and the world's sense of us. The horror of *Metamorphosis*, for example, comes from the remorseless exploration of the paradox the reader is made to live out from the first sentence on: how can I be *both* myself *and* a beetle? In comparison, **'Father's Last Escape'**, in which Father turns into a crab and is eventually boiled by Mother, suffers not merely from being derivative, but from the arbitrary nature of the event.

Schulz is probably closer to a fine minor writer like Robert Walser [than to Kafka himself]. . . .

Yet there are moments, in [Schulz' work] of magical achievement. . . . The intermixture of charlatanry and miracle, which is never far from genuine folk culture, has rarely been more accurately and humorously caught. At his best, Bruno Schulz can give us something we cannot find in any other modern writer. (p. 363)

> *Gabriel Josipovici, "Unrelieved Magic," in* The Listener *(© British Broadcasting Corp. 1979; reprinted by permission of Gabriel Josipovici), Vol. 101, No. 2601, March 8, 1979, pp. 362-63.*

JOHN UPDIKE (essay date 1979)

Bruno Schulz was one of the great *writers*, one of the great transmogrifiers of the world into words. In [*Sanatorium under the Sign of the Hourglass*], his second and final book, the writing, with its ardent accumulations of metaphor and unexpected launching of heavy objects into flight, seems even more rarefied than in his first. The magical town and family melt, shimmering, into the pageant of the calendar and the unfolding of a young consciousness. Sensitivity dawns as entirely artistic: "The fiery beauty of the world" is revealed through the translucent emblems of a schoolmate's stamp album, and the magnificent atmospheric effects of the changing seasons are conjured more than once in terms of deliberately staged theatrics, "a touring show, poetically deceptive, an enormous purple-skinned onion disclosing ever new panoramas under each of its skins." These panoramas disclose themselves to the author through the lens of memory, a cerebral elaboration peculiar to man and requiring the invention of language for its code. (p. xiii)

The pages are crowded with verbal brilliance, like Schulz's brimming, menacing, amazing skies. But something cruel lurks behind this beauty, bound up with it—the cruelty of myth. Like dreams, myths are a shorthand whose compressions occur without the friction of resistance that reality always presents to pain. In his treasured, detested loneliness Schulz brooded upon his personal past with the weight of generations; how grandly he succeeded can be felt in the dread with which we read even his most lyrical and humorous passages, the dread that something momentous approaches. Something alien may break through these dark, tense membranes of sensation. The scenery-mover, the laboring writer, might rescind his illusion. The rules that hold us safe are somehow awry.

I. B. Singer . . . said of Schulz, "He wrote sometimes like Kafka, sometimes like Proust, and at times succeeded in reaching depths that neither of them reached" [see excerpt above]. The striking similarities—Marcel Proust's inflation of the past and ecstatic reaches of simile, Franz Kafka's father-obsession and metamorphic fantasies—point toward an elusive difference: the older men's relative orthodoxy within the Judaeo-Christian presumptions of value, and the relative nakedness with which Schulz confronts the mystery of existence. Like Jorge Luis Borges, he is a cosmogonist without a theology. The harrowing effort of his prose (which never, unlike that of Proust or Kafka, propels us onward but instead seems constantly to ask that we stop and reread) is to construct the world anew, as from fragments that exist after some unnameable disaster.

What this disaster might be, our best guess would be his father's madness. "Madness" may be too strong a term— "retreat from reality," certainly. . . . The many metamorphoses of Schulz's fictional father-figure, culminating in the horrifying crab form he assumes in the last story of [*Sanatorium under the Sign of the Hourglass*], the sometimes magnificent delusional systems the old man spins, and the terrible war of diminishment versus enlargement in the imagery that surrounds this figure have their basis in an actual metamorphosis that must have been, to the victim's son, more frightening than amusing, more humiliating than poetic.

In Kafka, by contrast, the father threatens by virtue of his potency and emerges as less frail than he at first seems. In both cases the father occupies the warm center of the son's imagination. The mother is felt dimly and coolly and gets small thanks for her efficiency and sanity. At least, however, Schulz's mother is not entirely absent from his recreated world; in the writings of Sören Kierkegaard—another lonely bachelor son of a fascinating, if far from reassuring, father— the mother is altogether absent. From the mother, perhaps, men derive their sense of their bodies; from the father, their sense of the world. From his relationship with his father Kafka construed an enigmatic, stern, yet unimpeachable universe; Schulz presents an antic, soluble, picturesque cosmos, lavish in its inventions but feeble in its authority. In **"Tailors'**

Dummies'' (from *The Street of Crocodiles*) he has his father pronounce: "If, forgetting the respect due to the Creator, I were to attempt a criticism of creation, I would say 'Less matter, more form!'"

Sensitive to formlessness, Schulz gives even more attention than Samuel Beckett to boredom, to life's preponderant limbo, to the shoddy swatches of experience, to dead seasons, to those negative tracts of time in which we sleep or doze. His feeling for idle time is so strong that the adamant temporal medium itself appears limp and fickle to him. . . . [A] problematical feature of modern literature [is] its immurement in the personal. Abandoning kings and heroes and even those sagas of hearsay that inspired Joseph Conrad and Thomas Hardy, the writer seems condemned to live, like the narrator of **"Loneliness"** (in *Sanatorium under the Sign of the Hourglass*), in his old nursery. Limited, in a scientific age that has redefined verification, to incidents he has witnessed, to the existence he has lived minute by drab minute, the writer is driven to magnify, and the texture of magnification is bizarre. More purely than Proust or Kafka Schulz surrendered to the multiple distortions of obsessed reflection, giving us now a father as splendid as the glittering meteor, "sparkling with a thousand lights," who leaps into the spread canvas of the fire brigade, and in other places a father reduced to rubbish.

Schulz's last surviving work, the small novella **"The Comet"** (published at the end of *The Street of Crocodiles*), shows Father himself at the microscope, examining a fluorescent homunculus that a wandering star has engendered in the quiet of the stove's pitch-dark chimney shaft, while Uncle Edward, whom Father's sorcery has transformed into an electric bell, sounds the alarm for the end of the world, which does not come. In these vivid, riddling images an ultimate of strangeness is reached, and a degree of religious saturation, entirely heterodox, unknown in literature since William Blake. Indeed, Schulz's blazing skies, showing "the spirals and whorls of light, the pale-green solids of darkness, the plasma of space, the tissue of dreams," carry us back to the pagan astronomers, their wonder and their desolate inklings of a superhuman order. (pp. xiv-xvi)

The same eye that so greedily seizes upon the pictorial artifacts translucently afloat on the surface of creation sees symbolic intentions in natural formations like the stars, "the indifferent tribunal of stars, now set in a sky on which the shapes of the instruments floated like water signs or fragments of keys, unfinished lyres or swans, an imitatory, thoughtless starry commentary on the margin of music." Schulz's own illustrations to his stories, though skilled, do not participate in his fluid confusion of the graphic and the actual but, like illustrations by another man, sit athwart the text, obstructing our imagining. Idiosyncratically etched on spoiled photographic plates, the drawings make a dominant impression of shyness—the oversize heads habitually averted, foreshortened from above and unsmilingly wreathed in silence. These efficiently drawn dolls, which yet dwarf the toylike cityscapes they inhabit, disclose none of the radiant depths of their creator's prose; they do suggest the preceding centuries of illustrated fable that lie behind his fabulous relaying of his personal legends.

Personal experience taken cabalistically: This formula fits much modern fiction and, complain though we will, is hard to transcend. Being ourselves is the one religious experience we all have, an experience shareable only partially, through the exertions of talk and art. Schulz's verbal art strikes us—stuns us, even—with its overload of beauty. But, he declares, his art seeks to serve truth, to fill in the gaps that official history leaves. "Where is truth to shelter, where is it to find asylum if not in a place where nobody is looking for it . . .?" Schulz himself was a hidden man, in an obscure Galician town, born to testify to the paradoxical richness, amid poverty of circumstance, of our inner lives. (pp. xviii-xix)

John Updike, "Introduction" (copyright © John Updike 1979; reprinted by permission of the author), in Sanatorium under the Sign of the Hourglass *by Bruno Schulz, translated by Celina Wieniewska, Penguin Books, 1979, pp. xiii-xix.*

ADDITIONAL BIBLIOGRAPHY

"New in Paperback: *Sanatorium under the Sign of the Hourglass*." *Book World—The Washington Post* (4 November 1979): 13.
     Brief review that compares Schulz to André Gide, Jorge Luis Borges, Franz Kafka, Donald Barthelme, and Gilbert Rogin.

Hoberman, J. "Short Circuits: *Sanatorium under the Sign of the Hourglass*." *The Village Voice* XXIII, No. 51 (18 December 1978): 121.
     Review with plot outlines of some stories from this collection.

Tōson Shimazaki

1872-1943

(Pseudonym of Shimazaki Haruki) Japanese poet, novelist, short story writer, and essayist.

Tōson was one of the representative authors of the Japanese naturalist movement. His works reflect the changing way of life brought about by the Meiji Restoration, an era in Japanese history that saw wide acceptance of Western styles and conveniences. Although originally recognized as a poet, Tōson is now considered more important as a novelist. In his novels he depicted the effects on the people of Japan of the change from a feudal to a modern society.

Tōson was educated at a Christian missionary college; he became a school teacher, but later abandoned this profession to dedicate his life to literature. Tōson and his family suffered a series of personal tragedies, due in part to poverty caused by his refusal to work at anything but his writing.

The poems in Tōson's first collection of poetry, *Wakanashū*, were idealistic and romantic, and displayed his unusual ability for combining objectivity and lyricism. Although Tōson used pseudoclassical language and traditional meter, his poems were personal reactions to life in an era of change. Although his career as a poet was brief, critics regard Tōson's poems as "the fountainhead of the new Japanese poetry."

Tōson's first novel, *Hakai (The Broken Commandment)*, is one of the few Japanese novels of its era to deal with social themes. Concerned with the *eta*, or the outcasts of Japan, it is a pioneer work of modern Japanese realism. *The Broken Commandment*, his only novel that is not autobiographical, is Tōson's work of greatest interest to Western readers.

In his other novels Tōson examines the turmoil of his personal life against the backdrop of changing Japanese society. For example, *Ie (The Family)* gives an account of his marriage during the changes wrought by the rapid industrialization of Japan. *Yoaké Maé*, generally considered Tōson's most important work, is a long historical novel concerned with the effects of Western influences on older Japanese citizens. The central character, a provincial scholar in conflict with modern life, is reminiscent of Tōson's father.

Though little known in the West, Tōson is considered an important novelist in Japan. His works provide an excellent study of the problems that arise when a traditional culture encounters forces of change.

PRINCIPAL WORKS

Wakanashū (poetry) 1897
Hitohabune (poetry and prose) 1898
Natskusa (poetry) 1898
Rakubaishu (poetry and prose) 1901
Hakai (novel) 1906
  [*The Broken Commandment*, 1974]
Haru (novel) 1908
Ie (novel) 1910
  [*The Family*, 1976]
Sakura no mi no juku suru koro (novel) 1917

Shinsei (novel) 1919
Yoaké Maé (novel) 1935
Tôhô no mon (unfinished novel) 1943; published in
  journal *Chuo Koron*

JOSEPH ROGGENDORF (essay date 1951)

The transformation which Japanese literature underwent with the Meiji Restoration is, as the late Professor Oda Masanobu wrote some years ago, perhaps not sufficiently realized by foreign students of Japanese letters. To indicate the vast import of this "revolution," he says that well educated Japanese born around the beginning of this century "can read any early Victorian writer with greater ease" than a Japanese work of the same period. Nor is this "immense change" a matter of the language only. It has equally revolutionized a great number of traditional ideas on the technique and the structure of literature and its place within life and society.

And it is to a large extent responsible for the creation of an entirely new *genre* of literature, the modern Japanese novel.

The change happened, of course, under the impact of Japan's encounter with the West, and it is understandable that it is commonly attributed to Western influences. But, as Sir George Sansom . . . wisely remarks, "of all cultural influences, it is literary influences that are easiest to allege and hardest to measure."

When the work of "measuring" such "influences" is undertaken the imposing figure of Shimazaki Tôson . . . cannot be overlooked. "The story of his life and literary work symbolizes that of the entire era," an often quoted critic [Yamazaki Akira] has said. The statement is valid in the sense that his largely autobiographical work records the life of a peculiarly sensitive Japanese within a most disturbed and unsettled epoch. . . . [He] was actively present on the literary stage from the time the drama opened in the late 'eighties to the time the curtain fell after a decisive act in the Pacific War. In another sense, however, Tôson's life and work cannot be called "symbolical." He does not typify the average post-Meiji man of letters, always theorizing, debating, joining clubs and coteries, proclaiming and denouncing literary fads and schools. "The direction of post-Meiji Japanese letters," Professor Doi Mitsutomo has noted, "changes about every ten years. New trends appear, new leaders arise and wherever they carry their flags, the people follow them; but as the direction changes again, both leaders and followers disappear from the literary scene. Tôson alone is never carried away by these currents. He talks little outside his work: he calmly continues at his own improvement; he marches on along a winding and steep road, indeed a dark and lonely road."

That stubborn solitariness of Tôson makes him to the student of the modern novel a subject both fascinating and difficult. (pp. 40-1)

[The] most decisive event of his adolescence, [was his] friendship with Kitamura Tôkoku . . . and the "Romantic" movement of the early 'nineties. (p. 44)

With Tôkoku and his group we are in the presence of real poetic genius inspired, no doubt, by the contact with the Western literary tradition but not overwhelmed by it to the extent of losing touch with an indigenous heritage. Of Tôkoku's work very little is left; the other friends were soon overshadowed by the young Tôson who embodied their aspiration and also became the chronicler of the movement in his novel *Spring*.

We are not concerned here with an evaluation of the lyrical poetry which brought national fame to Tôson when he was still in his twenties. But it is important to probe into the impulse which his poetry may have given his prose. Japanese critics, analyzing the haunting rhythm of Tôson's verse, have noted the innovations which may have some bearing on his prose. There is, for instance, the arresting new technique of separating the conventional seven-syllable line not through the usual caesura between three and four or four and three, but to place it recurrently between two and five or five and two. There is again the unsparing use of particles and suffixes, frequently placed at the end of a line and thus slightly neutralizing the major caesura between seven and five. Through gently drawing the lines into each other, the impression of a spoken modern sentence is almost achieved, as in the *Ode on a White Porcelain Vase.*

It is difficult for a non-Japanese to pronounce judgment on such purely esthetic perfection which appeals to a fund of emotion held in common by the members of an old culture. These poems as well as much of Tôson's prose consist of style and atmosphere and these are the first things lost in the approach by the foreigner. And that is also true of the appreciation of the allusive imagery with which both Tôson's poems and novels abound. Edward Sackville-West speaks, in his *Inclinations,* of the influence on contemporary Western poetry of Mallarmé and Rimbaud "who suppressed metaphor in favour of an image, or chain of images, comporting both the idea and its evocations." He speaks of "the enormous risks to communication" which this procedure involves, and says that it is "probably the greatest invention of poetic technique which the last hundred years have to show." In Japan this is surely no invention of the last hundred years, nor does it seem to hamper the poetic communication of the *waka.* But in Japan, while the device is older, it is also more stereotyped. Tôson adopted it and gave it new life. Thus in the *Ode on a White Porcelain Vase* all the classical chains of images are there again—fountain, fragrance, whiteness, heart, root, flower, the beloved—, yet the evocation is modern. Here is perhaps the secret of the continuity of Japanese verse through the ages.

Professor Doi vividly recalls the impression which the first reading of Tôson's poems made on his mind in 1904, the year he went to college at Kyôto and Tôson's first Collected Edition appeared. It was the first encounter of the young student, trained in the Spartanic atmosphere of the Tosa clan's former military academy, with the richer and more humane tradition of an older Japan. Doi, wrestling for words to evoke the emotion he experienced, calls it *das ewig Weibliche.* He then recounts how, three years later, having entered Tôkyô University, he found the poems "dated" on opening them again. The atmosphere had changed. It was the time of the naturalistic novels, [Katai's *Futon* and Tôson's *Hakai*]. . . . "English literature was no longer *à la page*; Maupassant and Gorki began to have their turn." But on rereading the poetry three decades later, he confesses to having changed his mind. He discovered on reflection an "organic continuity" in the literary career of Tôson. The secret of this continuity he sees in the genuinely classical literary device of economy, reserve and allusiveness which is of the essence of Japanese lyrics. (pp. 45-7)

Tôson set to work on his first prose efforts with the deadly seriousness which is characteristic of him, taking literally the precepts of Doppo who was teaching the young to begin with "realistic sketches of nature" in order to learn the art of writing. He labored for years at the *Chikuma River Sketches* . . . , descriptions of the rugged landscape of his native Kiso . . . mountains in Shinshû and its rugged people. These cameo-like "poems in prose," as they have been called, are justly famous and still a favorite of anthologies. (pp. 49-50)

[*Suisaigaka* (**The Water Color Painter**)] gives, of all the early stories, the best idea of the author's characteristic gifts. . . .

The theme is partly autobiographical and recurs in the novel *The House.* The suspicion of the infidelity of his wife tormented Tôson for years, until after her death he discovered that it had been unfounded. The story is not naturalistic in any accepted sense of the term. It rather reveals the tender suggestiveness which we know from his lyrics. One scene is characteristic: the parrot, which Denkichi had brought with him from his foreign travels, is cheerfully and noisily present in the background, until suddenly and helplessly he dies one night, the image of the love between the two, alive till yesterday and now hopelessly dead. (p. 50)

It is hard to see why a discerning critic such as Shimamura Hôgetsu . . . could call [*Hakai* (**Disobedience**)] "the first naturalistic novel after Western standards in Japan." If naturalism consists in describing life without modification and pruning, this novel hardly falls into the category. The characters are arranged into an implausible black-white contrast; the whole background little corresponds to what one imagines as the realistic atmosphere of a Meiji village. But there is a dramatic urgency about the story which Tôson never reached again and which is rare in the Japanese literature of the time. The concentration on a simple and poignant plot, to the exclusion of anything outside the tightly knit little community, and the very articulate political message of the novel explain perhaps the appeal of the piece to Japanese readers and its repeated performance on stage and screen. It has also been called "the forerunner of the proletarian novel" and has had the honour of being translated into Russian. (p. 51)

Together with *Hakai* and *Ie* [*Haru* (**The Spring**)] is commonly considered to constitute Tôson's great "naturalistic trilogy." But *Disobedience* and *Spring* share less a naturalistic technique than a youthful discontent with the world at large and a certain melancholy moodiness. They both possess a remarkable felicity of phrase and diction, the result of laborious labor and experimentation. In conception and structure the novels are worlds apart. The dramatic vigor of the earlier novels is replaced by interminable dialogues and lachrimose sighing under the moon, as the friends of the *Bungakkai* group wearily move across the scene. The suicide of Aogi (the Tôkoku of the Romantics) lacks any kind of inner justification, and his friend Kishimoto Sutekichi makes his final exit with a tired and despairing gesture. . . .

This concluding scene is characteristic of the vaguely lyrical allusiveness of many other passages in the novel. But as an effective literary device it is not yet handled with the sureness of touch which Tôson later came to acquire. Some of the short stories of the period seem to reveal that, in a smaller and less ambitious frame, Tôson was already capable of producing veritable jewels of his peculiar prose style. [*Namiki* (**The Avenue**)] may serve as an example. (p. 52)

[It] is an example of modern Japanese prose at its best, and it shows Tôson at work to help make it. The underlying feeling of the story also reveals the problem that came to preoccupy the writer more and more, the questionable character of the rapidly industrialized Japan of his time, the emptiness of her culture, the *ennui*. His third novel [*Ie* (**The House**)] makes of this problem the central issue. . . .

The novel is epic in character—if we have to employ Western terms—rather than dramatic as *Hakai* or lyrical as *Haru*. As such it may be considered a forerunner of Tôson's masterpiece *Before the Dawn*. But Tôson is not yet able to view the destiny of his family as a part of the dramatic metamorphosis of Japanese society. He has not yet acquired the serene detachment which explains the greatness of his later work. He took enormous pains to write *Ie*. (p. 53)

Shinsei, however deplorable as a creation and an incident, had the effect of refreshing the air. A calmer and quieter tone, which had slowly and imperceptibly changed his style and technique, now also began to transform the subject-matter of his fiction and indeed his philosophy. Many of the

leading writers and critics had long been denouncing the aberrations of naturalism. With some of them, such as the brothers [Arishima of the Shirakaba group or Kubota Mantarê] . . . of the Neo-Romantics, Tôson had always been on friendly terms. It is possible that he underwent new "influences." Already the companions of his youth admired the amazing gift he had of assimilating while yet instantly reshaping impressions. But it is more true to say that he continued to inspire the evolution of the novel. In spite of all his lapses and failures, he had never at any time surrendered to the fads and fashions of the moment. He now performs the function of guardian and mentor against the threatening decline into estheticism and *décadence*. He insists that the task is still what it was at the beginning of the creative epoch in post-Meiji literature, to capture the complex reality of modern Japan in a language and in artistic forms which are themselves still in the making. As he spoke of romanticism when naturalism was *à la mode*, so he now has the courage to speak of realism. (pp. 57-8)

Nevertheless, the novelist feels that he has reached the end of a phase. . . . (p. 58)

More and more the problem of a Japan between two worlds comes to obsess him, of a civilization cut drift from its moorings and exposed to dangers that, helplessly floating, it cannot overcome. That, at any rate, is the subject of the fiction of his maturity. Everything he ever wrote was autobiographical. But now he begins to expand the circumference of his Self. He is still concerned with his own fate and that of the family from which he hails. Now he begins to see it as part of a larger world and he sets about to probe into the nature of the society into which he was born. The curtain of depressive fatalism begins to lift, the vista expands both into the past and into the future.

The publication of [*Yoake Mae* (**Before the Dawn**)] began in 1935. Since 1928, . . . Tôson had been working with his customary industriousness at the book which was to be his greatest achievement. The publication in the Review *Chûô Kôron* . . . where it was first serialized was preceded by a characteristic announcement.

> I cannot make any great promises to my readers concerning this work. It is my fifth novel, written, as far as I could manage, in the ordinary colloquial language. For the last few years I have lived a retired life and have written very little. This has caused all kinds of rumor, mostly exaggerations. I consider *Yoake Mae* as only a 'study,' nothing more.

Such understatements usually do not mean much in Japan. But it is perhaps significant that he insists, once more, on his two old cherished ideas, the 'colloquial language,' *heidan zokugo* . . . , and 'study' (he uses the English word). His greatest pride was in his conscientious craftsmanship, "Look well at things." . . . "Ever again look anew at the world." . . . The concern for the living language comes from the same preoccupation. In a probing essay *On Language* he had written, a few years before, that the beauty of literary language was not in its preciousness but in its ordinary plainness, much as Saigyô and Bashô had "drawn the language of their poetry from the daily language of the common people." But "study" also means the years he had spent in archives, libraries, farmers' cottages to look for the propelling forces behind the Meiji Restoration and its effects on modern Japan. The novel is proof that such love of artisan detail is capable of producing a masterpiece, provided a mature artist chooses a great subject. (pp. 59-60)

No mere summary can do justice to the grandiose sweep of the work, its inspired prose and subtle structure. For, the novel signifies the consummation of the labour of a lifetime. His ceaseless "sharpening of tools" had been put, at last, to good use, his horizon had been widened further than any of the great novelists of the period had ever dared to. It is understandable that the work received lavish praise when it was published. It stands as a monument to the literary endeavour of an epoch.

It is more difficult to range the novel in those categories of fiction with which a Westerner is more familiar. Japanese critics have compared *Before the Dawn* with Tolstoy's *War and Peace*, a hardly valid opinion. For what Tolstoy describes are not events but only the people in them. (p. 62)

Almost the reverse is true of Tôson's great novel. It is concerned with a society at a particular stage of transition, and characters which are only true in so far as they are representative of that society. The work is, therefore, nearer to the Period Novel of the type of *Die Buddenbrooks*, the *Forsyte Saga* or the *New Machiavelli*. The obvious difficulty of the period novel is that exactitude of contemporary detail becomes more important than exactitude of imagination; while the period lives, the men in it do not. Tôson has perhaps not quite evaded this pitfall, and in that respect, *Before the Dawn* is less of a success than some of his earlier novels, all period pieces, notably *The House*. A Japanese critic has spoken with some justice of the "lifeless figures on a China ink painting," as which some of the characters of *Before the Dawn* emerge.

Nevertheless, whatever time and labour the author spent on reconstituting the scenery and documenting his subjects, he has not thought lightly of the ardours of imagination. The reason is that he felt himself personally engaged in the events he described, he attempted to relive them, because they were of an intensely personal, not a mere academic interest to him. In that sense, none of his novels, not even his ambitious major work, is of the type of the fiction of Mann, Wells or Galsworthy to whom Society is essentially an abstract conception convenient for the illustration of an idea. To Tôson it is an imaginative reality; events are not recorded as having taken place, they take place before our eyes.

The very rigidity of [the protagonist] Hanzô explains in fact his tragic impact on the reader. Man is often conceived as a *type*, representing a province, a school, a tendency or trend, in Japanese literature and perhaps also in Japanese society. The petrification of their life during the rigid feudal rule of the Tokugawas must have accentuated this peculiarity. And Hanzô's description as a *type* is masterfully done.... (pp. 62-3)

Tôson [also wished to] undertake "what has never been attempted in Japanese literature," namely a reconstruction of the growth of a type, stretching over a lifetime or several lifetimes.

Whether Tôson was prompted by such suggestions or whether he felt within himself the need to probe even deeper into the reasons for his being and that of his time, the fact is that his last literary creation consists in the attempt to push the boundaries of his inquiry even further, both into the past and into the present. (pp. 63-4)

[Tôson] had little humour, it is true; but he possessed a burning love of truth, much gentleness and much compassion. (p. 66)

> *Joseph Roggendorf, "Shimazaki Tôson: A Maker of the Modern Japanese Novel," in* Monumenta Nipponica, *Vol. VII, Nos. 1 & 2, January, 1951, pp. 40-66.*

DONALD KEENE (essay date 1953)

The novel of the Meiji era which I believe has the greatest interest for the Western reader of today is *The Broken Commandment*.... This is the story of a young man who is a member of the *eta* or pariah class. Although discrimination against members of this class has long been prohibited by law, feeling is still rather strong among Japanese on the subject, and fifty years ago it must have been far more intense. The young man of the novel is commanded by his father never under any circumstances to reveal to others that he is an *eta*, and he manages in fact to conceal it from even his closest friends during the time that he is at school, and later, when he becomes a teacher.... Then, quite by chance, the director of the school, who is unfriendly to Ushimatsu, learns that the young man is an *eta*. The fact spreads among the teachers of the school, and finally to the pupils just at the moment when Ushimatsu decides that he must break his vow to his father. The effect is beautifully managed, the two currents meeting at the moment when Ushimatsu makes his supreme effort and tells the truth. What can the ending of the novel be, we wonder, as we approach the last few pages with no solution in sight. It comes, a pure *deus ex machina*. The *eta* who was driven from Ushimatsu's inn at the outset of the novel reappears with an offer of a job on a ranch in Texas, and Ushimatsu accepts, setting off with the young lady who has remained faithful to him in spite of the awful truth of his background. The ending vitiates the story for us, but it was perhaps the only possible one for Japan. I think it likely that in a European novel of the same date, it would be far more usual that the hero, offered the choice of a comfortable job in Texas or badly paid work as a battler for *eta* rights in Japan would have chosen the latter. In this the Japanese novel is realistic as European works are not.

The Broken Commandment is an example of one important result of European influence of Japanese literature, the increasing interest in social problems. On the whole Japanese poetry remained true to the old spirit, in spite of the innovations in the forms, but other branches of literature came increasingly to serve as vehicles for new thought. When we look at lists of European novels translated in the early years of Meiji, we are struck and perhaps amused by the preponderance of political novels, such as those of Disraeli or Bulwer Lytton, and in the works written under European influence this political element is equally conspicuous. The realism of such writers as Zola was, initially at least, not of great interest to the Japanese because many of the subjects which Zola treated were the most common themes of their own literature, and the realism with which he shocked Europe was quite matter-of-fact to the Japanese. The real challenge for them lay in the field of political and social writing, something quite new in their fiction. *The Broken Commandment* attempted to discuss the problem of the *eta* in such a way as to arouse sympathy for those unfortunate people, but always within the limits of an interesting story. Other attempts at social questions were usually more crudely done. (pp. 99-101)

Donald Keene, "Japanese Literature under Western Influence," in his Japanese Literature: An Introduction for Western Readers, *John Murray Publishers, Ltd.,* 1953, pp. 88-110.*

EDWIN McCLELLAN (essay date 1969)

[Shimazaki Tōson's] first collection of verse, *A Collection of Young Leaves (Wakanashū),* . . . immediately established him as a young poet of great promise. (p. 75)

These poems may strike the modern Western reader as being at best rather unoriginal. But what may seem to us today undistinguished lyrical verse—and here we are speaking merely of the content, not the language—can very easily have seemed novel and exciting to the Japanese public of 1897. Tōson himself was very conscious of having done something new. He suggests that he had tried to give new meaning to those Japanese words which had become shopworn in their traditional setting; and indeed, it would seem that such words as *koi* (love), *haru* (spring), *tabi* (journey), and *tabibito* (those that journey) gained a certain freshness under Tōson's handling. In verse which was surprisingly free and flowing, he used these words to express the sentiments of modern Japanese youth. "I went to Sendai," he tells us, "and there tried to make poetry come closer to the hearts of young people like myself."

It is extremely difficult to point with any precision to those qualities of sentiment which made Tōson's poetry "new." One can only hope, by reference to such words as "nostalgia," "heartache," and "loneliness," to convey an approximate idea of what they are. True, similar feelings are present in the haiku of Issa. . . . But what is significant is that Tōson found it necessary, and Issa did not, to escape from the confined, implicit world of traditional verse to the more flexible, explicit world of song. And in the very explicitness of the emotionalism of Tōson's poetry, we find a new kind of self-consciousness and, unavoidably perhaps, a new sentimentality which we do not find in Issa's poetry. In **"Pillow of Grass"** (**"Kusamakura"**), for example, which is one of the most successful of the poems in *Young Leaves,* the melancholy of the poet comes very close to seeming in our eyes a pose. But we find it expressed with that freshness which is characteristic of Tōson's best lyrics; and this freshness comes from the young poet's genuine sense of discovery of a new world of poetic articulation. (pp. 75-6)

One of the great weaknesses of the poetry in *Young Leaves* is its small emotional range. Of this Tōson himself was quite aware. In his essay, **"Diction and Poetry"** (**"Gagen to shika"**), Tōson complains of the limitations of sound and of vocabulary inherent in the Japanese poetic language, which must necessarily limit the variety of moods the poet may express. That Tōson should therefore have moved on to fiction is not altogether surprising. It would seem that no matter how hard he tried, he could not entirely break away from the restrictions imposed upon him by long-established poetic usage. For one thing, his ear had been attuned to the seven-and the five-syllable counts; and for another, he could not materially increase his vocabulary without violating his sense of proper poetic diction. In other words, with almost the same tools

that the seventeenth-century poet Bashō, for example, had used in his brief, suggestive poems, Tōson tried to bring to his own some of the range and explicitness of Western poetry. He was not altogether unsuccessful; there is in such a work as **"Pillow of Grass"** a sustained lyricism which is rare in Japanese poetry, and for this alone he deserves to be ranked amongst the most important of modern Japanese poets. But to Tōson, endowed as he was with great descriptive power, poetry must have come to seem very confining. Some years later, shortly after he wrote his first novel, he remarked: "I write novels because they are the best medium for what I want to say. . . ." (p. 77)

It may occur to the reader later that there is a world of difference between Tōson of *Young Leaves* and Tōson of *The House (Ie)* or of *Before the Dawn.* But actually there is not as sharp a separation between these phases of his career as may be imagined. There is of course a difference. First, the author of *The House* is more mature than the author of *Young Leaves;* and second, one literary form, such as the novel, may bring out certain qualities in a man which another form, such as lyrical verse, may not. But this is not to say that the "romantic" poet is suddenly transformed into a "realistic" novelist. The passionate lyricist in Tōson always remained. However conspicuous in his novels the labored detachment of his technique may become, we always sense the painfully suppressed emotionalism that lies beneath the surface; and what gives his sometimes heavily written novels their peculiar power is the seemingly incongruous presence of the poet in the background. (p. 78)

[*Broken Commandment*] was an immediate success, and Tōson's future as a full-time writer was assured.

Whatever differences of critical opinion regarding this first novel of Tōson's we may find among literary historians, there seems to be agreement on one point; namely that it constitutes a landmark in the history of modern Japanese realism. Indeed, whether or not we agree with the view that a new literary school—that of "naturalism"—was founded with its publication, we cannot deny that in *Broken Commandment* we find less melodrama and contrivance than in the works of those writers who had dominated the Japanese literary scene until the rise of such men as Tōson and Sōseki.

The hero of the novel is a young *eta* [the outcast caste of Japanese society] by the name of Segawa Ushimatsu. By keeping secret the fact of his unusual birth he has managed to go through the prefectural normal college in Nagano without mishap, and is now a schoolteacher in the fair-sized town of Iiyama, which is also in Shinshū. The main theme of the novel is concerned with the strain this deception places on Ushimatsu and his decision finally to confess his secret. The title *Broken Commandment* refers to Ushimatsu's breaking of his father's commandment, which was that he must never tell anyone of his eta birth.

Unfortunately the title tends to mislead the reader into assuming that the moral issue at stake for Ushimastsu is whether or not he should disregard his father's admonishment. But what makes *Broken Commandment* such a remarkable book for its time is the complexity of Tōson's handling of Ushimatsu's psychology. We find as we read the novel, that Ushimatsu's deception springs from motives far less conventional than the mere desire to obey his father. We begin to see quite clearly that though the consideration of filial obedience is indeed real enough for Ushimatsu, it becomes also a means of rationalizing his own fears of censure and ostracization. It is the presence of this added dimension in the interpretation of the protagonist's motives that makes **Broken Commandment** an essentially modern and historically important novel. The presence or absence of social consciousness in it does not seem to me to be a problem of great relevance. Tōson is more interested in Ushimatsu the eta than in the eta class as a whole.

The novel begins rather crudely. In less than ten pages Tōson tells us, with much explicitness, almost all we need to know about Ushimatsu's background and his present dilemma. (pp. 79-80)

The introduction . . . is rather too explanatory: it tells us too much too quickly. However, the manner in which Tōson begins his novel implies something about his intention. The bare outline of the story is in itself of little consequence to him. What he wants to do is to write a modern psychological novel, where the essential thing is not the situations themselves, but the way in which they affect the behavior of the protagonist. . . . This means that the success of **Broken Commandment** depends to a large extent on whether or not the author manages to convince the reader that given the peculiar characteristics of Ushimastsu and the initial set of circumstances in which he is put, the outcome of the plot is natural. Judged in this light, **Broken Commandment** is not entirely successful, for it collapses in the end in a heap of tasteless melodrama; nevertheless, the restrained realism that is characteristic of most of the novel represents a considerable achievement. (p. 81)

That **Broken Commandment,** for all the achievement that it represented, was made quite imperfect by the intrusion of melodrama towards the end, Tōson must have known. He later said that when writing **Broken Commandment** he had expended too much energy on useless things, and that with the next novel, he would try to write more naturally. What exactly he meant by this remark is not entirely clear; but at any rate, **Spring,** his second novel, has no plot to speak of, and it is more or less a loosely connected series of impressionistically described scenes.

After **Broken Commandment,** Tōson never wrote a novel around imaginary characters again. **Spring, The House, When the Cherries Ripen,** and **A New Life (Shinsei)** are all based, in varying degrees, on autobiographical material; and his last completed novel, **Before the Dawn,** is based on the life of his father. What seems likely is that Tōson simply felt more comfortable, less strained, when writing around his own personal experiences. There are certain writers who, no matter how talented they may be otherwise, seem to find it extremely difficult to avoid banality in imaginary situations. Tōson was perhaps one of these. (p. 93)

[**Spring**] is essentially a lyrical piece in which Tōson tries to capture in retrospect the emotions of his early manhood in the days of the *Bungakkai.* Years later, in 1930, Tōson wrote: "**Spring** is a work full of faults, but even today, when I take it out and read it, I find that there are passages here and there which bring tears to my eyes."

Spring indeed has faults. It is very loosely constructed, the characterizations are thin and motives obscure, and the attitude of the author is often far too uncritical and sentimental. One distinguished critic has remarked, not without justification, that its main interest is historical: were it not for the

information it contains about Kitamura Tōkoku and the *Bungakkai* group, he says, it would hardly be worth reading.

Spring is nevertheless a significant work for the student of Tōson. For despite its faults, it reflects the author's peculiarities far more clearly than **Broken Commandment** does. . . . Tōson at his best does not appeal to the intellect. His inclinations are lyrical and impressionistic rather than analytical, and his novels—with the exception of **Broken Commandment**—are singularly lacking in explicitness. When he is successful, he can suggest moods which seem to transcend the presence of the human actors. But when he is unsuccessful, he seems merely inarticulate and ponderously vague, and the characters begin to seem intolerably without form or meaning.

Tōson tells us that it was with **Spring,** and not with **Broken Commandment,** that he began to write in a way he could feel was his own. In other words, **Spring** may be considered an experimental work in which Tōson tried to give his impressionistic leanings free rein. All of his novels—again, with the exception of **Broken Commandment**—are characterized by loose construction and lack of narrative continuity. **The House** and **Before the Dawn** hold together because here there is no mistaking the author's over-all purpose, and the individual scenes, though often disconnected, are in mood and content related to it. The trouble with **Spring,** however, is that it seems to be totally without design, so that in many of the scenes the reader has no idea where he is being taken or precisely what emotional response is expected of him.

The central figure of **Spring** is Kishimoto (Tōson himself), who is in his early twenties. The novel for the most part describes the young man's struggle to overcome his growing sense of purposelessness. (pp. 93-4)

Unfortunately [none] of the other characters in the book ever seem to come into focus. Scene after scene flashes past our eyes, and we catch glimpses of Kishimoto, Aoki, and their friends doing and saying various things, but we cannot see the different aspects of their behavior as parts of a whole. The figures not only remain vague outlines—which would perhaps be forgivable—but they become annoyingly unintelligible. (pp. 94-5)

The novel, then, is weak because the characters' actions are never based on sufficient motive. Tōson describes but does not explain. This surely is a weakness inherent in the impressionistic technique, which by its very nature cannot be concerned with the examination of the complexities of human behavior. In writing a novel such as **Spring,** therefore, the author must be careful not to enter into the realm where searching questions as to why the characters behave as they do become relevant. **Spring** is a failure not because it is impressionistically written, but because Tōson raises questions in our minds which cannot be answered within the limits he has set for himself. In intention at least, **Spring** is an extended prose lyric. Yet in it Tōson unwittingly allows certain considerations to intrude on our consciousness which would more properly belong in a psychological novel with a well-defined plot.

For all its faults, however, **Spring** is an historically important work. It is an attempt, though not a very successful one, to introduce material of the sort that had never been associated in Japan with the novel before. Whatever else it may be, it is certainly not vulgar entertainment. In trying to write truthfully and lyrically about his own youth, Tōson was bringing to the novel a new kind of emotional commitment. He was bringing to it the truthfulness of the poet. And even if he did fail here, he succeeded in his next attempt, where we see his own peculiar conception of realism come to life with some power. (pp. 100-01)

[*The House*] is considerably longer than *Spring,* and shows much more careful planning. From the purely technical point of view, it is probably his most successful work: in it, we see a particular technique being applied with more consistency and perhaps more effectiveness than in any of his other novels. "When I wrote *The House,*" says Tōson, "I tried to ignore those things which took place outside the house, and to limit myself to scenes inside the house. . . . I wrote in the kitchen, in the front hall, and at night [i.e., in order to describe faithfully the time and place of each scene]. When I wished to describe the sound of the river, I went to the room where it was audible." For the author of *The House,* the details of the backdrop are as important as what the actors do or say. He is equally removed from both: the human voices are hushed and seem to merge with other sounds; and the people move only as distant figures, never intruding on our awareness of the surroundings. None of the characters is allowed to stand out in bold relief. Their thoughts and actions are described accurately but with extreme detachment, just as the details of the surrounding scene are, and they are delved into no further than the latter. Thus there is no personal tragedy in *The House,* but an all-pervading mood of quiet sorrow.

The House is therefore primarily a novel of description, where the author tries to describe accurately only that which his eyes see and his ears hear, and to express his emotions implicitly through detached observations of the surface scene. What Tōson tries to do in *The House* is to keep the interpretive role of the novelist to the absolute minimum and to render the novel as free as possible from an imposed rational construct. The result is what Tōson himself chose to call "impressionism." He once asked: "Does not observing carefully and seriously the incidents of daily life lead the writer naturally to impressionism?" And what he seems to be implying here is that in real life we see the scene around us in a series of separate impressions and that the novelist who imposes on what he has seen a rationalized thread of continuity is merely giving reality an arbitrary and personal interpretation. (pp. 101-02)

The novel covers a period of some twelve years beginning . . . from the time Tōson left Sendai to the time immediately preceding the publication of *The House.* However, unlike *Spring* or *A New Life,* the novel concerns Tōson's life only as it relates to his family, and there is hardly a reference in the entire work to himself as an individual personality or to his own private life as a writer. Nor can it be considered a family chronicle in any strict sense. There is no uniformity of pace in the chronological progression, and there is no attempt on Tōson's part to maintain narrative continuity. The time lapse between scenes may be a few years or it may be a few days; and often, a scene will end abruptly in the middle of a conversation, and the next scene may deal with a totally different situation involving different characters. Particular members of the family will claim our attention for a time, then suddenly fade into the background and remain forgotten until they appear again perhaps years later, having as likely as not undergone, during their absence from the scene, crucial experiences which in another kind of novel would have formed the core of the narrative.

In the scheme of the novel, neither the incidents nor the persons have much significance in themselves. They have proportionately no more content, say, than distant sounds and figures described in a lyrical poem about a lonely autumnal scene. If they are more detailed and possess more concrete reality, it is because *The House* is a novel—and a long one at that—and not a lyrical poem. *The House* is nevertheless a poet's novel. It abounds in scenes which are clearly rich in dramatic potential, yet nowhere does Tōson depart from his set purpose: the lyricist always remains in control, and the dramatist is never allowed to assert himself. For this reason, *The House* at times may seem to the reader far too uneventful, much too lacking in drama; but it is for this reason too that it is one of the best executed of modern Japanese novels. (pp. 102-03)

[*A New Life*] is an altogether different kind of novel from *The House,* in that it is an account of a single major experience in the author's private life. It is a confession, or a justification perhaps, of his illicit relationship with one of his nieces. Unlike *The House,* therefore, it is the kind of novel that demands, by the very nature of its content, a ruthless and articulate examination of the state of mind of the characters involved. Not surprisingly, it is as conspicuous a failure as *Spring.* Tōson is so heavyhandedly circuitous in his treatment of the delicate subject matter that we begin to find ourselves in sympathy with Akutagawa Ryūnosuke who, on reading it, was moved to comment that he had never encountered anyone so hypocritical as its hero.

Kishimoto (Tōson once more calls himself by that name) is in his early forties and has been a widower for almost three years. His household now consists of two young sons, Senta and Shigeru, an elderly maid, and a grown niece, Setsuko, who acts as both housekeeper and a kind of governess. It is a measure of Tōson's vagueness that for the first forty pages or so, he gives us no recognizable indication that there is anything unusual in the relationship between the uncle and niece; instead, he gives us a lengthy and very serious-minded discourse on Kishimoto's disillusionment with life in general. (pp. 123-24)

Such preliminary description of Kishimoto's condition is not in itself objectionable. But the reader quite naturally asks in what way it is intended to illuminate the nature of Kishimoto's relationship with his niece. That is, when the story actually begins with the sudden announcement by Setsuko that she is pregnant, the surprised reader is forced to presume that Tōson has, in the course of the preceding forty pages, somehow been trying to provide a basis for understanding why Kishimoto has seduced her. Was he having his revenge on womankind? But surely we are not expected to believe that an intelligent, mature man will seduce a girl twenty years his junior, and his niece at that, for so flamboyant a reason? Besides, we have not been quite convinced of the reality of this peculiar desire for revenge in the first place. Did he, then, seduce his niece because he was disillusioned with life? But without further clarification, such an explanation would be so obscure as to be absolutely meaningless. In short, Tōson offers us no intelligible explanation as to why or in what circumstances the unfortunate relationship was allowed to begin. And not unreasonably, we come to the conclusion that in the first few chapters of the book Tōson, whether consciously or unconsciously, is attributing to Kishimoto motives which are highly unrealistic. That Kishimoto was not in love with Setsuko becomes quite clear in the course of the novel. Perhaps he was simply lonely and needed a mistress; or perhaps living under the same roof with an unattached young woman proved too much of a temptation. But no such straightforward reason is given by Tōson.

Unfortunately, the whole novel abounds in obfuscations of this sort. And when judged in the light of what we presume to have been Tōson's primary intention of writing it—that is, to write a "confessional" novel—it is an obvious failure. For in such a novel as this, where self-examination is the chief concern of the author, a vague accounting for one's actions is inexcusable.

But it is not without its redeeming qualities. Despite the annoying lack of self-understanding that the author seems to manifest throughout the novel, for all the naïve and transparent posing, *A New Life,* perhaps because of the very solemnity of the content, invites our respect. And it is evidence of Tōson's peculiar strength as a writer that even the clumsiness, which becomes so conspicuous in his more explicit attempts to explain the conduct of his characters, begins to seem a necessary part of his individuality. At any rate, he does manage, in his tenacious fashion, to make the prolonged emotional ordeal that Kishimoto undergoes real enough for the reader. Moreover, in all those passages where Tōson's intention is to limit the reader's attention to the immediate, he writes unerringly. (pp. 125-26)

Kishimoto's behavior [after learning of his niece's pregnancy] is quite abject. Fear of censure and derision becomes, it would seem, the sole basis of all he does. In his frantic search for some way of averting disgrace, Setsuko is all but forgotten. His primary concern now is not how Setsuko may be protected from whatever unkindness she will be exposed to, but how he himself may avoid the acute embarrassment of having to face up to her family, in particular her father Yoshio (Morihiko in *The House*). There are not many alternatives. Abortion? Suicide? But surely, there must be a less extreme course of action open to him? Finally, he hits upon a solution which, from his point of view, is the only practicable one. He will run away. (p. 126)

We cannot help wondering by what devious process of rationalization Kishimoto has arrived at the conclusion that Setsuko would welcome the prospect of being deserted by her lover. Does Tōson intend us here to see the heartlessness and irrationality of Kishimoto? Or does he really believe that Kishimoto's decision to go away is at least in part prompted by a certain selfless regard for Setsuko's welfare? We are not sure; and we have the uncomfortable feeling that neither is Tōson. (p. 127)

Tōson's account of Kishimoto's three-year sojourn in France is perhaps the most satisfactory part of the book. It is here that Tōson's genius for description, which elsewhere in *A New Life* is almost completely obscured by his attempts at explanation, becomes most evident. In one important respect, indeed, the account is characteristically disappointing, for it fails to provide us with any additional insight into Kishimoto's motives; and at the end of it, we have no clearer picture of Tōson's attitude towards him than we ever had before. We were not certain how Tōson wished us to view Kishimoto's departure from Japan: was it to be understood as a shamefaced flight from the unpleasant consequences of a youthful *faux pas,* or was it a self-inflicted punishment in atonement for a serious moral offense? Similarly, Kishimoto's thoughts while in France are described with such

vagueness, with such lack of formulation, that when he finally decides to end his exile, we are not sure exactly what considerations have led him to this decision. However, despite this serious failing, Tōson's description of Kishimoto's lonely sojourn in an alien country is a remarkably well sustained piece of good writing. Here, more than in any other section of the book, we are reminded that whatever his various shortcomings may be, Tōson is finally a writer of distinction. It is not strictly a narrative but rather a lyrical expression of the forlornness, the pathos, of an exile's condition. (p. 131)

The second half of the book deals with Kishimoto's relations with Setsuko and her family after his return. Despite his great relief at seeing Japan again, there is still the air of the fugitive about him as he arrives in Tokyo. His long absence, after all, was only a temporary escape and not a real solution. (p. 133)

Yoshio gives him a warm welcome; we wonder, however, whether it is entirely sincere. [His sister-in-law, Kayo, also] appears pleased, but Kishimoto senses a certain bitterness in her, and he begins to suspect that she has somehow guessed the truth. Setsuko's manner is withdrawn and strained. It is altogether a strange family reunion. The occasion must after all be acknowledged to be a happy one; and everything that is said is friendly to the point of being hearty. Yet beneath the surface jollity and solicitousness, there is the scarcely concealed undercurrent of mutual suspicion and resentment. "An atmosphere of desperate suppression seemed to pervade the house," Tōson writes. "Even the expression on the children's faces seemed to Kishimoto to be stiff."

Kishimoto and his two sons must live for a while with their relations until the latter find a house of their own. It is during this short period when they are all living under one roof that Kishimoto and Setsuko repeat their old mistake. Kishimoto, however, is not the man he was before, we are told; and so his reasons for seducing his niece have also changed. "He had ceased," Tōson says, "to regard his own unmarried state as a kind of revenge on women; he no longer hated them so much." This comment is followed, not many lines later, by yet another abstraction: "In Kishimoto's breast there had begun to grow a profound sense of pity, a desire to save not only Setsuko but himself also." This time, then, Kishimoto becomes Setsuko's lover not for the sake of revenge but through some desire for mutual salvation.

From this point on until we reach the end of the novel, Tōson treats the whole problem of their relationship as though it were a religious experience. Unfortunately, he makes very little effort to convince us that Kishimoto is in any normally accepted sense in love with Setsuko. Rather, he almost blatantly presents Kishimoto in the role of a generous guardian, selflessly dedicating himself to the improvement of his ward's condition. We are led to infer that their relationship is an ennobling one for both Kishimoto and Setsuko. But since we never come to know Setsuko as a personality in her own right and since Kishimoto's attitude towards his mistress seems devoid of love, it is inevitable that our reaction should be tinged with skepticism. (pp. 134-35)

[The] strain of having to keep their unnatural relationship a secret becomes more and more oppressive to Kishimoto. Finally, he decides he cannot go on lying about himself and Setsuko. He will write his "confession" and publish it. (The work in question is of course *A New Life.*) (p. 136)

Yoshio is given no warning of the impending publication of his brother's new book. We cannot but wonder how Kishimoto can, with such blandness, behave quite so badly towards Yoshio. And we are inclined to agree with the latter when, upon the publication of the first part of the novel, he sends this message to Kishimoto: "What a sorry business writing must be, when in order to eat you have to wash your dirty linen in public."

The relationship between Setsuko and Kishimoto is now over. Yoshio will never permit them to see each other again. Setsuko will join her uncle Tamisuke (Minoru in *The House*) in Taiwan, and there live, we presume, the life of a religious recluse. It is a terrible predicament, yet it fails to affect us very deeply. Try as we may, we cannot bring ourselves to take her any more seriously than Kishimoto seems to have done throughout the novel. (p. 137)

[*Before the Dawn*, Tōson's last completed novel] has some conspicuous imperfections: it is even more loosely constructed than *The House;* it is written in a style so bereft of ornament that its determined inelegance sometimes begins to seem unnecessary; it is too frequently interrupted by extended historical discourses on the main events surrounding the Meiji Restoration; and of the many characters that appear in it, not one, not even the hero, seems to emerge as a fully rounded personality. Yet, for all its faults, *Before the Dawn* seems to deserve its fame. Indeed, it has two qualities so rarely to be found in modern Japanese fiction that their presence alone seems to give it a unique distinction. These two qualities are grandeur and a genuine sense of tragedy.

The scope of the novel is ambitious. The main intention of Tōson here is to trace the life of his father, whom he calls Hanzō, and to depict him as an idealist and a dedicated reformer whose hopes are inevitably destroyed by the ugly realities of the Meiji Restoration. But also, in the course of his depiction of Hanzō as a tragic figure betrayed by his own times, Tōson is careful to describe in great detail not only those major national events that took place in Japan during the years immediately before and after the Restoration, but the social conditions prevailing in the relatively remote Kiso Valley area at the time. *Before the Dawn*, then, is more than a novel written in piety by a son who had never really known his father; it is also an attempt to see the vast social and political upheaval which came to be known as the Meiji Restoration through his father's eyes. (pp. 137-38)

In the first part of *Before the Dawn*, . . . Tōson seems to do little more than set the scene for what is to follow. Considered as an introduction, it is perhaps too long and meandering, written at too leisurely a pace. Too much of the content, it seems, deals with history, and too little with Hanzō. Yet the patient reader who continues on to the second part will in time decide that without the detailed background provided in the first part, the final fate of Hanzō will not have seemed half so moving or meaningful. The reason for this perhaps is that the great historical events which Tōson describes so carefully in the first part lend weight to Hanzō and increase his personal significance. Tōson does not, or cannot, depend on intimate portrayal of Hanzō to convince us of his tragedy. Even in the second part, Hanzō remains a vague figure: his relationship with his family or friends, his understanding of his own desires and fears, the cause of his final madness—these are only broadly stated or merely hinted at, and never explained to our full satisfaction. Rather, what seems to give power to Tōson's portrayal of Hanzō is the utter seriousness of the author's attempt to understand the times in which his father lived. Hanzō for Tōson has become almost a symbol:

he is a dedicated idealist who is destroyed by a series of disillusionments. Tōson's memory of his father, one suspects, was little more complicated than this. And it may be for this reason that his characterization of Hanzō seems to us to be lacking in depth. However, a novel may be distinguished even if its protagonist is thinly drawn and its construction noticeably imperfect. It may possess, as *Before the Dawn* does, qualities which may fully compensate for such shortcomings. There is, we feel, great dignity in Tōson's devotion to the task he has set himself; and in the scale of the historical setting in which he has placed Hanzō, a certain magnificence. Thus we are persuaded of the significance of Hanzō's predicament by the dignity with which he has been conceived and by the magnitude of the events that affect him. (pp. 149-50)

Tōson's handling of [Hanzō's dismissal from the office of village headman] is markedly restrained. Hanzō is shown displaying so little emotion over his own misfortune that one is apt to feel either that he is not too deeply affected by his dismissal from office or that Tōson is not quite capable of making full dramatic use of the incident. But actually, the author is purposely understating here. Indeed, the whole of *Before the Dawn* is understated. This is perhaps why so many readers find it dull. So much of what Tōson might have said is left unsaid, so much is barely implied, that Tōson does sometimes, it is true, seem to be demanding more of the reader than he has a right to. But there is no mistaking the suggestion of emotional power, which, because of its very containment, seems all the more moving. Moreover, Tōson is trying to convey to the reader Hanzō's own enormous restraint. Hanzō is a deeply emotional man who cannot show, even to those who are close to him, what he really feels. This inability, or refusal, to give release to his innermost feelings increases his loneliness and becomes, as his suffering grows, an intolerable strain. Later, he does suddenly allow all the bitterness that he has been secretly harboring for so long to come to the surface; but by then he has become an eccentric who is soon to become a drunk and, in the end, a madman. (pp. 154-55)

Edwin McClellan, "Tōson," in his Two Japanese Novelists: Soseki and Tōson *(reprinted by permission of The University of Chicago Press; © 1969 by The University of Chicago), University of Chicago Press, 1969, pp. 73-163.**

JAMES R. MORITA (essay date 1970)

In compiling his first collection of poems, *Wakanashū (Seedlings)*, [Shimazaki Tōson] . . . placed in the beginning of the book six poems, all with women's names as titles. Prominent in the collection, the six poems dealt superbly with the different characters and situations of women who pursued love under adverse conditions. Evidently Tōson aimed at creating in this collection a special narrative effect—the poems are almost stories, or vignettes—which might be termed, for the purpose of examination, 'prose elements' in his verse. (p. 325)

[In the first poem of this group of six] the basic tone of Tōson's [poetry is established]—immature in places with traditional style and diction, but remarkably fresh and characterized by an overt romanticism. The inversion of words and the contracted expressions that color the monotony of the seven-five syllable pattern are exquisite, making the poem facile for both ear and voice. (p. 326)

The other five poems in the beginning of *Wakanashū* are equally fictionalized and dramatized. They are, however, variations on Tōson's sentiment, his joys in youthful loves. At a time when love generally was considered immoral, he embodied himself in the heroines of his poems and emancipated their hidden aspirations. The maidens are reflections of Tōson. (p. 327)

Retaining the traditional seven-five syllable combination, ['Osayo'] is in essence elementary: its vocabulary is limited and some words are repeated frequently. There is scarcely a single line or stanza that surprises the reader and entices him to memorize it. Characteristically, Tōson's poems are such that they are best appreciated if judged as a group: few lines or even stanzas in themselves contain deep thought, a theme in one poem is echoed in others; the same hero appears and reappears; and the mood of one poem is often carried on to another. 'Osayo', nevertheless, reads well in Japanese. It displays much of the mood of youthful melancholy which is common to many other works of Tōson.

Yet 'Okume' is the most passionate. This poem contains bold stanzas that amazed many Japanese. . . . This is the young Tōson's praise for a girl who deserted her parents to satisfy her passions. (pp. 329-30)

Otsuta, the heroine of the fifth poem, may also be considered as reflecting the young Tōson, who was baptized at the age of sixteen and had left the church several years afterwards. She is an orphan. Raised by a monk, she reaches her womanhood and then tempts the monk by offering him saké, songs, and, finally, herself. The poem includes dialogues which are dramatically established in a seemingly innocent mood. . . . This is a theme that reminds the reader of Tōson's *Ie (House)*, in which the protagonist desires his own niece while his wife is away. This also is a temptation to break a commandment, or to 'hakai', which Tōson later explored in his first long novel, *Hakai*. (pp. 331-32)

[Many] of the long poems are virtually stories written in divided lines for the sake of rhythm. For example, 'Niwatori' (**A Hen**) depicts a diabolic story in which a hen, after witnessing the grisly event of the killing of her husband, is curiously attracted by the strong cock who did the killing. (p. 336)

There are other poems consisting of dialogues between younger sisters and elder sisters. These poems are really too crude, in the strict sense of the term, to be called poetic dramas. . . . This sort of device, however, shows Tōson's interest in and perhaps his ability for more dramatic fiction, as well as his deficiencies in poetic techniques and imagination. (pp. 337-40)

Hitohabune (Small Leaf-Boat), includes nine prose works preceded by only five poems. (p. 340)

The prose works in *Hitohabune* . . . vary in style, subject matter, and the treatment of the subjects. Some of them are close to blank verse, containing such a refrain as 'Ah, I too am a child of Spring. You, young friend! My beautiful girl! If not you, whom should I tell of the coming of Spring in my heart?' They also contain much of the self-indulgent lamentations often found in his verse. It is as if the poet is trying to control his overwhelming sentiment by fitting it into the freer prose form. And yet, from the first of the nine works, a travelogue . . . , to the last work, which is virtually a novella in colloquial style, what is conspicuous is the author's

steadily growing interest in the form of the novel in the modern language. (p. 344)

[In *Natsuksa (Summer Grass)*] there is no longer the praise of springtime which Tōson so boldly sang in *Wakanashū*. Instead, he offers modest self-criticism of his earlier poems. . . . (p. 345)

Tōson's transformation to a novelist becomes more pronounced when he writes for *Natsukusa* a poem called '**Nōfu**' (**Farmer**). This poem consists of eight hundred and eighty-three lines, including eight different scenes, such as '**On the Bank of the Tone**', '**On a Path in the Field**', '**At the Blacksmith's House**', '**In the Woods**', '**Under an Evergreen**', and '**Midnight**'. In this group Tōson explores each of the ten characters and penetrates their psychology. (p. 350)

Rakubaishū (The Collection of Fallen Plums) . . . , the last of the four collections, was compiled in Komoro, a small castle town about one hundred miles northwest of Tokyo. There, while teaching English and Japanese, Tōson wrote '**Chikumagawa no suketchi**' (**Sketches of the Chikuma**), his 'exercise in depicting things in modern prose'. (p. 357)

Inclining further toward prose, Tōson at the same time deepens his poetic spirit and style. There are few poems which are as elementary as those in the earlier collections. '**Komoro naru kojo no hotori**' (**By the Old Castle of Komoro**), the first poem in the book, is probably one of the best of Tōson's poems. (p. 358)

Tōson's soul wandered, and wandering was a major theme of his poetry. Starting from the formless ardor of springtime, Tōson journeyed in search of a resting place for his soul, something more concrete and secure, the land to which he could return. He knew his search would continue. (p. 359)

Rakubaishū includes four prose works. One of them, '**Kumo**' (**Clouds**), clearly reveals Tōson's interest in realistic description. It contains two detailed tables showing the results of the writer's observation of the varying colors and shapes of clouds at different times of the day. It avoids any sentiment, merely describing what he saw in the sky of Komoro. Tōson writes that he did so 'as my attempt to break from the monotony of my thoughts', and continues to say that he tried this 'because of my love for nature that flows out like the spring current and because of my wish to solve the feverish and impossible problems of this life which is joyous and at the same time sad'. Tōson's commitment to transformation is here obvious. (p. 365)

From *Wakanashū* to *Rakubaishū* Tōson's career as a poet lasted only four years. During the short period, however, Tōson cultivated his plastic realism, a basis for the long novels that he published in the later years. His contribution to the development of modern Japanese poetry was also substantial. Through his springtime and his departure from it, along with his longing for love and his bitterness from love, Tōson brought his 'romantic spirit' to maturity, creating a solid foundation of both content and style on which other poets based their works. Those four years were the formative period of modern Japanese poetry.

Tōson was not merely a romantic poet who sang only in the spring, much less the ordinary naturalistic novelist he is sometimes remembered as. Behind his autobiographical novels lay the above poems, which contained elements that developed into his novels. It was the rare blend of these poetic qualities that distinguished his prose works from those of other novelists who lacked it. Writing these novels in his later years, Tōson must have often looked back to this period of poetry and found there the source for his enormous energy and inspiration. (p. 369)

James R. Morita, "Shimazaki Tōson's Four Collections of Poems," in Monumenta Nipponica *(copyright in Japan, 1970, by Monumenta Nipponica), Vol. XXV, Nos. 3 & 4, 1970, pp. 325-69.*

KENNETH STRONG (essay date 1972)

[In] the earlier stages of Japan's modern century, when the gap between Japanese and Western experience was obviously far wider than is the case today, some novels appeared that are . . . readily accessible to a reader used to Western fiction. Of these, Shimazaki Toson's *Broken Commandment* is probably the most memorable. In Japan its reputation is enduring. (pp. vii-viii)

The humanist intention of *The Broken Commandment* is apparent from even a brief summary of its plot. . . . But whether the implicit attack on a particularly Japanese form of social and class prejudice is to be taken as the sole, or even the main, intention of *The Broken Commandment* is open to doubt.

The novel is somewhat more complex than is evident at first sight. When it first appeared, most Japanese were puzzled by the "outcast" motif: though discrimination against the eta might have survived in some provincial areas, they persuaded themselves that essentially it was a feature of the feudal past, unknown in the new, modernized Japan. In this belief they were mistaken. Discrimination against the eta is not uncommon even today; in Shimazaki's time it was harsher and more widespread. (pp. viii-ix)

At the beginning of the twentieth century the modern Japanese novel, with one or two exceptions, had hardly begun to grow beyond the naïve political allegories and sentimental stories of the 1880s and 1890s. *The Broken Commandment* was not the first novel to display some social concern, nor was it the first to deal with the outcasts, but in its realism, its seriousness, and its humanism, however muted, it was wholly new. Yet the early Japanese critics, in playing down the eta theme of the story, were not influenced only by their ignorance of and lack of interest in the depressed minority. According to their interpretation of the novel (which is still generally accepted), its eta hero is primarily an embodiment of Shimazaki's own longing for inner, spiritual emancipation, an image that suggested itself to him from the life history of one particular eta that he heard from a friend: a symbol that by chance served his purpose, perhaps even better than he realized, but that could equally well have been replaced by some other figure burdened with Werther-like aspirations. (p. xiv)

Shimazaki's sympathy with outcasts who had to suffer . . . humiliation, or even brutal attack, was genuine. Yet just as certainly this sympathy was not his chief concern in writing the novel. . . . The reality of eta humiliation is dramatized only occasionally, and then only in a shadowy way . . . ; nor does the eta hero show any sign of wishing to carry on the fight for liberation that his mentor has so heroically launched.

The Broken Commandment might have been a more satisfying novel, in traditional Western terms, if it were not deficient in these respects. But to judge it too harshly for this reason would be to miss the author's intention, and to underestimate the degree to which the novel, not least by its apparent defects, mirrors the society of its time. The latter point is particularly worth making in regard to the "happy ending," the wholly unexpected manifestation of a *deus ex machina* in the shape of an invitation to Ushimatsu to emigrate to Texas. At first sight this seems preposterous. But as Donald Keene remarks, this "ending vitiates the story for us . . ." [see excerpt above]. (p. xxi)

"The tragedy of one who has awakened," Shimazaki called *The Broken Commandment:* the tragedy of an early twentieth-century Japanese outsider, who by deliberate decision reached only after a long struggle achieves spiritual freedom, but at the cost of cutting himself off irrevocably from society. It is the inner freedom that interests Shimazaki more than any notion of the freedom of the individual within the social framework, or of the absolute dignity of the individual. In this respect, he and his eta hero are the forerunners of a long line of novelists and fictional characters in modern Japanese literature whose lives have revolved around their perception of themselves and their own immediate circle, rather than their relation, if any, with the changing society and culture of which they have been, as it were, nonparticipatory members.

Behind the "awakening" Ushimatsu lie several Western literary models, notably the Rousseau of *Confessions* and Dostoevsky's Raskolnikov. It is possible, as one Japanese critic early noticed, to equate at least five of the characters in *The Broken Commandment* with their "originals" in *Crime and Punishment*—Ushimatsu with Raskolnikov, Keinoshin with Marmeladov, Ginnosuke with Rasmihin, Bunpei with Rugin, O-Shio with Sonia. But Shimazaki was no slavish imitator. In a letter to a friend in November 1903, written just after reading *Crime and Punishment* and a month or two before starting work on *The Broken Commandment*, he concludes that Dostoevsky's achievement lay in the creation of a "modern tragedy of passionate thought." Japanese literature was rich in emotion, short on intellect: Dostoevsky had fused the two into a perfect, organic whole, and it was this fusion that Shimazaki wanted to aim for in *The Broken Commandment*. Potentially, at least, and by Shimazaki's standards, Ushimatsu is a modern, self-conscious, and clear-thinking man. He knows how rational beings should behave, and slowly comes to realize that it is within his own power to free himself from the attitudes of subservience to which his birth condemned him.

Every word of Shimazaki's summing up of what he admired in Dostoevsky is relevant to *The Broken Commandment*. The Japanese bias toward emotion, with Shimazaki's own brand of lyricism, softens the harsh outlines of the story—too much so, no doubt, for some Western readers: Ushimatsu has at least his share of the tendency to gloomy or even mawkish introspection that balances the often lighthearted, hedonistic outlook of his countrymen. But that the tale should be a tragedy, in a peculiarly Japanese sense, is inevitable, given the role played by a character who has no counterpart in *Crime and Punishment* and whose influence is pervasive, though he never appears except as a corpse—Ushimatsu's father.

Through Ushimatsu's struggle of conscience to throw off the burden laid on him from boyhood, with wholly admirable intention, by the father whom he admires profoundly yet whose dearest wish he must in the end betray, Shimazaki effectively dramatizes the will of his generation to resist enslavement to the past. If there were any doubt about the strength of this determination, it is dispelled symbolically by the manner of Ushimatsu's father's death, murdered as he is by the prize bull of the herd he loves. Yet the sequel to the killing, the long description of the slaughter—ironically, by eta butchers—of the bull, the instrument of the father's end, is surely one of the most curious things in the novel.

The plot requires no such detailed account. Is Shimazaki implying—perhaps unconsciously—that while Ushimatsu may have succeeded in freeing himself from the authority of his father, the victory and the freedom may turn out to be sterile unless "freedom" is seen to have social implications beyond the narrowly personal, and the battle fought again on a much broader front? The point is not just academic. The authority of the "family" concept was all-powerful in Shimazaki's time, and survives in different forms today, in government as well as business life, offering valuable psychological support to the individual but operating not infrequently as a burdensome, coercive influence, as many writers—and more recently, film makers—have testified. Shimazaki himself was to take up the theme directly in his second novel, *Ie* [The House].

The interest of *The Broken Commandment*, therefore, lies partly in its attempt to articulate the difficult process of self-awakening in a young Japanese at a time when despite Japan's rapid transformation into a modern state, traditional and authoritarian attitudes remained predominant. The feeling of emancipation in the novel is far from complete. At the climax of the story, Ushimatsu's public confession of his outcast birth, Shimazaki makes him grovel before his pupils and colleagues—which may ring true, as a reflex action inculcated by centuries of oppression, but scarcely convinces the reader of the reality of Ushimatsu's hard-won independence of spirit. Nor does Ushimatsu ever confide in his friend Ginnosuke, though the latter would clearly not have rejected him had he done so.

But for all its inadequacies, *The Broken Commandment* remains a landmark in the development of the modern spirit in Japan. Ushimatsu's longings for a freer future reflected the aspirations of innumerable readers. . . . In style as in subject matter—its opening sentence, "Rengeji temple took in boarders," astonished contemporary readers, used to flowery diction, by its simple directness—and in its combination of the new realism with a poetic feeling for the austere splendour of the Shinshu landscape and compassion for the harsh lives of peasant and outcast, it opened new directions.

Later writers have explored particular aspects of the Japanese experience with greater subtlety and sophistication; few have attempted to probe as seriously into the problems that lie at the heart of *The Broken Commandment*. It deserves a place alongside the representative Japanese novels that are already well known in the West, such as Kawabata's *Snow Country*, Natsume Soseki's *Kokoro*, Tanizaki's *The Makioka Sisters*, Mishima's *The Golden Pavilion*, and Abe Kobo's *Woman of the Dunes*. Nor is it only a literary landmark. *The Broken Commandment* is as revealing as any Japanese novel of the psychology of a people who have changed much in the hectic century since they entered the modern world but remain even today largely conditioned by their unique history and culture. (pp. xxii-xxv)

Kenneth Strong, "Translator's Introduction" (1972), in The Broken Commandment *by Shimazaki Toson, translated by Kenneth Strong (translation © 1974 by the United Nations Educational, Scientific and Cultural Organization; reproduced by permission of UNESCO and University of Tokyo Press), The Japan Foundation, 1974, pp. vii-xxv.*

WILLIAM E. NAFF (essay date 1979)

The Broken Commandment has often been called the most important novel of the Meiji period from the point of view of literary and social history. Its pre-eminence as a work of art is somewhat less certain, although it has its supporters in this claim as well. (p. 785)

As Professor Strong points out in his very useful introduction, *The Broken Commandment* has often been treated as disguised autobiography by Japanese critics [see excerpt above]. This interpretation suggests that even though this is the first work by a major Japanese writer that attempts to deal with a social problem, the protagonist's pariah background is first of all an allegorical representation of the author's inner life as he struggles with certain dark secrets of his own. There is much in the novel that lends credibility to this thesis, and the pervasiveness of the autobiographical predilection in traditional Japanese criticism does not seem to be sufficient in itself to discredit such a reading. Yet there is also genuine social criticism; problems are finely observed and well presented. That the inner life of one who must live with a difficult secret is presented with such conviction and sensitivity reminds us that the author himself had a great deal of firsthand experience with such problems. If modern readers find the novel as a whole somewhat less than the sum of its many strengths, this is perhaps because the inner life of the protagonist paralleled the inner life of the author so closely that there were unresolved problems of distancing.

An exploration of the various levels of theme and organization in *The Broken Commandment* brings us first of all to a general structure and argument that owes much to *Crime and Punishment*. There is an examination of the institution of pariahism, an institution which seems to fill such a deep human need that Japan, a racially homogeneous society, has found it necessary to invent a spurious "race" to play a role normally played by minority peoples in other countries. There are unmistakable Biblical allusions in the protagonist's repeated denial of Inoko. Although the protagonist admires Inoko with a nearly religious intensity for his bravery in making no secret of his outcaste background, he cannot approach him with openness and honesty without endangering his own secret. There is the autobiographical element and, finally, there is a portrayal of provincial life in turn-of-the-century Japan. (pp. 785-86)

William E. Naff, "Book Reviews: 'The Broken Commandment'," in Journal of Asian Studies *(copyright 1979 by the Association for Asian Studies), Vol. XXXVIII, No. 4, August, 1979, pp. 785-86.*

ADDITIONAL BIBLIOGRAPHY

"Wakanashū (Collection of Young Herbs)." In *Introduction to Classic Japanese Literature,* edited by The Kokusai Bunka Shinokai, pp. 425-30. Tokyo: Kokusai Bunka Shinkokai (The Society for International Cultural Relations), 1948.

Briefly discusses Tōson's career and provides a prose version of an early poem.

McClellan, Edwin. "The Novels of Shimazaki Tōson." *The Harvard Journal of Asiatic Studies* 24 (1962-63): 82-174.
    Examines Tōson's writing and compares it to other modern Japanese novelists.

McClellan, Edwin. "The Impressionistic Tendency in Some Modern Japanese Writers." *Chicago Review* 17, No. 4 (1965): 48-60.*
    Discusses the changes that Tōson and Soseki made on the Meiji novel and focuses on their impressionism, a quality found in many modern Japanese writers exposed to Western influences.

Ninomiya, Takamichi and Enright, D. J. Introduction to *The Poetry of Living Japan,* edited by Takamichi Ninomiya and D. J. Enright, pp. 1-12. New York: Grove Press, 1957.*
    General survey providing background information on the poets of the Meiji era.

Shioda, Ryôhei. Afterword to "'Yoaké Maé' ('Before the Dawn') 1929-1935." In *Introduction to Contemporary Japanese Literature,* edited by The Kokusai Bunka Shinkokai, pp. 309-11. Tokyo: Kokusai Bunka Shinkokai (The Society for International Cultural Relations), 1939.
    A short examination of *Yoaké Maé* and appraisal of Tōson's talent.

Alfonsina Storni

1892-1938

Argentinian poet, dramatist, short story writer, and essayist.

Although little of her work is available in English, Storni was a literary figure of considerable importance in her native Argentina. She is remembered primarily for her poetry, yet she wrote numerous plays, short stories, and essays. An examination of Storni's entire corpus reveals a progression from passionate self-absorption to increasing detachment, and finally despair.

Storni's early years greatly influenced her writing. At age twelve, her father's fortune depleted, Storni worked to help support the family. Instilled with an early sense of independence and determined to become an actress, she toured for a year with a theatrical troupe when she was fifteen. Although she was soon convinced that acting was not her forte, this theatre experience undoubtedly inspired her dramas. The birth of her illegitimate son Alejandro, and the responsibility of supporting and raising him, also had a great effect on her art. The period following Alejandro's birth, when Storni lived alone in Buenos Aires, working at various jobs while trying to protect her son from the stigma of illegitimacy, was essential to the development of her unconventional ideas about love, marriage, illegitimacy, and motherhood. These ideas, evident throughout her work, but most explicit in her controversial play *El amo del mundo*, distinguish her from other women writers of her day, most of whom were privileged members of the educated bourgeoisie.

Although Storni never consciously allied herself with any literary school, her early collections of poetry contain elements of romanticism and reflect traces of the Hispanic modernist movement of Rubén Darío. Primarily autobiographical, her early poetry revolves around lyrical and sentimental themes, portraying the misunderstood, rebellious poet standing alone against the world. Her first collection, *La inquietud del rosal*, reflects the restlessness and emotional conflict which persisted throughout her life. Storni later renounced this volume, and critics generally feel that it is her least significant work.

Storni's next collections, *El dulce daño*, *Irremediablemente*, and *Languidez*, express her disillusionment with love and her desire to renounce physical passion. Much of the outrage and suffering evident in these verses resulted from her frustration with contemporary stereotypes of women, and in these collections she pleads for a more balanced and intellectual relationship between men and women. Her fifth collection, *Ocre*, demonstrates Storni's increasing maturity of concept and conciseness of style. She now steps outside of herself, observing her life more analytically and less emotionally. In contrast to the bitter resentment of her early confessional verse, these more cerebral, cynical, and ironic poems demonstrate Storni's increasingly caustic attitude towards men.

Storni's last two collections mark the final stage in her poetic development. The poems of *Mundo de siete pozos* describe moods and dreams in abstract language. Abandoning the literary conventions of her previous collections, Storni uses free verse to communicate her predominant themes through images

of the city, sea, and death. She had always favored the sea as a symbol, but Storni's obsession with sea and death imagery in *Mundo de siete pozos* intimates her forthcoming suicide. For *Mascarilla y trébol*, published posthumously, Storni created a new verse form which she called the "anti-sonnet." While contemporary critics who were fond of her early lyricism called this volume harsh and obscure, many critics now believe it contains her most original and interesting poetry.

PRINCIPAL WORKS

La inquietud del rosal (poetry) 1916
El dulce daño (poetry) 1918
Una golondrina (novella) 1919; published in journal
    Hebe
Irremediablemente (poetry) 1919
Languidez (poetry) 1920
Ocre (poetry) 1925
Poemas de amor (poetry) 1926
El amo del mundo (drama) 1927
"Catalina" (short story) 1933; published in journal *La nación*
Mundo de siete pozos (poetry) 1934

Cimbelina en 1900 y pico   (drama)   1938
Mascarilla y trébol   (poetry)   1938
Cinco cartas y Una golondrina   (letters and novella)
     1959
Obra poetica completa   (poetry)   1961
*Alfonsina Storni: Argentina's Feminist Poet; The Poetry in
     Spanish with English Translations*   (poetry)   1975

SIDONIA CARMEN ROSENBAUM (essay date 1945)

[Alfonsina Storni's] lyre, far from being monochord—as are those of so many other poetesses of lesser, or even equal, worth—has multiple and varied tones and themes. For not only does she sing of love without "the instinctive false blushes" which have curbed so many women through the ages; not only are her verses the cry of a sensitive, intelligent woman tortured by a gnawing, unsatisfied mental anguish, beset by an elusive, yet persistent ideal, parched by a spiritual thirst which this "impoverished century" cannot allay, but she reveals an aspect until then but little known in feminine poetry: a forceful and poignant interpretation of modern city life, with its piercing loneliness, its chilling indifference, its soulless uniformity and maddening monotony, its spiritual vacuity, its unending vulgarity . . . which rots and perplexes the soul. (p. 206)

Written under the fast-declining light of "the last gleams of Rubén Darío", and sounding still the familiar and distant echoes of a Romanticism long eschewed by more expert, pliant and alert hands and minds, her first book, *La inquietud del rosal* . . . , however many its deficiencies of form, style, and even content— opened heretofore difficult, or forbidding literary doors to women in the Argentine, and revealed a spirit unafraid, undaunted by the many prejudices which the free expression of feminine sufferings, yearnings, feelings still evoked. For when her book was published in Buenos Aires, people looked upon a woman who dared publicly to reveal intimate thoughts, intimate longings, as somewhat of a *déclassée*. (p. 210)

[Alfonsina's] book had resonance, mainly because of what was then termed its audacity, and the author's self depiction in verses that sounded a new note—the *feminine* note. . . . It served, at best, merely to reflect, as does its title, that restlessness—emotional and intellectual—so characteristic of her throughout her life. But as a work it is an isolated, sterile phase and does not bear any appreciable relation to her future and more personal production.

Other books followed with astonishing rapidity and fecundity. [*El dulce daño, Irremediablemente, Languide*] . . .—books which profiled and defined in each successive phase her many-faceted poetic personality, her indubitable talent, her keen mind. They were also the only means by which one could peer, at times, into her somewhat veiled life. . . . Written when *el dulce daño*—that "sweet torture" that was love— sounded the dominant note in her spirit; when she found sorrow and life irrevocably, *irremediably*, linked in her being; when she resigned herself, at times with indifference, at times with spiritual and moral *languidness*, to the relentless Nemesis which hounded her, these books comprise a definite and distinct phase in her poetic evolution.

El dulce daño, engendered in a far from happy mood . . . , seems to cull happiness only from the past. Its last part, called "Hielo," reflects a mood that in time becomes characteristic: an ironic, pseudosupercilious mood, in which she adopts an antagonistic, defiant and superior tone which people driven from the social pale so often assume. Life, with its tumult and its weariness, makes her sometimes long for the eternal silence, for the quieting sleep of death. And she feels weighed down by thought, oppressed by consciousness, overwrought by emotion. (pp. 210-11)

She knows the frailties of woman, her whims, her caprices; yet she feels very strongly against two distinct moral codes— one for man, and one for woman. . . . Death stalks through some of these lines, but not yet with the intensity that it assumes in later books. (p. 211)

Irremediablemente recaptures "humble, amorous, passionate" moments of her life—as the sub-sections indicate—as well as "bitter, sylvan and tempestuous" ones. (pp. 211-12)

The two initial poems, "Este libro" and "Alma desnuda"— which serve as preamble—bespeak the sincerity of the verses that follow. . . . The second poem graphically depicts her soul: a brave and dauntless one, a willing soul—sensitive, humble, restless, idealistic. . . .

With a plea to man to understand her suffering, her *madness*, she recounts the multiple phases of her love. . . . But man remains adamant and so, in a biting poem called "Hombre pequeñito", she asks him to free her—the bird—caught in his guileful and deceiving cage. . . .

Her "fight for freedom" rather than individual is collective. She feels that in liberating herself she is freeing all women from the "ancestral weight" of prejudice; for she has dared to unseal her lips and declare her desire openly—although, like Prometheus, she too had been "bound.". . . (p. 212)

Languidez sets its tone in its dedicatory note: "To those who, like myself, have never fulfilled a single one of their dreams." The discontent and dissatisfaction apparent in so many of her previous poems are even more evident and poignant now when she feels impotent to break from "the prison of the senses" that enslaves her; when she sees herself "consumed" in life within the four symmetrical walls of her house, and her love wasting away in useless and fruitless waiting; when she realizes that she has not yet said "the best" that is within her, and wonders if ever—in prose or verse—she will be able to "extract" it. . . .

[*Ocre*] which reveals greater maturity of mind, of concept, and more conscious form and style, heads the literary phase which, according to her own admission, she prefers.

In this book she is more bitter, yet more resigned to the poverty of her spiritual and amorous life. Her taunts at man are more caustic; her attitude more ironic. Her spirit, with the vintage of experience, has assumed the *ocher* or faded tone of aridity rather than the honeyed and mellow one of fruitfulness. Her laughter is more raucous and rings less true.

She takes whatever love—whatever life—is meted out to her, with spiritual and moral listlessness, for she is weary of hoping and of waiting. . . . She knows man to be faithless, vain, selfish, yet she continues to be cognizant of the power he has over her—for she cannot free herself from the need of that "rey devorante." But, rather than with resignation, she meets failure with cynicism, with irony, or with feigned in-difference. (p. 213)

[*Mundo de siete pozos* consists of] poems in "the new manner" which achieve a form polished and succinct and ingenious imagery, and which mark the beginning of a strange, new and bitter phase.

There seems now to be a depuration of certain familiar themes, and an exclusion of others. Those that persist with more trenchant contours are the city, and death—constantly associated in this prophetic book of hers with the sea. The style follows more closely the patterns of the times. She abandons rhyme and seeks expression in free verse and in a form scintillating with images—not always equally inspired. (p. 214)

[Some poems, like "**Uno,**"] again evince that admiration and cult—that strong desire—for the masculine physique and strength that recurs throughout her poems. . . . And although she can already discern the "black flocks" of death in the horizon, she still expresses the hope of finding the ideal lover. . . .

Never a poetess of joy and laughter, Alfonsina sinks still deeper into the bitter waters of sadness and hopeless-ness. The world is sour—she has learned—immature and stunted. . . . (p. 215)

If in other books she spoke of the sea, it seemed to be in a somewhat casual manner. Not so here where the sea and the thought of finding peace in its icy, turbulent depths, become almost an obsession. . . . And that world of seven wells—of seven doors—which is her head, registers all the emotions of city-life. Seldom has the city inspired more tortured, im-passioned, tragic poems. . . . (pp. 216-17)

The book closes with a group of sonnets and ends, appro-priately, with the dolorous "**Landscape of a dead love**" which leaves no doubt that even then her tongue was savoring the black taste of death. . . .

Her books, like her life, became progressively more bitter; and *Mascarilla y trébol (Círculos inmantados),* her last book, published but shortly before her death . . . , marks the high point in this route of grief which she was fated to traverse. This book is saturated with the brine of the sea which now, rather than an objective reality, becomes almost an integral, an intimate part of her; and with the turbid waters of that other sea—the disconsolate sea of woe, of discontent and tears—that lies, always agitated, within her. (p. 217)

But more poignant than the poems that speak of feeling mis-understood by the people in general are those which, like "**Hombre pequeñito**", bemoan a lack of understanding on the part of that "little man"—"little" in spirit, in moral worth—that fills her verses. It is, therefore, an unsatisfied love of which she sings: all suffering and yearning; never the joy of fulfillment one finds in Juana de Ibarbourou, for instance. For Alfonsina, like Delmira Agustini, like countless others, wanted a love such as no one could ever dream of; a love that would be all of life, all poetry. . . . (p. 221)

[She] had been "born for love" and, in her untiring search, she must have more than once surrendered to its tempes-tuousness. And although she loved—she says—until she wept, and unto death; although she loved until it turned to hate, and unto madness . . . she found "all love was meager." For she who gave her heart as does a flowing fount its water—

without reserve; she who had offered it pure—ere other hands had plucked its tempting fruit—found herself frozen in the icy breath of man's egotism. . . .

In *Mascarilla y trébol*, her last book, she takes vengeance on the mocking Eros; she seizes him by the neck, and tearing him apart she finds the deceiving trap which had so long ensnared her—Sex. . . . (p. 222)

And because in all—save in death—she met frustration, one senses a constant dissatisfaction in her; a feeling of "incom-pleteness" in life, in love, and in all things. . . . (p. 223)

Man is the ever-recurring theme of her poems, for he con-stitutes the constant "problem" in her femininity. And when she finds that neither "fervent breath" nor "yielding kiss" can penetrate the iron cast of his egotism, she masks her pain in irony and scorn. Still, in her verses, he is most often the object of her desire; and it is only when this desire of hers is thwarted because of his indifference, or when her pride is hurt because of his egotism, that she descends upon him with all the strength of her irony. Her scorn of man, therefore, is not that of a woman who is above temptation, and will not succumb to the pleasures which he seeks, but that of one who has yielded, yet does not feel spiritually satisfied.

She alludes, repeatedly, to their different approach to love. Man looks for "a bit of a feast in woman" and is not repelled by coldness or indifference. Woman, on the other hand—if Alfonsina is typical—has need of the warmth which only soul-inspired love can give. And although she herself is not wholly exempt from carnal desires . . . her idea of love was far from festive.

Like many intellectual women, she feels superior to the av-erage run of men who surround her and is humiliated when man seeks in her merely what he can find in any other woman. She realizes, bitterly, that "the women of intellect are the losers in matters of love." All this, however, does not make her shun "el dulce daño". Her idealism yields to the lure of the "somber man"—he of the strong hands with the hardness of steel! . . . (pp. 223-24)

Alfonsina Storni is the only one of these major poetesses who has in any way carried the feminist banner. She is the only one who has essayed the *woman-theme* in poems which sing of the bitterness that has been woman's lot since time immemorial. . . .

Yet she who ofttimes speaks of love with cynicism and with irony as when, in a mood that recalls one of Edna St. Vincent Millay's, she says: "little man, I loved you half an hour, do not ask for more"; she who is forever intent on proclaiming the final "liberation" of woman, is also the one who says to the lover: "I shall lay myself at your feet, humble and meek"; "sweetly, I shall fall at your feet, 'neath the full moon"; "take my life; make it, if you will, your slave," in a tone which is not *feminist* surely, but *feminine* to the ex-treme. For many of her poems disclose a meekness and submission in the face of the "sweet torture" of love for which she ever clamors; and what she admires most in man is his virility, his physical strength. She speaks of iron mus-cles, of hands of steel, of a voice that makes a woman cringe, and dominates—a man's voice: warm and feared. And before this tower of strength she likes to feel small and humble. (p. 224)

She never gives herself wholly to her passions, as do most women, for she is forever conscious of the mind—*the first nucleus,* as she calls it in ***Mundo de siete pozos***—whose weight she cannot elude, and which she feels nailed fast within her by a cruel destiny. For she is aware that were it not for this propensity of hers to think, to philosophize, to rationalize, she might have found more happiness in life, more freedom. And so more than once she bemoans this cerebral chain that has the power to bind her to the stolid, cold and restricting fetters of thought, and to keep her from roaming freely in the uninhibited plains of instinct.

Perhaps because of this, many of her poems seem somewhat prosaic and *intellectual;* to reflect preconceived mental attitudes, rather than spiritual or emotional needs. Such are the ones that pretend to depict her merely as a modern, cynical, urbane, "free" woman—bereft of plebeian emotions or femininity. But there are others that are born of a true duality of spirit, with her two selves—intellectual and emotional—constantly struggling to gain the upper hand. (p. 225)

One can say, therefore, that Alfonsina never achieved true happiness—nor spiritual repose—not only because Fortune was adverse, but because of the insurmountable contradictions within her; for there was a bitter war, as in so many other "idealists," between her aspirations and reality, between her art and her life, between her emotions and her intellect.

Her poetry frequently transcends the personal bounds and becomes, at times, almost social in character. In this she differs from most women poets whose work tends to be monotonously centripetal; for whereas others look only within to find the meaning of love, of life, of death . . . she attempts to probe problems which affect others besides herself. Her poems, too, may be called "cerebral"—as she once suggested—in that she captures in them not only emotional but mental states as well. Thus, we may well consider her the most intellectual, the most objective and the most social-minded of these modernist Spanish American poetesses. (pp. 225-26)

> *Sidonia Carmen Rosenbaum, "Alfonsina Storni," in her* Modern Women Poets of Spanish America: The Precursors, Delmira Agustini, Gabriel Mistral, Alfonsina Storni, Juana de Ibarbourou *(copyright 1945 by Sidonia C. Rosenbaum), Hispanic Institute in the United States, 1945, pp. 205-28.*

EDNA LUE FURNESS (essay date 1957)

In the feminine literature of twentieth-century Spanish America, some authors follow true feminine tradition by writing of subjects which have always had high priority with women, such as love, motherhood, and religion. Others have stepped out of their traditional role, and have written of social, political, and urban problems. To the latter group belongs Alfonsina Storni, who reportedly initiated in Argentina a new school of literature. . . . (p. 96)

Storni's strength lies in the preponderance of the rational and mental attitudes, rather than the sensory and instinctive qualities, which constitute the true essence of femininity. Consequently, Alfonsina Storni has often been considered the least feminine of the major poets of Spanish America. . . .

[If] Storni dwells on the "woman" theme, she also writes, at much greater length, of woman in the mental world. She is constantly conscious of the mind—the first nucleus, as she calls it in her book, [*Mundo de siete pozos*] *World of Seven*

Wells—whose weight clings like a barnacle, and to which, according to Rosenbaum [see excerpt above], she feels nailed fast by a merciless destiny. Storni is aware that were it not for a penchant of hers to think, to rationalize, to philosophize, she might have found more joy in life, more freedom, and more happiness. And more than once Alfonsina Storni bemoans this cerebration that has the power to bind her to the cold, harsh, and restraining fetters of thought, and even to keep her from "roaming freely in the uninhabited plains of instinct."

Storni is also conscious of the modern social world, of its attendant spiritual ills, and of the apathetic masses whose feelings have been numbed by their worldliness or materialism. In a poem entitled **"Cuadros y angulos" (Squares and Angles)** . . . the Argentine poet protests against the "maddening monotony" and the unending uniformity of modern mechanized cities. This uniformity and this spiritual vacuity victimize men and women, who, like herself, inevitably become mechanized members of that human herd that moves along the avenues past houses, more houses, and still more houses. The mathematical precision and impersonality of the houses in straight rows and in square blocks are complemented by people's right-angled ideas, by their square shoulders all in a line, and even, as Alfonsina Storni tells us at the end of her poem, by a square tear she shed one day. (pp. 97-8)

One of her most poignant poems is **"Faro en la noche" (Nocturnal Beacon).** Here Storni seems to be saying that the sea and the sky, on the one hand, and the raven and the black rock, on the other, all represent some form of despair. For those not given to despair, the lighthouse beam comes and goes. But a heart like hers already doomed to hopelessness, nailed to a black rock, is not touched even by intermittent hope sent forth by the lighthouse. For her, the wellsprings of life and hope have dried up. For her, all that remains is the torment of deep and dark despair, a raven's picking at the poet's heart, which no longer bleeds, and which is nailed to the cold, hard rock of fate, to the fetters of thought. (p. 98)

> *Edna Lue Furness, "A Woman and the World," in* Western Humanities Review *(copyright, 1957, University of Utah), Vol. 11, No. 1, Winter, 1957, pp. 96-8.*

FLORENCE TALAMANTES (essay date 1973)

[Alfonsina Storni,] a great Argentine poet who was born when Virginia Woolf was ten years old, mirrors in her life and art many of the same problems and concerns that can be seen in Woolf's work. Like her English counterpart, she too committed suicide by walking into the sea. . . . Disillusioned by an unsympathetic, materialistic society and afflicted with a fatal cancer, Alfonsina Storni chose to unite herself with the symbol of the sea which reappears continually throughout her works just as Virginia Woolf, afflicted with mental illness and recognizing the signs of its oncoming, chose also to unite herself in the same way with the same symbol. . . .

If one compares some of the prose writings of Woolf with the poetic works of Storni, one can see that although they were largely unknown to each other and living oceans apart, the sensitivities and feelings of the two women who shared the same century in different cultures and languages were amazingly similar. In Virginia Woolf's masterpiece, *The*

Waves, the reader is constantly reminded of change and movement—especially that of the sea, a favorite theme in the works of Storni. (p. 4)

The works of Alfonsina Storni, like those of Virginia Woolf, represent, although in somewhat different ways, an embodiment of the feminine point of view. Her early poems reveal a vast need for love, a need which stands in sharp contrast to the role which society, incapable of understanding the problems confronting woman, has forced her to assume. The poet wants to accept love, but only on an equal basis. In the final analysis, she concludes that she must substitute passion with intellectual indifference—with a lack of concern or compassion for others. Reason must replace emotion. Her reason triumphs; but the struggle leaves her tortured, beaten, and humiliated. She has lost her sensitivity; and as a result, her final works [*El Mundo de siete pozos* and *Mascarilla y trébol*] . . . , failed to gain wide acceptance.

The first five books of Alfonsina Storni's poetry belong to the period of Post-Modernism. These include [*La Inquietud del rosal, El dulce daño, Irremediablemente, Languidez,* and *Ocre*]. . . . The first three consist primarily of love poetry; however, *Languidez,* which Storni dedicated, ''To those who as I, never realized even one of their dreams,'' was to initiate a new mode of composition consisting primarily of the abandonment of subjective poetry. Nevertheless, there appear in *Languidez* remembrances from childhood as well as portraits of the poet's mother and sisters. Virginia Woolf's *To the Lighthouse* is similarly autobiographical. The dominant theme, however, is love and the overtones of bitterness and irony which appeared in her early works are practically non-existent. *Ocre* takes its name from an autumn shade—although Storni maintained that the title could have been ''Green,'' ''Purple,'' or any other color. The title suggests those tones of a beginning autumn of serenity, of acceptance, and often of desolation. The anguish and suffering, although present, is somewhat crystallized and more veiled. Of all her works, the poet showed a preference for *Ocre,* which reveals her joy in creating and, consequently, in the knowledge that she will continue to exist through that creation. (pp. 8-9)

In her later works [*Mundo de siete pozos,* and *Mascarilla y trébol*] . . . , we find poetry of an intellectual type with new forms and metaphors. These works reveal constant repetition of a favorite theme—the sea, which symbolizes the origin of all life. In these compositions we observe the poet's pantheistic regard for nature and her envy of the indifference of nature.

That Alfonsina Storni suffered humiliation and disillusionment is evident throughout her works. Love is the cause of that disillusionment which, as seen in *El dulce daño* and *Ocre,* terminates in utter despair. In *El Mundo de siete pozos* she has freed herself from the struggle by forsaking her sensitivity. . . .

Her art, which comprises the period of Post-Modernism, Expressionism, Futurism, Cubism, and even Dadaism, reflects the anti-materialism and the search for a reality independent of logic or intelligence characteristic of that era between the two world wars. (p. 9)

> Florence Talamantes, ''*Virginia Woolf and Alfonsina Storni: Kindred Spirits,*'' in Virginia Woolf Quarterly *(copyright © 1973 by Aeolian Press), Vol. I, No. 3, Spring, 1973, pp. 4-21.*

RACHEL PHILLIPS (essay date 1975)

Storni's development as a poet is not only that of the writer seeking individuality of style and voice (as is universally the case). It is vitally linked to the growth of the woman who gradually transcends her sex and circumstances and discovers the human possibilities within herself. (p. 6)

Though Alfonsina Storni wished to disown *La inquietud del rosal,* the differences between it and the three volumes which immediately followed it have to do with questions of poetic technique rather than with personal growth or range of theme. These volumes are bound by a common thread; their poetry is a poetry of emotional attitudes and of dramatic self-presentation. The ''yo'' is not only the speaking subject but also the object described, and while the attitudes adopted are varied and wide-ranging, the tone which is communicated is often inauthentic. The reader senses an insistence, bordering on the hysterical, that each poem be a mirror image of some new emotional trauma.

Yet this conviction as to the validity of the felt emotion often has the value of an antidote in the literary panorama of one or another period. Looking for poetic excellence, we find much in the early Storni to criticize, but it must be recognized that in a literary environment befogged by understatement, classical restraint and gentlemanly melancholy, Alfonsina Storni's belief in the relevance and interest of her sharply-outlined moods and emotions must have sounded a blaring, discordant but living note. (p. 18)

[The] taut expression of deeply-felt moods was an ingredient lacking in Argentinian poetry during the first decades of our century, and to Alfonsina Storni falls the credit of providing it. It is necessary that poetry should not separate itself for too long from its ground, the net of emotions and intensities which we call our spirit. Storni refused to allow her readers to forget that most ambiguous of human characteristics, the capacity for feeling both joy and sorrow. (p. 19)

The interest of *La inquietud del rosal* lies less in the individual poems than in the sense of inner conflict found in all four of Storni's early books, but least disguised here. The need to speak in a strong and personal voice shows in the careful way in which she worked her poems as close to technical perfection as she was able. Every poem is a finished work of art, and rarely does any one repeat the stanza pattern of that which precedes or follows it. Clearly each one is an act of transcendence, a declaration of the individual's right to take his/her being and give it the shape desired: the work of art is seen as an act of self-justification. But against this positive impulse some contrary force seems to be impelling Storni towards annihilation. It is as though immanence itself holds her back, forcing her constantly to seek a state of non-being, even though she expresses the conflict within her in the transcendent moment of the poem. Nature seems to represent for her a womb or shroud which will reclaim her as soon as she tires of life's struggle; the pantheistic vision of Nature as source of an emotional, if not metaphysical, nirvana will persist even through her later work. . . . (pp. 21-2)

Storni constantly uses the image of passive woman abandoned to the forces of Nature as a metaphor of the loss of identity in death, and also for the loss of self-awareness in physical passion. . . . The erotic moment is perceived not as rite of passage to a higher level of consciousness, but as loss of self in a-temporal peace and non-being. This attitude persists in Storni's love-poems, and is disconcerting in view of her final suicide, which was poetically expressed in her last sonnet as a blending into night and nothingness. (p. 22)

What might be seen as a coincidental use of symbols—loss of self in Nature expressing both death and sexual fulfilment—becomes instead one of the fundamental impulses behind Storni's poetry: the desire for annihilation, be it in sleep, passion or death. Always a cosmic metaphor is used—sea, sky, the heavens—and always the poem is fashioned with a care which is the very antithesis of this urge to non-being. (p. 23)

It is surely no coincidence that the main theme of [*El dulce daño, Irremediablement* and *Languidez*] is love, and that they therefore fit most easily into the category of "feminine" poetry. As such they pose no problems for the reading public, are predictable for the critics—and less interesting by far than the poetry which was to follow. Nevertheless, they contain poems of merit, some of them exceptional creations, and they are of great interest in their own right for the way in which they reveal the development of Storni's particular poetic voice.

Though all three volumes contain a preponderance of poems on variations of the theme of love, each has a distinct organization and tone. In the case of *El dulce daño* it is erotic love which compels into existence the majority of the poems. (p. 29)

[Most of the poems of *Irremediablement*] fit into the category of "feminine" poetry in so far as they present the theme of love from traditionally female points of view. Yet somewhat more often now than before, a text appears in which a more original voice is heard. This interchange of voices (Storni the poetess and Storni the poet, as we might categorize them) forms the true dialectic within the volume. (p. 35)

The now-familiar complaints of love still find expression in some poems, but the new voice is heard more often, and Storni's growing technical skill produces ever more successful poems.

The overall impression left by *Languidez* is that of depression. . . . Less than melancholy or anguish, a feeling of life-lessness pervades the book. Death appears as a motif in many poems, but not as the loss of self, identified previously with love; death is merely an alternative to life, both equally disappointing, and both devoid of importance. (p. 39)

Though only four years had passed between the publication of *Languidez* . . . and that of *Ocre* . . . , the latter volume shows a distinct change of atmosphere. . . . The thematic range and the technique of the earlier poems have not been replaced by a new poetic style. Rather it is the changed tone of the poetic voice that we notice. The change is a subtle one, yet pervasive, producing in us the feeling of contact with a more mature poet and person. The gaze of the poetic speaker is directed inwards, but not solely to the region of the emotions. An act of detachment seems to have occurred, so that we sense a separation between the poetic voice and the domain of subjectivity from which it draws its themes. This no-man's-land of uninvolved contemplation is illuminated by the light of understanding. Moreover it is shot through by disconcerting flashes of the irony which from now on will mark Storni's mature work, poetry and drama alike.

Introspection and self-awareness are the keys to *Ocre*'s position in Storni's creative development, and the sonnet provides the formal restrictions which she apparently deemed necessary for these adventures within her psyche. Fully three quarters of the poems are sonnets, or follow some variation of sonnet form. . . . [While] Storni still submits herself to a strict formal discipline, she continues to experiment with different metrical schemes. This characteristic remains with her through the last two volumes of her poetry. In the case of *Ocre*, it is as though the areas of introspection in which she wished to venture demanded strictness of form as a safeguard against the dangers of poetic as well as psychological freedom.

Many of the poems continue to create images of male-female tensions. Yet the poetic speaker now looks with less involvement at each amorous constellation. The male partner is dismissed in poem after poem as superficial, beautiful, inconstant and incapable of passion. The female self, however, is revealed in all the complexities of her physical nature and of her personality, these two conceived of as opposing forces in a struggle which exhausts and defeats the "yo" of these poems. (pp. 45-6)

Storni could never finally resolve her personal dilemma by persuading herself into a position of defence by irony. In *Ocre* she expanded her gamut of responses to this dilemma, but she could not escape the bedevilment of the dichotomy as she felt it. . . . So *Ocre*'s kinship with the earlier volumes announces itself in the recurrence of old attitudes, namely the tensions of frustrated love which give shape to fully half its poems. True to the moment of transition which it reflects, it echoes themes of an earlier day, though the poet has widened her range and varied her tone. (p. 48)

Where *Ocre* captures our interest is in the expression of new experiences conveyed by many of its poems. Some combine a heightened consciousness of self with a prosaic style happily replacing neoromantic rhapsodies and *modernista* opulence. (pp. 49-50)

[Use] of deliberately prosaic language, and . . . eschewing of abstraction are characteristic of the best poems in *Ocre*. The dramatic flair around which Storni's most impressive poems crystallize needed precisely this concreteness of detail and language, which was often obscured in the earlier volumes by romantic effusiveness. The more direct impact of the volume is due in part to a preference for the quotidian rather than the literary expression, and in part to a restraint in the use of the epithet. (p. 50)

[In] "**Versos a la tristeza de Buenos Aires**" . . . Storni sounds a note of deep despair. She speaks as one for whom existence has become a living death; there is no memory of past pleasures and no anticipation of relief. Her youthful illusions have been extinguished by the city's monolithic monotony, and her responses are deadened: should she hear her name called, she would no longer answer. (p. 58)

The absence of distance between the felt emotion and its aesthetic semblance links "**Versos a la tristeza de Buenos Aires**" to the poetry of Storni's earlier years. Yet the poet who resigned herself to solitude, and who overcame spiritual desolation, is speaking almost for the first time in this and similar poems in *Ocre*. There can be sensed, at this stage of Storni's life, her realization of her spiritual orphanhood in the world, and *Ocre*'s introspective mood seems to echo the poet's determination to explore herself and her circumstances, and to come to terms with both. "**Versos a la tristeza de Buenos Aires**" marks some of the more painful phases of this process. We suspect, however, that without this rigid account-taking, the return to the world, which *Mundo de siete pozos* represents, would never have been possible. (p. 59)

As in many of Storni's poems, man is dehumanized and subtly ridiculed in [Storni's play *El amo del mundo*]. The true conflict lies in the relationship of Márgara and the coquettish Zarcillo to each other and thus, incidentally, to Claudio. Both women's roles are well-developed and convincing, though they would have to be underacted in an actual performance if they were not to appear melodramatic. The male roles, on the other hand, are shadowy and unformed, even within the stereotypes they represent. (p. 63)

Márgara is what Storni clearly wanted to be: the dignified woman of the world, respected in society, sufficient unto herself, and not a prey to sexual desires, whose son is a glorious testimony of disinterested love. (pp. 65-6)

There is no distance between Storni and her work, so that the bitterness which pervades the play is that of remembered hurts, not yet transcended and transformed into the stuff of literature. What we witness is not an aesthetic spectacle bringing with it the catharsis which the ritual of the theater can produce. The play is more an act of self-immolation masquerading as rational justification. Emotions still control the pen, and not vice-versa. Thus the deadly seriousness of the action, the total lack of humor, of irony, of any perspective other than that of Márgara/Alfonsina. (p. 66)

The visual impact alone of *Mundo de siete pozos* suffices to alert the reader to a new direction in Storni's poetry; regularity of line-length and of strophic organization is abandoned in favor of a free-flowing structure with an unobtrusive and irregular rhythm. At the end of the collection there is a return to Storni's favorite form, the sonnet, but from the eponymous first poem to **"Haz de tus pies"** . . . poems are written in free form, occasionally with assonantal rhyme, more often with none at all, and only rarely with any kind of metrical symmetry. . . .

The open form of the *Mundo de siete pozos* poems places emphasis on two newly important aspects of Storni's verse: visual detail, and rhythm echoing sense. These poems attempt first to capture the visual and aural qualities of a scene or moment (only *then* relating them to the state of mind of the poet); in them line length is used to force attention upon each element of that which is re-created in the poem. . . . (p. 81)

In this volume Storni skilfully explored the many possibilities of re-creating meaning in rhythm by means of freer versification. It is in its new range of tempi and verbal rhythms that the haunting charm of the collection seems to lie. (p. 82)

[In] Storni's case the liberation of rhythm bespoke a liberation of vision also. The result is that, for almost the first time, Storni gives the impression of writing as a poet of the twentieth century. . . .

Mundo de siete pozos shows an even greater detachment of emotion from poetic material. The poet has not "lost her lyricism", as critics have suggested. Rather she has recognized that she has eyes to see the world, and music with which to express it, as well as emotions to be torn at by the vicissitudes of love affairs. . . .

Storni does look at the world of objective reality—much more than heretofore she describes what she sees beyond herself, able now to create a scene verbally, rather than merely to

use it as a vehicle for her emotional states. . . . [Anguish] does not disappear because it is not directly expressed; indeed it deeply affects the way in which the eye looks at what surrounds it. And there is a distortion in Storni's vision of the world in *Mundo de siete pozos*, and even more in *Mascarilla y trébol*, which points to an inner crisis of increasingly serious proportions.

Both volumes have also a vein of fantasy which had not been a characteristic of Storni's earlier work. In *Mundo de siete pozos* the reader is aware of a whimsical tone which produces some delightfully light-hearted images, though a certain surrealistic note is sounded from time to time. When Storni escapes from her immediate surroundings into an imaginative world of mermaids and sea-houses, the result is charming; sometimes the images evoked are more ominous, even sinister. At the same time, the artist's developing skill in the manipulation of her materials, combined with a resolution not to lose contact with the world of reality, make the poems of these volumes Storni's most transcendent creations. (p. 83)

It is [the] juxtaposition of inner and outer worlds from which comes the coherence of the apparently loose poems in *Mundo de siete pozos*. Without closing off her emotional responses Storni had discovered the magic of the world outside herself, which for almost the first time she chose to explore freely. (p. 100)

[*Mascarilla y trébol*] was Storni's conscious swan-song. It is a volume of fifty-two unrhymed sonnets, which Storni calls "antisonetos" and which include her most interesting and original poems. . . .

She now feels a fascination towards the world of objects, which she uses as imaginative springboards, delighting in their physical reality, yet wandering freely down the paths of association and suggestion which these objects open up for her. She looks with clarity at what surrounds her, but she allows her private world of dreams and symbols to merge with what her eye beholds. (p. 101)

The book is, in fact, intriguing. First of all there is the enigmatic quality of the title, its ominous evocation of death conjoined with the regenerative quality of Nature. But "mascarilla" is more than an image of death, for it implies the utter disappearance of human flesh, and the survival of only a haunting likeness of inanimate features. The image of the death-mask is an eerie reminder that the poems which survive their maker also bear witness to the annihilation of what was a human existent. The trefoil also survives, however, like the grass which covers graves in cemeteries, and thus forms part of the constant, though mindless and therefore unconscious, cycle of Nature.

The image of trefoil or clover recurs in the poems themselves, so that it acts as a linking symbol within the organic unity of the collection as a whole. However, it takes on a new coloration in the light of the subtitle, *Círculos imantados*. Echoes of superstition, folk-lore, even supernatural powers now haunt the poems which follow. If the symbolism of the circle in itself is complex, it seems here to draw together the seemingly disparate images of the title. . . . (p. 102)

There are poems in *Mascarilla y trébol* . . . which bear out the hint of the subtitle that the book, in an artistic and a spiritual sense, represents a moment of transcendence in Storni's perceptions and experience of reality; that it represents, in fact, not a new departure in her *oeuvre,* but a refinement of vision and poetic technique brought about by suffering. . . .

On a formal level the sonnet is the most closed poetic form, and is therefore the nearest equivalent to the circle in the visual arts, or the basic rondo form in music. Evidently after the more open organization of poems in *Mundo de siete pozos* Storni felt the need to return to a stricter formal discipline. While she ventured away from tradition by abolishing all rhyme, she used the hendecasyllable in every poem in the volume, which she had not done in *Ocre,* for instance. Obviously she wanted to exercise careful control over her subject matter in these poems of intense inspiration. The fact that Storni called them "antisonnets" does not lessen their essential sonnet-ness except to emphasize rhythm and meter in the absence of rhyme. (p. 103)

[With] very few exceptions, emotional states and sentimental regrets are banished from these poems—the moment is too serious for any but the most crucial expression. The control of form is accepted, but within it freedom is zealously maintained by the abandonment of rhyme. Hence Storni's coinage of a new term, incapable of hedging in an inspiration which has reached its moment of apocalypse. Many of these poems are strange, with that mixture of strangeness and marvel which Baudelaire called the "bizarre", and which he thought the essence of true poetry. In the antisonnets Storni lets herself venture into dangerous territory; she escapes all stereotypes, and anchors herself to the visible world in order not to lose the way back again. In the white heat of these poems she most nearly approaches the androgeny of the great artist, and speaks with her most powerful voice. In her moment of greatest anguish she opened her eyes and saw: the mysteries of both the inner and the outer world inspire these poems. (p. 120)

As a minor poet Storni produced work of merit, and within her own trajectory she developed personally and poetically to a remarkable degree. . . . By the end of her life she was in touch with a poetic intuition which is truly inspired and inspiring. For what she achieved she deserves attention and recognition. . . .

She is interesting precisely by reason of the inner pressures which forced out of her the poetry of her last volumes, that is, by reason of her growth as a human being, and her resultant growth as a poet. Interesting enough, in fact, to be able to survive a demotion—or rather promotion—from the upper ranks of women poets, into the place which is properly hers as a maker, a poet in the true sense of the word. (p. 122)

Rachel Phillips, in her Alfonsina Storni: From Poetess to Poet *(© copyright 1975 by Tamesis Books Limited), Tamesis Books, 1975, 131 p.*

JANICE GEASLER TITIEV (essay date 1976)

It seems safe to assume that by the time Alfonsina Storni published *Mundo de siete pozos*, in 1934, form had in general become more important to her than content. Her first four collections . . . contained a variety of structures, and all but the initial book had a principal theme, love. Love was also the favored subject in *Ocre* . . . , which consisted almost entirely of sonnets in consonant rhyme, and in *Poemas de amor* . . . , a justifiably neglected book of prose poems. In *Mundo de siete pozos*, however, there is no longer any pre-

dominant theme; there is a predominant form. It is form that gives a definable unity to the collection. Throughout her work Storni fluctuated between liberty and limitation in structure, and both of these directions are in evidence in this volume. The experiments with freedom which had reached an extreme in *Poemas de amor* give way here to the poems in free verse which make up most of the book. The trend towards rigidity again is expressed in sonnets, a group of ten at the end of the book, and scattered among the poems in free verse are a few which would not fall into this category because of some pattern within them, usually rhyme. The entire collection is characterized by an extreme simplicity which approaches the colloquial in the free verse. The poems of the first part are basically slow-moving and suggestive of thought, and each element in them is given time and importance of its own. (p. 185)

The general tone of the collection is a quiet, resigned pessimism. Only occasionally are there signs of rebellion, cynicism, or hope. Blame is seldom placed on anyone. Sometimes the negative feelings are all but hidden. . . . As in all of Storni's works, one occasionally finds here subjects which are still surprising today, if not as shocking as they must have been to her contemporaries. "**Canción de la mujer astuta**" is basically a sonnet about the menstrual cycle. . . . In short, this is an extremely eclectic collection as far as themes are concerned. (pp. 191-92)

In the light of what had been happening in poetry for some twenty years before *Mundo de siete pozos* appeared these poems are amazingly clear. There are indications of the conscious striving towards obscurity which became more pronounced in the poet's next, and last, book *Mascarilla y trébol* . . . , but there is another explanation for frustrations in trying to approach this book. An interesting, and for the most part new characteristic at this point, is a strong preference for pure fantasy. There are metaphors and entire poems which would certainly seem hermetic if one were to attempt to find a concrete meaning beyond what is actually stated. These are daydreams, fantasies. They were not bound to reality nor rationality when they were written and they should not be when they are read. They mean what they say, nothing more, and at times they are superb poetry. . . . The book as a whole is highly metaphorical, and the images profit greatly from the poet's flights of fancy. Most of the poems are series of metaphors. As part of this abundance of metaphors, or perhaps because of it, there is a constant fusion of the human and the non-human. This is particularly common with human characteristics and elements of the landscape. "**El mundo de siete pozos**" . . . , the poem which gives title to the book, is an extended metaphor in which the human head is a world with seven doors ("ojos como mares," ears that are "antenas" and "caracoles," a nose that is a mountain, a mouth that is a crater). When some natural element is being "humanized," the image takes the form of personification. . . . As in previous books there is a preoccupation with human anatomy. Aside from the frequent mentions of hands, eyes, the heart, *etc.,* that had long been familiar to the poet's readers, several poems are devoted entirely to a description of some part of a person—or of a person. . . . Perhaps the most constant presence here is the sea (and, despite some common misconceptions, this is the only one of Storni's books of which this can be said). The sea is the "scene" in all of the poems of the section labeled "**Motivos de mar**," but it is also used generously in the other sections both as scene and image. Aside from "**Crepúsculo**" there are other poems which indicate a desire for some sort of retreat into or union with the sea. (p. 192)

The theme [of **"Y la cabeza comenzó a arder"**] concerns the stuff of which daydreams are made—a fantasy in which the persona and the moon exchange roles. One could force a "meaning" on this fantasy, create an interpretation, by making associations with other poems of the poet or with general traditions, but working from within the poem a symbolic interpretation is impossible. . . . The poem, like so many of the collection, appears at first to be basically a third-person description of something outside of the persona. She is a witness to the moon's experience and rebellion in the first five stanzas, and only in the last two stanzas is it apparent that the poem is about the "yo," that the true subject is its effect upon her. Through the use of dialogue, the poem becomes a revelation of two personas. The "yo-tú" relationship reverses itself, reflecting the role reversal that is the theme of the poem.

In the first five stanzas the moon is the principal focus of attention—a personified moon in rebellion against her traditional routine. . . . The moon is taking on the role of a person. This first section of the poem occasions some lovely metaphors. The moon establishes herself like any humble flower in a hole in the wall of the house, but she is not just any flower. She is "infinita." She opens but will never close definitively. The images of the fourth and fifth stanzas play with antithetical points of view on the moon's role. One ordinarily thinks of the moon as giving out light. Here she appears as a butterfly sipping up the shadows. . . . The following image reverses the action. Here it is the "cúpulas" that drink in the moon as her rays fall upon them. Both images represent action. (pp. 194-95)

The first time the head is mentioned, in stanza six, it seems ordinary enough. The next stanza could also be a metaphorical treatment of common eyes. In these eyes full of flowing brown water, though, there is already an element of light. The fantasy again comes to the fore in the eighth stanza when the head begins to shine. It is significant that it shines like stars, as the stars are usually thought of as companions to the moon. When this star-like shining is transferred to the hands of the persona she takes on characteristics of the moon—albeit in a rather vehement fashion, judging by the verb used—"incendio." It is now the persona who has a panoramic view of the world, who can reach and light up houses and entire forests. (The repetition of the grammatical structure creates an incidental parallel between humans and beasts.) Although it is not clear whether this act of illumination is a negative or a positive situation, it seems to be positive. Fire, flame, or burning are used with a positive connotation in several other poems of the book. (p. 195)

Mundo de siete pozos was Alfonsina Storni's penultimate book, published four years before her last and eighteen years after her first. She was at this point well along in her gradual transition from straightforward, seemingly spontaneous confession to subtle, controlled revelation, as well as in the experiments with form which would lead her ultimately to the creation of a personal structure which she called the "antisoneto," a sonnet in unrhymed *endecasílabos*. Although the volume illustrates these changes in her work, it also shows many of the constants, such as basic clarity and simplicity, and a pessimistic view of life. The delayed recognition of new directions and the setting of poems in immediate surroundings, even when fantasy will take over, are also typical. Like most of her books of poetry, this one is very uneven in quality. She does prove here that she can do fine things with free verse. She was certainly more successful with this form than with poetry in prose, *Poemas de amor* having been a complete failure. Although she was obviously willing to accept prose poetry, her personal mode of expression apparently needed this minimum of verse form. (p. 196)

Janice Geasler Titiev, "Alfonsina Storni's 'Mundo de siete pozos': Form, Freedom, and Fantasy," in Kentucky Romance Quarterly *(© University Press of Kentucky; reprinted by permission of* Kentucky Romance Quarterly*), Vol. XXIII, No. 2, 1976, pp. 185-97.*

SONIA JONES (essay date 1979)

Any attempt to classify [Alfonsina Storni's] poetry by applying to it the usual literary labels is bound to fail. . . . Her early work reflects a predominantly Romantic tone, with its autobiographical elements, its lyrical and sometimes sentimental themes, and its overall tendency to portray the sensitive, rebellious, misunderstood poet standing alone against the world. Yet even in her first volume there is considerable influence from the Hispanic Modernist movement, which developed primarily as a reaction against the worn-out imagery of Romanticism. (p. 51)

In [**"Sábado"** (**"Saturday"**)] Alfonsina accomplished what was to become a hallmark of her later work: the creation of a poetic world based on scenes taken from everyday reality. The refined aristocratic setting, with its fountain and herons, brings to mind the imagery of the Modernists, but the wicker chair and the breakfast dishes were typical of the sort of objects that were to reappear often in her poetry. Like some of her contemporaries, she refused to make a distinction between "poetic" and "prosaic" vocabulary. She did not separate her inner and outer world—if a chair inspired a poetic association in her mind, then the chair appeared as part of the resultant creation. She was not concerned about whether a chair was more or less poetic than a swan.

Nor was she concerned, apparently, about whether or not it was considered fitting for a young lady unblushingly to express her amorous yearnings. Her poem "Sábado" already suggests, in a most subtle and delicate way, what was to become a constantly recurring theme in her poetry: the unfulfilled desire for love. . . .

Her attitude of defiance constitutes a theme that can be traced throughout her first volumes. (p. 58)

El dulce daño [*(Sweet Pain)*] expresses both the pleasure and the suffering of passionate love, and *Irremediablemente* [*(Irremediably)*] focuses on the feeling of disillusionment that inevitably follows. *Languidez* [*(Languor)*] is generally speaking a description of the poet's attempts to renounce the passion that caused her so many disappointments. . . . Together these three collections of poetry could well be considered a trilogy dedicated to the three fundamental stages of passionate love: hope, with its attendant pain and exaltation, then disillusionment, and finally, renunciation. . . . She had lived the three stages of passionate love, she had expressed every feeling and emotion associated with the various phases, and she could not go back to the beginning again. [*Languidez,* the final book in the trilogy,] might well be considered the supreme expression of her loss of innocence. (p. 64)

The poet's "worn out soul" is the key to the new tone which is evident everywhere in *Languidez*. She no longer has the strength to give herself freely to a new love, nor does she have the innocence to believe in the promise of happiness it offers. But in spite of the worldly knowledge she has acquired, she does not have the courage to abandon all thoughts of love, for the memory of passion's exaltation is too fresh in her mind. She becomes almost like an earthbound spirit, wandering about in a world which offers her nothing, but which she cannot give up. (p. 65)

Feeling drained and disillusioned, then, Alfonsina turned her thoughts to other forms of love. Poems dealing with filial, fraternal, and maternal love are especially powerful in this volume. (p. 68)

Alfonsina's own love for children is clearly evident in a number of poems in this volume, particularly in one called **"Miedo,"** (**"Fright"**) where the poet cradles a frightened child in her arms. The little boy's subsequent relief is described with great simplicity.... It is through her contemplation of children that it slowly begins to dawn on her that the disillusionment she feels cannot apply generally to the whole human species. (p. 69)

She is now able, as never before, to go beyond the limited world of her self-oriented passions and extend her love to include all humanity. One of the poems that best expresses this new freedom is **"El obrero"** (**"The Workman"**). (pp. 69-70)

In spite of its naïveté, ... this poem should be seen as an expression of the poet's new desire to seek freedom from the self, an assertion which she clearly states in the prologue of *Languidez*. (p. 70)

If, in general terms, it can be said that *Languidez* focuses on that moment of insight which led the poet to attempt a conscious renunciation of passion, then *Ocre* is in many ways a testimony to her failure. Instead, she resigns herself to the age-old struggle to harmonize the conflicting demands of reason and instinct, and from her personal defeat there emerges an artistic victory.... In the early collections the poet was the protagonist of the various dramas that unfolded. But in this volume something entirely new has happened: she has stepped outside herself, so to speak, and has become the rather analytical observer of her own life. She now views herself from a distance, with a perspective that allows her to place herself within a larger framework. (p. 71)

[The] cynical disillusionment expressed in *Ocre* has lost the bitterness it had in the trilogy. The poet has grown older, and she no longer blames her lover for falling short of her ideal.... Her experience and insight into the ways of men have given her a sense of humor that was almost entirely absent from previous collections of poetry. (p. 73)

The remarkable thing about *Poemas de amor* [(*Love Poems*)], ... is that it stands in such striking contrast to *Ocre*, which appeared only the year before....

In *Love Poems* Alfonsina drops her role as the cynical, solitary observer of other peoples' foolish illusions, and abruptly becomes an active participant in the sentimental dramas that had figured so prominently in her early books of verse. She no longer turns her back on the young women dancing under the stars. Instead, she feels a tender solidarity with them, for they share with her the ecstasy of passion. (p. 75)

The book contains sixty-seven short compositions inspired, no doubt, by the style of Baudelaire's "petits poèmes en prose" ("little poems in prose"). The comparison can go no farther, however. The quality of Alfonsina's work in this volume is very uneven, ranging from mini-letters that are frankly sophomoric to paragraphs that do succeed in capturing a poetic moment. Perhaps part of the failure of these compositions can be attributed to the fact that they were written in a prose that turned out to be too prosaic for the content. Baudelaire set out to prove that poetry did not necessarily have to be written in verse, and while Alfonsina may have wished to emulate him, her compositions give the impression of being poor prose translations of her poetry. (pp. 75-6)

The title of the collection [*Mundo de siete pozos (World of Seven Wells)*] is a metaphor in which the world is seen as a human head, whose "seven wells" are the eyes, ears, nose, and mouth. This image sets the tone of the volume, which describes man as being part of a larger universe, rather than being at the core of the universe as he was in previous books of verse. (pp. 77-8)

The very fact that it has become necessary to warn the reader that it is risky to hazard an interpretation of some of the poems in *Mundo de siete pozos* is in itself indicative of the new character of the poet's creation. Many of the poems have ceased to be a direct expression of her feelings and opinions; they have become instead the reflection of moods and dreams described with abstract symbols and occasionally obscure images. (p. 78)

In tracing the trajectory of [the] theme of despair, one notices a stylistic change that takes place as the volume progresses. In **"Ojo,"** one of the first poems in the book, the verses vary greatly in length, some having as many as nine syllables while others have as few as two. The short verses tend to focus attention on their content, with the result that the poem becomes a sort of catalogue of individual moments, each of which acquires a certain importance because it stands alone. One is forced, therefore, to acknowledge each part of the poem as a unit, and this serves to distract the attention from the whole. The reader is invited to give up the temptation to reason; instead, he must feel, hear, and see the images which dance in kaleidoscopic patterns. In **"Calle,"** however, although the verses continue to be irregular (varying from three to eleven syllables), the majority of them are longer than those in **"Ojo."** What is more, the poet has largely eliminated the constant punctuation that added to the staccato quality of **"Ojo,"** so the verses of **"Calle"** flow more smoothly and allow the reader to enter the poetic world without undergoing the constant interruption of duo-syllabic verses.... Finally, toward the end of the collection, she makes use of her favorite structure, the sonnet, and the lyrical world which this form traditionally expressed emerges once again in her poetry. (p. 80)

In spite of everything that has been said about the general tone of each of her various collections, Alfonsina periodically bursts out of the pervasive mood of a book of verse and creates a poem in direct contrast to the others.... In *Mundo de siete pozos, (World of Seven Wells)* whose title gave special emphasis to the human head, there are nevertheless a number of poems in which the poet's irrepressible heart springs up to challenge the cool world of the mind. (p. 81)

[Alfonsina's final book of verse, *Mascarilla y trébol (Mask and Clover)*,] was a testimony to the many changes that had taken place within her, and to the very different vision of the world which she had created as a result of her suffering. (pp. 81-2)

[A careful reading of this book reveals a poetry that] expresses the poet's deeply felt insights into the meaning of her life. . . . The most original aspect of this volume is found in her quiet triumph over the heretofore incessant demands of her active and frustrating life, a life to which, for better or for worse, she had always dedicated herself entirely. And there is irony in her triumph: all her disillusionment, her cynicism, her insight, her resolutions to control the passion which she had so often seen as a cruel deception, all her mental efforts to negate her physical and sentimental needs met with failure, until she accepted her impending death and so saw life in an entirely new perspective. There is no inner conflict, no tension, no sign of struggle in *Mascarilla y trébol* as there was in every one of the preceding volumes—only a sorrowful understanding of the "vanity of vanities," an understanding devoid of her former anger and rebelliousness.

It was perhaps only natural that her totally new orientation should be expressed in a different style. Finding the traditional verse forms of her previous collections too restrictive, and feeling dissatisfied with the unlimited scope afforded by free verse, she invented a new verse form which she called the "anti-sonnet.". . . [It] was the same as the classical sonnet with its fourteen hendecasyllabic verses, except without rhyme. The discipline of the traditional structure and the freedom of the unrhymed verse proved to be a happy combination. The sober, unconstrained hybrid offered her just the right medium in which to express her new perspective, which included both a minutely detailed description of a newly discovered microcosm and a panoramic view of the "outside" world and its symbolism. (pp. 82-3)

She started out by worshipping the god of love only to discover, finally, that passion was based on illusions and on repetitive situations which always led to the same dead end. . . . But it was not until the last year of her life that she found a replacement for her idol, and she knelt before Poetry just as she had once bowed down to Passion. She had seen that passion as an end in itself was a trap. Had she lived, she might well have discovered that intellect as an end in itself was also a deception. (p. 85)

The author had a message that she was anxious to convey [in her first three-act play, *El amo del mundo (The Master of the World)*], so she simply made her characters talk to one another about the various problems she had in mind, instead of creating a conflict that would allow the action to speak for itself. . . . The play consequently failed as a play, but there is certainly no reason why it should not be remembered as a piece of extremely interesting literature. If its technical defects have caused it to be considered a mediocre play, then it might be more profitably considered a novel in dialogue form, for example. . . . The important thing is what Alfonsina said in this composition, and not the fact that she had not yet learned to manipulate the genre. (p. 86)

[The protagonist, Margara,] had learned that the fundamental thing in the life of any human being, man or woman, was to establish a profound and loving relationship with another person. Márgara is finally able to bring this about at the end of the play when she confesses to her son that she is his mother. She at last found the courage she needed to get rid of all the falseness and hypocrisy which had existed in the only relationship that was really important to her. . . .

This very worthy play has been largely forgotten today, in part because Alfonsina's biographers and critics have tended to repeat the negative opinions that were expressed in the reviews that came out in 1927. The time for a reevaluation is long overdue. (p. 91)

It is ironic that each play she wrote turned out to be worse than the one before, and even more ironic that the critics should have panned *El amo del mundo*, her first and best play in terms of its content, while praising *Cimbelina*, one of her last and greatest failures. The irony here does not imply that the situation is in any way untrue to life—it is only a shame that Alfonsina should have put so much faith in the opinion of others when it came to writing plays. Her first play was the only one that had any real substance. (p. 100)

Judging from the content of both her poetry and her prose, 1919 was a year of crisis for Alfonsina, as she struggled with her new insights and with her need to tame the elusive god of love. The short story that best illustrates her frame of mind is given the appropriate title of "Una crisis" [("A Crisis")] an intriguing composition representing what might be understood as the confrontation of her ego and alter ego. (p. 111)

A detail in this story might well have passed unnoticed were it not for the fact that Alfonsina underlined it so often in her prose fiction of 1919 that it grew into a regular theme: the infidelity of a partner in an apparently *happy* relationship. This motif is not strongly delineated in "Una crisis" because Julia's sincerity is so obviously in question that the reader does not take seriously the so-called happiness of her marriage, and yet the situation described here by the author foreshadows her growing concern about passion's ability to devastate even the most stable partnerships. (p. 112)

The infidelity of one of the partners in an apparently happy relationship is the theme once again of . . . *Una golondrina (A Swallow)*. (p. 117)

In this story, as in many others, the modern reader will find that Alfonsina had a tendency to exaggerate the sentimental passages to an embarrassing degree. No matter how distasteful this may be, however, it should be kept in mind that her writing was largely autobiographical, based almost entirely on her own experience and observations, so it was inevitable that her characters should be a direct expression of the highly charged emotions she was feeling during that period of her life. . . . (p. 119)

The image of the swallow was one that appealed greatly to Alfonsina, for it appeared time and again throughout her poetry, especially in the early volumes. The best definition of what the swallow represented for her is found in her first book of poetry, *La inquietud del rosal* [*(The Disquietude of the Rosebush)*], in a poem called simply "Golondrinas" ("Swallows"). (p. 120)

Alfonsina identified with these birds, compelled as they were by some strange and relentless power of nature to abandon the nest and fly away over the sea, restlessly looking for a new life, a new love. Alfonsina herself was forever moving, both emotionally and in the most literal sense, trying to find a feeling of renewal by changing her surroundings at every opportunity. . . . She tended to see herself as forever soaring high above the stifling mediocrity of the world, and like the swallow she so admired, she could not tolerate the idea of being imprisoned in a cage. (pp. 120-21)

There was another kind of cage, however, that disturbed her a good deal more than the one that was so often fashioned by lovers who proved to be unworthy of her. This cage is so universally feared and desired that it has been described variously as "the tender trap," "the tie that binds," and the like. Nevertheless, it is one that should not be overlooked in Alfonsina's case, for it sheds further light on her preoccupation with the failure of the apparently happy relationship. Stability, she felt, could lead all too easily to stagnation, and nothing seemed to trouble her more than the idea of settling into a safe, predictable pattern. It was the very security of her life in the chalet that prompted Lucila, the protagonist of *Una golondrina,* to ask herself whether there might not be something more waiting for her somewhere else. And yet even after she fell in love with Ernesto, she struggled hard to remain in her gilded cage, for she felt understandably bound by Julián's generosity and her own gratitude for all he had given her. She was drawn more or less equally in both directions, and the tension was finally more than she could bear. (p. 121)

[The short story "Catalina"] may very well be Alfonsina's masterpiece in the genre. (p. 129)

It is lamentable that Alfonsina did not continue writing short stories, for "Catalina" is a small chef d'oeuvre of humor, style, and timing. Like many other artists, however, she probably attached no importance to what she was able to accomplish with so little effort, not realizing that her creation came easily to her precisely because it reflected the very core of her talent. (p. 130)

[Alfonsina's] ultimate significance as a writer rests not so much with how she expressed herself, as it does with what she stood for and what she was as a human being. Thousands of women readers saw her as a model of what they or their friends or daughters could hope to achieve some day. . . .

It is ironic, but perhaps not surprising, that she should be remembered today only for her poetry, when so much of value is to be found in her plays and prose fiction. It was in these latter genres that she revealed her best insights into social sham and human failure, and it was here that she made her most important contribution to her nation's culture. (p. 133)

[Much] of her writing, particularly the nonfictional prose, situates her in the mainstream of feminism. Her concern about women's rights and the servility to which women are condemned by years of conditioning is reminiscent of Mary Wollstonecraft; her views on marriage are similar to those of Lucy Stone; and it would be difficult not to draw comparisons between *El amo del mundo* and Ibsen's *A Doll's House.* Faithful to her own character, Alfonsina almost always treated problems of female emancipation from the point of view of the individual. . . . [She] preferred to analyze the purely psychological difficulties encountered by both men and women as a result of what must rightly be considered the ridiculous legacy of social custom and training that was handed down from generation to generation. . . . She was convinced that life could be infinitely improved by the institution of some real teamwork between men and women, and that both sexes would stand to gain intellectually, spiritually, and emotionally by dealing with each other as equals. It is a tribute to her depth of insight and the passion with which she expressed herself that so many men and women in Argentina agree with her today. (pp. 133-34)

Sonia Jones, in her Alfonsina Storni *(copyright © 1979 by Twayne Publishers, Inc.; reprinted with the permission of Twayne Publishers, a Division of G. K. Hall & Co., Boston), Twayne, 1979, 149 p.*

ADDITIONAL BIBLIOGRAPHY

Imbert, Enrique Anderson. "1910-1925." In his *Spanish American Literature,* translated by John V. Falconieri, pp. 327-420. Detroit: Wayne State University Press, 1963.*
    Briefly summarizes Storni's poetic development.

Georg Trakl

1887-1914

Austrian poet and dramatist.

Trakl is an important lyric poet in German literature of the early twentieth century. Critics associate his work with various modern artistic movements, and he is viewed as one of the principal writers to set the dark, introspective tone that later influenced the course of German expressionism. Affinities with imagism have also been noted in Trakl's strikingly visual style. In addition, the dreamlike flow of images in his poems has indicated to some commentators a compositional method similar to the automatic writing of the surrealists, with whom Trakl also shared a preoccupation with violence, perversity, and death. Trakl's strongest literary affiliation, however, is with the French symbolists of the nineteenth century, primarily Arthur Rimbaud, whose disordered and conflict-ridden genius is said to be incarnated in the Austrian poet.

Of great significance in Trakl's early homelife in Salzburg was his close, possibly incestuous, relationship with his sister Grete. Critics frequently identify her as the inspiration for "the sister," a multifaceted symbolic figure in the poems. Trakl attended a Catholic elementary school, while receiving Protestant religious instruction; he was an unsuccessful student and eventually dropped out of school. Later, however, he entered the University of Vienna for training as a pharmacist, a vocation which facilitated his lifelong use of drugs. Soon after leaving the university he was drafted into the Austrian army and assigned to the medical corps. Returning to civilian life, Trakl found a job in a pharmacy, failed to adjust to the routine of working life, and reenlisted in the army. In 1912, while stationed in Innsbruck, he met Ludwig von Ficker, editor of *Der Brenner*. Ficker became friend and mentor to Trakl for the remaining years of his short life, publishing the poet's work regularly in his literary journal. Though Trakl had been writing poetry from an early age, critics agree that his best work dates from this period.

The poetry of Trakl's last two years displays a noticeable development from his efforts prior to 1912. Personal torment and an unrelieved sense of horror and disintegration dominated the earlier poems. The tone of Trakl's later poems is more impersonal and ambiguous. In these works Trakl transcends the extreme subjectivity of his former poetic self, to evolve into what Jungian psychologist Erich Neumann calls a "transpersonal, archaic singer." Some critics describe this new quality in Trakl's mature poems as a mythic objectivity, while confronting the paradox that this poet's world is essentially private, resembling that of a schizophrenic. Critical analysis of Trakl's work has revealed its disjointed, fragmentary nature, summarizing it as a collection of often-repeated symbols and motifs without consistent meaning. These poems, however, are credited with a consistency of mood and attitude which unifies them into a cohesive, though nonrational, statement. In essence they form the poet's protest against the corrupt, fallen condition of humankind.

While Trakl's poetry is overwhelmingly negative, critics find in it a gesture of affirmation. Internal evidence of the poems and statements made by Trakl have indicated to many com-

mentators that he was a Christian, and thus balanced his visions of damnation with the possibility of ultimate redemption. Trakl died of a self-administered drug overdose in a Polish hospital while recovering from his battle experience during the First World War.

PRINCIPAL WORKS

Gedichte (poetry) 1913
Sebastian im traum (poetry) 1915
Die dichtungen (poetry) 1918
Aus goldenem kelch (poetry) 1939
Decline: Twelve Poems by G. Trakl, 1887-1914 (poetry) 1952
Twenty Poems of Georg Trakl (poetry) 1961
Selected Poems (poetry) 1968
Dichtungen und briefe (poetry, prose poems, and letters) 1969
In the Red Forest (poetry) 1973
Poems (poetry and prose poems) 1973

IRENE MORRIS (essay date 1949)

The problem of western man and the civilization he has built up, which in all its manifold spiritual, intellectual and cultural complexity is the theme of the greatest of modern German poets, Rilke and George, is also the content of Trakl's work, but in its basic and most terrifying form. His preoccupation with it, and the singleness of vision with which he saw it, while it limits the width of his appeal, gives him as a metaphysical poet a power and directness and solidity such as Hölderlin possesses. His verse, which is almost exclusively sensuous with its wealth of imagery and melody, and yet free from the cloying weight that usually goes with such verse, is peculiar to himself and perfectly at one with all he has to say. Rilke aptly speaks of the mirror-like character of Trakl's verse; the goodness and beauty, the ugliness and evil of life are there in all their earthly fullness, and yet wonderfully transfigured, as distant and unapproachable as the world in a hall of mirrors.

It is this peculiarly unearthly-earthly quality of his poetry as well as the experience of the problem of our age in its essentials, which gives Trakl a unique position in modern German literature. (pp. 122-23)

[One] can suggest a common denominator of the experiences behind his poems, and that is the dualism of life. He was painfully aware of the conflict within himself between the spiritual and the physical, which because of the extremes they drove him to and his inability to harmonize them he frequently equates with the good and evil in life respectively. Thus he speaks of 'das Böse' in his poems; no single interpretation is possible, but it generally refers to the sensual, and is often connected with a female figure or some sensuous experience. . . . In the autobiographical prose poems '**Verwandlung des Bösen**' and '**Traum und Umnachtung**' he gives a picture in frightening, strangely beautiful imagery of the struggle within him, of the ecstasies and horrors and annihilating sense of accursedness his unhappy disposition brought him. . . . The image of God's anger whipping him occurs more than once in his poetry; it is no mere figure of speech or poetic ornament but an example of the physical intensity of his emotion.

Trakl's horror of the sensual in himself was further intensified and perhaps caused by the relationship to his youngest sister. She appears in his poetry as 'die Schwester', the companion of his soul, but also bringing with her 'das Böse' and torment to the poet. . . . [At] times he seems to symbolize the saving grace that comes through suffering. (pp. 124-25)

In a poem like '**Die Raben**' Trakl's revulsion at the devilish destructiveness of unredeemed sensuality becomes a nightmare. Birds are a favourite image with him, but 'die Raben' and the 'hungertolle Krähen' of '**Winterdämmerung**' are personifications of 'das Böse', loathsome creatures which pollute the air, bringing disease and death with them, and whose shrill hissing cries and scurried flight destroy the 'Stille' when the world is open to the transcendental. . . .

The wrongness of natural man from the moment he is born, the suffering that life brings and the death that it is, is the content of the poem '**Geburt**'. There, as in other passages referring to birth, the 'moon' appears, the dead companion of the earth and a symbol. . .of the fearful, desolate regions the new-born child has entered. (p. 127)

The hypersensitivity which made Trakl scent evil in a flock of ravens or shudder at the smell of decaying leaves in autumn, made him ecstatically aware of the rich loveliness of Nature. Like the sunflower, one of his favourite images, his senses were ever open, eagerly following and drinking in the warmth and beauty of life. He rejoices particularly in the intoxicating fullness and rich colours of autumn, in the golden beauty of cornfields and vines ripening on the hillside. . . . But it is a delight enhanced by the signs of transience and death already visible in the plenteous splendour. Autumn is beloved of Trakl; only then are the two drives in his nature reconciled: his thirsting senses find refreshment in the ripeness and colour, his soul the promise of release from the weight of the physical world. '**Der Herbst des Einsamen**', one of Trakl's most beautiful poems and containing much of the 'experience of life', is full of a dark sweetness and rich beauty transfigured and spiritualized by the gentle decay of autumn. (pp. 128-29)

Trakl loved autumn because the transition to death was full of a magic beauty and gentle peace; it reconciled him with death from which he physically recoiled, and there are poems which express his horror and revulsion at 'die grüne Verwesung des Fleisches'. He saw death then not as opening life to God, but as the punishment for the sinfulness he sensed in the dualism of life.

The overwhelming experience of decay and death and the awareness of judgment and doom are not just the result of a maladjusted personality. Art can never be explained away by psychology as the expression of a purely subjective experience, and Trakl's sense of impending disaster points to something deeper and greater than his own early death. The motifs of the scythe, the linen and the carpenter . . . do not refer to the poet's fate alone. The decline of Western civilization . . . he felt approaching, [wrings] from him lamenting cries of horror and dread. . . . The isolation and desolation of a generation which according to Nietzsche had 'killed God', the disintegration and fragmentary nature of a world no longer theocentric, this 'sickness unto death' which still threatens modern civilization, is the theme of many poems. . . . (pp. 130-31)

Trakl seldom escapes from this consciousness of a terrifying doom hovering over the world. Even in '**Der Herbst des Einsamen**' where it is a beauteous death of ripeness and peace, he hears the rustling reed, reminding him of the soulless hollow land in men's hearts which is not transfigured. '**Die Ratten**' can be read as a nightmarish but nevertheless realistic description of a sordid scene and a purely subjective experience of loathing and horror. It has, however, a meaning beyond the surface value of this experience of which the poet himself may not be conscious. . . . Against a background of empty silence so different from the 'milde Stille' of '**Der Herbst des Einsamen**' the ghostly band of rats springs up, symbolical of the devilish powers ready to invade men's hearts, grown equally empty and silent, and consume the good that past generations have carefully garnered.

Trakl's recoil from life, a feeling which was intensified by the progressive secularization of spiritual things under the impact of science in the era which ended in 1914, is radically

Christian. The dualism of human nature, all the suffering and bitterness in the world were to him proof of a universal guilt man could never atone for by himself; he was convinced of the wrongness of life and that it can be put right only in the shadow of the Cross. Hence the frequent use of Christian symbols in their original biblical sense: the many compounds of Dornen, the ever-returning cross, so much a part of an Austrian landscape, the olive tree, . . . all express the Christian conception of sacrifice as the eternal principle of human life. The orphan, the leprous and diseased, social outcasts like prostitutes, are nearer salvation because of their suffering and degradation. Confusion, despair and suffering lead men to God, who in His mercy has prepared a home for them on earth in communion with Him through the grace of Jesus Christ, the bread and wine of life. That is the message expressed in simple language and homely imagery in the beautiful poem **'Ein Winterabend'**. . . . The Christian's sure hope of a final redemption beyond death, and the experience that it can be achieved 'in part' here on earth, are at the back of firmly positive poems like **'Gesang des Abgeschiedenen'** and **'Frühling der Seele'** with its conquest of death. . . . (pp. 131-33)

Trakl's last poems are completely visionary in style and apocalyptic in content, and that his only hope for the world is the Cross of Christ is brought out vividly in **'Nachtergebung'**, where a cross towers high in the visionary landscape, the symbol of the paradox that death is life, and the simple, metrical form conveys the complete and childlike submission to this death. . . . The poetic mood may vary, ranging from the dread of **'Der Schlaf'** with its ghostly garden . . . to the exultant affirmation of destruction in **'Die Nacht'** or the trusting surrender of **'Nachtergebung'**, the experience behind the visions is always the same: the 'end' is not just foreboded as in the main body of Trakl's work, it has actually come for the poet. The imagery . . . makes this clear: almost every poem has an image of darkness breaking upon the scene. . . . (pp. 135-36)

Trakl has a strictly personal style which makes his poems easily recognizable. His vocabulary with its frequent use of the same and similar images, while strangely beautiful, seems very limited until closer study reveals the amazing richness and variety within those limits. With few exceptions the language is pastoral, drawing on Nature and the simplest activities of human life for its images; this is in keeping with his concentration on only the central theme of the modern problem of mankind. He experienced everything in images and was said to be unable to understand people who mastered life by means of ideas. His poetry shows this: it is perhaps unique in its almost total lack of reflective thought or intellectual concepts. It is for the most part purely pictorial and descriptive, appealing directly to the senses like a painting set to music. The mellow beauty of the sensuous imagery, the sweet monotony of the rhyme and the gently falling rhythm have a narcotic effect, singing the excessive sadness of the poet more persuasively than any powerful, direct expression of what he felt or thought. The earliest poems are directly comprehensible, but the deeper significance and even the meaning of some are only gradually (and then not completely) revealed as the reader becomes better acquainted with the symbols and their approximate meaning. Snow which one ordinarily connects with purity, has become a private symbol of something hampering and yet in the end impermanent; it is mostly used in a figurative sense, but is

significantly part of the apocalyptic landscape in the last poems.

Trakl's place in German literature is not with the socialist poets of Expressionism. He was not primarily concerned with social ills and their cure, but with the spiritual sickness behind them. Along with the great German poets of the twentieth century he seeks beyond the material distress the solution to man's dilemma in metaphysical spheres. Hofmannsthal pleads finally for a new sense of responsibility within the stabilizing tradition of Roman Catholicism; George proclaims his 'kingdom of the spirit'; Rilke wins through to his mystical philosophy of 'Verinnerlichung'; Trakl's solution is the radical Christianity of Kierkegaard and the modern exponents of the 'theology of crisis'. It is, however, typical of the ebb and flow of his extremely lyric nature that he can seldom hold fast to the positive, practical values of Christianity which optimistically affirm life. (p. 137)

Irene Morris, "Georg Trakl" (revised by the author for this publication), in German Life & Letters, *n.s. Vol. II, No. 2, January, 1949, pp. 122-37.*

MICHAEL HAMBURGER (essay date 1957)

Of all the early Expressionists, Trakl was the least rhetorical and the least dogmatic; and he was an Expressionist poet only in so far as he was a modernist poet who wrote in German. . . . If Trakl had written in English—but, of course, it is inconceivable that he should have done—he would have been called an Imagist, though it is most unlikely that he ever heard or read this word. Neither label is very useful, but Imagist would at least have the virtue of indicating the most distinctive characteristic of Trakl's art: all poets express themselves, but Trakl expressed himself in images. To treat Trakl's poems as self-expression, that is to say, as fragments of an autobiography, is to misunderstand them: for Trakl's dominant aspiration was to lose himself. (p. 239)

Every interpretation of Trakl's works hinges on the difficulty of deciding to what extent his images should be treated as symbols. . . . This, of course, raises the question of his beliefs, for belief comes into play as soon we attempt to "interpret" an image at all; a purely existential image has no meaning other than itself. Since Trakl undoubtedly lent a symbolic significance to his images—or to some of them, at least—these two basic questions are bound to be raised. Trakl's poetry is so essentially ambiguous—so "laconic", as one of his interpreters has observed—that many different interpretations of its symbolism are possible. (p. 240)

The horizontal range of [Trakl's] poems is not wide: it is limited by Trakl's extreme introversion and by his peculiar habit of using the same operative words and images throughout his later work. But Trakl's introversion must not be mistaken for egocentricity. . . . Trakl's inner experience is "objectified" in images and in the symbolic extension of those images: his concern, as he says, was with general truths and with the rendering of general truths in a purely poetic manner. For that reason, the melancholy that pervades his work was only a premiss, not the substance, of what he wished to convey: it is as important, but no more important, than the key of a musical composition. It was certainly a limitation of Trakl's that he could compose only in minor keys; but the same could be said of [Giacomo] Leopardi and of other lyrical poets whose poetry conveys a distinct mood. Nor should Trakl be assessed in terms of optimism and pessimism, categories that are largely irrelevant to his vision. As Rilke was one of the first to point out, Trakl's work is essentially affirmative; but what it affirms is a spiritual order that may not be immediately perceptible in his poems, filled as they are with images pertaining to the temporal order which he negated.

"Trakl's poetry", Rilke wrote, "is to me an object of sublime existence.... It occurs to me that this whole work has a parallel in the aspiration of a Li-Tai-Pe: in both, falling is the pretext for the most continuous ascension. In the history of the poem Trakl's books are important contributions to the liberation of the poetic image. They seem to me to have mapped out a new dimension of the spirit and to have disproved that prejudice which judges all poetry only in terms of feeling and content, as if in the direction of lament there were only lament—but here too there is world again." This tribute is especially important for two reasons; because of Trakl's influence on Rilke's own work, and because Rilke interpreted Trakl's poetry existentially when other critics, less close to Trakl's way of thought, read it as a record of Trakl's morbid states of mind.... What Rilke meant by "world" in the letter cited is what professional Existentialists would call "being"; and he believed that it is the poet's business to affirm whatever aspect of being is manifested to him, whether it be bright or dark. The mood is incidental; what matters is the intensity of the poet's response to the world and his ability to render his perceptions in words and images.... It was Rilke's insight, then, which directed the attention of Trakl's readers away from the categories of optimism and pessimism and towards that "truth" which Trakl himself thought more important than his own predicament. As the work of so many of Trakl's contemporaries shows, optimism can be just as morbid a symptom as pessimism, because there is a kind of optimism that is a hysterical perversion of the truth; its premises give it the lie. Trakl, on the other hand, wrote of what he knew; he was true to his premises, and these premises were positive enough.

The temporal order which Trakl's poems negate was that of materialism in decay. That is the significance of the decaying household possessions in the first part of *Sebastian im Traum*. To this order, Trakl opposed an existential Christian faith akin to Kierkegaard's and an unreserved compassion akin to that of certain characters in Dostoievsky. (pp. 245-47)

What Trakl lamented was not the fact or the condition of death, but the difficulty of living in an age of cultural decline and spiritual corruption.... The dead who people his poems—the mythical Elis, for instance—are more vivid, more full of life, than the living. In the poem *An einen Frühverstorbenen* **(To One who Died Young)**, the surviving friend is haunted by the other.... It is the dying friend who smiles, the survivor who becomes obsessed with death and decay. The reason, it appears from other poems, is that those who die young preserve "the image of man" intact; wherever they appear in Trakl's poems they are associated with righteousness and with images of the good life; and this, in turn, is associated with an earlier stage of civilization, opposed to modern life in the large cities. One thinks of Rilke's cult of those who died young; but Trakl's dead are symbolic of a state of innocence which cannot be identified with youth or childhood, nor even with a rustic and pastoral stage of civilization. It is an innocence that precedes original sin. That is why, in his poem on the Kaspar Hauser legend, Trakl describes the murdered boy as "unborn". Kaspar Hauser

is murdered as soon as he reaches the city, after living in the woods in a wild state; the whole poem is an allegory of the relation between innocence and death, not, as one might easily think, a glorification of a "noble savage" murdered by the corrupt inhabitants of the city. (pp. 248-49)

Most of Trakl's later poems are written in a form of free verse that owes much to the elegies and hymns of Hölderlin. (p. 249)

In spite of a few innocent plagiarisms, Trakl's debt to Hölderlin should not be exaggerated; Trakl also borrowed a few devices and images from Rimbaud, but very much less has been made of this debt or of his no less obvious debt to Baudelaire. (p. 250)

[The] difficulty of summing up Trakl's work as a whole, and the much greater difficulty of interpreting it as a whole, are two reasons why his work stands out from the German poetry of his time. Trakl's plagiarisms—and especially his self-plagiarisms—lend a deceptive consistency to his work—deceptive, because his poems are essentially ambiguous. His ambiguities derive from the tension between image and symbol, the phenomenon and the Idea. Sometimes this tension remains unresolved, so that one cannot tell whether an image is to be taken descriptively or symbolically, an epithet synaesthetically or qualitatively. It is true that each of Trakl's poems offers some kind of clue to the next; but it is a clue that can be very misleading.

Trakl's ambiguities are not deliberate or cerebral; he was an imaginative poet, not a fanciful one. That is why his plagiarisms are never disturbing or offensive. His debt to Hölderlin alone was such that, by all the usual criteria, his work should be very nearly worthless. He appropriated Hölderlin's imagery, rhythms and syntax; yet Trakl's originality is beyond doubt. Any group of three lines detached from one of his later poems is immediately recognizable as his own. Trakl carried plagiarism further by continually quoting himself, repeating, varying and adding to his earlier poems. But there is no reason why a poet should not steal his own property in order to re-arrange it; and this very habit points to the harmlessness of Trakl's borrowings from other poets. (pp. 269-70)

Trakl's debt to Hölderlin is a curiosity of literature; it does not mean that his symbolism can be interpreted in terms of Hölderlin's or that his vision begins where Hölderlin's left off. Heidegger not only presupposes such a tradition of vision and prophecy, but reads his own philosophy into Hölderlin and applies this reading to Trakl. The result is a fascinating, but ruthless, gesture, which sweeps away all evidence of Trakl's own thought in order to turn him into the prophet of an Occident regenerated by the philosophy of pure being. It is true that existential creeds tend to look alike, especially if they have been expressed in poetry alone; and Trakl's Christian faith was an existential one. But this faith is essential to his poetry, as most of his critics agree. Heidegger's exegesis would not have been possible at all but for Trakl's imagist practice; because of the non-committal character of imagism, it would also be possible to argue that Trakl was an alchemist (as his astrological metaphors confirm!) or a Marxist (because of his vision of Capitalism in decay!).

In an age of conflicting creeds and sects, such openness is an advantage. Horizontally, Trakl's range is that of a minor poet, but his vertical range is out of all proportion to it. By "vertical" here I mean neither profundity nor sublimity, but a dimension related to harmony in music. Trakl's poetry is a series of microcosmic variations, poor in melodic invention, rich in harmonic correspondences. Another way of putting it is to say that his work is valid on many "levels" of meaning. It depends as little as possible on the poet's person, opinions and circumstances. One reason is that Trakl was conscious neither of himself nor of his reader; all his poems had his undivided attention. Of Mr. Eliot's "three voices of poetry", Trakl had only the first; but because it never even occurred to him to cultivate the others, his monologue was strangely quiet and pure. (pp. 270-71)

> *Michael Hamburger, "Georg Trakl," in his* Reason and Energy: Studies in German Literature *(reprinted by permission of the author; copyright © 1957 by Grove Press, Inc.), Grove Press, 1957, pp. 239-71.*

MARTIN HEIDEGGER (essay date 1959)

Every great poet creates his poetry out of one single poetic statement only. The measure of his greatness is the extent to which he becomes so committed to that singleness that he is able to keep his poetic Saying wholly within it.

The poet's statement remains unspoken. None of his individual poems, nor their totality, says it all. Nonetheless, every poem speaks from the whole of the one single statement, and in each instance says that statement. . . .

Since the poet's sole statement always remains in the realm of the unspoken, we can discuss its site only by trying to point to it by means of what the individual poems speak. (p. 160)

The fact that every one of Trakl's poems points, with equal steadiness though not uniformly, to the statement's one site, is evidence of the unique harmony of all his poems in the single key of his statement. (p. 161)

[Of what sort] is the language of Trakl's poetic work? It speaks by answering to that journey upon which the stranger is leading on ahead. The path he has taken leads away from the old degenerate generation. It escorts him to go under in the earliness of the unborn generation that is kept in store. The language of the poetry whose site is in apartness answers to the home-coming of unborn mankind into the quiet beginning of its stiller nature.

The language that this poetry speaks stems from this transition. Its path leads from the downfall of all that decays over to the descent into the twilit blue of the holy. The language that the work speaks stems from the passage across and through the ghostly night's nocturnal pond. This language sings the song of the home-coming in apartness, the home-coming which from the lateness of decomposition comes to rest in the earliness of the stiller, and still impending, beginning. In this language there speaks the journey whose shining causes the radiant, ringing music of the departed stranger's ghostly years to come forth. According to the words of the poem "Revelation and Descent" . . . , the "Song of the Departed" sings of "the beauty of a homecoming generation."

Because the language of this poetry speaks from the journey of apartness, it will always speak also of what it leaves behind in parting, and of that to which the departure submits. This language is essentially ambiguous, in its own fashion. We shall hear nothing of what the poem says so long as we bring to it only this or that dull sense of unambiguous meaning.

Twilight and night, descent and death, madness and wild game, pond and stone, bird's flight and boat, stranger and brother, ghost and God, and also the words of color—blue and green, white and black, red and silver, gold and dark—all say ever and again manifold things.

"Green" is decay *and* bloom, "white" pale *and* pure, "black" is enclosing in gloom *and* darkly sheltering, "red" fleshy purple *and* gentle rose. "Silver" is the pallor of death and the sparkle of the stars. "Gold" is the glow of truth as well as "grisly laughter of gold." . . . These examples of multiple meanings are so far only two-sided. But their ambiguousness, taken as a whole, becomes but one side of a greater issue, whose other side is determined by the poetry's innermost site.

The poetic work speaks out of an ambiguous ambiguousness. Yet this multiple ambiguousness of the poetic saying does not scatter in vague equivocations. The ambiguous tone of Trakl's poetry arises out of a gathering, that is, out of a unison which, meant for itself alone, always remains unsayable. The ambiguity of this poetic saying is not lax imprecision, but rather the rigor of him who leaves what is as it is, who has entered into the "righteous vision" and now submits to it.

It is often hard for us to draw a clear line between the ambiguous saying characteristic of Trakl's poems—which in his work shows complete assurance—and the language of other poets whose equivocations stem from the vagueness of groping poetic uncertainty, because their language lacks authentic poetry and its site. The peerless rigor of Trakl's essentially ambiguous language is in a higher sense so unequivocal that it remains infinitely superior even to all the technical precision of concepts that are merely scientifically univocal.

This same ambiguity of language that is determined by the site of Trakl's poetic work also inspires his frequent use of words from the world of biblical and ecclesiastical ideas. The passage from the old to the unborn generation leads through this region and its language. Whether Trakl's poems speak in a Christian fashion, to what extent and in what sense, in what way Trakl was a "Christian," what is meant here, and indeed generally, by "Christian," "Christianity," "Christendom" and "Christlike": all this involves essential questions. But their discussion hangs in a void so long as the site of his poetic work is not thoughtfully established. Besides, their discussion calls for a kind of thorough thinking to which neither the concept of a metaphysical nor those of a church-based theology are adequate.

To judge the Christianity of Trakl's poetic work, one would have to give thought above all to his last two poems, "Lament" and "Grodek." One would have to ask: If indeed this poet is so resolute a Christian, why does he not, here in the extreme agony of his last saying, call out to God and Christ? Why does he instead name the "sister's swaying shadow" and call her "the greeting one"? Why does the song end with the name of the "unborn grandsons" and not with the confident hope of Christian redemption? Why does the sister appear also in the other late poem, "Lament" . . . ? Why is eternity called there "the icy wave"? Is this Christian thinking? It is not even Christian despair.

But what does this "Lament" sing of? In these words, "Sister . . . Look . . . ," does not an intimate ardent simplicity ring out, the simplicity of those who remain on the journey toward the "golden face of man," despite the danger of the utter withdrawal of all wholeness?

The rigorous unison of the many-voiced language in which Trakl's poetry speaks—and this means also: is silent—corresponds to apartness as the site of his work. Merely to keep this site rightly in mind makes demands on our thinking. We hardly dare in closing to ask for the location of this site. (pp. 191-93)

Martin Heidegger, "Language in the Poem: A Discussion of Georg Trakl's Poetic Work," in his On the Way to Language, *translated by Peter Hertz (translation copyright © 1971 by Harper & Row, Publishers, Inc.; reprinted by permission of Harper & Row, Publishers, Inc.; originally published as* Unterwegs zur Sprache, *Verlag Günther Neske, 1959), Harper, 1971, pp. 159-98.*

T. J. CASEY (essay date 1964)

Trakl has come to be regarded as the oracular poet, at once visionary and victim, in a manner unparalleled in German literature since the Romantics. (p. 1)

Trakl's poetry is, to use terms applied to it by [Eduard Lachmann and C. Heselhaus] respectively, laconic and hermetic. His language is foreign in Novalis' sense, . . . demanding a great deal of patient attention, though making an immediate sensuous appeal. His poetry is essentially reflective, but by way of natural description. Always spiritual, it is never abstract, for all his abstractions are personified and the very soul seems to be localized in his ghostly landscape poetry. The obvious illustration is *Landschaft* itself, though it is not really typical, as it can be read more easily than most as 'mere' description. . . . *Landschaft* is compelling in the first place for the sheer compression of its colourful imagery, but the reader soon becomes aware that the landscape, realistic in detail, is as expressionistic in composition as any surrealism. (pp. 1-2)

Read in the context of Trakl's imagery generally, *Landschaft* is seen to proceed from a pastoral-elegiac beginning, through a sequence of chthonic and erotic images, to an ending in which daylight gives way to night-light and night-life.

It is not surprising that the critics have unanimously chosen as the proper and . . . only approach to Trakl's imagery the approach of cross-reference. Yet the conclusions drawn are various and in many cases contradict one another; indeed, the critic is foredoomed if we are to believe Michael Hamburger [see excerpt above], who takes the view that 'Trakl's use of imagery, on which every interpretation of his poems must rest, was not consistent'. . . . [It] is certainly true that the critic is bound to mislead if he does not cautiously contrast and compare, but flits as the spirit moves him from image to image in Trakl's bewildering landscape. (p. 3)

There is an element of chance in any attempt to establish the basic concepts of Trakl's work as a whole by following up the cross-references of his more frequent terms, according as they happen to occur in a few selected poems. This is so even if the selection is fairly representative of his mature poetry, and the method is only possible because Trakl has a very limited, if very pure and personal register. His work could be entered upon at almost any point and we should find the same ideas and images. At the same time, *Ein Winterabend* . . . is a comparatively simple poem, and as such

a more than usually secure basis for an examination by cross-reference that it needs less than most. At any rate it has that surface simplicity by virtue of which a poem is mysteriously clear rather than obscure, oblique rather than opaque. It is a serene poem that seems to inhabit, as it were, the harmony to which it bears witness in composite images of house, inn and chapel. That the atmosphere of well-being is radiated from within is not established until the last stanza, but is already suggested in the opening image. At the same time there is a discreet development, as the nature of the homecoming is gradually discovered. The image of a single house in winter is followed by the suggestion of many people, but of many treated as one, an idea already imaginatively implicit in bell and table, the secular image of communion imperceptibly assuming the religious significance of Holy Communion. That the imagery of the poem is transfigured in the mind of the reader at some invisible point is itself a hidden analogy to the religious act of 'Wandlung'. (pp. 11-12)

'Christian' interpretations [of Trakl] can be very misleading . . . where the writers confuse an already problematic terminology by seeming to equate Christian poetry with supposedly 'positive' poems—particularly inept in the case of Trakl, where the imagery of Christian Passion may seem very oblique and even twisted in contrast to the serene celebration of the 'blue flower'. It may be noted in passing that Trakl is invariably regarded as a Christian poet in the testimony of those who were closest to him, both in their own comments and in the remarks they report or the anecdotes they relate. But it is clear that evidence of this nature does not dispose of the problem. (p. 116)

Attempting to establish Trakl's basic terms is not [hopeless] . . . , but, however consistent they may be, neither the material itself nor the method of cross-reference admits of more than relative certainty. The endless proliferation of cross-references can only be arbitrarily limited, and if it is true of poetry generally that there is no such thing as a last analysis, Trakl's is probably more ambiguous than most. One could no more exclude the Christian reference of Trakl's Fall-imagery than deny the narcissistic nature of these same images of decline and reflection. In so far as there can be any definition of his subject, perhaps the least controversial is found in the negative form of *Klage*, the lament for the 'golden image of man'. (pp. 121-22)

T. J. Casey, in his Manshape That Shone: An Interpretation of Trakl *(© Basil Blackwell & Mott, Ltd., 1964; reprinted by permission of the author), Basil Blackwell, 1964, 128 p.*

J. M. COHEN (essay date 1966)

[Trakl's failure] arose from his close imprisonment in his own imaginary world. . . . [He] is obscure only because one is uncertain what value to attach to a particular symbol. (p. 93)

Trakl's poems do not develop; they lack argument. To Rilke it did not seem inevitable that he should have expressed his feelings through the medium of words. 'A Trakl who could have exercised his genius in painting or music,' he wrote, 'would not have perished under the over-great weight of his creation, and the darkness which it brought upon him.' But the darkness did not arise from Trakl's efforts to write; it had enveloped him in his childhood, before he was a poet at all. No deflection into another medium could have saved him.

Trakl's unrelieved gloom and his narrow range of intellectual interests limit his choice of subject, but heighten the intensity of his vision. By the very economy of his means he creates a landscape all his own. 'One quickly sees,' wrote Rilke of the poem **'Sebastian im Traum' (Sebastian in Dream)**, 'that the circumstances governing this rising and falling music were individual and unrepeatable, like the conditions giving rise to a dream. Even a close spectator sees the poet's vision and insights as through a window-pane, and as if shut outside. For Trakl's experience is like the reflexions in a glass; it fills the whole of his room, which is inaccessible, like the room in a mirror.' (pp. 94-5)

[In the poems written between 1909 and 1912] Trakl turned for examples to Baudelaire, Verlaine and Rimbaud's 'Bateau Ivre'.

Such a poem as **'Menschliches Elend' (Human Misery)**—which was later renamed **'Menschliche Trauer' (Human Grief)**, while it presents a scene of suburban squalor that might derive from Baudelaire, is free from that quality of self-dramatisation that pervades *Les Fleurs du Mal*. Either because his own personality was weak, as the result of drug-taking, or because he welcomed rather than fought against the horror he saw, Trakl succeeds in removing himself from the foreground of his poems. He remains oppressively present in his symbols, yet is apparently writing of the fate of his fellow-men rather than of his own. . . . (pp. 96-7)

Yet though the symbols are all drawn from Trakl's nightmares, there is, overflowing them, a pity for mankind, and also—a motive that develops in the poetry of his last years—some hint that the poet's personal disaster was matched by some external catastrophe which threatened the world. Trakl's apocalypticism has never the strength of [Alexander] Blok's; there is nevertheless present even in his Salzburg poems, some intimation of a fallen state common to himself and to the world. (p. 97)

There are aspects of Trakl's last poems that have lately been described as Existentialist. Certainly he had read Kierkegaard; certainly there are images from Christian myth in that enigmatic sequence, **'Helian'**, for which Rilke demanded a key. But the Christian symbols were mere arbitrary constituents of his own dreams. The crisis which he foresaw was not a crisis of faith, nor the threat to civilisation of the approaching war. It was rather the fear of his own approaching madness, a terror of the consequences of his own guilt. And in his fear he glimpsed a way back, not as Nikolaus Lenau had done under similar circumstances, to the innocence of childhood, but into his private dream-world. . . . (p. 99)

Trakl's power lies in the hallucinatory nature of his disordered dreams. The choice of his pictures is small, and his view of the outer world restricted by the narrow slit of his own temperament, through which he peers. With crazy simplicity, he presents this vision as if it shows rather more of known reality than it actually does. (p. 101)

> *J. M. Cohen, "The Vision of the Apocalypse," in his* Poetry of This Age: 1908-1965 *(© J. M. Cohen 1960 and 1966), revised edition, Hutchinson University Library, 1966, pp. 84-113.**

D. J. ENRIGHT (essay date 1968)

Trakl makes use of a quite constricted range of references and images . . . and many of his poems look like variations on each other. The range of meaning is much harder to assess, because Trakl's meaning is customarily difficult to establish. It is narrow, one would venture, but by no means superficial. The usual comparison is with Hölderlin, and the similarities are obvious enough and (I would say) not very significant. For one thing, Trakl is a miniaturist, whereas even Hölderlin's shortest poems convey a sense of spaciousness. Trakl is reminiscent of the older poet in the movement of his verse, in the dignity and solemnity of its tone, which modifies severely what otherwise would be a somewhat sensational subject-matter, and occasionally also in wording and in local statement. . . .

The chief difference with Hölderlin, and it far outweighs the similarities, is this: in the poetry of his sanity (which *is* his poetry), Hölderlin is pursuing a line of thought, he is what can legitimately be called a 'philosophical poet'. The thought is there, it is of prime importance, and it can be followed with no more difficulty than is to be expected in a serious-minded author who is also a poet. What holds Trakl's poems together, in as far as they do hold together, is not a continuity of thinking. Only occasionally are these poems truly self-sufficient wholes—and I will admit that those which are, such as **'Caspar Hauser Song'**, **'The Sun'**, **'Summer'**, **Eastern Front'**, and perhaps **'Grodek'**, seem to me the most unequivocally satisfying—but more often they are a succession of images, sometimes touching, sometimes chilling, interspersed with more or less enigmatic exclamations are arbitrary assertions ('The sun desires to shine black').

For Trakl the designation that springs to mind is 'Imagist'. . . . It must be added, though, that Trakl is radically unlike the Anglo-American poets whom we know by this title: their imagist poems are light, and the meaning (such as it is) is not hard to find; his poems, whose meaning is very hard to find, convey an impression of weightiness. The Imagists are rather self-consciously performing literary manoeuvres, whereas Trakl is doing what he is driven to do.

Trakl's work has numerous references to 'decay' and 'decline', corruption and putrescence both physical and spiritual, but the verse never mimes, it maintains at such moments a cold, almost clinical air, which however is warmed by other references to the point at which the total effect is one even of tenderness. Perhaps it was this which led Rilke to say of Trakl's work in his sacerdotal manner, that 'falling is the pretext for the most continuous ascension'. Trakl was most certainly no bard of the refuse bin or the garbage cart. . . .

[Set] beside Hölderlin, Trakl has the look of a minor rather than a major poet. He could well be overestimated today, when enigmaticness is considered a sign of superiority and the fully 'made' poem is looked down on. But he is a true poet and a unique voice. . . .

> *D. J. Enright, "Blue Fruits" (© British Broadcasting Corp. 1968; reprinted by permission of Bolt & Watson Ltd, as agents for D. J. Enright), in* The Listener, *Vol. 80, No. 2065, October 24, 1968, p. 542.*

THE TIMES LITERARY SUPPLEMENT (essay date 1970)

The classic comment on Trakl's poems was made in July, 1914, by his patron, Ludwig Wittgenstein: "I do not understand them, but their *tone* delights me. It is the *tone* of a man of real genius." . . .

On the surface Trakl's autumnal landscapes (they are really objective inscapes) appear romantic in the manner of Keats's "Season of mists and mellow fruitfulness"; Trakl too seems to "fill all fruit with ripeness to the core". But it is soon clear that his autumnal colours have an historical (Spenglerian) dimension that Keats's lack; what Trakl watches with morbid fascination are the "last oozings" of a symbolical season, a decadent, spiritually moribund society. In fact Trakl is far closer to the romanticism of the blue flower, for his poetry is essentially "hieroglyphics"—for Novalis the first and highest form of art. His poetry is inward-looking in the sense that the key-images are recurrent to the point of obsession and that—as Heidegger also said—all his poems are variations on a single unwritten and unwritable poem.

Trakl was concerned to express general truths (often of a theological-historical nature) in a purely poetic manner; the self-abnegation which this demanded did not come easily to him. Kafka's sympathetic comment that Trakl had "too much imagination" is true, for the radiant obscurity of his poetry comes from its purely imaginative quality; however considerable the influence of Rimbaud, Hölderlin and Dostoevsky, the writer with whom Trakl has most in common is certainly Kafka. Trakl described his own life as "an infernal chaos of rhythms and images"; in his poetry this chaos has been transmuted into a series of visionary pictures of the chaos of the spiritually degenerate modern world. . . .

Trakl's work poses precisely the same critical problems and dangers as Kafka's. The critic is in a cleft stick, for he is continually tempted to generalize and systematize, but once he does so, he violates the work; and yet without generalization he will do less than justice to it. It is true to say that Trakl's poem is invariably a combination of all possible interpretations of it; but this only highlights the problem. From the fact that his poems are all variations on a single poem, it follows that the interpretation of any given poem must also take all the other poems into account; the interpretation of a given image will be incomplete if it does not take into account all the serial variations on that image. All is relation. Trakl may not be a "deep" poet, but his work has greater "depth" (in purely verbal terms) than that of any other modern poet. . . .

[Trakl is one] of the few giants among modern German-language poets. . . .

> *"A Single Unwritten, Unwritable Poem," in The Times Literary Supplement (© Times Newspapers Ltd. (London) 1970; reproduced from* The Times Literary Supplement *by permission), No. 3567, September 7, 1970, p. 752.*

HERBERT LINDENBERGER   (essay date 1971)

Even a quick reading of Trakl's earlier poems gives the impression of warmed-over versions of works by the more respected writers of the period. The marks of Rimbaud, Hölderlin, and Dostoevsky, the three major formative influences on Trakl's mature work, can already be found in these early poems, although at this point their influence was quite undigested. . . . Hofmannsthal, Verlaine, and Maeterlinck not only contributed a number of themes and images, but in Trakl's hands their intense lyricism often turned into a facile and vague mellifluousness. (p. 30)

I shall use the terms "early poems" and "1909 collection" synonymously to refer to these poems. . . . Although little

is known of the occasions for these poems, one thing is certain: nobody could have used them to predict the emergence of a major poet.

Despite the poor quality of the 1909 collection, some of the central concerns of Trakl's later poetry are already evident in his earliest surviving work. (pp. 30-1)

Within these early poems, Trakl explores the negative side of his poetic world much more thoroughly than he does the positive; in fact, his most frequently recurring images are centered around sickness, decay, and personal torment. (p. 32)

Besides this play of opposites, the 1909 collection also displays the basic character types and dramatic situations which recur and are further developed in Trakl's later work. The two characters who dominate his poetic world from the start are, first, the speaker-protagonist, who assumes such semblances as criminal and sufferer as well as mere observer, and, second, the sister—in the early poems she is sometimes simply an anonymous woman—who appears variously as a victim of the protagonist's violence and as a partner in incest. The protagonist is often portrayed as a kind of double, as in the poem **"Das Grauen,"** in which, after describing poisonous flowers growing out of his mouth, he suddenly recognizes himself in the mirror as Cain and concludes, "Da bin mit meinem Mörder ich allein" ("Then I am alone with my murderer"). . . . In the poem **"Naturtheater"** (**"Nature Theater"**) . . . , moreover, he views the lost innocence of his childhood as though it were taking place before him on a stage. . . . For Trakl the polarities of character are at once polarities of the outer world. (p. 35)

Just as the protagonist in Trakl's later poems moves from one role to another, so the sister alternates among the extremes. Innumerable later poems, for instance, end with a vision of her transformed into a heavenly being. As in the case of Goethe's Gretchen, whose name Trakl's sister shares, the protagonist's guilt is assuaged, as it were, by his assigning his victim a divine role in the order of things. But this role is not yet discernible in the 1909 collection. Instead, Trakl concentrates on her role as victim, which sometimes takes the specific form of an angry, wronged woman who sets off a reaction of guilt in the protagonist as soon as she confronts him. (p. 36)

Although Trakl's major themes (one might almost say obsessions) are all present, in one way or another, in his early work, his way of treating them differs radically from that characteristic of his mature period. A conspicuous feature of the style of his early verse, for example, is the predominant use of the first person. . . . In most of the mature works, on the other hand, he maintains a posture of objectivity, recording images and events usually in the third person and without the explicit intrusion of a narrator. (pp. 36-7)

[Concreteness,] impersonality, and precision . . . are the dominant characteristics in all of Trakl's poetry from late 1909 until the end of 1912. . . . (p. 41)

[In 1912,] Trakl's writing entered a new phase, characterized by radical stylistic experimentation which, in turn, enabled him to explore and define a mode of visionary experience which he had only hinted at in his earlier work.

The transition to this new mode is marked by the poem **"Psalm,"** which is not only longer than any of his earlier poems but is his first attempt at free verse since his unsuccessful early experiments with this form. **"Psalm"** has many of the features that characterize a poet's transitional work. It extends themes from his earlier work—notably through its images of hospitals and sickness—yet is also full of literary echoes that are not completely assimilated. It tries out a new tone of voice but is unable to modulate this tone with the subtlety of the later poems. It does not, for one thing, know quite where to stop. Moreover, although it contains some very memorable lines and images, it has others which seem awkward and even embarrassing. (p. 58)

["**Psalm**" anticipates a] central aspect of Trakl's later work. Despite the diversity of images within the poem, one is even more strongly aware than in his earlier poetry of two general areas of imagery which shape the poem: on one side, "idyllic" images—sounds of music and the "lost paradise" of a South Sea island—and on the other, images of desolation. A sense of desolation, indeed, dominates the poem as a whole. . . . In historical terms, one could speak of **"Psalm"** as a typical early twentieth-century "wasteland" poem; its parallels with Eliot's famous poem of the following decade are by no means exhausted through the image they hold in common of the nymphs who have departed from the modern world.

Yet the contrast between idyllic and desolate states has not been worked out in **"Psalm"** with the drama and subtlety that characterize this conflict in Trakl's subsequent work. The poem, in fact, has little real development. Except for the first stanza, with its detailed description of the lost South Sea paradise, we find only a random dispersal of images centering about the same theme. Not until the final line, "Schweigsam über der Schädelstätte öffnen sich Gottes goldene Augen" ("Silently, above the place of skulls [Golgotha], God's golden eyes are opened"), are we aware of any larger framework through which we can view and interpret the events depicted. Here, with the introduction of an eternal realm behind all earthly things, the seemingly random images are placed within a single, all encompassing perspective. Trakl creates this perspective not only through his allusion to Golgotha and the notion of God's presence in the scene but also on the most literal, visual level through the image of the "golden eyes" which silently survey the bleak panorama all around. Yet these allusions to a higher reality scarcely work to undo the general effect of desolation with which the poem is shot through. God remains at best a distant observer, a *deus absconditus*, establishing no contact with the scene below, except, perhaps, by way of some sort of passive, vicarious suffering. (pp. 60-1)

[The] central formative influence on **"Psalm"** . . . was without doubt Arthur Rimbaud. (p. 62)

Rimbaud's significance in Trakl's literary development was principally that of a catalyst. And it was Rimbaud's example (largely through *Illuminations* and *Une Saison en Enfer* [*A Season in Hell*]) which inspired Trakl to develop a type of free verse new to German literature—a free verse without explicit rhetorical connectives, and one directed to dramatizing the processes of consciousness by means of concrete images rather than by comments *upon* these processes. Indeed, it was through Rimbaud's impact on Trakl that one of the central tendencies of French Symbolism—the conception that a poem makes its statement not by direct pronouncements but through the suggestive power of objects as they are set next to one another—entered the mainstream of German poetry. When Rilke praised Trakl for his contribution

to "the liberation of the poetic figure," he referred precisely to the type of innovation which Trakl had derived from Rimbaud. (p. 63)

The full flowering of Trakl's free-verse manner occurs in **"Helian"** . . . , one of his most celebrated and difficult poems. . . . **"Helian,"** together with those of Rilke's *Duino Elegies* that date back to 1912, is probably the first major poem in German written in an uncompromisingly Symbolist style. From beginning to end one senses the vitality that accompanies the discovery of a new way of expression. The poem's essential manner—its imagery, tone, syntax, progressions, its mode of organization—is more or less representative of the remainder of Trakl's work. (p. 65)

Most attempts to interpret **"Helian"** have come to nought through the insistence of critics to read the poem as though it were an example either of Christian allegory or of what the Germans call *Erlebnislyrik*, poetry describing the author's "experience." In all too many instances, Trakl's critics have failed to take into account the poem's Symbolist background and, instead, have approached it with much the same critical technique as they would use, say, to analyze a Goethe lyric or a nineteenth-century novel. Thus, they would search through the poem for a meaningful sequence of events which could be related, in one way or another, to Trakl's life or Christian religious experience. (p. 71)

[In **"Helian"**] there is no single protagonist or central character, at least not in the conventional literary sense; instead there is a group of analogous figures—some of them benign, other afflicted with death and dissolution—who are dispersed throughout the poem in accordance with the alternating visions of death and decay.

To speak of Helian as an example of self-portraiture, as some of Trakl's critics have done, is to put the question the wrong way. In one sense, of course, we can speak of Helian, as well as such figures in later poems as Elis, Sebastian, Kaspar Hauser, and the many unnamed wanderers, strangers, and dead men, as "masks" through which Trakl speaks or reflects aspects of himself. Such an observation, however, seems less relevant than one which would approach the poem from the opposite direction: it is remarkable, one could assert, how thoroughly Trakl manages to distance himself from the "characters" of the poem. The central fact about the protagonist is not that he is a monk or a savior or even a corpse but rather that he is fragmented into many beings at once. These beings exist as though in a dream, within a dreamers' mind, one might say, yet they remain strangely independent of him; it is as if the poet could portray himself only by fragmenting himself and projecting the fragments as far distantly as possibly. If anything, Trakl's mature verse shows an extreme reticence to engage in overtly personal utterance; like other poetry in the Symbolist tradition, it deliberately rejects the Romantic convention that a poem is the overt expression of the writer's personal experience. (pp. 76-7)

After **"Helian,"** Trakl's development was never again to show the astonishingly rapid growth which took place in late 1912 and early 1913. The work of the last eighteen months of his life was essentially a consolidation of the discoveries he had made in **"Helian"** and a gradual development of several new forms and tones of voice. If we define the last year and a half in terms of language, we can speak of an increasing degree of stylization and a tendency toward personal mannerism. If we approach it by way of influence, we note a sharply decreasing dependence on Rimbaud and—though no writer was to have a comparable effect—an increased interest in Hölderlin and Dostoevsky. Thematically, the later poems consolidate a private set of images whose traces were discernible from Trakl's earliest work, but whose central terms—a world polarized by idyllic landscapes and images of decay—come more consistently to control the organization of his poems in the period after **"Helian."** In terms of formal elements, the vast majority of Trakl's remaining poems are free-verse lyrics not radically different, in their total organization or their use of the stanza form, from **"Helian"** or the shorter lyrics that came out of the so-called "'Helian'-complex." (p. 81)

[Although] each of Trakl's poems gives the illusion of being a fragment of a myth, this myth itself must not be thought of in sequential terms. It does not, in other words, have a beginning, a middle, and an end, nor any of the conventions which we normally associate with narrative. What remains constant in Trakl's poetry is not a single line of events that governs the meaning of individual poems, but rather certain sets of images which keep reappearing throughout his work in varying relationships with one another. Instead of "using" the individual poems to extrapolate some such larger narrative which seems implied in the background, the critic is, I think, on firmer ground if he starts by asking himself to precisely what effect Trakl is combining his characteristic images in a particular poem. (p. 85)

Trakl's imagery can be divided roughly into two areas: benign, pastoral images, on the one hand, and malign, often demonic images, on the other. The most common type of benign imagery is the nocturnal landscape illustrated in **"An den Knaben Elis"** [**"To the Boy Elis"**], though it can also take the form of the South Sea paradise of "Psalm" or the traditional, ordered life of the countryman in "Helian" who "carries bread and wine in clean hands." . . . Benign imagery is associated sometimes with a past world of innocence, as in the "Elis" poems and sometimes with the process of expiation. Malign images intrude in varying ways from poem to poem, and, by the same token, the relationship between the two groups of images shifts from poem to poem. Sometimes the malign images destroy a landscape of innocence while at other times benign images work to overcome a demonic landscape. Sometimes the balance remains precarious throughout a poem. Benign images at times carry unpleasant overtones, while some malign images have an unexpectedly pleasing aspect to them. Instead of a single, all-pervasive narrative that "stands behind" all the poems, there are, in effect, as many "narratives" in Trakl as there are poems—or, for that matter, as there are drafts of poems. The individual poem—even the earliest sketch for a poem—is a means by which Trakl can effect a fresh interaction among his various strains of images. Each poem becomes a new means of coping with reality. From one poem to the next, the basic components are essentially the same, but their arrangement and the feelings with which they are presented change. They are like counters in a game, shifting their values according to their position on the board. (pp. 85-6)

By constructing his poetic world out of images which have a mythical aura about them, Trakl . . . succeeds in endowing each poem with a greater range of reference than he could by means of more discursive expression. On its most literal level, **"Elis"** is a poem about the gradual extinction of Elis' world. But a statement of this kind does not even begin to exhaust the poem's range of meaning, for the poem deals at once with the process of physical death, the death of poetic inspiration, cosmic disintegration, the change of seasons from summer to winter, and the declining condition of man in human history. The complex effect of such poems is dependent upon what might seem a contradictory set of intentions: Trakl's image patterns seek to define emotions precisely, yet at the same time they open up into a remarkably wide range of meanings within the context of the individual poem. (p. 95)

[The following poems] all represent significant aspects of the final phase of Trakl's poetry. The prose poem **"Traum und Umnachtung"** (**"Dream and Madness"**) . . . fuses the methods of prose narrative with Trakl's poetic techniques to create a personal drama of visionary proportions; **"Das Gewitter"** (**"The Thunderstorm"**) . . . is written in terse, exclamatory lines and attempts a new, more assertive mode of expression; and his last poems, **"Grodek"** and **"Klage"** (**"Lament"**), . . . use Trakl's characteristic private images to come to terms with the actual cataclysm which had been hovering in his imagination all along. . . . [Many] of Trakl's late poems contain an intense, peculiarly demonic quality that manifests itself in various new forms of language in which he was experimenting during his last year. (pp. 106-07)

The lofty stance, the cosmic range, and the haunting music of Trakl's poetry now mark him, with Rilke, as perhaps the last great representative of what could be called the sublime tradition in German. . . . (p. 143)

Herbert Lindenberger, in his George Trakl *(copyright © 1971 by Twayne Publishers, Inc.; reprinted with the permission of Twayne Publishers, a Division of G. K. Hall & Co., Boston), Twayne, 1971, 166 p.*

LUCIA GETSI (essay date 1973)

For Georg Trakl the process of poetic creation is dialectical; it functions in terms of dualities and opposites. Poetic creation springs from the awareness of the schism between the aesthetic "I" and all that is not the "I," between self and "other." In Trakl's early poetry this rupture and the resulting tension is manifested as the one common to most Western cultures, between the perceiving "I" and the external world of objects. However, in Trakl's mature poetry the tension between external and internal reality becomes so tightly knit that landscapes flow into inscapes; like images in a dream, Trakl's images in the mature poetry are already one step removed from the external world from which they sprang. Everything is drawn inward in an expression of a particular intensity of atmosphere in which the poet finds himself. The self becomes a multiplicity of selves and is dispersed into all its various component selves. However, as if in a dream, the dream eye, or the controlling poetic consciousness, looks on from a distant level of being and receives the essential tone of the drama enacted before it. In this manner, Trakl could in his poems simultaneously be the murderer (or that violent aspect of self which overwhelms the external object and destroys it) and the murderer's victim, himself as well as his brother, and he could become his sister or the reverse. And just as dreams have an inner coherence, not of logic, but of mood and tone, so do Trakl's poems. All stages of emotion, all moods and tones of feeling are objectified into images. These images function as metaphors which reveal the essence of one self from the poet's multiplicity of selves and also the particular tone of the situation in which this component personality finds itself. Even though Trakl wrote out the personal "I" from his mature poetry, substituting imagistic disguises like "the lonely man" or "a dead thing," Trakl's vision, and Trakl was a visionary in the full sense of the word, is himself; or rather, his inner essential selves. (p. 3)

[There] are very few real people in Trakl's work, and none whatsoever in his later poems. There are only shapes, figures, skeletons, phantoms, and those who are as yet unborn. These apparitions are generally in motion—when motion ceases, the effect is never one of tranquility, but of instant terror or dread or despair. This dialectical motion or rhythm between the images is what gives the poems unity, both within themselves and in terms of each other.

Trakl's phantom-like images, extensions of the poet's own divided personality, move in many instances from a containment within the nature images which comprise Trakl's inscapes toward a fusion with an essential aspect of the poet's being. But the mergence of selves can rarely ever be maintained, and thus the phantoms are dispersed outward to be again fused with the nature images of the inscape. In the prose poem **"Revelation and Decline"** the earth vomits up "a child's body, a shape of moonlight, which slowly stepped from . . . (the poet's) shadow, plunged with shattered arms down a stone cataract—flakes of snow." The child's body is one of the many images Trakl uses as a metaphor for his own lost childhood, for imagination, innocence and creativity. This phantom-like image of the child comes from within the earth of the inscape, this earth being a metaphor for the shadow of the poet's self, for the ground of being and the unconscious past, and moves into fusion with an aspect of the poet's being, that particular aspect which is a severed extension in the present of the child-image in the past. But this fusion cannot be maintained. The child-image plunges again into a fusion with nature, becomes "flakes of snow," an image of dispersal, even of death. And this suggests the inability to contain the pure creativity which the child at one time held intact.

These images of dispersal, of phantom-like extensions of the poet undergoing a metamorphosis into natural imagery and then splintering, occur repeatedly. This presents an overwhelming problem for the poet; for each time an aspect of the poet's self moves toward fusion with an internalized object, that object, or image, not only is immediately separated from the self, but is dispersed, splintered and changed in form, making the next attempt at union even more difficult. And from this comes the despair so evident in Trakl's poetry. Dispersal images suggest a kind of death, an inability to recapture for eternity a part of the poet's self. . . . All of these images are metaphors which move toward and merge with an essential aspect of Trakl; the movement is from solidified, contained images to ones of dispersal and death. And although this movement suggests despair, at the same time it suggests a kind of paradoxical affirmation. Even though images, internalized objects, may change, disperse, fade or momentarily disappear, they still have an existence in the poet's mind, an existence which is transmuted into other types of existence with which the poet may again seek union. Because nothing ever vanishes from the inscape, even though it may be changed in form, a harmony between disparate elements of self continues to remain in the realm of possibility.

Because all the phantoms in Trakl's poetry are internalized extensions or objectifications of essences in the poet's own personality, any love that is manifest in the poetry is a love of and for the self. Thus we find no real love poems, or poems in which the poet seeks a union with an external object and allows that object to speak for itself through the medium of his being. The closest Trakl's poems ever come to love is when the sister image occurs. Whether or not the poems refer to Trakl's own sister Margarete is beside the point, for in the poems the sister image becomes a feminine extension of part of the poet's personality. (pp. 4-5)

Trakl's treatment of the sister image in his poems is ambiguous. At times this image brings about a terrible guilt, a destruction, or a total engulfment in darkness. . . . In ["**Dream and Derangement**"] while the poem's speaker is thinking of passionate things ("his thoughts afire") the sister image appears as a "flaming demon in a coat of hair. . . . When they awoke, the stars died above their heads." Then, probably because of the union implied by the last sentence, images of guilt follow. . . . [Many] times the sister image occurs within this context of symbolic guilt. This is understandable if one keeps in mind that the sister image is but an extension of an essential aspect of the poet, and that any love union which happens does not arise from a need to give expression to the sister for herself, but rather from a need to obliterate the sister image by overwhelming it, bringing it into a forced union with the poet's self. However, there are other poems in which no physical union is implied, and in these the sister image appears in contexts of almost complete, if melancholy, serenity, as in . . . **"Revelation and Decline"**. (p. 6)

One of Trakl's most tranquil poems is in itself a hymn entitled **"To the Sister."** Although God has "twisted" her eyelids, has distorted her vision and has therefore, by implication, caused her madness, perhaps even because He has done this to her, she is a "child of the Passion," and "at night stars seek the arch of her brow." In this poem we can see the possibility of a redemptive function in the sister-image. As a "child of the Passion" she is born within sacrifice, born from the sacrifice of the poet's self as well as from the sacrifice, born from the sacrifice of herself in becoming an extension of the poet. She is his creation, and is therefore the symbolic embodiment of his sacrifice. She must, in order to yield a sense of tranquility, remain an extension of the "I." The "I" must remain fragmented, objectified into internalized objects, must continue to be sacrificed in order for the sister, functioning almost like a "Magna Mater" figure, to lead it to rebirth into a higher innocence. The "I" cannot return to the innocence of the primordial child; thus the guilt and damnation inherent in the attempt at a complete, almost physical, union with the sister. The poet must achieve innocence, creativity on a higher plane, even if it is a plane of inner reality cut off completely from the external world. Thus the sister-image brings guilt and violent destruction only when she, and her madness, is raped, is overwhelmed by a forced union with the poet's own. Her madness, the feminine projection of the poet's, is a madness in which creative energy and beauty are possible. The poet's own madness is filled with despair, with "Umnachtung," the decline of reason, insanity which lives in its own private, dark vision. When the sister image comes into direct contact with an aspect of the poet's being, the result is fear, guilt and damnation. This type of narcissism, an aesthetic love of self only and not a love of objects for themselves and their essential functions, brings about the guilt. The poet damns himself with each union he forces upon the sister image, for this means death to her existence and to the possibility of a higher form of innocence and creativity which she sustains. The sister image itself does not bring on the damnation; when allowed to remain at an aesthetic distance from the being of the poet, the function of the sister image is redemptive in nature. (p. 7)

The poem which would ultimately serve to unite all the disparate elements of Trakl's aesthetic self was never written. All the images which suggest the paradise of pure and natural, creative innocence are internal objectifications of the poet's self which are cut off from the external world of objects; and from this severance and the type of self love it generates arises the guilt so evident in the poetry. When the poet seeks to bring these extensions of self, all aspects of his personality, into the composite, conscious and symbolically physical union, which is the ultimate aim of this kind of aesthetic narcissism, damnation and despair result. Yet even within the damnation and the guilt, Trakl's images are still shadows of a paradise that, lost to external reality as it is, is transformed into psychic, creative energy within the inner reality of the poet's vision. And within this inner reality and in the midst of terrible disintegration and despair, harmony and even the way leading to a higher plane of innocence and creativity beyond both the primal child and the man are still affirmed possibilities. For Georg Trakl the dialectic of the poetic process was both his damnation and the method of attaining harmony and self-completion. The world of poetry became the only world which could give space back to being; the poem was being's affirmation. (pp. 11-12)

> *Lucia Getsi, "The Poetry of Georg Trakl," in Poems by Georg Trakl, translated by Lucia Getsi (copyright © 1973 by Lucia Getsi), Mundus Artium Press, 1973, pp. 3-12.*

MAIRE JAANUS KURRIK (essay date 1974)

Trakl's work starts out from silence. Every critic has been struck by Trakl's intimacy with silence and emptiness.... The void surrounding Trakl's words is the crucial dimension of his verse out of which things emerge as in the voided state of consciousness in sleep. Trakl's poetry presents the phenomenon of a transference to language, provoked by his existence in the void. He did not experience language as an objective given that can be used and molded, but as the shape of his true inner inexpressible self. From the first, all the words that did not express his inner being were abolished. They were less authentic than silence. However, silence was also terrifying, as terrifying in fact as it can only be when language is invested with all of reality and identified with self. (p. 9)

Even the juvenilia, Trakl's earliest, rather unoriginal, and aesthetically valueless poems, prose, and drama-fragments ... are interesting in what they reveal about his attitude to language. At this point Trakl experiments with a variety of verse forms and borrows heavily—but the very restlessness of the adolescent imitations and experimentations serves to point to his discontent with the poetic language that he inherits. The discontent emerges more clearly in the poetry itself as a continual lament and complaint about language as impotent, sterile, and incapable of incarnating experience or the self. (p. 10)

More valid for Trakl than the linguistic sphere are the verbally less easily definable semiconscious states of feeling, revery, intuition, and dream, and the voice of the sexual instincts. (p. 11)

[One of Trakl's letters] acknowledges that melody is a way of shutting out the voices of instinctual life Trakl hears "howling in his blood," and which he evidently cannot deal with.... Initially, Trakl's repression appears to be successful.

A number of [the poems from the 1909 to 1912 period] are harmonious, positively toned, and superficially they can be read as mood lyrics or romantic ballads, for example, **"The Beautiful City"** and **"The Young Maid."** Read glancingly they need not strike one as being particularly personal. But in the light of Trakl's own confession, a poem such as **"The Rats"** is clearly an example of the instinctual life returning in a derivative and distanced form. Also the tone of melancholy which insinuates itself even into the most harmonious and positive poems is too marked and persistent not to be noticed—and to be noticed especially as something that somehow always misses its object or is beyond it or in excess of it—a seemingly separate, objectless affect. Finally, in the latter half of this period a kind of anxiety about the ghostly, incomprehensible nature of a gyrating, unreal, or often senselessly repulsive or threatening reality seems to develop. And such anxiety is a sign that the repression is failing. This cycle of repression, its failure, and the return of the repressed in the form of anxiety or dread comes to be a fundamental one in Trakl's work. (pp. 12-13)

"Soul of Life," a rhymed poem written approximately in the middle of this first period, shows in a particularly discordant form some of the tensions and contradictory ways of representation that characterize this period. (p. 15)

The discourse in the first two stanzas is ... acausal, discontinuous, somewhat mysterious, and eerie ... [What] matters is the lack not only of obvious connections between lines and images but also of clear distinctions between nature and man, animate and inanimate, mobile and immobile, inside and outside, subject and object.... We are not in the presence of an ensouled landscape where subject and object interpenetrate each other or stand for each other, but have merely the suggestive remnant of such a process. We are rather in the world of dreams where transitions, events, and things simply occur, or appear, or are in their own reality. It is a world of irrational conjunctions where configurational perceptions are registered merely by contiguity. (p. 16)

If we study this poem in the context of his other poems from this period, we find that it is merely a new and different constellation of images that have already been constituted. Trakl's reservoir of analogies and imaginative stimulants is not the outer world or perception, but his inner world, his own poetry. For example, the line "The sister's mouth whispers in black branches" is a new and more striking formulation of a basic image of something taking place through trees which occurs in other poems.... Trakl's excessive dependence on self-repetition suggests a withdrawal into the self where the search continues for another reality, differently constituted, which would allow him to escape both the pressures of outer reality and those that arise from within. (pp. 17-18)

The second phase of Trakl's development, which begins late in the year 1912 and which includes all but a handful of poems written in the late spring and summer of 1914 before his death, is the most remarkable and most creative phase of his life; it is the period which makes him, in the words of a *Times Literary Supplement* reviewer [see excerpt above], one of "the few giants among modern German-language poets." On the whole, it is a period in which we see the elaboration of an increasingly fantastic substitute reality and its collapse. At first the substitute reality aims to construct an ideal imagined past. Later a violently antithetical fantasy world of good and evil seeks to replace the real world. (pp. 18-19)

Reading the poems of this and his final phase can make one feel as if Trakl had personally discovered the arbitrary character of linguistic signs. . . . We are stunned and confused by what appears to be an entirely willful use of language; we are tempted to pass Trakl's poems off as mere play with words together with the numerous critics who have done so. . . . (p. 19)

Trakl's words, isolated in silence, have both a vertical and a horizontal dimension. By horizontal I mean the inevitable rootedness of language in conventional meanings and associations and in an etymological, social, and mythical history. Here the word becomes "encyclopaedic," open to the totality of associations that can be made with it. On the horizontal level, Trakl's poetry is ambiguous, capable of multiple, uncertain, and ever doubtful interpretations. It is the horizontal dimension, for example, to which Trakl's aura of rootedness in a mythical and Christian tradition must be connected. . . . By vertical I mean the purely personal and psychic dimension of language which is rooted in the closed recollections of the person, in the depths of his own personal and secret mythology and biology. Here the individual determines what a word refers to by his own private and closed use of the word. (p. 22)

On the vertical level Trakl's poetry is not ambiguous, but ambivalent, under the sway of contrary impulses. Because it is the vertical level which dominates in Trakl, traditional, classical criticism with its emphasis on the horizontal dimension misses most of what is the essence of Trakl. However, the attempts to track down Trakl's private use of words by compiling concordances and by using cross-reference approaches in order to delimit and to define the associational complexes surrounding his words and thereby also their meaning for him have not been successful. We find that there are no distinct associational complexes because they all intertwine with each other in one undefinable and unlimited complex. Thus where we hope to find a limit and a definition we find arbitrariness or a mass of material too large to be digested. We also find that the meaning of some of his most characteristic words is determinably ambivalent, that "silver," for example, can signify both guilt and guiltlessness, but that the ambivalence of other words exceeds pure opposition, for both antithetical meanings may be displaced in yet another context of merely contiguous and undefinable words. Still, if we assume then that the words in Trakl are largely arbitrary and that their significance is to be critically determined anew in each poem, we find that they are definitely bound, if not to an absolute meaning, at least to one modality of feeling or another in the poem. . . . But to be harried back and forth between a sense of meaninglessness and meaning, a sense that the words are absolutely arbitrary and fixed in an undefinable meaning, is an experience in madness.

One difference between Trakl and the Symbolists is that he did not arrive at his modernist poetic practice with its emphasis on the word by any conscious theory or method. He also did not court the experience of derangement as Rimbaud did; it overwhelmed him. In theory the Symbolists stressed the necessity of separating the expressive capacity of words from their abstract, creative capacity. . . . The Symbolist poets sensed that there is an impersonal and objective dimension in language itself or a creative mechanism within it which is beyond our conscious control. However, in Trakl the word is purged of conventional language and meaning in order to reveal not the abstract, creative power of the word but the unconscious and censured dimension of the individual. Also, his identification with the word did not allow him to experience the "liberation" of the word or a language dominated by unconcious processes as a positive condition.

His art is not, like Rimbaud's or Blake's, an attempt at mystical experience and visions of another outer dimension. Nor is it a mere experiment, a game with words, or an arbitrary, willful art of combinations. For Trakl the world of unconscious discourse with its mechanisms of condensation and displacement involved being in touch with what was the opposite of willful: the world of involuntary statements. The experience of an uncontrollable, arbitrary, and yet compulsive language must only have exacerbated his feeling of isolation and unreality—his sense of helplessness, impotence, and enervation and the feeling that he lacked control over himself and the world. Thus it seems difficult to speak of this phase as one of "visionary freedom." The poetry shows that he experienced his visionary existence as a painful kind of compulsion to reflect on himself and to order what seemed incapable of being ordered. What has often been called Trakl's narcissism is appallingly similar to the unloving self-scrutiny and the compulsive inspection of one's own mental and bodily processes that R. D. Laing describes as common in schizophrenia. (pp. 22-5)

Just as Trakl's discontinuous images of his first phase originated partly from his discontinous relationship to himself and the real world, so the oneiric and alienated language of [his] later phase suggests a secondary, more radical split within the true, melodic self. The identifiable, definable ego—the pronoun "I"—loses its primacy and disappears from his verse altogether in this phase. The "I" becomes volatilized, unreal, and more and more engaged in fantasized relationships with its own phantoms. It sinks back into the greater anonymity and flux of the more impersonal and unindividuated state where the ego can be another, or an object, or a series of others, and have many names, but not that of the simple, unifying "I." Thus, it is in this phase that Trakl creates his series of, one could almost say, epiclike poems about his newly divided and, hence, in a sense enlarged self: **"Helian," "Elis," "Caspar Hauser Song,"** and **"Sebastian in Dream."** All these figures are projections of himself in a substitute, fantasy reality and passive purveyors of its visions. (pp. 27-8)

But for the visual-temporal structure that Trakl forged in his mature verse, his poems present us with a co-presence of things without fusion. The theme of self-reflection is distinguishable, but the reflection remains caught in itself and its self-fantasies, self-bounded, repetitious, vain, and incapable of delivering itself of its own magic circle of language. The effort to establish a coherent, continuous self is frustrated by interferences suggestive of internal conflicts that cannot be reached and hence, cannot be solved. The relations between the split parts of the self become extremely complex and, in part, sadomasochistic; the questions of guilt or innocence—which self is guilty of what?—become paradoxical and unresolvable. The problematic, diseased emotional life ruptures the conjoining, healing efforts of fantasy. . . . Trakl fought disintegration by an abiding musical and painterly sense. Thus it becomes comprehensible why Trakl's variants are often determined by sound, by the desire to retain, for example, a certain sequence of vowels. A vowel sequence is a form of containment and order, a remnant, moreover, of his beautiful world of melos. Order, albeit one of abstract formal relationships, and sublanguage coherence seem in any event to be more primary than meaning when the issue at stake is loss of being. (pp. 28-9)

Toward the latter half of this second phase Trakl's images break. The most basic metaphors of all, the bodily metaphors, are destroyed: eyes, mouth, head, arms, the human frame are shattered or broken. **"Sink"** comes to be the most common verb of his mature poetry and the transformation of images comes to be, as in **"Nightsong,"** an experience of their sinking away: "O how everything sinks into the dark." The phenomenon of sinking into the semiconscious state of harmony, which was observable in the first phase, together with the phenomenon of reduction and loss, is now dominant. (p. 31)

[A] tremendous ethical obsession in the latter part of Trakl's second phase . . . [is] an attempt to resolve his ambivalence in ethical and religious categories. (pp. 32-3)

Ambivalence, the fact that every tendency is balanced by a contrary one, is normal; the manifest struggle between opposites that we see in Trakl is not. He is in the grip of a compulsion to produce contrary associations—a phenomenon that E. Bleuler called "negative suggestibility"—where the control of the psyche is too weak to promote or inhibit either the positive or negative approach. (p. 33)

Trakl's prose poems **"The Transformation of Evil," "Dream and Benightedness,"** and **"Revelation and Decline"** are attempts to escape the intolerably exacerbated ambivalence by stressing the negative associations. In these poems Trakl presents himself relentlessly as guilty. They are a complete and stark autobiography of the nightmarish visions and hallucinations in which he lived. They are an account of the "black hell of his heart," "the stony hell" in which his "countenance died." (p. 34)

If the unbearable visions at the end of the second phase indicate a return of the repressed in a violent and dreadful form, with personal visions of punishment, murder predominating, then Trakl's terse, impersonal, and prophetic poems of 1914, with their visions of cosmic disaster, indicate the return of an expulsion from without in the form of visionary hallucinations. (p. 39)

It is the return of the expulsed powerfully from without that gives these poems their character of having won back a sense of reality, as most critics put it. But the sense of reality is there, not because Trakl reestablished a contact with the concrete things represented by words, but rather because he lost this contact utterly. His disease gives his language the status of the real. The experience of schizophrenia is most likely the tragic, psychic history behind what has often been called, not inaccurately but on other grounds, Trakl's unconscious signaling of the reality of the Great War in his last poems.

What distinguishes the handful of poems of Trakl's final phase in 1914 from the poems of the second phase is that in them we confront what may be called schizophrenic language

rather than dream language. The transference to language has now become an absolute and exclusive identification with words alone. Trakl's final substitution and reconstruction is the world and the self as the word. . . . Trakl's last style is a nominal style. Language is reduced primarily to nouns, which are closer to the roots of words and of language as such. On the one hand, the simplification reduces the possibility of ambivalence, the necessity and dread of word choices and sentence elaboration through verbs, adjectives, and so on. On the other hand, single words now stand for what were formerly entire images, or whole sentences, or possibly even poems. The word-condensation is extreme. The radically truncated style leaves no room for the earlier long, elegiac lines, or for the work of dream-formation: for the creation of strange time-spaces, the transformation of words into preverbal visual images, the theatrical staging of the self in various situations, or the self-perceptions of the libido in visions. . . . Trakl's last cathexis is to words. But by this final maneuver of reduction Trakl also possesses his world as never before. All obstruction is eliminated; the word is instinct and energy, essence and authority; it can exclaim, lament, or condemn in a demonic and prophetic way in its uninhibited power. (pp. 40-1)

The final Trakl poem is like a set of words caught in a space of mirrors. In the poems the word is cut off both from the images that the unconscious could bring it and from the concrete idea that consciousness could contribute. It is a language excommunicated from the interior and the exterior world; it designates nothing in any direction. But it is powerfully dynamic and dramatic, nonetheless, because it is naked primary process. (p. 44)

The deranged mind cannot create the intelligible symbolic discourse that is the privilege of the authentic indissoluble imagination, but it can without cessation strive to fasten the awfulness of derangement in formal patterns. It would seem important to accept and understand the mute radiance of Trakl's art not despite his disease, or by repressing the fact of his disease, but only together with it because we will better understand the art that we have always valued when we bring an art carved purely out of the unconscious into our total perspective of what art is. (p. 45)

Maire Jaanus Kurrik, in his Georg Trakl *(Columbia Essays on Modern Writers Pamphlet No. 72; copyright © 1974 Columbia University Press; reprinted by permission of the publisher),* Columbia University Press, *1974, 48 p.*

ADDITIONAL BIBLIOGRAPHY

Brown, Russell E. "Time of Day in Early Expressionist Poetry." *PMLA* 84, No. 1 (January 1969): 20-8.
    Uses time of day ("that imaginary time in which the poem is most likely to take place'") as a means for comparing Trakl, Georg Heym, and Ernst Stadler, stating that Trakl's poems "take place" mostly at evening.

Calbert, Joseph P. *Dimensions of Style and Meaning in the Language of Trakl and Rilke: Contributions to a Semantics of Style.* Tubingen, Germany: Max Niemeyer Verlag, 1974, 247 p.
    Linguistic analysis of Trakl's poetry, using the manner in which the language of his poems deviates from "normal" (non-poetic) language as a means to describe the nature of his literary "style."

This is a highly technical study employing a correspondingly technical vocabulary.

Harries, Karsten. "Language and Silence: Heidegger's Dialogue with Georg Trakl." *boundary 2* IV, No. 2 (Winter 1976): 495-511.
   Examines Heidegger's interpretation of Trakl's poetry from the perspective of the poet's "one unwritten poem" (see excerpt above).

Kritsch, Erna. "The Synesthetic Metaphors in the Poetry of Georg Trakl." *Monatshefte* LIV, No. 1 (January 1962): 69-77.
   Studies the use in Trakl's poetry of synesthesia, the description of one kind of sense impression in terms of another (loud color, for example).

Lindenberger, Herbert. "The Play of Opposites in George Trakl's Poetry." *German Life & Letters* XI, No. 3 (April 1958): 193-204.
   Sees opposition in Trakl's poetry characterized on the one hand "by images of decay and dissolution" and on the other by "idealized pastoral landscapes."

Lindenberger, Herbert. "A Study in Influence and Development." *Comparative Literature* X, No. 1 (Winter 1958): 21-35.
   Compares the lives and works of Trakl and the French symbolist poet Arthur Rimbaud.

Lyon, James K. "Georg Trakl's Poetry of Silence." *Monatshefte* 62, No. 4 (Winter 1970): 340-56.
   Examines Trakl's "near obsession with the phenomenon of silence" as a poetical means of expressing what is beyond the power of words to describe.

Marson, E. L. "Trakl's *Grodek*—Towards an Interpretation." *German Life and Letters* n.s. XXVI, No. 1 (October 1972): 32-8.
   Close reading of the images and language of this poem, considering it "some kind of 'final statement'" of Trakl's.

Schier, Rudolf D. "'Afra': Towards and Interpretation of Trakl." *The Germanic Review* XLI, No. 4 (November 1966): 264-78.
   Analysis of "Afra" as the interplay between romantic "natural language" and post-romantic "figural language," and Trakl's attempt to transcend both.

Sheppard, R. W. "Georg Trakl's *Grodek:* The Text and Two Translations." *Modern Languages* LII, No. 3 (September 1971): 124-32.
   Technical linguistic analysis of this poem.

Sokel, Walter H. "Poeta Dolorosus." In his *The Writer in Extremis: Expressionism in Twentieth-Century German Literature*, pp. 55-82. Stanford: Stanford University Press, 1959.*
   Biographical sketch and basic introduction to the major themes of Trakl's poetry.

Ramón (María) del Valle-Inclán (y Montenegro)

1866-1936

(Pseudonym of Ramón José Simón Valle y Peña) Spanish dramatist, novelist, poet, and essayist.

Valle-Inclán contributed more to the modernization of twentieth-century Spanish drama than any other artist except Federico García Lorca. He invented his own genre: the *esperpento*, in which all the elements of drama are satirically distorted to create Goyaesque worlds of horror and comedy. In addition to the *esperpentos*, Valle-Inclán is best known for his four *Sonatas*, the elegantly styled, fictive memoirs of the rakish Marquís de Bradomín.

Raised in a family of disinherited aristocrats, Valle-Inclán longed from the beginning for the dignity of his country's past. After spending his youth in Galicia, whose primitive Celtic customs and rugged landscape colored his early prose, he traveled to Mexico, where he worked as a journalist. Valle-Inclán returned to Galicia in 1893, becoming known as a bohemian eccentric, raconteur, and would-be writer, with a mysterious past and an impressive pen name.

Valle-Inclán's career can be divided into two periods. In the first, extending from 1895 until World War I, his writing is characterized by its polished *fin-de-siècle* decadence, reminiscent of Barbey d'Aurevilly and Gabriel D'Annunzio. His first book was a collection of stories entitled *Femeninas*, published in 1895. In the next few years Valle-Inclán presented the eroticism and adventure of the romantic past in a colorful, exquisitely crafted style that linked him with the decadents of the era, in sharp contrast to members of the socially conscious Generation of 1898. He projected an exaggerated portrait of himself in the Marquís de Bradomín of *Sonata de otoño*, the first and most accomplished of the *Sonatas* (collectively translated as *The Pleasant Memoirs of the Marquis of Bradomin*). The *Sonatas* brought him his first fame. Other prominent works of the first part of Valle-Inclán's career include: the first two *comedias bárbaras*, *Aguila de blason* and *Romance de lobos*, concerning his other great character, Don Juan Manuel de Montenegro; *Flor de santidad;* and the trilogy *La guerra carlista.*

World War I, with its technologically wrought mass-slaughter, aroused Valle-Inclán's wrath against industrialization, the military, and the customs by which people are manipulated and impoverished. This led to his second period. Valle-Inclán served as a war correspondent on the Western Front during World War I, recording his impressions in *La media noche*. After the war his attitudes and writings about society, its conventions, and Spain's past aligned more closely with the thinking of the Generation of 1898. The first *esperpento*, *Luces de bohemia (Lights of Bohemia)*, appeared in 1920. The others,—like the first, distorting their elements as would a funhouse mirror—are *Los cuernos de don Friolera*, *La hija del capitán*, and *Las galas del difunto*. Unlike his prewar work, Valle-Inclán's *esperpentos* deal with contemporary life, containing satire directed "against the army, against the preoccupation with outworn shibboleths, against the concept of patriotism propagated by cheap literature, against customs and institutions," according to J. L. Brooks. His novels continue in the same vein, the best of these being *Tirano Banderas (The Tyrant)*. Valle-Inclán did not live to complete a projected nine-volume series of novels subtitled *El ruedo ibérico*, which began as a blistering indictment of Isabella II's corrupt government.

Valle-Inclán was admired by the Spanish writers of his era, though many critics dislike his work for its eroticism, cruelty, and general bizarreness of theme and manner. Spain's government perceived seditious intent in Valle-Inclán's later work, and on one occasion he was jailed. Today, Valle-Inclán is recognized as one of the most influential Spanish writers of his time.

PRINCIPAL WORKS

Femeninas (short stories) 1895
Epitalamio (novella) 1897
La cara de Dios (novel) 1900
Sonata de otoño: Memorias del Marqués de Bradomín (novel) 1902
Jardín umbrio (short stories) 1903
Sonata de estío: Memorias del Marqués de Bradomín (novel) 1903
Flor de santidad (novel) 1904

*Sonata de primavera: Memorias del Marqués de
    Bradomín* (novel) 1904
Sonata de invierno: Memorias del Marqués de Bradomín
    (novel) 1905
**Aguila de blasón: Comedia bárbara* (drama) 1907
Aromas de leyenda (poetry) 1907
Los cruzados de la causa: La guerra carlista, I (novel)
    1908
Romance de lobos: Comedia bárbara (drama) 1908
Gerifaltes de antaño: La guerra carlista, III (novel)
    1909
El resplandor de la hoguera: La guerra carlista, II
    (novel) 1909
La marquesa Rosalinda (drama) 1912
Voces de gesta (drama) 1912
La lampara maravillosa: Ejercicios espirituales (essays)
    1916
La media noche (essays) 1917
La pipa de kif (poetry) 1919
**Divinas palabras* (drama) 1920
El pasajero (poetry) 1920
**Cara de plata: Comedia bárbara* (drama) 1923
Luces de bohemia (drama) 1924
    [*Lights of Bohemia* published in journal *Modern
        International Drama*, 1968]
Los cuernos de don Friolera (drama) 1925
Tirano Banderas (novel) 1926
    [*The Tyrant*, 1929]
La corte de los milagros: El ruedo ibérico, I (novel)
    1927
La hija del capitán (drama) 1927
Viva mi dueño: El ruedo ibérico, II (novel) 1928
Las galas del difunto (drama) 1930
Baza de espadas: El ruedo ibérico, III (unfinished novel)
    1958

*These four novels were translated and published as *The Pleasant
Memoirs of the Marquís de Bradomín* in 1924.

**These are the dates of first publication rather than first perfor-
    mance.

SALVADOR de MADARIAGA (essay date 1922)

[The] Gallegan and the Castilian types differ profoundly, both
in language and in character. The Gallegan language may be
shortly described as Portuguese free from the nasal developments which true Portuguese evolved under French influence. Gallegan is thus softer and more melodious than Castilian, and as superior to Castilian in lyrical quality as inferior
to it in dramatic power. (p. 129)

The admirable efflorescence of the Gallegan muse which took
place in the thirteenth and fourteenth centuries has been
sometimes explained as being due to the influence of Provençal poetry.... The hypothesis is both insufficient and
unnecessary, for ... it overlooks the fact that in its most
truly felt and moving, as well as in its most original, varieties,
Gallegan lyrical poetry was popular, that is, born in the layers
least likely to be reached by an art expressed in a foreign
language. There is, moreover, a striking difference in spirit
between the two kinds of poetry, for, while form in the art
of Provence is drawn out according to intellectual devices,

form in Gallegan poetry is inspired by a musical feeling which
is so closely in harmony with the character of the country
that its main features remain to this day as typically its own.
(pp. 129-30)

In its sense of melody, in its quaint grace, in its gift of emotion,
the poetry of Galicia is distinctly un-Castilian. Two remarks
made on its mediaeval forms remain true to this day. It is
a poetry concerned with love almost to the exclusion of any
other theme, and it is generally conceived from the point of
view of women, often indeed created by women. Thus, it is
three times feminine: in its point of view (if not in its actual
origin); in the predominance of the subject of love; and in
its tenderness. We may add another feminine feature, a sense
of form which is not external and intellectual, but internal
and musical, and directly due to emotion. (p. 130)

The Gallegan spirit is to-day admirably ... represented in
Spanish letters by a poet and novelist of great talent, imagination, and artistic ability: Don Ramón María del Valle Inclán. (p. 131)

Valle Inclán is, amongst contemporary Spanish poets, the
most gifted in musical and formal powers. The peculiar charm
of his poetry is largely due to the interplay, and to a certain
extent, the opposition, of two tendencies traceable to the two
features of old Gallegan poetry: a popular vein, rich in emotion and rhythm, and a knowing taste for the formal refinements evolved by the exquisite genius of France.... It is
the fresh country-like smell of apples which predominates
in his *Aromas de Leyenda*. In this book of poems ...,
Galicia—a Galicia perhaps a little old-fashioned and beau-
tified—is sung with its quiet hills, its wandering flocks and
shepherds, its hermits and pilgrims, its grey atmosphere,
which covers with a protective mantle dreams ever rising
and never-dying beliefs. In this, his most truly poetical mood,
Valle Inclán goes to the people for his inspiration. Every one
of the poems of the book rises as it were from the contemplation of a popular song, in Gallegan, which is quoted at the
end.... Together with [the] human emotion which he finds
in the earth of his native land, our poet reveals in these poems
his delicate sensibility for the perception of the most elusive
aspects of nature and an exceptional power of rendering them
without apparent effort, as if by the simplest possible device.
This device is indeed quite simple. It consists in giving to
each word its full poetic power ... but that cannot be done
unless the things themselves which the words represent have
impressed on the poet's soul all the poetic power which they
possess. And it is here, in his capacity for poetical impression,
that this Gallegan poet probably surpasses every poet that
ever wrote Castilian since Garcilaso. (p. 134)

He resembles Garcilaso also in his capacity for assimilating
foreign refinement. It is not Italy, nowadays, but France,
which leads the evolution of poetical forms. Valle Inclán
knows all the professional secrets of the art of ... Baudelaire
and Verlaine, of Régnier and Viellé-Griffin. And yet it can
hardly be said that he has studied them. The graces of French
art seem to flourish naturally in this poet.... It is this measure in emotion (which reminds us that *Gallegan* and *Gallic*
have the same root) that makes our poet, though Spanish in
temperament and vision, French in taste and in form. His
emotion, even though genuine, is easily mastered, and as it
were projected outwards into the world whence it came. The
poet knows how to place himself at the right distance for the
fashioning of his impression into a work of art. Valle Inclán
is in fact that *rara avis* in Spanish letters: an artist.

The masterpiece of his courtly 'French' style, is his ***Marquesa Rosalinda***. This little poetical comedy is a unique gem in Castilian poetry. It proves in most brilliant fashion that that masculine language which seems fit only for the forcible accents of the epic ballad, the intense lyricism of the mystics, the grandiloquence of the conventional ode and the metallic blasts of warlike songs, can be rendered as slim and graceful as a Versailles *marquise*, as subtle as an eighteenth-century *abbé*, as nonchalant as a Verlainian decadent, as exquisitely humorous as a musical comedy of Mozart. The plot is conceived and developed in that half-serious, half-jesting mood which is the real mood of true comedy, so easy, yet so difficult to attain. . . . [Valle Inclán's] playful mood, not entirely frivolous but nearly so, delicately intellectual though not devoid of feeling, is more complex, more *precious* than is usual in Spanish literature. (pp. 134-36)

In its rhythmical grace *La Marquesa Rosalinda* is without rival in the language. Every scene is sung in its right melody, every line rings true, every word weds sound and sense in most felicitous harmony. . . . Yet all is not Gallegan—whether rustic or courtly—in Valle Inclán. This name itself is too much in a major key to let us forget the heroic strain in the poetry which makes it illustrious. The poet who sang a pastoral rhapsody in his *Aromas de Leyenda*, who told a courtly and witty tale in his *Marquesa Rosalinda*, has proved that his voice can rise to the epic tone in a dramatic poem of great beauty: *Voces de Gesta*. . . . It is a poem, modern in the polish of its form, in the impeccable use of language and style, in the deliberate play of its effects, and in the skilful resources of its orchestration; but old in its primitive vision of the human soul, with its virtues still fresh in the light of man's morning and its passions still roaming free like wolves in the unexplored forests of new lands. This contrast between a tempestuous, primeval nature and the refined art which reflects it like an impassive, limpid glass, might have given to *Voces de Gesta* the cold perfection of Parnassian poetry, were it not, again, for the popular element which restores to it the humility, the movement, and the warmth of life.

Now the epic-dramatic genius is not typically Gallegan, but Castilian. Don Ramón María del Valle Inclán is thus a Gallegan assimilated by Castile. He brings to Castilian poetry the distinctive lyrical gift of his land, but the strong dramatic power of the Centre finds in him so quick a response that he becomes one of its most inspired exponents. Nor is it possible to consider *Voces de Gesta* as a mere incursion into a kind of poetry foreign to his usual bent. Far from it. Drama is an inherent and most important element in his genius, so much so that it is perhaps by the consideration of this side of his art that his literary personality can be best understood.

The three elements of the poetry of Valle Inclán—the lyrical-popular, the lyrical-courtly, and the epic-dramatic—reappear in his fiction. It is indeed doubtful whether a decision between poetry and fiction is possible in a work which is so imaginative in its poetical forms and so poetical in its novels. Our poet will have nothing to do with the humdrum world in which we all live. In the same haughty manner in which he passes through our modern matter-of-fact streets, . . . so he presents to the noisy and busy multitudes that struggle for comfort and thirst for justice and truth, an art indifferent to modern ideals and devoted to the glorification of the passions. . . . [The Marquis of Bradomín, the hero of the four *Sonatas* collected as *The Pleasant Memoirs of the Marquis of Bradomin*,] like the poet who created him, contemplates man in a purely

æsthetic attitude and admires the passions for their inherent beauty as forces of nature manifesting their prime vigour in that most noble of creatures, man. . . . He therefore recoils instinctively from the city, with its well-thought-out system of laws which impose upon every man a certain minimum of virtue and curb the passions under the weight of municipal regulations. His inspiration is kindled in those corners of Spain where there still lingers—or lingered when he wrote, for such things nowadays die out quickly—a life ruled by the primitive traditions of peasantry and chivalry: below, humility towards the lords of the land, stretching from heroic devotion to abject servility; above, a natural authority founded on courage and high traditions, an egotism degenerating towards licence and tyranny; and over all, high and low, the deeply rooted beliefs of a devotional religion enfolded in clouds of superstition, yet able to put the light of a meaning and the warmth of a hope into the most miserable life.

It is this primitive world in which the passions grow richer and purer than in our urban civilizations, where, like the trees of our cities, our passions are lightless and cheerless and covered with the grime and ashes of our hearths, it is this primitive world that Valle Inclán describes in his fiction. One of the three elements of his art will be found to predominate in each of three groups into which his novels naturally fall. The first, the model of which is *Flor de Santidad*, is inspired by the peasant-like and religious lyricism of *Aromas de Leyenda*. The second, which is best represented by his four *Sonatas*, is the prose parallel to the courtly lyricism of *La Marquesa Rosalinda*. The epic-dramatic strain is most powerfully rendered in his two *Comedias Bárbaras*, i.e. *Aguila de Blasón* and *Romance de Lobos*.

Flor de Santidad is a picture of peasant life in Galicia, conceived in a distinctly poetical mood. The passions described are the elementary passions which animate primitive man: avarice and charity, ferocity and kindness, self-denial and lust, all moving freely and darkly in an atmosphere of superstition. . . . It is a story told with that skill for emotional music which is the secret of our poet-novelist, simple and humble in its subject-matter like a village tale, yet on a level higher than the mere matter-of-fact narrative of events. The typical features of the Gallegan genius are to be observed in it—the musical sense, the predominance of women and their point of view, and that peculiar atmosphere of commonalty in mansion, kitchen, and road which makes Galicia so murmuring and social. Yet the tale leaves an unpleasant impression, as if the author had not been fair to the poor folk whose superstition he exhibits. Had we felt that he shared the limitations of his characters, the story would have been more moving; had he written from the outside of them, it would have been more convincing. As it is, the impression that remains is one of insincerity.

It is also the impression left after reading the four exquisitely written sonatas. Here, the sense of music and form prevails to the point of imposing the name and method on the work. These four sonatas, one for each season of the year, correspond to four moments in the life of Xavier de Bradomín, a kind of melancholy and decadent Don Juan, who in his old age writes his memoirs so that the world may know of his love-triumphs before he repents. The character of Don Juan is one which fascinates Valle Inclán. It is in fact almost the only masculine character which he has really worked out in his prose and verse. The explanation is simple, and springs from that other feature which we have observed in Gallegan poetry, the predominance of women and their point of view. Don Juan is the only man compatible with this feature, since he is himself obsessed by women and of women he has the central tendency, namely, that which makes love the most important affair of life. Don Juan, fundamentally, is a feminine character, and the Don Juan of the four sonatas is a typically feminine Don Juan. As for the hero's portrait, it is brushed in three words. . . . 'He was ugly, a Catholic, and sentimental. Very sentimental. Which means that he talks about feeling more than he feels. Yet it must be owned that he talks well, having at his disposal all the resources of his creator's art. The four sonatas are impeccable exercises of style, not of the burnished style, relentlessly accurate, wherewith Flaubert can raise headaches of a purely æsthetic origin, but rather of that perfectly fluid form which flows in rhythm with the emotions and faithfully reflects them. They are four songs of love. It is not, however, Xavier, the beloved, who gives them their emotional wealth, but the women whom he fascinated throughout his adventurous life. These women are admirably though lightly and delicately rendered by an observer who was admitted into the inmost chambers of their hearts yet who could keep cool enough to note love's movements. In the sonatas, all the women are in earnest, but the man they all love is not. Xavier is rather in that half earnest, half frivolous mood which inspired *La Marquesa Rosalinda*, only here the frivolous lies deeper down, hidden under a pool of sentiment, and loses in grace and attractiveness by being cut off from the fresh air of sincerity. There is a sceptical undercurrent in Xavier's character which makes his melancholy melodies sound false and deceiving. We feel that a frank cynicism would have been pleasantly honourable by the side of this sentimental cant! For this Don Juan, who goes about the world fascinating women, is not only incapable of repaying their love with love, however passing, but lives so low as not to be able to respect those souls who open themselves out to him. . . . This feature gradually grows upon the reader until it destroys the implicit nobility of the character. The manly animal qualities of aristocracy—courage, pride, and a kind of natural authority—are his and well rendered. But his generosity is external and showy; his loyalty for his king, the whim of a decadent dilettante: his sensibility, never higher than curiosity stimulated by lust; of religion he knows nothing but its picturesque side; and thus the type which the author meant to be noble has no real nobility in his heart.

Our poet-novelist has brushed a rougher, ruder, and altogether greater type of Spanish nobleman in his Don Juan Manuel Montenegro, the hero of his *Comedias Bárbaras*. The *Comedias Bárbaras* are two novels written in dialogue. The first of these stories—*Aguila de Blasón*—may be considered as a first attempt at what the author achieves in the second. *Romance de Lobos* is a masterpiece of dramatic vigour and concentration. It has all the violent quality of an etching by Goya. Don Juan Montenegro is a magnificent human beast, a kind of centaur of the passions—the noble as well as the low ones—a tyrant both loved and feared by the peasantry, who lets his fortune slowly go in grants to avaricious but complaisant husbands and fathers on his estates. The drama derives its barbaric strength from the opposition between his overpowering will and the brutal behaviour of his five sons, the heirs of all his unruly passions but not of his noble traditions. (pp. 136-42)

The closing scene in particular gives to the drama an earnestness and a gravity which saves it from mere picturesqueness. For the figure of Don Juan Manuel, like that of his five sons, suffers from the defect of its qualities. It is too simple in its romantic freedom from all restraint. It lacks subtlety. It is precisely this lack of subtlety in his characters which makes *Aguila de Blasón*, despite its vigour and the dramatic quality of its plot, somewhat unsatisfactory. In *Romance de Lobos,* however, that popular element which often comes to the rescue of our novelist when his fancy threatens to run away with his common sense, stands him in good stead, and for once also his religion, which is too often but a pretext for pretty sights and quaint feelings, becomes earnest and purposeful, and Don Juan Manuel is at last sincere and is at last a man. Yet, here and there, even in *Romance de Lobos*, we hear the jarring note of insincerity. It may be a metaphor a little self-conscious, it may be a bombastic phrase or an overstrained feeling, which appears as soon as the fury of action abates and the narrator can hear himself speak and has time to think of what he is doing. So that, even in this his masterpiece, Valle Inclán does not allow us to forget that the metal of his art is not so pure as its beautiful colour might lead us to expect. (pp. 143-44)

[While] acknowledging that the artist sings well and paints admirably, we feel that his art sounds hollow. Why?

Whenever the work of an artist appears to suffer from one dominant defect, it is wise to search for the root of this defect in the very region where the root of his main quality lies. The main quality of Valle Inclán, that which gives formal excellence and emotional music to his art, is the purity of his æsthetic attitude. He turns his soul on nature like a mirror, the limpidity of which is untarnished by any moral or philosophical preoccupation. He sees, feels, and reflects in perfect peace. Now, this is as it should be. A work of art should be—indeed, can only be—conceived in a purely æsthetic attitude, which neither the eagerness to learn nor the desire to teach should disturb. Neither proving nor improving have anything to do with art.

But when we have said that the mood in which the artist looks at life should be free from ethical or philsophical influences, we do not mean that the artist himself should be altogether free from ethical and philosophic preoccupations. Here lies the kernel of that most vexing question, art for art's sake. Yes, of course, art must be for art's sake. But provided the artist has a philosophic mind and an ethical heart. Let his mood, while creating, be wholly æsthetic, but not the soul which goes into that mood. (p. 145)

It is here, to my mind, that the flaw in the art of Don Ramón María del Valle Inclán is to be found. His æsthetic attitude is not merely the natural one of an artist intent on creation. It arises also from a real indifference towards the higher philosophical and moral issues. His emotion is purely æsthetic, and evokes no resonances in the recesses of his soul. The vacuum which surrounds the strings of his sensibility reflects back its inaneness on the sound that they yield. The æsthetic emotion itself, lacking the necessary resonance, becomes thin and false. Hence that jarring note of insincerity throughout his work. There is in it a literary preoccupation which savours too much of the *métier*. It comes out now and then in the use of bookish expressions. . . . (p. 146)

It explains the indifference with which man's most sacred passions are handled without leaving the slightest tremor in the hands of the artist, a circumstance which leads him to commit strange breaches of taste. It stimulates the search for the merely weird and picturesque, for the horrible and the morbid. It is, in fine, the manifestation of an æsthetic sensibility without philosophical guidance nor ethical ballast.

Nor is this meant to imply that Valle Inclán is lacking in mental powers and curiosity. Far from it. His work is full of most ingenious symbols, images, and ideas which reveal a penetrating mind. It is not from lack of ideas that his work suffers, nor do we here suggest that it is worthless because of its unmoral philosophy. This philosophy, which is that of the freedom of passion as opposed to the philosophy of repression and discipline, is perfectly defensible, and the deliberate choice of it implies in Valle Inclán a power for discernment and a capacity for high thought which no one thinks of denying him. He fails, not because he lacks a philosophy, nor because his philosophy is wrong, but because, once he has adopted it, he does not succeed in convincing us that he really believes in it inherently. Rather does he convey the impression that his choice is purely determined by the æsthetic advantages which he detects in the point of view which he adopts. And this impression is sufficient to sap the vitality of his æsthetic emotion itself. (pp. 146-47)

> *Salvador de Madariaga, "Ramón Maria del Valle Inclán" (originally published in* Hermes, March, 1922), *in his* The Genius of Spain and Other Essays on Spanish Contemporary Literature (© *Oxford University Press 1923; reprinted by permission of Oxford University Press), Oxford University Press, Oxford, 1923, pp. 128-47.*

WILLIAM A. DRAKE (essay date 1928)

In the whole of Europe, it would be difficult to discover another man who can create with words such limpid and ravishing beauty as [Ramon del Valle-Inclán]. Beneath his cunning hand, words take on a strange, unearthly luster; his phrases sing and palpitate with beauty, and the most commonplace scene which he describes is invested with fairy luminance, as in the glow of a rich sunset. But it would be difficult anywhere to find, at the heart of so much splendor, so much perverse cruelty, moral atrophy so complete, and such a decadence of every humane sentiment. This is the flaw which renders the art of Valle-Inclán ultimately sterile, which leaves its beauty devoid of the emotion of recognition which signifies masterpieces, and which makes it, to its would-be imitators, a leper pearl, which only tarnishes what it cannot lend its own superb luster. (pp. 130-31)

Although he is erroneously counted among the leaders of the modernist movement, Valle-Inclán in fact contributed nothing to the artistic progress of these early associates, save perhaps by the perfection of his form, which is their answer to the reproach of iconoclasm. His talent, his viewpoint, are valid for himself alone. But he learned from them the immemorial passion of art; and, learning meanwhile to savor the best productions of the writers of France and Italy, he found himself presently in the possession of a style.

If "style" were to be defined broadly and in its essence, and if the works of the author were to be judged in corresponding narrowness, it might justly be said of Valle-Inclán that he has hardly accomplished more than the perfection of his particular style. . . . [His] plagiarisms are so obvious that they hardly need to be mentioned. Barbey d'Aurevilly and Ga-

briele d'Annunzio, Maeterlinck, Casanova, Eça de Queiroz, and Pérez Galdós are all Valle-Inclán's literary creditors, and there are so many more besides, that to enumerate them would be as tiresome as it would be futile. For, like Anatole France, whom he resembles in many ways, and like "those ineffable poets, Homer," Valle-Inclán commits his plagiarisms openly and unabashedly. His is the type of adaptive talent which requires a stimulus to creation outside of itself; and what he finds that he can utilize, he takes, by the divine right of employment, without embarrassment and without attempting to dissemble what only pedants would consider as his shame. To observe how exquisitely he has adorned what he has borrowed, one has only to compare his *Sonata de Otaña* with its manifest source, the story "Le Rideau Cramoisi," in Barbey d'Aurevilly's *Les Diaboliques*, or the *Sonata de Primavera* with the passage of Casanova's *Mémoires* which inspired it. (pp. 133-34)

It would be difficult to term Ramón del Valle-Inclán a great novelist or a true poet. He is neither the one nor the other. He has made the figure of Xavier de Bradomín, "ugly, Catholic, and sentimental," the center of a series of ingenious episodes set in luscious prose; in *Aguila de Blasón* and *Romance de Lobos*, he has created, within the dark spirits of Don Juan Manuel Montenegro and his bestial sons, a vital drama of morbid and prodigious lives; in *La Guerra Carlista*, he has described the civil wars as the frenzy of base passion that they were; and in his novels of Galicia, he has preserved a medley of characters and episodes which the reader will never be able to forget. Yet, in reading his novels, one does not feel the flux of creative vigor which fills with life and substance the little world within the covers of a book. Nor, in reading his poetry, although it is exquisite, does one feel that Valle-Inclán is more than a gifted amateur at verse.

Somewhere in the creative faculty of Ramón María del Valle-Inclán there is concealed a flaw which prevents him from achieving even the debatable greatness of his French similar, Anatole France. For France was capable of moral indignation in the face of brutality or injustice; he was capable of emotional discretion, of humane impulses, of the precious quality of pity. Therefore, in spite of the thinness, the hypocrisy, and the frequent meretriciousness of his work, there are moments when it is filled with life, when it evokes tender emotions, when it even becomes noble. With Valle-Inclán, although his art, at its best, is a more perfect vehicle than that of Anatole France, there are no such moments. For Valle-Inclán is limited, in his artistic achievement, by a singular incapacity for any moral feeling, which places the seal of sterility upon the exquisite vessel of his art, distorts it with the lust of cruelty, and takes it as far from life as the beautiful enchanted princesses of Moorish legend.

Herein lies the limitation of Valle-Inclán as a creator. . . . [He] is inhuman, because there is a senseless and wanton quality in his perpetual cruelty that has no human answer, because he writes as if in an infernal void, with black hate, not in his heart, for there it might serve as a powerful creative force, but with the door of his heart closed and with black hate in his brain. Great artist as he is, he cannot create magnificently, because he cannot feel; because he cannot experience through any medium except his meticulously wrought style and his too subtle, sarcastic intellect. And the intellect is not enough. (pp. 135-37)

> *William A. Drake, "Ramon del Valle-Inclán," in his* Contemporary European Writers *(copyright,*

1927, by William A. Drake), John Day, 1928, pp. 130-37.

L. A. WARREN (essay date 1929)

Valle-Inclán comes after Rubén Darío as the leading modernistic writer. He is the most important man of letters in Spain to-day and is equal in aesthetic merit and interest to [Gabriel] D'Annunzio. Three main elements go to his making. The place: he is a Galician; the time: he is of the modernistic period; and the man: he has a striking character. It is as a modernist that he is famous in Spain to-day; but it is as a Galician that he is likely to endure in literature. His Galician qualities he gets entirely out of himself. His modernism is said to be borrowed or acquired. He claims to derive and model himself upon Casanova and Barbey d'Aurevilly. . . . [But he] is a far greater artist than either Casanova or Barbey d'Aurevilly, and so his books, on lines similar to theirs, are far superior. D'Annunzio possibly is the only author whom Valle-Inclán has followed so closely as to be in danger of neglecting the expression of himself. But his Galician nature has saved him from this and from being merely a follower of D'Annunzio.

La Lampara maravillosa does not seem to me a success. It is a sort of formless treatise of aesthetic, and sets up a Platonized ideal of beauty rather than the actual principles and feelings of its author. In all the other books of his that I have read Valle-Inclán expresses his personality.

Roughly these books divide into two groups: the group in which Galicia and its nature is most prominent, and the group in which modernistic qualities predominate; though Galician qualities such as the sense of horror, pervade the modernistic books, and modernistic qualities such as artificiality, pervade the Galician books. In some of his works the two elements are about equally mixed. *Sonata de Estio* is the book furthest removed from Galicia; *Flor de Santidad* is the one freest from modernism.

The four sonatas are Valle-Inclán's *magnum opus*. They are modernistic. They are called the *Sonata de Primavera,* the *Sonata de Estio,* the *Sonata de Otoño,* and the *Sonata de Invierno.* They deal with the love affairs of an aristocratic Don Juan, the Marquess de Bradomin, in the four seasons of life, spring, summer, autumn and winter.

The *Sonata de Primavera* is exotic and precious. An elaborate artificial style, but easy to read and rather beautiful. . . . Love is the theme; but an artificial love of kings' palaces, scented boudoirs and moonlit gardens, not the free and natural love of the streets and open country. There is a baroque air and one is stifled by heavy perfumes, drowsiness and hushed voices, and longs to escape to the open and fresh air; in the gardens one feels crushed by the cypresses and the air of mystery and wants to get out to nature. (pp. 256-58)

The second volume of the Marquess de Bradomin's memoirs is the *Sonata de Estio.* The subject is love, that is to say hot, voluptuous passion; and the setting is the tropical coast of Mexico. But more important than the matter is the manner. The book is written more for the pattern of words than for what the words say. It might be said that first in importance come the sketches, ribbons and fruit with which the pages are decorated, second comes the highly artificial patterned style, and last comes what it is all about. But in reality the decoration, the style and the subject are all suited to one

another. It is a work of decadence, a book that regrets the past ages without being of the past ages, a book that admires the Conquistadores and regrets the days of adventure are over, a book that regrets that the age of superb courtly aristocrats is past. It is sensuous and voluptuous, a book all of the senses and not of the understanding or imagination; it may show skill and experience in the senses, but there is no delicacy, and one can feel a certain hardness, callousness, cruelty, cynicism, through the beautiful style. This style is most deliberate and artificial, creating with a paucity of words and a careful selection of but few details the impression intended: it gives the heat, the brightness and the languor of nature in the Gulf of Mexico, and combines this with the passion and callousness of man. The general impression left is unhealthy and unpleasant.

In the first two or three pages of the *Sonata de Otoño* we are in a few lines enveloped in an atmosphere, an atmosphere of decadence. How is it created? A letter faintly scented with violet says: 'My adored love, I am dying and want to see you.' The hero kisses the letter, interviews two nuns, sisters of the lady, and then goes into a church. It is dark and gloomy there, a couple of austere women dressed in black flit about from altar to altar in the dim light of a few candles, while the hero thinks how devout his lady was at her prayers and how she would cease from them passionately to throw her arms round his neck and burst into sobs. With a careful selection of these facts and a still more careful and narrow selection of the attendant details we are placed in an atmosphere of decline and death; of gloom, hopelessness, and melancholy, of vain echoes of passionate love, with a religion in tone somewhere between the sensuous and the ascetic dim but all-pervading, foreboding, in the background.

The hero arrives at the old palace. His love-making with the dying heroine is extraordinarily unhealthy. If it were a case of affection and spiritual love it would be pathetic. But it is a case of passionate, carnal love, a hot feverish thing of nerves and sensations. To be in fleshly love with a dying body is unwholesome; this erotic and unpleasant feeling is raised to its height by the Marquess passing the night in bed side by side with the heroine. The Marquess has great skill and address in his love-making; he is a practised hand, a professional at the business. This again enhances the effect of the false, hollow, rotten and artificial; we long for something fresh, genuine and natural. The author is very skilled. (pp. 258-59)

The *Sonata de Invierno* is, as it says, an impression of winter: winter on the earth, and winter in the soul. . . . Old age is upon [the Marquess de Bradomin], his hair is white and he loses an arm in some Carlist skirmish. Now he has his last love affair, the experienced Don Juan wakens a first love in the heart of a young girl of fifteen; in spite of the age and reputation of the old roué and her inexperienced youthfulness, in spite of the hint that the Marquess is the girl's father, there is not in this love so much of the horrible and the unwholesome as in some of the other affairs. On the contrary, the love passages, although voluptuous, as in all of Valle-Inclán's, are tender and charming, and have grace and delicacy. (p. 260)

Valle-Inclán is admirable at impression. *Sonata de Estio* gives the burning heat of Mexico, the tropical life and the voluptuous frenzy of the fever of passion; *Sonata de Otoño* gives the quiet decline of the old manor-house in green, dreamy, rainy Galicia and with it the sad ending of an unhealthy love;

Sonata de Invierno gives a marvellous impression of winter in the Basque uplands with wintry old age descending upon the Marquess de Bradomin.

Valle-Inclán stands out among Spanish authors for his love passages and in writing love dialogues. (pp. 260-61)

The chief aim of Valle-Inclán's writing is to give the sensation of things. In his four sonatas he gives the sensations made on the nerves by the impact of the four seasons from nature outside and the mind inside. We have here the triumph of his style. I have suggested that he regards manner as more important than matter, form than substance; and a superficial, ornamental beauty as the highest of achievements. (p. 261)

Artificiality is prominent among Valle-Inclán's qualities. He lives in a scented and unwholesome world. . . . (p. 263)

Added to this artificiality, Valle-Inclán is aristocratic. Aristocracy is bred deep into him. It is hard to see how he ever can become a popular writer in any sense of the word. (p. 265)

The *Sonata de Otoño* is by far the best of Valle-Inclán's books. In it are combined in a fortunate mixture the qualities of Galicia and the modes of modernism. One would at first have thought fresh, green Galicia more suited as a setting for spring. With fine sense Valle-Inclán has placed it as a setting for autumn. In Galicia and Ireland, difficult of access, shut away at the extreme end of the world, a primitive race has existed from prehistoric times and has dwelt on untouched. . . . They have the power of seeing and feeling and sensing the spiritual beings immediately around them; it is not the fair powers of heaven above that they see, but petty creatures and for the most part dark and evil. As a possessor and an exponent of this Celtic nature Valle-Inclán is similar in nature to Celtic Irish writers such as Synge and Yeats, but far stronger, and artistically incomparably more gifted. (pp. 269-70)

Valle-Inclán is a modernist; his writing contains no long, detailed descriptions, his descriptions select and suggest; he is subjective rather than objective, he has Galicia inside him and his aim is to give us the feeling and sensation of the province and its people. (p. 270)

In Valle-Inclán's verse there is just a touch of the artificial, gold and roses are introduced; the words are rich and beautiful, the metre is most skilful and there are sonorous musical phrases. It is this artificiality which keeps him from being of the highest rank; music is more important than meaning, there is a lack of human interest, there is finally no depth of feeling and if there is feeling it is unhealthy; he has preferred ornamental beauty to human passion, and hence is both empty and sterile. However, as a decorative artist he is admirable, and gives tones and sensations, an aesthetic that is peculiarly his own; and he stands alone and peculiar in that he has combined the atavistic primitiveness of Galicia with the refined decadence of modernistic Paris. Here two opposite extremes are joined, the ultra-savage and the over-civilized, and strange to say the two extremes appear to have something akin. (p. 272)

> L. A. Warren, "Roman del Valle-Inclán," in his Modern Spanish Literature: A Comprehensive Survey of the Novelists, Poets, Dramatists and Essayists from the Eighteenth Century to the Present, Vol. 1, Brentano's Ltd, 1929, pp. 256-72.

PEDRO SALINAS (essay date 1936)

Valle-Inclán found unity only in his extremes. Led astray by the initial phase of his work. critics thought he was only a delicate artist, a painter of miniatures. But the real Valle-Inclán is rather the writer who treats barbarous themes with refinement, who stylizes violence. Crude human nature is violence, barbarity. And words are the divine power which elevates it to the quality of art. The art-process in Valle-Inclán, who always scoffed at the reality of the realist, lies in passing through a stylization of the real, concerned above all with the aesthetic, such as in the *Sonatas,* to another kind of stylization—mystic and profound—which we might call a stylization of psychological origin. At first he proceeded inwardly and dressed his characters in artistically designed costumes taken from literature and painting. But in his last period the characters emit from within themselves their own elements of stylization as they become their own caricature; and what accounts for the tragic element in the *esperpento* is precisely man's encounter with his own acts, with his own farce and grimace. He converts himself into a tragicomic motif as he encounters his own true character. At the beginning of his career Valle-Inclán may have indeed been a sensual contemplator and a sceptic, but in the end he is a man in anguish, and in his works, what he gives us is a plastic transcription—for Valle-Inclán could never be anything if not plastic—of man's conflict with his conscience.

> *Pedro Salinas, in his essay from "Valle-Inclán and Contemporary Spain," by José Luis Cano, translated by José Sánchez (originally published as "Valle-Inclán visto por sus coetáneos," in* Indice literario, *No. 1, 1936), in* Valle-Inclán Centennial Studies, *edited by Ricardo Gullón (copyright © 1968 by Board of Regents, The University of Texas at Austin), University of Texas, 1968, p. 101.*

MARY BORELLI (essay date 1961)

Valle-Inclán's poetry is contained in three volumes called *Aromas de Leyenda, El Pasajero* and *La Pipa de Kif.* This versatile writer, who is well-known as the creator of characters such as Bradomín, Montenegro and Tirano Banderas, published his books of poems in several editions, always seeking to give to his three volumes a final and definitive form. In the last version, he ended by placing them all together in one volume, under the general title of *Claves Liricas.* The linking element that binds these three collections of poems together is purely external, however, and merely indicates that they are poems, for, actually, each volume has a distinct character of its own. *Aromas de Leyenda* is the earliest, and, with its predominantly pastoral tone, it reflects Valle-Inclán's first manner, such as we find in his novel *Flor de Santidad* and in other works which led up to the *Sonatas.* The second volume, *El Pasajero,* could be said to represent his mystic period. *La Pipa de Kif,* which precedes the esperpentic play, *Luces de Bohemia,* and the novel, *Tirano Banderas,* would seem to contain, rather broadly, the style which Valle-Inclán himself later defined as *esperpento.*

The term *esperpento* is metaphorical and refers to certain concave and convex mirrors which in our author's day were placed for the amusement of the passers-by in a certain street in Madrid. With his use of this term, Valle-Inclán wished to indicate his own special attitude towards life—an attitude which he translated into art through the use of a measured deformation of ordinary things and people, so that they became grotesque images, with all the tragic feeling that can underlie them. It was a period of bitterness, of disillusionment, of despair, that immediately followed the First World War, and in the ruin of the old ideals, the obvious interpretation of life that presented itself to the artist could be summed up in one artistic expression: sarcasm.

It may be interesting to give brief consideration to the *Pipa de Kif* as a forerunner of the better-known *esperpento* in *Luces de Bohemia*. This volume of poems appeared in 1919. The search for poetic inspiration in artificial paradises of various kinds must have been by that date a mere reminiscence of earlier French readings, and the experiments of a De Quincey could hardly offer any explanation. Yet Valle-Inclán plays with the idea, and even informs us in the first poem that in the smoke of his oriental pipe (that is, La Pipa de Kif) he saw strange shapes: ["My consciousness reverted to that of a child"]—not completely "infantiles," since we read in the second poem that his verses . . . are written to ridicule such writers as Cotarelo, Ricardo León, Rubén Dario. Rather, we find ourselves here in full literary satire, with all the tone, the rhyming couplets, the pseudo-folkloristic rhythms that are so frequent in this type of poetry.

The following poems do not continue quite in this vein, but gradually become somewhat more elevated in tone, and ever more tragic. The poet sets his tone which, with his easy rhythm, prepares the mood of the reader for the grotesque and sardonic elements that are to follow.

Whereas in his earliest book of poems, *Aromas de Leyenda*, we found ourselves in the delightful setting of a gentle countryside, with peasants and saints and an atmosphere of legend and miracles, and then, in *El Pasajero*, we were transported to a suggestion of an Oriental Paradise and we were almost hypnotized with the insistent expressions of mysticism, here in *La Pipa de Kif*, the subjects of inspiration are grey and everyday. We are in the city. From the quiet peace of the Galician countryside, the poet has moved us to the dusty villages of Castile, and thence to Madrid, with increasing absorption in sordid human interests. His scenes acquire more people, people who live and suffer intensely under their own personal tragedy. (pp. 266-67)

Since he has revealed himself to be of the same nature as the men of the Generation of '98, the words of Laín Entralgo about this generation, with reference to landscape, may also be applied to Valle-Inclán [the landscapes drawn by the writers of '98 are closed by the nostalgia of childhood and the scenery of Castile]. . . . This is particularly true of a series of poems in which Valle is concerned with a highly tragic theme, set in the village of Medinica in Castile, and entirely expressed in images. Here the style has become almost that of prose and it is only the rhyme and the rather difficult rhythm that keep it in the realm of poetry. . . . With a vaguely folkloric background, the poet chooses his images and presents them with his new esperpentic technique. We find, as we gradually proceed through these poems, that the word *esperpento* can be applied sometimes to the inspiration, sometimes to the tone that the poet assumes, and sometimes to the choice of subject. But, whatever the angle, it always maintains its fundamental character of grotesqueness.

In *La Pipa de Kif* the poet is fascinated by the low characters that inhabit the underworld of Madrid and he now puts them sharply in the foreground of his poetry. His rhythm is always consistent, his rhymes are scrupulously observed, but in the

poetry there is, somehow, lacking the spirit which would make of it truly poetic material. Rather, there is an obvious intention on the part of the poet to make us feel that what he is stressing in his narration is the tragic, the ineluctable. This is in part also the result of his pictorial technique, which does not encourage meditation. In fact, Valle-Inclán here seems to proceed as though in front of a canvas, where he fixes his impressions in a completely static and two-dimensional manner. The poems in *La Pipa de Kif* are characterized by this static quality, and the continual use of the present tense renders them rather more contemplative than dramatic.

Valle-Inclán has always had a certain tendency to this type of descriptive writing, and his own aims in art, as we read them in his treatise, the *Lámpara Maravillosa,* are directed towards an ideal abolition of time. It is, however, interesting that this technique, which stresses the omnipresence of objects and things, is applied here, where the subject seems to spring from a feeling of tragedy, and hence of movement.

In the earlier volume, *Aromas de Leyenda*, it was its serenely legendary atmosphere that animated the poetry. In the *Pasajero*, it was the mystical or pseudo-mystical exclamations. But here, in the *Pipa de Kif*, the tragic feeling comes from within, and the poet seeks it and throws it into relief in his facts. Valle-Inclán never really narrates in his poetry: he does not feel any real development of events. He merely places them on the page and lets the situation make its own effect on the reader. . . . The poetic value of the compositions of the *Pipa de Kif* lies in this intimate fire, which the poet has moulded together with that spirit that will later become the full flowering of the *esperpento.*

It is a very special and highly original poetic value, in that it is almost plastic, reminiscent, in a sense, of the cubists, who were painting in France at the very same time, and one of whose leaders was the Spaniard Picasso. Their choice of technique, which is very bold in nature, makes them very close relations of the characters in Valle-Inclán's *Pipa de Kif*. Both are forms, symbols of a vision of life, of a period in history. This line of interpretation carries the experiment of Valle-Inclán in his *esperpento* to a European level of high art. (pp. 267-68)

Mary Borelli, "Valle-Inclan, Poet of Sarcasm," in Hispania (© 1961 The American Association of Teachers of Spanish and Portuguese, Inc.), Vol. XLIV, No. 2, May, 1961, pp. 266-68.

JEAN FRANCO (essay date 1962)

On first reading *La corte de los milagros* and *¡Viva mi dueño!* one has the impression of powerful but haphazard works, a series of brilliant, disconnected vignettes. These novels have, however, a carefully worked-out concentric plan which is so vastly different from the chronological time sequence usually employed by novelists that the reader is apt to find the construction disconcerting. The concentric structure was not chosen by Valle-Inclán merely from a desire to shock or even for the sake of experiment; it corresponds to philosophical and religious ideas about time which he had first set out in *La lámpara maravillosa.* . . .

La lámpara maravillosa has the sub-title *Ejercicios espirituales;* it is a record of Valle-Inclán's attempts to transcend fleeting sense experiences and intuit eternal truths. . . . The spiritual journey which Valle-Inclán describes in *La lámpara mara-*

villosa is one of escape from the "Satanic" time of the senses into an eternity in which past, present and future exist side by side. (p. 177)

[This] view of time is, as he himself acknowledges, derived from the Gnostics.

According to Hellenic belief time is cyclical; in Christianity, it is rectilinear. The Gnostics took the cyclical time of Hellenic belief but they attribute it only to the base world of what is created. Matter is inherently evil and cyclical time is bound up with the world of matter. The higher world is timeless but Sophia (wisdom) is exiled in the lower world of matter and cannot return to the Pleroma (plenitude) because there is an impassible limit, the Horus. It is to this that Valle-Inclán refers when he talks of Satan whirling eternally in the Horus of Pleroma.... If Valle-Inclán shared the Gnostic belief that matter was inherently evil, then this has interesting implications. In this article, however, I wish to confine myself to the Gnostic view of time and eternity first set out by him in 1916 and its influence on the structure of [*La corte de los milagros* and *¡Viva mi dueño!*]....

One of the most striking characteristics of *La lámpara maravillosa* is the frequency with which Valle-Inclán uses the symbolism of the circle. The circle symbolizes both Satanic time, which is likened to the coils of a serpent, and also states of completion and quietude. Whilst Valle-Inclán describes the world as imprisoning us in ["the circle of shadow that spreads with each hour,"] in memory images appear to us ["quietly and out of time, at the center of the circles of shadow."] (p. 178)

Eleven years passed between the publication of *La lámpara maravillosa* and *La corte de los milagros;* but in the latter book the concentric circle is the basis of the construction, and the ideas of Satanic time and eternity are repeatedly contrasted.... [In *La corte de los milagros*] he took a central chapter and built the rest of the novel in circles round this.

Both *La corte de los milagros* and *¡Viva mi dueño!* have nine books in which there is a relationship between the first and last books, between the second and the eighth, the third and the seventh and the fourth and the sixth with the fifth book forming the centre and giving meaning to the whole.... [*La corte de los milagros*] summarizes the state of Spain in the closing years of Isabel's reign and has a circular plan, beginning and ending with the same sentence.... [Book] five *La soguilla de Caronte* sets the theme of the whole book—the theme of death and destruction. The scene is the estate of the Marqués de Torre-Mellada where a storm has brought devastation, destroying a mill and the bridge across the river, so that the body of the overseer's wife who has died of cancer will now have to be drawn across the water to her burial on the end of a rope.... [Book five is] like the stone cast into the lake which starts a series of "círculos concéntricos" ... in it, death and corruption shadow all walks of society from the dead countrywoman to the courtiers and the ... figure of General Narváez. The rest of the novel shows the widening circles of death and corruption spreading through all Spain and even beyond.

Books four and six (*La jaula del pájaro* and *Para que no cantes*) describe the violence and corruption in the Andalusian countryside. (pp. 179-81)

Books three and seven (*El coto de los Carvajales* and *Malos agüeros*) describe journeys. In both, the trains are referred to as black coffins and the occupants of the carriages travel through a countryside that is sinister in the moonlight and haunted by rumours of banditry and violence. (p. 181)

Books two and eight (*Ecos de Asmodeo* and *Requiém del espadón*) open and close in the salon of the Marquesa de Torre-Mellada and the intervening sections take us through all walks of Madrid life, through theatres, cafés and clubs. In book two, while their elders gossip and conspire against the government, a group of young aristocrats throw a policeman from the window.... This act of violence is contrasted with the performance of *El alcalde de Zalamea* whose theme has lost all significance for the fashionable society before whom it is acted. In this society, the aristocrats get away with the killing of their inferiors and the seduction of their daughters. In book eight, the disorderly conduct of the aristocracy is now endemic. In the cafés, people openly flout the police, scandalous songs about the Queen and the court circulate freely. The Ateneo prostitutes itself by holding an absurd contest between the King Consort and the Duke of Montpensier (Isabel's brother-in-law and one of the aspirants to the throne), neither of whom can claim any literary ability. The complete bankruptcy of society is symbolized by the attempted suicide of the young son of the Marqués de Redín. (pp. 181-82)

The outer circle of the book is formed by the Queen and the court. The opening book (*La rosa de oro*) describes the ceremony in which a Papal order is presented to Isabel and the accompanying celebrations. The sections of the book alternate between the public appearances of Isabel and the privacy of her antechamber where she gossips, plans to take a new lover and worries about her poverty. The ceremony is overshadowed by the presence of General Narváez who is showing the first signs of a mortal illness.... In the last book [*Jornada régia*], Isabel who had set the pace in the first book, has become the victim. It is now apparent that she is not really in control. Disconcerted by the death of Narváez who has kept the government together for so long, she allows herself to be manipulated by Sor Patrocinio and her false miracles. She signs the list of promotions given to her by the nun, an action which will cause repercussions in *¡Viva mi dueño!*; as she signs, the cannons boom out a last salute to the dead General whose state funeral closes the novel.

¡Viva mi dueño! has a similar construction to *La corte de los milagros*, though the theme is slightly different. Discord is now added to death and violence, and this becomes the subject of the novel. The fifth book, *Cartel de ferias*, again provides the key to the whole novel. There are repeated acts of violence in the book. There is the fight between the gypsies on the one hand against Juan Caballero, the priest and Barón Bonifaz on the other.... In the knife fight, the gypsies, who represent the forces of anarchy, are pitted against a representative of the clergy, the aristocracy and a country gentleman who had once been a bandit of legendary fame. But while these forces are temporarily united against the gypsies, they are themselves torn by discord in exactly the same way as the ruling classes of Spain as a whole. Barón Bonifaz's seduction of the [priest's] niece earns him the bitter enmity of the priest and Juan Caballero is also shocked by this incident. Most significant of all, the fight during the fair is represented as a sterile repetition of an old feud. Juan Caballero finds himself fighting the nephew of Antonio el Tuerto, a man whom he had killed and whose family he had burned to death thirty years before. (pp. 182-83)

This is insisted upon several times in the novel: the repetition of what has happened thirty years before. Again there is a parallel with the fate of Spain, for the Carlist war of the 1830s will soon break out again. This eternal resurgence of discord not only corresponds to the Gnostic belief that the souls of the unenlightened return to earth. . . . According to Gnostic belief, the imperfect lower world will continue until all the particles of light are gathered up and returned to the Pleroma. Throughout *El corte de los milagros* and *¡Viva mi dueño!* acts of violence are repeated and engender other acts of violence in endless recurrence. (p. 183)

[Each] book in these novels is linked through having common characters, a common environment and parallel incidents with a sister book. It will also have been noticed that the events of the books that form the early part of the novels are often reflected ironically or exaggerated in the sister books. Thus in *La corte de los milagros* the book dealing with the train journey to Córdoba describes a gratuitous shooting by the Guardia Civil; on the return journey in the sister book bandits are rumoured to be on the train but the Guardia can do nothing about it. . . . In *¡Viva mi dueño!* this technique is amplified by the use of linking sections; the story of the crime of Solana, for instance, goes from mouth to mouth, though the criminals have only done on a small scale what others are doing on a much bigger scale. (pp. 184-85)

Valle-Inclán's special concept of time is not only shown in the structure of these two novels of the *Ruedo ibérico* but is also revealed in the attitudes of the characters as well as in the author's attitude to his creation. The two concepts of eternity and chronological time are continually contrasted: eternity in which all past, present and future happenings already co-exist and 'el absurdo satánico' of chronological time which he had previously [presented] in *La lámpara maravillosa*. . . . The characters of the novels are prisoners in time. There is no question of choice or free will: at best they dominate life as a skilful dancer dominates the figures of a dance. . . .

Death or the nearness of death alone makes the characters step outside this Satanic circle and consider their lives as if from a distance and in the light of eternity. (p. 185)

[For] a moment past, present and future coexist. (p. 186)

Since, according to Gnostic belief, the whole of the lower world is imperfect, there can be no escape into an idealized world of nature. The countryside suffers as do human beings. . . . The storm at the end of book four of La corte de los milagros disrupts the life of men and animals alike.

The only truth is then the insight that we gain at the moment of death or during contemplation. It is not surprising, therefore, that the central book of *La corte de los milagros*, which is on the theme of death, should echo the actual wording of *La lámpara maravillosa*. Since death closes the circle of life and allows us to solve its enigma, so contemplation also opens the 'visión cíclica'; and both these parallel experiences are presented against the same background of tolling bells. . . . (pp. 186-87)

From the foregoing, it will be evident that the constructions of *La corte de los milagros* and *¡Viva mi dueño!* are anything but haphazard. They correspond to a view of time which Valle-Inclán had formulated as early as 1916 and which he retained at least until 1931 when he published *Aires nacionales*. A recent critic has spoken of the ideas of *La lámpara mar-*

avillosa as leaving "un rastro leve pero preciso" in a passage of *La corte de los milagroso*. In fact the circular structure not only symbolizes the theme of *El ruedo ibérico* but shows us that the ideas set forth in *La lámpara maravillosa* were still very much in Valle-Inclán's mind when he came to write his later novels. (p. 187)

Jean Franco, "The Concept of Time in 'El ruedo ibérico'," in Bulletin of Hispanic Studies (© copyright 1962 Liverpool University Press), Vol. XXXIX, No. 3, 1962, pp. 177-87.

AZORÍN   (essay date 1966)

"We will not find in all our literature more radiant verbal invention than that by Valle-Inclán . . . he creates a language for his own use . . . Just as he has created a whole poetic world, so he has created, as well, a language adequate to that world."

"Precisely the greatest spell cast by Valle-Inclán consists in that incertitude of illusion in which the poet sinks us." . . .

[This] man we would see arguing in a café is the same man who, in the intimacy of his home, worked unabatedly hour after hour with untiring effort. . . . What seems agile and easy in the reading is the product of deep complication."

"For us he has the sorcery of style: a style which is refined, elegant, Attic, full of fantasy and poetry, like no other we have ever experienced."

Azorín [pseudonym of José Martínez Ruiz], "Comments by Valle-Inclán's Contemporaries: Azorín," in Valle-Inclán: Autobiography, Aesthetics, Aphorisms, edited and translated by Robert Lima (© copyright 1966 by Robert Lima), Limited Centennial Edition, 1966.

JACINTO BENAVENTE   (essay date 1966)

It would be reducing Valle-Inclán to place him in a definite genre. He was one of those sublime spirits of great stature in whom the least important aspect is the activity in which they manifest themselves. Valle-Inclán proceeds from the same lineage as Leonardo da Vinci, as Michaelangelo, as Benvenuto Cellini, and other magnificent artists of the Renaissance. His works like Greek tragedy, are a compendium of all the arts: poetry, music, painting. . . .

Jacinto Benavente, "Comments by Valle-Inclán's Contemporaries: Jacinto Benavente," in Valle-Inclán: Autobiography, Aesthetics, Aphorisms, edited and translated by Robert Lima (© copyright 1966 by Robert Lima), Limited Centennial Edition, 1966.

JOSÉ ORTEGA Y GASSET   (essay date 1966)

"There are men who penetrate into ancient epochs. Of some it is possible to state the age in which they should have been born . . . Don Ramón del Valle-Inclán is a Renaissance man. The reading of his books makes one think of those names and great days of human history.

"But above all his is an art which is exquisite and perfect; from within his spirit the artist watches, with the solicitude of a prudent virgin, that first lamp of which Ruskin speaks: the lamp of sacrifice."

"Impatient, Valle-Inclán runs, hunting for the picturesque in his compositions. It is the axis of production; I am told it is likewise the axis of his life, and I believe it." . . .

"I believe that he teaches better than anyone else that special knowledge which is the chemistry of phraseology."

"He is an original stylist and, at the same time, a worshipper of the national tongue, to the point of fetishism; he is an inventor of novelesque fiction with deeper roots in historical rather than contemporary humanity; he is an enemy of all transcendency, a naked artist and a laboring creator of new word associations."

> *José Ortega y Gasset, "Comments by Valle-Inclán's Contemporaries: José Ortega y Gasset," in* Valle-Inclán: Autobiography, Aesthetic, Aphorisms, *edited and translated by Robert Lima (© copyright 1966 by Robert Lima), Limited Centennial Edition, 1966.*

FELICIA HARDISON   (essay date 1967)

In the spring of 1963 two Paris theatres presented plays by a Spanish dramatist little known to most French theatregoers. . . . It may seem strange that Valle-Inclán's plays, most of which were written between 1910 and 1930, should have taken so long to find their way to France, where they may be readily related to the works of that long line of *poètes maudits*—Villon, Jarry, Lautréamont, Rimbaud, and Artaud. It is the latter—Antonin Artaud—whose thought bears a particularly strong resemblance to that of Valle-Inclán. Both men, whose writings shared a forty-year time span, developed their own individual styles of theatre, a comparison of which may prove interesting from a stylistic point of view and certainly as revelatory of the two separate but similar landmarks in European drama. (p. 455)

The overall comparison of the lives and works of Ramón del Valle-Inclán and Antonin Artaud is significant within the scope of European "pre-absurd" drama, but it is necessary to come to a more precise understanding of what is meant by *esperpentismo* and by *théâtre de cruauté*. . . . The *esperpento* is not a literary genre, but refers rather to a particular vision of the world. Valle-Inclán's own definition of the word is contained in the dialogue of Max in *Luces de Bohemia:* "Esperpentismo was invented by Goya. . . . Classical heroes reflected in concave mirrors result in the esperpento. . . . The most beautiful images in a concave mirror are absurd. . . . Deformation ceases to be such when it is subjected to a perfect mathematical law. My current aesthetics is to transform classical norms through the mathematics of a concave mirror." Characters thus subjected to concave mirrors lose all reference to objectivity in that the transformation depends upon the author's intention. Only the proportions are changed, not the object itself. In any case, it is not really the object itself that is subject to re-interpretation, but rather the artistic conception or "classical norms" by which it is viewed. Jean-Paul Borel explains that the traditional norms have always augmented what is great, and diminished or suppressed the small and lowly. The esperpento does not operate in such a uniform manner, but hypertrophies select aspects of characters and of life. The result is a caricaturized vision of things alternately comic and macabre, an inseparable combination of bloody sombreness and parody. . . . *Los Cuernos de Don Friolera,* for example, is . . . a comic distortion of the traditional theme of honor, and any social criticism which may

be implied is only incidentally woven in with the picaresque elements, verbal effrontery, and various ironies. The conflict is centered in the puppet figure of Don Friolera with his very human hesitations off-balanced by semi-comic heroic gestures and satirical grotesqueness. The terrible conclusion . . . mingles burlesque and horror so adroitly as to make this, in Valbuena Prat's opinion, perhaps the best of the esperpentos. (pp. 459-60)

Artaud's purpose in creating the Theatre of Cruelty was to bring back to the theatre the notion of a passionate and convulsive life, but this cruelty need not always be bloody. He did not wish to make a systematic cult of horror, for cruelty, in the broad sense—the pure sense—of the word, is a sort of rigid direction, an irreversible determination, and the absoluteness of necessity. This kind of cruelty cannot exist without a conscience. . . . Life must be lived to the fullest, passionately, cruelly, for the absence of life is death. There is no better illustration of this point in Artaud's theory than the case of Max Estrella in Valle-Inclán's *Luces de Bohemia.* Toward the end of the play, after a day and a night of almost picaresque wandering attended by Don Latino, Max—who had never ceased to declare, "The world is mine, everything smiles upon me, I am a man without troubles."—suddenly gives up and lies down on the doorstep of his own home [and dies]. . . .

Analogous to life and death in the artaudian order of things are good and evil. "Good is willed, it is the result, evil is permanent. . . . A play which does not have this will, this blind appetite for life capable of passing judgment on everything, visible in each gesture and in each act and in the transcendental side of the action, would be a useless and unsuccessful play." Max was just such a force of good superimposed on the permanent evil of his surroundings. Jean-Paul Borel says that Max's will represented the overcoming of the absurdity of existence. The last three scenes of the play, which take place after Max's death, are merely a description of the world without Max, and this is the most lucid indication of the poet's importance. (p. 461)

The use of "supernatural images" is one point where the dramatic practice of Artaud and Valle-Inclán . . . closely coincide. Artaud complained that people had lost contact with true theatre because theatre was being limited to the realm which everyday thought could attain, to the realm of realized or unrealized consciousness,—"and if we do address ourselves theatrically to the subconscious, it is hardly more than to borrow what it might have stored (or hidden) from accessible daily experience." Unknown to Artaud, hundreds of examples already existed in the work of Valle-Inclán to illustrate an intense preoccupation with forces that operate beyond our comprehension. . . . In the first two scenes of *Las Galas del difunto,* the witch flies across the stage on her way to deliver a letter. Later in the play, an angel appears blowing on a clarinet, her skirts moving in the breeze. In *Los Cuernos de Don Friolera,* at the moment of the murder, the stage direction is: "Several stars hide themselves in fright." . . .

Ghosts, witches, and miraculous events, however, do not alone create the magic of theatre: natural conflicts and commonplace occurences, when detached from their ordinary psychological frame of reference, may appear quite extraordinary. Artaud said that the object of theatrical magic is to sharpen the perception, to make the senses "more refined, more responsive than the intellect." Certainly, this is what Valle-Inclán intended in holding a concave mirror up to the procession of life. Thus, objects which the spectator had presumptuously assigned to a stabilized position in the order of things suddenly reveal an underlying vital force. It is our veneration of what already is that prevents us from making contact with this hidden energy. It was the wish of both Valle-Inclán and Artaud to help us to rediscover the prodigious aspect of everything that happens. (p. 462)

The greater part of Artaud's writings on theatre constitutes a tremendous effort to liberate the spoken work from a mere conceptual function and to give it an intrinsic reality. He asked why Western theatre must be considered as a theatre of dialogue, and insisted that the stage is a concrete and physical place that demands to be filled and to be made to speak its own concrete language independent of the spoken word and destined to the senses. That Valle-Inclán would have agreed with Artaud is evident by the number and length of stage directions in his plays; he too felt "the necessity for mime and an unconcern with the histrionic." Valle-Inclán frequently indicates movement without dialogue or at times with dialogue improvised by the actor. There is, for example, in *Los Cuernos de Don Friolera,* a stage direction for the dog Merlin, and as an aid to the actor, a suggestion of what is going on inside the character Don Friolera, even though those thoughts are not directly expressed in his subsequent speech. . . . Valle-Inclán makes use of stage directions in another way; he indicates actions that cannot conceivably be realized on the stage: in *Divinas Palabras* "there wafts the smell of extinguished candles that smoke on the altar . . . ," in *Los Cuernos de Don Friolera* "his moustache trembles like that of a cat sneezing . . ."—and all of these brief paragraphs are extremely lyrical. All of the scenic directions of *Voces de gesta,* in fact, are in rhymed verse. Of what use this is in a drama intended to be performed rather than read is most apparent to those who have had some practice in the theatre. The expressiveness with which the playwright conveys his intention is a direct source of inspiration to the director, actor, and designer, who will then transmit the poetry in dramatic terms. Thus, for the spectator, scenery, colors, light, sounds, mood—all those elements which create an atmosphere—will be the equivalent of the poetic stage directions.

Artaud, in denouncing strict adherence to a written text, does not entirely reject the spoken word. Apart from the theatre, Artaud was a published poet; in the theatre, however, words were significant to him not for their meanings, but for their sounds. According to Artaud, "words will be taken in an incantatory sense, truly magic,—and for their form, for their palpable emanations, and no longer only for their sense." . . . Once again, Valle-Inclán had anticipated Artaud's theorizing, for Max says quite simply in *Luces de Bohemia,* "Let's deform our speech in the same mirror that deforms our faces and the whole miserable life of Spain." Artaud argues that any true sentiment cannot be expressed exactly in words; to translate feeling into words is to hide it. Verbal expression is opposed to the overtness of nature, because it creates a surfeit in the mind. Clear language, which prevents any expansiveness, also prevents the appearance of poetry within the mind. "That is why an image, an allegory, or a figure which masks what it wants to reveal have more significance for the mind than the clarity of verbal analysis. It is thus that true beauty never strikes us directly. And that a sunset is beautiful because of all it takes away from us." It is thus that Valle-Inclán's base creatures and sordid environments have a strange kind of beauty—in that they are subjectively truer

and more real than they are by objective appearances. For Valle-Inclán, says Jean-Paul Borel, "there is in the world an order of things and events that escapes the grasp of rational intelligence, and before which 'the word in powerless.'" In searching to discover brutal reality beneath the polite veneer of society, Valle-Inclán relies on poetry as an escape from order. . . . "The mysterious truth that throbs just beyond what is directly perceptible"—this is what Valle-Inclán and Artaud sought to convey by means of expression utilizable on the stage—music, dance, plasticity, mime, gesture, intonation, architecture, light, and scenery. (pp. 463-64)

Both Artaud's and Valle-Inclán's use of poetry is calculated for a desired effect on the audience [an effect calculated to draw the audience into the play as participants]. Here again, their intentions are identical. . . . We share in the episodic journeying of Max Estrella and Don Juan Manuel; we become a part of the street crowds in *Divinas Palabras* and *Luces de Bohemia* or of the café crowd in *La Hija del capitán.* "The participation of the spectator is constantly solicited," says Borel, "and at the same time it is subjected to violent shocks." (pp. 464-65)

Further consideration of Valle-Inclán's drama must include a word about characterization. His grotesquely humorous cardboard figures are perhaps best evoked by Guillermo Díaz-Plaja: "Let's imagine as through a clouded crystal, as in fantastic chiaroscura, the silhouettes of the characters, their peculiar defects and their essential virtues sharply defined. Imagine a caricature that doesn't produce in you the least comic effect, but rather a penetrating feeling of reality." Valle-Inclán's characters, says Valbuena Prat, "are not of this century, nor of the last, nor of any concrete century. . . . These characters are people in the dramatic and perhaps philosophical sense of the word, not individuals. People, for him, represent states, planes of reality with different levels. . . . In the case of Valle-Inclán then, it is not a fixed preference for seeing ugliness, but it is a search for truth; he is willing to examine the rags in order to get at the human body beneath, to inspect the deformed body en route to the soul. However sordid or miserable or puppetlike his characters may be, they take on a human warmth as Valle-Inclán finds his way to their interior being. "The more Valle-Inclán penetrates the baseness and pettiness of man," says Borel, "the more he searches at the same time to love and understand him. . . . The poet's generosity is so overflowing that it gives birth to a sort of love where any other would have let scorn or rage triumph."

The ultimate similarity and point of difference between a Theatre of Cruelty and *esperpentismo* lies in the theatrical means of interpreting man's place in the universe. Both would liberate man from a world that has become too easy, too tranquil, too lacking in mystery. In order to attain his true dimensions and affirm himself in all his dramatic grandeur, man must rediscover and reexperience the extraordinary, the marvelous, and the horrible. Cenci, in Artaud's play [Les Cenci], poses the question, "Free? When the sky is ready to fall on our heads, who dares to speak to us of liberty?" Valle-Inclán would supply the answer to the question: in the words of Jean-Paul Borel: "The only valid solution is to accept this destiny in its totality, in its crushing grandeur, in its harshness. . . . Man becomes a wolf and the universe an ensemble of blind forces and menaces. He alone can triumph who becomes more wolf than the wolves, and of a measure to defy God and the devil." . . . The subtle difference between the two dramatic theories is the way in which they attempt to relate this human self-realization through cruelty to actual theatrical practice. For Artaud, theatre itself *is* the emanation of forces, the unleashing of possibilities, the mainspring for achieving the expansive life, however black it may be. It is *within* the theatre, on the other hand, that Valle-Inclán presents (rather than imposes) the transgression of ordinary limits and the possibility of experiencing the totality of life. (pp. 465-66)

> *Felicia Hardison, "Valle-Inclán and Artaud: Brothers under the Skin," in* Educational Theatre Journal *(© 1967 University College Theatre Association of the American Theatre Association), Vol. XIX, No. 4, December, 1967, pp. 455-66.*

RICARDO GULLÓN   (essay date 1968)

The *esperpento*, certainly, has the unreal reality of art. But if we speak of reality in more inclusive terms, we may say that the *esperpento* reveals it. Contrary to common opinion, the *esperpento*, either as Valle-Inclán or as others conceived it, was used to approach reality in a more lucid and open-eyed way than the so-called realistic way. The idea was to discover what we might call the "essence" of reality. If I hesitate to use this term it is because I am not sure that one may speak of such an "essence," since by its very nature the reality to which I am referring—that which interests the novelist—is a reality subject to time and space; it is an ever-changing historical reality. (p. 125)

As soon as we approach the *esperpento* we notice that its most obvious feature is its mechanization of character. The most affected and miserable are described variously, with a wealth of words, yet they are always defined by terms which express the same thing: mechanization; marionettes, puppets, automats, dummies, dolls—they are called, and that is how they behave.... The mechanical effect is unintentional. It recalls the process by which man, in modern society, becomes a mere thing. For the individual continually loses significance as he is dealt with more and more cynically, as a tiny piece of the collective mass to which he must subordinate himself. The very concept of the hero demands an autonomous behavior that contemporary society seldom allows for. (p. 126)

The man who has become a "thing" is like any other object in the world. It is not surprising that, in order to emphasize this likeness, Valle-Inclán should turn the technique around, describing an inanimate object—a piano, a toy car—as if it were animate. In *La corte de los milagros*, Adolfito Bonifaz and his friend toss a policeman out of a window, killing him. They think the act is insignificant, because in their minds the guard is not a human being but merely a handy thing for their entertainment. And naturally the act does more than turn the victim into a thing; it dehumanizes the spoiled boys, emphasizes their inhumanity. A man cannot remain human if he denies the humanity of other men. (pp. 127-28)

In using the *esperpento*, Valle-Inclán presents his imaginative vision of an ontological crisis directly related to a social phenomenon: the negation of the individual's freedom and even the individual himself. When this happens, there can be no genuine human behavior.... On the other hand, once a certain level of suffering has been reached, a victim of circumstances, a victim whose part in such circumstances is passive and accidental, can be humanized again. This is

the case of Zacarías. When he discovers the remains of his child half-devoured by the hogs, he is turned to stone by his silent, paralyzing grief which, in its sheer intensity, frees him from his social conditioning and allows him—unknowingly—to regain his freedom as a man.

If the *esperpento* is a vehicle for this type of intuition, then its negation of so-called realism (as a novelistic technique) represents an oblique means of restoring reality. It destroys our faith in ideas, values and methods by forcing us to face an ambiguity that makes us feel insecure. In his *Sonatas*, Valle-Inclán offered us a lie in disguise, fiction as imagination, romance as it might naturally be idealized. But from *Luces de Bohemia* on, he strives to present bare truth so as to show that the reality of the realists is unacceptable, whereas the *esperpentesque* caricature is a much less tricky approximation because it does not attempt to deceive the eye as the former method does.... What happened was that in the later works, the reader was more easily able to recognize fragments of everyday life. Instead of concealing anything, the deforming distortion actually emphasized the breakdown of traditional values. (pp. 128-29)

Ever since the *esperpento*, there has been a suspicion that reality may not be as real as our ancestors thought. The destructive effect of these works is exactly what was needed to reveal what lies under the make-up; how to find the depths of a reality which has been adulterated, buried under a beguiling superstructure. This revelatory intention necessarily submitted the subject matter to a degrading treatment. A myth cannot be destroyed unless the person who embodies it is belittled, brought down to a lower level—degraded.

The effects of Valle-Inclán's demythicizing technique in his *esperpentos* are swift and devastating. One example will suffice: "Robust and seductive, her Catholic Majesty [Isabella II] smiled in the manner of the woman who sells doughnuts in the church of the Virgen de la Paloma." What the author does, obviously, is condense in a short sentence two antithetical terms, producing a kind of oxymoron which emphasizes a manifold being and its natural contradictions while, at the same time, abolishing the myth of a "Divine, Catholic, Royal Majesty." (p. 129)

Thus one suddenly arrives at "the truth." ... [But] the truth is not that Queen Isabella is a common woman, that King Francis is a lap dog, or that the Marquis is a sissy. The truth is that although the Queen is a sexy wench, the King an impotent man, and the Marquis an effeminate cuckold, they are also what their titles indicate. They are the one and the other, both; not the simplification and schematization required by either myth or countermyth, both of which are equally conformist and indiscriminate. The "truth" offered by the *esperpento* is equivocal in its substance, as life is; both consist of a contradiction between the elements of being and the elements of seeming-to-be. If the *esperpento* is subversive, it is because it degrades myth, the idea of myth and its value or values, upon which the continuity of the bourgeois world, our world, depends.

The concept of character as a multiple being is basic to the creation of the *esperpento*. The demythicizing intent imposes one condition: not to take off the mask (which is impossible, since it sticks to the skin) but to show that the face itself is a mask and that whoever wears one plays a part for which he is sometimes prepared and sometimes not. In successive scenes, a character might appear wearing different masks, or not wearing one at all; but the result is that the reader or spectator cannot help wondering if the "definitive" face, more deceptive because of its naked appearance, is not just as superimposed or false.

My earlier remarks on the reduction of characters to automatons are confirmed by the titles of Valle's works (*Farsa de la enamorada del Rey, . . . Retablo de la avaricia, la lujuria y la muerte*) as well as by their generic definition: "plays for silhouettes", "melodramas for puppets". At the beginning of each work there is an indication of its meaning. The characters are presented as playing a part and being conscious of it. (pp. 130-31)

The awareness of playing a part in life which is not only fictitious but too well-known does not prevent a character from identifying with the part and living it as he is playing it. In *Los cuernos de don Friolera*, this kind of identification is achieved in a zig-zag manner, with the protagonist experiencing vacillations and oscillations; he would gladly be deceived into thinking himself a victim; but finally he must accept, though unwillingly, the role of defender or restorer of his own honor. Upon grasping such acceptance as something imposed from without and corresponding to an idea—or an image—wrought by social convention, the reader or spectator quickly draws a general rule from this particular case. The archetype of the "Calderonian" husband, a physician of his own honor, is fictitious at first and then becomes a reality under the pressure exerted by the concept of honor dictated by social custom and literary tradition.

In the same work, the reader may notice that the person-mask-character chain is not always the result of violence or social conditioning. It stems rather from the possible transformation of an actual prosaic being into an ideal one. When the individual becomes aware of such a possibility, the prestige of the role suddenly offered him is overwhelming and, together with other more worldly stimuli, it makes him behave as would the archetype. The aura surrounding the part arouses in him the wish to play it, as is the case with Doña Loreta and Pachequín, whose mutual attraction is reinforced when they imagine themselves as heavenly beings or, at least, dramatic personages of great renown. Play-acting becomes living when the puppets realize that their roles enable them to participate somehow in the prestige of the archetypes in whose orbit they move. The comic effect is due to the contrast between how they see themselves and what they are, between appearance and ambition. In view of the circumstances, the picture must seem grotesque to the spectator. (p. 132)

Now and then buffoonery comes to a halt, and in the sudden stillness of the moment, brought about by the intrusion of something unexpected and tragic (for example, in *Luces de Bohemia,* the murder of the revolutionary worker by the police), there is a change of atmosphere. And the reader, like the characters in the story, suddenly discovers he is in the presence of true drama. The puppets take on a human aspect when they learn that the absurd wandering through the streets at night is something which they share with archetypes; it is the natural way to live or act out the adventure to which poets are destined. On a symbolic level, *Luces de Bohemia* may be considered a descent into Hell which, despite the esperpentesque degradation, retains a pathetic magnificence.

In a sense it is also an exception to the rule. The degrading element, part and parcel of the genre, is not operative when Max Estrella's misadventures are seen at a deeper level. On the contrary: the myth of the poet descending into the darkness in search of truth is more pathetic when (as is the case here) he cannot return to the land of the living. As the end approaches, the darkness surrounding the blind poet gradually brings together the diverse tragicomic or simply grotesque elements. It may be that these, separately, add a touch of degradation to the situation. But the final result, achieved after scenes of sheer drama, in which all buffoonery is gone, is anything but predictable. The myth is not ultimately degraded; it is restored to the world of human values through parable.

Which is why I speak of an exception: the usually demythicizing *esperpento* does not function typically in this case. Instead, through unexpected and sordid ways, it rehabilitates the character of the nocturnal wanderer, Max Estrella. (pp. 133-34)

The unexpected revitalization and bringing up to date of myths should prove that Valle's supposed system of deformation is not really so systematic and does not always produce the same effects. The destruction of the myths, or beliefs and values, on which middle class society is based does not annihilate—though it does transform—other types of myths, especially that of the poet as clairvoyant and prophet. The poet may not be a "tower of God," as Darío put it, but he does end up as a blind prophet, the chosen one, although being chosen by the Gods may be more a punishment than a prize, from the standpoint of calm and security. The intensity of revelation that distinguishes the poet from other men is accompanied by an intensity of suffering, also imposed by the Gods. (pp. 134-35)

Something else must be said regarding the transformation of reality into an *esperpento*. Reality is naturally not grotesque; it simply *is*. If it seems grotesque, it is because our vision qualifies it as such. A shift in attitude or point of view alters the apparent character of what we behold. Our vision, then, creates the *esperpento,* in acting as a distorting mirror. (p. 135)

Visual distance is a decisive factor in the process of turning reality into an *esperpento*. From afar the individual is diminished and dehumanized. This, in turn, lets him be observed ironically, so that the onlooker does not participate in the movements and gestures which seem ridiculous or even senseless. The onlooker cannot participate in what he sees because he is incapable of distinguishing or discerning. It is by the grace of creative language that Ana de Ozores and Anna Karenina seem to be like us and to be present among us, while Doña Loreta and Lupita la Romántica simply make us laugh because they are only puppets; yet they aspire to conduct themselves like people.

The reader or spectator may see things from the viewpoint and in the perspective selected for him by the author. But he also sees—or imagines—things which the latter purposely omits. He comes to realize that to see things from the inside leads to tolerance, whereas to see them from the outside leads to criticism, distortion, and caricature. (pp. 135-36)

If an individual who is inside accepts the view as seen by one outside, what occurs is a voluntary transformation of reality into an *esperpento*. (p. 136)

*Ricardo Gullón, "Reality of the 'Esperpento',"
translated by Miguel Gonzalez-Gerth, in* Valle-Inclán Centennial Studies, *edited by Ricardo Gullón
(copyright © 1968 by Board of Regents, The Uni-*

versity of Texas at Austin), University of Texas, 1968, pp. 123-37.

ALBERTO ADELL   (essay date 1970)

Don Ramón Maria del Valle-Inclán y Montenegro, as he was usually known, appears now, 35 years after his death, more outstanding than ever.... His work was a unique progress towards the final expression of personal meaning—this is not true of the other writers [of the Generation of 1898] whose work reached its peak earlier in their lives.

Moreover he did not share his colleagues' fascination with Castile or with Castilian mysticism or with the Golden Ages of the XVI and XVII centuries. He was not the first Galician writer to put his native land on the map of Castilian letters. Here the novelist, Countess Pardo-Bazán, preceded him, though her Galician scene is less vivid, less full of literary significance, than Valle's. His Galicia is fraught with literary allusions and seen through romantic spectacles. It is a dream land of ghosts and nightmares chiefly inhabited by the barbarian scions of feudal families. In his pages the relics of a pseudo-mediaeval past are projected into a nineteenth century which is ideal rather than strictly temporal, and put into a literary shape which is reminiscent of Barbey d'Aurevilly, Maeterlinck and D'Annunzio. This assortment of faded names may look unpromising and outmoded now, but the opposite is the truth. Today when most of his models, especially Maeterlinck and D'Annunzio are almost beyond resuscitation, we are able to see that behind the Symbolist façade something real and living is at work. The trappings of Modernism or Art Nouveau may still be there but real strength and vitality are beginning to be visible too.

In style, Valle was more colourful than the rest of his literary generation. Most of them favoured a simple, almost bare style of prose, with short sentences and a near Spartan frugality of thought and feeling.... By comparison with [Azorín and Baroja], Valle looks almost Baroque. Not for him the sun-scorched world beneath the limitless sky of the Castilian plains or the Eastern Mediterranean lands, but the countryside which his native mists enshroud, adding their own strange tints to its colourful scenery. It is a mysterious and sensuous world and his way of describing it has a flavour of Rabelais—the verbal ingenuity and fecundity of language are in a class with Rubén Darío's. (pp. 108-09)

At the time of his death he was a very popular figure in the Madrid literary landscape, though for the wrong reasons. People found him amusing but they failed to grasp his literary stature.... At this time poetry was the thing in Spain. Theatre and fiction, in particular, were at a low ebb. Valle was considered mainly as a poet who happened to write plays, and sometimes wandered with them into the limelight—a strange kind of plays, while his fiction was poetically distorted.

Thirty-five years later the whole situation is different. Today nobody can ignore the value of Valle's poetry although nobody would classify him merely as a poet, even though that is what in reality he may have been. In the world of the theatre the old verdict has been reversed. More and more it looks as if the only real contribution Spain has made to the theatre in the first half of this century is in two names only—Valle-Inclán and Federico García Lorca. (p. 109)

In truth the plays did not do much on their own behalf. In style they are a cross between poetry and fiction, although they include some theatrical elements. The stage directions, for instance, are written in a luscious prose, as if they came straight out of a novel—and sometimes they are in verse. There is certainly no clear distinction between Valle's fiction and his theatre.... If the plays could be read like straight novels, without any loss of theatrical force, his novels could be acted like plays, so dramatic and visual is their conception. (pp. 109-10)

[Valle] began in a highly imitative fashion. About the turn of the century he was writing fiction of the Eighties and Nineties. There were sad longhaired consumptive heroines, misty settings, a somewhat declassé aristocracy inhabiting old houses, half of them shipping themselves off to the Antilles, half of them still hunting and whoring. It was more Barbey d'Aurevilly than Maupassant, but still saved by the elegance of the prose. These first attempts reached their close with the cycle of novels written to commemorate a partial, romantic and personal view of the Spanish Civil War of the XIX century—the Carlist War; and, still more successfully, with another cycle, the *Sonatas,* four short novels, each taking its name from one of the seasons, which were the fictional 'memoirs' of the Marquis of Bradomín, a character into which Valle projected a fanciful image of himself. He wrote them in this most sensuous, elegant prose and they have only slightest suspicion of the *outré* and perhaps of the sadistic. (p. 110)

From these relatively early works, Valle's career advanced towards a clear personal goal. When he was about fifty he suffered a critical change—his world vision turned sour. The irony, the melancholy, the delighted play with the ideas of love, beauty and honour, which he had learned from the French 18th century—everything suffered a sea-change. It has more to do with vision than with taste. The mirror in which Valle sees the world—*his* mirror—has been warped, and sends back weirdly comic, unnatural, horrid shapes. The world has been turned into an *esperpento. Esperpento* means a "fright", something, especially a person, whose appearance is both terrible and laughable. Like the distorted image in a convex mirror, *esperpento* produces grotesques in a moral as well as an aethetic sense.

Esperpento is not only the structure of the vision, it is the work itself, a form beyond drama or comedy. To be essentially good or nice is no way of escaping from it—it makes its grotesques from the young, the innocent or the beautiful, as well as from the old, the corrupted or the ugly. *Esperpento* belongs to the theatre—*is* theatre. Everything in its world is a theatrical image or toy, stylised and mechanical. From the theatre, *esperpento* invaded Valle's fiction which is increasingly *seen* by the writer, just as a playwright can see as well as hear his plays before they reach the stage.

Esperpento then, for Valle resulted from a change in his aesthetic and moral attitudes. The novel in which he first openly applied the new method or as we might rather say, *tactics,* is **Tirano Banderas....** It is a *rara avis* in Spanish fiction, in being set in South America.... Rather in the way of Conrad with his Costaguana, he put his typical South American tyrant, Santos Banderas, in a fictitious Santa Fe de Tierra Firme, which is mainly Mexico. Here the poet is in charge. The short sentences brim with colour and the writing is full of small significant details. The final effect is of a fine variegated jig-saw puzzle. But the moral feeling is depressed. The aboriginal Indian race sunk in its poverty forms a sort of background frieze for the cast—Generals plotting to succeed the current tyrant; the parasitical Spanish colony of petty shopkeepers; the degenerate diplomats—the only hope is a revolution which would go to the roots.

The last creative period in Valle's life was devoted to the composition of a set of novels woven round a "non-event"—the downfall of Queen Isabella II in 1868. Although at the time it looked portentous, nothing came of it—it was like a comic opera Bastille. Valle envisaged it as a sour and faded operetta—soiled ermine, pawned tiaras, grease-painted faces. The same period had been covered also by Benito Pérez Galdós's *Episodios Nacionales*. . . . But there was an important difference between both writers. Galdós, whose first novel takes place in 1805 (the battle of Trafalgar), was too bored with his subject when he reached the 1870s to take trouble with it and his narrative looks as flat and conventional as an official report. Valle's is quite another matter. He sees everybody and everything with the same sharp eye and nothing escapes his contempt. Royal characters and freemasons, *camarillas* and *carbonari,* aristocrats and beggars, all are reduced to puppets in a Punch and Judy show—not merely to exercize his fancy or his contempt but because they were all in fact very much like bad actors shouting their heads off in a foolish play. (pp. 110-11)

[*El Ruedo ibérico*] was conceived as a great historical panorama. The original plan comprised three series of three novels each, nine altogether, and was meant to extend as far as the Spanish-American War of 1898. But Valle died when only the first two novels had been completed. (p. 112)

> Alberto Adell, "A New Study of Valle-Inclán's Art," in International P.E.N. Bulletin of Selected Books, *Vol. XXI, No. 1, 1970, pp. 108-112.*

ROBERT LIMA (essay date 1972)

Insofar as it is possible to categorize the creative foundation of an author who produced twenty-four plays, twelve novels, seven collections of stories, three poetry books, and assorted other titles, not to mention numerous translations and adaptations from the French, Italian, and Portuguese, it can be said that Valle-Inclán's literature, like his life, was conceived and crystallized under self-imposed aesthetic parameters. The full exposition of his ideas on creativity is found in *The Lamp of Marvels*, subtitled "Spiritual Exercises." In this apologia Valle-Inclán develops fully the travails of the artist in rising above his humanity, in breaking the bondage of the body to set his creative spirit free, to the end of reaching the heights of Beauty. In Valle-Inclán's version of the agon, the artist becomes a mystic through a threefold aesthetic initiation: "There are three transits through which the soul passes before it is initiated into the mystery of Eternal Beauty. The first transit, painful love; the second transit, joyful love; the third transit, love with renunciation and quietude." . . . His commitment to the search for creative fulfillment is visible in the concerted effort he made to energize aesthetic principles into kinesis in his literature. This process can be traced back in the stories first issued in Spanish and Mexican periodicals prior to 1895. These early works disclose their author's dedication to stylistic perfection, the first hallmark of his aesthetic stance, for, as he believed, "Literary men will live in future anthologies because of a well-written page. Beauty resides only in form. Whoever fails to carve and

polish his style will be no more than a poor writer." This approach was carried through in all his writings.

In 1895 he published his first book, *Femeninas*, which contained six tales whose protagonists were amorous Latin women. The work showed the earliest polarity in Valle-Inclán's literature: a belated romanticism which paid homage to Zorrilla, author of *Don Juan Tenorio* and one of the idols of the emergent writer. Valle-Inclán's second book, *Nuptial Song* . . . , was a novelette with similar romantic emphasis. Issued in a handsomely designed book of sparse size, *Nuptial Song* marked the beginning of the author's dedication to the totality of creation; in it he integrated content and design to achieve an artistic whole. This personal attention to the physical aspect of his books was a second characteristic of Valle-Inclán's aestheticism.

While *Femeninas* passed largely unnoticed, *Nuptial Song* caught the attention of several prominent critics. Clarín devoted an entire column in a newspaper to the slim volume, concluding that its author was a man of imagination capable of achieving a personal style but regretting that the work looked back to innovations of an earlier era. Navarro Ledesma also pointed to this rearward view in a derogatory way, noting that Valle-Inclán was an exotic writer whose work contained "an excess of intellectual elegance or decadent refinement." But as Azorín was to note years later, these critics had not realized that the past was merely a springboard for Valle-Inclán and not a rut. (pp. 6-8)

Valle-Inclán achieved his first literary success as a novelist with the issuance of *Sonatas: Memoirs of the Marquis de Bradomin.* This series of four Modernist novels relates the sensual life of the protagonist in autobiographical episodes allied to each of the four seasons. The splendid, if anachronistic, figure of the Marquis recounts his amorous exploits from the spring of his youth to the winter of his old age; in the process he adds to the classic concept of Don Juan, who was affected solely by passion and death, the sensibility requisite to an appreciation of his surroundings and melancholy reminiscence of the women whose lives he has touched indelibly. (pp. 8-9)

The four *Sonatas* . . . are exemplary of the artistry of Valle-Inclán in his first novelistic period. On the one hand, the series of novels brought to fruition those stylistic and aesthetic elements first manifest in earlier works. On the other hand, the four books were freed from the anarchic tendencies, youthful bravado, and archaic penchant which marred many of Valle-Inclán's first stories. The tenets which guided this new maturity were those of Modernism. . . . (p. 13)

[*Flower of Sanctity,*] the most underrated of Valle-Inclán's novels yet one of his best, is another Modernist work. Its powerful plot, played against the mountainous landscape of Galicia, [states] the author's theme of folk superstitions. In the mind of Adega, the country girl who is the novel's protagonist, a deep sense of piety is transformed into sensuality when, convinced that the pilgrim before her is Christ, she gives herself to him. . . . Led by ignorance to accept a common sexual act as divinely instigated, Adega acquires an unshakeable, if mistaken, faith. Her devotion makes her heroic.

Subsequent novels showed a trend away from the erotic themes of the *Sonatas* and *Flower of Sanctity*, and a new literary concern with politico-historical topics. . . . Historical evidence, [Valle-Inclán] believed, showed that the only possible way of achieving humanitarian goals was to have the ideal imposed upon society by the disciplined and selfless ruler, be he monarch, president, or dictator. These Machiavellian views are reflected in those novels that studied politics in action.

The theme of Carlism, given its first ample treatment by Valle-Inclán in *Winter Sonata,* was to reappear in the play *Epic Voices* and in a series of novels collected under the title *The Carlist War.* The latter, a trilogy, began with *The Crusaders of the Cause.* . . . (pp. 13-15)

The novel, replete with movement and suspense, lacks expert treatment of its subject. Valle-Inclán was to gain this when, after the issuance of *The Crusaders of the Cause,* he made the first of many trips to the strongholds of Carlism. . . . The sequels to the first novel show the mastery of detail, history, and landscape which Valle-Inclán achieved during this sojourn.

Consequently, perhaps, *The Splendor of the Bonfire* . . . is less a plotted novel than a sequence of episodes set against the hostilities. And although only one battle scene is described, the presence of war is pervasive. Everywhere in the work there is evidence of the bloody and frustrated history of Carlism. Everywhere, too, is visible the impartiality of the author in recounting events or depicting characters. Valle-Inclán wrote the novel without recourse to fatiguing series of occurrences, outcomes, dates. His view penetrated to the core and the resultant is a sensation of the war as seen through the medium of selected characters and events. The vision and its presentation are poetic. Rather than make a protagonist act out his role with the war as a backdrop, the author brought the war itself into the foreground and made the human beings involved in it part of the over-all scheme. (p. 16)

The third novel in the series, however, has a historical protagonist of imposing stature in Manuel Santa Cruz, a controversial priest whom the author treats with deep psychological and sociological insight. The ferocious warrior-priest, who was more a bandit than a patriot in the eyes of both government and Carlist forces, is drawn in *The Ancient Gerfalcons* . . . with a sympathy born out of the recognition of his legendary viability. The cruel, despotic man is interpreted in the novel as a fanatic with a holy cause—his ideal—which makes him inflexible. In his willful dedication, he emerges in epic proportions. (p. 17)

Although the most successful of his writings were novels, Valle-Inclán's best work was done for the theater. (p. 23)

The high-spiritedness of most of [Valle-Inclán's early] plays belies the deep concern of their author with the social and political inequities that marked European life in the period of World War I. The times were too severe for reality to be relegated to a secondary role and Valle-Inclán recognized the need to write about anquish and frustration, both of which he knew intimately. As a poet he had already made his statement in *The Pipe of Kiff.* . . . He found it necessary to state his concern also in his dramas. He did so through a group of plays designated *Esperpentos.* . . . (p. 33)

It is in *The Lights of Bohemia* . . . that the process first takes dramatic form. This is a drama is fifteen scenes which traces the final hours in the bitter life of Máximo Estrella, a poet blinded by syphilis, who has struggled for recognition only to witness the deterioration of hope. His life moves steadily toward its pathetic denouement while the grotesqueries of existence become increasingly visible in the incidence of irony, cynicism, baseness, lewdness, opportunism, mockery, and alienation. The dissonance of life becomes the reality of Máximo Estrella. (pp. 33-4)

The bitterness of *The Lights of Bohemia* is never repeated again in the same tone in the drama of Valle-Inclán. But there are other plays which portray the range of human frailty and social vices with the satirical gusto and planned distortion of the *Esperpento. Divine Words* (1920) is exemplary. Valle-Inclán's interpretation of rural Galicia's reality (sorrow, drudgery, death) encompasses the grotesque, both in situation and in characterization. This tragicomedy shows that the bucolic, too, can be seen in the distortive mirror. *Divine Words* is a tale of sexuality told in terms of repression and license with the added spice of farcical elements. (p. 36)

Divine Words is one of the masterworks of Valle-Inclán. Not only does it give evidence of the playwright's control of dramatic form and dialogue, but it becomes universal in its sensitive treatment of the human condition through such finely drawn characters as Pedro Gailo and Mari-Gaila. In Lucero, he has created a memorable satyr—half-human, half-satanic—who, despite his erotic nature, has nothing in common with the finesse of a Bradomín; Lucero is the embodiment of the paganism that lies beneath the veneer of civilized man, more so than Arlequin in *The Marchioness Rosalinda* or Don Juan Manuel Montenegro in the *Comedias bárbaras.*

Among other plays that treat the theme of rural Galicia are three small works. (p. 39)

Macabre plays of avarice, lust, and death, *The Paper Rose, Sacrilege,* and *Blood Pact* are powerful pieces worthy of the Grand Guignol in their theatrical effects and interpretations of humanity's baseness. . . .

Yet another thematic vein was explored in *The Captain's Daughter, The Corpse's Regalia,* and *Don Friolera's Horns,* three plays collected in *Shrove Tuesday.* . . . These three *Esperpentos* are strongly antimilitaristic, deriving their inspiration from the abuses and corruption of the Primo de Rivera regime together with the foreign fiascos of Spanish arms. (p. 42)

Don Friolera's Horns . . . is the best of these three *Esperpentos.* The plot of the cuckold provides the framework for a satire which exposes the inanity of social conventions and debunks that drama which thrives on bastard thematics. The play, therefore, is both a social and a theatrical document. . . . Don Estrafalario and Don Manolito, peripatetic intellectuals, are seen conversing against the active background of a fair as the prologue commences. It is through the former that Valle-Inclán expresses his theory on laughter with statements that parallel those of his contemporary Bergson: "Tears and laughter arise from the contemplation of elements which are on a par with us. . . . We reserve our mockery for that which relates to us. . . . My aesthetic requires the surpassing of pain and laughter as in the case of dead men telling each other tales of the living." The treatment of emotions on the stage was a serious concern with Valle-Inclán and he vehemently opposed those writers who, like Echegaray, abused the comic and the tragic muse in order to achieve a momentary reaction from the audience. The sublimation of emotion, as Don Estrafalario stated, represented a first step in the preparation of the audience for objectivity. It is this process which *Don Friolera's Horns* implements. (pp. 42-3)

This and all the *Esperpentos* make caricatures of the characters. This dehumanization destroys all possibility of attachment or sympathy. But it is not the dramatist who creates the grotesqueness that the *Esperpento* contains; he merely takes a superior position, like the puppeteer, and surveys the activities below. What he observes is that modern man is unable to cope with his burden. . . . (p. 44)

Rather than encourage empathetic response in his audiences, as did classic tragedy, Valle-Inclán opted for their objective exploration of the enigma of human existence. This approach was more appropriate to the times, he believed. The *Esperpento* concerns itself with sociopolitical injustice, the instability of personal relationship, the oppressive reliance on tradition, the subservience of the populace to superstitions (including religion), the implausibility of selflessness in contemporary life. Because it attains its goals so admirably, the *Esperpento* is the apogee of the playwright's efforts and helps establish him as a major figure in Spanish drama; because it views life in an absurdist mode, the *Esperpento* marks Valle-Inclán as the precursor of Beckett and Ionesco. (p. 45)

> Robert Lima, in his Ramón del Valle-Inclán (Columbia Essays on Modern Writers Pamphlet No. 59; copyright © 1972 Columbia University Press; reprinted by permission of the publisher), Columbia University Press, 1972, 48 p.

VERITY SMITH (essay date 1973)

Valle-Inclán's later novels, *Tirano Banderas* (*The Tyrant*), *La corte de los milagros* (*The Court of Miracles*), *Viva mi dueño* (*Hurrah for my Owner*) and the unfinished *Baza de espadas* (*Military Tricks*), are without doubt the most complex, ambitious and rewarding of his prose works. The style Valle employs is taut and telegraphic. Furthermore, . . . he sometimes pares down descriptions to a bare minimum of words after the manner of a stage direction. This, however, does not mean that the later novels make for easy reading. Indeed, the reverse applies since Valle is as determined now as in his earlier *modernista* phase to enrich the Spanish language by every means available to him. When conventional linguistic resources are felt to be inadequate, Valle-Inclán offers words of his own coinage. Thus there are times when a dictionary is but an inadequate tool to clarify the meaning of certain passages. In addition, the *Iberian Ring* novels demand an extremely close acquaintance with the minutiae of Spanish nineteenth-century history if all the allusions are to be understood. (p. 127)

[*The Tyrant*] undoubtedly the masterpiece of the *esperpento* period of the 1920's, takes place in an imaginary Latin-American state, Tierra Caliente, in the second half of the nineteenth century. The country is intended as a synthesis of all the states in the Southern continent which explains why its landscape, as critics have noted, is composite and unreal. . . . [Valle] deliberately avoided identifying Tierra Caliente with any specific land because the theme of the novel—the downfall of a macabre dictator—is considered relevant to the continent as a whole. (pp. 127-28)

[The] events narrated in the prologue take place after those related in the body of the novel and immediately precede the events forming the climax of the novel contained in the epilogue. Much of the action related in the central sections should be interpreted as occurring simultaneously. Furthermore, Valle is concerned with the depiction of a social cross section and not with that of a handful of individuals. This is made abundantly clear when the author speaks of his desire in this novel to imitate El Greco's technique of cramming so many people onto the one canvas that it would take a Byzantine mathematician to replace them in their correct positions should these be disturbed. (p. 128)

Valle saw Latin-American society divided into three categories: the native, the Creole, and the foreigner. Each one of these categories is represented by three figures, the native by Santos Banderas himself, Zacarías and an anonymous Indian who is tortured at the tyrant's orders. The Creoles are represented by Filomeno Cuevas, Roque Cepeda and Sánchez Oncaña; the *gachupines* or Spaniards by the Spanish minister, the plump businessman Celes Galindo and the pawnbroker Quintín Pereda.

Santos Banderas, whose name is not without significance as it suggests authority resting on religion and military force, is at the very center of this novel, affecting in arbitrary fashion the lives of everyone in the country he dominates. He is not an extrovert, sybaritic dictator with a love of fast living; instead, he is ascetic, choosing to reside in a former monastery, prudish, pedantic, and mentally unstable. The last point is emphasized not only by the insanity of his daughter but also by numerous references to his hypochondria and to the unhealthy delight he takes in humiliating those who like Nachito or Doctor Polaco have no defense against him. . . . The deadly nature of the tyrant's rule and the menace his presence implies to the citizens of Tierra Caliente are brought home to the reader not only by examples of his callousness and brutality, but also by the constant use of images to dehumanize him and equate him with death.

The first book, in which the tyrant is watching an Indian being tortured in the monastery's parade ground, is called, appropriately enough, "Ikon of the Tyrant." The reference to an ikon together with descriptions equating him with a wooden doll and a sacred cow is present to underline his quasi-godlike status in Tierra Caliente. Passages in which he is described as a mummy, or his head is visualized as a skull or a piece of parchment add to the notion of divinity that of death, in other words, a god bearing an affinity to the Aztec gods of pre-Columbian Mexico.

Death hovers also in the background: the action of the novel takes place during the religious festivals of All Saints and All Souls; references to the Monastery of San Martín de los Mostenses, where the tyrant has his headquarters, remind one that in the country it is impossible to escape from his control; buzzards wing across the skies of Tierra Caliente; the corpses of political prisoners thrown to the sharks bob on the water at the base of the prison fortress. Even the pottery fashioned by the natives is described as "funereal," adding to the impression that the novel is a symphony to death.

Of the three racial groups mentioned by Valle, those who are treated with least sympathy are the *gachupines* and other foreigners, whether the members of the diplomatic corps who are incapable of taking a firm line, or the rapacious businessmen and landowners. The latter group is intent on enriching itself by the exploitation of a typical "banana republic." (pp. 130-32)

The Creoles are more sympathetically portrayed, with the exception of Sánchez Ocaña who, as the professional poli-.ician, is equipped for action with grandiloquent speeches, empty rhetoric and wilting platitudes. A contrast is established between the two remaining Creoles; Filomeno Cuevas is essentially a man of action, while Roque Cepeda is a dreamer with a marked mystical bent. Filomeno has the qualities of an epic hero. He is courageous, upright and generous of heart. Circumstances rather than inclination have turned him into an ardent revolutionary, for, as he says to his wife, he could not in time have faced their children had he not taken action to end the tyranny of Santos Banderas.

Roque Cepeda sees the revolution as but the necessary first step in the emancipation of the Indian, whose position in the social scale is barely higher than a serf's. It is ironical that don Roque is opposed to Santos Banderas in this respect, since the tyrant is an Indian who doubts the capacities of his own kind, while Roque Cepeda is a Creole and has forsaken his social position to take up arms for the Indian. It is obvious that don Roque has been influenced by Gnostic doctrines, for when the author comments on his religious beliefs, he indicates that in Cepeda's eyes man is a celestial being condemned to live in a world ruled by Time: "Men are exiled angels: the perpetrators of a celestial crime, they seek forgiveness for their theological sin along the ways of time which are those of the world."

The temperaments of the revolutionary leaders imply that Valle-Inclán was not overly optimistic about the political future of Tierra Caliente. Filomeno Cuevas is essentially a practical man who would be likely to retire from the scene as soon as his mission was accomplished; Roque Cepeda is too idealistic to compromise, placate and maneuver in the tough arena of politics, and Sánchez Ocaña's mind is as empty as his speeches imply. Thus it would seem that after a relatively short period the country would once more be the victim of a military coup followed by a further period of tyranny. (pp. 132-33)

The technical and stylistic excellence of *The Tyrant* is apparent not only in the elaborate structure and in the effects used to suggest simultaneity of action, but also in the exquisite descriptions which introduce and round off individual scenes together with the vivid imagery. . . . The techniques of dehumanization favored by Valle-Inclán in the *esperpento* period are much in evidence here. There is a variety of puppet metaphors including German automata, wire dolls and Chinese shadow puppets. Also apparent are certain techniques borrowed from the cinema, particularly in the episode concerning Domiciano de la Gándara's escape from the police. Here the cuts from the pursuers to the pursued have the lightning rapidity of a film sequence in which the technique of parallel cutting is being employed. One other detail which is very reminiscent of the movie is the description of a room as observed by the tyrant in a mirror.

Both in terms of theme and style, *The Tyrant* is an outstanding example of Valle-Inclán's mature production. It reveals the underlying unity of his work in that the sympathy shown formerly for the Galician social outcast, the beggar, is replaced here by his sincere championing of the Indian's cause. (pp. 133-34)

It is no easy matter to summarize the plots of the *Iberian Ring* novels because of the number of characters involved and the wealth of circumstantial detail. Although they appear fragmentary, this is not in fact the case since . . . both the completed novels of the cycle have a symmetrical structure which gives them unity despite the proliferation of characters and the variety of unrelated incidents. Valle seeks in the two novels to depict in breadth the social and political situation of Spain in 1868. It has been remarked by some critics, among them Pedro Salinas, that there is too much warmth and indignation in Valle-Inclán's blistering attacks on Isabeline Spain for him to be concerned with the past. It is thought, instead, that the nineteenth-century setting of these novels marks the author's intention to criticize the society of his own day. Bearing in mind that the censorship during Primo de Rivera's dictatorship was severe, it is quite likely that Valle availed himself of this subterfuge to wage a full-scale attack on the political and military corruption of his own period. (pp. 134-35)

It is worth considering the two completed volumes of the cycle simultaneously [*The Court of Miracles* and *Hurrah for My Owner*] since they are linked not only structurally but also thematically by the author's concentration on the Queen, her courtiers, and their dubious or nefarious activities. In the third book of *Military Tricks* the revolutionaries, whose position had already been more prominent in *Hurrah for My Owner,* completely dominate the scene and no space at all in the novel—which admittedly is incomplete—is allotted to the Queen.

Speaking of the *esperpento,* Ramiro de Maeztu observed that it was "the negative aspect of the world, a dance seen by the deaf, religion examined by a skeptic . . ." Certainly, this statement is applicable to the *Iberian Ring* novels whose devastating satire is of a totally negative order. Very little in this bleak panorama meets with the author's approval; when he does show sympathy for some of the characters, as in the case with Adolfito Bonafaz' charming sister and her elderly suitor Bradomín, the note that is struck is so unusual that it appears incongruous and out of harmony with the whole. Gone are the bold, upright country nobles of the Galician trilogies. They are replaced by . . . fatuous, sycophantic court aristocrats. . . . These city aristocrats are fundamentally ignorant and superficial; they are versed in nothing more profound than court intrigue and the sleight of hand most likely to improve their position in the eyes of the monarch. It might be thought that in his depiction of the Queen, her ministers and the aristocrats, Valle is guilty of exaggeration. . . . [But] Valle had little need to distort, for he chose a period which was by its very nature a parody of an equitable society.

It is above all Valle's intense dislike of the army which reveals that he is not solely concerned with a portrayal of the past in these novels. There are times when his comments are so acrimonious that they cease to be witty. At such times the author's normally impassive front, the "lofty vision" he sought to cultivate in his novels, is not in evidence, and the author speaks clearly with his own voice. By and large these are dramatic novels in which the author allows the characters to speak for themselves; but there is one extremely important passage in *Hurrah for My Owner,* reflective in tone, where the author gives his opinion on the course Spanish history had taken in the nineteenth century. He maintains that until after the Napoleonic Invasion Spain was united by a religious fervor whose instrument was the Holy Office. However, after the Peninsular War an attempt was made to supplant this with patriotism and the inspiration of the armed forces. Such an endeavor was vain, resulting in the regional divisions and the internecine warfare from which the Spanish nation had suffered in the nineteenth century. (pp. 141-42)

There is a remark in *The Crusaders of the Cause* which is pertinent to Valle's social appraisal of Spain in 1868. It is made by a tinker who comments that since Spain is led by ruffians and villains, it is only just that everyone be allowed to behave after the same fashion. This is precisely the philosophy carried into effect by the citizens of the *Iberian Ring*. What Valle reveals is that the corruption in the higher echelons of society has spread to the very humblest Spanish citizens. The bandits are protected by the large landowners; an officer of the law will beat up an innocent man because of the tempting prospect of promotion; a group of young bloods throw a policeman out of a window as a joke; a man cares more about a mare with a ticklish throat than about a dying woman. There is a fundamental disregard for human life which has very disturbing undertones. It suggests a society which has completely lost its standard of values and is about to be plunged into chaos. This sense of disquiet is underscored by the episodes of violence punctuating these novels: the devastating flood in the fourth book of *The Court of Miracles* and the affray at the Solana Fair in *Hurrah for My Owner*. (pp. 143-44)

It remains finally to assess the development of Valle-Inclán's novelistic technique from the *modernista* novels to those of the *esperpento* period. In many ways there is little change. Nearly all of Valle-Inclán's novels have a dramatic bias, and in all cases the author raises an artistic barrier which may be idealized (*modernismo*) or degraded (*esperpento*) between himself and the reader, preferring the indirect approach and believing that the characters should speak for themselves. However, novels such as those of the Carlist War trilogy are concerned with active Traditionalist propaganda, while in the *Iberian Ring* novels Valle is in a destructive, negative mood. Circumstances have turned him into an angry old man whose personal disillusionment with the state of his country is given concrete expression in his later novels. Something else which changes with the emergence of the *esperpento*—and this is as obvious in the novels as in the plays of the period—is the artistic stimulus; the jerky, telegraphic prose style of *The Tyrant* and the *Iberian Ring* cycle, coupled with their profusion of startling and complex images are much more modern than those of, say, *Saintly Flower* or the *Sonatas*. (p. 145)

> *Verity Smith, "The Later Novels," in her* Ramón del Valle-Inclán *(copyright © 1973 by Twayne Publishers, Inc.; reprinted with the permission of Twayne Publishers, a Division of G. K. Hall & Co., Boston), Twayne, 1973, pp. 127-45.*

THOMAS R. FRANZ (essay date 1974)

La cara de Dios is a long novel, originally published in [1900] and virtually unobtainable ever since. Ostensibly it is based on a play by Carlos Arniches, which in reality bears almost no resemblance to it. . . . [What] we have is a lengthy, sometimes well-written murder mystery which incorporates many of the constants in Valle-Inclán's production: violence, mystery, black magic, eroticism, degenerate aristocracy, political consciousness, and effective use of neologisms, abrupt juxtapositions, synesthesia, and onomatopoeia.

Although on the whole a poor novel, the work is technically and historically interesting for a variety of reasons. The narrator frequently destroys cause-and-effect relationships, while creating scenes of great irony, by presenting events out of chronological order. Numerous sections read like a naturalist novel, while a late segment involving the newspaper *El socialista* suggests a *roman à clef*. The author demonstrates a mature ability to analyze the causes of alienation

and anti-social behavior, particularly those with an economic base. At the same time he repeatedly pokes fun at those who employ the unwieldly tools of sociological analysis where intuition might provide simpler, more accurate results.

The novel's faults are many and derive in part from an agreement whereby the author's payment depended upon the length of his manuscript. Early details are continually repeated lest the reader forget, and at least fifteen or twenty powerful scenes are ruined through unnecessary dialogue or repetitious action. It is sometimes impossible to make stylistic distinctions between the characters' paraphrased thinking and the ever-present voice of the narrator. Late in the novel the narrator annoyingly interjects numerous "Dear Reader" asides in order to get himself out of untenable plot situations. If there is a saving grace in all of this, it may be found in occasional hints that all must not be taken too seriously. These range from a parody of the *Quijote's* opening lines, to seemingly deliberate melodramatic scenes and corny *double-entendres*.

One only need follow the characterization of Víctor Rey—one of the work's two chief actors—to recognize that Valle-Inclán has utilized liberal amounts of autobiographical detail in this novel. However intriguing this at first seems, it is soon apparent that the author not only fails to supply any indispensable new personal data, but quickly transforms whatever anecdote there is into pure fiction. . . . *La cara de Dios* cannot decide whether fiction is truer than fact, or fact more compelling than fiction. And amid this indecision, the murder mystery loses credibility and art becomes buried under a mass of details.

> *Thomas R. Franz, "Books of the Hispanic World," in* Hispania *(© 1974 The American Association of Teachers of Spanish and Portuguese, Inc.), Vol. 57, No. 3, September, 1974, p. 600.*

ADDITIONAL BIBLIOGRAPHY

Bell, Aubrey F. G. "The Novel." In his *Contemporary Spanish Literature*, pp. 39-150. New York: Alfred A. Knopf, 1925.*
　　A critical survey of Valle-Inclán's career, tracing his literary antecedents and praising his economical, highly-evocative writing style.

Boudreau, Harold L. "The Circular Structure of Valle-Inclán's *Ruedo iberico*." *PMLA* LXXXII, No. 1 (March 1967): 128-35.
　　A continuation of and elaboration on Jean Franco's seminal essay, "The Concept of Time in the *Ruedo iberico*" (see excerpt above).

Boyd, Ernest. "Ramón del Valle-Inclán." In his *Studies from Ten Literatures*, pp. 87-95. New York: Charles Scribner's Sons, 1925.
　　Discussion of the development of Valle-Inclán's work, and the ways in which his later fiction stems from his first group of stories, *Femeninas*. Boyd quotes a Spanish critic's remark that "so frequently have those first stories been reworked and elaborated that one book of 300 pages would actually contain all that is original in his writings, apart from some plays and his three novels dealing with the Carlist wars."

Brooks, J. L. "Valle-Inclan and the *Esperpento*." *Bulletin of Hispanic Studies* XXXIII (1956): 152-64.
　　An informative study of the characteristics of the *esperpentos*, tracing their development in light of the changes in Valle-Inclán's outlook following World War I.

Callan, Richard J. "Satire in the *Sonatas* of Valle Inclan." *Modern Language Quarterly* XXV, No. 3 (September 1964): 330-37.

An essay examining the *Sonatas,* finding the Marquís de Bradomín a figure used by Valle-Inclán to ridicule Calderonian honor and other aspects of Spanish society that he more blatantly attacked in the *esperpentos.*

Drake, William A. "Ramon del Valle-Inclan." In his *Contemporary European Writers,* pp. 130-37. New York: The John Day Co., 1928.

An appraisal of Valle-Inclán, praising his style but decrying the cruelty and hate suffusing his work.

Flynn, Gerard Cox. "The Adversary: Bradomín." *Hispanic Review* XXIX, No. 1 (January 1961): 120-33.

Examines elements in the four *Sonatas* suggesting an affinity between the Marquís de Bradomín and Satan.

Flynn, Gerard Cox. "Psiquismo: The Principle of the *Sonata* of Don Ramon del Valle-Inclan." In *Spanish Thought and Letters in the Twentieth Century: An International Symposium Held at Vanderbilt University to Commemorate the Centenary of the Birth of Miguel de Unamuno, 1864-1964,* edited by German Bleiberg and E. Inman Fox, pp. 201-06. Nashville: Vanderbilt University Press, 1966.

Relates Valle-Inclán's doctrine of "psiquismo"—communion among people through a vitalist life force—to his four *Sonatas.*

Greenfield, Sumner M. "Stylization and Deformation in Valle-Inclán's *La reina castiza.*" *Bulletin of Hispanic Studies* XXXIX, No. 2 (1962): 78-89.

Critical commentary upon the mocking *La reina castiza* and its relationship to the *esperpentos.*

Litvak, Lily. *A Dream of Arcadia: Anti-Industrialism in Spanish Literature, 1895-1905.* Austin: University of Texas Press, 1975, 278 p.

Examines Valle-Inclán's use of agrarian, medieval, and naturalistic elements in his work in reaction to the evils of industrial society.

Lyon, F. E. "Valle-Inclán and the Art of the Theatre." *Bulletin of Hispanic Studies* XLVI, No. 2 (1969): 132-52.

A study finding Valle-Inclán to be essentially a dramatist, whose vision anticipated subsequent trends in drama.

Penuel, Arnold M. "Archetypal Patterns in Valle-Inclán's *Divinas palabras.*" *Revista de estudios hispanicos* VIII, No. 1 (January 1974): 33-93.

An interpretation of *Divinas palabras* in terms of C. G. Jung's theories of archetypes.

Ramirez, Manuel D. "Valle-Inclan's Self-Plagiarism in Plot and Characterization." *Revista de estudios hispanicos* VI, No. 1 (January 1972): 71-83.

A study of Valle-Inclán's use of his earliest writings in the construction of his later works, particularly the *Sonatas* and the *Comedias bárbaras.*

Zahareas, Anthony, and Gillespie, Gerald. "Ramon Maria del Valle-Inclan: The Theatre of Esperpentos." *Drama Survey* 6, No. 1 (Spring-Summer 1967): 3-23.

An excellent essay on the intent and features of the *esperpentos,* notably *Los cuernos de don Friolera* and *Lights of Bohemia.*

(Sir) Hugh (Seymour) Walpole

1884-1941

English novelist, short story writer, biographer, critic, screenwriter, and dramatist.

Walpole was among England's most popular novelists writing just before World War II. His skill at painting the settings of his works, his gift for interesting plots, and his accessibility as a lecturer and public figure contributed to his wide readership in the United Kingdom and North America. Many readers preferred the familiarity of Walpole's traditional style rather than the literary experiments of Virginia Woolf, James Joyce, and other modernist writers.

The elements of several nineteenth-century styles appear in Walpole's work; Dostoyevsky, Trollope, Dickens, and Hardy all influenced him. Most important, however, is the romanticism of Sir Walter Scott, which pervades Walpole's entire canon, except for his earliest efforts. Of his more than three dozen novels, *Mr. Perrin and Mr. Traill*, *The Cathedral*, *Rogue Herries*, and *Judith Paris* are considered among his best books, while *The Old Ladies*, *Fortitude*, and the *Jeremy* books have been among his most popular.

The son of a cleric, Walpole was born in Auckland, New Zealand, moved to England at an early age, and attended school in several towns that provided scenes for his books. After studying for the clergy, he rejected his father's vocation, feeling drawn to writing. However, Walpole examined the nature of God and humanity throughout his work, most notably in *The Golden Scarecrow*.

Walpole's first novel, *The Wooden Horse*, barely repaid the cost of having it typed. His first success was *Mr. Perrin and Mr. Traill*, published in 1911. From then on his works were consistently popular. Henry James provided Walpole with guidance and encouragement during the latter's early years of literary effort. *The Green Mirror* and *The Duchess of Wrexe*, of all Walpole's books, most clearly demonstrate James's influence.

Major critics of the time, many of them proponents of modernism, disliked Walpole's works, objecting to unbelievable settings and characters, and to his outdated style. Furthermore, they criticized the vagueness of his philosophical passages and the carelessness of his writing. Walpole's reputation with critics and readers suffered throughout the 1930s, especially after Somerset Maugham, in *Cakes and Ale*, created a mocking portrait of Walpole in the character Alroy Kear, a romantic literary lightweight and opportunist. It is true that through his frequent lectures and autograph sessions Walpole sought to increase his popularity and prestige as a writer, and succeeded. But however much his reputation was inflated, he possessed strong talents. Among them were his versatility in describing varied settings and characters, and an ability to unobtrusively give eternal and spiritual import to commonplace scenes. An additional strength was his proficiency in using disparate novel forms. *The Herries Chronicle*, which sparked a resurgence of interest in historical novels during the 1930s, displays his boldest use of a neglected form.

Interest in Walpole's books, intimately tied to the author himself, dropped off sharply after his death in 1941. The advent

of World War II and subsequent changes in literary styles also contributed to a decline in critical and popular attention. Nevertheless, his books are still read, and his position as a prominent twentieth-century novelist remains secure.

PRINCIPAL WORKS

The Wooden Horse (novel) 1909
Mr. Perrin and Mr. Traill (novel) 1911; published in the
    United States as *The Gods and Mr. Perrin*
Fortitude (novel) 1913
The Duchess of Wrexe (novel) 1914
The Golden Scarecrow (novel) 1915
The Dark Forest (novel) 1916
The Green Mirror (novel) 1917
Jeremy (novel) 1919
The Secret City (novel) 1919
The Captives (novel) 1920
The Thirteen Travellers (short stories) 1921
The Cathedral (novel) 1922
Jeremy and Hamlet (novel) 1923
The Old Ladies (novel) 1924
Portrait of a Man with Red Hair (novel) 1925

Jeremy at Crale   (novel)   1927
Wintersmoon   (novel)   1928
*Rogue Herries   (novel)   1930
*Judith Paris   (novel)   1931
*The Fortress   (novel)   1932
*Vanessa   (novel)   1933
The Inquisitor   (novel)   1935
Head in Green Bronze and Other Stories   (short stories)
   1938
The Sea Tower   (novel)   1939
The Bright Pavilions   (novel)   1940
The Killer and the Slain   (novel)   1942

*These volumes were published as *The Herries Chronicle* in 1939.

THE ATHENAEUM   (essay date 1909)

The Colonial hero who, after an absence of twenty years, returns to the ancestral home to find himself unappreciated by his relations, including his own son, offers scope for originality of treatment. Here [in *The Wooden Horse*] Mr. Walpole has succeeded, if he has not altogether resisted the temptation to overdo the situation. The breezy Colonial has every right to be shocked and disappointed; and the manner in which, when his son behaves more like a cad than a Trojan, he seizes the opportunity to assert himself, is ingenious. As a satire of some modern manners, the story has good points, but it is overweighted by the classical allusion in the title.

> "'The Wooden Horse'," in The Athenaeum, *No. 4259, June 12, 1909, p. 697.*

HENRY JAMES   (essay date 1914)

[Mr. Hugh Walpole] enjoys in a high degree the consciousness of saturation, and is on such serene and happy terms with it as almost make of critical interference, in so bright an air, an assault on personal felicity. Full of material is thus the author of **"The Duchess of Wrexe,"** and of a material which we should describe as the consciousness of youth were we not rather disposed to call it a peculiar strain of the extreme unconsciousness. Mr. Walpole offers us indeed a rare and interesting case—we see about the field none other like it; the case of a positive identity between the spirit, not to say the time of life or stage of experience, of the aspiring artist and the field itself of his vision. **"The Duchess of Wrexe"** reeks with youth and the love of youth and the confidence of youth—youth taking on with a charming exuberance the fondest costume or disguise, that of an adventurous and voracious felt interest, interest in life, in London, in society, in character, in Portland Place, in the Oxford Circus, in the afternoon tea-table, in the torrid weather, in fifty other immediate things as to which its passion and its curiosity are of the sincerest. The wonderful thing is that these latter forces operate, in their way, without yet being disengaged and hand-free—disengaged, that is, from their state of *being* young, with its billowy mufflings and other soft obstructions, the state of being present, being involved and aware, close "up against" the whole mass of possibilities, being in short intoxicated with the mixed liquors of suggestion. In the fumes of this acute situation Mr. Walpole's subject-matter is bathed; the situation being all the while so much more his own and

that of a juvenility reacting, in the presence of everything, "for all it is worth," than the devised and imagined one, however he may circle about some such cluster, that every cupful of his excited flow tastes three times as much of his temperamental freshness as it tastes of this, that or the other character or substance, above all of this, that or the other group of antecedents and references, supposed to be reflected in it. All of which does not mean, we hasten to add, that the author of **"The Duchess of Wrexe"** has not the gift of life; but only that he strikes us as having received it, straight from nature, with such a concussion as to have kept the boon at the stage of violence—so that, fairly pinned down by it, he is still embarrassed for passing it on. On the day he shall have worked free of this primitive predicament, the crude fact of the convulsion itself, there need be no doubt of his exhibiting matter into which method may learn how to bite. The tract meanwhile affects us as more or less virgin snow, and we look with interest and suspense for the imprint of a process. (pp. 339-40)

> Henry James, "The New Novel, 1914" *(originally published under a different title in a slightly different form in* The Times Literary Supplement, *No. 635, March 18, 1914), in his* Notes on Novelists with Some Other Notes *(reprinted with the permission of Charles Scribner's Sons; in Canada by Alexander R. James, as literary executor to the Estate of Henry James; copyright 1914 by Charles Scribner's Sons; copyright renewed © 1942 by Henry James), Scribner's, 1914, pp. 314-61.**

KATHERINE MANSFIELD   (essay date 1920)

If an infinite capacity for taking pains were what is needed to produce a great novel, we should have to hail Mr. Walpole's [**"The Captives"**] as a masterpiece. But here it is— four parts, four hundred and seventy pages, packed as tight as they can hold with an assortment of strange creatures and furnishings; and we cannot, with the best will in the world, see in the result more than a task—faithfully and conscientiously performed to the best of the author's power—but a "task accomplished," and not even successfully at that. For we feel that it is determination rather than inspiration, strength of will rather than the artist's compulsion, which has produced **"The Captives."** . . . In a word, for all his devotion to writing, we think the critic, after an examination of **"The Captives,"** would find it hard to state with any conviction that Mr. Walpole is a creative artist. These are hard words; we shall endeavour to justify our use of them.

But first let us try to see what it is that Mr. Walpole has intended to "express" in his novel—what is its central idea. "If this life be not a real fight in which something is eternally gained for the universe by success." It is, we imagine, contained in these words of William James. A *real* fight—that is the heart of the matter—and waged in this life and for this life that something may be eternally gained. Maggie Cardinal, a simple, ardent creature with a passion to live, to be free, to be herself and of this world, is caught as she steps over the threshold of her Aunt Anne's house in a burning, fiery trap. . . . [She] is captured by . . . the fanatic religious sect to which her aunt belongs. The head of the Kingscote Brethren is Mr. Warlock, and Martin, his son, is the second captive. Martin's father and Maggie's aunt are determined, with all the passion of their fanatic souls, to offer these two to God when he descends, as they believe he may do at any moment, in his chariot of fire. . . . But when, after endless complications and separations, [the captives] are released from their fiery bonds, what happens? What has been the significance of all this to them? We are led to believe that both of them are conscious, while they are fighting the world of Aunt Anne and Mr. Warlock, that, nevertheless, they do acknowledge the power of some mysterious force outside themselves—which may . . . some day . . . what? We are left absolutely in the air. Maggie and Martin, together at last—Martin, a broken man, and Maggie happy because somebody needs her—are not living beings at the end any more than they are at the beginning; they will not, when Mr. Walpole's pen is lifted, exist for a moment.

But apart from the author's failure to realize his idea, the working out of **"The Captives"** is most curiously superficial. Mr. Walpole acts as our guide to these strange people, but what does he know of them? We cannot remember a novel where we were more conscious of the author's presence on every page; but he is there as a stranger, as an observer, as someone outside it all. How hard he tries—how painfully he fails! His method is simply to amass observations—to crowd and crowd his book with figures, scenes, bizarre and fantastic environments, queer people, oddities. But we feel that no one observation in nearer the truth than another. (p. 519)

But in spite of it all, the feeling that remains is the liveliest possible regret that Mr. Walpole should have misjudged his powers—so bravely. (p. 520)

> *Katherine Mansfield, "Observation Only," in* The Athenaeum, *No. 4720, October 15, 1920, pp. 519-20.*

J. MIDDLETON MURRY (essay date 1921)

The publishers of ["**The Thirteen Travellers**"] say no more than the truth on the dust-wrapper: "Mr. Walpole's work is too well known to need introduction; it has won high praise for its author in two continents, and has securely established his position in the very front rank of modern authors. . . . The author views modern times in a modern spirit."

It is all true, except that some may feel a little doubt of the "securely." Mr. Walpole himself is not quite sure of that, one imagines . . . [Still, we] will not quarrel about a word. In the nearer of the two continents Mr. Walpole's work has been praised in terms not inadequate to Tolstoy; and as for the remoter, his fame there is legendary here. What Mr. Walpole says in America, goes. It is rumored that he created Mr. Conrad there, and that on his next visit he may create Mr. Hardy.

The facts are not in question. What is worth a moment's investigation is the significance of the facts. . . .

Mr. Walpole's books are at the top of his readers' gamut, a rather intoxicating head note. In reading them they are being serious, almost intellectual; they have a sense of problems; they feel that life is not so simple, but that it is in the end "all right." They are in touch, but they are not disturbed. Mr. Walpole interposes his genial personality between them and the mysterious, passionate creatures who worry about truth and justice, and honesty and good writing; he waves a beneficent hand: "Do not be alarmed, ladies. . . . Cranks, of course. . . . But very lovable when you know them—very."

That is a very peculiar (and very comfortable) position to occupy. If Mr. Walpole had deliberately made it for himself, if he waved his hand with the true Pecksniffian unction, we should be compelled to admit that he was a clever and a wicked man; and we should be angry with him. But that is impossible. Mr. Walpole is not wicked. It is a thousand to one that he believes what he says. He is a true democratic leader of his public; he does not dictate to them, he represents them. They would like to know; he would like to know. They are mystified; he is mystified. They want to believe the best; he would like nothing better. They do not know the difference between good writing and bad; neither does he. They are a little snobbish, a little "romantic"; so is he.

The only important distinction between them is that Mr. Walpole does the writing. It is a distinction, and probably he knows misgivings and doubts that have never troubled them. He must ask himself sometimes: "What am I really doing? Is there anything in it?" His reply must be a little dubious. He may even (for he is, in a way, conscientious) compare his books with the real ones. What *can* the difference be? He looks round at his editions, is reassured, and sets vigorously to work again.

A writer ought to be serious. Well, he is serious. He will deal with England "in Nineteen-Nineteen." A queer England, after the armistice. He felt it was somehow queer, somehow different. But how? Why, people talked of Bolshevism. Labor was restive. People who had large incomes had small ones. Men came back from the war; they were changed. He could have got it from the ladies' page of any newspaper. Perhaps he did. Perhaps it was the result of his own unaided observation.

> He turned back and down into Jermyn Street. Next to the Hammam Baths they were painting a house light green. A nice young fellow in overalls stepped off a ladder as Clive passed.
> "Is that an easy job?" Clive asked him.
> "Oh yes, sir," the young fellow answered.
> "Could you manage it with one arm?" Clive asked.
> "Why, yes," the man said.
> "Could I pick it up quickly?"
> "Lord, yes."
> "Will you teach me?"
> . . . . .
> A young workman in yellow overalls, perched on a ladder, managed his brush adroitly with one arm. . . . The workman looked down and revealed to the astonished countenance of Mr. Nix the laughing eyes of his late tenant, the Hon. Clive Torby.

If Mr. Walpole had read a few more newspapers he might have learned that house-painting is not picked up in a week even by the son of a peer. But that is not the point. It is the silliness of the whole situation. A changed world! It is only an empty phrase to Mr. Walpole. It means dukes turned organ-grinders to him.

There are signs that Mr. Walpole thinks this is Romance. You feel that Mr. Walpole would never dream of being depressing. And yet if you come to think of it, that was what Nineteen-Nineteen chiefly was, and Nineteen-Twenty as well. It may possibly be that he, who is deliberately occupied with the changed world, was unable to convey the feelings of a typical inhabitant of it. Still, you guess that even if he had been able, he would not have done it, because he is an Optimist. (p. 584)

You see, Mr. Walpole does not let Imagination and Invention go for nothing; but that is hardly equivalent to writing a Romance. He has, however, a number of pleasant little romantic touches, of the same kind as the Hon. Clive Torby on the ladder. Sometimes they escape, sometimes they are detected by his vigilant, critical eye: and he begins to apologize for them. . . . But why apologize, Mr. Walpole, why apologize? On his behalf we reply that it is very embarrassing to feel that you are in the Ouida tradition, and at the same time to know that it is no longer the thing to be. We sympathize with him; yet we should like him better if he had the courage of his evident convictions. We should, but his growing and adoring public would not, for they know, as he knows, that Ouida's day is over. Her *décor* is *démodé:* Mr. Walpole's appointed function is to keep it up-to-date.

And yet we do not believe that he chose this part for himself. It happens by accident rather. He longs to let his Invention and Imagination go; but they refuse to budge. He has to help them out with the Hammam Baths and Scott's the hatters and Willis's Rooms. Unless he has those pegs to hang his characters on to they would disappear into the abysm. But that necessity places him in an awkward situation. He begins to look like a realist. That would be very depressing for everybody concerned. Instinct helps him out again. His reality is *soigné;* it is chosen between the Mall and Piccadilly. There he can use real names of real streets, real shops, real clubs without upsetting anybody.

Naturally, he is a little bewildered, and inclined to wonder what he is: Romantic, Realist, or Optimist? He is a little of all three, but not enough to matter. He is not sufficiently afflicted with imagination, or observation, or power of thought to be seriously involved in any of these undesirable things. For they are undesirable. If he were possessed by any one of them he would begin to forfeit the sympathy of that public to which he now so intimately speaks. Romance, created by the imagination, demands imagination; realism, born out of observation, calls for observation to respond to it; and even optimism needs to produce reasons for itself, and needs intelligence to appreciate them. Mr. Walpole is wiser than perhaps he knows in not asking for these things; he does well to keep his thought, his characters, his prophecies, and his writing vague. It is better, in the company he affects, to talk of a "newer and a better world" than to think about it. (pp. 584-85)

J. Middleton Murry, "The Case of Mr. Hugh Walpole," in The Nation and The Athenaeum, *Vol. XXIX, No. 16, July 16, 1921, pp. 584-85.*

JOSEPH HERGESHEIMER (essay date 1923)

It is a fortunate thing, here, that Mr. Walpole is a novelist, for a novelist and his novel are one, nothing can disentangle or separate them, one cannot be measured or praised aside from the other. I mean, of course, that the essential in the novelist is like his essential novel; and that, in Mr. Walpole, could hardly be better—he has humor and the qualities of the heart and, unlike me, he has no prejudices; nothing that is life is condemned by him. . . . And, because of all this,

even when I don't like a novel he has written I like it far better than a great many novels which I like. (p. 626)

That tenderness for singular characters, so obviously part of an older manner of story writing, Mr. Walpole is getting more and more to be without; the feeling that, while the mass moves on, human particles drop, unimportantly, is stronger in **"The Cathedral"** than in any of his previous books. He may, perhaps, deny this to me, for he is a link in a chain reaching back from the present; but exactly that is happening to him.

"The Cathedral", then, is not a character novel; the story does not depend on the sentimental or bitter projection of an individual, but has to do generally with people lost together on a whirling atom of fiery substance, It is about the church but it is not religious; the English clergy, clergymen at all failed to interest me until I read **"The Cathedral"**; but throughout its pages I was fascinated by the affairs of the church, I could scarcely wait to discover who would get the appointment to Pybus St. Anthony. Against that paramount decision both Brandon and Ronder were lost sight of; and my feeling in this was as it should be, for that appointment, finally, was bigger than either or both of the men, it absorbed and owned and infinitely harmed them. The Archdeacon it killed but the hurt to Canon Ronder was more secret and—though it didn't destroy his physical rotundity—perhaps even more fatal.

Archdeacon Brandon's defeat, the last bravery of his creed flung without effect against the obduracy of a new and unsympathetic dispensation, his heart's failure and death, has a breath of courage forever denied to Ronder's perversity of motives and power. But, in Mr. Walpole, there is no discrimination against Ronder, actually the Canon lives and the Archdeacon dies . . . it would not have fallen like that in the novel of yesterday.

"The Cathedral", then, is his best; it is Hugh Walpole, big, with a fine surface, and beautifully clothed; it is that rare thing today—rare in the comparatively young—a splendid Anglo-Saxon novel. (pp. 626-27)

The easy thing, of course, is to say that **"The Cathedral"** follows the spirit of Anthony Trollope; that is more obvious, more superficial, than true; but it would be correct to say that they belong to the same spirit. **"The Cathedral"** is disarming—on the surface it has small trace of absolute modernity, it seems to be bound into its tradition, more retrospective in form than advanced; but examine it carefully. . . . (p. 627)

On the surface **"The Cathedral"** is, again, a record of the perpetual dying of the past, the destruction of the past by the present; it would be possible, on that plane, to write a very profound study of the thematic structure of the novel. I might follow, with immense discernment, the symbolical importance of the Cathedral, now a vast interior of shuddering gloom and then a dominating fateful bulk against a burning sky; I could show it taking life into the coldness of its stone; but that would be—I have the strongest conviction—superficial; it would multiply vanity and be concerned with personal show.

The inner, the fundamental, fact about **"The Cathedral"** is that it is an admirable story; in spite of its apparent diversity of ends it is a simple story; anyone capable of reading may follow it to its beautiful end—a man in the pomp of high public circumstance and power is ruined by a seemingly modest individual. In the beginning the Archdeacon is up and Canon Ronder down and at the end the Canon is up and Brandon destroyed.

I had said that the Archdeacon was the principal in **"The Cathedral"**, but there are times when the interest, the anxiety, of the reader is wholly delivered to Frederick Ronder; and in that the skill, the purpose, of the story teller is revealed. The moment the Canon appears in Polchester he is significant, and this in spite of the fact that he is almost casually described as a man of a quite genial roundness, round of body and of spectacles. He is, apparently, eager to be no more than comfortable, to propitiate life and men; but at once his innocence is enveloped in darkness, at once the reader fears him . . . because of an art which shows the aunt who is his companion fearing him. At once Archdeacon Brandon is brought into the story on the very pinnacle of his glory, a pinnacle, seemingly as high and fixed as the utmost high thrust of the Cathedral, and beside him Ronder, with all his unpredictable qualities and hidden power, is thrust modestly into the scene.

All else that happens, settings and avocations and beliefs and philosophies, are subservient to a struggle which is the mirror of a larger and, at bottom, impersonal affair; I mean that in Brandon and Ronder other men, a measure of universality, are present; but that is there because the individuals are seen in relation to their purpose in **"The Cathedral"**, a novel. Mr. Walpole is not a sentimentalist about the individual, he understands that an individual is not of very great importance in his or herself—this is clear in his treatment of Annie Hogg—and, I believe, he realizes that one man is not very different from another, one woman's being from another's. (pp. 627-28)

> *Joseph Hergesheimer, "The Book of the Month: Hugh Walpole's 'Cathedral',"* in The Bookman, *New York (copyright, 1923, by George H. Doran Company), Vol. LVI, No. 5, January, 1923, pp. 625-28.*

JOSEPH CONRAD (essay date 1923)

Of the general soundness of Mr. Walpole's work I am perfectly convinced. Let no modern and malicious mind take this declaration for a left-handed compliment. Mr. Walpole's soundness is not of conventions but of convictions; and even as to these, let no one suppose that Mr. Walpole's convictions are old-fashioned. He is distinctly a man of his time; and it is just because of that modernity, informed by a sane judgment of urgent problems and wide and deep sympathy with all mankind, that we look forward hopefully to the growth and increased importance of his work. In his style, so level, so consistent, Mr. Hugh Walpole does not seek so much for novel as for individual expression; and this search, this ambition so natural to an artist, is often rewarded by success. Old and young interest him alike and he treats both with a sure touch and in the kindest manner. We see Mr. Walpole grappling with the truth of things spiritual and material with his characteristic earnestness, and we can discern the characteristics of this acute and sympathetic explorer of human nature: His love of adventure and the serious audacity he brings to the task of recording the changes of human fate and the movements of human emotion, in the quiet backwaters or in the tumultuous open streams of existence.

> *Joseph Conrad, "A Comment on Hugh Walpole,"* in Hugh Walpole: Appreciations *by Joseph Conrad, Arnold Bennett, and Joseph Hergesheimer, edited by Grant Overton, George H. Doran Company, 1923, p. 1.*

J. B. PRIESTLEY (essay date 1928)

A glance at the present state of fiction reveals [Hugh Walpole] in a happy position. He happens to be an intelligent storyteller at a time when so many writers of fiction either have the stories without the intelligence or have the intelligence without the stories. . . . He is also in a happy position because he is singularly well equipped as a novelist. It is significant that one of his earliest stories, written in his twenties, was that of a successful man of forty, and that one of his most recent novels, written when he knows what it is to be a successful man of forty, is the story of a young and naïve idealist, a Scandinavian professor of gymnastics. Here, it is obvious, is a writer of fiction who can at least escape from his own life, who is not—as so many are—serving up chapters of his autobiography, merely sprinkled with false names. Nor is he condemned to restrict himself to one side of life, to one little section of society. . . . He has no difficulty in presenting quite adequately a varied host of characters, from duchesses to charwomen, bishops to schoolboys; and he confidently takes us into schoolmasters' common rooms, Cornish inns, deaneries, . . . all manner of places from Penzance to Petrograd. That is one reason—and it is a good reason—why he has become so popular with readers in general. We like to know what all kinds of people are doing, to be taken to many different places, to feel that the novelist will not be compelled to ignore innumerable sides of life.

We might call this the Trollope motive in Walpole. It happens that he has provided us with two valuable little clues to his character as a novelist. He is an enthusiastic admirer of Trollope. . . . He is also an enthusiastic admirer of Dostoievsky. . . . A writer who puts before his mind such different ideals as the work of Dostoievsky and the work of Anthony Trollope would seem to be asking to be pulled in two opposite directions. Yet the fact remains that there can be found in Walpole's work what might be called a Dostoievsky motive and a Trollope motive, and perhaps the best way of understanding that work is to disengage these two motives. And actually we have already begun to do that with the second, the Trollope motive. Both novelists have that wide range and general "convincingness" of presentation; and both of them have their own special little world of the cathedral town and its surrounding country, something as essentially English as the Anglican church itself. There are differences, of course. Trollope is more thoroughly immersed in the world of fact. He achieves a solid realism, a "chunkiness" of character and scene to which the modern novelist never attains. We cannot put ourselves back in the easy sixties. A modern novelist who worked as Trollope worked would be either a queer anachronism or a mere fake, a creator of sham antiques. But there are times when Hugh Walpole would seem to have told himself that he wanted to be nothing more than an up-to-date and jollier Trollope.

At such times he appears to work to a theory rather than from any inner conviction, any needs of the spirit to express itself. He only asks to show us his tremendous zest for all the good things of this life, for all manner of people, for mountains and lakes and cities, for etchings and opera and football matches, and even for the works of his fellow-authors.... He has an eager and appreciative, rather than a soberly critical, intelligence.... Therefore we must not grumble when Hugh Walpole keeps alive a childlike sense of wonder and delight. Nevertheless it must be admitted that this sense is occasionally kept alive only by something that looks suspiciously like forcible feeding. His enthusiasm, in these lighter works, is rather too mechanical at times. His jolly young men are often too determinedly jolly, too naïve and uncritical, and we begin to long for other company.

We find this other company in the stronger novels. In them too we find what I have called the Dostoievsky motive. When we read them we understand why their author thinks *The Brothers Karamazov* the greatest novel in the world. He spent some time in Russia during the war, and two of his novels, **The Dark Forest** and **The Secret City,** are not only Russian in subject, but are Russian in manner. It is not simply of these that I am thinking, however, when I mention the Dostoievsky motive. It is there in them, of course, but it is also there in **Mr. Perrin and Mr. Traill, The Cathedral, The Old Ladies,** and **Harmer John.** It turns up elsewhere too—even in such things as **The Young Enchanted**—and suddenly it will transform the pleasant easy scene he is giving us into transparency behind which are bright stars and red hell-fire. It makes him see this life against a vast cloudy background of warring good and evil. I know no contemporary English (or American) novelist who is more deeply concerned with this central conflict. He is the Manichee among English writers of fiction. It is this side of his character as a novelist that is surprisingly seldom recognized and appreciated, at least in criticism. Everybody notices the Trollope motive, but few remark the Dostoievsky one, though all his strongest work reveals it almost at a glance.

No matter how jolly and zestful he may appear to be, the fact remains that he possesses an unusually sharp sense of evil. Now evil—real evil, devils' work—is something that has almost disappeared from the world that most contemporary fiction describes.... I do not say that Hugh Walpole believes that absolute evil exists. His sense of evil is not an intellectual matter, and may, for all I know, be at variance with his ideas about the universe. But it is there in his work, and it is something that cannot be kept out, rather than something that is deliberately introduced; in other words, it is a characteristic expression of his mind when it is fully creative; it is part of his nature. Thus it comes about that this enthusiastic admirer of Trollope is a master of sinister atmosphere, in which hate and cruelty stalk abroad, taking possession of the most unlikely persons. Walpole can move with startling and enthralling rapidity from a rather commonplace account of a commonplace scene to a picture of tortured nerves and thence to a drama of souls hurled into the battle of good and evil. At one moment we are watching some schoolmasters bickering in their common room, we are hearing something about little jealousies in a cathedral town, we are looking on at some poor old ladies having tea together, ... and then, the very next moment, all is changed; we are swinging dizzily between heaven and hell. It is the transition that is important. Other contemporary writers, Walter de la Mare, for example, may be able to achieve more subtle horror, are better at suggesting a poetically sinister magic in things, can perhaps present more circumspectly and movingly the crises in one individual mind, the drama of one soul. What distinguishes Walpole is his power of creating, with convincing and amusing realism, the ordinary social scene, and then of turning

it into a kind of transparency, illuminated by the hellish flares of cruelty and hate and the serene glow of pity and love. This is his chief characteristic, his capital virtue.

Another characteristic, next in importance, is his ability to diffuse the interest.... There is perhaps nothing harder in fiction than to turn a whole group of persons, almost a whole town, into your central figure, presenting the drama of a community, and not of a single person; and this Walpole has succeeded in doing more than once. Indeed, he began doing it very early. Thus, **Mr. Perrin and Mr. Traill** is not the story of Traill, a figure of no great interest, nor even of Perrin, though he is much better, but the whole school, through which the flame, fanned by Perrin's insane hatred, travels with terrible rapidity. The very crisis of the story, it seems to me, is a scene in which neither Traill nor Perrin appears, namely, that where Comber strikes his wife. This is an early novel, but the method, a swift netting of all the personages in the drama, is there, and is only carried a little farther in the best of the later novels. It is most fully revealed in the Polchester novels. **The Cathedral** may be said to describe a kind of duel between the proud and defiant Archdeacon Brandon and the subtle and mischievous Canon Ronder, both of whom are very powerful characters; but the novel is really the story of Polchester itself, of all the people whose lives are affected by that famous quarrel. **Harmer John** may be read as the story of that personage himself, the young naïve idealist who comes from afar to an old settled community and tries to make it reform itself; but the tale leaps into a far more vivid and enduring life if it is regarded as it should be regarded, as the story of that community itself, into which Harmer John is flung as a stone might be flung into a pool. It is really the people round him who are important, just as it is the reactions of the other characters to the Prince in Dostoievsky's *The Idiot* that really create that marvelous novel. Harmer John himself is only a touchstone, a symbolic figure, and his arrival is merely the signal for the old battle of good and evil to begin again in Polchester, which rapidly becomes a maze of passion and prejudice, timidity and cruelty, generosity and pity. The growing tide of rumor, the snaring of person after person, the darkening of the whole sky, the victory of evil that is no victory at all because the good remains unconquered—these things are very characteristic of their author. (pp. 530-35)

Hugh Walpole, then, has been able to combine a hearty and humorous realism with the power of creating a huge background of warring good and evil; and further, he has been able to avoid that concentration of the interest on one or at most two figures that is so characteristic of the introspective fiction of today. This means that he has done a great deal indeed. It means that he has staked out a claim far larger than that of any of his fellow-novelists, excluding the generation headed by Conrad. This is his strength; and naturally it is his weakness. Such a claim demands correspondingly great technical resources, and he does not always succeed in commanding them. Indeed, nowhere yet has he appeared in absolutely full command of them. I suspect that his natural gifts have been so great (consider how early he began and how well he worked) that he has never been compelled to grapple closely with the problems of his craft, that he has always been tempted to go soaring on to his final scene without taking much thought about the hundred and one little difficulties in the way.

In this connection it is worth remarking that the last novel, **Wintersmoon,** though by no means his best novel, has a better surface than any of the others: it is, you feel, really *written*, not merely turned out onto paper. That is one reason why it is so pleasant criticizing Walpole, for, unlike so many of his contemporaries, he does not give the impression that he has shot his bolt.... He is going on, and there is every reason to suppose that his best work is yet to come. He now occupies a very strong position, and it is, too, a happy middle position.... [It is] between the older sociological school of Wells and Bennett, the fiction that dealt with men chiefly as members of a social order, and the purely subjective or metaphysical school of the younger writers, whose fiction gives us one real person in a world of shadows. He is still moving on, finding his own way, and yet, I think, is already secure in the tradition of the English novel. (pp. 535-36)

J. B. Priestley, "Hugh Walpole," in English Journal *(copyright © 1928 by the National Council of Teachers of English), Vol. XVII, No. 7, September, 1928, pp. 529-36.*

PATRICK BRAYBROOKE   (essay date 1929)

If we take the bulk of Mr. Walpole's writings and endeavour to see in them something of his general standpoint we shall realise from what angle he seems to view human activity. Walpole does not start out on a search for the extraordinary. He does not even go in for very big events.... Walpole's theme more than anything else is ordinary life, for he knows only too well that if you want to find the extraordinary you must search most diligently amongst the ordinary. (p. 65)

Having said something of his general theme, that is, Walpole's interest in that substance or commodity which we so inaccurately define as ordinary life, we may ask of what nature is the background of this ordinary life in which Walpole is so interested. Without attempting to be too dogmatic, Walpole seems to view life as rather a cruel experience. It is cruel in the sense that it is inevitable and appears to lead so often from bad to worse. It is the type of cruelty which is the most deadly in that its infliction is quite often not apparent to the onlooker. Thus, when Walpole writes his most tragic book, **"The Old Ladies,"** the cruelty there displayed is not the cruelty of a sudden and devastating blow, but the cruelty of a deadening process of evolutionary misery. No one is particularly cruel to the old ladies. They are cruel to themselves, not perhaps wittingly, but because more often than not cruelty and being old and being a lady and being poor are intimately associated. The old ladies, so Mr. Walpole insists again and again, have nothing to look forward to. (p. 66)

But if Mr. Walpole sees that much of life is cruel he does not forget that there are compensations. Something of his attitude of the response that can be made to the challenge of existence is to be found in his book **"Fortitude"** when he remarks that the important thing in life is how much courage is brought into it.... [He] is optimistic in so far as he determines that mankind can make a fight and has the merit of refusing to give up without a struggle. (p. 67)

When Walpole sees, as in the case of Peter Westcott [in **"Fortitude"**], a fight being made against hardship, he is consistently sympathetic. He philosophises also about the strange fact that if people make a fight, life lets them continue to do it so that in the end we have the dualism that either we become such efficient fighters that life is beaten, or so tired that life beats us. I mean, in other words, Walpole sees

that if a person has courage he will always find himself in situations in which he has need to bring it out for his use. He is a novelist of the school of unrelenting realism.... His general philosophy seems to be ... that life in its ordinary progress can be more cruel than startling events of ferocity. At the same time, mankind is equipped with the attributes of endurance and courage and can make a fight even if the fight ends in a devastating and bloody defeat. (p. 69)

[Walpole's] outlook is perhaps a sombre one, sometimes his outlook is as melancholy as that of Hardy, but his theological position would probably always prevent him from joining those philosophers who emulate the doctrine of despair. Eager for truth, Walpole formulates his philosophy of life. If it is dark, it is because truth is dark. When it is light, it is because truth is also light. Altogether Walpole's philosophy postulates mankind enshrined in darkness, but a darkness that sometimes gives place to lesser darkness. (pp. 69-70)

Patrick Braybrooke, "Hugh Walpole," in his Philosophies in Modern Fiction, The C. W. Daniel Company, *1929 (and reprinted by Books for Libraries Press, 1965; distributed by Arno Press, Inc.), pp. 65-70.*

CLEMENCE DANE [Winifred Ashton]   (essay date 1929)

Innovations are to be expected from James Joyce, D. H. Lawrence, Mrs. Woolf, Wyndham Lewis, the Sitwells, and the rest of the literary airplanes and gliders, but not—surely not—from that coach-and-four Hugh Walpole!

Consider his style, his structure, his choice of material! If they prove him a born story-teller, with the Victorian virtues added of readableness and the power to draw character and characters, places as objects in the landscape, and places as living entities, has he not also the Victorian faults—length, leisureliness, carelessness, with an inborn disrespect for words as words? This, of course, is in the tradition.... [The traditional novelist] achieves style by the happy accidental combination of a gift for story-telling with passionate sincerity. Hugh Walpole can write beautiful simple English when he chooses. (pp. 82-3)

But he can also write, when he is in a hurry or when he is particularly excited by the plot of his story, like an earnest and sentimental schoolboy. At such moments "rathers," "verys," "awfullys," "wonderfuls," and "splendids" drip comfortably and confidentially from his pen, blotting his best work, he remaining the while serenely unconscious of messiness. On the same spread of page he is capable of remarking, "the scene was wonderfully beautiful," yet following it up, a line or two later, by living touches such as, "the sky was gray with little pools and rivers of watery blue," or, "the mouse-faced farm." And when he paints, as he constantly does, a vivid and convincing picture of some natural object and uses it then to serve some idea that he wishes to express, to illustrate a mood not easy to record directly, he constantly spoils it by some carelessness of structure. Take a sentence picked at random from the *Portrait of a Man with Red Hair:*

> "Do you believe in God, Mr. Harkness?" and the draught went whispering on hands and feet around the room. "Do you believe in God, Mr. Harkness?"

Was ever a sentence, perfect in its suggestion of things unwritten, unwritable, so recklessly dumped on to paper? But it is useless to protest against such criminal carelessness; because Mr. Walpole can triumphantly retort that, carelessness or no carelessness, he has contrived to etch on the brain of the reader exactly the impression which he intended to create, or the sentence would not be thus rousing me to indignation. (pp. 84-5)

And, of course, because he is primarily a storyteller, his point of view is justifiable. If the tale and the people of the tale and the moral of the tale come first, come last, come all the time with him, that after all is what the Gentle Reader likes and requires; for the Gentle Reader's concern has always been, always will be, the tale and the people of the tale. (p. 86)

As conservative as his style but much more carefully considered is Hugh Walpole's literary architecture. His usual ground plan is the ground plan of group life. Indeed, his whole method is rooted in the group. He uses the family community in his first novel, *The Wooden Horse:* he uses it in his latest novel, *Wintersmoon.* . . . Indeed it may be said that, except in . . . *The Crystal Box,* Hugh Walpole has never related the history of an individual apart from the crowd: that his individual should be related to the crowd is a condition of his storytelling, as it was a condition of all the traditive novelists before him. (pp. 87-9)

In one only of his typically traditional impulses does he in form break away from consecrated use. He becomes experimental so soon as he deals with the problem of the introduction of children into his book world. (p. 90)

[Walpole uses] children in a new way. His interest in them does not lead him to join forces with the children's novelists and to write books for children: he does not make occasional and exceptional ventures like *Kim* or *Cubwood* or *Bevis:* nor does he follow Charlotte Yonge and Miss Alcott in their incomparable inter-relations of the two planes, the adolescent and the mature: instead he confines children to a world of their own. He first sets spinning in the skies of his imagination his adult world, and then allows to revolve near it a second smaller world, a moon to his earth. (p. 100)

In these lesser worlds of childhood Hugh Walpole works out practically the same problems of character and environment as he does in his major world. He presents the same types, but in earlier stages of development: and he replaces the necessary frieze of external events, events which mould the adult—such as travelling, encounter with the herd, the sight of men and cities, passions, money problems, art—by a frieze of elders. The lives of these children of the ''little'' novels are walled in by their parents, governors, pastors, and masters, and they move in a much more restricted space; but otherwise this chronicle of a derived world is written with precisely the same care, gravity, and respect for its subject matter as is used in the larger series. There is no softening of outline, no prettifying, and above all no writing down. Exactly the same methods, carefully dwarfed, are employed. There is even a simplified use of symbolism.

This adaptation of the . . . novel to the scale of childhood and the running of such an experiment concurrently with a major series of adult romances is practically a new departure in novel writing. . . . Let us examine the simplest of the experiments, the novels about children. Hugh Walpole's ''little novels'' began with *The Golden Scarecrow,* a series of independent studies of children from babyhood to the age of twelve. His favourite use of symbolism was seen in the

strange and beautiful central character, the only one common to all the tales, of the children's Friend. The baby, half blind and groping in a monstrous new state of life, clings desperately to the Somebody who has accompanied it into this world from some already forgotten earlier one. The Somebody, the Friend, is drawn as a shadowy male figure, half Christ, half Santa Claus, part Conscience, part Pan. The figure is, however, as vividly alive as the little humans, so much so that its gradual withdrawal from the sight and the consciousness of the children as their mundane shells harden about them actually gives the reader also a curious and painful sense of loss. The whole series of tales is in fact a restatement in terms of the novel of certain passages in [Wordsworth's] ''Intimations of Immortality,'' for whatever Hugh Walpole's technical ancestry may be, spiritually he derives from Wordsworth via Hawthorne.

The Golden Scarecrow was followed by a book about a small boy called Jeremy: and *Jeremy* has been followed by *Jeremy and Hamlet* and *Jeremy at Crale.* It is hardly necessary to give a detailed synopsis of the *Jeremy* saga. It is obvious that the main difference between a chronicle of childhood and one of maturity lies in the fact that in the former there can be no dramatic plot. The natural second act, marriage or the equivalent, is missing. . . . A novel of childhood can be no more than a prologue, soon over or indefinitely prolonged according to the writer's belief in the importance of every incident belonging to the first ten years. But though an actual plot is absent from *Jeremy,* his story has plenty of plots. Remembering that a child's day is often an adult's year, Hugh Walpole has designed each chapter to cover a stage in the protracted pilgrimage of childhood: each chapter is, in fact, a novel in minature. In each Jeremy has his violent new experience and leaves it behind him as his elders leave at last behind them an agony of months. The *Jeremy* volumes, in consequence, though they are not closely written, do reproduce with extreme reality the agitated lengthiness of childhood, which resembles nothing so much as a concertina stretched out full. Now the usual type of child's book with its arbitrary climax and conclusion is much more like a concertina shut up: and a concertina shut up is not in the least like a concertina. But the book has very much more than mere technical and experimental interest for the reader. The children are worth meeting for their own sake. Jeremy, Mary, Helen, and the rest are drawn from the inside, and are imagined rather than recollected children, though it is clear from the resemblance between the child books and the various groups of the adult novels that recollection even more than observation plays a part in rounding these small circles. But the children are imagined from the point of view of the elder, the masculine novelists. They are all fixed characters acting on life and each other, and acted upon by life and each other. They are not new-formed every morning by their own emotions. (pp. 104-07)

> *Clemence Dane [pseudonym of Winifred Ashton], in her* Tradition and Hugh Walpole *(copyright © 1929 by Doubleday, Doran & Company, Inc.; copyright renewed © 1956 by Clemence Dane; reprinted by permission of Curtis Brown Ltd, London, as literary agents of the Estate of Clemence Dane), Doubleday & Company, Inc., 1929, 263 p.*

JOSEPH WARREN BEACH (essay date 1932)

[In James's handling of the restricted point of view,] the artistic intention calls for extremely extended passages [in which the character muses and reflects upon his situations, passages] much more extended than the patience of the average reader can bear. But there is, I think, no watering. The problem of the moment is often a very subtle one, and the author's imagination dwells upon it broodingly so as not to lose one shade of what it means to the character. In many writers under James's influence, the exploitation of this part of the narrative is carried to tedious lengths.

In Hugh Walpole, for example, there are pages upon pages of this sort of thing which the judicious reader will know how to skip. One trouble is that the characters are so much alike, all tarred with the same faint brush of suffering and soulfulness. In **"The Duchess of Wrexe"** . . . , which is probably his best novel, a large part of the narrative is given over to the thoughts and feelings of Rachel, of Breton, Roddy, Lizzie Rand, and Dr. Christopher. And while these people have very different parts to play in the story and the author has done his best to differentiate them in character, they all think alike, and, what is more, all feel alike. They are all so nice in their sentimental reactions, so troubled in spirit, going through so languidly and yet convulsively their exercises in the moral gymnasium which is life!

Opposed to them is a malignant old woman, Rachel's grandmother, the Duchess, who is supposed to sum up in some vague way all that is evil and mean in social life—the old, selfish, autocratic tradition of the Beaminsters. The duchess knows that her granddaughter is in tacit rebellion against her ideals, and she marries her to her favorite, the pagan Beaminster, Roddy, with the deliberate intention of crushing her spirit and bringing her to heel. (pp. 314-15)

Her motivation is anything but clear. Mr. Walpole always wants to make his characters too widely representative. **"The Duchess of Wrexe"** is one of the many novels of the time which were intended to chronicle the changing social order, with presumably the change in ideals. . . . Only, while it is perfectly clear, in Miss [Rose] Macaulay and Wells and Galsworthy, what changes in social custom and alignment, in economic theory and political ideals, are being discussed, and while none of these writers suggests that the soul of man is undergoing beneath our eyes some radical alteration, the whole matter is shrouded by Walpole in a mist of transcendental vagueness, in which we know only that, in some mysterious manner, the death of the Duchess signalizes the approach of the millennium and the emergence of Soul. Ethical terms which have no clear application (honesty and truth), metaphysical terms from Carlyle (shams, Real and Unreal), are all messed up with terms from social theory (progress, the new Individualism, the end of a Period); and throughout it is implied that the opposed terms of an ethical dualism are somehow to be assigned respectively to the old and the new generation. The relief of Mafeking, with the riotous London crowd, soberly enough interpreted by Soames Forsyte in "In Chancery," is made by Walpole's people the occasion for an orgy of confused speculations.

There is a speculative citizen of the world named Brun who has no part in the story but makes an occasional appearance for the sole purpose of putting strained interpretations on simple events. He has a curious generic resemblance to Gabriel Nash of [James's] "The Tragic Muse." In addition to his political-social theory, he has a picturesque and most elusive moral theory having to do with a Tiger which each one of us carries hidden somewhere in his heart, and which, if our soul is to live, we must sometime face and conquer.

This is not the first or last appearance of the Tiger in Walpole—a mythical beast lineally descended from James's Beast in the Jungle and Blake's "tyger burning bright in the forests of the night."

This Tiger belongs to a region of Mr. Walpole's imagination which makes him rather skilful in creating an atmosphere of mystery and terror. He has done this quite successfully, for example, in ["**Fortitude**," in "**The Dark Forest**" and "**The Secret City.**"] . . . (pp. 315-16)

Mr. Walpole has used somewhat the method of Conrad in "Heart of Darkness" . . . for gradually working up his mysterious terrors, and he has obviously been influenced by Dostoevski in the psychology of his characters. But the moral degradation of the ivory-hunter Kurtz in "Heart of Darkness," while so long a matter of shadowy guesses and intimations, is sufficiently real and itemized in the end to justify the shudders to which the reader is subjected. And the psychology of Dostoevski, while he keeps it obscure through long stretches of his story, is solidly enough based in a coherent religious philosophy. Strange as the Russians may seem to us, there is nothing in them so factitious and fantastic as these two pairs of men in **"The Dark Forest,"** rivals in each case for the love of a dead woman and racing each other to Death under the impression that the one who first arrives in the realm of the shades will possess the desired woman. If the idea is not so simple as this, that will be because it is more confused. (pp. 316-17)

It is this pretentious haziness of ideas that stands in the way of any serious study of human nature, and gives that air of unreality to the situations in which Mr. Walpole's characters find themselves. Mr. Walpole was a close friend of James, who evidently regarded him as one of his most promising disciples. And he perhaps considered that in **"The Duchess of Wrexe"** he was developing a James situation. We read of Rachel's "desperate efforts to analyze a situation that was, in definite outline, no situation at all." But the situations in James, while they are often baffling enough for the people involved, never want definite outline. What Mr. Walpole lacks, to be a proper disciple of James, is the imaginative precision which is maintained through all the windings and subtleties of thought, as well as James's freedom from the sentimental stress. (p. 317)

> *Joseph Warren Beach, "Critique of the Well-Made Novel," in his* The Twentieth Century Novel: Studies in Technique *(© 1932, renewed 1960; adapted by permission of Prentice-Hall, Inc., Englewood Cliffs, New Jersey), Appleton-Century-Crofts, Inc., 1932, pp. 307-20.**

MARGUERITE STEEN (essay date 1933)

Hugh Walpole in his Herries Saga so epitomises the new [historical novel] that we may take the four Herries novels as the text of our enquiry into the modern development of the historical novel. Although he was not the first of the modern novelists to experiment in the form, it may be generally conceded that *Rogue Herries* blazed the trail for the renaissance of the [historical novel]. (p. 244)

The elements which accounted for the decline of the old historical novel were, undoubtedly, its longwindedness, its pomposity, its museum atomosphere and the time barrier which it erected between the *then* and the *now*. In every possible way it emphasised the "long, long ago," and seemed at pains to impress upon its readers that its characters were now dust. (pp. 244-45)

The old historical novelist was too much in awe of his period, too deeply impressed by his historic motive, to come to grips with his subject. He was inclined to see his period through the wrong end of a telescope: so that all the subtler qualities, all the embroideries, were blurred out, and the things which remained were the big things: the big heroism, the big villainy: all the things which were exceptional and exaggerated and extravagant. He would not allow that human beings are far more often simply silly than they are either heroic or ignoble. (p. 245)

The first task which lay before the reformers of the historical novel was the clearance of ancient formulae, and the replacement of the ''long-long ago'' perspective with a sharper angle of vision. They had to convince their readers of a thing that everyone knows theoretically: that human nature in the eighth or the twelfth or the sixteenth century reacted to certain common stimuli in precisely the same manner in which it reacts in the present day: and that it expressed its feelings in exactly the same essence, albeit modified by certain turns of expression which, since they are superficial, may be ignored. They had to oust the false in order to make room for the true. (pp. 246-47)

What author was better able to understand this paradox than Hugh Walpole, who, from his first published work, had sedulously employed the realistic convention as the vehicle of his romance?

Thus it comes to pass that one can read *Rogue Herries*, which opens in the year 1720 and closes in 1774: *Judith Paris*, which carries us over to the second decade of the eighteenth century, and *The Fortress*, which ends on Judith's hundredth birthday in the year 1874 with the same sense of immediacy, of the living and eternal present with which one reads the war-time section of *Vanessa*, which, with its sequel, brings the narrative up to the year 1932.

Instead of making the path of the reader difficult by insistence upon the difference between the eighteenth century and the twentieth, Hugh Walpole employs every tacit means of making him realise that as it was, it now is, and ever shall be, world without end. Rogue Herries talking to his son David, is not an eighteenth-century marionette, with a mouthful of contemporary oaths and expletives, but any father talking to any son, whom he adores. (p. 247)

And, most vital of all points, the Herries Saga enshrines the apical difference between the old and the new historical novel by replacing plot with psychological development, the manufactured sensation with the spontaneous emotion. The business of the modern author is to put thought and action in their proper sequence, so that the former is seen to be unmistakably the more important, and the second exists only in the sense of a Q.E.D. to the mental processes. In applying this method to his Herries Saga Hugh Walpole redeemed history from the dustheap and set his characters and his incidents in the very foreground of his readers' consciousness, not as a group of people who lived very many years ago, and wore odd clothes, and used odd expressions. Their thoughts are the very thoughts of people who are living today; their aspirations, their fears, their sorrows and delights are the same: and if their actions are not identical, if they are in some degree conditioned by the times in which they lived (murder, for example, is no longer convenient or prac-

tical, under the present social regime), we who live in a more restricted age have certainly felt at some time or other that we would like to do the things they did. (p. 248)

It is impossible to do justice to the Herries Saga without some consideration of the material background of the four books.

To get their full bouquet they should be read, as I have just read them, one immediately after the other: three thousand odd pages, three days' reading, a fortnight's reading, according to whether one is fast or slow. It is an act of faith and enthusiasm, but richly worth while. Only in this way is it possible to feel every bit of history clicking into place, like the pieces of a Chinese puzzle: to link up town with country, generation with generation, to trace the silver thread of motive from volume to volume, to feel the full directive drive of heredity, to experience that moving on in time and space that is marked by the change in custom and manners. It is impossible by reading one volume in an isolated fashion to get the full force of the epic of country and family, or to appreciate that vast shifting background against which Hugh Walpole manoeuvres his characters, without comparing it with that which was before, that which is to come.

Some of the writing is in the highest degree coloratura; some Hugh Walpole himself dismisses as mere journalism—notably the Sayers-Heenan fight chapter in *The Fortress*, upon which practically every critic seized at the time of the book's publication for especial praise. It is not usual to applaud a book, or even a succession of books, on the score of physical energy which they represent, but it must be acknowledged that the Herries Saga represents a sum of intellectual and physical energy unequalled by any contemporary writer. (pp. 264-65)

A peculiar charm of the four books lies in the clear delight with which the author handles his vast dual background of town and country. . . . Mr. Walpole does not trouble us with his hatreds: it is therefore the more easy to share his enthusiasms.

There is, first and foremost, his enthusiasm for crowd depiction. Here Hugh Walpole stands absolutely without rival. There is that about his crowd scenes which no other writer achieves: a rustle, a surge, a throb of authentic apprehension, an excitement, a fullness, a genuine sense of jostle and thrust, something delightfully gay, dangerous or sinister as the occasion may warrant. . . .

There is his enthusiasm in the depiction of family celebrations. The Herries love vast hospitalities, and their creator abandons himself to these with an orgic rapture. (p. 265)

His familiar delight in colour and decorative detail scatters itself through the pages of the four books like a fountain of jewels. He shows the sensitiveness of a modern house decorator for ''period'' interiors. . . .

Then there is his enthusiasm for descriptions of masculine and feminine apparel. The four books afford almost a complete history of costume over the two centuries: we are made free of a delicious sensualism of materials and colours and silhouettes. . . . (p. 267)

Let us, in conclusion, consider the pattern of Hugh Walpole's epic, its theme, the unities that bind it together: for the four books are one book, and it remains for us to decide the secret of their oneness.

Somewhere there is a Lake, a Water still as life and death, green as the eternal hopes and aspirations of mankind. Into it a Hand—never mind whose—drops a stone; what happens? Circles and circles and circles: widening until the whole surface is rippled into rings that take their shape from the momentary whirlpool caused by the dropping of the stone: changing in size and colour, resurgent, turbulent, polemical, breaking into and out of one another, but weakening, weakening—until the last tremor dies; remains but a glaucous emerald. Somewhere there is a Lake. . . .

This, figuratively speaking, is the design followed by the Herries Saga—of concentric rings widening from a common centre. It takes two hundred years for the ripple to die out of the water; during those two hundred years the circles widen and widen, break into and out of one another, hold their shape by virtue of that magnetic force hidden in the centuries, tremble on the edge of dissolution, shudder and fade as they pass out of the radius of the controlling power.

And the controlling power itself? What is it but the fusion of Family and Locality that first takes place in a manor-house under Watendlath Fell? (p. 283)

Take a place, he says, in effect, and take a person; work them together until particles of the one mingle with particles of the other: until their friction generates a force so virile that it must go on propagating itself until that force is spent. The generated force will be stonger than either of the elements which caused it, and may prolong, *ad infinitum*, the influence of the generative elements. . . . The human soul pursues its eternity cycle for an age or two within the comprehended bounds of human intelligence, but sooner or later it completes its course by passing into the inapprehensible.

Thus mankind works out its liberation from the finite, and there remain only the scenes of Nature in which it has performed its *agon, pathos* and *anagnorisis.*

This is the spacious theme which Hugh Walpole has developed through the four novels. (pp. 283-84)

The shapeliness of the ending brings the Saga to a close on a note of high spiritual significance. Where there was one man only there is again only one man. The Place is getting ready to take possession again; all human passion, turmoil, defeat and strife float away like trails of mist up the mountainside. (p. 284)

> *Marguerite Steen, in her* Hugh Walpole: A Study *(Canadian rights by permission of A. M. Heath & Co. Ltd., as literary agents for the Estate of Marguerite Steen), Doubleday, Doran & Company Inc., 1933, 287 p.*

GRAHAM GREENE   (essay date 1939)

Sir Hugh Walpole occupies an official position among popular writers: he is the liaison officer between them and the arts: he has a pedigree. . . . [*The Sea Tower*] is his twenty-eighth novel and forty-fifth book, and nobody can help feeling sympathy for such unremitting pressure on the creative instinct. His style has not come through unimpaired, but he has remained readable; he writes loosely, carelessly, but with speed—his novels do move, and his plots have an enviable simplicity. One thinks of his rivals—new and old—in popularity: Mr. Priestley, Mr. [Charles Langbridge] Morgan, Mr. [George Warwick] Deeping, Mr. Brett Young; they all seem

a little stuffed beside him. Sir Hugh Walpole has remained young—too young, perhaps.

His prevailing mood has never changed, and the strict puritan may raise a dubious eyebrow at the part played by pain and cruelty: we remember the father beating his son in *Fortitude;* the woman driven nearly crazy with fear in *The Old Ladies;* the man with red hair. The new book ends in a positive orgy of red-hot poker, slipping pyjamas and naked flesh, when old Mrs. Field, driven mad with jealousy—that is the whole story—attacks her too lovely daughter-in-law. . . . It is a little crude and sensational (references to Hitler, Mussolini, the violent world outside fail to give a wider significance to the private fantasy); the physical explicitness is sometimes embarrassing—there are passages which would be erotic if they were not naïve; *The Sea Tower* certainly has neither the fastidiousness nor the general implications of a really good novel, but there remains something . . . something rather like a schoolboy's world, full of bullies and understanding older people and incredible day-dreams about girls, but still a world. When the nerve of fear and pain is touched Sir Hugh writes best. Sentimentality and foolishness creep in with virtue—the author's compassion has the false air of a father with a cane: "This hurts me more than it hurts you." Then the style becomes wordy, unbuttoned and grotesque. . . . Only once—in *The Old Ladies*—has he allowed himself to go all the way with his temperament, and we must suppose that he has gained in popularity by the long loose robes he drapes his nightmares in. We are reminded of his own excellent description of a too bluff, too literary sea-captain: "a kind of fake iridescence, shining and stretching over the hard true bone of . . . experience."

> *Graham Greene, "Fiction: 'The Sea Tower'" (© 1939 by Graham Greene; reprinted by permission of Lawrence Pollinger Limited), in* The Spectator, *Vol. 163, No. 5804, September 22, 1939, p. 420.*

L.A.G. STRONG   (essay date 1944)

Hugh Walpole was a romantic novelist. It was no accident that he chose the Lake District as the background for his most ambitious work. The essence of romanticism, as Mr F. L. Lucas has pointed out, is that it releases the less conscious levels of the mind. Coleridge had seen this, though he put it less concisely. Of Wordsworth's *Immortality* ode, he wrote . . . :

> In every work of art there is a reconcilement of the external with the internal; the conscious is so impressed on the unconscious as to appear in it.

If I labour this point, it is because it gives (I think) the clue to Walpole's merits and defects as a novelist. A true romantic in that he wrote from his unconscious mind, he distrusted the source of his inspiration, and often very much disliked what it said to him. At the same time, he was too knowledgeable not to be aware that his inspiration had narrow limits. He was dissatisfied with it, both in quantity and quality, and laboured to supplant it with a deal of deliberate and conscious craftsmanship. This anxiety was revealed in the anxious thoroughness with which he organised his career, in his almost hysterical sensitiveness to criticism, and in the pains he took to conciliate or silence hostile critics. (p. 222)

Thus we see in Walpole an artist developing his talent at both ends, the conscious and the unconscious, and leaving a gap in the middle. The two sides of his literary personality never met. In Coleridge's phrase, there was no reconcilement of the external with the internal. As a writer, we can liken him to a long avenue with a bright light at each end. In the darkness between crouches a terrified small boy, whom the craftsman at one end cannot reach, and to whom comes no ghostly comfort from the other. (p. 223)

A badly frightened man, [Walpole] excelled at depicting fear. Since Henry James, no one has surpassed him at anatomising fear, and at describing the slow disintegration of a character exposed to it. The numb fascinated helplessness of a person in its grip, the weakness that provokes cruelty and has no will to resist, the fatalistic misery of an ill-treated child: with such themes Walpole could not go wrong. But because he hated cruelty, and because he knew fear, his conscious mind rushed to a frantic affirmation of kindliness, to a robust, Brothers-Cheeryble optimism which rang hollow as the blows with which he noisily thumped his chest. His Christmas cheer, which Walpole the man loved and believed in, is far less convincing than Dickens's, though it comes out of the same box. The difference is not only Walpole's infirmity as an artist: it is that, on paper, he could not wholly believe in the good of life, and so had to keep on assuring himself of it all the time. For Hugh Walpole there was no problem of evil, but a problem of good.

His nearest approach in his work to an inspired belief in good was through the second quality in which he excelled, his knowledge of children. Here, too, he could hardly put a foot wrong. The terrors of childhood, its wonder, its fearful joys, he understood with real sensitiveness and love.... Nothing in the Herries chronicle has the magic of the first scene where the child in the inn bedroom watches the maid, Alice Press, sitting by the fire. In such passages Walpole stands for a moment beside the creator of David Copperfield: but he is liable to spoil them by an access of self-distrust which makes him bring on the deliberate craftsman. I do not deprecate the craftsman; heaven forbid. The trouble was that in Walpole he was not integrated with the creator.

The third department of writing at which Walpole excelled was the realisation of atmosphere and background. In his best novels the background is not only suggested: it dominates. He had a remarkable faculty of keeping the background vivid in the reader's mind even at the height of the most passionate and violent of the scenes enacted in front of it. Throughout *The Cathedral*, one is aware of the dark and soaring bulk above the roofs. After the happenings of the Herries books have faded from memory one sees still the violent dripping greens, the stiff uprush of bracken, the burns foaming and twisting down between the rocks. The scenery of the Lakes captured Walpole's imagination. His gifts cried yes to it, and, careless and inexact though his writing often was, he splashed the landscapes down with a vividness that often swamped the characters he set amongst them.

It is early yet to say which are his best books. Not any of the Herries saga, which reached its height in *Judith Paris*, and certainly not its conclusion, *Katherine Christian*. This is unfinished, but throughout it we see the craftsman working with assured skill, though getting little help from the man within. Let me repeat that as a craftsman Walpole was highly expert. With the possible exception of Mr Frank Swinnerton,

he knew more about the novelist's craft than any writer or critic I have met.... (pp. 223-25)

To show him at his best, I would pick a short story, *The Silver Mask*, a quite terrifying study of terror; *The Cathedral*—he always protested against my praise of this, saying very truly that it was melodramatic; and *The Dark Forest*, one of the two novels inspired by his visit to Russia in the last war. Melodrama was of the essence of his work. His recurring theme was the conflict between good and evil. Evil he understood, and feared, and showed in nightmare guise, dressed in the fantastic trappings of the romantic period. Of good as an artist he knew less, because his inspiration did not believe in it. Had it done so, had he been able to believe in sunlight as strongly as in darkness, he could have been a great novelist. (p. 225)

L.A.G. Strong, "Hugh Walpole" (originally published in Time and Tide, *Vol. XXV, No. 25, June 17, 1944), in his* Personal Remarks *(reprinted with the permission of Liveright Publishing Corporation; copyright 1953 by L.A.G. Strong), Liveright, 1953, pp. 222-25.*

ELIZABETH STEELE   (essay date 1972)

When Walpole, age twenty-four, arrived in London in 1909 impatient to begin his professional career, he had been writing novels for over a decade. (p. 26)

If, as some have thought, *The Wooden Horse* ... seems unusually mature for a first novel, this quality is attributable to two factors: the young author's long apprenticeship, and his having submitted the manuscript to three professional writers for suggestions. (p. 28)

The theme of *The Wooden Horse* concerns an important socio-economic issue for its time and place: the British law of primogeniture. (p. 29)

Walpole never boosted his first novel as he did some of the later ones. "So *mild* a book," he complained of it.... But *The Wooden Horse* is not bad. Seldom jejune, it is alert to human foibles; is often witty; and, except for a recapitulative monologue by Robin near the end (the confessional device that mars some of Walpole's later books also), is fairly well paced. Yet I would not suggest a new reprint: even in Britain, primogeniture is no longer a serious problem except in the royal family; and *The Wooden Horse* is not impressive enough in other ways to survive its out-of-date theme. (p. 30)

Commercially speaking, *Mr. Perrin and Mr. Traill* ... is Walpole's most long-lived novel. Critically speaking, until recently, it has been one of his best regarded works.... "About 1910 H. G. Wells gave his famous lecture at the Times' Book Club," Walpole later recalled, "in which he declared, that we had had enough of romantic nonsense and that novels must deal with real people and be afraid of nothing." This invitation, coming from one of his special mentors, was seized on by the young author, who emerged in two months with *Perrin and Traill*. Despite the Cornish setting, it was obviously a transcription of the year he had spent at Epsom College teaching French—except that he neither committed suicide like Vincent Perrin, nor like Archie Traill, caused anyone else to do so. (pp. 33-4)

A main reason for the kind reception may have been its brevity in a time when most novels ran much longer, for favorable analysts saw *Perrin and Traill* as a vignette making its point exquisitely and poignantly within a small compass. And the point made was new: the problems of the English schoolboy were a familiar subject in English fiction, but those of the English schoolmaster were not. Amazing as it seems today, *Mr. Perrin and Mr. Traill* was the first fictional treatment of English public-school life from the teacher's viewpoint since Dickens' *Nicholas Nickleby.* Walpole minced no words in describing the strained conditions in a typical public school, not only between teacher and pupil (the traditional angle) but also, and more importantly, between teacner and teacher and teacher and headmaster.

Finally, the critics admired its reality. Of course, as a roman à clef, it employed real people, events, and setting. But by "realism" they meant that it illustrated certain traits attributed by consensus to the Realistic novel: "natural" diction, an emphasis on life's tediums as experienced by the common man or woman in believable circumstances, and a reluctance on the writer's part to provide a happy ending. That Vincent Perrin is an antihero, sadly flawed, vulnerable, even physically unattractive, also assures the novel's "realism." "You cannot read it, and then say it isn't true," [Arnold] Bennett had written. You cannot read it and then say it isn't beautiful." Presumably this last adjective refers to the final scene where Perrin, with a Sidney Carton-like gesture of "It is a far, far better thing that I do than I have ever done," throws away his life in order to save the life of the youth he has viewed as his worst enemy. The reader, if he takes this kind of quasi-tragedy seriously, as the English critics and public apparently did, may find it elevating.

Walpole's American publishers, however, disliked the ending: they thought it too serious, too "morbid" for the tenderhearted American public. My own reasons for preferring the ending of the American edition, *The Gods and Mr. Perrin,* are the same as Walpole's, who wrote in his diary when making the change: "It will be *such* an improvement . . . much more logical and convincing—wish I had done it originally.". . . (pp. 34-5)

Still tingling from the excitement of writing fictionalized autobiography in *Mr. Perrin and Mr. Traill,* Walpole embarked next on a *Künstlerroman,* that is, the story of an artist—in this case a young writer whose experience in some ways again resembled Walpole's. . . . [The] novel was called *Fortitude.* (p. 42)

[*Fortitude*] is absorbing enough; and, except for attempts at dialect, the diction is well enough managed; but the constant sobriety is boring, and the unities in so long a work are hard for the reader to keep in mind. An abridged version was issued in 1938, edited apparently by Walpole himself, where the loss of discursive ramblings and supererogative vignettes constitutes a real gain. (pp. 44-5)

In *Fortitude,* Peter Westcott's career as a writer is viewed from two standpoints: the commercial, his relative earnings or lack thereof and how long it takes him to write; and the social, the reaction of his family and friends to his career as a writer, and his relationships with other writers, friendly or not. Overall, there hangs an air of excitement about the creative process itself; and, in this respect, Peter's attitude coincides with his author's. (p. 45)

Walpole's first Russian novel, *The Dark Forest.* . .is one of his best works; the second, *The Secret City.* . .won the first James Tait Black Memorial Prize. Although *The Dark Forest* is the better of the two, both are worth reading. *The Dark*

Forest, a love story, happens in East Galicia during the Great Retreat by the Russians in the face of the German offensive early in World War I; *The Secret City* is an atmosphere-shrouded tale of the March, 1917, "Provisional" Russian Revolution. (p. 55)

The strengths of *The Dark Forest* are its universal theme [of death], varied characters, and engrossing plot. To me, its greatest flaw is [the protagonist] Trenchard's diary, quoted from sporadically during the novel, extensively at the end. (pp. 57-8)

[Walpole's] comments on Russia and the Russian character [in *The Secret City*] are thought-provoking, but he does not pretend to expertness: "This business of seeing Russian psychology through English eyes has no excuse except that it *is* English. That is its only interest, its only atmosphere, its only motive . . . any one's ideas about Russian life are of interest." This fact alone would not suffice to keep *The Secret City* in the permanent Walpole canon. However, the slow-moving narrative is ultimately compelling, Durward's tone is for the most part sincere, and there are a variety of interesting characters. Add to these its uniqueness—Walpole's eyewitness position vis à vis the events described—and I would rank *The Secret City* among the upper 25 percent of his novels. . . . (p. 61)

The questions animating *Golden Scarecrow* . . . and *Prelude to Adventure* are identical: "How real is God?" "What is God like?" He is real, say both novels, because He can be felt, heard, even seen—by certain people; but *what* is felt, seen, and heard depends upon personal need. The God vouchsafed to Dune [in *Prelude to Adventure*] is relentless, as He must be to bring an erring soul into line; at the same time, He is beautiful and the source of all rapture. . . . (p. 79)

The protagonists of *The Golden Scarecrow* are children, and to most of them God is kind, benevolent, and comfortable. A series of related short stories, *The Golden Scarecrow* takes its theme from Wordsworth's famous "Ode on Intimations of Immortality from Recollections of Early Childhood." (p. 80)

From the naive mysticism of *Prelude to Adventure* and *The Golden Scarecrow,* Walpole in his evangelical role moved to the criticism of religious institutions, [as in] *The Cathedral.* Before this, he chose as his main butt in *The Captives* . . . the pentecostal church, its outward forms and the spirit which, he felt, animated it. (pp. 80-1)

[The] unpopularity of *The Captives* is probably due to its grim atmosphere which is seldom relieved by light or warmth.

Recalling George Gissing and Thomas Hardy, this approach was more compatible to Walpole's active temperament than the languorous Jamesian mode of *The Green Mirror.* But many readers find the 474 pages in fine print of unmitigated grimness in *The Captives* hard to take or even believe. (p. 81)

Admirers of Thomas Hardy and the Naturalist school, on the other hand, will probably enjoy the novel. Distinguished by its wealth of detail and by the fact that, having established his mood, Walpole consistently maintains it, *The Captives* ranks for me among Walpole's dozen "best.". . .

[Two London] novels were intended as serious studies of upper-class, urban society. In the first, *The Duchess of Wrexe,* Walpole's awkward handling of the milieu revealed that he did not understand it. Fourteen years later *Wintersmoon*

. . ., one of his best novels, shows how much he had learned. The sureness of his psychology as he moves among people whose type he has come to know so well is matched by a new suavity of style, one as smooth as cream that is appropriate to the setting. The novel's only problem is pace, a bit too slow to give the plot developments the excitement they deserve. (p. 104)

Neither the plot nor the characters makes *Wintersmoon* the champion of the London novels. For its supremacy we must thank the language; stately and gracious, it fits the story's theme, the value of gracious living, and its rhythms are such that the reader finds whole sentences lingering in his mind. (p. 106)

Hugh Walpole is most respected for his novels, and rightly so. His short-story collections—[*The Silver Thorn, All Souls' Night, Head in Green Bronze,* and *Mr. Huffam*]—received, on the whole, good reviews; but most of the stories are mediocre. Walpole's temperament contributed to his lack of success in this genre. . . . With his uncritical expansiveness, it was hard for him to concentrate on a single character in a single important episode for a single effect. (p. 136)

> *Elizabeth Steele, in her* Hugh Walpole *(copyright © 1972 by Twayne Publishers, Inc.; reprinted with the permission of Twayne Publishers, a Division of G. K. Hall & Co., Boston), Twayne, 1972, 178 p.*

ADDITIONAL BIBLIOGRAPHY

Adcock, A. St. John. "Hugh Walpole." In his *Gods of Modern Grub Street: Impressions of Contemporary Authors,* pp. 293-99. New York: Frederick A. Stokes, 1923.
    A sketch of Walpole's life and career, in which he is favorably compared to Anthony Trollope.

Chesterton, G. K. "Our Notebook." *The Illustrated London News* 172, No. 4645 (28 April 1928): 730.*
    A discussion of Walpole's treatment of the horrible in his work. Chesterton praises Walpole for handling the sinister with "a certain clean tact and sympathy, like the touch of a surgeon."

Dutton, George B. "Romance and Mr. Walpole." *The Sewanee Review XXXI,* No. 2 (April 1923): 178-86.
    An explication of Walpole's romantic beliefs as they appear in his novels, and critical reconciliation of those beliefs with *The Cathedral* and *The Captives.*

Edel, Leon. "Hugh Walpole and Henry James: The Fantasy of *The Killer and the Slain.*" *American Imago* 8, No. 4 (December 1951): 351-69.
    A discussion of the similarities between the characters in *The Killer and the Slain* and *The Turn of the Screw.* The critic sees, in the two main characters of *The Killer and the Slain,* portraits of Walpole and James. Further, he sees in the book's cycle of death Walpole's symbolic tearing away from his "master."

Frierson, William C. "The Postwar Novel, 1919-1929: Sophisticates and Others." In his *The English Novel in Transition: 1885-1940,* pp. 237-78. Norman: University of Oklahoma Press, 1942.*
    A brief introduction to Walpole's career.

Greicus, M. S. "Writing from the War Years." In his *Prose Writers of World War I,* pp. 7-14. Harlow, England: Longman Group, 1973.*
    An essay on *The Dark Forest* and *The Secret City* that discusses how they came to be written.

Hart-Davis, Rupert. *Hugh Walpole: A Biography.* New York: The Macmillan Co., 1952, 503 p.
    The definitive Walpole biography. The book contains many informative extracts from Walpole's journals and letters, as well as from the letters of Henry James, Arnold Bennett, Somerset Maugham, and others.

Hartley, L. P. "The Two Magics." *The Spectator* 133, No. 5026 (25 October 1924): 612, 614.*
    A review of *The Old Ladies.* Hartley finds the book a flawed expression of Walpole's fascination with childhood and second-childhood.

Hergesheimer, Joseph. *Hugh Walpole: An Appreciation.* New York: George H. Doran Co., 1919, 65 p.
    A laudatory overview of Walpole's canon through *The Secret City.* The second half of the book contains excerpted book reviews from various periodicals.

Noyes, Alfred. "Exit Hugh Walpole." In his *Two Worlds for Memory,* pp. 305-11. Philadelphia, New York: J. B. Lippincott Co., 1953.
    Remembrances of the author's brief associations with Walpole. Noyes reveals certain fabrications and distortions of fact that Walpole included in *Roman Fountain.*

(Adeline) Virginia Woolf

1882-1941

English novelist, critic, essayist, short story writer, and biographer.

Woolf is one of the most prominent literary figures of the twentieth century. Like her contemporary James Joyce, with whom she is often compared, Woolf is remembered as one of the most innovative of the stream of consciousness novelists. Concerned primarily with depicting the life of the mind, she revolted against the traditional narrative techniques of Bennett, Wells, and Galsworthy, and developed her own highly individualized style. Woolf's works, noted for their subjective exploration and delicate poetic quality, have had a lasting effect on the art of the novel.

The daughter of the eminent Victorian editor and critic Sir Leslie Stephen, Woolf was related to some of England's most distinguished scholarly families, including the Darwins and the Stracheys. She grew up in a cultured and literary atmosphere, receiving her education from her father's extensive library and from conversing with his friends, many of whom were prominent writers of the day. Following her father's death, Woolf settled in the Bloomsbury district of London and soon became a central figure of the Bloomsbury group. Within this intellectual circle, which included John Maynard Keynes, Vita Sackville-West, and Lytton Strachey, she met her husband, Leonard Woolf. Together she and her husband founded the Hogarth Press and published the early works of such writers as Katherine Mansfield, T. S. Eliot, E. M. Forster, and Sigmund Freud.

A discerning and influential critic and essayist as well as a novelist, Woolf began writing reviews for *The Times Literary Supplement* at an early age. Her critical essays, which cover almost the entire range of English literature, are praised for their insight and contain some of her finest prose. In *A Room of One's Own* and *Three Guineas* Woolf vigorously champions women's rights, emphasizing the importance of an independently creative life.

An examination of Woolf's fiction reveals her increasing concern with subjective exploration. Although her first novel, *The Voyage Out*, is relatively conventional, its emphasis on character analysis rather than plot foreshadows Woolf's later treatment of her characters' inner lives. It was not until her third novel, *Jacob's Room*, that she attempted a wholly individual technique and finally discovered her true voice. Minimizing external action, Woolf explores and illuminates her hero's personality with a series of impressions conveyed through his inner monologue. This stream of consciousness technique is further developed in *Mrs. Dalloway*, which demonstrates Woolf's complete rejection of traditional narrative form.

Regarded by many as her finest achievement, *To the Lighthouse* treats Woolf's favorite themes of marriage, time, and death. In a further maturation of her subjective mode, plot is completely abandoned, with unity and coherence provided instead by imagery, symbolism, and poetic elements. This technique reached its extreme in the prose poems of *The Waves*. Here Woolf depicts the passage of time through the impressionistic

Culver Pictures

interior monologues of her six characters, and again attempts coherence through recurrent imagery and symbol. While critics praise the beautifully poetic prose of *The Waves*, many argue that Woolf's method has become restrictive and artificial through a too-obvious imposition of pattern and significance upon her material.

Fearing she would be unable to overcome her recurring mental illness, Woolf took her own life. Her posthumous novel, *Between the Acts*, a combination of prose, poetry, and dialogue, demonstrates Woolf's continued desire to expand the novel's scope. Although numerous critics debate her ultimate importance, Woolf's position as a great literary innovator is assured.

(See also *TCLC*, Vol. 1)

PRINCIPAL WORKS

The Voyage Out (novel) 1915
Kew Gardens (short stories) 1919
The Mark on the Wall (short stories) 1919
Night and Day (novel) 1919
Monday or Tuesday (short stories) 1921
Jacob's Room (novel) 1922

E. M. FORSTER (essay date 1915)

[Perhaps] the first comment to make on [Virginia Woolf's] *The Voyage Out* is that it is absolutely unafraid, and that its courage springs, not from naiveté, but from education.... Here at last is a book which attains unity as surely as *Wuthering Heights*, though by a different path, a book which, while written by a woman and presumably from a woman's point of view, soars straight out of local questionings into the intellectual day. (pp. 52-3)

Mrs Woolf's success is more remarkable since there is one serious defect in her equipment; her chief characters are not vivid. There is nothing false in them, but when she ceases to touch them they cease, they do not stroll out of their sentences, and even develop a tendency to merge shadow-like. (p. 53)

[If] Mrs Woolf does not 'do' her four main characters very vividly, and is apt to let them all become clever together, and differ only by their opinions, then on what does her success depend? Some readers—those who demand the milk of human kindness, even in its tinned form—will say that she has not succeeded; but the bigness of her achievement should impress anyone weaned from baby food. She believes in adventure—here is the main point—believes in it passionately, and knows that it can only be undertaken alone. Human relations are no substitute for adventure, because when real they are uncomfortable, and when comfortable they must be unreal. It is for a voyage into solitude that man was created, and Rachel, Helen, Hewet, Hirst, all learn this lesson, which is exquisitely reinforced by the setting of tropical scenery—the soul, like the body, voyages at her own risk.... Mrs Woolf's vision may be inferior to Dostoieffsky's—but she sees as clearly as he where efficiency ends and creation begins, and even more clearly that our supreme choice lies not between body and soul, but between immobility and

motion. In her pages, body v. soul—that dreary medieval tug-of-war—does not find any place. It is as if the rope has broken, leaving pagans sprawling on one side and clergymen on the other.... (pp. 53-4)

[A] word must be said about the comedy: the book is extremely amusing. (p. 54)

The writer can sweep together masses of characters for our amusement, then sweep them away; her comedy does not counteract her tragedy and at the close enhances it, for we see that the Hotel and the Villa will soon be dancing and gossiping just as before, that existence will continue the same, exactly the same, for everyone, for everyone except the reader; he, more fortunate than the actors, is established in the possession of beauty. (p. 55)

> *E. M. Forster, within an essay in* Daily News and Leader *(reprinted by permission of King's College, Cambridge and the Society of Authors as the literary representative of the Estate of E. M. Forster), April 8, 1915 (and reprinted in* Virginia Woolf: The Critical Heritage, *edited by Robin Majumdar and Allen McLaurin, Routledge & Kegan Paul, 1975, pp. 52-5).*

P. C. KENNEDY (essay date 1925)

Mrs Dalloway is in many ways beautiful; but I think it sets out to be, and continues until the end to pretend to be, what it is not. I think it quite sincerely claims to employ a new method, and I think it employs an old one.... People will tell you, with a face of praise, that the whole action of *Mrs Dalloway* passes in one day. But it doesn't pass in one day. In order to create that impression, Mrs Woolf makes her characters move about London, and, when two of them come into purely fortuitous and external contact, she gives you the history of each backwards. She might just as well—better—have given it forwards. The novelty is not a novelty.... Mrs Woolf has really imposed on several quite different stories a purely artificial unity. (p. 165)

Mrs Woolf, too, has—or so it seems to me—a purpose: and a genuinely splendid one. The whole trouble is the incongruity between the apparent purpose and the distracting method.... I take it that Mrs Woolf means to show us the kaleidoscope of life shaken into a momentary plan; the vagueness, the casualness, the chaos, suffering the compulsion which gives orders and makes order. And that, I repeat, is splendid. All art aims, consciously or unconsciously, at that. But all the novelty of Mrs Woolf's technique simply distracts from it. And if, as I suspect, she has the subsidiary but still vital purpose of stressing the incoherence, of catching the bubble, the spark, the half-dream, the inexplicable memory, the doubt, the snare, the joke, the dread, the come-and-go of the moment on the wing—then again the needless links, the co-incidences, distract.

Mrs Woolf has extraordinary gifts; the only doubt is whether they are the specific gifts of the novelists. She excels in description of mood or sudden scene; but the mood might always be anybody's; anybody might occupy the scene. In all this brilliant novel (and the brilliance is at times quite dazzling) there are no people. It is like that ghostly world of Mr Bertrand Russell's philosophy, in which there are lots of sensations but no one to have them.... She understands a mood; she analyses it; she presents it; she catches its finer implications; but she never moves me with it, because she never makes me feel that the person credited with it is other than an object of the keenest and most skilful study. . . . [My] admiration for what Mrs Woolf has achieved outweighs my dislike of the fetters she has put on her achievement. Call *Mrs Dalloway* an intellectual triumph, and I agree. I could quote scores of fine and profound things from it. . . . But I want to weep with Peter Walsh and leap to death with poor Septimus Warren Smith; and my trouble is that I can't. (pp. 166-67)

P. C. Kennedy, "New Novels: 'Mrs. Dalloway'," in New Statesman *(© 1925 The Statesman Publishing Co. Ltd.), Vol. XXV, No. 632, June 6, 1925 (and reprinted in* Virginia Woolf: The Critical Heritage, *edited by Robin Majumdar and Allen McLaurin, Routledge & Kegan Paul, 1975, pp. 165-67).*

EDWIN MUIR   (essay date 1927)

To the Lighthouse is a novel difficult to judge. . . . [It] stands at the summit of the development of a remarkable writer. Its aim is high and serious, its technique brilliant; there are more beautiful pages in it than Mrs Woolf has written before; a unique intuition and intelligence are at work in it almost continuously, and at high pressure. The difficulties which the author surmounts in it are such as few contemporary novelists would even attempt. Its positive merits are thus very high. Yet as a whole, though showing an advance on many sides, it produces a less congruous and powerful effect than *Mrs Dalloway.* . . . The symbolism is plain enough; but in the novel, so entangled is it with other matters, interesting enough in themselves, that it becomes obscured. Actually it is obscured most by the device which should make it most clear: the intermediary book called 'Time Passes', which, to add to the difficulty, is the best of the lot, and could only have been written by a writer of profound imagination. For this section, composed in a different key, concerned with entities more universal than the human, entities which do not need human life, but, affecting everything, affect human life, too, inexorably and yet as if heedlessly, is not a real transition from the first section to the last, both conceived in human terms, but something outside them. The time which passes in this interval passes not for the characters in the story, but for everything; it is a natural, an astronomical, a cosmical transition, and not a human one except incidentally; and the result is that when Mrs Woolf returns to the human plane the sequence seems doubly abrupt. We are not only transported from James's childhood to his youth, we are switched from one dimension of time to another. That this was not the right means to mark the flight of time in his place is shown, I think, by the effect of the third section; for that effect is not intensified, it is, if anything, lessened by what has gone immediately before. Yet one cannot regret that Mrs Woolf wrote the second section in this book. For imagination and beauty of writing it is probably not surpassed in contemporary prose. But how this kind of imagination can be applied, as one feels sure it can, to the business of the novelist, the shadowing forth of human life, is still a problem to be solved. (pp. 209-10)

Edwin Muir, "Fiction: 'To the Lighthouse'," in The Nation And The Anthenaeum, *Vol. XLI, No. 13, July 2, 1927 (and reprinted in* Virginia Woolf: The Critical Heritage, *edited by Robin Majumdar and Allen McLaurin, Routledge & Kegan Paul, 1975, pp. 209-10).*

LOUIS KRONENBERGER   (essay date 1942)

[Virginia] Woolf forged her criticism into something quite as distinctive as her novels, and the best of it may well survive everything else she wrote except *To the Lighthouse* and *Mrs. Dalloway*, and may conceivably survive them. . . .

[Her] real strength did not lie in any remarkable powers of mind, any systematic principles of criticism. In fifty pages of any first-rank critic we shall find more inseminating ideas than in all three volumes of Mrs. Woolf. Where we do find a purely critical perception, it is likely to seem neither new nor old, and we are likely to value it for its pertinence rather than its originality, or for the light it throws on Virginia Woolf. (p. 245)

[With rare exceptions], Mrs. Woolf is hardly more a suggestive critic than she is a systematic one. She seldom reacts to literature in a purely critical way: to the writing of her own time she reacted as a writer; to the literature of the past she responded, for the most part, as a reader. . . . [She] had fine imagination and extraordinary sensibility; she was a born reader and could assimilate effortlessly, but she was also a very cultivated reader, and could correlate and compare. (pp. 245-46)

What she distills is much less the meaning of a writer or a period than the temperament, the savor, the personality: she is a kind of highly skillful portrait-painter who catches the style of her model while imposing a style of her own. We shall not learn from her just what the Greeks or the Elizabethans, Montaigne or Chaucer, signify, but we do know how they look. She reveals them, with beautiful clarity, in a mirror: it is for others to peer down at them through a microscope. Accordingly her best work, most of which will be found in the first *Common Reader*, has about it a real charm of artistry. One reads it a little less for profit than for pleasure, for its freshness, its shapeliness, its sensitiveness, for its language, its wit, its sense of poetry. The poet in Virginia Woolf constantly pleads for a hearing in these essays, as in her novels it ultimately insists on being heard.

After the first *Common Reader* the language becomes a little too fine; the style, at moments, tends to inflate the contents. . . . What had once been highly individual begins to seem, in *The Second Common Reader,* merely professional. There is less submerged poetry and more protruding rhetoric. . . . Mrs. Woolf still writes extremely well, but one feels that she has no desire to write differently. There is no sense here of trying to break the mold, to alter the pattern, as there always was in her fiction.

The Death of the Moth reveals a further decline, though some of it must be judged as early work and some as in not quite final form. But additional polish would hardly have given additional weight. Here, to be sure, are many things that give pleasure. . . . Here, indeed, is a good deal of the old skill. And yet there is far too much emptiness and inadequacy—nothing, for example, could be more disappointing than the essays on Henry James. Too many of these pieces are book reviews, lectures, *jeux d'esprit,* made-to-order things that disappoint even as they divert us. The style, moreover, is full of horrible Stracheyan flourishes. (pp. 246-48)

[Mrs. Woolf] was possibly a little undiscerning and literary about the past, a little too fascinated with its décor and not quite enough concerned with its large outlines. For acute as her historical sense clearly was, it pre-eminently reflected the student of manners; she was most at home, after all, in the eighteenth century. What almost equally drew her to the past, however, were its echoing corridors, its grace of distance, its poetry. Both these interests reveal that intense literary feeling which was so distinctive and valuable a part of Virginia Woolf, and which she could embody in entirely consonant prose. This is what she could do best, and what she could do better than anyone else of her time. She will survive, not as a critic, but as a literary essayist recording the adventures of a soul among congenial masterpieces. For on the whole she did not approach—modern authors excepted—what she could not in some real sense enjoy. Her taste in the classics was surprisingly catholic, and her range, at first glance, seems amazingly broad. Yet the writers who are most downright, and masculine, and central in their approach to life—a Fielding or a Balzac—she for the most part left untouched. (They fathered, of course, the contemporary fiction that she most disliked.) Her own approach was at once more subterranean and aerial, and invincibly, almost defiantly, feminine. (pp. 248-49)

> Louis Kronenberger, "Virginia Woolf as Critic," in The Nation, *Vol. 155, No. 16, October 17, 1942 (and reprinted in his* The Republic of Letters: Essays on Various Writers, *Alfred A. Knopf, 1955, pp. 244-49).*

DAVID CECIL (essay date 1949)

Through the eyes of one or more of her characters [Virginia Woolf] strove simply to record the actual process of living, to trace the confused succession of impression and thought and mood, as it drifted cloud-like across the clear mirror of consciousness. . . .

Instinctively she picks out for emphasis only those features of her subject which strike her as peculiarly significant. So that all the disordered matter of experience falls into a pattern imposed by the predominant motive force in her own inner life. This was her sensibility to the beautiful. Virginia Woolf was in the fullest, highest, extremest sense of the word, an æsthete. (p. 161)

The ugly and æsthetically insignificant she passes by; or admits only as they may serve as foil to the beauty that precedes and follows them. Thus she creates her perspective: thus she designs her pattern. (p. 162)

Æsthetic experiences are contemplative affairs. So also are the big moments in Virginia Woolf's books. Action, event, play hardly any part in them at all. . . . She will take a chapter to describe a casual stroll in which a woman feels quickened to a deeper apprehension of experience: her death or marriage Virginia Woolf may pass over in a parenthesis. Indeed the title of her last book, *Between the Acts,* indicates her feeling that active drama supplies only a superficial view of life. The things that really matter happen "between the acts". (pp. 162-63)

Virginia Woolf's characters are presented to us essentially as solitaries. Their inner life is what really matters about them. Even in company, they seem to be alone, absorbed in private unspoken trains of thought. Their relations to others are only valuable to them in so far as they feed and enrich their solitary experience, as they contribute to their moments of inner illumination and ecstasy. Not that their creator is only concerned to record moments of ecstasy. . . . When æsthetic receptiveness flags, when the imagination ceases to respond to the spectacle of the world, a terrifying sense of

universal emptiness, a chill, as of spiritual death, assaults the spirit. Some of Virginia Woolf's most memorable passages are concerned with describing this phenomenon. (p. 163)

Virginia Woolf's delight in beauty brings a correspondingly acute awareness of its frailty. Indeed, if her first impulse is to express life's loveliness, her second is to express its transience. . . . The fact of its fleetingness creates a sadness and bewilderment, a sense of unresolved discord at the very heart of her vision of experience. What is one to make of an existence in which what appears supremely significant and valuable is at the same time so ephemeral? (pp. 164-65)

Life, as shown in *Jacob's Room* and *Mrs. Dalloway,* is an insoluble mystery. But Virginia Woolf was too searching and too profound a spirit not to try and pierce deeper; and in her later works she seems to be feeling after some explanation for the enigma. There are hints that at moments she has attained to a vision of some ultimate principle of beauty, outside the flux of mortal things. (p. 165)

[At the end of *The Years*] in veiled, tentative fashion she suggests that there is a strain in the human spirit which is part of eternal reality, and which is inevitably unsatisfied as long as it is imprisoned in the wearisome condition of mortality: but which may, after it is freed from it, at last find fulfilment. (p. 166)

The end of life, so Virginia Woolf ponders, may be no blank, dark wall, but rather an opening into a region of light, where all is at last made clear. In *Between the Acts* she seems to be yet another step ahead nearer penetrating the mystery. (p. 167)

It is very unlike the vision presented by other novelists; and excludes some of the chief sources of their effects. There is no room for drama in it. Drama depends on the clash of character. . . . Imprisoned as they are, each in the solitary confinement of his own consciousness, the characters in Virginia Woolf's books never come into direct contact. Indeed, character, in the objective sense, hardly exists for her. Seen through the shifting haze of the observer's mood other people's individualities lose their clear-cut outline; while the observer's own self is dissolved into a succession of impressions.

Virginia Woolf's exclusive concentration on the æsthetic aspects of experience also prevents her from envisaging its moral aspects. People in her books are shown as happy and sad, beautiful and ugly but seldom as bad and good. Nor, in any consistent way, as loving or hating; the climate in which they live is cold and ethereal, the heart does not grow warm there for love or hate. . . . Even when Virginia Woolf describes a happy marriage like that of Mr. and Mrs. Ramsay in *To the Lighthouse,* she gets no further than indicating that at brief moments they felt an unusual harmony of soul one with the other. "We perish each alone," murmurs Mr. Ramsay to himself as he paces the beach. All Virginia Woolf's characters might have said the same thing. Not that she seems to regret it. On the contrary . . . , solitude is for her the condition of the richest experience of which the human spirit is capable. (pp. 168-69)

A novel without drama, without moral values, and without character or strong personal emotion—it is a hard thing to write: and it cannot be said that Virginia Woolf is always successful. Sometimes she fails because she goes outside our own self-appointed limitations, because her plot entails her presenting aspects of life which her vision inevitably excludes. . . . [At] times she attempts, unsuccessfully, to draw characters in the objective external convention of the traditional novel. Hugh Whitbread and Sir William Bradshaw [of *Mrs. Dalloway*] are carefully observed portraits; but because their creator does not draw them from the inside they never come to life. They are meticulously dressed dummies, mere conventional types of snobbish worldling and hard, power-loving careerist. Moreover they are drawn in a spirit of moral indignation. This puts them out of focus with the rest of Virginia Woolf's picture. What basis is there for moral indignation in a world not concerned with moral values? (pp. 170-71)

Elsewhere she errs in the other direction. Her picture is so concerned with the inner life as to destroy our sense of the reality of the outer. This surely stops her most ambitious venture, *The Waves*, from making the impression at which it aims. . . . Indeed the balance between the internal world, which is her subject, and the external, to which she must convince us that it is in fact related, is extremely delicate. Only in *To the Lighthouse* does she succeed in preserving it throughout a whole book. Elsewhere, like so many English novelists, Virginia Woolf impresses by the heights to which she rises, rather than by the level of perfection she maintains.

But what heights they are! As might be expected, they are heights of beauty, they reveal her æsthetic sensibility. (p. 171)

But Virginia Woolfs æsthetic response is not confined to the accepted, recognised and official objects of beauty. Not only does she illuminate our appreciation of what we already think beautiful, she opens our eyes to new sources of delight. Far more successfully than any contemporary poet has she disengaged the æsthetic quality in the modern scene. In the first chapter of *Mrs. Dalloway* a summer morning in Bond Street, all buses and policemen and clamouring shoppers, is made to glow with the splendour of a picture by Vermeer. (p. 173)

These pictures are so fully visualised as to seem the work of a painter rather than a writer. A realistic painter too; here we come to the second outstanding quality in her sensibility. . . . [Always] she combines beauty with accuracy, and gets her effect, not by idealising and decorating it, but simply by isolating and indicating those aspects of her subject that appeal to the æsthetic sense. (pp. 173-74)

She is by far the most satisfying of æsthetes. . . . There is nothing languid or academic about her æstheticism. Casual and zestful, it is the expression of an intense vitality, at home in the bustle and clamour of the modern age. . . . As presented by her, the æsthetic life is as vigorous and satisfying as any other kind of life. And for us too, while we are reading her books: as long as their spell is on use we do not bother about the limitations of her vision. Indeed these limitations are seen to be a necessary condition of her success. In order to concentrate our eyes on the æsthetic aspects of experience, she has to exclude its other aspects. And they seem more beautiful for being thus isolated. Her coldness, her detachment from the hot earth, add to her vision a sea-fresh purity, a pearly gleam which set the spirit astir with a sort of delicate exhilaration. . . . How cleansing to be transported, if only for an hour, to a region where it is more important to be clever than to be good, and more important to be beautiful than to be either! (pp. 179-80)

> *David Cecil, "Virginia Woolf," in his* Poets and Story-Tellers: A Book of Critical Essays *(reprinted*
> *by permission of David Higham Associates Limited, as literary agents for David Cecil; in Canada by Constable & Company Ltd), Constable, 1949, pp. 160-80.*

PHILIP RAHV (essay date 1949)

Mrs. Woolf no doubt made a very brave attempt to break through conventional realism and to create new forms for the novel. *Mrs. Dalloway* and *To the Lighthouse* are minor successes and unique in their way, but on the whole she failed. (p. 140)

[At] one time Mrs. Woolf thought of herself as an associate of Joyce, whereas actually there is little kinship between them. Consider to what totally different uses they put such a device as the interior monologue. While in Joyce the interior monologue is a means of bringing us closer to the characters, of telling us *more* about them than we could learn from a purely objective account of their behavior, in Mrs. Woolf it becomes a means of telling us *less* about them, of disengaging their ego from concrete situations in life and converting it into a vehicle of poetic memory. Her tendency is to drain the interior monologue of its modern content and turn it back to the habitual forms of lyrical expression—and reverie. Where Joyce performs a radically new act of aesthetic selection, Mrs. Woolf performs what is in the main an act of exclusion; for she retains no more fictional material than will suffice to identify the scene and its human inhabitants; beyond that all is sensation and impression of a volatile kind. And it is so volatile because only on the surface does it flow from the actual experience of the characters—its real source is the general tradition of English poetry and of the poetic sensibility. However, there is a crucial fault in Mrs. Woolf's grasp even of this tradition, for she comprehends it one sidedly, and perhaps in much too feminine a fashion, not as a complete order but first and foremost as an *order of sentiments*. (pp. 140-41)

> *Philip Rahv, "Sketches in Criticism: Mrs. Woolf and Mrs. Brown," in his* Image and Idea *(copyright 1949 by Philip Rahv; copyright renewed © 1976 by Betty T. Rahv, as widow of the author; reprinted by permission), New Directions, 1949, pp. 139-43.**

A. D. MOODY (essay date 1963)

Certainly [Virginia Woolf's *The Voyage Out*] is not to be dismissed as "the immature first book." It has too much life in its art for that, and too developed a form of life. The writing creates, with natural assurance and ease, an intelligent and amused insight into society and its manners, with all that implies for the direct and precise observation of character, speech and behaviour in social relations; it brings alive too a profoundly searching (though rather u formed) concern for ultimate meanings and values. . . . Nevertheless it has to be said that the novel is essentially immature.

The significant immaturity is manifest in its imperfect form. It is not a coherent and organic whole; indeed it seems scarcely to attempt any unified comprehension of its experience. It is, for the most part, simply a series of satiric observations of "civilised" living; and for the rest it gestures insubstantially towards a rather romantic ideal of passionate personal existence. (p. 11)

There are certain ironies and reserves in the writing which suggest that Virginia Woolf was uneasy about the novel's commitment to its heroine's romantic idealism. She was perhaps unwillingly aware that her death was not so much a price exacted by an adverse fate for nobility of soul, as the inevitable end of romantic dreaming. But for the matured and fully achieved recognition of that one has to wait for the treatment of Rhoda in *The Waves*. Virginia Woolf's development through her early novels up to *The Waves* is, in effect, a progressive and reluctant education of her imagination in the enmity to life of that kind of idealism, and in the necessity for human beings to seek fulfilment in a wholehearted engagement with their actual world, limited and limiting as it is bound to be.

In *Night and Day* . . . Virginia Woolf seems to have set out quite deliberately to prevent the tendency of her idealism to seek romantic and ultimately desperate forms, by committing herself to an attempt to achieve a form for the free and enlightened soul within the conventions and commonplaces of civilised society. (pp. 12-13)

[The novel] has the appearance of being a very Jamesian study, in the issues it raises and in the way it deals with them: so much seems to depend upon the tones and values of social behaviour, and yet the vital concern is always with the qualities of personal life which these manifest. . . . Virginia Woolf's adaptation of a relatively realistic mode manifests, beyond any merely technical concern, an attempt to engage with social conventions and traditions upon their own terms. . . . She is clearly attempting, in the mode of the novel as much as in its action, not to balance the claims of the individual and of society against each other, but instead to establish enlightened personal feeling as the more substantial and profound source of moral valuations. But with the failure of that feeling to grasp and penetrate the life of society, the novel breaks down into a comedy of the manners which are not accepted as morals, and a moral seriousness which, having failed of its object, can find expression only in the baffled rhetoric of aspiration. (pp. 14-15)

The main defects of *The Voyage Out* and *Night and Day* come from a kind of double-vision, an inability to bring into a single focus the ideal sense of the individual life, and the conventional image of itself entertained by the English middle class. The primary distinction of *Jacob's Room*. . . is that here for the first time Virginia Woolf caught both her society and her sense of the soul in a unified vision, and from a point of view and with an emphasis that were fully hers. (p. 15)

Jacob is not a character in the usual sense, of having significance as an individual identity—the sense in which Rachel Vinrace and Katherine Hilbery were characters. Instead the determination which distinguished *Night and Day* from *The Voyage Out*, to seek a form for the soul in the life of its world, is here more fully followed out. Jacob's existence is defined altogether by his participation in the life of his world, by his objective presence there. . . . For in *Jacob's Room* [Virginia Woolf] is concerned for the quality of life not simply of the individual but of a whole culture: the vital concern is to probe beneath the veneer put upon her civilisation by convention, commerce, and *The Times*, and to realise what she can of its inward life. (pp. 16-17)

[*Mrs. Dalloway*] is a direct and very considerable development from *Jacob's Room*. It is a minor and imperfect novel, yet the conception and writing are masterly to a degree which reveals the genius behind the immaturities. (p. 18)

The immediately relevant development upon the preceeding novels is in the perfection of the focus of the vision—the

achievement of a fully resolved and unified insight into the spiritual condition of a society; together with the avoidance of oversimplifying distinctions, as between the individual soul and the outward world, or between the actual and the absolute. . . . In *Mrs. Dalloway* Virginia Woolf meets the facts of "Society" culture quite squarely. Clarissa Dalloway isn't set off against her world; she is realised at its own valuation as one of its fine products; and by that very fact she exposes its bankruptcy the more absolutely. (pp. 18-19)

[*To the Lighthouse*] has been admired, deservedly, as an extremely fine work of art. At the same time it does have considerable limitations; and these make it less fully satisfying than the more mature *The Waves* and *Between the Acts*, though it remains a rare and invaluable achievement.

Its art is so perfectly refined because it has not had to contend very directly with life. The threat offered to the inward vision in the earlier novels, (and later again in *The Years*), by "society" and "civilisation," is here distanced into the comic and the cosmic—Mr Ramsay's rationalism, and the processes of Time and Nature. In these relatively distanced forms the destructive element is felt to stimulate the powers of the spirit, as much as to overcome them. The central characters, Mrs Ramsay and Lily Briscoe, truimph over the chaos of experience; and their triumphs constitute a compellingly positive vision of life and art. But that vision depends upon a relative simplification of the world, and a partial withdrawal from life into art. (p. 29)

It is a distinctive achievement of the novel that it does follow the laws of the mind's own inner processes, and not those of the external world. . . . The life that is dramatised is the life of the mind; and the values by which experience is criticised are those of the mind. All this reflects the main concern of the novel, which is to discover how the world which the mind creates and values may be established in the face of an indifferent and annihilating natural universe. (pp. 30-1)

[At the end], as throughout the novel, there remain both the persistent division between the inner and external realities, and the exaltation of the former over the latter. The conclusion is something less than a resolution in the full sense. It is a relationship established almost entirely from the point of view of the intuitive imagination, and on the terms most to its advantage. It is symptomatic that the longer first and final parts of the novel are given over to the workings of that imagination, and that the chaotic energies of the natural world are abstracted and isolated in the brief middle section. Whatever reality is not subjected to the mind's processes is not allowed it due weight and effect. In consequence, with all its excellence as a work of art, the novel is rather limited to the sphere of art. (p. 42)

The attempt stops short of a final resolution of this divided and limiting view of life. But it is a considerable advance beyond the near absolute division obtaining in the earlier novels; and a step towards the more engaged and mature achievements of *The Waves* and *Between the Acts*. (p. 43)

In *To the Lighthouse*, having recognised that in human life there is no ultimate stability or permanence, [Virginia Woolf] had shifted her attention from life to art and stressed such stability and permanence as art could offer. But this obviously was too partial to be fully satisfying. The full implications had still to be faced of the fact that it is not in art that we live, but in the flux of Nature; not in the security of the lighthouse but in the uncontrollable waves.

The basic difference between *To the Lighthouse* and *The Waves* . . . is that the latter is an attempt to comprehend human life in more ultimate terms—in the context of a universe which, against the human values of permanence and order, appears to oppose a relative, shifting, multivalent process. With this, and even more valuably, there is for the first time in Virginia Woolf's work an adequately convincing sense of the energies which constitute life beneath the mind's abstraction of it into "society" or "art" or "the soul"; a response to it in its wholeness and fullness, which shows up the attitudes and visions of all the previous novels as partial and relatively superficial. (p. 46)

[The] convention established [at the beginning of *The Waves*] and followed throughout the novel, whereby the characters are presented in quite sharply divided dramatic monologues, is a dramatisation of their relationship: it insists upon the relative isolation of the individual persons within the group, bringing up at once the reality of their separate identities and the shadowiness of the whole they potentially form. (pp. 51-2)

Virginia Woolf asked herself: "Who thinks it? And am I outside the thinker?" . . . The solution arrived at in the novel may be described as a form of relativistic objectivity. On the one hand the author appears not to enter into the work at all, but to be merely a recording intelligence, observing the six characters with complete impartiality. The characters seem to exist objectively, in complete detachment from the author. Yet at the same time there is that uniformity of style which insists that the novel is the action of a single comprehensive mind; and obviously the characters exist only as this mind selects and arranges the materials of which they are composed. There is after all, then, a single controlling viewpoint, which is in effect the author's own. However, the authority of this viewpoint is deliberately qualified by its being subordinated to the "objective existence" of the characters. While it remains the offered viewpoint through which the novel must be read, it doesn't claim omniscience, nor does it appear to pass judgment. (p. 52)

[The] novel traces the lives and relationships of the six characters, through their development from schooldays to the verge of old age and death. In broad outline, their lives individually and collectively assume the form of waves, at first gathering force and shape, rising to a crest, then breaking and dissolving finally in a thin spread of foam. This too is the form of the novel itself. As a statement about the shape of human existence this form is exact but obvious, undeniably true yet not in itself very interesting. What is interesting is human behaviour within this form; and what interests above all is the attempt to achieve a truly human form of life, within and in spite of this immitigable life and death cycle of the physical order. That is where the controlling interest of *The Waves* is to be found. (p. 53)

While we are made aware of the larger life which flows through [the characters] we do not *see* it in them, so that our actual perception of the world we experience is not altered, or not profoundly and fully altered. . . . Virginia Woolf's writing in *The Waves* makes one look at the world with enlarged interest and expectation, with a quickened consciousness of what it might offer and what might be made of it; and while this is a fine and valuable achievement it is a lesser one. (p. 67)

Beside the greatest novels—*Middlemarch, Anna Karenina,* considerable passages of Lawrence—it is seen to be in a

minor mode. That is to say that while its vision of life is profound and mature, and an invaluable achievement of the human mind, its power to enforce its vision within the imagination of its readers is relatively limited. (p. 68)

[*The Years*] is perhaps the least inspired or inspiriting of Virginia Woolf's novels. (p. 71)

The novel is divided into two parts. . . . First there is a panoramic view of what happens to the individual in this society; then there is an attempt to break through the social surface and to probe the resources of the individual personality in depth. But the two parts are very unequal in achievement and value. It is the first which makes the novel clearly unsatisfactory; the second is not altogether unworthy of the mature Virginia Woolf.

Throughout the first part of the novel the view of life is predominantly bleached and negative. (pp. 71-2)

[The] unmistakably serious and significant intention is not adequately realised. Where one looks for a solidly achieved social critique—George Eliot comes to mind—one finds a deeply felt and intensely perceptive indictment of an historical social order, based, quite incongruously, upon fragmentary and trivial details, upon a disablingly undeveloped awareness of social realities. Moreover, not only the weight but the internal coherence and force of the whole first part suffers from the pervasive slightness. (p. 73)

The significance and the value of the achievement of "Present Day" [the second part of *The Years*] can be defined most directly in terms of the caricature which is its main resource. . . . The caricature is the means by which the deadening social experience is controlled and brought into a manageable perspective. (pp. 79-80)

The caricature is the vital, the most creative function of this novel. It is in fact the strength exactly corresponding to the weakness observed in the first part. There, where the novel was attempting to deal directly with the realities of social experience, one had evidence only of the intractability of the experience, which is to say, evidence only of the mind's inability to comprehend it. In the second part the mind reasserts itself in its own terms and disengages itself, through its power of caricature, from the experience which only crushes it. The caricature is essentially an assertion of the mind's supremacy in its own sphere, of its power to image and judge external reality according to its own life and values. In this aspect the novel represents a prolonged contention against the oppressive social realities, on behalf of the freedom and rights of the individual spirit. (p. 80)

[In] relation to Virginia Woolf's development as a novelist [*The Years*] had probably a considerable therapeutic value, in the sense that by confronting and shaping towards caricature this body of her experience which was otherwise intractable, her imagination achieved a kind of release from it. Whether such terms are appropriate or not, it seems likely that if she had not laboured at this "failure," *Between the Acts* would not have been the extraordinarily fine and mature achievement that it is. (p. 81)

[*Between the Acts*] is at least among her best three novels, along with *To the Lighthouse* and *The Waves*; and it is more mature than either of those. Certainly *To the Lighthouse* is the more highly wrought work of art: but when it is put beside *The Waves* and *Between the Acts*, the refinement of the art seems not to effect a more valuable grasp on experience, but rather to compensate for an ultimate unwillingness to accept the human condition. . . . In *The Waves* Virginia Woolf had rejected the comforts of art's illusion, through Bernard and in the placing of Rhoda, and, accepting that the human condition is immitigably one of flux and process, had sought out and affirmed such positive powers as men have to control and construct their lives within nature. *Between the Acts* takes up the same concerns and significantly develops them.

For one thing it incorporates the historical dimension which in *The Waves* was barely noticed; so that instead of merely affirming the continuity of human life, it essays a critical scrutiny of the meaning and value of history for the present. Secondly, the function of the artistic imagination which was overstressed in *To the Lighthouse,* and deliberately played down in *The Waves*, is here established in a more justly balanced relationship with life. The artist, in this case Miss Latrobe, is not set like Lily Briscoe to cultivate an aesthetic sphere, outside and rather in opposition to the process and actuality of life. . . . Her pageant is strikingly not a perfected work of art, and the novel itself hardly strives for aesthetic perection as such. This lack of aesthetic finish, which is a response to the texture of life as it is actually known and experienced, marks an immensely difficult and valuable achievement. It represents Virginia Woolf's acceptance of life such as it is in a degree exceeding that of *The Waves,* which though it affirmed such an acceptance remained very self-consciously involved in its art. In *Between the Acts* she went her furthest towards that ultimate subordination of the interests of art to the interests of life which constitutes the maturity of the imagination. (pp. 84-5)

There is no reason to suppose that Virginia Woolf felt *Between the Acts* to be a conclusion to her work as a novelist. Yet without being unduly portentous one can see it as a fitting close, and a genuine completion of the tasks she had set her imagination from the start. For, whether deliberately or organically, it does achieve a resolution of the main difficulties and problems her experience had confronted her with through all her novels. Here at last, by resisting the simplicities of idealism with a mode of flexible and engaged irony, she had comprehended the relations of the soul and its society, of the artist and life itself, of civilisation and its natural universe. It was surely in quest of a conclusion of this sort that Rachel Vinrace had voyaged out to "the heart of darkness." The recurrence of that phrase from her first novel upon the last page of *Between the Acts* is a reminder of the deeper, subterranean connexions which run back through all the novels; and the difference in context marks how far Virginia Woolf's imagination had matured in the twenty-five years which separate them. (pp. 96-7)

> *A. D. Moody, in his* Virginia Woolf *(copyright © 1963 A. D. Moody; reprinted by permission of the author), Oliver and Boyd, 1963, 119 p.*

MITCHELL A. LEASKA (essay date 1970)

To the Lighthouse, generally considered [Virginia Woolf's] finest novel, bears eloquent testimony to her mastery of a complex and disciplined form. In it she was able to present, within severely circumscribed limits of time, a wide range and multiplicity of experience by subtle and constant movements in and out of the minds of her various *personae.* With lucidity and sureness, she selected out of the flux and chaos of appearances certain thoughts, feelings, and impressions

and arranged them in that skillful juxtaposition and sequence not only to produce a beautifully textured and formally composed whole, but also to render the fabric of experience which conformed to her own singular and sensitive vision. (p. 62)

Mrs Woolf was concerned with exploring the quality and complexity of human relationships; and to translate her explorations to the novel form, she had to abandon that series of dramatic events by which the conventional novel arrested and sustained interest and in its place to create moments of human consciousness. She had further to juxtapose those moments in such a way so as to effect a sequence, the arrangement of which would enlarge and enrich the moments already traversed as well as those to be encountered—in brief, to create an order in which the multiple contents of consciousness would, at any particular moment, illuminate the past and anticipate the future. Thus it was not for her to 'describe *what* we have all seen so that it becomes a sequence', but rather more to describe *how* her people have experienced what they have seen and *how* all of these experiences stand in relation to one another and to some central principle. It is out of this concern that she achieved a unity of design that crowns her triumph in *To the Lighthouse.* (pp. 63-4)

Mrs Woolf did not confine herself to *a* single point of view: she used many to fashion her novel; and the problem of studying these points of view is compounded, moreover, by the fact that the characters, through whose minds the material is being filtered, are not established for us at the beginning of the book; they are given to us piecemeal, elusively; so that even at the end, though we see them in their entirety, we do not necessarily see them conclusively. The fact is that, more often than not, when we have finished one of her novels, although our imaginative sympathy has been aroused and enlarged, our knowledge of the character remains incomplete; he remains the sum of our impressions, a fluid personality.

The method, then, of creating these fictional people is, in a sense, additive: our own impression grows as the character's reflections and impressions—as well as those he elicits from others—grow. Thus our understanding too, in a sense, is additive: it is a continual synthesis of accumulated impressions. . . . Mrs Woolf *creates* a point of view; she does not 'select' one. And we, as readers, are invited to recreate, through the process of reflexive reading, a portrait of the character in much the same creative manner. (pp. 64-5)

With great economy, Mrs Woolf [gives] us in less than three pages a small but vivid picture of Mrs Ramsay's relationship to her son and to her husband as well as a dab or two of the colours contained on her emotional palette; and a little further we are given some idea of her generosity for the Lighthouse keeper, her sympathy for his isolation, and, in general, her desire to comfort those less fortunate creatures needing her bounty. (pp. 65-6)

[We] are easily persuaded over to Mrs Ramsay's side because she represents the maternity, the sympathy, and the charity that we place high in our scale of values. And we tend to feel averse to Mr Ramsay (and to Tansley) for having contridicted and upset the person who has engaged our sympathy. (p. 66)

But Mrs Ramsay, for all her catalytic function in bringing people together, is herself an extremely isolated person. She is unable to share her deepest feelings with anyone, unable to open herself spontaneously to express freely her anger or her hurt or her love. Unlike her husband, she must conceal her moods. Her relationship to Mr Ramsay is, in fact, a fairly accurate index of the aloofness and estrangement which lurk at the very core of her 'wedge of darkness.' (p. 71)

Our first introduction to Mr Ramsay is not a sympathetic one. His relentlessness in the matter of the trip to the Lighthouse, indeed, strikes a negative chord. His intellectualism is harsh and uncompromising; his logic will not be tampered with; his opinions will not be questioned. (p. 77)

[For] all his harshness and severity, his seeming disregard for people, his outward sterility, we know that in his own company he is ruthlessly honest with himself; that his grandiose fantasies are compensatory measures to ward off the onslaught of feelings of inadequacy he experiences; further, that the sympathy and assurance he craves are, for him, urgent and human needs—the very needs which the others find degrading. (p. 78)

In the course of the novel Mr Ramsay repeatedly owns up to most of his many shortcomings; and in his sincerest reflections, we find little of the self-depreciation that permeates his wife's musing. Here rather we have self-evaluation, for good or ill, that is forthright without self-pity, at times, almost boyish in its naïveté. Despite the charges constantly brought against him for his sympathy-mongering, we might begin, legitimately to suspect that much of it is the result of Mrs Ramsay's distance, her solitude—that estrangement which inevitably exacts from him, too, the price of being alone. He knows that she will not permit him entry into her world; he knows as well that she can not share his. Their walk through the garden . . . supports eloquently the testament of her, and consequently his, enforced isolation. But even under these circumstances, he is not only acquiescent, but loyal and even grateful. . . . If we divest Mr Ramsay of all the judgements crowded on his image by the other *personae* and attend only to those reflections and impressions which originate in him, we find a very different image emerging. His intellectual life may seem austere, uncompromising, rigourously dedicated to fact; but as a husband and father, he is indeed not only more devoted than his wife to those who make up his world, but also more honest than she in his dealings with them. As egotistical or tryannical or cruel or barren as the others may choose to see him, his effectiveness as a man becomes apparent when he acknowledges James' steering. He has only to say two words: 'Well done!' to transform his sons' world, to establish finally the union between father and son. And with all this we might ponder the validity of his being the 'arid scimitar'; we might even begin to question the reliability of those *personae* who throughout the novel heap negative judgments on the man. The problem of deducing James Ramsay offers no special difficulty since emotionally he remains fairly constant throughout. (pp. 79-80)

If we consider James in terms of his possessiveness for his mother, his rivalry and jealousy for his father, his insatiable need for paternal recognition, his sense of impotence and rage, and the pervasive anxiety which conditions his introspection, we might easily attach to him a Freudian label and summarily dismiss him as a victim modelled after that prototype of antiquity. But to do so, to resort to that kind of verbal shorthand, would be to ignore the richness and sensitivity to detail with which he was created. (p. 82)

Lily Briscoe is of central importance in unifying the work. Hers is the principal consciousness through which Mrs Ramsay is kept vivid before the reader in the final movement of the novel. As deputy for the artist and as chief sentient centre, she is the reader's most reliable source of information and his most effective emotional and intellectual guide. More than any of the other *personae,* she expresses her ambivalence towards certain of the people, her inadequacy as human being and as artist, her sense of the strange admixture of emotional and intellectual and moral elements which undergirds human behaviour. (pp. 89-90)

One of the most significant aspects of Lily Briscoe's highly sophisticated sensibility, and one of ther most sharply individualizing traits, is her ability to translate her own experience of human relations into subtle and profound insights. She is aware of the depth and diversity of impulses which govern human behaviour, impulses which cast human activity in endless enigmatic shadows, so that the sensitive observer wonders 'how many shapes a person might wear'. . . . She is sensible to the imperfect vision one has of another; of the futility of attempting to know or to understand what goes on in another's 'wedge-shaped core of darkness'; of the inadequacy and obliquity of human relations. (p. 92)

Significantly the Ramsay's landing at the Lighthouse signifies that sudden order in life that Lily seeks to express in art. Thus it is only when James has united with his father—their communication realized and their harmony established—that Lily sees finally and vividly, in the pattern of relationship on her canvas, the fleeting harmony that constitutes her vision. And indeed it is a vision which 'must be perpetually remade', just as human relations must be kept in a constant state of repair. (p. 93)

That in this novel Mrs Woolf utilizes and modulates nine principal angles of perspective should indicate how intricate the balance must be to keep the experiential life suspended until the design is complete. The two most crucial aspects of the method are recording the *impressions of the moment* and simultaneously rendering the subjective impressions of the manifold consciousnesses—to show their relationships—so that the whole constellation of emotional and mental processes which make up human experience is revealed to the reader.

Because human experience is conceived as an indefinable, continous and fluid thing, it is important to remember that the impressions do not progress in a logical sequence; rather, they are ordered according to the emotional force of one experiencing consciousness in relation to another. The meaning of life, which Lily Briscoe wants to know, therefore, is not tendered in some 'great revelation'; its meaning comes in 'little daily miracles, illuminations, matches struck unexpectedly in the dark.' Consequently, the reader, always subject to each of the mind's vagaries, begins to see these 'illuminations' as dominant beats in the rhythm of each individual's experience. And from this rhythmic configuration of selected moments, emerges the *shape* within which the *persona* comes to terms with the concrete world and, in dealing with it, comes to know the *quality* of his experience. (p. 106)

[Virginia Woolf's] profound awareness of the nature of consciousness provided her with a feeling for the *moment*—that unique stretch of time when the past filters in and saturates the present; when the inner world is projected on and colours the outer . . . , when all emotion and sense and past and present and order and disorder and love and hate and joy and sorrow mingle together and give shape to that ineffable experience we call 'living'; and this experience is revealed primarily in Mrs Woolf's arrangement of the minds she chose to mirror their images, ideas, and feelings. (p. 107)

Critics generally agree that on the prose plane the novel deals with female intuition and male intellection; permanence and change; order and chaos; the art of living and the life of art. But critical consensus vanishes immediately an attempt is made to follow through these themes. . . .

To see the disparate, the contradictory elements, and to be unaware of their reconcilability is to miss the interpretive framework which, in fact, embraces these pervasive opposites. *That Virginia Woolf should have chosen to use multiple perspectives is indication enough that no interpretation can be arrived at which settles on one aspect at the expense of the other.* (p. 112)

Part I, made up of seventeen angles of perspective, amply demonstrates the complexity of the relationship betwen one individual and another, with no single character emerging as a set personality. . . . It becomes clear, as the section progresses, that each narrator is made up of numerous contradictory ingredients. Mrs Ramsay, for instance, maternal, generous, and loving as she is, is also a meddling, self-seeking, possessive affection-monger. (p. 113)

Part II, given primarily through the Omniscient Narrator, is a short poetic interlude dealing metaphysically with man's relation to nature. . . . The destructive forces of the natural world are dramatized; but equally dramatic is the human capacity to check and finally to defeat those chaotic energies through a stronger force—the will to endure. (p. 114)

Part III centres on the relationship of art to life, and Lily Briscoe is its governing consciousness. In the boat Mr Ramsay, James, and Cam are struggling with the problem of human relations, while on shore Lily is struggling with the problem of the formal relations in her picture. . . . She begins to fathom the Ramsay's relationship as husband and wife, an understanding which bears with it a clearer grasp of the art of human relations—something she had not understood before.

While these moments of illumination are occurring on shore, long since disturbed relations are being resolved on the trip to the Lighthouse: Cam's antagonism for her father vanishes; James' hatred disappears with his father's words of praise. Mr Ramsay's anxieties are being resolved. Integrity in the family is finally being realized. And runnning parallel with it is Lily's final apprehension that in harmonious human relations there is a deep involvement in life; she realizes that for the artist such involvement is necessary before he can become objectively detached from it to seize its harmony and translate it into the aesthetic relations of art. Only when she grasps these strange entanglements of human intercourse can she complete herself as a human being and fulfil herself as an artist. (pp. 114-15)

The novel, however, also operates on the plane of poetry. On that plane, language, heightened by various poetic devices, is the basic instrument informing the work's intensity and integrity and authority. The novel does not progress on the 'what-happens-next' basis. Rather it moves forward on

the arrangement of scenes, on the sequence of selected moments of consciousness.

By moving into the province of poetry, Virginia Woolf was able to overcome many of the difficulties indigenous to prose expression. (p. 116)

[On] both the literal and symbolic levels—the prose and poetic planes—the novel, in its most general meaning, organizes around the need for both human involvement and artistic detachment in life, which is the very centre of art. Only then does that mysterious principle effect the proper relationships which reveal the complex nature of reality and at the same time realize, aesthetically, the chaotic reality of nature. (p. 123)

> Mitchell A. Leaska, "The Rhetoric of 'To the Lighthouse'," in his Virginia Woolf's Lighthouse: A Study in Critical Method (copyright © Mitchell A. Leaska 1970; reprinted by permission of the publisher), Columbia University Press, 1970, pp. 61-123.

JAMES NAREMORE   (essay date 1973)

The difference between the "surface" and the "depths" of life in [Virginia Woolf's] *The Voyage Out* is much the same as the difference between England and the South American country Rachel voyages to. (p. 30)

The Latin American landscape is set off against the English landscape through a series of basic contrasts—night and day, for example, or water and land. By means of these contrasts, Virginia Woolf develops a kind of metaphor for her view of experience. . . . [The] human personality is divided, having both a civilized exterior of manners and routine, of tea cakes and prime ministers, and a profound, obscured inner life of passion and feeling. So in the novel there is a light half of the world and a dark half—on the one hand a world of manners, politics, and reason, where the masculine will dominates and where a few individuals like the Tory politician Richard Dalloway wield power; and on the other hand a world of primitive feeling, where the more feminine impulse toward being is strongest and where individuals, usually isolated, desire to be united and subordinated under a natural law. In departing from the brightly-lit, busy streets of London and voyaging to a village with the exotic, watery name of Santa Marina, the characters of the novel enter a strange, passionate, half-obscured world which is analogous to the private self. Thus the literal voyage out represents a psychological or spiritual voyage inward.

Significantly, the South American landscape is depicted as both frightening and beautiful. . . . In this nether-world we are closer in spirit to what Virginia Woolf saw as an intense and true form of experience, an ultimate reality. But at the same time we are very close to extinction as individuals: there is a frightening and destructive quality in all this beauty, which is not very far from death itself. (pp. 31-2)

[Even] the prose style of the novel ranges back and forth as the writer attempts to capture two views of experience. On the one hand is a personable narrator with an elegant, somewhat ironic style and a more or less detached view of life (visible in the opening paragraphs of the novel), and on the other is a dreamy, poetic voice which expresses a muted awe toward nature and a desire to be united with it. (p. 32)

A great deal of *The Voyage Out* is made up of the internal, purely subjective experience of the characters, especially the experience of Rachel. . . . Early in the book, Rachel is seen drifting toward sleep in a state of "dreamy confusion.". . . In this case, as in many scenes where Mrs. Woolf presents an inner view of her characters . . . , we are caught on a borderline between sleeping and waking. (p. 33)

Something in this sort of moment seems to have exerted a powerful hold over [Mrs. Woolf's] imagination. Such occasions, when the vestiges of individuality begin to fall away and the character is pulled toward a somewhat erotic communion with the world itself, can be found everywhere in her fiction. (p. 34)

[In depicting Rachel's thoughts as she falls asleep] Virginia Woolf begins with the Proustian moment only to take it a step further, to report a state of almost pure feeling, something beneath words and ideation. Indeed, the mature stages of her career are marked by an increasing tendency to render purely emotional states, where she is less interested in what her characters think than in how they feel. The Proustian novel shows the personality being liberated from time and space, but Mrs. Woolf goes even further until the personality itself becomes dissolved in total communion with what is "out there." Ultimately, the sense of being in contact with "reality" is replaced by a vast and peaceful darkness. (p. 36)

[The settings of the novel] are always used in a symbolic fashion. This is not to deny that they have some realistic qualities, but only to insist that details like the crowded London streets, the wide sea, the boxlike rooms of the hotel at Santa Marina, and the winding river that carries the party of Europeans into a tropical forest are meant to objectify a kind of internal landscape. Terence and Rachel's love scene, for example, is set in a richly sensual bower. . . . [The] sexual passion of the two young people has been transferred to the landscape; there is no doubt of the sexuality in the surroundings, but the characters' behavior has been etherealized. (pp. 46-7)

Here, as in every other comparable passage in Virginia Woolf, there is a hypersensitivity to rhythm, prose verging upon poetry, and in this case the rhythms and indeed the whole pacing of the scene are designed to roughly approximate the curve of passion in sexual intercourse. (p. 48)

In Virginia Woolf's fiction the more intense and meaningful states of feeling are always associated with dimness and depth, with some sort of drowsiness or hypnotic effect, with a blurring or effacing of the ordinary visible world, and with something very near to a death of the self. In their first euphoric recognition that they are in love, Rachel and Hewet are said to feel that they have "dropped to the bottom of the world together.". . . [They] are described almost as if they were stirring in the peace of the womb, only dimly aware of the world outside. (pp. 49-50)

Death, like sleep and intense union in love, has the attraction of the return to the womb. And ultimately, death has the power to bring about an intense communion; at the moment when Rachel dies, Terence feels that "their complete union and happiness filled the room with rings eddying more and more widely.". . . (p. 53)

The sleepy, hypnotic moods that [Virginia Woolf] renders so lovingly in all of her writings exerted a powerful hold on her imagination; so much so that often her novels can be understood in terms of the uneasy compromises the characters make between the will to live in the world and the temptation to dissolve all individuality and sink into a death-like trance. Her first novel seems an unconscious reflection of these compromises, wavering between two kinds of experience: the rational, orderly, mannered world of regular proportions and social relationships, and the deeper world of intense feeling where individuals lose their sense of separateness and blend with nature. Very clearly, however, it is the latter emotional, feminine world that attracts Virginia Woolf most powerfully. She finds that this world represents something more real and intense than ordinary life can afford; or, to put it another way, it represents what ordinary life is all about. Her novel is not, therefore, simply about Rachel Vinrace. It concerns the elemental forces of sexuality, of life and death, that stir far down beneath the civilized and orderly exterior of British life. Rachel is a personification of that theme—a young virgin who journeys out to meet a bridegroom who is death. And Rachel's experience is seen ultimately in relation to the community at large, so that through her death that community, including its most rational member, Hurst, is able to sense the elemental affinities which are the pattern and meaning of life. (p. 55)

[It] is characteristic of Virginia Woolf to interpret the mental life of a character rather than transcribe it. Hence in the first pages of *Mrs. Dalloway* the technique is fairly realistic, but while the author refrains from analysis of the action, there is nevertheless a feeling that all the materials have been given form by a controlling authorial personality that is sometimes self-consciously artistic. It is true that a sense of random thought pervades the opening pages of the book, but this quality is barely suggested. . . . Even when Clarissa Dalloway is busy and relatively gay, as in these opening pages, the style has a high degree of order. It is a polished, elegant, rhythmic prose; not even the literary, Hamletesque young Dedalus in *Ulysses* thinks in such beautifully modulated periodic sentences. The reason for this quality in the style is obvious enough from the brief authorial asides: Mrs. Dalloway and the other characters are seen as third persons, and all the thoughts are rendered by an ever-present narrator, who endows the novel with its poetic rhythms and unity of style. (pp. 78-9)

Because so much of the novel is given over to the relatively uninterrupted flow of daydreams and meditations controlled by an authorial voice, the book has an almost seamless quality. (p. 82)

[The steady, almost uninterrupted flow] obviously depends upon the author's ability to make orderly transitions. One thinks immediately of the motorcar travelling down Piccadilly, carrying the thoughts of the crowd with it; also of the skywriting airplane which, like the car, "grazed something very profound" in the emotions of the crowd. For a moment everyone is united by an elemental emotion of wonder and curiosity, and we move easily from Clarissa to Sara Bletchely to Mrs. Coates to Mr. Bowley to Rezia and finally to Septimus Smith again. (pp. 82-3)

The whole conception of the skywriting scene is perhaps a bit arty. Nevertheless it is in some ways a very typical moment in Mrs. Woolf's fiction, an important manifestation of the emotional undercurrent that seems to dissolve the boundaries between people. Most of the transitions in the novel contribute to just such an effect. Not all are so spectacular, but nearly every one of them enables the author to move discreetly from one character to another, to shift our viewpoint from one scene to another. (p. 85)

These transitions entail no major change in prose style between the meditations of one character and those of another, and the characters sometimes seem to feel the same rhythmic pulse; but this does not mean that the prose has a monotonous regularity or that the rhythms remain the same. . . .

Significant changes of style emerge, however, when there is an important change in the emotional lives of the characters; as on the first page, where the brisk, short sentences that accompany Mrs. Dalloway's departure from her house give way to the long and complex section that describes her memory of Bruton. (p. 88)

Mrs. Woolf recorded in her *Diary* a desire to make *Mrs. Dalloway* a finished work of art which yet retained the quality of a sketch. In scenes of potentially dramatic interplay between characters her intent is especially clear; but her reports of consciousness are also somewhat generalized, refined, indirect.

And the authorial voice, which often supplies what might be called indirect interior monologues, is not by any means an impersonal voice. . . .

[Only] in *The Waves* is she totally noncommittal. In her other works, Virginia Woolf and the reader are always face to face, and while usually far from assertive, she sometimes engages in traditional analysis or makes lofty ironic judgments about her characters. . . . Sometimes, when an objective outlook is required or an ironic point needs to be made, the novelist simply shifts the viewpoint. (pp. 91-2)

[In] spite of the indirection, the sketchy details, and the occasional open declarations of an authorial personality, *Mrs. Dalloway* fits Robert Humphrey's definition of stream-of-consciousness writing. Clearly the book is designed to present the flux of several character's thoughts; but, granted that the conventional terminology may be applied here, it may also tend to obscure or oversimplify Virginia Woolf's technique. True, she tries to approximate the aimless pattern of consciousness, but her voice is often so far removed from the actual contents of a mind that it verges on a traditional omniscience. The result is an unusually flexible method, well-suited to the novelist's special purposes. (p. 95)

[Often] Mrs. Woolf employs the same method to present her character's thoughts as in *The Voyage Out,* using image, metaphor, and rhythm to evoke a special emotional state resembling hypnosis or sleep. Mrs. Dalloway working at her knitting is an example of this method, as is the description of Lady Bruton's mind after lunch. . . . [The] minds of the characters can be shown to have a unity not only through subtle transitions and a consistent prose style, but also by means of the very images which are used to evoke their states of mind. (p. 98)

The primary motive behind *Mrs. Dalloway* . . . is the same one already detected in *The Voyage Out.* Clarissa Dalloway, like so many of Virginia Woolf's characters, is beset by the problem of aloneness and separateness in life. . . . This, in fact, is the central problem that Mrs. Woolf tries to deal with in all her fiction. It is intimately related, of course, to the problem of death, the ultimate separation and from one point of view the ultimate confirmation of the separateness of things. (p. 102)

Mrs. Dalloway, disturbed by her inability to really "know" people, troubled by the transitoriness of love, and haunted by a fear of death, feels somehow that there remains a vague transcendental unity. One consolation for her is that she feels she can live on through others, that life is a shared web of experience. (p. 103)

Septimus Smith is, of course, a concrete demonstration that Mrs. Dalloway is a part of "people she had never met." (p. 106)

[Smith,] like Rachel Vinrace and Mrs. Ramsay, has a partially redemptive death, in that he gives to Mrs. Dalloway, quite unawares, an acute sense of her unity with life. He is also in a way the "scapegoat" he considers himself, since Mrs. Dalloway experiences his death vicariously and gains a consolation from it. (pp. 106-07)

[She] seems to absorb Septimus' experience, and as a result she comes to terms with death. The novel, like so much of Virginia Woolf's fiction, is elegiac. Mrs. Dalloway, aging and in poor health, no longer fears death but embraces it. Indeed nearly all of Virginia Woolf's characters seem to be drawn toward a kind of death. (p. 110)

> *James Naremore, in his* The World without a Self: Virginia Woolf and the Novel *(copyright © 1973 by Yale University), Yale University Press, 1973, 259 p.*

CLIFTON SNIDER   (essay date 1979)

[Apart from Bernard in *The Waves*], the character in the fiction of Virginia Woolf who probably best exemplifies her idea of the androgynous—and, therefore, whole—personality is Orlando. (p. 263)

To the extent that *Orlando* draws on what [Carl] Jung terms the collective unconscious, in its use of archetypal patterns and symbols, *Orlando* is a myth for the twentieth century. So far as we know, Virginia Woolf never read Jung or Freud and was aware of their ideas only from what she heard in conversation, but if this is the case, it makes a book such as *Orlando* all the more extraordinary. It is her most light-hearted book, and it indicates that, as an artist, Woolf has learned, so to speak, to laugh. . . . (p. 265)

In order for a writer to be balanced, he or she should have both humor and seriousness. Psychic balance is the great aim of Jungian analytical psychology, and that is why Orlando, apart from Bernard, seems the most psychically whole of the characters of Virginia Woolf. At times, Orlando can be the most extreme kind of introvert. . . . At other times Orlando manages to behave as an extrovert, as when he is the Ambassador to Constantinople. On the whole, however, he/she is at heart an introvert who treasures his/her solitude.

In his psychology of the conscious mind, Jung calls introversion and extraversion psychological types. In addition to these are the four functions of consciousness: sensation, thinking, feeling, and intuition. Most people are able to develop one or two of these functions to a high degree, but Orlando, by the end of her "biography," has been able to develop all four functions of consciousness.

The sensation type of individual perceives the world through his conscious senses. Early in the novel, as a boy of sixteen, Orlando has already developed this function: "He loved . . . to feel the earth's spine beneath him. . . ." [Immersed] in nature, he feels "as if all the fertility and amorous activity of a summer's evening were woven web-like about his body." . . . The "earth's spine" is "the hard root of the oak tree." "The Oak Tree" is the title of the poem Orlando works on for some three hundred years, and, as we shall see, it is symbolic of Orlando's psyche. As it grows, so does Orlando.

Orlando, as a poet and man—and later woman—of letters, must be able to think. . . . And think Orlando most assuredly does, for "months and years of his life" he ponders such questions as "What is love? What friendship? What truth?". . .

Traditionally, the thinking and sensation functions have been placed in the sphere of "masculine" activities, and it is no accident, I think, that it is as a male that Orlando develops these functions. When he becomes a woman, at the age of thirty, he develops the more traditionally "feminine" functions: feeling and intuition. (pp. 265-66)

The intuition function is perhaps the hardest to understand or to develop. Orlando is, nevertheless, able near the end of the novel to perceive the world intuitively, that is, through the unconscious. (p. 266)

[Orlando] has experienced the contrasexual, male and female, in her own body and psyche, and, therefore, at the end of the novel she is "a single self, a real self," . . . and she is "one and entire." . . . No one is ever fully individuated in life, but Orlando reaches Selfhood for the first time in her life and stands with Bernard as Woolf's most androgynous character.

That this is so is reinforced by the two symbols that unite the novel: the house and the oak tree. . . . Woolf clearly intends that [The house, Knole] should stand for the history of the Sackvilles and of England and its literature. Unconsciously, however, she has created a symbol that stands for the psyche of her heroine. The roots of the psyche reach into the unknown, into the collective unconscious. The branches are in the open air of the known, the conscious. And as Knole grows, as Orlando furnishes it, so grows the psyche of Orlando.

"The Oak Tree," the poem and the actual tree itself, is perhaps the most important symbol, apart from Orlando herself, in the novel. Based on Vita Sackville-West's prize-winning poem, "The Land," it is the only piece of her writing Orlando preserves throughout the centuries. As a work of art, it is a product of the unconscious shaped by the conscious mind. As a tree, it stands for the *coniunctio,* the joining of opposites. Like the house itself, its roots go down to the collective unconscious, and its branches breathe the air of consciousness. . . . The successful completion of the poem symbolizes that Orlando has, for the time being, reached that union of opposites, of anima/animus, of the Self. Because of this fusion of the contrasexual she has become androgynous, her mind and her psyche, to use Woolf's own words, "fully fertilised," able to use "all its faculties." (pp. 267-68)

> Clifton Snider, "'A Single Self': A Jungian Interpretation of Virginia Woolf's 'Orlando'," in Modern Fiction Studies (© copyright 1979 by Purdue Research Foundation, West Lafayette, Indiana), Vol. 25, No. 2, Summer, 1979, pp. 263-68.

EDWIN J. KENNEDY, JR. (essay date 1981)

Over the years of publication of the individual volumes of *The Letters of Virginia Woolf,* many reviewers have praised

them as "vibrant," "brilliant," "enchanting," and "wicked." But the most pervasive characteristic of the collected *Letters* is their ordinariness. Woolf's is not a literary correspondence, for she does not openly discuss her fiction; it is not philosophical, and it certainly does not demonstrate any historical or political comprehension of world events. However, this ordinariness is so powerful that it must be understood not as a lapse, which a few critics have charged, but as an achievement, an act of will.

In *Moments of Being* Woolf reveals that she always felt life on two distinct levels, which she called "being" and "non-being." She defined non-being as the "nondescript cotton wool" of daily life. She considered the painful "sledge-hammer" blows of fate as "being," not only because they were intense, but also because she believed that such blows were "tokens of some real thing behind appearances." Virginia was ambivalent about both non-being and being. Non-being might be nondescript appearance, but it was safe and reassuring; being might be the "revelation of some order," but the revelation was threatening and the order was uncertain. In non-being the self was the author of the action. In being the self was only an actor, only a part of a work of art, whose creator and whose end were unknown, for "certainly there is no God."

In her letters more than in any of her other writing, Virginia Woolf confined herself to the cotton wool of daily life, without discussing her "mountain summit moments" of revelation. . . . This deliberate limitation of scope is especially apparent in the last volume of letters [*The Letters of Virginia Woolf, Vol. VI: 1936-1941*], written during the time of Virginia's mourning the deaths of her friend Roger Fry and her nephew Julian Bell, her anxieties at the destruction of Britain during the war, and her growing fears of insanity. In her letters Woolf characteristically and obsessively focuses on the minor irritations of daily domestic life. . . . Woolf is crotchety and often funny about these matters, but the overwhelming impression is that she is willfully restricting her attention to the ordinary to avoid "blows" that were terrible and deeply felt. . . . If one did not know that Woolf killed herself, one would not consider these letters those of a deeply disturbed person. But in hindsight, the knowledge that these letters lead up to and end with her suicide both allows and encourages the reader to seek the "pattern" behind all this cotton wool of daily life, to ascertain what she felt as terrible and tried to control. (pp. 23-4)

[The] issues of death, loss, sex, madness, and suicide were emotionally clustered in [the] years of Virginia's childhood and prolonged adolescence.

During the years covered by Volume VI of the *Letters,* Virginia was continually being drawn back to this harrowing time of her life. *The Years* . . . [is] in part directly about this period. . . .

She writes to Stephen Spender that the trouble with *The Years* is that it includes too many dates and facts and too much action, which she thinks "generally unreal." . . . Woolf had contrasted her fiction of "vision" to the traditional realistic (and traditionally masculine) novel of "fact"—a distinction which echoes that between cotton wool and pattern. Woolf was right to follow the inclination of her temperament, and her greatest achievements in the novel (a word she also found unacceptable), *To the Lighthouse* and *The Waves,* are the best defense of her choice. But in the case of *The Years,* all her talk of "facts" tends to conceal what the facts are about. *The Years* examines more realistically some of the frightening experiences of her early life: the death of her mother, emotional anesthesia, sexual molestation, sexual frigidity. This novel lacked the protective transformation of "vision," and she was left to confront "a loathsome lump of fact." Most likely it was the fear and loathing of the facts of her life, not simply the aesthetic decision to be factual, which almost broke her down. (p. 24)

Virginia Woolf's extreme desperation in her last days becomes fully evident only when the *Letters* are placed within the context of her other writings, particularly the diary and autobiographical memoirs. Her letters to friends right until the day before her suicide are matter-of-fact. . . . The two suicide notes to Leonard and the one to Vanessa are therefore interspersed in this final volume with perfectly ordinary letters to old friends, such as Lady Cecil, Lady Tweedsmuir, V. Sackville-West, and to business associate John Lehmann, who was arranging for the publication of *Between the Acts*. These letters show, for the last time, how she could maintain the surface appearance of the ordinary while confronting her psychic disintegration and contemplating her own death. This final element of control, manifested in her letters, is the best suggestion of how to understand her motive for suicide. . . .

To her there did seem to be a pattern to her life which now with its sledge-hammer blows was breaking through the cotton wool and forcing her to act the part of a madwoman. Even though there is not a single letter in this volume about Virginia Woolf's writing of *Between the Acts*, this last work of fiction shows her anxious fascination with being forced to act a part in a drama one does not know the meaning of. Rather than become merely an actor, an object of fate, Woolf chose not to suffer madness and the strict and humiliating regime of treatment that accompanied it. . . . This premeditation, now emphasized by the re-dating of the suicide notes, shows that Woolf's death was not an insane or impulsive act, but rather her last desperate act of free will. By choosing to take her own life she authored, as well as acted, her fate. Her death was the final expression of her "spirit" in response to that terrible hardness of life which again seemed to be closing in on her in her last years. . . .

For the common reader of the life and letters of Virginia Woolf, her death completes and reveals the whole pattern contained within all the fragments. But the pattern does not allow us to know with absolute certainty the extent to which

Virginia Woolf's life and death may have been determined by forces beyond her control even in her assertion of some control over them. Virginia was so ground down by the harshness of her fate that finally the only expression of her spirit was to choose death over madness, fusing permanently in a single action her life and death, her character and her fate. (p. 27)

Edwin J. Kennedy, Jr., "Enemies Within and Without," in The New Republic *(reprinted by permission of* The New Republic; *© 1981 The New Republic, Inc.), Vol. 184, No. 5, January 3, 1981, pp. 23-7.*

ADDITIONAL BIBLIOGRAPHY

Bell, Quentin. *Virginia Woolf: A Biography.* New York: Harcourt Brace Jovanovich, 1972, 314 p.

    A definitive account of Woolf's life and career.

De Araujo, Victor. "'A Haunted House'—The Shattered Glass." *Studies in Short Fiction* III, No. 2 (Winter 1966): 157-64.

    Examines Woolf's poetic exploration of a series of relationships, including life and death, past and present, and intellect and intuition, in her short story "A Haunted House."

Eliot, T. S. "Virginia Woolf." *Horizon* III, No. 17 (May 1941): 313-16.

    A tribute to Woolf upon her death. Eliot laments the loss of a great writer, stating that "a whole pattern of culture is broken."

Graham, J. W. "A Negative Note on Bergson and Virginia Woolf." *Essays in Criticism* VI, No. 1 (January 1956): 70-4.

    Disputes the influence of Bergson's central ideas on Woolf's fiction.

Hafley, James. "On One of Woolf's Short Stories." *Modern Fiction Studies* II, No. 1 (February 1956): 13-16.

    A detailed study of Woolf's short story "Moments of Being" from the collection *A Haunted House*.

Majumdar, Robin. *Virginia Woolf: An Annotated Bibliography of Criticism 1915-1974*. New York: Garland Publishing, 1976, 117 p.

    The most exhaustive bibliography of criticism on Woolf to date.

Wellek, René. "Virginia Woolf as Critic." *The Southern Review* XIII, No. 3 (Summer 1977): 419-37.

    Examines the overriding concerns organizing Woolf's critical essays, and outlines Woolf's assessment of numerous literary figures.

Woolf, Leonard. "Virginia Woolf: Writer and Personality." *The Listener* LXXIII, No. 1875 (4 March 1965): 327-28.

    Personal reminiscences by Woolf's husband.

Alexander (Humphreys) Woollcott

1887-1943

American critic, journalist, essayist, dramatist, and short story writer.

A master of the withering insult and a mawkish sentimentalist, Woollcott is best known as one of America's most eccentric wits and raconteurs, as well as an influential pioneer of modern drama criticism. During his years as a critic for *The New York Times*, *New York Herald*, *New York Sun*, and *New York World*, he brought such performers as Paul Robeson, the Marx Brothers, and Fred Astaire to the public's attention. With his gossipy approach to reviewing, a style that focused on personalities, trivia, and general impressions of the plays, Woollcott attained and wielded the power of success or failure over Broadway's offerings.

Woollcott took an interest in reviewing during his youth. After founding the drama club at Hamilton College, New York and publishing several drama reviews, he joined the reporting staff of *The New York Times* in 1909. Becoming drama critic five years later, Woollcott quickly found himself involved in a legal battle with Jake and Lee Shubert, a team of Broadway producers, in a trial that eventually determined the right of critics to attend and criticize, kindly or adversely, the dramas of their choice.

Drafted and sent overseas during World War I, Woollcott established himself as an aggressive reporter with *The Stars and Stripes*, the newspaper of the American Expeditionary Forces. His news stories, like his drama reviews, concentrated on the personal, anecdotal side of the conflict. One of these became one of America's most popular dog stories: "The Story of Verdun Belle."

Back in New York, Woollcott dominated Broadway as its most influential critic throughout the 1920s. His reviews, noted for their gushing admiration for performers and performances he liked, and the cruel blasts he reserved for those he did not, drew ridicule from George Jean Nathan, whose article "The Seidlitz Powder in Times Square," delighted Woollcott and brought him wide attention. With a personality as flamboyant as his prose, he quickly developed his public image as a foppish eccentric.

Woollcott's first book, *Mrs. Fiske: Her Views on Actors, Acting, and the Problems of Production*, was a record of several interviews with one of his lifelong idols, actress Minnie Maddern Fiske. Charles Dickens, the Marx Brothers, Irving Berlin, and other artists he admired, as well as Woollcott's other widely varied interests, appeared in the books he published throughout the twenties. These books, composed of essays, stories, and sketches from his newspaper columns, are mostly forgotten today. Woollcott also served as one of the ringleaders of the Algonquin Round Table, a lunchtime gathering of prominent journalists, authors, and show business people, including Dorothy Parker, James Thurber, Harpo Marx, and Robert Benchley, who met daily at the Algonquin Hotel to tell stories, discuss the news of the day, and playfully insult each other.

The Bettmann Archive

Retiring from drama criticism in 1928, Woollcott turned to reviewing books as a much sought-after magazine columnist and radio personality. His stature and influence as a book reviewer both on the air and in the pages of *The New Yorker* soon rivalled that which he had earlier enjoyed as a theater critic. His radio broadcasts as "The Town Crier" and his writings also contained retellings of his favorite sentimental stories, horror tales, and gossip, all of which were later reworked, retold, and republished many times, giving critics cause to believe that Woollcott's talent, though well executed, was quite limited. *While Rome Burns*, containing his favorite stories, appeared in 1934 and proved his most popular book. His two efforts as a playwright, though—*The Channel Road* and *The Dark Tower*, both written with George S. Kaufman— were unsuccessful.

While Woollcott's contribution to American literature is minimal, he did much to raise drama criticism from an insignificant trapping to a legitimate feature of journalism. He remains the colorful personality immortalized in Kaufman's and Moss Hart's comedy *The Man Who Came to Dinner*: "an improbable character," according to Louis Untermeyer, "unaccountably in love with his own portly shadow."

PRINCIPAL WORKS

*Mrs. Fiske: Her Views on Actors, Acting, and the
    Problems of Production* (interviews) 1917
The Command Is Forward (journalism and sketches)
    1919
Mr. Dickens Goes to the Play (biographical essay) 1922
Shouts and Murmurs (criticism) 1922
Enchanted Aisles (essays and sketches) 1924
The Story of Irving Berlin (biography) 1925
Going to Pieces (essays and sketches) 1928
Two Gentlemen and a Lady (short stories) 1928; also
    published as *Verdun Belle*, 1928
The Channel Road [with George S. Kaufman] (drama)
    1929
The Dark Tower [with George S. Kaufman] (drama)
    1933
While Rome Burns (essays, legends, and sketches) 1934
The Woollcott Reader [editor] (short stories) 1935
Woollcott's Second Reader [editor] (short stories and
    prose) 1937
Long, Long Ago (legends and sketches) 1943
The Letters of Alexander Woollcott (letters) 1944
The Portable Woollcott (essays, letters, sketches, and
    short stories) 1946

THE NEW YORK TIMES BOOK REVIEW (essay date 1917)

Alexander Woollcott's book about Mrs. Fiske ["**Mrs. Fiske: Her Views on Actors, Acting, and the Problems of Production**"] is concerned almost wholly with her theories, conclusions, and convictions as to many phases of the arts of the theatre. He records a series of talks with her in which by means of an occasional question he leads her on to reveal some of the much wisdom as to the theatre, plays, acting and audiences she has acquired during the years since, as a baby of three, she made her debut.... The book is full of interesting exposition, nuggets of wisdom, conclusions clearly thought out and forcibly presented. No one who is in the least interested in the theatre, either as a place of mere amusement or as one of the important means of the expression of daily life, can fail to find the book fascinating and stimulating.

> *"The Modern Theatre and Its Problems," in* The New York Times Book Review *(© 1917 by The New York Times Company; reprinted by permission), December 30, 1917, p. 578.**

GEORGE JEAN NATHAN (essay date 1921)

[Today Mr. Ochs, publisher of *The New York Times*,] has the satisfaction of knowing that there is perhaps not a schoolboy or schoolgirl in the eastern part of the United States who wouldn't rather read a single piece of his theatrical criticism than the entire works of Ezra Kendall, Irvin Cobb, and Daisy Ashford. To achieve this end, the good Ochs had, of course, to try out many fancy prancers, but he at last found the True Pumpkin in an effervescent young neo-Acton Davies from a small upstate college [named Alexander Woollcott], and his reward was immediate. (pp. 66-7)

Let us proceed [to **Mr.** Woollcott's] decisions on the mimes. These are, for the most part, stage-struck. The appraisals of Mrs. Fiske, estimable comedienne, of Ethel Barrymore, com-

petent actress, and of Emily Stevens, dinner-party giver, read like a bewitched college boy writing to the Elsie Ferguson of *Liberty Belles* days and beseeching a lock of hair. Of a pleasant but not unusual young acrress in a Clare Kummer play, is not the appended "criticism," for instance, like a valentine to one's best prep-school girl?

> This most beguiling role ... is played to incredible perfection by Lotus Robb, the April charm of whose delicate performance seemed in the confusion of last evening a thing which only lyric verse could adequately describe. Etc. ...

Miss Robb is probably an intelligent woman, and capable now and then of a self-grin. I should like to know what such a woman thinks when, after a good performance of a very incomplex and easy role, she reads such vanilla as this, with its irrelevant ravings about spring and its inability to describe in simple straightforward prose the performance of an ingenue, however pretty. (pp. 67-8)

I do not set myself bumptiously to say that the *Times* Hazlitt's estimates are always wrong (it is not a question of their rightness nor wrongness; they may often be fully right); the style in which they are expressed is the particular bouquet that I invite you to sniff. This style presents an interesting study. It never strikes a mean; it is either a gravy bomb, a bursting gladiolus, a palpitating missa cantata, an attack of psychic hydrophobia, or a Roman denunciation, unequivocal, oracular, flat, and final.... A style, in brief, that is purely emotional, and without a trace of the cool reflectiveness and contagious common sense suited to criticism. It is not that enthusiasm and impatience are not on occasion valuable critical attributes, but that [Woollcott's] particular species of enthusiasm is less the enthusiasm of criticism supported by cultural background and experience than that of a small boy at his first circus, and that [Woollcott's] species of abrupt impatience is less that of the same school of criticism than that of a fox-trot dancer who has had his toe stepped on. (pp. 71-2)

> *George Jean Nathan, "Alexander Woollcott: The Seidlitz Powder in Times Square" (originally published in* The Smart Set, *Vol. 64, No. 2, February, 1921), in his* The Magic Mirror, *edited by Thomas Quinn Curtiss (copyright 1921 by George Jean Nathan; reprinted by permission of Alfred A. Knopf, Inc.),* Knopf, 1960, pp. 64-74.

CLAYTON HAMILTON (essay date 1922)

"**Mr. Dickens Goes To the Play**" is a book that every lover of the great Victorian novelist will wish to add to the collection on his shelves.... This material has been carefully culled and piously arranged, and the resultant book is pleasant to read and handy to have around.

It has long been generally known that Dickens was an amateur actor of large enthusiasm and considerable ability [and] that there was a great deal of the histrionic in his widely patronized appearances on the platform as a reader of his own novels.... But a contemplation of these facts has led Mr. Woollcott to exaggerate the importance of Dickens in relation to the history of the English drama and even in relation to the history of the English theatre....

[For example], we are told of Dickens's commentaries on the theatre. "Implicit in that record is some of the best dramatic criticism in the language." One can only wish that Mr. Woollcott had chosen to append an answer to the obvious question, "Where?" One of the points that are most likely to strike a disinterested student on rereading the material that has been gathered into this book is the strange fact that Dickens, despite his lifelong enthusiasm for the theatre on both sides of the footlights, never devoted any systematic thought to it which may be defined as critical. . . .

But the compiler of this amiable book grows even more extravagant when he writes about Dickens in the jargon of the "new" psychology and "analyzes" him, in Freudian terms, as a "thwarted actor" who suffered all his life from "an exhibition complex." This, we are told was "the secret of his heart." It seems rather a pity that this secret should at last be revealed: one would so much prefer to remember Dickens as an unthwarted novelist who was as free from complexes as his stories were free from complexities—to continue to think of him as a success, instead of being taught to regard him as a failure. . . .

In his own delightful book of commentaries on the current theatre, entitled **"Shouts and Murmurs,"** Mr. Woollcott evinces a passion for the playhouse which is just as eager, though not quite so undiscriminating, as that which he has ascribed to Dickens. . . .

It is only in jest that a friendly reviewer would pretend to "analyze" Mr. Woollcott in the barbarous jargon of the "new" psychology; but if every great passion is to be regarded as an indication of a great inhibition, it would be difficult to refrain from classing Mr. Woollcott with the late Mr. Dickens as a thwarted actor or a disappointed dramatist. He is always a readable, often a witty, and at times a charming writer; but can it be that the secret of his heart is that he does not really want to be an essayist at all, but is suffering from a suppressed desire to be Mrs. Fiske?. . .

"Shouts and Murmurs," though a book about the theatre, is not a contribution to dramatic criticism. It was not intended to be so. Its general purpose has been indicated by the author in the following sentence: "I am suggesting rather an excursion among the circumstances which have determined certain of the plays to-day, a look into the biographies of certain tragedies and comedies which are alive now in the theatre here or abroad.". . . . Along these chosen lines Mr. Woollcott writes entertainingly, with ample insight and abundant zest. . . . Considering the lively interest and the literary excellence of many of these papers, one wonders how Mr. Woollcott has managed to keep company with Dickens in avoiding any deliberate assumption of the critical attitude in his comments on the theatre. His book is a literary record of enjoyments; but it makes no critical attempt to measure them and weigh them by the test of any theory of the theatre, however pragmatical such a theory might be. In fact, in a playful chapter, Mr. Woollcott speaks rather scornfully of dramatic criticism and says that "the tradition of prolixity and the dulness in all such writing is as old as Aristotle and as lasting as William Archer." Thus is Aristotle accused, at least by implication, of prolixity. One wonders if Mr. Woollcott has ever read the "Poetics." Or has he forgotten how brief that treatise is—how succinct and how sententious? And if Archer is by implication dull, yet the dulness of his disinterested and successful endeavor to introduce the plays of Ibsen to the English speaking theatre has resulted in many

moments that Mr. Woollcott has found enlivening during the course of his thousand and one nights of theatregoing.

It is not always possible to agree with Mr. Woollcott's opinions. . . . But, for the most part, one may read these "shouts and murmurs" without any desire to halt the author and shout back. Enjoyment is one of the most contagious, as well as one of the most healthy, of emotions, and Mr. Woollcott so enjoys the theatre and all its ways and writes about it at once so briskly and so lovingly that his book at nearly every moment is a charmingly companionable volume.

> *Clayton Hamilton, "Woollcott Goes to the Plays,"*
> *in* The Literary Review *(copyright, 1922 by N.Y.*
> *Evening Post, Inc.), December 9, 1922, p. 288.*

JOSEPH WOOD KRUTCH (essay date 1929)

Everyone who has ever taken a course in the short-story or owned a "Library of the World's Best Literature" knows Maupassant's old shocker "Boule de Suif." Alexander Woollcott and George Kaufman have now turned it into an entertaining play which will doubtless never be as famous as the original, but which might reasonably be called a good deal more sensible. By completely changing the mood while retaining the main incidents they have afforded a very pretty illustration of the fact that a plot is hardly more than a challenge to the intelligence of an author. . . .

[When Maupassant] hit upon the story of the patriotic prostitute who refuses to bed with a Prussian officer he accomplished one of the things which seem most difficult for a modern writer: he invented a new situation. Complicate it by adding a group of conventional people in the power of the officer who are led by their interests to persuade the prostitute to ply her trade; show them reverting to their original self-righteousness when the momentous transaction has been completed, and you have a story which, in its outline, is as unforgettable as any of the best traditional tales. . . .

Now the story is so obviously dramatic as to invite retelling on the stage, but any sensitive person who undertook to retell it would soon perceive not only that it is blatantly obvious but that one can hardly propose the stubborn prostitute as a modern Joan of Arc to an audience whose sense of proportion does not happen to be, as Maupassant's was, considerably disturbed by the fevers of a war-time hatred. The story is not tragic and neither can it be transformed by pathos into that species of demi-tragedy which constitutes one of the varieties of the sentimental drama. Like the juggler of Notre Dame, Tallow Ball expressed her loyalty by the manner in which she proposed to practice her profession, and she had ethical scruples about entertaining an enemy alien, but this pathos is tinged with the ridiculous. The more seriously one attempts to tell the story the more comic it becomes, and to discover that is to discover that the situation actually belongs to the realm of comedy. The man who invented it did not realize the fact, and it requires a good deal of boldness to borrow his story for purposes so different from his own, but that is exactly what Messrs. Woollcott and Kaufman have done. They have taken most of the main incidents but none of the spirit. They have very skilfully transposed the whole thing into the key of comedy, and the fact that their play will stand analysis far better than the original story is proof that they were right in so doing.

They have called it **"The Channel Road"**.... The action begins when the party of fugitives arrives at the inn which serves as headquarters for the Prussian lieutenant, and it ends when, by a slight twist, the prostitute has been enabled to depart with the last laugh on her righteous companions. But the important thing is that with the change of little except the point of view the whole has been lifted out of the murky region of patriotic melodrama into the serene atmosphere of comedy. As soon as one forgets to be in a rage because the Germans instead of the French are winning the war; as soon, that is to say, as one uses one's head instead of Maupassant's heart, all the events fall into a new perspective. One perceives that they constitute a contretemps rather than a calamity and that the occasion is one rather for wit than for either indignation or tears. Messrs. Woollcott and Kaufman supply the lightness of touch which is necessary and the whole thing goes off with a ripple of laughter. Doubtless many serious persons will accuse them of having perverted the story but it was the original author who did that. "Boule de Suif" is startling, unforgettable, and preposterous; **"The Channel Road"** is slight and not tremendously important, but it uses intelligence to deflate a melodrama and it puts Maupassant's ingenious situation in exactly the category where it belongs.

> Joseph Wood Krutch, "Drama: 'Boule de Suif'," in The Nation (copyright 1929 The Nation magazine, The Nation Associates, Inc.), Vol. 129, No. 3357, November 6, 1929, p. 530.

RICHARD DANA SKINNER (essay date 1933)

Messrs. Alexander Woollcott and George S. Kaufman have put their heads together to write a melodrama, but I would hardly say that it is a case of two heads proving better than one. The mystery [*The Dark Tower*] depends largely on a situation that is not bullet-proof, and one can never tell whether an acute audience will or will not pierce to the bottom of things and spoil the suspense. Then, too, the joint authors, in their excessive efforts to be sophisticated, have given the play a dose of degenerate verbiage and implication which has nothing to do with the plot but a great deal to do with a vaguely foul atmosphere—at least as long as one Stanley Vance is alive and on the stage. Perhaps it is all supposed to be part of the comedy relief, but it succeeds chiefly in creating a comedy of errors in taste and judgment.

Stanley Vance is a Svengali in the modern spirit, a species of quite odious worm who, as the husband of Jessica Wells, an actress, succeeds in hypnotizing her quite completely and literally. By making him sufficiently slimy, the authors lay the groundwork for a merry murder with which the audience is expected to sympathize heartily. Thus, when the murderer is caught, there is little else than jubilation on the stage. For my part, I wondered just why the play had been written at all. One of the final wise-cracks did not seem an entirely sufficient explanation. The murderer is asked if he is not worried at having broken one of the ten commandments. His gay reply is to ask his questioner if he, the questioner, has ever worried about breaking the commandment, "Thou shalt not commit adultery." That, in the opinion of the authors, seems to settle everything and make further comment unnecessary. In one sense, of course, it does!

There is, however, one character in the play worth all of the best fiction detectives rolled together in one bundle. That is Inspector William Curtis.... I should like to see a whole play written around William Curtis, around that benign and vacuous smile and that impenetrable skull. He trembles on every thin edge of discovery, but discovers nothing. But **"The Dark Tower"** is not about William Curtis, and is not, in fact, about much of anything at all.

> Richard Dana Skinner, "The Play: 'The Dark Tower'," in Commonweal (copyright © 1933 Commonweal Publishing Co., Inc.), Vol. XIX, No. 6, December 8, 1933, p. 160.*

LEONARD BACON (essay date 1934)

Mr. Woollcott's **"While Rome Burns"** arouses in this reviewer mingled emotions. The book in question is a selection from Mr. Woollcott's contribution to literature over a period of six years, and unquestionably has much in it to divert or to edify.

Mr. Woollcott is without doubt an entertaining, and at times a stimulating writer. He has fine admirations which do him honor and to offset them splenetic and dubious vagaries. It is good to hear him speak up heartily and eloquently in praise of Mrs. Richards, Maxine Elliot, or the Marquis of Villalobar. It is perhaps not so pleasant to follow him into those regions of Platonic sadism, where he apes but does not attain the performance of his acknowledged master, Mr. Edmund Pearson. Where Mr. Pearson produces something with a family resemblance to Goya, Mr. Woollcott achieves the emotional effects which I personally connect in my thoughts with Madame Tussaud's bust of Marat. Nor can I forget a character in "Pickwick" who wanted to make your flesh creep.

Two of his characteristics have been economically glanced at. His interest in the theatre is another which may be touched in passing. As a dramatic critic he seemed to me formerly, as he seems to me now, occasionally entertaining and sometimes effective, the last, of course, when he agreed with me.... But I think, as I thought six years back, that his esthetic judgments are far too highly colored by his private likes and dislikes. I don't mean that his opinions are dishonest, but I do mean that sentimental considerations bias his estimates to an inordinate degree. (p. 553)

[He] does one thing which I find hard to forgive, worse than his studies in the vulgar macabre, ... worse than his idiosyncratic injustice to better men than himself. It is this. He can write straightforward, cleanly, hard-hitting English, yet never was there such a crawling slave of the cliché. Not since writing began have there been so many quirks dependent on a vague and inapposite allusiveness.... Mr. Woollcott is among the most criminal of literary gangsters in this connection.

The reason is easy to find. It is his audience. He writes for the imperfectly educated, for the sort of person who has enjoyed every advantage, but complains about highbrows when an Italian lady quotes Dante. Such persons have vague half-memories of jewels five words long, that on the stretched forefinger of all time sparkle forever. When they hear phrases of this kind they feel a vague half-thrill of half-recognition, and a conscious pleasure in seeing something good put to base uses. (pp. 553, 557)

But it is sad that an able and ready writer should have injured his own vigorous, pleasing, and natural style. The stale catchword, the metallic cliché, the cant phrase of a metropolitan (and as they would put it) sophisticated clique, do infinite wrong to a writer who, in spite of being a critic and in spite of constant association with others just like him, retains traces of life and originality. To conclude:

It's the kind of a book that would please Jimmy
    Walker,
There's much spurious swank and much tittle and
    tattle.
It was made for palookas who love the *New Yalker*,
    Ed Wynn, Groucho Marx and inferior cattle. . . .
And I haven't a doubt that he's perfectly charming
And that socially he's uncommonly nice,
That his manners are finished and poised and
    disarming,
And that he won't relish this final advice,—
That his book would be better were it not so ungentle.
The flattery so fulsome, the jests so jejune,
Were it not so sadistic, or so sentimental,
Were it less like the juice of the tenderized prune.

(p. 557)

> *Leonard Bacon, "The Juice of the Tenderized Prune," in* The Saturday Review of Literature *(copyright © 1934 by* Saturday Review*), Vol. X, No. 35, March 17, 1934, pp. 553, 557.*

LOUIS KRONENBERGER   (essay date 1935)

Mr. Woollcott is not only a best-seller in his own right, but with a sentence or two he can make best-sellers of other men. At present he is by far the most influential salesman of books in the United States. . . . (p. 720)

Now there is perhaps no better way of attracting followers than by suggesting that they, like oneself, have a superior sense of humor, and I have no doubt that Mr. Woollcott's ripe appreciation of anecdote has helped pave the way for his dictatorship over literature. But he is by no means one-sided, and if he has a lively turn for laughter, he has an even livelier turn for tears. I even suspect that weepsiness is his true love and that he would rather have a good cry than a good laugh. And I further suspect that literature has no meaning for him beyond providing one or the other.

It is very seldom, of course, that a critic who becomes widely influential with the general public is a good critic. He is usually its superior in articulateness, not acumen. If he has virtues, they are only tolerated for the sake of his vices. Thus Mr. Woollcott's immediate predecessor in the land, Professor [William Lyon] Phelps, really liked good books as well as bad, but won his spurs entirely through recommending the bad ones. . . . But Mr. Woollcott is a very different kind of critic. He is vastly harder on dull books than Mr. Phelps, and vastly harder on good books. He does not like a great many things, and all the things he likes have points in common. Thus the prose had better be more like French pastry than bread, the sentiment bountiful and lush, the characters exceedingly wicked or noble or salty, the scene distant if not downright exotic. But Mr. Woollcott will not approve of such productions if there is anything naive or blundering about them: they must be executed with all possible cunning and sophistication. Their true character must not be obvious; it must not only steal upon you that they are hokum.

Yet hokum they are, high-grade, streamlined hokum if you will, but hokum. There is not much in **"The Woollcott Reader"** that any well-known critic of our time except Mr.

Woollcott will wish to see preserved. Here is, I say boldly, second-rate taste at its most formidable and deceptive, tricked out in its Sunday best, beckoning and easy to take. It is second-rate in a number of respects, but I am satisfied to rest my case on the fact that there is scarcely a thing in this anthology which does not, at bottom, falsify or run away from life. Like all sentimentalists and easy scoffers, Mr. Woollcott can be quickly spotted as an escapist; and in this compilation of modern writing he has escaped to the strongholds of all those who bruise easily and think with difficulty— to the world of children and animals and triflers and people easy to laugh and cry over. I count it of some significance that in a book of 1,011 pages, exactly 72 are laid in the United States. I count it of some significance that in a volume running over with pathos, there is exactly one story that might by any standards be considered to treat of tragedy. I count it of some significance that Mr. Woollcott's leviathan does not include one living writer interpreting the current scene.

It would no doubt be more than enough if Mr. Woollcott sent this book forth to his hundred thousand or so admirers merely with the statement that it contained things which he had enjoyed. But he is at all times the critic: these selections are called "minor masterpieces"; one of them is "as simple and modest and perfect as a Vermeer" and another is "the most moving and uplifting tale ever told in the English language." His critical dicta, furthermore, are set down in a prose which I do not hesitate to describe as nauseating. Mr. Woollcott loves perfumed words, but knows no better how to use them than certain women know how to use an atomizer. This sentence from one of his recent indorsements may indicate what many times awaits a reader of this book: "You, I think, will find Carrie mysteriously warming to the cockles of your foolish heart." When such a writer comes along and compiles such a book as **"The Woollcott Reader,"** I am not afraid to put my own sense of humor to the touch and get up in the pulpit as a reformer. While Rome, by Mr. Woollcott's bland admission, is burning, I should like to see practically everything that he has written and most of what he has compiled and recommended thrown as further fuel upon the conflagration. At least while Rome is burning, let it fumigate. (pp. 720-21)

> *Louis Kronenberger, "Down with Woollcott," in* The Nation *(copyright 1935 The Nation magazine, The Nation Associates, Inc.), Vol. 141, No. 3676, December 18, 1935, pp. 720-21.*

ODELL SHEPARD   (essay date 1936)

Mr. Woollcott is one of those persons for whom we should like to lift the adjective "elegant" out of the gutter and cleanse it as best we can; and in him, as in all such persons, there is always an echo and a reflection of that most ancient irrecoverable time called yesterday. His wit, his air of omniscience, his imperturbable poise, and most of all the beauty of his fastidious prose, relate him to certain English writers who adorned the last age of literary style; but he reminds us of the Nineties with a refreshing difference. When his expert care for prose rhythm has made us think of Walter Pater, we soon find that his cadences are never languid and that his eyelids are not even "a little weary." Compared with Max Beerbohm, he is far gentler and more neighborly. He has a head grown old in this wicked world, but a heart as young as any sophomore's, stuffed with enthusiasms, and wholly American.

523

Not the least American trait in Mr. Woollcott is his regret for a day that is dead—for some golden American day, of rather uncertain date, that comes not back again. He has an eye for spring and summer beauty, but the faces that he most loves are autumnal. . . . At the dance of life he prefers, like young Romeo, to "be a candle-holder, and look on." So always he manages to be up-to-date in a charmingly old-fashioned way.

This effect is due, partly, to his prose style. The elegant Englishmen named above never wrote a prose at once so brilliant and yet so even in texture as this of his, so meticulous and nicely calculated and yet so free of mannerism. To find in our raucous America a man who writes by ear, using every delicate chime and nuance of which the old rich language is capable, is a delightful surprise. Mr. Woollcott's prose is as expert, in its very different kind, as Santayana's own. He has captured his large audience by the ear, and his fame reveals in us certain unsuspected traits of civilization.

Or perhaps it is not so much his prose style as his great skill in the art of the raconteur that explains his reputation. "**While Rome Burns**" contains a score of stories not very remarkable for the events narrated but nearly perfect in the skill of the narration, and "**The Woollcott Reader**" has some fifteen tales from other pens in which this same skill is everywhere apparent. It is clear that the man who wrote the one book and selected the other is definitely turning away from the "objective reporting" of much recent fiction towards the elegant old fashion of telling a story with all the art and all the charm one can muster. Often his stories are little more than anecdotes, but there is a finish and finality about them that promises long life. Other story-tellers of the day may delve in coal mines; Mr. Woollcott cuts diamonds. And yet his work is not hard, and it does not glitter. In the book that he has written as well as in the one he has compiled the outstanding characteristic is not brilliancy but tenderness. Human courage and gallantry, human patience, human love, are what touch him most deeply and hold his lasting admiration. These books of his have been made by an agile, witty, and well-stored mind, but already they have been taken home to the American heart. (pp. 647-48)

> *Odell Shepard, "The Art of Story-Telling," in* The Yale Review *(© 1936 by Yale University; copyright renewed © 1964 by Yale University; reprinted by permission of the editors), Vol. XXV, No. 3, March, 1936, pp. 647-48.*

SAMUEL HOPKINS ADAMS (essay date 1945)

[With the publication of *While Rome Burns*, Woollcott] attained his highest status in the world of letters. Through skillful and patient showmanship he had theretofore established himself as a personage, whether distinguished or notorious depending upon one's viewpoint or prejudice; but his literary repute had been both ephemeral and circumscribed. At last, here was Woollcott, in bulk; take him or leave him. The public took him with acclaim.

How far the best-seller lists are a criterion of merit is debatable. The Woollcott collection of random pieces was more than a best seller; it marked the emergence of a form new to the period: the smooth art of the raconteur-essayist: a sort of twentieth-century *Colloquia*. (p. 250)

That, within his limitations, Woollcott is a stylist, is undeniable. He can be as nostalgic as wood smoke on a frosty

morning. He is infinitely artful in the contriving of that literary device so ineptly employed by many imitators of O. Henry, the "snapper" that ends a narrative. Sometimes a line of his sings, as of the dead actor, Moissi: "I know not who is heir to all his dreams." He speaks with Emerson's "sad lucidity of soul," in the nobly sincere letter in which he views his own character as it would appear "when the sentries we all post to warn us that the world is looking . . . no longer do their duty." Many of his characterizations, sentimental and other, would be hard to better: witness the double-barreled description of Vermont and its favorite son, Calvin Coolidge, "small, lean, and crabbed; frugal, and addicted to old ways"; [and] of Mrs. Patrick Campbell, in her desperately resentful decline, "a sinking ship firing upon her rescuers." . . . In his later work, the thumbnail introductions to his selections are models of compact and luminous composition.

But, to the mind of this reader (and admirer), the prime virtue of Alexander Woollcott's method lies in its informing personality and pervasive friendliness. He is not pointing a pen at you and narrating at long range something that may or may not interest you. He is talking to you confidentially about friends of his—fascinating people, distinguished people: you ought to know them—passing on to you a good story that he picked up in some unlikely place; making you free of intimate childhood or college or war or professional experiences; this with a cherubic confidence that you will enjoy hearing them as much as he enjoys telling them. All his method is pointed to this end of making the public his confidant.

The Woollcott ideal is expressed in a letter to President Hutchins of Chicago, complimenting him upon his skill of authorship:

"Your pieces sound like you, creating by the printed word the illusion that you are actually present and speaking. That is all a writer can ask."

He had the newspaperman's sensitiveness to what would catch the general reader. People are sentimental; he gave them sentiment to the verge of bathos and sometimes beyond it. People love dogs. There was always a dog in the Woollcott memorabilia. People thrill to ghosts, mysteries, murders, crimes; Woollcott can wallow in blood until the sanguine hue tinges his ink. The public is interested in prominent personalities. Woollcott deals lavishly and intimately with them, nearly always in the first and second person, and this without pretense or exaggeration, for he knew them, as likely as not, by their first names. His is not the callow pretentiousness of the elbow-rubbing type of reporter who gloats in his column over the proximity of the glittering great. When he tells you wryly that he will feel like a fool at the entrance gate of heaven if Saint Peter happens to remember his refusing a dime to a needy beggar on the same evening when he paid for the dinner of the richest girl in the world, you know that he is dealing in fact. What he said to Bernard Shaw or H. G. Wells said to him, or he wrote to Chief Justice Holmes, or wired to Helen Keller, rings true because it is true. Snobbery of one kind or another is innate in most of us. Woollcott's writings appeal to that as to other susceptibilities. The curious part is that he does not write about people like a snob, but simply and unaffectedly.

Much of his matter is gossamer-light, but so amiably set forth, with such balmy smoothness and so radiant a faith in the reader's enjoyment, that it persuades one's engrossed attention where weightier matters might fail of it. If he slops over into sentimentality, it is a fault readily condoned by the vast majority of his cult . . . , however painful to the judicious. (pp. 251-52)

Fervor was both his virtue and his vice. Only under self-induced emotional pressure could he produce his best effects. He lived in the superlative degree. Everything was *in extremis*, whether for praise or blame. Of all the nicknames whereby his correspondents addressed him, the late John H. Finley's was the most apt, "My dear Stentor."

Woollcott's judgments tended to the superoracular. It was not enough to extol Paul Robeson's voice; he must record "the indisputable fact that he is the finest musical instrument wrought by nature in our time.". . . Lizzie Borden, a pretty dull and sordid murderess when all is said and done, is, to Woollcott's mind, "America's most interesting woman," and the saga of her axe "on the plane with Shakespeare and Sophocles." (p. 253)

All this tumult and shouting served a purpose: it beguiled the generality of his readers. Because he saw everything so magnified, so irradiated, Woollcott was able to communicate his self-hypnosis to his public, which not only accepted him as a mentor, but wept or cheered with him over his extremest ecstasies. So artfully were his overstatements set forth that they seldom palled or cheapened. He was that rare example of virtuosity, a soloist on the bass drum.

"When Aleck found something he liked," says Marc Connelly, "he seldom qualified his enthusiasm. He not only liked it; he loved it. And with the ardor of his affection dominating him completely, he occasionally—like all wholehearted lovers—did things which seemed absurd to less stimulated people."

The keyword here is "stimulated." His was the authentic *furor scribendi*. Only its sincerity saved it. In the heat of composition he believed everything he said. Later he might have his doubts. But later he was doing something else equally fervent. (p. 254)

> *Samuel Hopkins Adams, "'I Am Sir Oracle'," in his A. Woollcott: His Life and His World (reprinted by permission of Brandt & Brandt Literary Agents, Inc.; (copyright 1945, by Samuel Hopkins Adams; copyright renewed © 1973 by Katherine A. Adell), Reynal & Hitchcock, 1945, pp. 248-60.*

JOHN MASON BROWN (essay date 1946)

Woollcott, the critic, was never the Woollcott who mattered. . . . Read as a critic, he was often disappointing; read as Woollcott, he seldom failed to be diverting. He had as little interest in the dull orthodoxies of nightly reporting as he had in the so-called higher criticism.

There has always been a recruitable army of sobersides equipped to release the jargon of pedestrian reviewing. I mean aisle-seat occupants in every city of every land, who can write with a certain grave competence about what they have just seen. With them their opinions matter; with Woollcott his copy did. Due to the cruel pressure of their deadlines, these reviewers are tempted to feel they have done their duty when they dash off such phrases as, "To the Longacre last night came a bright little comedy produced with George Spelvin's *usual* skill." (pp. xx-xxi)

Woollcott did not belong to this tribe. Clichés were not the natural language of his spirit. He scarcely ever resorted to tired words. He did not write *about* the theater. His reviews, in addition to being one of the most delectable breakfast foods on the market, *were* in themselves theater. To verify this, you have only to consult the ones printed in [*The Portable Woollcott*].

The heat with which Woollcott fueled his copy was his substitute for criticism. A. B. Walkley once contended that, just as one solid body cannot collide with another without creating heat, so one mind cannot impinge upon another without generating criticism. In Woollcott's case the warmth of his reviews was created less by the friction of two minds than by the impact of another mind on Woollcott's heart. Though admirably equipped to think, Woollcott preferred to feel. Ideas did not interest him as much as people. He rejoiced in personalities, and left principles alone. Never a slave to theory, he confessed more and more in his writings that the anecdote was his master. Before long, it was of the anecdote itself that he became a master.

I dwell on Woollcott's days as a dramatic critic because a part of Woollcott dwelt ever after in the theater. (pp. xxi-xxii)

Although his horizons widened, the world through which he subsequently moved—even as a foreign correspondent—continued to be lighted by a spotlight. The ribbon on his typewriter remained dipped in grease paint. He never touched life without rouging it. He insisted upon seeing it with its make-up on. His subjects continued to be theater people. When they were not, they were men and women who appealed to him because their lives were dramatic or their personalities theatrical.

Woollcott's dish was trivia. Dish? More precisely, his caldron. He could ladle it out, endlessly, enchantingly. He had the skill to make it seem important, and the wisdom to recognize that it was so.

He was the most creative uncreative person imaginable. He can be described as the man who couldn't write fiction but who did. No journalist of our time could so clothe an episode in the trappings of the novelist. All of his pieces have a fairy-tale quality about them. One of their chief surprises is that they do *not* begin with "Once upon a time." Although they are fairy tales of facts, they are filled with as much wonder as if their origins were fanciful. Woollcott's mind was filled with entertaining oddments no less than with pressed flowers. He saw life in terms of curtain lines, delayed arrivals, and O. Henry twists. He was able to distend a minor incident until it became a story, and to tell a short story merely by withholding a person's name.

He loved to have the past and present meet, to give them a double exposure, to see them through bifocal lenses. Places were for him always peopled by the shades of those who had been there and by the bodies of those present. One of the fascinations Paris held for him was that "the twisted alleys of the Marais" were "murmurous with the footfalls of two thousand years."

Woollcott rejoiced in coincidence. He was never happier than when giving its long arm a tug. In his own phrase, "we love to catch life in the very act of rhyming." In his pages he saw to it that life did rhyme. He liked when the impossible proved to be not only a probability but an actuality.

He was Shakespearean, and romantic, enough to believe that the heavens were concerned with the fate of his characters. Woollcott was a great one to dignify his coincidences with celestial repercussions. When, for example, he tells us how Anne Parrish found on the quais in Paris the very copy of *Jack Frost and Other Stories* which she had read as a child in Colorado Springs, and in which she had scrawled her name, Woollcott cannot resist appealing to a higher echelon than the Planetarium. "Somewhere," writes he, regrettably, "in fathomless space a star chuckled—chuckled and skipped in its course." (pp. xxii-xxiii)

[Woollcott] was far too good a writer to be forgotten. He was one of the best yarn-spinners of his time. He was a raconteur who could achieve the miracle of seeming to talk in print. None of his contemporaries could use an adjective with his lethal precision. None of them tossed his hat so high in the air, or danced so happily in the streets. None squandered superlatives with his abandon. He was a buoyant enthusiast.

Beyond all this, however, he was an instinctive writer. The rich juices of his spirit course through his prose. . . . Our world and our public prints are the paler for his going. (pp. xxvii-xxviii)

> *John Mason Brown, in his introduction to* The Portable Woollcott, *edited by Joseph Hennessey (copyright 1946 by The Viking Press, Inc.; copyright renewed © 1973 by The Viking Press; reprinted by permission of Viking Penguin, Inc.), Viking Penguin, 1946, pp. xi-xxviii.*

WAYNE CHATTERTON (essay date 1978)

[Had Woollcott] maintained an unbroken tenure as drama critic without ever having served on the *Stars and Stripes* during the First World War, . . . it is less likely that his talents would have matured as they did or that his later career would have been so spectacular. (p. 56)

Woollcott's service with the American Expeditionary Force was a broadening, deepening, and highly satisfying experience. . . . [He] learned that his readers would respond to his heightened and intensified sentiments only if they were genuine. If his stories for *Stars and Stripes* are told "in the manner of Ernie Pyle with an overlarding of Elsie Dinsmore," they are nonetheless charged with unmistakable conviction. "It was all in the superlative mood, all under high pressure," explains Samuel Hopkins Adams, "but it was saved by its utter sincerity. Woollcott more than believed every word he wrote: he felt it."

In Woollcott's prefatory remarks to the collected *Stars and Stripes* despatches, which he published in 1919 under the title *The Command Is Forward*, his sincerity is unmistakable. Not ghoulishly, but with gratitude for the luck of the professional newspaperman, he speaks of the fortuitous circumstances by which he attained "a reserved seat at the war." At the same time, he also realizes that the handy metaphor of war as drama is, after all, only a figure of speech, that war is not an art form, but the grimmest of realities that is to be properly written about only by one who is part of it. . . . For Woollcott, then, the "theater of war" was real life seen in its most dramatic terms. (pp. 57-8)

What he felt when he wrote the *Stars and Stripes* stories, and what he intended that his readers should feel every bit as keenly, were national pride and the highest degree of patriotic fervor. . . . But transcending this . . . were other emotions that Woollcott felt just as deeply—ones that were even more fundamental to the human condition at large. "In that strange simple country which was called the front," he observed with a touch of awe in "A Letter to the Folks" at the end of *The Command Is Forward*, there were no artificial lines separating human beings from each other, no superficial values, no sectional or geographical distinctions. (p. 58)

Of the thirty-five newspaper stories that constitute *The Command Is Forward*, ten can be categorized as panoramic reports of the major military engagements marking the advance of the American Expeditionary Force. . . . Though these reports are the most purely reportorial of all the items in the collection, these stories provide a basic pattern for what would otherwise be a random and heterogeneous assortment of impressions, ones without focus or progression. In pulling all his despatches together into a single collection, Woollcott demonstrated that, even as he wrote the stories chronologically day by day, his eye had never lost track of the vast movements of men and material under which were subsumed all the smallest individual thoughts, feelings, and actions of the war.

In writing these panoramic chapters, Woollcott tended to adopt the tone and spirit of the individual battles of the Classical epics; and while his accounts were appropriate to current taste, he adapted to these stories many of the tested devices of the epics: an elevated tone, a sense of massive simultaneous movements, individual heroics, quick glimpses of revealing and humanizing minutiae, and at times even the sense of cosmic or supernatural forces at work. The heroes of these small epic engagements, however, were no classic supermen or demigods; they were the American infantryman, the doughboy, who, as Woollcott declares in his preface, "bore the greatest burden, suffered the greatest hardship and privation, earned the greatest glory."

In his earliest panoramas, Woollcott experimented with ways by which he might employ varieties of restricted viewpoint to localize his material, even while that same viewpoint suggested the full scope of the action. (pp. 58-9)

The single characteristic of these panoramic war studies is that, collectively, though they capture the sweep and movement of the whole front, the memorable things are preserved in the details—in the dog's search, in heroic actions by individual soldiers, in lines of dialogue, in postures and attitudes, in unconsciously revealing words and gestures. True to form, Aleck was incapable of seeing the war in terms of maps and charts, strategy and statistics. To him, these were not the war at all. The people were the war. Only the people, both military and civilian, mattered.

For this reason, the basic structure of *The Command Is Forward* emerges as a chronological sequence of these panoramic stories, to each of which adheres a cluster of more highly specialized stories devoted to dramatizing the peculiar ways in which each of the major military engagements affected both the troops and the native inhabitants. (p. 60)

Of all the stories which comprise the thirty-five chapters of *The Command Is Forward*, those that caught the fancy of the general reading public were the three or four representatives of a Woollcottian literary formula that did much to establish his success in later years—the sentimental and the nostalgic sketch. (p. 62)

By far the most successful [of these] . . . was **"Verdun Belle,"** a touching tale "of a trench dog who adopted a young leatherneck, of how she followed him to the edge of the battle around Chateau-Thierry, and was waiting for him when they carried him out." (pp. 62-3)

This story has been anthologized and otherwise reprinted many times. For Woollcott, its tone and method became a model for the sentimental tales he wrote with adroitness and effect throughout his career as a free-lance writer and as a radio raconteur. . . .

With such narratives as **"Verdun Belle,"** Woollcott became something more than a converted drama critic and something more than a superior journalist. He was emerging as a superb storyteller whose best tales were to be founded upon actual occurrences or upon the reworking of legendary materials. (p. 63)

Despite the only modest commercial success of his earliest anthologies, Woollcott felt by the summer of 1921 that the best of his contributions to [his regular columns in *The New York Times*], as well as some of his earliest magazine sketches about theatrical subjects, might be successfully recycled. Under the title *Shouts and Murmurs*, this compilation reached the bookshops early in 1922. . . .

[The] pieces that appear in *Shouts and Murmurs* are unsurpassed in the long tradition of the stage anecdote. As ancient as the stage itself, this highly esoteric and largely oral kind of anecdote had awaited only a professional writer who was saturated with stage lore and who had a flair for developing anecdotes into full-blown tales. No other writer in the history of the American theater, perhaps in the history of any theater, was better equipped than Woollcott to make this traditionally oral and esoteric kind of tale both permanent and popular. In *Shouts and Murmurs*, as well as later in *Enchanted Aisles* and *Going to Pieces*, and in the "Program Notes" of *While Rome Burns* and *Long, Long, Ago*, Woollcott came very close to making the stage anecdote a distinctive literary type, one that appeals to the general reader but was previously reserved for the initiated. (p. 101)

Of all Woollcott's books, *Shouts and Murmurs* is the only one that is derived wholly from his drama columns, and it is therefore the only one devoted exclusively to his criticism of the drama. Both *Enchanted Aisles* and *Going to Pieces*, though drawn largely from his newspaper and magazine essays about the theater, are really transitional collections that mark the earliest phases of his development from a drama critic to a wide-ranging essayist and eventually to a man of letters. (p. 108)

In *Enchanted Aisles* . . . Woollcott openly concedes the power of his personal biases and splits his essays and sketches into two sections—"Enthusiasms" and "Resentments." Though most of the essays deal with the theater, his "Enthusiasms" are represented by several magazine pieces that belong more properly among his mature and whimsical essays upon personalities or character types outside the theater world. . . .

But the rest of the pieces in *Enchanted Aisles* are an extension of Woollcott's long experience as drama critic; and, even more than *Shouts and Murmurs*, this collection helped to make the stage anecdote a popular literary form. As one might expect, most of Woollcott's "Enthusiasms" take the form of biographical essays about theater people. (p. 109)

But, to balance his enthusiasms, Woollcott provides also a dozen "Resentments." These mature essays in dramatic criticism afford the reader a concentrated exposure to Woollcott's special blend of acerbity and wit. Together with the "Enthusiasms," these "Resentments" are an honest reflection of Woollcott's personal preferences in theatrical matters. Though nearly half of his "Enthusiasms" are concerned with particular actors and actresses, not a single performer and only one playwright, Maeterlinck, are among his "Resentments." Most of his resentment is directed at theater advertising, types of plays, and misconceptions about the theater, especially on the part of critics. (p. 112)

[Woollcott's] next collection of previously published works is ostensibly a theatrical volume with a theatrical title, even though more than a third of the book is devoted to essays that roam freely among such trivial or sensational subjects as are suggested by these last two section titles: "On Croquet, Murder, Old Magazines and the Like" and "City-Room Memories." By this time, however, Woollcott seems to have made a distinction between his work as a drama critic and his career as a general essayist; he no longer mixes his pieces indiscriminately, as he did in *Enchanted Aisles* but deliberately separates them and gives each group its own heading. In this respect, *Going to Pieces* is the last bridge on a long route that leads to his two best-selling collections of broadly miscellaneous but carefully grouped essays, tales, and sketches, *While Rome Burns* and *Long, Long Ago*. (pp. 113-14)

A considerable number of the theatrical essays in *Going to Pieces* are biographical sketches of famous theater personalities, though most of the pieces are by this time less like reviews or dramatic criticism than like the mature personal essays of his later collections. Many of them are documents on stage history that are no less valuable for the charming fashion in which they are told. (p. 114)

Though *Going to Pieces* is Woollcott's last appearance as a professional play reviewer, he actually "quit the routine but never the practice." In his switch to the magazine market, he was simply adapting his carefully wrought reviewing techniques to his growing interest in famous crimes, bizarre personalities, nostalgia, whimsy, and the literary criticism that he had already mastered in his constant evaluation of the fictional forms that had been adapted to the theater. Free to try anything, he turned his talents toward playwriting, radio, lecturing, and book reviewing, but he also maintained a staggering production of top quality magazine material. If anything, his public image became as bizarre and as attention commanding as any that he drew in his most bizarre character sketches, whose popularity became almost a cult among American readers. (pp. 116-17)

Except for Woollcott's early biography of Irving Berlin . . . he did not actually "write" his books in the conventional sense. The day-by-day writing he generally produced, the circumstances under which he habitually wrote, and the nature of his popularity as a writer made it almost unavoidable that most of his books would simply accumulate. The best and most felicitous of his pieces rose from the mass of his newspaper columns or from his magazine offerings and thereby presented themselves as candidates for successive compilations. Nonetheless, he could not resist from time to time the temptation to prove himself capable of deliberately crafting a book; and, when the subject of such a book was to be one of his idols like Mrs. Fiske, Charles Dickens, or Irving Berlin, he was willing to forego his usual activities and even isolate himself in the interests of getting the job done; and, to a lesser extent, the same procedure was used to write plays. But his talent was not suited to sustained writing projects of any kind, and though many of his early attempts to harness his powers for the long pull may have added a cubit to his height as a literary figure, none of these volumes proved as lucrative as his highly marketable shorter pieces. (p. 118)

Everything in [Woollcott's] training as a writer, every rhetorical device and trick of organization, had suited him for the high specialty of the short essay, and particularly for the quick "personalized" sprint in prose. . . .

[But in 1924 he] prepared himself to write a biography that—though not so long as biographies often go—would require that he sustain a single piece of writing for two or three hundred pages. His choice of subject [was] the early and as yet unfinished life and career of Irving Berlin. . . . (p. 124)

[Woollcott] stuffed his head full of information gleaned from interviews with friends of Berlin in New York, from letters from composers, and from his own well-stocked memories of the era when Berlin had risen from poverty to prominence in the best Horatio Alger tradition.

The result is a crowded panoramic study of the sometimes half-lit, sometimes garish and brassy world that could spawn an Irving Berlin, a world of which Berlin was an integral part, but one in which the central figure is seen always from the outside. In an attempt to tell the story of Irving Berlin without offending the living subject by speculating upon his conflicting motives and inner struggles, Woollcott falls back upon the story-telling device he had always used supremely well—the anecdote. Indeed, he tries to write biography by means of anecdote; and he should not have been surprised that the result is not really biography but a lively, colorful, fast-paced, entertaining study in the social and cultural history of an era, with Irving Berlin as its central figure. Had he far more accurately used the title *The World of Irving Berlin*, he would have satisfied his critics better. (p. 125)

Altogether, Berlin emerges as a kind of current legend; he is a fabulous and unlikely figure whose inexplicable talent serves as the bottomless well-spring of words and melodies so often heard in every corner of the world—ones that are so thoroughly imbued with the quality of folklore that they seem not to have been written by a man at all but to have sprung spontaneously from the lives of the people. . . . In Woollcott's book the reader can momentarily share the world in which [the songs] came to life. But relative to Irving Berlin, as Douglas Moore points out, "the reader wonders vainly what he is really like."

One cannot know, for in Woollcott's book Berlin becomes a living legend without having quite come to life as a man. The reason for this peculiar shortcoming is only partly to be explained by Woollcott's declaration that he had consciously done no more than compile "a source book for the wiser historian who will put the facts in permanent form.". . . A deeper reason . . . is that to do so Woollcott would have had to submerge his own personality—and, of all the writers of his day, he was one of the least likely to possess this special capability.

After writing his book on Irving Berlin, Woollcott never again attempted a full-sized biography, or, for that matter, any other sustained writing projects except two plays with which he rather fondly hoped to achieve success in those Broadway theaters where he had served for years as a critic. (pp. 126-27)

To Woollcott, it seemed sensible—but as a practical matter it did not prove entirely fortunate—that he should enter the [theater] with the expert help of Broadway's most successful and most versatile collaborator, George S. Kaufman, with whom, eventually, he wrote and produced both [*The Channel Road* and *The Dark Tower*]. . . .

As wits, critics, journalists, literary men, and unique personalities, these men were worthy of each other; and the close association they maintained throughout their lives was characterized as much by incessant intellectual contest as by mutual respect for each other's uniqueness. (p. 127)

In a collaboration, this interaction of personalities was unlikely to create the intricate balance necessary to success. As a result, both of the plays that emerged from the Kaufman-Woollcott teamwork suffer from imbalances that suggest that the melding of their talents was impossible. In each play, for instance, Kaufman seems to have devoted most of his attention to the technical aspects of the composition and to have done so without making use of Woollcott's keen sense of dramatic timing. On the other hand, Woollcott seems to have worked mostly with dialogue and characterization; and he committed excesses because he did not call upon Kaufman's spare and pointed sense of verbal economy in stage writing. Moreover, Woollcott could not have been the easiest of collaborators since he had spent a lifetime establishing himself as incontrovertible authority upon certain matters, and it was hardly worth chancing his wrath to suggest that he might need advice in these areas. (pp. 127-28)

The job that Woollcott had in mind was a dramatization of de Maupassant's widely read story "Boule de Suife" ("Ball-of-Fat" or "Tallow-Ball"), a biting and cynical tale about a group of self-righteous and self-seeking French people who, for profiteering motives of their own, try to escape the German occupation of 1870 by hiring a common stagecoach to take them from occupied Rouen to the channel city of Le Havre. (p. 128)

In *The Channel Road*, the German lieutenant emerges as a more complex and subtle character than the German officer of [Maupassant's] narrative. . . . This officer does not desire the prostitute, but lets the group believe that he does; for he is really awaiting authority from his superior to arrest them as profiteers seeking escape to England. He is amused and disgusted at their behavior; and to go through with the farce, he accepts the prostitute into his bed on Christmas Eve but arrests the group the next morning—and permits only the scorned prostitute and the two nuns to go on their way to Le Havre. As a result of this twist, the play acquires a moral force that is altogether lacking in de Maupassant's narrative. Since Kaufman had never felt himself a "literary" man, the selection of this story was probably left to Woollcott, who must also have been largely responsible for shifting its basic mood from the brutally realistic to the satirically comic and for devising the alterations of incident that made possible that tonal shift. (p. 129)

Four seasons later, undeterred by . . . mixed reviews and frustrated by a feeling that the run of *The Channel Road* had been stunted by the 1929 market crash, Kaufman and Woollcott wrote and produced another Broadway play, *The Dark Tower*. . . . A revenge play, its success depends entirely upon a villain so monstrous that his murderer seems a hero and a liberator. It is also a play in which the important element of suspense requires the withholding of the murderer's identity until the last few moments.

Since 1929, Woollcott had been writing his "Shouts and Murmurs" column for *The New Yorker,* where his lightly told accounts of famous murders had found a strong vogue. *The Dark Tower* was Woollcott's attempt to contrive a successful play by using the sly tone of his retold murders as a vehicle to reenact the old and reliable Svengali story. Once more, however, Woollcott found that he could not achieve the same effects when he transferred these subtle qualities to other literary forms. . . . Woollcott wisely avoided collaboration hereafter and made the most of his unique talents as essayist, tale-teller, and sketch-artist. (pp. 130-31)

In one sense, everything Woollcott wrote was a form of trivia. Early in his career he had realized that his strength as a writer lay in his extraordinary command of the minor forms of literature rather than in what lies at the top of the "hierarchy of the genres," and he was not apologizing or rationalizing but accepting the proven limits of his talents when he characterized himself as a great writer with nothing to say. He was well aware, however, that a keen eye for trivia had been the special gift of all the best-loved familiar essayists, and he worked with satisfaction in the literary tradition that had . . . enabled Dickens to take a reader along with him on a night walk; and that had inspired Washington Irving to weave a suspenseful sketch upon the identity of a half-seen fellow lodger or to ruminate upon the ravages of time. Woollcott truly loved trivia, and his trivial pieces at their best possess a rare quality of illumination.

To Woollcott, the delight of trivia was that subjects were numberless and that their appeal was limitless. But, since he could not repeatedly fill large spaces with pure trivia, no matter how pleasingly he wove the material, he found the thousand word space of the "Shouts and Murmurs" page the ideal medium for his infinitely various observations upon the small highlights of human life. There he might . . . muse upon pirated volumes of Barrie and other bookish tidbits, upon the early American self-appointed "aristocracy," upon the hoarding of old theater programs, or upon linguistic quibbles, card playing, curious names, versions of ubiquitous tales, croquet—or he might simply pull together an array of jokes and anecdotes that were so loosely connected as to make his *New Yorker* editors speculate that radio broadcasting had ruined him.

Most of the best of Woollcott's trivia was gathered into his books, beginning with *Going to Pieces,* which contained three or four such pieces in a section titled "On Croquet, Murder, Old Magazines, and the Like." (pp. 135-36)

Among the fifty-two widely assorted pieces in *While Rome Burns,* seven are sheer trivia, of which **"The Editor's Easy Chair"** and **"This Thing Called They"** can be classed as the most interesting sketches in the collection. (p. 136)

In each of these finely spun pieces of literary trivia, the Woollcott touch is unmistakable. Here, as in no other area of his writing, he demonstrates his extraordinary versatility in the sheer variety with which he presents his material. No sketch or essay is quite like any other. His endless anecdotes and relevant digressions afford limitless combinations and permutations in style and structure. At his best, Woollcott is unique in his capacity to mold a trivial idea into an entertaining as well as a valuable piece of literature.

Of all the inconsistencies in Woollcott's character, none is more revealing than the strain of unabashed sentimentalism in a man whose public image has been a combination of the "ultimate sophisticate" and the "fabulous monster." Though in any other writer these qualities might appear to be irreconcilable contradictions, in Woollcott they were thoroughly acceptable to a reading public that had gradually become accustomed to regarding him as "a congress of opposing parties." (pp. 137-38)

Woollcott reserved his most passionate strain of sentiment for the profiles and biographical sketches that he wrote about the people he knew and loved best. (p. 139)

Besides the special *New Yorker* profiles that he wrote about such people as Kaufman, Connelly, and Harpo Marx, Woollcott wrote dozens of similar ones for other magazines. The general tone of these pieces is a combination of admiration, affection, and nostalgia that appears at its best in his brief sketch about the life and career of Stephen Foster, **"Dear Friends and Gentle Hearts."** (pp. 139-40)

In his prose, Woollcott shared his friendships with his readers, and, as Edward Weeks observed upon the appearance of *Long, Long Ago* after Woollcott's death, "In the attic of his mind were hundreds of little boxes . . . and these boxes held the souvenirs of his friends past and present." In the word "souvenirs" lies the key to the mood of nostalgia that prevails in much of Woollcott's writing. The nostalgia lurked just below the surface of everything that he wrote, prompting one reviewer to say, "He has an eye for spring and summer beauty, but the faces he loves most are autumnal." (p. 140)

If Woollcott's trivia sometimes seems too trivial and his sentiment too sentimental, the wonder is that the vast number of his devotees never seemed to worry about his excesses. During that sometimes sophisticated, sometimes despairing, largely materialistic era between the wars, when sentiment could be so easily misunderstood or distrusted, even the most cynical reader sensed that the "honest moisture" on Woollcott's "old lashes" was the unabashed expression of real emotion in one who was not afraid to admit that he was a man of feeling as well as wit. When John Mason Brown declared that Woollcott's "heart is one of the country's largest public gardens," he also spoke for a nation of readers who were prepared to find in that garden from time to time a splash of too-bright color or an unmodified strain of "Ah-shall-we-ever-forget-the-glamor-of-those days." They knew the garden to be of hues that could be riotous as well as soft, and that the music from the hidden alcove was often sad. It was their garden, and they liked it the way it was. (pp. 141-42)

Wayne Chatterton, in his Alexander Woollcott *(copyright © 1978 by Twayne Publishers, Inc.; reprinted with the permission of Twayne Publishers, a Division of G. K. Hall & Co., Boston), Twayne, 1978, 191 p.*

ADDITIONAL BIBLIOGRAPHY

Cerf, Bennett. "The Woollcott Myth: A Minority Report." In his *Try and Stop Me: A Collection of Anecdotes and Stories, Mostly Humorous,* pp. 77-87. New York: Simon and Schuster, 1945.
  A humorous essay discussing Woollcott's life and relationships.

Gibbs, Wolcott. "Big Nemo." In his *More in Sorrow*, pp. 79-125. New York: Henry Holt and Co., 1958.

A Woollcott portrait, featuring many entertaining anecdotes.

Hoyt, Edwin. *Alexander Woollcott: The Man Who Came to Dinner; A Biography*. New York: Abelard-Schuman, 1968, 357 p.

An excellent biography.

Klee, Bruce B. "Woollcott vs. Shubert: Dramatic Criticism on Trial." *Educational Theatre Journal* XIII, No. 4 (December 1961): 264-68.

An account of *The New York Times* suit against the producers Jake and Lee Shubert. The lawsuit was brought when the Shuberts banned that newspaper's drama critic, Alexander Woollcott, from attending their productions because of his unfavorable reviews.

Teichmann, Howard. *Smart Aleck: The Wit, World, and Life of Alexander Woollcott*. New York: William Morrow and Co., 1976, 334 p.

A biography containing many anecdotes about Woollcott's life and career.

Thurber, James. "Dishonest Abe and the Grand Marshall." In his *The Years with Ross*, pp. 273-91. Boston, Toronto: Little, Brown and Co., 1959.

An account of Woollcott's long, tumultuous relationship with Harold Ross, founder and long-time editor of *The New Yorker*.

West, Rebecca. "Woollcott." *The Spectator* 177, No. 6175 (1 November 1946): 452.

A heated letter written in response to a *Spectator* review of Samuel Hopkins Adams's biography of Woollcott. West calls the book "crude and silly and irrelevant in nearly everything except its anecdotes of his personal life," then defends Woollcott's vitriolic bearing as the understandable result of his ill health.

Wilson, Edmund. "Alexander Woollcott of the Phalanx." In his *Classics and Commercials: A Literary Chronicle of the Forties*, pp. 87-93. New York: Farrar, Straus and Co., 1950.

Wilson's personal reminiscences of his friendship with Woollcott, finding him a sensitive, self-conscious man who used bluster and insult as a defense against all who might find him unattractive.

Winterich, John T. "Came the War." In *Squads Write! A Selection of the Best Things in Prose, Verse and Cartoon from "The Stars and Stripes": Official Newspaper of the A.E.F.*, edited by John T. Winterich, pp. 52-85. New York: Harper & Brothers Publishers, 1931.*

Tells how Woollcott wrote "The Story of Verdun Belle."

Appendix

THE EXCERPTS IN TCLC, VOLUME 5, WERE REPRINTED FROM THE FOLLOWING PERIODICALS:

The Academy
American German Review
American Literature
American Quarterly
The American Review
The American-Scandinavian Review
The American Scholar
The Athenaeum
The Atlantic Monthly
Book Week—New York Herald Tribune
The Bookman (London)
The Bookman (New York)
Books Abroad
Bulletin of Hispanic Studies
Colby Library Quarterly
The Colorado Quarterly
Commonweal
Comparative Drama
Contemporary Review
The Critic
Daily News and Leader
The Dial
Drama Survey
Educational Theater Journal
English
English Journal
English Studies in Africa
Essays and Studies
The Fortnightly Review
Forum
The Freeman
The Georgia Review
German Life & Letters
The German Quarterly
The Germanic Review
Harper's

Hermes
Hispania
Horizon
Indice Literario
International P.E.N. Bulletin of Selected
  Books
Italian Studies
Italica
Journal of Asian Studies
Kansas Quarterly
Kentucky Romance Quarterly
Leader
Life and Letters
The Listener
The Literary Review (New York)
The Living Age
London Magazine
The London Mercury
The Mississippi Quarterly
Modern Drama
Modern Fiction Studies
The Modern Language Journal
Modern Language Notes
Modern Language Quarterly
The Modern Language Review
Monumenta Nipponica
The Nation
The Nation and The Athenaeum
The New Republic
New Statesman
The New Statesman & Nation
New York Herald Tribune Book Review
The New York Review of Books
The New York Times
The New York Times Book Review
The New Yorker

The Nineteenth-Century
Novel: A Forum on Fiction
Papers on Language and Literature
PMLA
Poetry
Polish Perspectives
The Polish Review
Punch
Renascence
Review of National Literatures
The Russian Review
The Saturday Review (London)
The Saturday Review (New York)
The Saturday Review of Literature
Scandinavian Studies and Notes
The Sewanee Review
Slavic and East European Journal
The Slavonic Review
The Smart Set
The Southern Literary Journal
The Spectator
Studies in the Novel
Studies in Short Fiction
The Texas Quarterly
Texas Studies in Literature and Language
Time & Tide
The Times Literary Supplement
Transition
The Tulane Drama Review
The University of Michigan Papers in
  Women's Studies
Virginia Woolf Quarterly
Western Humanities Review
World Literature Today
Yale French Studies
The Yale Review

THE EXCERPTS IN TCLC, VOLUME 5, WERE REPRINTED FROM THE FOLLOWING BOOKS:

Adams, Samuel Hopkins. A. Woollcott: His Life and His World. *Reynal & Hitchcock, 1945.*

Allen, Walter. Arnold Bennett. *Alan Swallow, 1949.*

Barnard, Ellsworth. Edwin Arlington Robinson. *Macmillan, 1952.*

Bates, H. E. The Modern Short Story: A Critical Survey. *Nelson, 1941, Joseph, 1972.*

Beach, Joseph Warren. The Twentieth Century Novel: Studies in Technique. *Appleton-Century-Crofts, 1932.*

Benet, Mary Kathleen. Writers in Love. *Macmillan, 1977.*

Bergonzi, Bernard. Heroes' Twilight: A Study of the Literature of the Great War. *Constable and Co., 1965.*

Bettinson, Christopher. Gide: A Study. *Rowman and Littlefield, 1977.*

Beyer, Harald. A History of Norwegian Literature. *New York University Press, 1956.*

Bogan, Louise. Achievement in American Poetry: 1900-1950. *Henry Regnery, 1951.*

Bone, Robert A. The Negro Novel in America. *Yale University Press, 1965.*

Bowra, C. M. The Heritage of Symbolism. *Macmillan, 1943.*

Boyd, Ernest. Ireland's Literary Renaissance. *Barnes & Noble, 1922, Barnes & Noble, 1968.*

Boyd, Ernest. Studies from Ten Literatures. *Scribner's, 1925.*

Boyesen, Hjalmar Hjorth. Essays on Scandinavian Literature. *Scribner's, 1895, Scribner's, 1911.*

Braybrooke, Patrick. Philosophies in Modern Fiction. *Daniel, 1929, Books for Libraries Press, 1965.*

Briggs, Julia. Night Visitors: The Rise and Fall of the English Ghost Story. *Faber and Faber, 1977.*

Brown, Sterling. The Negro in American Fiction. *Associates in Negro Folk Education, 1937, Kennikat Press, 1968.*

Bunin, Ivan. Memories and Portraits. *Doubleday, 1951.*

Cairns, Christopher. Italian Literature. *Barnes & Noble, 1977.*

Casey, T. J. Manshape That Shone: An Interpretation of Trakl. *Basil Blackwell, 1964.*

Cather, Willa. The World and the Parish: Willa Cather's Articles and Reviews, 1893-1902. 2 vols. *Edited by William M. Curtin. University of Nebraska Press, 1970.*

Cecil, David. Poets and Story-Tellers: A Book of Critical Essays. *Constable, 1949.*

Cestre, Charles. An Introduction to Edwin Arlington Robinson and Selected Poems. *Macmillan, 1958.*

Chatterton, Wayne. Alexander Woollcott. *Twayne, 1978.*

Ciholas, Karin Nordenhaug. Gide's Art of the Fugue: A Thematic Study of "Les faux-monnayeurs." *U.N.C. Department of Romance Languages, 1974.*

Cohen, J. M. Poetry of This Age: 1908-1965. *Hutchinson University Library, 1966.*

Colby, Vineta. The Singular Anomaly: Women Novelists of the Nineteenth Century. *New York University Press, 1970.*

Cooper, Frederic Taber. Some English Story Tellers: A Book of the Younger Novelists. *Holt, 1912.*

Cross, Wilbur L. Four Contemporary Novelists. *Macmillan, 1930, Books for Libraries Press, 1966.*

Daiches, David. New Literary Values: Studies in Modern Literature. *Oliver and Boyd, 1936, Books for Libraries Press, 1968.*

Dane, Clemence. Tradition and Hugh Walpole. *Doubleday, 1929.*

Darton, F. J. Harvey. Arnold Bennett. *Holt, 1915, Scholarly Press, 1971.*

Davies, J. C. Gide: "L'immoraliste" and "La porte étroite." *Arnold, 1968.*

Davies, Margaret. Colette. *Grove, 1961.*

Davis, Oswald H. The Master: A Study of Arnold Bennett. *Johnson, 1966.*

Deutsch, Babette. This Modern Poetry. *Norton, 1935, Kraus, 1969.*

Deutsch, Babette. Poetry in Our Time. *Holt, 1952, Columbia University Press, 1956.*

Dickey, James. Babel to Byzantium: Poets and Poetry Now. *Farrar, Straus, 1968.*

Drake, William A. Contemporary European Writers. *John Day, 1928.*

Drew, Elizabeth A. The Modern Novel: Some Aspects of Contemporary Fiction. *Harcourt, 1926.*

Erlich, Victor. The Double Image: Concepts of the Poet in Slavic Literature. *Johns Hopkins University Press, 1964.*

Fallis, Richard. The Irish Renaissance. *Syracuse University Press, 1977.*

Field, Frank. Three French Writers and the Great War: Studies in the Rise of Communism and Fascism. *Cambridge University Press, 1975.*

Fowlie, Wallace. André Gide: His Life and Art. *Macmillan, 1965.*

Fraser, G. S. The Modern Writer and His World. *Verschoyle, 1953.*

Gass, William H. The World within the Word. *Knopf, 1978.*

Gohdes, Clarence, ed. Essays on American Literature in Honor of Jay B. Hubbell. *Duke University Press, 1967.*

Gregory, Horace. Spirit of Time and Place: Collected Essays of Horace Gregory. *Norton, 1973.*

Guerard, Albert J. André Gide. *Harvard University Press, 1951, Dutton, 1963.*

Gullón, Ricardo, ed. Valle-Inclán Centennial Studies. *University of Texas, 1968.*

Gunn, Peter. Vernon Lee: Violet Paget, 1856-1935. *Oxford University Press, 1964.*

Gustafson, Alrik. Six Scandinavian Novelists: Lie, Jacobsen, Heidenstam, Selma Lagerlöf, Hamsun, Sigrid Undset. *Princeton University Press, 1940, American-Scandinavian Foundation, 1940.*

Hamburger, Michael. Reason and Energy: Studies in German Literature. *Grove, 1957.*

Heermance, J. Noel. Charles W. Chesnutt: America's First Great Black Novelist. *Archon Books, 1974.*

Heidegger, Martin. On the Way to Language. *Harper, 1971.*

Heller, Erich. The Disinherited Mind: Essays in Modern German Language and Thought. *Barnes & Noble, 1971.*

Hibberd, Dominic. Wilfred Owen. *British Council, 1975.*

Hockey, Lawrence. W. H. Davies. *University of Wales Press, 1971.*

Hytier, Jean. Andre Gide. *Translated by Richard Howard. Editions Charlot, 1938, Doubleday, 1962.*

Iggers, Wilma Abeles. Karl Kraus: A Viennese Critic of the Twentieth Century. *Martinus Nijhoff, 1967.*

Jackson, Robert Louis. Dostoevsky's Underground Man in Russian Literature. *Mouton Publishers, 1958.*

James, Henry. Notes on Novelists, with Some Other Notes. *Scribner's, 1914.*

Jones, Sonia. Alfonsina Storni. *Twayne, 1979.*

Keene, Donald. Japanese Literature: An Introduction for Western Readers. *John Murray Publishers, 1953.*

Kettle, Arnold. An Introduction to the English Novel: Henry James to the Present Day, Vol. II. *2d. ed. Hutchinson University Library, 1967.*

Klein, Holger, ed. The First World War in Fiction: A Collection of Critical Essays. *Barnes & Noble, 1976.*

Kridl, Manfred. A Survey of Polish Literature and Culture. *Columbia University Press, 1956.*

Kronenberger, Louis. The Republic of Letters: Essays on Various Writings. *Knopf, 1955.*

Krzyzanowski, Jerzy R. Wladyslaw Stanislaw Reymont. *Twayne, 1972.*

Kurrik, Maire Jaanus. Georg Trakl. *Columbia University Press, 1974.*

Lafourcade, Georges. Arnold Bennett: A Study. *Frederick Muller, 1939, AMS Press, 1973.*

Landeira, Ricardo, ed. Critical Essays of Gabriel Miro. *Society of Spanish-American Studies, 1979.*

Lavrin, Janko. From Pushkin to Mayakovsky: A Study in the Evolution of Literature. *Sylvan Press, 1948.*

Lavrin, Janko. A Panorama of Russian Literature. *Harper, 1973.*

Leary, Lewis. Southern Excursions: Essays on Mark Twain and Others. *Louisiana State University Press, 1971.*

Leaska, Mitchell A. Virginia Woolf's ''Lighthouse'': A Study in Critical Method. *Columbia University Press, 1970.*

Lemaitre, Georges. Four French Novelists. *Oxford University Press, 1938, Kennikat, 1969.*

Lewis, R.W.B. The Poetry of Hart Crane. *Princeton University Press, 1967.*

Lima, Robert. Ramón del Valle-Inclán. *Columbia University Press, 1972.*

Lima, Robert, ed. Valle-Inclán: Autobiography, Aesthetics, Aphorisms. *Translated by Robert Lima. Limited Centennial Edition, 1966.*

Lindenberger, Herbert. Georg Trakl. *Twayne, 1971.*

Littlejohn, David, ed. Gide: A Collection of Critical Essays. *Prentice-Hall, 1970.*

Lowell, Amy. Tendencies in Modern American Poetry. *Macmillan, 1917, Haskell House, 1970.*

Lowry, Malcolm. Selected Letters of Malcolm Lowry. *Edited by Harvey Breit and Margerie Bonner Lowry. J. B. Lippincott Company, 1965.*

Lucas, F. L. Authors Dead and Living. *Macmillan, 1926.*

Lucas, John. Arnold Bennett: A Study of His Fiction. *Methuen, 1974.*

Luker, Nicholas. Alexander Kuprin. *Twayne, 1978.*

Lyngstad, Sverre. Jonas Lie. *Twayne, 1977.*

Macdonald, Ian R. Gabriel Miró: His Private Library and His Literary Background. *Tamesis Books, 1975.*

Mackenzie, Compton. Literature in My Time. *Cowan, 1933, Arno Press, 1967.*

Madariaga, Salvador de. The Genius of Spain and Other Essays on Spanish Contemporary Literature. *Oxford University Press, 1923.*

Majumbdar, Robin, and McLaurin, Allen, eds. Virginia Woolf: The Critical Heritage. *Routledge & Kegan Paul, 1975.*

Marble, Annie Russell. The Nobel Prize Winners in Literature: 1901-1931. *D. Appleton and Company, 1932.*

Marcus, Phillip L. Standish O'Grady. *Bucknell University Press, 1970.*

Marks, Elaine. Colette. *Rutgers, 1960.*

Maskaleris, Thanasis. Kostis Palamas. *Twayne, 1972.*

McCarthy, Justin, ed. Irish Literature, Vol. VII. *John D. Morris, 1904.*

McClellan, Edwin. Two Japanese Novelists: Soseki and Toson. *University of Chicago Press, 1969.*

McFarlane, James Walter. Ibsen and the Temper of Norwegian Literature. *Oxford University Press, 1960.*

Mirsky, D. S. Contemporary Russian Literature, 1881-1925. *Knopf, 1926, Routledge, 1926.*

Monroe, Harriet. Poets and Their Art. *Macmillan, 1926.*

Moody, A. D. Virginia Woolf. *Oliver and Boyd, 1963.*

Muchnic, Helen. From Gorky to Pasternak: Six Writers in Soviet Russia. *Random House, 1961.*

Murphy, Francis. Edwin Arlington Robinson: A Collection of Critical Essays. *Prentice-Hall, 1970.*

Naremore, James. The World without a Self: Virginia Woolf and the Novel. *Yale University Press, 1973.*

Natan, Alex, ed. German Men of Letters, Vol. III. *Wolff, 1964.*

Nathan, George Jean. The Theatre in the Fifties. *Knopf, 1953.*

Nathan, George Jean. The Magic Mirror. *Knopf, 1960.*

O'Connor, Frank. The Lonely Voice: A Study of the Short Story. *World Publishing, 1963.*

O'Conor, Norreys Jepson. Changing Ireland: Literary Backgrounds of the Irish Free State, 1889-1922. *Harvard University Press, 1924.*

O'Grady, Hugh. Standish James O'Grady, the Man & the Writer: A Memoir by His Son, Hugh Art O'Grady, Litt.D., with a Foreword by Alfred Perceval Graves, and Contributions by A. E. & Others. *The Talbot Press, 1929.*

Olgin, Moissaye J. A Guide to Russian Literature (1820-1917). *Harcourt, Brace and Howe, 1920.*

Overton, Grant, ed. Hugh Walpole: Appreciations. *Doran, 1925.*

Pattee, Fred Lewis. The Development of the American Short Story: An Historical Survey. *Harper, 1923.*

Penzoldt, Peter. The Supernatural in Fiction. *Neville, 1952, Humanities Press, 1965.*

Peyre, Henri. The Contemporary French Novel. *Oxford University Press, 1955.*

Peyre, Henri. French Novelists. *Oxford University Press, 1967.*

Phelps, William Lyon. Essays on Russian Novelists. *Macmillan, 1911.*

Phillips, Rachel. Alfonsina Storni: From Poetess to Poet. *Tamesis Books, 1975.*

Poggioli, Renato. The Poets of Russia: 1890-1930. *Harvard University Press, 1960.*

Politis, Linos. A History of Modern Greek Literature. *Oxford University Press, 1973.*

Pollard, Percival. Their Day in Court. *Neale, 1909, Johnson, 1969.*

Povey, John. Roy Campbell. *Twayne, 1977.*

Pritchett, V. S. The Living Novel and Later Appreciations. *Rev. ed. Random House, 1964.*

Quinn, Vincent. Hart Crane. *Twayne, 1963.*

Rahv, Philip. Image and Idea. *New Directions, 1949.*

Raknes, Ola. Chapters in Norwegian Literature. *Gyldendal, 1923, Books for Libraries Press, 1969.*

Rankin, Daniel S. Kate Chopin and Her Creole Stories. *University of Pennsylvania Press, 1932.*

Redding, J. Saunders. To Make a Poet Black. *University of North Carolina Press, 1939, McGrath, 1968.*

Reeve, F. D. Aleksandr Blok: Between Image and Idea. *Columbia University Press, 1962.*

Reilly, Joseph J. Of Books and Men. *Julian Messner, 1942.*

Rexroth, Kenneth. Assays. *New Directions, 1961.*

Rickword, Edgel, ed. Scrutinies by Various Writers. *Wishart, 1928.*

Robinson, W. R. Edwin Arlington Robinson: A Poetry of the Act. *The Press of Western Reserve University, 1967.*

Rosenbaum, Sidonia Carmen. Modern Women Poets of Spanish America: The Precursors, Delmira Agustini, Gabriel Mistral, Alfonsina Storni, Juana de Ibarbourou. *Hispanic Institute in the United States, 1945.*

Sartre, Jean-Paul. Situations. *Braziller, 1965.*

Saul, George Brandon. A. E. Coppard: His Life and His Poetry to the Publication of the "Bibliography." *University of Pennsylvania, 1932.*

Saul, George Brandon. In Praise of the Half-Forgotten and Other Ruminations. *Bucknell University Press, 1976.*

Segel, Harold B. Twentieth-Century Russian Drama: From Gorky to the Present. *Columbia University Press, 1979.*

Seyersted, Per. Kate Chopin: A Critical Biography. *Louisiana State University Press, 1969.*

Sherman, Stuart P. On Contemporary Literature. *Holt, 1917.*

Simons, J. B. Arnold Bennett and His Novels: A Critical Study. *Basil Blackwell, 1936.*

Sitwell, Edith. Aspects of Modern Poetry. *Duckworth, 1934, Books for Libraries Press, 1970.*

Slonim, Marc. Modern Russian Literature from Chekhov to the Present. *Oxford University Press, 1953.*

Smith, Rowland. Lyric and Polemic: The Literary Personality of Roy Campbell. *McGill-Queen's University Press, 1972.*

Spalter, Max. Brecht's Tradition. *The Johns Hopkins University Press, 1967.*

Spender, Stephen. The Destructive Element: A Study of Modern Writers. *Jonathan Cape, 1935, Jonathan Cape, 1938.*

Starkie, Enid. André Gide. *Yale University Press, 1954.*

Steele, Elizabeth. Hugh Walpole. *Twayne, 1972.*

Steen, Marguerite. Hugh Walpole: A Study. *Doubleday, 1933.*

Stonesifer, Richard J. W. H. Davies: A Critical Biography. *Jonathan Cape, 1963.*

Strong, L.A.G. Personal Remarks. *Liveright, 1953.*

Sullivan, Jack. Elegant Nightmares, the English Ghost Story from Le Fanu to Blackwood. *Ohio University Press, 1978.*

Swinnerton, Frank. The Georgian Scene: A Literary Panorama. *Farrar & Rinehart, 1934.*

Swinnerton, Frank. Arnold Bennett. *British Council, 1961.*

Symonds, John Addington. The Letters of John Addington Symonds: 1869-1884, Vol. II. *Edited by Herbert M. Schueller and Robert L. Peters. Wayne State University Press, 1968.*

Tate, Allen. On the Limits of Poetry. *William Morrow, 1948.*

Thomas, Dylan. Quite Early One Morning. *New Directions, 1954.*

Thomas, Lawrence. André Gide: The Ethic of the Artist. *Secker & Warburg, 1950.*

Thompson, William Irwin. The Imagination of an Insurrection; Dublin, Easter, 1916: A Study of an Ideological Movement. *Oxford University Press, 1967.*

Tolton, C.D.E. André Gide and the Art of Autobiography: A Study of ''Si le grain ne meurt.'' *Macmillan, 1975.*

Trotsky, Leon. Literature and Revolution. *Russell & Russell, 1925, Russell & Russell, 1957.*

Unterecker, John, ed. Approaches to the Twentieth-Century Novel. *Crowell, 1965.*

Untermeyer, Louis. Lives of the Poets: The Story of One Thousand Years of English and American Poetry. *Simon & Schuster, 1959.*

Waggoner, Hyatt Howe. The Heel of Elohim: Science and Values in Modern American Poetry. *University of Oklahoma Press, 1950.*

Wain, John. Arnold Bennett. *Columbia University Press, 1967.*

Warren, L. A. Modern Spanish Literature: A Comprehensive Survey of the Novelists, Poets, Dramatists and Essayists from the Eighteenth Century to the Present, Vol. 1. *Brentano's, 1929.*

Waters, Brian. The Essential W. H. Davies. *Jonathan Cape, 1951.*

Welland, Dennis. Wilfred Owen: A Critical Study. *Chatto & Windus, 1978.*

West, Geoffrey. The Problem of Arnold Bennett. *Joiner and Steele, 1932.*

West, Rebecca. The Strange Necessity. *Doubleday, 1928.*

Will, Frederic, ed. Hereditas: Seven Essays on the Modern Experience of the Classical. *University of Texas Press, 1964.*

Williams, Harold. Modern English Writers: Being a Study of Imaginative Literature 1890-1914. *Sidgwick & Jackson, 1919.*

Wilson, Colin. The Outsider. *Houghton, 1956.*

Wilson, Donald. A Critical Commentary of André Gide's ''La symphonie pastorale.'' *Wilson, 1971, Macmillan, 1971.*

Wilson, Edmund. The Shores of Light: A Literary Chronicle of the Twenties and Thirties. *Farrar, Straus & Giroux, 1952.*

Wilson, Edmund. Patriotic Gore: Studies in the Literature of the American Civil War. *Oxford University Press, 1962.*

Winters, Ivor. Edwin Arlington Robinson. *New Directions, 1946.*

Woodcock, George, ed. Malcolm Lowry: The Man and His Work. *University of British Columbia Press, 1971.*

Woolf, Virginia. 'The Captain's Death Bed' and Other Essays. *Harcourt, 1950.*

Yeats, W. B. Letters on Poetry from W. B. Yeats to Dorothy Wellesley. *Edited by Dorothy Wellesley. Oxford University Press, 1940, Oxford University Press, 1964.*

Yershov, Peter. Science Fiction and Utopian Fantasy in Soviet Literature. *Research Program on the U.S.S.R., 1954.*

Ziff, Larzer. The American 1890s: Life and Times of a Lost Generation. *Viking Penguin, 1966.*

Zohn, Harry. Karl Kraus. *Twayne, 1971.*